PLAYBOY'S
NEW
HOST & BAR
BOOK

PLAYBOY'S
NEW
HOST & BAR
BOOK

Thomas Mario

ЯⱯP

A Playboy Press Book

Copyright © 1971, 1979 by Thomas Mario

Designed by Tere LoPrete

Library of Congress Cataloging in Publication Data

Mario, Thomas.
    Playboy's new host and bar book.

    First ed. published in 1971 under title:
Playboy's host & bar book.
    Includes index.
    1. Alcoholic beverages. 2. Cocktails.
I. Title.
TX951.M266 1979   641.8'74   79-4880
ISBN 0-87223-541-6

CONTENTS

INTRODUCTION

Drinking habits come and go. The old Teutonic custom of quaffing beer out of drinking vessels made from the skulls of your enemies would raise a few eyebrows at any beer party today. And, skipping a few centuries, President John Adams's daily tankard of hard cider (rough apple wine) before breakfast would hardly be the drink of one's choice at a chichi brunch nowadays. Indeed, even in the short span of ten years since Playboy's first *Host & Bar Book* was written, new drinking habits have been fomenting with revolutionary fervor.

Any host wetting his fingers to the winds knows, for example, that the once-traditional Saturday night boozefest with straight shots of anything from white corn liquor to Peruvian pisco has seeped into oblivion; and the two- or three-martini rite before the business lunch has in many cases been disfranchised by cold dry white wine. Ten years ago Americans were drinking a gallon of wine per capita annually; they now drink double that amount. If, ten years ago, someone mentioned Riesling, you thought of the luscious white wine of the Rhine valley. Today you can drink magnificent rival Rieslings not only from California and New York State but from the state of Washington. Tequila, once a primitive curio among potables, is flowing north of the Rio Grande in an ever-surging river, the fastest-growing liquor in the States. And vodka, white knight of spirits, which long ago nosed out gin, now has top possession of the hard-liquor field, leaving bourbon in the rear.

This isn't to imply that hosts have stopped pouring brandy, gin, rum, or whiskey. But instead of the shots of stiff, straight liquor at the highest possible proof, they're enjoying lighter proofs and turning to easy-sail entertaining with mixed drinks. The old orange-juice crowd who daringly mixed Sunkist with Smirnoff is now making screwdrivers with anything from rum to sherry to Pernod. They carry picnic jugs of salty dogs for the afternoon's cruise. From the tailgates of their station wagons you'll be offered anything from stingers to sparkling Beaujolais. And at the beach or at their own poolsides, the number of new tall

coolers is countless. In tune with these trends, *Playboy's NEW Host &
Bar Book* has expanded its recipes for mixed drinks and appetizers
from approximately 700 to 1000.

For those who are being introduced to the fine art of hosting, endless
avenues are opened by the fact that our own country now distills some
of the best spirits and makes some of the best wines in the world. The
United States is also the world's largest clearinghouse for wines and
spirits shipped from almost every corner of the earth. Any man, for
instance, contemplating whiskeys for his bar can choose—for better or
worse—among no less than 500 different brands, not to mention the
hundreds of gins, rums, vodkas, schnapps, brandies, and liqueurs of
such kaleidoscopic variety of strengths, flavors, ages, and colors as to
boggle eyes, nose, and taste buds. A newcomer to wines, faced with the
10,000 wine labels now being sold in this country, could be excused
for being unable to see the cellar for the *vins*.

Obviously, in all this surging maze, a roadbook is important. But
in stocking your cellar or liquor cabinet, you hardly need one of those
encyclopedic tomes describing in harrowing detail the chemistry of
distillation and the world's vineyards and vintages. What is helpful is
a down-to-earth guide that tells hosts how wines and spirits are *used*:
when age in a wine or liquor is important and when it is not; how to
store and pour; what drinking vessels to use; how drinks should be
chilled, mixed, stirred, shaken, frappéed, garnished, blended in a
pitcher, or brewed in a bowl.

The author hopes the present volume will be useful for these needs
and other party purposes, for blowing away the haze of formality,
for the subtle chemistry of good fellowship.

PLAYBOY'S
NEW
HOST & BAR
BOOK

1

THE CODE OF CONVIVIALITY

Meticulous planning, comfortable digs, an alluring patio, elaborate platters may be important to your reputation as a host, but *vital* to it is your understanding that every prearranged drinking session calls for two kinds of alchemy: The first is mixing potables; the second, mixing people.

Whether your drinks are as potent as arrack or as gentle as fino sherry, whether they be frosty coolers or steaming punches, their purpose is to create fun and amity. As for guests—whether lads or lassies, foreigners or natives, water skiers or beach combers, anecdotists or listeners—all should be carefully blended in your mind beforehand, and during the party reblended—like a true Spanish solera—in the most stimulating proportions. To this end, as a good host you need, first and always, to be a resourceful mind reader.

You should start with the proposition that friends who are warm toward you are not necessarily going to be warm toward each other. Mindful of this kind of sensitive interplay, you'll naturally choose for small gatherings guests who'll be as compatible as gin and tonic. For larger parties, two or three abrasive acquaintances may provide just the catalytic force needed to transform a low-key soirée into an uninhibited revel—like yeast in small quantities, they often guarantee the lively but controlled fermentation on which good parties rise. In any event, guests—however diverse—who share wisely chosen libations do become *simpatico*. Whether arriving as friends or strangers, they leave with a glowing feeling, having found and fathomed the same warm company.

In recent years, partying and party manners have undergone a ruthless shakeout by simply moving from the parlor to the patio. Weather permitting, the indoor soirée all over the land has abdicated in favor of the outdoor barbecue, and former rites of etiquette have been laughed away. The question of whether the female guest of honor should be seated at the host's right or left becomes academic when the female guest of honor is happily sprawled on a terrace chair, tearing apart a grilled fresh lobster.

But whether your friends are sitting around a table at a black-tie dinner or sitting on the floor munching hero sandwiches, the host must still remember that his guests' pleasure comes before his own. If you're inviting a half-dozen skiers to your private lodge after a day on the slopes, at least an hour before your friends arrive you'll get back to your quarters, however reluctantly, to build the fire, start the fondue pot, and begin mulling the rum. If you've asked some friends to spend an afternoon on your motor cruiser, it's your duty to see that everything in your galley, from the casserole to the cordials, is stowed aboard before your party arrives.

If you're seized with minor anxieties about the preparation of your party, or are concerned about making the grade after the crowd arrives, remember the one essential ingredient of modern civility—a sense of humor. Any gesture on the part of host or guest, even heel clicking if you can imagine that at a modern bash, becomes acceptable with a genial tongue-in-cheek attitude. If the temporary coatrack collapses under an overload, don't sweat and swear silently while trying to keep a stiff front; let the quips fall where they may and calmly go about restoring order.

Invitations

Don't plan to invite twenty-four people if your pad, pool, or cruiser can only accommodate twelve, unless it's a combination indoor/patio party where guests can move freely from one place to another.

—After drawing up your guest list, extend your invitations, allowing at least a week's prior notice for most parties and two to three weeks for important or outstanding gatherings.

—Except for formal parties or events like weddings, when printed invitations might be sent, it's best to telephone your friends or, when practical, ask them in person. Don't slight friends by issuing invitations through a third party.

—If for some special or rare occasion invitations are to be mailed, your printer or stationer will supply you with samples showing styles of makeup and RSVP forms. The language on the invitations needn't be traditional or rigid; make it as easy and cordial as if you were inviting your friends in person.

—When inviting people to an outdoor party, give whatever information is important: If it's a poolside party, tell guests to bring swimwear; if it's tennis, tenniswear, etc.

—You don't have to recite a complete guest list along with your invitations, but invitees often appreciate knowing that other mutual friends will be joining the shindig.

—If you're having a cocktail party supplemented only by the usual salted nuts, dips, and what the French call *crudités*, let your friends know that they're coming for drinks so they can make their own arrangements for dinner later.

—If cocktails are to be followed by a cold, or cold and hot buffet, make this understood so that guests won't make other plans for dinner.

—For your own as well as your guests' convenience, specify the time of your party—such as cocktails with buffet from 5:00 to 9:00; brunch from 11:00 to 3:00; pizza and beer from 9:00 to midnight. If it's a sit-down dinner, the starting time is sufficient, such as dinner at 8:00.

—If you want to keep a nucleus of friends on after the mob has departed, arrange this privately when extending your invitations.

—You may have a few dreamy acquaintances who chronically forget the time of your party; telephone them the day before to remind them, or send them a note.

Preliminaries

Most guests at a party will unbend only if the host himself can relax, and this means taking care of party details hours before the party or frequently a day or days in advance. After phoning your invitations, go through a dry run of all phases of the party, and make a list of the spadework that can be comfortably done beforehand.

—Take an inventory of your glassware, china, silverware, linen, chairs, etc., and make sure they're adequate for the number you've invited.

—Equipment such as glassware, platters, punch bowls, etc., may be rented for special occasions, but be sure the equipment you rent is compatible with what you have; don't use gold-rimmed coffee cups on Mexican pottery saucers.

—For outdoor bashes, be sure there's an ample supply of towels and other amenities for ablutions.

—In a crowded area, move out small objects that clutter the floor, like footstools, plants, etc.

—Choose the discs or cartridges for your stereo, and have them within easy reach.

—Set up the hors d'oeuvres or buffet table as well as the bar in an accessible spot, but don't use a low coffee table that will be monopolized by those guests at adjacent chairs or sofa.

—Enjoy your party, but don't drink intemperately before or during the party.

—For an al fresco party, arrange beforehand for all outdoor supplies—charcoal, bottled gas, outdoor chairs, cushions, debugger, etc., but also make alternative preparations for indoor partying in case of rain.

—If it's going to be a smallish get-together for no more than five or six couples, you'll probably be able to handle the drinks and food yourself, without having to spend half your time in the kitchen or behind the bar. But if you're planning a grand gala for more than twelve, you'll be well advised to arrange for outside help—unless you want to make do with premixed punch and prepared finger food.

Party Help

Although hiring help to take care of mixing drinks, serving food, and cleaning is the simplest way for a host to become a guest in his own house, certain guidelines are important.

—Hire only experienced help who, if possible, come recommended by someone you know.

—Explain the kind of party you're hosting, the number of people, time, menu, drinks, etc., and make sure they will be able to handle the work. If they are to look after extra details such as taking coats at the door, tidying the bathroom, etc., explain these duties beforehand. If additional help is required, discuss this now, too.

—If you have a special assignment such as unmolding an aspic, taking care of a chafing dish, or mixing a special punch recipe, make sure they understand and are able to handle it.

—Check their fee beforehand, after spelling out the duties and working hours.

—Make sure their uniforms are appropriate.

—Go over the menu, drink list, table setting, etc., at least an hour before the party.

—Pay them only after all cleanup has been completed.

A few duties may have to be held off to the last moment. Keep them at a minimum so that you'll be available for greeting guests and making introductions. Cold canapés, cold sandwiches covered with a damp cloth, and cold salads or meat should be on platters in the refrigerator ready for the hors d'oeuvres or buffet table. Hot foods in casseroles or on baking sheets should be ready to be popped into the preheated oven. Sometimes a job is best handled in several stages beforehand. For instance, if you're planning to serve Irish coffee on a cold day, buy the whiskey, coffee, and cream the day before, whip the cream about a half-hour before guests arrive, have the coffee maker filled but don't plug it in until the last moment.

Another key to relaxation for the thoughtful host is simply rehearsing. If, for instance, you're concocting a wine cup you've never made before, or a punch, it's a good idea to swizzle up a half-pint or so the day before the party. Even if you're going to use a tried and tested recipe, a quick run-through can be useful; you may be using a different gin than you formerly used, or the lemons may not be as tart in the fall as in the spring. The practice run gives you the polish and assurance that every skillful host enjoys.

If you're planning a bacchanalia to start at three o'clock on a weekend afternoon, set your bedside alarm for an early hour in the morning rather than noontime; it'll take longer than you think to wrap up all the last-minute details. You'll be doing yourself and your guests another favor if you not only write out a work agenda beforehand but refer to it frequently along the way, starting long before partytime. All such schedules are only worth the paper they're written on unless they're checked and carried out. And make sure those bunches of watercress that were so hard to find are actually decorating the platters of cold cuts and not buried in the refrigerator for you to stumble over next week.

When the revelers arrive, remind yourself that no matter how busy the whirl, everyone appreciates a congenial word of welcome at the door. Shake the hands of the men *and* the women, a charming European custom that American men should adopt. And a gracious kiss is appropriate for all women whom you've previously met.

Expect that each guest will arrive with parched throat and ravenous appetite; offer drinks within moments, trays of hors d'oeuvres within minutes. Since the greeting of guests at the door and first-round dispensing of drinks is always fast-moving, it's a good idea to have a friend or inamorata act as cohost. The load is lightened, of course, if you've hired a bartender.

Introductions depend entirely on the size of the party. At small gatherings, it may be feasible to introduce newcomers all the way around; but in a larger crowd, introducing each new arrival to all present becomes increasingly time-consuming and stiff, and names and faces usually become a blur after four or five exchanges. If possible, make two or three strategic introductions for latecomers—preferably to those with whom they'll have something in common—or, if this means fighting your way across the room, introduce them to whomever is nearest at hand. Again, a cohost can ease your burden.

At an outdoor barbecue, a cohost or cochef is almost essential if the host is to fill his customary role of presiding over the fire ritual. If there are both host and hostess, it's usually and quite blindly taken for granted that she's too frail an understudy to care for an outdoor fire—although she's considered perfectly capable of handling a galley on a cruising yacht or any other indoor cooking job, however strenuous. Happily, both men and women are kicking over the traces of this old notion. At many outdoor parties even the guests tend to pitch in—basting meat, husking corn, pouring beer, and even grilling their own steaks and chops, thus adding to their own fun while reducing the host's ordeal by fire.

Hosts, like verbs, are either active or passive, with the active much to be preferred. The passive host is one who feels obliged only to line up his bottles of liquor and then point the way. However pleasant this may be for him, it's not appreciated by the guest who must then do battle with a half-dozen other eager drinkers, all vying for the bottle of Scotch. (There *are* times when a self-serve bar is welcome—at the end of a long, cold drive, for drop-ins at an impromptu drinking party, when the host is unavoidably shunted elsewhere.)

For a planned festivity, an active host enjoys doing rather than merely waiting on the sidelines, whether he's offering his own mint juleps, his Rhine-wine punch, or his midnight fondue. He'll naturally spot the dwindling rocks in an old-fashioned glass and offer renewals. His vigilant eye, undeterred by his own double Scotch, will tell him that a coaster is needed here, a napkin there. He'll check the air conditioning in the summer or toss an extra log on the fire in the winter. Instead of emptying ashtrays, his or his waiter's sleight of hand will simply put fresh ashtrays in place while the old unobtrusively disappear.

Even if he sponsors a catered party, the active host sees to it that the caterer's drinks provide a special éclat that sets them off from the routine drinks poured at committee meetings or the straight firewater tossed down at nightly commuters' bars. Every active host has a simple test for his drink offerings: Will his guests spot their special excellence? In almost everyone's drinking career, one is bound to meet up sooner or later with a memorable potable—a Ramos gin fizz in New Orleans, an outsize derby daiquiri on a tropical beach, a special champagne cocktail under countless stars. Such drinks don't just happen; the drinkmaster thoughtfully calls the shots or creates them. There are many hosts who, when it comes to food, will move heaven and every gourmet shop in the hemisphere if necessary to serve a barbecued blue-ribbon shell of aged beef, a platter of braised pheasant in sour cream, or a curry of fresh Maine lobster. The active host at his bar will do no less.

Talk about active hosts—in the South there are partisans who specialize in old-fashioneds. Before partytime they'll line up their old-fashioned glasses. In the bottom of each glass, lemon peel, sugar, and a trickle of boiling water are worked and reworked by hand with a muddler until the zest of the peel and the syrupy liquid in each glass turn to a rich, almost aged mellowness, when the best bourbon in the land is added. The glasses are stashed in the refrigerator or freezer for further ripening until the guests pile in, and then rocks are placed in each glass just before serving. A host with an aide or two will think nothing of building up two or three dozen glasses in this manner. Neither he nor his guests ever need an excuse for toasting. They drink to the drink itself.

But while a host should be active and should generously offer his punches, his pitchers or trays of cocktails, he should remember at the height of his wassailing that he's a host and not a hustler. The host should rely on his sixth sense to tell him that bibbers here and there are getting too much of a glow on and the moment has arrived when the restoratives of food and hot coffee are needed to provide the mellow slowdown in which every good drinking party basks. Guests know their own capacities. Let them be pleased with, not plied with, drinks.

A talented drinking host, the kind who's born with a barspoon in his mouth, always feels free to create his own drinking customs. Guests will invariably stretch out their hands to welcome his offerings at almost any hour of the day or night. If a man decides to serve champagne at eleven o'clock in the morning rather than at midnight, his guests will hail the novelty as the host's inalienable right. Generations ago, a bottle of vintage port would be opened late at night, before a fireplace and under the frowns of ancestors preserved in oil and canvas. But a host today, if he wishes, may tap his vintage port after eighteen holes of golf, or carry it to his ski lodge, or sip it in a secluded picnic spot, in each case with mellow contentment. Bachelors these days frequently find themselves serving breakfast or brunch, and few if any guests would question the host's judgment in mixing his fresh orange juice with vodka or tequila or Madeira. If called upon, the host could cite numerous precedents for serving spirits in the morning. Besides John Adams's aforementioned tankard of hard cider before breakfast, there are the Germans, who now, as of yore, serve their Steinhäger gin or schnapps and their thin Westphalian ham on a wooden plate as regular matutinal fare. Novelty for novelty's sake is hardly the aim of the modern host at his bar, but novelty that becomes an unexpected pleasure turns everybody on.

As for tradition, that, too, has its place. Take toasting: No host in his right mind would rise like a stuffed phoenix from the dining table and toast a guest just because his renowned pedigree or station in life made him theoretically toastable. But if one of his guests had just stepped into a new job, was about to fly to the other side of the globe, had just completed his Ph.D. thesis, was just engaged or just married, a toast in his honor would add to the general merriment. The strict tradition prescribing that the one toasted responds or toasts in return needn't be followed unless the toastee desires it. Traditionally this give-and-take applies to men toasted; women (another putdown?) are supposed to merely smile with lowered eyelids. In any case, raising glasses can be immense fun without speech following speech like two sides of a debating team. The Scandinavian custom of intimate toasting, in which the man looks fondly into the eyes of the woman beside him or across the table and then silently raises his glass, is sometimes the most articulate of all toasts.

Au Revoir

Your interest in your guests and sincere care for them should be evident even as they are leaving.

—Although you may have set an hour for the party's end, it shouldn't be an ironclad schedule—some dawdling is to be expected and even encouraged in the fond farewells, and a brief chat at the door or on the terrace adds a pleasant glow to the festivities.

—Help guests with their clothes or sporting gear, or arrange for a cohost to help them.

—If single people are leaving unaccompanied and do not have a car, and if someone is driving in their direction, arrange, if possible, for them to share the ride.

—In an apartment, take guests to the elevator, and wait till they've entered.

—Alert the apartment doorman beforehand or tip him in advance so that if a cab is needed he'll be ready for your departing guests.

—At a suburban home, walk your guests to their car if feasible; provide an umbrella if necessary.

—If someone is too deeply in his cups, arrange for a taxi to take him home, or drive him home yourself.

All in all, inviting guests for drinks is a perfect way for a man living alone to entertain. Your bachelor apartment may be comparatively small, but if your food and drink are keyed for intimate fun, your friends will happily embrace the chance to crowd into your cozy quarters. More and more hosts nowadays—bachelors as well as non-bachelors—are getting away from the stodgy notion that parties attended must be parties repaid, like meeting a bank note on a certain date. The whole idea isn't to load your guests down with both liquor and an obligation to return the liquor, but simply to share fun and friendship.

2

GLASSWARE

The Long and Short of It

Because fine glasses make drinking surprisingly more pleasurable, you should acquire those that are both functional and elegantly shaped. They should be so handsome that the mere sight of the sparkling, clear glasses on the shelf makes you want to pour liquor into them and begin quaffing. In choosing them, it isn't necessary to spend months delving into the drinking customs of Roman nobles, who fashioned wine cups after the most beautiful breasts of the day, or attempt to acquire gilt-decorated goblets made by Venetian glassmakers in the seventeenth century. It is helpful, however, to understand crystal and lime glass.

Crystal is glassware that contains lead, and the lead gives it weight, a bell-like tone, magnificent luster, and also a magnificent price.

Lime glass (or soda-lime glass) lacks lead as one of its components and, while comparatively inexpensive, lacks the brilliance of crystal.

Crystal made in Europe is about twenty-five percent lead. In the United States the lead content may fall below twenty percent, and such crystal is sometimes called "half-lead" glassware. For fine entertaining, for displaying the rich color of a fine wine, crystal drinking vessels and the liquid poured into them are mutually flattering. For more casual entertaining, lime glassware not only costs less but in some cases is more durable than its elegant cousin.

A label that says "hand-blown" or "mouth-blown" is usually the guide to the handsomest of all glassware. *Hand-blown* simply refers to the method wherein the glassmaker dips a long tube into a pot of molten glass, picks up a blob at one end of his pipe, and then, with his lips and breath as tools, blows until the bowl takes shape. He twists, turns, rubs, and paddles the blown bubble until it reaches its final perfect curve. *Blown* glassware is similar but made by machine. *Pressed* glassware—the least expensive—is made by pouring molten glass into molds from which it takes its shape. Today you can find drinkware of pressed glass with heavenly lines and limpid forms. Finally there's *cut glass*—that is, glass cut or engraved and polished to reflect as much prismatic light as possible—the darling of conservative drinkers and very impressive when used for an old-fashioned cocktail or whiskey and soda.

Regardless of the quality of glassware you decide on, you'll find it available in three basic shapes:

(1) *Tumblers*—glasses of cylindrical shape, sometimes with a heavy or "sham" bottom which makes them stable.

(2) *Footed glasses*—glasses of cylindrical or bowl shape which rest on a round pedestal or foot but with no stem.

(3) *Stemware*—glasses consisting of a bowl, stem, and foot.

Stemware is not only gracious to the eye but can be held in the hand without warming the contents of the bowl and is also easier on furniture, since condensation on the cold glass rarely makes its way down to the base or foot. Tumblers are less formal, more secure, and usually less expensive than the other two types, although some cut-glass tumblers are in the Rolls-Royce category.

If you want to limit yourself to only two kinds of glasses, the first one to buy is the on-the-rocks glass. It's simply an old-fashioned-cocktail glass, with or without a short stem. In our time it's become the bearer for any potable from ale to Zinfandel. It's practical not only for cocktails but for whiskey, rum, gin, and vodka, and every now and then— to everyone's intense surprise—it is used for the old-fashioned cocktail of bourbon or Scotch, the drink for which it was originally designed. The other most sought-after glass is the tulip-shaped wineglass, holding from 8 to 11 ounces, allowing ample space for swirling and releasing the wine's bouquet. It, too, has leaped way beyond its birthright and is now the vehicle for any liquid from champagne to stout.

Oddball hosts, game for anything, have even been known to pour water into it.

You'll want to supplement your glass supply with such specialized vessels as sour glasses, steins and Pilsners, highball glasses, ponies, jiggers, and hollow-stemmed champagne glasses (see the photographs of glittering glassware and descriptions of each), but it's no longer necessary to stock an infinite variety of glassware. Although it was once customary for the proper host to set out an assortment of glasses at the dinner table in anticipation of the wines that were offered with each course, now, even at black-tie dinners, you seldom see four different kinds of wineglasses arrayed like four empty-headed guardsmen. Nine times out of ten there will be one all-purpose glass for one carefully chosen wine. If a Sauternes or champagne is passed with the dessert or if port follows the demitasse, another appropriate glass can be brought on at that time.

It's also unnecessary to have all your glassware in the same pattern. Matching beverageware should be used at the dining table, but before or after dinner the patterns may vary. Dry sherry on the rocks can be poured on your patio in lightweight old-fashioned glasses; whiskey and soda by the hearth in stately, heavy-bottomed highball glasses.

How many glasses should you own? It depends on the maximum number of people your pad can comfortably contain at any one time. Double it for drop-ins and for normal glassware breakage. Thus, if you normally invite eight for a party, stock sixteen of each kind of glass you'd most likely use.

Buying Tips

When stocking your bar glassware for the first time or replenishing the odd or incomplete assortment of glasses you may now own, keep the following guides in mind:

—Ask if the glass is crystal or lime glass; no reputable shop will represent a glass as crystal if it is not genuine.

—Ask if it is hand-blown or machine-made; the former is more expensive although not necessarily more suitable for your own needs.

—When selecting crystal, you cannot analyze a glass for its lead content. Look instead for its clarity and brilliance; hold it up to the light—there should be no bubbles, wavy lines, uneven edges, or other obvious imperfections.

—Test crystal for its bell-like tone. Using a pencil, tap the top of the glass near the edge; crystal glasses of slightly different shape from the same manufacturer will give off tones of different pitches; when you tap lime glass, the sound will be flat and edgy.

—Ask if the glass is open stock—that is, a standard product continuously available for a reasonable period of time so that replacements can be made to keep a full set. Some bargain lines of imported glassware available during the midwinter holidays are sometimes one-time offerings, and cannot be replaced; even some American open-stock items aren't available indefinitely, and you may be frustrated if you try to replace several glasses from a set you bought five years ago.

—If you are selecting cut-crystal glassware, check to see that the cut edges of the design are distinct and uniform and that the glass when held to the light has a sparkling prismatic effect.

—Consider the glasses you are buying in relation to your table, linen, and china to be sure they are compatible or complementary.

—Hold the glass you are considering to make sure it has a balanced feel and that the stem is comfortable; if it is a glass with a narrow top —such as a dock glass for sherry or port—make sure it is adequate for "nosing" the wine.

—Ask if the glassware is dishwasher-safe; some extremely expensive glasses of gossamer weight, or glasses with a gold band, must be washed by hand.

The higher mathematics of whether a drinking glass should hold 6 or 8½ or 10⅝ ounces isn't important if you're pouring punch from a bowl, or beer from a bottle or keg; you merely pour until you have what your thirst says is a reasonable amount and stop. But if you're concocting a particular cocktail following a particular recipe and the ingredients are designed to fill a 4½-ounce cocktail glass and your glass holds a miserly 3 ounces, you'll find yourself with more drinks than you intended or with seconds that slosh around with ice until they're too weak to serve. If you're buying champagne for a party and you don't know whether your glasses hold 5½ ounces or 7 ounces, you can miscalculate badly. For special concoctions and for mass drinking, you really should know the capacity of the drinking vessels you own. If necessary, fill them with water and pour the contents into a measuring glass or beaker from the chem lab. Make a note of their capacity and use it as a guide for the next party.

Among offbeat drinking vessels you may want to consider, there are special glasses emblazoned with hens, tomatoes, or oranges designed for hosts who respectively specialize in bullshots, bloody marys, and screwdrivers; for the aquatic cocktail hour there are swimming-pool glasses that float; glacier tumblers with walls that retain the cold can be prechilled in the freezing section of your refrigerator for long icy chills of gin and tonics, cuba libres, etc.; moscow-mule copper cups are available for husky drafts of ginger beer and vodka; the Irish-coffee goblet with thick stem is designed for comfortably grasping the hot brew of coffee, Irish whiskey, and cream; for warm wassail in the wintertime, you'll need capacious beverage mugs with handles that stay cool; finally, for extra-large parties of fifty to a hundred people, particularly outdoor bashes, you'll probably want the disposable, well-designed, very thin plastic drinkware with no fear of insufficient glasses or cleanup problems. How many kinds of specialized beverageware you'll need depends entirely on your life-style.

Taking Care of Glassware

Whether you use a bartender at a party or do your own pouring, there are a few practical rules for handling glassware.

—Wash glasses in warm water with detergent as soon as possible after each use; use a dishwasher if glasses are dishwasher-safe, but stack them in the machine with special care. If glasses are expensive crystal, it may be prudent to wash them by hand no matter what the label says.

—Avoid putting cold glasses in scalding water; temperature extremes may crack them.

—Glasses that may be sticky on the bottom after being used for liqueurs should be soaked before washing.

—Cut glass sometimes shows a film on the cut areas and may have to be soaked in warm water with detergent and scrubbed with a small brush in the crevices of the design.

—Do not stack glasses in the sink or on the shelf. If by any chance glasses have been stacked and are locked, place the bottom glass in warm water and fill the top with cold; the resulting expansion and contraction should separate them safely.

—If hand-washed, dry glasses with a lint-free towel or, better yet, if thirsty guests aren't waiting for another round of drinks, let the glasses drain dry upside down on a ridged drainboard.

—Use a paper towel or tissue paper to give added brilliance to crystal.

—Glasses may be stored on the shelf either right side up or upside down, but in either case never crowd the glasses, allowing a margin of about an inch if possible between them.

—If glasses have been stored on the shelf for months and have been unused, they may be covered with a dusty or sticky film sometimes caused by cooking fumes; check them before partytime and wash them if necessary.

—Be sure all glasses used for wine tasting are immaculate, with no trace of detergent from a previous washing.

3

KEEP YOUR SPIRITS UP

Let's assume you're planning to stock a home bar and you don't as yet own an ounce of straight stuff. You may remember the time when mixed drinks meant martinis, manhattans, and highballs. A host of that period acquiring the rudiments of the *ars bibendi* knew that if he owned gin, whiskey, and vermouth, he had the basic trio for serving the popular mixed drinks of his day. In recent years one single drink, the vodka martini, has moved gin to a second-fiddle position. And in less time than it takes to say margarita or daiquiri, you realize that tequila and rum are now indispensable for the starting lineup.

It's always a comfortable if not sumptuous feeling to buy your liquor leisurely rather than under the pressure of some sudden emergency at the liquor cabinet. It's good to know that your supply of spirits is varied and ample, and that it's at your elbow for drop-ins as well as for pre-arranged dinners. But in stocking a bar for the first time or building up your present liquor inventory, don't attempt to range the gamut of the spirit world from anisette to zubrovka; consider rather the tastes of the group that socializes casually with you. Every host soon learns that a special Scotch provides a warm afterglow for some of his comrades, a certain bourbon is preferred by others. If the drinking companions in your neck of the woods have a habitual thirst for sloe gin fizzes, you'll want to have sloe gin on hand even though it isn't mentioned in any of the combinations below. If there are those in your crowd who are only happy with Harvey Wallbangers (orange juice, vodka, and Galliano liqueur), you'll need Galliano, and ignore the liquor adviser who tells you Galliano is only an after-dinner liqueur.

You'll save money on any liquor by buying the large size, 1¾ liters (formerly ½ gallon), whenever possible, and if you regularly use a large amount of a specific liquor, the case price is usually more economical than the bottle price. But at the outset, a typical supply might reasonably consist of the following bottled goods in what are still called quarts but are now liters, 33.8 ounces.

3 Vodka
2 Bourbon
2 Blended whiskey, U.S.
2 Scotch
1 Canadian whisky
2 Gin
2 Rum
2 Tequila
1 Dry vermouth
1 Sweet vermouth
1 Brandy, U.S.
3 Assorted liqueurs (fruit, coffee, crème de menthe, etc.)
1 Aperitif (Campari, Dubonnet, etc.)
Total cost: about $140.

As your spirit world expands, you'll begin to think of diversifying this basic closet with a variety of other potables. If, for example, your basic vodka is American, you'll add Finnish or Russian vodka, or one of the imported flavored vodkas like zubrovka. You may want to add one of the high-proof English gins or perhaps a bottle of Holland genever gin. If you started with light Puerto Rican rum, you might want to enhance your offering with an aged Puerto Rican añejo rum or one of the 151-proof rums. Thus your starting repertory might reasonably be expanded to include varieties like these:

Whiskey—Irish
Scotch—twelve-year-old blend or single-malt (unblended)
Gin—English, Dutch, German Steinhäger

Vodka—Finnish, Russian, Polish, zubrovka, pepper-flavored

Rum—Martinique, Virgin Islands, Jamaican, añejo, 151-proof

Brandy—Cognac, Armagnac, apple, German, Greek Metaxa, ouzo

Liqueurs—from straight flavors like apricot or banana to pro-
prietary brands like Southern Comfort, Wild Turkey, Grand
Marnier, Cointreau, Chartreuse, Drambuie, Benedictine, Peter
Heering, etc.

Apéritifs—Cynar, Amer Picon, Byrrh, Punt e Mes

Going still further one might wish to add:

Whiskey—Japanese Suntory

Unaged brandies—aquavit, slivovitz, kirschwasser

For the average bar host, $120 would cover a reasonable selection
from the two preceding categories.

Having stocked your bar with potables calculated to satisfy the tastes
of your most sophisticated guests, you may wonder whether, under
any circumstances, you should consider stocking and serving any of
the imposing list of bottled premixed cocktails.

Premixed drinks are especially useful if you're hiring a bartender
of doubtful talent for an evening's work, or when, at the end of a long,
dusty day, you may not have fresh lemons for your Tom Collins thirst;
the bottled gin sours made into tall drinks with ice and club soda will
perform well as understudies, while bottled whiskey sours elongated
with ice and soda are quickly transformed into whiskey collinses. On
boat trips, in cramped galley quarters, at wayside picnics, for tailgate
bars at football or ski sites, the premixed partymates are most welcome.
But the fact is that little labor is saved by using them. If you're serving
a bottled martini, for example, you still have to prechill the glasses,
take ice out of the freezer, mix and stir the makings in a shaker, pour
them, and adorn each martini with an olive or a lemon twist.

Nevertheless, effort aside, there are some premixed cocktails that
will serve you well. The number of such mixes cramming the shelves
in liquor stores has grown from a few standard combos to such specialty
items as mai tais and stingers—and a few of them are actually first-
rate. Among the best of the lot is the bottled manhattan, which may be
even better than the one you make yourself. When the two ingredients
—whiskey and vermouth—not only mingle but marry, as they do in
the bottle, the result is as superior to the fresh-made mixture as a curry

on the third or fourth day. And no one would presume to fault—or imitate—the excellence of English Pimm's No. 1 Cup, the definitive premixed base for a gin sling; or the subtlety of that aristocrat of after-dinner drinks, B & B, an epicurean admixture of brandy and Benedictine.

But be warned that there are limits to these distillery-born combinations. While manufactured manhattans, martinis, Rob Roys, and black russians may turn up winners, the great majority of premixes made with fruit juice draw an average-to-poor grade, simply because bottled orange or lemon juice can't begin to match the fresh. Our advice: Be as selective about the premixes you purchase as you are about the appropriate occasions to serve them. For most purposes—and people—it's more fitting (and more fun) to do it yourself.

There will be times when your normal bar supply will be temporarily expanded for mass drinking—a big cocktail celebration, a holiday blowout, or similar affair where the number of heads and the possible number of drinks must be estimated. In such cases, the slide rule works like this: A fifth of hard liquor will be enough for seventeen 1½-ounce (standard-size) drinks. A liter (formerly quart), will provide twenty-two drinks. At a dinner party, count on two to four jiggers of hard liquor per person, dispensed in either straight or mixed forms. At a bachelor party, allow from three to six jiggers.

Finally, a few sensible reminders to all custodians of liquor:

Your bar may be a movable one on wheels, a built-in piece of sectional furniture, the shelves above a clothes closet, a tea wagon, or a wicker hamper in the back of your station wagon. Reserve supplies may be stashed away wherever it's convenient—in cellar or attic. But within easy reach, close to your mixing counter, there should be one bottle of each commonly used liquor. Your inventory isn't an old rock collection to be hunted behind bookshelves, nor is a host normally able to pop fifths Houdini-like out of a silk hat. Keep everything arranged so conveniently that you can find the liquor you're looking for without fumbling or squinting at labels. For big blowouts, punch-bowl and holiday parties, fill in your stock well in advance of the fest itself. Don't get caught scrounging for replacements at the eleventh hour.

A host may commence many things; he may finish few. But every host at his home-bar base learns that the one thing that always gets finished is liquor. Still, you may now and then find an odd bottle that has reached the aged-in-the-coffin stage. Take such oddments, supplement them with fresh liquors, and turn them into coolers, pitchers, or punches. It's fun to invent them and to make room simultaneously for new liquors that may readily become a going concern.

Filling a wine rack or a wine cellar is a separate avocation dealt with in Chapter 17.

4

ALL THE TRIMMINGS

The applied art of mixing alcoholic drinks depends on many things that aren't alcohol. There would be no screwdrivers without orange juice, no daiquiris without limes, and Irish coffee without coffee and whipped cream would be just a glass of whiskey. Alcohol must be made tart, sweet, rich, bitter, foamy, and in countless other ways congenial to sophisticated taste buds. Frequently it's garnished in a manner that accents a drink's appearance as well as its flavor and aroma, as with the olive in the martini, the cucumber peel in the Pimm's Cup, or the strawberry in the champagne cocktail.

Quantities of accessories for mixing will depend upon whether you're going in for mass drinking or for more modest quenching. As a rule, small containers of seasonings like bitters are less likely to lose their zest than larger bottles that hang around on the shelf too long. Large bottles of syrups like Falernum or red-currant syrup will lose their bright color and flavor if untouched for months. If this occurs, don't hesitate to discard the old stock and buy fresh replacements. Fruits or other perishables should be emphatically fresh.

The checklist which follows should be consulted not only for setting up a basic bar stock but every time you're hosting a drinking party of sizable dimensions. Normal bar items that belong in any basic bar are marked with an asterisk to differentiate them from those less frequently used.

Mixing Aids

Almonds   Use them whole for Scandinavian glögg, sliced or julienne for floating on punches and tall summer drinks.

Almond syrup   Called orgeat when made in France, orzata when made in Italy. Some liqueurs with a vivid almondlike flavor such as amaretto, made from apricot pits, may be used in place of the non-alcoholic almond syrup.

Apple juice   Often found in congenial company with vodka. The space-saving frozen concentrated variety is handy for parties. (See also Cider.)

Apricots   Whole peeled canned apricots are better than the fresh for velvety blender drinks.

Bananas   Should always be speckled ripe for bar purposes. They're turned to best account in banana daiquiris.

*Bitter lemon   A superior mixer in high esteem among the gin-and-tonic crowd.

Bitter lemon concentrate   An essence that may be added to plain club soda in an emergency.

*Bitters   Best-known is Angostura from Trinidad, but orange bitters are sometimes preferred for drinks that benefit from a soupçon of citrus. It's a good idea to keep Peychaud's bitters (obtainable in some areas only in liquor stores) on hand for making New Orleans sazeracs.

Butter   Use fresh sweet butter for a mellow glow in hot buttered rum.

Cassis   This black-currant syrup—simpatico with vermouth—is similar to crème de cassis, except that it contains no alcohol.

*Cherries   Most common are the maraschino, with or without stems. Mint-flavored cherries provide a green decorative note; brandied pitted red cherries and pitted black cherries, with or without rum flavor, complete the cherry constellation.

Cider In groceries, "apple cider" and "apple juice" are synonymous terms for pasteurized juice of the apple. Country cider, sold at roadside stands, is often partially fermented apple juice. Hard cider is apple juice fermented to the wine stage.

Cinnamon sticks (or stick cinnamon) Used for both stirring and flavoring hot mulled mixes. Buy the extra-long sticks for drinks in deep mugs.

Cloves Add them whole (not ground) to hot winter wassail.

*Club soda Buy it in splits for individual drinks, the 12-ounce size for several highballs, and quarts for parties or punch bowls. Most national brands have good bite and can keep their fizz locked up overnight or even several days. Generally, club soda provides more zing than seltzer water despite the convenience of the siphon.

Cocktail mixes (Not to be confused with bottled premixed cocktails.) Nonalcoholic mixes are never the equal of the fresh ingredients, but many hosts like to keep them on hand as reserve ammunition. Mixes for the bloody mary, daiquiri, mai tai, manhattan, navy grog, scorpion, and whiskey sour have become standard items in many home bars. While all bottles have specific mixing directions on them, try varying the alcohol/mix ratio to suit your own taste.

Coffee Brew it fresh and strong for steaming Irish coffee.

Cranberry juice Adds brilliant color and eye-opening tartness to punches and vodka drinks.

Cream Use heavy sweet cream for alexanders and dessert drinks.

Currant syrup Red currants (rather than black cassis berries) go into this tart extract. It's not a substitute for grenadine but a flavoring component in its own right.

Eggs There would be no nog without them—nor a number of frothy confections such as clover clubs, silver fizzes, and the like. Use small size for individual drinks.

Falernum A delightful West Indian syrup made from almonds and spices.

*Frothee Creamy Head   A few dashes will give mixed drinks the creamy cap supplied otherwise by egg whites; however, the head tends to disappear faster than an egg-white head.

*Ginger ale   The drier the better for modern tastes.

Ginger beer   The second-fiddle catalyst in a moscow mule.

Grape juice   One of vodka's many compatible consorts. The frozen concentrated form is a space saver.

Grapefruit juice   The one fruit juice that's better canned or frozen than fresh, undoubtedly because the latter is often so insipid and varies so much in flavor. The unsweetened variety is best for drink making.

Grenadine   A bright-red syrup made from the pulp of pomegranates, it's used in Jack Rose, clover club, Bacardi, and many other cocktails, as well as in punches and tall drinks. Unlike most additives, it can be stored on the shelf for long periods without losing its tint or tartness. Grenadine liqueur, made by Leroux, may be used in place of its non-alcoholic cousin.

Guanabana nectar   The luscious juice of the soursop, moderately sweetened, makes a delicious partner in rum drinks.

Guava jelly   Melted down to a syrup, it's used for sweetening Caribbean rum drinks.

Honey   Use a light-colored honey for bar purposes. If granulation occurs, place the jar in hot water for a few minutes and then stir until the granules disappear.

*Lemons   They should be firm and green-stemmed. The size of the fruit is not too important, since most recipes using lemon juice are most successful following ounce measurements. Before squeezing, using the palm of the hand, lean on the fruit on a cutting board, rolling it back and forth to make squeezing easier and to extract more juice.

Lemon juice   The bottled juice, whether in glass or plastic containers, never equals the fresh-squeezed variety and should be kept on hand for emergency use only.

*Limes   A far from silent partner in almost all rum drinks. Choose limes with smooth green skin rather than yellow.

Lime juice As with lemon juice, the bottled product should be used only in emergencies.

*Lime juice, sweetened The best-known brand, Rose's, is actually a tart syrup rather than a substitute for fresh lime juice, and is an essential ingredient in a gimlet.

Mangoes or mango nectar An exotic ingredient in certain tall rum drinks.

Maple syrup Occasionally used as a drink sweetener.

Milk Essential in many brandy drinks, milk punch, and eggnogs. Use whole milk rather than skimmed for best results.

Mint Fresh mint leaves are best if taken from the mint patch directly to julep cups or glasses. In buying them, choose mint leaves that are deep green rather than yellowed, small tender leaves rather than large.

Nutmeg For flips, nogs, mulls, and other hot cold-weather drinks, buy the whole nutmeg for grating rather than the ground.

*Olives Although the small pitted variety is a standard bar ingredient, many martini men prefer the unpitted, stuffed colossal, or supercolossal. There are also almond-, anchovy- and onion-stuffed olives, all of which are delightful; and even pitted black olives are used in certain martini-type drinks. Be sure to store recapped jars in the refrigerator; olives should be kept in their own brine and washed just before serving. If stored opened more than several weeks, flavor will deteriorate.

*Onions, cocktail or pearl The *sine qua non* of the gibson cocktail. Buy them in small jars and store in the refrigerator after opening. Bottled in vinegar or in vermouth and vinegar.

Orange-flower water An essential ingredient in Ramos gin fizz—sometimes labeled *fleur d'orange*. Available on gourmet shelves as well as drugstores and some liquor shops.

*Oranges Juice from fresh oranges is always better than frozen juice or the kind that comes in cartons or bottles, even though the fresh fruit varies widely in sweetness and color during the year. (Frozen juice also varies widely in quality from one brand to the next. If you must use it, say, for large blowouts, select the best brand you can find.)

Orange slices   Actually wedges rather than slices, they're packed in syrup in jars. They provide a rich garnish for old-fashioneds.

Orgeat   (from France) or
Orzata (from Italy)   Nonalcoholic almond syrups. (See above.)

Papaya syrup or nectar   One of the tropical juices occasionally called for in Polynesian rum drinks.

Passion-fruit juice or nectar   A pleasantly tart mixer used in rum drinks.

Peaches   Sliced fresh in season, they make an elegant adornment for champagne, sparkling Rhine wine, and wine cups. Elbertas—frozen or canned—are best for crushed-ice blender drinks.

Pineapple   When buying, check for ripeness: The top center leaves should come out easily and the fruit should have a heavy, musky pineapple aroma. Pineapple cocktail sticks in syrup are a pleasant cocktail garnish.

Pineapple juice   Best for bar purposes is the frozen concentrated juice, canned unsweetened next. If canned juice is stored in the refrigerator after opening the can, be sure to pour it into a glass jar and cover tightly to ward off other refrigerator aromas.

Quinine concentrate   Used for making quinine water by adding to siphon water or club soda; it's useful on boats and in other cramped bar quarters.

*Quinine water   A staple bar item that you should keep on hand in quantity for warm-weather drinks.

Raspberries   Use fresh or frozen in summer wine cups, punch bowls, and blender drinks.

Raspberry syrup   This bar sweetener, not as tart as grenadine, has its own distinctive fruit-with-a-punch flavor.

Salt   Keep a saltcellar at your bar for bloody marys, bloody marias, etc. Celery salt is widely appreciated both in the bloody genre and in pick-me-ups. A special margarita salt flavored with lemon is packed in wide containers for rim dipping.

Seltzer water   Fizz from a seltzer bottle seldom has the liveliness of club soda, but it's convenient. A cartridge charge for permanent siphon equipment is a modern space saver.

*7-Up   The most popular of all light carbonated lemon drinks, this one can be mixed with almost any conceivable potable.

Soft drinks   Besides cola drinks and ginger ale, such flavors as pineapple, coffee, and grapefruit are pleasant tall-drink extenders.

Strawberries   Fresh berries make a colorful garnish for May wine, wine cups, fancy drinks, and summer fruit bowls. Frozen ones can be used in blender drinks with crushed ice.

Strawberry syrup   One of the brightest members of the family of red bar sweeteners. Be sure it's a natural, not artificial, fruit flavor—and don't keep it too long on the shelf.

*Sugar   For bar purposes, superfine sugar, which dissolves quickly, is preferred to plain granulated; but if kept too long after the box is opened, it will tend to lump, in which case it should be put through a fine sieve. Do not use confectioners' sugar. Brown sugar is rarely called for except in hot mulled drinks.

Sugar syrup   Some of the commercially prepared table syrups may be too thick for blending easily. Exceptions are Wuppermann's bar syrup and rock candy syrup. Make your own (see page 40).

Tea   Punch bowls of colonial times, now happily being revived, often called for brewed tea as part of the liquid. Brew it for five minutes, then let it cool at room temperature to prevent the drink from clouding.

*Tomato juice   The base for bloody marys and many other pick-me-ups. Buy straight tomato juice rather than tomato-juice cocktail. Jars, rather than cans, are best for refrigerator storage.

Vegetable juice   Sometimes preferred to tomato juice in a bloody mary because its blend of flavors gives a somewhat livelier, more interesting flavor to the drink.

*Water   At out-of-the-way picnic nooks and lonely beach sites, a bottle of this offbeat ingredient is sometimes desirable as an additive to Scotch. In localities where tap water is rusty or has a pronounced taste of chlorine, use bottled spring water.

Worcestershire sauce A snappy accent for prairie oysters, bloody marys, and the like.

Besides accessories for mixing drinks, a host's larder should contain a reasonable supply of appetizers in jars, cans, or packages which can be tapped on a moment's notice. It isn't necessary to enumerate the king-size list of chips, nuggets, wafers, spreads, and other ready-to-munch snacks piled high in deli shops and supermarkets. But for the host who likes to offer his drop-ins something better than the old peanut-and-potato-chip alms, and who doesn't have time for the preparation of his own freshly made hors d'oeuvres, there are distinguished delicacies, many of them imported, one can store in the larder. Most of them require no refrigeration. They are cited in the checklist below.

Prepared Hors d'Oeuvres for Drinks

(To make your own fresh hors d'oeuvres, see Chapter 24).

Anchovies *Flat fillets in oil, or rolled with capers, pimientos, or nuts*

Anchovy paste *A concentrated puree used for mixing with butter, cream cheese, etc.*

Artichoke hearts *Tiny, in olive oil*

Caviar *Best and most expensive is giant-grain fresh beluga, followed by sevruga and pressed caviar. Fresh caviars must be refrigerated; others in hermetically sealed jars may be kept on pantry shelves. Besides the above caviars from sturgeon, there are less expensive caviars processed from salmon, whitefish, and lumpfish.*

Cheese *Best types for laying in the hold and offering with drinks are the hard rather than the semisoft or soft cheeses. Best representatives: New York State aged Coon cheese; aged cheddar from U.S., Canada, and England; Cheshire from England; Welsh Caerphilly; French Tomelait; Swiss Emmentaler or natural Gruyère; Italian provolone or caciocavallo.*

Clams *Smoked in oil*

Cockles *Small English clams in vinegar or water*

Cocktail crackers, snacks, etc.   *Banana chips; biscuits for cheese such as Carr's, Jacob's, etc.; coconut chips; cheese sticks; salt sticks; onion sticks; Japanese rice crackers; pumpernickel in cans; Twiglets*

Cod liver   *Smoked in oil*

Eels   *Smoked fillets in oil*

Fish balls   *Swedish, small cocktail-size in lobster sauce*

Frogs' legs   *Smoked in oil*

Ham   *Deviled Smithfield; sliced prosciutto in cans or cryovac packages*

Herring   *Tidbits (Norwegian gaffelbiter)—in wine sauce, dill sauce, mustard sauce, etc.; fillets—Swedish, schmaltz, or matjes; sprats in oil*

Meatballs   *Small cocktail-size in sauce*

Mushrooms   *Tiny in olive oil; in olive oil, vinegar, and spices*

Mussels   *Smoked in oil; marinated; in butter; in tomato sauce*

Nuts   *Almonds, smoked; cashews, salted; macadamias; mixed nuts, roasted and salted*

Olives   *Martini; queen, ripe; stuffed with almonds, anchovies, or onions*

Oysters   *Smoked in oil*

Pâtés   *Pâté de foie gras (goose liver) with truffles in crocks or cans; pork pâté with truffles; pâté maison (loaf shape) of pork, eggs, spices, etc.; pâtés (purees for spreading) of anchovies, chicken livers, game, goose, sardines, smoked rainbow trout, smoked salmon, and smoked sturgeon*

Salami   *Narrow hard types such as salamini alla cacciatora and pepperoni, unsliced; sliced Genoa in cryovac packages*

Salmon, smoked   *Scandinavian, sliced in oil*

Sardines   *Boneless and skinless, French or Portuguese, in olive oil; bristling in olive oil, tomato sauce, or mustard*

Sausages   *Small cocktail-size in brine*

Shrimp   *Smoked in oil; tiny Scandinavian in brine*

Sprats   *In oil*

5

SAY WHEN

A Short Course in the New Math of Mixology

Y ou don't normally use a lab beaker marked in milliliters for pouring your Tennessee sour mash into an old-fashioned glass. Nor are you likely to plug in your calculator to verify that the quart of tonic water you're chilling holds 32 ounces. But whenever a resourceful barman plans a drink party for a dozen or two dozen people rather than the couple or foursome around a cocktail table, he makes it his business to know in advance the capacity of his bottles and glasses. You could always assume that a "fifth" was a fifth of a gallon whether it was bourbon or California brandy. But until recently whenever you began reading the fine print on the labels of some of the imported swig in liquor stores, you were likely to become numb with confusion before you were soothed by the swig itself. If you were selecting amaretto, you'd have noted that one bottle held 23 ounces, another 24 ounces, while a third contained 25 ounces. Not one corresponded to the traditional U.S. fifth (25.6 ounces). You'd pick up a bottle of apricot liqueur and it was 25 ounces; a bottle of triple sec was 24 ounces; Chartreuse turned out to be 23.6 ounces; while Cherry Marnier dipped to 22 ounces. Most likely you still have some of these bottles acquired in the liquid shell game.

Happily the wine-and-spirits wheel of chance will stop spinning in 1980, when all wines and spirits sold in the United States will, by federal regulation, be bottled in a limited set of specific sizes. Wines (except for those bottled abroad before 1979) will be sold in seven sizes instead of the previous sixteen sizes for American wines and twenty-seven for imports. Spirits will be available in six standard sizes only. The new bottles are part of the wider move to metrics. It may take years before you read the number of grams on a package of wild rice or the milliliter size of a can of tomato juice. But in 1980, whether you buy a bottle of domestic gin or German Jägermeister, you'll own a standard size from which there will be no deviation.

Undoubtedly the traditional 1½-ounce bar jigger will continue to be the standard unit for mixing or measuring individual drinks. Other units of liquid measurement from dash to demijohn, as well as old and new bottle sizes, are described below. They should help you take a recipe for a single drink and magnify it at will or reduce a giant-size punch bowl to the desired amount of wassail.

Dash   For all drink recipes in this book, a dash means ⅛ teaspoon; two dashes will thus fill a ¼-teaspoon measure. Theoretically, a dash is the amount of liquid that squirts out of a bottle equipped with a dash stopper. Stoppers, however, vary in size, and to different liquor dispensers a dash means anything from three drops up; but dashes have potent flavor or they wouldn't be dashes, so it's important to be as accurate as possible. Thus, if you're making sazeracs for sixteen people and you need sixteen times a dash of Pernod, a little calculating will quickly tell you that you need two teaspoons of Pernod, and it's best to measure it exactly rather than to take a clumsy guess.

Teaspoon   ⅓ tablespoon, or ⅙ ounce. Use a measuring teaspoon, not a long-handled barspoon, which is designed for mixing rather than measuring.

Tablespoon   3 teaspoons, or ½ ounce.

Pony   1 ounce, or the small end of a double-ended measuring jigger. Also the usual capacity of the liqueur glass or the pousse-café glass.

Jigger   1½ ounces. Also called a bar measuring glass, it's the standard measure for mixing individual drinks, though generous hosts use a 2-ounce jigger. Although jiggers are supposed to provide exact measurements, they're sometimes grossly inaccurate, so it's a good idea, if possible, to check any new jigger you buy with a lab measuring glass.

Wineglass   Used as a measuring term, it means 4 ounces, which is the old-fashioned wineglass filled to the brim. Though today wine is generally served in a much larger glass—one-third full to permit the wine to be swirled for releasing its bouquet—*wineglass* as a 4-ounce measure still appears in some drink recipes and in food recipes.

Hosts attempting to get the hang of the metric system should start with an old point of reference, namely the U.S. quart or 32 ounces. It will be replaced by the liter, which is slightly larger—33.8 ounces. The liter is subdivided into milliliters; there are 1000 in a liter, and they're shown in Table 1 and 2 as *ml.* Here then are the new bottle sizes and their closest corresponding old sizes.

Table 1

Spirits (Six Sizes)

(Now used for some bottlings. Mandated after December 31, 1979.)

Old Size Names	Old Size Fluid Oz.	New Metric Sizes Fluid Oz.	New Metric Sizes
Miniature	1.6	1.7	50 ml.
½ Pint	8.	6.8	200 ml.
Pint	16.	16.9	500 ml.
Fifth	25.6	25.4	750 ml.
Quart	32.	33.8	1 liter
½ Gallon	64.	59.2	1.75 liters

Table 2

Wines (Seven Sizes)

(Conversion must be complete by 1980 except for wines bottled abroad before January 1, 1979.)

Old Size Names	Old Size Fluid Oz.	New Metric Sizes Fluid Oz.	New Metric Sizes
Miniature	2, 3, or 4	3.4	100 ml.
⅖ Pint	6.4	6.3	187 ml.
⅘ Pint	12.8	12.7	375 ml.
Fifth	25.6	25.4	750 ml.
Quart	32.	33.8	1 liter
⅖ Gallon	51.2	50.7	1.5 liters
⅘ Gallon	102.4	101.4	3 liters

Needless to say, such colorful old containers as the demijohn—a narrow-necked bottle of either glass or stoneware containing from one to ten gallons—are out. Ditto for the tappit hen (about ⅗), the jeroboam (about ⅘), and the rehoboam (about 1⅕ gallons). Travelers to Europe may occasionally notice massive bottles of wine seldom shipped to the United States. These range from the Methuselah (1⅗ gallons) to the Nebuchadnezzar (about four gallons). Bottles of these huge dimensions are hard to fabricate in uniformly exact capacities. The U.S. government is proposing to allow some bottles of these lusty sizes to be used provided they are in exact liter sizes such as four liters, five liters, etc.

For the quantities of liquor, mixers, etc., to buy for party purposes, see the drink calculators (Tables 3, 4, and 5) in Chapter 25.

6

BARMANSHIP

Given a choice selection of spirits, fresh and flavorful mixing ingredients, and attractive glassware, the host at home is still several steps away from the professional bartender's finesse, an art that is public property for every drinker astride a barstool to behold. It looks deceptively easy, especially to the eye that's been mellowed by two or three dry martinis. But there are skills, tricks of the trade, and tips in creating and serving drinks—icemanship, mixing, stirring, garnishing, and others—which can be briefly explained in the same way that a pro on the golf course can make a detailed analysis of each of the strokes and positions he's carefully mastered. Familiarize yourself with the basic barman's skills that follow, consult them for special potables, and every time you pour drinks you'll generate among your guests the mood described superlatively by novelist Henry Fielding as "one universal grin."

Icemanship

There was a time when rocks were really rocky, when a bartender armed with an ice pick hacked away at his block of ice until it eventually disappeared. On a summer's day you'd ask for a gin rickey and it would come to you with one or two tottering crags of ice. It looked cool, but it couldn't possibly stand up to a contemporary gin rickey, because of a simple undisputed fact: Ice is now much colder than it once was. Frozen water may be 32°F. or, just as possibly these days, −32°F. Most of the cubes in the present ice age range from 0 to −10°F. Needless to say, for fast cooler-offers, the colder the ice the better. Crushed ice or cracked ice is chillier in a bar glass than the cubed variety, because more cooling ice surface comes into intimate contact with the drink.

The number of muscle-powered as well as plug-in ice crushers seems to have kept pace with the population explosion. There are ice-crusher blender attachments that can reduce a tray of ice cubes to crushed ice or snow ice in twenty to thirty seconds. Even simple ice trays are now designed not only for cubes but for ice slices, thirty-eight to a tray, and, perhaps most useful of all, for cracked ice. Lacking this equipment, a man needn't find the technique for cracking or crushing ice too difficult. Simply place the ice cubes in a canvas bag designed for this purpose or in a large, clean kitchen towel (wrap the towel around the ice so that there is a double thickness of cloth); on a carving board, bang the bag or towel with a mallet or the smooth side of a meat tenderizer. Keep your banging somewhat restrained if you want fair-size pieces of cracked ice; for crushed ice, whack away with abandon.

Every barman—amateur or pro—should insist that his ice be clean, hard, and dry and should make each drink or batch of drinks with fresh ice. Hoard your ice in the freezing section of your refrigerator until you actually need it. Use ice buckets with vacuum sides and lids; plastic-foam ice tubs are convenient for throwaway service. When you empty your ice trays, don't run water over them unless it's absolutely necessary to spring the ice free; the water will cause them to stick together after they're put into the bucket. Most new ice trays, especially those with nonstick surfaces, discharge their cargo with a single swift yank. There are also refrigerators that not only make ice cubes automatically but turn them out and store them night and day— a comforting thought when one is party-planning. If the water in your fiefdom is heavily chlorinated, use bottled spring water for ice. Finally, as a host, be the most prodigal of icemen. If you're gambling on the fact that you may just possibly get by with two buckets of ice at a summer fling, don't gamble. Provide at least three or four bucketfuls for supercooling your crowd. If your ice-making equipment is somewhat limited, find out before your rumpus takes place just where you can buy or borrow additional ice.

Here are three icy ideas you might want to try:

Punch-bowl ice   There are still commercial icehouses where you can buy a chunk of ice tailored to fit your punch bowl. But you can make your own ice floe by filling a deep pot or plastic bucket with water—at least a day in advance of the party—and placing it in the freezer. The top of the ice may congeal in a hump as the water expands. When you're ready to use it, run warm water over the sides of the pot and invert it, permitting the round glacier, with its smooth bottom upright, to slide into your bowl.

Aquavit in ice   At smorgasbord parties, it's a delightful custom to serve a bottle of aquavit (or sometimes straight vodka) encased in a block of ice. The job's simple: Place the bottle of liquor in an empty two-quart paper milk container with the top removed; fill the container with water; then set it in the freezer. The alcohol will keep the liquor from solidifying as the surrounding water freezes. Finally, tear off the paper or remove it with a knife. The long robe of ice with its rectangular sides should be partly covered with a napkin for serving and then returned to the freezer to preserve it for second skoals.

Frappéed ice cap   After-dinner frappés—refreshing alternatives to cloying desserts—are made by drizzling a liqueur or liqueurs over finely crushed ice in a saucer champagne glass. A cool and convenient variation is to make them beforehand and store them a few hours or even overnight in the freezer. In time the liqueur settles to the bottom and the ice forms a solid cap on top; after you remove it from the freezer, the cap will loosen slightly, allowing the icy liqueur to be sipped from the rim of the glass sans straw.

Glass Preparation

There are three basic ways to prepare glasses beforehand—chilling, frosting, and sugar-frosting.

Chilling glasses Every cocktail glass should be chilled before it's filled. There are three ways: (1) Before drinking time, store glasses in the refrigerator or freezer until they're cold; (2) bury the glasses completely in cracked ice; (3) fill them with cracked ice and stir the ice a few times before pouring drinks.

Frosting glasses For a longer-lasting frost, dip the glasses into water and, while still dripping, place them in your refrigerator's freezer section (set at its coldest point) for two or three hours.

Sugar-frosting glasses Glasses for appropriate cocktails, coolers, and liqueurs can be made more fascinating to the eyes and lips by frosting their rims with sugar. To administer this fancy finishing touch, make sure, first of all, that you use superfine sugar—not the regular granulated or confectioners'. Moisten the rim of each glass, inside and out, to a depth of about ¼ inch before dipping into sugar. There are four easy rites: (1) Anoint the rim with a small wedge of lemon or orange, invert the glass to shake off extra juice, then dip into sugar; (2) rub rim with lemon or orange peel, using the outside of the rind, then dip into sugar; (3) dip rim into grenadine, Falernum, or any other syrup—or any desired liqueur—then into sugar; (4) moisten rim with coffee liqueur, then dip into a mixture of 3 teaspoons superfine sugar mixed well with 1 teaspoon powdered instant coffee.

The contents of all sugar-frosted glasses, needless to add, should be sipped without benefit of a straw. For party purposes, a large number of glasses may be sugar-frosted and stored in the refrigerator or freezer until drinktime.

(Margarita glasses are often salt-frosted, which I consider a bit too much of an otherwise good thing. Some alternative suggestions are offered in Chapter 12, "Tequila.")

Some Basics to Have on Hand

Simple syrup In many drinks, such as the whiskey sour, some barmen prefer sugar syrup to loose sugar, since it makes drinks velvety smooth and—because alcohol is a notoriously poor solvent for sugar— is often easier to use because it blends without prolonged stirring or shaking. Others object to syrup on the grounds that, in such potables as the daiquiri, sugar adds to the bite of the drink. In the final analysis, your own taste should dictate the sweetener best suited for your drink.

To make a batch of simple syrup, bring 1 cup water to a boil and stir in 1 cup sugar; simmer for 1½ minutes. By that time, the mixture will have been reduced to approximately 1 cup, making it possible to subtitute equal amounts of syrup for sugar in any bar recipe where it may be preferred. Pour it into a bottle or syrup container and store at room temperature. After a while, there may be some crystallization of sugar, but it won't affect the syrup's usefulness.

Cream   For drink making, particularly as an ingredient in liqueur cocktails for dessert, cream should be heavy, not light. And if it's been standing for a day or two, check it for freshness. Note that when it's mixed with lemon juice, as it is in a clover-club cocktail, it tends to turn after a few minutes; that is, while not actually spoiling, it does become thickish and somewhat clotted. Therefore, when using cream with tart fruit juices, mix your drinks as closely as possible to serving time. Like cream, milk for eggnogs and milk punch should be checked for freshness; ditto for butter in hot buttered rum.

A good egg   When a whole egg is used in a single drink, its richness is sometimes overpowering, particularly in one as small as a sherry flip. To avoid this, use a small pullet egg for a single drink, or two large eggs for three drinks. Eggs, of course, must be strictly fresh; to double-check, empty the egg into a dish before dropping it into the shaker or blender. If it's fresh, the yolk will remain whole and the white will be thick, not runny.

To separate whites from yolks, place two small dishes or cups on your work surface. Holding the egg over one dish, crack the shell in the center with a knife; then pour the yolk back and forth between shell halves while the white slips into the dish below. Drop the yolk into the second dish. Occasionally the yolk alone is used in a drink; it may also be saved for an omelet or hollandaise sauce or other use.

The Mechanics of Mixing and Pouring

Filling the shaker   Ice should always go into the shaker first; alcohol last. By giving ice first place, all the ingredients that follow will be cooled on their way down. Furthermore, once you acquire the habit of adding the liquor last, it's unlikely that you'll inadvertently double the spirits or, worse yet, forget them altogether, both possible errors for hosts taking jolts along with their guests. The order of ingredients between ice and alcohol follows no dogmatic ritual; whether sugar should precede the lemon juice or vice versa isn't important as far as the final drink is concerned. One useful control for drinking hosts is to put the correct number of glasses for the needed drinks in front of the shaker before adding *anything*—a clear reminder of how many dashes of bitters, how many spoons of this or jiggers of that are necessary. Finally, never fill a shaker to the brim; allow enough room for all ingredients to be tossed back and forth, to set up the clear, pleasant rattle of ice.

Measuring   Guests at a pour-it-yourself bar should feel free to pour as many fingers as they please; but if the host himself is preparing any kind of mixed drinks, he should trust the jigger rather than his eye, just as the best professional barmen always do. In simple drinks such as Scotch and soda, as well as in more complicated tipple, too much liquor can be unpleasant and, in a way, as inhospitable as too little.

Stirring   To keep their icy clarity, cocktails such as martinis, manhattans, Rob Roys, and gimlets should always be stirred, not shaken (though it's no major disaster if you unwittingly shake rather than stir a martini; it will turn cloudy, but only for a few minutes). For proper dilution, stir every batch of cocktails at least twenty times. When carbonated water is added to tall drinks, stir as briefly as possible; most of the liquor rises to the top automatically, and excessive stirring only dissipates the sparkle in the water.

Shaking   Shake the shaker, not yourself. Don't just rock it—hold it well out in front of you and move it diagonally from lower left to upper right, or in any other convenient motion, with a pistonlike rhythm. In time the cold, icy feel of the cocktail shaker will tell you that the drinks have a creamy head and are ready for pouring. Shake one round of drinks at a time and rinse the shaker thoroughly after each use.

Pouring   When drinks have been shaken, pour them at once; don't let the cocktail shaker become a watery grave. If extra liquid is left in the shaker, strain it off at once; the so-called dividends left standing in ice will be weak replicas of the original drinks. Never pour drinks higher than ¼ inch from the rim of the glass. In the case of wine, a large glass should never be more than ⅓ to ½ full to permit swirling of the wine and liberation of its aromas. In large brandy snifters, a 1½-ounce drink is the maximum. When garnishes such as orange slices and pineapple sticks are being used, allow sufficient room to add them without causing the drink to overflow. When pouring more than one mixed drink, line up the glasses rim-to-rim, fill them half-full, then pour again to the same height in each glass.

Special Effects

Floating liqueurs   Drinks are sometimes served with a spoonful of liqueur or 151-proof rum floating on top; usually such toppings are merely poured slowly from the spoon against the side of the glass. The pousse-café, on the other hand, is a multilayered after-dinner drink whose rainbow effect can be created in any one of four ways: (1) First pour the heaviest liqueur slowly against the side of the glass, following it in turn with progressively lighter liqueurs, a procedure that can be learned by trial and error or by following the drink recipes on page 223; (2) pour the liqueurs over an inverted small spoon held at the top of the glass; (3) pour the liqueurs down the side of a mixing rod held in the glass; (4) pour liqueurs slowly into the glass in any sequence you desire, place the glass in your refrigerator, and in time each liqueur will find its own weight level, forming distinct layers.

Flaming liquors   Occasionally brandy or liqueurs are set aflame in a drink. For this bit of showmanship, the liquor should be preheated briefly—not boiled, which causes the alcohol to evaporate, but simply made hot enough so that when a flame is held to the liquor, it will begin quietly to blaze.

Homemade Garnishes

There are two kinds of garnishes. Some, like the twist of lemon in the martini or the cucumber peel in the Pimm's Cup, actually transform the drink's aroma and savor; others are frankly adornments for bedecking the festive glass but, like neckties, which are also dispensable, should be tastefully chosen. Some of the main garnishes—like the cherry in the manhattan—are purchased in bottles or jars and are listed in Chapter 4. The guide below tells you how to prepare your own drink garnishes and put them to best use.

Almonds   Sliced almonds or almonds julienne are sometimes floated on tall drinks or punches. They're best if toasted beforehand and slightly cooled: Spread the almonds in a shallow pan with a small amount of melted butter. Toast them in a moderate oven ten to fifteen minutes or until light brown, stirring from time to time to avoid charring; then sprinkle generously with salt and cool before adding to drinks.

Bananas   Cut firm, ripe bananas into slices and immediately dip into tart fruit juice to keep the fruit from darkening. Slices cut from rim to center and fastened onto the rim of a glass make a delicious adornment for banana daiquiris.

Fresh cherries   Remove the stems from fresh Bing or Royal Anne cherries; then remove the pits with a sharp-pointed paring knife or cherry pitter.

Whole coconut   Like the whole pineapple, the whole coconut is sometimes used as a bearer for rum potations. The end *opposite* the eyes should be cut off. Holding the eye end in one hand, strike the opposite end a sharp, glancing blow with a heavy French knife. Pour off liquid. Place the coconut cup in a deep dessert dish with cracked ice to keep the cup in a stable position.

Cucumber peel   A cool complement to Pimm's No. 1 Cup as well as wine cups and other slakers of summer thirsts. Using a sharp paring knife or a lemon-twist cutter, slice the peel about ½ inch wide, but use it sparingly; it's surprisingly pungent.

Flowers   Tame or wild orchids, gardenias, roses, and hibiscus blossoms not only ornament drinks but their exotic fragrance also enhances the flavors of rum and fruit juices in tall potables as well as summer punch bowls.

Lemon, lime or orange slices   Cut the fruit crosswise just before adding to your drinks. Whenever possible, place the slice on the rocks so that the nostrils almost meet the fruit when the drink is sipped. Or you may cut each slice from rim to center and affix it to the rim of the glass.

Lemon or orange peel These should be cut just before using to save volatile oils. Use a lemon-twist cutter or a very sharp paring knife for the job. And, if possible, avoid cutting a large amount of peel before partytime.

Drink recipes sometimes call for the peel of an entire orange or lemon in one continuous spiral—called a horse's neck. To prepare it, use a small, sharp paring knife (not a lemon-twist cutter) and, starting at the stem end, cut a continuous ½-inch swath around the fruit; avoid breaking the "neck" as the piece becomes longer.

Melons Any thick, ripe melon, such as honeydew, Persian, casaba, or Cranshaw, may be cut into round balls (using a Parisienne potato cutter or a melon-baller).

Mint leaves You may not be able to reach out of your penthouse window and grab fresh mint leaves, but mint should be as close to garden-fresh as possible, with tender young, rather than overgrown, leaves. The leaves may be dipped into syrup and then into superfine sugar before planting in drinks.

Nutmeg Though most spices for hot winter drinks, like cinnamon sticks, whole cloves, and whole allspice, are simply dropped into the drink, nutmeg is generally ground. You can buy it that way, but for best effect, buy it whole and grate it fresh, either by using a nutmeg grater or by rubbing it over the fine side of a square metal grater.

Pineapple Like the coconut, pineapple can serve both as a garnish and as a fancy substitute drinking vessel for outsize rum drinks—when the fruit is part of the drink. To prepare a whole pineapple as a drinking vessel, lop off the leafy top and cut out the deep core of fruit with a long narrow-bladed knife or meat-boning knife; then remove more of the interior with a grapefruit knife—but be careful not to pierce the shell, or your drink will spring a leak.

To make pineapple sticks or wedges, start by lopping the cap off with a heavy, sharp knife, then cut off and discard a bottom slice about ½ inch thick. Holding the fruit upright, slice off the skin from top to bottom and gouge out the remaining pieces with a pointed paring knife to make sure that the outside is completely edible. Finally, cut it in half from top to bottom, place fruit flat side down, and cut lengthwise into equal wedges of any desired thickness; then slice off the core end of each wedge. Cut each long wedge into smaller ones—about 2½ inches to make pineapple sticks, ¾ inch thick to make chunks.

If the fruit is very tart, sprinkle it heavily with sugar and marinate three to four hours, or even overnight, before using in drinks.

Pomegranate seeds   In drinks made with grenadine, a few seeds of the pomegranate, from which the syrup is made, are sometimes added for their tart succulence.

Strawberries   Some prize strawberries come with their own long stems, perfect for plucking from a bar glass. Strawberries may be dipped into red syrup such as grenandine or into beaten jelly. Outsize berries may be cut in half through the stem end.

Tropical fruit   For rum libations, fresh mangoes or papayas may be cut into long pieces like pineapple sticks or into chunks about ¾ inch thick.

Finally, a note on retrieving fresh-fruit garnishes: No strict code of etiquette, fortunately, exists; small pieces of fruit like melon balls, strawberries, etc., may be dropped directly into a drink and later retrieved with a spoon, cocktail spear, or, for that matter, the bare hand. But for convenience as well as eye appeal, the fruit may be affixed to a cocktail spear, which can then be placed into the end of a straw (if the drink is a tall cooler) or across the rim of the glass.

BOTTLED WATER

Despite formidable filtration plants in the major cities, most tap water today is barely palatable—which presents a problem to those who don't wish to mix good whiskey with chlorine on the rocks, who like their rocks to be clear rather than cloudy, and who enjoy their coffee strong and fresh rather than something akin to wormwood. The solution: bottled aqua—domestic and imported, sparkling and still—now offered at supermarts, gourmet shops, and health-food stores across the country. From a purely aesthetic standpoint, bottled waters are beautifully free from the offensive color and odor of waters flowing from most city taps.

The prodigious success of Perrier, a naturally sparkling water from France, has chagrined liquormen no end who see guests at cocktail parties not only drinking Perrier but drinking it straight, unmixed with whiskey, gin, or vodka. Indeed the number and variety of bottled waters have now reached floodlike proportions. Many of them in this country are regional, taken from springs running beneath the earth or from city water systems and then carefully processed. Some prestige waters have been served for generations in superposh restaurants and private clubs, and cost as much as some wines. At the other extreme are waters allegedly purified on the spot by vending machines at twenty cents a gallon.

Among all this variety, the best way to keep your head above water is to hold a tasting session, using three or four waters from different countries and sources. You can make a party out of it. If the people you've invited don't show the same spontaneous enthusiasm they'd normally feel for a wine- or Cognac-tasting affair, quickly explain that, after a variety of straight waters have been judged, the same liquids will then be tested for their mixability with fine bourbons or whatever potables you select. Most panelists who for the first time taste waters consecutively are surprised at the differences. Occasionally, there's an individual with an uptight palate, to whom all water is simply something wet in the mouth, but most people with normally sensitive taste buds will easily and consistently spot the differences in waters.

In practical terms, the technique of a water-tasting party is simple. Be sure to include your tap water as one of the samples. Provide spotlessly clean glasses marked for identification. Bottles should be covered with paper bags or kept out of sight. Pour the water at room temperature, not iced. Suggest that each water be taken in two or three consecutive mouthfuls before going to another sample. The water may be swallowed or merely held in the mouth briefly.

In theory, tasting water should follow the reverse procedure of tasting wine. When you enjoy the latter, you look for its lovely "robe" (color), its deep aroma, its unique bacchic flavor. By contrast, when you taste water, if there's a perceptible color in the glass, you'd be advised to toss it down the sink; any pronounced aroma is wrong; and if your taste buds detect any vivid flavor, you'll want to turn your back on it. By definition, water is colorless, odorless, and tasteless. That definition would be correct if water were merely H_2O. But all drinking water (undistilled) contains traces of dissolved minerals—from sodium ions to sulfur ions—and even though they show up in minuscule quantities, like the small amount of congeners in whiskeys, their presence or absence is sufficient to make water from one spring taste different from that of another. In other words, you can expect the flavor profiles of different waters to be low—just as they are in such foods as lettuce or potatoes—but they're *there*.

When you taste four waters chosen at random, say two French waters such as Evian and Celestins Vichy and two American waters such as Mountain Valley and water from your own tap, the differences are marked. Evian is extremely soft and gentle; Celestins Vichy has a saline flavor that can startle you but for some reason is quite acceptable; the American Mountain Valley is mildly alkaline and mellow; your own tap water, depending on where it's drawn, may be lovely or may cause you to hold your nose as you swallow it.

Some of the oldest, most distinguished bottled waters are those that are naturally sparkling just as they're drawn from the spring—organic club sodas, if you please. In the United States, the best-known is Saratoga Vichy Water from the famous New York State spa, commendable because of its high alkaline content, long appreciated as a specific against the morning after. Ramlösa from Sweden is lightly carbonated and completely free of iron and lime. More robust are Appolinaris from Germany and Perrier from France, both with fine-size bubbles; they can be quaffed straight for a vibrant lift at any time or may be used as mixers with spirits. It's unfair to compare these waters with our own club sodas, which have much more zing per ounce but lack the subtle softness of the naturally carbonated waters. Pellegrino water from Italy does in fact contain added carbon dioxide in small quantities.

As in buying wine, a bottle briefing helps in selecting waters. On the label you'll often see the phrase "Mineral Water," which means nothing in itself since all drinking waters contain minerals. However, many brands with this designation are waters from old health spas such as Saratoga, or Fiuggi in Italy, beloved by Michelangelo; their waters, unchanged from one generation to the next, deserve their eminence.

And in choosing a *spring* water, make certain it was bottled at the spring whose name it so proudly hails, just as when you buy a château wine you want to be sure it was bottled at the château. It is always a pleasure to open a bottle of Perrier water and read, *"Mise en bouteille à la source."* Even the words "springwater" can be deceptive, since half the bottled waters now being sold are nothing more than city tap water cleaned up and sometimes mixed with a small quantity of spring water to justify the use—or misuse—of the word "spring." Don't be conned by the rhetoric on a label. Such phrases as "pure as a porpoise's heart," "clear as a lookout's eye" provide little guidance to urban hosts who've never had heart-to-heart chats with porpoises or whose lookouts from their penthouse terraces normally reveal a sea of dense smog.

Beyond labels, it pays to check the bottle cap, which should be as securely fitted as that on a bottle of beer or brandy. When you lift or unscrew it, it should be clean. Some waters are now put up in plastic containers, which are cheaper than glass; however, many astute water tasters insist that water from plastic containers often leaves a synthetic, nonwater aftertaste that registers on the roof of the mouth.

In any case, once you've chosen a water that pleases you, whether you mix it with spirits, with a spritzer, or with *sangria*, whether you pour it into a coffeepot or a stockpot or take it straight, it's comforting to know that you don't have to depend on what comes out of your tap. And that's a watery groove.

8

WHISKEY

In the battle of the booze between white goods and brown goods—that is to say, between white distillates like vodka, gin, tequila, and rum versus whiskey—one of the whites has hung up a decisively winning score. Vodka now outsells U.S. straight whiskey, the former lord of the heavies. But when spirit statisticians quit racing their motors and the last ice cube has melted away, 45 percent of our national spirit drinking still consists of whiskey—not only whiskey but blended whiskey, bottled-in-bond, Scotch, Canadian, Irish, and Japanese—while 39 percent of the spirits we quaff are white.

What really matters when friends of whiskey touch glasses is not the latest gallonage figures of distilled spirits, but how the battle has affected the *kind* of whiskey we now pour. Thankfully, many whiskeys aren't what they used to be. One only has to remember some of the blended whiskeys offered in the Thirties after Repeal, with their unique aftertaste of a dusty stone fence, or some of the more expensive straights which frequently reminded you of raw barrel staves in liquid form, to realize how smooth and richly mellow whiskeys have become over the years.

In whiskeydom there are now two distinct schools of drinkers, at times polarized, at times within friendly distance of each other. First, there's the large majority who want low-proof whiskeys with balanced, gentle flavors. They idealize lightness, with one firm reservation—they don't want their whiskey to be so gentle it rolls over and plays dead. When a new federally classified type of whiskey was introduced in 1972, officially designated as "Light Whiskey," it was hailed as the oncoming of a new planetary system in the spirit universe. Instead, it turned out to be a small falling meteor. It was distilled at very high proofs where flavor begins to disappear. After aging and cutting to normal proofs, most of the new light whiskeys were very low-pitched in aroma and taste. Some were positively pallid. Only a few brands ever became popular, and these few were good whiskeys before they joined the "light" category.

In the meantime a rebellious minority has broken away from the light parade, and their spirit philosophy is that they want their whiskey to be truly whiskeyish, with rousing rather than merely satisfying flavors. As a result, while whiskey sales generally have been dipping year after year, one prominent distillery in the South, Jack Daniel's, is not only bottling more whiskey than in previous years but is hard put to keep up with the demand for its Old Time Tennessee Sour Mash whiskey, a 90-proof specimen of an extremely mellow but deeply flavored spirit. Sales of Wild Turkey bourbon, another whiskey known for its impressively vivid savor, have tripled in the past five years. Among Scotch drinkers, an increasing number have picked up the scent of the original and oldest type of Scotch—the single malts, unblended whiskies renowned for their deep, uncompromising flavors.

As a host, it's possible for you to stock the lighter blends and the strapping straights as well as whiskeys in the middle of the spectrum. All of this is to remind you that, as a knowledgeable owner of a liquor cabinet, you can get by with one kind of gin, one kind of vodka, one kind of brandy, and one, maybe two, kinds of rum, but you should be able to dispense at least four, and preferably five, different kinds of whiskey: U.S. blended, bourbon, Canadian, Scotch, and Irish. And if your whiskey outlook is liberal, you'll offer two from each class and also consider the smooth Suntory whisky from Japan.

Americans may be puzzled about the uses of aquavit, ouzo, or sake; but when it comes to their own whiskeys, there's no such puzzlement. Most of us know how to serve them in the old ways and are ready and willing to mix them in new ways. From the old colonel with his icy mint julep to the young skier with his mug of hot buttered bourbon and ginger, Americans find in their native whiskeys anything from stimulant to solace. When we *buy* whiskeys, however, we tend to be diehards about the same old brand X we've been buying for years, forgetting that brand Y or Z could not only furnish the pleasure of a newfound potation but could ignite the same gentle flame of surprise that guests find in a new piece of Art Deco on the shelves.

In aspiring to be a judge of good whiskey, don't let color influence your judgment. It has little to do with what we mean by lightness in flavor. Some whiskeys receive their tint from the barrels in which they're aged; others, with the outstanding exception of bourbon, from added caramel coloring.

The first step in judging a whiskey is to nose it. If your nose is reasonably sensitive, it's a more accurate and objective instrument for appraising whiskey flavor than the mouth.

Pour the whiskey to be sampled into a tulip-shaped glass or a dock glass, which helps to fence in the aroma. Add a little water so that the proof is cut in half—that is, a 90-proof whiskey, for example, is reduced to about 45-proof, the strength which professional whiskeymen find best for nosing spirits. (Whiskey on the rocks, well stirred, usually drops to half its bottle proof.) Swirl it around the sides of the glass, then hold it to the nostrils for a few seconds and breathe deeply. Repeat the nosing with a second kind of whiskey of the same proof, and note the differences, not necessarily for better or worse but in order to scan the features of the whiskey's flavor, its profile. (Don't repeat the procedure too frequently at one sitting or you may suffer nose fatigue.) In time, with repeated nosings, one develops a flavor memory, so that at the first whiff you'll notice the subtle twists of one whiskey's flavor as compared to another.

Of course, your ultimate object in appraising whiskey is not merely to judge it but to enjoy it, and that means the pleasure of whiskey in the mouth. An old-fashioned taste test still ritually observed by some whiskey lovers is to pour whiskey into a glass, swirl it around, and empty the glass. A richly flavored whiskey will leave its aroma for several hours, while a more pallid whiskey will fade into nothingness. A somewhat more primitive test is to rub whiskey between the palms of the hands, just as chefs do when testing herbs or other flavoring ingredients. A pungent, heavy aroma will indicate the whiskey's flavor strength.

The making of whiskey in all countries follows steps that are essentially the same: A mash is made of grain, malt turns it to sugar, yeast turns it to alcohol, heat vaporizes the alcohol, it cools into whiskey, and wood ages it. But the subtle variations in the finished product are virtually limitless. The things that make up whiskey flavor, that give it its essence, are called congeners—products other than alcohol that result from distillation. To recruit the pleasant congeners and stave off the poor ones is the real science and sorcery of whiskey making. In a fifth of whiskey there is, all told, only about a teaspoon of congeners, but without them it would be plain alcohol and water.

Some congeners are born in the kind of grain used. Others owe their genes to the yeast's paternity. They must be controlled during the whiskey's stormy adolescence in the big fermenting vats, and in the still they're carefully hoarded by drawing off the liquor at low proofs. By federal regulation, bourbon, the principal whiskey in this country, must be taken out of the still at 160 proof or less. Actually, most of it is drawn off at considerably lower proofs and is cut to drinking strength later. The higher the proof when the liquor leaves the still, the weaker the flavor. If liquor trickling out of the still goes above 190, much of the gusto of the grain simply disappears. You then have grain neutral spirits, the basis for vodka or gin. It's like a steak cooked rare retaining its magnificent flavor and a steak cooked well done losing its juices. The comparison must be amended, however, because whiskey begins to flash its good stuff only when the congeners become mellow—after aging in the wood, which eliminates the unpleasant and refines the pleasant congeners.

Let us hastily add, however, that you can't judge a whiskey's personality exclusively by age. Some whiskeys mature earlier than others. Weaker-flavored spirits age more quickly than stronger ones. Whiskey in a large hogshead takes longer to mature than the same whiskey in a small cask, because less of it is in contact with the wood. If certain whiskeys are left too long in the wood, for age's sake alone, they sometimes begin to show the "casky" flavor of old age.

Whiskey flavor is coaxed out of a grain mash by either a pot still or a column still. The pot still isn't a yawning soup pot but a huge onion-shaped metal flask having a blazing fire beneath it and a narrow outlet at the top for trapping and delivering the whiskey vapors into a coil where they're cooled back to a liquid. Some pot stills in Ireland today are monsters holding over 20,000 gallons each. The other, more modern utensil is the column still, a lanky affair three or four stories high in which the alcohol is wheedled out by live steam inside the column rather than by flames beneath it. Column stills are like modern coffee makers—the slaves of science rather than art—producing a suave, controlled flavor. Pot stills are like old-fashioned enamel coffeepots in which the ground beans have been dumped into the boiling water and swirled around to bring out all the robust coffee essence. Pot stills are generally used for heavy-flavored spirits; column stills for lighter spirits.

Some bourbons today are made, as they were generations ago, in pot stills. Others flow from the column stills. Most of the Scotch and Irish whiskeys exported to this country are now combinations of pot- and column-stilled spirits.

U.S. Whiskey

The history of American whiskey predates the rebellion of the American colonies against England, and was later marked by another uprising correctly called the Whiskey Rebellion. When Scotch and Irish farmers in western Pennsylvania were told that the rye whiskey they were making would henceforth be taxed, they rose in arms against the government that would penalize them for practicing the Old World art they had brought to the new. This time, however, the rebellion was put down not by a foreign monarch but by President George Washington. Discouraged, small bands of farmer-whiskeymen left Pennsylvania and settled in Bourbon County, Kentucky, where they discovered magnificent limestone water, a prime ingredient for whiskey making. The section of northeastern Kentucky called Bourbon honored Louis XVI for his help in freeing the colonies from Britain. Among the most eminent of those early whiskeymen was the well-known distiller the Reverend Elijah Craig, a Baptist minister.

Good whiskey was always aged in oak barrels, but around the middle 1800s someone discovered that it aged faster and acquired a melodious mellowness when it was kept in *charred* oak barrels. As legend has it, some distillerymen found themselves at that time with no available barrels except ones used for transporting salted fish. To get rid of the fishy smell, the insides of the staves were burned, and thus bourbon— something like the whiskey we know today—was born.

For practical purposes, American whiskey production can be grouped into six categories:

Straight whiskey   Whiskey distilled at 160 proof or less and aged for at least two years in new, charred oak barrels; most brands are aged for four years or more. Bourbon is a straight whiskey, concocted from a grain mixture that is at least 51 percent corn; bourbon's counterpart, rye whiskey, is similarly made from a mixture of at least 51 percent rye. Straight bourbon is the best-selling U.S. whiskey.

Blends of straight whiskey   Two or more straights united to combine their best features—some for mellowness, some for strength, some for aroma.

Bottled-in-bond whiskey   Straight whiskey required to be aged at least four years (actual age is usually higher), recognized by its green rather than red stamp on the bottleneck, produced by a single distillery in one year, bottled at 100 proof, and kept under more or less constant surveillance by Internal Revenue men. Theoretically it can be a poor whiskey and still be bottled in bond; the revenuers don't care about quality. It represents about 2 percent of current U.S. whiskey sales.

Light whiskey   Whiskey distilled at 161 to 189 proof, a range that results in lighter flavor and lighter body; may be aged in used barrels in the same way that Canadian and Scotch whiskies are aged. Much of it is now used as the big component in blended whiskey (see below).

Blended whiskey   A blend of about ⅓ straight whiskey (regulations say ⅕ is enough) and ⅔ grain neutral spirits or light whiskey (see above); it's often misnomered rye. Second-best seller among U.S. whiskeys.

Tennessee whiskey   Although only a small part of U.S. whiskey gallonage, this cousin of bourbon, with corn the leading ingredient, is famed for its luscious mellowness brought about by slow filtering through a special charcoal of Tennessee maple. Jack Daniel and George Dickel are Tennessee's emissaries to the world of fine spirits.

Like a stubborn gate-crashing ghost, the word "rye" keeps weaving in and out of bars and drinking parties when what's really meant is blended whiskey. Actually, less than one-half of 1 percent of the whiskey wetting American throats is straight rye. In the finer liquor stores you may still find a distinguished old bottling of straight rye, but that is decidedly the exception. To be sure, rye, the grain, is used in many American whiskeys as a minor ingredient along with other grains such as wheat and barley, but to call for rye in a bar today is as illogical as asking for an onion stew when you really want beef, on the grounds that onions are used for seasoning purposes.

At the end of World War II, three out of four jiggers of whiskey were the neutral-flavored blended whiskey. Shortly thereafter, bourbonmen began to cut their traditional 100-proof liquors down to 86. Many of them started to spin out lighter flavors. But it was still bourbon, made from the seraphic oils of the corn, its new, easier flavor as perfectly burnished as ever. Bourbon sales blasted off and have now eclipsed blended whiskey.

The terms "sweet mash" and "sour mash" can stand clarification. First of all, there's absolutely nothing sour-tasting in a sour-mash whiskey. The "sour" refers to a step in the fermentation process, and not the end product—whiskey. A sour-mash whiskey is produced when the liquid grain mixture or mash (also called beer) contains some spent beer from a previous run of whiskey, usually about 25 percent. Like the base or starter used to make sourdough bread, it's the kind of leftover that makes for controlled fermentation, and up- rather than downgrades the new batch. Most straight whiskeys nowadays are made by the sour-mash method during a three-day fermenting period. When whiskeys are made this way, you don't normally see the term "sour mash" on the label. If, however, you see the phrase "old-time," "old-fashioned," or "genuine sour mash" on the label, it indicates that the mash used for that whiskey contained at least 50 percent spent beer, the fermenting period was at least four days, and the resulting flavor was indeed unique. In the mouth, a sweet-mash whiskey is light in flavor; a sour mash medium-bodied; while an "old-time," "old-fashioned," or "genuine" sour mash is the heaviest in flavor.

Scotch Whisky

When Bobbie Burns, liquordom's Scottish laureate, said, "O whisky, soul o' play and pranks,/Accept a bardie's gratefu' thanks," he was talking about the primitive, high-voltage spirits of his day, a dose fit for doughty laird and rough peasant alike. It was all pot-stilled, and became known as a "self" whisky because it had barley's single, strong flavor unmixed with any other grain. Barley is to Scotch as corn is to the flavor of bourbon.

Beginners tasting Scotch for the first time are often puzzled if not dismayed by what some consider its oddly medicinal flavor. The taste of Scotch is due not only to barley but to the fact that the barley is smoked before it's crushed and fermented in a mash. At one time all peat was used for smoking, and different Scotches were described as having more or less of the peat reek. Nowadays, coal is used as the first step in smoking, and later peat—which is expensive—is burned to give the grain its characteristic Scotch aroma. In some distilleries, fans are used to blow the peat smoke over the grain for a more rapid infusion.

But if it were only the barley and the peat that made Scotch, Scotch could theoretically be made anywhere. Efforts were made to make "Scotch" in other countries, using barley and imported peat, and they were disasters. Even when they used imported water taken from Scotland's highland streams, they were unable to duplicate it, proving that you can import everything that goes into Scotch except the weather—the highland dew and sunshine, as well as the winds, the wet, and the cold that surround Scotch during its long sleep in the casks. Fortunately all of the elements that go into Scotch can be found bottled at your nearest liquor store.

The modern Scotch that Englishmen, Americans, and other non-Scotsmen drink is an amalgam of two kinds of spirits. The first is the modern grain whisky, made mostly of corn, a small amount of barley, and sometimes rye and oats. It flows out of tall column stills, and in flavor is as light as thistledown, but doesn't become the Scotch we know until it's first aged and later fortified with the old-time "self" whisky, also known as single-malt or malt whisky.

Note that the Scots spell their whisky without an "e," the absence of which is usually attributed to the alleged Scottish parsimony. Since the Canadians also spell their whisky without an "e," the theory must go down the drain, although Scottish whiskymen love to encourage foreign legends of Scottish tightfistedness. "It's guid," one old maltster boasted to me. "It gives us individuality."

But young American drinkers who taste Scotch for the first time don't have to be told that it's a breed apart from the American whiskey they've known. It's such a long jump that many of them are torn between what they think they should like and what they actually like.

Eventually, after they taste different Scotches under different circumstances, many of them find themselves in tune with the great Highland fling.

Scotches coming to this country are blends not of one heavy malt whisky with one light grain, but of as many as a dozen heavies with a dozen lights. Some Scotch blends imported in the United States are now 80 percent light grain whisky and 20 percent heavy malt whisky; the average is perhaps 60 and 40. (Men who keep an assortment of Scotches in their liquor cabinets sometimes assume that most of the light Scotches are now leveled out to a common plateau where one light Scotch doesn't differ noticeably from another. It's a mistaken conclusion, and the host who tastes one light versus another at the same sipping session will discover that any Scotch, no matter how light, shows its own strong profile. The malt still dominates the whisky in the same way that onions dominate an onion soup—you can use one, two, or three cups of onions in the same pot; it will still emerge as onion soup and not a colorless consommé.) Whatever the relative amounts of heavies and lights, the breeding and crossbreeding of these whiskies is a process so refined and complex that it can rightly be called a Scottish art. And what's amazing is that, year after year, Scottish shippers, some of whom blend their whisky but don't own a distillery, can turn out a spirit that seldom varies, as purebred in flavor as bottles of a vintage wine from the same grapes on the same hillside of the same château.

Before World War II, almost all Scotches coming to this shore were at least eight years old. U.S. law says they must be a minimum of four years old; i.e., the youngest of the blend must be four years old. Now they're running between five and seven years, even though many labels indicate no age at all. If you're in a mood for taste exploration, try the same brand of Scotch in an eight- and a twelve-year-old version. The satiny smoothness of the older Scotch is roamin' in the gloamin' at its best. Now and then a label will read, "Liqueur Scotch Whisky." It's not a sweet liqueur in the literal sense, but indicates an older Scotch which the shipper presents as his gilt-edged potation.

At liquor stores, you can choose from any of the four great clans of Scotch being imported:

Blends, twelve years and older. These are the prestige Scotches such as Chivas Regal, Johnny Walker Black Label, etc., renowned for their luscious mellowness and subtle balance of malt and grain whiskies.

Blends up to eight years of age. Most of them are 86 proof, but a few 80-proof specimens are in the pack. *Caveat emptor:* The reduced proof means not merely that alcohol has been taken away but that Scotch whisky itself has been removed and water added. If no age is shown on the label, you can assume it's between five and seven years, since the youngest of the blend must be four years old by U.S. regulations. Included in this largest of the categories are all the well-known labels like Cutty Sark, J & B, Dewar's, Black & White, Teacher's, White Horse, etc.

Blends bottled in the United States. To reduce high duty imposed on bottled-in-Scotland whiskies, these are imported in bulk and bottled here, saving about 15 percent in duty, shipping costs, etc. They make up about 40 percent of our Scotch imports and are typified by such brands as Passport, Old Smuggler, etc.

Single malts. These are the traditional and original type of Scotches, made from malted barley alone, pot-stilled, and the product of one distillery. They are the cream of the Scotch sippin' whiskies.

An increasing number of Americans have been finding their whisky hobby in the single malts, and are riding them happily. Two decades ago they were virtually unknown in this country except in some of the crusty men's clubs—and even there they were considered an odd dram to be sipped on a rare occasion, certainly not an everyday drink. Today single malts are on liquor shelves everywhere. American visitors to Scotland, sampling the single malts, soon learn that their spectrum of flavors is immense, ranging from the light Highland malts to the extremely heavy peaty malts of Campbeltown which Scotsmen say "go down singing hymns."

All of them are notably self-assertive. They are the least mixable of whiskies, not just because of their smoky overtones but because their subtlety is instantly annulled by such mixers as ginger ale, lemon juice, or vermouth. (Scotches—the blended variety—can, of course, be used in dozens of mixed drinks.) Once you're at home with the somewhat complex flavors of single malts, you may want to take them with an ice cube or two, or a little water rather than soda. In Scotland, single-malt connoisseurs insist that the best possible water for adding to their whiskies is the same spring water that was used in distilling the whisky itself. Avoid at any cost a noticeably chlorinated tap water. Like Cognac, a single malt is a magnificent postprandial drink served in a brandy inhaler or a tulip-shaped wineglass in which the spirits can be swirled, nosed, and intimately appreciated.

In the past fifteen years the quality of many single malts has become much more consistent thanks to modern instrumentation used in malting, distilling, and vatting. The best-selling single malt in the world is Glenfiddich. It's distinguished not only by its bottle with three sides but by its haunting, dry aftertaste and gentle peatiness. Scotsmen sometimes call it sweet—not sweet in the sugary sense but sweet in the sense that it carries the kind of aroma you remember for its amiability and graciousness. Another well-known malt whisky is Smith's The Glenlivet. The article "the" is allowed only with this one brand to distinguish it from other Scotches—at least twenty-three—which have the word "Glenlivet" hyphenated in their brand names, provoking Scotsmen to ironically refer to Glenlivet as the longest glen in Scotland. The Glenlivet is renowned for its deep mellow flavor and subtle, subdued peatiness. Another single malt, less well known in this country but available, is Mortlach, with only a trace of peatiness and an opulently rich flavor.

Canadian Whisky

If, in spelling "whisky," the Scot in the Canadian seems to have taken charge, in distilling it the French-*canadien* is obviously the creative force—for Canada turns out the world's lightest, most delicate of spirits, a marvelous balance of corn, rye, and barley. While every bottle of Canadian whisky seems to reflect the icy clarity of the Arctic, you can depend upon its eventual effect to be as warming as any 86-proof potable in the world.

Just how Canadian distillers achieve their subtle flavor balances is both the secret and the fine art of the distillers themselves. Unlike the U.S. Bureau of Tobacco, Alcohol, and Firearms which regulates the minimum amount of corn that goes into bourbon, the maximum proof beyond which it can't be distilled, and the kind of barrels (only new charred oak) in which the bourbon must be aged, Canadian excisemen follow a policy of *laissez-faire* when it comes to whisky making. As long as they collect their taxes, they don't see any reason for insisting that more corn or less rye or more barley and less wheat are necessary to make their whisky truly Canadian.

We do know that Canada is the second-best customer for our used cooperage (Scotland is the number-one consumer), yet we also know that they use some new barrels, too. But what American distillers can never duplicate are the local waters and the special Canadian weather conditions of cloudiness, sunshine, heat, cold, and humidity in which Canadian whiskies mellow during their approximately six years in the wood. Throughout their aging, the whiskies evaporate in the barrels, leaving headspace at the top. Canadian whiskymen normally replace this headspace with newer whiskies; therefore all Canadian whiskies are sold as blends.

If Scotch malts are the least mixable of whiskies, Canadian whiskies are probably the most mixable. It would be hard to create a better whiskey sour, for example, than one made with Canadian spirits. The same goes for a whiskey collins. A manhattan is usually made with a rich U.S. blended whiskey or a bourbon. But if you prefer a dry manhattan made with dry vermouth, then Canadian whisky is your best bet. For liquor to take along when traveling, for tailgate parties, or for any occasion at the journey's end when you want a bracer-upper, Canadian whisky is perfect taken as a straight shot or with any impromptu mixers on hand. Finally, for gift giving, when you don't know the specific heisting habits of the person for whom the gift is intended, Canadian whisky has a special giftlike aura which makes it universally pleasing.

Irish Whiskey

In sharp contrast to the light Canadian spirits are Ireland's hearty whiskeys. After a few sturdy drams, amateur whiskey genealogists often trace Irish whiskey to its first maker, Patrick, patron saint of Ireland. When literal-minded whiskey historians insist that Saint Patrick in the fifth century was a brewer of beer rather than a distiller of whiskey, Irishmen aren't in the least bit rattled. They simply point out that whiskey is only distilled beer, just as brandy is distilled wine; and the whole history of distilling, they add, from the ancient Arabs onward, is such a barmy tale that Saint Patrick might just as well be credited as less worthy benefactors.

When impertinent Sassenachs claim that Irish whiskey is like Canadian but more robust, they make a comparison that may be partly true but is nevertheless odious to any true Irishman, who can point out that the very word "whiskey" is a derivative of the Gaelic *uisge beatha*, "water of life." For there's something regal in the flavor of Irish whiskey that sets it apart not only from Canadian but from any other whiskey in the world. As best described in Holinshed's *Chronicles* in 1577, "Trulie it is a soverigne liquor if it be orderlie taken."

Before World War I, Irish whiskey heavily outsold Scotch in this country. Over 400 brands were registered in the U.S., and in England it was the drink of those who dined *en famille* at Buckingham Palace. Between the two wars, the canny Scots stepped in with their new, lighter blends and ran away with the foreign-whiskey market in both England and this country. The Irish, who considered themselves perfectionists in making whiskey—particularly that which they exported —resisted change. In the nineteenth century, when John Jameson's foremen were planning to build a new fence in the courtyard of his Dublin distillery, Jameson objected strongly. "It may change the taste of the whiskey," he warned. But in whiskey making, the perfectionists of one era are all too often the reactionaries of a succeeding one. Over the years, Irish whiskey did change, but only at a drop-by-drop pace.

In 1970, however, it was remodeled noticeably and notably. The difference between the old and the modern is that the previous Irish whiskey was made in old-fashioned pot stills, and the new Irish whiskey, like most of the Scotch coming to this country, is a blend of pot and column stills. Any pot still produces pungent, low-proof, intense flavor; a column or continuous still yields high-proof, light, buoyant whiskey.

Don't assume that the new Irish whiskey is simply Scotch in a Gaelic guise. It's an easy assumption to make, since both whiskeys are made from barley, but actually the two barley-born whiskeys are worlds apart in taste. Scotch barley is dried over kilns where the smoke of peat gives it an unforgettably smoky flavor. Irish barley is dried over smokeless anthracite coal. There are other variations, but that alone is enough to make Irish as different from Scotch as a harp from a haggis.

As far as mixability is concerned, the new Irish whiskeys leave the old ones far behind. The best-known mixture in which Irish whiskey is "orderlie taken" is, of course, Irish coffee—a drink as good cold as hot (see page 438). Of the standard bar drinks, an Irish old-fashioned or an Irish sour on the rocks bring out the best of the new Irish blends.

Japanese Whisky

It may come as an odd surprise to Americans to discover that the single best-selling whisky in the world is neither a vigorously trumpeted U.S. blend nor one of those renowned Scotches whose name is boundlessly commended to the whole world, but instead a Japanese product—Suntory Old whisky. If you've never tasted it and you were to sip it blindfolded, you'd swear you were drinking a fine Scotch. At the most recent count, it was being whisked off liquor-store shelves at the rate of over ten million cases a year—most of it, of course, sipped in Sakeland.

Like Scotch, Japanese whisky is spelled without an "e." And like Scotch, its base of peat-smoked barley is fermented, aged, and blended with grain whiskies, the youngest of which is at least four years old. But while it's like Scotch generically, it's as different from the old-fashioned single-malt Scotches as a happicoat is from a kilt. While most Scotches are doughty in flavor, Suntory's chief feature is its rare elegance. Its subtly balanced flavor leaves a gentle but vivid aftertaste.

Scotch depends for its character not only on its smoked barley but on the special small clear streams of water flowing through granite in the Highlands. Japanese whiskeymen, realizing that they couldn't move Scotland's streams to the Orient (although they once transported a shipload of water as a trial), built their first big distillery in the placid misty valley of Yamazaki where the famed spring water was originally chosen for a sixteenth-century tearoom nearby. Most Scotches are blends from numerous small distilleries. By contrast, Suntory whisky is made in two huge distilleries, one of which houses twenty-four monster pot stills, the largest malt distillery in the world. Finally, while hundreds of old Scotch maltmen depend on their noses and their mouths for blending whiskies, the Japanese take advantage not only of their noses and mouths but, as you might expect, of chromatograph-coupled mass spectrometers, nuclear magnetic resonance analyzers, and electron microscopes, devices that seem to be consistent with Japanese success in so many other fields. Undoubtedly it's this happy coupling of art and the latest technology that makes Suntory amazingly consistent from one year to the next.

It's not the fault of Japanese whisky makers that so little of it is now seen in American public and private bars. Those who sip it the first time may cry, "*Imitation*," but the same response was heard from those who years ago first tasted California Cabernet Sauvignon and sneered that it was a fake Bordeaux. As the California wines gradually came of age, more and more wine drinkers began recognizing the greatness of California wines in their own right. Something of the same eventual response might be expected of consumers of Japanese whisky in the United States.

In Japan, cocktails and mixed drinks aren't popular. The Japanese prefer to drink their whisky merely mixed with water. Served this way, their delicately balanced whisky acts as a perfect counterpoint to the simple but very artful Japanese cuisine.

In the whiskey world, two significant shifts occurred in recent years. Drinking strengths in many cases were lowered from 100 to 86, and some whiskeys that always were 86 proof were in some instances trimmed down to 80—incidentally chopping distillers' costs somewhat while gratifying the popular move toward lightness in potables. The second change is the substantial improvement of U.S. blended whiskey. At one time the best of it was one-third straight whiskey and two-thirds straight white eye—that is, raw white alcohol, just as it came from the still, cut to drinking strength. It's this two-thirds that was radically transformed. Some U.S. whiskeymen, in an effort to turn out the best blended whiskey, began to age all of it. A good blended whiskey such as Seagram's 7 Crown is made up of about seventy-five different spirits, all of them mellowed by years in the wood.

Drinking tastes are always in ferment, and where future whiskey tastes are destined is still any bar philosopher's guess. Many whiskeymen believe that the worldwide ebb toward lightness has reached a plateau and is rippling to a halt. As a matter of fact, federal regulations that forbid whiskey to be bottled at less than 80 proof automatically bring to a dead end any effort toward further lightening.

But be it heavy in flavor or light, 86 proof or 80, the real proof of any whiskey is in the drinking. And having discovered this, more and more men find themselves in felicitous accord with the canny Scotsman who said, "There's whusky and there's guid whusky, but there's nae bad whusky."

9

GIN

The next time someone asks, "Who is Sylvius?" be prepared with the answer: He was the inventor of gin. Sylvius's proper name was Franciscus de Boë. He was a professor of medicine at the Dutch University of Leiden, and the pure lab alcohol that Dr. Sylvius distilled with the oil of juniper berries was intended as a blood cleanser for sale in apothecaries rather than taverns. It was the seventeenth century, when drinking most distilled liquors snapped the neck and left a lingering ball of fire in the throat. The professor's comparatively smooth and inexpensive nostrum soon not only cleansed the blood of countless native Hollanders but also juiced up the minds and bodies of English soldiers campaigning in the Lowlands. Englishmen brought the new Dutch formula back to their cold, foggy isle, and a great mass warming of an entire nation took place over the next several centuries.

Beginning in England with the reign of William of Orange, gin drinking became a mark of the highest patriotism. The number of amateur gin makers mushroomed until eventually every fourth house in London was a ginshop; English workmen were even paid a share of their wages in gin. In the late nineteenth century, the elaborate gilded and mirrored Victorian gin palaces came into being and gin rose to a peak of glamour, reaching its apex with the introduction to England of the American cocktail. Not even Prohibition's bathtub gin, generations later, nor the runaway rise of vodka, could cause gin to fall again.

All dry gins made in England or the United States are created almost equal. They start out as neutral spirits made from grain. These spirits which form the base of gin are close to, but not quite, vodka. They're later redistilled in the presence of juniper berries and about ten to fifteen other forms of flavor sorcery such as coriander, bitter almonds, cardamom, cassia (cinnamon) bark, angelica, and lemon and orange peel. It's this second flavoring step that reveals the gin maker's art and accounts for most of the differences in gins.

Deepest-flavored of all is the imported Holland gin called genever or Hollands. (The English word "gin" is a contraction of the Dutch *genever*, which means "juniper.") Holland gin makers use fresh juniper berries chopped and added right into the fermenting mash before distillation takes place, and they distill their gins at rather low proofs. This technique imparts an odd, impressive flavor which is so assertive that Hollands is seldom used in a mixed drink; it's always taken biting cold and neat. While the first gulp is always somewhat surprising to Americans, it leaves a rich aftertaste much like an old *eau de vie*. Like Germany's Steinhäger gin—which is very much like it in flavor—genever is sold in stone crocks.

English gins differ from one another just as American gins do. When the gin maker uses spices, he becomes something of a cook. The spices he uses vary from season to seaon in flavor potency, so that too much of this or a little less of that can make a perceptible difference. You can almost bet that two gin makers with the same formula, like two chefs working with the same recipe, will come up with two different products. The gin gap between England and America, although not as wide as it used to be, is still there. The main differences between English and American gins are these:

—English gins cost about one-third more because of duties, shipping charges, handling, etc., and the fact that many of them are 94 proof as against an American high of 90 proof.

—The starting spirits of English gins, before they're juniper flavored, are distilled at about 180 proof, ten less than their American counterparts. It's a small segment in the proof range but just enough to make the English base flavor more pronounced.

—English starting spirits contain less corn and more barley than their American counterparts which also makes for eventual flavor differences.

—English water differs from American, and this affects both the alcoholic base for gin and the water used to later cut the gin to bottle proof.

In both countries some gins are now distilled under vacuum, permitting the flavors of the spices to be liberated at low temperatures rather than the pugnaciously high ones of normal stills, which sometimes cause flavors to be rough. Other gins are flavored not by immersing the botanicals right in the still but by passing the final alcohol vapors, as they come from the still, through a separate chamber, called a gin head, where the juniper and other spices convey a pleasant subtlety to the spirits before they're condensed. How "ginny" a gin you select—how vividly flavored—is a matter of personal taste.

At least ten different gins in the United States carry the phrase "London Dry." The phrase is meaningless, although at one time in England, when sweet gin was widely sold, it could have been significant. Today it may evoke some geographical fascination but has nothing whatever to do with London itself. Most English gin makers, in fact, seem to avoid the phrase.

Whatever the manner in which they're flavored, both American and English gins are considered to be dry. Until recently that meant unsweetened, but virtually all gins today are unsweetened. When barmen speak of dry gin these days, they mean one which is more muted in flavor, though not pallid, and, above all, smooth. Actually, the only nondry gin is English Old Tom, which is made with added sugar as a sweetener and is exported mostly to the Orient. There are also a few fruit-flavored gins on the market, but they're not a significant segment of the gin world. And sloe gin isn't gin at all but a liqueur made with the sloe plum of the blackthorn.

In addition to being dry, most gins in England and America are unaged, but a few in both countries are mellowed in the wood for further blending and flavor development. Although American liquor laws don't permit gin labels to carry any statement of age, these elder statesmen can be recognized by their clear straw color.

Over the centuries, English gin drinkers have created their own terminology, and some of it has spilled across the ocean. "Pink gin," for instance, is simply gin with a dash of Angostura bitters; "gin and it" is a blend of gin and Italian vermouth; and the gin sling, which has been a British standby since General Gordon drank it at the officers' mess in Khartoum, will probably outlast the final expiration of the Empire. It's sold bottled as Pimm's No. 1 Cup.

About the only class of mixed drinks in which you don't find gin are hot grogs, although skiers have been known to sip a hot gin toddy now and then after a vigorous run on the slopes. Otherwise, if you're a gin partisan, you can use it in almost any mixed drink into which vodka is normally poured. One of the most delightful cocktails is a gin sour on the rocks. The best-known tall gin drink is the Tom Collins, while the perennial lion among short drinks for generations has been the martini. For some reason which sociologists might study, a drinker who doesn't mind taking his whiskey or brandy straight will hesitate to honor gin in the same way. The exceptions are Holland gin, or gin that is icy cold. Gin drinkers have been known to keep a bottle at all times in the refrigerator or even the freezer (it won't freeze because of the alcohol) and to take a nip now and then in the same way they'd drink aquavit or other schnapps neat. All those wags who joke about how little vermouth they use in a martini—just a drop from an eye dropper or a tiny spritz from an atomizer—are simply gin fans who are too embarrassed to admit that they love gin straight.

Wherever it comes from and whatever company it keeps, Sylvius's venerable and versatile nostrum remains among the best possible medicines for the treatment of the common thirst. It is written that Elijah the prophet once derived sublime comfort from sitting under a juniper tree. It's not surprising that most men today prefer to take their juniper through the lips in the comfort of an armchair.

10

VODKA

Vodka's amazing success (for years it's been outselling any other spirits in the United States) is no longer news, but what is incredible is that it reached the top of the liquor heap despite all the false witnesses who originally baptized it in this country and springboarded it with phony descriptions. Foremost of the mis-leaders was the U.S. government, which issued Standards of Identity that distillers must follow both when they make vodka and when they later describe it in their advertising. With well-intended but somewhat fuddled reasoning the government said vodka (a Russian word mean-ing "little water") cannot be sold as vodka unless it is free from "dis-tinctive character, aroma, taste, or color."

Now nothing that passes over the taste buds (including water) is free from taste. To demonstrate how false the injunction is, pour orange juice into two glasses, add a jigger of vodka to one of them, and ask one or any number of tasters to note the difference if any. Unless the tasters' taste buds are completely paralyzed, they consistently spot the screwdriver from the plain orange juice. Vodka obviously has con-siderably less taste than whiskey, brandy, rum, or ouzo, but when added to any other potable—from beef bouillon to branch water—it distinctly modifies the flavor of that to which it is added.

"Free from aroma"? Take two tulip-shaped glasses. Pour water into one and vodka into the other. Submit them for nosing to anyone present—a child, a nondrinker, or whom you will. Notice the instant jolt as the glass with vodka is sniffed.

"Free from character"? If, by character, you mean something that confers distinctiveness, then all vodkas should be exactly alike. How far this parts company with the facts can easily be shown by simply tasting two or three different vodkas side by side. You'll notice that while they're all from the same breed, small but notable differences stand out. You'll notice deviations in smoothness, graininess, or traces of sweetness, and in some vodkas you may even detect flavors mildly reminiscent of various herbs and spices.

As vodka drinking continues to mount, old myths continue to dissolve. The claim that vodka is undetectable on the breath is seldom touted anymore. Drink too much vodka and your breath unfortunately will proclaim that there's a full cargo aboard. The old fable about vodka's abnormal potency—a handful of people still compare it to bottled dynamite—is also rapidly disappearing as drinkers realize that 80-proof or 100-proof vodka is no more of a stiff glass than 80- or 100-proof whiskey. In fact, the next morning vodka seems to leave fewer cranberry eyes and somewhat smaller heads than other liquors.

When a distiller makes vodka, his goal is to make "pure" ethyl alcohol, which he will later cut to drinking strength by adding water. By "pure" the distiller means as free as possible from congeners, the substances that give flavor to whiskey, rum, brandy, etc. Vodkamen have several ways of eliminating congeners. The first is to distill vodka at the highest possible proof, always above 190. It must be distilled with such artful care that only the smoothest fraction of spirits is accepted; the balance of the run is rejected or redistilled. It may be distilled several times, i.e., rectified in order to eliminate traces of residual congeners. Often the vodka is filtered through charcoal for further purifying, and the kind and amount of charcoal is important. Sometimes vodka is agitated by special devices for flavor elimination. Finally it's put through filter pads. These finishing processes are a fine art indeed, and the subtle differences between vodkas are the result of the sensitive skill with which these final steps are handled.

Vodkas are usually made from grain. The one recent notable exception is Turkish Izmira vodka made from white beets, which give it a subtle distinction. Stories of vodka made from potatoes were true to a limited extent in Europe. During World War II, middle-European moonshiners made vodka from potato peelings, since potatoes were desperately needed as food. Theoretically you can distill vodka from any fermented mash, but large distillers use corn, wheat, rye, and other grains normally used in whiskey.

Because the quality of the water used to make vodka is important, advertisers naturally stress this component. Finnish vodka, for instance, is made from Ice Age water. Extremely deep wells, the importer says, tap a moraine formation left by glaciers eons ago. Another vodka from Denmark is, the producer says, made from glacial ice collected from a Greenland ice cap. Since many vodka advertisers can no longer beard each other on the raw ingredients, some of them resort to boasting of their conspicuously high prices. For several years Russian vodka was the most expensive sold in this country. Now, importers who handle vodka from the People's Republic of China claim that *theirs* will put an even deeper dent in your pocketbook.

Liquor stores now carry many vodkas prominently marked as "Flavored Vodka." Most of the American specimens, flavored with mint, cherry, orange, etc., and often sold in half-pints, are "sneaker drinks," taken on the side. The best of the flavored vodkas are from Europe, and are highly useful for party purposes. Perhaps the best-known is zubrovka, a vodka from Poland with a yellowish-greenish cast. In the bottle you will see several blades of an herb popularly known as buffalo grass. Zubrovka is somewhat sweetish, although by no means a liqueur, and is best appreciated served straight and biting cold.

From Russia there are a number of vodkas with unique and fascinating flavors. They should be sipped rather than killed, bottoms-up. They include:

> Pertsovka—pepper-flavored
> Starka—aged vodka with a brandylike flavor
> Okhotnichya—herb-flavored

The art of flavoring your own vodkas or using vodkas as a base for homemade liqueurs has now become a national hobby. To make pepper-flavored vodka, it is only necessary to steep slightly crushed peppercorns (whole black or white pepper) in vodka for three or four days, and then strain the spirits through cheesecloth or filter paper. The more peppercorns used, the more pungent the flavor. About 2 tablespoons to a pint of vodka give it a resounding zing. For kümmel liqueur, steep 2 tablespoons kümmel, pounded in a mortar, ½ teaspoon crushed coriander seeds, ¼ cup sugar syrup, and a 2-inch piece of orange rind in a pint of vodka for about two weeks, then strain. Star anise can be used in the same way for anise liqueur. To make tea vodka, place 2 tea bags in 4 ounces of vodka for several hours. It may be sweetened if desired. Apricots, cherries, and other fruits can be employed for your own imaginative combinations.

Because of its vivacious and seemingly endless versatility, vodka gives the inventive host unbridled rein to concoct new drinks indefinitely. When the spirit world was suddenly stirred up by screwdrivers about thirty years ago, it wasn't a question of loving vodka less but of loving orange juice more. Someone discovered a magnificent combination in vodka and ginger beer, the moscow mule. Shortly thereafter, longshoremen who liked to follow their straight whiskey with a beer chaser (the boilermaker) found that vodka could be poured right into the foamy suds of their beer mugs and the results were a liquid joyride. It was the time when hosts were discovering the brunch as the right meal at the right time of the weekend for easy entertaining, and they stretched out their hands to their guests with such vodka drinks as bloody marys, bullshots, and salty dogs. Vodka has since thrown down the gauntlet to gin in the vodka martini, the vodka and tonic, and the vodka gimlet. The black russian (vodka and Kahlúa liqueur) has a foamy cousin in the black cossack (vodka and Guinness Stout).

Finally there's the Russian and Scandinavian rite of skoaling you with a neat vodka, upending the glass in a single swallow. A good deal of high-go macho is involved in the custom. If repeated too frequently within too short a time span, both toaster and toastee will, as light is swallowed up by darkness, simply flicker out in the here's-looking-at-you routine. The best defense in this kind of situation is to make sure that every skoal is followed by a spoonful of caviar on toast, an anchovy canapé, a chunk of cheese, or any other hors d'oeuvre capable of delaying action. If the bottoms-up routine is repeated during the meal, it's wise to busy yourself playing a good knife and fork as assiduously as possible.

If you, as the host, are planning to offer vodka in this manner, use pony glasses, holding no more than one ounce. Fill each glass no more than three-quarters full. Serve your vodka icy cold, preferably enrobed in ice as described in Chapter 6. As the *arbiter bibendi*, be sure to keep the water goblets full, and drink unto others as you would have them drink unto you.

11

AND A BOTTLE
OF RUM

One of rum's most memorable
qualities is that it never lets you forget where it comes from. Bourbon,
Scotch, or gin drinkers don't necessarily think of corn-covered prairie-
land, peat bogs, or verdant groves of juniper shrubs while imbibing
their pet potations. But as soon as the first drop of rum is poured,
tropical touches inevitably begin to appear—plump mangoes, passion
fruit, ripe papayas, green limes, cool coconut milk, and pineapples as
heavy and musky as the jungle itself. Even without such exotic em-
bellishments, there's something in the sheer aroma and brandylike
smoothness of distilled sugarcane that spurs every mixmaster's imagination.

While making rum is an art, the secret of which is well guarded by
the few who hold it, the basic steps in the process can be described
simply: Remember, first of all, that rum is a by-product of sugar.
Sugarcane is crushed; it turns to cane juice; and in a small number of
distilleries this original juice is used to make rum. Most rum, however,
is made from molasses: The sugarcane juice is boiled down; part of
the rummish stew turns to crystallized sugar and is removed; the rest,
the "mother liquor" or molasses, is first fermented, then distilled. In
the big rum distilleries, the molasses is fermented by special strains
of yeast developed for specific rums and kept alive by lab technicians

who hover over their yeast dynasty like guardian angels, believing it's the inscrutable secret that makes their rum different from all other rums.

All rums are aged. The youngest blend of the prominent rums from Puerto Rico must, by law, be aged at least a year. Most of them are somewhat older. One would assume that the clear—"white"— rums were younger than those with a yellow tint called "golden." Actually, in some cases, the difference is merely the addition of caramel coloring. Some of the better-known rums don't attempt to attract the buyer with color but with age, plainly indicated on the label. Ronrico, for example, is four years old. Bacardi añejo is six years old. Other rare rums from some of the Caribbean islands range in age up to ten years or older, and some rank with the finest of velvety old brandies in flavor. In the aging warehouses of Don Q Puerto Rican rums, the casks are handled in a solera system, whereby a cask is never completely emptied; part of the old rum always remains to mingle with the new in such proportions that the new merges with the old and takes on its best features.

At least three-fourths of the yo-ho-ho sold in the States is Puerto Rican, a light, dry spirit in favor with contemporary freebooters. An oligarchy of Puerto Rican distillers takes more pride in their rum formulas than a Kentucky colonel takes in his bed of mint leaves. Warehouses in which the rum is kept for aging are patrolled day and night by armed government guards. The lock to each warehouse contains two keyholes, one for the owner and one for the government guard, so that neither can tamper with the sleeping golden distillate. And the government, in cooperation with the University of Puerto Rico, carries on a research program to keep the rum *ne plus ultra* in every drop that leaves the island.

Most of the white rum naturally finds its way into daiquiris, rum sours, rum martinis, and similar drinks. The rums with more flavor accent, the true golden rums, are the mainstays of rum on the rocks, rum and Coke, rum collinses, and other drinks where a distinct but not overpowering rum aftertaste is desirable. The sturdy, heavy-bodied rums with pungent flavors—typified by Jamaican rums—may in a few cases be taken straight, but are more likely to find their eventual homes in rum swizzles, planter's punch, winter punch bowls, and in mixed tropical drinks combined with lighter rums. Finally, 151-proof rums are now offered by many major distilleries. Rum of this strength has not only almost twice as much alcohol as the 80-proof rums but almost twice as much flavor concentrated in the bottle. At one time the best-known representative of this particular form of kill-devil was the Demerara rum from British Guiana, designed primarily to thaw the frozen veins of Canadian lumberjacks. Today 151-proof rums serve more urbane needs; their high proof makes them perfect accents for any dessert from *baba au rhum* to crêpes flambée. In mixed drinks the 151-proof rums, in small quantities, add a piquant note of concentrated rumminess. A bottle belongs in every man's rum library.

The personality of every rum, no matter how old it may be, depends upon its birthplace. The following guide may be helpful in making your selections:

Puerto Rican rum   At least three-fourths of the rum sold in the states is Puerto Rican—the prototype of lightness and dryness. Because the Puerto Rican government lays down the law controlling rum standards, all Puerto Rican rums—even the aged ones—are remarkably consistent in quality from one year to the next. Flavors range from the very gently flavored white or silver labels to the more mellow golden rums and on to the six-year or older añejo rums.

Virgin Islands rum   Although also in the light dry class, its flavor is slightly more reminiscent of molasses. Some of it seems to lack sufficient aging. Since some brands are shipped in bulk and bottled in the States, prices are generally lower than Puerto Rican rums.

Dominican rum   Ron Bermudez, distilled by a firm over 125 years old, is in the light dry class.

Barbados rum   Intermediate in flavor and color, Barbados rum is known for its soft finish and gentle aftertaste.

Cuban rum   Since normal trade relations do not now exist between Cuba and the States, no rum is imported, but visitors returning from Cuba usually bring back some of the famed rum from the island. Cuba was the original home of Bacardi—the daddy of light rums, now made in Puerto Rico and elsewhere and the third-best-selling hard liquor in the United States. Cuban rums have a light, dry but luscious flavor with just a trace of sweetness. If and when relations are resumed, one can see the Cuban rums rapidly flowing to the States.

U.S. rum   The three labels of rums made on mainland U.S.A. are La Conga, Libre Straight, and Pilgrim; all are of intermediate flavor, well suited for hot winter grog.

Demerara rum Rum from Guiana, named after the Demerara River and its large sugar fields, is intermediate to heavy in flavor and color; much of it is made from a combination of pot-stilled and column-stilled spirits; widely known in the states is the 151-proof variety.

Haitian rum Although there are a number of rum distilleries in Haiti, the best-known brand in the States is the famed Barbancourt rum, in the three-star and special-reserve five-star varieties, both 86 proof. The latter, an intermediate-bodied rum, is a magnificent brandy-like but mellow rum.

Martinique rum There are nearly fifty distilleries in the French colony, producing rums that range from white to heavily dark. The most eminent brand in the States is Rum Saint James. It is a heavy-bodied rum, well aged, bottled at 94 proof, and has been the darling of rum-sipping connoisseurs for years.

Jamaican rum At one time all Jamaican rum was known for its extremely heavy, pungent flavor. It was all made in pot stills from a mash fermented over a period of three weeks using only the wild yeast of the air. Today, yeast cultures are used, and rums are made from a combination of pot stills and modern column stills. Colors range from a pure white rum to extremely dark ones. In spite of these recent variations, the best-known Jamaican rums imported to this country are the traditional heavy-bodied types. Myers's rum and Appleton Punch rum, although both are only 80 proof, are still the sturdy, heavy-bodied, pungent rums indispensable to planter's punch and to those fans who like their rum really rummy with a lingering aftertaste. Other freebooters who want not only pungency but power can select Lemon Hart at 86 proof or Old Sea Dog twelve-year-old rum at 97 proof.

Trinidad rum Trinidad, best known in the States for its Angostura bitters, produces an intermediate-bodied rum veering to the light side, represented by Siegert's Bouquet 86 proof.

Batavian arak This pungent dry rum distilled and aged on the island of Java is seen very little in the States, although now and then a bottle is obtainable in specialty liquor stores. Its offbeat, far from gentle flavor is due to special molasses, local water, and the addition of Javanese rice in the fermenting vats.

Whether one chooses light or heavily flavored rums is sometimes a matter of the age of the drinker. Just as white wines are a pleasant introduction to Bacchus, while the more complex red wines appeal to older drinkers, so the dry white rum via a fruity mai tai or a frozen banana daiquiri seems to make its best impression on rum drinkers in the bloom of youth. As one gets older, rums with greater age and more intricate flavors, best savored in a leisurely way, seem more felicitous.

Any young man today who has learned to wet his lips with something other than water knows that rum has a peculiarly persuasive effect. Whiskey makes a girl stop arguing. Beer soothes her. Gin disarms her. But rum cajoles. No one has described the effect better than William James when he philosophized about alcohol: "It is in fact the great exciter of the Yes function in man. It brings its votary from the chill periphery of things to the radiant core."

12

TEQUILA

Visitors to Mexico thirty or forty years ago described the native hard liquor as somewhat akin to rattlesnake venom with an aftertaste carrying the impact of a thousand blackjacks. There was a measure of truth in what they said. Then, as now, you could go into rough village bars and order what was supposed to be tequila. In many cases it wasn't tequila made by the well-known Mexican distillers but a version turned out by local moonshiners. The powerful white fun water was unaged and uncut, tossed down just as it trickled out of the still. It was instant machismo at the highest possible proof, and gringos naturally associated it with the flavors of Mexican chilies and their explosive effects on the taste buds. Of course at that time Margarita was just a girl's name rather than a mixture of tequila, triple sec, and lime juice.

The tequila now flowing to the States, much of it aged and most of it bottled at 80 proof (the lowest proof allowed under U.S. federal regulations), bears no more resemblance to the legendary Mexican tarantula juice than Grand Champagne Cognac bears to Prohibition's bathtub gin. Its flavor is derived from a special agave plant grown in a delimited area about a hundred miles in circumference around the town of Tequila, near Guadalajara. The Mexican government keeps a tight hand on the type of plant, its harvesting, distillation, and labeling, just as the French government calls the signals on the brandy distilled and aged in or near the town of Cognac in the Charente.

First of all, one should clear up the little semantic matter of the words used to identify Mexico's hard liquor and the desert plant with long sharp leaves from which the liquor is made. Spanish explorers from Columbus on called the plant *maguey*. Later, the Swedish botanist Linnaeus called it *agave*, and this is the word that Statesiders and many Mexicans now use. The liquor derived from the plant is called tequila only if the plant is a certain blue species known as *agave azul* that flourishes in the special soil and climate near the town of Tequila. If the liquor is made from any other species growing in other parts of Mexico, it is called *mescal*.

For centuries, Mexicans have tapped the growing agave in the field, and have used the sweet juice to make a beerlike beverage called *pulque*. Pulque is *not* the base used for distilling tequila, and since the beverage is not suitable for shipping, it's not sold outside of its native habitat.

It takes between eight and twelve years for the agave to ripen to the stage where it's ready for distillation. But don't worry about the farmers growing it; in between the wide-spaced rows of agave, they grow corn, alfalfa, and other annual crops while waiting for the agave to reach adulthood. When the plant is ripe, the leaves are lopped off and the core, looking like a monster pineapple and weighing anywhere from 80 to 400 pounds, is separated from the plant and carried from the fields to the distillery. There it's steam-cooked for nearly three days until the woody pulp tastes something like a sweet potato— its starch has been turned to sugar. To convert the sugar to alcohol, the pulp is chopped and pressed for its juice, which is then mixed with yeast and fermented. Finally it is pot-stilled twice, and drawn off at a proof slightly above 100.

What isn't widely known in the States is the fact that most of the tequila we drink nowadays is actually a distillate of two principal ingredients. The first, naturally, is the agave plant, which comprises about 55 percent of the blend. The remaining 45 percent is a distillate of sugar or what's normally considered a rum base with an almost neutral flavor. One brand, Herradura, is made from 100 percent agave. The best tequilas, like many whiskeys and vodkas, are now charcoal-filtered, providing additional sauvity. Finally, tequilas coming to the States are now aged anywhere from several months to four years, and this adds to their civilized mellowness.

For most mixed drinks, you'll undoubtedly use the standard white tequila. But if you take tequila straight or on the rocks, you'll probably enjoy the older tequilas, often bearing the word "añejo" on the label and distinguished by their gold color. José Cuervo, for instance, the best-selling tequila in the States, turns out not only the standard white tequila but one called gold, aged a year in wood. Their most expensive, designated *1800*, is aged three to four years in oak barrels. It's a silky smooth tequila that one could proudly offer after dinner in a brandy snifter.

Gringos are somewhat startled by certain brands of mescal with a fat dead worm at the bottom of the bottle. This isn't just a display of Mexican machismo; rather, it is intended as a symbol of authenticity, since the worm—called the *gusano de maguey*—normally grows in the plant, and in Mexico has a certain fame as a food delicacy with a seafoodlike flavor akin to snails. The *gusano* doesn't alter the flavor of the mescal; rather, the mescal tunes up the flavor of the *gusano* according to *gusano* gourmets. At a party, the pickled *gusano* is a showstopper whenever margaritas or brave bulls are being poured.

Though much of it is golden in color, tequila is still listed by liquormen in the "white goods" category. But there's no identity crisis whatever as far as the flavor of tequila is concerned. Some drinkers, in the futile game of trying to describe it, see in it a resemblance to Dutch genever gin. To others the flavor is somewhat reminiscent of freshly ground peppercorns—and to still others there's a reminder of salt and perhaps sugar. Actually, like any distinguished liquor, tequila asserts its own individuality, and it can't and shouldn't be shoved into a simple descriptive slot. It's one of those acquired tastes, and it not only stands up extremely well but obviously keeps drawing more and more converts, since tequila sales continue to mount astronomically.

Indeed, if tequila sales continue to soar at the present rate, the restricted zone around the town of Tequila may not be able to appease the expanding thirst of tequila drinkers in both Mexico and elsewhere. To meet future needs, the Mexican government has given permission to grow the blue agave in another state, Tamaulipas, where the special climate and soil seem congenial to its healthy growth.

Although tequila, north of the Rio Grande, has come into wide use as a cocktail base, Mexicans and other tequila purists still toss it down using their famed here's-blowing-the-lid routine. Before hoisting the glass, the aficionado tilts his head back; squints in the direction of the camera, the spotlights, or the sun; and squeezes the freshest lime he can find directly into his mouth—and sometimes actually eats part of the lime. Then he swallows his straight tequila in a lightning chugalug, and finally laps up a dab of salt from the soft fleshy hollow between thumb and first finger. Sometimes the order is reversed, with the salt first and the lime last. But however the ritual is performed, all he's actually bolted down is a straight jigger of liquor with less potency than an American boilermaker (a shot of whiskey followed by beer). As much fun as it is to indulge in such drinking histrionics, tequila is equally enjoyable without lime, salt, or dramatics, served either icy cold or at room temperature, sipped and rolled about in the mouth as though you were tasting a fine bourbon or Scotch.

When Christopher Columbus wrote about the Indian drink made from the "marrow of the maguey," he may have been referring to pulque—the fermented juice of the maguey, or the distilled beverage we know as tequila. Quibblers may argue that the art of distillation was introduced to the New World from the Old, but scholars of potable spirits aren't so sure; some believe that the Mexican Indians may indeed have discovered distillation independently. If they did, tequila was undoubtedly the weapon they used to conquer their Spanish conquerors. As early as the 1700s the Mexicans, in the true spirit of imaginative bartenders, were not only drinking their spirits straight but were making countless mixed drinks including a mixture of mescal, lemon juice, cloves, and nutmeg; another of mescal stirred with honey; and a third of mescal and the juice of the prickly pear.

Today, tequila's camaraderie with anything from tomato juice to tonic water makes it a wonderful prop for imaginative hosts who like to offer their guests bloody marias instead of marys, and tequila, instead of Tom, collinses. The best-known mixed drink, the margarita, sometimes miscarries because of the heavy rim of salt around the glass in which it's served. Actually, salt and tequila are a wonderful compound, just as a light spray of salt on grapefruit or a pinch of salt in a hot chocolate acts as a natural flavor pick-me-up. But too much salt is *muy malo*. A sensible way to offer the margarita is to rub about an inch of the rim of a prechilled cocktail glass with lemon or orange peel and dip that inch in salt. Then make your margarita, and let the drinker take or leave the salt. Or, omit the salt entirely on the glass, and offer a small open saltcellar with the drink, permitting the guest to sprinkle as much or as little as he wants directly into the glass.

Travelers in Mexico are often introduced to *sangrita*. It's sold as a liquid mix in bottles and looks like the tomato-juice mix for a bloody mary. Generally there's no tomato juice in it—the principal ingredients being orange juice, sweetened and colored red with grenadine and made piquant with assorted spices including the hottest Mexican chili peppers. Tequila veterans in Mexico order their tequila straight with a glass of sangrita on the side, and then toss down the sangrita and tequila in alternate gulps. In many Mexican homes, however, a fresh sangrita is made which does include tomato juice as well as orange juice, onion, and spices. (See the version on page 293.) It joins hands beautifully with tequila taken straight and is delightful with many mixed drinks, one of the most popular of which is the vampiro, a tall drink of tequila, sangrita, and grapefruit juice (see page 387).

As a mixer in short, medium, or tall drinks, tequila has sumptuous possibilities. Whatever associations the taste of tequila brings to you, and however you choose to drink it, the pleasant afterglow is always *muy simpatico.*

13

APÉRITIFS

Preprandial Potations

oo often in the conviviality of the cocktail hour, drinks are gulped as indifferently as one clinks ice in a highball. But apéritifs, straight or mixed, are never taken for granted. Observe, for example, the Frenchman in his natural habitat, as each afternoon he sits at his favorite café table and partakes of his Byrrh, Amer Picon, or vermouth cassis with attentive enjoyment. To him, each day's apéritif is an excitingly different experience. He observes its color, savors its scent, and samples it with a relish one usually associates with newfound pleasures. His senses then undergo the most salutary of metamorphoses: Taste buds tingle in anticipation of the evening repast; the local scenery becomes more vivid; and the passing *mesdemoiselles*, though they may be the same *jeunes filles* who promenade daily past his table, are surveyed with fresh appreciation.

Even the etymology of "apéritif" evokes its appetite-awakening effects. Though the word is French, it's best understood by going back to its Latin source, *aperio*, meaning "to open, to lay bare." Swallow a jigger of Campari with soda on ice; its unabashed bitterness may cause you to shake your head dubiously over what has been proclaimed a prime libational pleasure, but soon waves of hunger sweep over you, and you can hardly wait for the antipasto tray; thoughts of the anticipated anchovy fillets, cracked black olives, prosciutto, roasted-pepper salad, and wafer-thin slices of Genoa salami are almost overpowering.

The apértif's ancient origins are a reminder that the world's first great wines were sharp potations. In 400 B.C., Hippocrates stopped prescribing medicines long enough to conjure up a lusty elixir of wine, resin, and bitter almonds. Pliny, an antiapéritif man, called the consumption of such concoctions before meals "an outlandish fashion recommended by doctors who are always trying to advertise themselves by some newfangled ideas." Undaunted, adventurous Romans began to create preprandial potations not only from the grape but from turnips, radishes, asparagus, parsley, thyme, mint, hyssop, and almost anything else that sprang up around the villa. Even seawater was added for tang. Often, grapevines were surrounded by other plants placed close enough to the roots so that their insinuating essences would seep through the soil into the fruit before it was plucked. If, now and then, a decidedly toxic plant like wormwood worked its way into a wine, pleasure-seeking Romans didn't hesitate to drink it anyway—as long as it didn't offend their aesthetic sensibilities.

Modern apéritifs, happily, are admixtures of wine, spirits, and as many as forty different kinds of harmless but equally exotic spices, roots, barks, herbs, buds, and flowers from every corner of the earth. The family is a surprisingly large one with several distinct branches: the wine-based apéritifs (such as Byrrh, Dubonnet, and Punt e Mes); the vermouths (sweet and dry); the distilled apéritifs (Amer Picon, Pernod, pastis, and the like); and such stomach-settling bitters as Dutch Boonekamp.

In American frontier days, plainsmen mixed a pint of water with two tablespoons of buffalo gall for a "wholesome and exhilarating drink." Some years later, Kansans refined the formula, combining a mere ounce of wahoo (bark of the winged elm tree, also used for making string and rope) with a quart of whiskey. Somewhat more sophisticated American traditions are observed, along with the European, in the following roster of contemporary wines and liquors used as apéritifs.

Amer Picon   A bittersweet French apéritif liqueur of quinine, orange, and gentian, sometimes mixed with ice, soda, and grenadine, served as an apéritif punch in an eight-ounce glass.

Boonekamp bitters   Dutch-style bitters taken neat before a meal as a stomachic.

Byrrh (pronounced *beer*)   A French proprietary apéritif wine with a tangy aftertaste.

Campari   An Italian *aperitivo*, 48 proof, taken with soda and often with a twist of orange peel. Mixed half-and-half with Italian sweet vermouth, you get an americano; with Italian sweet vermouth and gin, a negroni.

Chambery Fraise   One of the lightest and most delicately flavored of all French dry vermouths, with a hint of wild strawberries.

Chambraise   Strawberry-flavored French vermouth.

Crème de cassis   Made from black currants, it's actually a liqueur because of its sweetness. In the best-known version, it's combined with vermouth, ice, and soda as a vermouth cassis, or with white wine as a *vin blanc cassis*.

Cynar   An Italian apéritif liqueur made from artichokes.

Dubonnet   A quinine-flavored apéritif wine originally imported from France, now made in the United States, in both red and white types. One or two parts Dubonnet to one part gin is a Dubonnet cocktail.

Fernet Branca   Of Italian origin, now made in the United States, it combines compatibly with gin or Cognac and vermouth as a pre-prandial cocktail.

French Kiss   A French blend of dry and sweet vermouths.

Kir Gallique   A blend of crème de cassis and white wine—a combination, when mixed to order, also known as kir or *vin blanc cassis*.

Lillet   This French red or white apéritif wine has a subtle orange flavor with a subdued bitterness.

Muscari   A sweet-tart apéritif wine imported from Portugal, with flavors of orange and almond.

Ouzo   A Middle Eastern high-proof anise liqueur taken before or after dinner.

Pastis   An anise-flavored apéritif liqueur that, like ouzo, turns milky white when mixed with water. It's a favorite of Marseilles fishermen and Riviera jet-setters.

Pernod   A 90-proof French anise-flavored apéritif liqueur reminiscent of absinthe (which is now illegal). When used in place of vodka in a screwdriver, it's called the tiger's tail.

Pinot des Charente   A French blend of wine from the Cognac region plus a small amount of Cognac brandy; may be either white or rosé.

Port wine, white   In its white version, this consummate Portuguese product, with its full-bodied flavor and bouquet, is immensely popular in France and Belgium as a sundown apéritif; one of its best representatives here is Sandeman's porto branco.

Positano   A semidry apéritif vermouth with a pleasant, decisive aftertaste.

Punt e Mes   A deep, dark Italian apéritif wine known for its provocative bitterness.

Quinquina   A French apéritif wine with the subtly bitter taste of quinine.

Raki   A brandy-based, high-proof, anise-flavored apéritif liqueur from the Middle East.

St.-Raphaël   A proprietary French apéritif wine noted for its full body and clean flavor.

Sherry, fino   Bone-dry Spanish sherry, served as an apéritif with or without ice. Even medium-dry sherries are now appearing as appetite sharpeners.

Shogun   A blend of sake and white wine.

Suze   A dry, 40-proof French apéritif flavored with orange and gentian.

Vermouth   An herb-flavored wine, fortified with brandy, containing 16 to 19 percent alcohol. May be either red, white, or rosé. At one time, French vermouth was light, dry, almost white; Italian vermouth, sweet, heavy, red. Nowadays, both types are produced in Italy, France, South America, and the United States. For mixing purposes, dry vermouth should be light in color with subtle overtones; sweet vermouth, round in flavor, sweet but not cloying. But both should be able to stand in their own right as straight iced drinks, trenchant, tantalizing, never tiresome.

It should be obvious even from this basic list that the choice of appetite arousers is as diverse as it is diverting. Sipped straight from the bottle or elaborately combined, any of these lively potations will turn on your taste buds with delightful dispatch.

14
LIQUEURS
Cordially Speaking

Centuries ago, liqueurs weren't just sweet little drams to be sipped around a fireplace but wondrous philters believed capable of conjuring all kinds of supernatural feats. Distillers in those days weren't ordinary stillmen moonshining for a living but alchemists whose cordials, it was claimed, "strengtheneth any weake member of man's body" and keep "evil cogitations coming to minde." A certain sweet potion, it was said, "refreshes the spirits and corroborates the brains" (a wonderful solace for those men whose brains occasionally needed corroboration), cured assorted ills, and, above all, restored feeble oldsters to the vigor of their youth.

Professional liquormen today see their elixirs playing a role which in one important respect is diametrically opposite to their medieval predecessors. Rather than restoring youth, liqueurs—according to an analysis of modern buying habits—seem to be opening the buds of youth to the full flower of maturity. As liqueur sales zoom to ever-rising heights (in the past twenty years they've quadrupled), more and more young people are discovering that the easiest way of jumping the generation gap is to switch from a Hershey Bar to a pony of chocolate almond liqueur.

Chocolate addicts of all ages, in fact, who once had to confine themselves to crème de cacao, can now roam over a field that includes such liqueur combinations as chocolate mint; chocolate banana; chocolate raspberry; chocolate cherry; Choclair—a combination of chocolate and coconut; as well as imported Sabra from Israel, made of chocolate and orange; and Verana, a chocolate, orange, and almond combination from Spain.

And it's not only the liquid chocolate bar that's humming with new varieties; the whole arena of liqueurs seems to be seething with as many new and old varieties as there are people to sip them. Traditional liqueurs concocted from tender rose petals or flakes of twenty-carat gold are challenged by a new one from Japan with the refreshing cool flavor of honeydew melon, and another from Germany faithfully duplicating the subtle flavor of Darjeeling tea.

While the younger crowd today seems to go for the relatively simple liqueurs with one or two dominant flavors, the more mature drinkers continue to find pleasure in the great French monastery liqueurs, spirits that are moderately sweet but with richly complex flavors. Hosts know that a simple pony of Benedictine, or Benedictine and brandy, will make a routine dinner memorable. Liqueurs like Chartreuse, Benedictine, and Izarra, although no longer in the exclusive hands of monks, are status liqueurs not just because of their price but because their flavors never seem to become tiresome. Their formulas, naturally, are kept secret, although it's acknowledged that Benedictine is based on twenty-seven herbs and plants; that Izarra is made of forty-eight herbs, spices, and flowers; while Chartreuse contains no less than 130 ingredients. The macho minority who still think that liqueurs are made for softies should try Yukon Jack, a liqueur with a Canadian whisky base at 100 proof, or green Chartreuse at a stunning 110 proof.

Even many of the seemingly simple liqueurs often reveal flavor complexities and bouquets that vary drastically from one label to another. One need only compare Kahlúa coffee liqueur from Mexico to the espresso-coffee liqueur from Italy to see the vast gulf between liqueurs derived from a similar source. Even as presumably simple a liqueur as the blackberry-flavored brandy made in this country by Leroux contains no fewer than seven different kinds of blackberries: Each must be balanced from crop to crop each year and from batch to batch; and to make the final blend even more deliciously fruity, a small stream of fresh raspberries, with their soft but lush savor, or rich-scented loganberries, may be added as artful supporting flavors.

Liqueurs are infusions, percolations, or distillations made from fantastically complex formulas containing—besides a base of brandy or other spirits and sugar—fruits, flowers, herbs, seeds, spices, roots, bark, and kernels gathered from every corner of the world. Infusion is the same as making tea: Fresh apricots, for example, are steeped in a tank with spirits till both fruit and spirits are intimately united. Percolation is like making coffee: Sloes, for example, are placed in a basket, and spirits from the bottom of the percolator are pumped over them to make sloe gin (which, as noted earlier, isn't a gin at all but a liqueur). For many liqueurs, infusion or percolation are only beginning steps. After flavor extraction, they're distilled into a subtly flavored final product. Certain liqueurs are distillations alone, through a flavor head containing, in the case of curaçao for example, sweet and bitter orange peels. White crème de cacao is made by distillation alone. Brown crème de cacao is made by all three forms of legerdemain.

Men shopping for liqueurs are often bewildered by the nomenclature on the bottles. In the first place, let it be understood that the words "liqueur" and "cordial" mean exactly the same thing. For many generations, both English and American puritans shunned the word "liqueur," thinking it would identify them too closely with the hard-liquor set; if a drink was called a "clove cordial" or a "conserve of Cowslips Good Against Melancholie," it was considered perfectly respectable. Early liqueur drinkers in Europe used both words together, *liqueurs cordialis*—meaning liqueurs of the heart—to describe the mellifluous compounds invented by monks and dispensed in monasteries for all whose spiritual comfort was miraculously braced by a small potion of bodily comfort. To add to the confusion, some French liqueurs, in France, are still called *digestifs*.

Besides the words "liqueur" and "cordial," the phrase "fruit-flavored brandy" appears on many American products these days. This term also refers to a sweet type of after-dinner drink, but with this basic difference: Fruit-flavored brandy must be made with a brandy base, while other liqueurs can be made with a base of any distilled spirits. Also, fruit-flavored brandies are generally somewhat less sweet than liqueurs and crèmes and somewhat higher in proof.

The word "crème" normally means a liqueur of special smoothness and with a flavor having pronounced body. The word "liqueur" is all-inclusive, taking in the crèmes, the fruit-flavored brandies, and the cordials. Outstanding Cognacs, rums, and Scotches sometimes bear the word "liqueur" on their labels, but don't be misled; it's a boast of excellence rather than a literal description of the contents, which have no resemblance to a true sweet liqueur.

Finally, one more semantic misdemeanor: In the New York–New Jersey area, local liquor regulations forbid selling hard liquor in half-pint bottles. To fill the needs of drinkers on the run, whiskeys, gins, vodkas, and such are slightly sweetened and bottled in half-pints, ready for the coat or hip pocket; they're sometimes called "dry liqueurs." However silly the term may sound, it simply means a spirit with as little sweetness as possible that still stays within the federal definition of a liqueur.

For hosts who don't have the shelf room to store a wide assortment of liqueurs, the compartmented bottle containing from two to four assorted liqueurs is a convenient asset. If you like to pass a tray of assorted liqueurs with or after the coffee, the new 16.9-ounce (500 ml.—formerly a pint) bottles are more easily handled than fifths. If there's a new imported or domestic liqueur that seems intriguing but whose flavor is unknown to you, buy the miniature 1.7-ounce size for taste exploration before you invest in a large bottle. If you're starting a liqueur collection from scratch and want to be able to offer a reasonable assortment, a bottle each of a coffee liqueur, an anisette, one of the peppermint family like crème de menthe, and one of the proprietary liqueurs like Chartreuse or Peter Heering would be a good starting collection. Of course, if your own fancy runs to something special like one of the chocolate liqueurs or one of the orange family, by all means indulge yourself.

Often you'll want to buy a liqueur for use in a mixed drink. On the West Coast where margaritas (tequila, triple sec, and lime juice) are almost as popular as martinis on the East Coast, a bottle of triple sec or other orange liqueur would be part of your basic bar supply. There are parts of the country where sloe gin and Coke, or peppermint schnapps and soda, are favorites, and where these liqueurs are always kept on hand for private as well as party bashes. There are vogues in liqueurs, and in many quarters none is now more glittering than amaretto, a relative unknown a few years back, a liqueur made from either almonds or apricot pits and now available under at least three dozen labels. For years, one of the eminent American liqueurs was Forbidden Fruit, made with a West Indian citrus fruit resembling grapefruit. Forbidden Fruit is still on the shelves, but it is now a delightful apple liqueur. One of the most recent in the long parade of liqueurs is Vaklova, vodka-based spirits with pleasant herblike overtones, bottled at 80 proof.

At impromptu parties, hosts who dust off the old bottle of anisette just because it happened to have lingered on the shelf for too many years should be advised that any bottle of liqueur, after it's opened, has a limited shelf life. It won't turn sour like wine or otherwise become a drinking hazard, but its flavor in some cases after six months will go downhill. Low-proof liqueurs like a 40-proof triple sec will tend to deteriorate more readily than a liqueur at 80 or 100 proof.

In recent years liqueur cocktails—icy mixtures of liqueurs, fruit juices, and in many cases sweet cream—have all but supplanted the heavier, more conventional desserts at many party tables. (See Chapter 19). They're easy, exciting, and the number of possible creative combinations add up to what Milton called "a wilderness of sweets."

Here now, from abisante to zitronen, is our lexicon of the principal liqueurs available to Americans.

Abisante   One of the modern replacements for the now outlawed absinthe. The pale-green anise-flavored liqueur turns opalescent when allowed to drip slowly over ice.

Abricots, crème d', or Abricotine   French cream-of-apricot liqueur. It's luscious when drizzled over cracked ice in a champagne glass.

Absinthe   This anise-flavored liqueur was originally 136 proof and made with wormwood, and it was hard to tell whether the proof or the poison was more shattering. It is now illegal in most countries. The firm of Pernod, which originally made absinthe in France, still turns out a luscious 90-proof liqueur in its own name.

Advokaat   An eggnog liqueur, originally from Holland and now concocted in the United States. This 40-proof mixture of grain neutral spirits, egg yolks, and sugar usually goes into holiday tipple, accented with rum or brandy. It comes in a thick type of almost custard consistency as well as a thinner version.

Afri Koko   A 65-proof liqueur of coconut and chocolate imported from Africa.

AK: 49-proof Japanese plum liqueur.

Allasch   A sweet, cumin-flavored version of kümmel, it takes its name from the Latvian town where it originated; the name since appropriated by other kümmel makers means little now.

Almond, crème d' A pink liqueur flavored with almonds and/or fruit pits; similar to crème de noyaux. It's been almost pushed out of the picture by amaretto (see below).

Almondrado A Mexican almond liqueur with a tequila base.

Amaretto The reigning queen of the nut-flavored liqueurs. The original version was made from almonds; other amarettos are made with apricot pits. It's also available in combinations such as chocolate amaretto, amaretto and brandy, amaretto and coffee, amaretto and orange, etc.

Ambrosia A 56-proof liqueur from Canada.

Amer Picon A French apéritif liqueur of quinine, oranges, and gentian, served as an apéritif rather than a postprandial liqueur.

Anise; Anisette; Anesone Liqueurs flavored with anise seeds, reminiscent of licorice; they're usually white but may be colored red. Although anise is the principal feature of the flavor profile, other spices are used by individual bottlers. Proofs range from the 60s to 100; anesone is usually higher in proof and less sweet than anise.

Apple-flavored brandy An apple liqueur, used in drinks calling for applejack such as the Jack Rose cocktail; since it's sweet, sugar is omitted from the mixed-drink recipe.

Apricot-flavored brandy A somewhat less sweet version of cream-of-apricot liqueur.

Apricot liqueur; apry; crème d'abricots; abricotine All are names for the liqueur made from the pulp and pits of apricots.

Aurum Italian orange liqueur with overtones of herbs, made with a brandy base.

Bahai A 50-proof Brazilian coffee liqueur.

Balsam Haitian banana liqueur.

Banana liqueur; bananes, crème de Buy American labels marked "true fruit flavor" which are known for their fidelity to original banana flavor; most brands are quite sweet; may be used in place of the fresh fruit for a banana daiquiri.

Benedictine One of the greatest of the monastery liqueurs, made of herbs, roots, and sugar, with a Cognac base. It started reviving tired monks in 1510. Now a proprietary liqueur, the letters D.O.M. on the label stand for *Deo Optimo Maximo*, "to God, most good, most great." The B & B is brandy and Benedictine, one of the most urbane of after-dinner potions.

Ben Shalom   Israeli orange liqueur, 64 proof.

Black currant liqueur   Normally labeled crème de cassis (see below).

Blackberry-flavored brandy   Less sweet and usually of higher proof than blackberry liqueur (below); not to be confused with completely dry Hungarian blackberry brandy.

Blackberry liqueur   One of the most successful of the berry liqueurs, usually either 50 or 60 proof as opposed to the 70-proof blackberry-flavored brandy; makes a superb blackberry sour by shaking a jigger of the liqueur with ½ ounce lemon juice and ice, no sugar required.

Cacao, crème de   Liqueur with a base of cacao (chocolate) and vanilla beans. It is available in both brown and white versions, the latter always used in grasshopper cocktails, the former in alexanders.

Cacao Mit Nuss   Crème de cacao with a hazelnut flavor.

Café Benedictine   A 60-proof liqueur that's a combination of coffee liqueur and Benedictine (see above).

Café, crème de   The French name for coffee liqueur is used both by American and foreign distillers. See coffee liqueur below.

Café de love   A 53-proof coffee liqueur from Mexico.

Café orange   A combination of coffee and orange liqueurs.

Calisay   Quinine-flavored liqueur from Spain, of medium sweetness.

Caramella   Caramel-and-vanilla-flavored liqueur, decidedly sweet.

Cassis, crème de   A low-proof liqueur made from French black currants. Although sweet, it's used as an apéritif in vermouth cassis or white-wine cassis.

Cerise, crème de   French name for cherry liqueur.

Chartreuse   Green 110 proof or yellow 86 proof, it has been made by the Carthusian monks since 1605. The green, most eminent of all liqueurs, contains 130 herbs. The Carthusian order, twice expelled from France, took the secret formula with them to Spain but couldn't find the precise herbs, and Chartreuse in exile never came up to the one produced on native soil. A few bottles of pre-expulsion Chartreuse, made before 1903, were sold at $125 per bottle.

Cheri-Suisse A liqueur flavored with chocolate and cherries, extremely well balanced.

Cherristock A popular Italian cherry liqueur from the Stock distillery; known for its fresh fruity flavor.

Cherry-flavored brandy Of higher alcoholic content than most cherry liqueurs, sometimes made with wild black cherries.

Cherry Heering Former name of Peter Heering, famed Danish cherry liqueur.

Cherry liqueur Somewhat sweeter than cherry-flavored brandy (above); often made with both sweet and wild cherries.

Cherry blossom liqueur A Suntory Japanese liqueur, 44 proof, with very light cherry flavor.

Cherry Marnier A French cherry liqueur made by the distillers of famed French Grand Marnier, with hint of almond in flavor.

Cherry- and peach-flavored brandy Well-balanced 70-proof flavor duo.

Cherry Rocher A French cherry liqueur known for its true fruit flavor.

Cherry with rum German 48-proof cherry liqueur with a rum base.

Cherry vanilla A U.S. 54-proof liqueur combining cherry and vanilla flavors, with the cherry predominating.

Choclair U.S. coconut-and-chocolate liqueur with herbal overtones.

Chococo A Virgin Islands liqueur also combining coconut and chocolate.

Chu Yeh Ching Chien A clear 92.9-proof liqueur with sharp herbal flavors from mainland China.

Claristine Spicy herbal U.S. liqueur made by Leroux, who follows the formula once used by the Clarisse nuns of Belgium.

CocoRibe   A combination of coconut and rum in a 60-proof liqueur.

Coffee liqueur   It comes under many names, including Kahlúa from Mexico, Tia Maria from Jamaica, Espresso from dark-roasted Italian coffee, crème de café, Brazilia, Pasha from Turkey, etc. Any of the large galaxy is delightful ice-cold with heavy sweet cream floating on top.

Coffee and ginger brandy   Moderately sweet coffee liqueur livened with ginger flavor.

Coffee sambuca   A combination of coffee liqueur and sambuca; the latter is an Italian liqueur made from the elder bush.

Cognac and orange   A combination of triple-distilled orange liqueur and French Cognac is made by Leroux in the United States.

Cointreau   An eminent French liqueur made by maceration and double distillation of bitter and sweet orange peels; one of the best-selling in the world's family of orange liqueurs.

Cordial Médoc   A French liqueur made from a blend of oranges, cherries, brandy, and crème de cacao.

Cranberry liqueur   A U.S. liqueur with the tart-sweet flavor of fresh cranberries.

Cuarenta y Tres   The words mean 43 in Spanish, signifying the number of ingredients in this vanilla-accented, mildly herbal, decidedly sweet liqueur.

Curaçao   A liqueur made of the dried peel of small green oranges grown in the Dutch West Indies, plus spices and sometimes port wine and rum. It may be white, blue, or green, although it is normally orange in color from the maceration of bitter orange peels.

Danziger Goldwasser   Goldwasser liqueur (see below) which originated in the city of Danzig, Poland.

Delecta   The U.S. version of a Benedictine-type liqueur, made from herbs and spices.

Drambuie   Originally from a recipe presented to the Mackinnon family, present guardians of its formula, by Bonnie Prince Charlie, this liqueur, made from Scotch whisky at least ten years old, heather honey, and herbs, gets its name from the Gaelic phrase *an dram buid-heach,* or "the drink that satisfies."

Escorial   A German herbal liqueur of Green Chartreuse type, 112 proof, two degrees higher than the French prototype.

Enzian   A Bavarian 80-proof liqueur made from the yellow enzian plant; always served ice-cold.

Fior di alpi; fiore d'alpe; flora di alpi; flora alpina   All four spellings refer to an Italian liqueur of herbs and spices. The bottle contains a twig covered with crystallized sugar.

Forbidden Fruit   Now a U.S. apple liqueur, 64 proof; the name was formerly used for a liqueur of West Indian grapefruit-type fruit.

Fraises, crème de; fraisette   Liqueur of either wild or cultivated strawberries; Dolfi fraise de bois is the most prestigious brand of the wild-strawberry category.

Framboise, crème de   This raspberry liqueur—not to be confused confused with framboise, a white, unsweetened raspberry brandy— makes a refreshing summer highball with lemon juice, soda water, and ice. It also takes the place of Melba sauce in peach Melba.

Frangelico   An Italian hazelnut liqueur with flavors of berries and flowers.

Galliano   A mildly spicy but extremely smooth liqueur from Solaro, Italy, with flavor overtones of anise and vanilla; one of principal ingredients in the Harvey Wallbanger cocktail.

Gebirgs Enzian   A German liqueur with the flavor of gentian root; decidedly on the bitter side; used as stomachic.

George M. Tiddy's Canadian Liqueur   A 72-proof liqueur of medium sweetness and citrusy overtones.

Gilka   German kümmel liqueur.

Ginger-flavored brandy   An infusion of fresh ginger root and brandy, usually taken straight or on crushed ice.

Glayva   A liqueur with a Scotch-whisky base, flavored with honey, anise, and herbs.

Goldwasser, Danziger; gold liqueur   Goldwasser is the German version of an aromatic liqueur made since 1598. Gold liqueur is the modern U.S. rendition. It contains specks of gold leaf so light they leave no sensation in the mouth. The gold is harmless and makes the orange-herbal liqueur a sensational conversation piece as an after-dinner drink. In spite of the price of gold, a bottle of gold liqueur costs less than $6.00 a fifth, perhaps a clue to the amount of gold you ingest with each sip.

Grand Marnier   Distinguished French orange liqueur with a Cognac base, aged in oak casks; famed not only as an after-dinner liqueur but as an ingredient in haute cuisine desserts.

Grasshopper   A green-colored liqueur made of white crème de cacao and green crème de menthe; may be sipped straight or shaken with cream and ice for a grasshopper cocktail.

Green tea liqueur   A Japanese Suntory liqueur, 50 proof, with a velvety, true green-tea flavor.

Grenadine   Normally a nonalcoholic sweetener made of pomegranates, the liqueur is a 25-proof version, available in liquor shops, which saves the job of searching for it in supermarkets; used in the sunrise cocktail.

Halb und Halb   A mildly bitter German liqueur with citrusy accents.

Herbsaint   Another substitute for absinthe, without harmful worm-wood.

Honey liqueur   A liqueur usually from central Europe, the first sip of which will remind you of easily flowing honey. It's a natural mixer in brandy milk punch, eggnog, etc.

Hungarian pear liqueur   A 60-proof liqueur of a fruit usually distilled as a nonsweet eau de vie.

Irish Mist   Irish whiskey, honey, and orange make this mellifluous liqueur a delightful after-dinner drink; its subtlety is somewhat lost when used in Irish coffee.

Izarra   A French herbal liqueur of the Chartreuse type, which includes Armagnac in its base. The green version is 100 proof; the yellow, 86 proof.

Jägermeister   German 70-proof liqueur with bitter overtones, made from fifty-six herbs.

Kahlúa   Mexican coffee liqueur, richly sweet with a vanilla overtone, famed for the black russian cocktail.

Kirsch, crème de; kirschwasser liqueur   A sweet white cherry liqueur, not to be confused with the completely dry kirschwasser, a white brandy or eau de vie.

Kümmel   A caraway-flavored liqueur, usually colorless, varying considerably in sweetness depending on brands; the best continental versions are on the dry side.

Lemonique   A liqueur with zest-of-lemon flavor.

Liqueur d'Or   Gold-flecked liqueur of Goldwasser type (see above).

Lochan Ora   Scotch-based liqueur of medium sweetness and delicate herbal flavors.

Macadamia   Liqueur of the famed Hawaiian nuts, available in Hawaii but not widely distributed on the U.S. mainland.

Mandarine   An 80-proof liqueur of tangerines with a Cognac base.

Maraschino   A heavily sweet liqueur of cherry and almond flavors, widely used in fruit compotes and other desserts.

Mastic; mastikha; mastika   A Greek liqueur made of the mastic shrub; extremely pleasant, high-proof, on the dry side, but there's very little available in the United States.

Menthe, crème de   This liqueur made of mint leaves may be white, green, pink, or gold. The small amount of menthol in fresh mint leaves gives it its refreshing coolness. Most versions are heavily sweet in contrast with peppermint schnapps below.

Midori   A Japanese liqueur with the flavor of honeydew melon.

Moka, crème de   Coffee liqueur.

Noisette   A liqueur of hazelnuts usually combined with herbal flavors.

Noyaux, crème de, or crème de noya   Pink liqueur made with the stones of such fruits as plums, cherries, peaches, and apricots, producing a predominantly almond flavor.

O-Cha   Japanese green-tea liqueur with a bitter aftertaste; the perfect finale for an Oriental dinner.

Ojen   A colorless anise-flavored Spanish liqueur. There are some high-proof bottlings in both sweet and dry varieties.

Ouzo   A high-proof Greek apéritif liqueur, somewhat on the dry side; it's similar to the French pastis with its anise base and is usually mixed with ice water, in which it turns milky-looking.

Parfait amour   Although the words *parfait amour* mean "perfect love," liqueurmen have never agreed on the formula for perfection. One kind is made of lemon, citron, and coriander; another of anisette, vanilla, and orange; a third is produced from flowers, including violets. The only constant is its purple color.

Pasha   Richly flavored, spicily accented coffee liqueur from Turkey, vividly reminiscent of Turkish coffee itself.

Passion fruit liqueur   A Hawaiian product with the intriguing tart flavor of fresh passion fruit, reminiscent of peach or mango.

Pastis; pastis de Marseille   An aniselike liqueur used as both an apéritif and a thirst quencher; it makes an immensely refreshing on-the-rocks drink. The best-known brand in this country is Ricard 90 proof.

Peach-flavored brandy   Of higher alcohol content and less sweet than peach liqueur (below).

Peach liqueur   Made from an infusion of whole fruit, sometimes fresh, or fresh and dried mixed, with brandy or neutral spirits as a base. It is an essential, though small, ingredient in fish-house punch.

Peanut Lolita   America's newest nut liqueur, launched during the term of our first peanut-farmer president.

Pear liqueur   A 60-proof liqueur from Hungary with the hard-to-capture flavor of fresh pears.

Peppermint schnapps   Mint liqueur of higher alcoholic content and less sweet than crème de menthe; often taken on the rocks or with soda and ice.

Peppermint Get   A very popular French mint liqueur, heavily sweet, 60 proof, noted for mint-flavor fidelity.

Pernod   A 90-proof licorice-flavored liqueur which is served both as an apéritif and postprandial liqueur; refreshing when served in a high-ball glass with ice and water.

Peter Heering   Formerly Cherry Heering; a famed 49-proof Danish liqueur with vivid, tart, natural cherry flavor.

Pimento Dram   Jamaican rum liqueur with peppery, spicy overtones.

Pineapple liqueur; licor de pina; crème d'ananas   Liqueur from the Caribbean or Hawaii with straight, uncomplicated pineapple flavor.

Pistachio liqueur; pistasha   Medium-sweet green liqueur with the flavor of pistachio nuts.

Ponche   Heavily sweet liqueur with pronounced sherry brandy taste and raisiny overtones.

Prunella; prunelle, crème de   Liqueur with the predominant flavor of small tart plums, sometimes blended with prunes and sometimes with figs and vanilla.

Raki   High-proof anise-flavored liqueur from the Middle East.

Raspail   French herbal liqueur of the Benedictine type.

Raspberry liqueur; framboise   Liqueur made from fresh or wild raspberries.

Ratafia   A general term for apéritif liqueurs from France, made of assorted fruits and fruit pits.

Rock and rum   The same as rock and rye (below), except with a rum base; superb in milk punch.

Rock and rye   Rye whiskey, rock-candy syrup, and fruit juices, with slices of fruit in the bottle. Another type contains crystallized sugar and no fruit. This old-fashioned winter solacer is a natural for hot drinks in mugs.

Roiano   An amber Italian liqueur with the flavor of anise and vanilla.

Ron Coco   A 60-proof liqueur of rum and coconut.

Rose, crème de   A liqueur of vanilla, spices, and the aroma of rose petals. An enchanting end for a shish-kebab party.

Rosémint   A pink-hued mint liqueur.

Rosolio   Similar to crème de rose above but less sweet, flavored with spices and orange-blossom water.

Rumona   A 63-proof liqueur from Jamaica with a rum base and flavors reminiscent of coffee and chocolate.

Sabra   A chocolate-orange liqueur from Israel.

Sambuca   Italian liqueur made from the sambuca plant whose fruit is close to anise in flavor; usually served with a few coffee beans for munching. **Caffé Sambuca** combines coffee and sambuca liqueurs.

Sciarada   Italian 80-proof liqueur with the color of lime and the flavors of orange and lemon that manage to be both subdued and lively at the same time.

Sloe gin   This red liqueur, made from the sloe plums of the blackthorn bush, is not a gin at all, though juniper berries are sometimes used in its manufacture. It is probably called gin after the European holiday drinks made of gin, crushed sloe, and sugar. Some types, as indicated on the label, will produce a creamy head when shaken with ice.

Southern Comfort   A famed American liqueur of whiskey base and peaches, it's excellent as a mixer in tall and short drinks. Its 100 proof adds to its comforting qualities.

Strawberry liqueur   Called fraise or fraise de bois (wild strawberries) if imported; look for a bottle that says "true fruit" flavor; usually low proof.

Strega Liquore   Pale yellow Italian liqueur of the monastery type, subtly blended with numerous herbs and spices of which no single one has a predominant flavor.

Swedish punsch   Also known as Caloric punsch, it's popular in Scandinavian countries; made of a rum or arrack base, spices, and citrus flavors.

Tangerine   Liqueur of tangerines with a mild herbal flavor. (See Van Der Hum below.)

Tea Breeze   A French tea-flavored liqueur.

Tia Maria A medium-sweet Jamaican coffee liqueur made from noted Blue Mountain coffee and spices.

Tiffin German liqueur with flavor of Darjeeling tea; has a mildly tannic aftertaste.

Tilus A 70-proof liqueur with truffles as one of its ingredients.

Trappastine A French herbal liqueur of the Chartreuse type, in both green and yellow types.

Triple Sec A popular colorless orange-flavored liqueur; may be flavored with orange-flower water, orris root, and other fragrances. It's widely used in the United States for sidecars, margaritas, etc.

Tuaca Subtly flavored, medium-sweet Italian liqueur known as "milk brandy" in Tuscany because milk, oddly, is one of its ingredients; made with a brandy base, the primary flavors are citrusy.

Vaklova Moderately sweet, vodka-based liqueur with herbal accents; 80 proof.

Van der Hum Literally, "What's his name?" An African liqueur flavored with native tangerine peel and spices.

Van der Mint Dutch chocolate-mint liqueur.

Vanille or Vanilla, crème de This once extinct liqueur, made in the Caribbean, is again on the shelves.

Verana Spanish liqueur of chocolate and orange flavors.

Vieille Cure A French monastic-type liqueur in both green and yellow types.

Violette, crème de; Yvette, crème de Very sweet purple liqueur made from petals of violets and spices.

Visnoka Wild-cherry liqueur from central Europe.

Wild Turkey liqueur An American 80-proof liqueur in which the base flavor—bourbon—clearly dominates the mild, spicy overtones.

Wishniak; Wisniowka Cherry-flavored liqueur, moderately spiced, from Poland or other Slavic countries.

Yukon Jack 100- and 80-proof liqueur with Canadian-whisky base, moderately sweet, citrusy with herbal overtones.

Yvette, crème de, or Violette, crème de Liqueur of extract of violets.

Zamoura Liqueur with predominant flavor of cloves.

Zitronen Eis German liqueur whose principal flavor is lemon.

15

BRANDY

The Eau de Vie

"Claret is the liquor for boys, port for men; but he who aspires to be a hero must drink brandy."

Either Samuel Johnson's classic eighteenth-century dictum no longer applies, or the fact that U.S. Cognac consumption has tripled in recent years suggests that heroes have proliferated of late at an unparalleled rate. In any case, Dr. Johnson was on the right track to this extent: Brandy taken neat is in itself heroic. There is something about brandy's finesse that caresses the senses and even the palm of your warming hand. Frenchmen call it *largeur*, a spreading glow that suffuses the whole body.

Whatever your brandy persuasion, discount the myth that it's necessary to sate your palate with a formal twelve-course dinner before a great brandy can make its presence truly felt. Though it outshines almost any flavor or aroma that has gone before it, it's an impressive finale for even the most informal casserole dinner or buffet supper.

It's a quality achieved simply by distilling wine. Those who passed Chem I may recall that alcohol has a lower boiling point than water and that when wine is heated in a still, the vapors rise—leaving the water behind—and then later condense to become the *eau de vie*. The first raw spirits trickling out of medieval European alembics were properly used for treating battle wounds rather than drinking. How they evolved into what we now know as brandy is explained in a number of well-aged, well-blended myths.

One story concerns a Dutch sea captain who had been shipping wine from France to Holland and was rowing in the Charente River near the area which now produces Cognac. He dropped his hat into the water, fished it out, and noticed that it was twice as heavy. As he wrung it out, he reasoned: Why not extract the water from his vinous cargo, save a fortune in shipping costs, and then later restore the water to the wine? He arranged to have the wine distilled, only to discover, upon tasting it, a new kind of Dutch courage so stunning that he couldn't possibly think of restoring the water to his *brandewijn* (Dutch for "burnt wine").

Or perhaps you prefer this legend: In England during the sixteenth century, importers often received wine from the same area of France. It didn't travel well and was frequently spoiled upon arrival at the English docks. To salvage their investment, they distilled the wine into brandywine, a product which Chaucer had long before identified as the "water of immortality." It was a reasonable name because the powerful distillate, stored in wooden kegs, seemed, unlike wine, to live on and on for years without spoiling.

Italian specialists in drinking mythology easily explain how brandy came to be aged in wood. The way they tell it, an alchemist in the fifteenth century stored his aqua vitae in a cellar barrel. To keep it out of the hands of mercenary soldiers about to plunder his village, he buried the barrel of raw brandy. He died, however, before he could retrieve his trove. Years later, someone discovered the hidden barrel of grappa, half-empty from evaporation, its raw white liquid now infused with a golden color and an indescribably noble flavor.

Cognac

However accidental its beginnings, the method of making and aging brandy has evolved over the centuries into an art of the highest order —an art that achieves its supreme expression in the creation of Cognac. Finest of the brandies, Cognac is as unique as its old home, the countryside astride the Charente and Gironde rivers of which the sleepy town of Cognac is the center. Sixty-four thousand grapegrowers, each with his little plot of land, toil in a land saturated with more sun than any other grape region in France. An odd freak of nature makes the otherwise unfriendly soil—a dour mixture of chalk and pebbles—just about perfect for growing the tart grapes that turn into greenish wine and eventually into aged brandy. Pot stills, kept under government lock and key when the distilling season is over, are identical with those used three centuries ago. Just as important as the grapes and stills is the wood, from the nearby Limousin forest, in which the Cognac is put to sleep. So heady are the vapors around the ancient brandy casks that workmen wear safety belts to keep them from tumbling into the vats. No railroad has ever been permitted to go into the Cognac region. The old distillers fear that a spark might accidentally cause the whole countryside to go up in flames; for during its long hibernation, enough brandy is released as fumes into the air each day to provide Cognac for all France.

When buying Cognac it's well to be familiar with the inscriptions and annotations printed on the labels. The phrase "fine champagne Cognac," for example, has no allusion whatever to the bubbly wine produced in an altogether different section of France. The French word *champagne* also means "an open stretch of land," and on a Cognac label it's the tip-off that the grapes used came mainly from two of the finest open sections in the heart of the Cognac region, identified on the map as Grande Champagne and Petite Champagne. (There are five other sections of Cognac, but these are of less importance.) To be labeled "fine champagne," Cognac must contain grapes of which at least 60 percent came from the Grande Champagne. To be labeled "grande fine champagne," the Cognac must have been made from grapes 100 percent of which came from the Grande Champagne heartland.

Stars on Cognac labels, and other brandy labels as well, don't offer any really meaningful information to the buyer. You can, for instance, buy a bottle of French brandy with no fewer than five stars on the label for less than $4.00; it's a good mixing brandy for sidecars and brandy sours, but it's not from the Cognac region and it's completely out of the major-league class. For those interested in myth and mystique, a single star was once used by vintners to mean a good vintage after a poor year. Two stars meant the bottle represented a succession of two good years, and so on. According to one old Cognac tale, the good year was 1811, the Year of the Comet, which was succeeded by two more wonderful years. Some Cognac houses themselves take credit for having originated the three stars, since stars, like pearls, were symbols of the gems of Cognacland. From a practical standpoint, stars are only the Cognac maker's way of giving a subjective nod to what *he* considers a better than average quality. You're not likely to come across a well-known label with less than three stars. In recent years, such distinguished firms as Hennessy have dropped the stars entirely from their Cognac labels, since they consider them meaningless.

A somewhat more meaningful method of coding employs initials. The most common are V.O. (very old) and V.S.O.P. (very superior old pale or particular). The most interesting thing about these initials is that they represent English rather than French designations, obviously coined for the export trade. As with stars, they can't always be taken as a strict code of quality, but bottles marked V.S.O.P. by a particular brandy shipper are usually finer spirits than a bottling from the same shipper's Cognac without these initials. The V.S.O.P. signet is usually an assurance that the brandy thus marked is largely composed of twenty- to twenty-five-year-old stock. V.V.S.O.P. (very, very superior old pale) signifies stock about forty years old. X.O. (extra old), *cordon bleu,* and *La Reine* are also designates of old Cognacs of the finest quality. Sometimes these are called liqueur Cognacs, though they have no relation to sweet liqueurs or cordials.

Interestingly, in a blind tasting of Cognac by professional Cognac tasters, a Cognac marked with three stars was given a higher rating than the Cognac marked V.S.O.P. by the same distinguished shipper. A great Scotch such as Chivas Regal doesn't need the myth or mystique of stars or initials to tell its story; Cognac makers are beginning to come around to the same sensible viewpoint.

The whole question of age is disposed of very simply by American import laws. *No* age is permitted to be printed on a bottle of Cognac, except a very insignificant amount of vintage Cognacs made from grapes of a specific year. The quantity of these vintage Cognacs is so small, and their quality so dubious, that they seldom become a significant item even in a Cognac collector's library. The American ruling is reasonable since the greatest Cognacs are blends of different vineyards, different distilleries, and different years. In mixing their artful blends, the Cognac masters choose one for mellowness, another for virility, another for finesse.

Naturally, a superb Cognac contains more liquid age than youth. One sagacious brandyman, when asked for the perfect age of a Cognac, said it was the same as that for a woman—somewhere between twenty-five and forty. Brandy connoisseurs all agree that waters of immortality beyond the age of fifty begin to slip in quality. Stories about the excellence of a dusty bottle taken from Napoleon's footlocker are so much romantic nonsense; in the cellars of the old Cognac houses, there may be a cask here and there containing Cognac a hundred years old, but these are museum pieces from which most of the glory has gone with the years. And remember that Cognac ages only in the wood, never in the bottle. When you buy it, therefore, the best advice is, use it. It will never attain a greater quality. And once opened, don't keep it around too long. Frequent uncorking will eventually cause it to lose its original glow.

You may confidently forget all about stars, initials, and other identification tags when you buy Cognac bearing the labels of the eminent old brandy shippers. Generally speaking, price is one of the better yardsticks. Two others are equally dependable—your nose and mouth: In the last analysis, Cognac can be properly assessed only as it trickles down your throat. You should find yourself not only drinking it but drinking to it.

Non-Cognac Grape Brandies

The only other French brandy one can talk about in the same breath with Cognac is Armagnac. Though it's distilled from the same type of grapes grown in the Cognac region, the earth of its home, Gascony, is unlike that of the Cognac area, and the black oak used in making Gascon casks results in a different marriage of wood and spirits. The taste is somewhat harder and more pungent than Cognac, but the brandy of Armagnac is still in the pantheon of great spirits and has immense appeal to the brandy-faithful everywhere.

Marc, a common brandy in France, is distilled from the stems and skins of grapes and has a woody, rustic flavor. Although you aren't likely to find it at your corner liquor store, you'll meet it in many French bistros. Other French grape brandies exported to this country are light-tasting and excellent for mixing purposes.

German brandies from the valley of the Rhine are superb distillates with a faintly sweet perfume, due to the fact that the Rhenish grapes are left on the vine longer than the French. While the best-known ambassadors of Spain and Portugal are sherry and port, both countries produce brandies as fortifiers for their wines. Each has its own bouquet and, to many brandy noses, is reminiscent of the national wine. Metaxa, from Greece, the richest-tasting of all brandies, is made from the sweet muscat grape and is a semiliqueur. Greek ouzo, with its pronounced anise flavor, is called a brandy in some quarters but, because of its sweetness, a liqueur in others.

Pisco is a nearly clear 90-proof Peruvian brandy distilled from the muscat or mission grapes of Chile and Peru. It is aged briefly in paraffin-lined containers to keep the brandy from acquiring the color or flavor of the wood. The youthful, high-proof spirit gives you a sensation somewhat akin to a slight earthquake. It usually finds its way into the Peruvian pisco sour, a brandy sour made from pisco with a small amount of egg white and a few drops of bitters.

California Brandy

Despite Cognac's monumental prestige in the field of sipping brandies, the fact remains that four out of every five bottles of brandy poured in the United States come from California. In a sense it's as unfair to compare the flavors of the two brandies as to compare Scotch with bourbon although both are whiskeys. The aging process of Cognac transforms the original flavor of the grape into something altogether different. California brandy, after aging, retains the fruity, light flavor of the grape. Like U.S. blended whiskey, it's one of the most mixable of spirits and can be successfully used in any mixed-drink recipe calling for whiskey, from a manhattan to a hot toddy. The prominent California brandies are now aged about four years in the wood, and then blended for balanced flavor.

Until 1972 no brandy maker in the world ever had sufficient cheek to stand his product up against Cognac for comparative tasting. In that year, however, a California brandy was introduced which, to the astonishment of drink experts, hurled a provocative challenge to the French brandymen of the Charente. The newcomer was Christian Brothers X.O. Rare Reserve brandy, made half from eight-year-old pot-stilled brandies and half from column-stilled brandies five to six years old. Only a limited amount of this exceptional brandy is produced each year, and its exquisitely developed aroma (not grapy), complex flavor, and mellow aftertaste with minimal sweetness make it a really great sipping brandy. Its price may seem extravagant for an American brandy, but it still costs considerably less than any of the well-known Cognacs.

White Fruit Brandies

Great brandies aren't all derived from the meat within a grapeskin. Superb distillations are extracted from other fruits and are generally white, fiery, and unaged in order to preserve their straight fruity essence. Usually not a trace of sugar is apparent. The most noted of these is kirsch (or kirschwasser), a white brandy made of cherries and cherry pits. Crushed plums are used to make quetsch or mirabelle in France and slivovitz in central Europe; the latter is an exception to the no-aging rule and develops a light golden aura after six or eight years in the wood. The lush flavor of red raspberries is drawn into framboise in France and Himbeergeist in Germany. Perhaps the most spectacular of the white fruit brandies is Switzerland's pear brandy, which comes with a large whole pear in the bottle. When the pear on the tree is still in its infancy, it is slipped through the neck of the bottle. The bottle is attached to the tree, and the pear blooms and eventually grows to natural size. Later, both bottle and pear are detached from the tree, and the bottle is filled with white pear brandy, which, incidentally, seems to have more of the pear fragrance than the fresh pear itself.

Apple Brandy

Long before George Washington wrote to Samuel Laird asking for his apple-brandy recipe, Americans were distilling what we now call applejack. Currently used as a cocktail mixer, it is famed particularly for its role in the Jack Rose cocktail. Its French counterpart, calvados, is a suave postprandial potation. Applejack, although aged, keeps a vivid perfume of the apple. Calvados retains a subtler hint of the fruit, perhaps because of its longer aging. Vets of World War II who remember the Normandy invasion shouldn't confuse the white lightning surreptitiously made in the cellars of French apple growers with the present-day extremely suave ten-year-old calvados.

The newest form of liquid apple made in the United States, called blended apple brandy, is a union of aged apple brandy and neutral grain spirits. It's lighter and more satiny than straight apple brandy, and, as a mixer in drinks like the Jack Rose or applejack and ginger ale, dances rings around its older version.

16

OLD-AGE FOLLIES

Age in Wine and Spirits

Ecclesiaticus said, "When it is old, thou shalt drink it with pleasure." If he'd said, "When it is mature," rather than merely old, he might have prevented a lot of confusion.

Promoters of spirits have long fostered the obstinate, almost blind homage to age for age's sake. At least twenty-six brands of American straight whiskey are called Old this or Old that, ranging from Olde Bourbon by J. W. Dant through Old Charter and Old Hickory to Old Weller. Scotch whiskeymen genuflect in the same direction with their Ancestor and Antiquary brands, proceeding to Old Rarity and Old Smuggler, up to Grand Old Parr, a whisky whose label pictures a Scotsman who allegedly lived to the age of 152 even though the Scotch in the bottle is one year short of a teen-ager. The name Napoleon keeps on appearing on the labels of French brandy, conjuring up images of *eau de vie* drawn from pot stills in the 1800s. Around the New York area you can buy a variety of French brandies all bearing the name of Napoleon, in a price range that rises from about $5.00 a fifth to $27.00 a fifth—an incredible price range for Bonapartean excellence. Some are from the Cognac region, some not. Actually, by French government regulations, the designation "Napoleon" only guarantees that the brandy was aged in wood for a minimum of five and a half years.

Quality in wines or spirits is a complex thing of which age is only one of the ingredients. Age may give pronounced body to a wine; but if one cares less about body and more about fruitiness, freshness, and aroma, age loses its alleged glamour. In the instance of wine, quality depends not only upon the grape variety as well as the continent, soil, air, and water on which the grape feeds, but upon the skill of the wine maker. In whiskey making, it depends not only on the distiller's expertise but upon the type of still he uses, the corn or other grain, the local waters, the cooperage, the storage conditions, and other factors which, from the consumer's standpoint, at times would seem to be set in quicksand.

All of this isn't to say that maturation doesn't count in the world of wines and spirits. Alcoholic beverages reach their maturity when they attain their optimum flavor. Vodka, gin, the colorless white fruit brandies like kirschwasser, as well as most tequilas, are as mature as they will ever be the moment they flow from the still. The same goes for most liqueurs. Whiskeys, brandies, and rum are a different story: A twelve-year-old Scotch is indeed a different kind of wassail from an eight-year-old bottled by the same distiller or shipper. When it comes to wines, professional winemen have always pointed out that at least three-fourths of the world's wines should be drunk within two to three years after they're bottled. On the other hand, the famed Bordeaux château red wines of great vintage years are almost undrinkable at the beginning of their life, being rough, high-spirited, and in some cases downright unpleasant. They *must* age to develop the mellow, complex flavors of their prime. Eventually they're great wines if they've made good use of their ten, fifteen, or twenty years in the bottle, and if they're uncorked at that ideal time when they've ripened to rich adulthood rather than mistakenly kept in the cellar until they've tottered to a watery grave.

Although the process of aging wines and spirits is centuries old, scientists concerned with oenology or distilled beverage spirits aren't completely sure of what takes place. It should be explained that many wines are aged for a year or two in the wood—a few longer—after which they are aged in the bottle. Red wines generally need more time to "grow up" than whites; certain other spirits may hibernate from two to twelve years or longer in their wooden dens. During that time three things take place:

1. Extractives from the wood add flavoring and color as well as mellowness to the contents of the barrel;

2. Oxygen, seeping very slowly through the wood, modifies the wine or spirits;

3. Organic substances present in the wine or spirits react to one another and aid the job of attaining adulthood.

After wines and spirits leave the wood and enter the bottle, each behaves in a different way.

Spirits like whiskey, brandy, and rum do *not* continue to mature in the bottle; time stops as soon as the bottle is sealed. That seven-year-old bottle of bourbon, still unopened ten years from now, will be seven years old, not seventeen.

All wines *do* change in the bottle. The distinguished French red Bordeaux and Burgundy wines; some Italian reds, especially Chiantis; red wines of the Rioja in Spain; and the late-picked white wines of Germany, as well as some eminent California reds, all need years of slow transformation in the bottle to evolve their prime flavors. Wines not meant for prolonged age—such as the California jug wines, the rosés of all countries, and fruity wines like Beaujolais, Sancerre, etc.— will maintain their quality for months after being bottled, but, if kept for years, will only darken and go downhill. They are meant for your mouth, not the bottle.

One thing you can usually count on when it comes to spirit age: The majority of distillers of respected brand names—not all—bottle their goods at the summit of their best age. If you're considering a bottle of six-year-old bourbon on the shelves, you can usually count on the fact that the bourbon came to full flower at six years. To have kept it in the wood a seventh year would have meant no jump ahead, and possibly a slide downhill.

People obsessed with age are often equally haunted by color. A bottle of dark whiskey, however it tastes, looks older and heavier in flavor than a bottle of light whiskey. To adjust the color, the whiskey maker simply adds more caramel coloring (the same kind of coloring used to darken sauces and stews) when he thinks the appearance of age will add status to his product. If, on the other hand, he wants to appeal to the light dry crowd, he uses less coloring or none at all.

Whatever the color or whatever the age, remember that the age on a bottle of blended spirits is always the minimum age. Thus a bottle of eight-year-old blended Scotch will contain a number of Scotches eight years old or older, but none younger.

Like beauty in the eyes of the beholder, the age that strikes your fancy in any wine or spirits depends upon your own tastes. No other person can ever possibly tell you what age is best for you as an individual. The old Portuguese farmer quaffing his *vinho verde*—green young wine—at the end of a hot day's labor slakes his thirst and finds the tart pale *vinho*—which outsiders might consider disagreeably sour and almost tasteless—the sprightliest pleasure of his table. When you are twenty, you may taste that single-malt Scotch rather skeptically; at two-score years, you may look forward to sipping it at the end of a meal like a rare brandy.

The list that follows gives age its due in the realm of spirits. (For a more detailed discussion of age and vintages in wine, see Chapter 17.)

U.S. blended whiskey The federal definition of this grade simply states that 20 percent must be straight whiskey—that is, at least two years old—while the balance may be neutral spirits, theoretically without any age. As a matter of actual practice, the finer grades of blended whiskey these days, such as Seagram's 7 Crown, contain *all* whiskeys of varying unstated ages. In a fiercely competitive segment of the liquor trade, this is one of the outstanding instances in which the whiskey makers far exceed the minimum requirements. Since no statement of age is allowed on the label, your nose and taste apparatuses are the only and best guides.

U.S. straight whiskey Straight whiskeys made in this country are almost entirely bourbons, with only a tiny fraction of straight ryes in the lineup. Although the government requires only two years' aging, the best-known brands range from four to fifteen years, with many of the most popular labels in the six-year-old range. If you are one of those seeking pronounced body or intensity of flavor, select the high-proof specimens, since higher proof means more whiskey and less water per bottle. Thus, if the same label bourbon is available in both 86 and 100 proof, the latter will not only provide an additional jolt but more concentrated flavor per shot.

U.S. bottled-in-bond whiskey All whiskey marked "bottled in bond" must be 100 proof and must have been aged a minimum of four years in the wood. Actual ages range from four to about thirteen years. Since modern taste habits have moved to lighter, softer spirits, the bottled-in-bonds are now in a downswing and their age is a much less impressive factor than it used to be.

Scotch whiskey   No Scotch blended whisky imported to the States is allowed to be less than four years old, a designation you're not likely to see on a bottle of Scotch—importers obviously regard four years old as too fresh from the cradle to boast of. Since many popular Scotches indicate no age, one can assume they are mixtures of anything from four to eight years. If the minimum age in the blend is eight years, you'll undoubtedly see that on the label. Most of the best-selling prestige Scotch blends are twelve years old. Unblended Scotches in this country (see page 59) are in the ten- to twelve-year-old range.

Cognac   Federal regulations don't permit any age to appear on a bottle of Cognac, a very sensible rule since Cognacs are blends of many ages from many sources. There are nearly 6000 small and large distillers in the Cognac area of France. The small distillers sell their Cognac to well-known shippers and blenders for further aging, blending, and bottling. It is generally thought that the most expensive brands of Cognac contain some brandies from twenty-five to forty years old, although how many of such older Cognacs are combined with how many younger ones is anybody's guess. Price can sometimes be a very treacherous guide in buying liquor; but among great Cognac house names like Remy Martin, Courvoisier, Hennessy, and Martell, usually the higher the price, the greater the amount of aged Cognacs in the bottle.

Rum   Light, almost white, Puerto Rican rums, by far the lion's share of the rums consumed on the mainland, must be aged a minimum of one year. Somewhat more flavorful rums, called golden, are aged about three years in the wood. If your rum drinking consists mostly of daiquiris, rum screwdrivers, rum and tonic, etc., either of the above types works out beautifully. The darker, deeper-flavored rums with a pronounced molasses flavor from Jamaica and other Caribbean islands, aged from five to fifteen years, are used in rum eggnogs, rum flips, planter's punches, and other drinks where a pronounced rum flavor is appreciated.

WINE

In Vino Felicitas

The outstanding difference between wine drinking in the Sixties and today is that wine is no longer the libation poured mostly for the grand bash, the black-tie dinner, and the champagne breakfast; it's something we're taking more and more with our daily bread. If we're hosts, we offer wine whether we're dishing out spaghetti marinara or sweetbreads *sous cloche*. If we're guests, we recognize the capable host as one who prepares a table in the presence of his red and white table wines. A surprising number of those superb French *premiers crus*, at one time only available in Madison Avenue shops, are now conspicuously displayed on supermarket shelves in all those states sufficiently civilized to allow supermarkets to sell wine.

While we now drink two gallons of wine a year instead of the one gallon we each drank ten years ago, we're mere babes compared to the French, who drink twenty-seven, and the Italians, who outstrip even the French by a gallon. Nevertheless, we've managed to become the best-informed, and at the same time the most obviously self-conscious, wine drinkers in the world. The endless deluge of books on wine, magazine pieces and entire magazines devoted to wine, news columns, seminars and summer courses, cruises and foreign tours, all engulfing us with wine information, have made U.S. wine drinkers infinitely more knowledgeable than their European counterparts. It's a good guess

that more wine drinkers on this side of the ocean are familiar with the French Official Classification of the Great Growths of the Gironde, Classification of 1855, than are Frenchmen themselves. Few natives of Burgundy, who naturally drink the illustrious wines of their country-side, would be able to talk at any length about the wines of the Alsace, a few hundred miles away. A meeting of growers and shippers in Bordeaux, the most eminent wine region in the world, was once challenged by one of its members to name five estate-bottled wines from either Germany or Italy, and, as you may guess, not one of the distinguished members of this outstanding French professional group was able to do so. Wine retailers in the New York area will not hesitate to place huge advertisements in New York papers listing hundreds of different wine labels, confident that you will read the ads in all their myriad detail and come to their shops. You do—and by your mere appearance cut the figure of one who knows each label intimately.

The best clue to the present American way with wine is the wine-tasting party—a social institution which, among groups of friends in France or Italy, is almost unheard of and anyhow unthinkable (although professional European winemen, importers and exporters, will naturally have tastings among themselves from time to time). Why don't Americans have bourbon-tasting parties, or, moving from the field of drink, steak-tasting parties or clam-chowder-tasting parties? The answer is simple security. We're not just satisfied with our personal choice of bourbons, steaks, and chowders, we revel in it, and we'd fight to the death anyone who claimed the right to tell us which bourbons, which steaks, or which chowders rated superior on a scale of one to twenty. It could be argued that wine is different because it changes from one year's vintage to the next, but so do the 2000 varieties of apples we eat from year to year. Even if we were learning to eat apples for the first time, as we're learning to drink wines, apple tasting could never possibly qualify as a chichi event because apples lack the one ingredient which promoters of wine tastings somehow don't emphasize and pretend to put out of mind, but which can be counted upon to energize any wine-tasting party anywhere—alcohol.

Wine-tasting parties can generate immense fun. (They are described in Chapter 26.) If you're in the mood, you can run a beer-tasting party or even a water-tasting party. The important thing never to forget is, of course, the word "party." The real purpose is to have fun. If a wine-tasting session gives some intellectuals a feeling of being better stocked with oenological information, okay. But only by drinking wine abundantly over the years will their taste buds tell them what they're trying to learn in a cram course.

Responsibility for the special American attitude about wine can be laid at the door of some of the very people whose self-appointed role it is to explain wines to Americans; that is, certain—not all—wine writers and wine publicists. Promoters of wine have done their job so well in encouraging Americans to become wine encyclopedists that they've created a class of connoisseurs inevitably frustrated because the subject of oenology is indeed so vast, and still developing, that any amateur who tries to view the whole world of wine will always wind up as someone on the outside looking in. Few of those who promote the endless wine tastings, debates, and discussions stop to realize that beyond their well-informed but timorous following there are millions of potential wine drinkers who would accept wine in the same way they accept their bourbons, steaks, and chowders—as sensuous, untiring pleasures to be enjoyed in the mouth the same way a lieder recital or a rock concert is enjoyed by the ears. If they enjoy it, they really don't care what the critics say the next day in their probing newspaper analyses.

This is not to argue that wine isn't a subject for discussion; as with any source of pleasure—a party, a card game, a special weekend on the ski slopes—our tongues should run loose in contemplating the fun. But when the persistent, comparative analysis goes on before, during, and after drinking it, when a journal takes it upon itself to classify certain wines as X-rated because they don't meet the magazine's allegedly objective ratings, their sententious rant takes on the puritanical rigidity of a straitjacket. Aeschylus said wine was the mirror of the heart—he didn't say mirror of the mind. What he meant was that it reflected our gut feelings, our taste sensations and pleasures. When all the swirling dust has settled, it's good to remember what's been said from ancient times onward: Wine is the catalyst turning strangers into friends, rounding the edge of trouble, enabling us to step back from the daily commotion to a delightful recess. And at the dinner or buffet table it can always be counted upon for its hedonic role, providing a rich, tart counterpoint to the meat, bird, seafood, or casserole.

Happily, winemakers as businessmen (although they love to receive gold medals at fairs and other events that help to promote their wines) only on rare occasions participate in the ceremonial gaff, the wine rhetoric, and the elaborate scorekeeping. Generally, winegrowers and winemakers, exporters and importers have a few sensible categories for judging wine. It may be acceptable or unacceptable, good or out-standing—the few large but realistic classifications into which any bottle of wine will fit. Within each of these groups, it's every wine drinker for himself or herself. But some wine writers and pundits, confusing the hundreds of taste buds in their individual mouths with an exact science, insist on grading the color, bouquet, and flavor of a wine in exact quality slots from one to ten or one to twenty. One luminary in a prominent magazine claims he can take any wine—an evanescent, changing product that, like a sunset, can evoke thousands of personal reactions—and rate it on an exact scale from one to fifty, no less. He goes on to describe a certain wine as having "an ambience of the purity of gold in its bouquet, its taste, its balance, the firm con-struction of its liquid body."

Let any young person who likes drinking and serving wine—and doesn't mind making a complete jackass of himself—just go to a wine merchant and ask for a bottle of wine recommended for "the firm con-struction of its liquid body."

Another prominent magazine-and-book wine writer describes a red that he found disappointing because it hadn't "aged gracefully." He explains that "although its monotone, somewhat chocolatey flavor had a surprisingly long finish, it had developed a not altogether attractive rotting-vegetable pungency in the nose." Few young wine drinkers are likely to have chocolate on the brain before or after they taste a glass of red wine; but if, after sipping the wine, they ask themselves whether it leaves an attractive or unattractive rotting-vegetable pun-gency, they can hardly be blamed for feeling that somehow or other their noses must be out of commission.

The whole point of this is not to berate those wine writers whose semantics have gone berserk, but to stress the fact that the best and only way to judge wine is to rely completely on what your eyes, your nose, and your mouth tell you. Only four taste sensations fit into words —acid, bitter, salty, and sweet. The rest of our taste experience, and perhaps the biggest part of it, depends on modifications of these four sensations and even more importantly on our sense of smell. Words only permit us to describe taste experiences comparatively: An orange tastes like a lemon except that it's sweet, and it tastes like a grapefruit but it's not bitter. Forced thus to rely on similes, wine writers turn verbal somersaults, describing wines that leave an echo of honeysuckle or are reminiscent of wild mushrooms or Russian leather—rhetoric that can only confound readers exploring the subject of wine.

Even when it comes to the service of wine at the table, the advice of many prominent wine authorities can fog up the picture terribly. For instance, many winemen will tell you that when you open a bottle of vigorous red wine, not a very old one, you should let the wine "breathe"—that is, you should pull the cork considerably in advance of the time you plan to pour the wine in order to expose the wine for this all important breathing period. What do noted wine writers say on this point?

Alexis Lichine, author of *The Encyclopedia of Wines & Spirits* (1974) says, "Red wines which are young and full bodied . . . should be uncorked several hours before dinner; a very young one may even benefit from being opened the day before."

Alexis Bespaloff, author of *The Signet Book of Wine* (1971), says in that book, "Open red wines half an hour before pouring them." In his later book *Guide to Inexpensive Wines* (1973), he explains *why* exposure to the air is beneficial: "Any mustiness that may be present will disappear, the wine's bouquet will develop, and the tannic astringency typically found in many young red wines will be softened." But in an article in the magazine *New York* (May 23, 1977), he completely reverses himself, saying the results of tastings show that young red wines do not benefit from being opened beforehand.

Hugh Johnson, author of *Wine* (revised edition, 1974) says, "By and large the younger and/or bigger a red wine is, the more it will benefit from contact with the air before drinking, so the longer ahead you should decant it. Twenty-four hours is often none too long for wine with plenty of vigour and personality."

Edouard Kressman, author of *The Wonder of Wine* (1968) and former president of the Bordeaux Wine Merchants' Syndicate, says, "Personally I never do that, as I have never noticed the effectiveness of it. If, as is said, the purpose of it is to give the wine a chance to 'breathe' a little, what, I ask you, can be the effect of air on a bottle it attacks over an area about as large as a postage stamp, other than to damage the top few centilitres of the bottle . . . and have no effect on the rest?"

If four of the greatest authorities, all identified with fine French wines, can't agree on the simple subject of breathing, the lowly amateur should take heart. For the judgment of the professionals turns out to be subjective rather than scientific, and therefore the amateur's much less lofty opinion is as good as the best of them. As far as I'm concerned, I'm inclined to agree with Edouard Kressman that wine breathing beforehand does nothing significant; in very old and delicate wines, it might in fact be harmful. Kressman points out that when you pour the wine into the glass and swirl the glass, the mixture of air and wine creates as much breathing as possible, and gives you the opportunity, of course, to enjoy the wine's bouquet.

If the subject of breathing were the only one on which wine cognoscenti disagreed, it would be a minor matter. But they differ on dozens of other topics, including, first of all, which wines are greater than which other wines. When it comes to the rating of individual years, experts do agree on those years which are out-and-out disasters or unquestioned successes. But when grape harvests turn out in the intermediate ranges, the experts play at cross-purposes all over the place. The oenological moral is clear: When you listen to authorities or read them, you should do so skeptically; they may be of some help, but the only authority you can eventually submit to is your own.

You can turn to books on wine for information in the same way you'd consult a dictionary or encyclopedia; you can read about wine for amusement or simply because it's a lively new subject. But when you seek guidance in buying wines for your own use, you want down-to-earth information shedding light on wines you'll now find in your local shops rather than descriptions of wines that titillated a reporter in a cave on another continent. Such a book is *Which Wine?* by Peter M. F. Sichel and Judy Ley Allen, a careful study which is not molded on authoritarianism but rather along the style of *Consumer Reports*, with prices indicated for each wine. Instead of scoring wines from one to twenty, or describing them in pretentious verbiage, the panels responsible for this book's reports simply graded them into three sensible categories: Best Wines, Highly Ranked Wines, and Other Recommended Wines. Wines are judged by cross-continental types such as the French Pouilly-Fuissé and the California Pinot Chardonnay. The tasting panels were made up of professional wine people and what the authors call "thoughtful consumers," the latter being the most decisive judges in the long run in any country.

In taking a tour through the wine world, you'll find four main classifications: red and white table wines; sparkling wines; dessert wines; and fortified wines. Looking at the whole field in terms of these four basic categories will eliminate a lot of confusion.

RED AND WHITE TABLE WINES

They're called table wines because generally they're poured at the dining table, usually with the main course, although they're sometimes served with the soup or appetizer. The white-wine explosion in this country, however, demonstrates that they needn't be served at the table. Dry white wines, usually recommended with seafood or poultry, are now offered before the meal, dislodging cocktails from their previously unchallenged eminence in this country. Even fruity red wines like Beaujolais or Zinfandel are now being poured at the cocktail hour.

Most table wines are dry, although the white wines from the Alsace and Germany, as well as the Rieslings, Chenin Blancs, and others from California, are semidry. There are dry or semidry table wines not only from Europe and the United States but from vineyards as far away as South Africa, Argentina, and Australia, and at times these latter wines are worth exploring.

The three subdivisions that follow are arbitrarily divided by price, keeping in mind that price is always based on scarcity and not necessarily on desirability. In any case, to many wine drinkers, that $40 bottle of red Bordeaux with its huge, mouth-filling flavor may be less desirable than a gentler, fruitier wine that complements the meal rather than lords it over the roast beef or the duckling.

—*Older red and white wines from great vintage years*   Most of them are from famed châteaus or estates in France, and most now sell above $10 a bottle. It isn't necessary to know each château's wines intimately before buying them, but you should have had some taste exposure to the type of wine you're buying. In fine wine shops you may find some guidance talking with the owner. In those cities where all wines and spirits are under state monopoly control, clerks are usually forbidden to make recommendations.

—*Table wines priced at $10 and under*   By far the biggest chunk of the world's table wines are now selling for $10 a bottle or less, many of them for less than $5. They may come from noted estates when the harvest was plentiful or from noted estates and great vintage years while the wine is young, and you buy them for cellaring rather than serving at once. If they are foreign wines, they may be distinguished by the name of the shipper—such as B & G, or Sichel—or in

this country their labels may carry the name of an outstanding winery
—such as Robert Mondavi in California or Great Western in New York
State. They may range in flavor from the magnificent Chianti Classicos
of Italy to lovely white wines from the state of Oregon. They are served
with *intime* meals or large buffets, with brunches, lunches and dinners,
picnics, tailgate parties, midnight suppers, and galley dinners when
boats tie up at sunset.

—*Red or white jug wines in half-gallons or two liters*   These, from
both California and Italy, are in many cases equal or superior to the
vins ordinaires of Europe. Those with generic names, such as Chablis,
Rhine wine, etc., bear little resemblance to their European counterparts but make pleasant drinking. If you can forget names and taste
them for their sturdy, delightful flavors, their possibilities for pleasure
at the table are unlimited. As has been said of the music of Rachmani-
noff, long the butt of critics' sneers but still adored over the world, the
only ones who like his music are the people.

Sparkling Wines   The white-tie-and-tails class of these wines are
the French champagnes, even though you may want to drink them
wearing Levi's or ski pants around a roaring fire. They include the
nonchampagne sparkling wines from Italy, Germany, and the United
States. Besides their obvious use at celebrations from wedding breakfasts to ship launchings, they may be served at any meal and with any
course, from soup to nuts, and they're also magnificent apéritif wines
before a meal.

Dessert Wines   Hosts and hostesses who are on edge about how rich
or how elaborate their desserts should be could relax if they'd occasionally forget about pastries and baked Alaskas and think instead
of the world's fine dessert wines. A cheese tray, a fruit bowl, and a
lovely dessert wine are an easy, amiable trio.

Most of the dessert wines (with the exception of port in the Fortified
Wines section below) are white. They're made from late-picked grapes
in which a great deal of the normal water in the grapes has evaporated,
leaving a rich concentrated juice heavy with natural sugar. In France
the great specimens of this class are the Sauternes with their marvelous
balance of tartness and sugar, lively as any table wine but leaving the
rich aftertaste you'd expect of any fine dessert, whether it be a fresh
fruit sherbert or a fruit tart. Germany is renowned for its sweet rare
specimens known as *auslese* or *trockenbeerenauslese*. Hungary produces the classical Tokay wines. In recent years some of the California

Rieslings have equaled or surpassed the best of the European white dessert wines.

Fortified Wines   These include apéritif wines such as Dubonnet, Lillet, Cynar, vermouths, etc., as well as sherries and ports. All of them are wines to which brandy has been added for stability. If you open a bottle of red or white table wine, you normally drink it the same day; only in rare cases would you save it for drinking the next day or several days later. Once opened, the wine deteriorates and may even spoil if not refrigerated. But if you open a bottle of fortified wine such as sherry or port, you may keep it for days or weeks before the bottle is empty. Brandy not only makes the wine shelf-stable but increases its alcohol content and gives it its traditional character. Sherries are served both as appetizers and as after-dinner or dessert wines, and your guests take them in sips rather than gulps. In Europe more than in this country, white port is served as an appetizer, while the red or tawny ports are offered at the end of the meal or with the coffee.

Wine Making

Wine is fermented grape juice. Special grape varieties—often, in this country, recently developed new styles of old varieties—are planted in soils and climates friendly to those varieties. Some of the so-called hospitable soils are stony and rough, and some of the best vineyards in Europe are on hillsides so steep wild goats would blanch before climbing them.

As grapes ripen on the vine, sugar develops in the juice. Shortly before the grapes reach their optimum ripeness, nature, in an act of benediction, settles wild yeast on their skins. When the grapes are crushed, the juices and yeast begin fermenting and from then on the wonderwork of sugar changing to alcohol takes place. When a certain percentage of alcohol is reached, the yeast dies, and the juice is now wine. Sometimes the winemaker deliberately stops the fermenting to save some of the residual sugar, if he's making a semisweet or sweet wine. Frequently he supplements the wild yeast with special strains of yeast for greater control of the fermentation.

As the new wine stands, solid matter, called lees, falls to the bottom of the tanks and the wine becomes less murky. Periodically it's drained off or pumped into empty clean tanks or barrels, leaving the lees behind.

If the wines are made from red grapes, or if the grapes are white and strong like the Burgundy Pinot Chardonnays, the wines are aged in wood. People don't normally think of wood as a flavoring ingredient, but the kind of wood used is extremely important. When a California winemaker, for instance, wants to match the flavor of a French wine, he uses French oak for his casks instead of American oak. During the aging process, oxygen, slowly seeping through the wood, as well as extractives from the wood itself, begin to round out the wine's adolescent harshness and reduce its acid. Strong wines may be wood-aged for several months to several years, acquiring woody overtones, bringing the wine to the first stages of its manhood—or womanhood, since the French are always comparing their best wines to beautiful women. Such wines only reach the full flower of their development later in the bottle.

Wine drinkers these days, particularly Americans, don't like the taste of wood in most of their white wines and even in many of the fruity red wines that are so popular. Many American red wines, therefore, are only aged briefly in wood, and almost all white wines are instead aged in stainless-steel tanks or tanks lined with plastic or glass in which, while the wines mature, they retain as much as possible of the original fruitiness of the grapes. Gone are the old days when California winemakers said their first job was to "oak the hell out of the wines as soon as possible."

Most wines are carefully filtered before they're bottled. Some American wines in recent years, however, are unfiltered. Careful racking ensures that they're clear; and by skipping the filtering process, as much as possible of their natural flavor remains in the bottle. In some cases wines are "fined," which simply means that a substance like beaten egg whites is added to the cask and, as it precipitates to the bottom, causes solid particles to adhere to it.

Red wine results when dark grapes are crushed and the dark skins are permitted to remain in the juice until their pigments are extracted.

If the dark skins are only allowed to remain briefly with the juice, overnight or a few hours longer, the wine becomes a rosé. The French call the rosés *vins de nuit* or wines of the night.

If the dark skins of red or black grapes are quickly removed from the juice, the wine may be white—as in the case of white champagne made from dark grapes, like the Pinot Noir.

If white grapes are used, the wine is called a white wine although the color may vary from pale greenish yellow to deep gold.

Bottle Age

While age fetishists will sometimes spend hundreds, and in some cases thousands, of dollars for a single bottle of old wine (so old it may be undrinkable), an infinitely greater number of wine connoisseurs look to youth for their wine pleasure. Beaujolais Nouveau is the shining example of a wine that couldn't be any younger. In France, it's shipped to Paris right after it's fermented; waiting trucks race with one another to deliver the infant Beaujolais for gulping the next day. Parisians love it not for its rich body or intense flavor—those qualities that are supposed to make a wine "great"—but for its racy, young, natural fruitiness. If you can imagine eating ripe grapes off the vine, their sugar magically converted into alcohol, you can picture the joy of Beaujolais. Most of the Beaujolais you see in wine shops is aged only until the next spring and then bottled; it may be drunk immediately or in some cases may be held for several years. Many other extremely popular wines—like liebfraumilch, Gewürztraminer, rosés, and others—are dedicated to the festival of youth; keep them two or three years and they usually fall on the shady side of their wine life. Bottle aging, therefore, is a process that helps certain wines and may harm others.

Most of the table wines destined for prolonged aging are the expensive reds from Bordeaux and Burgundy in France; some of the white Burgundies such as Montrachet or Meursault; the sweet wines made from late-picked grapes in both France and Germany; the Chiantis Reserva of Italy; the red wines from Rioja, Spain; and the California Cabernet Sauvignons, as well as some of the late-picked California Rieslings. But when you recite this list, remember that you're talking about less than one-quarter of the world's wine production. The other three-fourths are ready for drinking a year after they're bottled, and shouldn't be kept more than three years at the maximum.

The changes that take place during bottle aging aren't too clearly understood. Winemakers and wine technologists agree that red wines, after aging in the bottle, become less harsh; their tannin, which is necessary for aging, becomes less puckerish, their acid less aggressive. The strong white wines become smoother and more deeply mellow.

As a very important footnote on the subject of bottle age, many French winemakers and drinkers, as well as a considerable number of Americans, like their strong red wines a little on the rough side, often enjoying them at five years rather than the idealized ten years or longer. All wines, red and white, after considerable bottle aging develop flavors that are regarded as complex rather than simple—that is, flavors in which you recognize multiple rather than single hallmarks. As a camp example, a coffee ice cream soda made with coffee syrup is looked upon as a simple flavor experience; take away the coffee syrup and substitute chocolate syrup and the flavor becomes complex, and to many people more interesting.

Most people, lacking space or inclination for cellaring wines, buy wines for their weekly or monthly needs or wines for special parties, and they can usually find young or old wines that are ready for pouring immediately; the job of aging has been adequately handled both by the winegrower and the shipper. Those individuals who want to lay down wines for future use, gambling on higher values a few years or a decade hence, unless they intimately know a certain vintage and are reasonably confident of how much further bottle aging is needed, should only buy wines for cellaring under the guidance of a wine merchant who knows what the score is. The trouble has been in finding such a knowledgeable wine seller. But in recent years, shops that specialize in wines for laying away have recruited or trained salesmen who know their wines, who can guide you, and who, in some cases, are more interested in being honest than in putting dollars in the till. If your own wine palate and nose are sufficiently educated in aged reds or whites for you to make your own decisions for cellaring wines, it's still sometimes a good idea to buy a bottle and try it it (making allowances for its youth) before you buy a case.

When you're ready to serve that wine you've carefully hoarded for years, your instincts as a host will naturally cause you to invite guests who can appreciate the pleasure of an aged wine.

Vintages

A vintage is the produce of the vine for a specific year. The word is loudly noised each year, particularly in Europe where the ups and downs of the grape harvest each fall are prone to greater extremes than in this country. Certain European vintages turn out to be dramatically better than others, and for these wines you pay a premium. But what a premium! Too often wine consumers are both awed and intimidated by such phrases as "great vintage," "vintage of the decade," or "vintage of the century." Privately some prestigious winemakers will acknowledge that the phrase "great vintage" is often a synonym for "great price," and that "greatness" is what the traffic will bear.

Each fall, when the grape harvests are in, the yields are announced and the click-clacking of the wine prophets' tongues begins. The yield may be full, moderate, or poor, or in some years a disaster. There are years when the yield may be small but the quality of the grapes excellent. The vintages of southern France, Italy, and Spain vary, but not nearly as much as other parts of France and Germany. In California the uniformly beneficent climate accounts for even smaller changes in vintage qualities. Keep in mind that in all these areas there are microclimates, sometimes on two different sides of a hill belonging to the same vineyard, so that in one year the same variety of grapes yields wines of different qualities. The grapes from old vines will also be different from those of young vines in the same year. And finally, different winemakers, because of the individual art, technology, and equipment that each possesses, inevitably come up with different wines from the same year even though each grows the same grape. Time and again a so-called poor year will yield some fine, even magnificent, wines, and the great year—a decade later—will in some cases turn out to be so-so.

For some wine lovers waiting to see how the cat will jump, the very undependability of vintage prognostications and even vintage charts is the exciting witchery of wine. Wine is a living thing that changes in the wood and the bottle, and this becomes an extremely popular indoor game. Those who follow the vintage charts don't mind being kept holding the bottle.

But for the great majority of wine buyers, the word "vintage" is about as useful as a discarded cork. French champagnes, for instance, only carry a vintage year on the label if the year is fine. Vintage port is only made in a year when the vintage is outstanding. In this country a wine marked with a vintage year must contain at least 95 percent of the year indicated, but a wine from Germany need only contain 75 percent of the vintage printed on the label. While theoretically, each year's harvest in any country means a shuffle of the cards for the winemaker, most of the eventual wines in wine shops do not reflect these dramatic ups and downs. Winemakers everywhere have mastered the art of blending—that is, taking wines from different vats in the same cellar or from different vineyards in the same area and, like chefs balancing flavors, merging them into a unified product. Most importantly, the well-known and responsible shippers of wine to this country will never allow a poor-vintage wine to be sold under their label.

All of this isn't to imply that all vintage designations should be ignored. The vintage wines from the great châteaus in Bordeaux or the famed estates in Burgundy and Germany, as well as certain Chiantis from Italy, vary widely in price, depending on the year on the label. If you've decided to cellar a case or several cases of a particular wine, and if you're paying a premium price for it, you should know if the year was outstanding.

Among French wines from Bordeaux '61, '66, '70, '71, and '75 are prestigious.

French Burgundies are renowned for the years '61, '66, '69, '71, and '76.

From Germany for the late-picked wines, spätlese or better, '67, '71, and '76 are the present prizewinners.

In California, it's now the practice of many of the smaller premium wineries to indicate a vintage on every bottle, even though vintages in that state do not vary as drastically as in European wineries. A vintage marking may be useful for several reasons. For one thing, if you like a particular year over another for a certain varietal wine, you can buy it or cellar it as long as it's available. For another, it helps in choosing the fruity reds or dry white wines, which shouldn't be bought if they're more than five years old, since most likely they'll have gone over the hill. The same advice applies to all young fruity reds and most of the dry whites from France, Italy, or Spain, as well as German wines not marked spätlese or better.

Wine Tasting

No phase of the wine experience is camouflaged with more mumbo jumbo than wine tasting. So deep is the mantle in which it's wrapped that the novice, feeling his way around wines, is made to feel that he must of necessity turn to the wine expert or panel of experts or wine judges at fairs and other places, the admonishing angels telling him what he should or should not like.

If you are a beginner, the best way to learn to judge wine is to drink wine—not guzzle it in huge quantities but repeatedly taste the same type of wine, even in small amounts, day after day. In a reasonably short time, you'll find yourself noticing changes in wines the same way you'd spot changes in soups, sauces, or stews. Whether you're looking for an intense or light flavor, whether you're trying to associate the flavor of the raw grape with the finished wine, whether you're comparing American with European wines made from the same grape, the technique is a simple one. You do *not* have to go through the ritual slurping, sloshing, and spitting. That method should be reserved for the vineyards and the movies—it's ridiculous in your home. Wine-makers don't do it in *their* homes.

First of all you want a thin, clear, tulip-shaped glass with at least eight-ounce capacity. Fill the glass one-third full; then, grasping it securely by the foot of the stem and using a white tablecloth as a background or holding the glass to the light, look at the wine's color and clarity, since both are clues to the soundness of a wine. A young red wine may range from a light to deep-purplish red. If it's an old red wine, it may have a brownish tinge around the edge of the glass. If it's a rosé, it should look like a rosé, neither rusty nor a dark garnet. If it's a white wine, it may range from the lightest pale yellow, sometimes tinged with green, to deeper straw-colored yellow to deep gold. In both red and white wines, color is the guide to the wine's body (intensity of flavor). The lighter the color, the lighter the body; the deeper the color, the more heavy-bodied, or robust.

After assessing the clarity and color, set the glass on the table and, holding the bottom of the stem, revolve the glass carefully so that the wine swirls and laps against the side of the glass and releases its bouquet. Raise the glass and nose it, breathing deeply. In time you'll learn to recognize the smell that's technically called the aroma, the smell of the raw grape rather than the finished wine.

Next, sip the wine, taking a small amount, holding it briefly at the front of the mouth on the tongue, and then slowly swallowing it. Note the aftertaste—give it several moments to develop before you take more wine or food. The aftertaste, or finish, is considered by some wine-men the most important of any of the taste sensations. In time, after drinking and tasting many wines, the aftertaste becomes the wine memory that you retain and recognize when you taste the same kind of wine again.

Storing, Aging, and Decanting Wines

If there's a wine you particularly like, you may choose to buy it by the case. If you intend to use it up within a month or two, you can store it in any cool dark place away from a source of heat. (Almost any place in the kitchen is bad because of the adjacent heat.) Use wine racks so that bottles are stored on their sides, keeping the cork wet to prevent air entering the bottle.

If you are storing wines for aging purposes and intend to keep them longer than a year, you should have a cellar where the temperature is between 55° and 60°F. or as close to that range as possible. Again, use wine racks, or simply store the unopened cases so that the bottles are on their sides, or with the bottlenecks slightly elevated to keep any sediment at the bottom of the bottle. The benefits from aging only come if the wine is aged slowly, and any very warm room or excessive summer heat causes wine to age quickly. Sturdy red wines can withstand some of the summer heat, but lighter wines can't take the temperature ups and downs of some homes and apartments. Unless you live in a building where there is underground garage space with adjacent storage units for tenants, the best advice for apartment dwellers is to forget aging wines and simply purchase them as needed.

Whether you're storing wines for a few months or for years, buy wines from wine shops where bottles are properly stored on their sides. They may be in cases on the floor, but the respectful wine seller keeps them in a horizontal rather than vertical position. Some shops bend the knees to all foreign wines by placing them on their sides, but stand on no such ceremony when it comes to California wines, which are all unhappily standing upright at attention.

Some strong red wines, including vintage port, after a number of years may require decanting to remove the sediment that has formed in the bottle. The sediment is perfectly natural, but it should be removed before serving. This is the procedure:

1. Be sure your decanter is clean; rinse and drain well if necessary.

2. Stand the wine upright for at least a day so that the sediment flows from the side of the bottle to the bottom.

3. Draw the cork very carefully to avoid spreading the sediment.

4. Hold the bottle in front of a light bulb or candle placed near the shoulder of the bottle so that you can watch the wine as it is being poured into a decanter.

5. Very slowly and steadily pour the contents of the bottle into the decanter, stopping just before the sediment emerges.

Serving Wine

When you pour wine at your own table, you don't assume the role of the restaurant sommelier, fluttering over the bottle, awaiting your guests' approval as though it were a life-or-death verdict. As a host, your first job is to make sure you've bought enough wine for two rounds at least. If it's a hot day and guests haven't been drinking cocktails, it's possible for two people to finish a single bottle (three or four drinks apiece) of a chilled white wine, but this is the exception. Most likely before mealtime your guests will have had their cocktails, highballs, or apéritif wines; subsequent wine drinking at the dinner table will usually average out to two glasses per person, some taking more, some less.

So much for the basics. Now for the actual service.

1. If it's a white wine, champagne, or dessert wine, it should be chilled beforehand. Some fruity young red wines like Beaujolais, Zinfandel, or rosés are often preferred chilled, too. *How* chilly is a matter of personal choice. Here again, wine authorities can be counted on to confuse you: One will tell you to chill wine to a temperature between 31° and 41°F.; another says to serve it between 41° and 45°F.; and two California professors say, "Most dessert wines require a slight chilling to about 60°F." I myself don't recommend that you run around with a thermometer to take its temperature. At a small party, you can chill wine in a champagne bucket; at very large parties, washtubs filled with ice are sometimes put on display. Fill the bucket or tubs with cracked ice and twirl the bottles occasionally. About a half-hour's chilling is enough; if ice cubes rather than cracked ice are used,

add water to the bucket or tub to hasten the chilling. Wine can also be chilled in the refrigerator for an hour or two (most are set between 35° and 40°F.) or in the freezer for about a half-hour.

2. If white wine or any other wine is chilled in a bucket, wipe the entire bottle with a towel to prevent dripping at the table. If it's a red wine served at room temperature and is taken from the cellar with the dust of ages on it, wipe it well, too. Don't, however, wrap the bottle in a towel; guests are often as interested in the wine label as they are in the food that's being served. If you're serving a jug wine, pouring it from a carafe is easier and more attractive than attempting to handle the two-liter bottle at the table.

3. With a paring knife, cut off the foil capsule over the cork. Don't merely cut it level with the top of the bottle but at least an inch below, or remove it entirely. Sometimes it's grimy, and wine poured over it may pick up off-flavors.

4. Wipe the top of the bottle with a clean towel. Moisten the towel if necessary to remove any grime.

5. For opening, use a corkscrew, which should always be longer than the cork. Insert the end of the corkscrew at the very center of the cork. Turn the corkscrew evenly; do not push it or attempt to force it in by leaning on it or you may force the cork into the bottle. If the cork seems to be slipping into the bottle, stop turning it or, again, the cork might be forced into the bottle. Withdraw the corkscrew as steadily as possible. Don't attempt to make it pop like a champagne bottle. If the cork seems to be breaking while you're withdrawing it, grasp its top with your fingers to keep it intact. If you are opening champagne, hold the cork covered with a towel in your right hand, and twist the the bottle with your left hand.

6. Smell the cork. It should smell of wine. If it's a strong old wine, the cork will have a strong smell, which is natural. (Don't confuse the wine smell with the smell of a rotten cork—a very rare occurrence. Such a cork has an out-and-out putrid smell that causes both the wine's odor and taste to be unmistakably bad, or "corky.") Wipe the rim of the bottle. Wipe the inside of the neck of the bottle if necessary.

7. If the cork breaks or falls into the bottle, or if there's an abundance of cork crumbs in the wine, the wine must be strained. Use a clean linen or silk cloth in a funnel, or use filter paper. Straining never helps the flavor of any wine, but in some cases it's unavoidable. If the neck of the bottle breaks (a very rare occurrence), the wine shouldn't be used.

8. Pour a little wine into your own glass for your own nosing and tasting. If there are a few cork crumbs, they will fall into your glass rather than your guests' glasses. If you'd like your wife, inamorata, or any guest to share in the tasting beforehand, do so. The preliminary glass for good humor as well as tasting is a good way of throwing off the yoke of convention, and guests are invariably flattered when you ask them to offer *their* judgment.

9. Pour the wine at each place at the table. (The old custom of formally filling the glasses of all the ladies before the men seems a bit quaint in the age of women's lib.) If you're serving wine at a buffet party, the glasses may be on the buffet table and should be filled just before the food is offered. Offer refills to guests, but don't ply them with wine, and don't insist that they kill the bottle just to avoid leftover wine.

10. The custom of keeping wine at the table in a wine basket with the bottle on its side has never caught on in this country. The original idea of the wine basket (a device for keeping the bottle at a forty-five-degree angle, and with a handle at the top for passing the wine) was to keep the sediment of the wine, if any, from flowing into the glasses. This proves an impractical idea because some sediment can still flow into the glass. The basket is useful—sediment or no sediment—for allowing guests to pass the wine around the table.

11. If you're serving sweet sherry or port with the coffee at the end of the dinner, and you're using dock glasses (page 16) rather than the conventional tulip-shaped wineglasses, you might bring the glasses to the table with the coffee rather than clutter the table beforehand. It's an old custom among port lovers to pass the bottle from one guest to the next rather than have the host pour it at each place; the bottle is passed clockwise around the table in deference to an old superstition that the port would turn sour if passed otherwise.

Wine and Food

In posing the question of what wine to serve with what food, honest hosts will admit they're governed by habit more than anything else, and no one would dare fault them. After all, food combinations *without* wine are strongly traditional: We eat yams with turkey and not with roast beef, for example, because we're following a well-trodden track we've loved since childhood. The conventional guideline says red wines are to be served with dark meat and game; white wines with light meat, poultry, or seafood. But the standing order begins wobbling when you ask, What's a dark meat? Is lamb, for instance, light or dark? When it's raw, it's red in color like beef, and yet, if it's fine spring lamb, its flavor when cooked is considerably tamer than beef, definitely on the gentle side.

Lamb is the perfect opportunity to toss the rule overboard and serve, if you will, anything from a light-bodied red like Valpolicella to a full-bodied white like Meursault. Duck is another example. It's poultry, yet people all over the place wash it down with red wine, not because the flesh of duck is dark but because a dry, tart red wine seems the perfect foil for the rich, fatty duck. In France where domestic ducks are much leaner than in this country, either red or white wine is served.

There are countless instances when hosts would do well to shut their eyes to the red wine–dark food and white wine–light food dictum and realize that either wine would do. If you're serving deviled shrimp in a rich brown sauce, any medium-bodied wine—even a semidry Rhine wine—would flatter the dish. If you've prepared a corned-beef hash (red meat), a red or white would go equally well. At those festive holiday dinners where you go all out, loading the table with appetizers, a roast, stuffing, relishes, pies and puddings, champagne is the angel at the table whether you're serving light turkey, dark goose, or roast pork. At the festive board, no one stops to think that the bubbly is a white wine or attempts to match it with anything else on the menu's color spectrum.

There was a period in this country when hosts solved the dilemma by simply pouring rosé, a wine that is neither red nor white and can serve for either of them. The rosé craze in the Fifties and Sixties worked as a safe compromise, but as wine tastes continued to develop everywhere, the fad diminished. The point was eventually reached where some hosts would be painfully embarrassed to be caught serving a rosé at any meal lest it be construed as an inability to choose the right wine with the right food. It's a pity because good rosés are wonderful accompaniments to many soups, quiches, cold platters, sandwiches, soufflés, and other dishes.

The wine/food question seldom arises in wine-growing regions where local wines or *vins du pays* are naturally served with any and almost all food of the neighborhood or province where the wines are made. In this country certain purists would raise their eyebrows if one were to serve a white wine with boiled beef, sauerbraten, or venison. But if they were living in a village along the Rhine, they'd find the natives happily pouring their Rieslings (white and semidry) with any of these foods. Yes, they down beer, too, but many of them are just as happy, or happier drinking the lovely white wines bred in their own soil and bottled in their own cellars. If you criticized the Rhinelanders for serving their slightly sweet wines with meat, they could remind you of your apple sauce with pork, your cranberry sauce with turkey, and your chutney with curry.

In this country the two chief wine-growing regions are California and New York; and the residents of those states, particularly California, are known for their hearty wine drinking and their sensitive appreciation of local wines. They serve their American *vins du pays* with a wide variety of foods, no holds barred by red or white colors.

Hosts who habitually pair wines and foods in traditional ways would do well to explore some of the more offbeat combinations. For instance, when you're offering a tureen of hearty soup as the main course at a postfootball supper on an après-ski supper, try a Barbera from California with the minestrone, a Moselle with the yellow split-pea soup with ham, or a New York State Diamond Chablis with the clam chowder. Brunch dishes like ham and eggs or creamed finnan haddie or chicken hash browned take kindly to crisp white wines like Pouilly-Fumé or the New York State Chelois. And for that summer picnic, no matter what's in the picnic basket, a bottle of one of the new "soft" wines, red or white, from San Martin Vineyards in Monterey would be luscious.

Finally, there's the hoary old advice that if two wines are served at a meal, the lesser (less expensive) wine should precede the better (either heavier or more expensive) wine. Thus, if you were serving an Italian Soave—a very pleasant white wine—with the fish, you'd be expected to serve a rich, costly Burgundy with the roast fillet of beef. The two wines would be analogous to a woman's informal slacks at lunch and her costly dinner gown for the impressive evening meal.

This advice, too, can hardly be taken literally. For one thing; our menus these days don't always include a modest first act followed by a theatrical second-act high spot. For another thing, suppose you're serving with your main course at dinner a great red Burgundy like Romanée-Conti from one of the famed vintage years, which cost you $18 a bottle, and you're also planning to buy a sweet white wine for your fruit dessert which will be strawberries Romanoff. Should you now go out and buy several bottles of Château d'Yquem, at $35 a bottle, just to keep up the crescendo until the last guest staggers from the table? In this day and age, reaching for this kind of flash point, purely for show purposes, is asinine. Your dessert wine could be one of the extremely late-picked California Rieslings; it would be luscious drinking—proving that a lovely diminuendo can be as beautiful as the crowning stroke of that Romanée-Conti priced higher than the roof.

Wines of France

Even an absolute neophyte in wines knows that France is the home of the most prestigious, and in some cases the most expensive, wines in the world. What the neophyte may not know is that France is not only one of the world's largest exporters of wine but also one of its largest importers, with a huge river of wine flowing into the country each year from Algeria and even from Italy. Also, the French government and French winemakers work under laws that are perhaps the most stringent in the world, designed to control not only the words on their wine labels but the kinds and amounts of grapes that can be grown on a hectare (2.47 acres), the amount of wine made per hectare, and even how the wine can and cannot be made. With all of this wine flowing in and out of the country, and with thousands of regulations which each winegrower and winemaker may say to himself are maybe good for the wine drinker but not good for me, there's bound to be a horrendous amount of hanky-panky.

The inevitable major scandal surfaced in the notorious trial several years back when the firm of Cruse Fils et Frères was charged with substituting a cheap wine from Languedoc in southern France for the far more expensive and distinguished wine of Bordeaux. The realism or cynicism of the defendants' lawyers—who maintained that even an expert can't tell the difference between a Languedoc and a Bordeaux when they're young—caused wine experts from every country to explode in fire and fury. As far as Americans were concerned, the worst indictment against the Cruse firm was the fact that in their cellars there was found a vat of especially inferior wine marked "Salable as Beaujolais to Americans." Cruse, of course, was found guilty, and for one year French wine prices plummeted downward. But they've since risen astronomically, and this simply reflects that France is still at the first-fiddle desk when it comes to wines, playing tunes for which, happily, no matter what your nationality, you'll never need a translator. You may need a little guidance, however, in understanding French wine laws and labels.

In the United States and many other countries that produce wines, there are regulations controlling the way wine is made and what the label can and cannot say. But France for over a century has gone a giant step further and, in the case of the famed old vineyards of Bordeaux, tells you which wine is *better* than another one. They do it by classifying certain vineyards in terms of "growths." In 1855 the wines of the Médoc, a section of Bordeaux famed for its red wines, as well as Sauternes and Barsac, renowned for their white wines, were classified into five growths, with four wines in the *premier cru*, or First Growth, and fifty-eight in the Second to Fifth Growths. The list was amended in recent years so that there are now five wines in the First Growth and fifty-six in the Second to Fifth Growths.

Naturally, from 1855 on, French winegrowers, wine sellers, and wine drinkers have been in a perpetual knockdown and drag out verbal battle, differing first of all with their presumptive government and then with each other on which château should be in which growth, claiming that in some cases a *premier cru* wine costing five times as much as the wine of the adjoining vineyard was actually inferior to the wine in the lower echelon. To mollify winegrowers that were left out of the 1855 elite classification, the government's wine experts then drew up an even larger list of *crus exceptionnels, crus bourgeois supérieurs,* and *crus bourgeois* of the Médoc. Wines not in the official classifications could be assumed by foreigners and kindergartners in the sophisticated realm of wines to range anywhere from *crus ordinaires* to *crus lousy,* but this would be a gross mistake; unclassified wines, often bearing just the shipper's name, can be delightful.

A century later, in the 1950s, the French government classified the wines of two other Bordeaux districts—St. Emilion and Graves—in a hierarchy of *premiers grands crus, grands crus,* and just plain *crus,* again demonstrating the odd confidence that the French wine bureaucracy can be what all other human beings can't be—uninfluenced by past prejudices and scientifically objective in judging and ranking wines.

The 1855 and 1955 lists are shown on page 146 to page 149, not to encourage you to indelibly print each and every one of the names on your memory but to enable you to occasionally check the prestige and price of individual Bordeaux wines sold in this country. When you pay a premium for any wine on these lists, you can count on receiving a wine ranking from just pleasant to immensely enjoyable. It's hard to imagine a wine bearing any of these labels turning out to be an out-and-out disaster. Still, many buyers of French wines, in Europe as well as in this country, derive much of their drinking pleasure from comparing the wines in their mouths to the official classifications and proving to themselves how wide of the mark the official classifications can sometimes be.

Another set of French wine regulations is considerably more useful to wine buyers. These are the wine-labeling rules called A.O.C., or *Appellation d'Origine Contrôlée*, put into effect in 1935, which apply to all French wines rather than just those of Bordeaux. They stipulate that the labels on all French wines must indicate the general area where the wine was produced, since most wines depend for their excellence on their birthplace—the special spot in the countryside, with its special soil and microclimate, where the grapes are grown. Thus, on the label you may note, first of all, the general area where the grapes were grown, such as Bordeaux. The label may go on to list smaller, more specific localities—but the more delimited and specific the place names, the more stringent are the regulations for permission to print them. If the winemaker is permitted to specify a district within an area —such as Médoc—the wine is probably of special or superior quality. If he's permitted to specify a parish or town within a district, this indicates the wine's special character or prestige. And if he is allowed to print the name of the estate or château where the wine was made— especially if it's a noted estate or château—so much the better. It's like entering a building with an impressive lobby, proceeding on to an even more sumptuous apartment, and there finding a fine old cabinet holding a priceless rarity.

The A.O.C. regulations also govern the grape variety that may be planted in a specific vineyard, since experience has shown that in certain localities certain varieties of grapes do better than others. They specify the minimum alcohol content for wines—since the ripeness of the grapes and their sugar content (resulting in a corresponding volume of alcohol) is at the top of the quality scale. They limit the quantity of grapes per acre the winegrower can grow—since the more grapes grown per given space, the lower the final quality of his wine in many cases. They tell him how to prune his vines and how to crush, ferment, strain, bottle, and label his wine.

To an outsider, all of these complex regulations would seem like Big Brother arbitrarily bringing the poor winemaker to his knees. But actually the regulations for growing and vinification are accepted, albeit with much grumbling, as indispensable for keeping French wines in the high esteem they enjoy worldwide. In the great Bordeaux area, only one-fourth of the wines are not given an A.O.C. designation.

BORDEAUX WINES

The most distinguished wines of Bordeaux bear the name of a château. Americans must understand, however, that our concept of a château as a feudal castle or seignior's mansion doesn't always hold true in Bordeaux. There are more than 4000 wine-producing châteaus in Bordeaux, registered with the French government, and while some of them are famed structures such as Château Margaux, in many cases they are simply plots of an individual owner's land, some with nothing more than a shack on the property.

On a wine label, when you see the phrase *mis en bouteilles au Château*—meaning the wine was bottled on the particular property where the grapes were grown—the wine's authenticity is assured.

The principal, best-known districts of Bordeaux are Médoc, St. Emilion, and Pomerol, all north of Bordeaux and all producing mostly red wines; Graves, south of the city, producing both reds and whites; Sauternes and Barsac in the most southerly section, homes of some of the richest dessert white wines in the world.

Médoc, on top of the area with its 240 square miles, is known for the delicacy and fine balance of its wines, which, long before feminism, were called "queens" of the wine world.

St. Emilion, beloved by all tourists because of its medieval architecture, is considered by some Bordeaux-wine lovers to produce the largest gallonage of exceptional wines in the whole Bordeaux area. Among the many great châteaus there is Château Ausone named after the Latin wine lyricist Ausonius who was growing grapes there in the fourth century and boasted that the wines of his neighborhood were a special favorite of Julius Caesar.

Pomerol, a much smaller area than St. Emilion and directly above it, is known for the extremely smooth but firm quality of its wines. In it is the famous Château Petrus, whose wines (unlike most other reds made from the sturdy Cabernet Sauvignon grape) are made from the Merlot grape, the same grape that produces some of the smoothest California reds.

Graves is an area south of Bordeaux and it produces both red and white wines. The French word *graves* is associated with our word "gravelly," which aptly describes the loose, pebbly soil in which these grapes flourish. Some of the reds have greater body than many of the Médoc wines, but for some reason are not as well known or appreciated in the United States. The whites are distinguished by their dry but very smooth grape flavor, the kinds of wines that are now riding at the crest of our American white-wine explosion.

Sauternes and **Barsac,** at the bottom or southern end of the Bordeaux area, produce mellifluous sweet wines, some of which are complete desserts in themselves; you don't need fruit or other sweets because they are the essence of both—though Barsacs are not quite as sweet as the Sauternes. In this area is the great Château d'Yquem whose wines now sell at $30 to $40 a bottle, a show-off price but one fully justified because of the labor that goes into their wines. Normally grapes in a vineyard are picked in one harvest lasting a few days, and in some vineyards a mechanical picker can remove the grapes in a matter of hours. But Château d'Yquem workers wait until their grapes develop the mold *Botrytis cinerea,* called *pourriture noble* or noble rot, a condition that causes the fruit to shrivel as the water evaporates and the sugar becomes concentrated. Not bunches of grapes but single grapes are picked as they reach this stage, and the job takes three months to complete as the vintagers comb the vineyard day after day.

There are other wines from Bordeaux of lesser importance, such as those of Blaye, Premières Côtes de Blaye, and Côtes de Bourg, all red wines. Occasionally they appear in American wine shops, sometimes for less than $5 a bottle. In many cases their quality doesn't reach the best of the California reds.

Finally, for the huge numbers of Americans who are confused and frequently bored by château and estate names but enjoy French wines from great districts, there are wines of blender-shippers who bottle wines under their own names, sometimes called *monopole* wines. Some of the most dependable and remarkably consistent wines are not bottled in great châteaus but are blends compounded by a shipper in his own cellars, carefully selecting the best features of many different vineyards. The names of such shippers—B & G, Kressman, Sichel, and others—for years now have meant assurances of top-quality French wines. Tasters employed by these companies will sample thirty to fifty wines a day in order to buy one or two. On their staffs are not only experienced wine buyers but trained oenologists. Through careful blending and aging in their own cellars, they actually breed the type of wine whose sum is greater than any of its parts. For those hosts who haven't the time or the energy to travel thirty miles to a special wine shop to buy that *premier cru* but love to entertain and be entertained at impromptu dinners and suppers, the *monopole* wines vastly simplify the sometimes exasperating game of wine shopping.

The Classified Growths of Bordeaux

(*Note*: Château Mouton-Rothschild, always listed as a second growth, was belatedly moved into first position in 1973. Château Haut-Brion, located in Graves, was relisted among the Médocs because of its great prestige.)

MEDOC WINES

First Growths

Château Lafite-Rothschild
Château Margaux
Château Latour
Château Haut-Brion
Château Mouton-Rothschild

Second Growths

Château Rausan-Ségla
Château Rauzan-Gassies
Château Léoville-Lascases
Château Léoville-Poyferré
Château Léoville-Barton
Château Durfort-Vivens
Château Gruaud-Larose
Château Lascombes
Château Brane-Cantenac
Château Pichon-Longueville,
  Baron de Pichon
Château Pichon-Longueville,
  Comtesse de Lalande

Château Ducru-Beaucaillou
Château Cos d'Estournel
Château Montrose

Third Growths

Château Kirwan
Château d'Issan
Château Lagrange
Château Langoa-Barton
Château Giscours
Château Malescot-Saint-Exupéry
Château Boyd-Cantenac
Château Cantenac-Brown
Château Palmer
Château La Lagune
Château Desmirail
Château Calon-Ségur
Château Ferrière
Château Marquis d'Alesme-
  Becker

Fourth Growths

Château Saint-Pierre
Château Talbot
Château Branaire-Ducru
Château Duhart-Milon-
   Rothschild
Château Pouget
Château La Tour-Carnet
Château Lafon-Rochet
Château Beychevelle
Château Prieuré-Lichine
Château Marquis de Terme

Fifth Growths

Château Pontet-Canet
Château Batailley
Château Haut-Batailley
Château Grand-Puy-Lacoste
Château Grand-Puy-Ducasse
Château Lynch-Bages
Château Lynch-Moussas
Château Dauzac
Château Mouton-Baron-Philippe
Château du Tertre
Château Haut-Bages-Libéral
Château Pédesclaux
Château Belgrave
Château Camensac
Château Cos-Labory
Château Clerc-Milon-Mondon
Château Croizet-Bages
Château Cantemerle

SAUTERNES AND BARSAC

First Superior Growth

Château d'Yquem

First Growths

Château La Tour-Blanche
Château Lafaurie-Peyraguey
Clos Haut-Peyraguey
Château de Rayne-Vigneau
Château Suduiraut
Château Coutet
Château Climens
Château Guiraud
Château Rieussec
Château Rabaud-Promis
Château Sigalas-Rabaud

Second Growths

Château Myrat
Château Doisy-Daene
Château Doisy-Dubroca
Château Doisy-Védrines
Château d'Arche
Château Filhot
Château Broustet
Château Nairac
Château Caillou
Château Suau
Château de Malle
Château Romer-Farges
Château Romer-du Hayot
Château Lamothe
Château Lamothe-Bergey

Later Classifications of Bordeaux

(*Note*: Graves wines were classified in 1953 and amended in 1959. The wines of St. Emilion were classified in 1955. The wines of Pomeral have never been officially classified although Château Petrus is ranked among the very greatest wines of Bordeaux.)

GRAVES

1959 OFFICIAL CLASSIFICATION

Crus Classés—Red
Château Bouscaut
Château Carbonnieux
Domaine de Chevalier
Château Fieuzal
Château Haut-Bailly
Château Haut-Brion
Château La Mission Haut Brion
Château La Tour Haut Brion
Château La Tour-Martillac
Château Malartic-Lagravière
Château Olivier

Château Pape-Clément
Château Smith-Haut-Lafitte

Crus Classés—White
Château Bouscaut
Château Carbonnieux
Domaine de Chevalier
Château Couhins
Château La Tour-Martillac
Château Laville Haut Brion
Château Malartic-Lagravière
Château Olivier

SAINT-EMILION

1955 OFFICIAL CLASSIFICATION

**Premiers Grands Crus
Classés**
Château Ausone
Château Cheval-Blanc
Château Beauséjour-Lagrosse
Château Beauséjour-Fagouet
Château Belair
Château Canon
Château Figeac
Château La Gaffelière
Château Magdelaine
Château Pavie
Château Trottevieille
Clos Fourtet

Grands Crus Classés
Château L'Angélus
Château L'Arrosée
Château Balestard-La Tonnelle
Château Bellevue
Château Bergat
Château Cadet-Bon
Château Cadet-Piola
Château Canon-La Gaffelière
Château Cap-de-Mourlin

Château Chapelle-Madeleine
Château Chauvin
Château Corbin-Giraud
Château Corbin-Michotte
Château Coutet
Château Croque-Michotte
Château Curé-Bon
Château Fonplégade
Château Fonroque
Château Franc-Mayne
Château Grand-Barrail-
    Lamarzelle-Figeac
Château Grand-Corbin-Despagne
Château Grand-Corbin-Pécresse
Château Grand-Mayne
Château Grand-Pontet
Château Grandes-Murailles
Château Guadet-Saint-Julien
Château Jean-Faure
Château La Carte
Château La Clotte
Château La Couspaude
Château La Dominique
Château La Gluzière
Château Lamarzelle

Grands Crus Classés (*cont'd.*)
Château Larcis-Ducasse
Château Larmande
Château Laroze
Château Lassere
Château La Tour-du-Pin-Figeac-
  Bélivier
Château La Tour-du-Pin-Figeac-
  Moueix
Château La Tour-Figeac
Château Le Châtelet
Château Le Couvent
Château Le Prieuré
Château Mauvezin
Château Moulin-du-Cadet
Château Pavie-Décesse
Château Pavie-Macquin

Château Pavillon-Cadet
Château Petit-Faurie-de-
  Souchard
Château Petit-Faurie-de-Soutard
Château Ripeau
Château Sansonnet
Château Saint-Georges-Côte-Pavie
Château Soutard
Château Tertre-Daugay
Château Trimoulet
Château Trois-Moulins
Château Troplong-Mondot
Château Villemaurine
Château Yon-Figeac
Clos des Jacobins
Clos La Madeleine
Clos Saint-Martin

BURGUNDY WINES

If the wines of Bordeaux are known for their beautiful finesse, the wines of Burgundy are known for their richness and hearty flavor, their fuller body. Charles Montague put it well when he said, "Burgundy was the winiest wine, the greatest common measure of all the kindly wines of the earth." But to measure it in gallonage, Burgundian wines are less than 2 percent of all wines produced in France. It follows, therefore, that they are normally in scarce supply and mightily expensive.

When you buy a Burgundy wine, you'll note that the word "château" doesn't appear on the label, but instead the vineyard—frequently called an estate and often made up of dozens of individual owners of small parcels of land. The phrases used in Burgundy for wine bottled on the premises are "*Mis En Bouteilles Par Le Proprietaire*" or "*Mis Au Domaine*" or "*Mis En Bouteilles Dans Nos Caves.*"

The two grapes for which Burgundy is famed are the red Pinot Noir and the white Pinot Chardonnay. Both, incidentally, are grapes that flourish in California, and now represent some of the best American wines being produced.

Burgundy on the map of France is the old duchy of Bourgogne. Starting southeast of Paris, it spreads 225 miles to Lyons. Most of the region is known as the Côte d'Or, or "Slope of Gold," which has two main divisions: the Côte de Nuits and Côte de Beaune.

The Côte de Nuits is famed for such red wines as Chambertin (Napoleon's favorite); Musigny (a wine that reminds imaginative wine drinkers of violets and depends for its finesse on a small amount of white grapes in the red must); Vougeot or Clos de Vougeot (a vineyard whose workmen were once instructed to shake the dirt from their shoes before leaving the estate in order not to lose any of the incomparable soil); Romanée-Conti (one of the highest-priced and most renowned of all red Burgundies, famous for its full velvety flavor and longevity); and Richebourg, known for its sumptuous bouquet and complex flavors.

The Côte de Beaune, known for both red and white wines, is represented first of all by its northernmost village, Aloxe Corton. (Frequently just Corton, minus the Aloxe, appears on the label.) The city of Beaune is the home of the famous Hospices de Beaune, a charity hospital whose wine auctions in November are a celebrated annual event. Among the reds in this area, Pommard has always enjoyed an extraordinary popularity outside of France. Cynical statisticians once estimated that the amount of red wines bearing the word "Pommard" exceeded ten times the amount of wine made in this section of Burgundy; but when winemakers have a good thing, the *contrôle* doesn't always control their enthusiasm.

Among Burgundy whites, the name Chablis has become almost a household word in the United States. (The California version of Chablis bears little if any resemblance to the French Chablis whose name it has appropriated.) It's a greenish-tinged white wine, extremely dry and always served chilled, and therefore has all the elements that stimulate easy wine drinking in this country. A label marked *Petit Chablis* is a light version and should be drunk as young as possible. *Premier Cru Chablis* is ranked a grade higher, while *Grand Cru Chablis* is the most full-bodied of all.

Two other Burgundy wines, Meursault and Montrachet—both white —are names of immense prestige. Meursault is a green-gold wine, racy but with rich body and magnificent aftertaste. Montrachet, representing about a thousand cases a year, is the most elegant and most expensive of white Burgundies. Over the years the wine has acquired such fame that its name on labels is joined to two adjoining communes, Puligny and Chassagne. Even two vineyards adjoining Montrachet— Chevalier and Bâtard—are allowed to bear the Montrachet name hyphenated on the labels of the remarkable white wines they produce.

Going south in Burgundy, the wines of Mâcon appear. They're

made from the Pinot Chardonnay grape and may be called simply Macon or Pinot Chardonnay Macon. Like our California Pinot Chardonnays, the wines of Macon, pale gold and usually very dry, serve magnificently with any seafood, light meats, or poultry.

Finally, in the southernmost region of Burgundy you find Beaujolais, a red wine whose name defies everything that implies "greatness." It doesn't have that big expansive body elitists call "chewy." People don't talk about its finesse, elegance, or subtle balance. It's fresh, fruity, easy, and can be enjoyed at any time of the day or night with almost any food. In France certain Beaujolais wines, as soon as they are finished fermenting, are enjoyed like the first fresh raspberries or strawberries. In this country a Beaujolais bottled in the spring following the wine's harvest the previous fall should be drunk as fresh as possible. While dealers tell you of the remarkable life of one vintage over another, mainly to palm off their old stock, you'd do best to buy the freshest Beaujolais available. Certain villages in Beaujolais are noted for their wines, and their names are a guide to quality. They include Brouilly, Chenas, Fleurie, Julienas, Morgan, Moulin-à-Vent, and St. Amour.

RHONE WINES

Leaving Burgundy and going south from Lyons, the great culinary center, is the wine country along the banks of the Rhône. The section called *Côte Rôtie*, or "Roasted Slope," produces red wines that seem perfectly adapted to the fat poultry, the rich pâtés, sausages, and quenelles for which Lyons is famed. The hillside known as Hermitage produces about two-thirds rich, strong red wine; the white is not popular in the United States. Certainly the most eminent Rhône wine in this country is Châteauneuf-du-Pape, a wine of abundant alcoholic strength and robust body. For those who want a strong red wine with assertive flavor, Châteauneuf-du-Pape fills the bill at comparatively modest prices. This area is also the home of Tavel, a delightful rosé.

LOIRE WINES

The 600-mile stretch of the Loire valley, alongside the broad river of the same name, is not only lovely countryside but also the scene of old fortresses and châteaus built by the French nobility of the seventeenth and eighteenth centuries. The word *château* in the Loire, unlike its use in Bordeaux, actually means a historical mansion.

Loire wines are light and supple in flavor. They include dry and sweet, still and sparkling, red, white, and rosé wines, although in this country the whites enjoy top billing. One of the most pleasant Loire wines is Pouilly-Fumé from the eastern section of the Loire, a lively white wine whose fresh flavor seems a perfect adjunct to any fish or shellfish. Sancerre, known for its crisp flavor, is another white wine as popular in France as in this country. From Touraine come two excellent reds—Chinon and Bourgueil. The famed white wine from Touraine is Vouvray. Both Vouvray and Saumur produce charming white wines from the Chenin Blanc grape—a California favorite. If you're in the mood for a comparative tasting session, be sure you buy the dryest California Chenin Blancs you can get to make the comparison fair. Finally, made in the most westerly part of the Loire, near the Atlantic, is Muscadet, another light, tart white wine, sometimes slightly bubbly, a young, fresh wine with immense appeal for lovers of seafood.

ALSATIAN WINES

The Alsace, a long chunk of northeast France, historically has been fought over, traded, and exchanged between Germany and France for generations. In conversations with natives of the Alsace, you'll often hear them switch—sometimes in midsentence—from French to German and vice versa. But if the language, politics, and culture of the Alsatians are a whimsical amalgam, their wines have no such identity problem. They're all like the German white wines, except in one important particular: While the German wines lean to the sweet side, the Alsatian wines are mostly dry. Their grapes are those that flourish in Germany, and even their tall, slender wine bottles follow the German tradition.

The beautiful thing about Alsatian wines isn't just their fruitiness and charm but the fact that, like the best of the California wines, they're identified by the grape. All of the confusing terminology of châteaus, townships, districts, and other gobbledygook is quickly resolved by the grape name. The most eminent of their wines is the Riesling, the grape used for the fine German Rhine and Moselle wines.

Next in prestige is the Gewürztraminer, the wine you recognize by its spicy overtones. (The flowery aroma of these grapes sometimes conveys the feeling that the wines are sugary when this isn't the case.) Sylvaner, Muscat d'Alsace, and Pinot Blanc are other Alsatian wines that might be looked upon as cousins of the Riesling in their luscious fruitiness.

Most of the fruity Alsatian wines are bottled and drunk young, although some may last for three or four years without slipping in flavor. When you're serving a party of young people, and you're in a dilemma about which wines will go with which foods or which wines will please which people, the Alsatian wines flow in a happy channel with any course on the bill-of-fare from pâté through seafood, red or light meat, birds, or game, to desserts and cheese.

The Wines of Germany

It's often said that people learn to appreciate wines by starting with the sweet and eventually graduating to the semidry or dry. In Germany, really bone-dry wines are rare phenomena. You start with the semidry (or semisweet, which means the same thing), and as your wine experience continues, you reach the summit of their vinous treasures, which are extremely sweet—and extremely expensive.

Germany, on a latitude with Labrador and Newfoundland, is the northernmost limit of European vineyards. That they're able to grow any grapes in some sections seems a Bacchic miracle. Sometimes snow is falling in the Black Forest when the German vintagers along the Moselle and Rhine rivers (their two chief wine-growing sections) begin their harvest. Long after Californian, Italian, and French wines have been pressed and are fermenting, the Germans are still climbing the slopes alongside their rivers collecting grapes.

Almost all German wines are made from white grapes of which the Riesling is the patriarch. The other main varieties—the Sylvaner and the Mueller-Thurgau—like the Riesling, produce wines so fruity and filled with such rich bouquet that you imagine you're biting into fresh grapes rather than the fermented juice of those grapes. What gives German wines their outstanding zest isn't just fruitiness or sweetness but a dexterous balance: The fruit and sugar, as though walking a tightrope, strike a heavenly balance with the wine's acidity so that the net effect is luscious, seductive drinking.

Many of their wines are of low alcoholic content, so low that in California, for example, they wouldn't qualify as wines. Some of them actually contain less alcohol than certain English ales. But since they're always served chilled, they're immensely refreshing. If you're not yet a German wine buff, wait till a thirsty moment when perhaps you're a little done in from the day's work, and try one of the semidry German wines to see how lightly uplifting it is. While, generally speaking, German wines are short on alcohol, they're long on flavor (a situation often reversed in other countries), which makes for extremely pleasant drinking.

Since World War II, German technology in wine making has established a beachhead as one of the most advanced in the world. The amount of German wines produced during the past several decades has risen from 60 million gallons a year to over 200 million gallons. Much of the German wine that Americans drink is *liebfraumilch*, a term that originally identifed a wine from a specific vineyard near the Church of Our Beloved Lady, in Worms. Over the years it's become a catchall term for almost any German white wine, fair or good—although the more expensive liebfraumilchs, like Blue Nun, are delightful and well worth their price. *Moselblumchen*, meaning "little flower of the Moselle," is another general term for wine from the Moselle region. Rhine wine is always in a green bottle, Moselle in a brown bottle.

Because it takes so long for the grapes in Germany to reach adulthood, "ripeness" is the word that lifts the veil from the rather confusing gamut of German wine terminology. The less ripe the grapes, the lower the alcohol content, quality, and price of their wines. Many of the lower grades of German wines are made with added sugar in the must. The sugar is converted into alcohol in order to reach even the low minimum required in German wines. Among the highest grades of German wines, there is residual sugar in the bottle—that is, sugar left over when the grapes stopped fermenting—which gives them their characteristic sweetness.

In 1971, German wine labels were an intolerable muddle of conflicting terms even if you knew the German language perfectly. In that year the German government drastically changed the regulations governing wine and wine labeling. It simplified the labels and, more importantly, provided for a uniform government grading of the main types of wine. There are now three broad categories of German wines permitted to carry specific labels:

1. **German Table Wine** *(Deutscher Tafelwein)*: Most of these wines are consumed in Germany and would correspond to the *vins ordinaires* of France or the jug wines of California. Most of them have sugar added to the must to raise their alcoholic content. However, *tafelwein* must be made only from approved grape varieties in one of the six table-wine regions of Germany: Mosel, Rhein, Main, Neckar, Oberrhein Burrengau, and Oberrhein Roemertor. These regional wine names will always appear on the label, and 75 percent of the wine must be made from the named grape in the named area. If a vintage is indicated, at least 75 percent of the wine must be made from grapes picked in that year. Finally, the name of the bottler *(abfüller)* must appear on the label. These are normally all young wines; and if a vintage is shown, be sure the vintage is not more than two years old.

2. **German Quality Wine** *(Deutscher Qualitätswein)*: By the book, this second class of German wines need only have a minimum alcohol content of 8.5 percent, although many reach 10 percent or over. They must come from one of the eleven German Quality Wine Regions—Mittelrhein, Rheingau, Hessische Bergstrasse, Ahr, Mosel-Saar-Ruwer, Nahe, Franken, Rheinhessen, Rheinpfalz, Baden, and Wuerttemberg. The label on each bottle must be printed with a control number—proof that the wine was officially tasted, judged, and analyzed by a government agency and found worthy of, and conforming to, the label information. Quality wine may be labeled by region, subregion, collective vineyard, or vineyard, provided that 75 percent of the wine was made in the smallest named area. It must indicate the community name, and may indicate a grape type only if 75 percent of the named variety was used. Liebfraumilch is now a Quality Wine, thus assuring that none of it is of doubtful status.

3. **German Quality Wine with Special Attributes** *(Deutscher Qualitätswein Mit Prädikat)*: This is the top pick of the finest German wines. Wines in this class must have a minimum alcohol content of 10 percent, although most of them exceed it. It includes a number of subcategories, each of which must be indicated.

a. *Kabinett*: Years ago a *Kabinettwein* was a special one a winemaker would set aside as one of the casks which was head and shoulders above all his other wines and which he'd keep for his own personal use in his private cabinet. Today the term means the first of a number of superior wines made from grapes sufficiently ripe so that no added sugar is used in the must.

b. *Spätlese*: The German word *spät* means tardy or late, and in vineyards *spätlese* indicates a wine made from grapes picked after the normal harvest.

c. *Auslese*: Only individually selected ripe bunches are selected and pressed for this wine; some of them may have the *Botrytis* or "noble rot" (called *edelfäule* in German) found in the great Sauternes of France.

d. *Beerenauslese*: *Beeren* is, as you've probably guessed, the word for berry, and the grapes in this *lese,* or picking, are picked individually for the wine that bears this name.

e. *Trockenbeerenauslese*: *Trocken* means dried, and, therefore, the grapes for this top rung of the German wine aristocracy are grapes so ripe they've dried and shriveled almost to the raisin state.

f. *Eiswein*: Ice wine is really a rare phenomenon, prized for its rarity rather than its superiority. Sudden frosts in the late harvest may actually freeze the grapes. Many of them are frozen solid, but those with extremely high sugar content are usually not completely frozen, and are used to produce a rich, extremely sweet wine.

German wine labels in this country are a mixture of German and English words, mostly the former. Why they don't print an English translation in a legend on the back of the bottle can perhaps be answered simply: They'd lose the special mystique of foreignness that wine exporters, advertisers, and promoters obviously treasure above the wine itself. In any case, for non-Teutonic wine drinkers, here are a few translations:

Abfüller	bottler
Abgefüllt durch	bottled by
Burg	castle
Domäne	domain or vineyard
Erzengerabfuellung	bottled on the estate or premises
Fass or *fuder*	cask in which a special wine was matured; often the cask number is indicated
Freiherr	baron

Gebrüder	brothers
Grosslage	cooperative vineyard
Halbtrocken	semidry
Keller	cellar
Lage	individually owned vineyard
Natur	natural wine, unsugared
Schloss	castle or palace
Süss	sweet
Wachstum	growth of a single vineyard
Weinhändler	wine merchant or shipper
Weinkellerei	wine cellar, winery
Winzergenossenschaft	cooperative grape-growers' association

Finally, German wine labels often list the towns renowned for the wines in their district. They include:

Deidesheim	Piesporter
Erbach	Rüdesheim
Geisenheim	Urzig
Oppenheim	Zeltingen

The Wines of Italy

Making and drinking more wine than any other nation, probing into it less but loving it more, most Italians would simply laugh their way through all the affectedly judicial wine tastings and tests that now attract hordes of amateur wine savants in this country. Accustomed to look upon it as a food, a comfort more than an intoxicant, they'd no more chatter about last night's wine than they'd chatter about last night's pasta. To the Italian, wine is something for which the whole body thirsts. Now and then an Italian businessman will slip out of his office for a quick glass of vermouth and some salted almonds. But at mealtime he wants his full bottle of *vino* on the table; and if it's not there, it's as though someone had snatched away his roast, his bread, or his salad.

Most of the billion-gallon river of Italian wine runs red each year, though there are some excellent specimens among the whites as well. If you travel through Italy, you'll see some areas of planted vineyards, all in neat rows, all tended by careful vintagers. But there are thousands of other winegrowers among whose vines one will find tomatoes, potatoes, squash, olives, and lemons growing, and some of the vines are trellised to trees, barns, or fences. The Italian word for this kind of grape growing is *promiscura*, and it represents well over half of the wine produced in Italy. Such vines can't be sprayed, cultivated, and pruned in an artful manner, and much of the Italian wine made in Italy, but not shipped abroad, suffers from this kind of promiscuous treatment.

Italian wines that arrive in this country bearing prominent shippers' names are another story. In recent years Italian winemakers have begun to use stainless-steel tanks and have adopted controlled fermentation and every modern method for filtering and bottling their wines. The Italian government, too, has put into effect a system for guaranteeing the place names of their wines; called D.O.C. (*Denominazione Di Origine Controllata*), it is found on labels from nineteen controlled wine regions of Italy. Only a comparatively small number of Italian wines have ever been able to challenge the eminence of the greatest French Bordeaux and Burgundy wines, but the fact that many of the noted Italian wines sell for a fraction of the cost of the French *premiers crus* makes them worth investigating.

Italian wines vary considerably from one region to another, with the most prestigious wines flowing from the top of the Italian boot. The following regions produce noted Italian wines available to Americans:

Piedmont, in the northwest section of Italy, is known for wines from the Nebbiolo grape. The name is derived from the Italian *nebbia*, meaning mist, and the grapes are normally gathered very late in the season when the autumn mist is in the air. Most outstanding of the Piedmontese wines is Barolo, a rich red wine that ages long and well and is magnificent with roasts, steaks, and game. Julius Caesar was said to have been enamored of Barolo, and, according to Piedmontese historians at least, the Gallic invaders of the Roman Empire were specifically motivated by their special thirst for Barolo—as good a pretext as many others for starting war. It's the wine whose aftertaste reminds some connoisseurs of violets, an odd comparison since Barolo's flavor is hardly shy; indeed, it's a wine of huge flavor and alcohol content. Barolo Riserva must have at least four years' aging before it's sold, and some Barolos only reach their prime at eight to ten years.

Barbaresco is another so-called big wine—meaning it develops slowly, and reaches a stage of complex powerful flavors. Barbera wine from the grape of the same name is made in Piedmont, but ironically it's somewhat on the rough side when compared to some of the Barbera wines of California.

Gattinara, somewhat softer than Barolo, has lately stirred the interest of Americans even though the volume reaching our shores is comparatively small.

Piedmont is also the home of Italy's wonderfully festive sparkling wine, Asti spumante.

Lombardy, east of Piedmont and at the top center of Italy, is best known for Valtellina, produced east of Lake Como. Somewhat lesser-known wines such as Grumello, Inferno, Sassella, and Valgella originate here—all of them pressed from the Nebbiolo grape, all of them hearty, full-bodied red wines. One thinks of them as macho wines, keeping in mind the crusty Italian tradition that any man who drank white wine was weak.

Veneto, an area in the northeastern part of Italy, within which is the city of Venice, is the home of two of the most beloved Italian red wines, Bardolino and Valpolicella. Both of them are light- to medium-bodied and made mainly from the Corvina and Molinara grapes. They can take a few years' aging, but beyond five years their charm and fruitiness begin to slip. Sometimes they are served just slightly chilled. They make extremely pleasant predinner drinks as a switch from the ubiquitous light white wines.

Veneto is also the home of Soave, a white wine that is literally suave. While pale in color, the best Soaves are delicate in flavor, and serve as all-purpose wines not only for predinner drinking but for picnics, buffets, tailgate parties, or midnight bashes. There's no American wine corresponding to it exactly since the grapes for Soave are the Garanega and Trebbiano, not grown here.

Emilia produces several wines, but Lambrusco tops them all. It's the slightly sparkling, slightly sweet red wine that displaced our native "pop" wines when they began tailspinning in 1976. Lambrusco is especially popular among younger crowds who are tasting wine for the first time and are repelled by dry or heavy-bodied wines from any country. A large part of the 23 million gallons of Italian wine imported to the United States (now holding a two-to-one edge over French wine imports) is accounted for by Lambrusco. In Emilia they drink Lambrusco as the natural accompaniment to their somewhat fatty foods like sausage *cotechino*, stuffed pigs' feet, and boiled pork. Among the college crowds in the States, you're likely to see it gulped down with anything from buttered popcorn to porterhouse steaks.

Tuscany, according to some Italians who claim to have evidence proving it, had grape vines before mankind itself appeared. In any event, it's a region of both undulating hills and rocky, harsh terrain, and is the home of Chianti, a word that to many Americans has always meant the archetype of the best Italian wines. Even in the Thirties at the beginning of Repeal, when Italian wines were contemptuously referred to as coal tar or red ink, the few Chiantis that had arrived were recognized for their zestful superiority. In those days most of the Chiantis coming here were packed in raffia-covered bottles, or *fiaschi*, many of which were quickly emptied and converted into table lamps. Over the years the cost of the *fiaschi* has become prohibitive—they were always a problem anyway when you wanted to store the bottles on their sides on a wine rack. Today most of the best Chiantis are those in conventional Bordeaux-style bottles. They're labeled Chianti Classico, are made in a delimited region of Tuscany near Florence and Siena, and represent about 12 percent of the total Chianti output. On the label you'll see a black cockerel or *Gallo Nero*, symbol of the Chianti League whose members pledge themselves to follow strict procedures for vineyard planting and harvesting.

Chianti is made from a mixture of grapes, the dominant one being Sangiovese. About one-fifth of the must is the black Canaiolo grape, and one-tenth is Malvasia and Trebbiano grapes. (It's always a surprise to outsiders to learn that the Malvasia is a white grape, which is added for its softening effects.) After Chianti has stopped fermenting, a small proportion of sun-dried grapes is added so that a second fermentation starts, and this additional step (called the *governo* process) helps reduce the biting acidity of the original mixture.

Travelers in Tuscany often come across young Chiantis of rather low alcohol content, bright rather than deep red wines that are enjoyed —as any young red wine like Beaujolais would be—for their attractive fruitiness. The older Chianti Classicos, ranging from an alcohol content of 11½ to 13 percent, which were harsh when young, will age beautifully in the bottle, sometimes for a decade, when their color becomes garnet and their flavor highly developed and complex.

Tuscany is also the home of two other distinguished red wines, Brunello di Montalcino and Vino Nobile di Montepulciano (the latter made as far back as the 1300s), but you'll have to search out a shop specializing in Italian wines to acquire either of these.

Marche is an east central region whose best-known wine, for Americans, is Verdicchio. Made from the white grape of the same name, it comes in a slender amphora-type bottle. It's a medium-bodied dry white wine with a somewhat pungent aftertaste, and is a beautiful partner for such Italian dishes as vermicelli with clams, fresh ham with capers, etc.

Umbria, a region just north of Rome, produces the well-known white wine Orvieto. Like the Chiantis in the Thirties, Orvietos were famed as much for their straw-covered bottles as the contents of the bottles. Orvieto may be *secco* (dry) or *abboccato* (semidry). Some Orvietos may come from vineyards previously described as *promiscura,* and when this is the case, wines even of the same label may have a somewhat checkered quality.

Latium, an area close to Rome, produces two outstanding wine names, Frascati and Est!Est!Est! Frascati from vineyards southeast of Rome is a white wine of medium body, and if you've ever had it in Rome you can understand why it's extremely popular there. Like many other wines that are delightful in their native habitat but deteriorate noticeably when they travel, Frascati is a wine that has never prominently fraternized with the white-wine parade in this country.

Est! Est! Est! is a wine whose name seems to arouse more interest than the wine itself. The Latin word *est* means "it is." In the fourteenth century a German bishop traveling in Italy instructed his valet, who moved a day or so ahead of the bishop scouting for the best accommodations, to scribble the word *Est!* on the wall of any wayside tavern where the wine and food were good. In Montefiascone the valet reached an inn where the wine and food so impressed him that he chalked *Est!* three times on the wall. The bishop not only later agreed with his valet's judgment but made his permanent home in Montefiascone. The wine is a semidry white, pleasant for light spring or summer drinking.

Southern Italy is the home of many wines. From this area comes the name Lacrima Christi—which translates as "tears of Christ"—a white wine from grapes grown on the slopes of Mt. Vesuvius. Legend has it that Lucifer fell into the Bay of Naples, and brought a little piece of Paradise along with him. Later the Saviour visited the paradise on earth only to find that its inhabitants were somewhat fiendish. He shed tears of divine pity, and where the tears fell, vines flourished. There is also a red Lacrima Christi, but the whites are the softest, and to American tastes perhaps the most pleasant.

Beyond the tip of the Italian boot is Sicily, famed for its Marsala (from the Arabic *Marsh-el-Allah,* or God's Harbor, for which the city of Marsala in western Sicily was named). Marsala is a sweet dessert wine fortified with brandy, best served bitingly cold and best drunk as an accompaniment to a cheese platter and bowl of fruit rather than a rich dessert such as a soufflé or tart. It's the vital ingredient in the frothy Italian dessert, zabaglione. Marsala comes in both sweet and dry types, the latter being less sweet but still a far cry from the bone-dry red or white table wines. If you've traveled in Sicily, you've probably discovered that many of the local table wines are on the rough side. In this country, however, in recent years we've been receiving the red and white wines with the name Corvo di Casteldaccia on the label; both the strong red Corvo and the medium-bodied white Corvo rival the best wines of northern Italy.

The Wines of Rioja, Spain

For many years the wines of Spain, to Americans, meant either sherry or sangria; the latter of course is a wine punch that can be made from the dry red wine of any country. In recent times, however, as premium imported and domestic wines have risen sharply in price, the wines of Rioja have drawn extravagant attention. They are wines of sturdy body with a smooth finish, and their prices are startlingly low, selling often for less than four dollars a bottle.

Often they are compared to the wines of Bordeaux and Burgundy. It's an unfair comparison because Riojas are made from different grapes, some of which are not grown in France. But a resemblance does exist, and it's due to a historical event. When the French vineyards were virtually destroyed in the 1870s by *phylloxera,* French winemen emigrated to the Rioja area in north central Spain, which had been growing wine grapes for centuries. They took their vinification techniques with them, and started to make wine that in certain respects bore an uncanny resemblance to the great wines of France. In those days wines were only bottled after long aging in wood, and this practice is still followed in Rioja. While modern Bordeaux wines and California wines are aged for two years or less in wood, Riojas are kept in the barrel from a half dozen to a dozen or more years, and this is the clue to their flavor. Whether you like this kind of wood-developed flavor is a matter of personal taste, and if you sample a Rioja you should expect this feature in the wine's taste profile.

Rioja produces both red and white wines. The white wines are a mixed bag and don't cause much excitement in this country. You may buy a bottle of red Rioja marked "light red wine" only to find that what the shipper considers lightweight has middleweight strength or better. Some Riojas are marked *Riserva* with a year beside the word. This does not have the same meaning as our vintage year. The year indicated may have been a great vintage in Rioja, but during the long aging process in wood, as the wine evaporates, the Rioja wine-makers refill the evaporated portion of the barrel with new wine or wine of any year that they feel will enhance the blend. Often this blend-ing of new with old is successful, but at the same time it makes the *Riserva* year meaningless. Do not look for the name of a vineyard on a Rioja label. All Riojas are made from grapes or wine that are bought by large shippers, and the shipper's name is your guide to quality.

Sherry, Port, and Madeira

That port is the exclusive indulgence of doddering London clubmen and that sherry is designed mainly for elderly distaff tea parties are stubborn stereotypes that should be laid to rest. White ports are now among the most popular of all apéritifs sipped at sundown in Parisian and Belgian cafés. There are watering spots where ice-cold fino sherry has supplanted the martini, and still others where it's used in place of vermouth in the martini pitcher. Even the semisweet and sweet sherries flow over the rocks regularly at the cocktail hour.

The most important thing on the labels of both sherry and port is the shipper's name, and when you look at a bottle of either one, you'll find less pretentious terminology than on almost any other bottling of fine wine. The great sherries are all blends, as are all ports—outside of vintage ports—and the blending arts in Spain and Portugal are the accumulated knowledge of centuries of training and skill. Consequently, when you see names like Sandeman, Harvey's, Gonzalez Byass, Cockburn, Robertson Bros., Pedro Domecq, Williams and Humbert, Duff Gordon, and others, you can invariably count on wines that are amazingly consistent in spite of snowstorms, withering heat, hail, and good, bad, and indifferent years.

Both sherry and port are fortified—that is, wines whose fermentation has been arrested at a desired point by adding brandy to them. Years ago both suffered from cloudiness, the result of sedimentation in the bottle. A new process called supercooling, wherein the wines are held at low but not below-zero temperatures just before bottling, eliminates this annoying problem.

Bottles of port and sherry, unlike table wines, may be opened, recorked, and then left in your liquor cabinet without any fear of spoiling. But both are at their best shortly after they're opened the first time. In Spain, for instance, a host wouldn't think of pouring from the bottle opened yesterday. Instead, he'll open a new one—perhaps a bone-dry fino sherry—to start his party and then continue serving it through soup and fish courses like any other table wine. If there's any left over, it's used for cooking.

Sherries run the spectrum from the palest of finos or manzanillas, usually served as apéritifs, to the medium-dry amontillados, all the way to the deep olorosos or cream sherries, which are magnificent dessert wines. Spanish sherries are developed, aged, and blended in the solera system, whereby young wines are gradually moved into casks containing older wines. The younger wines thus take on the rich flavor, deep color, and full-bodied maturity of the senior sherries much sooner than if they had remained alone, leading the indeterminate asocial life followed by most table wines in their own casks.

In contrast to sherries, which darken with age, ports lose color as they get older. All young ones, outside of white ports, are a deep, intense purple. As they ripen, they turn ruby, indicating a fine port that is mature but not terribly old. In time, they become tawny, with brown overtones and still deeper flavor. Most of the ports sent to this country from Portugal are either ruby or tawny, and both are complicated blends that somehow remain remarkably consistent in quality over the years.

Vintage ports are those of a particularly good year, kept in casks for two years and then bottled; names like Da Silva, Rochas, and Hooper represent the finest of these. During their long bottle life, they throw off a crust, and most of them until recently required decanting. A few vintage ports, those of the war years, have been decanted in Portugal and shipped in new bottles, thus eliminating a formerly tedious job. If you make a hobby of vintage ports, recent vintages selected for bottling include '27s, '34s, '35s, '42s, '43s, '45s, '47s, '50s, '55s, '58s, '60s, '62s, '63s, '67s, '70s, and '73s. Different shippers may have some of these years or different years. Vintages from '66 on will now (1979) need additional aging for full maturity. Although one can still buy 1890 and early-1900 ports, most collectors nowadays seem to prefer vintages not quite as ancient as in other generations. For the young bachelor who doesn't have the space to lay down bottles for future years—or the patience to wait for them—there are bottlings of vintage reserve ports, blends of old ports of different vintage years, which needn't be decanted and are great for after-coffee sipping. White ports from Portugal (not the California variety) are apéritif wines with a lively bouquet but very little sugar—a welcome change-of-pace drink for those who want to be stimulated, not stunned, at the cocktail hour.

The Portuguese island of Madeira became famous as a source of American wines during colonial days. But in cookbooks even today, particularly in France, Madeira is often the wine called for rather than sherry, which it resembles in color, flavor, and the solera system in which it's made. Though only a small amount is imported to America, all the Madeiras (from Sercial, the lightest, to Verdelho or Bual, of medium sweetness, to the rich, dark Malmsey) are pleasant and warming wines to be sipped on a lazy winter afternoon in the States.

American Wines:
Generic and Varietal

Wines made in the United States bear labels that fall into two well-beaten paths. The first are *generic* wine titles, names referring to regions of Europe, such as Rhine Wine, Burgundy, Chablis, etc. You may find some very palatable American wines bearing these generic names but also bearing little or no resemblance to the native wines of those specific European areas. For instance, you can buy a New York State Chablis or a California Chablis, but the wine you drink will be made from grapes unknown to the little town in Burgundy, France, and its surrounding district. Like French Chablis, it may be a crisp, white wine that goes well with light meats and seafood, but it tastes no more like French Chablis than French Chablis tastes like sherry.

Some of the generic wines are imitators, but they're not worthless. In many instances they are *not* imitations at all but simply blended red or white wines, often sold in jugs, whose names in this country have become simple conveniences over the years—like King Street or Queen Street in an American town that never saw a king or queen. People drink them like they drink beer, with little analysis but great enjoyment. They are marvelous for making wine punches, wine cups, and sangria, and they make great cooking wines. Even some French wines use generic names, such as Ecu Royal Claret Reserve; "claret" is the old English term for red wines from Bordeaux. A few American wines bear simple trade names—such as the Paul Masson Rubion, which happens to be an excellent dry red wine from California.

For Americans learning American wines, the second category— *varietal* wines—is the most important. They demonstrate that what's in a name throws all else into the shade when the wine's name is the name of the grape. No wine lover, however devoted he or she may be to Bacchic pleasures, can ever possibly know all the names of grapes that have been grown. Besides the countless grapes native to Europe that have been transplanted to California, there are about 2000 varieties of native American grapes called *Vitis labrusca*, grapes growing on this continent before white men landed, used for wines conveying those "foxy" flavors reminiscent of bottled blue grape juice or a jar of grape jelly. Then there are about 5000 known varieties of native European grapes, the kind transplanted in California to produce wines with the traditional flavors we associate with wines from Germany, France, Italy, etc.

For practical purposes, however, only a few dozen grape names are important. When it comes to American wines, knowing the name of the grape uncomplicates the task of selecting, buying, or tasting wines, and makes it a far simpler thing than it is with European wines. French and German wine labels, as we have seen, are an intolerably muddled business because it's so easy to become confused by all the foreign names—châteaus, townships, estates, *clos*, *schlosses*, etc.

By contrast, an American wine bearing the word "Zinfandel," one knows, is made from the Zinfandel grape. This doesn't mean that one Zinfandel doesn't differ from another. A bottle of David Bruce Zinfandel may cost twice the price of a bottle of another California Zinfandel. Different bottlings may be older or younger. Regulations now say that Zinfandel, like other varietal wines, may be called Zinfandel if 51 percent of the contents of the bottle is made from the named grape. Usually the percentage is much higher, but the proportion of non-Zinfandels may affect the wine's quality.

When you've been drinking Zinfandels for a reasonable period of time, you learn to recognize their varietal flavor, the feature that makes the wine different from a Barbera or a Pinot Noir. You may decide that an older and more expensive Zinfandel is, to your taste, less desirable than the younger one with its fresher, fruitier flavor. Beginners, however, should be advised that when they taste a varietal, dry red wine for the first time, it may be difficult to separate their taste experience from other red wines. As they continue to drink specific red wines, their taste memory develops, and then the special flavor of a red wine like Zinfandel (often described as berrylike or brambly) will come into focus.

Some varietal white wines can also be instantly spotted. For instance, if you were to taste the fresh juice pressed from Riesling grapes for white wine before the juice is fermented, you'd instantly identify the aroma of the fresh grape with the finished wine you know as a Riesling.

In the following list of grapes used for varietal American wines, there are some whose names do not appear as the name of the wine on the bottle's front label. They may be grapes used in small amounts for blending with the principal grape; sometimes there's a label on the back of the bottle naming both the major and the minor grapes; sometimes wine labels will have a legend sketching the origin of the grape and the features of the wine as far as they can be expressed in words. Like leading a horse to water, the descriptive list below helps you to identify wines; to really learn them, to plumb their true pleasure, you must, of course, drink them.

Aurora   A French-American hybrid white wine grape used in making medium-sweet New York State wines.

Baco Noir   A French-American hybrid red wine grape; very successful New York State wines with surprisingly well-developed flavors are now made with this grape.

Barbera   An Italian red wine grape that flourishes in California; it produces earthy wine best drunk young, although some outstanding bottlings may be aged for five years and develop into rounded, mellow wines.

Cabernet Sauvignon   The principal red wine grape for the great French Bordeaux wines; in California it's also on the top rung of the ladder. Wines of this grape are tart and tannic when young, but age into mellow wines with complex full flavors; California Cabernet Sauvignons generally (though there are exceptions) tend to age faster than their French counterparts. Because the yield per acre of this grape is low and because its wines must be aged longer than other red wines in both wood and bottle, prices are higher than other reds.

Carignane   You're not likely to see the name of this red grape featured on a bottle of California wine, although it's one of the most widely planted wine grapes in the state; it's known for its sturdy flavor, but even more important to winegrowers is its high yield per acre; widely used as a blending ingredient in generic red wines.

Catawba   A light red native American grape used in New York State for white wines with distinct "foxy" flavor; sometimes used in sparkling wines from New York State.

Chelois   A red French-American hybrid grape producing medium-bodied New York State wine.

Chenin Blanc   A great white wine grape of the Loire in France, used for Vouvray and similar wines; also known as the *Pineau* (not Pinot) *de la Loire*, a varietal name that may appear in California. Chenin Blanc is one of California's most popular white varietal wines with pronounced individual flavor; unlike their European counterparts, most Chenin Blancs here are made slightly sweet. It's also one of the principal ingredients in California Chablis.

Concord   Known to most Americans as a blue-skinned table grape, the Concord is the constituent in many very sweet New York State wines, including kosher wines.

Delaware   A pink American native grape that takes its name from Delaware, Ohio, where it originally flourished; it makes a flowery tart wine often used in eastern champagne.

Diamond   Known also as Moore's Diamond, this eastern grape has been used for a spicy, tart white wine and eastern champagne.

Emerald Riesling   A cross between Riesling (see below) and Muscat grapes, a variety grown in Bordeaux for flavoring Sauternes; produces fruity white wine resembling Alsatian or Germanic wines; popular because of its good sugar/acid balance.

Folle Blanche   The French name of this grape literally means crazy white; actually it was for generations the staid white grape used for making the acidy wine from which Cognac was distilled. In California it's turned to good account as a blending ingredient in Chenin Blanc (see above).

Gamay Beaujolais   One would expect the California red wine made from this grape to resemble wine of the grape used in Beaujolais, France, for its fruity fresh flavor, but actually this grape, after much research and debate, turns out to be a variety of the Pinot Noir (below). If you want the counterpart of the French wine, you should buy a bottle marked *Napa Gamay* (below). This is an instance where a varietal name has been so tossed about in the storm of oenological semantics that the best thing is to simply follow the guidance of your own nose and taste buds rather than the words printed on the label. Most of the California wines called Gamay Beaujolais are fresh and sprightly in flavor, and enjoyed best when young.

Gewürztraminer   The German word *gewürz* means spice, and the California white wine of this grape has overtones which have been called spicy but don't really convey the intensity of such spices as cloves, nutmeg, or cinnamon. To many people the wine has a mildly pungent but easygoing floweriness, at once similar to the Alsatian and Germanic Reislings, yet different. This is a wine of such individuality that even a rank beginner would be unlikely to confuse it with any other wine.

Grenache   A red wine grape used in making some dessert wines but best-known for its distinctive rosé; other red grapes such as the Gamay, Petite Sirah, Cabernet Sauvignon, etc., are also used for rosés.

Grey Riesling   In France this white wine grape is called the Chauché Gris and is held in rather low esteem; in California its flavor is more vivid and satisfying; the wine is often compared to Sylvaner (below).

Grignolino A red wine grape whose home is Piedmont, Italy; it seems to do better in California than in its native habitat, but is used mostly for blending with other red wines.

Isabella A native blue-skinned grape of the Labrusca type, used in eastern wineries for both still and sparkling wines.

Johannisberg Riesling A famed white wine grape that is called simply *Riesling* in Germany has somehow in California acquired the word "Johannisberg" after the famous castle and winery overlooking the Rhine; also known as the White Riesling—not to be confused with Emerald or Grey Riesling, both wines of tamer flavor. The intense cultivation of this grape in California and new, progressive methods of vinification have resulted in California Rieslings that truly rival their German ancestors. Aroma is flowery, and flavor extremely fruity with a subtle balance of sweetness and tartness; California Rieslings range from semidry to sweet or heavily sweet.

Merlot A red wine grape famed in Bordeaux as the minor partner in many illustrious château wines; it's softer, more mellow, and fruitier than the major partner, Cabernet Sauvignon. In California it plays the same role. Recently some varietal Merlots have appeared—that is, red wines labeled Merlot in which Merlot is the principal grape. The new varietal Merlots are wines of fine body and excellent bouquet.

Muscat A type of sweet grape of which there are both black and white varieties; in France a white one called the Muscat de Frontignan is used for a delicious dessert wine named after the town of Frontignan on the Mediterranean coast; the same variety in California is employed for several delicate sweet wines of which Louis Martini's Moscato Amabile and Christian Brothers Château La Salle are examples; not to be confused with the cheap Muscatel wine of the winos made from the Muscat of Alexandria.

Napa Gamay The same red wine grape used in France for Beaujolais is grown in California under this name, and produces fresh young wines for which there seems to be an ever larger audience.

Niagara A white New York State native Labrusca grape used for a semidry white wine; the best-known label is Widmer's Lake Niagara.

Petite Sirah A California variation of a grape thought to have been brought from the Middle East to the Rhône Valley, where it's used in making robust wines such as Hermitage and Châteauneuf-du-Pape. California Petite Sirah is a vigorous red wine; some versions may be drunk young; others should be aged at least five years for optimum flavor. Some oenologists think that what we call the California Petite Sirah is actually another Rhône grape called the Duriff, although this name never appears as a varietal labeling.

Pinot Blanc A white grape not as well known as the Pinot Noir (below); a number of California wines erroneously called Pinot Blanc are made from the Chenin Blanc grape. When used as a varietal, which is not often, it can become a fine white wine of the Burgundy type, similar to Pinot Chardonnay.

Pinot Chardonnay A white wine grape from which the great French white Burgundies are made; shy-bearing vines yield a comparatively small harvest, and the wines are therefore expensive. At their best, California Pinot Chardonnays are dry, ranging in color from light yellow to light or medium gold, with rich, pronounced body and aroma; the best are aged in oak just long enough to bring out the wine's marvelous complexity.

Pinot Noir A red grape used for the famed French red Burgundies, renowned for their velvety, full flavors. Most California Pinot Noirs have not reached the eminence of the California Pinot Chardonnays in challenging the top French red Burgundy estate wines, but they are improving; recently in Monterey County, Pinot Noirs have been made with the full, mouth-filling flavors winemen call "meaty." This red grape, incidentally, is the main one used for making French champagne.

Pinot St. George A California grape of the Pinot family, sometimes called Red Pinot; a successful specialty of the Christian Brothers winery.

Ruby Cabernet A hybrid of the Cabernet Sauvignon and the Carignane, a grape with high yield per acre (see both above); the cross maintains the tart, intense flavor of the Cabernet Sauvignon, a comparatively shy-bearing grape.

Sauvignon Blanc A white grape that sometimes appears on label as just Sauvignon; used in France for Graves and as a partner with Semillon in making French Sauternes and other sweet wines of Bordeaux; also used in the Loire for making the delightfully dry Pouilly-

Fumé. In California this grape is the principal one for the sweet wine labeled Sauvignon Blanc or the dry one labeled Blanc Fumé, an increasingly popular wine.

Semillon A white wine grape used in combination with Sauvignon Blanc (above) for French Sauternes; in California it's employed for a medium-bodied white wine in both sweet and dry versions.

Seyval A white French-American hybrid grape that results in a fruity, very dry wine; it appears on labels sometimes as Seyval Blanc; grown in the eastern United States.

Sylvaner The common white grape of the Alsace and Germany, sometimes called the Franken Riesling, famed for its soft, fruity flavor; in California it's often sold as a Riesling wine or used in blending with the Johannisberg Riesling grape; somewhat less complex and less assertive than Johannisberg Riesling.

Zinfandel A red wine grape whose European ancestry is acknowledged but can't be traced; the grape is not now grown in Europe but flourishes in California. As a wine, its flavor overtones are frequently described as berrylike or brambly, and it's both an extremely attractive young fruity wine and one with the capacity for aging into a rich complex wine. One of the oldest California wines, some vineyards that specialize in it—like Foppiano in the Russian River Valley of California—make rich Zinfandels from grapes of which one-third were planted nearly a hundred years ago.

CALIFORNIA WINES

Many young wine hobbyists find it hard to believe that there was a time when the chief customers for California wines were the denizens of skid row or park flops anywhere, when the best thing you could say about California Burgundies was that they'd do for some cooking purposes but Bacchus forgive you if you ever poured them into a Baccarat glass. (As for the first New York State wines, they had all the complexity of a jar of Aunt Maude's grape jelly.)

We're talking about the middle 1930s when Repeal ended thirteen years of Prohibition, and when the drinking savants of the day seriously discussed the subtleties of various bathtub gins and ether beers. It was a period when old established vineyards had been grubbed out or abandoned, when skilled American winemakers were forced to find other livelihoods, and when a whole nation forgot the meaning of such foreign words as *Zinfandel* or *Pinot Noir.*

Oddly—and fortunately—the winemakers of a few eminent old California wineries whose haciendas were flourishing in the last century never lost their skill. Beaulieu Vineyards in the Napa Valley of California is a prime example. All during Prohibition, Georges de Latour, the eminent former French citizen who owned Beaulieu, continued to grow grapes and to supply—quite legally—altar wines for the Catholic church. Soon after Repeal, Beaulieu wines and their BV insignia were among the first American wines to be spotted for their rare excellence. Today the Beaulieu Private Reserve Cabernet is one of the most distinguished red wines in the world.

To aid the renascent wine industry, the University of California at Davis, in its Department of Viticulture, began training a new generation of winegrowers and winemakers, and its faculty and research program in a few decades has hoisted American wines to a point where they are more than a match for European wines whose traditions go back to Roman times. You can now visit small wineries in Napa and Sonoma counties—whose winemakers are young people in their twenties or thirties, graduates of the University of California—and taste wines that would warm the blood and rouse the envy of some of France's oldest *vignerons.*

During the late Fifties and the Sixties, California wine producers, now masters in their own vineyards, had the brass to begin conducting large-scale blind wine tastings in which California varietal wines were compared to French wines made from the same type of grapes. To the astonishment of the testers, the testees often showed a preference f r the California wines. French wine importers in this country noted that some of the audiences were college students, and what could you expect of the closed taste buds of youngsters, who'd naturally go for wines with simple flavors rather than the subtly complex Gallic wines? When similar results later occurred with American wine-and-food writers, one American importer of French wines said the whole ritual had no validity because lackluster French wines were being poured, while only the best of the Californias were put on show. The debate seethed back and forth for years, and is still actively fermenting.

Looking for literal equals in European and U.S. wines is like trying to find identical rivers. Each breathes its own prevailing atmosphere, is hugged and colored by its own soil, and flows along its own course.

Juice crushed from grapes on one hill can be quite different from the product of the very same variety grown on another hill of the same vineyard. There are not only different climates on different continents but countless microclimates that affect the wine's eventual flavor. When a specific grape, such as the Pinot Chardonnay, is transplanted from the Côte d'Or in Burgundy to the Sonoma Valley in California, it's destined to yield a subtly different cup of cheer.

But you can't stop people from viewing wines alongside each other any more than you can stop them from talking about wine. Americans have their games in the Rose Bowl, Sugar Bowl, and Cotton Bowl, and, at very irregular times, a Wine Bowl with French and American competitors. Undoubtedly the biggest blow to Gallic supremacy occurred in 1976 when the owner of a prominent Parisian wine shop invited nine eminent French judges of the grape—including Raymond Olivier, owner of Le Grand Vefour restaurant, and noted French oenologists associated with Grand Cru wines—to compare French white Burgundies against California Pinot Chardonnays (the same variety of grape), and French red Bordeaux wines versus California Cabernet Sauvignons (again the same grape). There were twenty wines in the lineup. This time the contest was conducted on French soil, with every wine carefully chosen to put its best foot forward in its class. In accordance with the high principles of the French *code d'honneur*, the wine was poured from bottles on which no label was visible.

When all the glass twirling, eyeing, nosing, inhaling, mouth rolling, swishing, and swallowing ended, the inconceivable happened: California wines took first place in both the red and the white categories. Stag's Leap Napa Valley '72 was a clear winner against the French Mouton-Rothschild '70 for the reds. Among the whites, the California Château Montelena '73 bested the French Meursault-Charmes '73. In the runners-up, too, the Californias were bottleneck to bottleneck with their French adversaries.

Admittedly, ranking wines in contests of this type is one of those rites which some mature wine lovers consider ridiculous. It requires an objective grade for a subjective experience, and often, like a beauty contest, tells you more about the judges than the winners. But the Paris scores and others in this country make it abundantly clear that, in the four decades since Repeal, American wines have become more than a match for the finest in Europe.

If one were to generalize about American and European wine qualities—and this now is the *author's* ostensibly subjective viewpoint, throwing in his own two cents—one might say that generally French wines have more bite (not alcohol), more of the tang that comes from the acid of the grape, and more of the concentrated grapiness that stays in your mouth after you've swallowed the wine. But this is no sooner said than one begins thinking of an endless parade of exceptions, permitting any dissenter to prove what he/she set out to prove.

On somewhat safer grounds, one can state that a disproportionate amount of California table wines (compared with those of France and Italy) are on the slightly sweet side. Vineyard tourists in the California tasting rooms often talk "dry" as they sit around sipping wines, and then buy sweet or semisweet wines to take home. In the Fifties and Sixties, European winemakers shipping wines to this country were well aware of our national sweet tooth. No matter that we loudly insisted on dry beer, dry whiskey, and dry gin; when it came to wines, they could always bait us with sweetness. One Italian vineyard owner, who was then making an excellent rosé, each year turned out a dry one for his compatriots and the same rosé slightly sweetened for export to America. California winemakers, always on their oenopoetic toes, know that in the coming years they'll probably make less sweet and semisweet wines as more and more Americans awaken to the adulthood of dry table wines.

Robert Frost once wrote about the Californian who, boasting of his state's climate, said it was "so blessed . . . none had ever died there a natural death." Wine-wise students of Sunny Cal can readily understand the boast, for it's indeed a state blessed with comfortably equable weather, a long growing season with relatively small danger of damaging storms, and with microclimates that allow every great grape in the world to flourish. By contrast, weather conditions in Europe drastically limit the number and kinds of wines from a given area. If you travel through the Rhineland, you'll find wines like Riesling and Sylvaner but not much else that you'll remember. In southern Burgundy you'll find Beaujolais and little else of distinction. But in California a single winemaker, drawing on grapes from his own or neighboring valleys, will make wines representing all the major areas of Europe and, in some instances, produce wines like those of Spain, Portugal, and the island of Madeira.

Because of the climate, some prominent California winemen used to boast (to non-Californians usually) that there were no vintage years in their state—every year was a great vintage year, and that was why their bottles never carried a vintage date. To a certain extent the boast was true. But while California doesn't suffer the wildly capricious weather changes of European vineyards, the fact remains that California vineyard harvests have their ceaseless ups and downs nonetheless. The total yield of the vineyard, the ripeness of the grapes, their color, sugar, and acid are in many senses a fluid phenomenon, subject to the sport of sun, wind, fog, frost, mildew, and other factors well known in the Golden State.

California wineries are of three types. The first, and in recent years the most exciting to American oenophiles, are those known as boutique wineries. The word "boutique" is more than a little ridiculous when you've visited one of these small wineries, seen men struggling with casks of wine piled to the ceiling, and recognized the smell of grapes that permeates the rafters, the floor, and even the jeans the workmen wear as they toil all year long. They're called boutiques not just because they're small in output but because at exhibitions and tastings they carry off so many of the gold medals.

As an example of this type of winery, consider Château St. Jean in California's Sonoma Valley, distinguished for late-picked Riesling wines of the German *beerenauslese* or *trockenbeerenauslese* types. The German words don't appear on their labels because this isn't allowed, but these are the very rare wines from overripe grapes on which, until recent years, Germany had a monopoly. Château St. Jean is so comparatively young that the grapes planted on its own land are not yet yielding harvests. They buy their grapes from small vineyards just as they do in Burgundy. But getting the very select grapes that Château St. Jean uses isn't quite like going to neighboring farmers to buy a crop of oats, peas, beans, or barley. For the particular Rieslings they require, it's necessary to have grapes picked way after the normal harvest. The grapes must achieve the kind of ripeness resulting from the beneficent *Botrytis* mold. The grower must gamble on the weather being sunny; if the weather suddenly becomes too wet or too cold, the entire crop may be destroyed in a matter of hours.

Château St. Jean contracts with the grape growers to share the risk. The growers are paid double for grapes kept an additional month or month and a half, since half the grapes' moisture will be lost from dehydration. They are also paid double the normal 20-percent bonus for high sugar content. In the event of a total crop loss, a grower is paid half of what he'd have received if he'd simply harvested his grapes for the ordinary Riesling. It's this kind of intelligent gambling that has paid off beautifully.

After the grapes are pressed, the difficult and sensitive job of vinification continues until the wine is eventually bottled. For this, Château St. Jean employs a noted winemaker, Richard Arrowwood.

You're not likely at this time to find Château St. Jean wines on mass-market shelves; for a boutique wine of this type, you'll have to find a boutique wine shop. With almost space-age speed, Château St. Jean has reached the eminence of some of the finest and oldest wineries of the Rheingau. In a New York blind tasting session of California versus German Rieslings, judges chose the St. Jean wines in every category tasted.

The second type of winery is one that doesn't confine itself to a few boutique specialties, nor attempt to match the output of the king-size winemakers shipping wines in the millions of cases. Mirassou Vineyards of San Jose, California, are an outstanding model of this intermediate species. The Mirassou family is one of those California dynasties that were making wine over a century ago. After Repeal they concentrated on bulk wine for other producers. Unlike some of the patriarchal families of France who bequeath a fortune, an eminent château, and a prestigious label to their offspring, the Mirassous inherited a certain know-how and the opportunity to pioneer.

Before the Mirassous started to bottle wine in the Sixties, most of the premium California wine had been coming from areas like Napa and Sonoma, north of San Francisco. Mirassous owned 300 acres in the Santa Clara area, and they were among a handful of winemakers who opened a new vista south of San Francisco in the Salinas Valley in Monterey County, until then better known for salad greens than Cabernet Sauvignon. Viticultural specialists had predicted years before that the Salinas Valley would be a Garden of Eden for grapes even though the area was known to have the benefit of little rainfall. And indeed, when the juice that "first from out the purple grape" flowed, the Mirassous discovered that the grapes grown here were grapier—that is, the varietal characteristics were more intense—than in other areas.

The Mirassous initiated an innovative sprinkling system. And instead of fermenting their Cabernet Sauvignon grapes at high temperatures (the old-fashioned way of getting good color and tannin from their skins), they experimented in reducing temperatures and fermenting for a longer time. While their first wines for several years were varied in quality, their efforts eventually hit the jackpot. All their wines are vintage-dated. Certainly their Petite Rosé is one of the best specimens anywhere. One would be tempted to pin medals all over them for their Harvest Selections Zinfandel, Pinot Noir, and Gewürztraminer.

Finally, there's the American type of mammoth winery, unknown in Europe, producing an assortment of approximately fifty different products of the grape, including varietal and generic wines, dessert wines, vermouth, and brandy. When you look over the lists of such wineries as Paul Masson, E. & J. Gallo, Almaden, and Christian Brothers, you realize that each represents not a large or small grape patch but an elaborate industry. It might be tempting to call these huge operations jacks-of-all-trades, masters of none, but it would be absolutely false. They make their popular jug wines, but they also make some superb varietal wines.

As an example, consider Christian Brothers sweet Château La Salle, a dessert wine made from the Muscat de Frontignan grape. It does not have the heavy richness of a French Sauterne or a late-picked German Riesling, but its flavor is distinguished by an intensity and liveliness that are delightful. Their Napa Valley Pinot St. George is a match for some of the best specimens of Châteauneuf-du-Pape.

No Christian Brothers wines are marked with a vintage date at the present time, since their wine making is all built around what the French call the art of the *cuvée*, or blending. Christian Brothers winemakers not only blend different grapes and the grapes of different vineyards but vintages as well to achieve a steady range of quality that many European winemakers of moderately priced table wines might well emulate. The Christian Brothers, incidentally, are a religious order, and their specialists include graduates in oenology of the University of California at Davis. It's possible that one day they may bottle vintage-dated wines or the so-called boutique wines of strong individuality, but for the huge number of wine drinkers who are more interested in wines that are dependably uniform rather than in those rare wines that arrive with an eleven-gun salute, the Christian Brothers Estate Bottled Wines or Brother Timothy's Special Selections are very pleasurable drinking.

NEW YORK STATE WINES

Thomas Jefferson, after serving two bottles of wine sent to him as a gift, wrote to the donor saying that his guests could not tell the difference between them and "the far famed Burgundy named Chambertin." Today, the only conclusion you can draw from Jefferson's comment is that his guests must have been sloshed to the ears, for American wines made from native American grapes are as different from European wines as chocolate is from vanilla.

There's always been this immense chasm between the two wines—the European representing the *Vitis vinifera* (just as California wines do) and the native American representing the grapes Leif Ericson found here, which prompted him to call the country in which he first beat the bush Vineland the Good. These native grapes are the *Vitis labrusca.*

While California, with its transplanted European grapes, produces about four-fifths of U.S. wines (a small amount of vinifera is also made in other states, including recently some lovely wines from the Northwest), the balance of it is largely New York State wines, which are bred from three types of grapes.

The first are the aforementioned Labruscas or crosses of Labrusca, grapes that were flourishing before white men shuffled onto the stage of the New World. The flavor of these grapes has traditionally been described as "foxy"—though just what "foxy" means hasn't been, and perhaps can't be, adequately described. Foxes in the vineyard, of course, are ancient legends. And a foxy wine, at one time, always meant a coarse wine. To "fox" someone is to stupefy him with drink. Today a foxy wine is more or less taken to mean one with a flavor unmistakably like the flavor of grape jelly or grape juice—an intense, perfumy taste which has been analyzed as produced by methyl anthranilate, an ingredient used in making grape soda. Whether you like foxy wines depends entirely on your wine-drinking background. There are millions of easterners who love these wines and proudly serve them not only for mealtime entertainment but for anything from christenings to wedding breakfasts to funeral suppers. Many Europeans or Americans who regularly drink European or California wines find them of petty breed, quickly tiresome and eventually intolerable.

The second type of eastern U.S. grapes are the comparatively new hybrid French-American grapes, such as the red Baco Noir or the white Seyval Blanc. To wine drinkers able to keep their taste buds open to new things, wines made from these grapes can indeed be fascinating drinking. Some of the aged wines of this type seem to lose their foxy Labrusca flavor after a few years of wood and bottle aging, and emerge as well-rounded, complex wines.

The third type are European grapes transplanted to New York State. The wines from these grapes, if you didn't see the label, might come from France, Germany, or California. They were pioneered in recent years by Dr. Konstantin Frank, a Russian émigré familiar with wine making in very cold climates. Frank, after much skeptical resistance from local winemakers, proved that European grapes, especially the Riesling, could not only survive the harsh northeastern winters but flourish, substantiating his theory that it wasn't the cold weather but plant diseases (now under control) that were the problem. His first wines, made at the Gold Seal Vineyard, turned out to be magnificent testimony to one man's unwearying patience. Today Dr. Frank's grapes are grown in his own Vinifera Wine Cellars and include such European classics as Riesling, Gewürztraminer, Chardonnay, and Pinot Noir.

The best guides to New York State wines are the wineries, old and new; there aren't so many of them that the buyer becomes lost in a snowstorm of names, and the *vins du pays* of the Empire State are remarkably consistent from one year to the next. Here's a list of them:

Benmarl   A small vineyard in the Hudson River region which describes itself as a kind of private experiment station producing limited amounts of dry table wines from hybrid grapes.

Bully Hill Vineyards   Founded by members of the Taylor wine family, no longer associated with the Taylor Wine Co. (below), Bully Hill produces its own estate-bottled, vintage-dated wines, including Baco Noir, Chelois Noir, Seyval Blanc, and other hybrid wines, as well as brut champagne.

Gold Seal Winery   Founded in 1865, the Gold Seal stone winery is the home of the distinguished Gold Seal champagne and Charles Fournier wines. Charles Fournier is the French-trained wineman who introduced French-American hybrids to New York State and in the 1940s developed a brut champagne that has become an American classic. Among other Gold Seal wines of note are the Catawba Pink (a rosé), Pinot Chardonnay, and Riesling.

Great Western Winery   The oldest winery in the Finger Lakes region is best known for a remarkably superior champagne; although made with Labrusca grapes, its dry, intense, mouth-filling flavor puts it at the very top of the world's great bubblies. Their first winemaker, Joseph Masson, was a French champagne maker, and the tradition of the *méthode champenoise*, with its slow fermentation, is combined with modern, streamlined finishing and bottling. Besides champagne, Great Western produces a number of Labrusca as well as hybrid wines, and, surprisingly, an excellent New York State sherry made in the classical Spanish solera tradition.

Taylor Wine Company   This biggest of the New York State wineries, producing 4½ million cases a year, recently started an impressive California winery in Monterey County, California, making Vinifera wines. They now include in their New York State list no less than twenty-eight wines, champagnes, and vermouths made from both Labrusca and hybrid grapes. Most of their labels are generic rather than varietal wines, with such names as Lake Country White or Lake Country Red, and all are plainly identified as New York State wines. For those who are happy with Labruscas, Taylor wines are dependably consistent and obviously extremely satisfying not only to hordes of easterners but to customers in all the fifty states and over eighty countries.

Widmer's Wine Cellars   When one thinks of the way so many businesses come and go, it's always astonishing to learn of the New York State wineries that were founded in the last century and, in one way or another, survived the thirteen years of Prohibition. Widmer's winemakers, of Swiss extraction and training, were making wines in 1888. They feature both generic and varietal wines among their Naples Valley wines—wines which, of course, bear no resemblance to the *vinos* of Naples, Italy. Widmer's is noted for its Rieslings, which while made with native American grapes, have an uncanny resemblance to the true German Rieslings. It's best known perhaps for its semidry Lake Niagara, a varietal white. At Naples, New York, Widmer's "cellar on the roof" is a tourists' landmark. Here casks exposed to the icy blasts of winter and summer's heat contain sherries made by the classical solera system in which the wines of older casks are systematically blended with younger ones during the aging process. Widmer's believes that exposure to the extremes of the seasons is beneficial to wines of the sherry type, and while their sherries have an unmistakable New York State flavor, they *are* remarkably good for their genre.

Champagne

If ever a single symbol immediately and unmistakably meant luxurious living, it's the scintillant wine known variously as nosetickler, gigglewater, fizz, bubbly, and sometimes even as champagne. One would not drink gin out of a lady's slipper or christen a ship with a bottle of Scotch; occasions that call for gaiety and celebration require a special drink, a brilliant drink, a bravura drink. But, fortunately, champagne is no longer exclusively tied to Lucullan feasts and to hidebound formal occasions. Lord Chesterfield's favorite toast is more pertinent than ever: "Give me champagne and fill it to the brim,/I'll toast in bumpers every lovely limb!" Today the pop of the cork is heard just as frequently at an *intime* table for two as in a big banquet hall. Its unparalleled flavor, tingle and chatoyance go equally well with beluga caviar or a platter of cheese, with breast of guinea hen or glazed Virginia ham.

Although great age doesn't mean great gigglewater (after about ten years the bubbly loses its zest), great price usually does. With few exceptions, you pay for what you get in champagne, and the more it costs, the better it usually is. There are a few important clues to excellence the knowing champagne taster will seek. One of the first is the champagne's vinosity. It's simply the essential and natural flavor of the grape; call it "grapiness" if you will, keeping in mind that it's not the flavor of the raw grape but the finished flavor of the fermented juice. Time and again a taster sampling a poor champagne will say that it tastes like water, meaning it lacks the deep, straight, unmistakable flavor of the fruit—the flavor that fills your mouth and stays there after your glass is empty. It's just like a man eating a tender steak complaining that it's less "beefy" than it should be. Dryness is often a valuable clue, too, since sugar is often, but not always, used to mask poor champagne. Aroma is important, and as in tasting wine, the best way to train both nose and palate is to taste three or four champagnes slowly, one after another. Such qualities as finesse and mellowness are learned only through long and happy practice. The effervescence of a fine champagne is shown in small steady bubbles, sometimes so small they're barely visible.

If you're wondering when champagne should be served, stop wondering. It can be served any time. It has been called a dessert wine, and indeed it is wizard at meal's end, but it's also the only potation that can be tippled before dinner as a cocktail and during dinner as an accompaniment to every course as well. It flatters all food and is indispensable with caviar. Some say it is grand stuff on certain mornings, too, as a specific against the horrors.

How to serve? There's no mystery. Prior to pouring, it should, of course, be thoroughly chilled—but not frozen to death. The best serving temperature is between 40° and 50°F.; to achieve it, place the bottle in the refrigerator for an hour or two—as far from the freezing section as possible—or for about a half-hour in the ice of a champagne bucket. Don't jostle the bottle unnecessarily before opening it or the contents will fizzle out as soon as the cork is pulled. Old hands at removing champagne corks follow this ritual: Twist off the wire muzzle. Hold the cork in your left hand, and grasp the bottom of the bottle with your right. Keep the bottle inclined slightly, but don't aim it at your guests. Be sure your grip on the cork is firm; you want it to stay in your hand, not take off like an unguided missile. Turn the bottle with your right hand, holding the cork until it pops. Make sure the cork smells of wine and has no off-odor; then wipe the rim of the bottle with a napkin.

The best glass for savoring both flavor and bouquet is the 8-ounce tulip-shaped glass; fill it no more than one-third to one-half full. Opinions appear to coincide in regard to the saucer-shaped champagne glass with the solid stem: Although it is almost universally used for champagne cocktails and other mixed champagne drinks, it dissipates the bubbles too quickly. The best glass for showing off the sparkle is the hollow-stemmed champagne glass, although many experts claim that it, too, tends to debubble the bubbly. Ladies in the upper stratum of Continental society have discovered a trick for "storing" champagne bubbles. They scratch the inside bottom of the glass with a diamond ring, and while the tiny scratches can't be seen, they provide a kind of cache for the bubbles, and the drink's sparkle lasts longer—or at least it seems that way to ladies with sparkles on their fingers. While we're on the subject of effervescence, it's worth noting that some of the cheaper champagnes which show a great surge of froth actually have less bite than greater champagnes whose fine bubbles are literally imprisoned in the wry smile of the liquid.

Whence those heady bubbles in the bubbly? They come about when yeast and sugar are added to the wine in the bottle, producing a second fermentation and a second colony of bubbles now trapped in the bottle. During the bottle fermentation a sediment forms. To eliminate it, the bottles, neckdown, are turned by hand day after day for months until the sediment eventually slides down to the cork. At this juncture the wine is disgorged—that is, each bottle is opened, causing the pressure in the bottle to eject the sediment. The wine is now clear champagne. Before the bottles are recorked, all champagnes—except the one called *naturel* (see below)—are given a dose of sugar mixed with wine or wine and brandy, called *dosage*. The amount of sugar determines how sweet the champagne will be. The long procession of steps is an extremely expensive manual job. It's called the *méthode champenoise* and is the process followed for all the best French and American champagnes.

A cheaper method of making champagne—some of which is surprisingly good—is the bulk process, wherein wines are fermented a second time in tanks rather than bottles, and drawn off into bottles under pressure. In this country, champagne made in this manner is labeled "bulk process" or *Charmat*.

The whole *sec/brut*/extra-dry scene is a puzzler, probably because although *sec* is the French word for "dry," champagne labeled *sec* is actually semisweet. Compounding the confusion, extra dry is not the driest. Here's the way it goes: Champagne with the word *naturel* on the label is the driest of all champagnes and may taste almost sour to a virgin palate; it is champagne made without the *dosage* (see above). *Brut* is what most people drink as very dry since it contains the minimum amount of *dosage*. Extra dry is next in line with a little more sweetness. *Sec* is definitely sweet, but not cloying. You may also run across *doux*, which is very sweet.

Few American champagnes bear a vintage year, but those that do are usually estimable bottlings. When French champagne carries a vintage year, it simply means that in that particular year grapes were produced that gave the champagne a unique flavor. The salient fact to remember is that most old French firms use the same fine wines for their nonvintage as for their vintage champagnes. They keep their quality uniformly high by an elaborate and artful system of blending wines from different vineyards and different years.

Frenchmen naturally take umbrage when non-French winemakers label their product "champagne," and they sometimes take legal action, with varying results. *Champagne*, after all, *is* a French word, and it means a flat body of land like the wide stretch of plain country east of Paris whence all French champagne comes. In this country the word "champagne" can be used legally provided the section in which it was produced is named, such as New York State champagne or California champagne. Most other countries keep clear of the word, but just the same produce a large variety of bubbly wines. Since the import duty on all sparkling wines is a large part of the price squeeze, few foreign bottlings are imported to the United States; but among those that are, here are some corking examples of the best:

Sparkling red Burgundy   Made in France from a quality of grapes not normally used in the still red Burgundies; on the soft, sweet side.

Sparkling Saumur   A sparkling white wine from the Loire with rather good body.

Sparkling Vouvray   Perhaps the best of the French nonchampagnes; at bottling time, extra sugar is added, which means extra bubbles as the sugar changes to alcohol.

Sparkling rosé   Imported from France; also produced in the United States; it's often called "pink" champagne.

Crackling rosé   A well-known import from Portugal having the quality which the French call *pétillant*—that is, with a very subdued sparkle.

Sekt   German sparkling white wine; like the German still wines, it conveys the same soft but vivid flavors of the grape.

Asti spumante   Most of it is on the sweet side, but alluring when served cold with Gorgonzola cheese and a bowl of ripe fruit.

Wine Cellars

Collecting wines is the kind of indoor hobby you can indulge in your whole life long, and it's really the best possible means of sipping your way to expertise, remembering of course that expertise isn't an end in itself but a step to pleasure. Some hobbies are lonely, but keeping a wine cellar is the most convivial of avocations. It flatters both the collector and guests of all persuasions, since wine, like music, speaks a tongue all men understand. A cellar can be a case of assorted wines resting on its side or a subterranean vault ennobled with cobwebs. Whatever your tastes and facilities, you'll find something to your liking among the following three suggested cellars—containing from 18 to 112 bottles each. Remember, they are suggestions, not dicta. We've also included two all-American cellars for those who may want to excel in the fine wines now flowing from American vineyards. Because of the wide variation in prices, costs of individual bottles are not indicated. Totals, however, are approximated for each cellar.

Use will determine the rate and kind of your replacements. For general guidance: A bottle of wine (25.4 ounces) serves three to four; a half-bottle is enough for two. If you average one dinner party a week, two large parties a month, and you drink wine with meals, your annual needs should be well covered by ten cases.

A note about storage: It's unlikely that you live in a manor house with its own wine vaults to provide ideal conditions for the maturation and keeping of wine, but you should do the best you can to approximate these conditions. Avoid sunlight, strive for evenness of temperature (perhaps of greater importance, even, than coolness—which is highly desirable), and pick a closet or cupboard where the wine can rest quietly—away from slamming doors and stored gear to which there must be daily access. Place white wines (which are most delicate) in the coolest spot (probably closest to the floor), Burgundies above the whites, red Bordeaux on top. Never store bottles standing; lay them on their sides so that the entire cork stays wet, which will prevent its crumbling and keep the seal airtight.

The Modest Cellar (18 bottles, under $80)

2 Champagne (California)
3 Red (Burgundy or Bordeaux)
3 White (Alsatian, Rhine, or Moselle)
2 Rosé (French, Italian, Portuguese, or U.S.)
4 California red
3 New York white
1 Sherry (Spanish)

The Superior Cellar (36 bottles, under $200)

3 Champagne (French or California)
3 Red Bordeaux
3 Red Burgundy
3 Red Italian
3 White Bordeaux (Graves or Sauternes)

3 White Burgundy (Chablis or Pouilly-Fuissé)
3 White (Alsatian, Rhine, or Moselle)
3 Rosé (French, Italian, Portuguese, or U.S.)
3 California red
3 California white
3 New York white
1 Sherry (Spanish, dry)
1 Sherry (Spanish, medium or sweet)
1 Port

The Munificent Cellar (112 bottles, under $800)

6 Champagne (French)
6 Champagne (American)
4 Sparkling red Burgundy
4 Sparkling white (German or Italian)
6 Red Bordeaux (regional)
6 Red Bordeaux (château-bottled)
6 Red Burgundy (Beaujolais)
6 Red Burgundy (estate-bottled)
4 Red Italian
4 White Bordeaux (Graves)
4 White Bordeaux (Sauternes)
4 White Burgundy (Chablis or Pouilly-Fuissé)
4 White Burgundy (estate-bottled)
4 White Alsatian (Riesling or Gewürztraminer)
4 White Moselle
4 White Rhine
4 White Italian
6 California red
6 California white
6 California rosé
6 New York white
2 Sherry (Spanish, dry)
2 Sherry (Spanish, medium or sweet)
2 Port
2 Madeira

The Modest American Cellar (24 bottles, under $125)

3 Cabernet Sauvignon
2 Pinot Noir
1 Gamay Beaujolais
2 Rosé
2 Zinfandel
1 Barbera
2 Delaware
2 Diamond
1 Sauvignon Blanc
2 Johannisberg Riesling
2 Dry Emerald Riesling
1 Champagne *blanc de blancs*
3 Champagne *brut*

The Munificent American Cellar (97 bottles, under $600)

8 Cabernet Sauvignon
6 Pinot Noir
3 Gamay Beaujolais
4 Rosé

8 Zinfandel
5 Barbera
8 Delaware
8 Diamond
5 Sauvignon Blanc
8 Johannisberg Riesling
8 Dry Emerald Riesling

5 Champagne *blanc de blancs*
8 Champagne *brut*
2 Sherry
5 Pinot Chardonnay
3 Chenin Blanc
3 Dry Semillon

The Language of Wine: A Glossary

The *vignerons* who work in the noted wine estates of Europe and America are artists with a magnificent background of experience, and they have a professional jargon which appears in long wine tomes and short essays, is heard in wine shops and in wine cellars as well as in the ordinary conversation of people who believe that wine is one of the purest forms of liquid pleasure. While their phraseology is more meaningful than that of the dilettante, it's often equally incomprehensible to the uninitiated; hence the following glossary of the most frequently used terms in the wineman's vocabulary, which should help enhance not only your expertise but also your appreciation of the fermented grape.

Acidity   The pleasant bite and natural tartness of fruit, not to be confused with sourness; without it, wines would be insipid.

Amabile   An Italian term used to describe a wine that is very pleasing, often sweet.

Aroma   The smell of a wine when it's young that reveals its grape but is not a duplicate of the fresh grape flavor; as wine ages, it develops its bouquet (see below).

Astringency   A quality produced by tannin, particularly in red wines; as wines mature, tannin tends to mellow out. In all dry reds, a reasonable amount of tannin and, therefore, astringency is on the plus side.

Balance   To understand balance in wine, one should think of a common fruit such as an orange. At its best, it's both sweet and tart in such proportions that both qualities complement each other; the pungent aroma that rises when you peel it is both sharp and pleasant; and its flesh is firmly pliant, neither pulpy as an orange will sometimes be nor so soft that it's spoiling. So, too, with wine; it may be tart or very sweet, but its body, bouquet, smoothness, and all other salient qualities must combine and counterbalance so that the total effect is like a scale in balance—tip one quality too much one way or the other and the wine will be out of balance.

Big   A significant amount of body (see below), often with high alcohol content and deep color.

Body   Intensity rather than quality of flavor; good body is the opposite of wateriness.

Bouquet   As wine ages, its original aroma changes with maturity; the finished fragrance of wine in the glass is its bouquet.

Breed   A wine whose original type was great and whose present quality reflects the superior type of which it is the progeny.

Brilliant   Said of wines whose colors shine brightly as opposed to cloudy, murky, or dull-looking wines.

Character   A wine with character need not be great, but it must be one whose qualities are so definite and vivid as to be unmistakable; a rosé with its own color and fresh fruity flavor has rosé character, even though you wouldn't talk about it in the same breath with one of the great Bordeaux.

Chewy   Used to describe red wines of great body with mouth-filling flavor and pronounced aftertaste.

Clean   Leaving an uncluttered and distinct flavor in the mouth.

Coarse   A lot of flavor but not necessarily good flavor; a wine with no finesse—one to accompany a salami-and-onion sandwich.

Complex   Having a number of perceivable flavors; when you add lemon juice to a Coke drink, you make it more *complex* in the taster's jargon. When fruity young wines with the relatively simple flavor of the grapes become older, their flavors acquire overtones and are then said to be more complex.

Corky or corked   When you draw a cork from a bottle of wine, the cork should smell of wine. Very rarely the cork will have spoiled, giving off an almost rotten aroma and spoiling the wine. Again, it's an extremely rare defect.

Delicate   Subtle, smooth, not very assertive but not devoid of flavor; true of many German wines.

Doux   The French term for "sweet," but not used with most naturally sweet wines such as Sauternes. It is sometimes applied to champagnes that have been given a heavy *dosage* of sweet syrup.

Dry   The opposite of sweet. The greatest champagnes are dry; most notable table wines are on the dry side.

Earthy   A solid flavor, reminiscent of freshly turned earth, in a complimentary sense.

Finesse   Just as a delicious consommé is consummate with modest but not overbearing flavor accents, a wine with finesse has great distinction and subtlety.

Finish   Aftertaste or lingering sensations in the mouth after the wine has been swallowed.

Flabby   Used to describe wines with no definite flavor accents.

Flat   Describes sparkling wines that have lost their effervescence; also still wines with low acidity or dull flavor.

Flinty   Hard but not harsh.

Flowery   Evocative of fragrant flower blossoms, but not perfumy in the artificial sense. A flowery wine is easy and delicate on the nostrils.

Foxy   A term that describes the flavor of wines made from indigenous American grapes that Leif Ericson found in Vineland the Good. The fact that the finished wines taste so much like the original grapes makes them anathema to European wine drinkers. California wines from European root stocks do not have this foxy flavor. That the flavor is loved by millions of Americans in the eastern half of the country only goes to prove the adage that wine is good if it tastes good.

Fresh   There are wines famed for the patina of great age; others— like the Beaujolais wines, the rosés, and many of the whites—are treasured for their fresh young flavor. Thus, millions of gallons of native Italian wines are eagerly gulped down within months of their pressing; like fresh asparagus or warm bread, they're enjoyed as fresh food in the form of drink.

Green　A term used to describe young wines somewhat rough in flavor and often with strong acidity.

Growth　The word "growth" in connection with French wines is the English word for *cru*. It refers to a classification by quality—usually a high quality—and not a state in growing. To Americans it can be a misleading word, but it's been used so long by Frenchmen and Englishmen that it can't be ignored.

Hard　A stubborn flavor which time, in the case of many fine wines, softens; if it fails to soften, hardness becomes harshness.

Long　Leaving a pronounced, pleasant aftertaste.

Maderisé　When a white wine turns brown or a rosé turns deep orange, oxygen has done its dirty work and the wine is over the hill; it may look like Madeira, a great fortified wine, but the end result in the case of table wines is most unfavorable.

Mellow　The winemaker uses this word just as everyone else does; a mellow wine is soft and full, may or may not be sweet, and of course has survived a stormy adolescence.

Mousseux　A French term for sparkling wines which are not champagne, such as *Bourgogne mousseux*, or "sparkling Burgundy."

Musty　Unpleasant flavor reminiscent of old or moldy wood.

Nerveux　A French term meaning well balanced and vigorous.

Nose　The effect of a wine on the nose; therefore, its bouquet. It's also a verb meaning to judge a wine via the olfactory sense.

Nutty　Most often used to describe sherries of medium dryness; they're somewhat reminiscent of walnuts.

Oxidize　When wine is exposed to the oxygen of the air too long, the wine may darken and the flavor becomes lazy.

Pétillant　With a very slight sparkle; wines like some of the Swiss, the Portuguese crackling rosé, and the German Perlwein are examples.

Piquant　With lively acidity and vivid flavor, but not coarse.

Rough   Unlike the term "earthy," "rough" is not a compliment. The wine may lack maturity, be puckerish, and, although drinkable at an outdoor fishing party, would not be the kind you'd present at a leisurely dinner.

Rounded   Like the term "balance," "rounded" describes a wine whose qualities complement each other. The wine may not be illustrious, but no one quality can be said to be notoriously wrong.

Sec   French term for "dry," although *sec* when used to describe champagne means on the sweet side, if not the very sweetest.

Short   Leaving a brief flavor or no flavor in the mouth.

Soft   A pleasing, harmonious wine but not an insipid one.

Spicy   Although cloves, nutmeg, and cinnamon don't normally go into wine making, a wine is called spicy when its flavor is young, provocative, and pleasant, characteristic of many of the young Alsatian and German wines.

Spritzig   German term for a wine with a small, light natural sparkle.

Sulfury   Sulfur dioxide, widely used in making wines to prevent flavor deterioration and spoilage, is normally harmless and important in quality control; if used excessively, however, its flavor intrudes and the wine is said to be sulfury.

Tannin   The elements in a wine that make it puckerish; grapes vary in their tannin content, but the red wines that become memorable with age all contain it.

Tart   As in food, a tart wine has a pleasant acidity which is one of its main attractions.

Vigorous   Of pronounced assertive flavor; applied to both young strong wines and older ones.

Vitis labrusca   Grapes indigenous to North America. (See **foxy** above.)

Vitis vinifera   Grapes indigenous to Europe; cultivated and used in California wine making.

Woody   The literal flavor of wood in wines held too long in the cask, or in casks whose wood conveyed an unacceptable flavor.

18

BEER AND ALE

A Hopfest

Ask some of our more solemn pundits what Noah took along on the ark and nine times out of ten they'll begin reciting names of animals. They're right, of course, but how many of these Biblical experts know of the Sumerian tablet which describes the rest of Noah's cargo as well and reads, ". . . with beer and stronger brews, oil and wine, I filled large jars"? Latin scholars might well be reminded of the fact that Julius Caesar not only crossed the Rubicon in 49 B.C. but climaxed the feat by serving the drink he admired above everything else—beer. Surely there are no horn-rimmed pedants who haven't heard of Charlemagne; yet how many know that he once interrupted affairs of state long enough to call all able beer-masters to his court and lecture them on how to brew beer for the best results? Thousands of Shakespearean scholars have studied the Bard's genius with awe and perseverance, but without discovering one of the keys to Shakespeare's greatness: His father was the official ale taster of Stratford-on-Avon. When Catherine the Great felt she was beginning to lose some of her pepper, she followed the advice of her Scottish physician, Dimsdale, and drank English-brewed beer.

Ask students of American history why the Pilgrims landed at Plymouth Rock on their way to Virginia. The average crammer will answer, "Because they ran out of provisions." Give the groggy boy a zero for vagueness. Explain to him that the colonists on the *Mayflower* boarded a vessel that was well stocked with beer and that they had to cut their voyage short, as the ship's journal tells us, because of "our victuals being much spent, especially our beere." Ask another history major what John Alden was most noted for. Instantly he'll respond, "He won Priscilla Mullens's hand while speaking on behalf of Captain Miles Standish." Wrong again. A cooper by trade, Alden was asked to join the *Mayflower* company for the extremely important task of caring for the vessel's beer kegs.

Down through history to modern times, beer continued to attract the brains and the pacesetters of society: Washington in his own hand wrote a recipe for small beer; Madison among other notables was a brewery owner; in France, Pasteur wrote his famous *Etudes sur la bière*; and the first air-conditioning unit ever installed was in a brewery in Virginia in the latter part of the nineteenth century.

Today beer still weaves its rare and special magic. It may be a common brand put up in millions of gallons annually. You may drink it from a bottle or bucket, from an exquisite blue crockery stein or from a cool pewter mug. It may be unique or taste like many other brands of beer. And yet, though you drink it night after night, in fraternity houses, saloons, or penthouses, the first grand gulp always revives the same singular sensation of unexampled goodness. You can drink too much beer, but you can hardly get tired of it. It's difficult to convey in words the qualities that give gusto to a fine glass of brew, but the elixir of all beer, the very soul of its flavor, is the refreshing bite which comes from the hops and which is always damned by non–beer drinkers because it's bitter, as though that quality were unpalatable. Now, it's a fact that most youngsters dislike things that are bitter. But as we grow and our taste buds become more experienced, we begin to savor goods that may be sour, salty—and frequently bitter. Among the many kinds of bitterness we've welcomed in this country are the astringency of quinine water in a gin and tonic, the soft bitterness of Italian black olives, the sweet bitterness of the dark-chocolate fondant on an éclair, the subtlety of bitters in an old-fashioned cocktail, and the deep bitterness of an imported stout.

When you taste beer slowly and deliberately, the earthy tang of the hops rests on your tongue as the beer goes slowly down. There's a mild aftertaste, too, and this is most important to recognize when you're learning to discriminate between one kind of beer and another. If it's a fine, well-balanced beer with a good body, the subtle aftertaste lingers on. If it's a watery beer, there's hardly any aftertaste at all.

This echo of the original flavor is somehow quite stimulating to the appetite, and almost automatically you find yourself reaching for the pretzels, the anchovy canapés, or the Swiss cheese. When the icebox is raided and the remains of the cold roast turkey are torn apart and laid between thin slices of rye bread, only one thing is needed for perfection itself—the Pilsner glass of cold beer, sparkling and happy as hops. No man needs to be told that the only partner for a dozen cherrystone clams or a fried deviled crab is a bottle of dry, pale ale. Even such saucy dishes as Hungarian beef goulash or hot curried shrimp are best sent on their way with mugs of foamy beer. Certainly the annual alumni steak dinner would be incomplete without two or three kegs freshly tapped for the occasion.

Every beer drinker should know a few simple facts about the art of the brewmaster. Beer is made from malt, hops, yeast, and water, with an alcoholic strength of about 3.5 percent by weight. The malt in beer is made by germinating barley. The actual brewing process consists of four main steps: First, the malt is boiled with water; the liquor thus produced is called wort (rhyming with curt). Then hops are added and boiled; as we've already noted, they give the brew its snappy, bitter flavor. In the third step, the hops are removed and yeast is added to start fermenting the brew. Finally, after the fermentation period, the beer is aged.

Most of the beer we drink in this country is lager beer, a pale, light brew introduced into the United States from Germany during the middle of the last century. Besides malt, other grains, such as corn and rice, are frequently used to make the wort for lager; they give the brew its light body. The German word *Lager* means "storehouse," and all lager beers are stored for several months before going into bottle, can, or keg.

The difference between lager beer and ale is that in brewing beer a yeast is used that settles to the bottom of the vat during fermentation, and it's fermented at a low temperature. Ale, on the other hand, is fermented at high temperatures—between 50° and 70°F.—and the yeast used to make it remains at the top of the liquid during fermentation. These differences give ale a racier and more pronounced hop flavor than beer. It's also sometimes higher in alcohol content.

Beers are often designated by type. In some cases the designation is very loose and almost meaningless. For instance, some U.S. beers are called *Pilsner* after the famed Pilsner Urquell brew of Czechoslovakia, a country that enjoys the reputation of growing the finest hops in the world. Pilsner Urquell is indeed a magnificent beer, light in color but rich in flavor, dry, with an alcohol content above 4 percent. Unfortunately the American beers which attach the name Pilsner to their labels come nowhere near the old-world model. *Munchener* is another name for beer made in Munich, Germany, and beers so designated are deep brown in color, accented with some sweetness, and aim for a strong, pure malt flavor. The best-known beer from Munich was Löwenbräu, which came in both light and dark varieties. Löwenbräu today is made in the United States, and the domestic version seems to be a disappointment to connoisseurs of foreign beers, especially to those who drank Löwenbräu in its city of origin. *Weisse*, or white, beer is a German beer made from wheat, light but not pallid in flavor, and very refreshing.

In many states the alcohol content of beer is limited to a range of 3 to 4 percent. *Malt liquor* is a brew that circumvents this restriction. Malt liquors are simply beers whose alcohol content ranges from 4 to 6 percent. The additional wallop is sometimes, but not always, an assurance of additional flavor.

Dark Beer

Velvety dark beer is noted by those who drink it for the rich flavors of the malt and hops; it is not for guzzling. You pour it at the *gemütlich* dinner when you're serving roast tenderloin of beef, at the special board when you're carving a crown of lamb, or at the season's first feast of cold fresh Kennebec salmon. Even with fare as casual as Roquefort cheese and sourdough French bread, or with bowls of fresh lump crab and mayonnaise, it's an extremely pleasant turn of the beer tide to be able to ask your guests whether they'd prefer dark Danish Carlsberg or Oyster Stout from the Isle of Man. Understandably, beer drinkers are fiercely loyal to one kind of brew. But when four good men of different loyalties are sitting around a pinochle table, the most convivially ubiquitous balm you can dole out, after dealing the cards, is tankards of rich black beer.

There's no exact point on the beer spectrum that separates light from dark. Beers range in color from the palest American blonds to the blackest of British stouts—but even the latter aren't literally black. Hold a glass of Guinness up to the light and you'll see ruby threads among the ebony. Then there are in-between hues like the Mexican Cerveceria Moctezuma, which leans toward the dark side. What makes a beer turn from light to dark when it's brewed is largely a matter of heat. During the brewing process, the barley malt is roasted. At a low temperature, its color is light; at a higher temperature, the color is deeper brown and the resulting beer is dark. Like dark-roasted coffee, it captures that special crowd that appreciates espresso or *café noir* rather than just another cup of coffee.

In rare instances, you may encounter a phony dark beer. It's simply a light beer to which color has been added. You can spot it first by its flavor and sometimes by its head. If the head is a deep brown and collapses quickly, a fake pigment has been introduced. If it is light brown and the flavor lingers, then the beer is the genuine dark brew worthy of Gambrinus himself. Needless to say, the foam on any great beer is creamy thick and holds itself proudly to the last drop.

Dark beers, like certain women, mature beautifully. Most light beers are at their peak of flavor about two to three weeks after they've come from the brewery; because their shelf life is so short, they should be bought at a shop with a rapid turnover. But the dust on a bottle of dark beer, like the cobwebs on bottles of rare red Burgundies, is often a badge of quality. Why? Oxidation. The small amount of air in the headspace at the top of the bottle actually helps age a dark beer to perfection, whereas it weakens its lighter liquid brethren. Britain's Guinness in bottles will handily survive eighteen months—a far cry from the suds Queen Elizabeth I drank, so strong "no man durst touch," and which the good queen insisted should be matured at least seven or eight hours before she would drink it.

Once a year American and European brewers genuflect to the goat that heralds spring and the bock-beer season. Bock is a dark beer with more than usual body and is hoppier—that is, with the added pleasant bitterness that comes from hops rather than malt, a captivating prelude for a man learning to savor the brunet brews.

The darkest and boldest in flavor of imported brews are the British stouts. Mackeson's, once called milk stout because it's brewed with milk sugars, will actually float on top of certain British beers that are lighter in color. Guinness speaks the brogue of its old Dublin dynasty. You may be somewhat less than ecstatic the first time you sip it; like that first sip of an Italian bitter apéritif, stout's rich and insolent flavor will probably take your taste buds by storm. But then, as it slowly flames your appetite and lingers in the back of your mouth, you'll inevitably want more and more. When Guinness is finished brewing, fresh wort (beer with unspent yeast) is added just before the stout is poured into bottles or kegs. As with champagne, the fermentation is then completed in the container, giving the stout its rare ebullience.

Serving Beer

Among enlightened bibbers, beer excites quite different reactions at different temperatures. Extremely quick cooling in the freezing section of your refrigerator will cause it to lose flavor and acquire a harsh edge in taste. Extreme heat is just as harmful. When professional beer tasters in our country do their thing, the brew is usually from 40° to 50°F. At these temperatures, the aromatic qualities are more easily detected. This doesn't mean you must stick a thermometer into the next mug you serve. But if you remove the cans or bottles from your refrigerator fifteen to twenty minutes before you pour, your beer will probably reach a most pleasant temperature for civilized guzzling.

When pouring beer, some hosts tip the mouth of the bottle or can gingerly against the side of the glass, pouring slowly so the glass is filled up with as much liquid and as little head as possible. The trouble is, when beer is poured in this manner, most of the carbon dioxide is trapped in the glass, and the head turns out to be a thin wafer instead of the snowy high collar it should be. It's true that the carbon dioxide is what gives the beer its tingle and revival power, but too much of it is stultifying. When, on the other hand, beer is poured straight to the bottom of the glass, with the bottle or can held one or two inches above the rim, it builds a rich, creamy cap and loses just enough of its carbonation to make its softness and mellowness much more evident. When poured in this manner, a superior beer will not only form a deep, dense head, but as the beer is slowly sipped, a lace of foam will cling to the sides of the glass.

Equally important in serving beer correctly are clean glasses, for the smallest trace of foreign matter will affect both the taste of the beer and the formation of the head. Wash beer glasses in very hot water with detergent, followed by hot rinse water. But don't towel them. Just before pouring the beer, rinse them again in clear, cold water. If you belong to the ferocious fraternity that uses beer glasses for stressing points during an argument, you'll want heavy seidels or steins. If you enjoy drinking your beer in curvaceous company, you'll want thin Pilsner glasses, or perhaps the large tulip-shaped goblets which show off the brilliant clarity of a superb beer. The glass bottoms on old pewter mugs were designed for the same purpose.

To set up your own beer-tasting criteria, you don't have to emulate the original ale tasters in London, known there as conners. These august connoisseurs always wore leather trousers. To test a brew, they'd pour a little on a wooden bench and then sit down. If, after three minutes, their trousers stuck to the bench, the ale was deemed "good for man's body in lawful measure."

A better way to explore three or four different brands of beer or ale is to pour them into large tulip-shaped glasses, just as you would wine at a wine-tasting party. All first-rank beers, particularly the dark members of the tribe, have a definite malty aroma that is part of their taste profile. Don't try to taste them immediately after a meal. Wait an hour or so, or taste them before the meal. Beer tasters, unlike wine savants, don't sip their brew; and to savor its complete flavor, they drink it through the foam. A single swallow is enough to give you the beer's flavor—don't down it in uncontrolled gulping if you're studying its flavor. Along with the beers your guests are tasting, keep a pile of breadsticks or unsalted crackers (water crackers, if possible) and wedges of hard cheese nearby. Take small nibbles of each between tasting to clear the palate.

You'll probably be surprised at the extent of your own flavor-consciousness. You'll notice such characteristics as hop flavor, body (that is, intensity of flavor), sweetness, mellowness, sharpness, blandness, and many other qualities that you never expected to be able to identify.

BEER AND FOOD

When it comes to combinations of food and wine to be served at the same table, there are some traditions that should not only be questioned but soundly rebuffed. The old dictum of white wine with white food, for example, has happily been kicked in the teeth. But when it comes to the combination of food and beer, tradition is the big throbbing bosom we all seek.

It's traditional and still wonderful to wash down big thick sausages like knackwurst, bratwurst, and kielbasa with mugs of foamy beer. And those hot Szechuan, Mexican, and Indian dishes Americans now love are natural go-togethers with huge drafts of cold beer. It's almost impossible to imagine a big platter of corned beef and cabbage or the French choucroute of pork chops, frankfurters and sauerkraut served without beer. When you're serving seafood of any kind, from broiled scrod to bouillabaisse to butterfly shrimp, and you've argued yourself to a standstill over which wine to serve, solve the whole thing very quickly by offering schooners of light or dark beer; no one will question your choice. Finally, for all those outdoor charcoal-broiled shell steaks, mixed grills, shish kebabs, and barbecued spareribs, every host has an obligation to keep his guests well primed on beer. At a big patio party, if you happen to own an old-fashioned large wooden washtub, fill it with ice and an assortment of light and dark beers, including the light U.S. brews as well as the imported scuttles now reaching our shores.

U.S. and Foreign Brews

It's easier to describe U.S. beer than almost any other beer in the world: It's the Napoleon of thirst quenchers, which reached its high spot by eliminating rather than emphasizing flavor. The U.S. beer kingpins—Budweiser, Schlitz, Pabst, Miller, and Coors—make the lightest and dryest beers in the world, and Americans quaff them as cold as possible since the closer you get to the freezing temperature of water when chilling your beer, the less discernible will be whatever taste of the malt and hops remains in the highly carbonated brews we prefer. In contrast to wine drinkers, the majority of native beer drinkers are indifferent to—or simply have never tasted—rich, dark, or deeply flavored brews. Their philosophy seems to be that if you're enjoying magnificent roast prime ribs of beef, you shouldn't dilute the pleasure with any deeply flavored beer, ale, or stout; you want your beer to literally wash your food down and call as little attention to itself as possible. There's a dissident minority, of course. You'll find them drinking the Pabst Andeker beer or the magnificent San Francisco Anchor beer called steam beer because of the hiss emitted whenever kegs were opened.

One of the phenomena of the American brewing scene has been the disappearance of small local breweries, some of which maintained their properties and brewing equipment all through Prohibition. Not all of the small breweries made distinctive beer; some did. But the 750 breweries operating when Repeal allowed Americans to drink beer again have shrunk to less than four dozen in the gobbling-merging of the beer industry, and the giants that remain seem determined to be carbon copies of each other when it comes to beer flavor.

If you're one of the small but fast-growing minority looking for beers with memorable flavor, your best bet is one of the foreign imports. Not all imports are great brews; beer from mainland China, for instance, would benefit from some Teutonic expertise. But generally speaking, beers like the Dos Equis from Mexico and others make many American beers taste like watered-down facsimiles of what fine beer could be. Visitors to Cuba return home talking about the rich-tasting local beers they sampled there. But several foreign beers, like Tuborg from Denmark, are now being made in the States, and many beer drinkers who tasted the original versions in their native lands are sadly let down by the transfer of citizenship.

One of the main reasons for the differences is the fact that many foreign beers use, or are legally required to use, only the simple, natural ingredients of beer—malt, hops, yeast, and water. In this country, so-called adjuncts or substitutes for malt—like corn products, rice, and soybeans—are introduced. The amount of these adjuncts, plus a host of other additives, can guarantee that beer will keep its color as well as its head, have a long shelf life, and at the same time an anemic flavor. A. E. Housman once said, "And malt does more than Milton can/ To justify God's ways to man." If some American brewers would concentrate on using malt—malted barley—instead of some of the five dozen additives that now go into beer, Housman's paean to beer would again become true.

The number and variety of foreign beers coming to the States are staggering. In exploring them, one must remember that they do not have an indefinite shelf life, thus it's best to buy the better-known and better-moving brands rather than those with the dust of the ages on their bottle caps. Often a delicatessen will have a larger selection of imported brews than a mass-market outlet. In some states there are shops that specialize in carbonated bottled drinks and beers, and these are usually the best source for exploring beers of the world.

Besides foreign beers previously mentioned, the following should be cited for beer drinkers beating the bush:

> Pilsner Urquell (Czechoslovakia)
> Würzburger (Germany)
> Holsten (Germany)
> Beck's (Germany)
> Ringnes (Norway)
> Carlsberg (Denmark)
> Elephant Malt Liquor (Denmark)
> Heineken's (Netherlands)
> Grolsch (Netherlands)
> Kirin (Japan)
> San Miguel (the Philippines)

Note to American beer drinkers traveling in the British Isles: Americans are often completely broken up by British beer terminology. To the Briton, the words "beer" and "ale" are now synonymous, like "car" and "automobile" in the U.S. At one time the English word "ale" meant a brew made without hops, but today ale and beer in Britain are both made with malt and hops. The British word "bitter" means a beer with a very heavy hop flavor: "mild," darker and less strong than bitter. "Burton" refers to a strong dark beer (not black and not necessarily made at Burton on Trent). If you want American-type beer in Britain, be sure to ask for lager, fermented at a low temperature with a light hop flavor. It's served at a temperature that the British call cool and that most Americans living on the pleasures of the ice age call tepid.

19

COCKTAILS

The most overwhelmingly popular of all potables, the open sesame to brunch parties, lunch parties, dinner parties, midnight supper parties, and the next morning's revival parties, the cocktail is undoubtedly America's most noted contribution to the world of bibulous pleasure. The stories concerning the origin of the word "cocktail" are nearly as many and varied as the mixtures themselves. Among them, the following legends have enjoyed long vintage life:

The word came from the French word *coquetel*, once used to describe a mixed drink in the Bordeaux region.

Southern army officers were once served a luscious mixed drink by a lovely southern belle. Her name? Octelle, suh!

A distinguished American general was invited to the court of a Mexican monarch whose daughter appeared with a drink in the royal cup of gold encrusted with rubies. When the obvious question of who would drink first racked all the king's men, the daughter solved the problem very intelligently by drinking the libation herself. The stunning princess's name was, of course, Coctel.

Western horse traders whose nags weren't worth the price of their pelts, on sale day, fed their horses liquor whose effects made them cock their tails and come to life with incredible spirit.

Morning tipplers in New Amsterdam, visiting inns for a pick-me-up, would invariably run into Dutch barmaids who (you guessed it) used the tails of roosters for sweeping away last night's litter.

A young Irish lass (this one by James Fenimore Cooper) not only managed to procure and roast chickens from Tory farmers for her Revolutionary guests, but decorated their drinks with feathers from the cocks' tails.

Whether or not these stories are any truer than Bunyan's blue ox, it's clear that the cocktail goes deep into America's drinking heritage. And even today, Americans remain the foremost masters and idolaters of the cocktail.

Cocktails range from appetite-awakening bone-dry martinis to velvety dessert cocktails that correctly climax a rich feast. Men taking the lead at their own cocktail parties should weigh the counsel in Chapter 6, "Barmanship." In time, as your cocktail repertoire expands, the ups and downs of the cocktail shaker will become second nature. But even the most polished perfectionists at their bars follow certain well-tested guidelines for cocktails, hence the following review of the more important considerations in drink making:

1. Inferior liquors aren't masked in cocktails. A fine gin will seem even finer in a martini. The same goes for whiskeys, rums, vodkas, and vermouths.

2. Don't imitate free-pouring bartenders in public bars. Use standard measures, whether they be teaspoons, jiggers, ounces, cups, or quarts. When you multiply quantities for party drinking, be mathematically accurate.

3. Ice must be hard, cold, and clean—not weeping. Fresh ice at $0°$F. or below will produce a much brisker drink than lazy ice turning to water.

4. Though cocktails must be icy cold (proper dilution is part of the art), they shouldn't be watery. Anyone can begin shaking cocktails. An artist knows when to stop. Normally 2 to $2\frac{1}{2}$ ounces poured into a cocktail shaker will grow to approximately 4 ounces after proper shaking. Use a $4\frac{1}{2}$-ounce glass or 6-ounce glass for larger cocktails.

5. Use the proper glass for each cocktail, and be sure that it's sparkling clean and prechilled. The glass should first chill the hand and then the lips; the icy cocktail itself will take care of the rest.

6. You should, of course, use fresh ingredients in your cocktails, especially when it comes to fruit juices.

7. Cocktails with fruit juices, eggs, syrups, etc., are normally shaken; those containing only liquor and vermouth are stirred (although one of the most eminent martini men of modern times, Somerset Maugham, insisted that his martinis be *shaken*). The stirred cocktail is clear; the shaken cloudy.

8. Make your own personal recipe changes only with the greatest care, remembering that some cocktails are dominated by a single straight, powerful flavor—the martini by gin, for instance, or the negroni by Campari—while others are a medley of flavors: liquors, fortified wines, juices, bitters, fruits, etc. A fine cocktail of the latter type is always in delicate balance; even its aftertaste leaves a pleasant sense of the tart and the sweet, the strong and the weak. Sometimes adding or subtracting an eighth of a teaspoon will make a noticeable difference. Be creative if you will, but create slowly and deftly. A new drink is always an evolution.

The cocktails that follow are designed for a 4½-ounce cocktail glass, except in those cases where an old-fashioned or other glass is used. The parsimonious 3-ounce cocktail glasses are now skeletons in most liquor closets; not only does the larger cocktail provide more sumptuous bliss for guests, but it's a boon to the host since it means fewer refills and the coveted chance to sit down, drink, and enjoy the revels.

After-Dinner Cocktails

On a dinner or late-supper menu, the after-dinner cocktail can take the place of the dessert or supplement it. As a libation, it's frankly sweet and toothsome. It goes perfectly with a platter of cheese and crackers, a fresh fruit bowl, or both. It graciously replaces the ubiquitous pie and the gooey ice cream. For the harried host who has neither the time to make nor the energy to shop for a fresh dessert, it's a deliverance. Freshly concocted, any of the following are an imaginative way to conclude a brunch, lunch, or dinner.

AFTER-DINNER CHARADE

1 oz. Sciarada
½ oz. peppermint
schnapps
½ oz. heavy cream

Shake extremely well with ice. Strain into prechilled cocktail glass.

AMARETTO CREAM

1 oz. amaretto
1 oz. Muscari
½ oz. heavy cream

Shake well with ice. Strain into cocktail glass or over rocks.

BANSHEE

1 oz. banana liqueur
½ oz. white crème de
cacao
1 inch ripe banana,
sliced
½ oz. cream or milk
½ cup crushed ice

Put all ingredients in blender. Blend 10 seconds. Pour into deep-saucer champagne glass.

BERRIES AND CREAM

1 oz. blackberry-
flavored brandy
1 oz. strawberry
liqueur
1 oz. nondairy creamer
½ oz. lime juice

Shake well with ice. Strain into prechilled cocktail glass or serve over rocks. Fresh heavy sweet cream may be used, but it tends to curdle when mixed with the lime juice.

BLUE ANGEL

½ oz. blue curaçao
½ oz. parfait amour
½ oz. brandy
½ oz. lemon juice
½ oz. heavy cream

Shake well with ice. Strain into prechilled cocktail glass. Cool and incredibly smooth.

BOURBON CREAM

1 oz. bourbon
½ oz. Wild Turkey
  liqueur
1 oz. heavy sweet
  cream

Shake well with ice. Strain into prechilled cocktail glass.

BRAVE BULL

1 oz. Kahlúa
1 oz. tequila
1 piece lemon peel

Pour Kahlúa and tequila over rocks in an old-fashioned glass. Stir well. Add ice if necessary to fill glass. Twist lemon peel over drink and drop into glass.

CADIZ

¾ oz. amontillado
  sherry
¾ oz. blackberry
  liqueur
½ oz. triple sec
½ oz. heavy cream

Shake well with ice. Strain over rocks in prechilled old-fashioned glass.

CALM VOYAGE

½ oz. Galliano or
  Roiano
½ oz. passion-fruit
  syrup
2 teaspoons lemon
  juice
½ oz. light rum
½ egg white
⅓ cup crushed ice

Put all ingredients into blender. Blend at low speed 10–15 seconds. Pour into prechilled deep-saucer champagne glass. Mendelssohn is good accompaniment on this trip.

CARAMEL COW

2 ozs. (¼ measuring
  cup) vanilla ice
  cream
1 oz. Caramella
½ oz. crème de cacao
1½ ozs. milk

Pour all ingredients into blender. Blend at high speed 10 seconds. Pour over rocks in 8-oz. old-fashioned glass. Stir well.

CARA SPOSA

1 oz. coffee liqueur
1 oz. curaçao
½ oz. heavy cream
⅓ cup crushed ice

Put all ingredients into blender. Blend at low speed 10–15 seconds. Pour into pre-chilled deep-saucer champagne glass. Although any kind of coffee liqueur may be used in this drink, the espresso-coffee liqueur is especially pleasant.

CHERRY RUM

1¼ ozs. light rum
¾ oz. cherry liqueur
½ oz. heavy cream
⅓ cup crushed ice

Put all ingredients into blender. Blend at low speed 10–15 seconds. Pour into pre-chilled deep-saucer champagne glass.

CHIQUITA PUNCH

1½ ozs. banana
    liqueur
1½ ozs. orange juice
1½ ozs. cream
¾ oz. grenadine
¾ cup crushed ice

Put all ingredients into blender. Blend at high speed 10 seconds. Pour into prechilled old-fashioned glass.

CHOCOLATE BLACK RUSSIAN

2 ozs. (¼ measuring
    cup) chocolate ice
    cream
1 oz. Kahlúa
½ oz. vodka
1½ ozs. milk

Pour all ingredients into blender. Blend at high speed 10 seconds. Pour over rocks in 8-oz. glass. Stir well.

CHOCOLATE ÉCLAIR

2 ozs. (¼ measuring
    cup) chocolate ice
    cream
1 oz. Choclair
½ oz. light rum
1½ ozs. milk
1 tablespoon sweet
    chocolate shavings

Pour chocolate ice cream, Choclair, light rum, and milk into blender. Blend at high speed 10 seconds. Pour over rocks in 8-oz. glass. Stir well. Sprinkle chocolate shavings on top.

CHOCOLATE MINT

2 ozs. (¼ measuring cup) chocolate ice cream
1 oz. peppermint schnapps
½ oz. vodka
1½ ozs. milk

Pour all ingredients into blender. Blend at high speed 10 seconds. Pour over rocks in 8-oz. glass. Stir well.

CHOCOLATE RUM

1 oz. light rum
½ oz. white crème de cacao
½ oz. white crème de menthe
½ oz. heavy cream
1 teaspoon 151-proof rum

Shake light rum, crème de cacao, crème de menthe, and cream well with ice. Strain into prechilled cocktail glass. Float 151-proof rum on top.

CHOCOLATIER

2 ozs. (¼ measuring cup) chocolate ice cream
1 oz. dark Jamaica rum
½ oz. crème de cacao
1½ ozs. milk
1 tablespoon sweet chocolate shavings

Pour chocolate ice cream, rum, crème de cacao, and milk into blender. Blend at high speed 10 seconds. Pour over rocks in 8-oz. glass. Stir well. Sprinkle chocolate shavings on top.

COCO AMOR

1 oz. CocoRibe
½ oz. amaretto
½ oz. lemon juice

Shake extremely well with ice. Strain into prechilled cocktail glass with sugar-frosted rim.

COCO BANANA

1 oz. CocoRibe
½ oz. banana liqueur
½ oz. heavy cream

Shake extremely well with ice. Strain into prechilled cocktail glass.

COCONUT MINT

1 oz. CocoRibe
½ oz. peppermint
 schnapps
½ oz. heavy cream
1 tablespoon chocolate
 shavings

Shake CocoRibe, peppermint schnapps, and cream extremely well with ice. Strain into prechilled cocktail glass. Float chocolate shavings on drink.

COFFEE CREAM

1 oz. coffee liqueur
1 oz. California brandy
1 oz. heavy cream

Shake well with ice. Strain into large cocktail glass or over rocks.

COFFEE GRASSHOPPER

¾ oz. coffee liqueur
¾ oz. white crème de
 menthe
¾ oz. cream

Shake well with ice. Strain into prechilled cocktail glass.

COFFEE ROIANO

1½ ozs. Roiano
½ oz. coffee liqueur
½ oz. heavy cream
⅓ cup crushed ice

Put all ingredients into blender. Blend at low speed 10–15 seconds. Pour into prechilled deep-saucer champagne glass. May be served not only at the end of a meal but at any time of the day.

CREAMY CHARADE

1 oz. Sciarada
½ oz. vodka
½ slightly beaten egg
 white
½ oz. lemon juice
½ oz. heavy sweet
 cream

Shake all ingredients extremely well with ice. Strain into prechilled large cocktail glass.

DULCET

1 oz. vodka
½ oz. curaçao
½ oz. anisette
½ oz. apricot liqueur
1 teaspoon lemon juice
½ brandied apricot

Shake vodka, curaçao, anisette, apricot liqueur, and lemon juice well with ice. Strain over cracked ice or rocks in prechilled old-fashioned glass. Add brandied apricot.

FROZEN BANANA MINT

1 oz. banana liqueur
1 oz. peppermint
    schnapps
⅓ cup sliced ripe
    banana
¾ cup crushed ice
2 large mint leaves

Pour banana liqueur, peppermint schnapps, sliced banana, and crushed ice into blender. Blend at high speed 10 seconds. Pour into 8-oz. glass. Float mint leaves on drink.

FROZEN BLACK CURRANT

1 oz. crème de cassis
1 oz. pineapple juice
½ oz. brandy
⅓ cup crushed ice
1 slice orange

Put crème de cassis, pineapple juice, brandy, and crushed ice into blender. Blend at low speed 10–15 seconds. Pour into prechilled deep-saucer champagne glass. Add orange slice.

FROZEN COCO BANANA

2 ozs. CocoRibe
⅓ cup sliced ripe
    banana
½ cup crushed ice
½ oz. lemon juice

Whirl all ingredients in blender at high speed 10 seconds. Pour into deep-saucer champagne glass.

GINGERMAN

2 ozs. (¼ measuring
    cup) chocolate ice
    cream
1 oz. ginger-flavored
    brandy
½ oz. light rum
1½ ozs. milk

Pour all ingredients into blender. Blend at high speed 10 seconds. Pour over rocks in 8-oz. glass. Stir well.

GOLD CADILLAC

¾ oz. crème de cacao
¾ oz. Galliano
¾ oz. heavy cream
⅓ cup crushed ice

Put all ingredients into blender. Blend at low speed 10–15 seconds. Pour into prechilled deep-saucer champagne glass. For another version, omit crushed ice, shake well with ice, and strain into prechilled cocktail glass.

GOLDEN FROG

½ oz. Strega
½ oz. Galliano
½ oz. vodka
½ oz. lemon juice
¾ cup crushed ice

Put all ingredients into blender. Blend at high speed 10 seconds. Pour into prechilled old-fashioned glass.

GRASSHOPPER

¾ oz. white crème de cacao
¾ oz. green crème de menthe
¾ oz. heavy cream

Shake well with ice. Strain into prechilled cocktail glass.

GRASS SKIRT

1 oz. CocoRibe
½ oz. light rum
1 oz. pineapple juice
½ oz. lime juice

Shake well with ice. Strain into prechilled large cocktail glass with sugar-frosted rim.

IL MAGNIFICO

¾ oz. Tuaca liqueur
¾ oz. curaçao
¾ oz. heavy cream
⅓ cup crushed ice

Put all ingredients into blender. Blend at low speed 10–15 seconds. Pour into prechilled deep-saucer champagne glass. May be served before, with, or after the espresso.

IRISH ALEXANDER ON THE ROCKS

¾ oz. blended Irish
   whisky
¾ oz. Irish coffee
   liqueur
¾ oz. heavy cream

Shake all ingredients well with ice. Pour into prechilled old-fashioned glass. Add ice cubes to fill glass to rim. Stir.

KALANI WAI

1 oz. Midori
1 oz. green crème de
   menthe
1 oz. heavy cream

Shake well with ice. Strain into large cocktail glass or over rocks.

LADY IN GREEN

1 oz. pistachio liqueur
1 oz. green crème
   de menthe
½ oz. heavy cream

Shake well with ice. Strain over rocks in 8-oz. glass. Stir.

MAUI

1 oz. Midori
1 oz. Cointreau or
   triple sec
½ oz. lemon juice

Shake well with ice. Strain into large cocktail glass or over rocks.

MOCHA MINT

¾ oz. coffee liqueur
¾ oz. white crème
   de menthe
¾ oz. crème de cacao

Shake well with ice. Strain into prechilled sugar-and-coffee-frosted cocktail glass.

NUMERO UNO

1 oz. amaretto
1 oz. tequila
1 oz. heavy cream
Ground cinnamon

Shake well with ice. Strain into large cocktail glass. Sprinkle with cinnamon.

ORACABESSA

1 oz. banana liqueur
½ oz. lemon juice
½ oz. 151-proof rum
1 slice banana
1 slice lemon

Dip banana slice into lemon juice or orange juice to prevent discoloration. Shake banana liqueur, lemon juice, and rum well with ice. Strain over rocks in old-fashioned glass. Add banana and lemon slices.

ORANGE COMFORT

½ oz. Southern
  Comfort
½ oz. anisette
¾ oz. orange juice
½ oz. lemon juice
1 slice cocktail orange
  in syrup

Shake Southern Comfort, anisette, orange juice, and lemon juice well with ice. Strain into prechilled cocktail glass. Garnish with cocktail-orange slice.

ORANGE FLOWER

1 oz. curaçao
½ oz. cherry liqueur
½ oz. orange juice
1 teaspoon lemon
  juice
1 dash orange-flower
  water
⅓ cup crushed ice

Put all ingredients into blender. Blend at low speed 10–15 seconds. Pour into prechilled deep-saucer champagne glass. Exhilarating finale for a roast-goose dinner.

PARSON WEEMS

2 ozs. (¼ measuring
  cup) chocolate ice
  cream
½ oz. cherry-flavored
  brandy
½ oz. maraschino
  liqueur
½ oz. California
  brandy
1½ ozs. milk

Pour all ingredients into blender. Blend at high speed 10 seconds. Pour over rocks in 8-oz. glass. Stir well.

PAYOFF

2 ozs. (¼ measuring
    cup) vanilla ice
    cream
¾ oz. amaretto
¾ oz. California
    brandy
1½ ozs. milk
1 tablespoon toasted
    slivered almonds

Pour vanilla ice cream, amaretto, California brandy, and milk into blender. Blend at high speed 10 seconds. Pour over rocks in 8-oz. glass. Stir well. Sprinkle almonds on top.

PINK ALMOND

½ oz. crème de noyaux
½ oz. orgeat or orzata
1 oz. blended whiskey
½ oz. kirschwasser
½ oz. lemon juice
1 slice lemon

Shake crème de noyaux, orgeat, whiskey, kirschwasser, and lemon juice well with ice. Strain over rocks in prechilled old-fashioned glass. Add lemon slice.

PINK CARNATION

2 ozs. (¼ measuring
    cup) vanilla ice
    cream
½ oz. cranberry
    liqueur
½ oz. cherry-flavored
    brandy
½ oz. California
    brandy
1½ ozs. milk

Pour all ingredients into blender. Blend at high speed 10 seconds. Pour over rocks in 8-oz. glass. Stir well.

PINK COCONUT

1½ ozs. CocoRibe
½ oz. nondairy
    creamer
½ oz. lime juice
1 teaspoon grenadine

Shake all ingredients extremely well with ice. Strain into prechilled cocktail glass.

PINK RIBBON

1 oz. strawberry
   liqueur
½ oz. triple sec
½ oz. California
   brandy
½ oz. lemon juice

Shake all ingredients well with ice. Strain into sugar-frosted cocktail glass.

PINK SQUIRREL

1 oz. crème de noyaux
1 oz. white crème de
   cacao
¾ oz. heavy cream

Shake all ingredients well with ice. Strain into prechilled sugar-frosted cocktail glass. Pinker and smoother than a pink lady.

PISTACHIO CREAM

2 ozs. (¼ measuring
   cup) vanilla ice
   cream
1 oz. pistachio liqueur
½ oz. California
   brandy
1½ ozs. milk

Pour all ingredients into blender. Blend at high speed 10 seconds. Pour over rocks in 8-oz. glass. Stir well.

RUSSIAN CARAMEL

1 oz. Caramella
1 oz. vodka
1 oz. heavy cream
Freshly grated nutmeg

Shake Caramella, vodka, and cream well with ice. Strain into large cocktail glass. Sprinkle nutmeg on drink.

RUSSIAN COFFEE

¾ oz. coffee liqueur
¾ oz. vodka
¾ oz. heavy cream
⅓ cup crushed ice

Put all ingredients into blender. Blend at low speed 10–15 seconds. Pour into prechilled deep-saucer champagne glass.

SHERRIED COFFEE

1¼ ozs. oloroso sherry
1¼ ozs. coffee liqueur
2 teaspoons heavy
cream

Shake sherry and coffee liqueur well with ice. Strain over rocks in prechilled old-fashioned glass. Float cream on top.

SNIFTER

¾ oz. Galliano
¾ oz. brandy
1 teaspoon white
crème de menthe
⅓ cup finely crushed
ice

Pour liquors into prechilled brandy snifter. Add crushed ice. Stir. May be served with or without straw.

SOUTHERN PEACH

1 oz. Southern Com-
fort
1 oz. peach liqueur
½ oz. heavy cream
1 slice fresh or
brandied peach

Shake Southern Comfort, peach liqueur, and cream well with ice. Strain over rocks or coarsely cracked ice in prechilled old-fashioned glass. Add peach slice. It's peaches and cream brought up to date.

STRAWBERRY KISS

1 oz. strawberry
liqueur
½ oz. kirschwasser
½ oz. light rum
½ oz. orange juice
1 teaspoon lemon juice
1 large strawberry

Shake strawberry liqueur, kirschwasser, rum, orange juice, and lemon juice well with ice. Strain into prechilled sugar-frosted cocktail glass. Add strawberry.

SWEET OFFERING

1 oz. Caramella
½ oz. crème de cacao
½ oz. light rum
½ oz. lime juice

Shake all ingredients well with ice. Strain into large cocktail glass.

SWEET TALK

1 oz. blackberry-
flavored brandy
½ oz. California
brandy
½ oz. heavy cream

Shake all ingredients very well with ice.
Strain into cocktail glass.

SWEET WILLIAM

¾ oz. pear brandy
¾ oz. apricot liqueur
¾ oz. heavy cream
Ground cinnamon

Shake pear brandy, apricot liqueur, and
cream very well with ice. Strain into prechilled cocktail glass. Sprinkle with cinnamon.

YELLOW FINGERS

1 oz. gin
1 oz. blackberry
brandy
½ oz. banana liqueur
½ oz. heavy cream

Shake all ingredients well with ice. Strain
into prechilled saucer champagne glass.

FRAPPÉS

Frappés are even more pleasing than ice cream and cake as a finale
for a feast. Cool, clean, and rich, they're a mixture of liqueurs poured
over finely crushed ice. You can serve them freshly made, but we prefer
to swizzle them up beforehand and store them in the freezer until the
drinking lamp is lit. When you take them out, you'll find that an ice
cap has formed on top of each drink. But the cap will loosen after a
minute or two and the drink can be sipped from the rim with or without
a short straw.

ALL-WHITE FRAPPÉ

½ oz. anisette
¼ oz. white crème de
menthe
½ oz. white crème de
cacao
1 teaspoon lemon juice

Stir without ice. Pour over crushed ice in
deep-saucer champagne glass.

BANANA RUM FRAPPÉ

½ oz. banana liqueur
½ oz. light rum
½ oz. orange juice

Stir without ice. Pour over crushed ice in deep-saucer champagne glass. Cool postscript for an Oriental dinner.

BRANDY APRICOT FRAPPÉ

¾ oz. California
brandy
½ oz. apricot-flavored
brandy
¼ oz. crème de
noyaux

Stir without ice. Pour over crushed ice in deep-saucer champagne glass.

CRANBERRY FRAPPÉ

½ oz. cranberry
liqueur
½ oz. cherry brandy
½ oz. orange juice

Pour ingredients over crushed ice in deep-saucer champagne glass.

CHARTREUSE COGNAC FRAPPÉ

¾ oz. yellow Char-
treuse
¾ oz. Cognac

Stir without ice. Pour over crushed ice in deep-saucer champagne glass.

CHERRY GINGER FRAPPÉ

1 oz. cherry liqueur
¼ oz. kirschwasser
¼ oz. ginger-flavored
brandy
1 brandied cherry
1 piece preserved
ginger in syrup

Stir cherry liqueur, kirschwasser, and ginger-flavored brandy without ice. Pour over crushed ice in deep-saucer champagne glass. Pierce brandied cherry and preserved ginger with cocktail spear and place over rim of glass.

CHOCOLATE ORANGE FRAPPÉ

¾ oz. white crème de cacao
¾ oz. orange juice
1 teaspoon Galliano or Roiano

Stir without ice. Pour over crushed ice in deep-saucer champagne glass.

COFFEE GRAND MARNIER

½ oz. coffee liqueur
½ oz. Grand Marnier
½ oz. orange juice
1 slice orange

Stir coffee liqueur, Grand Marnier, and orange juice without ice. Pour over crushed ice in deep-saucer champagne glass. Add orange slice.

COGNAC MENTHE FRAPPÉ

1 oz. green crème de menthe
½ oz. Cognac
2 large mint leaves

Stir crème de menthe and Cognac without ice. Pour over crushed ice in deep-saucer champagne glass. Tear each mint leaf partially and place on drink.

DUTCH PEAR FRAPPÉ

1¼ ozs. pear brandy
¾ oz. Vandermint liqueur
½ oz. heavy cream
½ cup finely crushed ice
Sweetened whipped cream

Pour pear brandy, Vandermint, heavy cream, and ice into blender. Blend at low speed 20 seconds. Pour into prechilled old-fashioned glass. Add ice cubes if necessary to fill glass to rim. Top with dollop of whipped cream. Make this drink just before serving.

GRAND MARNIER QUETSCH

1 oz. Grand Marnier
¼ oz. quetsch
¼ oz. orange juice
1 slice lemon

Stir Grand Marnier, quetsch, and orange juice without ice. Pour over crushed ice in deep-saucer champagne glass. Add lemon slice. Mirabelle or slivovitz may be used in place of quetsch, since all are plum brandies.

KÜMMEL BLACKBERRY FRAPPÉ

¾ oz. kümmel
¾ oz. blackberry
   liqueur or
   blackberry-flavored
   brandy
1 teaspoon lemon juice

Stir without ice. Pour over crushed ice in deep-saucer champagne glass.

MIXED MOCHA FRAPPÉ

¾ oz. coffee liqueur
¼ oz. white crème de
   menthe
¼ oz. crème de cacao
¼ oz. triple sec

Sugar-frost rim of deep-saucer champagne glass. Fill with crushed ice. Stir liqueurs without ice and pour over ice in glass.

PERNOD CURAÇAO FRAPPÉ

¾ oz. Pernod
¾ oz. curaçao
1 teaspoon lemon
   juice
2 teaspoons orange
   juice
1 thin slice orange

Stir Pernod, curaçao, lemon juice, and orange juice without ice. Pour over crushed ice in deep-saucer champagne glass. Add orange slice.

SAMBUCA COFFEE FRAPPÉ

1 oz. sambuca
½ oz. coffee liqueur
Roasted coffee beans

Stir the sambuca and coffee liqueur without ice. Pour over crushed ice in deep-saucer champagne glass. Place the glass on a saucer along with about a half-dozen coffee beans to munch while sipping. It's an Italian custom; the more distinguished the guest, the more coffee beans placed alongside his sambuca.

SHERRIED CORDIAL MÉDOC FRAPPÉ

1 oz. Cordial Médoc
½ oz. amontillado
   sherry

Stir without ice. Pour over crushed ice in deep-saucer champagne glass.

SLOE LIME FRAPPÉ

1 oz. sloe gin
½ oz. light rum
1 slice lime

Stir sloe gin and light rum without ice. Pour over crushed ice in deep-saucer champagne glass. Add lime slice. Sip without straw.

SOUTHERN COMFORT STRAWBERRY FRAPPÉ

¾ oz. Southern Comfort
¾ oz. strawberry liqueur
Orange peel
1 slice lemon

Stir Southern Comfort and strawberry liqueur without ice. Pour over crushed ice in deep-saucer champagne glass. Twist orange peel above drink and drop into glass. Add lemon slice. Sip on a summer evening under the stars.

POUSSE-CAFÉ

This showy little drink is one of the oldest bits of nonsense known to bartenders—and, needless to say, the number of drinkers who never stop loving nonsense is greater than ever. If not a cocktail by definition, it is for after-dinner imbibing and thus we include it here.

The pousse-café is a series of liqueurs poured into a small, straight-sided pousse-café glass so that each forms a layer. Since the liqueurs are of different weights or densities, the heaviest stays on the bottom, the next heaviest directly above it, and so on. The main problem that bedevils the pousse-café specialist is that the densities of liqueurs of the same flavor often vary from one brand to the next. One man's menthe may not rise above another man's parfait amour. Since the density of a liqueur is not indicated on the bottle's label, a certain amount of trial and error may be necessary in building a pousse-café. As a general guide, remember that frequently the higher a liqueur's alcohol content, the lower its density. This doesn't apply in all cases, but it's something of a help. The so-called *demi-sec* liqueurs are lighter than the sweet crèmes, and U.S. fruit-flavored brandies are lighter than liqueurs. If you're in doubt about a recipe, make an experimental pousse-café before the guests arrive, and when you find a formula that works, stick to it as long as you're using the same brands of liqueurs.

To keep the ingredients from mingling, pour them slowly over the back of a teaspoon, with the tip of the spoon held against the inside of the glass. Pour slowly and steadily, keeping your eye on the liquid as it flows. If you follow this procedure carefully, the layers should stay separate; you may find, in fact, that a liqueur poured in the wrong order will seep down or rise up to its proper level and stay there intact. For a party, you can make a large number of pousse-cafés beforehand, and if you place them carefully in the refrigerator, each small rainbow will remain undisturbed until you need it.

A pousse-café may be of three, four, or five layers. Each layer needn't be equal, but each should be of a distinctly different color when held at eye level. Nonalcoholic liquids such as syrups and cream may be poured along with the liqueurs or other spirits. Here are twelve pousse-café combinations, with the heaviest liquid listed first and the lighter ones in ascending order. To both create and divert conversation, make an assortment with several combinations on the same tray.

1. White crème de cacao, cherry liqueur, kümmel, and a dab of whipped cream.
2. Green crème de menthe, Galliano, blackberry liqueur, and kirschwasser.
3. Banana liqueur, Peter Heering or Cherry Karise, and Cognac.
4. Peach liqueur, kirsch liqueur (not kirschwasser), and Pernod.
5. Orzata or orgeat, crème de noyaux, curaçao, and sweet cream mixed with enough crème de noyaux to make cream pink.
6. Passion-fruit syrup, green crème de menthe, strawberry liqueur, and ouzo.
7. Grenadine, brown crème de cacao, Drambuie, and sweet cream flavored with crème de menthe.
8. Crème de noyaux, anisette, Tuaca, and a dab of whipped cream.
9. Grenadine, brown crème de cacao, triple sec, and Sciarada.
10. Brown crème de cacao, maraschino liqueur, Rosémint, yellow Chartreuse, and Cognac.
11. Parfait amour, cherry liqueur, anisette, and sweet cream flavored with a small amount of parfait amour.
12. Strawberry liqueur, cream, Cointreau, and Sciarada.

Apéritifs

AMERICANO

1¼ ozs. Campari
1¼ ozs. sweet
    vermouth
Lemon peel
Club soda (optional)

Stir Campari and sweet vermouth well with ice. Strain into a prechilled cocktail glass. Twist lemon peel above drink and drop into glass. If you prefer, a Delmonico or old-fashioned glass may be used instead—with a rock or two and a splash of soda.

APPLE BYRRH

1 oz. calvados
½ oz. Byrrh
½ oz. dry vermouth
½ teaspoon lemon
    juice
Lemon peel

Shake calvados, Byrrh, vermouth, and lemon juice well with ice. Strain into prechilled cocktail glass. Twist lemon peel above drink and drop into glass. Then pass the Gruyère and anchovy canapés.

BASTARDO

1 oz. dry vermouth
1 oz. sweet vermouth
½ oz. California
    brandy
Two dashes Angostura
    bitters
Iced club soda
1 slice lemon

Pour dry vermouth, sweet vermouth, brandy, and bitters over rocks in old-fashioned glass. Stir well. Add splash of soda. Add lemon slice.

BITTERSWEET

1¼ ozs. sweet
    vermouth
1¼ ozs. dry vermouth
2 dashes Angostura
    bitters
1 dash orange bitters
Orange peel

Stir both kinds of vermouth and both kinds of bitters well with ice. Strain into prechilled cocktail glass. Twist orange peel above drink and drop into glass. Salted shelled pistachios go well with this taste teaser.

BUTTERFLY

¾ oz. dry vermouth
¾ oz. sweet vermouth
½ oz. red Dubonnet
½ oz. orange juice

Shake everything well with ice. Strain over rocks into prechilled old-fashioned glass. This combination of orange juice and three fortified wines is extremely light.

BYRRH BRANDY

¾ oz. Byrrh
¾ oz. Cognac
¾ oz. dry vermouth

Combine and stir well with ice. Strain into prechilled cocktail glass.

BYRRH CASSIS

1½ ozs. Byrrh
¼ oz. crème de cassis
½ oz. lemon juice
1 slice lemon
Iced club soda
   (optional)

Shake Byrrh, crème de cassis, and lemon juice well with ice. Strain over rocks in pre-chilled old-fashioned glass. Add lemon slice —and a splash of soda if desired.

BYRRH COCKTAIL

1¼ ozs. Byrrh
1¼ ozs. gin
Lemon peel

Stir Byrrh and gin well with ice. Strain into prechilled cocktail glass or over rocks in prechilled old-fashioned glass. Twist lemon peel above drink and drop into glass.

CALIFORNIAN

1½ ozs. sweet
   vermouth
1 oz. blended U.S.
   whiskey
2 ozs. orange juice
1 teaspoon orgeat

Combine and shake well with ice. Strain over large ice cube in prechilled old-fashioned glass. Be sure the orange juice is freshly squeezed from ripe California navels or Valencias in midseason.

CANADIAN AND CAMPARI

1 oz. Canadian whisky
½ oz. Campari
1 oz. dry vermouth
Lemon peel

Stir whisky, Campari, and vermouth well with ice. Strain into prechilled cocktail glass. Twist lemon peel above drink and drop into glass. A perfect drink to sip while anticipating the antipasto.

CARDINAL I

¾ oz. gin
¾ oz. Campari
¾ oz. dry vermouth
Lemon peel

Stir gin, Campari, and vermouth well with ice. Strain into prechilled cocktail glass. Twist lemon peel above drink and drop into glass. (If you're wondering where and what Cardinal II is, you'll find it in Rum Cocktails, p. 271.)

COMBO

2½ ozs. dry vermouth
½ teaspoon curaçao
¼ teaspoon
  Angostura bitters
½ teaspoon sugar
1 teaspoon Cognac

Shake everything well with ice. Strain over rocks in prechilled old-fashioned glass. An elusive, but not illusive, glow is created by this combination of apéritif flavors.

CYNAR SOUR

1 oz. Cynar
1 oz. California
  brandy
2 ozs. orange juice
1 oz. lemon juice
½ slice orange

Shake Cynar, California brandy, orange juice, and lemon juice well with ice. Strain into old-fashioned glass. Garnish with orange slice.

DIABOLO

1½ ozs. imported dry
  white port
1 oz. dry vermouth
¼ teaspoon lemon
  juice
Lemon peel

Shake port, vermouth, and lemon juice well with ice. Strain into prechilled cocktail glass. Twist lemon peel above drink and drop into glass.

DUBONNET COCKTAIL

1¼ ozs. red Dubonnet
1¼ ozs. gin
Lemon peel

Stir Dubonnet and gin well with ice. Strain into prechilled cocktail glass. Twist lemon peel above drink and drop into glass.

FINO

1¼ ozs. fino sherry
1½ ozs. sweet
   vermouth
1 slice lemon

Stir sherry and vermouth well with ice. Strain over rocks in prechilled old-fashioned glass. Garnish with lemon slice.

FLORIDIAN

1½ ozs. dry vermouth
½ oz. Forbidden Fruit
1 teaspoon Falernum
2 ozs. grapefruit juice
2 dashes orange bitters
1 slice lime

Shake vermouth, Forbidden Fruit, Falernum, grapefruit juice, and bitters well with ice. Strain over large ice cube in prechilled old-fashioned glass. Garnish with lime slice.

GIN AND CAMPARI

1¼ ozs. gin
1¼ ozs. Campari
Orange peel

Stir gin and Campari well with ice. Strain over rocks in prechilled old-fashioned glass. Twist orange peel above drink and drop into glass. Savor it in sips.

LILLET COCKTAIL

1½ ozs. Lillet
1 oz. gin
Lemon peel

Stir Lillet and gin well with ice. Strain into prechilled cocktail glass. Twist lemon peel above drink and drop into glass.

LILLET NOYAUX

1½ ozs. Lillet
1 oz. gin
¼ teaspoon crème de
   noyaux
Orange peel

Stir Lillet, gin, and crème de noyaux well with ice. Strain into prechilled cocktail glass. Twist orange peel above drink and drop into glass. The scintillating flavor of Lillet is even more pleasant when this drink is poured on the rocks.

MANHATTAN MILANO

1 oz. kirschwasser
2 ozs. sweet vermouth
1 brandied cherry

Pour kirschwasser and vermouth into mixing glass with ice. Stir very well. Strain into prechilled large cocktail glass. Add cherry. Use regular maraschino cherry if brandied cherries are unavailable.

NEGRONI

¾ oz. Campari
¾ oz. gin
¾ oz. sweet vermouth

Stir well with ice. Strain into prechilled cocktail glass. Similar to the Cardinal I except that the vermouth is sweet instead of dry. May be served on the rocks with a twist of lemon or splash of soda or both.

PICON ON THE ROCKS

1½ ozs. Amer Picon
½ oz. lemon juice
Club soda
1 slice lemon

Pour Amer Picon and lemon juice over rocks in prechilled old-fashioned glass. Add a splash of soda. Stir. Garnish with lemon slice.

PICON PUNCH

1½ ozs. Amer Picon
¼ teaspoon grenadine
Iced club soda
1 tablespoon Cognac
Lemon peel

Pour Amer Picon, grenadine, and a splash of soda over rocks in a prechilled old-fashioned glass. Stir. Float Cognac on top of drink. Twist lemon peel above drink and drop into glass. Although Amer Picon is a sweet liqueur, Frenchmen for over a century have sipped it avidly before mealtime. There's just enough bitterness to balance the sweet.

PLUM APÉRITIF

1½ ozs. dry vermouth
½ oz. Cognac
¼ oz. prunelle
1 slice lemon

Stir vermouth, Cognac, and prunelle well with ice. Strain over rocks in prechilled old-fashioned glass. Add lemon slice. A small jar of fresh beluga caviar will make the *mise en scène* perfect.

PUNT E MES NEGRONI

¾ oz. Punt e Mes
¾ oz. gin
¾ oz. sweet vermouth

Stir well with ice. Strain into prechilled cocktail glass. May be served on the rocks with a twist of lemon or splash of soda or both. Punt e Mes is one of those Italian apéritifs that cause you first to shudder, then instantly to ask for more.

RUM APÉRITIF

1 oz. dry vermouth
1 oz. light rum
1 teaspoon dark
  Jamaican rum
1 teaspoon raspberry
  syrup
½ oz. lemon juice
Lemon peel

Shake vermouth, both kinds of rum, raspberry syrup, and lemon juice well with ice. Strain into prechilled cocktail glass. Twist lemon peel above drink and drop into glass. This apéritif could just as well be included among the rum cocktails. The effect in either case is the same: a ravenous appetite.

SANCTUARY

1 oz. red Dubonnet
½ oz. Amer Picon
½ oz. Cointreau
½ oz. lemon juice
1 slice lemon

Shake Dubonnet, Amer Picon, Cointreau, and lemon juice well with ice. Strain over rocks in prechilled old-fashioned glass. Add lemon slice. Pass hot hors d'oeuvres.

SILVER KIRSCH

1½ ozs. Positano
1 oz. kirschwasser
½ oz. lemon juice
½ egg white
1 teaspoon sugar
⅓ cup crushed ice

Mix all ingredients in blender for 10 seconds at high speed. Pour into prechilled old-fashioned glass.

SLOE VERMOUTH

1 oz. sloe gin (creamy
  cap)
1 oz. dry vermouth
½ oz. lemon juice

Shake well with ice. Strain into prechilled cocktail glass. A soft *divertissement* on a lazy afternoon.

SOUTHWEST ONE

¾ oz. vodka
¾ oz. orange juice
¾ oz. Campari bitters

Shake well with ice. Strain into prechilled glass. Named after the London district in which the popular drink originated.

TRIO

¾ oz. dry vermouth
¾ oz. sweet vermouth
¾ oz. gin

Stir well with ice. Strain into prechilled cocktail glass. A drink for rebels from the dry-martini crowd.

VERMOUTH CASSIS

2¼ ozs. dry vermouth
½ oz. crème de cassis
Iced club soda

Pour vermouth and crème de cassis over one or two rocks in a prechilled old-fashioned glass, a large wineglass, or an 8-oz. highball glass. Stir. Add soda, which Frenchmen use to stretch the drink into a long apéritif. Americans seem to prefer the drink less diluted. A *vin blanc* cassis is the same drink with dry white wine used instead of vermouth. A slice of lemon may be used as a garnish if desired.

VERMOUTH MARASCHINO

2 ozs. dry vermouth
½ oz. maraschino
   liqueur
½ oz. lemon juice
2 dashes orange bitters
1 maraschino cherry

Shake vermouth, maraschino liqueur, lemon juice, and bitters well with ice. Strain over large ice cube in prechilled old-fashioned glass. Garnish with cherry.

VERMOUTH SCIARADA

2½ ozs. chilled dry
   vermouth
½ oz. Sciarada
1 slice lemon

Pour vermouth and Sciarada over rocks in 8-oz. tall or squat glass. Stir well. Add lemon slice. May also be served in large stemmed wineglass.

VERMOUTH TRIPLE SEC

1 oz. dry vermouth
½ oz. triple sec
1 oz. gin
2 dashes orange bitters
Lemon peel

Shake vermouth, triple sec, gin, and bitters well with ice. Strain into prechilled cocktail glass. Twist lemon peel above drink and drop into glass.

ZAZA

2 ozs. red Dubonnet
1 oz. gin
1 slice orange

Stir Dubonnet and gin well with ice. Strain over rocks in prechilled old-fashioned glass. Place the orange slice on the rocks. Your nose should catch the aroma of the orange before your lips meet the drink. While there are many versions of this Dubonnet cocktail, these are the proportions we like best.

Apple-Brandy Cocktails

APPLE AND GINGER

1½ ozs. applejack
¾ oz. ginger-flavored brandy
½ oz. lemon juice
½ teaspoon sugar

Shake well with ice. Strain into prechilled cocktail glass. A cool alfresco drink.

APPLE BLOSSOM

1½ ozs. applejack
1 oz. apple juice
½ oz. lemon juice
1 teaspoon maple syrup
⅓ cup crushed ice
1 slice lemon

Put applejack, apple juice, lemon juice, maple syrup, and crushed ice into blender. Blend at low speed 10–15 seconds. Pour into prechilled deep-saucer champagne glass. Add lemon slice.

APPLE DUBONNET

1 oz. calvados
1 oz. red Dubonnet
1 slice lemon

Stir calvados and Dubonnet well with ice. Strain over rocks in prechilled old-fashioned glass. Add lemon slice.

APPLE GRAND MARNIER

1 oz. calvados
½ oz. Grand Marnier
½ oz. Cognac
Lemon peel
Orange peel

Stir calvados, Grand Marnier, and Cognac well with ice. Strain over rocks in prechilled old-fashioned glass. Twist lemon peel and orange peel above drink and drop into glass.

APPLE LILLET

1 oz. calvados
1 oz. Lillet
1 slice orange

Stir calvados and Lillet well with ice. Strain over rocks in prechilled old-fashioned glass. Add orange slice. A perfect drink to kill time while waiting for the hot onion soup.

APPLECAR

¾ oz. applejack
¾ oz. Cointreau or curaçao
¾ oz. lemon juice

Shake well with ice. Strain into prechilled cocktail glass. The appleman's sidecar.

APPLEHAWK

1¼ ozs. applejack
1¼ ozs. unsweetened grapefruit juice
½ teaspoon sugar

Shake well with ice. Strain into prechilled cocktail glass.

APPLEJACK MANHATTAN

1¾ ozs. applejack
¾ oz. sweet vermouth
1 dash orange bitters
1 maraschino cherry

Stir applejack, vermouth, and bitters well with ice. Strain into prechilled cocktail glass. Add cherry.

APPLEJACK RABBIT

1½ ozs. applejack
½ oz. lemon juice
½ oz. orange juice
1 teaspoon maple syrup

Shake well with ice. Strain into prechilled sugar-frosted cocktail glass. Salted nuts or toasted coconut chips are good companions.

APPLEJACK SOUR

2 ozs. applejack
½ oz. lemon juice
1 teaspoon sugar
½ slice lemon

Shake applejack, lemon juice, and sugar well with ice. Strain into prechilled whiskey-sour glass. Add lemon slice.

APPLE SUISSESSE

Grenadine
Superfine sugar
2 ozs. applejack
½ slightly beaten egg
   white
½ oz. heavy sweet
   cream
½ cup crushed ice

Dip rim of old-fashioned glass in grenadine, then in superfine sugar to make frosted rim. Place in freezer to chill. Pour applejack, 1 teaspoon sugar, egg white, cream, and crushed ice into blender. Blend at high speed 10 seconds. Pour into prechilled glass.

BITTER APPLE

2 ozs. applejack
2 dashes Angostura
   bitters
Iced club soda
Lemon peel

Pour applejack and bitters into prechilled old-fashioned glass. Add ice slices or cubes to fill glass. Add a splash of soda. Stir well. Twist lemon peel over drink and drop into glass. Aromatic, potent, and dry.

BLENHEIM

1 oz. applejack
½ oz. apricot-flavored
   brandy
¾ oz. lemon juice
1 teaspoon grenadine
1 dash orange bitters

Shake well with ice. Strain into prechilled sugar-frosted cocktail glass.

FROZEN APPLE

1½ ozs. applejack
½ oz. lime juice
½ egg white
1 teaspoon sugar
⅓ cup crushed ice

Put all ingredients into blender. Blend at low speed 10–15 seconds. Pour into prechilled deep-saucer champagne glass. A cocktail to pave the way for a roast suckling pig.

FROZEN APPLE AND BANANA

1½ ozs. applejack
½ oz. banana liqueur
½ oz. lime juice
⅓ cup crushed ice
1 slice banana

Put applejack, banana liqueur, lime juice, and ice into blender. Blend at low speed 10–15 seconds. Pour into prechilled deep-saucer champagne glass. Add banana slice.

FROZEN APPLECART

1½ ozs. applejack
¼ cup diced Delicious apple, peeled
⅓ cup crushed ice
½ oz. lemon juice
1 teaspoon sugar

Put all ingredients into blender. Blend at high speed 10 seconds. Pour into deep-saucer champagne glass or outsize cocktail glass.

JACK ROSE

2 ozs. applejack
½ oz. lime juice or lemon juice
1 teaspoon grenadine

Shake well with ice. Strain into prechilled cocktail glass. The classic applejack drink.

POLYNESIAN APPLE

1¼ ozs. applejack
¾ oz. pineapple juice
½ oz. California brandy
1 pineapple stick

Shake applejack, pineapple juice, and brandy well with ice. Strain over rocks in prechilled old-fashioned glass. Add pineapple stick. A standby cocktail when spareribs are slowly turning on the spit over charcoal.

PUERTO APPLE

1¼ ozs. applejack
¾ oz. light rum
½ oz. lime juice
1½ teaspoons orgeat
 or orzata
1 slice lime

Shake applejack, rum, lime juice, and orgeat well with ice. Strain over rocks in prechilled old-fashioned glass. Add lime slice.

RABBIT'S FOOT

¾ oz. applejack
¾ oz. light rum
½ oz. orange juice
½ oz. lemon juice
¼ oz. grenadine
1 slice orange

Shake applejack, rum, orange juice, lemon juice, and grenadine well with ice. Strain into prechilled old-fashioned glass. Add ice to fill glass. Garnish with orange slice.

Brandy Cocktails

ALABAMA

1¾ ozs. brandy
½ oz. lemon juice
1 teaspoon curaçao
½ teaspoon sugar
Orange peel

Shake brandy, lemon juice, curaçao, and sugar well with ice. Strain into prechilled sugar-frosted cocktail glass. Twist orange peel above drink and drop into glass.

APRICOT AND RASPBERRY SOUR

1 oz. apricot-flavored
  brandy or apricot
  liqueur
½ oz. framboise
  (white raspberry
  brandy)
½ oz. lemon juice
1 oz. orange juice
Iced club soda
½ slice orange
1 fresh raspberry or
  maraschino stem
  cherry

Shake apricot-flavored brandy, framboise, lemon juice, and orange juice well with ice. Strain into whiskey-sour glass. Add splash of soda. Stir. Garnish with orange slice and raspberry.

APRICOT SOUR

1½ ozs. apricot-
  flavored brandy or
  apricot liqueur
½ oz. lemon juice
1 oz. orange juice
Iced club soda
½ slice orange
1 maraschino stem
  cherry

Shake apricot-flavored brandy, lemon juice, and orange juice well with ice. Strain into whiskey-sour glass. Add splash of soda. Stir. Garnish with orange slice and cherry.

BAYOU

1¾ ozs. brandy
¼ oz. peach liqueur
½ oz. mango nectar
2 teaspoons lime juice
1 slice fresh or
  brandied peach

Shake brandy, peach liqueur, mango nectar, and lime juice well with ice. Strain over rocks in prechilled old-fashioned glass. Garnish with peach slice.

BOMBAY

1 oz. brandy
½ oz. dry vermouth
½ oz. sweet vermouth
½ teaspoon curaçao
¼ teaspoon Pernod
1 slice fresh or canned
  mango

Shake brandy, both kinds of vermouth, curaçao, and Pernod well with ice. Strain over rocks in prechilled old-fashioned glass. Add mango slice. Serve before a curry dinner.

BRANDIED APRICOT

1½ ozs. brandy
½ oz. apricot-flavored
  brandy
½ oz. lemon juice
Orange peel

Shake brandy, apricot-flavored brandy, and lemon juice well with ice. Strain into prechilled sugar-frosted cocktail glass. Twist orange peel above drink and drop into glass.

BRANDIED CORDIAL MÉDOC

1½ ozs. brandy
½ oz. Cordial Médoc
½ oz. lemon juice
Orange peel

Shake brandy, Cordial Médoc, and lemon juice well with ice. Strain into prechilled cocktail glass. Twist orange peel above drink and drop into glass. Either California brandy or Cognac may be used with good results.

BRANDIED GINGER

1½ ozs. brandy
½ oz. ginger-flavored
  brandy
1 teaspoon lime juice
1 teaspoon orange
  juice
1 piece preserved
  ginger in syrup

Shake brandy, ginger-flavored brandy, lime juice, and orange juice well with ice. Strain over rocks in prechilled old-fashioned glass. Garnish with preserved ginger.

BRANDTINI

1½ ozs. brandy
1 oz. gin
1 teaspoon dry
    vermouth
Lemon peel or cocktail
    olive

Stir brandy, gin, and vermouth well with ice. Strain into prechilled cocktail glass. Twist lemon peel above drink and drop into glass, or serve with cocktail olive.

BRANDY ALEXANDER

¾ oz. brandy
¾ oz. crème de cacao
¾ oz. heavy cream

Shake well with ice. Strain into prechilled cocktail glass.

BRANDY AND AMER PICON

2 ozs. Cognac
½ oz. Amer Picon
Lemon peel
Orange peel

Stir Cognac and Amer Picon well with ice. Strain over rocks in prechilled old-fashioned glass. Twist lemon peel and orange peel above drink and drop into glass.

BRANDY CASSIS

1¾ ozs. brandy
½ oz. lemon juice
2 teaspoons crème de
    cassis
Lemon peel

Shake brandy, lemon juice, and crème de cassis well with ice. Strain into prechilled cocktail glass. Twist lemon peel above drink and drop into glass.

BRANDY CRUSTA

Peel of ½ lemon, in
    one spiral
2 ozs. brandy
½ oz. curaçao
2 teaspoons lemon
    juice
1 dash bitters
1 teaspoon maraschino
    liqueur

Place lemon peel and cracked ice or rocks in prechilled sugar-frosted old-fashioned glass. Shake brandy, curaçao, lemon juice, bitters, and maraschino liqueur well with ice. Strain into glass.

BRANDY FINO

1½ ozs. brandy
½ oz. very dry sherry
½ oz. Drambuie
½ slice orange
Lemon peel

Shake brandy, sherry, and Drambuie well with ice. Strain over rocks in prechilled old-fashioned glass. Add orange slice. Twist lemon peel above drink and drop into glass.

BRANDY GUMP

2 ozs. brandy
½ oz. lemon juice
½ teaspoon grenadine

Shake well with ice. Strain into prechilled cocktail glass. A good one to relax with after an all-day sail.

BRANDY MANHATTAN

2 ozs. brandy
½ oz. sweet vermouth
1 dash bitters
  (optional)
1 maraschino cherry

Stir brandy, vermouth, and bitters well with ice. Strain into prechilled cocktail glass. Add cherry. For a dry brandy manhattan, use dry instead of sweet vermouth.

BRANDY MELBA

1½ ozs. brandy
¼ oz. peach liqueur
¼ oz. raspberry
  liqueur
½ oz. lemon juice
2 dashes orange bitters
1 slice fresh or
  brandied peach

Shake brandy, peach liqueur, raspberry liqueur, lemon juice, and bitters well with ice. Strain into prechilled cocktail glass. Add peach slice. If raspberry liqueur isn't available, raspberry syrup may be substituted.

BRANDY SOUR

2 ozs. brandy
½ oz. lemon juice
¼ oz. orange juice
½ to 1 teaspoon sugar
½ slice lemon

Shake brandy, lemon juice, orange juice, and sugar well with ice. Strain into prechilled whiskey-sour glass. Add lemon slice. Softer than a whiskey sour.

CHAMPS-ELYSÉES

1½ ozs. Cognac
½ oz. yellow Char-
treuse
½ oz. lemon juice
1 dash Angostura
bitters (optional)

Shake well with ice. Strain over rocks in prechilled old-fashioned glass. Bitters may be omitted for a more pronounced Chartreuse flavor.

CHERRY BLOSSOM

1¼ ozs. brandy
¾ oz. wild-cherry
liqueur
2 teaspoons lemon
juice
¼ teaspoon curaçao
¼ teaspoon grenadine

Shake well with ice. Strain into prechilled sugar-frosted cocktail glass. Dip rim of glass into wild-cherry liqueur before dipping into sugar.

CLASSIC

1½ ozs. brandy
½ oz. lemon juice
¼ oz. maraschino
liqueur
¼ oz. curaçao

Shake well with ice. Strain into prechilled cocktail glass. More tart than earlier versions of the brandy classic.

DAME MELBA

¾ oz. peach-flavored
brandy
¾ oz. framboise
(unsweetened
raspberry brandy)
½ oz. lemon juice

Shake very well with ice. Strain into sugar-frosted cocktail glass.

DEAUVILLE

1 oz. brandy
½ oz. lemon juice
½ oz. apple brandy
½ oz. triple sec

Shake well with ice. Strain into prechilled cocktail glass.

DRY COLD DECK

1¾ ozs. brandy
½ oz. dry vermouth
¼ oz. white crème de
menthe

Shake well with ice. Strain into prechilled cocktail glass. A sophisticated stinger.

FEMINA

1½ ozs. brandy
½ oz. Benedictine
½ oz. orange juice
1 slice cocktail orange
in syrup

Shake brandy, Benedictine, and orange juice well with ice. Strain over rocks in prechilled old-fashioned glass. Add orange slice. Not biting in the "sour" tradition, but cool and comforting.

FOXHOUND

1½ ozs. brandy
½ oz. cranberry juice
1 teaspoon kümmel
1 teaspoon lemon juice
½ slice lemon

Shake brandy, cranberry juice, kümmel, and lemon juice well with ice. Strain over rocks in prechilled old-fashioned glass. Add lemon slice. Serve before a dinner of pheasant or partridge.

FRAMBOISE SOUR

1 oz. framboise
¾ oz. lime juice
2 level teaspoons sugar
1 wedge prepared
cocktail orange in
syrup
1 fresh raspberry
if available

Pour framboise, lime juice, and sugar into cocktail shaker with ice. Shake about double the usual time for proper dilution. Pour into prechilled whiskey-sour glass. Garnish with cocktail orange and raspberry.

FROUPE

1¼ ozs. brandy
1¼ ozs. sweet
vermouth
1 teaspoon
Benedictine

Stir well with ice. Strain into prechilled cocktail glass. Like a sunset's afterglow.

FROZEN BRANDY AND PORT

1½ ozs. brandy
1 oz. port
1 small egg
1 teaspoon powdered
   sugar
⅓ cup crushed ice
Grated nutmeg

Put brandy, port, egg, sugar, and ice into blender. Blend 20 seconds at low speed. Pour into prechilled saucer champagne glass. Sprinkle with nutmeg. Also known as coffee flip when crushed ice is omitted and drink is shaken with ice in regular cocktail shaker.

FROZEN BRANDY AND RUM

1½ ozs. brandy
1 oz. golden rum
½ oz. lemon juice
1 egg yolk
1½ teaspoons sugar
⅓ cup crushed ice

Put all ingredients into blender. Blend 15–20 seconds at low speed. Pour into prechilled saucer champagne glass. Soothing.

HARVARD

1½ ozs. brandy
½ oz. dry vermouth
1 teaspoon grenadine
2 teaspoons lemon
   juice

Shake well with ice. Strain into prechilled cocktail glass. Drier than earlier versions, but still crimson.

HILLSBOROUGH

1 oz. California brandy
1 oz. Muscari
½ oz. lemon juice
Lemon peel

Shake brandy, Muscari, and lemon juice well with ice. Strain into cocktail glass. Twist lemon peel above drink and drop into glass.

JAPANESE

2 ozs. brandy
¼ oz. orgeat or orzata
¼ oz. lime juice
1 dash Angostura
   bitters
Lime peel

Shake brandy, orgeat, lime juice, and bitters well with ice. Strain into prechilled cocktail glass. Twist lime peel above drink and drop into glass.

LA JOLLA

1½ ozs. brandy
½ oz. banana liqueur
2 teaspoons lemon
   juice
1 teaspoon orange
   juice

Shake well with ice. Strain into prechilled sugar-frosted cocktail glass.

McBRANDY

1½ ozs. brandy
1 oz. apple juice
1 teaspoon lemon juice
1 slice lemon

Shake brandy, apple juice, and lemon juice well with ice. Strain into prechilled cocktail glass. Add lemon slice. Serve before a dinner of roast ham or duck.

PHOEBE SNOW

1¼ ozs. brandy
1¼ ozs. red Dubonnet
¼ teaspoon Pernod

Shake well with ice. Strain into prechilled cocktail glass.

PICASSO

1½ ozs. Cognac
½ oz. red Dubonnet
½ oz. lime juice
1 teaspoon sugar
Orange peel

Shake Cognac, Dubonnet, lime juice, and sugar well with ice. Strain into prechilled cocktail glass. Twist orange peel above drink and drop into glass.

POLONAISE

1½ ozs. brandy
½ oz. blackberry
   liqueur or
   blackberry-flavored
   brandy
½ oz. very dry sherry
1 teaspoon lemon juice
2 dashes orange bitters

Shake well with ice. Strain over rocks in prechilled old-fashioned glass.

QUAKER

1½ ozs. brandy
½ oz. rum
½ oz. lemon juice
1 teaspoon raspberry
　　syrup or grenadine
Lemon peel

Shake brandy, rum, lemon juice, and raspberry syrup well with ice. Strain into prechilled cocktail glass. Twist lemon peel above drink and drop into glass. Two rounds of these and all will be Friends.

SANTA FE

1½ ozs. brandy
½ oz. grapefruit juice
½ oz. dry vermouth
1 teaspoon lemon juice

Shake all ingredients well with ice. Strain into prechilled sugar-rimmed cocktail glass.

SARATOGA

2 ozs. brandy
½ oz. pineapple juice
1 teaspoon lemon juice
½ teaspoon
　　maraschino liqueur
1 dash Angostura
　　bitters

Shake well with ice. Strain into prechilled cocktail glass.

SIDECAR

¾ oz. brandy
¾ oz. Cointreau,
　　curaçao, or triple
　　sec
¾ oz. lemon juice

Shake well with ice. Strain into prechilled cocktail glass. All three ingredients may be varied to suit one's taste. For a strong brandy accent, use 1½ ozs. brandy, ½ oz. Cointreau, and ½ oz. lemon juice. One of the most venerable of traditional cocktails.

SLOE BRANDY

2 ozs. brandy
½ oz. sloe gin (creamy
　　cap)
1 teaspoon lemon juice
Lemon peel

Shake brandy, sloe gin, and lemon juice well with ice. Strain into prechilled cocktail glass. Twist lemon peel above drink and drop into glass.

SOUTH PACIFIC

1½ ozs. brandy
½ oz. lemon juice
¼ oz. crème d'ananas
¼ oz. white crème de menthe
1 pineapple stick

Shake brandy, lemon juice, crème d'ananas (pineapple liqueur), and crème de menthe well with ice. Strain over rocks in prechilled old-fashioned glass. Garnish with pineapple stick.

STINGER

1¼ ozs. brandy
1¼ ozs. white crème de menthe

Shake well with ice. Strain into prechilled cocktail glass. For a dry stinger, increase brandy to 2 ozs. and reduce crème de menthe to ½ oz. May be offered before or after dinner. It is frequently served with a glass of ice water on the side.

THUMPER

1¾ ozs. brandy
¾ oz. Tuaca liqueur
Lemon peel

Stir brandy and Tuaca well with ice. Strain into prechilled old-fashioned glass. Add ice cubes or ice slices to fill glass. Stir well. Twist lemon peel above drink and drop into glass. One of Italy's oldest liqueurs shines in this drink.

VIA VENETO

1¾ ozs. brandy
½ oz. sambuca
½ egg white
2 teaspoons lemon juice
1 teaspoon sugar

Shake well with ice. Strain over rocks in prechilled old-fashioned glass. An engaging patio drink that's a little on the sweet side.

WATERBURY

1½ ozs. brandy
½ oz. lime juice
½ egg white
½ teaspoon grenadine
½ teaspoon powdered sugar

Shake well with ice. Strain into prechilled sugar-frosted cocktail glass.

Champagne Cocktails

AMERICANA

1 teaspoon 100-proof
   bourbon
½ teaspoon sugar
1 dash bitters
4 ozs. iced brut
   champagne
1 slice fresh or
   brandied peach

Stir bourbon, sugar, and bitters in pre-chilled champagne glass. Add champagne and peach slice.

CARIBBEAN CHAMPAGNE

½ teaspoon light rum
½ teaspoon banana
   liqueur
1 dash orange bitters
4 ozs. iced brut
   champagne
1 slice banana

Pour rum, banana liqueur, and bitters into prechilled champagne glass. Add champagne. Stir very gently. Add banana slice.

CHAMPAGNE FRAISE

½ teaspoon
   strawberry liqueur
½ teaspoon
   kirschwasser
4 ozs. iced brut
   champagne
1 large fresh
   strawberry

Pour strawberry liqueur and kirsch into prechilled champagne glass. Tilt glass so that liqueurs coat bottom and sides of glass. Add champagne. Float strawberry on drink. (Measure ½ teaspoons precisely—don't overpour.)

CHAMPAGNE MANHATTAN

1 oz. Canadian whisky
¼ oz. sweet vermouth
1 dash bitters
3 ozs. iced brut
champagne
1 brandied cherry

Stir whisky, vermouth, and bitters well with ice. Strain into prechilled champagne glass. Add champagne and brandied cherry.

CHAMPAGNE NORMANDE

1 teaspoon calvados
½ teaspoon sugar
1 dash Angostura
bitters
4 ozs. iced brut
champagne

Stir calvados, sugar, and bitters in prechilled champagne glass. Add champagne. Stir very gently.

CHAMPAGNE NOYAUX

½ oz. crème de noyaux
1 teaspoon lime juice
1 large toasted almond
4 ozs. iced brut
champagne
1 slice lime

Stir crème de noyaux and lime juice in prechilled champagne glass. Add almond. Pour champagne into glass. Stir slightly. Float lime slice on top.

CHAMPAGNE OLD-FASHIONED

½ oz. Grand Marnier
½ oz. Forbidden Fruit
1 dash orange bitters
4 ozs. iced brut
champagne
1 slice lemon

Into prechilled old-fashioned glass, pour liqueurs and bitters. Add champagne. Stir very gently. Launch with lemon slice.

CHAMPAGNE POLONAISE

1 teaspoon blackberry
liqueur
½ teaspoon Cognac
4 ozs. iced brut
champagne

Pour blackberry liqueur and Cognac into prechilled sugar-frosted champagne glass. Add champagne. Stir very gently.

CHARTREUSE CHAMPAGNE

½ teaspoon green
  Chartreuse
½ teaspoon Cognac
4 ozs. iced brut
  champagne
Lemon peel

Pour Chartreuse, Cognac, and champagne into prechilled champagne glass. Stir very gently. Twist lemon peel above drink and drop into glass. Toast the Carthusian order.

CHERRY CHAMPAGNE

½ oz. iced Peter
  Heering
4 ozs. iced brut
  champagne
½ pitted fresh cherry

Pour Peter Heering into stem of prechilled hollow-stemmed champagne glass. Add champagne. Float cherry on drink.

CLASSIC CHAMPAGNE COCKTAIL

½ teaspoon sugar
1 dash Angostura
  bitters
4 ozs. iced brut
  champagne
Lemon peel

Stir sugar and bitters in prechilled champagne glass. Add champagne. Usually, the sparkle of the champagne will blend the ingredients, and little if any stirring is necessary. Twist lemon peel above drink and drop into glass.

MELBA CHAMPAGNE

½ oz. Himbeergeist
  (raspberry brandy,
  not liqueur)
4 ozs. iced brut
  champagne
1 fresh or thawed
  frozen raspberry
Raspberry sherbet,
  hard-frozen

Pour Himbeergeist into prechilled champagne glass. Add champagne and the raspberry. With a fruit-baller, scoop out a single small ball of sherbet. Float on champagne.

ORANGE CHAMPAGNE

Peel of ½ orange, in
    one spiral
2 teaspoons curaçao
4 ozs. iced brut
    champagne

Place orange peel in prechilled champagne glass. Add curaçao and champagne. Stir very gently.

SPARKLING GALLIANO

½ oz. Galliano
½ teaspoon lemon
    juice
4 ozs. iced brut
    champagne
Cucumber peel, 1½
    inches long, ½ inch
    wide

Pour Galliano and lemon juice into prechilled champagne glass. Stir. Add champagne and cucumber peel. Drink to the stars.

Gin Cocktails

ALEXANDER WITH COFFEE

¾ oz. gin
¾ oz. coffee liqueur
¾ oz. heavy cream

Shake well with ice. Strain into prechilled sugar-frosted cocktail glass. Moisten rim of glass with coffee liqueur before dipping into sugar. Especially good with espresso-coffee liqueur. Like all alexanders, which are really sweet cocktails, this one is both a pre- and postprandial drink.

ALEXANDER WITH GIN

¾ oz. gin
¾ oz. crème de cacao
¾ oz. heavy cream

Shake well with ice. Strain into prechilled cocktail glass. (An Alexander made with a brandy base instead of gin will be found among brandy cocktails.)

ALEXANDER WITH PRUNELLE

¾ oz. gin
¾ oz. prunelle
¾ oz. cream
Ground cinnamon

Shake gin, prunelle, and cream well with ice. Strain into prechilled cocktail glass. Sprinkle lightly with cinnamon.

ALEXANDER'S SISTER

¾ oz. gin
¾ oz. white or green
  crème de menthe
¾ oz. heavy cream

Shake well with ice. Strain into prechilled cocktail glass.

BENNETT

1½ ozs. gin
½ oz. lime juice
1 teaspoon sugar
2 dashes Angostura
  bitters
Lime peel

Shake gin, lime juice, sugar, and bitters well with ice. Strain into prechilled cocktail glass. Twist lime peel above drink and drop into glass.

BERLINER

1½ ozs. gin
¼ oz. dry kümmel
½ oz. dry vermouth
¼ oz. lemon juice

Shake well with ice. Strain into prechilled cocktail glass. Best appreciated with freshly made, well-buttered smoked-salmon canapés.

BISCAYNE

1 oz. gin
½ oz. light rum
½ oz. Forbidden Fruit
½ oz. lime juice
1 slice lime

Shake gin, rum, Forbidden Fruit, and lime juice well with ice. Strain over rocks in prechilled old-fashioned glass. Add lime slice.

BISHOP'S COCKTAIL

1 oz. gin
1 oz. Stone's ginger
  wine
1 slice lemon

Stir gin and ginger wine well with ice. Strain over rocks in old-fashioned glass. Add lemon slice.

BLUE DEVIL

1½ ozs. gin
½ oz. blue curaçao
½ oz. lemon juice
1 slice lemon

Shake gin, curaçao, and lemon juice well with ice. Strain into prechilled cocktail glass garnished with lemon slice. A gentle blues chaser.

BONNIE PRINCE

1¼ ozs. gin
½ oz. Lillet
¼ oz. Drambuie

Shake well with ice. Strain into prechilled cocktail glass. Inspired by gin drinkers with both French and Scottish blood in their veins.

BRITTANY

1½ ozs. gin
½ oz. Amer Picon
¼ oz. orange juice
¼ oz. lemon juice
Orange peel

Shake gin, Amer Picon, orange juice, and lemon juice well with ice. Strain into prechilled cocktail glass. Twist orange peel above drink and drop into glass.

BRONX

1½ ozs. gin
½ oz. orange juice
¼ oz. dry vermouth
¼ oz. sweet vermouth

Shake well with ice. Strain into prechilled cocktail glass. For a drier bronx, omit sweet vermouth and increase gin to 1¾ ozs. One of the few inventions of the Prohibition era really worth retaining when made with fine gin rather than the notorious bathtub variety.

CHATHAM

1¼ ozs. gin
½ oz. ginger-flavored brandy
¼ oz. lemon juice
1 small piece preserved ginger in syrup

Shake gin, ginger-flavored brandy, and lemon juice well with ice. Strain into prechilled cocktail glass. Garnish with preserved ginger.

CHERRY SLING

1½ ozs. gin
½ oz. cherry liqueur
½ oz. lime juice

Shake well with ice. Strain into prechilled cocktail glass. Use a tart cherry liqueur such as Peter Heering or Cherry Karise for best results.

CLOISTER

1½ ozs. gin
½ oz. grapefruit juice
¼ oz. lemon juice
¼ oz. yellow
   Chartreuse

Shake well with ice. Strain into prechilled cocktail glass. A contemplative kind of drink, perfect for an autumn sundown.

CLOVER CLUB

1½ ozs. gin
¾ oz. lemon juice
1 teaspoon grenadine
   or raspberry syrup
½ egg white

Shake well with ice. Strain into prechilled cocktail glass.

CLOVER CLUB ROYAL

1½ ozs. gin
¾ oz. lemon juice
1 teaspoon grenadine
   or raspberry syrup
½ egg yolk

Shake well with ice. Strain into prechilled cocktail glass. A trifle richer than the clover club, above, this velvety cocktail is even smoother when made with ⅓ cup crushed ice in a blender and poured over the rocks in an old-fashioned glass.

COCONUT GIN

1½ ozs. gin
½ oz. lemon juice
¼ oz. maraschino
   liqueur
¼ oz. cream of
   coconut

Cream of coconut, from the can, should be well mixed before using. Shake all ingredients well with ice. Strain into prechilled sugar-frosted cocktail glass. Sets up a beautiful indoor tropical breeze.

COLD GIN TODDY

2 ozs. gin
½ teaspoon sugar
Lemon peel

Shake gin and sugar well with plenty of ice and strain into old-fashioned glass filled with large cubes or slices of ice. Twist lemon peel above drink and drop into glass.

COPENHAGEN

1 oz. gin
1 oz. aquavit
¼ oz. dry vermouth
1 large stuffed olive

Stir gin, aquavit, and vermouth well with ice. Strain into prechilled cocktail glass. Add olive.

CORDIAL MÉDOC

1 oz. gin
½ oz. Cordial Médoc
½ oz. dry vermouth
¼ oz. lemon juice

Shake well with ice. Strain into prechilled cocktail glass. For a bon-voyage cocktail party before flying to Paris.

CORDIAL MÉDOC SOUR

1½ ozs. gin
½ oz. Cordial Médoc
½ oz. lemon juice
½ slice orange

Shake gin, Cordial Médoc, and lemon juice well with ice. Strain into prechilled whiskey-sour glass. Garnish with orange slice.

DUNDEE

1 oz. gin
½ oz. Scotch
½ oz. Drambuie
¼ oz. lemon juice
Lemon peel

Shake gin, Scotch, Drambuie, and lemon juice well with ice. Pour over rocks in prechilled old-fashioned glass. Twist lemon peel above drink and drop into glass.

FOGGY DAY

1½ ozs. gin
¼ oz. Pernod
1 slice lemon
Lemon peel

Shake gin and Pernod well with ice. Strain over rocks in prechilled old-fashioned glass. Rub outside of lemon peel around rim of glass and drop peel into glass. Add lemon slice.

GENOA

¾ oz. gin
¾ oz. grappa
½ oz. sambuca
½ oz. dry vermouth
1 cocktail olive

Stir gin, grappa, sambuca, and vermouth well with ice. Strain into prechilled cocktail glass. Add olive.

GIMLET

2 ozs. gin
½ oz. Rose's lime juice

Stir extremely well with ice. Strain into prechilled cocktail glass. Long stirring is absolutely essential to present this English classic in its best light. The above formula, 4-to-1, may be made 5-to-1, if desired, by adding ½ oz. gin. Glass may be sugar-frosted by moistening rim with Rose's lime juice before dipping into sugar.

GIN AND LIME

1½ ozs. gin
½ oz. fresh lime juice
½ oz. orange juice
1 teaspoon Rose's lime
   juice
Lime peel

Shake gin, fresh lime juice, orange juice, and Rose's lime juice well with ice. Strain into prechilled cocktail glass. Twist lime peel above drink and drop into glass. A superb cocktail to sip with English potted shrimp or anchovy-paste canapés.

GIN AQUAVIT

1½ ozs. gin
½ oz. aquavit
½ oz. lemon juice
1 teaspoon sugar
½ egg white
1 teaspoon heavy
   cream

Shake well with ice. Strain into prechilled old-fashioned glass containing two or three ice cubes. A light, foamy drink to serve before passing a platter of Danish open sandwiches.

GIN CASSIS

1½ ozs. gin
½ oz. lemon juice
½ oz. crème de cassis

Shake well with ice. Strain into prechilled cocktail glass, or into prechilled old-fashioned glass with one or two rocks.

GIN DAIQUIRI

1½ ozs. gin
½ oz. light rum
½ oz. lime juice
1 teaspoon sugar

Shake well with ice. Strain into prechilled sugar-frosted cocktail glass.

GIN OLD-FASHIONED

¼ teaspoon sugar
1 or 2 dashes
  Angostura bitters
1¾ ozs. gin
Lemon peel

Put sugar and bitters into prechilled old-fashioned glass. Stir until sugar dissolves, adding a teaspoon of water if necessary to complete the process. Add gin and two or three ice cubes or large pieces of coarsely cracked ice. Stir well. Twist lemon peel above drink and drop into glass. Old-fashioneds are frequently garnished with orange slice, lemon slice, pineapple, cherry, etc., but knowledgeable old-fashioned men shun the fruit salad.

GIN SIDECAR

¾ oz. high-proof
  English gin
¾ oz. triple sec
¾ oz. lemon juice

Shake well with ice. Strain into prechilled cocktail glass. The gin substitutes for brandy in this version of the sidecar.

GIN SOUR

1½ ozs. gin
½ oz. lemon juice
¼ oz. orange juice
1 teaspoon sugar
½ slice orange
1 maraschino cherry

Shake gin, lemon juice, orange juice, and sugar well with ice. Strain into prechilled whiskey-sour glass. Garnish with orange slice and cherry.

GIN SOUTHERN

1½ ozs. gin
½ oz. Southern
  Comfort
¼ oz. grapefruit juice
¼ oz. lemon juice

Shake well with ice. Strain into prechilled cocktail glass. For drinking men who appreciate verandas and magnolia blossoms.

GOLDEN HORNET

1½ ozs. gin
½ oz. amontillado
  sherry
½ oz. Scotch
Lemon peel

Stir gin and sherry well with ice. Strain over two rocks in prechilled old-fashioned glass. Float Scotch on top. Twist lemon peel over drink and drop into glass.

GRANVILLE

1½ ozs. gin
¼ oz. Grand Marnier
¼ oz. calvados
¼ oz. lemon juice

Shake well with ice. Strain into prechilled cocktail glass.

GREEN DEVIL

1½ ozs. gin
½ oz. lime juice
¼ oz. green crème de
  menthe
2 sprigs mint

Shake gin, lime juice, and crème de menthe well with ice. Strain over two or three rocks in prechilled old-fashioned glass. Tear several mint leaves to release aroma before adding to drink as garnish.

HUDSON BAY

1 oz. gin
½ oz. cherry liqueur
½ oz. orange juice
¼ oz. lime juice
¼ oz. 151-proof rum
1 slice lime

Shake gin, cherry liqueur, orange juice, lime juice, and rum well with ice. Strain into prechilled cocktail glass. Add lime slice. A winter or summer cocktail with prodigious thawing powers.

JAMAICA GLOW

1½ ozs. gin
½ oz. dry red wine
½ oz. orange juice
1 teaspoon dark
  Jamaica rum
1 slice lime

Shake gin, wine, orange juice, and rum well with ice. Strain into prechilled sugar-frosted cocktail glass. Add lime slice. This relic of plantation days is still a magnificent reviver for surf riders and scuba divers.

JOULOUVILLE

1 oz. gin
½ oz. apple brandy
½ oz. lemon juice
¼ oz. sweet vermouth
¼ teaspoon grenadine

Shake well with ice. Strain into prechilled cocktail glass.

KEY COCKTAIL

1½ ozs. gin
½ oz. lime juice
¼ oz. dark Jamaica rum
¼ oz. Falernum
1 pineapple stick

Shake gin, lime juice, rum, and Falernum well with ice. Strain into prechilled cocktail glass. Garnish with pineapple stick.

MARTINI

(See p. 263 for a separate discussion of this immensely popular cocktail and its many variations.)

MATINÉE

1 oz. gin
½ oz. sambuca
½ egg white
1 teaspoon heavy cream
½ oz. lime juice

Shake all ingredients well with ice. Strain into prechilled cocktail glass. A comfortable midafternoon cocktail. May also be served as a pick-me-up the morning after with a spray of freshly ground nutmeg.

MINTED GIN

1½ ozs. gin
½ oz. lemon juice
1 teaspoon sugar
2 sprigs fresh mint
1 slice lemon
½ slice orange

Shake gin, lemon juice, and sugar well with ice. Strain into prechilled old-fashioned glass with rocks. Garnish drink with lemon and orange slices. Tear mint leaves before placing on rocks. A perfect drink for unwinding after eighteen holes on the fairway.

MOLDAU

1½ ozs. gin
½ oz. plum brandy
¼ oz. orange juice
¼ oz. lemon juice
1 brandied cherry

Shake gin, plum brandy, orange juice, and lemon juice well with ice. Strain into prechilled old-fashioned glass with two or three ice cubes. Garnish with brandied cherry.

MORRO

1 oz. gin
½ oz. golden rum
½ oz. lime juice
½ oz. pineapple juice
1 teaspoon sugar

Shake well with ice. Strain into prechilled sugar-frosted glass. Moisten rim of glass with Falernum before dipping into sugar. Once tasted, the marriage of gin and rum is one of those unions that no man in his right drinking sense would dream of putting asunder. Fruit juices in this drink help fortify the nuptials.

ORANGE BLOSSOM

1½ ozs. gin
1 oz. orange juice
½ slice orange

Shake gin and orange juice well with ice. Strain into prechilled sugar-frosted cocktail glass. Glass may be sugar-frosted by moistening rim with orange peel before dipping into sugar. Add orange slice.

ORANGE BLOSSOM FROZEN

1½ ozs. gin
2 ozs. orange juice
½ oz. curaçao
½ oz. lemon juice
2 drops orange-flower water
¼ cup cracked ice
½ slice orange

Put gin, orange juice, curaçao, lemon juice, orange-flower water, and ice into blender. Spin 5–8 seconds. Pour into deep-saucer champagne or old-fashioned glass. Place orange slice on top.

PINK GIN

2 ozs. gin
2 dashes Angostura
bitters

In Britain, the custom is simply to stir these ingredients at room temperature in a small cocktail glass. For American tastes, it's more pleasant if the gin and bitters are well stirred with ice and then poured into a prechilled glass. This is one of the drinks that sustained Sir Francis Chichester so beautifully on his long, lonely trip round the world.

PINK LADY

1½ ozs. gin
¼ oz. lime juice
1 teaspoon heavy
cream
1 teaspoon grenadine
½ egg white

Shake well with ice. Strain into prechilled cocktail glass. Glass may be sugar-frosted by moistening rim with grenadine before dipping into sugar.

PIROUETTER

1 oz. gin
½ oz. Grand Marnier
1 oz. orange juice
1 teaspoon lemon juice
Orange peel

Shake gin, Grand Marnier, orange juice, and lemon juice well with ice. Strain into prechilled cocktail glass. Twist orange peel above drink and drop into glass.

POLISH SIDECAR

¾ oz. gin
¾ oz. Polish or Polish-
style blackberry
liqueur
¾ oz. lemon juice

Shake well with ice. Strain into prechilled cocktail glass. A large fresh blackberry, if available, is a pleasant garnish for this drink.

POMPANO

1 oz. gin
½ oz. dry vermouth
1 oz. grapefruit juice
4 dashes orange bitters
1 slice orange

Shake gin, vermouth, grapefruit juice, and bitters well with ice. Strain over rocks in prechilled old-fashioned glass. Garnish with orange slice. A perfect cocktail for Florida- or Caribbean-bound vacationers.

PRINCETON

1¼ ozs. gin
¾ oz. dry vermouth
½ oz. lime juice

Shake well with ice. Strain into prechilled cocktail glass. Like the bronx (page 251), it's one of very few drinks born in Prohibition days really worth retaining. Named for the great seat of learning which, during the Noble Experiment, distinguished itself even more for its prowess in soaking up bathtub gin.

RED CLOUD

1½ ozs. gin
½ oz. apricot liqueur
½ oz. lemon juice
1 teaspoon grenadine
1 dash bitters

Shake well with ice. Strain into prechilled cocktail glass.

RENAISSANCE

1½ ozs. gin
½ oz. dry sherry
½ oz. heavy cream
Freshly grated nutmeg

Shake gin, sherry, and cream well with ice. Strain into prechilled cocktail glass. Spray with nutmeg. A drink to savor after a lengthy tour of art galleries.

RENDEZVOUS

1½ ozs. gin
½ oz. kirschwasser
¼ oz. Campari
Lemon peel

Shake gin, kirschwasser, and Campari well with ice. Strain into prechilled cocktail glass. Twist lemon peel above drink and drop into glass. An appetite arouser best sipped while a double-thick filet is browning over the charcoals.

ROCKY DANE

1 oz. gin
½ oz. dry vermouth
½ oz. Peter Heering
¼ oz. kirsch
Lemon peel

Shake gin, vermouth, Peter Heering, and kirsch well with ice. Strain over rocks in prechilled old-fashioned glass. Twist lemon peel above drink and drop into glass.

ROSE

1 oz. gin
½ oz. apricot-flavored
   brandy
½ oz. dry vermouth
½ oz. lemon juice
1 teaspoon grenadine
Lemon peel

Shake gin, apricot-flavored brandy, vermouth, lemon juice, and grenadine well with ice. Strain into prechilled cocktail glass. Twist lemon peel above drink and drop into glass.

ST.-LÔ

1½ ozs. gin
½ oz. calvados
½ oz. lemon juice
1 teaspoon sugar

Shake well with ice. Strain into prechilled cocktail glass.

SAN SEBASTIAN

1 oz. gin
¼ oz. rum
½ oz. grapefruit juice
¼ oz. curaçao
½ oz. lemon juice

Shake well with ice. Strain into prechilled cocktail glass. Recommended for galley bartenders after a lazy Sunday-afternoon sail.

SEVILLE

1 oz. gin
½ oz. fino sherry
½ oz. orange juice
½ oz. lemon juice
½ teaspoon sugar

Shake well with ice. Strain into prechilled sugar-rimmed glass.

SOUTH SIDE

2 ozs. gin
½ oz. lemon juice
1 teaspoon sugar
2 sprigs fresh mint

Shake gin, lemon juice, and sugar well with ice. Strain into prechilled cocktail glass. Tear several leaves of each mint sprig before adding to drink. Although not as well known as the mint julep, the south side is a delightful summery cocktail with a delicate mint accent.

STRAWBERRY SWIG

1½ ozs. gin
½ oz. strawberry
   liqueur
¼ oz. lime juice
1 dash orange bitters
1 slice lime

Shake gin, strawberry liqueur, lime juice, and bitters well with ice. Strain into prechilled old-fashioned glass with several rocks. Garnish with lime slice.

STREGA SOUR

1½ ozs. gin
½ oz. lemon juice
½ oz. Strega
1 slice lemon

Shake gin, lemon juice, and Strega well with ice. Strain into prechilled sugar-frosted cocktail glass. Moisten rim of glass with Strega before dipping into sugar. Garnish with lemon slice.

TURF

1 oz. gin
1 oz. dry vermouth
¼ oz. Pernod
¼ oz. lemon juice
1 slice lemon

Shake gin, vermouth, Pernod, and lemon juice well with ice. Strain over rocks in prechilled old-fashioned glass. Add lemon slice.

VERBOTEN

1 oz. gin
½ oz. Forbidden Fruit
½ oz. lemon juice
½ oz. orange juice
1 brandied cherry

Shake gin, Forbidden Fruit, lemon juice, and orange juice well with ice. Strain into prechilled cocktail glass. Garnish with brandied cherry.

WHITE ROSE

1¼ ozs. gin
½ oz. orange juice
½ oz. lime juice
1 teaspoon sugar
½ egg white

Shake well with ice. Strain into prechilled cocktail glass. There are dozens of different recipes bearing the name white rose. This balmy concoction is designed for sipping in the vicinity of a glowing fireplace.

WOODSTOCK

1½ ozs. gin
1 oz. lemon juice
¼ oz. maple syrup
1 dash orange bitters

Shake well with ice. Strain into frosty cocktail glass. A drink from the ski country.

THE MARTINI

Over the years, the martini, most famous of all cocktail-hour thoroughbreds, has evolved into a drink that is practically all gin with only the faintest hint of vermouth. This preference for drier and drier martinis (while "dry" usually means less sweet, in reference to martinis it means less vermouth) has spawned some strange equipment and a countless number of jokes. Some barmen ritualize the exacting vermouth formula with a long ℞ dropper; some spray their vermouth from atomizers. The fanatical, reaching the *reductio ad absurdum*, claim they waft the vermouth bottletop over the gin or mutter the word "vermouth" under their breath while stirring their raw concoction in the mixing glass. It would be unfortunate if the use of vermouth in the martini became extinct, for its bite, however faint, is trenchant. It turns cold gin into a civilized cocktail.

Most top-flight barmen make their martinis with about ten or twelve parts gin to one part dry vermouth. The drink may be served "up," meaning in a regular stemmed cocktail glass, or on the rocks in an old-fashioned glass. You can drop a twist of lemon peel into the glass or rub the rim with the peel before adding it to the drink. The martini's most common garnish is an olive, pitted or stuffed. With a cocktail-onion garnish, it turns into a gibson.

A martini must be piercingly cold; at its best, both gin and vermouth are prechilled in the refrigerator, well stirred with ice, and poured into a prechilled glass. Energetic stirring with the ice is all-important; the dilution makes the drink both smooth and palatable. Those who merely combine gin and vermouth beforehand and then refrigerate without stirring wind up serving raw slugs to guests who are quickly cargoed and who completely miss the pleasure of a well-made martini.

Although vermouth is the spirited minor ingredient, a bottle opened for pouring and left standing in the liquor cabinet for weeks will lose its bell-ringing zest. To retain as much as possible of the flavor of the aromatic herbs used in making vermouth, store the opened bottle in the refrigerator. It's a good idea for the martini man to buy his vermouth in pint bottles and make frequent replacements.

Here are several variations on the familiar martini theme:

12-to-1 MARTINI

2 ozs. gin
1 teaspoon dry
  vermouth

8-to-1 MARTINI

2 ozs. gin
¼ oz. dry vermouth

4-to-1 MARTINI

2 ozs. gin
½ oz. dry vermouth

GIBSON

As noted, any of the above martini mixtures garnished with a cocktail onion.

BLENTON

1½ ozs. gin
¾ oz. dry vermouth
1 dash Angostura
  bitters

Stir well with ice. Strain into prechilled cocktail glass. A martini variation so old that it's new. Total effect on the palate: warming and elevating.

BLOODHOUND

1 oz. gin
½ oz. dry vermouth
½ oz. sweet vermouth
½ oz. strawberry
  liqueur
1 large strawberry

Shake gin, both kinds of vermouth, and strawberry liqueur well with ice. Strain into prechilled cocktail glass. Drop strawberry into glass. The best dry vermouth for this one is Chambery Fraise.

CORDIAL MARTINI

1¼ ozs. gin
¼ oz. dry vermouth
¼ oz. Cordial Médoc
Lemon peel

Stir gin, vermouth, and Cordial Médoc well with ice. Strain into prechilled cocktail glass or over rocks. Twist lemon peel over drink and drop into glass.

FINO MARTINI

2 ozs. gin
½ oz. fino sherry

Stir well with ice. Strain into prechilled cocktail glass. Add olive or lemon twist. Serve with a side dish of freshly toasted, salted almonds.

FLYING DUTCHMAN

2 ozs. gin
¼ oz. dry vermouth
Curaçao

Into a prechilled cocktail glass, pour enough curaçao so that when the glass is slowly twirled, it will coat the sides. Stir gin and vermouth well with ice. Strain into glass.

GIN AND IT

2 ozs. gin
Italian sweet vermouth

Stir gin well with ice. Into a prechilled cocktail glass, pour enough vermouth so that when the glass is slowly twirled, it will coat the sides. Add the gin. The English drink is often served at room temperature. The It stands for the Italian vermouth. A gin and French is the same drink with French dry vermouth instead.

KNICKERBOCKER

2 ozs. gin
½ oz. dry vermouth
¼ oz. sweet vermouth

Stir well with ice. Strain into prechilled cocktail glass. Serve without benefit of cherry, olive, or lemon twist. This version of the martini appeals to those who like vermouth in both sweet and dry forms.

MARSALA MARTINI

¾ oz. gin
¾ oz. dry vermouth
¾ oz. dry Marsala
Lemon peel

Stir gin, vermouth, and Marsala well with ice. Strain into prechilled cocktail glass. Twist lemon peel above drink and drop into glass.

MARTINEZ

2 ozs. gin
½ oz. dry vermouth
½ teaspoon
  maraschino liqueur
2 dashes orange bitters

Stir well with ice. Strain into prechilled cocktail glass. Martini men with a strain of Spanish in their veins go for this one. Alleged to have been the original martini.

MARTINI, HOLLAND-STYLE

2 ozs. Dutch genever
  gin
½ oz. dry vermouth
Lemon peel

Stir gin and vermouth well with ice. Strain into prechilled cocktail glass. Twist lemon peel above drink and drop into glass.

PAISLEY MARTINI

2¼ ozs. gin
¼ oz. dry vermouth
1 teaspoon Scotch

Stir well with ice. Strain into prechilled cocktail glass. The flavor of the Scotch in this 9-to-1 martini is just subtle enough to let the drinker know that something delightfully offbeat is in his glass.

PERFECT

1½ ozs. gin
½ oz. dry vermouth
½ oz. sweet vermouth

Stir well with ice. Strain into prechilled cocktail glass. Add olive or twist of lemon peel if desired. Modern martini men would call this an "imperfect" martini, but "*perfect*" is its traditional name.

PERNOD MARTINI

2 ozs. gin
½ oz. dry vermouth
⅛ teaspoon Pernod

Stir well with ice. Strain into prechilled cocktail glass. Very pleasant with an onion-stuffed olive. Some bartenders pour a soupçon of Pernod into the glass, swirl it around, and then add the martini.

RACQUET CLUB

2 ozs. gin
½ oz. dry vermouth
2 dashes orange bitters

Shake, don't stir, with ice in silver cocktail shaker until shaker is completely frosted. Strain into cocktail glass so cold it's some-what uncomfortable to hold.

SAKETINI

2 ozs. gin
½ oz. sake

Stir well with ice. Strain into prechilled cocktail glass. If desired, an olive or twist of lemon peel may be added. The saketini is a reminder that dry vermouth and rice wine bear an uncanny resemblance to each other.

SWEET MARTINI

2 ozs. gin
½ oz. sweet vermouth
Orange peel

Stir gin and vermouth well with ice. Strain into prechilled cocktail glass. Twist orange peel above drink and drop into glass. While *"sweet martini"* sounds like a contradiction in terms, the drink is not only tolerable but titillating.

Rum Cocktails

ACAPULCO

1½ ozs. light rum
½ oz. lime juice
¼ oz. triple sec
½ egg white
½ teaspoon sugar
2 fresh mint leaves

Shake rum, lime juice, triple sec, egg white, and sugar well with ice. Strain into prechilled cocktail glass. Tear each mint leaf partially and drop into glass.

APRICOT LADY

1½ ozs. light rum
1 oz. apricot-flavored brandy
½ oz. lime juice
½ teaspoon curaçao
½ egg white
¼ cup crushed ice
½ slice orange

Put rum, apricot-flavored brandy, lime juice, curaçao, egg white, and ice into blender. Blend 15 seconds at low speed. Pour into prechilled old-fashioned glass. Add ice cubes or ice slices to fill glass to rim. Place orange slice on top.

APRICOT PIE

1 oz. light rum
1 oz. sweet vermouth
½ teaspoon apricot-flavored brandy
½ teaspoon lemon juice
¼ teaspoon grenadine
Orange peel

Shake rum, vermouth, apricot-flavored brandy, lemon juice, and grenadine well with ice. Strain into prechilled cocktail glass. Twist orange peel above drink and drop into glass.

BACARDI

1½ ozs. light or golden
  Bacardi rum
½ oz. lime juice
1 teaspoon grenadine

Shake well with ice. Strain into prechilled cocktail glass or over rocks in a prechilled old-fashioned glass. The proprietary name Bacardi, a rum originally distilled in Cuba but now made in Puerto Rico and other Spanish-speaking lands, has long been the title of this classic rum cocktail.

BANANA DAIQUIRI

1½ ozs. light rum
½ oz. lime juice
1 oz. orange juice
1 oz. banana liqueur
⅓ cup finely crushed
  ice

Mix all ingredients in blender at high speed 10 seconds. Pour into 6-oz. saucer champagne glass or outsize cocktail glass.

BANANA MANGO

1½ ozs. light rum
¼ oz. banana liqueur
½ oz. mango nectar
½ oz. lime juice
1 slice fresh mango

Shake rum, banana liqueur, mango nectar, and lime juice well with ice. Strain over rocks in prechilled old-fashioned glass. Add mango slice.

BEACHCOMBER

1½ ozs. light rum
½ oz. lime juice
½ oz. triple sec
¼ teaspoon mara-
  schino liqueur

Shake well with ice. Strain into prechilled sugar-rimmed cocktail glass.

BEACHCOMBER'S GOLD

1½ ozs. light rum
½ oz. dry vermouth
½ oz. sweet vermouth

Stir well with ice. Strain into prechilled deep-saucer champagne glass. Add cracked ice or ice slices to fill glass. The same mixture of rum and both kinds of vermouth is also known as the rum perfect, usually served in a regular cocktail glass without added ice. Either way, it's delightful.

BEE'S KNEES

1½ ozs. light rum
¾ oz. orange juice
½ oz. lime juice
1 teaspoon sugar
2 dashes orange bitters
Orange peel

Shake rum, orange juice, lime juice, sugar, and bitters well with ice. Strain into prechilled cocktail glass. Twist orange peel above drink and drop into glass. A speakeasy heirloom whose orange accent is most mellow.

BETWEEN THE SHEETS

¾ oz. light rum
¾ oz. California brandy
¾ oz. Cointreau
½ oz. lemon juice

Shake well with ice. Strain into prechilled cocktail glass. An exhilarating variation on the rum sidecar.

BLACK DEVIL

2 ozs. light rum
½ oz. dry vermouth
1 black olive

Stir rum and vermouth well with ice. Strain into prechilled cocktail glass. Add black olive.

BOLERO

1½ ozs. light rum
¾ oz. apple brandy
¼ teaspoon sweet vermouth
Lemon peel

Stir rum, apple brandy, and vermouth well with ice. Strain into prechilled sugar-frosted cocktail glass. Twist lemon peel above drink and drop into glass.

BOLO

1½ ozs. light rum
½ oz. lemon juice
½ oz. orange juice
½ teaspoon sugar
½ slice lemon

Shake rum, lemon juice, orange juice, and sugar well with ice. Strain into prechilled cocktail glass or prechilled whiskey-sour glass. Garnish with lemon slice.

BORINQUEN

1½ ozs. light rum
½ oz. passion-fruit
  syrup
¾ oz. lime juice
½ oz. orange juice
1 teaspoon 151-proof
  rum
½ cup crushed ice

Put all ingredients into blender. Blend at low speed 10 seconds. Pour into prechilled double old-fashioned glass. Add ice cubes or cracked ice to fill glass. Garnish with gardenia if available.

BUSHRANGER

1 oz. light rum
1 oz. red Dubonnet
2 dashes Angostura
  bitters
Lemon peel

Shake rum, Dubonnet, and bitters well with ice. Strain into prechilled cocktail glass. Twist lemon peel above drink and drop into glass.

CARDINAL COCKTAIL II

2 ozs. light rum
¼ oz. orzata
1 teaspoon grenadine
¼ oz. triple sec
1 oz. lime juice
1 slice lime

Shake rum, orzata, grenadine, triple sec, and lime juice well with ice. Strain into prechilled old-fashioned glass. Add ice cubes to bring liquid to rim. Garnish with lime slice.

CARIB

1 oz. light rum
1 oz. gin
½ oz. lime juice
1 teaspoon sugar
1 slice orange

Shake rum, gin, lime juice, and sugar well with ice. Strain over rocks in prechilled old-fashioned glass. Garnish with orange slice.

CASABLANCA

2 ozs. golden rum
1 dash Angostura
  bitters
1 teaspoon lime juice
¼ teaspoon curaçao
¼ teaspoon mara-
  schino liqueur

Shake well with ice. Strain into prechilled cocktail glass.

CHERRY DAIQUIRI

1½ ozs. light rum
½ oz. lime juice
½ oz. tart cherry
  liqueur
¼ teaspoon kirsch-
  wasser
Lime peel

Shake rum, lime juice, cherry liqueur, and kirschwasser well with ice. Strain into prechilled cocktail glass. Twist lime peel above drink and drop into glass.

CHINA

2 ozs. golden rum
¼ teaspoon grenadine
¼ teaspoon passion-
  fruit syrup
1 teaspoon curaçao
1 dash Angostura
  bitters

Shake well with ice. Pour into prechilled cocktail glass. A slightly sweet drink, but not a dessert cocktail; one to set the mood for a roast-duck dinner.

COLUMBIA

1½ ozs. light rum
½ oz. strawberry
  syrup
½ oz. lemon juice
1 teaspoon kirsch-
  wasser

Shake well with ice. Strain into prechilled sugar-frosted cocktail glass. The kirschwasser, though small in proportion, comes through vividly.

CONCH SHELL

4 ozs. light rum
½ oz. lime juice

Shake well with ice. Strain over rocks in prechilled double old-fashioned glass. Allow at least an hour for polishing this one off.

CONTINENTAL

1¾ ozs. light rum
½ oz. lime juice
½ teaspoon sugar
½ teaspoon green
   crème de menthe

Shake well with ice. Strain into prechilled cocktail glass. A light bracer before a seafood dinner.

CORKSCREW

1½ ozs. light rum
½ oz. dry vermouth
½ oz. peach liqueur
1 slice lime

Shake rum, vermouth, and peach liqueur well with ice. Strain into prechilled cocktail glass. Add lime slice.

CREOLE

1½ ozs. light rum
1 dash Tabasco sauce
1 teaspoon lemon juice
Iced beef bouillon or
   consommé (un-
   diluted)
Salt and pepper

Put two large ice cubes into prechilled old-fashioned glass. Add rum, Tabasco, and lemon juice. Stir well. Fill glass with beef bouillon. Sprinkle with salt and pepper. Stir again. A pleasant pick-me-up or prebrunch cocktail.

CUBA LIBRE COCKTAIL

1 oz. light rum
½ oz. 151-proof rum
½ oz. cola drink
½ oz. lime juice
½ teaspoon sugar
Lime peel

Shake both kinds of rum, cola drink, lime juice, and sugar well with ice. Strain into prechilled cocktail glass. Twist lime peel above drink and drop into glass. Not to be confused with cuba libre, a tall rum-cola drink that's somewhat slower in its liberating effects.

CULROSS

1½ ozs. golden rum
½ oz. Lillet
1 teaspoon apricot-
  flavored brandy
1 teaspoon lime juice

Shake well with ice. Strain into prechilled cocktail glass as a straight-up drink or over the rocks in a prechilled old-fashioned glass. Equally good either way.

DAIQUIRI

2 ozs. light rum
½ oz. lime juice
½ teaspoon sugar

Shake well with ice. Pour into prechilled sugar-frosted cocktail glass or over the rocks in an old-fashioned glass. Sugar may be increased if a sweeter daiquiri is desired.

DERBY DAIQUIRI

1½ ozs. light rum
½ oz. lime juice
1 oz. orange juice
½ oz. simple syrup
⅓ cup crushed ice

Put all ingredients into blender. Blend 10–15 seconds at low speed. Pour into prechilled oversize cocktail glass or deep-saucer champagne glass.

DEVIL'S TAIL

1½ ozs. golden rum
1 oz. vodka
½ oz. lime juice
¼ oz. grenadine
¼ oz. apricot liqueur
⅓ cup crushed ice
Lime peel

Put rum, vodka, lime juice, grenadine, apricot liqueur, and ice into blender. Blend at low speed 10–15 seconds. Pour into prechilled deep-saucer champagne glass. Twist lime peel above drink and drop into glass. Powerful, but pleasant rather than pugnacious.

EL PRESIDENTE

1½ ozs. golden rum
½ oz. dry vermouth
1 teaspoon dark
  Jamaica rum
1 teaspoon curaçao
2 teaspoons lime juice
¼ teaspoon grenadine

Shake well with ice. Strain into prechilled cocktail glass. Hail to the chief.

FERN GULLY

1 oz. dark Jamaica rum
1 oz. light rum
½ oz. cream of
  coconut
½ oz. lime juice
2 teaspoons orange
  juice
1 teaspoon orzata
⅓ cup crushed ice

Put all ingredients into blender. Blend 10–15 seconds at low speed. Pour into prechilled deep-saucer champagne glass. More rummy than the usual frozen daiquiri, but delicious.

FORT LAUDERDALE

1½ ozs. golden rum
½ oz. sweet vermouth
¼ oz. orange juice
¼ oz. lime juice
1 slice cocktail orange
  in syrup

Shake rum, vermouth, orange juice, and lime juice well with ice. Strain over rocks in prechilled old-fashioned glass. Add orange slice.

FROSTY DAWN COCKTAIL

1½ ozs. light rum
1 oz. orange juice
½ oz. Falernum
¼ oz. maraschino
  liqueur

Shake well with ice. Strain over rocks in prechilled old-fashioned glass.

FROZEN APPLE DAIQUIRI

1½ ozs. light rum
½ oz. apple juice
½ oz. lemon juice
⅓ cup crushed ice
1 teaspoon sugar
1 wedge apple, with
  skin

Put rum, apple juice, lemon juice, crushed ice, and sugar into blender. Blend 10–15 seconds at low speed. Pour into prechilled deep-saucer champagne glass. Add apple wedge.

FROZEN BANANA DAIQUIRI

1½ ozs. light rum
½ oz. lime juice
½ medium-size very ripe banana, sliced
½ cup finely crushed ice
1 to 2 teaspoons sugar, to taste

Mix all ingredients in blender at low speed 10–15 seconds. Pour into 6-oz. saucer champagne glass or outsize cocktail glass.

FROZEN BERKELEY

1½ ozs. light rum
½ oz. California brandy
½ oz. passion-fruit syrup
½ oz. lemon juice
⅓ cup crushed ice

Put all ingredients into blender. Blend 10–15 seconds at low speed. Pour into prechilled deep-saucer champagne glass.

FROZEN DAIQUIRI

1½ to 2 ozs. light rum
½ oz. lime juice
½ to 1 teaspoon sugar
½ cup crushed ice

Put all ingredients into blender. Blend at low speed 10–15 seconds. Pour into prechilled deep-saucer champagne glass. May be served with a small straw. The drink may be made rummier by floating a teaspoon of 151-proof rum on top of the daiquiri in the glass, or the drink may be made with golden rum or any of the heavier-bodied rums such as Jamaican, Barbados, or Martinique.

FROZEN GUAVA DAIQUIRI

1½ ozs. light rum
1 oz. guava nectar (not syrup)
½ oz. lime juice
1 teaspoon banana liqueur
⅓ cup crushed ice

Put all ingredients into blender. Blend 10–15 seconds at low speed. Pour into prechilled deep-saucer champagne glass.

FROZEN GUAVA-ORANGE DAIQUIRI

1½ ozs. light rum
¾ oz. guava syrup
½ oz. lime juice
½ oz. orange juice
⅓ cup crushed ice

Put all ingredients into blender. Blend 10–15 seconds at low speed. Pour into prechilled deep-saucer champagne glass.

FROZEN MINT DAIQUIRI

2 ozs. light rum
½ oz. lime juice
6 large mint leaves
1 teaspoon sugar
½ cup crushed ice

Put all ingredients into blender. Blend 20 seconds at low speed. Pour into prechilled deep-saucer champagne glass. Perfect prelude to a lamb-chop dinner.

FROZEN PASSION-FRUIT DAIQUIRI

1½ ozs. light rum
½ oz. passion-fruit
   syrup
½ oz. lime juice
½ oz. orange juice
¼ oz. lemon juice
⅓ cup crushed ice

Put all ingredients into blender. Blend at low speed 10–15 seconds. Pour into prechilled deep-saucer champagne glass.

FROZEN PEACH DAIQUIRI

1½ ozs. light rum
½ oz. lime juice
¼ cup frozen sliced
   peaches, thawed
½ oz. syrup from
   frozen peaches
⅓ cup crushed ice

Put all ingredients into blender. Blend at low speed 10–15 seconds. Pour into prechilled deep-saucer champagne glass. You'll find the rich flavor of the frozen peaches and their syrup peachier than the fresh fruit for this drink.

FROZEN PINEAPPLE DAIQUIRI

1½ ozs. light rum
½ oz. lime juice
½ teaspoon sugar
4 canned pineapple
   chunks, drained
⅓ cup crushed ice

Put all ingredients into blender. Blend 10–15 seconds at low speed. Pour into prechilled deep-saucer champagne glass. The canned pineapple is actually better than the fresh for this fruity cocktail.

FROZEN SESAME DAIQUIRI

1½ ozs. rum
½ oz. sesame-seed
  syrup (*ajonjoli*)
½ oz. lime juice
½ oz. dry vermouth
½ oz. orange juice
⅓ cup crushed ice

Put all ingredients into blender. Blend at low speed 10–15 seconds. Pour into prechilled deep-saucer champagne glass.

FROZEN SOURSOP DAIQUIRI

1½ ozs. light rum
¼ oz. dark Jamaica
  rum
1 oz. guanabana
  (soursop) nectar
¼ oz. lime juice
¼ cup sliced banana
⅓ cup crushed ice

Put all ingredients into blender. Blend 10–15 seconds at low speed. Pour into prechilled deep-saucer champagne glass. The delicious soursop is now shipped to the States as a canned nectar.

GAUGUIN

2 ozs. light rum
½ oz. passion-fruit
  syrup
½ oz. lemon juice
¼ oz. lime juice
⅓ cup crushed ice
1 maraschino cherry

Put rum, passion-fruit syrup, lemon juice, lime juice, and ice into blender. Blend at low speed 10–15 seconds. Pour into prechilled deep-saucer champagne glass. Add cherry.

GOLDEN GATE

¾ oz. light rum
¾ oz. gin
1 teaspoon 151-proof
  rum
½ oz. lemon juice
½ oz. crème de cacao
½ teaspoon Falernum
1 slice orange

Shake light rum, gin, 151-proof rum, lemon juice, crème de cacao, and Falernum well with ice. Strain over rocks in a prechilled old-fashioned glass. Add orange slice. It leaves a rich afterglow.

GUANABANA

1½ ozs. light rum
1 oz. guanabana
  (soursop) nectar
1 teaspoon lime juice

Shake well with ice. Strain into prechilled cocktail glass. Drink must be icy cold.

HURRICANE

1 oz. light rum
1 oz. golden rum
½ oz. passion-fruit
  syrup
2 teaspoons lime juice

Shake well with ice. Strain into prechilled cocktail glass. Quantities may be doubled and drink poured over rocks in a coconut shell or double old-fashioned glass.

ISLE OF THE BLESSED COCONUT

1½ ozs. light rum
½ oz. cream of
  coconut (canned
  coconut syrup)
½ oz. lime juice
¼ oz. lemon juice
¼ oz. orange juice
½ teaspoon sugar
⅓ cup crushed ice

Put all ingredients into blender. Blend at low speed 10–15 seconds. Pour into prechilled deep-saucer champagne glass. Serve with a bowl of toasted coconut slices.

JADE

1¾ ozs. golden rum
½ teaspoon green
  crème de menthe
½ teaspoon curaçao
1½ teaspoons lime
  juice
1 teaspoon sugar
1 slice lime

Shake rum, crème de menthe, curaçao, lime juice, and sugar well with ice. Strain into prechilled cocktail glass. Add lime slice. Minty, but not overpowering.

LEEWARD

1½ ozs. light rum
½ oz. calvados
½ oz. sweet vermouth
Lemon peel

Shake rum, calvados, and vermouth well with ice. Strain over rocks in prechilled old-fashioned glass. Twist lemon peel above drink and drop into glass. Pass anchovy canapés sprinkled with chopped hard-boiled egg.

MAI TAI

3 ozs. light rum
½ oz. lime juice
¼ teaspoon triple sec
¼ teaspoon orzata
½ teaspoon sugar
1 slice lime
1 sprig mint
1 pineapple stick

Shake rum, lime juice, triple sec, orzata, and sugar well with ice. Strain into prechilled double old-fashioned glass. Add enough cracked ice or ice cubes to fill glass. Tear one or two mint leaves partially to release flavor. Garnish with lime slice, mint sprig, and pineapple stick.

MANDEVILLE

1½ ozs. light rum
1 oz. dark Jamaica rum
¾ oz. lemon juice
1 teaspoon Pernod
½ oz. cola drink
¼ teaspoon grenadine
1 slice orange

Shake both kinds of rum, lemon juice, Pernod, cola drink, and grenadine well with ice. Strain over rocks in prechilled old-fashioned glass. Add orange slice.

MUSKMELON

1½ ozs. light rum
¼ cup sliced ripe cantaloupe meat
⅓ cup crushed ice
½ teaspoon sugar
½ oz. lime juice
½ oz. orange juice
1 cube cantaloupe meat on cocktail spear

Put rum, sliced cantaloupe, ice, sugar, lime juice, and orange juice into blender. Blend at low speed 10–15 seconds. Pour into prechilled old-fashioned glass. Add ice cubes or ice slices, if necessary, to fill glass to rim. Garnish with cantaloupe cube.

NAVY GROG

1 oz. dark Jamaica
   rum
½ oz. light rum
½ oz. lime juice
½ oz. orange juice
½ oz. pineapple juice
½ oz. guava nectar
¼ oz. Falernum
½ cup crushed ice
4 large mint leaves

Put both kinds of rum, lime juice, orange juice, pineapple juice, guava nectar, Falernum, and crushed ice into blender. Blend at low speed 15 seconds. Pour into double old-fashioned glass. Add ice to fill glass to rim. Tear mint leaves partially and float on drink. Serve with straw.

OCHO RIOS

1½ ozs. Jamaica rum
1 oz. guava nectar
½ oz. heavy cream
½ oz. lime juice
½ teaspoon sugar
⅓ cup crushed ice

Put all ingredients into blender. Blend at low speed 10–15 seconds. Pour into pre-chilled deep-saucer champagne glass. A creamy, rummy drink recommended after a spearfishing expedition.

PAGO PAGO

1½ ozs. golden rum
½ oz. fresh lime juice
½ teaspoon green
   Chartreuse
¼ teaspoon white
   crème de cacao
½ oz. pineapple juice

Shake well with ice. Strain into prechilled cocktail glass. Pineapple comes through beautifully.

PENSACOLA

1½ ozs. light rum
½ oz. guava nectar
½ oz. orange juice
½ oz. lemon juice
⅓ cup crushed ice

Put all ingredients into blender. Blend 10–15 seconds at low speed. Pour into pre-chilled deep-saucer champagne glass.

PINK CREOLE

1½ ozs. golden rum
½ oz. lime juice
1 teaspoon heavy
  cream
1 teaspoon grenadine
1 black cherry, soaked
  in rum

Shake rum, lime juice, cream, and grenadine well with ice. Strain into prechilled cocktail glass. Add cherry.

PINK VERANDA

1 oz. golden rum
½ oz. heavy
  Jamaica rum
1½ ozs. cranberry
  juice
½ oz. lime juice
1 teaspoon sugar
½ egg white

Shake well with ice. Strain into prechilled old-fashioned glass. Add ice slices or ice cubes, if necessary, to fill glass to rim.

POLYNESIA

1½ ozs. light rum
1 oz. passion-fruit
  syrup
¼ oz. lime juice
½ egg white
⅓ cup crushed ice

Put all ingredients into blender. Blend 10–15 seconds at low speed. Pour into prechilled deep-saucer champagne glass.

POLYNESIAN PARADISE

1½ ozs. golden rum
1 teaspoon brown
  sugar
¾ oz. lime juice
½ oz. sweet vermouth
¼ oz. triple sec
⅓ cup crushed ice

Put all ingredients into blender. Blend at low speed 10–15 seconds. Pour into prechilled deep-saucer champagne glass. Paradise enow.

PONCE DE LEON

1½ ozs. light rum
½ oz. grapefruit juice
½ oz. mango nectar
1 teaspoon lemon juice

Shake well with ice. Strain into prechilled sugar-frosted cocktail glass.

PORT ANTONIO

1 oz. golden rum
½ oz. dark Jamaica
   rum
½ oz. lime juice
½ oz. coffee liqueur
1 teaspoon Falernum
1 slice lime

Shake both kinds of rum, lime juice, coffee liqueur, and Falernum well with ice. Strain over rocks in prechilled old-fashioned glass. Add lime slice.

PORT MARIA

1½ ozs. light rum
¾ oz. pineapple juice
½ oz. lemon juice
1 teaspoon Falernum
Grated nutmeg

Shake rum, pineapple juice, lemon juice, and Falernum well with ice. Strain into prechilled cocktail glass. Sprinkle nutmeg on top.

PUERTO RICAN PINK LADY

1¾ ozs. golden rum
¾ oz. lemon juice
½ egg white
1 teaspoon grenadine
⅓ cup crushed ice

Put all ingredients into blender. Blend at low speed 10–15 seconds. Pour into prechilled sugar-rimmed deep-saucer champagne glass.

ROSE HALL

1 oz. dark Jamaica
   rum
1 oz. orange juice
½ oz. banana liqueur
1 teaspoon lime juice
1 slice lime

Shake rum, orange juice, banana liqueur, and lime juice well with ice. Strain over rocks in prechilled old-fashioned glass. Add lime slice.

RUM AND SHERRY

1½ ozs. light rum
¾ oz. sherry
1 maraschino cherry

Stir rum and sherry well with ice. Strain into prechilled cocktail glass. Add cherry. The felicitous blend of rum and sherry may be made with very dry cocktail sherry, medium amontillado, or rich cream sherry to meet your own choice of dryness or sweetness. All are good.

RUM CASSIS

1 oz. light-bodied rum
1 oz. dry white wine
  or dry vermouth
2 teaspoons crème
  de cassis
Chilled club soda
1 slice lime

Pour rum, wine, and crème de cassis over rocks in 8-oz. tall glass or old-fashioned glass. Stir well. Add a splash of soda. Stir lightly. Add lime slice.

RUM DUBONNET

1½ ozs. light rum
¾ ozs. red Dubonnet
1 teaspoon lime juice
Lime peel

Shake rum, Dubonnet, and lime juice well with ice. Strain into prechilled cocktail glass. Twist lime peel above drink and drop into glass.

RUM OLD-FASHIONED

½ teaspoon sugar
1 or 2 dashes
  Angostura bitters
1 teaspoon water
2 ozs. light, golden, or
  dark Jamaica rum
Lime peel
1 teaspoon 151-proof
  rum

Mix sugar, bitters, and water in old-fashioned glass until sugar is completely dissolved. Add two ice cubes or several pieces of cracked ice. Add 2 ozs. rum. Stir well. Twist lime peel above drink and drop into glass. Float 151-proof rum on top.

RUM SCREWDRIVER

1½ ozs. light rum
3 ozs. cold fresh
 orange juice
1 slice orange

Put rum and orange juice (without ice) into blender. Blend 10–15 seconds at low speed. Pour over rocks in old-fashioned glass. Garnish with orange slice. A drink sometimes known as the aunt agatha, though it's the most un–aunt agathaish drink we can imagine. A perfect brunch beginner.

RUM SIDECAR

1½ ozs. golden rum
½ oz. Cointreau or
 triple sec
½ oz. lemon juice
¼ oz. dark
 Jamaica rum

Shake golden rum, Cointreau, and lemon juice well with ice. Strain into cocktail glass or over rocks. Float dark rum on top.

RUM SOUR

2 ozs. light or golden
 rum
½ oz. lemon juice
1 teaspoon orange
 juice
1 teaspoon rock-candy
 syrup or sugar
½ slice orange

Shake rum, lemon juice, orange juice, and syrup or sugar well with ice. Strain into prechilled whiskey-sour glass. Add lemon slice. A teaspoon of 151-proof rum may be floated on the drink for a more rummish accent. For a heavier-bodied but richly mellow rum sour, use dark Jamaica rum.

SAGUENAY

1 oz. light rum
1 oz. dry vermouth
1 teaspoon lemon juice
2 teaspoons crème
 de cassis

Shake well with ice. Strain over rocks in prechilled old-fashioned glass. Add a splash of club soda if desired.

ST. AUGUSTINE

1½ ozs. light rum
1 oz. grapefruit juice
1 teaspoon Cointreau
Lemon peel

Shake rum, grapefruit juice, and Cointreau well with ice. Strain into prechilled sugar-frosted cocktail glass. Twist lemon peel above drink and drop into glass. Perfect before a pompano dinner.

SAN JUAN

1½ ozs. light rum
1 oz. grapefruit juice
1 teaspoon cream
  of coconut
2 teaspoons lime juice
⅓ cup crushed ice
2 teaspoons 151-proof
  rum

Put 1½ ozs. light rum, grapefruit juice, cream of coconut, lime juice, and ice into blender. Blend at low speed 10–15 seconds. Pour into prechilled deep-saucer champagne glass. Float 151-proof rum on top.

SCORPION

2 ozs. light rum
2 ozs. orange juice
½ oz. lemon juice
1 oz. California
  brandy
½ oz. orzata
⅓ cup crushed ice
1 slice orange

Put rum, orange juice, lemon juice, brandy, orzata, and ice into blender. Blend at low speed 10–15 seconds. Pour into prechilled double old-fashioned glass with enough ice cubes to fill glass to rim. Add orange slice.

SEPTEMBER MORN

1½ ozs. light rum
½ oz. lime juice
1 teaspoon grenadine
½ egg white

Shake well with ice. Strain into prechilled sugar-frosted cocktail glass. Glass rim may be moistened with grenadine before dipping into sugar.

SESAME

1½ ozs. light rum
½ oz. lime juice
½ oz. sesame-seed
  syrup (*ajonjoli*)

Shake well with ice. Strain into prechilled cocktail glass. Sesame is a versatile seed. It's available in syrup form in stores featuring Caribbean products. A rummy and off-beat drink.

SHARK'S TOOTH

1½ ozs. golden rum
¼ oz. lemon juice
¼ oz. passion-fruit
   syrup
¼ oz. sweet vermouth
¼ oz. sloe gin
1 dash Angostura
   bitters
Orange peel
1 maraschino cherry

Shake rum, lemon juice, passion-fruit syrup, vermouth, sloe gin, and bitters well with ice. Strain into prechilled sugar-frosted cocktail glass. Twist orange peel above drink and drop into glass. Add cherry.

SHAW PARK

1 oz. golden rum
½ oz. Cointreau or
   triple sec
¼ oz. apricot liqueur
½ oz. lime juice

Shake well with ice. Strain into prechilled cocktail glass or pour over rocks.

SOUTHERN BANANA COMFORT

1 oz. golden rum
1 oz. Southern
   Comfort
¼ cup sliced banana
½ oz. lime juice
1 teaspoon sugar
⅓ cup crushed ice

Put all ingredients into blender. Blend at low speed 10–15 seconds. Pour into prechilled saucer champagne glass. The best possible way to usher in a platter of fried or barbecued chicken.

STRATOSPHERE

1 oz. rum
½ oz. California
   brandy
¼ oz. tart cherry
   liqueur
½ oz. lemon juice
1 teaspoon sugar

Shake well with ice. Strain into prechilled cocktail glass. Pleasant to drink around a cheese fondue.

STRAWBERRY FROZEN DAIQUIRI

1½ ozs. light rum
¼ cup thawed frozen
   strawberries in syrup
½ oz. lime juice
1 teaspoon sugar
½ oz. heavy cream
½ teaspoon
   maraschino liqueur
⅓ cup crushed ice

Whirl all ingredients in blender at high speed 10 seconds. Pour into prechilled deep-saucer champagne glass or old-fashioned glass.

TAHITI CLUB

2 ozs. golden rum
½ oz. lime juice
½ oz. pineapple juice
1 teaspoon maraschino
   liqueur
1 slice orange

Shake rum, lime juice, pineapple juice, and maraschino liqueur well with ice. Strain into prechilled old-fashioned glass. Add cracked ice or ice cubes to fill glass. Add orange slice.

TOBAGO

1 oz. golden rum
1 oz. gin
1 teaspoon 151-proof
   rum
2 teaspoons lime juice
1 teaspoon guava
   syrup (not nectar)
⅓ cup crushed ice
Lime peel

Put golden rum, gin, 151-proof rum, lime juice, guava syrup, and ice into blender. Blend at low speed 10–15 seconds. Pour over rocks in prechilled old-fashioned glass. Twist lime peel above drink and drop into glass.

TORRIDORA COCKTAIL

1½ ozs. light rum
½ oz. coffee liqueur
¼ oz. heavy cream
1 teaspoon 151-proof
   rum

Shake light rum, coffee liqueur, and cream well with ice. Strain into prechilled cocktail glass. Float 151-proof rum on top. In the Caribbean, the dinner hour commences rather late, about nine o'clock in the evening. By this time, the sweetness of the cocktail hour will have passed on, and one will be left with a rummy repose and a fine appetite.

TRADE WINDS

2 ozs. golden rum
½ oz. lime juice
½ oz. plum brandy
1½ teaspoons sugar
⅓ cup crushed ice

Put all ingredients into blender. Blend at low speed 10–15 seconds. Pour into pre-chilled deep-saucer champagne glass. Potent with plum flavor but not a scalp raiser.

UNISPHERE

1½ ozs. golden rum
1 teaspoon grenadine
½ oz. lime juice
½ teaspoon
  Benedictine
½ teaspoon Pernod

Shake well with ice. Strain into prechilled cocktail glass. Small amounts of liqueurs come through beautifully without over-powering flavor.

Tequila Cocktails

APRICOT AND TEQUILA SOUR

1½ ozs. tequila
¾ oz. apricot liqueur
½ oz. lemon juice

Shake well with ice. Strain into cocktail glass or over rocks in 8-oz. glass.

BLOODY MARIA

1½ ozs. tequila
2 ozs. ice-cold
  tomato juice
1 teaspoon lemon juice
1 dash Tabasco sauce
1 dash celery salt
1 slice lemon

Pour tequila, tomato juice, lemon juice, Tabasco, and celery salt into prechilled old-fashioned glass. Add rocks or ice slices to fill glass. Stir very well. Add lemon slice. Viva Maria!

BUNNY BONANZA

1½ ozs. tequila
1 oz. apple brandy
½ oz. lemon juice
1 teaspoon sugar
½ teaspoon curaçao
1 slice lemon

Shake tequila, apple brandy, lemon juice, sugar, and curaçao well with ice. Strain into prechilled old-fashioned glass. Add ice to fill glass. Garnish with lemon slice.

CHAPALA

1½ ozs. tequila
½ oz. orange juice
½ oz. lemon juice
1 dash orange-flower
   water
2 teaspoons grenadine
1 slice orange

Shake tequila, orange juice, lemon juice, orange-flower water, and grenadine well with ice. Strain over rocks in prechilled old-fashioned glass. Add orange slice.

COCONUT TEQUILA

1½ ozs. tequila
½ oz. cream
   of coconut
½ oz. lemon juice
1 teaspoon
   maraschino liqueur
½ cup crushed ice

Put all ingredients into blender. Blend 20 seconds at low speed. Pour into prechilled deep-saucer champagne glass. Perfect before a Polynesian brunch.

FROZEN BLACKBERRY TEQUILA

1½ ozs. tequila
1 oz. blackberry
   liqueur
½ oz. lemon juice
⅓ cup crushed ice
1 slice lemon

Put tequila, blackberry liqueur, lemon juice, and crushed ice into blender. Blend 10–15 seconds at low speed. Pour into prechilled old-fashioned glass. Add rocks to fill glass. Add lemon slice.

FROZEN MATADOR

1½ ozs. tequila
2 ozs. pineapple juice
½ oz. lime juice
⅓ cup crushed ice
1 cocktail pineapple
   stick

Put tequila, pineapple juice, lime juice, and crushed ice into blender. Blend at low speed 10–15 seconds. Pour into prechilled deep-saucer champagne glass. Add pineapple stick. Or pour over rocks in prechilled old-fashioned glass. Add ice cubes to fill glass. Garnish with pineapple stick.

FROZEN SUNSET

1½ ozs. tequila
½ oz. lime juice
½ oz. grenadine
½ cup crushed ice
1 slice lime

Put tequila, lime juice, grenadine, and ice into blender. Blend at low speed 10–15 seconds. Pour into prechilled old-fashioned glass. Add ice slices or cubes to fill glass. Garnish with lime slice.

MARGARITA

1½ ozs. tequila
½ oz. Cointreau,
   triple sec
   or curaçao
½ oz. lemon or lime
   juice

Shake well with ice. Strain into prechilled salt-rimmed cocktail glass. (See pp. 40 and 83 on salt-frosting glasses.) To prepare glass, rub rim with outside of lemon peel; then dip into salt and shake off excess. Although traditionally the glass for a margarita is salt-rimmed, it may also be sugar-rimmed. A twist of lime or lemon peel may be added if desired.

MEXICAN CLOVER CLUB

1½ ozs. tequila
¾ oz. lemon juice
½ oz. grenadine
½ oz. heavy
   sweet cream
½ slightly beaten
   egg white

Shake all ingredients extremely well with ice. Strain into prechilled cocktail glass.

MEXICAN CONNECTION

1 oz. Amer Picon
1 oz. tequila
Chilled orange juice

Place 2 large ice cubes in 8-oz. glass. Add Amer Picon and tequila. Stir well. Add orange juice to fill glass. Stir.

MEXICO PACIFICO

1½ ozs. tequila
½ oz. lime juice
1 oz. passion-fruit
  syrup
⅓ cup crushed ice
1 slice lime

Put tequila, lime juice, passion-fruit syrup, and crushed ice into blender. Blend 10–15 seconds at low speed. Pour into prechilled deep-saucer champagne glass. Add lime slice. Exotico!

MIA VIDA

1 oz. tequila
½ oz. Kahlúa
½ oz. crème de cacao
½ oz. heavy cream
Sweet chocolate

Shake tequila, Kahlúa, crème de cacao, and cream well with ice. Strain into prechilled large cocktail glass. Grate chocolate over large holes of metal grater, and sprinkle on drink.

MINT TEQUILA

1½ ozs. tequila
6 large mint leaves
½ oz. lemon juice
1 teaspoon sugar
½ cup crushed ice

Put all ingredients into blender. Blend at low speed 15–20 seconds. Pour into prechilled old-fashioned glass. Add a rock or two to fill glass to rim. Lively and minty.

NORTEAMERICANO

1½ ozs. tequila
½ oz. very dry sherry
  (manzanilla
  if possible)
Olive or lemon peel

Stir tequila and sherry very well with ice. Strain into prechilled cocktail glass or over rocks. Add olive, or twist lemon peel above drink and drop into glass.

PETROLEO

1½ ozs. tequila
½ oz. lemon juice
½ teaspoon Maggi
  sauce
1 slice lemon

Shake tequila, lemon juice, and Maggi sauce well with ice. Strain over rocks in old-fashioned glass. Stir well. Add lemon slice.

PRADO

1½ ozs. tequila
¾ oz. lime juice
½ egg white
½ oz. maraschino
  liqueur
1 teaspoon grenadine
½ slice lemon
1 maraschino cherry

Shake tequila, lime juice, egg white, maraschino liqueur, and grenadine well with ice. Strain into prechilled whiskey-sour glass. Add lemon slice and cherry.

SANGRITA *(makes 2¼ cups)*

12 ozs. tomato juice
4 ozs. orange juice
2 ozs. lime juice
2 tablespoons
  diced onion
¼ teaspoon salt
1 small hot chili
  pepper

Mix all ingredients in blender at high speed 10 seconds. Chill several hours and stir well before serving. Sangrita is a Mexican non-alcoholic drink that is served with tequila, each in a separate glass; guests sip sangrita and tequila alternately. To make a bloody-mary-type drink, combine 4 ozs. sangrita and a jigger of tequila, shake well, and serve on rocks.

SEÑOR STINGER

1½ ozs. tequila
¾ oz. peppermint
  schnapps

Shake extremely well with ice. Strain into prechilled cocktail glass. Serve glass of ice water on the side, or pour stinger over cracked ice in deep-saucer champagne glass. For a somewhat sweeter drink, use white crème de menthe instead of peppermint schnapps.

SLOE TEQUILA

1 oz. tequila
½ oz. sloe gin
½ oz. lime juice
½ cup crushed ice
Cucumber peel

Put tequila, sloe gin, lime juice, and ice into blender. Blend 10–15 seconds at low speed. Pour into prechilled old-fashioned glass. Add cucumber peel and fill glass with cubed or cracked ice.

SUNRISE

1½ ozs. tequila
½ oz. lime juice
4 ozs. chilled
  orange juice
1 teaspoon grenadine
Wedge of lime

Pour tequila, lime juice, and orange juice over rocks in squat or tall 8-oz. glass. There should be enough rocks to fill glass to rim. Stir well. Pour grenadine on top and let guest stir sunrise, or stir grenadine with other ingredients before serving. Fasten wedge of lime to glass. Grenadine up to ½ oz. (3 teaspoons) may be used, but drink tends to become cloying. Slice of lime may be used instead of wedge. Crème de cassis may be used in place of grenadine.

SUNRISE ANISE

1½ ozs. tequila
½ oz. anise
4 ozs. chilled
  orange juice
1 teaspoon grenadine

Pour tequila, anise, and orange juice over rocks in 8-oz glass. Stir well. Pour grenadine on top and let guests stir it when served. For a somewhat snappier sunrise, use Pernod instead of anise.

TEQUILA DUBONNET

1 oz. tequila
1 oz. red Dubonnet
1 slice lemon

Pour tequila and Dubonnet into prechilled old-fashioned glass. Add cubed or cracked ice to fill glass. Stir. Garnish with lemon slice.

TEQUILA FRESA

1½ ozs. tequila
¾ oz. strawberry
  liqueur
½ oz. lime juice
¼ teaspoon orange
  bitters
1 slice lime
1 fresh strawberry

Shake tequila, strawberry liqueur, lime juice, and bitters well with ice. Strain over rocks in old-fashioned glass. Add lime slice and strawberry.

TEQUILA FROZEN SCREWDRIVER

1½ ozs. tequila
3 ozs. iced orange juice
⅓ cup crushed ice
1 slice orange

Put tequila, orange juice, and crushed ice into blender. Blend at low speed 10–15 seconds. Pour into prechilled old-fashioned glass. Add orange slice.

TEQUILA GUAYABA

1½ ozs. tequila
½ oz. guava syrup
½ oz. orange juice
½ oz. lime juice
Orange peel

Shake tequila, guava syrup, orange juice, and lime juice well with ice. Pour into prechilled old-fashioned glass. Add a rock or two to fill glass. Twist orange peel above drink and drop into glass. Pass a guacamole dip.

TEQUILA OLD-FASHIONED

½ teaspoon sugar
2 dashes Angostura
  bitters
1 teaspoon water
1½ ozs. tequila
Iced club soda
Lemon peel
1 cocktail pineapple
  stick

Stir sugar, bitters, and 1 teaspoon water in prechilled old-fashioned glass until sugar is dissolved. Add tequila. Add rocks or cracked ice to glass. Stir well. Add a splash of soda and stir. Twist lemon peel above drink and drop into glass. Garnish with pineapple stick.

TEQUILA SOUR

2 ozs. tequila
½ oz. lemon juice
1 teaspoon sugar
½ slice lemon
1 maraschino cherry

Shake tequila, lemon juice, and sugar well with ice. Strain into prechilled whiskey-sour glass. Add lemon slice and cherry.

TEQUINI

1½ to 2 ozs. tequila
½ oz. dry vermouth
Lemon peel
1 cocktail olive
  (optional)

Stir tequila and vermouth well with ice. Strain into prechilled cocktail glass. Twist lemon peel above drink and drop into glass. A Mexican martini. Olive may be added for a salty accent.

Vodka Cocktails

AQUEDUCT

1½ ozs. vodka
¼ oz. curaçao
¼ oz. apricot liqueur
½ oz. lime juice
Orange peel

Shake vodka, curaçao, apricot liqueur, and lime juice well with ice. Strain into prechilled cocktail glass. Twist orange peel above drink and drop into glass. Make book on this drink without any qualms.

BLACK RUSSIAN

1½ ozs. vodka
¾ oz. Kahlúa coffee
  liqueur

Shake well with ice. Strain over rocks in prechilled old-fashioned glass. Serve at poolside during the cocktail hour or by candlelight at the witching hour.

BLOODY MARY

1½ ozs. vodka
3 ozs. tomato juice
½ oz. lemon juice
1 teaspoon catsup
1 dash Worcestershire
  sauce
1 dash celery salt
1 dash Tabasco sauce

Shake all ingredients well with ice. Strain into tall or squat 8-oz. glass.

BUCKEYE MARTINI

2¼ ozs. vodka
¼ oz. dry vermouth
1 large ripe black olive

Stir vodka and vermouth well with ice. Strain into prechilled cocktail glass. Add olive.

BULLSHOT

4 ozs. beef bouillon
1½ ozs. vodka
1 teaspoon lemon juice
Dash Tabasco sauce

Pour ingredients over rocks in squat 10-oz. glass. Stir well. Add ice if necessary to fill glass. Sprinkle, if desired, with freshly ground pepper.

CHERRY VODKA

1¼ ozs. 100-proof
  vodka
½ oz. lime juice
½ oz. Peter Heering
  or Cherry Karise

Shake well with ice until the shaker is almost too cold to hold. Strain into prechilled cocktail glass.

CHIQUITA

1½ ozs. vodka
½ oz. banana liqueur
¼ cup sliced ripe
  banana
½ oz. lime juice
1 teaspoon sugar
¼ cup finely
  crushed ice

Put all ingredients into blender. Spin at low speed for 15 seconds. Pour into deep-saucer champagne glass.

FLYING GRASSHOPPER

1 oz. vodka
½ oz. green crème de menthe
½ oz. white crème de cacao

Stir well with ice. Strain into prechilled cocktail glass. More potent and less rich than the plain grasshopper (p. 212).

FROZEN APPLE

1½ ozs. vodka
¼ oz. calvados or applejack
½ oz. lime juice
¼ cup diced fresh apple
¼ cup finely crushed ice
½ teaspoon sugar

Put all ingredients into blender. Spin at low speed for 15 seconds. Pour into deep-saucer champagne glass. A north-country version of the frozen daiquiri.

GYPSY

2 ozs. vodka
½ oz. Benedictine
1 teaspoon lemon juice
1 teaspoon orange juice
1 slice orange

Shake vodka, Benedictine, lemon juice, and orange juice well with ice. Strain over rocks in prechilled old-fashioned glass. Add orange slice.

KREMLIN COLONEL

2 ozs. vodka
½ oz. lime juice
1 teaspoon sugar
2 large fresh mint leaves

Shake vodka, lime juice, and sugar well with ice. Strain into prechilled cocktail glass. Tear each mint leaf in half to release aroma and drop into glass.

KRETCHMA

1 oz. vodka
1 oz. crème de cacao
½ oz. lemon juice
½ teaspoon grenadine

Shake well with ice. Strain into prechilled cocktail glass. Serve to girls with a deep addiction to chocolate.

LORENZO

1 oz. vodka
1 oz. Tuaca liqueur
½ oz. lime juice

Shake well with ice. Strain into prechilled sugar-frosted cocktail glass. Rim of glass may be moistened with Tuaca before dipping into sugar. One sip of this and you'll understand why Lorenzo de'Medici was called Il Magnifico.

RED APPLE

1 oz. 100-proof vodka
1 oz. apple juice
½ oz. lemon juice
½ teaspoon grenadine
1 dash orange bitters

Shake well with ice. Strain into prechilled cocktail glass. Not to be confused with a vodka and apple juice, a lowball rather than a cocktail.

RUSSIAN BEAR

1 oz. vodka
½ oz. crème de cacao
½ oz. heavy cream

Shake well with ice. Strain into prechilled cocktail glass.

RUSSIAN ESPRESSO

1½ ozs. vodka
½ oz. espresso-coffee
  liqueur
½ teaspoon lemon
  juice
Lemon peel

Pour vodka, coffee liqueur, and lemon juice over rocks in prechilled old-fashioned glass. Stir well. Twist lemon peel above drink and drop into glass. A coexistence cocktail.

SALTY DOG

1½ ozs. vodka
3 ozs. unsweetened
  grapefruit juice
1 teaspoon lemon juice
Salt

Pour vodka, grapefruit juice, and lemon juice over rocks in old-fashioned glass. Sprinkle with salt. Stir.

SCREWDRIVER

1½ ozs. vodka
4½ ozs. ice-cold
 orange juice, freshly
 squeezed
1 teaspoon lemon juice
 (optional)

Shake extremely well with ice or pour into blender and blend with ice at high speed for 5 seconds. Strain into prechilled tall or squat 10-oz. glass. Lemon juice gives the screwdriver an extra twist.

SOVIET

1½ ozs. vodka
½ oz. amontillado
 sherry
½ oz. dry vermouth
Lemon peel

Stir vodka, sherry, and vermouth well with ice. Strain over rocks in prechilled old-fashioned glass. Twist lemon peel above drink and drop into glass. Liquid tranquilizer.

SVETLANA

1½ ozs. 100-proof
 vodka
½ oz. sweet vermouth
¼ oz. kirsch
¼ oz. orange juice
Orange peel

Shake vodka, vermouth, kirsch, and orange juice well with ice. Strain into prechilled cocktail glass. Twist orange peel above drink and drop into glass. Serve biting cold. No *nyets* will be heard.

TOVARICH

1½ ozs. vodka
½ oz. kümmel
½ oz. lime juice
Lime peel

Shake vodka, kümmel, and lime juice well with ice. Strain into prechilled cocktail glass. Twist lime peel above drink and drop into glass.

VODKA FRAISE

¾ oz. vodka
¾ oz. light rum
½ oz. strawberry
 liqueur
½ oz. lime juice
½ teaspoon grenadine
½ large fresh
 strawberry

Shake vodka, rum, strawberry liqueur, lime juice, and grenadine well with ice. Strain into prechilled sugar-frosted cocktail glass. Float strawberry on top.

VODKA GIMLET

2 ozs. vodka
½ oz. Rose's lime
    juice

Stir well with ice. Strain into prechilled cocktail glass.

VODKA GRAND MARNIER

1½ ozs. vodka
½ oz. Grand Marnier
½ oz. lime juice
1 slice orange

Shake vodka, Grand Marnier, and lime juice well with ice. Strain over rocks in prechilled old-fashioned glass. Garnish with orange slice.

VODKA MARTINI

2 ozs. vodka
¼ oz. dry vermouth

Stir well with ice. Strain into prechilled cocktail glass or serve over rocks. Garnish with twist of lemon peel or olive. Lacks the zip of the gin-based martini, but is wonderful midday solace for vodka partisans.

VODKA OLD-FASHIONED

½ teaspoon sugar
2 dashes Angostura
    bitters
1 teaspoon water
2 ozs. vodka
Lemon peel

Dissolve sugar with bitters and water in old-fashioned glass. Add vodka. Fill glass to rim with cubes, slices, or coarsely cracked pieces of ice. Stir very well. Twist lemon peel above drink and drop into glass.

VODKA SOUR

1¾ ozs. vodka
¾ oz. lemon juice
1 teaspoon sugar
1 slice lemon
1 maraschino cherry

Shake vodka, lemon juice, and sugar well with ice. Strain into prechilled whiskey-sour glass. Garnish with lemon slice and cherry.

VODKA STINGER

1½ ozs. vodka
½ oz. white crème
    de menthe

Shake extremely well with ice. Pour into prechilled cocktail glass. Drink must be extremely cold. May be pre- or postprandial.

WARSAW

1½ ozs. vodka
½ oz. blackberry
  liqueur
½ oz. dry vermouth
1 teaspoon lemon juice
Lemon peel

Shake vodka, blackberry liqueur, vermouth, and lemon juice well with ice. Strain into prechilled cocktail glass. Twist lemon peel above drink and drop into glass.

Whiskey Cocktails

ALLEGHENY

1 oz. bourbon
1 oz. dry vermouth
¼ oz. blackberry
  liqueur
¼ oz. lemon juice
1 dash Angostura
  bitters
Lemon peel

Shake bourbon, vermouth, blackberry liqueur, lemon juice, and bitters well with ice. Strain into prechilled cocktail glass. Twist lemon peel above drink and drop into glass.

BLACK HAWK

1 oz. blended whiskey
1 oz. sloe gin (creamy
  cap)
½ oz. lemon juice
1 maraschino cherry
  (optional)

Shake whiskey, sloe gin, and lemon juice well with ice. Strain into prechilled cocktail glass. Garnish with cherry.

BOURBONNAISE

1½ ozs. bourbon
½ oz. dry vermouth
¼ oz. crème de cassis
¼ oz. lemon juice

Shake well with ice. Strain over rocks in prechilled old-fashioned glass. A perfect way to introduce a French girl to American bourbon.

CANADIAN APPLE

1½ ozs. Canadian
   whisky
½ oz. calvados
¼ oz. lemon juice
1 teaspoon sugar
Ground cinnamon
1 slice lemon

Shake whisky, calvados, lemon juice, sugar, and a spray of cinnamon well with ice. Strain over rocks in prechilled old-fashioned glass. Add lemon slice. A delight before a holiday dinner of roast turkey or goose.

CANADIAN CHERRY

1½ ozs. Canadian
   whisky
½ oz. Peter Heering
   or Cherry Karise
¼ oz. lemon juice
¼ oz. orange juice

Shake well with ice. Strain into prechilled sugar-frosted cocktail glass. Glass rim may be moistened with cherry liqueur before dipping into sugar.

CANADIAN COCKTAIL

1½ ozs. Canadian
   whisky
½ oz. lemon juice
¼ oz. curaçao
1 teaspoon sugar
2 dashes bitters

Shake well with ice. Strain into prechilled cocktail glass or over rocks in old-fashioned glass.

CANADIAN OLD-FASHIONED

1½ ozs. Canadian
   whisky
2 dashes Angostura
   bitters
½ teaspoon curaçao
½ teaspoon lemon
   juice
Lemon peel
Orange peel

Pour whisky, bitters, curaçao, and lemon juice into prechilled old-fashioned glass. Add rocks. Stir. Twist lemon peel and orange peel above drink and drop into glass. More suave than the conventional old-fashioned made with U.S. blended whiskey.

CANADIAN PINEAPPLE

1½ ozs. Canadian
   whisky
½ oz. pineapple juice
½ oz. lemon juice
½ teaspoon
   maraschino liqueur
1 cocktail pineapple
   stick

Shake whisky, pineapple juice, lemon juice, and maraschino liqueur well with ice. Strain over rocks in prechilled old-fashioned glass. Add pineapple stick.

CHAPEL HILL

1½ ozs. blended
   whiskey
½ oz. curaçao
½ oz. lemon juice
1 slice cocktail orange
   in syrup

Shake whiskey, curaçao, and lemon juice well with ice. Strain over rocks in prechilled old-fashioned glass. Garnish with orange slice. Pass freshly toasted, salted pecans.

COMMODORE

1¾ ozs. blended
   whiskey
2 teaspoons lime juice
1 teaspoon orange
   juice
1 teaspoon strawberry
   liqueur
1 dash orange bitters

Shake well with ice. Strain into prechilled cocktail glass. A subtle blend of whiskey and fruit flavors that's appreciated at the end of a lazy Sunday sail.

COMMONWEALTH

1¾ ozs. Canadian
   whisky
¼ oz. lemon juice
½ oz. Van der Hum
   liqueur
Tangerine peel or
   orange peel

Shake whisky, lemon juice, and Van der Hum well with ice. Strain into prechilled sugar-frosted cocktail glass. Twist tangerine peel above drink and drop into glass. Serve before a dinner of grilled lobster tails.

CROTON

1¾ ozs. bourbon or
  blended whiskey
¼ oz. cocktail sherry
Lemon peel

Stir whiskey and sherry well with ice. Strain into prechilled cocktail glass. Twist lemon peel above drink and drop into glass. A patio or terrace cocktail to be served with a bowl of fresh iced shrimp and a tangy cocktail sauce.

CURRIER

1½ ozs. blended
  whiskey
½ oz. kümmel
¼ oz. fresh lime juice
¼ oz. Rose's lime juice
1 slice lime

Shake whiskey, kümmel, and both kinds of lime juice well with ice. Strain into prechilled cocktail glass. Add lime slice. A cocktail to savor between the fox hunt and breakfast.

DELTA

1½ ozs. blended
  whiskey
½ oz. Southern
  Comfort
½ oz. lime juice
½ teaspoon sugar
½ slice orange
1 slice fresh peach

Shake whiskey, Southern Comfort, lime juice, and sugar well with ice. Strain over rocks in prechilled old-fashioned glass. Garnish with orange and peach slices. A drink to accompany Gershwin on the hi-fi.

GLASGOW

1½ ozs. Scotch
¾ oz. lemon juice
¼ oz. dry vermouth
¼ oz. orzata

Shake well with ice. Strain into prechilled cocktail glass. Serve with thin slices of Nova Scotia salmon on hot buttered toast.

HABITANT COCKTAIL

1½ ozs. blended
    Canadian whisky
1 oz. lemon juice
1 teaspoon
    maple-sugar syrup
1 slice orange
1 maraschino cherry

Shake whisky, lemon juice, and syrup well with ice. Strain over rocks in prechilled old-fashioned glass. Garnish with orange slice and cherry.

INDIAN RIVER

1½ ozs. blended
    whiskey
½ oz. unsweetened
    grapefruit juice
¼ oz. raspberry
    liqueur
¼ oz. sweet vermouth

Shake well with ice. Strain over rocks in prechilled old-fashioned glass.

IRISH ALMOND

1½ ozs. blended
    Irish whiskey
½ oz. orange juice
½ oz. lemon juice
2 teaspoons orgeat or
    orzata (almond
    syrup)
1 teaspoon toasted
    almond slices

Shake whiskey, orange juice, lemon juice, and orgeat well with ice. Strain into prechilled whiskey-sour glass. Sprinkle almond slices on top. (To toast almonds, place sliced almonds in shallow pan in oven preheated to 350°. Bake 8 to 10 minutes or until medium brown, stirring occasionally. Sprinkle with salt. Cool.)

JACKSON SQUARE

1½ ozs. bourbon
½ oz. peppermint
    schnapps
3 dashes Peychaud's
    bitters
Iced club soda
Lemon peel

Pour bourbon, peppermint schnapps, and bitters over rocks in old-fashioned glass. Stir. Add soda. Stir. Twist lemon peel over drink and drop into glass.

KENTUCKY

1½ ozs. 86-proof
  bourbon
½ oz. lemon juice
½ oz. pineapple juice
1 teaspoon maraschino
  liqueur

Shake well with ice. Strain into prechilled sugar-frosted cocktail glass.

LAWHILL

1¼ ozs. blended
  whiskey
¾ oz. dry vermouth
¼ teaspoon Pernod
¼ teaspoon
  maraschino liqueur
½ oz. orange juice
1 dash Angostura
  bitters

Shake well with ice. Strain into prechilled cocktail glass. A superb cocktail to mix beforehand, strain into a Thermos, and tote along on a picnic.

MANHASSET

1½ ozs. blended
  whiskey
½ oz. lemon juice
¼ oz. dry vermouth
¼ oz. sweet vermouth
Lemon peel

Shake whiskey, lemon juice, and both kinds of vermouth well with ice. Strain into prechilled cocktail glass. Twist lemon peel above drink and drop into glass.

MANHATTAN

(See p. 314 for a separate discussion of this longtime favorite and its variations.)

MAY COCKTAIL

1½ ozs. blended
  whiskey
¼ oz. kirschwasser
¼ oz. strawberry
  liqueur
Chilled May wine
1 slice lemon

Shake whiskey, kirschwasser, and strawberry liqueur well with ice. Strain into prechilled old-fashioned glass with a large ice cube. Fill glass with May wine. Stir. Garnish with lemon slice.

NEVINS

1½ ozs. bourbon
½ oz. grapefruit juice
¼ oz. apricot liqueur
¼ oz. lemon juice
1 dash Angostura
  bitters

Shake well with ice. Strain into prechilled sugar-frosted cocktail glass.

NEW WORLD

1¾ ozs. blended
  whiskey
½ oz. lime juice
1 teaspoon grenadine
Lime peel

Shake whiskey, lime juice, and grenadine well with ice. Strain into prechilled cocktail glass. Twist lime peel above drink and drop into glass. Drink this one while listening to Dvořák before a midnight supper.

NEW YORK SOUR

2 ozs. blended
  whiskey
½ oz. lemon juice
1 teaspoon sugar
Chilled dry red wine
½ slice lemon

Shake whiskey, lemon juice, and sugar well with ice. Strain into prechilled 6-oz. sour glass. Fill glass with dry red wine. Stir. Garnish with lemon slice. A miniature punch in a sour glass.

NEW YORKER

1½ ozs. blended
  whiskey
½ oz. lime juice
1 teaspoon sugar
¼ teaspoon grenadine
Lemon peel
Orange peel

Shake whiskey, lime juice, sugar, and grenadine well with ice. Strain into prechilled sugar-frosted cocktail glass. Twist lemon peel and orange peel above drink and drop into glass. A fruity terrace cocktail appreciated equally under sun or stars.

NIGHT SHADE

1½ ozs. bourbon
½ oz. sweet vermouth
½ oz. orange juice
¼ teaspoon yellow
  Chartreuse
½ slice orange
½ slice lemon

Shake bourbon, vermouth, orange juice, and Chartreuse well with ice. Strain over rocks in prechilled old-fashioned glass. Add orange and lemon slices. Pass freshly fried, generously salted shrimp chips.

OLD-FASHIONED

½ teaspoon sugar
1 or 2 dashes
  Angostura bitters
1 teaspoon water
1½ to 2 ozs. blended
  whiskey
Lemon peel

Stir sugar, bitters, and water in prechilled old-fashioned glass until sugar dissolves. Fill glass with ice cubes or large pieces of cracked ice. Add whiskey. Stir well. Twist lemon peel above drink and drop into glass. An old-fashioned may be made with U.S. blended whiskey, Canadian, Irish, or Scotch. In smart men's clubs, the words *"garnish"* and *"garbage"* were once synonymous; orange and lemon slices, cherries, cocktail sticks, etc., were considered female diversions for filling a glass with fruit instead of the cocktail itself. Over the years, this attitude has been somewhat mitigated. Generally, however, most men and women appreciate the old-fashioned unencumbered with superfluous fruit.

PRINCE EDWARD

1¾ ozs. Scotch
½ oz. Lillet
¼ oz. Drambuie
1 slice cocktail orange
  in syrup

Shake Scotch, Lillet, and Drambuie well with ice. Strain over rocks in prechilled old-fashioned glass. Garnish with orange slice.

QUEBEC

1½ ozs. Canadian
  whisky
¼ oz. Amer Picon
¼ oz. maraschino
  liqueur
½ oz. dry vermouth

Shake well with ice. Strain into prechilled sugar-frosted cocktail glass.

ROB ROY

1½ to 2 ozs. Scotch
½ oz. sweet vermouth
1 dash orange bitters
(optional)

Stir well with ice. Strain into prechilled cocktail glass. The Rob Roy is, of course, simply a Scotch manhattan, and variations in whisky and vermouth proportions may be made to your own drinking taste. A light rather than a smoky Scotch is preferred by most people. A brandied cherry may be added for a special flourish. For a dry Rob Roy, use dry vermouth; add a twist of lemon if desired.

ROB ROY, HOLIDAY STYLE

½ teaspoon Drambuie
2 ozs. Scotch
¼ oz. dry vermouth
¼ oz. sweet vermouth
1 maraschino or
   brandied cherry

Pour Drambuie into a prechilled cocktail glass and swirl it around to coat bottom and sides of glass. Stir Scotch and both kinds of vermouth well with ice. Strain into glass. Add cherry.

RUSTY NAIL

¾ oz. Scotch
¾ oz. Drambuie

Pour over rocks in prechilled old-fashioned glass. Stir.

SAZERAC

¼ teaspoon abisante,
   anesone, or any
   other absinthe
   substitute
½ teaspoon sugar
¼ teaspoon bitters
   (Peychaud's, if
   possible)
1 tablespoon water
2 ozs. blended
   whiskey or bourbon
Lemon peel

Swirl abisante around in prechilled old-fashioned glass until inside is completely coated. Add sugar, bitters, and 1 tablespoon water. Stir until sugar is dissolved. Add a large ice cube and whiskey. Stir well. Twist lemon peel above drink and drop into glass. A New Orleans specialty and a magnificent prebrunch drink.

SAZERAC À LA PLAYBOY

¼ teaspoon Pernod
1 small sugar cube
2 dashes Peychaud's
   bitters
1 dash Angostura
   bitters
Water
1½ ozs. straight rye
Lemon peel

Pour Pernod into prechilled old-fashioned glass and roll glass until inside is entirely coated. Add sugar, both kinds of bitters, and enough cold water to barely cover sugar. Muddle until sugar is completely dissolved. Add whiskey and a large ice cube. Stir well. Twist lemon peel above drink and drop into glass.

SCOTCH HOLIDAY SOUR

2 ozs. light Scotch
1 oz. cherry liqueur
½ oz. sweet vermouth
1 oz. lemon juice
½ egg white
1 slice lemon

Shake Scotch, cherry liqueur, vermouth, lemon juice, and egg white well with ice. Strain into prechilled oversize sour glass or into prechilled old-fashioned glass with a large rock. Garnish with lemon slice.

SEABOARD

1 oz. blended
   whiskey
1 oz. gin
½ oz. lemon juice
1 teaspoon sugar
2 sprigs mint

Shake whiskey, gin, lemon juice, and sugar well with ice. Strain over rocks in prechilled old-fashioned glass. Tear several leaves of each mint sprig before dropping into drink.

THE SHOOT

1 oz. Scotch
1 oz. dry sherry
1 teaspoon lemon juice
1 teaspoon orange
   juice
½ teaspoon sugar

Shake well with ice. Strain into prechilled cocktail glass. Serve before a dinner of roast pheasant or partridge.

SINGAPORE

1½ ozs. Canadian
   whisky
¼ oz. sloe gin
¼ oz. Rose's lime
   juice
½ oz. lemon juice
Cucumber peel

Shake whisky, sloe gin, Rose's lime juice, and lemon juice well with ice. Strain over rocks in prechilled old-fashioned glass. Add cucumber peel.

SOUTHERN GINGER

1½ ozs. 100-proof
   bourbon
1 oz. ginger ale
¼ oz. lemon juice
½ teaspoon ginger-
   flavored brandy
Lemon peel

Shake bourbon, ginger ale, lemon juice, and ginger brandy well with ice. Strain into prechilled cocktail glass. Twist lemon peel above drink and drop into glass.

STONYBROOK

1½ ozs. blended
   whiskey
½ oz. triple sec
¼ teaspoon orzata
½ egg white
Lemon peel
Orange peel

Shake whiskey, triple sec, orzata, and egg white well with ice. Strain into prechilled cocktail glass. Twist lemon peel and orange peel above drink and drop into glass. A drink to accompany *barquettes* of hot deviled crab meat.

TROIS RIVIÈRES

1½ ozs. Canadian
   whisky
½ oz. red Dubonnet
¼ oz. Cointreau
Orange peel

Shake whisky, Dubonnet, and Cointreau well with ice. Strain into prechilled cocktail glass. Twist orange peel above drink and drop into glass. Perfect before a midnight collation.

TWIN HILLS

2 ozs. blended
  whiskey
¼ oz. lemon juice
¼ oz. lime juice
2 teaspoons
  Benedictine
1 teaspoon sugar
½ slice lemon
½ slice lime

Shake whiskey, lemon juice, lime juice, Benedictine, and sugar well with ice. Strain into prechilled whiskey-sour glass. Garnish with lemon and lime slices. Offbeat but a very superior sour.

WARD EIGHT

2 ozs. blended U.S.
  whiskey or Canadian
  whisky
½ oz. lemon juice
1 teaspoon sugar
½ teaspoon grenadine
1 slice lemon

Shake whiskey, lemon juice, sugar, and grenadine well with ice. Strain into tall 8-oz. glass. Add cracked ice or ice slices to fill glass. Stir. Garnish with lemon slice. A pleasant tall cocktail that survived Prohibition.

WHISKEY SOUR

2 ozs. blended
  whiskey
¾ oz. lemon juice
1 teaspoon sugar
½ slice lemon
1 maraschino cherry
  (optional)

Shake whiskey, lemon juice, and sugar well with ice. Strain into prechilled whiskey-sour glass. Garnish with lemon slice and cherry, if desired. For a more tart drink, reduce amount of sugar. For a more mellow whiskey sour, use ½ oz. lemon juice and ¼ oz. orange juice. Sours made with Canadian or Scotch whiskies are pleasing variants, the former having a strong appeal for the distaff side.

WHISKEY TODDY, COLD

½ teaspoon sugar
2 teaspoons water
2 ozs. bourbon or
  blended whiskey
Lemon peel (optional)

Put sugar and water into prechilled old-fashioned glass. Stir until sugar dissolves. Fill glass with ice cubes or large pieces of cracked ice. Add whiskey. Stir well. Twist lemon peel above drink and drop into glass. Must be stinging cold.

WHISKEY MAC

1½ ozs. Scotch whisky
1½ ozs. Stone's
  ginger wine

Pour whisky and ginger wine over rocks in 8-oz. glass. Stir. In Scotland this drink is usually served at room temperature without ice. Americans prefer the chilled version. May also be served with lemon twist.

MANHATTAN

In the national drink derby, two or three cocktail generations ago, the manhattan and the martini always wound up in a dead heat. At the present time, the manhattan occupies the second spot. Manhattanites, though less demanding than martini fans, have nevertheless stirred up many spirited variations on the whiskey-vermouth theme. In public pouring houses, the usual manhattan is made with 1½ ounces of whiskey. At private bars, a more generous allowance of whiskey is likely. Here's what most manhattanites expect:

MANHATTAN

1½ to 2 ozs. blended
  whiskey
½ oz. sweet vermouth
1 dash bitters
  (optional)
1 maraschino cherry

Stir whiskey, vermouth, and bitters well with ice. Strain into prechilled cocktail glass. Add cherry.

Dry Manhattan: Use dry instead of sweet vermouth; a twist of lemon peel or an olive may be substituted for the cherry.

Bourbon Manhattan: Use 86- or 100-proof bourbon instead of blended whiskey; if 100-proof bourbon is used, a little extra stirring is in order.

Canadian Manhattan: Use Canadian instead of U.S. blended whiskey; don't overstir or the delicate flavor of the Canadian spirits will become pallid.

Muscari Manhattan: Use Muscari (an apéritif wine) instead of vermouth.

Wine Cocktails

Wine cocktails are for those who like wine and also enjoy pleasantly odd combinations of cold mixed drinks that help unwind the day and provoke appetites for dinner, but who don't want the fast, sometimes staggering, jolt of a martini or an old-fashioned. There are bottled wine cocktails now on the market, but making your own is no formidable task, and the results are extremely pleasant unless you're one of those wine zealots who spend more time appraising one wine versus another than they do drinking them.

The wine cocktails that follow are made from red and white dry table wines. California jug wines are perfect for this kind of bartending. Both red and white wines should be well chilled, and should be served in stemmed wineglasses holding 8 to 10 ounces each. The kind of wine you use will naturally determine the final results of the mixed drinks: A medium-bodied California mountain Burgundy will become a cocktail with sturdy flavor; a Beaujolais nouveau used for the same recipe will result in a lighter, fresher-tasting cocktail. Among the whites, any light-bodied dry wine—from an Italian soave to a dry California Chablis—will do beautifully.

BASES FILLED

4 ozs. chilled dry
   white wine
½ oz. Cointreau
   or triple sec
½ oz. Cognac
1 piece of orange peel

Pour wine, Cointreau, and Cognac into large wineglass. Add 2 ice cubes. Stir well. Twist orange peel above drink and drop into glass.

BERMUDA BLANC

4 ozs. chilled dry
   white wine
½ oz. light rum
1 teaspoon Rose's
   lime juice
1 slice lime

Pour wine, rum, and Rose's lime juice into large wineglass. Add 2 ice cubes. Stir well. Add lime slice.

BRIGHT BERRY

4 ozs. chilled dry
   red wine
½ oz. strawberry
   liqueur
1 teaspoon Cognac
1 fresh strawberry

Pour wine, strawberry liqueur, and Cognac into large wineglass. Add 2 ice cubes. Stir well. Add strawberry.

COOL JAZZ

1 oz. dry white wine
¾ oz. banana liqueur
½ oz. lime juice
1 slice banana

Shake wine, banana liqueur, and lime juice well with ice. Strain into cocktail glass. Float banana slice on drink.

CRANBERRY EYE

4 ozs. chilled dry
   red wine
½ oz. cranberry
   liqueur
½ oz. California
   brandy
1 slice orange

Pour wine, cranberry liqueur, and brandy into large wineglass. Add 2 ice cubes. Stir well. Add orange slice.

FRENCH CURVE

4 ozs. chilled dry
   white wine
1 teaspoon Pernod
1 teaspoon maraschino
   liqueur
1 slice lemon
½ slice orange

Pour wine, Pernod, and maraschino liqueur into large wineglass. Add 2 ice cubes. Stir well. Add lemon slice and orange slice.

ITALIAN PERFUME

4 ozs. chilled dry
   white wine
½ oz. Italian brandy
1 teaspoon amaretto
1 slice lemon

Pour wine, brandy, and amaretto into large wineglass. Add 2 ice cubes. Stir well. Add lemon slice.

MONK'S WINE

4 ozs. chilled dry
   white wine
1 teaspoon green
   Chartreuse
1 slice lemon

Pour wine and Chartreuse into large wine-glass. Add 2 ice cubes. Stir well. Add lemon slice.

PIKE'S PICON

4 ozs. chilled dry
   red wine
½ oz. Amer Picon
1 teaspoon grenadine
1 piece of orange peel

Pour wine, Amer Picon, and grenadine into large wineglass. Add 2 ice cubes. Stir well. Twist orange peel above drink and drop into glass.

RED CARPET

1 oz. dry red wine
1 oz. Chambery Fraise
   (strawberry-flavored
   French vermouth)
½ oz. strawberry
   liqueur
Iced club soda
1 slice lemon

Stir red wine, Chambery Fraise, and strawberry liqueur well with ice. Strain into 6- or 8-oz. wineglass. Add small splash of soda. Stir. Add lemon slice.

RED KIR

4 ozs. chilled
   dry red wine
½ oz. crème de cassis
1 slice lemon

Pour wine and crème de cassis into large wineglass. Add 2 ice cubes. Stir well. Add lemon slice.

RED LIGHT

4 ozs. chilled dry
   red wine
½ oz. Cordial Médoc
½ oz. Cointreau or
   triple sec
1 slice lemon

Pour wine, Cordial Médoc, and Cointreau into large wineglass. Add 2 ice cubes. Stir well. Add lemon slice.

RED MANHATTAN

Dash Angostura bitters
1 teaspoon sugar
Iced club soda
4 ozs. chilled dry
   red wine
½ oz. sweet vermouth
1 piece of orange peel

Pour bitters and sugar into large wineglass. Add a small splash of soda. Stir until sugar dissolves. Add wine and vermouth. Add 2 ice cubes. Stir well. Twist orange peel above drink and drop into glass.

RUBY

2 ozs. red wine
½ oz. maraschino
   liqueur
½ oz. lemon juice
1 dash Angostura
   bitters
1 slice lemon

Stir wine, maraschino liqueur, lemon juice, and bitters well with ice. Strain into 6- or 8-oz. wineglass. Add lemon slice.

SOFT TOUCH

1½ ozs. dry
   white wine
½ beaten egg white
½ oz. heavy
   sweet cream
½ oz. lemon juice
1½ teaspoons sugar

Shake all ingredients extremely well with ice. Strain into prechilled cocktail glass.

VESUVIO

3 ozs. dry white wine
1 teaspoon apricot
   liqueur
1 teaspoon amaretto
1 slice cucumber

Stir white wine, apricot liqueur, and amaretto well with ice. Strain into 6- or 8-oz. wineglass. Add cucumber slice.

WINE AND BITTERS

1 teaspoon sugar
2 dashes
    Angostura bitters
Iced club soda
4 ozs. chilled dry
    white wine
1 slice lemon
½ slice orange

Pour sugar, bitters, and a small splash of soda into large wineglass. Stir until sugar dissolves. Add wine and 2 ice cubes. Stir well. Add lemon and orange slices.

Miscellaneous Cocktails

ANDALUSIA

1½ ozs. very dry
    sherry
½ oz. Cognac
½ oz. light rum
1 dash Angostura
    bitters

Stir well with ice. Strain into prechilled cocktail glass.

BLOODY SAKE

3 ozs. tomato juice
2 ozs. sake
2 teaspoons lemon
    juice
Dash Tabasco sauce
Dash Worcestershire
    sauce
Salt, celery salt, pepper

Pour tomato juice, sake, lemon juice, Tabasco sauce, and Worcestershire sauce into cocktail shaker with ice. Add a sprinkling of salt, celery salt, and pepper. Shake very well. Strain into 8-oz. glass. Add a sprinkling of freshly ground pepper if desired.

BRANDIED MADEIRA

1 oz. Madeira
1 oz. brandy
½ oz. dry vermouth
Lemon peel

Stir Madeira, brandy, and vermouth well with ice. Pour over rocks in prechilled old-fashioned glass. Twist lemon peel above drink and drop into glass.

BRANDIED PORT

1 oz. tawny port
1 oz. brandy
½ oz. lemon juice
1 teaspoon maraschino
  liqueur
1 slice orange

Shake port, brandy, lemon juice, and mara-schino liqueur well with ice. Strain over rocks in prechilled old-fashioned glass. Add orange slice.

CLARET COCKTAIL

1 oz. dry red wine
1 oz. brandy
¼ oz. curaçao
¼ oz. lemon juice
½ teaspoon anisette
Orange peel

Shake wine, brandy, curaçao, lemon juice, and anisette well with ice. Strain into pre-chilled cocktail glass. Twist orange peel above drink and drop into glass.

CREAMY ORANGE

1 oz. orange juice
1 oz. cream sherry
½ oz. heavy cream
2 teaspoons brandy

Shake well with ice. Strain into prechilled cocktail glass. A gentle introduction to a brunch omelet.

FIORD

1 oz. brandy
½ oz. aquavit
½ oz. orange juice
½ oz. lime juice
1 teaspoon grenadine

Shake well with ice. Strain into prechilled cocktail glass.

FLORIDA

1¼ ozs. orange juice
½ oz. gin
¼ oz. kirschwasser
¼ oz. triple sec
1 teaspoon lemon juice

Shake well with ice. Strain into prechilled sugar-frosted cocktail glass. A drink with less hard liquor than citrus juice, but one that always clears up the fog.

FROZEN AQUAVIT

1½ ozs. aquavit
½ oz. lime juice
½ egg white
½ cup crushed ice
1 teaspoon sugar
1 teaspoon kirschwasser

Put all ingredients into blender. Blend at low speed 10–15 seconds. Pour into prechilled deep-saucer champagne glass.

GENEVER COCKTAIL

1½ ozs. Dutch genever gin
½ oz. lime juice
½ oz. orange juice
1 teaspoon sugar
1 dash Angostura bitters

Shake well with ice. Strain over rocks in prechilled old-fashioned glass. Odd but very obliging.

GRAPPA STREGA

1 oz. grappa
1 oz. Strega
¼ oz. lemon juice
¼ oz. orange juice
Lemon peel

Shake grappa, Strega, lemon juice, and orange juice well with ice. Strain into prechilled cocktail glass. Twist lemon peel above drink and drop into glass.

GREAT DANE

1½ ozs. aquavit
¼ oz. dry vermouth
¼ oz. sweet vermouth
2 cocktail onions

Stir aquavit, dry vermouth, and sweet vermouth well with ice. Strain into prechilled cocktail glass with onions, or serve on rocks.

KIR

3½ ozs. ice-cold dry white wine
½ oz. ice-cold crème de cassis

Pour into prechilled 7- or 8-oz. wide-bellied wineglass. Add an ice cube or two if desired. Proportions may be varied, but the 7-to-1 *vin blanc*-cassis ratio above (actually a variation of the vermouth cassis) is the most commonly accepted version.

MARY KÜMMEL

3 ozs. tomato juice
1 oz. kümmel
1 oz. vodka
1 tablespoon lemon
juice
Dash Tabasco sauce
Dash Worcestershire
sauce
Salt, celery salt, pepper

Pour tomato juice, kümmel, vodka, lemon juice, Tabasco sauce, and Worcestershire sauce into cocktail shaker with ice. Add a sprinkling of salt, celery salt, and pepper. Shake very well. Strain into 8-oz. glass. Add a sprinkling of freshly ground pepper if desired.

MIDNIGHT SUN

1½ ozs. aquavit
½ oz. unsweetened
grapefruit juice
½ oz. lemon juice
1 teaspoon sugar
½ teaspoon grenadine
½ slice orange

Shake aquavit, grapefruit juice, lemon juice, sugar, and grenadine well with ice. Strain into prechilled whiskey-sour glass. Add orange slice. Keep herring tidbits within reach.

NORTHERN LIGHTS

1 oz. aquavit
1 oz. light
Canadian whisky
1 dash Angostura
bitters
½ teaspoon grenadine
Iced club soda
1 slice lemon
½ slice orange

Pour aquavit, Canadian whisky, Angostura bitters, and grenadine into old-fashioned glass three-quarters filled with ice cubes. Stir well. Add splash of soda. Add lemon slice and orange slice.

PERNOD DRIP

1½ ozs. Pernod
1 cube sugar

The first requirement for this drink is an absinthe drip glass. If you don't own a drip glass, you can use a tea strainer over an old-fashioned glass as a substitute. First pour the Pernod into the glass. Place the strainer on the glass. Put the sugar over the drip section on top of the glass. Pack a mound of crushed or finely cracked ice atop the sugar. When the ice has melted, the drip is ready. Strictly for curio seekers in the spirit world.

PISCO SOUR

1½ ozs. pisco brandy
½ oz. lemon juice
1 tablespoon sugar
1 tablespoon egg white
Angostura bitters

Shake pisco, lemon juice, sugar, and egg white well with ice. Strain into prechilled cocktail glass with sugar-frosted rim. Float a few drops bitters on top. May also be poured into small punch cups.

ROCKY GREEN DRAGON

1 oz. gin
¾ oz. green
   Chartreuse
¾ oz. Cognac

Shake extremely well with ice. Strain over rocks in prechilled old-fashioned glass. A potent dragon to be slowly sipped, not gulped.

SAKE SOUR

2 ozs. sake
½ oz. lemon juice
1½ ozs. orange juice
1 teaspoon sugar
½ slice orange

Shake sake, lemon juice, orange juice, and sugar well with ice. Strain into whiskey-sour glass. Garnish with orange slice.

SAKE STINGER

1 oz. sake
½ oz. white crème
   de menthe or
   peppermint
   schnapps
½ oz. California
   brandy
Lemon peel

Shake sake, crème de menthe, and brandy well with ice. Strain into cocktail glass. Twist lemon peel above drink and drop into glass.

SEA ROVER

1½ ozs. aquavit
½ oz. strawberry
   liqueur
½ oz. lime juice
1 piece of lime peel

Shake aquavit, strawberry liqueur, and lime juice well with ice. Strain into prechilled cocktail glass. Twist lime peel above drink and drop into glass.

SHERRY GIMLET

2 ozs. very dry sherry
1 oz. gin
1 oz. Rose's lime juice

Stir sherry, gin, and Rose's lime juice well with ice. Strain into 8-oz. glass. Add ice cubes to fill glass. Stir.

SHERRY SOUR

2 ozs. very dry sherry
2 teaspoons sugar
½ oz. lemon juice
1 oz. orange juice
½ slice orange

Shake sherry, sugar, lemon juice, and orange juice well with ice. Strain into whiskey-sour glass. Garnish with orange slice.

SHINTO

2 dashes Angostura
   bitters
½ teaspoon sugar
Iced club soda
1 oz. sake
1 oz. Suntory whisky
1 slice lemon

Pour bitters, sugar, and splash of soda into old-fashioned glass. Stir until sugar dissolves. Add sake, Suntory whisky, and three large ice cubes. Stir well. Add splash of soda. Stir. Add lemon slice.

SUISSESSE

1½ ozs. Pernod
½ oz. anisette
¼ oz. heavy cream
½ egg white

Shake well with ice. Pour into prechilled cocktail glass. Perfect midnight cocktail that's really more Mediterranean than Swiss.

SWEDISH SIDECAR

1 oz. aquavit
½ oz. Cointreau or
  triple sec
½ oz. lemon juice
½ oz. orange juice

Shake aquavit, Cointreau, lemon juice, and orange juice well with ice. Strain into prechilled sugar-frosted cocktail glass.

YELLOW PLUM

1½ ozs. quetsch,
  mirabelle or slivovitz
½ oz. lemon juice
½ oz. orange juice
1 teaspoon maraschino
  liqueur
1 teaspoon sugar

Shake well with ice. Strain into prechilled cocktail glass. Tart, triumphant, titillating.

20

HIGH SPIRITS

Medium-Tall and King-Size Potables

If the word "highball" is heard less and less frequently these days, the drink itself is called for more and more often. Drinkers everywhere now ask for Scotch and soda, bourbon and water, applejack and ginger ale, and other happy mixtures suited to their own thirst specifications. Although the highball is the easiest drink in the world to define—a small amount of something strong with a larger amount of something weak in a tall glass with ice —it's the one potable for which you seldom see a recipe. As a matter of fact, a host who, in the intimacy of his own digs, strictly follows a highball recipe is inhospitable. It's the one drink guests themselves expect to mix to their own tastes, in the same way that they salt and pepper their food. No two-finger measurements are alike and no two guests will ever say "when" at the same point on the stopwatch. Even at commuter stand-up bars, where whiskey is carefully measured in a standard jigger, the bubbly water usually remains in the hands of the highballer pouring his soda, 7-Up, or tonic water to his own level.

But the highball is only one of countless potables in tall glasses. A tall drink at the end of a long, tiring day can do things no short drink can ever hope to do. A wilted worthy need only look at a lofty drink clinking with ice, and miraculous changes take place within him. His collar seems to cling less tenaciously. He begins to talk in more relaxed, civilized tones. And then, as the first sip of a tall drink passes over his tongue and throat, like springwater gurgling into a hot arroyo, he feels the unparalleled pleasure of a long-delayed thrill.

One of the obvious virtues of tall mixed drinks is that they never seem to get in the way of food, or vice versa. A man may hesitate to eat a trout *au bleu* while drinking a manhattan, but he won't hesitate to drink a tall spritzer of Rhine wine and soda before, during, or after the trout. Although Europophilian wine pundits will be horrified at the thought, many a tall cooler at many a fine feast supplants *both* the cocktail and the wine. Ounce for ounce, a tall cooler with club soda is actually no stronger than wine. But in the final analysis, tall drinks are made not for debating but for happy guzzling.

In preparing tall drinks, whether they be 8, 12, or 20 ounces, the host should follow this modern code for presenting them:

Use a fine liquor. The flavor of a poor liquor is actually intensified in a tall drink; you have time to scrutinize it more carefully than when you down it in one gulp. This doesn't mean that you must buy a sixteen-year-old bonded whiskey the next time you serve a round of whiskey collinses, but you should seek one of the eminent brands of liquor that are mellow, smooth, and pleasing whether taken straight or in a tall drink.

Be meticulous about the quality of the iced club soda or the ginger ale. For a small number of highballers, serve splits of soda or ginger ale. Larger bottles of carbonated waters, except for a party, just stand around going quietly flat unless you and your guests are unusually speedy drinkers.

Add bubblewater just before drinks are delivered. For optimum sparkle and so that it retains its fizz as long as possible, pour it against the inside of the tilted glass. Be sure the effervescent water is ice-cold.

Plain tap water, if used, must be clear and clean, without evidence of rust, lime, iron, chlorination, or other urban evils. Use bottled springwater, if necessary, when your guests decline bubbles.

Use enough liquor in a tall drink, at least 1½ ounces in an 8-ounce glass and up to 2 ounces or more in 12- to 20-ounce glasses.

Use thin glassware with heavy bottoms to avoid the well-known sliding drink.

The gin and tonic has not only joined the tall-drink derby, but in many circles is way out in front both in summer and winter. Bitter lemon has joined the same fraternity. While the British Empire was shrinking, the British-inspired bubblies became more and more popular.

Among simple highballs, the whiskey highball is the best-known. But there's no dogma that interdicts the use of any liquor in a highball, from aquavit to zubrovka. One of the best contemporary highballs is light, dry rum and iced club soda or iced tonic water.

So-called lowballs are actually served in glasses which hold as much as their taller cousins but which are squat in shape rather than long; old-fashioned-type glasses ranging from 7 to 11 ounces are considered lowballs.

Bucks

Bucks are medium-long drinks—served in tall 8-ounce glasses—that always contain ginger ale and fresh lemon or lime juice. Traditionally the fruit was squeezed and dropped into the glass. You'll find you get better bucks if the lemon or lime juice is measured into the glass and the drink then garnished with a slice of fruit as its crowning touch.

APPLE BUCK

1½ ozs. applejack
1 teaspoon ginger-
    flavored brandy
½ oz. lemon juice
Iced ginger ale
1 chunk preserved
    ginger in syrup

Shake applejack, ginger brandy, and lemon juice well with ice. Strain into 8-oz. glass half-filled with ice. Add ginger ale. Stir. Add preserved ginger.

BRANDY BUCK

1½ ozs. brandy
1 teaspoon crème de
    menthe
½ oz. lemon juice
Iced ginger ale
Fresh grapes

Shake brandy, crème de menthe, and lemon juice well with ice. Strain into 8-oz. glass half-filled with ice. Add ginger ale. Stir. Add three or four seedless grapes or two large pitted black grapes cut in half.

GIN BUCK

1½ ozs. gin
½ oz. lemon juice
Iced ginger ale
1 slice lemon

Shake gin and lemon juice well with ice. Strain into 8-oz. glass half-filled with ice. Add ginger ale. Stir. Add lemon slice.

GREEK BUCK

1½ ozs. Metaxa
  brandy
½ oz. lemon juice
Iced ginger ale
1 teaspoon ouzo
1 slice lemon

Shake Metaxa and lemon juice well with ice. Strain into 8-oz. glass half-filled with ice. Add ginger ale. Stir. Float ouzo on top of drink. Add lemon slice.

NEW ORLEANS BUCK

1½ ozs. light rum
½ oz. lime juice
½ oz. orange juice
2 dashes Peychaud's
  bitters
Iced ginger ale
1 slice lime

Shake rum, lime juice, orange juice, and bitters well with ice. Strain into 8-oz. glass half-filled with ice. Add ginger ale. Stir. Add lime slice.

ORANGE BUCK

1½ ozs. gin
1 oz. orange juice
½ oz. lemon juice
Iced ginger ale
1 slice cocktail orange
  in syrup

Shake gin, orange juice, and lemon juice well with ice. Strain into 8-oz. glass half-filled with ice. Add ginger ale. Stir. Add orange slice.

PEACH BUCK

1¼ ozs. vodka
2 teaspoons peach-
    flavored brandy
½ oz. lemon juice
Iced ginger ale
1 slice lemon
1 slice fresh or
    brandied peach

Shake vodka, peach-flavored brandy, and lemon juice well with ice. Strain into 8-oz. glass half-filled with ice. Add ginger ale. Stir. Garnish with lemon and peach slices.

RUM BUCK

1½ ozs. light rum
½ oz. lime juice
Iced ginger ale
1 slice lime
Toasted slivered
    almonds

Shake rum and lime juice well with ice. Strain into 8-oz. glass half-filled with ice. Add ginger ale. Stir. Add lime slice and about a teaspoon of almonds.

SCOTCH BUCK

1 oz. Scotch
½ oz. ginger-flavored
    brandy
Iced ginger beer or
    ginger ale
½ medium-size lime

Fill a tall 8-oz. glass with ice cubes. Add Scotch and ginger-flavored brandy. Stir well. Add ginger beer to fill glass. Stir. Squeeze lime above drink and drop into glass.

Cobblers

Like a fix (see page 394-396), of which it is a larger version, a cobbler is concocted in the glass and drunk without club soda, quinine water, or any other sparkling diluents. Though the recipes that follow are designed to fill a 12-ounce glass—including the cracked ice that forms the base of each—they can be extended or abbreviated to fit your own glassware. The cracked ice in a filled glass will usually collapse somewhat when stirred with liquor; an ice refill is then necessary.

AMARETTO COBBLER

1½ ozs. gin
2 ozs. orange juice
1 oz. lemon juice
½ oz. amaretto
½ slice orange

Fill a 12-oz. glass with finely cracked ice. Add gin, orange juice, lemon juice, and amaretto. Stir well. Add more ice to fill glass almost to rim. Stir. Add orange slice.

BRANDY COBBLER

1½ ozs. brandy
½ oz. curaçao
½ oz. lemon juice
1 teaspoon sugar
1 teaspoon
  kirschwasser
1 cocktail-pineapple
  stick

Fill a 12-oz. glass with finely cracked ice. Add brandy, curaçao, lemon juice, sugar, and kirschwasser. Stir well until sugar is dissolved. Add more ice to fill glass to rim. Stir. Garnish with pineapple stick.

CHERRY COBBLER

1½ ozs. gin
½ oz. Peter Heering
  or Cherry Karise
½ oz. crème de cassis
1 teaspoon sugar
½ oz. lemon juice
1 slice lemon
1 maraschino cherry

Fill a 12-oz. glass with finely cracked ice. Add gin, Peter Heering, crème de cassis, sugar, and lemon juice. Stir well until sugar dissolves. Add more ice to fill glass to rim. Stir. Add lemon slice and cherry.

CHERRY RUM COBBLER

1½ ozs. light rum
1 oz. cherry-flavored
  brandy
½ teaspoon sugar
½ oz. lemon juice
1 slice lemon
1 maraschino stem
  cherry

Fill a tall 12-oz. glass with coarsely cracked ice. (Ice from a "chipper" tray is good for this drink.) Add rum, cherry-flavored brandy, sugar, and lemon juice. Stir very well until sugar dissolves. Add ice, if necessary, to fill glass to rim. Stir. Add lemon slice and cherry.

CLARET COBBLER

4 ozs. dry red wine
½ oz. lemon juice
½ oz. orange juice
½ oz. maraschino
   liqueur
½ slice orange
½ slice lime

Fill a 12-oz. glass with finely cracked ice. Add wine, lemon juice, orange juice, and maraschino liqueur. Stir well. Add more ice to fill glass to rim. Stir. Garnish with orange and lime slices.

PORT COBBLER

4 ozs. tawny port
¾ oz. brandy
½ teaspoon sugar
Lemon peel
Orange peel
2 large mint leaves

Fill a 12-oz. glass with finely cracked ice. Add port, brandy, and sugar. Stir well. Add more ice to fill glass to rim. Stir. Twist lemon peel and orange peel above drink and drop into glass. Tear mint leaves partially and drop into glass.

SHERRY COBBLER

2½ ozs. sherry
1 oz. brandy
½ oz. orange juice
½ teaspoon sugar
1 slice cocktail orange
   in syrup

Fill a 12-oz. glass with finely cracked ice. Add sherry, brandy, orange juice, and sugar. Stir well until sugar dissolves. Add more ice to fill glass to rim. Stir. Garnish with orange slice.

WHISKEY COBBLER

2½ ozs. blended
   whiskey
¾ oz. lemon juice
½ oz. grapefruit juice
1½ teaspoons orgeat
   or orzata
½ slice orange
1 slice fresh or
   brandied peach

Fill a 12-oz. glass with finely cracked ice. Add whiskey, lemon juice, grapefruit juice, and orgeat. Stir well. Add more ice to fill glass to rim. Stir. Garnish with orange and peach slices.

Collinses

Among the oldest and best-known tall summer drinks, collinses always start with liquor, lemon juice, and soda and bear a striking resemblance to fizzes (page 396). A Tom Collins and a gin fizz are for all practical purposes the same drink. A lemon slice is an accepted garnish. Some bartenders dress up the collins with orange slices, cherries, and other bits of fruit, although this practice is frowned upon by veteran benders at the bar.

APPLEJACK COLLINS

2 ozs. applejack
1 teaspoon sugar
1 oz. lemon juice
2 dashes orange bitters
Iced club soda
1 slice lemon

Shake applejack, sugar, lemon juice, and bitters well with ice. Strain into tall 14-oz. glass half-filled with ice. Add soda. Stir. Add lemon slice.

B & B COLLINS

2 ozs. Cognac
½ oz. lemon juice
1 teaspoon sugar
Iced club soda
½ oz. Benedictine
1 slice lemon

Shake Cognac, lemon juice, and sugar well with ice. Strain into tall 14-oz. glass half-filled with ice. Add soda. Stir. Float Benedictine on drink. Add lemon slice. California brandy may be used in place of Cognac.

BOURBON COLLINS

2 ozs. 100-proof
   bourbon
2 dashes Peychaud's
   bitters
½ oz. lemon juice
1 teaspoon sugar
Iced club soda
1 slice lemon

Shake bourbon, bitters, lemon juice, and sugar well with ice. Strain into tall 14-oz. glass half-filled with ice. Add soda. Stir. Add lemon slice.

BRANDIED BANANA COLLINS

1½ ozs. brandy
1 oz. banana liqueur
½ oz. lemon juice
Iced club soda
1 slice lemon
1 slice banana

Shake brandy, banana liqueur, and lemon juice well with ice. Strain into tall 14-oz. glass half-filled with ice. Add soda. Stir. Add lemon and banana slices.

COEXISTENCE COLLINS

2 ozs. vodka
½ oz. lemon juice
1 teaspoon sugar
1 teaspoon kümmel
Iced club soda
Cucumber peel, 2
  inches long, ½ inch
  wide
Lemon peel

Shake vodka, lemon juice, sugar, and kümmel well with ice. Strain into tall 14-oz. glass half-filled with ice. Add soda. Stir. Add cucumber peel. Twist lemon peel above drink and drop into glass.

CUERNAVACA COLLINS

1 oz. tequila
1 oz. gin
1 oz. lime juice
2 teaspoons sugar
Iced club soda
1 slice lime

Shake tequila, gin, lime juice, and sugar well with ice. Strain into tall 14-oz. glass half-filled with ice cubes. Add soda to fill glass. Stir lightly. Add lime slice.

DRY SHERRY COLLINS

3 ozs. very dry sherry
1 oz. gin
1 oz. lemon juice
1 teaspoon sugar or
  more to taste
Iced club soda
1 slice lemon

Shake sherry, gin, lemon juice, and sugar well with ice. Strain into 14-oz. glass half-filled with ice cubes. Fill glass with soda. Add lemon slice.

MINT COLLINS

2 ozs. gin
4 large mint leaves
½ oz. lemon juice
1 teaspoon sugar
½ cup crushed ice
Iced club soda
1 slice lemon

Put gin, mint leaves, lemon juice, sugar, and crushed ice into blender. Blend at high speed 15 seconds or until mint leaves are finely chopped. Pour into tall 14-oz. glass. Add soda to fill glass. Stir. Add lemon slice.

PISTACHIO LIME COLLINS

1½ ozs. gin
1 oz. pistachio liqueur
1 oz. lime juice
3 large ice cubes
Iced club soda
1 slice lime

Pour gin, pistachio liqueur, and lime juice over ice cubes in tall 12-oz. glass. Stir well. Add soda. Stir. Add lime slice.

PORT COLLINS

2 ozs. white port such as Porto Branco
1 oz. gin
1 oz. lemon juice
1 teaspoon sugar
Iced club soda
1 slice lemon

Shake port, gin, lemon juice, and sugar well with ice. Strain into tall 14-oz. glass half-filled with ice cubes. Add soda. Stir. Add lemon slice.

TOM COLLINS

2 to 2½ ozs. gin
1 to 2 teaspoons sugar
½ to 1 oz. lemon juice
Iced club soda
1 slice lemon
  (optional)
1 slice orange
  (optional)
1 maraschino cherry
  (optional)

Shake gin, sugar, and lemon juice well with ice. Strain into tall 14-oz. glass half-filled with ice. Add soda. Stir. Add lemon slice and/or orange slice and/or cherry.

JOHN COLLINS

Same drink as Tom Collins except made with Dutch genever gin.

Coolers—Miscellaneous Tall Drinks

For every taste, for every mood, for every summer day, the following potpourri of coolers and icy tall drinks will be as welcome as the trade winds to becalmed vessels on a sweltering sea.

ALLA SALUTE!

1 oz. Sciarada
1½ ozs. light rum
½ oz. lime juice
3 ozs. pineapple juice
Iced club soda
1 slice lime

Pour Sciarada, rum, lime juice, and pineapple juice into tall 12-oz. glass filled with rocks. Stir well. Add soda to fill glass. Stir. Add lime slice.

ALMOND EYE

1 oz. gin
1 oz. California
  brandy
½ oz. amaretto
1 oz. lemon juice
1 teaspoon grenadine
Iced club soda

Shake gin, brandy, amaretto, lemon juice, and grenadine well with ice. Strain into 8-oz. glass. Add 2 ice cubes. Add splash of soda. Stir.

ALOHA

1 oz. light rum
½ oz. Midori liqueur
½ oz. lime juice
½ oz. dry vermouth
1-inch cube papaya

Shake rum, Midori liqueur, lime juice, and vermouth well with ice. Strain over rocks in 8-oz. glass. Fasten papaya on cocktail spear and place over rim of glass.

AMER PICON COOLER

1½ ozs. Amer Picon
1 oz. gin
½ oz. cherry liqueur
½ oz. lemon juice
1 teaspoon sugar
Iced club soda

Shake Amer Picon, gin, cherry liqueur, lemon juice, and sugar well with ice. Strain into tall 14-oz. glass half-filled with ice. Add soda. Stir.

APPLE BRANDY COOLER

2 ozs. brandy
1 oz. light rum
3 ozs. apple juice
½ oz. lime juice
1 teaspoon dark
   Jamaica rum
1 slice lime

Shake brandy, light rum, apple juice, and lime juice well with ice. Strain into tall 14-oz. glass. Add ice to fill glass. Stir. Float dark rum on drink. Add lime slice.

APPLE KNOCKER

2½ ozs. applejack
½ oz. sweet vermouth
3 ozs. orange juice
½ oz. lemon juice
1½ teaspoons sugar
½ cup crushed ice

Put all ingredients into blender. Blend at high speed 15–20 seconds. Pour into tall 14-oz. glass. Let drink settle a moment. Add ice cubes to fill glass. Stir.

BARBADOS PLANTER'S PUNCH

2 ozs. Barbados
   Mount Gay rum
½ oz. heavy dark rum
1 oz. lime juice
2 teaspoons sugar
3 dashes Angostura
   bitters
Freshly ground nutmeg
1 slice lime

Shake both kinds of rum, lime juice, sugar, and bitters well with ice. Strain into tall 12-oz. glass three-quarters filled with coarsely cracked ice. Stir well. Add ice if necessary to fill glass to rim. Sprinkle with nutmeg. Add lime slice.

BATTERING RAM

1 oz. light rum
1 oz. dark
    Jamaica rum
4 ozs. orange juice
½ oz. Wild Turkey
    liqueur
½ oz. lime juice
Iced tonic water
1 slice lime

Shake light rum, dark rum, orange juice, Wild Turkey liqueur, and lime juice well with ice. Strain into tall 14-oz. glass half-filled with ice cubes. Fill glass with tonic water. Stir. Add lime slice.

BEER BUSTER

1½ ozs. ice-cold
    100-proof vodka
Ice-cold beer or ale
2 dashes Tabasco
    sauce

Pour vodka, beer, and Tabasco sauce into prechilled tall 14-oz. glass or beer mug. Stir lightly. A drink for those who like to key up with beer rather than with cocktails before dinner; for football fans hoarse from cheering; for men who like a long, cold drink with their bubbling-hot Welsh rabbit; and for cheese connoisseurs with a thirst.

BELFRY BAT

1 oz. Sciarada
1 oz. dark Jamaica
    rum
2 ozs. papaya nectar
2 dashes Angostura
    bitters
Iced club soda
1 slice lemon

Pour Sciarada, rum, papaya nectar, and bitters into tall 14-oz. glass three-quarters filled with ice cubes. Stir well. Add club soda to fill glass. Stir. Add lemon slice.

BITTER BANANA COOLER

1½ ozs. light rum
¼ cup sliced banana
¼ cup pineapple juice
½ oz. lime juice
2 dashes Peychaud's
    bitters
½ cup crushed ice
Iced bitter-lemon soda

Put rum, sliced banana, pineapple juice, lime juice, bitters, and crushed ice into blender. Blend 10–15 seconds at high speed. Pour into tall 14-oz. glass. Let foamy cap of drink settle somewhat. Add two ice cubes. Fill glass with bitter-lemon soda. A tall drink in the frozen-daiquiri tradition.

BITTER BOURBON LEMONADE

2 ozs. bourbon
1 oz. lemon juice
½ oz. lime juice
1 teaspoon grenadine
1 teaspoon sugar
Iced bitter-lemon soda
1 slice lemon

Shake bourbon, lemon juice, lime juice, grenadine, and sugar well with ice. Strain into tall 14-oz. glass. Add two ice cubes. Fill glass with bitter-lemon soda. Garnish with lemon slice. A bittersweet pleasure.

BITTER BRANDY AND SHERRY

1 oz. brandy
1 oz. oloroso (cream) sherry
½ oz. cherry liqueur
1 teaspoon lemon juice
Iced bitter-lemon soda
1 slice lemon

Shake brandy, sherry, cherry liqueur, and lemon juice well with ice. Strain into tall 14-oz. glass with two large ice cubes. Add soda. Stir. Add lemon slice.

BITTER-LEMON BRACER

2 ozs. vodka
2 ozs. orange juice
½ oz. lemon juice
Iced bitter-lemon soda
1-in. piece orange peel
1-in. piece lemon peel
1 slice orange

Fill 14-oz. glass with ice cubes. Add vodka, orange juice, and lemon juice. Fill with bitter lemon and stir very well. Twist orange and lemon peels over drink and drop into glass. For a drier bracer, use tonic water instead of bitter lemon. Cut orange slice and fasten onto rim of glass.

BITTER-LEMON COOLER

1½ ozs. dry vermouth
1 oz. gin
1 teaspoon strawberry syrup
1 teaspoon lemon juice
Iced bitter-lemon soda
Lemon peel

Shake vermouth, gin, strawberry syrup, and lemon juice well with ice. Strain into tall 14-oz. glass containing two large ice cubes. Add bitter-lemon soda. Stir. Twist lemon peel above drink and drop into glass.

BITTER-ORANGE COOLER

3 ozs. sweet vermouth
2 dashes Angostura
  bitters
2½ ozs. orange juice
½ oz. lemon juice
½ oz. cherry-flavored
  brandy
Orange soda
1 slice orange

Shake vermouth, Angostura bitters, orange juice, lemon juice, and cherry-flavored brandy well with ice. Strain into tall 14-oz. glass half-filled with ice cubes. Add soda. Stir. Garnish with orange slice.

BITTER PERNOD

1 oz. Pernod
1 oz. vodka
1 oz. lemon juice
Iced bitter-lemon soda
1 slice lemon

Fill tall 14-oz. glass with rocks. Add Pernod, vodka, and lemon juice. Stir very well. Fill with bitter-lemon soda. Add lemon slice.

BITTER PLANTER'S PUNCH

2 ozs. golden rum
1 teaspoon sugar
1 teaspoon grenadine
½ oz. lemon juice
Iced bitter-lemon soda
1 slice lemon

Shake rum, sugar, grenadine, and lemon juice extremely well with ice. Strain into tall 14-oz. glass three-quarters filled with ice cubes. Stir well. Fill glass with bitter-lemon soda. Stir lightly. Add lemon slice.

BLENDED COMFORT

2 ozs. blended whiskey
½ oz. Southern Comfort
¼ cup thawed frozen
  peaches
½ oz. dry vermouth
1½ ozs. lemon juice
1 oz. orange juice
½ cup crushed ice
1 slice lemon
1 slice cocktail orange in
  syrup

Put whiskey, Southern Comfort, peaches, vermouth, lemon juice, orange juice, and crushed ice into blender. Blend 10–15 seconds. Pour into tall 14-oz. glass. Add ice to fill glass. Garnish with lemon and orange slices.

BORDER CROSSING

1½ ozs. tequila
½ oz. cranberry
  liqueur
½ oz. lime juice
1 teaspoon sugar
1 slice lime

Shake tequila, cranberry liqueur, lime juice, and sugar well with ice. Strain over rocks in 8-oz. tall glass. Add lime slice.

BOURBON-AND-MADEIRA JULEP

1½ ozs. bourbon
1½ ozs. Madeira or
  amontillado sherry
¼ oz. lemon juice
Sugar (optional)
1 cocktail-pineapple
  stick
4 sprigs mint

Fill double old-fashioned glass with coarsely cracked ice. Add bourbon, Madeira, and lemon juice. Stir well. Add sugar if desired. Add more ice if necessary to fill glass to rim. Garnish with pineapple stick and mint.

BOURBON MILK PUNCH

2 ozs. bourbon
1 teaspoon sugar
8 ozs. (1 measuring
  cup) milk
Freshly grated nutmeg

Shake bourbon, sugar, and milk well with ice. Strain into 12-oz. glass. Sprinkle with nutmeg.

BOURBON RUMBO

1 teaspoon sugar
Dash Angostura
  bitters
Chilled club soda
¾ oz. bourbon
¾ oz. golden rum
½ oz. sweet vermouth
1 slice cocktail orange
  in syrup, drained

Pour sugar, bitters, and a small splash of soda into 8-oz. tall glass. Stir until sugar dissolves. Add bourbon, rum, vermouth, and several ice cubes. Stir well. Add a splash of soda. Stir. Add orange slice.

BUENAS TARDES

1½ ozs. tequila
5 ozs. chilled
 apple juice
1 oz. lemon juice
1 slice lemon

Pour tequila, apple juice, and lemon juice into tall 12-oz. glass. Add ice cubes to fill glass. Stir well. Add lemon slice.

BRANDIED PEACH SLING

1¾ ozs. brandy
½ oz. peach-flavored
 brandy
¾ oz. lemon juice
1 teaspoon sugar
Iced club soda
1 slice brandied or
 thawed frozen peach
Lemon peel

Shake brandy, peach-flavored brandy, lemon juice, and sugar well with ice. Strain into tall 14-oz. glass half-filled with ice. Add soda. Stir. Add peach slice. Twist lemon peel above drink and drop into glass.

BRIGHTON PUNCH

1 oz. bourbon
1 oz. Cognac
¾ oz. Benedictine
1 oz. orange juice
½ oz. lemon juice
1 oz. iced club soda
½ slice orange
1 slice lemon

Shake bourbon, Cognac, Benedictine, orange juice, and lemon juice well with ice. Strain into tall 14-oz. glass. Add soda and enough ice to fill glass. Stir. Garnish with orange and lemon slices. An individual punch brewed outside a punch bowl.

BUNNY MOTHER

1¼ ozs. vodka
1 oz. orange juice
1 oz. lemon juice
1 teaspoon sugar
¼ oz. grenadine
¼ oz. Cointreau
½ slice orange
1 maraschino cherry

Shake vodka, orange juice, lemon juice, sugar, and grenadine well with ice. Strain into prechilled 12-oz. mug. Add coarsely cracked ice to fill mug to ½ inch from top. Float Cointreau on top. Garnish with orange slice and cherry.

BYRRH CASSIS COOLER

2 ozs. Byrrh
½ oz. crème de cassis
Iced club soda
1 slice lemon

Put ice cubes up to the rim in a tall 14-oz. glass. Add Byrrh and crème de cassis. Add soda. Stir. Garnish with lemon slice. Quickens the appetite even though slightly sweet. Nice to hold in your hands when the *blanquette de veau* is simmering in the kitchen.

CABALLO

6 ozs. ice-cold
   grapefruit juice
1½ ozs. tequila
1 oz. amaretto

Pour into tall 14-oz. glass three-quarters filled with ice cubes. Stir well. Add ice cubes if necessary to fill glass to rim. Stir.

CALYPSO COOLER

2½ ozs. light rum
1 oz. frozen
   concentrated
   pineapple juice,
   thawed but not
   diluted
½ oz. lime juice
1 teaspoon sugar
Iced club soda
1 thin slice fresh
   pineapple
1 slice lime

Shake rum, pineapple juice, lime juice, and sugar well with ice. Strain into tall 14-oz. glass. Add a splash of soda and enough ice to fill glass. Stir. Garnish with pineapple and lime slices.

CARIBBEAN COFFEE

1 oz. light rum
½ oz. crème de cacao
6 ozs. cold strong
   coffee, sweetened
   to taste
1 oz. heavy sweet
   cream
Dollop of whipped
   cream

Pour rum, crème de cacao, and coffee into tall 12-oz. glass three-quarters filled with ice cubes. Add heavy cream. Stir well. Add dollop of whipped cream.

CARIBBEAN MULE

1½ ozs. light rum
½ oz. dark Jamaica
　rum
½ oz. lime juice
¼ oz. triple sec
¼ oz. maraschino
　liqueur
Iced ginger beer
　or ginger ale
1 slice lime
1 sprig mint

Shake both kinds of rum, lime juice, triple sec, and maraschino well with ice. Strain into tall 12-oz. glass half-filled with ice cubes. Add ginger beer to almost fill glass. Stir lightly. Garnish with lime slice and mint.

CARIBBEAN SLING

2 ozs. light rum
½ oz. lime juice
½ oz. lemon juice
½ oz. triple sec
1 teaspoon sugar
Iced club soda
1 piece cucumber rind
　½ in. wide, 4 inches
　long

Shake rum, lime juice, lemon juice, triple sec, and sugar very well with ice. Strain into tall 14-oz. glass half-filled with ice cubes. Stir well. Add soda to fill glass. Place cucumber rind in glass.

CARTHUSIAN COOLER

1 oz. yellow Chartreuse
1 oz. bourbon
Iced club soda

Put three large ice cubes into a tall 14-oz. glass. Add Chartreuse and bourbon. Fill glass with soda. Stir.

CHABLIS COOLER

½ oz. grenadine
½ oz. lemon juice
¼ teaspoon vanilla
　extract
1 oz. vodka
Iced Chablis

Sugar-frost a tall 14-oz. glass. Pour grenadine, lemon juice, vanilla extract, and vodka into glass. Stir well. Add three large ice cubes. Fill glass to rim with Chablis. Stir.

CHARTREUSE COOLER

2 ozs. yellow
   Chartreuse
3 ozs. orange juice
1 oz. lemon juice
Iced bitter-lemon soda
1 slice orange

Shake Chartreuse, orange juice, and lemon juice well with ice. Strain into tall 14-oz. glass half-filled with ice. Fill glass with bitter-lemon soda. Add orange slice.

CHERRY ISLE

1 oz. aquavit
1 oz. Peter Heering
   liqueur
Iced tonic water
1 slice lime

Pour aquavit and Peter Heering into 10-oz. glass half-filled with rocks. Stir well. Add tonic water. Stir. Add lime slice.

CHERRY PLANTER'S PUNCH

1 oz. kirschwasser
½ oz. dark Jamaica
   rum
½ oz. lime juice
2 dashes Angostura
   bitters
1 teaspoon sugar
Freshly grated nutmeg
1 slice lime
½ slice orange

Shake kirschwasser, rum, lime juice, bitters, and sugar extremely well with ice. Strain over rocks in 8-oz. glass. Add ice if necessary to fill glass to rim. Stir well. Sprinkle with nutmeg. Garnish with lime slice and orange slice.

CHERRY RUM COLA

1½ ozs. golden rum
¾ oz. Peter Heering
   liqueur
1 teaspoon lemon juice
Iced cola
1 slice lemon

Fill a 12-oz. glass three-quarters full with ice cubes. Add rum, Peter Heering liqueur, and lemon juice. Stir very well. Add cola to fill glass to rim. Add lemon slice.

CHICO

1 oz. tequila
1 oz. blackberry-
    flavored brandy
½ oz. lemon juice
1 teaspoon sugar
Iced club soda
1 slice lemon

Shake tequila, blackberry-flavored brandy, lemon juice, and sugar well with ice. Strain into tall 14-oz. glass half-filled with ice cubes. Stir. Add club soda to fill glass. Stir. Add lemon slice.

CLARET COOLER

4 ozs. chilled dry red
    wine
½ oz. brandy
1 oz. orange juice
½ oz. lemon juice
3 ozs. iced club soda
Orange rind, 3 inches
    long, ½ inch wide
1 slice lemon

Pour wine, brandy, orange juice, lemon juice, and soda into tall 14-oz. glass. Add ice cubes or cracked ice to fill glass. Stir. Place orange rind in drink. Float lemon slice on top.

CLARET RUM COOLER

3 ozs. chilled dry red
    wine
1 oz. light rum
½ oz. kirschwasser
½ oz. Falernum
3 ozs. iced club soda
1 slice orange
1 large fresh
    strawberry

Pour wine, rum, kirschwasser, Falernum, and soda into tall 14-oz. glass. Add ice cubes or cracked ice to fill glass. Stir. Garnish with orange slice and strawberry.

COCONUT COOLER

1½ ozs. CocoRibe
½ oz. California
    brandy
1½ ozs. papaya nectar
½ oz. lemon juice
1 slice lemon

Shake CocoRibe, brandy, papaya nectar, and lemon juice well with ice. Strain into tall or squat 8-oz glass. Add ice cubes to fill glass. Stir. Add lemon slice.

COCONUT COOLER IN SHELL

1 coconut
½ cup crushed ice
1 oz. canned cream of
  coconut
1½ ozs. light rum
1 oz. heavy cream

Remove end of coconut opposite coconut eyes. The best procedure is to hold the base of the coconut firmly in the left hand. With a very heavy French knife or cleaver, chop top off by striking coconut glancing blows diagonally. Several whacks may be necessary. Avoid spilling coconut juice if possible. Pour out coconut juice and save it. Into blender, pour ¼ cup coconut juice, ice, cream of coconut, rum, and cream. Blend at high speed 10 seconds. Pour into coconut shell. Place coconut shell in large dish surrounded with finely crushed ice. There will usually be enough juice from one coconut for three or four drinks. Reserve drinks may be made up beforehand, poured into a pitcher, and stored in the refrigerator. Coconut shells may then be refilled when necessary. Byron once said nothing calmed the spirit as much as rum and true religion. The balmy beneficence of the preceding recipe will bear out that astute poet to the fullest.

COCONUT FIZZ

2 ozs. CocoRibe
1 oz. lemon juice
½ slightly beaten
  egg white
Iced club soda
1 slice lemon

Shake CocoRibe, lemon juice, and egg white extremely well with ice. Strain into tall 12-oz. glass half-filled with ice cubes. Fill with club soda. Stir. Add lemon slice.

COCONUT GROVE

1½ ozs. CocoRibe
½ oz. triple sec
½ oz. lime juice
Iced club soda
1 slice lime

Shake CocoRibe, triple sec, and lime juice well with ice. Strain into 8-oz. glass. Add 2 ice cubes. Add soda to fill glass. Stir. Add lime slice.

COCORIBE MILK PUNCH

2 ozs. CocoRibe
4 ozs. milk
1 small egg
Ground cinnamon

Shake CocoRibe, milk, and egg extremely well with ice. Strain into 10-oz. glass. Sprinkle with cinnamon.

COFFEE COOLER

4 ozs. cold coffee
1½ ozs. vodka
1 oz. heavy cream
1 oz. coffee liqueur
1 teaspoon sugar
1 small dip coffee
   ice cream

Shake coffee, vodka, cream, coffee liqueur, and sugar well with ice. Strain into tall 14-oz. glass. Add ice cream. A sweet cooler that serves as both iced coffee and dessert in one glass.

COFFEE EGGNOG

1½ ozs. Canadian
   whisky
1 oz. coffee liqueur
1 small egg
4 ozs. milk
½ oz. heavy cream
1 teaspoon sugar
½ teaspoon instant
   coffee
Ground coriander seed

Shake whisky, coffee liqueur, egg, milk, cream, sugar, and instant coffee with ice extremely well—about twice the usual mixing time. Strain into tall 14-oz. glass. Sprinkle with coriander.

COFFEE MILK PUNCH

1 oz. coffee liqueur
1 oz. dark Jamaica
   rum
1 small egg
1 teaspoon sugar
5 ozs. milk
½ oz. heavy sweet
   cream
Freshly grated nutmeg

Pour all ingredients except nutmeg into cocktail shaker with ice. Shake extremely well to blend egg with other ingredients. Strain into 12-oz. glass. Sprinkle with nutmeg.

COFFEE RUM COOLER

1½ oz. dark
    Jamaica rum
1 oz. coffee liqueur
½ oz. lime juice
Iced club soda
1 slice lime

Shake rum, coffee liqueur, and lime juice well with ice. Strain into tall 14-oz. glass three-quarters filled with ice. Fill glass with club soda. Stir. Add lime slice.

COLD IRISH

1½ ozs. Irish whiskey
2 teaspoons Irish Mist
    liqueur
Iced coffee soda
Whipped cream
Crème de cacao

Pour whiskey and Irish Mist into tall 14-oz. glass. Add one large ice cube. Fill glass to within 1 inch of top with soda. Stir. Flavor whipped cream with crème de cacao, using ½ oz. crème de cacao for each ½ cup heavy cream used for whipping. Add a large dollop of whipped-cream topping to each drink.

COLD TURKEY

1½ ozs. cream sherry
½ oz. Wild Turkey
    liqueur
1 oz. orange juice
1 slice orange

Pour sherry, Wild Turkey liqueur, and orange juice over rocks in 8-oz. glass. Stir well. Add orange slice. An after-dinner drink that's not too cloying.

COOL COLONEL

1½ ozs. bourbon
1 oz. Southern
    Comfort
3 ozs. chilled strong
    black tea
2 teaspoons lemon
    juice
2 teaspoons sugar
Iced club soda

Pour bourbon, Southern Comfort, tea, lemon juice, and sugar into tall 14-oz. glass. Stir until sugar dissolves. Add two large ice cubes and a splash of soda. Stir. Breathe deeply. Tilt head. Bend elbow.

COOL GUANABANA

Grenadine
Superfine sugar
1½ ozs. light rum
½ oz. dark
   Jamaica rum
½ oz. lime juice
4 ozs. iced guanabana
   nectar
1 slice lime

Dip rim of tall 14-oz. glass into grenadine and then into superfine sugar to frost rim. Fill glass with ice cubes. Add both kinds of rum, lime juice, and guanabana nectar. (Guanabana nectar—made from the pulp of the soursop—is available in gourmet shops and in those featuring Puerto Rican foods.) Stir well. Cut lime slice halfway to center and fasten to rim of glass.

CORDIAL MÉDOC CUP

1 oz. Cordial Médoc
½ oz. Cognac
1 oz. lemon juice
½ teaspoon sugar
Iced brut champagne
1 slice orange

Shake Cordial Médoc, Cognac, lemon juice, and sugar well with ice. Strain into 10-oz. glass with two large ice cubes. Fill glass with champagne. Stir very slightly. Add orange slice. A tall drink for toasting.

CRANBERRY COOLER

1 oz. cranberry
   liqueur
1 oz. California
   brandy
½ oz. triple sec
Iced tonic water

Fill 14-oz. glass three-fourths with ice. Add cranberry liqueur, brandy, and triple sec. Stir well. Fill glass with tonic water. Stir.

CRANBERRY RUM PUNCH

1 oz. light rum
1 oz. dark
   Jamaica rum
4 ozs. chilled
   cranberry juice
2 ozs. orange juice
½ oz. lemon juice
1 slice lemon

Shake light rum, dark Jamaica rum, cranberry juice, orange juice, and lemon juice well with ice. Strain into tall 14-oz. glass three-quarters filled with ice cubes. Stir. Add lemon slice.

CRANBOURBON

2 ozs. bourbon
Dash Angostura bitters
1 teaspoon sugar
½ oz. lemon juice
Iced cranberry-juice
  cocktail
1 long strip cucumber
  rind

Shake bourbon, bitters, sugar, and lemon juice well with ice. Strain into 12-oz. glass half-filled with ice cubes. Add cranberry-juice cocktail to fill glass. Stir. Place cucumber rind in glass.

CREAMY SCREWDRIVER

6 ozs. orange juice
1 small egg yolk or
  ½ large yolk, lightly
  beaten
2 ozs. vodka
¾ cup finely cracked
  ice
1 teaspoon sugar

Put all ingredients into well of blender. Blend about 20 seconds. Pour over two or three ice cubes in tall 14-oz. glass. Add more ice cubes if necessary to fill glass. A pre-brunch potation.

CUBA LIBRE

2 ozs. golden rum
½ lime
Iced cola drink

Half-fill a tall 14-oz. glass with coarsely chopped ice or ice cubes. Add rum. Squeeze lime above drink and drop into glass. Fill with cola. Stir well. Heavier rums such as Jamaican or Martinique may be used in place of golden rum or may be mixed half-and-half with it. A teaspoon of 151-proof rum may be floated on top of drink for a rummy bite.

CUCUMBER CHAMPAGNE

Cucumber peel
1 oz. Benedictine
½ oz. lemon juice
8 ozs. iced brut
  champagne

Prechill a 10-oz. Pilsner glass. Wash cucumber, rubbing with a vegetable brush or towel if necessary to remove any waxy coating. Cut a long strip of peel, about ½ inch wide, the entire length of the cucumber. Place in glass. Pour Benedictine and lemon juice into glass. Slowly add champagne. Stir very slightly. Let drink set a few minutes for flavors to ripen.

CURAÇAO COOLER

1 oz. blue curaçao
1 oz. vodka
½ oz. lime juice
½ oz. lemon juice
Iced orange juice
Lemon peel
Lime peel
Orange peel

Shake curaçao, vodka, lime juice, and lemon juice well with ice. Strain into tall 14-oz. glass. Add two large ice cubes. Fill glass with orange juice. Stir well. Twist each of the peels above the drink and drop into glass. Cool as the blue-green Caribbean itself.

CYNAR CALYPSO

1 oz. Cynar
1 oz. light rum
1 oz. pineapple juice
1 oz. lime juice
1 teaspoon grenadine

Shake extremely well with ice. Pour into tall or squat 10-oz. glass. Add ice cubes to fill glass. Stir well.

CYNAR SCREWDRIVER

1 oz. Cynar
1 oz. vodka
4½ ozs. ice-cold
    orange juice

Shake ingredients well with ice. Strain into prechilled tall or squat 10-oz. glass.

DEEP END

1 oz. Cordial Médoc
½ oz. gin
2 ozs. chilled
    papaya nectar
2 ozs. chilled
    orange juice
Iced club soda
½ slice orange

Pour Cordial Médoc, gin, papaya nectar, and orange juice into tall 14-oz. glass three-quarters filled with ice cubes. Stir well. Add soda to fill glass. Stir. Add orange slice.

DOUBLE DERBY

2½ ozs. bourbon
2 ozs. cold strong
  black tea
2 ozs. claret
1 oz. red-currant
  syrup
1 oz. orange juice
½ oz. lemon juice
1 slice cocktail orange
  in syrup

Pour bourbon, tea, claret, red-currant syrup, orange juice, and lemon juice into double old-fashioned glass. Add ice cubes to fill to brim. Stir well. Add orange slice. If red-currant syrup is not available, red-currant jelly to which a teaspoon of hot water has been added may be heated over a low flame and stirred constantly until jelly is liquid.

DOWN YONDER

1 oz. bourbon
½ oz. peppermint
  schnapps
2 ozs. peach nectar
½ oz. lemon juice
1 slice fresh peach

Shake bourbon, peppermint schnapps, peach nectar, and lemon juice well with ice. Strain into 8-oz. glass. Add ice cubes to fill glass. Stir. Fasten peach on cocktail spear and rest on rim of glass.

DRACULA

1½ ozs. light rum
2 dashes Angostura
  bitters
4 ozs. cranberry-juice
  cocktail
1 oz. lemon juice
½ teaspoon grenadine

Shake well with ice. Strain into 14-oz. glass. Add ice cubes to fill glass to rim. Stir.

DRY-MANHATTAN COOLER

2 ozs. blended whiskey
1 oz. dry vermouth
2 ozs. orange juice
½ oz. lemon juice
½ oz. orgeat or orzata
Iced club soda
1 maraschino cherry

Shake whiskey, vermouth, orange juice, lemon juice, and orgeat well with ice. Strain into tall 14-oz. glass. Add a splash of soda and ice to fill glass. Stir. Add cherry.

EAST-WEST

2 ozs. sake
2 dashes Angostura
   bitters
Iced cranberry-juice
   cocktail
1 slice lemon

Place 3 large ice cubes in 8-oz. glass. Add sake and bitters. Fill glass with cranberry-juice cocktail. Stir well. Add lemon slice.

EAU DE VIE CAMPARI

½ oz. framboise
½ oz. kirschwasser
1 oz. Campari
½ oz. lemon juice
½ teaspoon grenadine
Iced club soda
Orange peel

Pour framboise, kirschwasser, Campari, lemon juice, and grenadine into mixing glass with ice. Stir very well. Strain into 8-oz. glass with 1 or 2 ice cubes. Add a splash of soda. Stir lightly. Twist orange peel above drink and drop into glass.

EGGNOG FRAMBOISE

4 ozs. milk
1 small egg
1 oz. framboise
½ oz. Cognac
½ oz. dark Jamaica
   rum
2 level teaspoons sugar
Freshly grated nutmeg

Shake milk, egg, framboise, Cognac, rum, and sugar extremely well with ice. Strain into 10-oz. glass. Sprinkle with nutmeg.

ELEPHANT'S EYE

1 oz. dark
   Jamaica rum
1 oz. sweet vermouth
½ oz. triple sec
½ oz. lime juice
Iced tonic water
1 slice lime

Shake rum, sweet vermouth, triple sec, and lime juice well with ice. Strain into tall 14-oz. glass half-filled with ice cubes. Add tonic water to fill glass. Stir. Add lime slice.

ENGLISH MULE

3 ozs. ice-cold
   green-ginger wine
1½ ozs. gin
2½ ozs. ice-cold
   orange juice
Iced club soda
1 piece preserved
   ginger in syrup

Put three ice cubes into tall 14-oz. glass. Pour wine, gin, and orange juice into glass. Stir well. Fill glass with soda. Stir slightly. Fasten preserved ginger, well drained, onto cocktail spear. Fit spear into straw in glass.

FINLANDIA

1 oz. aquavit
½ oz. Vaklova liqueur
Chilled orange juice

Pour aquavit and Vaklova into 10-oz. glass half-filled with ice cubes. Stir well. Add orange juice to fill glass. Stir well.

FRENCH COLONIAL

1½ ozs. golden rum
½ oz. crème de cassis
½ oz. Cointreau or
   triple sec
½ oz. lemon juice
Iced tonic water
1 slice lemon

Shake rum, crème de cassis, Cointreau, and lemon juice well with ice. Strain into tall 14-oz. glass three-quarters filled with ice cubes. Add tonic water. Stir. Add lemon slice.

FRENCH FOAM

1 teaspoon sugar
1 dash Angostura
   bitters
1 teaspoon brandy
1 teaspoon
   kirschwasser
1 split ice-cold brut
   champagne
Lemon sherbet

Put sugar, bitters, brandy, and kirschwasser into 10-oz. Pilsner glass. Stir with a tall stirring rod until sugar dissolves. Fill glass three-quarters full with champagne. Float a small scoop of sherbet on top. The scoop should contain no more than 2 liquid ounces (a parfait scoop). If such a scoop is not available, use a tablespoon to add the small amount of sherbet.

FRENCH 75

1½ ozs. Cognac
1 oz. lemon juice
1 teaspoon sugar
Iced brut champagne

Shake Cognac, lemon juice, and sugar well with cracked ice. Strain into 10-oz. glass with two large ice cubes. Fill to rim with champagne. Stir very slightly. Gin is sometimes substituted for Cognac, making a champagne collins out of this tall classic.

GASPÉ

2 ozs. very dry sherry
1 oz. Canadian
  whisky
½ oz. Vaklova liqueur
1 piece lemon peel

Stir sherry, whisky, and Vaklova liqueur well with ice. Strain over rocks in 8-oz. glass. Twist lemon peel above drink and drop into glass.

GEORGIA RUM COOLER

2½ ozs. light rum
1 teaspoon salted
  peanuts
½ oz. lemon juice
1 teaspoon grenadine
1 teaspoon Falernum
½ cup crushed ice
Iced club soda
Ground cinnamon

Put rum, peanuts, lemon juice, grenadine, Falernum, and crushed ice into blender. Blend at high speed 30 seconds. Pour into tall 14-oz. glass. Let froth on drink settle. Add two ice cubes and a splash of soda. Stir. Sprinkle lightly with cinnamon. Pass a platter of cold country ham sliced paper-thin.

GIN AND GINGER COOLER

1 oz. gin
1 oz. ginger-flavored
  brandy
½ oz. lemon juice
1 teaspoon sugar
4 ozs. ginger beer or
  ginger ale
1 slice lemon
1 small chunk
  preserved ginger
  in syrup

Shake gin, ginger-flavored brandy, lemon juice, and sugar well with ice. Strain into tall 12-oz. glass half-filled with ice. Stir. Add ginger beer. Stir. Add ice if necessary to fill glass. Stir. Garnish with lemon slice and preserved ginger.

GIN SWIZZLE

2 ozs. gin
½ teaspoon Angostura
  bitters
½ oz. lime juice
1 teaspoon sugar
Iced club soda

Shake gin, bitters, lime juice, and sugar well with ice. Strain into tall 14-oz. glass half-filled with ice. Add soda. Stir. A patriarchal drink invented when swizzle sticks were smart. Toothsome tipple now best handled in cocktail shaker and tall glass.

GOLD COASTER

1 oz. dry vermouth
1 oz. California
  brandy
½ oz. lemon juice
2 ozs. pineapple juice
1 teaspoon maraschino
  liqueur
1 slice fresh pineapple

Shake vermouth, brandy, lemon juice, pine-apple juice, and maraschino liqueur well with ice. Strain into 10-oz. glass. Add ice cubes to fill glass. Stir. Fasten pineapple on cocktail spear and place on rim of glass.

GRANADA

1 oz. very dry (fino)
  sherry
1 oz. brandy
½ oz. curaçao
Iced tonic water
1 slice orange

Shake sherry, brandy, and curaçao well with ice. Strain into tall 14-oz. glass. Add two large ice cubes. Add tonic water. Stir. Add orange slice.

GRAPEFRUIT COOLER

2 ozs. blended whiskey
4 ozs. unsweetened
  grapefruit juice
½ oz. red-currant
  syrup
1 teaspoon lemon juice
½ slice orange
½ slice lemon

Shake whiskey, grapefruit juice, red-currant syrup, and lemon juice well with ice. Strain into tall 14-oz. glass. Add ice to fill glass. Stir. Garnish with orange and lemon slices.

GRAPEFRUIT NOG

½ cup unsweetened
   grapefruit juice
1 oz. lemon juice
1 tablespoon honey
1½ ozs. brandy
1 small egg
½ cup crushed ice

Put all ingredients into blender. Blend 20 seconds. Pour into double old-fashioned glass or tall 14-oz. glass. Add ice cubes to fill glass.

GRINGO

1½ ozs. tequila
4 ozs. Clamato juice
1 teaspoon catsup
1 teaspoon lemon juice
½ teaspoon
   horseradish
Tabasco sauce
Worcestershire sauce
Freshly ground black
   pepper

Pour tequila, Clamato, catsup, lemon juice, and horseradish into cocktail shaker. Add a dash or two each of Tabasco and Worcestershire. Shake very well with ice. Strain into old-fashioned glass. Sprinkle with ground black pepper.

GUANABANA COOLER

2 ozs. light rum
4 ozs. chilled
   guanabana nectar
1 oz. chilled orange
   juice
Chilled club soda
½ slice orange
1 slice lime

Pour rum, guanabana nectar, and orange juice into tall 14-oz. glass three-quarters filled with ice cubes. Stir well. Add soda to fill glass to rim. Add orange and lime slices.

GUAVA COOLER

1½ ozs. rum
1½ ozs. guava nectar
½ teaspoon sugar
½ oz. maraschino
   liqueur
½ oz. lemon juice
½ oz. pineapple juice
Iced club soda
1 canned guava shell
½ slice lemon

Shake rum, guava nectar, sugar, maraschino liqueur, lemon juice, and pineapple juice well with ice. Strain into tall 14-oz. glass half-filled with ice. Add soda. Stir. Garnish with guava shell and lemon slice. Wonderful cooler before or with a jambalaya feast.

HARVEY WALLBANGER

1½ ozs. vodka
4½ ozs. ice-cold
   orange juice
¾ oz. Galliano

Put 3 large ice cubes into tall or squat 10-oz. glass. Add vodka and orange juice. Stir well. Float Galliano on top. Or shake vodka, Galliano, and orange juice with ice and strain into glass. Add ice cubes to fill glass. Stir.

HIGH POCKET

2 ozs. dry vermouth
½ oz. cherry-flavored
   brandy
½ oz. California
   brandy
½ oz. lemon juice
Iced apricot nectar

Be sure apricot nectar is well chilled beforehand. Shake vermouth, cherry-flavored brandy, California brandy, and lemon juice well with ice. Strain into tall 14-oz. glass half-filled with ice cubes. Add apricot nectar to fill glass. Stir.

HONEYDEW COOLER

⅓ cup diced ripe
   honeydew melon
1½ ozs. gin
¼ teaspoon Pernod
1 tablespoon heavy
   cream
¾ oz. lemon juice
½ teaspoon sugar
½ cup crushed ice
Iced club soda

Put honeydew, gin, Pernod, cream, lemon juice, sugar, and crushed ice into blender. Blend at low speed 15–20 seconds. Pour into tall 14-oz. glass. When foam settles, add a splash of soda and enough ice to fill glass to rim, if necessary.

HONKY TONIC

1 oz. Sciarada
1 oz. gin
½ oz. lemon juice
Iced tonic water
1 slice lemon

Pour Sciarada, gin, and lemon juice into tall 12-oz. glass half-filled with ice cubes. Stir well. Fill with tonic water. Stir. Add lemon slice.

HORSE'S NECK WITH GIN

Peel of whole lemon
2 ozs. gin
½ oz. lemon juice
Iced ginger ale

To peel lemon, start at stem end, using a sharp paring knife, and cut peel about ½ inch wide in a continuous strip until lemon is completely peeled. Place peel in a 14-oz. highball glass so that the top of peel overlaps rim of glass, with the rest spiraling down into glass. Fill glass with coarsely cracked ice. Pour gin and lemon juice into glass. Fill with ginger ale. Stir.

ICED RUM COFFEE

1½ ozs. light rum
1 teaspoon dark
   Jamaica rum
6 ozs. iced
   double-strength
   coffee
Sugar
2 tablespoons
   sweetened
   whipped cream

Pour rums and coffee into tall 14-oz. glass. Add ice to fill glass. Add sugar to taste. Top with whipped cream.

ICED RUM TEA

1½ ozs. light rum
½ oz. 151-proof rum
6 ozs. iced strong
   black tea
1 teaspoon sugar
1 teaspoon Falernum
1 teaspoon lemon juice
1 slice lemon
2 large mint leaves

Pour rums, tea, sugar, Falernum, and lemon juice into tall 14-oz. glass. Add ice to fill glass. Stir. Garnish with lemon slice and mint leaves partially torn. To prevent tea clouding, let it cool to room temperature before combining with ice.

INDEPENDENCE SWIZZLE

2 ozs. dark
    Trinidad rum
3 dashes Angostura
    bitters
1 teaspoon honey
1 teaspoon sugar
½ oz. lime juice
1 slice lime

In tall 14-oz. glass, stir rum, bitters, honey, sugar, and lime juice until honey is blended with other ingredients. Add finely cracked ice to fill glass. Twirl with a swizzle stick if you have one, or stir and churn with a barspoon or iced-tea spoon. As drink is stirred, ice will melt. Add more ice as necessary to fill glass to rim, swizzling or stirring until ice and liquids reach top of glass. Add lime slice. A drink used to celebrate the independence of Trinidad and Tobago.

IRISH MILK-AND-MAPLE PUNCH

2 ozs. blended
    Irish whiskey
8 ozs. milk
1 tablespoon maple
    syrup
Freshly grated nutmeg

Shake whiskey, milk, and maple syrup very well with ice. Strain into tall 14-oz. glass. Sprinkle with nutmeg.

JAMAICA ELEGANCE

1½ ozs. golden
    Jamaica rum
½ oz. brandy
½ oz. pineapple juice
1 oz. lime juice
1 teaspoon simple
    syrup or rock-candy
    syrup
1 slice lime

Shake rum, brandy, pineapple juice, lime juice, and syrup well with ice. Strain into prechilled tall 14-oz. glass. Add ice to fill glass. Add lime slice.

JAMAICA GINGER

1½ ozs. light rum
½ oz. dark Jamaica
  rum
½ oz. 151-proof rum
½ oz. Falernum
½ oz. lime juice
Iced ginger beer
½ slice pineapple in
  crème de menthe
1 cube preserved
  ginger in syrup

Shake the three kinds of rum, Falernum, and lime juice well with ice. Strain into tall 14-oz. glass half-filled with ice. Fill glass with ginger beer. Stir. Garnish with pineapple and ginger.

JOCOSE JULEP

2½ ozs. bourbon
½ oz. green crème
  de menthe
6 mint leaves
1 teaspoon sugar
1 oz. lime juice
Iced club soda
3 tall mint sprigs

Put into blender, without ice, bourbon, crème de menthe, 6 mint leaves, sugar, and lime juice. Blend 10–15 seconds or until mint is very finely chopped. Pour into tall 14-oz. glass half-filled with ice. Add soda. Stir. Insert mint sprigs. Serve to nearest belle.

KERRY COOLER

2 ozs. Irish whiskey
1½ ozs. Madeira or
  sherry
1 oz. orgeat
1 oz. lemon juice
Iced club soda
1 slice lemon

Into tall 14-oz. glass, pour whiskey, Madeira, orgeat, and lemon juice. Stir well. Add three large ice cubes. Fill glass with soda. Stir. Float lemon slice on top.

KIRSCH CUBA LIBRE

1½ ozs. kirschwasser
½ lime
Iced cola drink

Put three large ice cubes into a tall 14-oz. glass. Add kirschwasser. Squeeze lime above drink and drop into glass. Fill with cola. Stir.

LAIT DE VIE

2 ozs. Cognac or
   California brandy
4 ozs. milk
½ oz. heavy cream
½ oz. grenadine
Freshly grated nutmeg

Shake Cognac, milk, cream, and grenadine with ice. Strain into tall 14-oz. glass filled with ice cubes. Stir. Sprinkle with nutmeg.

LATIN DOG

½ oz. Sciarada
½ oz. Pernod
Chilled grapefruit juice

Fill 8-oz. glass with ice cubes. Add Sciarada, Pernod, and enough grapefruit juice to fill glass. Stir well. Very pleasant brunch drink.

LEMON RUM COOLER

2 ozs. light rum
1 teaspoon 151-proof
   rum
2 ozs. pineapple juice
½ oz. lemon juice
½ oz. Falernum
Iced bitter-lemon soda
1 slice lemon

Shake both kinds of rum, pineapple juice, lemon juice, and Falernum well with ice. Strain into tall 14-oz. glass. Add two ice cubes. Fill glass with bitter-lemon soda. Add lemon slice.

MADAMA ROSA

1½ ozs. light rum
½ oz. cherry-flavored
   brandy
2 ozs. orange juice
½ oz. lime juice
Iced tonic water

Shake rum, cherry-flavored brandy, orange juice, and lime juice well with ice. Strain into tall 12-oz. glass. Add 2 large ice cubes. Fill with tonic water. Stir.

MANGO COOLER

3 ozs. ice-cold mango
 nectar
1½ ozs. vodka
½ oz. ice-cold lemon
 juice
1½ ozs. ice-cold
 orange juice
½ oz. Cointreau
1 slice orange
1 slice mango, if in
 season

Into tall 14-oz. glass, pour mango nectar, vodka, lemon juice, orange juice, and Cointreau. Add ice to fill glass. Garnish with orange and mango slices. A fruity libation to serve before an Oriental or Polynesian menu.

MEXICAN MILK PUNCH

1 oz. tequila
1 oz. dark rum
4 ozs. milk
1 oz. heavy cream
1 small egg
2 teaspoons sugar
Freshly ground nutmeg

Shake all ingredients except nutmeg extremely well with ice. Strain into tall 12-oz. glass. Sprinkle with nutmeg.

MEXICAN MULE

1½ ozs. tequila
Iced ginger beer
½ lime

Place 3 large ice cubes in tall 12-oz. glass or 12-oz. mug. Add tequila. Fill glass with ginger beer. Stir. Squeeze lime over drink and drop into glass.

MINT JULEP

12 mint leaves on stem
1 teaspoon sugar
2 teaspoons water
2½ ozs. 86- or
 100-proof bourbon
6 mint leaves on stem

Tear the 12 mint leaves partially while leaving them on stem. Place in tall 12-oz. glass or silver julep mug with sugar and water. Muddle or stir until sugar is completely dissolved. Fill glass with finely cracked ice. Add bourbon. Stir. Ice will dissolve partially. Add more ice to fill glass to rim, again stirring. Tear the 6 mint leaves partially to release aroma and insert into ice with leaves on top. Serve with or without straw.

MINT JULEP, DRY, PARTY-STYLE (Serves 8)

1 quart bourbon
1 pint finely chopped
   mint leaves
8 sprigs mint

Steep mint leaves in bourbon for 1 hour at room temperature. Fill eight tall 14-oz. glasses with finely cracked ice. Strain bourbon and pour into glasses, allowing 4 ozs. minted bourbon per glass. Stir. Add more ice to fill glass to rim. Tear a few leaves of each of the mint sprigs and fit a sprig into each glass. If your party is late getting started, store prepared juleps in freezer. A few sips of this unsweetened julep should turn the longest of hot summer days into the coolest.

MISTY IRISH

1 oz. blended
   Irish whiskey
½ oz. Irish Mist
   liqueur
1 oz. orange juice
½ oz. lemon juice
1 teaspoon sugar
½ cup crushed ice
1 brandied cherry

Pour whiskey, Irish Mist, orange juice, lemon juice, sugar, and ice into blender. Blend at high speed 10 seconds. Pour into old-fashioned glass. Add ice cubes to fill glass to rim. Add brandied cherry.

MOBILE MULE

2 ozs. light rum
½ lime
Iced ginger beer

Pour rum into tall 12- or 14-oz. glass or copper mug with ice cubes or cracked ice. Squeeze lime above drink and drop into glass. Fill with ginger beer. Stir. A switch on the vodka-inspired moscow mule.

MOCHA COOLER

6 ozs. cold freshly
   brewed strong coffee
1 oz. light rum
½ oz. Galliano
1 teaspoon sugar or
   more to taste
Heavy cream

Pour coffee, rum, Galliano, and sugar into tall 12-oz. glass. Stir well until sugar dissolves. Add ice to nearly fill glass and stir well again. Float heavy cream on top by pouring it over the back of a spoon so that cream flows to rim of glass.

MOLOKAI

1 oz. sake
1 oz. cranberry
  liqueur
2 ozs. orange juice
1 slice orange

Pour sake, cranberry liqueur, and orange juice into 8-oz. glass. Add ice cubes to fill glass. Stir very well. Add orange slice.

MOSCOW MULE

1½ to 2 ozs. vodka
½ lime
Iced ginger beer

Pour vodka into tall 12- or 14-oz. glass or copper mug with ice cubes or cracked ice. Squeeze lime above drink and drop into glass. Fill with ginger beer. Stir. A variation on the moscow mule includes a long spiral of lemon peel in the mug.

MUSCARI COOLER

1½ ozs. gin
1 oz. Muscari
1 oz. lemon juice
1 teaspoon sugar
Iced club soda
1 slice lemon

Shake gin, Muscari, lemon juice, and sugar well with ice. Pour into tall 14-oz. glass half-filled with rocks. Add club soda. Stir. Add lemon slice.

NECTARINE COOLER

2 ozs. vodka
3 ozs. iced orange juice
¼ cup cold sliced
  ripe nectarine
1 teaspoon sugar
⅓ cup crushed ice
Iced club soda
1 slice fresh nectarine
1 slice lemon

Put vodka, orange juice, nectarine, sugar, and crushed ice into blender. Blend at low speed 15–20 seconds. Pour into tall 14-oz. glass. Add a splash of soda and enough ice to fill glass. Stir. Garnish with nectarine and lemon slices.

OAHU GIN SLING

2 ozs. gin
½ oz. crème de cassis
½ oz. Benedictine
1 oz. lime juice
1 teaspoon sugar
Iced club soda
Lime-rind spiral

To make lime-rind spiral, cut continuous strip of lime peel from stem end to bottom of fruit. Place peel in tall 14-oz. glass, hooking it to rim. Shake gin, crème de cassis, Benedictine, lime juice, and sugar well with ice. Strain into glass and add ice cubes until three-quarters full. Fill glass with soda. Stir.

OLD-FASHIONED ARTICHOKE

1 oz. gin
½ oz. dry vermouth
½ oz. Cynar
Iced club soda
1 slice lemon

Pour gin, vermouth, and Cynar over rocks in old-fashioned glass. Stir well. Add splash of soda. Add lemon slice.

OLD-FASHIONED RUM AND MUSCARI

1 oz. light rum
1 oz. Muscari
Angostura bitters
Iced club soda
Lemon peel

Pour rum, Muscari, and two or three dashes Angostura bitters into old-fashioned glass. Fill glass with rocks. Stir well. Add splash of soda. Twist lemon peel over drink and drop into glass.

ORANGE OASIS

4 ozs. ice-cold fresh
    orange juice
1½ ozs. gin
½ oz. cherry liqueur
Iced ginger ale
1 slice orange

Pour orange juice, gin, and cherry liqueur into tall 14-oz. glass. Add ice cubes or ice slices to rim of glass. Add ginger ale. Stir. Garnish with orange slice.

ORANGE COOLER IN SHELL

1 extra-large
    California orange
1 oz. 151-proof rum
½ oz. curaçao
½ oz. lime juice
1 teaspoon sugar
1 slice cocktail orange
    in syrup

Cut a cap off top of orange about ½ inch from top. With a sharp grapefruit knife, gouge out the meat, leaving orange shell intact. Squeeze enough juice from meat to make 1½ ozs. Shake orange juice, rum, curaçao, lime juice, and sugar well with ice. Strain into orange shell. Place orange shell in a bowl or soup dish about 7 inches in diameter. Pack finely crushed ice around orange. Fasten orange slice onto cocktail spear and place across orange cup. Serve with a short colored straw. A show-off concoction for drink hobbyists and rum specialists.

ORANGE COLADA

4 ozs. orange juice
1 oz. light rum
1 oz. dark
   Jamaica rum
1 tablespoon
   Coconut Snow
1 teaspoon sugar
1 cup crushed ice

Pour all ingredients into blender. (Coconut Snow is a powdered coconut mixture.) Blend at high speed 10 seconds. Pour into tall 14-oz. glass. Add 1 or 2 ice cubes if necessary to fill glass. To make piña colada, substitute pineapple juice for the orange juice.

PALMETTO COOLER

2 ozs. bourbon
½ oz. apricot liqueur
½ oz. sweet vermouth
3 dashes Angostura
   bitters
Iced club soda
Fresh mint

Fill a tall 14-oz. glass with ice cubes. Add bourbon, apricot liqueur, vermouth, and bitters. Stir well. Fill glass almost to top with club soda and stir lightly. Place generous bouquet of mint sprigs in glass. Tear a few leaves to release aroma.

PANAMA COOLER

2 ozs. iced Rhine wine
2 ozs. iced very dry
   sherry
1 oz. orange juice
1 teaspoon lime juice
½ oz. maraschino
   liqueur
1 dash Angostura
   bitters
1 oz. iced club soda
1 slice lemon

Shake Rhine wine, sherry, orange juice, lime juice, maraschino liqueur, and bitters well with ice. Strain into tall 14-oz. glass. Add soda. Fill glass with ice. Stir. Add lemon slice.

PASSION-FRUIT COOLER

4 ozs. passion-fruit
   nectar (not syrup)
1½ ozs. light rum
1 oz. gin
½ oz. lemon juice
1 oz. orange juice
2 sprigs mint

Shake passion-fruit nectar, rum, gin, lemon juice, and orange juice well with ice. Strain into tall 14-oz. glass. Add enough coarsely cracked ice or ice cubes to fill glass. Decorate with mint after partially tearing several leaves to release fragrance.

PERNOD AND PEPPERMINT

1 oz. Pernod
1 oz. peppermint
  schnapps
1 oz. lime juice
Iced club soda
1 slice lime

Fill tall 14-oz. glass with ice cubes. Add Pernod, peppermint schnapps, and lime juice. Stir well. Fill with club soda. Add lime slice.

PIMM'S CUP

1½ ozs. Pimm's No. 1
  Cup
Iced 7-Up or lemon soda
1 slice lemon
Cucumber peel

Pour Pimm's Cup into 8- or 10-oz. glass or Pimm's glass tankard with ice. Fill with 7-Up. Add lemon slice and cucumber peel. Stir. The old English gin sling is bottled as Pimm's No. 1 Cup, made with a gin base and fruit flavors. Other prepared Pimm's Cups are bottled with other liquor bases, but the No. 1 is the best-known in the States.

PINEAPPLE MINT COOLER

2 ozs. gin
½ oz. white crème
  de menthe
3 ozs. pineapple juice
1 oz. lemon juice
Iced club soda
1 cocktail pineapple
  stick
1 green cocktail cherry

Shake gin, crème de menthe, pineapple juice, and lemon juice well with ice. Strain into tall 14-oz. glass. Add a splash of soda and enough ice to fill glass. Stir. Garnish with pineapple stick and cherry.

PINK LEMONADE A LA PLAYBOY

5 ozs. chilled
  rosé wine
2 ozs. chilled lemon
  juice
2 ozs. chilled orange
  juice
½ oz. kirschwasser
2 teaspoons sugar
1 slice lemon
1 maraschino cherry

Into tall 14-oz. glass, pour wine, lemon juice, orange juice, kirschwasser, and sugar. Stir well until sugar dissolves. Add two large ice cubes and enough ice-cold water (not club soda) to fill glass. Stir. Garnish with lemon slice and cherry.

PINK RUM AND TONIC

2½ ozs. light rum
½ oz. lime juice
1 teaspoon grenadine
Iced tonic water
1 slice lime

Shake rum, lime juice, and grenadine well with ice. Strain into tall 14-oz. glass half-filled with ice. Add tonic water. Stir. Add lime slice. Curiously refreshing yo-ho-ho.

PINKY

2 ozs. ruby port
1 oz. strawberry
    liqueur
½ oz. heavy cream
1 large fresh
    strawberry

Shake port, strawberry liqueur, and cream well with ice. Strain over rocks in 8-oz. glass. Fasten strawberry on cocktail spear and place over rim of glass.

PLANTER'S PUNCH

1½ ozs. dark
    Jamaica rum
3 ozs. orange juice
½ oz. lemon juice
1 teaspoon sugar
¼ teaspoon grenadine
½ slice orange
1 slice lemon

Shake rum, orange juice, lemon juice, sugar, and grenadine well with ice. Strain over rocks in tall 10-oz. glass. Stir well. Add ice, if necessary, to fill glass. Garnish with orange and lemon slices.

PLANTER'S PUNCH WITH FALERNUM

2 ozs. dark
    Jamaica rum
Dash Angostura bitters
½ oz. Falernum
1 teaspoon sugar
½ oz. lime juice
Iced club soda
1 slice orange
Maraschino cherry

Shake rum, bitters, Falernum, sugar, and lime juice extremely well with ice. Strain into tall 14-oz. glass three-quarters filled with ice cubes. Stir. Add club soda to fill glass. Garnish with orange slice and cherry.

PLAYBOY COOLER

1¼ ozs. golden Jamaica
  rum
1¼ ozs. Jamaica
  coffee liqueur
3 ozs. pineapple juice
2 teaspoons lemon
  juice
Cola drink
1 slice pineapple

Shake rum, coffee liqueur, pineapple juice, and lemon juice well with ice. Strain into prechilled tall 14-oz. glass. Add ice to fill glass to 1 inch from top. Add cola. Garnish with pineapple slice.

PLUM AND TONIC

¾ oz. mirabelle
  or quetsch
1 oz. gin
½ oz. lemon juice
Iced tonic water
1 slice lemon

Pour mirabelle, gin, and lemon juice over 3 large ice cubes in tall 10-oz. glass. Add tonic water to fill glass. Stir lightly. Add lemon slice.

PORTAMENTO

2 ozs. tawny port
1 oz. bourbon
2 dashes Peychaud's
  or Angostura bitters
½ egg white
1 teaspoon lemon
  juice
1 slice lemon

Shake port, bourbon, bitters, egg white, and lemon juice extremely well with ice. Strain over rocks in 8-oz. old-fashioned glass. Add lemon slice.

PORT AND COGNAC MILK PUNCH

2 ozs. white port
  such as **Porto Branco**
1½ ozs. Cognac
4 ozs. (½ measuring
  cup) milk
1 small egg
Freshly grated nutmeg

Shake port, Cognac, milk, and egg extremely well with ice. Strain into 12-oz. glass. Sprinkle with nutmeg.

PORT ARMS

3 ozs. California port
1 oz. California brandy
1 oz. orange juice
½ oz. lemon juice
1 teaspoon triple sec
Iced club soda
½ slice orange
1 slice lemon

Shake port, brandy, orange juice, lemon juice, and triple sec well with ice. Strain into tall 14-oz. glass half-filled with ice cubes. Add soda. Stir. Add orange and lemon slices.

PORT CASSIS

2½ ozs. chilled white
    port such as
    Porto Branco
½ oz. crème de cassis
½ oz. lemon juice
Iced club soda
1 slice lemon

Pour port, crème de cassis, and lemon juice over rocks in 8-oz. glass. Stir well. Add splash of soda. Add lemon slice.

PORTCULLIS

2 ozs. ruby port
1 oz. cherry-flavored
    brandy
4 ozs. cranberry-juice
    cocktail
1 oz. lemon juice
1 slice lemon

Pour port, cherry-flavored brandy, cranberry-juice cocktail, and lemon juice into tall 14-oz. glass half-filled with ice cubes. Stir well. Add ice cubes to fill glass. Stir well. Add lemon slice.

PUNT E LEMON

3 ozs. Punt e Mes
Iced bitter lemon
1 wedge old-fashioned-
    cocktail orange in
    syrup

Pour Punt e Mes into tall 12-oz. glass three-quarters filled with ice cubes. Add bitter lemon to almost fill glass. Stir very well. Pierce orange wedge with cocktail spear and rest across top of glass.

QUADRUPLE PINEAPPLE   (4 single or 2 double drinks)

1 large chilled
   pineapple
½ cup pineapple
   sherbet
6 ozs. light rum
3 ozs. orange juice
1½ ozs. lime juice
½ oz. maraschino
   liqueur

The pineapple should measure at least 7 inches from base to top of fruit, not including stem. Cut a cap off pineapple about ½ inch from top. To remove meat from pineapple, cut a deep circle around edge of pineapple about ½ inch from rim, leaving a large cylinder of fruit which must then be gouged out. A very sharp boning knife is a good instrument for the job. Cut wedges of fruit loose by slicing diagonally toward rim of fruit. Use a grapefruit knife or large Parisienne-potato cutter to remove small pieces of fruit. Do not pierce shell of fruit or it will not hold liquid. The cavity of the pineapple should be large enough to hold 2 measuring cups of liquid. Test it for size. Cut hard core of fruit away and discard it. Cut enough tender pineapple meat to make ½ cup fruit in small dice. Into well of blender, put the ½ cup diced pineapple, sherbet, rum, orange juice, lime juice, and maraschino liqueur. Blend 5 seconds. Pour into pineapple shell. Place pineapple in deep dish or bowl surrounded with finely crushed ice. Place two or four colored straws in drink, allowing for two or four pineapple sippers. An elaborate production, beloved by rum barons. A second round may be prepared beforehand from the same pineapple and blended just before refilling pineapple.

RANCHO CONTENTO

1½ ozs. tequila
4 ozs. orange juice
¼ oz. dry vermouth
¼ oz. sweet vermouth
1 slice orange

Shake tequila, orange juice, and both kinds of vermouth well with ice. Strain into 10-oz. glass. Add 2 large ice cubes and orange slice.

RASPBERRY CLARET CUP

4 ozs. dry red wine
1 oz. brandy
1 oz. Himbeergeist
(dry white raspberry
brandy)
¾ oz. raspberry syrup
1 oz. lemon juice
Iced club soda
2 or 3 fresh or frozen
whole raspberries

Be sure wine and brandies are ice-cold before mixing drink. Put three ice cubes into tall 14-oz. collins glass. Pour wine, brandy, Himbeergeist, raspberry syrup, and lemon juice into glass. Stir until all ingredients are very well blended. Fill glass with soda. Stir slightly. Float raspberries on top.

RED BAIT

1 oz. sloe gin
½ oz. dark
Jamaica rum
2 ozs. chilled guava
nectar
½ oz. lime juice
Iced tonic water
1 slice lime

Pour sloe gin, rum, guava nectar, and lime juice into tall 14-oz. glass three-quarters filled with ice cubes. Stir well. Add tonic water to fill glass. Stir. Add lime slice.

RED DANE

1½ ozs. aquavit
2 ozs. cranberry-juice
cocktail
½ oz. lime juice
1 teaspoon sugar
1 slice lemon

Shake aquavit, cranberry-juice cocktail, lime juice, and sugar well with ice. Strain into 8-oz. glass with rocks. Stir. Add lemon slice.

RED PERIL

1 oz. sloe gin
½ oz. vodka
2 ozs. chilled papaya
nectar
½ oz. lime juice
Iced club soda
1 slice lime

Pour sloe gin, vodka, papaya nectar, and lime juice into tall 14-oz. glass three-quarters filled with ice cubes. Stir well. Add soda to fill glass. Stir. Add lime slice.

RHENISH RASPBERRY

2 ozs. Riesling
1 oz. vodka
¼ cup frozen
    raspberries in syrup,
    thawed
2 teaspoons grenadine
½ oz. lemon juice
½ cup crushed ice
Iced club soda

Put raspberries with their syrup, Riesling, vodka, grenadine, lemon juice, and ice into blender. Blend at high speed 10 seconds. Pour into tall 14-oz. glass. Add a splash of soda. Add ice if necessary to fill glass to brim. Stir lightly.

ROCK-AND-RYE COOLER

1½ ozs. vodka
1 oz. rock-and-rye
½ oz. lime juice
Iced bitter-lemon soda
1 slice lime

Shake vodka, rock-and-rye, and lime juice well with ice. Strain into tall 14-oz. glass half-filled with ice. Add bitter-lemon soda. Stir. Add lime slice.

ROMAN COOLER

1½ ozs. gin
½ oz. Punt e Mes
½ oz. lemon juice
1 teaspoon sugar
Iced club soda
Lemon peel

Shake gin, Punt e Mes, lemon juice, and sugar well with ice. Strain into tall 14-oz. glass. Add soda and ice to fill glass. Twist lemon peel above drink and drop into glass.

ROMAN FRULLATI

3 ozs. gin
¼ cup diced Delicious
    apple, with skin
¼ cup diced ripe pear,
    with skin
¼ cup frozen sliced
    peaches, thawed
1 oz. maraschino
    liqueur
1 oz. orzata or orgeat
½ cup crushed ice

Put all ingredients into blender. Blend at high speed 20 seconds. Pour into tall 14-oz. glass. Add ice, if necessary, to fill glass to rim.

RUM AND COCONUT COOLER

2½ ozs. light rum
1 oz. cream of coconut
½ oz. lemon juice
Iced club soda
1 slice lemon
1 maraschino cherry

Shake rum, cream of coconut, and lemon juice well with ice. Strain into tall 14 oz-glass half-filled with ice. Add a splash of soda. Garnish with lemon slice and cherry.

RUM AND PINEAPPLE COOLER

2½ ozs. light rum
2 ozs. pineapple juice
½ oz. lemon juice
1 teaspoon 151-proof rum
1 teaspoon sugar
1 dash Angostura bitters
Iced club soda
1 pineapple chunk
1 papaya chunk in syrup

Shake rum, pineapple juice, lemon juice, 151-proof rum, sugar, and bitters well with ice. Strain into tall 14-oz. glass. Add a splash of soda and enough ice to fill glass. Garnish with pineapple and papaya chunks fastened onto a cocktail spear.

RUM CITRUS COOLER

2 ozs. light rum
1 oz. orange juice
½ oz. lime juice
½ oz. Cointreau
1 teaspoon sugar
Iced 7-Up
1 slice lime
½ slice lemon

Shake rum, orange juice, lime juice, Cointreau, and sugar well with ice. Strain into tall 14-oz. glass half-filled with ice. Add 7-Up. Stir. Garnish with lime and lemon slices. Solace or celebration after eighteen holes on the fairway.

RUM CURAÇAO COOLER

1 oz. dark Jamaica rum
1 oz. curaçao
½ oz. lime juice
Iced club soda
1 slice lime
½ slice orange

Shake rum, curaçao, and lime juice with ice. Strain into tall 14-oz. glass. Add a splash of soda and ice to fill glass. Garnish with lime and orange slices.

RUM ROYALE

1 oz. light rum
2 ozs. Sauternes
1½ ozs. lemon juice
2 ozs. pineapple juice
1 teaspoon sugar
1 dash Peychaud's
 bitters
1 cube pineapple
1 maraschino cherry

Shake rum, Sauternes, lemon juice, pineapple juice, sugar, and bitters well with ice. Strain into prechilled tall 14-oz. glass. Add ice to fill glass. Affix pineapple cube and cherry to cocktail spear and rest on rim of glass.

ST.-CROIX COOLER

Peel of ½ large orange
2 ozs. light rum
½ oz. dark Jamaica
 rum
1 oz. brandy
1 tablespoon brown
 sugar
2½ ozs. orange juice
1½ ozs. lemon juice
1 dash orange-flower
 water
Iced club soda

Cut orange peel from stem end in one continuing spiral about ½ inch wide. Place peel in tall 14-oz. glass, permitting one end to overhang rim. Shake both kinds of rum, brandy, brown sugar, orange juice, lemon juice, and orange-flower water well with ice. Strain into glass. Fill glass to rim with coarsely cracked ice or ice cubes. Add a splash of soda. Stir. A rich tropical cooler that will easily outlast two ordinary cocktails.

SAKE CASSIS

1 oz. sake
1 oz. vodka
½ oz. crème de cassis
Iced club soda
1 slice lemon

Pour sake, vodka, and crème de cassis over rocks in 10-oz. glass. Stir well. Add a splash of soda. Stir. Add lemon slice.

SAKE SUNRISE

1 oz. sake
1 oz. California brandy
Chilled grapefruit juice
1 teaspoon grenadine

Place 4 ice cubes in squat or tall 10-oz. glass. Add sake, brandy, and enough grapefruit juice to almost fill glass. Stir well. Pour grenadine on top of drink. Guests stir drink to blend grenadine with other ingredients.

SAN JUAN SLING

¾ oz. light rum
¾ oz. cherry liqueur
¾ oz. Benedictine
½ oz. lime juice
Iced club soda
Lime peel

Shake rum, cherry liqueur, Benedictine, and lime juice well with ice. Strain into tall 14-oz. glass half-filled with ice. Add soda. Twist lime peel above drink and drop into glass.

SARASOTA

2 ozs. cream sherry
3 ozs. papaya nectar
1 oz. light rum
½ oz. lime juice
1 slice lime

Shake sherry, papaya nectar, rum, and lime juice well with ice. Strain into tall 14-oz. glass three-quarters filled with ice cubes. Add lime slice.

SCOTCH APPLE

1½ ozs. Scotch
½ oz. apple brandy
4 ozs. apple juice
½ oz. orange juice
½ oz. lemon juice
Orange peel
Lemon peel

Shake Scotch, apple brandy, apple juice, orange juice, and lemon juice well with ice. Strain into tall 12-oz. glass half-filled with ice cubes. Stir well. Add ice if necessary to fill glass to rim. Twist orange and lemon peels above drink and drop into glass.

SCOTCH HORSE'S NECK

Peel of whole lemon
  in one spiral
3 ozs. Scotch
½ oz. sweet vermouth
½ oz. dry vermouth

Place lemon peel in tall 14-oz. glass with one end of peel overhanging rim. Add Scotch and both kinds of vermouth. Fill glass with cracked ice. Stir. Add more ice if necessary to fill glass. Every horse's neck is improved if it ages about 10 minutes before sipping.

SCOTCH SOLACE

2½ ozs. Scotch
½ oz. honey
½ oz. triple sec
4 ozs. milk
1 oz. heavy cream
⅛ teaspoon freshly
  grated orange rind

Pour Scotch, honey, and triple sec into 14-oz. glass. Stir until honey is thoroughly blended. Add milk, cream, and orange rind. Add ice cubes to fill glass to brim. Stir well. Cold, creamy, and soothing.

SCREWDRIVER WITH SHERRY

½ cup orange juice
2 ozs. oloroso sherry
1 oz. vodka
½ cup crushed ice

Put all ingredients into blender. Blend 20 seconds. Pour into double old-fashioned or tall 14-oz. glass. Add ice cubes to fill glass. An outsize screwdriver especially suited for the brunchboard.

SHOO-IN

1 oz. California brandy
½ oz. dark Jamaica rum
1 oz. light rum
½ oz. maraschino liqueur
2 ozs. chilled grapefruit juice
2 ozs. chilled pineapple juice

Pour all ingredients into tall 14-oz. glass half-filled with ice cubes. Stir well. Add ice cubes if necessary to fill glass. Stir.

SHORE LEAVE

1 oz. sloe gin
1 oz. light rum
½ oz. lime juice
Iced tonic water
1 slice lime

Shake sloe gin, rum, and lime juice well with ice. Strain into tall 12-oz. glass three-quarters filled with ice cubes. Fill glass with tonic water. Stir. Add lime slice.

SIMPATICO

2 ozs. peppermint schnapps
1 oz. white rum
Iced bitter lemon
1 slice lemon

Pour peppermint schnapps and white rum into tall 14-oz. glass three-quarters filled with ice cubes. Stir well. Add bitter lemon to fill glass. Stir. Add lemon slice.

SINGAPORE GIN SLING

1½ ozs. gin
1 oz. cherry-flavored brandy
1 oz. lime juice
Iced club soda
1 slice lime

Shake gin, cherry-flavored brandy, and lime juice well with ice. Strain into tall 14-oz. glass half-filled with ice cubes. Fill glass with soda. Add lime slice.

SKI JUMPER

1½ ozs. aquavit
1 teaspoon kümmel
  liqueur
1 teaspoon lemon juice
Iced bitter lemon
1 slice lemon

Pour aquavit, kümmel, and lemon juice into tall or squat 10-oz. glass three-quarters filled with ice cubes. Stir well. Fill glass with bitter lemon. Stir. Add lemon slice.

SLOE AND BITTER

1 oz. sloe gin
1 oz. tequila
½ oz. lemon juice
Iced bitter lemon
1 slice lemon

Shake sloe gin, tequila, and lemon juice well with ice. Strain into tall 12-oz. glass three-quarters filled with ice cubes. Fill glass with bitter lemon. Stir. Add lemon slice.

SLOE CRANBERRY COOLER

2½ ozs. ice-cold
  sloe gin
6 ozs. ice-cold
  cranberry juice
1¼ ozs. lemon juice
1 slice lemon

Pour sloe gin, cranberry juice, and lemon juice into tall 14-oz. glass. Add ice cubes to fill glass. Stir well. Add lemon slice.

SLOE DOG

1 oz. sloe gin
½ oz. gin
2 ozs. grapefruit juice
1 slice lime

Shake sloe gin, gin, and grapefruit juice well with ice. Strain over rocks in 8-oz. glass. Add lime slice.

SLOE SWEDE

1½ ozs. aquavit
½ oz. sloe gin
½ slightly beaten
  egg white
1 teaspoon sugar
¾ oz. lemon juice
Iced club soda
1 slice lemon

Shake aquavit, sloe gin, egg white, sugar, and lemon juice extremely well with ice. Strain into tall 14-oz. glass three-quarters filled with ice cubes. Stir well. Add soda to fill glass. Stir. Add lemon slice.

SOUTHERN RASPBERRY

¾ oz. framboise
¾ oz. Southern
  Comfort
½ oz. lemon juice
1 teaspoon sugar
Iced club soda
1 slice lemon

Shake framboise, Southern Comfort, lemon juice, and sugar extremely well with ice. Strain over rocks in tall or squat 8-oz. glass. Add splash of soda. Add ice if necessary to fill glass to rim. Stir. Add lemon slice.

STEEPLEJACK

2 ozs. apple brandy
2½ ozs. iced apple
  juice
2½ ozs. iced club soda
1 teaspoon lime juice
1 slice lime

Pour apple brandy, apple juice, soda, and lime juice into tall 14-oz. glass. Add ice to fill glass. Stir. Add lime slice.

STONE FENCE

1½ ozs. bourbon
Chilled apple juice

Pour bourbon and apple juice over rocks in 10 oz. glass. Stir well. Add ice cubes if necessary to fill glass.

STRAWBERRY BLONDE

3 fresh strawberries
1 oz. strawberry
  liqueur
6 ozs. well-chilled
  Rhine wine
½ oz. kirschwasser
Iced club soda
1 slice lime

Marinate strawberries in strawberry liqueur for 1 hour. Fasten strawberries onto cocktail spear. Pour Rhine wine, strawberry liqueur, and kirschwasser into tall 14-oz. glass. Add a splash of soda and ice to fill glass. Stir. Add lime slice. Place speared strawberries over rim of glass.

STRAWBERRY CREAM COOLER

1½ ozs. gin
¼ cup frozen sliced
   strawberries (fruit
   and syrup), thawed
1 oz. lemon juice
2 tablespoons heavy
   cream
1 teaspoon sugar
Iced club soda

Put gin, strawberries, lemon juice, cream, and sugar into blender. Blend 10–15 seconds at high speed. Pour into tall 14-oz. glass. Add a splash of soda and enough ice to fill glass. Stir.

STRAWBERRY VERMOUTH COOLER

2½ ozs. dry vermouth
¼ cup fresh
   strawberries, hulled
   and sliced
1 oz. gin
2 teaspoons
   strawberry syrup
½ cup crushed ice
Iced club soda
1 slice lemon

Put vermouth, strawberries, gin, strawberry syrup, and ice into blender. Blend 10–15 seconds at low speed. Pour into tall 14-oz. glass containing two ice cubes. Add a splash of soda. Stir. Garnish with lemon slice.

STRAWBERRY VIN BLANC

4 ozs. chilled dry
   white wine, Graves
   if possible
1 oz. strawberry
   liqueur
2 large ice cubes
Iced club soda
1 slice lemon
1 fresh large
   strawberry

Pour wine and strawberry liqueur over ice cubes in tall 12-oz glass. Stir. Add soda to fill glass. Garnish with lemon slice and strawberry.

STRAWBERRY WHITE PORT

4 ozs. imported
white port
Iced tonic water
½ oz. strawberry
liqueur
1 slice lemon
1 large fresh
strawberry with
long stem if possible

Be sure port is a dry imported wine, such as Sandeman's extra-dry Porto Branco. Fill tall 14-oz. glass with ice cubes. Add port. Fill glass to within ½ inch of rim with tonic water. Float strawberry liqueur on top by pouring it over the back of a spoon held against the inside of the glass. Place lemon slice so that it rests on top of ice cubes. Place strawberry on lemon slice.

SUMMER LIGHT

2 ozs. dry vermouth
3 ozs. dry white wine
Iced bitter lemon

Pour vermouth and wine into tall 14-oz. glass half-filled with ice cubes. Fill glass with bitter lemon. Stir.

SURF RIDER

2 ozs. sake
1 oz. light rum
3 ozs. pineapple juice
Iced bitter lemon soda

Shake sake, rum, and pineapple juice well with ice. Strain into tall 14-oz. glass half-filled with ice cubes. Fill glass with bitter lemon.

TALL BLONDE

1 oz. aquavit
½ oz. apricot liqueur
Iced bitter lemon
1 slice lemon

Pour aquavit and apricot liqueur into tall 12-oz. glass three-quarters filled with ice cubes. Stir well. Add iced bitter lemon to fill glass. Stir. Add lemon slice.

TALL DUTCH EGGNOG

1½ ozs. Advokaat
liqueur
1½ ozs. light rum
½ oz. 151-proof rum
1 oz. orange juice
6 ozs. milk
1 teaspoon sugar
½ cup finely cracked
ice
Ground cinnamon

Put Advokaat, both kinds of rum, orange juice, milk, sugar, and ice into blender. Blend at high speed 10 seconds. Pour into tall 14-oz. glass. Sprinkle with cinnamon. The Dutch way of getting the new year rolling as merrily as possible.

TALL HAOLE

2½ ozs. CocoRibe
3 ozs. orange juice
2 ozs. apricot nectar
1 oz. lemon juice
Iced club soda
½ slice orange

Shake CocoRibe, orange juice, apricot nectar, and lemon juice well with ice. Strain into tall 14-oz. glass half-filled with ice cubes. Add soda to fill glass. Stir. Add orange slice.

TALL ISLANDER

2 ozs. light rum
3 ozs. pineapple juice
1 oz. lime juice
1 teaspoon dark
   Jamaica rum
1 teaspoon sugar syrup
Iced club soda
1 slice lime

Shake light rum, pineapple juice, lime juice, dark rum, and syrup well with ice. Strain into tall 14-oz. glass. Add a splash of soda and enough ice to fill glass. Stir. Add lime slice. Bound to make natives unrestless; equally at home in a high-rise or down among the sheltering palms.

TALL LIMONE

1 oz. Sciarada
1 oz. gin
½ oz. lemon juice
Iced bitter lemon
1 slice lemon

Pour Sciarada, gin, and lemon juice into a tall 12-oz. glass three-quarters filled with ice cubes. Stir well. Fill glass with bitter lemon. Stir. Add lemon slice.

TALL MARGARITA

1½ ozs. tequila
½ oz. Cointreau or
   triple sec
¾ oz. lemon juice
Iced bitter lemon
1 slice lemon

Shake tequila, Cointreau, and lemon juice well with ice. Strain into 12-oz. glass three-quarters filled with ice cubes. Fill glass with bitter lemon. Stir. Add lemon slice.

TALL MIDORI

1 oz. Midori
1 oz. dark Jamaica
   rum
½ oz. lime juice
Iced tonic water

Pour Midori, rum, and lime juice into a tall 14-oz. glass three-quarters filled with ice cubes. Stir well. Fill with tonic water.

TALL MUSCARI

1½ ozs. Muscari
1 oz. vodka
3 ozs. orange juice
Iced tonic water

Pour Muscari, vodka, and orange juice into a tall 14-oz. glass three-quarters filled with ice cubes. Stir well. Fill glass to top with tonic water.

TALL ORDER

3 ozs. dry vermouth
4 ozs. chilled
   strawberry nectar
Iced club soda

Pour vermouth and strawberry nectar into tall 14-oz. glass three-quarters filled with ice cubes. Stir very well. Fill glass with soda. Stir lightly.

TALL SACK

3 ozs. cream sherry
2 ozs. apricot nectar
3 ozs. orange juice
½ oz. lemon juice
½ slice orange

Shake sherry, apricot nectar, orange juice, and lemon juice well with ice. Strain into tall 14-oz. glass. Add ice cubes to fill glass. Stir. Add orange slice.

TALL SARDINIAN

1 oz. Cynar
1 oz. vodka
2 ozs. orange juice
Iced tonic water
1 slice orange

Put 4 large ice cubes into a tall 14-oz. glass. Add Cynar, vodka, and orange juice. Stir well. Fill with tonic water. Add orange slice.

TALL SUNRISE

2 ozs. tequila
½ oz. lime juice
½ oz. curaçao
1 teaspoon crème de
   cassis
Iced club soda
1 slice lime

Shake tequila, lime juice, curaçao and crème de cassis well with ice. Strain into tall 14-oz. glass half-filled with ice. Fill glass with soda. Stir. Garnish with lime slice. One to contemplate while waiting for the hot chili.

TALL TAWNY

3 ozs. tawny port
1 oz. white rum
2 ozs. papaya nectar
2 ozs. chilled orange
    juice
Iced club soda
1-inch square
    of papaya

Pour port, rum, papaya nectar, and orange juice into tall 14-oz. glass half-filled with ice cubes. Add soda. Stir. Fasten papaya on cocktail spear and place over rim of glass.

TAMARIND COOLER

3 ozs. chilled
    tamarind nectar
2 ozs. chilled
    mango nectar
1 oz. chilled orange
    juice
1 oz. chilled
    pineapple juice
1½ ozs. light rum
½ oz. 151-proof rum
1 slice lemon
2 large sprigs mint

Pour all ingredients except lemon slice and mint into tall 14-oz. glass. Add ice cubes to fill glass. Stir well. Add lemon slice and mint. (Note: nectars such as tamarind, mango, guanabana, etc., are available in shops featuring Puerto Rican specialties.)

TEE OFF

1 oz. California brandy
½ oz. peppermint
    schnapps
2 ozs. chilled
    pineapple juice
2 ozs. chilled
    orange juice

Shake brandy, peppermint schnapps, pineapple juice, and orange juice well with ice. Strain over rocks in 10-oz. glass. Stir.

TEQUILA COLADA

1½ ozs. tequila
4 ozs. pineapple juice
1 oz. cream of coconut
½ cup crushed ice

Pour tequila, pineapple juice, cream of coconut, and crushed ice into blender. Blend at high speed 10 seconds. Pour into tall or squat 12-oz. glass.

TEQUILA COOLER

1½ ozs. tequila
2 ozs. Stone's ginger
   wine
2 ozs. orange juice
½ oz. lime juice
Iced tonic water
1 slice lime
½ slice orange

Pour tequila, ginger wine, orange juice, and lime juice into tall 14-oz. glass three-quarters filled with ice cubes. Stir very well. Add tonic water to fill glass. Add lime and orange slices.

TEQUILA MIEL

1½ ozs. tequila
½ oz. honey liqueur
4 ozs. grapefruit juice

Shake well with ice. Strain over rocks in squat or tall 10-oz. glass.

TIGER TAIL

4 ozs. ice-cold fresh
   orange juice
1 oz. Pernod
1 slice lime

Pour orange juice and Pernod into tall 12- or 14-oz glass. Add cracked ice to fill glass. Stir. Add lime slice. Magnificent breakfast first course.

VAMPIRO

1½ ozs. tequila
3 ozs. *sangrita*
   (page 293)
3½ ozs. grapefruit
   juice
¼ teaspoon lime juice

Shake tequila, *sangrita*, grapefruit juice, and lime juice well with ice. Strain into tall 12-oz. glass. Add ice cubes to fill glass to rim. Stir. The reigning queen of tall tequila drinks in Guadalajara.

VERMOUTH COOLER

2 ozs. sweet vermouth
1 oz. vodka
½ oz. lemon juice
1 teaspoon sugar
Iced club soda
1 slice lemon

Shake vermouth, vodka, lemon juice and sugar well with ice. Strain into tall 14-oz. glass half-filled with ice. Add soda. Stir. Add lemon slice.

VERMOUTH AND GINGER

1 oz. dry vermouth
1 oz. ginger-flavored brandy
Iced ginger ale
1 slice lemon

Pour vermouth and ginger-flavored brandy into an 8-oz. glass with several ice cubes. Stir well. Add ginger ale. Stir. Add lemon slice.

VILLA NOVA

1½ ozs. ruby port
1 oz. California or Spanish brandy
Angostura bitters
Iced club soda
Lemon peel

Pour port, brandy, and several dashes bitters over rocks in old-fashioned glass. Stir well. Add splash of soda. Stir. Twist lemon peel above drink and drop into glass.

VOLUPTUOSO

1 oz. tequila
1½ ozs. banana liqueur
⅓ cup sliced ripe banana
1 cup crushed ice
1 teaspoon sugar
½ oz. lemon juice

Put all ingredients in blender. Blend 10 seconds at high speed. Pour into tall 12-oz. glass.

WATERMELON CASSIS

2 ozs. gin
½ cup diced watermelon, seeds removed
½ oz. crème de cassis
¾ oz. lemon juice
½ cup crushed ice
Iced club soda
1 slice lemon

Put gin, watermelon, crème de cassis, lemon juice, and crushed ice into blender. Blend at low speed 10–15 seconds. Pour into tall 14-oz. glass. Let drink settle for a few moments. Add two ice cubes and a splash of soda. Add lemon slice.

WATERMELON COOLER

½ cup diced
   watermelon,
   sans seeds
2¼ ozs. light rum
½ oz. lime juice
¼ oz. maraschino
   liqueur
1 teaspoon sugar
½ cup crushed ice
1 slice lime

Put watermelon, rum, lime juice, maraschino liqueur, sugar, and ice into blender. Blend 10–15 seconds at low speed. Pour into tall 14-oz. glass. When foam subsides, add ice to fill glass. Stir. Add lime slice.

WHITE-WINE COOLER

6 ozs. chilled dry
   white wine
½ oz. brandy
2 dashes orange bitters
1 teaspoon kümmel
2 teaspoons sugar
½ oz. lemon juice
Iced club soda
Cucumber peel, 2
   inches long, ½ inch
   wide

Put wine, brandy, bitters, kümmel, sugar, and lemon juice into tall 14-oz. glass. Stir until sugar dissolves. Add a splash of soda and enough ice to fill glass. Stir. Add cucumber peel.

YUCATAN TONIC

1½ ozs. tequila
½ oz. crème de cassis
½ lime
Iced tonic water

Fill a tall 10-oz. glass with ice cubes. Add tequila and crème de cassis. Stir well. Squeeze lime over drink and drop into glass. Stir. Fill with tonic water.

PICNIC COOLERS

The following nine drinks are planned for serving from the tailgate, whether it's a day in the dunes, at the dockside, or near a shady grove. All nine are designed for picnic jugs. Soda, rocks, etc., should be taken in insulated containers.

BITTER BOURBON
(6 drinks)

7½ ozs. bourbon
5 ozs. orange juice
1½ ozs. peppermint
   schnapps
1 teaspoon Angostura
   bitters
Iced tonic water

Shake bourbon, orange juice, peppermint schnapps, and bitters well with ice. Strain into prechilled picnic jug. Serve over rocks in 10-oz. glass. Add tonic water.

BLACK-CURRANT COOLER
(6 drinks)

9 ozs. blended whiskey
3 ozs. crème de cassis
7 ozs. lemon juice
7 ozs. orange juice
Iced club soda

Combine—but do not mix with ice—whiskey, crème de cassis, lemon juice, and orange juice. Chill in refrigerator. Pour into prechilled picnic jug. Serve over rocks in 10-oz. glass. Add splash of soda.

CARTHUSIAN CUP
(6 drinks)

1 fifth iced dry
   white wine
6 ozs. chilled orange
   juice
3 ozs. chilled yellow
   Chartreuse
Iced club soda
6 slices orange

Pour orange juice and Chartreuse into prechilled picnic jug. Carry iced dry white wine in another insulated container. Pour 1½ ozs. orange juice-Chartreuse mixture into 12 oz. glass. Add 4 ozs. wine and about 2 ozs. soda. Add ice cubes to fill each glass. Stir lightly. Add orange slice.

CELTIC CUP
(6 drinks)

9 ozs. Scotch
1½ ozs. cherry-
   flavored brandy
1½ ozs. sweet
   vermouth
1½ ozs. lemon juice
Iced club soda

Shake Scotch, cherry-flavored brandy, vermouth, and lemon juice well with ice. Strain into prechilled picnic jug. Serve over rocks in 10-oz. glass. Add splash of soda.

ICED COFFEE OPORTO

(6 drinks)

12 ozs. tawny port
6 ozs. brandy
24 ozs. (1½ pints)
strong black coffee,
sweetened to taste
Heavy cream

Combine port, brandy, and coffee, and chill in refrigerator. Do not shake with ice. Pour into prechilled picnic jug. At picnic site, divide among six tall 12-oz. glasses, allowing about 7 ozs. for each glass. Add ice cubes to fill glasses. Top with sweet cream and stir. A tall potable which, for some picnickers, takes the place of dessert.

PEACH CUP WITH CHABLIS

(6 drinks)

10-oz. package frozen
peaches in syrup
2 ozs. California
brandy
3 ozs. lemon juice
1 fifth iced Chablis
Iced club soda

Be sure you have an outsize picnic jug to hold all ingredients. Thaw peaches slightly. Put peaches together with their syrup, brandy, and lemon juice in blender. Blend until smooth. Pour into prechilled picnic jug. Add Chablis. At picnic site, divide contents of jug among six 12-oz. highball glasses. Add several ice cubes to each glass. Add soda. Stir lightly.

RUM AND SOURSOP

(6 drinks)

9 ozs. light rum
6 ozs. lime juice
2 7-oz. cans guanabana
nectar
Iced club soda
6 slices lime

Combine rum, lime juice, and guanabana nectar (made from the pulp of the soursop —a delightful tropical fruit—and available in specialty food shops). Chill in refrigerator, but do not shake with ice. Pour into prechilled picnic jug. At picnic site, pour into tall 10-oz. glasses, allowing about 5 ozs. of the chilled mixture for each drink. Add 2 large ice cubes to each and a splash of soda. Stir. Add lime slice.

RUMBO

(6 drinks)

7 ozs. golden rum
1½ ozs. banana
liqueur
3 ozs. lime juice
1½ ozs. orange juice
1½ ozs. guava syrup
6 slices lime

Shake rum, banana liqueur, lime juice, orange juice, and guava syrup well with ice. Strain into prechilled picnic jug. Serve over rocks as a cocktail rather than as a long drink. Garnish with lime slice.

TALL FRENCH GIMLET   (6 drinks)

9 ozs. gin
1½ ozs. Rose's
   lime juice
1½ ozs. Amer Picon
1½ teaspoons
   grenadine
Iced tonic water

Shake gin, lime juice, Amer Picon, and grenadine well with ice. Strain into pre-chilled picnic jug. At picnic site, divide gimlets among six 10-oz. glasses, allowing about 3 ozs. to each glass. Add ice cubes and tonic water. Stir lightly.

Daisies

The daisy, which originated in the mauve decade, is a medium-tall drink served if possible in knob glassware, a silver mug, or any vessel that conveys a feeling of sumptuousness. An amalgam of spirits and fruit juice, it is invariably sweetened with a red agent such as grenadine or raspberry syrup and usually topped with a float of some compatible liqueur—a last-minute touch that adds to its subtlety and good humor.

APPLEJACK DAISY

1½ ozs. applejack
½ oz. lime juice
1 teaspoon raspberry
   syrup
Iced club soda
1 teaspoon ginger-
   flavored brandy
1 slice lime

Shake applejack, lime juice, and raspberry syrup well with ice. Strain into tall 8-oz. glass half-filled with ice. Add soda. Stir. Float ginger-flavored brandy on drink. Add lime slice.

BOURBON DAISY

1½ ozs. bourbon
½ oz. lemon juice
1 teaspoon grenadine
Iced club soda
1 teaspoon Southern
   Comfort
½ slice orange
1 cocktail pineapple
   stick

Shake bourbon, lemon juice, and grenadine well with ice. Strain into tall 8-oz. glass half-filled with ice. Add soda. Stir. Float Southern Comfort on drink. Garnish with orange slice and pineapple stick.

CANADIAN DAISY

1½ ozs. Canadian
   whisky
½ oz. lemon juice
1 teaspoon raspberry
   syrup
Iced club soda
1 teaspoon Metaxa
   brandy
2 fresh or thawed
   frozen raspberries

Shake whisky, lemon juice, and raspberry syrup well with ice. Strain into tall 8-oz. glass half-filled with ice. Add soda. Stir. Float Metaxa on drink. Add raspberries.

GIN DAISY

1½ ozs. gin
½ oz. lemon juice
1½ teaspoons
   raspberry syrup
Iced club soda
1 slice lemon
2 sprigs mint

Shake gin, lemon juice, and raspberry syrup well with ice. Strain into tall 8-oz. glass half-filled with ice. Add soda. Garnish with lemon slice and mint sprigs.

HAWAIIAN DAISY

1½ ozs. light rum
½ oz. pineapple juice
1 teaspoon lime juice
1 teaspoon grenadine
Iced club soda
1 teaspoon 151-proof
   rum
1 papaya chunk in
   syrup

Shake light rum, pineapple juice, lime juice, and grenadine well with ice. Strain into tall 8-oz. glass half-filled with ice. Add soda. Stir. Float 151-proof rum on drink. Add papaya chunk.

WHISKEY DAISY

1½ ozs. blended
   whiskey
1 teaspoon red-currant
   syrup
½ oz. lemon juice
Iced club soda
1 teaspoon yellow
   Chartreuse
1 slice lemon

Shake whiskey, red-currant syrup, and lemon juice well with ice. Strain into tall 8-oz. glass half-filled with ice. Add club soda. Stir. Float Chartreuse on drink. Add lemon slice.

Fixes

Fixes are medium-tall drinks in which the ingredients are "fixed" in the glass itself, which is then packed with crushed or finely cracked ice. As with the cobbler, no club soda or other extender is added, and shaking or straining is unnecessary. The simple fix of liquor, sugar, ice, and a slice of lemon is an heirloom from Victorian drinking days. Modern variations make gloriously refreshing summer libations.

APPLE GINGER FIX

½ teaspoon sugar
1 teaspoon water
1 oz. applejack
1 oz. ginger-flavored
   brandy
½ oz. lemon juice
1 slice lemon

Dissolve sugar in 1 teaspoon water in an 8-oz. glass. Add applejack, ginger-flavored brandy, and lemon juice. Fill glass with crushed ice. Stir well. Add more ice to fill glass to rim. Stir. Garnish with lemon slice.

BOURBON SLOE-GIN FIX

½ teaspoon sugar
1 teaspoon water
1½ ozs. bourbon
½ oz. sloe gin
½ oz. lemon juice
1 slice lemon
1 slice fresh or
   brandied peach

Dissolve sugar in 1 teaspoon water in an 8-oz. glass. Add bourbon, sloe gin, and lemon juice. Fill glass with crushed ice. Stir well. Add more ice to fill glass to rim. Stir. Garnish with lemon and peach slices.

BRANDY BERRY FIX

1 teaspoon sugar
2 teaspoons water
2 ozs. brandy
1 teaspoon strawberry
   liqueur
½ oz. lemon juice
1 slice lemon
1 large strawberry

Dissolve sugar in 2 teaspoons water in an 8-oz. glass. Add brandy, strawberry liqueur, and lemon juice. Fill glass with crushed ice. Stir well. Add more ice to fill glass to rim. Stir. Garnish with lemon slice and strawberry.

CANADIAN BLACKBERRY FIX

1½ ozs. Canadian
 whisky
½ oz. blackberry-
 flavored brandy
½ teaspoon sugar
½ oz. lemon juice
1 slice lemon
1 fresh blackberry
 if available

Pour whisky, blackberry-flavored brandy, sugar, and lemon juice into tall 8-oz. glass. Stir very well until sugar dissolves. Fill glass with coarsely cracked ice, or ice from an ice-tray chipper, and stir well. Add ice if necessary to fill glass to rim, and stir. Garnish with lemon slice and blackberry.

CHERRY RUM FIX

1 teaspoon sugar
2 teaspoons water
1½ ozs. light rum
½ oz. Peter Heering
 or Cherry Karise
½ oz. lemon juice
1 slice lemon
1 brandied cherry

Dissolve sugar in 2 teaspoons water in an 8-oz. glass. Add rum, Peter Heering, and lemon juice. Fill glass with crushed ice. Stir well. Add more ice to fill glass to rim. Stir. Garnish with lemon slice and cherry.

DERBY RUM FIX

1 teaspoon sugar
2 teaspoons water
2 ozs. light rum
½ oz. lime juice
1 oz. orange juice
1 slice cocktail orange
 in syrup
1 maraschino cherry

Dissolve sugar in 2 teaspoons water in an 8-oz. glass. Add rum, lime juice, and orange juice. Fill glass with crushed ice. Stir well. Add more ice to fill glass to rim. Stir. Garnish with orange slice and cherry.

GIN MINT FIX

1 teaspoon sugar
2 teaspoons water
2 ozs. gin
½ oz. lemon juice
1 teaspoon white
 crème de menthe
2 large mint leaves

Dissolve sugar in 2 teaspoons water in an 8-oz. glass. Add gin, lemon juice, and crème de menthe. Fill glass with crushed ice. Stir well. Add more ice to fill glass to rim. Stir. Tear mint leaves slightly and float on drink.

IRISH FIX

1 teaspoon sugar
2 teaspoons water
2 ozs. Irish whiskey
½ oz. lemon juice
½ slice orange
½ slice lemon
2 teaspoons Irish Mist

Dissolve sugar in 2 teaspoons water in an 8-oz. glass. Add whiskey and lemon juice. Fill glass with crushed ice. Stir well. Add more ice to fill glass to rim. Stir. Garnish with orange and lemon slices. Float Irish Mist on top.

SCOTCH ORANGE FIX

1 teaspoon sugar
2 teaspoons water
1 3-inch piece orange
   peel, in one spiral
2 ozs. Scotch
½ oz. lemon juice
1 teaspoon curaçao

Dissolve sugar in 2 teaspoons water in an 8-oz. glass. Place orange peel in glass. Add Scotch and lemon juice. Fill glass with crushed ice. Stir well. Add more ice to fill glass to rim. Stir. Float curaçao on drink.

WHISKEY OUZO FIX

1 teaspoon sugar
2 teaspoons water
2 ozs. blended whiskey
½ oz. lemon juice
1 teaspoon ouzo
Lemon peel

Dissolve sugar in 2 teaspoons water in an 8-oz. glass. Add whiskey and lemon juice. Fill glass with crushed ice. Stir well. Add more ice to fill glass to rim. Stir. Float ouzo on top of drink. Twist lemon peel above drink and drop into glass.

Fizzes

Fizzes are effervescent cooling agents all built on lemon or lime juice and iced club soda. They're designed here for tall 14-ounce glasses, but they can easily be stretched into 16-, 18-, or 20-ounce portions for further appeasement of parched throats.

APRICOT ANISE FIZZ

1¾ ozs. gin
½ oz. apricot-flavored
   brandy
¼ oz. anisette
½ oz. lemon juice
Iced club soda
½ brandied or fresh
   apricot
Lemon peel

Shake gin, apricot-flavored brandy, anisette, and lemon juice well with ice. Strain into tall 14-oz. glass half-filled with ice. Fill glass with soda. Stir. Add brandied apricot. Twist lemon peel above drink and drop into glass.

AQUAVIT FIZZ

2½ ozs. aquavit
½ oz. lemon juice
1 teaspoon sugar
½ egg white
1 teaspoon Peter
   Heering or Cherry
   Karise
Iced club soda
Lemon peel
1 brandied cherry

Shake aquavit, lemon juice, sugar, egg white, and Peter Heering well with ice. Strain into tall 14-oz. glass half-filled with ice. Fill glass with soda. Stir. Twist lemon peel above drink and drop into glass. Add brandied cherry.

BAYARD FIZZ

2 ozs. gin
½ oz. lemon juice
2 teaspoons
   maraschino liqueur
1 teaspoon raspberry
   syrup
Iced club soda
1 slice lemon
2 fresh or thawed
   frozen raspberries

Shake gin, lemon juice, maraschino liqueur, and raspberry syrup well with ice. Strain into tall 14-oz. glass half-filled with ice. Fill glass with soda. Stir. Add lemon slice and raspberries.

BLUEBERRY RUM FIZZ

2½ ozs. light rum
1 teaspoon triple sec
½ oz. blueberry syrup
¾ oz. lemon juice
Iced club soda
1 slice lemon
3 large fresh
   blueberries

Shake rum, triple sec, blueberry syrup, and lemon juice well with ice. Strain into tall 14-oz. glass half-filled with ice. Fill glass with soda. Stir. Add lemon slice and blueberries.

BRANDIED PEACH FIZZ

2 ozs. brandy
½ oz. peach-flavored
   brandy
½ oz. lemon juice
1 teaspoon sugar
1 teaspoon banana
   liqueur
Iced club soda
1 slice fresh or
   brandied peach

Shake brandy, peach-flavored brandy, lemon juice, sugar, and banana liqueur well with ice. Strain into tall 14-oz. glass half-filled with ice. Fill glass with soda. Stir. Garnish with peach slice.

BRANDY MINT FIZZ

2 ozs. brandy
2 teaspoons white
   crème de menthe
1 teaspoon crème de
   cacao
½ oz. lemon juice
½ teaspoon sugar
Iced club soda
2 large fresh mint
   leaves

Shake brandy, crème de menthe, crème de cacao, lemon juice, and sugar well with ice. Strain into tall 14-oz. glass half-filled with ice. Fill glass with soda. Stir. Tear mint leaves partially and place on top of drink.

CALVADOS FIZZ

2 ozs. calvados
½ oz. lemon juice
1 teaspoon sugar
½ egg white
1 teaspoon heavy
  cream
Iced club soda
1 slice lime
1 maraschino cherry

Shake calvados, lemon juice, sugar, egg white, and cream well with ice. Strain into tall 14-oz. glass half-filled with ice. Fill glass with soda. Stir. Add lime slice and cherry. A fine wintertime fizz while waiting for the roast suckling pig.

CRANBERRY FIZZ

1 oz. cranberry
  liqueur
1 oz. vodka
¾ oz. lemon juice
½ egg white
1 teaspoon sugar
Iced club soda
1 slice lemon

Shake cranberry liqueur, vodka, lemon juice, egg white, and sugar well with ice. Strain into tall 14-oz. glass half-filled with ice. Fill glass with soda. Stir. Add lemon slice.

DANISH GIN FIZZ

1½ ozs. gin
½ oz. Peter Heering
  or Cherry Karise
¼ oz. kirschwasser
½ oz. lime juice
1 teaspoon sugar
Iced club soda
1 slice lime
1 maraschino cherry

Shake gin, Peter Heering, kirschwasser, lime juice, and sugar well with ice. Strain into tall 14-oz. glass half-filled with ice. Fill glass with soda. Stir. Add lime slice and cherry. A single round will pave the way for a Danish open-sandwich party.

DUBONNET FIZZ

1 oz. red Dubonnet
1 oz. cherry-flavored
brandy
1 oz. orange juice
½ oz. lemon juice
1 teaspoon
kirschwasser
Iced club soda
1 slice lemon
1 fresh or canned
pitted black cherry

Shake Dubonnet, cherry-flavored brandy, orange juice, lemon juice, and kirschwasser well with ice. Strain into tall 14-oz. glass half-filled with ice. Fill glass with soda. Stir. Add lemon slice and cherry.

FERN GULLY FIZZ

1 oz. dark
Jamaica rum
1 oz. light rum
1 oz. pineapple juice
¾ oz. lime juice
1 teaspoon sugar
Iced club soda
1 slice or chunk fresh
pineapple
1 slice lime

Shake both kinds of rum, pineapple juice, lime juice, and sugar well with ice. Strain into tall 14-oz. glass half-filled with ice. Fill glass with soda. Stir. Garnish with pineapple and lime slices.

FRAISE FIZZ

1½ ozs. gin
1 oz. Chambery Fraise
½ oz. lemon juice
1 teaspoon sugar
Iced club soda
Lemon peel
1 large strawberry,
sliced in half

Shake gin, Chambery Fraise, lemon juice, and sugar well with ice. Strain into tall 14-oz. glass half-filled with ice. Fill glass with soda. Stir. Twist lemon peel above drink and drop into glass. Add strawberry. Perfect as an apéritif.

GIN FIZZ

2 ozs. gin
½ oz. lemon juice
1 teaspoon sugar
Iced club soda
1 slice lemon

Shake gin, lemon juice, and sugar well with ice. Strain into tall 14-oz. glass half-filled with ice. Fill glass with soda. Stir. Add lemon slice. Brandy, whiskey, rum, or vodka may be used in place of the gin. A 10- or 12-oz. glass may be used instead of the 14-oz., but any diminution in its size only shortens the pleasure of the long, lazy drink implied by a fizz.

GOLDEN GIN FIZZ

2¼ ozs. gin
1 oz. lemon juice
1 egg yolk
2 teaspoons sugar
Iced club soda
1 slice lemon
Freshly ground nutmeg
  (optional)

Shake gin, lemon juice, egg yolk, and sugar well with ice. Strain into tall 14-oz. glass half-filled with ice. Fill glass with soda. Stir. Add lemon slice. Sprinkle with nutmeg if desired.

JAPANESE FIZZ

2¼ ozs. blended
  whiskey
¾ oz. port
½ oz. lemon juice
1 teaspoon sugar
Iced club soda
Orange peel
1 cocktail pineapple
  stick

Shake whiskey, port, lemon juice, and sugar well with ice. Strain into tall 14-oz. glass half-filled with ice. Fill glass with soda. Stir. Twist orange peel above drink and drop into glass. Add pineapple stick.

MORNING-GLORY FIZZ

2 ozs. Scotch
1 teaspoon Pernod
½ oz. lemon juice
1 teaspoon sugar
½ egg white
1 dash Peychaud's
   bitters
Iced club soda
1 slice lemon

Shake Scotch, Pernod, lemon juice, sugar, egg white, and bitters well with ice. Strain into tall 14-oz. glass half-filled with ice. Fill glass with soda. Stir. Add lemon slice. A drink for the elite of the fizz fraternity.

NEW ORLEANS GIN FIZZ

2½ ozs. gin
1 oz. lemon juice
½ egg white
1 teaspoon heavy
   cream
¼ teaspoon orange-
   flower water
2 teaspoons sugar
Iced club soda
1 slice lemon

Shake gin, lemon juice, egg white, cream, orange-flower water, and sugar well with ice. Strain into tall 14-oz. glass half-filled with ice. Fill glass with soda. Stir. Garnish with lemon slice. A variation of the Ramos gin fizz (page 403).

ORANGE FIZZ

2 ozs. gin
1½ ozs. orange juice
½ oz. lemon juice
2 teaspoons triple sec
1 teaspoon sugar
2 dashes orange bitters
Iced club soda
1 slice orange

Shake gin, orange juice, lemon juice, triple sec, sugar, and bitters well with ice. Strain into tall 14-oz. glass half-filled with ice. Fill glass with soda. Stir. Add orange slice.

OSTEND FIZZ

1½ ozs. kirschwasser
½ oz. crème de cassis
½ oz. lemon juice
1 teaspoon sugar
Iced club soda
1 slice lemon

Shake kirschwasser, crème de cassis, lemon juice, and sugar well with ice. Strain into tall 14-oz. glass half-filled with ice. Fill glass with soda. Stir. Add lemon slice. Splendid with a summer smorgasbord.

PEACHBLOW FIZZ

2 ozs. gin
½ oz. strawberry
   liqueur
½ oz. lemon juice
½ teaspoon sugar
1 teaspoon heavy
   cream
Iced club soda
1 slice lemon
1 large fresh
   strawberry

Shake gin, strawberry liqueur, lemon juice, sugar, and cream well with ice. Strain into tall 14-oz. glass half-filled with ice. Fill glass with soda. Stir. Garnish with lemon slice and strawberry. A classic old fizz—and a semantic mystery, since there's no peach in the recipe—but a joy for parched throats.

RAMOS GIN FIZZ

2 ozs. gin
1 egg white
½ oz. heavy cream
2 teaspoons sugar
½ oz. lemon juice
¼ oz. lime juice
½ teaspoon orange-
   flower water
1 cup crushed ice
Iced club soda

Put gin, egg white, cream, sugar, lemon juice, lime juice, orange-flower water, and crushed ice into blender. Blend at high speed 5 seconds. Pour into tall 14-oz. glass. Add enough club soda to fill glass. Stir. In the old days, no New Orleans bartender would think of serving a Ramos gin fizz if the drink hadn't been shaken at least 5 minutes. The electric blender does a better job in 5 seconds.

ROYAL GIN FIZZ

2¼ ozs. gin
1 oz. lemon juice
1 whole egg
2 teaspoons sugar
Iced club soda
1 slice lemon

Shake gin, lemon juice, egg, and sugar well with ice. Strain into tall 14-oz. glass half-filled with ice. Fill glass with soda. Stir. Add lemon slice.

RUM COCONUT FIZZ

2¼ ozs. light rum
½ oz. cream of
   coconut
½ oz. lime juice
Iced club soda
1 slice lime

Shake rum, cream of coconut, and lime juice well with ice. Strain into tall 14-oz. glass half-filled with ice. Fill glass with soda. Stir. Add lime slice. Sip while the teriyaki is browning over the charcoal.

RUM PINEAPPLE FIZZ

2 ozs. golden rum
½ oz. 151-proof rum
⅓ cup fresh
    pineapple, small
    dice
½ egg white
2 teaspoons sugar
½ oz. lemon juice
½ oz. lime juice
½ cup crushed ice
Iced club soda
1 slice lime

Put both kinds of rum, pineapple, egg white, sugar, lemon juice, lime juice, and ice into blender. Blend at low speed 10–15 seconds. Pour into tall 14-oz. glass. Add ice cubes to almost fill glass. Add a splash of soda and lime slice.

SLOE GIN FIZZ

1 oz. sloe gin (creamy
    cap)
1 oz. gin
¾ oz. lemon juice
Iced club soda
1 slice lemon

Shake sloe gin, gin, and lemon juice well with ice. Strain into tall 14-oz. glass half-filled with ice. Fill glass with soda. Stir. Add lemon slice.

TEQUILA FIZZ

2 ozs. tequila
1½ ozs. lemon juice
2 teaspoons sugar
2 dashes Angostura
    bitters
1 small egg
Iced club soda
Salt

Shake tequila, lemon juice, sugar, bitters, and egg well with ice. Strain into tall 14-oz. glass half-filled with ice. Fill glass with soda. Stir. Sprinkle very lightly with salt.

WHISKEY CURAÇAO FIZZ

2 ozs. blended whiskey
½ oz. curaçao
1 teaspoon sugar
1 oz. lemon juice
Iced club soda
½ slice orange

Shake whiskey, curaçao, sugar, and lemon juice well with ice. Strain into tall 14-oz. glass half-filled with ice. Fill glass with soda. Stir. Add orange slice.

Rickeys

The first time you try a rickey, your reaction may be the same kind of shudder you get with the first taste of Campari or Greek olives. But the instant shock of pleasure to a heat-weary body will draw you back again and again. Rickeys are made without sugar.

The word "rickey" evokes an immediate association with gin. But the gin rickey—though it's a justifiably renowned classic among warm-weather coolers—is only one among a multitude of these refreshingly effervescent lime libations. Other rickeys can be made by substituting other liquors for gin. Bourbon, blended whiskey, Canadian whisky, Scotch, apple brandy, vodka, and rum all make interesting and refreshing rickeys. But more imaginative rickeys may be created, too, as witnessed by these tried and tested formulas.

APPLE RUM RICKEY

¾ oz. applejack
¾ oz. light rum
¼ large lime
Iced club soda
Orange peel

Put three ice cubes into an 8-oz. glass. Add applejack and rum. Squeeze lime above drink and drop into glass. Add soda. Stir. Twist orange peel above drink and drop into glass.

AQUAVIT RICKEY

1½ ozs. aquavit
1 teaspoon extra-dry
    kümmel
¼ large lime
Iced club soda

Put three ice cubes into an 8-oz. glass. Add aquavit and kümmel. Squeeze lime above drink and drop into glass. Add soda. Stir.

FINO RICKEY

¾ oz. very dry (fino)
    sherry
¾ oz. gin
¼ large lime
Iced club soda

Put three ice cubes into an 8-oz. glass. Add sherry and gin. Squeeze lime above drink and drop into glass. Add soda. Stir. Serve with something salty—such as a bowl of assorted stuffed olives or anchovy canapés.

GIN RICKEY

1½ ozs. gin
¼ large lime
Iced club soda

Put three ice cubes into an 8-oz. glass. Add gin. Squeeze lime above drink and drop into glass. Add soda. Stir.

KIRSCH RICKEY

1½ ozs. kirschwasser
¼ large lime
Iced club soda
2 large fresh or canned pitted black cherries

Put three ice cubes into an 8-oz. glass. Add kirschwasser. Squeeze lime above drink and drop into glass. Add soda. Stir. Cut fresh cherries in half, remove pits, and fasten halves to cocktail spear; or fasten canned cherries to spear. Place spear across glass.

OUZO COGNAC RICKEY

1 oz. ouzo
1 oz. Cognac
¼ large lime
Iced club soda

Put three ice cubes into an 8-oz. glass. Add ouzo and Cognac. Squeeze lime above drink and drop into glass. Add soda. Stir. Ouzo has a delightful but forceful flavor, and Cognac is one of the few liquors that can stand up to it and live compatibly with it in the same drinking glass. A plate of freshly toasted, salted almonds on the side really brings the ouzo-Cognac combination into proper perspective.

PEAR RICKEY

1½ ozs. dry pear brandy (Birnebrande)
¼ large lime
Iced club soda
2 wedges fresh ripe pear

Put three ice cubes into an 8-oz. glass. Add pear brandy. Squeeze lime above drink and drop into glass. Add soda. Stir. Fasten the pear slices to a cocktail spear and place across rim of glass. Munch pear piecemeal while you drink.

PLUM RICKEY

1½ ozs. plum brandy (quetsch, mirabelle, or slivovitz)
¼ large lime
Iced club soda
3 wedges fresh ripe plum

Put three ice cubes into an 8-oz. glass. Add plum brandy. Squeeze lime above drink and drop into glass. Add soda. Stir. Fasten the plum slices to a cocktail spear and place across the rim of glass.

RASPBERRY RICKEY

1½ ozs. Himbeergeist
¼ large lime
Iced club soda
3 fresh or thawed
　frozen raspberries

Put three ice cubes into an 8-oz. glass. Add Himbeergeist. Squeeze lime above drink and drop into glass. Add soda. Stir. Float frozen raspberries on drink or fasten fresh raspberries to cocktail spear as garnish.

TEQUILA RICKEY

1½ ozs. tequila
¼ large lime
Iced club soda
Salt
1 sliced cocktail orange
　in syrup

Put three ice cubes into an 8-oz. glass. Add tequila. Squeeze lime above drink and drop into glass. Add soda. Stir. Sprinkle lightly with salt. Fasten orange slice to cocktail spear. Munch it before or after each swallow.

Sangarees

Sangarees are slightly sweet lowball drinks on the rocks. Unlike an old-fashioned, the sangaree contains no bitters. Each drink receives a benediction of freshly grated nutmeg and should be very well stirred for proper dilution.

APPLE GINGER SANGAREE

1½ ozs. apple brandy
½ oz. green-ginger
　wine
1 slice lemon
Freshly grated nutmeg

Pour apple brandy and ginger wine over rocks in old-fashioned glass. Stir. Add lemon slice. Sprinkle lightly with nutmeg.

BRANDY SANGAREE

½ teaspoon sugar
Iced club soda
2 ozs. brandy
1 teaspoon Madeira
Orange peel
Freshly grated nutmeg

Stir sugar and 1 tablespoon soda in prechilled old-fashioned glass until sugar dissolves. Add brandy and Madeira. Add ice to rim of glass. Stir. Add a splash of soda. Stir. Twist orange peel above drink and drop into glass. Sprinkle lightly with nutmeg.

CRANBERRY SANGAREE

1 oz. cranberry liqueur
1 oz. U.S. blended
   whiskey
Orange peel
Freshly grated nutmeg

Fill old-fashioned glass with ice cubes. Pour cranberry liqueur and whiskey into glass. Stir well. Sprinkle with nutmeg. Twist orange peel over glass and drop into drink.

IRISH CANADIAN SANGAREE

1¼ ozs. Canadian
   whisky
½ oz. Irish Mist liqueur
1 teaspoon orange juice
1 teaspoon lemon juice
Freshly grated nutmeg

Pour whisky, Irish Mist, orange juice, and lemon juice into prechilled old-fashioned glass. Stir. Add ice to rim of glass. Stir. Sprinkle lightly with nutmeg.

SANGAREE COMFORT

1 oz. bourbon
1 oz. Southern Comfort
1 teaspoon lemon juice
1 teaspoon peach-
   flavored brandy
½ teaspoon sugar
Iced club soda
Freshly grated nutmeg

Stir bourbon, Southern Comfort, lemon juice, peach-flavored brandy, and sugar in prechilled old-fashioned glass. Add ice to rim of glass. Add splash of soda. Stir. Sprinkle lightly with nutmeg.

SCOTCH SANGAREE

½ teaspoon honey
Iced club soda
2 ozs. Scotch
Lemon peel
Freshly grated nutmeg

Stir honey, 1 tablespoon soda, and Scotch in prechilled old-fashioned glass until honey dissolves. Add ice to rim of glass. Add a splash of soda. Stir. Twist lemon peel above drink and drop into glass. Sprinkle lightly with nutmeg.

21

ODDBALLS

This chapter contains drinks that, like some of those who drink them, refuse to be classified in conventional categories. But each of the offbeat offerings that follow has a special appeal that sets it apart as a perfect potation to please that special someone or to make a fête more festive: the creamy smoothness of a sherry flip sipped next to a blazing fire; the reviving effects of an eye-opening pick-me-up the mornin' after a long night; the crowning touch that a mist adds to any dinner. The only thing these drinks have in common—with those we've already discussed as well as with one another—is their excellence as libations for discriminating drinkers.

Flips

Flips, like pousse-cafés and frappés, prove that good liquids often come in small glasses. A flip is simply a liquor or wine with egg and sugar, shaken to a gay froth. Flips are rich; too much egg makes them overrich. Thus, for each drink it's best to use a small pullet-size egg, or one large egg for two flips. A classic brandy flip, for instance, is made like this: 2 ounces brandy, 1 small egg, and 1 teaspoon sugar are shaken with plenty of ice, strained into a Delmonico glass, then lightly topped with freshly grated nutmeg. Following the same pattern, standard flips are made by substituting whiskey, gin, rum, applejack, port, sherry, or Madeira for the brandy.

The following snug comforts are for winter holidays, mornings after, and long, carefree brunches near a glowing fireplace.

BRANDIED APRICOT FLIP

1 oz. brandy
1 oz. apricot-flavored brandy
1 small egg
1 teaspoon sugar
Grated nutmeg

Shake brandy, apricot-flavored brandy, egg, and sugar well with ice. Strain into prechilled Delmonico glass. Sprinkle with nutmeg.

CARAWAY FLIP

1½ ozs. aquavit
½ oz. lemon juice
½ oz. orange juice
1 small egg
2 teaspoons sugar
Freshly ground nutmeg

Shake aquavit, lemon juice, orange juice, egg, and sugar extremely well with ice. Strain into 6-oz. glass. Sprinkle with nutmeg.

COFFEE FLIP

1 oz. Cognac
1 oz. tawny port
1 small egg
1 teaspoon sugar
Grated nutmeg

Shake Cognac, port, egg, and sugar well with ice. Strain into prechilled Delmonico glass. Sprinkle with nutmeg.

CRANBERRY FLIP

1 oz. cranberry liqueur
1 oz. California brandy
1 small egg
Freshly grated nutmeg

Shake cranberry liqueur, brandy, and egg extremely well with ice. Strain into prechilled Delmonico glass. Sprinkle with nutmeg.

MADEIRA MINT FLIP

1½ ozs. Madeira
1 oz. chocolate-mint
   liqueur
1 small egg
1 teaspoon sugar
Grated nutmeg

Shake Madeira, chocolate-mint liqueur, egg, and sugar well with ice. Strain into prechilled Delmonico glass. Sprinkle with nutmeg.

PERNOD FLIP

1 oz. Pernod
½ oz. Cointreau
2 teaspoons lemon juice
1 small egg
1 teaspoon sugar
Grated nutmeg

Shake Pernod, Cointreau, lemon juice, egg, and sugar well with ice. Strain into prechilled Delmonico glass. Sprinkle with nutmeg.

SPICED APPLE FLIP

(2 drinks)

3 ozs. applejack
1 egg
1 tablespoon sugar
2 teaspoons lemon juice
⅛ teaspoon ground
   cloves
⅛ teaspoon ground
   cinnamon
Freshly grated nutmeg

Shake applejack, egg, sugar, lemon juice, cloves, and cinnamon with ice. Strain into prechilled whiskey-sour glasses. Sprinkle with nutmeg.

STRAWBERRY RUM FLIP

1 oz. strawberry liqueur
1 oz. light rum
1 teaspoon lemon juice
1 small egg
1 teaspoon sugar
Grated nutmeg

Shake strawberry liqueur, rum, lemon juice, egg, and sugar well with ice. Strain into prechilled Delmonico glass. Sprinkle with nutmeg.

STREGA FLIP

1 oz. Strega
1 oz. brandy
½ oz. orange juice
1 teaspoon lemon juice
1 small egg
1 teaspoon sugar
Grated nutmeg

Shake Strega, brandy, orange juice, lemon juice, egg, and sugar well with ice. Strain into prechilled Delmonico glass. Sprinkle with nutmeg.

TOKAY FLIP

2½ ozs. imported
  Tokay wine (Tokaji
  Aszu)
1 teaspoon sugar
1 small egg
Grated nutmeg

Shake Tokay, sugar, and egg well with ice. Strain into prechilled Delmonico glass. Sprinkle with nutmeg. It may cause another Hungarian revolution to suggest that the magnificent imported Tokay be turned into a flip. Actually the wine turns into sweet bliss.

Mists

A mist is simply straight liquor poured over crushed ice. The normal proportions are 1½ ounces of liquor poured into an 8-ounce old-fashioned glass filled with crushed ice. Sometimes a twist of lemon is added. Mists are cousins of frappés, which are sweet liqueurs poured over crushed ice. Actually, the large amount of fine ice in a mist doesn't befog the liquor's intrinsic flavor; the quality of a fine whiskey in a mist will seem more vivid than the same shot bolted straight down. We now draw the veil from ten of the best-known mists.

Brandy Mist The triumphant flavor of Cognac makes the non-Cognac brandies seem pallid by comparison. (In mixed drinks the story may be different.) Metaxa, the Greek semisweet brandy, creates a velvety, tremulous mist.

Scotch Mist Best when made with a full-bodied twelve-year-old Highland dew. When it comes to mists, some of the lighter Scotches turn into ordinary fog.

Vodka Mist   Ice and vodka emerge as just ice and vodka, nothing more; but an added dram of dry vermouth (a mere teaspoon or so) and a twist of lemon turn the mist into an instant vodka martini. Zubrovka vodka makes a subtle mist.

Kirschwasser Mist   A happy, silvery mist with a hauntingly dry aftertaste of cherries.

Bourbon Mist   Either 86 or 100 proof is fine, but more important than proof is a quality aged bourbon with a smooth, ripe flavor. Half bourbon and half Southern Comfort create a heavenly mist.

Rye Mist   One of the best ways of appreciating genuine straight rye.

Blended U.S. Whiskey Mist   As in bourbon, smoothness shows up in the very first sip. A slice of lemon is a pleasant garnish.

Canadian Mist   Use top Canadian whisky, but increase portion to 1¾ ounces to keep the cool north-country flavor from dissipating too soon.

Gin Mist   It's surprising how close a gin mist is to the modern martini. Add a tiny splash of dry vermouth for a martini mist. A good way to introduce Dutch genever gin to someone who's never tasted it is via the mist.

Rum Mist   The potent flavors of Martinique and Jamaica rums emerge beautifully in mists. Light rum is extremely pleasant with a slice of lime or a small gardenia as garnish. For a more rummy accent, float a teaspoon of 151-proof rum on a light-rum mist.

Pick-Me-Ups

The ancient Egyptians thought that boiled cabbage would prevent a big head after an all-night drinking session. A ground swallow's beak blended with myrrh was recommended by the Assyrians. In South America the Warau Indian women took care of their overindulgent males by deftly tying them like mummies in hammocks until their hangovers passed. In this country the "hair of the dog"—the very thing that caused you to see double—may be the shot in the arm that will straighten your sight. For generations, experienced barmen, especially in men's clubs, where hangover victims can be observed and treated at close range, have vouched for the hair-of-the-dog therapy. Naturally, the danger of taking a swig of liquor the morning after is that the stimulus and relief it brings may provide just enough narcosis to set you right back on the rocky road to ruin. Nevertheless, the effect of a small amount of liquor, especially if combined with citrus juice or tomato juice, seems in many cases to have an extremely salutary effect. The following are from PLAYBOY's repertory of classic and modern pick-me-ups.

CANADIAN STAVE

2 ozs. Canadian whisky
1 oz. red Dubonnet
½ egg white
¼ teaspoon
  Angostura bitters
2 teaspoons lemon juice
2 dashes Tabasco sauce

Shake all ingredients well with ice. Strain into prechilled old-fashioned glass. Add ice cubes to fill glass. Stir well.

CLAM-JUICE COCKTAIL

4 ozs. clam juice
½ oz. catsup
¼ oz. lemon juice
1 dash Worcestershire
  sauce
Salt and pepper
Celery salt

Shake clam juice, catsup, lemon juice, Worcestershire sauce, salt and pepper well with ice. Strain into prechilled Delmonico glass. Sprinkle with celery salt. Nonalcoholic but a wonderful bracer.

COGNAC COUPLING

2 ozs. Cognac
1 oz. tawny port
½ oz. Pernod
1 teaspoon lemon juice
½ teaspoon Peychaud's
  bitters

Shake well with ice. Strain into prechilled old-fashioned glass. Add ice cubes to fill glass. Stir well.

FRENCH PICK-ME-UP

1½ ozs. Pernod
1 oz. Cognac
1 small egg
½ oz. lemon juice
2 teaspoons sugar
Freshly grated nutmeg

Shake Pernod, Cognac, egg, lemon juice, and sugar extremely well with ice. Strain into 8-oz. glass. Sprinkle with nutmeg. Fine tranquilizer for the moaning after.

GIN BRACER

2 ozs. gin
½ oz. catsup
½ oz. lemon juice
1 dash Tabasco sauce
1 dash celery salt
¼ teaspoon Worcester-
   shire sauce
1 cup crushed ice

Put all ingredients into blender. Blend at low speed 15–20 seconds. Pour into tall 10-oz. glass. Add ice cubes to fill glass.

MORNING FIZZ

2 ozs. blended whiskey
½ egg white
½ oz. lemon juice
1 teaspoon sugar
½ teaspoon Pernod
Iced club soda

Shake whiskey, egg white, lemon juice, sugar, and Pernod well with ice. Strain into tall 8-oz. glass. Add a splash of soda and enough ice to fill glass. Stir.

ORANGE WAKE-UP

4 ozs. cold freshly
   squeezed orange
   juice
½ oz. Cognac
½ oz. light rum
½ oz. sweet vermouth
1 slice orange

Pour all liquid ingredients into a squat 8-oz. glass. Add ice cubes to fill glass almost to rim. Stir well. Add orange slice.

POLYNESIAN PICK-ME-UP

½ cup pineapple juice
1½ ozs. vodka
½ teaspoon curry
   powder
½ teaspoon lemon juice
1 tablespoon heavy
   cream
2 dashes Tabasco sauce
½ cup crushed ice
Cayenne pepper

Put pineapple juice, vodka, curry powder, lemon juice, cream, Tabasco sauce, and crushed ice into blender. Blend 10 seconds at high speed. Pour into prechilled old-fashioned glass. Dust very lightly with cayenne.

PRAIRIE OYSTER

1½ ozs. Cognac
2 teaspoons cider
   vinegar
½ oz. Worcestershire
   sauce
1 teaspoon catsup
½ teaspoon Angostura
   bitters
1 egg yolk
Cayenne pepper

Shake Cognac, vinegar, Worcestershire sauce, catsup, and bitters well with ice. Strain into prechilled old-fashioned glass. Add an ice cube or two to fill glass almost to rim. Place egg yolk on top of drink without breaking it. Sprinkle yolk lightly with cayenne. This oldest and most stunning of all morning-after drinks should be swallowed in one long, determined gulp. Grit your teeth. Then open your eyes very slowly.

RUDDY MARY

1½ ozs. aquavit
½ cup tomato juice
1 tablespoon heavy
   cream
1 dash Tabasco
½ egg yolk
¼ oz. lemon juice
¼ oz. catsup
½ cup crushed ice

Put all ingredients into blender. Blend at high speed 20 seconds. Pour into old-fashioned glass. When foam settles, add ice to fill glass to rim.

22

THE BRIMMING BOWL

In the world of entertaining, there is no more delightfully flexible potable than a good punch. This protean party favorite can assume any festive task to which it's put. Made with light Moselle or Rhenish wines, it can beguile your guests with a light, delicate flavor that rests easily on the tongue. Switch to the heavier-duty brandies and rums and it can single-handedly catalyze jolly high spirits and flowing conversation.

Nevertheless, for some time the punch bowl was trotted out only at the year-end saturnalia, when it was filled with a hot wassail or a rich whiskey eggnog, emptied a few times, and then stashed away in dry storage for the next twelve months. But today, more and more hosts are reviving the reigns of the four Georges of England, when men like David Garrick and Samuel Johnson vied with each other all year round to invent newer and stronger punch recipes as they ladled their way through clubs and taverns all over England, and when punch bowls in numerous shapes and sizes sparkled invitingly and were the center of conviviality at celebrations of everything from weddings to military triumphs.

Now, as then, there are a few punch recipes in which fruit has to be marinated in liquors for a day or two, but—happily—those are the exceptions. Generally, an hour or so is all you need for ripening the strong and the weak, the tart and the sweet into a really superior punch. And yet, for all its simplicity, the punch bowl, with its gleaming island of ice in a sea of liquor, turns any casual affair into a gala occasion. The mere sight of the brimming bowl seems an irresistible enticement to drinkers of all persuasions, be they light, moderate, or heavy.

Punch is made cold in two ways—by prechilling all the ingredients from the brandy to the bitters, and by placing a floating island of ice in the bowl itself to both cool and properly dilute the liquid—though a few cold punches, such as some of the champagne varieties, aren't diluted with ice but instead are sometimes ice-girt in a surrounding vessel of crushed ice. These days, when the iceman no longer cometh, it's sometimes difficult to buy a really good-sized chunk. However, in our age of the cube, this is no particular problem; in fact, cubes are faster in their chilling effect than a block. But to serious punch-makers, they are puny craft alongside the traditional icy blockbuster in the punch bowl. You can make your own by simply freezing water in a metal or plastic container, a deep saucepan, or metal mixing bowl. For each gallon of punch, you'll normally need a chunk of ice made with two quarts of water. After freezing, dip the sides of the bowl in warm water for a few seconds and the ice will slide free. The top may form a slight peak and reveal a crack or two, but the inverted iceberg will be smooth and should float serenely.

The punch recipes that follow each make approximately a gallon of potables, enough for eight bibulous guests at three rounds apiece.

APPLE EGG BOWL

12 eggs
½ cup sugar
1 quart applejack
3 quarts milk
1½ cups heavy sweet cream
1 tablespoon vanilla extract
Ground cinnamon

Pour eggs and sugar into blender, and blend at low speed 2 minutes. Pour into punch bowl. Gradually add applejack and beat with wire whip until well blended. Stir in milk, cream, and vanilla. Let mixture ripen in refrigerator at least 1 hour for flavors to blend. Stir well before serving. Serve in punch cups. Sprinkle with cinnamon.

APPLE GINGER PUNCH

24 ozs. apple brandy, either calvados or applejack

2 ozs. maraschino liqueur

2 ozs. kirsch

1 quart pineapple-grapefruit juice

24 ozs. green-ginger wine

1 quart plus 1 pint ginger beer or ginger ale

2 red apples

2 yellow apples

Chill all ingredients. Pour all liquids except ginger beer over large block of ice in punch bowl. Stir well. Let mixture ripen 1 hour in refrigerator. Cut unpeeled apples into wedgelike slices, discarding core. Just before serving, pour ginger beer into bowl. Float apple slices on top.

ARTILLERYMEN'S PUNCH

1 quart 86-proof bourbon

9 ozs. light rum

4 ozs. dark Jamaica rum

6 ozs. apricot-flavored brandy

12 ozs. lemon juice

24 ozs. orange juice

1 quart strong black tea

¼ cup sugar

Pour all ingredients over a large block of ice in punch bowl. Stir well to dissolve sugar. Let mixture ripen 1 hour in refrigerator before serving.

BARBADOS BOWL

8 medium-size ripe bananas

1 cup lime juice

1 cup sugar

1 fifth light rum

8 ozs. 151-proof rum

1 quart plus 12 ozs. pineapple juice

12 ozs. mango nectar

2 limes, sliced

Chill all ingredients except bananas. Cut 6 bananas into thin slices and place in electric blender with lime juice and sugar. Blend until smooth. Pour over block of ice in punch bowl. Add both kinds of rum, pineapple juice, and mango nectar. Stir well. Let mixture ripen in refrigerator 1 hour before serving. Cut remaining 2 bananas into thin slices. Float banana and lime slices on punch.

BERMUDA BOURBON PUNCH

3 tablespoons jasmine
   tea leaves
3 cups boiling water
1 fifth bourbon
8 ozs. Madeira
8 ozs. lemon juice
1½ ozs. Pernod
4 ozs. Falernum
1 quart plus 1 pint
   ginger ale
3 lemons, thinly sliced

Pour boiling water over tea leaves. Steep for 5 minutes; strain, cool to room temperature, and chill in refrigerator. Over large block of ice in punch bowl pour tea, bourbon, Madeira, lemon juice, Pernod, and Falernum. Stir well. Let mixture ripen 1 hour in refrigerator. Add ginger ale and sliced lemons. Add several spiced walnuts (recipe below) to each drink after pouring it into punch cup.

Spiced Walnuts

1 egg white
2 teaspoons cold water
½ lb. shelled walnut
   halves
1 cup sugar
1 tablespoon ground
   cinnamon
¼ teaspoon ground
   cloves
⅛ teaspoon ground
   nutmeg

Beat egg white until slightly foamy but not stiff. Add the water and mix well. Combine egg white and walnuts in a bowl; stir to coat nuts; drain thoroughly in colander to remove excess egg white. In another bowl, combine sugar, cinnamon, cloves, and nutmeg. Preheat oven to 325° F. Dip walnuts, a few pieces at a time, into sugar mixture (they should be coated thoroughly but should not have thick gobs of sugar adhering to them), place them on a greased baking sheet, and bake 20 minutes, or until medium brown. Remove from baking sheet with spatula, separating them from sugar coating on pan. Cool to room temperature.

BLACK-CHERRY RUM PUNCH

1 fifth light rum
4 ozs. 151-proof rum
4 ozs. dark Jamaica rum
2 17-oz. cans pitted black cherries in heavy syrup
8 ozs. fresh lemon juice
4 ozs. fresh orange juice
4 ozs. fresh lime juice
8 ozs. Peter Heering
8 ozs. crème de cassis
2 limes, thinly sliced
1 quart club soda

Put all ingredients except soda into punch bowl. Add block of ice. Stir well. Refrigerate 1 hour. Add soda. Stir well.

BRANDY EGGNOG BOWL

12 eggs
½ cup sugar
1 fifth Cognac or non-Cognac brandy
4 ozs. Jamaica rum
3 quarts milk
8 ozs. heavy cream
Grated nutmeg

Carefully separate egg yolks from whites. In punch bowl, combine egg yolks and sugar. Beat well with a wire whisk. Gradually add Cognac, rum, milk, and cream. Beat well. Taste. Add more sugar if desired. Place the bowl in the refrigerator for at least 2 hours. Just before serving, beat egg whites in a separate bowl or in mixer, in two batches if necessary, until stiff. Fold whites into punch; that is, do not mix them with a round-the-bowl movement but use the wire whisk in a down-over-up stroke until whites are thoroughly blended. Ladle into cups. Sprinkle with nutmeg.

CAPE COD CRANBERRY PUNCH

2 quarts plus 6 ozs. cranberry juice
1 quart 100-proof vodka
6 ozs. cherry liqueur
1 tablespoon orange-flower water
24 ozs. orange juice
1 teaspoon ground cinnamon
½ teaspoon ground allspice
¼ teaspoon ground nutmeg
2 limes, thinly sliced

Chill all liquid ingredients. Mix cinnamon, allspice, and nutmeg with a small amount of vodka until a smooth, lump-free paste is formed. Pour the paste and all other liquids over large block of ice in punch bowl. Stir well. Refrigerate 1 hour before serving. Float lime slices on top of punch.

CHAMPAGNE BLUES

1 fifth blue curaçao
8 ozs. lemon juice
4 fifths dry champagne
Peel of 2 lemons

Chill all ingredients. Cut lemon peel into strips 1½ to 2 inches long and ¼ inch wide. Pour curaçao and lemon juice into glass punch bowl. Stir well. Add champagne and stir lightly. Float lemon peel, yellow side up, in bowl. Do not use ice in bowl. It may be surrounded by cracked ice, if desired, by placing glass bowl in vessel of larger diameter.

CHAMPAGNE PUNCH WITH KIRSCH

4 fifths iced brut champagne
5 ozs. iced kirsch liqueur (not dry kirschwasser)
5 ozs. iced oloroso (cream) sherry
4 ozs. iced lemon juice
16 ozs. iced orange juice

Pour all ingredients into prechilled punch bowl. Stir lightly. Bowl may be surrounded by ice in larger bowl, or punch may be made in pitchers surrounded by ice.

CHAMPAGNE PUNCH WITH MARASCHINO

6 ozs. maraschino
 liqueur
6 ozs. Cognac
1 teaspoon orange
 bitters
2 oranges, thinly sliced
1 lemon, thinly sliced
4 fifths iced brut
 champagne

Put maraschino, Cognac, orange bitters, and sliced fruit into punch bowl. Let mixture brew about 1 hour in refrigerator. Place large chunk of ice in bowl. Pour champagne over ice. Stir lightly.

CHAMPAGNE SHERBET PUNCH

2 quarts lemon sherbet
 or lemon ice, frozen
 very hard
5 fifths iced brut
 champagne
1½ teaspoons
 Angostura bitters

Be sure lemon sherbet has been in freezing section of refrigerator set at the coldest point for at least 1 day. Place lemon sherbet in prechilled punch bowl. Pour champagne over sherbet. Add bitters. Stir. Let mixture ripen in refrigerator for about 15–20 minutes before serving.

EMERALD BOWL

3 quarts chilled
 emerald Riesling
⅔ cup California
 brandy
⅔ cup apricot-flavored
 brandy
1½ pints chilled apple
 juice
16 slices cucumber peel,
 each 1 inch long and
 ½ inch wide

Pour Riesling, California brandy, apricot-flavored brandy, and apple juice over large block of ice in punch bowl. Add cucumber peel. Stir. Refrigerate 1 hour.

FISH-HOUSE PUNCH I

1½ cups sugar
1 quart cold water (not carbonated water)
1 fifth Cognac
1 fifth golden rum
1 fifth Jamaica rum
24 ozs. lemon juice
6 ozs. peach-flavored brandy

A traditionally high-proof punch. Put sugar into punch bowl. Add about 1 cup of the water and stir until sugar is dissolved. Add all other ingredients, including balance of water. Let mixture ripen in refrigerator about 1 hour. Place large chunk of ice in bowl. Ladle punch over ice. Add more cold water if a weaker mixture is desired.

FISH-HOUSE PUNCH II

2 12-oz. pkgs. frozen sliced peaches, thawed
1 quart golden rum
1 fifth Cognac
1 pint lemon juice
1 cup sugar
1 quart ice water

Put peaches into blender. Blend 1 minute at high speed. Pour over large block of ice in punch bowl. Add rum, Cognac, lemon juice, sugar, and water. Stir well to dissolve sugar. Let punch ripen in refrigerator for about 1 hour before serving. A modern version of the colonial recipe fish-house punch I.

FLORENTINE PUNCH

2 21-oz. bottles coffee-cream Marsala wine
2 24-oz. bottles Italian rosé wine
1 fifth plus 8 ozs. brandy
4 ozs. lemon juice
2 oranges

Chill all ingredients. Pour both kinds of wine, brandy, and lemon juice over large block of ice in punch bowl. Stir well. Refrigerate 1 hour. Cut oranges into thin rounds. Slice in half and float atop punch.

GUAVA MILK PUNCH

2½ quarts milk
1 quart (32 ozs.) guava nectar
1 cup light cream
1 pint plus 4 ozs. light rum
6 ozs. golden rum
3 ozs. 151-proof rum
¼ cup sugar
12 1-inch pieces lemon peel
12 1-inch pieces orange peel

Pour all ingredients except lemon and orange peel into punch bowl. Stir very well to dissolve sugar. Add a large block of ice, lemon peel, and orange peel. Place bowl in refrigerator 1 hour for flavors to ripen. A good low-proof punch to serve the morning after, either before or with brunch; also pleasant on a lazy afternoon on deck.

INTERPLANETARY PUNCH

1 fifth light rum
4 ozs. dark Jamaica rum
12 ozs. peppermint schnapps
1 quart mango nectar
12 ozs. (1½ cups) heavy sweet cream
1 quart orange juice
8 large sprigs mint
1 large ripe fresh mango, if available
6 thin slices orange

Prechill all ingredients including liquors. Place large block of ice in punch bowl. Add both kinds of rum, peppermint schnapps, mango nectar, cream, and orange juice. Stir very well. Tear mint leaves from stems. Peel and cut mango into small slices. (Canned mango may be used in place of fresh; canned fruit, however, will not float.) Cut orange rounds into quarters. Float mint leaves and fruit on punch. Refrigerate for 1 hour for flavors to ripen.

IRISH APPLE BOWL

20 ozs. applejack
20 ozs. blended Irish whiskey
10 ozs. Rose's lime juice
4 limes sliced thin
2 large red Delicious apples
2 quarts plus 1 pint ginger ale

All ingredients, including spirits, should be prechilled. Apples should be cored, but not peeled, and cut into ½-inch dice. Pour applejack, whiskey, and lime juice over large block of ice in punch bowl. Add lime slices and apples. Stir well. Let mixture ripen in refrigerator 1 hour. Pour cold ginger ale into bowl. Stir lightly.

MOSELLE BOWL

1 very ripe medium-size
 pineapple
½ cup sugar
12 ozs. Grand Marnier
16 ozs. brandy
4 24-oz. bottles Moselle
 wine
1 quart large ripe
 strawberries

Cut ends off pineapple, remove shell and all "eyes," and cut lengthwise into 4 pieces. Cut away hard core from each piece; then cut crosswise into thin pieces. Place pineapple, sugar, Grand Marnier, and brandy in salad bowl or mixing bowl. Marinate, covered, in refrigerator at least 24 hours—48 hours if possible. Pour well-chilled wine into punch bowl with large block of ice. Add pineapple mixture and stir well. Let mixture ripen in bowl ½ hour before serving. Cut stems off strawberries. Cut lengthwise in half and float on punch.

MOUNTAIN RED PUNCH

3 quarts chilled
 California mountain
 red wine
½ cup amaretto
½ cup California
 brandy
½ cup cherry-flavored
 brandy
1 pint ginger ale
2 ozs. julienne almonds,
 toasted

Pour wine, amaretto, California brandy, and cherry-flavored brandy over large block of ice in punch bowl. Refrigerate 1 hour. Add ginger ale. Stir lightly. Float almonds on top. (Note: Almonds may be toasted by placing in shallow pan in moderate oven for about 10 minutes; avoid scorching.)

ORANGE ALMOND BOWL

6 ozs. slivered almonds
2 tablespoons melted
 butter
Salt
18 ozs. blended whiskey
12 ozs. Danish aquavit
1 quart plus 8 ozs.
 orange juice
8 ozs. sweet vermouth
1 teaspoon orange
 bitters
Peel of 2 large California
 oranges
1½ quarts quinine
 water

Preheat oven to 375° F. Place almonds in shallow pan or pie plate. Pour butter over almonds, mixing well. Place pan in oven and bake until almonds are medium brown, about 8 to 10 minutes, stirring once during baking. Avoid scorching. Sprinkle with salt. Chill almonds and all other ingredients. Pour whiskey, aquavit, orange juice, vermouth, and bitters over large block of ice in punch bowl. Refrigerate mixture for 1 hour. Cut orange peel into narrow strips about 2 inches long. Pour quinine water into bowl. Stir. Float orange peel and almonds on punch.

PHI BETA BLUEBERRY

1 fifth 100-proof vodka
16 ozs. Metaxa brandy
16 ozs. bottled
    blueberry syrup
12 ozs. lemon juice
2 quarts club soda
2 lemons, thinly sliced
1 pint cultivated
    blueberries

Chill all ingredients. Pour vodka, Metaxa, blueberry syrup, and lemon juice over large block of ice in punch bowl. Let mixture ripen in refrigerator 1 hour before serving. Pour club soda into bowl and stir. Float lemon slices and blueberries on punch.

POLYNESIAN PUNCH BOWL

1 fifth light rum
6 ozs. cream of coconut
1 quart plus 1 cup
    pineapple juice
3 cups orange juice
8 ozs. sloe gin
5 ozs. peppermint
    schnapps
1 cup lemon juice
12 thin slices very ripe
    fresh pineapple
12 thin slices orange
1 pint iced club soda

Pour rum, cream of coconut, pineapple juice, orange juice, sloe gin, peppermint schnapps, and lemon juice into punch bowl. Stir well until all ingredients, particularly cream of coconut, are well blended. Add a large block of ice and pineapple and orange slices, and place in refrigerator for about 1 hour for flavors to ripen. Add soda, and stir lightly just before serving.

ROSÉ PUNCH

3 quarts chilled rosé
    wine
1 cup cranberry liqueur
½ cup California
    brandy
16 thin slices ripe
    fresh pineapple
1 quart large ripe
    strawberries
1 pint iced club soda

Pour wine, cranberry liqueur, and California brandy over large block of ice in punch bowl. Add pineapple slices and strawberries. Refrigerate 1 hour. Add iced club soda. Stir lightly.

RUM CUP WITH WHITE WINE

(8–10 punch cups)

1 pint plus 4 ozs. light rum
10 ozs. very dry white wine
1 cup (8 ozs.) orange juice
½ cup (4 ozs.) lime juice
2 ozs. orgeat (almond syrup)
2 ozs. Falernum
2 ozs. triple sec
6 slices lime
6 large sprigs mint

Pour all ingredients except lime slices and mint into 2-quart pitcher. Add lime slices and mint. Chill 1 to 2 hours. Fill pitcher almost to rim with ice cubes. Stir very well. Pour into punch cups or 6-oz. fruit-juice glasses.

SANGRIA

(6 servings of 6–8 ozs.)

1 fifth light dry red wine
1 whole orange
1 ripe Elberta peach, peeled and sliced
6 slices lemon
1½ ozs. Cognac
1 oz. triple sec
1 oz. maraschino liqueur
1 tablespoon or more sugar to taste
6 ozs. iced club soda

Cut entire peel of orange in a single strip, beginning at stem end and continuing until spiral reaches bottom of fruit. White part should be cut along with outer peel, so that orange fruit is exposed. Leave peel attached to orange bottom, so that fruit may be suspended in pitcher. Pour wine into glass pitcher. Add peach, lemon, Cognac, triple sec, maraschino liqueur, and sugar. Stir to dissolve sugar. Carefully place orange in pitcher, fastening top end of peel over rim. Let mixture marinate at room temperature at least 1 hour. Add soda and 1 tray of ice cubes to pitcher. Stir.

WHISKEY PUNCH

3 cups orange juice
1 cup lemon juice
1 cup sugar
2 lemons, thinly sliced
2 quarts blended whiskey
1 quart iced club soda

Put fruit juices and sugar into punch bowl. Stir until sugar dissolves. Add lemon slices. Place a large chunk of ice in bowl. Add whiskey. Refrigerate 1 hour. Add club soda. Stir. Additional club soda may be added if desired.

WHITE SANGRIA

(6 servings of 6–8 ozs.)

1 fifth dry white wine
1 whole orange
2 slices lemon
2 slices lime
1 oz. Cognac
2 tablespoons sugar
1 piece stick cinnamon
8 large strawberries,
   stems removed, halved
6 ozs. iced club soda

Cut entire peel of orange, following procedure for Sangria recipe above. Pour wine into glass pitcher. Add lemon, lime, Cognac, sugar, cinnamon, and strawberries. Stir to dissolve sugar. Carefully place orange in pitcher, fastening top end of peel over rim. Let mixture marinate at room temperature at least 1 hour. Add soda and 1 tray of ice cubes to pitcher. Stir.

WHITE WINE PUNCH

3 quarts chilled dry
   white wine
½ cup triple sec
½ cup kirschwasser
½ cup California
   brandy
8 slices orange
8 slices lemon
1 pint iced club soda

Pour wine, triple sec, kirschwasser, and brandy over large block of ice in punch bowl. Add orange and lemon slices. Place bowl in refrigerator for 1 hour for flavors to blend. Add club soda. Stir lightly.

23

HOT CHEER

When hot drinks had to wait on icy weather, the ideal accompaniments for a hot-toddy party were a raging blizzard and a roaring fireplace. They're still picturesque backdrops, but nowadays any cool evening in the fall or winter is reason enough for filling the cups to the brim with grogs and nogs—and not just at the hearthside. Almost any casual brisk-weather get-together— a tailgate party at a football or soccer field, a caravan to the ski country —is perfect for tapping the cordial pleasures of the Thermos. And a demitasse cup filled with a blend of warm blackberry liqueur, Cognac, and lemon is the most tranquil joy we can imagine before sinking into an unbroken night's sleep.

Hot drinks should be just warm enough so that the flavors seem to float like the soft clouds on an old silk painting—but not so hot that they burn the lips. Heat them in a saucepan or chafing dish to just short of the boiling point; then turn off the flame and let them cool somewhat before pouring.

One of the oldest bar tools for making drinks hot was the loggerhead —a long iron tool with a cup or ball at one end. In colonial days the cup was used, among other purposes, for melting pitch to be poured upon the crews of attacking naval vessels; those were the days when men at loggerheads weren't kidding. It's now remembered as a fireplace device for the much more advanced purpose of heating rum flips. In time the loggerhead was succeeded by the poker, which serves just as well for those who feel like indulging in a bit of showmanship. Find one that's ash-free—old pokers with the soot of ages upon them aren't nearly as practical as clean ones that have never seen a fireplace —and heat it glowing hot in a normal gas flame. For reviving drinks that have become coolish from standing too long, keep the poker in the flame for at least three minutes before plunging it into the waiting mug.

The recipes that follow require no such fiery baptism (though it may win applause, it won't improve the drinks); nor are they intended to be enjoyed only at a bibbing party. Just as they can be served day or night, indoors or out, in fair weather or foul, they'll be the best of drinking companions with a colorful variety of meals: a warm Danish toddy of aquavit and Peter Heering before a smorgasbord or smørrebrød, a buttered bourbon and ginger before a chafing dish of creamed chicken hash, a blackberry demitasse after an urban luau.

Several of the recipes in this chapter depart from the usual one-drink formula. The reason: For some hot potations the nature of the ingredients makes the preparation of a single drink impractical. The blue blazer, for example, should be prepared for two in order to create a decent blaze. The taste of the gin and jerry becomes unpleasantly eggy unless two are made with each egg. The average *café brûlot* set serves eight, so the *café diable* recipe is for that number. And so on; wherever a recipe makes more than a single drink, it's because careful party and taste testing have shown that the number specified is the minimum for best results. But whichever recipes you try, and for however many people, you'll find that all create warm contentment.

APPLE GROG

1½ ozs. applejack
1 tablespoon brown
  sugar
4 ozs. water
2 whole allspice
1 piece stick cinnamon
2-inch strip lemon peel
½ oz. 151-proof rum

Pour applejack, sugar, and water into saucepan. Add allspice and cinnamon. Bring to boiling point but do not boil. Pour into preheated mug. Twist lemon peel above mug and drop into drink. Float rum on top (pour it over the back of a tablespoon held along inside of mug). Set rum aflame. Let it burn for about a half-minute, then stir to stop flaming. Warn guests not to burn lips on mug (take the first sip with a spoon).

APRICOT TOM AND JERRY

1 egg, white and yolk
  separated
Salt
⅛ teaspoon ground
  allspice
⅛ teaspoon ground
  cinnamon
1½ teaspoons sugar
1 oz. apricot-flavored
  brandy
1 oz. blended whiskey
1 oz. milk
1 oz. heavy cream
Freshly grated nutmeg

Beat egg yolk until light. Add a pinch of salt and the allspice, cinnamon, and sugar, blending well. Beat white separately in a small, narrow bowl until stiff. Slowly fold yolk into white. Put egg mixture into a 10-oz. tom-and-jerry mug. Heat apricot-flavored brandy, whiskey, milk, and cream until bubbles appear around edge of pan. Do not boil. Pour into mug slowly, stirring as liquid mixture is added. Sprinkle with nutmeg.

BLACKBERRY DEMITASSE

1 oz. blackberry liqueur
  or blackberry-flavored
  brandy
1 tablespoon blackberry
  jelly
½ oz. Cognac
½ oz. water
½ teaspoon lemon
  juice
¼ thin slice lemon

Heat blackberry liqueur, jelly, Cognac, water, and lemon juice without boiling. Stir well until jelly is completely dissolved. Pour into demitasse cup. Add lemon slice.

BLUE BLAZER

(Serves 2)

6 ozs. Irish whiskey or
Scotch
2 tablespoons honey
¼ cup boiling water
Lemon peel

Both nightcap and toast, the blue blazer should be served steaming hot and sipped slowly. (And to create a decent blaze, it should always be made for two.) For mixing it you need two heavy and rather deep mugs, about 12-oz. capacity. Rinse them with hot or boiling water before mixing the drink. Then pour honey and boiling water into one mug and stir until honey is dissolved. Heat whiskey in a saucepan until it's hot but not boiling. Pour into second mug. Light it. Pour the whiskey—carefully—back and forth between the mugs. The flowing blue-flaming stream will be best appreciated in a dimly lit room. Since a few drams of the blazing whiskey may spill, it's best to pour it over a large silver or china platter. When flames subside, pour the blazer into two thick cut-glass goblets. Twist the lemon peel over the blazer and drop it into the drink. Some bartenders wear asbestos gloves when making a blue blazer.

BUTTERED APPLE GROG

1 oz. apple brandy
1 oz. dry vermouth
2 ozs. apple juice
2 whole cloves
¼ baked apple, fresh
or canned
1 teaspoon syrup from
canned baked apple,
or sugar to taste
1 teaspoon sweet butter
1 slice lemon
Sugar

Heat apple brandy, vermouth, apple juice, and cloves until hot but not boiling. Into an old-fashioned glass or coffee cup put baked apple, butter, and lemon slice. Pour apple-brandy mixture into the glass. Add 1 teaspoon syrup if canned baked apple is used, or add sugar to taste. Stir until butter dissolves.

BUTTERED BOURBON AND GINGER

1½ ozs. bourbon
1 oz. ginger-flavored
    brandy
1 teaspoon sweet butter
1 cinnamon stick
6 ozs. apple juice
Freshly grated nutmeg

Into a 10-oz. mug or silver tankard pour bourbon and ginger-flavored brandy. Add butter and cinnamon stick to mug. Heat apple juice to boiling point, but do not boil. Pour into mug. Stir until butter dissolves. Sprinkle with nutmeg.

CAFÉ DIABLE   (8 demitasse cups)

2½ measuring cups
    extra-strong fresh
    black coffee
2 cinnamon sticks,
    broken in half
8 whole allspice
4 whole cardamom
    seeds, removed from
    shell
Grated rind of ½ orange
5 ozs. Cognac
3 ozs. Grand Marnier
2 ozs. sambuca
    (anise-flavored Italian
    liqueur)
2 tablespoons sugar

In a deep chafing dish or *café brûlot* set, simmer ½ cup coffee, cinnamon sticks, allspice, cardamom seeds, and orange rind about 2 or 3 minutes to release spice flavors, stirring constantly. Add Cognac, Grand Marnier, and sambuca. When liquors are hot, set ablaze. Stir with a long-handled ladle or spoon until flames subside. Add balance of coffee and sugar. When *café diable* is hot, ladle or spoon it into demitasse cups. A delightful postprandial drink—but you'd best rehearse it before debuting for guests. Once learned, it's an amiably engaging routine.

CRÈME DE CACAO NIGHTCAP   (Serves 4)

¼ cup heavy cream
2 teaspoons sugar
1 tablespoon crème de
    cacao
10 ozs. milk
4 ozs. crème de cacao
2 ozs. California
    brandy
3 tablespoons sugar
Cocoa

Beat cream in small, narrow bowl until whipped. Stir 2 teaspoons sugar and 1 tablespoon crème de cacao into whipped cream. Store in refrigerator until needed. Heat milk, 4 ozs. crème de cacao, brandy, and 3 tablespoons sugar until hot but not boiling. Pour hot milk mixture into four footed whiskey-sour glasses or small goblets. Spoon whipped cream on top. Put a small quantity of cocoa into a small fine wire strainer. Shake strainer above each drink, sprinkling lightly with cocoa. Place glass on saucer for serving.

DANISH TODDY

2 whole cloves
2 whole allspice
1 cinnamon stick
1 slice orange
2 ozs. Peter Heering or Cherry Karise
1 oz. aquavit
½ oz. kümmel
5 ozs. cranberry juice

Put cloves, allspice, cinnamon stick, and orange slice into a 10-oz. mug. Heat Peter Heering, aquavit, kümmel, and cranberry juice until hot but not boiling. Pour into mug.

GIN AND JERRY

(Serves 2)

4 ozs. gin
1 oz. yellow Chartreuse
3 ozs. orange juice
1 teaspoon sugar
1 egg
Ground cinnamon

Pour gin, Chartreuse, orange juice, and sugar into saucepan. Heat almost to boiling point, but don't boil. Beat egg in narrow bowl with rotary beater until egg is very light and foamy. Slowly, while stirring constantly, pour hot liquid into bowl. Pour into preheated tom-and-jerry mugs or punch cups. Sprinkle lightly with cinnamon.

HOT BUTTERED APPLE

2 ozs. applejack
½ oz. Stone's ginger wine
4 ozs. water
1 piece stick cinnamon
2 whole cloves
1 teaspoon sugar
1 teaspoon sweet butter
Freshly grated nutmeg

Pour applejack, ginger wine, and water into saucepan. Add cinnamon, cloves, and sugar. Stir until sugar dissolves. Bring to boiling point, but do not boil. Pour into preheated mug. Add butter and stir until butter melts. Sprinkle with nutmeg.

HOT BUTTERED IRISH

1½ ozs. blended Irish
   whiskey
½ oz. orange juice
½ oz. lemon juice
4 ozs. water
1 teaspoon sugar
2 dashes Angostura
   bitters
2 whole cloves
1 teaspoon sweet butter
1 piece lemon peel
Grated fresh nutmeg

Pour whiskey, orange juice, lemon juice, water, sugar, and bitters into saucepan. Add cloves. Heat to boiling point, but do not boil. Pour into preheated mug. Add butter and stir until butter melts. Twist lemon peel over drink and drop into mug. Sprinkle with grated nutmeg.

HOT BUTTERED RUM

2 whole cloves
2 whole allspice
1 inch stick cinnamon
1 teaspoon sugar
1½ ozs. hot light rum
½ oz. hot dark Jamaica
   rum
Boiling water
1 teaspoon sweet butter

Put the cloves, allspice, stick cinnamon, and sugar into a mug with a tablespoon or two of boiling water. Let the mixture stand 5 minutes. Add the hot rum (both kinds), 2 ozs. boiling water, and butter. Stir until butter dissolves. Add more sugar if desired.

PLAYBOY'S HOT BUTTERED RUM

2 ozs. dark Jamaica
   rum
½ teaspoon
   maraschino liqueur
1 oz. lemon juice
1 teaspoon sugar
1 pat butter, equal to 2
   teaspoons
Boiling water
1 slice lemon
Freshly grated nutmeg

Pour rum, maraschino liqueur, and lemon juice into 12-oz. mug. Add sugar and butter. Fill with boiling water. Stir to dissolve butter and sugar. Add lemon slice. Grate nutmeg on top.

HOT COCONUT COFFEE

2 ozs. CocoRibe
6 ozs. strong fresh hot
   coffee
Whipped cream

Pour CocoRibe and coffee into mug. Add dollop of whipped cream. Because of the sweetness of CocoRibe, sugar is usually not necessary in this drink.

HOT COCORIBE ORANGEADE

2 ozs. CocoRibe
4 ozs. orange juice
2 ozs. water
Stick cinnamon
½ slice orange

Pour orange juice and water into saucepan. Bring to a boil, but do not boil. Pour into mug. Add CocoRibe. Stir with stick cinnamon, and leave stick cinnamon in mug. Add orange slice.

HOT DRAMBUIE TODDY

2 ozs. Drambuie
½ oz. lemon juice
1 slice lemon
1 slice orange
4 ozs. boiling water
1 piece stick cinnamon

Pour Drambuie and lemon juice into preheated mug or punch cup. (To preheat mug, fill with boiling water for about a minute; then discard water.) Add lemon slice, orange slice, and 4 ozs. boiling water. Stir with cinnamon stick—and leave it in the mug.

HOT EGGNOG

1 egg
Salt
1 tablespoon sugar
¾ cup (6 ozs.) hot milk
2 ozs. hot Cognac
1 teaspoon dark Jamaica rum
Ground nutmeg

Put whole egg and dash of salt into mixing bowl. Beat egg until it is very thick and lemon yellow in color. Add sugar and beat until sugar is blended in. Add hot milk, Cognac, and rum. Stir well. Pour into mug. Sprinkle lightly with a dash of ground nutmeg.

HOT GRAPEFRUIT MUG

4 ozs. unsweetened grapefruit juice
2 ozs. orange juice
1½ ozs. gin
½ oz. rock-and-rye
1 tablespoon honey
2 teaspoons sweet butter
Freshly ground nutmeg

In saucepan heat grapefruit juice, orange juice, gin, rock-and-rye, honey, and 1 teaspoon butter. Bring to boiling point, but do not boil. Pour into warm 10-oz. mug. Add remaining teaspoon butter and stir until butter dissolves. Sprinkle lightly with nutmeg.

HOT IRISH AND PORT

1½ ozs. blended Irish
   whiskey
3 ozs. tawny port
2 ozs. water
1 piece stick cinnamon
1 slice orange

Pour whiskey, port, and water into saucepan. Heat to boiling point, but do not boil. Pour into mug. Add stick cinnamon and orange slice. Let drink stand about 3 minutes before serving.

HOT PORT FLIP

3 ozs. port wine
1 oz. Cognac
1 teaspoon sugar
¼ teaspoon instant
   coffee
1 small egg
1 tablespoon heavy
   cream
Freshly grated nutmeg

Pour wine and Cognac into saucepan. Add sugar. Stir well. Heat but don't boil. Stir in instant coffee. In a narrow bowl, beat egg with rotary beater until egg is very foamy. Stir in cream. Very slowly, while stirring constantly, pour hot liquid into egg mixture. Pour into preheated mug. Sprinkle with nutmeg.

HOT TODDY

1 teaspoon sugar
3 whole cloves
1 inch stick cinnamon
1 thin slice lemon
3 ozs. boiling water
2 ozs. bourbon
Ground nutmeg

Into a heavy mug put the sugar, cloves, stick cinnamon, and slice of lemon. Add 1 oz. of the boiling water. Stir well. Let the mixture stand about 5 minutes. Add the bourbon and the remaining 2 ozs. boiling water. Stir. Sprinkle lightly with nutmeg.

IRISH COFFEE

5 or 6 ozs. fresh, hot
   black coffee
1½ ozs. Irish whiskey
1 teaspoon sugar
Sweetened whipped
   cream

Warm an 8-oz. thick goblet or Irish-coffee glass by rinsing it in very hot or boiling water. Pour coffee and whiskey into goblet. Add sugar. Stir until sugar is dissolved. Add a generous dab of whipped cream.

IRISH TEA

1½ ozs. blended
   Irish whiskey
6 ozs. freshly brewed
   hot Irish black tea,
3 whole cloves
3 whole allspice
1 piece stick cinnamon
1 teaspoon sugar
2 teaspoons honey
1 slice lemon
Freshly grated nutmeg

Put whiskey, tea, cloves, allspice, cinnamon, sugar, and honey into mug. Stir well. Add lemon slice. Sprinkle with grated nutmeg.

JACK AND JERRY

(4 drinks)

2 eggs, separated
2 tablespoons sugar
1 cup milk
1 oz. heavy cream
Dash salt
¼ teaspoon ground
   cinnamon
⅛ teaspoon ground
   mace
⅛ teaspoon ground
   ginger
8 ozs. applejack
1 pint hot milk
Freshly grated nutmeg

Beat egg yolks and sugar in top part of double boiler until well blended. Slowly stir in 1 cup milk, cream, salt, cinnamon, mace and ginger. Cook over simmering water, stirring constantly with wire whip, until mixture thickens to the consistency of a light sauce. Remove from fire. Beat egg whites until stiff. Slowly stir cooked mixture into beaten egg whites. Divide among 4 preheated mugs. Pour 2 ozs. applejack into each mug. Fill mugs with hot milk. Stir. Sprinkle with nutmeg.

KIRSCH NIGHTCAP

1 oz. kirschwasser
3 ozs. Stone's ginger
   wine
4 ozs. water
1 piece stick cinnamon
2 whole cloves
1 teaspoon sugar
Lemon peel

Slowly heat ginger wine and water to boiling point, but do not boil. Pour into mug. Add kirschwasser, cinnamon, cloves, and sugar. Stir well. Twist lemon peel above drink and drop into mug.

MEXICAN COFFEE

1 oz. Kahlúa coffee
    liqueur
4 ozs. fresh, hot black
    coffee
Ground cinnamon
Sweetened whipped
    cream

Pour liqueur and coffee into Irish-coffee glass. Sprinkle with cinnamon. Stir. Top with whipped cream.

MULLED CLARET
(8 drinks)

1 cup boiling water
½ cup sugar
1 lemon, sliced
1 orange, sliced
12 whole allspice
12 whole cloves
4 inch cinnamon stick
1 fifth dry red wine

In large saucepan combine the boiling water, sugar, sliced lemon, sliced orange, allspice, cloves, and stick cinnamon. Bring to a boil. Reduce flame and simmer 5 minutes. Add the wine. Bring to the boiling point. Do not boil, but simmer 10 minutes. Pour the hot mulled wine into thick glasses or mugs. Place a slice of lemon, a slice of orange, and a few whole spices in each glass.

MULLED KÜMMEL

2 ozs. kümmel
1 oz. vodka
½ oz. lemon juice
1 teaspoon sugar
5 ozs. water
2 teaspoons butter
1 piece stick cinnamon
1 thin slice lemon
½ slice orange
½ oz. aquavit

In saucepan stir kümmel, vodka, lemon juice, sugar, water, and 1 teaspoon butter. Heat to boiling point, but do not boil. Place cinnamon in warm 10-oz. mug. Pour mulled kümmel into mug and add remaining teaspoon butter. Stir until butter dissolves. Add lemon and orange slices. Float aquavit on top.

MULLED MADEIRA AND BOURBON

2½ ozs. Madeira
1 oz. bourbon
1 oz. Lillet
¼ teaspoon orange
   bitters
4 ozs. water
1 tablespoon brown
   sugar
1 cinnamon stick
2 whole cloves
½ slice lemon
Orange peel

Heat Madeira, bourbon, Lillet, orange bitters, water, and brown sugar until hot but not boiling. Put cinnamon stick, cloves, and lemon slice into 10-oz. mug or metal tankard. Fill mug with Madeira mixture. Twist orange peel above drink and drop into mug.

MULLED PORT

4 ozs. ruby port
1 oz. dark Jamaica rum
4 ozs. water
½ oz. lime juice
1 teaspoon sugar
2-inch piece of orange
   peel
1 long piece stick
   cinnamon

Pour port, rum, water, lime juice, and sugar into saucepan. Stir. Bring to boiling point, but do not boil. Pour into mug. Twist orange peel over mug and drop into drink. Add stick cinnamon.

MULLED SCOTCH

2 ozs. hot Scotch
1 oz. hot Drambuie
2 dashes bitters
1 oz. boiling water
1 maraschino cherry
Lemon peel

Into an old-fashioned glass, pour the Scotch, Drambuie, bitters, and boiling water. Stir. Add the cherry. Twist lemon peel over the drink and drop into glass.

MULLED SHERRY

4 ozs. amontillado
  sherry
2 ozs. orange juice
½ oz. brandy
½ oz. lemon juice
1 to 2 teaspoons sugar
1 teaspoon butter
1 piece stick cinnamon

Heat sherry, orange juice, brandy, and lemon juice in saucepan over low flame until hot. Do not boil. Pour into mug. Add sugar to taste. Add butter. Stir with stick cinnamon until butter melts. Leave cinnamon stick in mug.

ROCK-AND-RYE TODDY

2 ozs. rock-and-rye
2 dashes Angostura
  bitters
1 slice lemon
3 ozs. boiling water
1 cinnamon stick
Grated nutmeg

Pour rock-and-rye and bitters into old-fashioned glass. Add lemon slice. Add boiling water and cinnamon stick. Stir. Sprinkle with grated nutmeg.

SCIARADA TEA

1 mug hot black tea
1½ ozs. Sciarada
1 slice lemon
1 cinnamon stick

Pour Sciarada into tea. Add lemon slice. Stir with stick cinnamon. An après-ski warmer.

SIMMERING PLUM

5 ozs. hot black tea
2 ozs. plum brandy
  (slivovitz, quetsch, or
  mirabelle)
1 oz. white crème de
  menthe
1 teaspoon sugar or
  more to taste
½ oz. heavy cream
1 piece stick cinnamon
Ground coriander

Stir tea, plum brandy, crème de menthe, sugar, and cream in saucepan. Heat to boiling point, but do not boil. Pour into warm 10-oz. mug with stick cinnamon. Stir. Sprinkle coriander on top.

SNOWBERRY

1½ ozs. strawberry
   liqueur
1 oz. vodka
½ oz. rock-candy
   syrup, or simple
   syrup (page 40)
1 oz. lemon juice
5 ozs. water
½ large strawberry
   cut in half lengthwise
1 thin slice lemon
½ oz. kirschwasser

In saucepan heat strawberry liqueur, vodka, rock-candy syrup, lemon juice, and water to boiling point, but do not boil. Pour into warm 10-oz. mug. Dip strawberry into rock-candy syrup. Float lemon slice, strawberry half, and kirschwasser on drink.

SNOWSHOE

1 oz. aquavit
½ oz. blackberry-
   flavored brandy
1 mug hot black tea
Stick cinnamon
Sugar
1 slice lemon

Pour aquavit and blackberry-flavored brandy into tea. Stir with cinnamon stick; leave cinnamon in mug. Add sugar to taste. Add lemon slice.

24

HORS
D'OEUVRES

Martinis are martinis, but martinis in the vicinity of a terrine of *pâté de foie gras* are a feast. Sydney Smith, eighteenth-century English wit, said, "My idea of heaven is eating *pâté de foie gras* to the sound of trumpets." A trumpet may be all right as a garnish, but the best modern orchestration for such luxury items is the soft rattle of a martini pitcher or the rhythm of a cocktail shaker—for one of the best things about drinking is eating. Liquor allows people to unwind; hors d'oeuvres *and* liquor make them soar. Although the phrase *hors d'oeuvre* is French, meaning literally "apart from the work," the prestigious art of amassing and presenting luscious appetizers reaches its pinnacle in the Scandinavian countries of the midnight sun, where the appetizing board is often in fact the *whole* works. In this country also—no longer a nation of mere nibblers—the cocktail and the appetizer have become partners in equal standing.

The number of magnificent imported and domestic hors d'oeuvres in cans, jars, bottles, and vacuum packs has reached Croesuslike proportions, as a brief trip to your nearest gourmet shop will show you. But a tray of four items—such as tiny cocktail mushrooms, caviar, Westphalian ham, and Roquefort cheese in brandy—will normally provide sufficient appetizers for eight to ten people.

Cold hors d'oeuvres must be cold, and in furtherance of reaching this end you must be a monomaniac. The serving platter or bowl, the plates, and every ingredient in the appetizer must be thoroughly pre-chilled. Cold appetizer salads are best when served surrounded by crushed ice in a large shrimp server or caviar server designed for that purpose. Hot hors d'oeuvres in a sauce should be offered in a chafing dish, fondue dish, or casserole over a spirit lamp. Small, dry, hot hors d'oeuvres should be placed on a platter lined with a linen napkin or paper doily, or on an electric hot tray—provided they're in a single layer in contact with the heat. If hot hors d'oeuvres are to be placed under the broiler or in the oven at the last moment, be sure the broiler is preheated, and keep it going for later use. But remember that a pre-heated broiler works fast; avoid scorching small filled tartlets and *bouchées.*

Both freshly made and prepared spreads should be placed on cock-tail crackers or canapé bases with a bland flavor. Be wary of crackers accented with bacon or barbecue seasonings, which sometimes over-power delicate seafood flavors. All crackers or cocktail biscuits should be tasted for freshness even when the box is freshly opened. If in doubt, replace them. If in semidoubt, place them in a warm oven for revival. Bread, too, should be almost oven-fresh, merely firm enough to spread without tearing.

Perhaps the easiest and most impressive of all hors d'oeuvres for intimate parties is the whole article of food, such as a large, well-aged Gouda cheese, a smoked turkey, or a smoked Smithfield ham. You can buy the latter completely cooked and glazed. Such centers of attention should be placed on a large carving board flanked with appropriate carving knife, meat fork, or cheese scoop, as well as a large basket with thin slices of French bread, salt rye bread, or cock-tail-size pumpernickel rounds.

At a small cocktail party, frequently one hot and one cold hors d'oeuvre are all the variety you need. Don't be the host with too much too soon, particularly when drinking *intime.* At larger revels, of course, hors d'oeuvres may be expanded to take in the astronomical and still-expanding world of gourmandise.

When, in his *Canterbury Tales,* Chaucer speaks of "the hors that hadde winges for to flee," he refers, of course, to "The Pegasee." But try the following hors, and see if they don't have the wings it takes to get your party off the ground.

(Note: Portions indicated in the next section are hors d'oeuvre–size.)

Caviar

Caviar can be neatly divided into two classes—the roe of the sturgeon and the roe of all other fish. Actually, the top of the sturgeon hierarchy is the beluga (Russian for the white color of the fish). It's called black caviar but, at its best, is actually gray. There's hardly a trace of saltiness in it, and although each tiny egg is intact, its texture is almost semiliquid in the mouth. There are excellent caviars of other sturgeons, such as the sevruga, in fresh forms and in sealed jars. So-called pressed caviar, made from the roe of several sturgeons, is always useful for emergency entertainment. Connoisseurs quite justly resent the fact that the word "caviar" can be used to describe the roe of the salmon, the whitefish, and the lumpfish—spreads which are nevertheless widely used for canapés. The price of fresh beluga caviar is hardly extortionate when you consider that a beluga sturgeon doesn't produce eggs until it's about twenty years old, that only the most sensitive fingers can force the eggs through the sieve that separates the large eggs from the small, that caviar must be aged three months at 30°F., and that it must be kept refrigerated like fresh crab lump or any other fresh food until the moment it's devoured. For entirely too many generations, caviar was the symbol of conspicuous gourmandizing, enjoyed only by the top carriage trade. Now foodshops and gourmet stalls everywhere have taken it out of the dowager's class and turned it over to people who simply dig good eating.

At the cocktail table, the caviar jar should rest atop crushed ice held in a commodious bowl. To keep the eggs intact, an ivory or glass spoon is used. Garnishes should be kept to simple chopped egg, chopped onion, or sour cream. Caviar may be served on fresh toast fingers, canapé biscuits, tiny tartlet shells, or tiny patty shells, but the most famed of all caviar vehicles are blini.

BLINI FOR CAVIAR (Makes 25–30)

3 tablespoons salad oil
3 eggs
½ cup milk
¾ cup water
¾ cup whole-wheat flour
½ cup sifted white flour
2 teaspoons baking powder
½ teaspoon salt

Blini are tiny pancakes, each about the size of a silver dollar, used as canapé bases. Originally made by a slow yeast process, this modernized version is easier and actually more toothsome.

Pour oil, eggs, milk, and water into blender. Add whole-wheat flour, white flour (sifted before measuring), baking powder, and salt. Blend until batter is smooth, stopping when necessary to scrape sides. Preheat electric skillet to 390° F. Grease lightly with salad oil. Wipe off excess oil with paper toweling. Drop batter into skillet by tablespoonfuls. When the edges of the blini are dry-looking and bubbles begin to appear in the center, turn and brown on the other side. Grease skillet lightly again before cooking second batch. Serve on white napkin. At cocktail table, spoon sour cream onto each blini. Add a dollop of caviar.

Shrimp

Shrimps make ideal canapés. Served whole, they're neatly bite-size, firm enough to spear securely, and lend themselves to a variety of sauces. They can also be ground and served up as fritters—called *beignets*. Either way, they're sure to please guests.

SHRIMP BEIGNETS

(Makes about 4 dozen)

½ lb. (cooked weight)
   boiled, peeled,
   deveined shrimp
1 cup water
2 tablespoons butter
¾ teaspoon salt
⅛ teaspoon celery salt
⅛ teaspoon white
   pepper
1 cup all-purpose flour
4 eggs
1 small onion
Deep fat for frying

Put shrimp through meat grinder, using fine blade. Bring water to a boil in a heavy saucepan. Add butter, salt, celery salt, and pepper. When butter melts, add flour all at once. Stir well. Remove from flame. Stir until no dry flour is visible; batter will be very stiff. Transfer batter to electric mixer. Gradually add unbeaten eggs, one at a time, mixing well after each addition. Grate onion into batter. Add ground shrimps and mix well. Keep batter covered in refrigerator until very cold—at least 2 hours. Heat deep fat to 370° F. or until it shows the first wisp of smoke; or heat 1 inch of fat in electric skillet preheated to 370° F. Drop batter by heaping teaspoonfuls into fat. Turn once to brown on both sides. Drain on absorbent paper. Sprinkle with salt and serve with Chinese-style mustard.

SHRIMP AND WATER CHESTNUTS IN DILL SAUCE

(Serves 6)

2 tablespoons butter
1 lb. (cooked weight)
   boiled, peeled,
   deveined shrimp
1 8-oz. can whole water
   chestnuts, drained
1 cup milk
2 tablespoons instant-
   dissolving flour
2 tablespoons very
   finely chopped fresh
   dill
½ teaspoon dill salt
2 tablespoons capers in
   vinegar, drained,
   chopped very fine
Salt, pepper, and
   cayenne pepper
¼ cup sour cream

Melt butter in saucepan over low flame. Add shrimp and water chestnuts. Sauté briefly, stirring frequently only until shrimp are heated through. Season with salt and pepper. In small mixing bowl combine milk and flour. Stir until flour is dissolved. Add to saucepan. Slowly bring to a boil. Reduce flame so that sauce merely simmers. Add dill, dill salt, and capers. Season to taste with salt, pepper, and a dash of cayenne. Remove from flame. Stir in sour cream. Keep warm in chafing dish over simmering water. Provide fondue forks or cocktail spears for serving.

SHRIMP WITH OREGANO   (Serves 6)

2 tablespoons butter
1 lb. (cooked weight)
  boiled, peeled,
  deveined shrimp
1 teaspoon oregano
Salt, pepper, and
  cayenne pepper
1 oz. California brandy
1 8-oz. can tomato sauce
1 tablespoon Dijon
  mustard
1 teaspoon dry
  mustard
1 oz. dry vermouth
1 tablespoon parsley,
  chopped very fine

Melt butter in saucepan over low flame. Add shrimp. Sauté, stirring constantly, until heated through. Crumble oregano between fingers over shrimp. Sprinkle with salt, pepper, and a dash of cayenne. Add brandy. When brandy is hot, set aflame. When flames subside, add tomato sauce. Combine Dijon mustard, dry mustard, and vermouth, blending well. Add to saucepan. Add parsley. Correct seasoning if necessary. Serve with cocktail spears or fondue forks.

FANTAIL-SHRIMP COCKTAIL   (Serves 10)

3 lbs. shrimps (12 to 16
  per lb.)
½ cup catsup
2 teaspoons Pernod
2 teaspoons paprika
½ cup sour cream
2 tablespoons chives or
  scallions, minced
Juice of ½ lemon
Light cream
Salt and pepper
½ cup mayonnaise
2 teaspoons curry
  powder
⅛ teaspoon Tabasco
  sauce
1 clove garlic
1 7-oz. bottle sauce
  diable

Boil shrimps in salted water. Shrimps of this large size will require 5 to 7 minutes' boiling time. Cool, then chill in refrigerator in own cooking liquid. Balance of ingredients are used for four separate cocktail sauces. All must be icy cold for serving. Mix catsup and Pernod. Chill in refrigerator. In small mixing bowl, dissolve paprika in 3 tablespoons hot water. Add sour cream, chives, and lemon juice, mixing well. Gradually add light cream, in very small quantities, until sauce flows very slowly. Sauce must be thick enough to adhere to shrimps and not be "soupy." Add salt and pepper to taste. Chill in refrigerator. In another mixing bowl, combine mayonnaise, curry powder, and Tabasco. Force garlic through garlic press into curry sauce. Again, add light cream in very small quantities until sauce has lost its stiffness. Chill in refrigerator. Chill sauce diable in small bowl in refrigerator. If sauce diable is not available, substitute any thick bottled

(Continued on following page)

savory sauce for meat or fish. Remove shells from shrimps, leaving bottom segments and tails intact. Remove back veins and cut a slit in shrimps between head and tail. Do not, however, separate them into halves. Hold each shrimp open, book-fashion, in one piece—facing you. Turn tail end and force it through back of shrimp until tail stands between the two cut sides of shrimp. It may be necessary to cut farther to permit tail to go through completely. Avoid making a large hole or shrimp will separate into halves. Press cut sides of shrimps so that they can rest flat on platter. Drain, using paper toweling if necessary to pat dry. Divide shrimps into four equal lots. Coat one fourth with catsup mixture, dipping shrimps into sauce or spreading sauce with a spoon. All the flesh of shrimps, top and bottom, must be thoroughly covered. Coat the second fourth with the sour-cream mixture, the third fourth with the curry mixture, and the balance with the sauce diable. Arrange the shrimps on a large silver or china platter. Keep cold in refrigerator until serving time.

Pâté de foie gras

Foie gras means "fat liver." *Pâté de foie gras* is the seasoned liver of a force-fed goose. The labor of stuffing grain or noodles down a goose's gullet every three hours, day and night, is rewarded with livers that sometimes weigh over two pounds apiece. The best-quality goose liver, from Strasbourg, is creamy rose in color. Although *foie gras* is available fresh in France and is sometimes airmailed to the States, we usually buy it here in tins or *terrines*. Each *pâté de foie gras* is overlaid with a rich stratum of goose or pork fat to keep the *pâté* moist and fresh-tasting. For hors d'oeuvres, *pâté de foie gras* should be biting cold. A sharp knife dipped into hot water helps to liberate thin, uniform slices.

OTHER PÂTÉS

LOBSTER PÂTÉ
(Serves 6)

2 tablespoons shallots
   or onion, chopped fine
½ cup dry white wine
1 cup cooked lobster cut
   into ½-inch dice
¼ cup melted butter
2 tablespoons
   mayonnaise
½ teaspoon dry
   mustard
1 teaspoon Dijon
   mustard
1 tablespoon lemon
   juice
1 teaspoon horseradish
Salt and pepper

Put shallots and wine into small saucepan. Simmer slowly until wine is reduced to no more than 2 tablespoons. Put shallot mixture and all other ingredients except salt and pepper into blender. Blend until pureed, stopping blender when necessary to scrape sides with spatula. Turn mixture into bowl. Add salt and pepper to taste. Chill well before serving, overnight if possible.

CLAM AND EGG PÂTÉ
(Serves 6)

1 8-oz. can minced
   clams, well drained
1 hard-boiled egg,
   diced
¼ cup diced sweet red
   pepper
2 tablespoons diced
   onion
¼ cup melted butter
¼ cup mayonnaise
1 teaspoon Dijon
   mustard
½ teaspoon
   Worcestershire sauce
Salt and pepper

Put all ingredients except salt and pepper into blender. Blend until pureed, stopping when necessary to scrape sides with spatula. Turn mixture into bowl. Add salt and pepper to taste. Chill well before serving, overnight if possible.

Cheese

Cheese, served alone or as a major ingredient in combination with other foods, is a host's staple. In fact, a cheeseboard alone, with an assortment of breads and crackers, will suffice for many get-togethers. Here are some other tasty ways to use cheese.

GRUYÈRE AND EMMENTALER FONDUE   (Serves 4–6)

2 large cloves of garlic, halved
2 cups dry white wine
3 tablespoons instant-dissolving flour
2 tablespoons butter
¾ lb. natural Swiss Gruyère cheese, shredded
½ lb. Swiss Emmentaler cheese, shredded
1 tablespoon lemon juice
2 tablespoons kirschwasser (dry, not the liqueur)
Ground nutmeg
Salt and pepper
French bread cut into 1-inch chunks with crust

(Prepare the fondue in a double boiler in the kitchen. When ready to serve, pour it into a fondue pot or chafing dish.) Rub top section of double boiler with garlic pieces. Discard garlic. Pour wine into top section of double boiler. Stir in flour until flour dissolves. Add butter. Heat over direct low flame, stirring well with wire whip, until liquid thickens. Simmer slowly five minutes. Place top of double boiler over simmering water in bottom section. Add cheese by handfuls, stirring well after each addition until cheese melts. Add lemon juice and kirschwasser. Sprinkle lightly with nutmeg. Add salt and pepper to taste. Turn fondue into chafing dish or fondue pot set over flame. Serve with French bread, providing a fondue fork for each guest.

FONDUE WITH PROSCIUTTO (Serves 6)

French bread
½ lb. prosciutto ham,
  sliced paper-thin
½ lb. Swiss Emmentaler
  cheese, shredded
½ lb. natural Gruyère
  cheese, shredded
4 tablespoons flour
1½ cups dry white wine
2 cloves garlic
4 tablespoons
  kirschwasser
Salt and pepper
Freshly grated nutmeg

Cut bread into chunks about 1 inch thick, taking care that each chunk of bread includes crust. Cut ham slices in half. Roll up each half, cornucopia-fashion. Pile bread into breadbasket. Arrange ham slices on platter. Shred cheese by forcing it through large holes of square metal grater. Put cheese and flour into mixing bowl, tossing until cheese is coated with flour. Heat wine in top part of double boiler over direct flame until bubbles appear around edge of pan. Do not boil. Place over simmering water in bottom section of double boiler. Add cheese by handfuls to wine, stirring well. When each handful of cheese is melted, add another, stirring well, until all cheese is used. Squeeze garlic through garlic press over fondue. Stir in kirschwasser. Add salt and pepper to taste. Pour fondue into chafing dish or *caquelon* and sprinkle with nutmeg before bringing it to cocktail table. Keep fondue hot over spirit lamp. Guests spear bread or ham, and dip.

HOT GRUYÈRE AND ANCHOVY CANAPÉS (Makes 24)

4 slices white bread
Sweet butter, at room
  temperature
4 ozs. Gruyère cheese,
  shredded
8 flat anchovy fillets,
  finely minced
½ cup mayonnaise
4 tablespoons grated
  Parmesan cheese
Paprika

Preheat oven to 450° F. Toast bread under broiler on one side only. Spread untoasted side with butter. Mix Gruyère cheese with minced anchovy fillets, mayonnaise, and Parmesan cheese. Spread cheese mixture evenly on untoasted sides of bread. Sprinkle with paprika. Place bread, cheese side up, on a baking sheet or the back of an inverted baking pan. Bake 5 minutes. Cut each slice into six pieces. Serve very hot.

HOT MOZZARELLA AND ANCHOVY APPETIZERS

(Makes 32)

2 eggs, well beaten
½ cup light cream
⅛ teaspoon salt
8 ozs. mozzarella
    cheese, thinly sliced
8 square slices white
    bread
1 2-oz. can flat anchovy
    fillets, drained
1 3-oz. can sliced
    mushrooms, drained
Olive oil

Combine eggs, cream, and salt, and beat well. Place cheese on four slices of bread. Place anchovies and mushrooms on cheese and top with remaining bread to make sandwiches. In large, heavy frying pan, heat ⅛ inch of oil. Holding sandwiches with both hands to keep intact, dip into egg mixture, as in making French toast. Fry sandwiches until golden brown on both sides and cut each one into eighths before serving.

PROSCIUTTO AND PROVOLONE ROLLS

(Serves 8)

6 ozs. provolone cheese,
    thinly sliced
6 ozs. prosciutto ham,
    sliced paper-thin
¼ cup olive oil
¼ cup dry vermouth
3 large cloves garlic
1 tablespoon finely
    minced parsley

Cut provolone cheese into strips about ¾ inch wide and 2 inches long. Fold lengthwise. Cut pieces of prosciutto about 1 inch wide and 3 inches long. Roll prosciutto around cheese. Fasten rolls with toothpicks. Smash cloves of garlic with flat side of heavy knife. Into a small shallow casserole or baking dish, put olive oil, vermouth, garlic, and parsley. Mix well. Place rolls in casserole. Marinate rolls 3 to 4 hours in refrigerator, turning to marinate evenly. Place rolls on thin bread or cocktail crackers for serving, after removing toothpicks.

DEVILED HAM AND CHEESE BALLS

(Serves 4)

6 ozs. sharp cheddar
    cheese
2 ozs. deviled Smithfield
    ham
¼ cup softened butter
1 oz. bourbon
½ cup toasted bread
    crumbs

Put cheese through meat grinder using fine blade. In mixing bowl combine cheese, ham, butter, and bourbon, stirring until well blended. Chill slightly. Shape into balls of 1 tablespoon each. Roll in crumbs. Keep chilled until served.

CRAB MEAT AND GRUYÈRE BALLS (Serves 4)

4 ozs. fresh crab meat
or deluxe canned crab
meat
4 ozs. natural Gruyère
cheese
1 tablespoon chives
chopped extremely
fine
2 tablespoons softened
butter
1 tablespoon dry sherry
¼ lb. walnut meat
chopped in electric
blender

Carefully pick over crab meat and remove any pieces of shell or cartilage. Put crab meat and cheese through meat grinder using fine blade. Add chives, butter, and sherry, blending well. Chill mixture. Shape into balls of 1 tablespoon each. Roll in chopped walnuts. Keep chilled until served.

HOT PARMESAN AND MOZZARELLA CANAPÉS (Makes 16)

2 ozs. prosciutto ham,
sliced paper-thin
2 ozs. mozzarella
cheese
Grated Parmesan cheese
½ cup mayonnaise
1 tablespoon brandy
1 tablespoon dry white
wine
4 square slices white
bread
Butter, at room
temperature
Paprika

Cut prosciutto into ¼-inch dice. Put mozzarella cheese through the large holes of a square metal grater. Combine ham, mozzarella, ⅓ cup Parmesan, mayonnaise, brandy, and white wine. Mix well. Toast bread lightly. Spread with butter. Cover bread uniformly to edge with mayonnaise mixture. Sprinkle lightly with paprika and Parmesan cheese. Place under preheated broiler flame until golden brown. Cut each slice into quarters.

GORGONZOLA CREAM (Serves 6–8)

12 ozs. Gorgonzola
cheese
6 tablespoons sweet
butter, at room
temperature
Grated Parmesan cheese
Finely minced fresh
chives

Crumble cheese. Force it through a wire strainer or colander. Add butter. Mix well. Shape into round or oval cake, ¾ inch thick. Place on serving plate. Sprinkle with Parmesan cheese and chives. Wipe rim of plate. Spread on cocktail crackers.

ROQUEFORT AND WINE CANAPÉS (Makes 16)

4 ozs. Roquefort cheese
2 tablespoons dry white wine
1 tablespoon Cognac
16 small canapé-type crackers
Butter, at room temperature
Cayenne pepper
2 tablespoons very finely chopped chives

Break cheese into small lumps and force through colander or wire sieve. Mix cheese with wine and Cognac until very well blended. If cheese seems too soft for spreading, place in refrigerator until it's firmer. Spread crackers generously with butter. Spread with cheese uniformly to edge of crackers. Sprinkle very lightly with cayenne, then with chives. Refrigerate until serving time.

CAMEMBERT TOAST MALAGA (Makes 16)

¼ cup large raisins
¼ cup Cognac
1 8-oz. pkg. soft ripe Camembert cheese
8 slices French bread, about 3 inches in diameter
¼ cup sweet butter, at room temperature

Put raisins into small saucepan. Cover with cold water. Slowly bring to a boil. Simmer a minute. Drain. Put raisins into cup or glass and cover with Cognac. Marinate overnight. Camembert cheese should be removed from refrigerator about an hour before preparation. Cut cheese into wedges and force cheese, including rind, through a colander. Toast bread. Drain raisins, saving Cognac. Sprinkle one side of each slice with reserved Cognac. Don't douse bread so liberally that it falls apart when handled. Turn bread on opposite side. Spread with butter. Spread evenly with Camembert cheese. Cut each slice in half. Place raisins on top of cheese, pressing slightly to keep in place. Arrange slices in rows on serving platter.

CHEDDAR AND ONION CANAPÉS (Makes 16)

4 square slices white
  bread
1 tablespoon salad oil
2 tablespoons butter
2 cups very thinly
  sliced onion
2 medium cloves garlic,
  finely minced
¾ cup dry red wine
1 teaspoon beef extract
Salt and pepper
4 slices sharp Cheddar
  cheese, large enough
  to cover bread
Paprika

Preheat broiler. Under broiler flame, toast bread on one side only. Heat oil and butter in saucepan until butter just melts. Add onion and garlic. Sauté over low flame, stirring frequently, until onion is soft and yellow, not brown. Add wine and beef extract. Simmer until wine has almost completely evaporated. Season onions with salt and pepper. Preheat oven to 350° F. Divide onions, spreading them on untoasted side of bread. Place cheese on onions. Sprinkle with paprika. Place bread on baking sheet or on bottom of inverted baking pan. Bake only until cheese is soft. Do not use broiler flame for heating cheese. Cut each slice into four triangles or squares. Serve immediately.

CROÛTES WITH MOZZARELLA AND ANCHOVIES (Serves 4)

4 slices white sandwich
  bread
Butter
6 to 8 ozs. sliced
  mozzarella cheese
  (amount of cheese
  will depend upon
  thickness of slices)
16 flat anchovy fillets in
  oil, drained
¼ cup finely chopped
  pepperoni (pepper
  salad in oil)

Toast bread on one side only, under broiler flame. Remove bread and lower oven temperature to 350°. Spread untoasted sides of bread with butter. Arrange mozzarella cheese on buttered side of bread, cutting cheese if necessary to cover bread completely. With heavy sharp knife, cut off crusts. Arrange 4 anchovy fillets on each slice of bread. Sprinkle with pepperoni. Place bread on cookie sheet. Bake croûtes 5 to 8 minutes or until cheese softens. Cut each croûte into 4 pieces with an anchovy on each piece.

CHEESE AND TONGUE CROÛTES (Serves 4)

4 slices white sandwich
bread
Butter
¼ lb. sharp cheddar
cheese, shredded
¼ lb. sliced smoked
beef tongue
2 tablespoons
mayonnaise
1 teaspoon Dijon
mustard
1 tablespoon bread-
crumbs
Grated Parmesan cheese
Paprika

Toast bread on one side only under broiler flame. Spread untoasted side with butter. Set aside. Cut beef tongue into 1-inch julienne strips as narrow as possible. In mixing bowl combine cheese, tongue, mayonnaise, mustard, and breadcrumbs. Spread mixture over buttered side of bread up to crust. Sprinkle with Parmesan cheese. Sprinkle lightly with paprika. With heavy sharp knife cut off crusts of bread. Place croûtes on cookie sheet and heat under broiler flame. Broil only until light brown. Cut each croûte into 4 pieces for serving.

Dips

Dips are another party standby. They may range from creamy liquids to spreadlike consistency, and be either cold or hot. (The fondues listed in the cheese section are, of course, hot dips.) If you're tired of onion soup–sour cream, try these:

CURRIED-EGG DIP (Serves 8)

2 hard-boiled eggs,
shelled
1½ cups sour cream
¼ cup mayonnaise
2 teaspoons curry
powder
1 teaspoon grated onion
2 tablespoons celery,
very finely minced
2 tablespoons green
pepper, very finely
minced
1 tablespoon fresh dill,
very finely minced
Salt and pepper

Cut eggs into large dice. Force through a fine wire strainer into mixing bowl. Add sour cream, mayonnaise, curry powder, onion, celery, green pepper, and dill. Mix very well. Add salt and pepper to taste. Chill thoroughly. Serve, if possible, with freshly fried shrimp chips or freshly fried pappadums.

SMOKED-OYSTER DIP

(Serves 8)

1 3⅔-oz. can smoked
  oysters
1 pint sour cream
1 teaspoon onion,
  grated
1 teaspoon fresh
  chives, minced
2 teaspoons lemon
  juice
4 dashes Tabasco sauce
Salt and pepper

Drain oysters very well, discarding oil. Put all ingredients into blender. Blend at high speed about 30 seconds, or until oysters are thoroughly pureed.

DEVILED-EGG DIP

(Serves 8)

4 hard-boiled eggs,
  shelled
1 tablespoon Dijon or
  Dijon-style mustard
1 teaspoon dry
  mustard
4 tablespoons sweet
  butter, at room
  temperature
1 cup sour cream
2 teaspoons anchovy
  paste
1 tablespoon fresh
  chives, minced
2 teaspoons fresh
  parsley, minced
Salt, pepper, and
  cayenne

Cut eggs into large dice. Force through fine wire strainer into mixing bowl. Add both kinds of mustard, butter, sour cream, anchovy paste, chives, and parsley. Mix very well. Season generously with salt and pepper. Add a dash of cayenne.

EGGPLANT CAVIAR

(Serves 8)

1 large eggplant
2 medium-size fresh
  tomatoes
¼ cup salad oil
2 medium-size onions,
  very small dice
1 small clove garlic,
  finely minced
½ green pepper, very
  small dice
1 tablespoon lemon
  juice
2 tablespoons finely
  minced fresh dill
Salt and pepper

Place eggplant in shallow pan in oven preheated to 450° F. Bake 45 minutes, turning once to bake evenly. Remove from pan and cut in half lengthwise. With sharp paring knife or grapefruit knife, remove pulp from eggplant shell; avoid tearing shell. Cut pulp into very small dice and set aside. Set the eggplant shells aside. Lower tomatoes into a pot of rapidly boiling water for 20–30 seconds; then hold them under cold running water for a few seconds, peel off the skin, and remove stem ends. Press tomatoes to squeeze out excess liquid, then cut them into very small dice. In a shallow saucepan, heat oil. Add onions, garlic, green pepper, eggplant, and tomatoes. Sauté slowly, stirring frequently, for 10 minutes, or until all vegetables are tender. Add lemon juice, dill, and salt and pepper to taste. Spoon cooked mixture into eggplant shells. Chill in refrigerator until ice-cold. Serve with sesame crackers.

MELON AND PROSCIUTTO WITH CREAM DIP

(Serves 8)

½ large ripe Cranshaw
  or honeydew melon
½ lb. prosciutto ham,
  sliced paper-thin
¼ cup heavy sweet
  cream
1 cup sour cream
3 tablespoons Peter
  Heering liqueur
2 teaspoons lemon juice
2 teaspoons sugar

Cut melon into long wedges about 1 inch wide. Cut skin off. Cut crosswise into slices about 1 inch thick. Wrap each piece with prosciutto. (Large slices of prosciutto may be cut in half if necessary.) Place melon on large serving platter and refrigerate until serving time. Beat sweet cream in narrow chilled bowl with rotary eggbeater until cream is whipped. Fold whipped cream into sour cream, using a down-over-up stroke with mixing spoon. Gradually fold in Peter Heering, lemon juice, and sugar. Serve cream as a dip for melon. Cocktail spears may be inserted in melon pieces for easy handling.

SOUR-CREAM MEDLEY

(Serves 6–8)

1 pint sour cream
1 tablespoon fresh
   chives, finely minced
1 teaspoon fresh
   parsley, finely
   minced
¼ teaspoon fresh basil,
   finely minced
¼ teaspoon fresh
   tarragon, finely
   minced
2 teaspoons horse-
   radish
1 8-oz. can water
   chestnuts, drained
2 2-oz. cans button
   mushrooms, drained
12 small red radishes
   or 6 large radishes
   cut in half
1 large green pepper,
   cut into ½-inch
   squares
Salt and pepper

(Technically, not a dip, since vegetables are already in it. However, guests must dip in to get them out.) Mix sour cream with chives, parsley, basil, tarragon, and horseradish, stirring thoroughly until well blended. (If fresh basil and tarragon are unavailable, don't substitute dried herbs; simply increase parsley by ½ teaspoon.) In fondue dish or casserole, combine sour-cream mixture with water chestnuts, mushrooms, radishes, and green pepper, tossing thoroughly. Chill in refrigerator at least 2 hours. Season generously with salt and pepper. Let guests serve themselves with long fondue forks. Serve with small squares of freshly buttered black bread.

BAGNA CAUDA

(Serves 6–8)

1 medium-size bunch
celery
1 large cucumber
2 green peppers
2 sweet red peppers
¼ lb. Belgian endive
1 bunch thin scallions
1 pkg. small bread-
sticks
¼ lb. sweet butter
4 large garlic cloves,
partly crushed
2 tablespoons anchovy
paste
½ pint heavy cream
Ground white pepper

Trim leaves from celery. Cut off root end and separate bunch into pieces. Run a vegetable peeler along outside of celery pieces to remove tough strings. Cut celery into pieces approximately 4 inches long and ½ inch wide. Peel and cut cucumber into pieces the same size as the celery. Cut peppers in half through stem ends. Discard seeds and stem ends. Cut peppers lengthwise into ½-inch pieces. Separate endive into pieces for dipping. Cut root end off scallions, allowing about 1 inch of green part to remain. Place vegetables on top of ice in a large salad bowl. Place breadsticks near chafing dish. In the chafing dish, over a low flame, melt butter. Add garlic. Sauté only until garlic begins to brown. Remove garlic and discard. Add anchovy paste. Mix well. Add cream. Add a generous dash of pepper. Let liquid simmer about 5 minutes before guests dip vegetables and breadsticks into bagna cauda (Italian for "hot dip").

Bouchées

Miniature puff-pastry shells called *bouchées* (which means "a mouthful" in French) are understandably popular bases for canapés since both the container and its tasty contents are edible and guests aren't left holding even so much as a toothpick. Puff pastry is a bit tricky to make yourself, but fortunately the shells are available pre-baked, ready to fill with your own creamed or curried mixture and pop into the oven to heat at the last minute. Here are two fillings to try—one made with chicken, the other with lobster.

CHICKEN BOUCHÉES

(Makes 24)

1 whole breast of
chicken
3 tablespoons finely
minced shallots
2 medium mushrooms,
extremely small dice
3 tablespoons butter
2 tablespoons brandy
2 tablespoons dry
white wine
3 tablespoons flour
1 packet instant
chicken bouillon
½ cup heavy cream
1 teaspoon yellow
Chartreuse
½ teaspoon Worcester-
shire sauce
Salt and freshly ground
pepper
24 hors d'oeuvre–size
patty shells or
barquettes

Simmer chicken in salted water until tender, 30 to 40 minutes. Remove skin and bone from chicken. Cut into cubes ¼ inch or less. Set chicken broth aside. Sauté shallots and mushrooms in butter until mushrooms are tender. Add brandy and white wine. Set it aflame. When flames subside, remove pan from fire and stir in flour, mixing well. Combine ¾ cup chicken broth with instant chicken bouillon in another saucepan. Add cream. Bring to boiling point. Slowly add to pan containing mushrooms, mixing well. Return to a moderate flame. Add chicken. Simmer, stirring frequently, for 5 minutes. Add Chartreuse and Worcestershire sauce. Add salt and pepper to taste. With small, sharp knife, hollow out centers of patty shells, if necessary, to hold chicken mixture. Fill patty shells and serve immediately, or set aside and warm in preheated oven just before serving.

DEVILED LOBSTER BOUCHÉES

(Makes 24)

24 very small hors
d'oeuvre–size patty
shells
1 9-oz. pkg. frozen
lobster tails
3 tablespoons instant-
dissolving flour
1 cup cold milk
2 tablespoons butter
2 teaspoons sherry
1 teaspoon brandy
½ teaspoon lemon juice
⅛ teaspoon anchovy
paste
1 teaspoon prepared
mustard
Salt, pepper, and
cayenne

If necessary, remove insides of patty shells with small, sharp knife to create cavities for the lobster. Cook lobster, following directions on package. Drain. Remove meat from lobster shells and cut into very small dice. Put flour and milk into saucepan. Stir until flour is dissolved. Add butter. Simmer until sauce is thick and no floury taste remains. Add lobster, sherry, brandy, lemon juice, anchovy paste, mustard, and salt and pepper to taste. Add a dash of cayenne. Mix very well. Fill patty shells with lobster mixture. Serve at once. If not served immediately, place on baking sheet. At serving time, place baking sheet in preheated moderate oven (375° F.) for 5 to 8 minutes, or until heated through.

Chicken Livers

Chicken livers make excellent cocktail-party fare. Served whole, they're delicious and firm enough to spear securely. Chopped, they make savory spreads for crackers or bread rounds. You've no doubt encountered them in this guise at other people's parties, or wrapped in bacon, grilled, and skewered. Here are two chicken-liver canapés you may not have met up with.

FRIED CHICKEN LIVERS WITH APPLE-BRANDY SAUCE
(Serves 8)

6 ozs. chicken livers
½ cup apple jelly
¼ cup apple brandy, either calvados or applejack
2 tablespoons orange juice
¼ cup pineapple juice
1 teaspoon lemon juice
1 teaspoon Dijon mustard
1 teaspoon grated lemon rind
2 teaspoons cornstarch
1 teaspoon butter
½ cup sifted flour
½ teaspoon baking powder
2 egg whites, beaten stiff
Salad oil
Salt, pepper, and onion powder

Put chicken livers into a saucepan and cover with cold water. Bring to a boil. Simmer 1 minute. Drain livers. Cut livers in half—or into three or four pieces if they're extra large. Chill. In a saucepan, heat apple jelly, apple brandy, orange juice, pineapple juice, lemon juice, mustard, and lemon rind. Stir well to blend mustard with other ingredients. When sauce boils, dissolve cornstarch in 2 tablespoons cold water. Slowly stir into sauce. Simmer 2 minutes. Remove from flame. Stir in butter. Add salt and pepper to taste. Set aside. Sift flour, ½ teaspoon salt, and baking powder. Add ¼ cup cold water, mixing well. Fold in beaten egg whites until blended. Small lumps in batter are permissible. Heat ½ inch salad oil in electric skillet preheated to 370°F. Sprinkle chicken livers with salt, pepper, and onion powder. Dip into batter. Fry until medium brown on both sides. Serve with warm apple-brandy sauce (reheated if necessary) as a dip. Fasten cocktail spears to chicken livers for easy handling.

CHICKEN LIVERS AND PEPPERS BORDELAISE

(Serves 4)

¼ lb. chicken livers
2 tablespoons butter
2 sweet red peppers cut into 1-inch dice
¼ cup shallots or onions, chopped extremely fine
1 cup dry red wine
2 tablespoons red wine vinegar
1 teaspoon Dijon mustard
Salt, pepper, and cayenne pepper

Cut chicken livers into 1-inch pieces. Wash and dry well. Melt butter over moderate flame in wide saucepan. Add livers. Sprinkle with salt and pepper. Sauté until medium brown. Remove from pan. Add peppers. Sauté, stirring frequently, only until semi-tender. Remove from pan. Add shallots to pan. Sauté briefly, stirring constantly, no more than one minute. Add wine, wine vinegar, and mustard. Stir well with wire whip, scraping pan bottom to loosen drippings. Simmer until liquids are reduced to approximately ¼ cup. There should be just enough gravy in pan to coat livers and peppers. Return livers and peppers to pan. Cook only until heated through. Add salt and pepper to taste and a dash of cayenne. Serve with cocktail spears.

Mushrooms

Mushrooms are an elegant addition to any canapé tray. They may be served whole, either sauced or stuffed; or chopped and combined to enhance other ingredients. The following recipes illustrate these three ways of using mushrooms and are particularly good party fare.

STUFFED MUSHROOMS WITH BLUE CHEESE
(Serves 4)

16 medium-size fresh
mushrooms
2 tablespoons cooking
oil
Salt, pepper, cayenne
pepper, and paprika
4 ozs. blue cheese
2 tablespoons softened
butter
1 teaspoon lemon juice
1 tablespoon heavy
cream
¼ teaspoon Worcester-
shire sauce
Tabasco sauce

By hand, carefully remove stem of each mushroom so that hollow mushroom caps are available for stuffing. (Stems may be used for omelets, sauces, etc.) Wash and dry mushroom caps. Heat oil in saucepan and sauté mushrooms until just barely tender—do not brown. Sprinkle with salt and pepper. Remove from pan and set aside to cool. In mixing bowl, break blue cheese apart with fork. Add butter, lemon juice, cream, Worcestershire sauce, and several dashes Tabasco sauce. Stir with spoon until mixture is very smooth. With spoon or pastry bag, fill mushroom caps with cheese mixture, making mounds uniform. Sprinkle lightly with cayenne and paprika. Chill well before serving.

DEVILED MUSHROOMS
(Serves 8)

1 lb. button mushrooms
with very short stems
4 tablespoons butter, at
room temperature
2 tablespoons salad oil
1 12-oz. can chicken
broth with rice
2 tablespoons flour
1 teaspoon prepared
mustard
½ teaspoon dry
mustard
2 tablespoons dry
sherry
1 tablespoon brandy
1 tablespoon white-
wine vinegar
Browning sauce
Salt and pepper

Cut stems off mushrooms. Melt 2 tablespoons butter with oil. Sauté mushroom caps and stems until tender. Remove stems, leaving caps in pan. Put chicken broth and mushroom stems into blender. Blend until smooth. Pour into pan with mushroom caps. Bring to a boil. Combine remaining 2 tablespoons butter with flour, mixing to a smooth paste. Add to pan and simmer, stirring, until sauce is thick and smooth. Add prepared mustard, dry mustard, sherry, brandy, vinegar, and enough browning sauce (brown color) to make sauce medium brown. Add salt and pepper to taste. Serve from chafing dish with cocktail spears, or place mixture in tiny tartlet shells if desired.

BAKED OYSTERS WITH MUSHROOMS (Makes 24)

24 large oysters on half
    shell, deep side
1 cup or less clam broth
¼ cup light cream
¼ lb. fresh mushrooms
¼ cup plus 3 table-
    spoons butter
3 tablespoons flour
2 tablespoons brandy
1 teaspoon Pernod
Salt and pepper
¾ cup bread crumbs
1 tablespoon finely
    minced chives

Preheat oven to 400° F. Remove oysters from shells, reserving liquid. Measure and add enough clam broth to total 1 cup. Combine with cream in saucepan and heat to boiling point, but do not boil. Set aside. Slice mushroom caps and stems very thin and sauté in 3 tablespoons butter until just tender. Stir in flour, mixing well. Slowly add clam-broth mixture, stirring constantly with wire whisk. Bring sauce to a boil, then reduce flame and simmer very slowly, stirring frequently, for about 10 minutes. Add brandy and Pernod. Add salt and pepper to taste. Remove from flame and divide half the mixture among the 24 shells. Place an oyster in each shell. Spoon balance of mushroom mixture on top of oysters. Melt ¼ cup butter in saucepan. Remove from flame and stir in bread crumbs and chives, mixing well. Place bread-crumb mixture on top of oysters, smoothing tops with spoon or spatula. Place oysters on a ½-inch bed of rock salt in shallow pan or casserole. (The rock salt isn't absolutely necessary, but it keeps oysters in an upright position so that as little juice as possible escapes.) Bake 15–20 minutes.

MUSHROOM SOUR-CREAM CANAPÉS (Serves 8)

6 ozs. fresh button
   mushrooms
2 tablespoons butter
1 cup sour cream
1 tablespoon kümmel
1 tablespoon brandy
2 teaspoons dry sherry
1 teaspoon lemon juice
⅛ teaspoon Tabasco
   sauce
1 scallion, white and
   green part, very finely
   minced
Salt and pepper
French dressing
Cocktail crackers or
   melba-toast rounds

Separate mushroom stems from caps. Set aside four of the caps for later use. Cut balance of mushrooms into extremely small dice. Sauté in butter until no liquid remains in pan. Cool mushrooms. Combine with sour cream, kümmel, brandy, sherry, lemon juice, Tabasco sauce, and scallion. Season generously with salt and pepper. Chill in refrigerator at least 3 hours. Cut raw mushroom caps in thinnest possible slices. Marinate in French dressing in refrigerator. Place spread on cocktail crackers or melba-toast rounds. Drain mushroom slices. Place one on top of each canapé.

Assorted Other Canapés

CANNIBAL CANAPÉS BURGUNDY   (Serves 8)

¼ cup red Burgundy
2 tablespoons bread
  crumbs
2 tablespoons melted
  butter
1 lb. freshly ground
  prime boneless shell
  steak
1½ teaspoons salt
¼ teaspoon freshly
  ground pepper
½ teaspoon Dijon
  mustard
1 tablespoon catsup
4 dashes cayenne
  pepper
1 small onion minced
  extremely fine
2 egg yolks
½ oz. lemon juice
2 tablespoons drained
  capers
Rye Melba-toast rounds
4 sour gherkins, thinly
  sliced
2 tablespoons finely
  minced parsley

Combine Burgundy, bread crumbs, and melted butter. Mix well. Add to meat in bowl. Add salt, pepper, mustard, catsup, cayenne, onion, egg yolks, lemon juice, and capers. Mix very well. Spread carefully and evenly on Melba toast. Place a slice of gherkin on each canapé. Sprinkle with parsley. Arrange on platter and refrigerate until serving time. A good way to introduce steak tartare to those who have never tasted raw beef.

HOT PIMIENTO CANAPÉS WITH BOURBON (Makes 16)

1 small onion, finely minced
1 medium clove garlic, minced extremely fine
Butter
1 cup bread crumbs (freshly made if possible)
3 tablespoons bourbon
Salt, pepper, and paprika
4 square slices white bread
1 4-oz. can pimientos, drained
Parmesan cheese

Sauté onion and garlic in ⅓ cup butter over very low flame. As soon as onion begins to turn light yellow, remove from flame. Combine with bread crumbs and bourbon, mixing well. Season with salt and pepper. Toast bread lightly. Spread generously with butter. Cut pimientos in half and divide among the four slices of toast. If pimientos do not cover bread, they may be cut into strips and divided among the four slices. Cover evenly with bread-crumb mixture. Sprinkle with Parmesan cheese and paprika. Preheat broiler. Broil until cheese browns lightly. Cut each slice into four triangles or squares.

CLAM AND STOUT CANAPÉS AU GRATIN (Makes 16)

1 8-oz. can minced clams
⅓ cup stout
2 tablespoons butter
1 medium onion, finely minced
1 medium clove garlic, finely minced
2 tablespoons finely minced green pepper
1 tablespoon finely minced parsley
½ teaspoon chervil
2 tablespoons flour
¼ teaspoon Worcestershire sauce
¼ cup bread crumbs
Salt, pepper, and cayenne pepper
4 square slices white bread
Grated Parmesan cheese
Paprika
Salad oil

Drain clams, reserving juice. Add stout to juice. Set aside. Melt butter in saucepan over low flame. Add onion, garlic, green pepper, parsley, and chervil. Sauté slowly, stirring frequently, until onion turns yellow. Remove from flame. Stir in flour, mixing until no lumps are visible. Heat clam broth to boiling point. Slowly add to onion mixture, stirring well. Return to moderate flame. Simmer 10 minutes, stirring frequently. Add clams, Worcestershire sauce, bread crumbs, salt and pepper to taste, and a dash of cayenne. Chill mixture in refrigerator. At serving time, preheat broiler. Toast bread under broiler flame on one side only. On untoasted side, spread clam mixture to edge of each slice. Sprinkle generously with Parmesan cheese, lightly with paprika and oil. Place under broiler flame. Broil until cheese browns lightly. Cut each slice of bread into four triangles.

STURGEON AND AQUAVIT CANAPÉS   (Makes 16)

4 slices light
    pumpernickel bread
Aquavit
Sweet butter, at room
    temperature
4 scallions, white part
    and 1 inch of green,
    thinly sliced
¼ lb. sturgeon, thinly
    sliced
2 tablespoons finely
    minced fresh dill
1 canned pimiento

Sprinkle bread on one side with aquavit. The aquavit should just barely penetrate the opposite side of the bread; take care that the bread doesn't become too soggy to handle. Turn bread over. Spread generously with butter. Sprinkle with scallions. Cover with one layer of sturgeon. Bread should be completely covered with sturgeon, but sturgeon should not overlap sides of bread. Sprinkle two of the four pieces with dill. If dill is wet from washing, squeeze it dry in a clean towel. Cut the four slices of bread into four finger-shaped pieces. Cut pimiento into eight long, thin strips. Place a strip on each piece of sturgeon not sprinkled with dill. Arrange pieces alternately on platter. Serve ice-cold.

For *smoked salmon and aquavit canapés*—use thinly sliced Nova Scotia salmon instead of sturgeon.

For *anchovy and aquavit canapés*—cover bread with flat anchovy fillets. Sprinkle two slices with finely chopped hard-boiled egg instead of dill.

For *caviar and aquavit canapés*—cover two slices of bread with black caviar and two slices with red caviar rather than with sturgeon. Sprinkle red caviar with dill. Place pimiento strips on black caviar.

ANCHOVY PIROSHKI

(Makes 14)

1 small onion, finely minced
2 tablespoons butter
⅔ cup mashed potatoes made without milk
10 anchovy fillets, finely minced
Salt and pepper
2 prepared unbaked 9-inch pie shells
1 egg, beaten
2 tablespoons milk

Although not literally canapés, piroshki are eaten as such. Preheat oven to 425° F. Sauté onion in butter until onion turns yellow. Combine onion, potatoes, and anchovies, and season to taste. Place pie shells on floured board and cut each into seven round pieces, using standard old-fashioned glass, 3 inches in diameter across top, for cutting. On each piece of dough, place about 2 teaspoons potato mixture. Lift one end of dough over potato mixture to make crescent-shaped turnovers. Press edges of dough with fingers, sealing tightly. Press again with tines of fork. Trim off any ragged edges. Combine egg and milk, mixing well. Brush top of each turnover with egg mixture and place on lightly greased cookie sheet or in shallow pan. Bake 20 minutes, or until well browned. Serve warm.

CHICKEN MOUSSE

(Serves 8)

1 whole chicken breast, boiled till tender
1 envelope plain gelatin
¼ cup cold chicken broth
1 cup hot chicken broth
4 tablespoons melted sweet butter
2 tablespoons brandy
1 teaspoon lemon juice
1 teaspoon prepared horseradish
1 tablespoon diced onion
4 dashes Tabasco sauce
Salt and white pepper

Remove skin and bones from chicken. Cut chicken into dice. Soften gelatin in cold chicken broth. Dissolve in hot chicken broth. Put diced chicken, chicken broth, butter, brandy, lemon juice, horseradish, onion, and Tabasco into blender. Blend at low speed for 2 minutes, or until chicken is thoroughly pureed. Season generously with salt and pepper. Turn into bowl or small mold and refrigerate until mixture is completely jelled and very cold. At serving time, run a knife around edge of mousse, dip bowl into warm water for a moment or two, and unmold onto serving dish. Serve with thin, crisp crackers (chicken-flavored if possible) or melba toast.

FRESH SALMON AND PEPPER SPREAD (Serves 8)

1 lb. fresh salmon,
 boiled
¾ cup mayonnaise
¼ cup green pepper,
 diced
2 tablespoons canned
 pimiento, diced
2 teaspoons lemon juice
1 teaspoon tarragon
 vinegar
1 teaspoon prepared
 horseradish
1 tablespoon fresh dill,
 minced
Salt and pepper

Remove skin and bones from salmon. Chop salmon with heavy French knife until finely minced. Put mayonnaise, green pepper, and pimiento into blender. Blend at low speed about 30 seconds, or until no solid pieces of pepper or pimiento are visible. Turn into mixing bowl. Add salmon, lemon juice, vinegar, horseradish, and dill. Mix very well, adding salt and pepper to taste. Chill thoroughly in refrigerator. Serve with party rye bread or rye melba toast.

25

PARTY
BRIEFINGS

Parties share several characteristics with rivers: They're of all lengths, and each flows on a different course. Some parties dry up at a comparatively early hour; others keep rolling along. A party can be anything from an hour's breathing spell on an apartment terrace to a year-end bacchanal. There are brunch parties where food rather than liquor becomes the feast of reason and the flow of the soul, and drinks are limited to a round or two of eye-openers. On the other hand, each day when the evening sun goes down, cocktail parties throughout the length and breadth of the land revolve almost completely around potables while food plays only a small supporting role. And, for the ambitious host, there are full-dress dinner parties where drinks begin with the preprandial cocktails and stretch on through the amontillado with the soup, the Rhine wine with the sea-food, the Burgundy with the roast, the Sauternes with the dessert, the brandy with the demitasse to the postprandial liqueurs and the midnight highballs.

But whatever course a party takes, its source begins with bottles and a bar. When a few congenial people meet privately to bend elbows, the first thing the host asks is simply and correctly, "What'll you have?" He then turns to his liquor cabinet and prepares his potations one by one. In the free play that follows, someone is bound to ask for an extra rock, a splash of soda, or a sprinkling of salt on his tequila-sour glass. It's all completely *gemütlich* and easy. For mass drinking parties, however, the proceedings must be changed. If a man's to be a host and not a walking computer, he must eschew the drinking whims of each of his assorted visitors. It may be gallant for him to run to his bar or kitchen and carefully mix a not too sweet gimlet with a twist of temple orange for the second lady on the right-hand side of the fireplace, but when seventeen other fierce thirsts remain unappeased, the only kind of bar to set up is one with all of its offerings—or a single offering, as the case may be—prominently in the spotlight atop the bar. This virtually guarantees that the assembled imbibers will adapt themselves to the available liquors just as naturally as they accept their host's creamed-chicken hash or lobster salad at the buffet table. If, for instance, there are several bottles of vodka on view, together with pitchers of orange juice and tomato juice, the crowd, without any prompting, will call for bloody marys and screwdrivers. When they see bottles of gin, they'll ask for martinis or gin and tonic. While all drinks are theoretically poured with the advice and consent of the entertainees, there's usually a minimum of advice, mostly consent, while the host and his guests settle into the same happy groove.

Party pourings are either straight or mixed. How diversified each kind should be depends on the kind of entertainment you've planned. Generally, the bigger the party, the more limited the selection. Consider the mixed libation first. One of the best examples is the punch bowl—a single offering that's often the master key to the happiest kind of big drinking party and that frees the host from the constraint of serving and his guests from the constraint of being served. At smaller parties, if you or some of your crowd are known to have a whale of a time with Zubrovka martinis, you might place a bottle of Zubrovka as well as a bottle of gin alongside your vermouth. But you must set reasonable limits on your martini variations. You could conceivably place on your party bar an American gin, an English-style gin made in America, an English gin made in England, a Dutch genever gin, and a German Steinhäger gin. You could, that is, if you were running a gin-tasting party and nothing else. But if you're tempted to match your gin assortment with a similarly expansive whiskey assortment, rum assortment, brandy assortment, and vodka assortment—all for converting into mixed drinks—you'll be running a party with all your bottletops as well as your reason unscrewed. Keep in mind the fact that a host often catapults into fame during a single party not by serving as many mixed long and short drinks as possible, but by serving one drink so superb, so perfectly balanced in flavors, so numbingly cold in the summer or pleasantly hot in the winter, so lively with the best liquors and freshest juices, in such handsome drinking vessels, that none of his guests can possibly forget its excellence.

When you're serving straight drinks at parties, it's thoughtful to take into account your guests' drinking preferences, but, again, don't go overboard, and don't jump to easy conclusions too hastily. For example, if you're throwing a party for a group of visiting Frenchmen, you might assume that wine apéritifs like St.-Raphaël, Dubonnet, or Lillet would be ideal preludes. Your guess might be right, and it would be sensible to have at least one such apéritif ready for pouring. But it would also be a good idea to have a bottle of Scotch on tap, since many Frenchmen, particularly those on the international circuit, regularly take Scotch and soda before mealtime. If you happen to know of some members in your party whose eyes always dance when they see a bottle of twelve-year-old Scotch, as well as others who are happy only with the lighter Highland dew, you might place a bottle of each on your bar table to add to the general enchantment. If, at a buffet table, you're serving a standing rib roast and you know that some of your crowd have always had a special partiality for dark brews, you might offer bottles of both stout and dark Münchener. If you're serving espresso and even though not a single guest knows of sambuca, the Italian anise-and-elderberry-flavored liqueur served with coffee beans, this might be the perfect opportunity to introduce the velvety sweet liqueur to everyone. If there's a simmering casserole of beef *bourguignon*, then bottles of red wine, anything from California mountain red to French Beaujolais, would be perfect.

As a practical guide for party potables (excluding the wines or spirits served with food, and champagne, which is in a class by itself), the ingredients for two short drinks and two tall drinks should be the outside limit for any party above a dozen people. The short drinks may be one mixed (sidecar) and one straight (bourbon on the rocks). The tall may be one mixed (Tom Collins) and one straight with a carbonated water (brandy and soda). Often the short and the tall are combined. Thus, if you're offering frozen daiquiris, which are made with rum, then rum and tonic in tall glasses would be a cool way of burning the candle at both ends. If you're offering Rob Roys, made with Scotch and vermouth, orders for Scotch and soda or vermouth on the rocks would be simply a matter of pouring the spirits already on hand.

The important thing to remember is not to try to serve too many different drinks at one party. At the same time, if you can possibly introduce one original or offbeat mixed drink along with the standard cocktails or highballs, you'll kindle the pulse for additional party fun.

Bars

The qualifications for a party bar are two: It must be big and it must be reachable. It may be a corner bar, a bar on wheels, or a built-in saloon with footrest. If it's a liquor cabinet, it should be high enough for mixing, pouring, and serving. If the ends of the cabinet have drop-leaf extensions that can be raised or lowered to fit party needs, so much the better. The bar may be a medium- or large-size dining table covered first with a pad and then with a snowy white linen or other attractive tablecloth. If the space under the table is to be used for reserve spirits and carbonated waters, the covering should be floor-length. Using bridge tables for bar mixing purposes may be adequate if your bartender happens to be Toulouse-Lautrec, but for any man of normal height they're entirely too low. Breakfast tables or dining-room sideboards can both be put into service at the party bar. A long, narrow table with all liquors, bar equipment, glassware, and carbonated waters on top is preferable to a wide table with limited access. Chafing-dish or platter food is best offered at another buffet table. At really big levees, hosts sometimes set up two bars strategically placed so that the crush of traffic at any one spot is never too great.

Bartenders

Just when a small crowd becomes a big one is one of those twilight distinctions that depend on your own party experience, your bar space, and your floor space. If, as the host, you're also your own bartender, chef, maître d'hôtel, waiter, and coat-check attendant all rolled into one, then a party of ten to twelve people is just about as large as you'll want to handle alone. If the drinking party is eighteen to twenty-four or above, you'll find it best to hire a bartender-waiter—i.e., one who mixes and serves drinks and takes care of the normal cleanup as the party proceeds, as well as the after-party cleanup. Sometimes the owner of your favorite bistro or manager of your club restaurant will suggest one of his staff who's willing to work on a day or evening off. Perhaps a friend or a friend of a friend will know of an available party bartender. Public agencies as well as college employment services are both sources of supply for single engagements.

When you hire a bartender, remember to spell out beforehand precisely what his duties will be. Fifteen minutes' or a half-hour's orientation will pay off well. If a special mixed drink is to be offered, it's a good idea to actually go through a test run beforehand. For mixing any offbeat drinks, the bartender should use a measuring jigger, following proportions exactly. For standard martinis, manhattans, and on-the-rocks drinks, he may pour freehand only if his hand is sufficiently trained to pour with accuracy. He may ask guests to "say when." But nothing—absolutely nothing—at a drinking party will cause guests to feel as ill starred and unhappy as drinks poured freehand that are irritatingly weak or unmercifully strong. If the bartender is unsure of his pouring hand, it's a good idea to have him use the measuring jigger, and then simply and quietly ask each guest served if he'd care for a dividend or a double.

Ice for Parties

Knowing that you're about to prepare for a wet holiday, you should begin making and collecting ice cubes several days (not hours) in advance of your party. If you don't have sufficient ice-making equipment or storage space, arrange with a local ice dealer to get ice from him or have him deliver it—as close to partytime as possible. If you're in need of an ice block for your punch bowl, the iceman will supply it, or you can make your own punch-bowl glacier (see page 418). Time and again at otherwise fine parties, the host finds himself scraping the bottom of the ice bucket, draining cocktail shakers for used ice, while his freezer works furiously to keep pace with his party's demands. At any cocktail party, count on at least a half-tray of ice per person. For long, drawn-out parties or for outdoor parties in warm weather, count on a full tray per person. If you're buying ice cubes, count on a minimum of ¾ pound and a maximum of 1½ pounds per person.

Party Drinking Equipment

Priming the pumps for a drinking party is more than playing with the multiplication table. If your only cocktail shaker is one of those cozy two-drink types, you'll obviously need a more commodious piece of barware for a dozen or eighteen people. If, on the other hand, your mixing glass or shaker has a capacity of six drinks and you've invited eighteen people for cocktails, it doesn't follow that you must rush out and hastily buy two more mixing glasses. Most likely the eighteen celebrants won't arrive en masse. Batches of drinks can be quickly stirred or shaken from time to time for those present. But if you plan to offer a choice of martinis and rum sours, the same mixing glass can be used continuously only if your bar is in the kitchen or right along-side a sink where the mixing glass can be washed as often as necessary; otherwise, two mixing glasses with strainers or one martini pitcher and one cocktail shaker are indicated.

Assume, again, that eighteen drinking comrades are coming for a fling of tall coolers or on-the-rocks drinks and that you own six highball stirrers. Here, you *should* shoulder drinking arms and multiply six times three at least, or, to be more practical, about six times ten. Stirrers—like cocktail or canapé spears—disappear fast and irretrievably. There should always be legions of them, along with coasters and cocktail napkins for any possible deluge. There should also be mountains of cocktail napkins not only for drinks but every time you serve hot or cold hors d'oeuvres for handpicking.

If you're planning party libations made with fresh fruit juice, then your small hand squeezer should retire in favor of the latest electrical equipment.

At least two large ice buckets should be on hand for any party above ten. At patio and picnic parties, plastic-foam ice buckets are completely serviceable and acceptable, but for indoor use you'll probably want to use something more elegant.

Finally, you should have two or three bottle openers, since this piece of bar gadgetry is inevitably misplaced. Whenever a party brings large numbers into your drinking circle, check the bar equipment in the color illustration section for mass imbibing.

Party Glassware

Not even Lloyd's of London would be likely to bet on the glassware needed for a bachelor party. When the bride's health is being toasted and retoasted and all the glasses are dutifully smashed in the nearest fireplace after each round because they cannot be raised for any purpose more worthy, the amount of glassware needed obviously becomes astronomical. It's the only drinking occasion where cheap dime-store glassware might be justified. For the usual cocktail party, there should be at least two glasses per drinker. Caterers who supply glassware for private parties will furnish from three to five glasses per person on the theory that it's not practical to wash glasses after each round of drinks. But in your own kitchen, particularly if you've hired someone for glass washing, two-per-cocktailer is a practical formula that allows ample time for washing, refills, etc. If you're serving tall drinks, from gin rickeys to rum collinses, you can again safely count on two glasses per person. For other merry-go-rounds, the host should set special sights for his glassware needs, depending on the particular kind of liquid cheer being offered. If, for instance, you're mapping out a wine-tasting party, there should be a complete set of clean glasses for each different wine, so that tasters making the rounds of pleasure from one wine to the next can sip comparatively without running into their neighbors' drinking vessels. Thus, eight people sipping four different clarets should have access to thirty-two wineglasses. Consider the opposite extreme: At a midnight hot-grog party, a single mug per person—with a 25-percent surplus for possible breakage or spur-of-the-moment guests—will usually be enough. Guests particularly treasure their mulled or blazed drinks. They sip them as slowly as possible and will very peacefully wait for refills. At a punch-bowl party, most of the crowd wanting seconds or thirds simply take their own punch cups to the bowl and ladle out their refills. The same formula of one glass per person (plus a reserve of 25 percent) also goes for dinner-table wineglasses, brandy glasses, and liqueur glasses.

Drink Calculator

As a rule, the drinking curve rises headlong on holidays and weekends and descends at other times. Also, as men get older, their capacity for hoisting and draining the glass increases. Seniors drink more, and can hold more, than freshmen. The class of 1940 at its annual midwinter reunion polishes off considerably more than the class of 1970. The '70s raise more thunder about their drinking, but at the end of the evening, when the actual liquor tally is made, the older imbibers will be far ahead of the more youthful alumni. A party around a punch bowl will normally drink at least 50 percent more than a party where the host laboriously mixes drinks one by one to order. Furthermore, the place where one cracks his bottles often determines the amount of liquid cheer consumed. Liquor is downed at a dockside party in far greater volume than when dispensed from a boat's galley. Ale or beer drinkers cavorting at an outdoor lobster barbecue will kill kegs rather than the bottles of an indoor seafood party.

In estimating how much liquor to buy for any party where mixed drinks are served, you must start out with the specific recipes you have in mind. If, for instance, you plan to serve brandy sours, you must decide beforehand whether each drink will have a 1½-ounce or a 2-ounce base. If you're serving tall coolers with rum and other spirits, you must go back to the base recipe, check each kind of spirit called for, and then expand it to any number up to infinity. Even when your goal isn't infinity, it's always best in your calculations to err on the side of too much. Certainly, if you're buying for your party the same spirits you'd normally stock in your liquor cabinet, additional bottles left over are good liquid assets. And in buying a half-dozen or dozen bottles at a time, you can usually tuck away a noticeable saving under the single-bottle price.

A useful guideline for parties, tested over and over, is simply this: Most of the crowd will consume two to three drinks at the usual cocktail hour at sundown, before a buffet, or before a sit-down dinner. After dinner, if you're serving highballs, you can again reasonably estimate two to three drinks per person, depending on how long guests remain after the dinner table has been cleared. At a knock-down, drag-out bachelor party, the two-to-three formula will expand to four-to-six. At a pre-theater party, where everyone wants to keep an especially clear head, the formula may dip to one to two drinks per guest. The drink-calculation guide in Table 3 covers cocktails before dinner or post-prandial highballs. If you're serving both, calculate both.

(**Note:** As of January 1980 all distilled spirits must be bottled in metric measurements, outlined on page 35. In the measurements below, the word "fifth" [fifth of a gallon] is used even though the old-fashioned fifth is $2/10$ ounce more than the new metric measurement replacing it. Since the word "fifth" is still used in this country by both customers and shopmen, it is indicated below and makes no difference in calculations for party requirements. To be on the plus side, however, quarts may be purchased instead of fifths; often there's a saving in the larger bottles.)

Table 3
Cocktail and Highball Calculator

If you're the host for a party of	as a rule, they'll consume	if drinks are 1½ ozs., you'll need at least	if drinks are 2 ozs., you'll need at least
6	12–18 drinks	2 fifths	2 fifths
8	16–24 "	2 "	2 "
10	20–30 "	2 "	3 "
12	24–36 "	3 "	3 "
20	40–60 "	4 "	5 "
30	60–90 "	6 "	8 "

In buying wines for a party, the host should allow 3 ounces for a serving of an apéritif wine, sherry, or port. Red and white table wines, including champagne, are usually poured in 4-ounce portions, assuming that you're using generous 11-ounce tulip glasses or wide-bellied wineglasses. If a single wine is served throughout the dinner, count on two or three glasses per person. If several wines are served with individual courses, count on one or two glasses of each wine per person. The wine schedule in Table 4 also applies to champagne or other sparkling wines served during the dinner. If the bubbly is served before the dinner as cocktails or after the dinner for toasting, the same guide may be followed.

Table 4
Apéritif and Table-Wine Calculator

If you're serving predinner apéritif wines, not apéritif cocktails, or if you're serving sherry or port for a party of	*Your guests will generally average*	*You should buy or have on hand ready for serving*
6	6–12 drinks	2 fifths
8	8–16 ”	2 ”
10	10–20 ”	3 ”
12	12–24 ”	3 ”
20	20–40 ”	5 ”
30	30–60 ”	8 ”
When serving a single red or white table wine throughout the meal and your party consists of	*Your guests will generally average*	*You should buy or have on hand ready for serving*
6	12–18 drinks	3 fifths
8	16–24 ”	4 ”
10	20–30 ”	5 ”
12	24–36 ”	6 ”
20	40–60 ”	10 ”
30	60–90 ”	15 ”

Brandy and liqueurs are in a special category when served straight and not as an ingredient in dessert cocktails, liqueur frappés, etc. The usual serving in the small brandy glass as well as the larger brandy snifter is 1 ounce per person; the same goes for liqueurs served straight. (See Table 5.)

Table 5
Brandy and Liqueur Calculator

When pouring brandy or liqueurs as after-dinner drinks for a party of	*As a rule they'll consume*	*You'll need the following fifths of brandy or liqueurs*
6	6–12 drinks	1 fifth
8	8–16 ”	1 ”
10	10–20 ”	1 ”
12	12–24 ”	1 ”
20	20–40 ”	2 ”
30	30–60 ”	3 ”

In estimating carbonated waters such as club soda, tonic water, ginger ale, cola drinks, etc., a generous guideline is to allow a 28-ounce bottle for every two persons. Thus, a person consuming three gin and tonics would usually pour from 12 to 14 ounces for his three drinks. The smaller 12-ounce bottles of carbonated waters are easy when guests are pouring their own drinks at cocktail tables. Larger-size bottles are used when a bartender is doing the honors. If you're using your own soda water made with soda charges, keep plenty of charges in reserve. The usual charge makes one quart of soda.

At an all-beer party—a picnic, barbecue, or steak party—count on an average of three bottles of beer, ale, or stout per person.

So much for a general guide to successful party planning; we now recommend to you several specific party ideas that we've found enjoyable. The following fêtes don't, of course, represent a comprehensive listing of all party plans—they're merely intended as a sampling of the many possible courses to follow. And this is as it should be. Our purpose is to suggest enough ideas to spark your own imagination. Glean those that complement your style of living and then embellish them with personal touches that will make each party very much your own thing.

26

PARTIES

16 Plans for an Extra Measure of Pleasure

The Brunch Party

Of all formulas concocted to cast off the post-Saturday-night pall, none is more likely to recapture the previous night's camaraderie and smooth the rumpled features of the late-rising night owl quicker than a festive early-afternoon array of good food and drink. There are winter brunches before a blazing log fire, spring brunches for inaugurating the new cabin cruiser, summer after-tennis fêtes held at courtside, and autumn brunches offered either indoors or on your terrace, to mention just a few of the species and subspecies.

Although your agenda may be scheduled for a noonish kickoff, the whole day's docket should be as flexible as possible. A bon-voyage brunch, for instance, before a sailing or a plane flight may be given on the midmorning or midafternoon of departure. And brunchers who love the pleasant preamble of a jog, a swim, a short drive, or just the indulgence of breathing in the cool morning zephyrs before brunch-time are entitled to the privilege of eating when they're hungry and drinking when they're dry—in either order.

One of the first duties of the brunchmaster is to set a sumptuous table, and the first step toward that end is to acquire tableware that's vivid and inviting. A single glass of orange juice or a screwdriver is a somewhat humdrum sight, but the same drinks become munificent and inviting when they're served from deep glass pitchers resting in an iced champagne bucket. Highly burnished Sheffield platters and coffee sets, once of interest mainly to antiquarians, are now sought after as modern graces of the brunch table. At an alfresco brunch, a hibachi or a portable charcoaler with a smoker top is perfect for conquering early-afternoon appetites with mixed grills of lamb chops, sausages, tomatoes, ham steaks, mushrooms and kidneys. Scrambled eggs should arrive on imposing platters or nestled in warm chafing dishes. Corned-beef hash or chicken hash-browned should be kept warm on hot trays or in casseroles over a trivet flame or candle lamp.

One of the most auspicious sights at any brunch table is a commodious breadbasket piled high with warm quick breads. Today, this kind of prodigality is merely a matter of shopping at the right bakeries. If you've access to a French baker, you can garner fresh *brioches*, the richest and silkiest of soft rolls, flaky *croissants* so tender they seem to float away when you sample them, long salt sticks and crisp club rolls. Italians will revel in their huge *panettone*, a billowy mound of a yeast cake with raisins and candied fruit. For partisans of Americana there are blueberry muffins, corn muffins, and pecan buns, all from the bakery or frozen-food counters. All quick breads or buns require no more toil than brief baking or warming in the oven. And the best coffee in the world will taste even better if you own an electric grinder and use it just before brewing.

Many dedicated brunchmen look to the Scandinavian smorgasbord for inspiration: cold rare roast beef, ox tongue, ham, rolled pork, sautéed kidneys, herring with boiled potatoes, hard and semisoft cheeses, and a selection of rich fruit jams. One of the best things about a smorgasbord brunch is that it can take care of itself; after the platters are set out, you simply join your guests in the waiting line.

Sunday brunches start with pick-me-ups that have the effect of alternately stimulating and soothing; the usual screwdrivers with vodka may be varied with rum, sherry, or Pernod. And be sure to lay in a stock of after-brunch liqueurs—especially a fine coffee liqueur with a float of heavy cream, served ice-cold. We know of no potion that so gently makes the clock stand still.

The Post-Football Fête

For one of October's most inviting recipes, take a cool Saturday afternoon, stir in approximately two hours of gridiron grandstanding, moisten to taste with *eau de vie* from a hip flask, then simmer down to a leisurely evening repast in the mellow light of your own digs. Ever since Englishmen in the eleventh century engaged in the manly sport of kicking around old skulls on battlefields, *futballe* has been one of the most uninhibited forms of ordered mayhem known to man. Happily, it has its own highly civilized safety valve—the convocation at cocktails and dinner following the game, when the afternoon's formations and strategies are all relived calmly in the vicinity of home bar and ice bucket. Only a fiercely loyal alumnus returning home from his own campus can appreciate the rich colors of fall—the scarlet of a bloody mary, the harvest yellow of a 16-ounce mug overflowing with frosty ale, the autumnal haze surrounding a double old-fashioned glass filled with whiskey and rocks.

One of the best things about football is that it starts with the September oyster season and its fried-oyster platters, oysters on the half shell, and creamy oyster stews. Coolish nights bring out the carnivore in men, best satisfied by such hearty fare as rich oxtail stews, calf's liver sautéed with calvados, and Swiss steaks simmered with Spanish onions, peppers, and tomatoes.

Every chef planning to tackle an after-football party is automatically guided by one obvious ground rule: All preliminaries for the party must take place either before or after the game. You can't retire to the kitchen between halves. A dinner that's cooked before the game and held for serving time can be as elaborate as you wish as long as it doesn't keep you from reaching your seat before the first whistle blows. An after-game menu naturally must consist of ready-in-a-minute foods. Wise kitchen strategists often combine both styles into winning combinations. An oxtail stew, for instance—cooking time, four hours— may be simmered a day or two before the game; stews always taste better when reheated, anyway. Hot smoked-oyster canapés can be broiled while guests are still making their first sweep toward the ice bucket.

The protracted cheering and jeering that goes on at any big tilt always creates a special symptom diagnosed as pigskin thirst. The most obvious kind of first aid is the double highball. Very prominently favored in the post-football pharmacopoeia is the Rob Roy, served either cold or hot—in an old-fashioned glass or in a mug with boiling water and stick cinnamon. For those of pure Scotch blood who'd rather skip the vermouth, a hot old-fashioned made with two ounces of Scotch will provide instant comfort. Many college men, past and present, simplify the whole problem of entertaining both their friends and some of their gridiron adversaries by offering the oldest of Anglo-Saxon potables—liquid malt. It was no accident that, for many centuries, breweries were located right on the campuses of English colleges. But even today, as the fall deepens into winter, a thirst doth rise for nut-brown ale and creamy stout. Both of them blend beautifully when poured together into tall seidels. Gambrinus's brew may flow with any food when men move from gridiron to groaning board.

An Après-Ski Party

Few things on this earth put a more ravenous edge on a man's appetite than a bracing, frost-nipped day on the slopes. When the day's skiing is over, Valhalla seems near at hand as the mountain air becomes suffused with the aromas of hot seafood chowder, strong coffee, and steaming rum toddies.

There are a number of techniques for hosting a ski feast. You can muster the whole meal ready-made, from quiche Lorraine to Cognac, using any first-class restaurant or club kitchen as your commissary, and then transport it intact to your lodge, where the simple chore of reheating is all that's required. Of course, if your lodge's larder and kitchen facilities lend themselves to on-the-scene cookery, you may prefer starting from scratch. Or you can cook a stew or glaze spareribs in your own kitchen beforehand, pack them in wide-mouthed vacuum jugs and insulated picnic bags, then simply unpack when you're ready to serve the hungry snowmen and their snow bunnies. If you're a ski host of the one-day-sojourn-to-a-nearby-slope persuasion, you might take along the raw ingredients in your station wagon, drop the tailgate for a buffet table, light the hibachi or gasoline stove, and broil the teriyaki or sauté the steaks to order.

There was a time when buying cooked collations meant a lot of bother. Advance shopping these days requires about as much effort as a trip on a chair lift. If you've access to a Swedish foodshop or café, Swedish meatballs as well as sweet-and-sour baked beans seem especially designed for modern appetites. Neapolitan Italy may not be the habitat for skiing, but any of the small pastas in rich cheese sauce or tomato sauce are perfect for relishing under the open sky. For cooking on the station-wagon barbecue, tender meats such as tournedos or shish kebab are all quickly done over a crackling fire. Turn such foods frequently, since the frigid air above the fire cools them quickly.

If all this begins to sound like a summer picnic, it's not coincidental —but you'll soon discover major differences. There are no ants, for example, in the winter, and there are some ski stamping grounds where Klondike temperatures cause cutlery, dinner plates, and mugs to become so frostbitten they can hardly be handled. To avert such a cold fate, it's wise to protect your dinnerware in an insulated picnic box—the kind that's used in summer to keep things cold. And if you're carrying hot grog, remember that winter drinks are made with boiling water, and the mugs in which they're served make for really tall drinks; consequently, a gallon vacuum-jugful is just about enough to warm the cockles and soothe the muscles of four to six skiers. To keep the grog hot, of course, you should preheat the jug by pouring boiling water into it and letting it remain for about five minutes before replacing it with your hot potation. For hot-drink recipes, see Chapter 23.

The Intimate Sundown Party

Americans are generally agreed that the best way to watch the evening sun go down is through a cocktail glass. The most frequent and fashionable way to celebrate that heavenly event is the small, intimate cocktail party, where a few friends gather to skoal each other in the congenial setting of one's home, rather than at the kind of mass drinking session where cocktailers are as crowded as the hold of a slave ship.

For such an intimate assemblage, no radical rearrangement of furniture is necessary. But if your studio or apartment is the scene of frequent predinner gatherings, it's a good idea to own cocktail tables that are alcohol-proof; otherwise cover them with glass tops. So that each guest will have a spot within arm's reach where he can easily rest his glass, small folding tables or stack tables should be distributed wherever necessary.

If you're addicted to spur-of-the-moment cocktail parties, your basic bar inventory should be well stocked at all times. Take a quick check of your hard and soft bar supplies once or twice a week, particularly before weekends. Don't be caught in the all too common spot of the host who undertakes to mix three frozen daiquiris only to find that he has about two ounces of light rum left in his bottle, or plenty of sweet vermouth but an embarrassingly small supply of dry vermouth for the six guests who opted for martinis.

As for the finger food, millions of toasties, tidbits, hot and cold hors d'oeuvres, canapés, and quiches are sold all ready for the oven, bowl, or tray. When making your selection, simply ask yourself: Are they decidedly provocative in flavor—salty, peppery, or in some way piquant? They needn't be so spice-laden that they take your scalp off, but they should spur rather than dampen both the thirst apparatus and the taste buds. Ordinary boiled ham, for instance, merely pacifies the taste juices; genuine razorback Smithfield ham, cured with pepper, sets them flowing.

If you want your canapés or hors d'oeuvres to be as showy as possible, buy them already prepared. If you're an hors d'oeuvre hobbyist and want your appetizers to bear your own culinary signature, consult Chapter 24. In any event, remember that hot hors d'oeuvres should be so hot as to make you hesitate before you take the second bite; cold hors d'oeuvres, with the exception of cheese which should be at room temperature, should taste as though they were just removed from an ice block on the North Pole.

A sensible custom is to place on the buffet or cocktail table two or three platters of really distinguished sundown goods, such as Stilton cheese, *pâté de foie gras*, beluga caviar, Westphalian or prosciutto ham, smoked turkey, and other high-stepping dishes that don't normally appear on the boardinghouse table. Guests can then scoop out the cheese or pâté and spread it on crackers or toast while the host sits Buddha-like in the background.

When you ask your friends to a simple cocktail party and not a cocktail supper, be sure to tell them in the clearest terms that they're invited to cocktails *before* dinner. Cocktail parties sometimes lead to spur-of-the-moment expeditions to a restaurant or potluck parties in your own pad, but a host should encourage such spontaneous suggestions only after a down-to-earth assessment of what's likely to be both practical and pleasurable for both himself and his guests.

The Bachelor Dinner Party

Judgment day doesn't necessarily coincide with one's wedding day; it often occurs several nights before the nuptials are celebrated, during the trial by alcohol, the riotous rite identified as the bachelor dinner party. Seldom is a bachelor dinner a do-it-yourself bacchanalia in your own pad, however; it is a pay-it-yourself affair, although sometimes the prospective father-in-law or the best man and some of his buddies will pick up the tab. In any case, a private room in a hotel or club is infinitely more practical than your own digs for absorbing the shock of baked Alaskas crashing on the floor, martinis poured into grand pianos, and champagne glasses sailing at supersonic speed into fireplaces. Those about to give up their bachelorhood should be guided by the following straight steers on the last supper.

Choose a private dining room in a club, hotel, or restaurant that can best be described as clubbable—that is, a *gemütlich* room with absolute privacy where the dinner and service are handled by top-flight pros. Avoid the type of men's clubs that have always been inhabited by live corpses. In many cities there are university clubs, among others, where the atmosphere is intimate, easy, and jovial. A nonmember of a particular club may often use the club's facilities simply by asking one of his acquaintances who is a member to sponsor him as a guest. Some clubs and all hotels include bedroom facilities, where guests who lose all power of locomotion can be quietly transported and stashed away until their heads resume normal size.

A bachelor dinner, in spite of all the ribbing and riling, should allow trenchermen to get together and enjoy an evening of reminiscences and sociability. Although the party may start with martinis, switch to beer or wine with the steak, champagne with the dessert, Cognac with the coffee, and resume with champagne, toasting on into the night, it shouldn't be designed to turn men into human drainpipes. One way to divert the drinkers to eating is to escort guests vigorously to the table right after the second round of cocktails. Additional drinks may be served at the table, but they'll soon be phased out by the crab-meat or jumbo-shrimp cocktails as serious eating begins. Offer the kind of soup guests simply can't ignore—bowls of velvety black-bean soup or baked onion soup au gratin. Avoid a fillet of sole marguery with its opulent sauce and order instead a simple broiled striped bass or Kennebec salmon. Beefsteak is the traditional meat course at a bachelor dinner. It can be dressed up as a planked steak surrounded with vegetables, but the most impressive and practical is the thick shell steak, a boneless cut of about six portions, which is sliced before serving. Draw the dinner to a close with a platter of assorted cheeses and salted crackers, or, if you have a sweet tooth, with a warm wedge of apple pie topped with cheddar cheese, or vanilla ice cream and warm brandied peaches.

The old custom of toasting the bride by breaking the glass against the fireplace symbolizes a number of things—the love of the bride and groom, which will continue to last until the glass is made whole again, or the fact that the glass can't possibly be used for any worthier purpose. Whatever tradition lies behind the custom, there's no doubt about its consequence: It costs like hell. Most clubs and hotels will furnish inexpensive glasses for breaking rather than hand-blown crystal etched with their own crest.

A young groom who receives a bill for his bachelor party sometimes goes into a state of deep shock. The best way to avoid being rolled is to ascertain all possible charges beforehand. Ask the steward or manager if there is any reduction when drinks are ordered beforehand in volume. Frequently there is. Ask for sample menus. When you make your choice at a stated price, ask what charges there will be for room rental, if any; the number of covers you must guarantee; how many additional covers the kitchen can take care of in the event there's a last-minute increase in the number of cronies attending; the cost of flowers, cigars, cigarettes, glassware breakage, and other so-called incidentals. Count on the usual 15- to 20-percent tip. It's a good idea to slip the headwaiter a five- or ten-spot before the dinner, explaining that he'll receive the main gratuity later for dividing among the help. A prepayment of this kind not only encourages him to give the best possible service during the dinner, but often is insurance against later hijacking. Remember simply that while marriages are sometimes made in heaven, bachelor dinners require more earthly considerations.

An Alfresco Party

Something marvelously metaphysical takes place when an indoor meal, no matter how magnificent, is carried outdoors. Simply by crossing the threshold between living room and terrace, vichyssoise suddenly becomes creamier, champagne bubblier, and fruit juicier. An alfresco dining room can be a terrace high above a city street, a stretch of bluestone beside a swimming pool, or a grass carpet beneath a patio umbrella. There were terraces long before there were tranquilizers. Guests stretched out on your leisure chairs, feeling charitable toward the whole world, may be predisposed to find whatever food and drink you proffer to be perfect. No effort must be spared, of course, to make the menu match their expectations, but there's no reason that a host can't enjoy his own hospitality. To help keep him as carefree as possible, there are now many models of food carts available, all designed to quickly and quietly transport food and drink from indoors to outdoors. Some come with movable shelves and drawers, some with hot-table surfaces that merely require plugging in to keep soup marmites and casseroles bubbling hot. There are others with recessed condiment racks, with insulated compartments for crushed ice, or even with beds for charcoal fires.

Quite often a meal served under the heavens will include an old classic, such as cold chicken Jeanette—boneless cooked breast of chicken in a velvety jellied sauce, flanked with slices of *pâté de foie gras*. It's not new, but, like the charm of baroque music reaching ears for the first time, it comes as a fresh discovery whenever it's served. Alfresco menus on the grand scale tend to be an appetizing amalgam of hot and cold. Hot consommé with a feathery garnish of spun eggs will provide all the benefits of a kitchen comfortably beyond the range of its heat. Cold peaches in champagne will take the edge off the most torrid summer day.

Like coffee and Cognac, alfresco dinners and summer wine cups glorify each other. Two good examples are raspberry claret cup (page 374) and white wine cooler (page 389). The Spanish are past masters at this art, as anyone can testify who's ever slaked his thirst with the countless species of *sangrías* in the Iberian Peninsula. (See pages 428–429). All good wine cups in the summertime seem to share one common fault: They're never big enough. Even non–wine drinkers find themselves drinking on and on. Hours will pass, and the wine cup is still *fresco*.

The Cocktail Supper Party

The cocktail supper is based on the theory that it takes more than peanuts to make a party. As a meal, it stands midway between the tidbittery of a mere drinking session and a full-fledged sit-down dinner. The appetites that always stir wherever drinks are served may be temporarily appeased with hot and cold hors d'oeuvres, but the most satisfying provender the gods can possibly provide is casseroles of chicken, bowls of herbed rice, beef stew in red wine—the cordial elements of an easy buffet. In planning a cocktail supper, the host must make sure that his guests are otherwise uncommitted for the evening. He should clearly spell out the fact that hunger as well as thirst will be exorcised, and he shouldn't draw the line for winding up the party at any particular time.

At a cocktail supper, let your food be ample, your menu brief. Instead of caravans of rich canapés with more garnishes than you can shake a cocktail spear at, the appetizers should feature a single cold and a single hot hors d'oeuvre of unrivaled goodness. The main dish that follows may be hot or cold or a seasonable combination of the two. Cold glazed ham, for example, and hot Swedish brown beans form a compatible partnership along with a mushroom-and-asparagus salad with curried mayonnaise. Or a hot beef or veal goulash may be served with hot buttered noodles or with a cold noodle salad and a julienne of radishes, green peppers, and scallions, and a French dressing with Parmesan cheese. Desserts should be the noncooked type such as strawberries Romanoff or a fresh-fruit compote with kirsch, supplemented with a tray of assorted small specialties from the best pastry shop within driving distance.

As for the drinking at a cocktail supper, anything goes. If you want to accompany food with wine, of course you may, but it's not necessary; American devotees of the cocktail will find a sazerac or a bourbon mist quite gratifying with their food as well as before it. Wine-oriented conservatives from the Continent may writhe, but Americans who blissfully drink their 11-to-1 martinis with the appetizers will be gloriously happy to continue downing them with the meal.

Hosts should also face the fact that at the cocktail hour these days the most important things aren't necessarily cocktails. They may be highballs, lowballs, or drinks of any variety from fino sherry to shandygaff. Finally, men who confidently offer one main dish at a cocktail supper shouldn't hesitate to offer one main drink, perfectly balanced and served, for which they've won their bar spurs.

The Galley Party

It's hard to imagine surroundings more felicitous for a party than topside on a boat moored in a quiet cove, the summer stillness broken only by the gentle lapping of gin and tonics against frosty tumblers.

The kind of victuals you stow aboard depends for the most part on the length of your cruise and the size of your galley. If you're speed-boating from one yacht club to another, of course, you can pick up food and drink wherever you happen to tie up. Slightly longer trips are simply floating picnics. You pack your portable cooler with unsliced rare roast beef, corned beef brisket, or barbecued chickens, fill a deep bowl with German potato salad, stack the fresh rye and the pumpernickel, remember the mustard, add the necessary amount of cold lager to your cargo, and shove off. But for an all-day or weekend cruise, you'll want hot and hefty fare from your own galley. The sailor assigned to the job may have a misgiving or two when he or she lights the ministove, but when the aroma of crisp bacon or hashed-brown potatoes or hot clam chowder first rises on deck, all hands will know that the real master of the vessel is stationed below.

Cruising schedules on rivers, lakes, and seas all over the world are alike in one respect: The best-laid schemes gang aft agley in the face of becalmed waters or ailing engines. Anticipating these normal de-lays, an experienced commodore sees to it that there are always extra rations in cans. The entire crew will welcome a canned cured ham as readily as a fresh one. Buy the type, if possible, that requires no refrigeration. Canned Canadian-style bacon—another name for smoked boneless pork loin—is equally good hot or cold, at sea as well as on land. In the canned-chicken department, large cans containing whole birds are a better bet than the small cans or jars filled with trimmings. Corned-beef hash or roast-beef hash, both staunch nautical standbys, can go into the frying pan without any additions, although you can enhance them mightily with a few beaten egg yolks, cream or melted butter, and a spray of Worcestershire sauce. Among canned meats and seafood, the field is unlimited—from galantine to *gaffelbiter*. Just remember, though, that some of the foods that sound exotic—kangaroo steak or canned wild boar—aren't likely to satisfy a ravenous seafaring party as readily as generous helpings of chili con carne, meat-stuffed ravioli, and other time-tested pleasures. There are days when nothing, not even 151-proof rum, can warm a crew like mugs of hot thick soup, many of which now come in foil envelopes.

Since most cruising for party purposes takes place in warm or comparatively warm climates, tall coolers fit in perfectly with offshore outings. But the gross tonnage of corkscrews, cans, bottles, ice buckets, tongs, racks, and ice picks can sometimes present a formidable obtacle course twixt the gent who's drawn the duty as bartender and his wares. To avoid this kind of overstocking, carry one superb totable potable, premixed on land, needing in some cases only the addition of carbonated waters. If you decide on straight drinks, try to carry no more bottles and glassware than fit into a mounted bar rack. Finally, insulated unbreakable bar glasses conserve ice and are the mainstay of many a waterborne party.

The Indoor Picnic

The best season for an indoor picnic is late winter, after you've recovered from end-of-the-year revelries and before the promise of a warm outdoors has become more than a pipe dream. The most natural site for such a celebration is directly in front of a glowing fireplace. Guests can gather near the hearth, preferably picnic-style on the floor, and grill to their hearts' content.

Like any well-bred picnic, your party should be a communal cook-in. Too many cooks can spoil a broth, but not a picnic. In fact, to keep a picnicker from joining in the cooking is an implied insult. While some of the party thread shrimp onto skewers, others can be basting the split squabs, the sirloin or tenderloin steaks. Martini mixers can twirl away while others open bottles of wine, and the couple in the corner, oblivious to the world, brew their own version of Irish coffee. Skewered beef, ham, or spareribs, even chunks of boned and skinned breast of chicken, are all magnificent fireside fare, basted with soy sauce, barbecue sauce, or olive oil flavored with herbs, mustard, and garlic.

On such occasions, the hibachi is perfect for the man who likes to play with fire. You'll need two double-size grills for a picnic party of from eight to ten. If you lack a fireplace, the best technique is to light your hibachi outdoors. When smoke no longer gets in your eyes, bring the fire equipment inside and place it on a stove or near a ventilating fan or hood. If your barbecue party stretches into several hours, build a double bed of charcoal two inches thick. Stack extra coals on the right and left sides of each brazier to provide even fire at the flared ends.

As host, it's your job to supply at least the main course; co-picnickers can be called upon to furnish a tasty bean salad or a box of delicious mignon éclairs. You should also furnish all the necessary accouterments—the hibachis, tableware, bar tools, brushes for basting, extra-long tongs, spatulas, and forks for scooping food from the grill.

Guests bearing liquid gifts will probably show up with whiskey, gin, and vermouth, which do yeoman's service on any bibbing occasion. But you'll be prepared for all comers—with or without bottles—if you have a gallon vacuum jug filled with bloody marys that have been premixed with ice, then drained into the jug for subsequent serving on the rocks in old-fashioned glasses. Chilled all-purpose wines such as Sylvaner should come to the party with the cold bloom still on the bottles. Among reds, the eye-opening flavor of Zinfandel is the perfect complement for charcoal-broiled meats and seafood.

The Catered Party

Sheer numbers aren't in themselves a guarantee that a party will be a howling hit, but for mounting a saturnalia featuring both food and drink, a crowd of a dozen or so well-matched pairs is just about big enough to be unbridled in a civilized way. The host who wants to have as good a time as his guests, however, keeps in mind that when the guest list goes above a score of people, party planning should be turned over to the pros. Caterers are masters of movable feasts. An experienced caterer is always happy to listen to the most inquisitorial host, confer with him, guide him, and even on rare occasions yield to him, provided he accepts the caterer's guiding philosophy: Don't do it yourself.

Hosts in search of caterers are usually guided by that oldest and most dependable of media—word of mouth. Some caterers are justly renowned for their pasta dishes. Others are luau specialists. There are hors d'oeuvre monarchs and canapé czars. So don't hesitate to ask a caterer which dish he considers his finest opus—and invite him, if possible, to offer samples. Many caterers have specialties such as beef stroganoff stashed away in their refrigerators or freezers. Naturally, no caterer will be able to snap his fingers and produce an instant twelve-pound cold stuffed lobster in aspic while you're waiting in his reception room. But many of them keep on file a gallery of colored photos and slides of their decorative culinary art. And most caterers are usually more than pleased to display their china, silverware, linen, chafing dishes, and other components of their *mise en scène*.

Prices for a catered affair will, of course, depend on your locale and your caterer, and always be higher than the same meal in a restaurant. In terms of time, temper, and money saved by not having to make all of the arrangements yourself, it's a sound investment.

If it's your first adventure in large-scale regalement, you'll want the caterer's counsel on how many celebrants your apartment or town house can comfortably hold for party purposes. In warm climates, terraces are often put to use. An adjoining study can sometimes be opened as an extension of the main party room, but the best parties are those that are not fragmented too noticeably. Keep in mind that you needn't provide seating for all your guests, since practically all large at-home parties today are combination stand-up and sit-down affairs. Guests help themselves and are helped at bountifully stocked buffet tables. Bar waiters circulate among both sit-downers and standees. The informal wall table and the light movable chair are indispensable for easy conversational islets and for keeping hot food and coffee on an even keel.

When the caterer's truck pulls up to your digs, one of the first pieces of equipment he's likely to deliver is a portable bar. In apartments where space is at a premium, however, it's sometimes best to eliminate this option in favor of additional dance-floor or dining space. A working bar can always be improvised in an adjoining room, where drinks are prepared out of sight and passed by waiters to the merry-makers.

In choosing your drinks, the simplest of all bar services is naturally the punch bowl—a perfect choice when drinking is the main focus of attention. But for rejoicing around a buffet, where stacked platters and bubbling chafing dishes are the big centers of interest, the punch bowl is frequently bypassed in favor of the regular bar repertory. In some cases, you may supply the bar stock yourself, but the caterer usually provides all the necessary makings and mixes—as well as the bartender.

As your professionally prepared party moves into high gear, it will take on a special warmth as the catered spirits raise those of the assembled celebrants. It's a glow that will be more than matched by the one you get when, in the midst of your limited duties as master of the revels, you realize that you're not only unruffled and unharried but are enjoying yourself immensely.

An Urban Luau

Staging an indoor luau is as easy as poi. Even being sky-high in an apartment can have some built-in blessings: Guests don't have to scour about for volcanic rocks, ti leaves, and palm fronds, and you don't have to dig a pit to roast the traditional whole suckling pig. Instead, just ask a butcher to wrap up his juiciest pork-loin roasts, which you can start sizzling on an indoor rotisserie. If naught but the entire pig on a platter will suffice, you can order one from a professional catering service.

Don't get hung up adorning your pad with fishnets and colored-glass globes. Concentrate on laying out a properly Polynesian bar and buffet, which is, after all, where the action is. Begin by visiting your friendly florist. He won't be able to duplicate all 4000 varieties of hibiscus growing on Oahu, but he can supply you with quantities of lush greenery. Tell him the size of your luau table and ask for enough flat ferns to cover it. Order one or two centerpieces of short-stemmed flowers—long-stemmed beauties are quite acceptable as buffet decorations, but at a sit-down feast they invariably create a junglelike atmosphere that inhibits cross-table conversation. Scatter fruit among the flowers and fronds: Pineapples cut lengthwise, with the meat removed, sliced, and returned to the shells; stalks of yellow and red bananas, grapes, citrus fruits, and mangoes—all make for delicious tropical tidbits that can also serve as decorations. Set the stage as well with plenty of condiments such as chutneys, some mild, others peppery hot. As sideshows, include chopped hard-boiled eggs and chives, tomatoes with basil, cucumbers in yogurt and dill, sliced bananas sprinkled with lime juice and brown sugar, and green salad with avocado and papaya chunks. Tiny morsels of browned coconut meat, called Coco Bits, taste great with coconut-cream or curry dishes.

The potable to proffer at any luau is rum. A stock of light, dark, and 151-proof rum will be the base for rum cocktails (Chapter 19), as well as many of the tall coolers (Chapter 20). For a special after-dinner tipple, try a sweet Polynesian change of pace such as a pineapple–crème de menthe frappé. Fill saucer champagne glasses three-fourths full with finely crushed ice and pour in a shot of undiluted frozen pineapple juice. Stir it in the glass, then add an ounce of green crème de menthe.

The key to a luau feast is neither pig nor poi but *hoomanawanui*, which means "take it easy." Let the party choose its own speed. A luau isn't an organized affair that requires careful supervision by the host. If you've done your preplanning well, the night can virtually run itself. As you and your guests dream and dance after dinner, you'll find that a luau never really seems to end but slowly drifts off into the moonlight.

The Progressive Dinner Party

For those who may not yet have caught up with this kaleidoscopic form of culinary sport, the progressive dinner party is one in which the hosting chores are divided into courses. Everybody may meet at one house for the hors d'oeuvres and cocktails, travel to another for the guinea hen and champagne, to a third for the crepes and demitasse, to a fourth for dancing and highballs, and finally, as the rosy-fingered dawn creeps round, gather in a breakfast room for the comforting stimuli of ice-cold bloody marys and soft-scrambled eggs on toast.

Nobody is ever really invited to a progressive dinner; a compatible crowd—eight or ten usually—gathers together and agrees to an eat-and-drink party. It may be necessary for a ranking member to take phone in hand and make a few initial calls. Some planning is needed, but the preliminary huddle around a cocktail table invariably turns into the kind of relaxed fun that the party itself always generates. Each host has the right to select his own course, lest the preliminary planning session turn into a gourmandial Great Debate as smoked salmon is voted or vetoed, Bibb lettuce sent back to the salad committee, or the main course filibustered into the night. Each host, of course, is responsible for one of the five acts in the dinner drama. The provider of the main course takes on a somewhat disproportionate share of work, but in this case the unequal share of the labor is one that is coveted by every devoted amateur chef who enjoys showing off.

Too many martinis have been known to seriously stall a progressive dinner at its very first port of call; so moderation in pursuit of the progressive dinner party is no vice. Let all those who have doubts about leaving a cozy apartment after the hors d'oeuvres be assured that the cold, bracing air will only make the *pièce de résistance* all the more irresistible. Appetites are worked up anew, and while the canapés may have been wonderful, the main course will be even more appetizing at the next way station. For long distances, a chauffeur-driven limousine is a worthwhile luxury. The host of each party segment should see to it that the troops leave his predecessor's within a reasonable amount of time and arrive at his own digs en masse. The old, hardened rule that the dinner and diner shall both be ready at the same time is here thrown overboard: Only the dinner waits. The acid test of a good host at a progressive dinner is doing so much in advance that he has practically nothing left to do when his guests arrive.

The host for each course is also the libation pourer for that course. Glassware for the cocktails should be prechilled, frosty cold. The champagne or white wine to be served with the main course should have been chilled beforehand, or the château red wine decanted if necessary. With the dessert and demitasse, brandy snifters or liqueur glasses or both should be within arm's reach. At the fourth anchorage, the highball host takes over. If ever a highball should be commandingly tall, it's late at night, during the witching hour, when thirsts are at their peak. The party reaches its happy apogee by the dawn's early light at breakfast headquarters, where vodka and gin, orange juice, tomato juice, and clam juice (a nifty addition to your bloody mary) should be ready alongside the bowl of eggs, the electric skillet, and the coffee-maker.

The Theater Party

Modern epicures have a perfect definition of theater: It's the interlude between the snack before and the supper afterward. The idea of pre-theater appeasement rather than a full trencherman's dinner bolted down in time to make the curtain gets a big hand from performers and audiences alike. And for generations the midnight supper *after* the show has been one of the most gracious of all ways to entertain.

If your theater party is to be really successful, you'll first pick a play cued to the tastes of your guests. You'll offer them the prologue of cocktails and the kind of food that takes the edge off their hunger but still lets them sit through Ionesco or Beckett with a clear head. Your potables should allow them to roll in the aisles with the play's fun rather than with the aftereffects of five martinis. And when the show's over, your party will taxi to the armchair comfort of your own hearth, where fine food and wine will help make a bomb tolerable and a superb play bewitching. In the fall and winter, there are all kinds of dialogues for fireplace suppers, but none more engaging than the chatter over cast, staging, sets, and story.

While one man can manage this kind of party, there are times when dual hosting works out best. The first producer gets the tickets and is responsible for the early snack and for taxi or limousine service. The second impresario hosts the leisurely after-theater supper and drink. The division of labor needn't follow these specifications to the letter, but it's the one we've found best for intimate theater parties of six to twelve people. If you belong to a theater-subscription club, members naturally take turns throughout the season in hosting the party.

Ironically, the scene of action that hangs up most hosts the first time they stage a two-act theater party isn't the sumptuous supper after the show but the small snack before. Bachelors in the land of plenty still seem to suffer from a pronounced phobia of not appeasing the belly slave that theoretically rules every civilized man about town. The question of how to allay the appetite without overwhelming it can be answered in very practical terms: Serve the first course of a dinner.

Would you normally offer cherrystone clams and an onion soup, a mulligatawny or a cheese fondue? Present any of these, and the first mouthful will assuage the pangs of hunger. Another delightful solution is the smørrebrød—or Danish open sandwiches—eaten with knife and fork. The toppings range from boneless sardines and sliced tomato to smoked cod liver with scrambled eggs, or raw chopped steak with onions and capers.

In planning your after-theater menu, the first rule is to avoid duplicating the party of the first part. If there were lobster cocktails beforehand, don't serve coquille of seafood to the captive crowd at midnight. Let your supper program fit the changed mood with dishes of substance such as chicken breasts in a cream sauce flavored with bourbon and sherry, or filet mignon garnished with mushrooms and artichoke bottoms and a red-wine sauce. Avoid avant-garde cookery, dishes that require elaborate carving, and food conversation pieces that try to steal the scene from the show itself. Last-minute preparation, even in your black tie, is perfectly feasible, provided all behind-the-scenes work has been put out of the way beforehand and your labors are limited to little more than simply sautéing and reheating of sauces.

Before the theater, those who want light cocktails will elect the negroni, vermouth cassis, or white-wine cassis. Cocktails on the rocks will appease those who want to make long drinks of short ones. When you return to your apartment after the theater, throw open the full resources of your bar. And for the final program note, what could possibly be better than a tray of liqueurs such as Chartreuse, Benedictine, or Grand Marnier poured over rocks or finely shaved ice?

The 12-to-12 Holiday Party

There are festive times round about the holiday season when you and other merrymakers wish the jollification could somehow last and last—that time could really be made to stand still. What we here propose as a means of accomplishing this miracle—or something close to it—is a twelve o'clock party, or, more precisely, a 12-to-12 one. The idea is this: Thanks to global time zones, it's midnight—or noon—somewhere in the world every hour on the hour. What you do as host to prolong the pleasure of the holiday is to follow the sun around the world, arresting time by celebrating twelve o'clock—wherever it may be—every hour on the hour for twelve hours. Practically speaking, you serve forth food and drink to your guests hourly, each offering reflecting the ethnic best of some part of the world where the hands of the clocks are pointing straight up. There's no set cocktail time, no set dining time. Your guests may nibble and swig as much or as little as they wish, when they wish, for as long as they wish, and the variety of victuals and potables you proffer will keep the most sylphlike birds and the huskiest trenchermen returning to your bar and buffet for renewed refreshment and high spirits from first arrival to last departure.

Sound like a hell of a lot of work for beleaguered hosts? Rest ye merry, gentlemen; the fun eclipses the toil, and preplanning precludes your being a kitchen slavey. Furthermore, the stopped-clock informality of your fête (the fact that your guests may drop in, drop out —and return as the holiday moves them) guarantees that your party participants, at any given moment, are *chez vous* because they want to be, not because they've accepted a time-binding invitation.

The wise way to invite friends to your party is to send out written invitations two or three weeks in advance. On each, list the dishes you'll be serving at the hour they're to be offered. By letting your guests know that there will be new manna from your kitchen every hour, your batting average for acceptances will come close to a thousand.

The best plan for most bachelors who've earned their own personal *cordon bleu* is to whip up a few of the thirteen courses that have won your friends' loudest bravissimos in the past and purchase the balance of the feast. Buy or prepare enough food for two-thirds the total number of guests invited. Hors d'oeuvre portions such as shrimp or pâté should be larger than normal. Chefs d'oeuvre, meats and poultry, should be smaller than normal. Leftovers can be converted into frozen assets.

To complete your preparations, bedeck the table with candles, flowers or centerpieces, and a fruit bowl or basket. Food plates should be no larger than salad-size. Provide the largest possible stockpile of forks and, at midnight, enough fondue forks for all present. Napkins should be amassed at the buffet table and other strategic spots throughout the apartment. There should be trays of assorted small, split, buttered rolls or small bread-and-butter sandwiches, allowing one and a half servings per guest. Store most of the bread and rolls, covered with moistened towels, in the refrigerator. You'll want to hire three helpers or recruit some of your friends—one who will act as custodian of the punch bowls, bar, and buffet table; the others to take care of cooking and cleanup.

At 12 noon you should start the buffet with something like a cold glazed ham, a potato-and-apple salad flavored with calvados, and a chafing-dish specialty such as wild rice and mushrooms. These standbys should be kept available through the whole party, replenished and refreshed from time to time, to be enjoyed for themselves or combined with subsequent courses.

Among foods which make their hourly appearance, and which you can buy in one grand taxi circuit, are: gnocchi, the Italian dumplings, with Parmesan cheese from your favorite trattoria; *pâté maison*; quiche Lorraine, warmed just before serving; cooked, shelled, deveined shrimp on a platter with Russian dressing and cocktail sauce; cold smoked turkey, sliced thin but not transparent; Chinese roast duck and roast pork; beef *bourguignon*; beef stroganoff; cheese fondue all ready for the chafing dish; curry of chicken from Indian and many American restaurants; a caviar platter of fresh beluga and red-salmon caviar, supplemented with a sturgeon-and-radish salad with sour cream.

Courses that might be prepared at your own range could include: whole fillet of beef, roasted in a very hot oven for thirty to forty minutes; thick shell steaks, broiled, sliced crosswise, and served on toast or buns; crab meat *diavolo*, cooked in a brandy-flavored, unstrained tomato sauce; sausages, small links browned in the oven and then simmered in a brown sauce with white wine.

For the bar, provide a fish-house punch (page 424) and a champagne punch (page 422) and/or the standard ingredients for hard drinks, as well as assorted light and dark beers.

A Wine-Tasting Party

There's no reason in the world why a party-bent host couldn't throw a whiskey-tasting party or a rum-tasting party or even a vodka-tasting party, since vodka, along with everything else that enters the mouth, *does* leave a taste impression. But it's doubtful if any of these hypothetical events could whip up the fun, the wild, hilarious prattle, the endless sippings and soundings off, the mellow feeling of having become well versed bacchanalogically, and the pleasant afterglow that are the natural result of every wine-tasting party.

Note if you will the happy judicial grin of people arriving at a wine-tasting party, each guest knowing that he holds the scales of judgment in his own mouth. There are, of course, self-conscious and sometimes pretentious wine drinkers—especially in England and America—who look upon a wine-tasting session as a court trial. (Some French and German wine promoters encourage this kind of mumbo jumbo in the interests of foreign trade.) The trial hopefully tests the sipper's ability to agree with the price of the wine. But let the host in any blind wine tasting pour his treasured Piesporter *Trockenbeerenauslese* 1959 costing $28 a bottle, and if the wine creates no more excitement than a Bernkasteler Doktor costing $7 a bottle—as may well happen—the host, if not his guests, learns that a wine costing four times the price of another wine doesn't necessarily multiply the pleasure by four. The price of wine, like other things, depends on its supply and the thirsty demand for it. In a blind wine tasting, the mouth sees no dollar signs. For instance, there are home-grown grapes in Italy and in this country which are pressed into home-made wines, and the pleasure they generate can't possibly be expressed in lire or dollars.

From a practical standpoint, wine tasting not only serves party purposes well but gives the host the chance to test candidates for his own cellar. In setting the sights for your party, invite those friends who don't mind forsaking hard liquor for the pleasures of the noble grape, and shun the sort of man whose concept of Nirvana is a half-dozen martinis in a row. Eight to twelve guests is a good number for a wine-tasting party. More than a dozen tends to cloud the issue and befuddle the tasting. Invite as many people as you'd normally ask to a buffet supper, since a supper normally follows a private wine tasting in a studio or apartment.

The best time for a wine-tasting party is sundown. At that time the taste apparatus will be at its keenest—freed from the cantankerousness of the breakfast table and fully recovered from every trace of lunch fatigue. Don't serve the elaborate assortment of hot and cold hors d'oeuvres that normally goes with cocktails at this hour. Provide instead, in modest quantities, breadsticks, unbuttered slices of thin French bread or whole-wheat Italian bread, soy crackers, and small wedges of mildly aged hard cheese such as Edam or cheddar. Avoid rich, pungent cheeses such as Gorgonzola which stick to the palate.

Provide pitchers of cold water. In other words, offer palate-clearing rather than palate-stultifying items: the kind of food that will clean the taste between sips of different wines and tempt the guest to sip and sample more.

For your first wine-tasting party, you may have to buy or rent glassware. If you've invited eight people, you should have at least thirty-two stemmed wineglasses so that guests can compare three or four wines at one tasting. They should be tulip-shaped with a minimum 8-ounce capacity, preferably larger. At a champagne-tasting party, glasses should again be tulip-shaped rather than the common saucer-shaped glasses, to conserve bubbles as well as bouquet. For red or white table wines, round-bellied Burgundy glasses serve well, permitting comfortable nosing. For sherries, Madeiras, or ports, the smaller dock glass is preferable. Glasses should be thin, crystal-clear, without the ropelike edge of glasses designed to prevent nicking.

At wine tastings in public eating places, a battery of four glasses is usually placed before each judge. When the four have been used, the contents of the glasses, if any, are then dumped into a container on the table. The glasses are sometimes rinsed at the table, readied for a second tasting. It's reminiscent of the rough-and-ready brass-spittoon era. In your own digs, an infinitely more gracious way is to hire a kitchen helper, if you need one, for washing glasses between tastings. He or she can later help with the buffet supper and cleanup.

In selecting wines for a tasting party, you can range from spicy apéritif wines through red and white table wines, rosés, and sparkling wines, on to the sweetest cream sherries, vintage ports, and Madeiras. But when your party becomes a jack-of-all-wines, it often leaves your guests feeling like masters of none. Infinitely more fun is to cover one or two segments of the huge wine scene with a selective sampling of the most interesting bottlings you can find.

Discuss your plans with your wine merchant—assuming you've found a reliable one who really knows his wines and isn't just another neighborhood dispenser of package goods. Choose new wines you're curious about as well as some you've already tried. You might have to visit the shelves of several stores to get three different Cabernet Sauvignons or three tawny ports. The wines to be judged should be both alike and different. One wouldn't compare a sweet Hungarian Tokay and a sweet Marsala. But one definitely would compare a French Sauternes with a California made from the same grapes. As a general guideline, you can select for party tastings:

Wines of the same grape: Rieslings from the Alsace, Germany, and California, and perhaps the Rieslings now being bottled in New York State, made from European grapes grown in an eastern state.

Wines of the same region: French red Graves and French Médocs.

Nonvintage wines versus vintage wines, assuming the latter aren't too hoary with age.

The same wines of different vintages: 1971s, say, versus 1975s.

Wines of similar processing: French versus California champagnes, or German *Sekts* versus Italian Asti spumantes.

Before the party starts, be sure that red table wines are at room temperature, not higher than 70°F. (Some people like reds at a cellar temperature—about 60°F.) Beaujolais, rosés, and sherries are often served chilled. White table wines and white dessert wines, as well as champagne or other sparkling wines, should be chilled to about 40° to 50°F. Place them in the refrigerator for one to two hours, or chill them in a champagne bucket with ice for fifteen minutes to a half-hour. Old vintage reds or vintage ports should be decanted if necessary.

Set up a rectangular or square table with a snowy white cloth. Space bottles between glasses or on a large lazy Susan. Wines should be uncorked, and corks placed beside the bottles for those wishing to inspect them. The corks should smell of wine, not cork. Naturally, any wine that might have been spoiled because of a defective cork—a very rare occurrence—wouldn't be on the table for sampling.

If your wine tasting is to be blind, then all bottles should be covered with paper bags, each numbered for refills and later identification. At home, the hide-and-seek game of a blind wine tasting may be fun if it doesn't make the guests feel that *they* rather than the wines are being judged. By exposing the labels in an open wine tasting, guests guide themselves from one pleasure to the next rather than engage in the mumbo jumbo of identification. For some people, it may be interesting to be seated in a Porsche racer blindfolded and driven around town to test the car's riding qualities; for others it's much more instructive to see and feel what's going on.

Don't worry about unfinished bottles as a result of your wine-tasting party. Recork them or empty them into decanters. Keep them chilled until served at another time. Some may be used for cooking. Naturally, once any bottle of wine is opened and the wine is exposed to the air, something of its original glamour evaporates. There are sherry experts who will always insist on opening a fresh bottle for tasting purposes. But sherry and other fortified wines can, in fact, last for weeks or months on the shelf after being opened.

Finally, when the tasting is completed and second-guessers as well as Monday-morning quarterbacks have had their say, the wine-tasting party may end or may continue with buffet food or a sit-down dinner, along with the wine that the host selects as *his* prize specimen. There's a whale of a difference between tasting wine alone and tasting it with meat or seafood. A soft white Burgundy, for instance, like a Meursault, will be both velvety and nutty in its flavor impressions. But the same wine later with a roast stuffed duckling or a dish of terrapin will be remembered for its odd, romping dryness. The quality of any wine is a marriage of the human palate and a subtle combination of alcohol, pigments, aromas, bouquets, acids, tannins, sugars, and countless other components that Bacchus himself couldn't name. When food is added, the list of components grows. The fact that they're seemingly infinite and infinitely arguable simply means that a wine-tasting party can never be dull. The more differences, the more opinionated the re-actions, the merrier.

Wine-and-Cheese Party

In spite of Fitzgerald's poem, a jug of wine, a loaf of bread, and thou aren't quite Paradise enow. You also need cheese. At any wine-tasting party there's usually some kind of hard cheese like Edam or cheddar, which, for tasting purposes, can be used like a pencil eraser: A little swipe of the cheese in your mouth causes the aftertaste of the previous wine to vanish so that you can go on and render monumental judgment on the next wine.

A wine-and-cheese party, by contrast with a wine-*tasting* party, isn't a quiz at all. You're not there to play blind wineman's bluff, you're there simply to gratify your palate. It's the ideal party for hosts who don't have the time to work at entertaining. One or several wines and several cheeses or a large platter of assorted cheeses are assembled, and these are the main components of your party. You can schedule your wine-and-cheese party at sundown—it's a pleasant diversion at the cocktail hour for gin-jaded drinkers—or it can be planned for after dinner, when sweet wines like the late-picked Rieslings or cream sherries or ports may be opened for postprandial fun. At a midnight after-theater party, a few bottles of Gewürztraminer and a ripe Port du Salut cheese will set a mellow conversational mood.

It's best to allow from one-third to one-half bottle of wine per person, and plan on a quarter-pound of cheese per person. If you offer more than one wine, they may be wines of completely different types—like an amontillado sherry and a California dry Sauvignon Blanc, or a California sparkling Gamay Beaujolais and a rich Marsala from Italy. Cheeses also should be varied, and may include soft, semisoft, and hard varieties. Don't fall into the trap of trying to match cheeses to wines; they're not meant to match like socks and shoes but to provide polarity. You simply want excellent specimens of each. If there's a cheese specialty shop in your area, explore it for domestic and imported varieties. If it's the kind of shop where stock moves rapidly, don't be afraid to try cheeses that are not normally in your larder—like Welsh Caerphilly, Belgian Limburger, American coon cheese, Greek casseri or English Stilton. Remember, though, that cheeses vary in flavor throughout the year, and a fine cheese that is insufficiently ripe should be avoided if you're going to serve it the same day. If possible, sample any cheese about which you may have a doubt.

Besides wine and cheese, you'll want a variety of breads and crackers. Crackers should be the crisp type made with as little shortening as possible, such as the English water crackers or others of this kind often available in cheese shops. Melba toast rounds are good, but make sure they're fresh. The best bread is the long, narrow French bread called a flute. If it's unavailable, the regular long French or Italian bread, well baked with a deep crust if possible, may be sliced and then cut in halves or quarters for easy handling. There should be at least one kind of dark bread like thinly sliced pumpernickel or other dark whole-grained bread.

An hour before partytime, take the cheeses out of the refrigerator, since their flavor is best at room temperature. Finally, set out your glasses, cheese, wine, and breadbasket on a dining table, rather than a cocktail table, so that guests don't have to fight their way to reach the island of wine and cheese, and can comfortably return for continued pouring, sipping, and munching.

INDEX

This index is designed to guide the reader to specific categories of wines and spirits.

Mixed drinks are indexed under *all* their alcoholic ingredients, whether they are major flavors or fillips.

Student Quick Tips

Use this Student Quick Tips guide for a quick and easy start with McGraw-Hill Connect. You'll get valuable tips on registering, doing assignments, and accessing resources, as well as information about the support center hours.

Getting Started

TIP: To get started in Connect, you will need the following:

- Your instructor's Connect Web Address

> Sample of Connect Web Address:
>
> http://www.mcgrawhillconnect.com/class/instructorname_section_name

- Connect Access Code

TIP: If you do not have an access code or have not yet secured your tuition funds, you can click "Free Trial" during registration. This trial will provide temporary Connect access (typically three weeks) and will remind you to purchase online access before the end of your trial.

Registration and Sign In

1. Go to the Connect Web Address provided by your instructor
2. Click on **Register Now**
3. Enter your email address

TIP: If you already have a McGraw-Hill account, you will be asked for your password and will not be required to create a new account.

4. Enter a registration code or choose **Buy Online** to purchase access online

(Continued: **Registration and Sign In**)

5. Follow the on-screen directions

TIP: Please choose your Security Question and Answer carefully. We will ask you for this information if you forget your password.

6. When registration is complete, click on **Go to Connect Now**

7. You are now ready to use **Connect**

Trouble Logging In?

- Ensure you are using the same email address you used during registration

- If you have forgotten your password, click on the "Forgot Password?" link at your Instructor's Connect Course Web Address

- When logged into Connect, you can update your account information (e.g. email address, password, and security question/answer) by clicking on the *"My Account"* link located at the top-right corner

Home (Assignments)

TIP: If you are unable to begin an assignment, verify the following:

- The assignment is available (start and due dates)

- That you have not exceeded the maximum number of attempts

- That you have not achieved a score of 100%

- If your assignment contains questions that require manual grading, you will not be able to begin your next attempt until your instructor has graded those questions

(Continued: **Home Assignments**)

TIP: Based on the assignment policy settings established by your Instructor, you may encounter the following limitations when working on your assignment(s):

* Ability to Print Assignment

* Timed assignments – once you begin a "*timed assignment*," the timer will not stop by design

TIP: "*Save & Exit*" vs. "*Submit*" button

* If you are unable to complete your assignment in one sitting, utilize the "*Save & Exit*" button to save your work and complete it at a later time

* Once you have completed your assignment, utilize the "*Submit*" button in order for your assignment to be graded

Library

TIP: The *Library* section of your Connect account provides shortcuts to various resources.

* If you purchased ConnectPlus, you will see an *eBook* link, which can also be accessed from the section information widget of the *Home* tab

* *Recorded Lectures* can be accessed if your instructor is using *Tegrity Campus* to capture lectures. You may also access recorded lectures when taking an assignment by clicking on the projector icon in the navigation bar

* Many McGraw-Hill textbooks offer additional resources such as narrated slides and additional problems, which are accessible through the *Student Resources* link

Reports

TIP: Once you submit your assignment, you can view your available results in the *Reports* tab.

* If you see a dash (-) as your score, your instructor has either delayed or restricted your ability to see the assignment feedback

* Your instructor has the ability to limit the amount of information (e.g. questions, answers, scores) you can view for each submitted assignment

Need More Help?

CONTACT US ONLINE

Visit us at:

www.mcgrawhillconnect.com/support

Browse our support materials including tutorial videos and our searchable Connect knowledge base. If you cannot find an answer to your question, click on "Contact Us" button to send us an email.

GIVE US A CALL

Call us at:

1-800-331-5094

Our live support is available:

Mon-Thurs:	8 am – 11 pm CT
Friday:	8 am – 6 pm CT
Sunday:	6 pm – 11 pm CT

Contemporary Management

Eighth Edition

Gareth R. Jones

Jennifer M. George
Jesse H. Jones Graduate School of Business
Rice University

BADM 310
Management

Special Edition for University of Illinois

Mc Graw Hill Education

4 5 6 7 8 9 0 CCI CCI 15

ISBN-13: 978-1-259-16411-8
ISBN-10: 1-259-16411-X

Learning Solutions Consultant: Bridget Hannenberg
Associate Project Manager: Kaitlin Weig
Cover Photo Credits: AA039353.jpg © Photodisc/Punchstock

BRIEF CONTENTS

CONTENTS

Chapter 3

Values, Attitudes, Emotions, and Culture: The Manager as a Person   64

A MANAGER'S CHALLENGE

Kevin Plank's Determination Pays Off at Under Armour 65

Topics

Chapter 4

Ethics and Social Responsibility   98

A MANAGER'S CHALLENGE

Apple and Foxconn Protect Its Products and the Workers Who Make Them 99

Topics

Chapter 5

Managing Diverse Employees in a Multicultural Environment

A MANAGER'S CHALLENGE

Sodexo and Principal Financial Group Effectively Manage Diversity in Multiple Ways 133

Topics

Chapter 6

Managing in the Global Environment

A MANAGER'S CHALLENGE

Nokia Flips Its Approach to Managing the Global Environment 165

Topics

Management in Action

Examples

Management in Action

Chapter 7

Decision Making, Learning, Creativity, and Entrepreneurship

194

A MANAGER'S CHALLENGE

Decision Making and Learning Are the Keys to Entrepreneurial Success 195

Topics

Chapter 8

The Manager as a Planner and Strategist

226

A MANAGER'S CHALLENGE

Groupon's Strategy to Become the Leader in the Online Coupon Market 227

Topics

Examples

Management in Action

Examples

Management in Action

Chapter 11

Organizational Control and Change

A MANAGER'S CHALLENGE

United Technologies Has an "ACE" Up Its Sleeve 333

Topics

Chapter 12

Human Resource Management

A MANAGER'S CHALLENGE

Happy Employees Provide Exceptional Service at Zappos 367

Topics

Chapter 13   Motivation and Performance   402

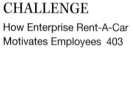

A MANAGER'S CHALLENGE

How Enterprise Rent-A-Car Motivates Employees 403

Topics

Chapter 14   Leadership   432

A MANAGER'S CHALLENGE

Doreen Lorenzo Leads Frog Design 433

Topics

Chapter 15   Effective Groups and Teams

A MANAGER'S CHALLENGE

Teams Innovate at Boeing 465

Topics

Chapter 16   Promoting Effective Communication

A MANAGER'S CHALLENGE

Fostering Effective Communication and Collaboration at Salesforce.com 497

Topics

Examples

Management in Action

Examples

Management in Action

PREFACE

Since the seventh edition of *Contemporary Management* was published, our book has strengthened its position as a leader in the management market. This tells us that we continue to meet the expectations of our existing users and attract many new users to our book. It is clear that most management instructors share with us a concern for the need to continuously introduce new and emerging issues into the text and its examples to ensure that cutting-edge issues and new developments in the field of contemporary global management are addressed.

In the new eighth edition of *Contemporary Management,* we continue with our mission to provide students the most current and up-to-date account of the changes taking place in the world of business management. The fast-changing domestic and global environment continues to pressure organizations and their managers to find new and improved ways to respond to changing events in order to maintain and increase their performance. Today, increases in the fortunes of global leaders such as Apple, Samsung, and Google and the challenges facing some of their competitors such as Nokia, Dell, and Microsoft show how fast the success and even survival of companies can change. In particular, the continuing global recession as well as the increasing complexity of the exchanges between global companies has profoundly affected the management of both large and small organizations. Today, there is increased pressure on managers to find new management practices that can increase their companies' efficiency and effectiveness and ability to survive and prosper in an increasingly competitive global environment.

In revising our book, we continue our focus on making our text relevant and interesting to students—something that we know from instructor and student feedback engages them and encourages them to make the effort necessary to assimilate the text material. We continue to mirror the changes taking place in management practices by incorporating recent developments in management theory and research into our text and by providing vivid, current examples of how managers of companies large and small have responded to the changes taking place. Indeed, we have made the way managers and organizations have responded to recent global economic events a focus of the new edition, and following the last edition many more examples of the opportunities and challenges facing founders, managers, and employees in a variety of types of organizations are integrated into the text.

The number and complexity of the strategic, organizational, and human resource challenges facing managers and all employees has continued to increase throughout the 2000s. In most companies, managers at all levels are playing catch-up as they work toward meeting these challenges by implementing new and improved management techniques and practices. Today relatively small differences in performance between companies, such as in the speed at which they can bring new products or services to market or in how they motivate their employees to find ways to reduce costs or improve performance, can combine to give one company a significant competitive advantage over another. Managers and companies that use proven management techniques and practices in their decision making and actions increase their effectiveness over time. Companies and managers that are slower to implement new management techniques and practices find themselves at a growing competitive disadvantage that makes it even more difficult to catch up. Thus many industries have widening gaps between weaker competitors and the most successful companies, whose performance reaches new heights because their managers have made better decisions about how to use a company's resources in the most efficient and effective ways.

The challenges facing managers continue to mount as changes in the global environment, such as increasing global outsourcing and rising commodity prices, impact organizations large and small. In the eighth edition, we extend our treatment of global outsourcing and examine the many managerial issues that must be addressed when millions of functional jobs in information technology, customer service, and manufacturing are sent to countries overseas. Similarly, increasing globalization means managers must respond to major differences in the legal rules and regulations and ethical values and norms that prevail in countries around the globe. Many companies and their managers, for example, have been accused of ignoring "sweatshop" working conditions under which the products they sell are manufactured abroad.

Moreover, the revolution in information technology (IT) has transformed how managers make decisions across all levels of a company's hierarchy and across all its functions and global divisions. The eighth edition of our book continues to address these ongoing challenges as IT continues to evolve rapidly, especially in the area of mobile digital devices such as smartphones and tablet computers that can access ever more sophisticated software applications that increase their functionality. Other major challenges we continue to expand on in the new edition include the impact of the steadily increasing diversity of the workforce on companies, and how this increasing diversity makes it imperative for managers to understand how and why people differ so they can effectively manage and reap the performance benefits of diversity. Similarly, across all functions and levels, managers and employees must continuously search out ways to "work smarter" and increase performance. Using new IT to improve all aspects of an organization's operations to boost efficiency and customer responsiveness is a vital part of this process. So too is the continuing need to innovate and improve the quality of goods and services, and the ways they are produced, to allow an organization to compete effectively. We have significantly revised the eighth edition of *Contemporary Management* to address these challenges to managers and their organizations.

Major Content Changes

Once again, encouraged by the increasing number of instructors and students who use each new edition of our book, and based on the reactions and suggestions of both users and reviewers, we have revised and updated our book in the following ways. First, just as we have included pertinent new research concepts in each chapter, so too have we been careful to eliminate outdated or marginal management concepts. As usual, our goal has been to streamline our presentation and keep the focus on the changes that have been taking place that have the most impact on managers and organizations. Our goal is to avoid presenting students with excessive content in too many and too long chapters just for the sake of including outmoded management theory. In today's world of instant sound bites, video uploading, text messaging, and tweets, providing the best content is much more important than providing excessive content—especially when some of our students are burdened by time pressures stemming from the need to work long hours at paying jobs and fulfilling personal commitments and obligations.

Second, we have added significant new management content and have reinforced its importance by using many new relevant small and large company examples that are described in the chapter opening cases titled "A Manager's Challenge"; in the many boxed examples featuring managers and employees in companies both large and small in each chapter; and in the new (from 2011 and 2012) "Case in the News" closing cases.

Chapter 1, for example, contains new and updated material on the way changes in IT and the products and services that result from it are affecting competition among companies. The chapter includes a new opening case about the way Tim Cook, Apple's new CEO is changing the way Apple is managed, and how his approach to the four functions of management differs from that adopted by Steve Jobs. It also contains a new discussion of insourcing, as opposed to outsourcing, and why some companies are bringing jobs back to the United States from abroad to increase performance. It also includes coverage of ethics and social responsibility using examples from the not-for-profit sphere. In addition, an expanded discussion about global crisis management is provided including an update on the consequences arising from the way BP handled the 2010 explosion of its Deepwater Horizon drilling rig that resulted in a huge oil spill in the Gulf of Mexico. Chapter 2 has updated coverage of changing manufacturing practices in the carmaking industry and of the way traditional management theories, such as Theory X and Theory Y, have been modified to suit changing work conditions today.

Chapter 3 updates material about the manager as a person and the way personal characteristics of managers (and all members of an organization) influence organizational culture and effectiveness. There is also new in-text discussion of why job satisfaction was at a record low in the United States during the recent recession and which factors employees and groups were most dissatisfied with. Also included is a discussion of how emotions can be triggers for change in organizations and a new "Management Insight" box on the factors that can affect this and their consequences.

Public concern over the ethical behavior of managers has continued to increase as a result of the major problems caused by the financial crisis that began in 2008. Chapter 4, "Ethics and Social Responsibility," provides updated material about the unethical and illegal behaviors of managers that helped to produce the crises in the banking and financial services industry including the many fund managers who engaged in insider trading. It also examines how regulators are striving to find new and better ways to reduce the likelihood of such unethical behavior in the future. We have expanded our coverage of the many issues involved in acting and managing ethically throughout the book. And Chapter 4 also examines the behavior of Apple towards its stakeholders as it became one of the world's most valuable companies. We also discuss new issues in ethics and ethical dilemmas and provide more conceptual tools to help students understand better how to make ethical decisions. We continue to highlight issues related to the high pay of CEOs, issues concerning regulations to protect consumer safety, and the problems caused by bribery and corruption in companies at home and overseas. Finally, we have expanded coverage of the ethics of nonprofits and their managers as well as how formerly ethical companies, such as Johnson & Johnson, began to behave in unethical ways in order to boost their returns to shareholders and benefit their managers. The ethical exercise at the end of every chapter continues to be a popular feature of our book.

Chapter 5, "Managing Diverse Employees in a Multicultural Environment," focuses on the effective management of the many faces of diversity in organizations for the good of all stakeholders. We have updated and expanded the text material and examples for such issues as age, gender, race and ethnicity, socioeconomic background, disabilities, and sexual orientation. We also discuss ways to effectively manage diversity and include an updated discussion of women's earnings in comparison to men's earnings. Methods to prevent discrimination and sexual harassment in an era when many companies face discrimination lawsuits involving hundreds of millions of dollars are also considered. The chapter provides expanded coverage on the way managers can take advantage of the increasing diversity of the population and workforce to reap the performance benefits that stem from diversity while ensuring that all employees are treated fairly and are not discriminated against.

Chapter 6 contains an integrated account of forces in both the domestic and global environments. It has also been revised and updated to reflect the way increasing global competition and free trade have changed the global value creation process. The chapter includes an updated account of competition in the global electronics industry, for example, among smartphone providers Apple, Samsung, and Nokia, and flatscreen TV and computer makers such as Sony, Dell, and Sharp to illustrate these issues. The chapter also has expanded discussion of issues related to global outsourcing and of the movement to insource production back to the United States as well as to find ways for companies to become powerful suppliers to emerging leading global companies in Korea and China. Finally, it continues to update the treatment of the changing dynamics of global competition—particularly in relation to how newly dominant global companies have developed successful new strategies to customize products to the tastes of customers in countries abroad.

Chapter 7, "Decision Making, Learning, Creativity, and Entrepreneurship," discusses new developments on these important issues. For example, we include a new discussion of the position of chief sustainability officer and examine how managers can make decisions to help ensure decisions contribute to sustainability. Also, we continue our discussion of social entrepreneurs who seek creative ways to address social problems to improve well-being by, for example, reducing poverty, increasing literacy, and protecting the natural environment. More generally, we discuss how managers in organizations large and small can improve decision making, learning, and creativity in their organizations. For example, we discuss ways of curbing overconfidence in decision making and how to use contests and rewards to encourage creativity and give examples of companies that use them.

As in the last edition, Chapter 8 focuses on corporate-, global-, and business-level strategies, and Chapter 9 discusses functional strategies for managing value chain activities. These two chapters make clear the links between the different levels of strategy while maintaining a strong focus on managing operations and processes. Chapter 8 contains a revised discussion of planning and levels of strategy with an increased focus on how companies can use vertical integration and related diversification to increase long-term profitability. It also includes a revised treatment of business-level strategy that focuses on the importance of low-cost strategies in a world in which the prices of many products are falling or under pressure because of recession, increased global competition, or because new dot-coms such as Zynga and Groupon find new strategies to reach customers more cost effectively. In Chapter 9 we continue to explore how companies can develop new functional-level strategies

to improve efficiency, quality, innovation, and responsiveness to customers. For example, beyond increased coverage of TQM, including the Six Sigma approach, we include an expanded discussion of the importance of customer relationship management and the need to retain customers during hard economic times. We focus on the ways Internet startups and dot-coms such as Zynga, Groupon, and Dropbox have developed new functional strategies.

Chapters 10 and 11 offer updated coverage of organizational structure and control and discuss how companies have confronted the need to reorganize their hierarchies and ways of doing business as the environment changes and competition increases. In Chapter 10, for example, we discuss how companies such as UPS, Walmart and Pier 1 have reorganized to improve their domestic performance. We also discuss how Nokia has been forced to reorganize its global operating structure to slow down its declining performance and avoid bankruptcy. Because of hard economic times, we give an increased discussion of how to design global organizational structure and culture to improve performance—and we focus on the experience of Japanese companies such as Toyota. In Chapter 11 we continue this theme by looking at how companies are changing their control systems to increase efficiency and quality, for example. More generally, how to use control systems to increase quality is a theme throughout the chapter.

We have updated and expanded our treatment of the many ways in which managers can effectively manage and lead employees in their companies. For example, Chapter 12 includes an updated discussion of how treating employees well can lead to exceptional customer service. The chapter also discusses best practices to recruit and attract outstanding employees, the importance of training and development, pay differentials, and family-friendly benefit programs. In addition, there is an updated and revised text discussion of the use of background checks by employers, the use of forced ranking systems in organizations, and issues concerning excessive CEO pay and pay comparisons between CEOs and average workers and statistics on U.S. union membership. Chapter 13 continues coverage of prosocially motivated behavior including examples of people who are motivated to benefit others. It also discusses the many steps managers can take to create a highly motivated workforce and how advances in IT have dramatically simplified the administration of piece-rate pay systems.

Chapter 14 highlights the critical importance of effective leadership in organizations and factors that contribute to managers being effective leaders, including an updated discussion of servant leadership. There is a new discussion of how managers with expert power need to recognize that they are not always right. The chapter also discusses how emotional intelligence may help leaders respond appropriately when they realize they have made a mistake, and it gives updated examples of how they can use reward and expert power to increase motivation and performance.

Expanded and updated coverage of the effective management of teams, including virtual teams, is provided in Chapter 15. The chapter also has coverage of the problems that arise because of a lack of leadership in teams.

Chapter 16 includes updated coverage of effective communication and how, given the multitude of advances in IT, it is important to create opportunities for face-to-face communication. There is also updated and revised information on the ethics of monitoring e-mail and Internet use, including statistics on increased Internet use in the United States. Finally, there is increased discussion of social networking sites and why some managers attempt to limit employees' access to them while at work. Chapter 17 includes an updated discussion of the vital task of effectively managing conflict and politics in organizations and how to negotiate effectively on a global level. There are many new examples of how managers can create a collaborative work context and avoid competition between individuals and groups.

Lastly, Chapter 18 has once again been substantially revised and updated to discuss the changing nature of companywide total computing solutions—including a new opening case that discusses the growing importance of cloud computing for Microsoft. There is also an expanded discussion of the nature of bricks & mortar and mobile server computers and how "server farms" can be used to connect to mobile digital devices such as tablet computers and smartphones to enhance competitive advantage. Recent developments in mobile and tablet computing and their many uses in global communication and coordination are also a focus of discussion—as is the growing competition between global IT suppliers.

We feel confident that the major changes we have made to the eighth edition of *Contemporary Management* reflect the changes that are occurring in management and the workplace; we also believe they offer an account of management that will stimulate and challenge students to think about their future as they look for opportunities in the world of organizations.

Unique Emphasis on Contemporary, Applied Management

In revising our book, we have kept at the forefront the fact that our users and reviewers are supportive of our attempts to integrate contemporary management theories and issues into the analysis of management and organizations. As in previous editions, our goal has been to distill new and classic theorizing and research into a contemporary framework that is compatible with the traditional focus on management as planning, leading, organizing, and controlling but that transcends this traditional approach.

Users and reviewers report that students appreciate and enjoy our presentation of management—a presentation that makes its relevance obvious even to those who lack exposure to a real-life management context. Students like the book's content and the way we relate management theory to real-life examples to drive home the message that management matters both because it determines how well organizations perform and because managers and organizations affect the lives of people inside and outside the organization, such as employees, customers, and shareholders.

Our contemporary approach has led us to discuss many concepts and issues that are not addressed in other management textbooks and it is illustrated by the way we organize and discuss these management issues. We have gone to great lengths to bring the manager back into the subject matter of management. That is, we have written our chapters from the perspective of current or future managers to illustrate, in a hands-on way, the problems and opportunities they face and how they can effectively meet them. For example, in Chapter 3 we provide an integrated treatment of personality, attitudes, emotions, and culture; in Chapter 4, a focus on ethics from a student's and a manager's perspective; and in Chapter 5, an in-depth treatment of effectively managing diversity and eradicating sexual harassment. In Chapters 8 and 9, our integrated treatment of strategy highlights the multitude of decisions managers must make as they perform their most important role—increasing organizational efficiency, effectiveness, and performance.

Our applied approach can also be clearly seen in the last three chapters of the book, which cover the topics of promoting effective communication; managing organizational conflict, politics, and negotiation; and using information technology in ways that increase organizational performance. These chapters provide a student-friendly, behavioral approach to understanding the management issues entailed in persuasive communication, negotiation, and implementation of advanced information systems to build competitive advantage.

Flexible Organization

Another factor of interest to instructors is how we have designed the grouping of chapters to allow instructors to teach the chapter material in the order that best suits their needs. For example, the more micro-oriented instructor can follow Chapters 1 through 5 with Chapters 12 through 16 and then use the more macro chapters. The more macro-oriented professor can follow Chapters 1 and 2 with Chapters 6 through 11, jump to 16 through 18, and then use the micro chapters, 3 through 5 and 12 through 15. Our sequencing of parts and chapters gives instructors considerable freedom to design the course that best suits their needs. Instructors are not tied to the planning, organizing, leading, and controlling framework, even though our presentation remains consistent with this approach.

ACKNOWLEDGMENTS

Finding a way to integrate and present the rapidly growing literature about contemporary management and make it interesting and meaningful for students is not an easy task. In writing and revising the various drafts of *Contemporary Management,* we have been fortunate to have the assistance of several people who have contributed greatly to the book's final form. First, we are grateful to Michael Ablassmeir, our senior sponsoring editor, for his ongoing support and commitment to our project and for always finding ways to provide the resources that we needed to continually improve and refine our book. Second, we are grateful to Trina Hauger, our developmental editor, for so ably coordinating the book's progress; and to her and Elizabeth Trepkowski, our senior marketing manager, for giving us concise and timely feedback and information from professors and reviewers that have allowed us to shape the book to the needs of its intended market. We also thank Cara Hawthorne for executing an awe-inspiring design; Bruce Gin for coordinating the production process; Margaret Richardson de Sosa (Rice University) and Patsy Hartmangruber (Texas A&M University) for providing excellent word-processing and graphic support; and Iliya Atanasov (Rice University) for his assistance with research. We are also grateful to the many colleagues and reviewers who gave us useful and detailed feedback and perceptive comments and valuable suggestions for improving the manuscript.

Producing any competitive work is a challenge. Producing a truly market-driven textbook requires tremendous effort beyond simply obtaining reviews of a draft manuscript. Our goal was simple with the development of *Contemporary Management:* to be the most customer-driven principles of management text and supplement package ever published! With the goal of exceeding the expectations of both faculty and students, we executed one of the most aggressive product development plans ever undertaken in textbook publishing. Hundreds of faculty have taken part in developmental activities ranging from regional focus groups to manuscript and supplement reviews and surveys. Consequently, we're confident in assuring you and your students, our customers, that every aspect of our text and support package reflects your advice and needs. As you review it, we're confident that your reaction will be, "They listened!"

We extend our special thanks to the faculty who gave us detailed chapter-by-chapter feedback during the development of the eighth edition:

Professor Susan Blumen, Montgomery College Department of Business and Economics

Edwin L. Bowman, Principal, Manhattanville College, Purchase, NY

Reginald Bruce, College of Business, University of Louisville

Stewart W. Edwards, Northern VA Community College–Annandale

William Eichenauer Northwest State Community College

Bagher Fardanesh, Piaget Consulting

Jim Glasgow, Instructor, Villanova School of Business

Monica Godsey, PhD, University of Nebraska

Selina Griswold, The University of Toledo

Kathy Hastings, Greenville Technical College

Perry Hidalgo, Gwinnett Technical College

Gwendolyn Jones, The University of Akron

Susan Kowalewski, MBA, PhD, D'Youville College

Jane Murtaugh, College of DuPage

Nanci D. Newstrom, Eastern Illinois University

Dr. Michaeline Skiba, Monmouth University–Leon Hess Business School

Frederick J. Slack, Indiana University of Pennsylvania

Velvet Weems-Landingham, Kent State University

John Weiss, Associate Professor, Daytona State College

Elizabeth Wilson, Georgia Southwestern State University

And our thanks also go to the faculty who contributed greatly to the fourth, fifth, sixth, and seventh editions of *Contemporary Management:*

Jerry Alley, Aspen University

M. Ruhul Amin, Bloomsburg University of Pennsylvania

Gerald Baumgardner, Pennsylvania College of Technology

Charles W. Beem, Bucks County Community College

James D. Bell, Texas State University

Danielle R. Blesi, Hudson Valley Community College

Jennifer P. Bott, Ball State University

Charley Braun, Marshall University

Professor Murray Brunton, Central Ohio Technical College

Judith G. Bulin, PhD, Monroe Community College, Rochester, New York

Barry Bunn, Valencia Community College

Gerald Calvasina, Southern Utah University

Bruce H. Charnov, Hofstra University

Jay Christensen-Szalanski, University of Iowa

Cheryl Cunningham, Embry-Riddle Aeronautical University–Daytona Beach

Brad Cox, Midlands Technical College

Marian Cox Crawford, University of Arkansas–Little Rock

Teresa A. Daniel, Marshall University

Thomas W. Deckelman, Owens Community College

Tom Deckelman, Owens Community College

Richard S. DeFrank, University of Houston

Fred J. Dorn, University of Mississippi

D. Harold Doty, University of Southern Mississippi

Max E. Douglas, Indiana State University

Sandra Edwards, Northeastern State University

Scott Elston, Iowa State University

Richard Estrella, California Polytechnic University

Valerie Evans, Kansas State University

Andrea Foster, John Tyler Community College

Travis Lee Hayes, Chattanooga State Technical Community College

Samuel Hazen, Tarleton State University

Kim Hester, Arkansas State University

Anne Kelly Hoel, University of Wisconsin–Stout

Robert C. Hoell, Georgia Southern University

Irene Joanette-Gallio, Western Nevada College

Carol Larson Jones, Cal Poly Pomona, California

Gwendolyn Jones, University of Akron

Coy A. Jones, The University of Memphis

Kathleen Jones, University of North Dakota

Dr. Jordan J. Kaplan, Long Island University School of Business

Joanne E. Kapp, Siena College

Renee N. King, MBA, Eastern Illinois University

Mike Knudstrup, Florida Southern College

Jim Long, Southwestern Oklahoma State University

Margaret Lucero, Texas A&M–Corpus Christi

Nicholas Mathys, DePaul University

Daniel W. McAllister, University of Nevada–Las Vegas

Christy McLendon Corey, University of New Orleans

Chrisann Merriman, University of Mary Hardin–Baylor

Douglas L. Micklich, Illinois State University

Sandra Jeanquart Miles, DBA, SPHR, Professor, Murray State University

Carol T. Miller, Community College of Denver

Don C. Mosley Jr., University of South Alabama

Clive Muir, Stetson University

Bahaudin G. Mujtaba, Nova Southeastern University

Catherine Nowicki, International Business College

John Overby, The University of Tennessee at Martin

Karen Overton, Houston Community College

Professor K. E. Overton, Houston Community College, Houston, Texas

Fernando A. Pargas, James Madison University

Marc Pendel, SPHR, Instructor, Miller College of Business, Ball State University

Susan A. Peterson, Professor of Business, Scottsdale Community College

Gary Renz, Webster University

L. Jeff Seaton, University of Tennessee–Martin

Gregory J. Schultz, Carroll University

Marc Siegall, California State University–Chico

Fred Slack, Indiana University of Pennsylvania

Randi L. Sims, Professor, Nova Southeastern University

M. James Smas, Kent State University

Professor Gerald Smith, University of Northern Iowa

Marjorie Smith, Mountain State University

Dr. Susan D. Steiner, The University of Tampa

Cynthia L. Sutton, Metropolitan State College of Denver

Sabine Turnley, Kansas State University

Isaiah O. Ugboro, North Carolina A&T State University

Please note that these lists do not include the more than 160 faculty members who reviewed or contributed to earlier editions of the text.

Finally, we are grateful to two incredibly wonderful children, Nicholas and Julia, for being all that they are and for the joy they bring to all who know them.

Gareth R. Jones

Jennifer M. George
Jesse H. Jones Graduate School of Business
Rice University

Rich and Relevant Examples

An important feature of our book is the way we use real-world examples and stories about managers and companies to drive home the applied lessons to students. Our reviewers praised the sheer range and depth of the rich, interesting examples we use to illustrate the chapter material and make it come alive. Moreover, unlike boxed material in other books, our boxes are seamlessly integrated into the text; they are an integral part of the learning experience and are not tacked on or isolated from the text itself. This is central to our pedagogical approach.

A Manager's Challenge opens each chapter, posing a chapter-related challenge and then discussing how managers in one or more organizations responded to that challenge. These vignettes help demonstrate the uncertainty and excitement surrounding the management process.

Our box features are not traditional boxes; that is, they are not disembodied from the chapter narrative. These thematic applications are fully integrated into the reading. Students will no longer be forced to decide whether or not to read boxed material. These features are interesting and engaging for students while bringing the chapter contents to life.

Additional in-depth examples appear in boxes throughout each chapter. **Management Insight** boxes illustrate the topics of the chapter, while the **Ethics in Action, Managing Globally, Focus on Diversity, and Information Technology Byte** boxes examine the chapter topics from each of these perspectives.

Further emphasizing the unique content covered in Chapter 3, Values, Attitudes, Emotions, and Culture: The Manager as a Person, the **Manager as a Person** boxes focus on how real managers brought about change within their organizations. These examples allow us to reflect on how individual managers dealt with real-life, on-the-job challenges related to various chapter concepts.

Small Business Examples To ensure that students see the clear connections between the concepts taught in their Principles of Management course and the application in their future jobs in a medium or small business, Jones and George have included a number of examples of the opportunities and challenges facing founders, managers, and employees in small businesses.

Experiential Learning Features

We have given considerable time and effort to developing state-of-the-art experiential end-of-chapter learning exercises that drive home the meaning of management to students. These exercises are grouped together at the end of each chapter in a section called "Management in Action." The following activities are included at the end of every chapter:

- **Topics for Discussion and Action** are a set of chapter-related questions and points for reflection. Some ask students to research actual management issues and learn firsthand from practicing managers.

- **Building Management Skills** is a self-developed exercise that asks students to apply what they have learned from their own experience in organizations and from managers or from the experiences of others.

- **Managing Ethically** is an exercise that presents students with an ethical scenario or dilemma and asks them to think about the issue from an ethical perspective to better understand the issues facing practicing managers.

- **Small Group Breakout Exercise** is designed to allow instructors in large classes to use interactive experiential exercises.

- **Exploring the World Wide Web** requires students to actively search the web to find the answers to a problem.

- **Be the Manager** presents a realistic scenario where a manager or organization faces some kind of challenge, problem, or opportunity. These exercises provide students with a hands-on way of solving "real" problems by applying what they've just learned in the chapter.

Each chapter ends with a

- **Case in the News** that is an actual or shortened version of an article from a major publication such as *Bloomberg Businessweek, The Wall Street Journal,* or *Fortune.* The concluding questions encourage students to think about how real managers deal with problems in the business world.

Assurance of Learning Ready

Many educational institutions today are focused on the notion of assurance of learning, an important element of some accreditation standards. *Contemporary Management, Eighth Edition,* is designed specifically to support your assurance of learning initiatives with a simple yet powerful solution.

Each test bank question for *Contemporary Management* maps to a specific chapter learning outcome/objective listed in the text. You can use our test bank software, EZ Test and EZ Test Online, or *Connect Management* to easily query for learning outcomes/objectives that directly relate to the learning objectives for your course. You can then use the reporting features of EZ Test to aggregate student results in similar fashion, making the collection and presentation of assurance of learning data simple and easy.

AACSB Statement

The McGraw-Hill Companies are a proud corporate member of AACSB International. To support the importance and value of

AACSB accreditation, *Contemporary Management, Eighth Edition*, recognizes the curricula guidelines detailed in the AACSB standards for business accreditation by connecting selected questions in the text and/or the test bank to the six general knowledge and skill guidelines in the AACSB standards.

The statements contained in *Contemporary Management, Eighth Edition*, are provided only as a guide for the users of this textbook. The AACSB leaves content coverage and assessment within the purview of individual schools, the mission of the school, and the faculty. While *Contemporary Management* and the teaching package make no claim of any specific AACSB qualification or evaluation, we have within *Contemporary Management* labeled selected questions according to the six general knowledge and skill areas.

Integrated Learning System Great care was used in the creation of the supplementary material to accompany *Contemporary Management*. Whether you are a seasoned faculty member or a newly minted instructor, you'll find our support materials to be the most thorough and thoughtful ever created:

- **Instructor's Manual (IM)** The IM supporting this text has been completely updated to save instructors' time and support them in delivering the most effective course to their students. For each chapter, this manual provides a chapter overview and lecture outline with integrated PowerPoint® slides, lecture enhancers, notes for end-of-chapter materials, video cases and teaching notes, and more.

- **PowerPoint® Presentation** 40 slides per chapter feature reproductions of key tables and figures from the text as well as original content. Lecture-enhancing additions such as quick polling questions and company or video examples from outside the text can be used to generate discussion and illustrate management concepts.

- **Test Bank and EZ Test** The test bank has been thoroughly reviewed, revised, and improved. There are approximately 100 questions per chapter, including true/false, multiple-choice, and essay. Each question is tagged with learning objective, level of difficulty (corresponding to Bloom's taxonomy of educational objectives), AACSB standards, the correct answer, and page references. The new AACSB tags allow instructors to sort questions by the various standards and create reports to help give assurance that they are including recommended learning experiences in their curricula.

McGraw-Hill's flexible and easy-to-use electronic testing program **EZ Test** allows instructors to create tests from book-specific items. It accommodates a wide range of question types, and instructors may add their own questions. Multiple versions of the test can be created, and any test can be exported for use with course management systems such as WebCT or BlackBoard. **EZ Test Online** (**www.eztestonline .com**) allows you to access the test bank virtually anywhere at any time, without installation, and it's even easier to use. Additionally, it allows you to administer EZ Test–created exams and quizzes online, providing instant feedback for students.

McGraw-Hill
Connect Management

Less Managing. More Teaching. Greater Learning.

McGraw-Hill *Connect Management* is an online assignment and assessment solution that connects students with the tools and resources they'll need to achieve success.

McGraw-Hill *Connect Management* helps prepare students for their future by enabling faster learning, more efficient studying, and higher retention of knowledge.

McGraw-Hill *Connect Management* Features

Connect Management offers a number of powerful tools and features to make managing assignments easier, so faculty can spend more time teaching. With *Connect Management*, students can engage with their coursework anytime and anywhere, making the learning process more accessible and efficient. *Connect Management* offers you the features described below.

Diagnostic and Adaptive Learning of Concepts: LearnSmart

Students want to make the best use of their study time. The LearnSmart adaptive self-study technology within *Connect Management* provides students with a seamless combination of practice, assessment, and remediation for every concept in the textbook. LearnSmart's intelligent software adapts to every student response and automatically delivers concepts that advance the student's understanding while reducing time devoted to the concepts already mastered. The result for every student is the fastest path to mastery of the chapter concepts. LearnSmart

- Applies an intelligent concept engine to identify the relationships between concepts and to serve new concepts to each student only when he or she is ready.

- Adapts automatically to each student, so students spend less time on the topics they understand and practice more those they have yet to master.

- Provides continual reinforcement and remediation, but gives only as much guidance as students need.

- Integrates diagnostics as part of the learning experience.

- Enables you to assess which concepts students have efficiently learned on their own, thus freeing class time for more applications and discussion.

Online Interactive Applications

Online Interactive Applications are engaging tools that teach students to apply key concepts in practice. These Interactive Applications provide them with immersive, experiential learning opportunities. Students will engage in a variety of interactive scenarios to deepen critical knowledge of key course topics. They receive immediate feedback at intermediate steps throughout each exercise, as well as comprehensive feedback at the end of the assignment. All Interactive Applications are automatically scored and entered into the instructor gradebook.

Student Progress Tracking

Connect Management keeps instructors informed about how each student, section, and class is performing, allowing for more productive use of lecture and office hours. The progress-tracking function enables you to

- View scored work immediately and track individual or group performance with assignment and grade reports.
- Access an instant view of student or class performance relative to learning objectives.
- Collect data and generate reports required by many accreditation organizations, such as AACSB.

Smart Grading

When it comes to studying, time is precious. *Connect Management* helps students learn more efficiently by providing feedback and practice material when they need it, where they need it. When it comes to teaching, your time also is precious. The grading function enables you to

- Have assignments scored automatically, giving students immediate feedback on their work and side-by-side comparisons with correct answers.
- Access and review each response; manually change grades or leave comments for students to review.
- Reinforce classroom concepts with practice tests and instant quizzes.

Simple Assignment Management

With *Connect Management,* creating assignments is easier than ever, so you can spend more time teaching and less time managing. The assignment management function enables you to

- Create and deliver assignments easily with selectable end-of-chapter questions and test bank items.
- Streamline lesson planning, student progress reporting, and assignment grading to make classroom management more efficient than ever.
- Go paperless with the eBook and online submission and grading of student assignments.

Instructor Library

The *Connect Management* Instructor Library is your repository for additional resources to improve student engagement in and out of class. You can select and use any asset that enhances your lecture. The *Connect Management* Instructor Library includes

- Instructor Manual.
- PowerPoint® files.
- TestBank.
- Management Asset Gallery.
- eBook.

Student Study Center

The *Connect Management* Student Study Center is the place for students to access additional resources. The Student Study Center

- Offers students quick access to lectures, practice materials, eBooks, and more.

- Provides instant practice material and study questions, easily accessible on the go.

- Give students access to self-assessments, video materials, Manager's Hot Seat, and more.

Lecture Capture via Tegrity Campus

Increase the attention paid to lecture discussion by decreasing the attention paid to note taking. For an additional charge, Lecture Capture offers new ways for students to focus on the in-class discussion, knowing they can revisit important topics later.

McGraw-Hill *Connect Plus Management*

McGraw-Hill reinvents the textbook learning experience for the modern student with *Connect Plus Management*. A seamless integration of an eBook and *Management, Connect Plus Management* provides all of the *Connect Management* features plus the following:

- An integrated eBook, allowing for anytime, anywhere access to the textbook.

- Dynamic links between the problems or questions you assign to your students and the location in the eBook where that problem or question is covered.

- A powerful search function to pinpoint and connect key concepts in a snap.

In short, *Connect Management* offers you and your students powerful tools and features that optimize your time and energies, enabling you to focus on course content, teaching, and student learning. *Connect Management* also offers a wealth of content resources for both instructors and students. This state-of-the-art, thoroughly tested system supports you in preparing students for the world that awaits.

For more information about *Connect*, go to **www.mcgrawhillconnect.com**, or contact your local McGraw-Hill sales representative.

 # Tegrity Campus: Lectures 24/7

Tegrity Campus is a service that makes class time available 24/7 by automatically capturing every lecture in a searchable format for students to review when they study and complete assignments. With a simple one-click start-and-stop process, you capture all computer screens and corresponding audio. Students can replay any part of any class with easy-to-use browser-based viewing on a PC or Mac.

Educators know that the more students can see, hear, and experience class resources, the better they learn. In fact, studies prove it. With Tegrity Campus, students quickly recall key moments by using Tegrity Campus's unique search feature. This search helps students efficiently find what they need, when they need it, across an entire semester of class recordings. Help turn all your students' study time into learning moments immediately supported by your lecture.

Lecture Capture enables you to

- Record and distribute your lecture with a click of a button.
- Record and index PowerPoint® presentations and anything shown on your computer so it is easily searchable, frame by frame.
- Offer access to lectures anytime and anywhere by computer, iPod, or mobile device.
- Increase intent listening and class participation by easing students' concerns about note taking. Lecture Capture will make it more likely you will see students' faces, not the tops of their heads.

To learn more about Tegrity, watch a two-minute Flash demo at **http://tegritycampus.mhhe.com**.

McGraw-Hill Customer Care Contact Information

At McGraw-Hill, we understand that getting the most from new technology can be challenging. That's why our services don't stop after you purchase our products. You can e-mail our product specialists 24 hours a day to get product training online. Or you can search our knowledge bank of Frequently Asked Questions on our support website. For customer support, call **800-331-5094**, e-mail **hmsupport@mcgraw-hill.com**, or visit **www.mhhe.com/support**. One of our technical support analysts will be able to assist you in a timely fashion.

McGraw-Hill's Management Asset Gallery

McGraw-Hill/Irwin Management is excited to now provide a one-stop shop for our wealth of assets, making it quick and easy for instructors to locate specific materials to enhance their courses.

All of the following can be accessed within the Management Asset Gallery:

Manager's Hot Seat

This interactive video-based application puts students in the manager's hot seat, builds critical thinking and decision-making skills, and allows students to apply concepts to real managerial challenges. Students watch as 15 real managers apply their years of experience when confronting unscripted issues such as bullying in the workplace, cyber loafing, globalization, intergenerational work conflicts, workplace violence, and leadership versus management.

Self-Assessment Gallery   Unique among publisher-provided self-assessments, our 23 self-assessments give students background information to ensure that they understand the purpose of the assessment. Students test their values, beliefs, skills, and interests in a wide variety of areas, allowing them to personally apply chapter content to their own lives and careers.

Every self-assessment is supported with PowerPoints® and an instructor manual in the Management Asset Gallery, making it easy for the instructor to create an engaging classroom discussion surrounding the assessments.

Test Your Knowledge   To help reinforce students' understanding of key management concepts, Test Your Knowledge activities give students a review of the conceptual materials followed by application-based questions to work through. Students can choose practice mode, which gives them detailed feedback after each question, or test mode, which provides feedback after the entire test has been completed. Every Test Your Knowledge activity is supported by instructor notes in the Management Asset Gallery to make it easy for the instructor to create engaging classroom discussions surrounding that materials that students have completed.

Management History Timeline This web application allows instructors to present and students to learn the history of management in an engaging and interactive way. Management history is presented along an intuitive timeline that can be traveled through sequentially or by selected decade. With the click of a mouse, students learn the important dates, see the people who influenced the field, and understand the general management theories that have molded and shaped management as we know it today.

Video Library DVDs McGraw-Hill/Irwin offers the most comprehensive video support for the Principles of Management classroom through course library video DVDs. This discipline has library volume DVDs tailored to integrate and visually reinforce chapter concepts. The library volume DVDs contain more than 90 clips! The rich video material, organized by topic, comes from sources such as *Bloomberg Businessweek* TV, PBS, NBC, BBC, SHRM, and McGraw-Hill. Video cases and video guides are provided for some clips.

Destination CEO Videos

Bloomberg Businessweek produced video clips featuring CEOs on a variety of topics. Accompanying each clip are multiple-choice questions and discussion questions to use in the classroom or assign as a quiz.

Online Learning Center (OLC)

www.mhhe.com/jonesgeorge8e
Find a variety of online teaching and learning tools that are designed to reinforce and build on the text content. Students will have direct access to the learning tools while instructor materials are password protected.

 eBook Options eBooks are an innovative way for students to save money and to "go green." McGraw-Hill's eBooks are typically 40% off the bookstore price. Students have the choice between an online and a downloadable CourseSmart eBook.

Through CourseSmart, students have the flexibility to access an exact replica of their textbook from any computer that has Internet service without plug-ins or special software via the online version, or to create a library of books on their hard drive via the downloadable version. Access to the CourseSmart eBooks lasts for one year.

Features CourseSmart eBooks allow students to highlight, take notes, organize notes, and share the notes with other CourseSmart users. Students can also search for terms across all eBooks in their purchased CourseSmart library. CourseSmart eBooks can be printed (five pages at a time).

More info and purchase Please visit **www.coursesmart.com** for more information and to purchase access to our eBooks. CourseSmart allows students to try one chapter of the eBook, free of charge, before purchase.

 Create Craft your teaching resources to match the way you teach! With McGraw-Hill Create, **www.mcgrawhillcreate.com**, you can easily rearrange chapters, combine material from other content sources, and quickly upload content you have written, like your course syllabus or teaching notes. Find the content you need in Create by searching through thousands of leading McGraw-Hill textbooks. Arrange your book to fit your teaching style. Create even allows you to personalize your book's appearance by selecting the cover and adding your name, school, and course information. Order a Create book and you'll receive a complimentary print review copy in three to five business days or a complimentary electronic review copy (eComp) via e-mail in about one hour. Go to **www.mcgrawhillcreate.com** today and register. Experience how McGraw-Hill Create empowers you to teach *your* students *your* way.

AUTHORS

Gareth Jones currently offers pro bono advice on solving management problems to nonprofit organizations in Houston, Texas. He received his BA in Economics Psychology and his PhD in Management from the University of Lancaster, U.K. He was formerly Professor of Management in the Graduate School of Business at Texas A&M University and earlier held teaching and research appointments at Michigan State University, the University of Illinois at Urbana–Champaign and the University of Warwick, UK.

He continues to pursue his research interests in strategic management and organizational theory and his well-known research that applies transaction cost analysis to explain many forms of strategic and organizational behavior. He also studies the complex and changing relationships between competitive advantage and information technology in the 2010s.

He has published many articles in leading journals of the field and his research has appeared in the *Academy of Management Review*, the *Journal of International Business Studies*, and *Human Relations*. An article about the role of information technology in many aspects of organizational functioning was published in the *Journal of Management*. One of his articles won the *Academy of Management Journal*'s Best Paper Award, and he is one of the most cited authors in the *Academy of Management Review*. He is, or has served, on the editorial boards of the *Academy of Management Review*, the *Journal of Management*, and *Management Inquiry*.

Gareth Jones has used his academic knowledge to craft leading textbooks in management and three other major areas in the management discipline: organizational behavior, organizational theory, and strategic management. His books are widely recognized for their innovative, contemporary content and for the clarity with which they communicate complex, real-world issues to students.

Jennifer George is the Mary Gibbs Jones Professor of Management and Professor of Psychology in the Jesse H. Jones Graduate School of Business at Rice University. She received her BA in Psychology/Sociology from Wesleyan University, her MBA in Finance from New York University, and her PhD in Management and Organizational Behavior from New York University. Prior to joining the faculty at Rice University, she was a professor in the Department of Management at Texas A&M University.

Professor George specializes in organizational behavior and is well known for her research on mood and emotion in the workplace, their determinants, and their effects on various individual and group-level work outcomes. She is the author of many articles in leading peer-reviewed journals such as the *Academy of Management Journal,* the *Academy of Management Review,* the *Journal of Applied Psychology, Organizational Behavior and Human Decision Processes, Journal of Personality and Social Psychology,* and *Psychological Bulletin.* One of her papers won the Academy of Management's Organizational Behavior Division Outstanding Competitive Paper Award, and another paper won the *Human Relations* Best Paper Award. She is, or has been, on the editorial review boards of the *Journal of Applied Psychology, Academy of Management Journal, Academy of Management Review, Administrative Science Quarterly, Journal of Management, Organizational Behavior and Human Decision Processes, Organization Science, International Journal of Selection and Assessment,* and *Journal of Managerial Issues;* was a consulting editor for the *Journal of Organizational Behavior;* was a member of the SIOP *Organizational Frontiers Series* editorial board; and was an associate editor of the *Journal of Applied Psychology.* She is a fellow in the Academy of Management, the American Psychological Association, the American Psychological Society, and the Society for Industrial and Organizational Psychology and a member of the Society for Organizational Behavior. She also has coauthored a textbook titled *Understanding and Managing Organizational Behavior.*

Contemporary
Management

CHAPTER 1

Managers and Managing

Learning Objectives

After studying this chapter, you should be able to:

LO1-1 Describe what management is, why management is important, what managers do, and how managers utilize organizational resources efficiently and effectively to achieve organizational goals.

LO1-2 Distinguish among planning, organizing, leading, and controlling (the four principal managerial tasks), and explain how managers' ability to handle each one affects organizational performance.

LO1-3 Differentiate among three levels of management, and understand the tasks and responsibilities of managers at different levels in the organizational hierarchy.

LO1-4 Distinguish between three kinds of managerial skill, and explain why managers are divided into different departments to perform their tasks more efficiently and effectively.

LO1-5 Discuss some major changes in management practices today that have occurred as a result of globalization and the use of advanced information technology (IT).

LO1-6 Discuss the principal challenges managers face in today's increasingly competitive global environment.

A MANAGER'S CHALLENGE

Tim Cook Succeeds Steve Jobs as CEO of Apple

What is high-performance management? In 2011 Tim Cook took full management control of Apple as its CEO six weeks after Steve Jobs stepped down as its CEO before his untimely death. Cook had been Apple's long-time chief operating officer and had been responsible for organizing and controlling its global supply chain to bring its innovative products to market as quickly and efficiently as possible.[1] One of Apple's major strengths is to continuously introduce new and improved products such as its iPhones and iPads, often at six-month and yearly intervals, to offer customers more options and to stay ahead of the competition. Cook was acknowledged as the leader who controlled Apple's purchasing and manufacturing operations, and of course he had intimate knowledge of Apple's new product design and engineering. However, Steve Jobs had been the manager who ultimately decided what kinds of new products Apple would develop and the design of their hardware and software.

Starting with Apple's founding in 1977, Jobs saw his main task as leading the planning process to develop new and improved PCs. Although this was a good strategy, his management style was often arbitrary and overbearing. For example, Jobs often played favorites among the many project teams he created. His approach caused many conflicts and led to fierce competition, many misunderstandings, and growing distrust among members of the different teams.

Jobs's abrasive management style also brought him into conflict with John Sculley, Apple's CEO. Employees became unsure whether Jobs (the chairman) or Sculley was leading the company. Both managers were so busy competing for control of Apple that the task of ensuring its resources were being used efficiently was neglected. Apple's costs

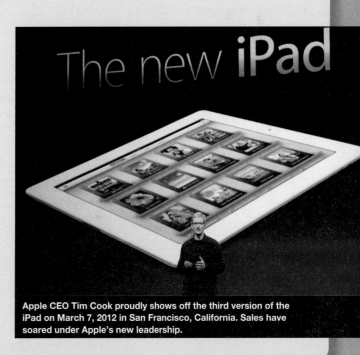

The new iPad

Apple CEO Tim Cook proudly shows off the third version of the iPad on March 7, 2012 in San Francisco, California. Sales have soared under Apple's new leadership.

soared, and its performance and profits fell. Apple's directors became convinced Jobs's management style was the heart of the problem and asked him to resign.

After he left Apple, Jobs started new ventures such as PC maker NEXT to develop powerful new PCs and Pixar, the computer animation company, which become a huge success after it made blockbuster movies such as *Toy Story* and *Finding Nemo,* both distributed by Walt Disney. In both these companies Jobs developed a clear vision for managers to follow, and he built strong management teams to lead the project teams developing the new PCs and movies. Jobs saw his main task as planning the companies' future product development strategies. However, he left the actual tasks of leading and organizing to managers below him. He gave them the autonomy to put his vision into practice. In 1996 Jobs convinced Apple to buy NEXT and use its powerful operating system in new Apple PCs. Jobs began working inside Apple to lead its turnaround and was so successful that in 1997 he was asked to become its CEO. Jobs agreed and continued to put the new management skills he had developed over time to good use.

The first thing he did was create a clear vision and goals to energize and motivate Apple employees. Jobs decided that, to survive, Apple had to introduce state-of-the-art, stylish PCs and related digital equipment. He delegated considerable authority to teams of employees to develop all the many different hardware and software components necessary to build the new products, but he also established strict timetables and challenging "stretch" goals, such as bringing new products to market as quickly as possible, for these teams. Moreover, he was careful to keep the different teams' activities separate; only he and his chief designers knew what the new products would actually look like and their capabilities—and his demand for secrecy increased over time.[2]

In 2003 Jobs announced that Apple was starting a new service called iTunes, an online music store from which people could download songs for 99 cents. At the same time Apple introduced its iPod music player, which can store thousands of downloaded songs, and it quickly became a runaway success. By 2006 Apple had gained control of 70% of the digital music player market and 80% of the online music download business, and its stock price soared to a new record level. The next milestone in Jobs's product strategy came in 2007 when he announced that Apple would introduce the iPhone. Once again he assembled different teams of engineers not only to develop the new phone's hardware and software but also to create an online iPhone applications platform where users could download applications to make their iPhones more valuable. In 2010 Jobs announced that Apple planned to introduce a new iPad tablet computer and after its release in April 2010 its stock rose to a new record high of $219.

Since Cook assumed leadership of Apple, it has become apparent to its employees and shareholders that he brings a new more open and participative approach to managing the company. While Jobs was respected as a guru, magician, and ruler—someone to be revered as well as feared—Cook makes himself available to employees in Apple's cafeteria and talks directly to shareholders and analysts, something that Jobs had no time for. Cook has also worked to integrate Apple's global supply chain and project management functions with its engineering functions to break down the barriers between teams in the company and increase the flow of information between product units as the company grows and becomes more complex. Following Jobs, Cook's goal is for Apple to focus on introducing innovative new products and not to lose its commitment to being the leader in every market in which it competes. However, while Cook is a demanding boss, he is down to earth, approachable, and well respected, as opposed to Jobs who became increasingly isolated, forbidding, and secretive as time went on.

Overview

The story of Tim Cook's approach to managing Apple after Steve Jobs illustrates the many challenges facing people who become managers: Managing a company is a complex activity, and effective managers must possess many kinds of skills, knowledge, and abilities. Management is an unpredictable process. Making the right decision is difficult; even effective managers often make mistakes, but the most effective managers, like Jobs and Cook, learn from their mistakes and continually strive to find ways to increase their companies' performance.

In this chapter we look at what managers do and what skills and abilities they must develop to manage their organizations successfully. We also identify the different kinds of managers that organizations need and the skills and abilities they must develop to succeed. Finally, we identify some challenges managers must address if their organizations are to grow and prosper.

What Is Management?

When you think of a manager, what kind of person comes to mind? Do you see someone who, like Tim Cook, can determine the future prosperity of a large for-profit company? Or do you see the administrator of a not-for-profit organization, such as a community college, library, or charity, or the person in charge of your local Walmart store or McDonald's restaurant, or the person you answer to if you have a part-time job? What do all these people have in common? First, they all work in organizations. **Organizations** are collections of people who work together and coordinate their actions to achieve a wide variety of goals or desired future outcomes.[3] Second, as managers, they are the people responsible for supervising and making the most of an organization's human and other resources to achieve its goals.

organizations Collections of people who work together and coordinate their actions to achieve a wide variety of goals or desired future outcomes.

management The planning, organizing, leading, and controlling of human and other resources to achieve organizational goals efficiently and effectively.

Management, then, is the planning, organizing, leading, and controlling of human and other resources to achieve organizational goals efficiently and effectively. An organization's *resources* include assets such as people and their skills, know-how, and experience; machinery; raw materials; computers and information technology; and patents, financial capital, and loyal customers and employees.

Achieving High Performance: A Manager's Goal

One of the most important goals that organizations and their members try to achieve is to provide some kind of good or service that customers value or desire. The principal goal of CEO Tim Cook is to manage Apple so it creates a continuous stream of new and improved

organizational performance A measure of how efficiently and effectively a manager uses resources to satisfy customers and achieve organizational goals.

efficiency A measure of how well or how productively resources are used to achieve a goal.

effectiveness A measure of the appropriateness of the goals an organization is pursuing and the degree to which the organization achieves those goals.

goods and services—such as more powerful PCs, more versatile iPhones and iPads, and the ability to easily download diverse kinds of digital content from the Internet—that customers are willing to buy. In 2012 Apple dominates the field in many of these areas; its managers are currently working to make its new iMacs and iPads the industry leaders. Similarly, the principal goal of doctors, nurses, and hospital administrators is to increase their hospital's ability to make sick people well—and to do so cost-effectively. Likewise, the principal goal of each McDonald's restaurant manager is to produce burgers, salads, fries, and shakes that people want to pay for and eat so they become loyal return customers.

Organizational performance is a measure of how efficiently and effectively managers use available resources to satisfy customers and achieve organizational goals. Organizational performance increases in direct proportion to increases in efficiency and effectiveness (see Figure 1.1). What are efficiency and effectiveness?

Efficiency is a measure of how productively resources are used to achieve a goal.[4] Organizations are efficient when managers minimize the amount of input resources (such as labor, raw materials, and component parts) or the amount of time needed to produce a given output of goods or services. For example, McDonald's develops ever more efficient fat fryers that not only reduce the amount of oil used in cooking, but also speed up the cooking of french fries. UPS develops new work routines to reduce delivery time, such as instructing drivers to leave their truck doors open when going short distances. Tim Cook instructed Apple's engineers and supply chain managers not only to develop ever more compact, powerful, and multipurpose models of its iPad and iPhone but also to find new cost-effective ways to do so, such as by outsourcing manufacturing to China. A manager's responsibility is to ensure that an organization and its members perform as efficiently as possible all the activities needed to provide goods and services to customers.

Effectiveness is a measure of the *appropriateness* of the goals that managers have selected for the organization to pursue and the degree to which the organization achieves those goals. Organizations are effective when managers choose appropriate goals and then achieve them. Some years ago, for example, managers at McDonald's decided on the goal of providing breakfast service to attract more customers. The choice of this goal has proved smart: Sales of

Figure 1.1

Efficiency, Effectiveness, and Performance in an Organization

EFFICIENCY

	LOW	**HIGH**
HIGH	Low efficiency/ high effectiveness Manager chooses the right goals to pursue, but does a poor job of using resources to achieve these goals. Result: A product that customers want, but that is too expensive for them to buy.	High efficiency/ high effectiveness Manager chooses the right goals to pursue and makes good use of resources to achieve these goals. Result: A product that customers want at a quality and price they can afford.
LOW	Low efficiency/ low effectiveness Manager chooses wrong goals to pursue and makes poor use of resources. Result: A low-quality product that customers do not want.	High efficiency/ low effectiveness Manager chooses inappropriate goals, but makes good use of resources to pursue these goals. Result: A high-quality product that customers do not want.

EFFECTIVENESS

High-performing organizations are efficient *and* effective.

breakfast food now account for more than 30% of McDonald's revenues and are still increasing. Jobs's goal was to create a continuous flow of innovative PC and digital entertainment products. High-performing organizations such as Apple, McDonald's, Walmart, Intel, Home Depot, Accenture, and Habitat for Humanity are simultaneously efficient and effective. Effective managers are those who choose the right organizational goals to pursue and have the skills to utilize resources efficiently.

Why Study Management?

Today more students are competing for places in business courses than ever before; the number of people wishing to pursue master of business administration (MBA) degrees—today's passport to an advanced management position—either on campus or from online universities and colleges is at an all-time high. Why is the study of management currently so popular?[5]

First, in any society or culture resources are valuable and scarce, so the more efficient and effective use that organizations can make of those resources, the greater the relative well-being and prosperity of people in that society. Because managers decide how to use many of a society's most valuable resources—its skilled employees, raw materials like oil and land, computers and information systems, and financial assets—they directly impact the well-being of a society and the people in it. Understanding what managers do and how they do it is of central importance to understanding how a society creates wealth and affluence for its citizens.

Second, although most people are not managers, and many may never intend to become managers, almost all of us encounter managers because most people have jobs and bosses. Moreover, many people today work in groups and teams and have to deal with coworkers. Studying management helps people deal with their bosses and their coworkers. It reveals how to understand other people at work and make decisions and take actions that win the attention and support of the boss and coworkers. Management teaches people not yet in positions of authority how to lead coworkers, solve conflicts between them, achieve team goals, and thus increase performance.

Third, in any society, people are in competition for a very important resource—a job that pays well and provides an interesting and satisfying career; and understanding management is one important path toward obtaining this objective. In general, jobs become more interesting the more complex or responsible they are. Any person who desires a motivating job that changes over time might therefore do well to develop management skills and become promotable. A person who has been working for several years and then returns to school for an MBA can usually, after earning the degree, find a more interesting, satisfying job that pays significantly more than the previous job. Moreover, salaries increase rapidly as people move up the organizational hierarchy, whether it is a school system, a large for-profit business organization, or a not-for-profit charitable or medical institution.

Indeed, the salaries paid to top managers are enormous. For example, the CEOs and other top executives or managers of companies such as Apple, Walt Disney, GE, and McDonald's receive millions in actual salary each year. However, even more staggering is the fact that many top executives also receive bonuses in the form of valuable stock or shares in the company they manage, as well as stock options that give them the right to sell these shares at a certain time in the future.[6] If the value of the stock goes up, the managers keep the difference between the price at which they obtained the stock option (say, $10) and what it is worth later (say, $33). When Tim Cook joined Apple in 1998, a year after Steve Jobs became its CEO, he was awarded stock options that, with the fast rise in Apple's stock price throughout the 2010s, are worth billions of dollars today (he declined to accept the $75 million dividend that he was entitled to based on his stock ownership in 2012).[7] In 2010 Goldman Sachs paid its top managers stock bonuses worth $16.2 billion, and its CEO Lloyd Blankfein received Goldman Sachs stock worth over $8 billion—but this was only half the value of the stock that JPMorgan Chase CEO Jamie Dimon received from his company![8] These incredible amounts of money provide some indication of both the responsibilities and the rewards that accompany the achievement of high management positions in major companies—and go to anybody who successfully creates and manages a small business. What is it that managers actually do to receive such rewards?[9]

Essential Managerial Tasks

The job of management is to help an organization make the best use of its resources to achieve its goals. How do managers accomplish this objective? They do so by performing four essential managerial tasks: *planning, organizing, leading,* and *controlling.* The arrows linking these tasks in Figure 1.2 suggest the sequence in which managers typically perform them. French manager Henri Fayol first outlined the nature of these managerial activities around the turn of the 20th century in *General and Industrial Management,* a book that remains the classic statement of what managers must do to create a high-performing organization.[10]

Managers at all levels and in all departments—whether in small or large companies, for-profit or not-for-profit organizations, or organizations that operate in one country or throughout the world—are responsible for performing these four tasks, which we look at next. How well managers perform these tasks determines how efficient and effective their organizations are.

LO1-2 Distinguish among planning, organizing, leading, and controlling (the four principal managerial tasks), and explain how managers' ability to handle each one affects organizational performance.

planning Identifying and selecting appropriate goals; one of the four principal tasks of management.

Planning

To perform the **planning** task, managers identify and select appropriate organizational goals and courses of action; they develop *strategies* for how to achieve high performance. The three steps involved in planning are (1) deciding which goals the organization will pursue, (2) deciding what strategies to adopt to attain those goals, and (3) deciding how to allocate organizational resources to pursue the strategies that attain those goals. How well managers plan and develop strategies determines how effective and efficient the organization is—its performance level.[11]

As an example of planning in action, consider the situation confronting Michael Dell, founder and CEO of Dell Computer, who in 2012 was struggling to increase the PC sales of his company given competition from HP, Apple, and IBM. In 1984 the 19-year-old Dell saw an opportunity to enter the PC market by assembling PCs and selling them directly to customers. Dell began to plan how to put his idea into practice. First, he decided that his goal was to sell an inexpensive PC, to undercut the prices charged by companies like Apple, Compaq, and HP. Second, he had to choose a course of action to achieve this goal. He decided to sell PCs directly to customers by telephone and so bypass expensive computer stores that sold Compaq and Apple PCs. He also had to decide how to obtain low-cost components and how to tell potential customers about his products. Third, he had to decide how to allocate his limited funds (he had only $5,000) to buy

Figure 1.2

Four Tasks of Management

Michael Dell sits in the dorm room at the University of Texas–Austin, where he launched his personal computer company as a college freshman. When he visited, the room was occupied by freshmen Russell Smith (left) and Jacob Frith, both from Plano, Texas.

strategy A cluster of decisions about what goals to pursue, what actions to take, and how to use resources to achieve goals.

labor and other resources. He hired three people and worked with them around a table to assemble his PCs.

Thus to achieve his goal of making and selling low-price PCs, Dell had to plan, and as his organization grew, his plans changed and became progressively more complex. After setbacks during the 2000s that saw HP, Apple, and a new Taiwanese company, Acer, achieve competitive advantage over Dell in performance, styling, or pricing, Dell and his managers actively searched for new strategies to better compete against agile rivals and help the company regain its position as the highest-performing PC maker. In 2010 Dell was still locked in a major battle with its competitors, and its performance had not recovered despite attempts to introduce innovative new models of laptops and digital devices. Dell needed a new approach to planning to compete more effectively; and new strategies Dell has followed in the 2010s include more powerful customized lines of new laptops, and a major focus on providing computer hardware, software, and consulting geared to the need of corporate customers.

As the battle between Dell, HP, Acer, and Apple suggests, the outcome of planning is a **strategy**, a cluster of decisions concerning what organizational goals to pursue, what actions to take, and how to use resources to achieve these goals. The decisions that were the outcome of Michael Dell's original planning formed a *low-cost strategy*. A low-cost strategy is a way of obtaining customers by making decisions that allow an organization to produce goods or services more cheaply than its competitors so it can charge lower prices than they do. Throughout its history, Dell has continuously refined this strategy and explored new ways to reduce costs. Dell became the most profitable PC maker as a result of its low-cost strategy, but when HP and Acer also lowered their costs, it lost its competitive advantage and its profits fell. By contrast, since its founding Apple's strategy has been to deliver to customers new, exciting, and unique computer and digital products, such as its iPods, iPhones, and its new iPads—a strategy known as *differentiation*.[12] Although this strategy almost ruined Apple in the 1990s when customers bought inexpensive Dell PCs rather its premium-priced PCs, today Apple's sales have boomed as customers turn to its unique PCs and digital products. To fight back, Dell has been forced to offer more exciting, stylish products—hence its decision to introduce powerful customized PCs.

Planning strategy is complex and difficult, especially because planning is done under uncertainty when the result is unknown so that either success or failure is a possible outcome of the planning process. Managers take major risks when they commit organizational resources to pursue a particular strategy. Dell enjoyed great success in the past with its low-cost strategy; but presently Apple is performing spectacularly with its differentiation strategy and hurting competitors such as HP, Sony, Nokia, and Blackberry maker Research in Motion. In Chapter 8 we focus on the planning process and on the strategies organizations can select to respond to opportunities or threats in an industry. The story of the way Joe Coulombe, the founder of Trader Joe's, used his abilities to plan and make the right decisions to create the strategies necessary for his, and his new organization's success, is discussed in the following, "Manager as a Person" box.

Manager as a Person

Joe Coulombe Knows How to Make an Organization Work

Trader Joe's, an upscale specialty supermarket chain, was started in 1967 by Joe Coulombe, who owned a few convenience stores that were fighting an uphill battle against the growing 7-11 chain. 7-11 offered customers a wider selection of lower-priced products, and Coulombe had to find a new way to manage his small business if it was going to survive. As he began planning new strategies to help his small business grow,

Pictured is Trader Joe's first New York City store that opened in 2006. Founder Joe Coulombe's approach to motivating and rewarding his employees to provide excellent customer service paid off in a city where the prices of food and drink are so high that customers were delighted to shop in stores with a great ambiance and friendly customer service.

he was struck by the fact that there might be a niche for supplying specialty products, such as wine, drinks, and gourmet foods, which were more profitable to sell; moreover, he would no longer be competing against giant 7-11. Coulombe changed the name of his stores to Trader Joe's and stocked them with every variety and brand of California wine produced at the time. He also began to offer fine foods like bread, crackers, cheese, fruits, and vegetables to complement and encourage wine sales.

From the beginning Coulombe realized that good planning was only the first step in successfully managing his small, growing company. He knew that to encourage customers to visit his stores and buy high-priced gourmet products, he needed to give them excellent customer service. So he had to motivate his salespeople to perform at a high level. His approach was to decentralize authority, empowering salespeople to take responsibility for meeting customer needs. Rather than forcing employees to follow strict operating rules and to obtain the consent of their superiors in the hierarchy of authority, employees were given autonomy to make decisions and provide personalized customer service. Coulombe's approach led employees to feel they "owned" their supermarkets, and he worked to develop a store culture based on values and norms about providing excellent customer service and developing personalized relationships with customers. Today many employees and customers are on first-name terms.

Coulombe led by example and created a store environment in which employees were treated as individuals and felt valued as people. For example, the theme behind the design of his stores was to create the feeling of a Hawaiian resort: He and his employees wear loud Hawaiian shirts, store managers are called captains, and the store decor uses lots of wood and contains tiki huts where employees give customers food and drink samples and interact with them. Once again, this helped create strong values and norms that emphasize personalized customer service.

Finally, Joe Coulombe's approach from the beginning was to create a policy of promotion from within the company so that the highest-performing salespeople could rise to become store captains and beyond in the organization. He had always recognized the need to treat employees (people) in a fair and equitable way to encourage them to develop the customer-oriented values and norms needed to provide personalized customer service. He decided that full-time employees should earn at least the median household income for their communities, which averaged $7,000 a year in the 1960s and is $48,000 today—an astonishingly high amount compared to the pay of employees of regular supermarkets such as Kroger's and Safeway. Moreover, store captains, who are vital in helping create and reinforce Trader Joe's store culture, are rewarded with salaries and bonuses that can exceed $100,000 a year. And all salespeople know that as the store chain expands, they may also be promoted to this level. In 2012 Trader Joe's has over 365 stores in 30 states and is still expanding because Coulombe's approach to managing his small business created the right foundation for an upscale specialty supermarket to grow and prosper.

Organizing

organizing Structuring working relationships in a way that allows organizational members to work together to achieve organizational goals; one of the four principal tasks of management.

Organizing is structuring working relationships so organizational members interact and cooperate to achieve organizational goals. Organizing people into departments according to the kinds of job-specific tasks they perform lays out the lines of authority and responsibility between different individuals and groups. Managers must decide how best to organize resources, particularly human resources.

organizational structure A formal system of task and reporting relationships that coordinates and motivates organizational members so they work together to achieve organizational goals.

The outcome of organizing is the creation of an **organizational structure**, a formal system of task and reporting relationships that coordinates and motivates members so they work together to achieve organizational goals. Organizational structure determines how an organization's resources can be best used to create goods and services. As his company grew, for example, Michael Dell faced the issue of how to structure his organization. Early on he was hiring 100 new employees a week and deciding how to design his managerial hierarchy to best motivate and coordinate managers' activities. As his organization grew to become one of the largest global PC makers, he and his managers created progressively more complex forms of organizational structure to help it achieve its goals. We examine the organizing process in detail in Chapters 10 through 12.

Leading

leading Articulating a clear vision and energizing and enabling organizational members so they understand the part they play in achieving organizational goals; one of the four principal tasks of management.

An organization's *vision* is a short, succinct, and inspiring statement of what the organization intends to become and the goals it is seeking to achieve—its desired future state. In **leading**, managers articulate a clear organizational vision for the organization's members to accomplish, and they energize and enable employees so everyone understands the part he or she plays in achieving organizational goals. Leadership involves managers using their power, personality, influence, persuasion, and communication skills to coordinate people and groups so their activities and efforts are in harmony. Leadership revolves around encouraging all employees to perform at a high level to help the organization achieve its vision and goals. Another outcome of leadership is a highly motivated and committed workforce. Employees responded well to Michael Dell's hands-on leadership style, which has resulted in a hardworking, committed workforce. Managers at Apple appreciate the way Steve Jobs, and now Tim Cook, have adopted a leadership style based on a willingness to delegate authority to project teams and to help managers resolve differences that could easily lead to bitter disputes and power struggles. We discuss the issues involved in managing and leading individuals and groups in Chapters 13 through 16.

Controlling

controlling Evaluating how well an organization is achieving its goals and taking action to maintain or improve performance; one of the four principal tasks of management.

In **controlling**, the task of managers is to evaluate how well an organization has achieved its goals and to take any corrective actions needed to maintain or improve performance. For example, managers monitor the performance of individuals, departments, and the organization as a whole to see whether they are meeting desired performance standards. Michael Dell learned early in his career how important this is; if standards are not being met, managers seek ways to improve performance.

The outcome of the control process is the ability to measure performance accurately and regulate organizational efficiency and effectiveness. To exercise control, managers must decide which goals to measure—perhaps goals pertaining to productivity, quality, or responsiveness to customers—and then they must design control systems that will provide the information necessary to assess performance—that is, determine to what degree the goals have been met. The controlling task also helps managers evaluate how well they themselves are performing the other three tasks of management—planning, organizing, and leading—and take corrective action.

Michael Dell had difficulty establishing effective control systems because his company was growing so rapidly and he lacked experienced managers. In the 1990s Dell's costs suddenly soared because no systems were in place to control inventory, and in 1994 poor quality control resulted in a defective line of new laptop computers—some of which caught fire. To solve these and other control problems, Dell

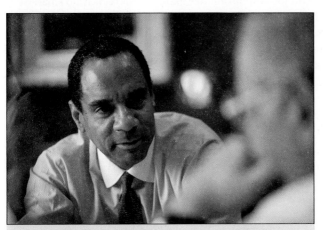

Ken Chenault, pictured here, is the president and CEO of American Express Company. Promoted in 1997, he climbed the ranks from its Travel Related Services Company thanks to his even temper and unrelenting drive. Respected by colleagues for his personality, most will say they can't remember him losing his temper or raising his voice. His open-door policy for subordinates allows him to mentor AmEx managers and encourages all to enter and speak their minds.

hired hundreds of experienced managers from other companies to put the right control systems in place. As a result, by 2000 Dell was able to make computers for over 10% less than its competitors, which created a major source of competitive advantage. At its peak, Dell drove competitors out of the market because it had achieved a 20% cost advantage over them.[13] However, we noted earlier that through the 2000s rivals such as HP and Acer also learned how to reduce their operating costs, and this shattered Dell's competitive advantage. Controlling, like the other managerial tasks, is an ongoing, dynamic, always-changing process that demands constant attention and action. We cover the most important aspects of the control task in Chapters 10, 11, 17, and 18.

The four managerial tasks—planning, organizing, leading, and controlling—are essential parts of a manager's job. At all levels in the managerial hierarchy, and across all jobs and departments in an organization, effective management means performing these four activities successfully—in ways that increase efficiency and effectiveness.

Performing Managerial Tasks: Mintzberg's Typology

Our discussion of managerial tasks may seem to suggest that a manager's job is highly orchestrated and that management is an orderly process in which managers rationally calculate the best way to use resources to achieve organizational goals. In reality, being a manager often involves acting emotionally and relying on gut feelings. Quick, immediate reactions to situations, rather than deliberate thought and reflection, are an important aspect of managerial action.[14] Often managers are overloaded with responsibilities and do not have time to analyze every nuance of a situation; they therefore make decisions in uncertain conditions not knowing which outcomes will be best.[15] Moreover, top managers face constantly changing situations, and a decision that seems right today may prove to be wrong tomorrow. The range of problems that managers face is enormous; managers usually must handle many problems simultaneously; and they often must make snap decisions using the intuition and experience gained through their careers to perform their jobs to the best of their abilities.[16] Henry Mintzberg, by following managers and observing what they actually *do* hour-by-hour and day-by-day, identified 10 kinds of specific roles, or sets of job responsibilities, that capture the dynamic nature of managerial work.[17] He grouped these roles according to whether the responsibility was primarily decisional, interpersonal, or informational; they are described in Table 1.1.

Given the many complex, difficult job responsibilities managers have, it is no small wonder that many claim they are performing their jobs well if they are right just half of the time.[18] And it is understandable that many experienced managers accept failure by their subordinates as a normal part of the learning experience and a rite of passage to becoming an effective manager. Managers and their subordinates learn from both their successes and their failures.

Levels and Skills of Managers

To perform the four managerial tasks efficiently and effectively, organizations group or differentiate their managers in two main ways—by level in hierarchy and by type of skill. First, they differentiate managers according to their level or rank in the organization's hierarchy of authority. The three levels of managers are first-line managers, middle managers, and top managers—arranged in a hierarchy. Typically first-line managers report to middle managers, and middle managers report to top managers.

Second, organizations group managers into different departments (or functions) according to their specific job-related skills, expertise, and experiences, such as a manager's engineering skills, marketing expertise, or sales experience. A **department**, such as the manufacturing, accounting, engineering, or sales department, is a group of managers and employees who work together because they possess similar skills and experience or use the same kind of

department A group of people who work together and possess similar skills or use the same knowledge, tools, or techniques to perform their jobs.

Table 1.1

Managerial Roles Identified by Mintzberg

Type of Role	Specific Role	Examples of Role Activities
Decisional	Entrepreneur	Commit organizational resources to develop innovative goods and services; decide to expand internationally to obtain new customers for the organization's products.
	Disturbance handler	Move quickly to take corrective action to deal with unexpected problems facing the organization from the external environment, such as a crisis like an oil spill, or from the internal environment, such as producing faulty goods or services.
	Resource allocator	Allocate organizational resources among different tasks and departments of the organization; set budgets and salaries of middle and first-level managers.
	Negotiator	Work with suppliers, distributors, and labor unions to reach agreements about the quality and price of input, technical, and human resources; work with other organizations to establish agreements to pool resources to work on joint projects.
Interpersonal	Figurehead	Outline future organizational goals to employees at company meetings; open a new corporate headquarters building; state the organization's ethical guidelines and the principles of behavior employees are to follow in their dealings with customers and suppliers.
	Leader	Provide an example for employees to follow; give direct commands and orders to subordinates; make decisions concerning the use of human and technical resources; mobilize employee support for specific organizational goals.
	Liaison	Coordinate the work of managers in different departments; establish alliances between different organizations to share resources to produce new goods and services.
Informational	Monitor	Evaluate the performance of managers in different tasks and take corrective action to improve their performance; watch for changes occurring in the external and internal environments that may affect the organization in the future.
	Disseminator	Inform employees about changes taking place in the external and internal environments that will affect them and the organization; communicate to employees the organization's vision and purpose.
	Spokesperson	Launch a national advertising campaign to promote new goods and services; give a speech to inform the local community about the organization's future intentions.

knowledge, tools, or techniques to perform their jobs. Within each department are all three levels of management. Next we examine why organizations use a hierarchy of managers and group them, by the jobs they perform, into departments.

Levels of Management

LO1-3 Differentiate among three levels of management, and understand the tasks and responsibilities of managers at different levels in the organizational hierarchy.

Organizations normally have three levels of management: first-line managers, middle managers, and top managers (see Figure 1.3). Managers at each level have different but related responsibilities for using organizational resources to increase efficiency and effectiveness.

At the base of the managerial hierarchy are **first-line managers**, often called *supervisors*. They are responsible for daily supervision of the nonmanagerial employees who perform the specific activities necessary to produce goods and services. First-line managers work in all departments or functions of an organization.

first-line manager A manager who is responsible for the daily supervision of nonmanagerial employees.

Examples of first-line managers include the supervisor of a work team in the manufacturing department of a car plant, the head nurse in the obstetrics department of a hospital, and the chief mechanic overseeing a crew of mechanics in the service function of a new car dealership. At Dell, first-line managers include the supervisors responsible for controlling the quality of its computers or the level of customer service provided by telephone salespeople. When Michael Dell started his company, he personally controlled the computer assembly process and thus acted as a first-line manager or supervisor.

middle manager A manager who supervises first-line managers and is responsible for finding the best way to use resources to achieve organizational goals.

Supervising the first-line managers are **middle managers**, responsible for finding the best way to organize human and other resources to achieve organizational goals. To increase efficiency, middle managers find ways to help first-line managers and nonmanagerial employees better use resources to reduce manufacturing costs or improve customer service. To increase effectiveness, middle managers evaluate whether the organization's goals are appropriate and suggest to top managers how goals should be changed. Often the suggestions that middle managers make to top managers can dramatically increase organizational performance. A major part of the middle manager's job is developing and fine-tuning skills and know-how, such as manufacturing or marketing expertise, that allow the organization to be efficient and effective. Middle managers make thousands of specific decisions about the production of goods and services: Which first-line supervisors should be chosen for this particular project? Where can we find the highest-quality resources? How should employees be organized to allow them to make the best use of resources?

Behind a first-class sales force, look for the middle managers responsible for training, motivating, and rewarding the salespeople. Behind a committed staff of high school teachers, look for the principal who energizes them to find ways to obtain the resources they need to do outstanding and innovative jobs in the classroom.

Figure 1.3
Levels of Managers

top manager A manager who establishes organizational goals, decides how departments should interact, and monitors the performance of middle managers.

In contrast to middle managers, **top managers** are responsible for the performance of *all* departments.[19] They have *cross-departmental responsibility.* Top managers establish organizational goals, such as which goods and services the company should produce; they decide how the different departments should interact; and they monitor how well middle managers in each department use resources to achieve goals.[20] Top managers are ultimately responsible for the success or failure of an organization, and their performance (like that of Michael Dell or Tim Cook) is continually scrutinized by people inside and outside the organization, such as other employees and investors.[21]

The *chief executive officer (CEO)* is a company's most senior and important manager, the one all other top managers report to. Today the term *chief operating officer (COO)* often refers to the top manager, such as Tim Cook, who is being groomed to take over as CEO when the current CEO becomes the chair of the board, retires, or leaves the company. Together the CEO and COO are responsible for developing good working relationships among the top managers of various departments (manufacturing and marketing, for example); usually these top managers have the title "vice president." A central concern of the CEO is the creation of a smoothly functioning **top management team**, a group composed of the CEO, the COO, and the vice presidents most responsible for achieving organizational goals.[22] Tim Cook is currently working to build such a team at Apple.

top management team A group composed of the CEO, the COO, the president, and the heads of the most important departments.

The relative importance of planning, organizing, leading, and controlling—the four principal managerial tasks—to any particular manager depends on the manager's position in the managerial hierarchy.[23] The amount of time managers spend planning and organizing resources to maintain and improve organizational performance increases as they ascend the hierarchy (see Figure 1.4).[24] Top managers devote most of their time to planning and organizing, the tasks so crucial to determining an organization's long-term performance. The lower that managers' positions are in the hierarchy, the more time the managers spend leading and controlling first-line managers or nonmanagerial employees.

Managerial Skills

Both education and experience enable managers to recognize and develop the personal skills they need to put organizational resources to their best use. Michael Dell realized from the

Figure 1.4

Relative Amount of Time That Managers Spend on the Four Managerial Tasks

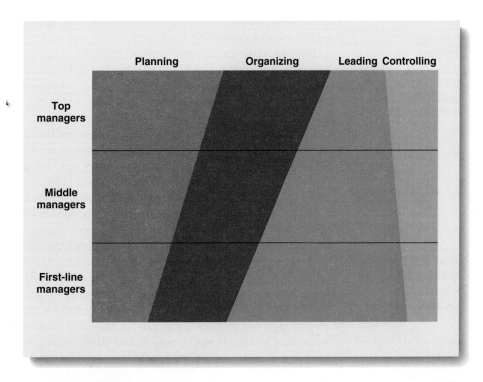

LO1-4   Distinguish between three kinds of managerial skill, and explain why managers are divided into different departments to perform their tasks more efficiently and effectively.

conceptual skills The ability to analyze and diagnose a situation and to distinguish between cause and effect.

start that he lacked sufficient experience and technical expertise in marketing, finance, and planning to guide his company alone. Thus he recruited experienced managers from other IT companies, such as IBM and HP, to help build his company. Research has shown that education and experience help managers acquire and develop three types of skills: *conceptual, human,* and *technical.*[25]

Conceptual skills are demonstrated in the general ability to analyze and diagnose a situation and to distinguish between cause and effect. Top managers require the best conceptual skills because their primary responsibilities are planning and organizing.[26] By all accounts, Steve Jobs was chosen as CEO to transform Apple, and he then picked Tim Cook to succeed him, because of his ability to identify new opportunities and mobilize managers and other resources to take advantage of those opportunities.

Formal education and training are important in helping managers develop conceptual skills. Business training at the undergraduate and graduate (MBA) levels provides many of the conceptual tools (theories and techniques in marketing, finance, and other areas) that managers need to perform their roles effectively. The study of management helps develop the skills that allow managers to understand the big picture confronting an organization. The ability to focus on the big picture lets managers see beyond the situation immediately at hand and consider choices while keeping in mind the organization's long-term goals.

Today continuing management education and training, including training in advanced IT, are an integral step in building managerial skills because new theories and techniques are constantly being developed to improve organizational effectiveness, such as total quality management, global supply chain management, and cloud computing and virtual business-to-business (B2B) networks. A quick scan through a magazine such as *Bloomberg Businessweek* or *Fortune* reveals a host of seminars on topics such as advanced marketing, finance, leadership, and human resources management that are offered to managers at many levels in the organization, from the most senior corporate executives to middle managers. Microsoft, IBM, Oracle, and many other organizations designate a portion of each manager's personal budget to be used at the manager's discretion to attend management development programs.

In addition, organizations may wish to develop a particular manager's abilities in a specific skill area—perhaps to learn an advanced component of departmental skills, such as international bond trading, or to learn the skills necessary to implement total quality management. The organization thus pays for managers to attend specialized programs to develop these skills. Indeed, one signal that a manager is performing well is an organization's willingness to invest in that manager's skill development. Similarly, many nonmanagerial employees who are performing at a high level (because they have studied management) are often sent to intensive management training programs to develop their management skills and to prepare them for promotion to first-level management positions.

human skills The ability to understand, alter, lead, and control the behavior of other individuals and groups.

Human skills include the general ability to understand, alter, lead, and control the behavior of other individuals and groups. The ability to communicate, to coordinate, and to motivate people, and to mold individuals into a cohesive team, distinguishes effective from ineffective managers. By all accounts, Tim Cook and Michael Dell possess a high level of these human skills.

Like conceptual skills, human skills can be learned through education and training, as well as be developed through experience.[27] Organizations increasingly utilize advanced programs in leadership skills and team leadership as they seek to capitalize on the advantages of self-managed teams.[28] To manage personal interactions effectively, each person in an organization needs to learn how to empathize with other people—to understand their viewpoints and the problems they face. One way to help managers understand their personal strengths and weaknesses is to have their superiors, peers, and subordinates provide feedback about their job performance. Thorough and direct feedback allows managers to develop their human skills.

technical skills The job-specific knowledge and techniques required to perform an organizational role.

Technical skills are the *job-specific* skills required to perform a particular type of work or occupation at a high level. Examples include a manager's specific manufacturing, accounting, marketing, and increasingly, IT skills. Managers need a range of technical skills to be effective. The array of technical skills managers need depends on their position in their organizations. The manager of a restaurant, for example, may need cooking skills to fill in for an absent cook, accounting and bookkeeping skills to keep track of receipts and costs and to administer the payroll, and aesthetic skills to keep the restaurant looking attractive for customers.

As noted earlier, managers and employees who possess the same kinds of technical skills typically become members of a specific department and are known as, for example, marketing managers or manufacturing managers.[29] Managers are grouped into different departments because a major part of a manager's responsibility is to monitor, train, and supervise employees so their job-specific skills and expertise increase. Obviously this is easier to do when employees with similar skills are grouped into the same department because they can learn from one another and become more skilled and productive at their particular jobs.

Figure 1.5 shows how an organization groups managers into departments on the basis of their job-specific skills. It also shows that inside each department, a managerial hierarchy of first-line, middle, and top managers emerges. At Dell, for example, Michael Dell hired experienced top managers to take charge of the marketing, sales, and manufacturing departments and to develop work procedures to help middle and first-line managers control the company's explosive sales growth. When the head of manufacturing found he had no time to supervise computer assembly, he recruited experienced manufacturing middle managers from other companies to assume this responsibility.

core competency The specific set of departmental skills, knowledge, and experience that allows one organization to outperform another.

Today the term **core competency** is often used to refer to the specific set of departmental skills, knowledge, and experience that allows one organization to outperform its competitors. In other words, departmental skills that create a core competency give an organization a *competitive advantage.* Dell, for example, was the first PC maker to develop a core competency in materials management that allowed it to produce PCs at a much lower cost than its competitors—a major source of competitive advantage. Similarly, 3M is well known for its core competency in research and development (R&D) that allows it to innovate new products at a faster rate than its competitors, and Dell has been working to develop a competency to provide a full range of computer hardware and software that is customized to the specific needs of each company it serves.

Figure 1.5

Types and Levels of Managers

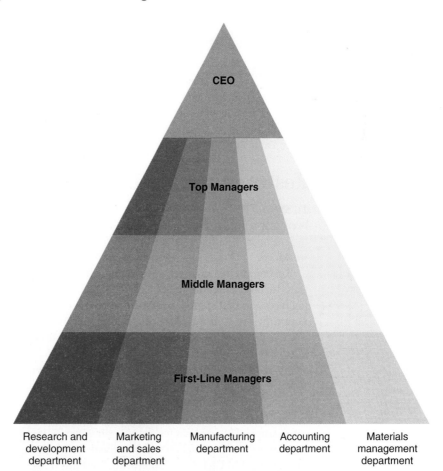

Effective managers need all three kinds of skills—conceptual, human, and technical—to help their organizations perform more efficiently and effectively. The absence of even one type of managerial skill can lead to failure. One of the biggest problems that people who start small businesses confront, for example, is their lack of appropriate conceptual and human skills. Someone who has the technical skills to start a new business does not necessarily know how to manage the venture successfully. Similarly, one of the biggest problems that scientists or engineers who switch careers from research to management confront is their lack of effective human skills. Ambitious managers or prospective managers are constantly in search of the latest educational contributions to help them develop the conceptual, human, and technical skills they need to perform at a high level in today's changing and increasingly competitive global environment.

Developing new and improved skills through education and training has become a priority for both aspiring managers and the organizations they work for. As we discussed earlier, many people are enrolling in advanced management courses; but many companies, such as Microsoft, GE, and IBM, have established their own colleges to train and develop their employees and managers at all levels. Every year these companies put thousands of their employees through management programs designed to identify the employees who the company believes have the competencies that can be developed to become its future top managers. Most organizations closely link promotion to a manager's ability to acquire the competencies that a particular company believes are important.[30] At Apple and 3M, for example, the ability to successfully lead a new product development team is viewed as a vital requirement for promotion; at Accenture and IBM, the ability to attract and retain clients is viewed as a skill its consultants must possess. We discuss the various kinds of skills managers need to develop in most of the chapters of this book.

Recent Changes in Management Practices

The tasks and responsibilities of managers have been changing dramatically in recent years. Two major factors that have led to these changes are global competition and advances in information technology (IT). Stiff competition for resources from organizations both at home and abroad has put increased pressure on all managers to improve efficiency and effectiveness. Increasingly, top managers are encouraging lower-level managers to look beyond the goals of their own departments and take a cross-departmental view to find new opportunities to improve organizational performance. Modern IT gives managers at all levels and in all areas access to more and better information and improves their ability to plan, organize, lead, and control. IT also gives employees more job-related information and allows them to become more skilled, specialized, and productive.[31]

Restructuring and Outsourcing

To utilize IT to increase efficiency and effectiveness, CEOs and top management teams have been restructuring organizations and outsourcing specific organizational activities to reduce the number of employees on the payroll and make more productive use of the remaining workforce.

restructuring Downsizing an organization by eliminating the jobs of large numbers of top, middle, and first-line managers and nonmanagerial employees.

Restructuring involves simplifying, shrinking, or downsizing an organization's operations to lower operating costs, as Dell, Nokia, and Xerox have been forced to do. The continuing recession that started in 2009 has forced most companies—large and small, and profit and nonprofit—to find ways to reduce costs because their customers are spending less money, so their revenues decrease. Restructuring can be done by eliminating product teams, shrinking departments, and reducing levels in the hierarchy, all of which result in the loss of large numbers of jobs of top, middle, or first-line managers, as well as nonmanagerial employees. Modern IT's ability to improve efficiency has increased the amount of downsizing in recent years because IT makes it possible for fewer employees to perform a given task. IT increases each person's ability to process information and make decisions more quickly and accurately, for example. U.S. companies are spending over $100 billion a year to purchase advanced IT that can improve efficiency and effectiveness. We discuss the many dramatic effects of IT on management in Chapter 18 and throughout this book.

Restructuring, however, can produce some powerful negative outcomes. It can reduce the morale of remaining employees, who worry about their own job security. And top managers of many downsized organizations realize that they downsized too far when their employees complain they are overworked and when increasing numbers of customers complain about poor service.[32] Dell faced this charge in the 2010s as it continued to reduce the number of its customer service representatives and outsource their jobs to India to lower costs.

outsourcing Contracting with another company, usually abroad, to have it perform an activity the organization previously performed itself.

Outsourcing involves contracting with another company, usually in a low-cost country abroad, to have it perform a work activity the organization previously performed itself, such as manufacturing, marketing, or customer service. Outsourcing increases efficiency because it lowers operating costs, freeing up money and resources that can be used in more effective ways—for example, to develop new products.

The need to respond to low-cost global competition has speeded outsourcing dramatically in the 2000s. Over 3 million U.S. jobs in the manufacturing sector have been lost since 2000 as companies have moved their operations to countries such as China, Taiwan, and Malaysia. Tens of thousands of high-paying IT jobs have also moved abroad, to countries like India and Russia, where programmers work for one-third the salary of those in the United States. Dell employs over 12,000 customer service reps in India, for example.[33]

Large for-profit organizations today typically employ 10% to 20% fewer people than they did 10 years ago because of restructuring and outsourcing. Ford, IBM, AT&T, HP, Dell, and DuPont are among the thousands of organizations that have streamlined their operations to increase efficiency and effectiveness. The argument is that the managers and employees who have lost their jobs will find employment in new and growing U.S. companies where their skills and experience will be better utilized. For example, the millions of manufacturing jobs that have been lost overseas will be replaced by higher-paying U.S. jobs in the service sector that are made possible because of the growth in global trade. At the same time, many companies have experienced growing problems with outsourcing in the 2010s, and the move to insource jobs (that is, to bring them back to the United States) has been increasing as discussed in the following "Managing Globally."

Managing
Globally

First Outsourcing, Now Insourcing

Outsourcing has become a major global strategic imperative over the last decades; to survive against low-cost competitors U.S. companies have been forced to find ways to reduce costs by moving manufacturing overseas. First, millions of unskilled manufacturing jobs were outsourced to countries in Asia and Central America; then semiskilled and skilled jobs in engineering and information technology (IT) followed. There is a huge talented workforce in countries such as India and China, where millions of workers have the skills to satisfy job requirements and are willing to work for a fraction of what companies must pay workers in the United States.

In some areas, such as the production of clothes and shoes and the assembly of electronic devices such as iPhones and PCs that are labor intensive, countries such as the United States will never be able to regain a competitive advantage because of low labor costs overseas. However, there are other areas in which companies that depend on a reliable supply of high-quality components and finished products have experienced problems with outsourcing production abroad, and many companies have or are in the process of moving back production to the United States—the process of insourcing. There are many reasons for this: Some relate to quality issues and some relate to the enormous problems that most electronics companies experienced after the disastrous

Boeing embraces insourcing: the first Boeing 787 Dreamliner is being built at Boeing's Paine Field near Everett, Washington.

flooding in Thailand and the tsunami that struck Japan cut off the supply of vital components. Thousands of U.S. companies were unable to obtain the chips and memory circuits necessary to maintain production, and they became backlogged with orders and lost billions in potential sales.

Boeing experienced firsthand the problems in controlling quality and product development during the building of the Boeing 787 Dreamliner that was finally delivered to its first customer in 2011. Boeing had experienced great success with outsourcing the production of many important components when it developed its previous new airliner, the 777. To tap into the skills of engineers in countries abroad and to reduce costs, Boeing decided early in development of the 787 to work closely with its suppliers who invested in the equipment and facilities necessary to meet Boeing's demands. Its Dreamliner team has about 50 suppliers from the United States and around the world; the partnership features six companies from Japan, six from Britain, five from France, two from Germany, two from Sweden, and one each from South Korea and Italy.[34] They make sections of the fuselage, landing gear, parts of the wing, pumps, valves, engines, brakes, doors, waste systems, escape slides, tires, tubing, cabin lighting, and ducts.

Boeing announced the first of several important delays in delivery dates of key components with overseas suppliers in 2007.[35] A major setback was a problem that arose in 2009 when major structural problems were found in the design of the assembly connecting the wing to the fuselage. Boeing was forced to postpone the date of introduction of the innovative new 787, and when it was finally delivered, it was over two years late to market. This was a major blow to Boeing since the 787 had a record 1,000 orders, although Boeing lost over 100 orders because of the delay as customers turned to its major competitor, Airbus.

In 2012 it was still having the problem of obtaining components fast enough to ramp up production of the 787 in order to better meet customer demand. It is reevaluating its outsourcing strategy and has already decided to insource production of more components in order to obtain more control over its global supply chain. Like many other companies Boeing has seen the disadvantages of offshore production, including shipping costs, logistical problems, and quality issues. And many U.S. companies are working with their employees and unions to establish pay rates that will make it practical to insource production of many complex or bulky products. For example, GE worked with its unions to establish an agreement that would allow it to bring back to the United States the manufacturing of water heaters and many of the complex components that go into its appliances. Similarly, Caterpillar announced that it would reorganize global production of excavators and triple the volume of excavators made in the United States for export to the Americas. Every manufacturing job brought back to the United States is valuable, especially in a recession.[36] The growing rate of insourcing provides a signal to all U.S. companies that they need to have a second source of supply to ensure they do not suffer when unexpected problems from natural and political factors arise quickly and disrupt their manufacturing activities.

LO1-5 Discuss some major changes in management practices today that have occurred as a result of globalization and the use of advanced information technology (IT).

empowerment The expansion of employees' knowledge, tasks, and decision-making responsibilities.

Empowerment and Self-Managed Teams

The second principal way managers have sought to increase efficiency and effectiveness is by empowering lower-level employees and moving to self-managed teams. **Empowerment** is a management technique that involves giving employees more authority and responsibility over how they perform their work activities. The way in which John Deere, the well-known tractor manufacturer, empowered its employees illustrates how this technique can help raise performance. The employees who assemble Deere's vehicles possess detailed knowledge about how Deere products work. Deere's managers realized these employees could become persuasive salespeople if they were given training. So groups of these employees were given intensive sales training and sent to visit Deere's customers and explain to them how to operate and service the company's new products. While speaking with customers, these newly empowered "salespeople" also collect information that helps Deere develop new products that

Lonnie Love, an Illinois farmer, checks out the custom wiring job on his John Deere tractor. Technicians, such as the one working on Love's tractor, add irreplaceable know-how to help John Deere's sales force.

better meet customers' needs. The new sales jobs are temporary; employees go on assignment but then return to the production line, where they use their new knowledge to find ways to improve efficiency and quality.

Often companies find that empowering employees can lead to so many kinds of performance gains that they use their reward systems to promote empowerment. For example, Deere's moves to empower employees were so successful that the company negotiated a new labor agreement with its employees to promote empowerment. The agreement specifies that pay increases will be based on employees' learning new skills and completing college courses in areas such as computer programming that will help the company increase efficiency and quality. Deere has continued to make greater use of teams throughout the 2010s, and its profits have soared because its competitors cannot match its user-friendly machines that are the result of its drive to respond to its customers' needs.

IT is being increasingly used to empower employees because it expands employees' job knowledge and increases the scope of their job responsibilities. Frequently IT allows one employee to perform a task that was previously performed by many employees. As a result, the employee has more autonomy and responsibility. IT also facilitates the use of a **self-managed team**, a group of employees who assume collective responsibility for organizing, controlling, and supervising their own work activities.[37] Using IT designed to give team members real-time information about each member's performance, a self-managed team can often find ways to accomplish a task more quickly and efficiently. Moreover, self-

self-managed team A group of employees who assume responsibility for organizing, controlling, and supervising their own activities and monitoring the quality of the goods and services they provide.

managed teams assume many tasks and responsibilities previously performed by first-line managers, so a company can better utilize its workforce.[38] First-line managers act as coaches or mentors whose job is not to tell employees what to do but to provide advice and guidance and help teams find new ways to perform their tasks more efficiently.[39] Using the same IT, middle managers can easily monitor what is happening in these teams and make better resource allocation decisions as a result. We discuss self-managed teams in more detail in Chapters 2, 10, and 15.

Challenges for Management in a Global Environment

global organizations Organizations that operate and compete in more than one country.

Because the world has been changing more rapidly than ever before, managers and other employees throughout an organization must perform at higher and higher levels.[40] In the last 20 years, rivalry between organizations competing domestically (in the same country) and globally (in countries abroad) has increased dramatically. The rise of **global organizations**, organizations that operate and compete in more than one country, has pressured many organizations to identify better ways to use their resources and improve their performance. The successes of the German chemical companies Schering and Hoechst, Italian furniture manufacturer Natuzzi, Korean electronics companies Samsung and LG, Brazilian plane maker Embraer, and Europe's Airbus Industries are putting pressure on companies in other countries to raise their level of performance to compete successfully against these global organizations.

Even in the not-for-profit sector, global competition is spurring change. Schools, universities, police forces, and government agencies are reexamining their operations because looking at how activities are performed in other countries often reveals better ways to do them. For example, many curriculum and teaching changes in the United States have resulted from the study of methods that Japanese and European school systems use. Similarly, European and Asian hospital systems have learned much from the U.S. system—which may be the most effective, though not the most efficient, in the world.

Today managers who make no attempt to learn from and adapt to changes in the global environment find themselves reacting rather than innovating, and their organizations often become uncompetitive and fail.[41] Five major challenges stand out for managers in today's world: building a competitive advantage, maintaining ethical standards, managing a diverse workforce, utilizing new information systems and technologies, and practicing global crisis management.

Building Competitive Advantage

What are the most important lessons for managers and organizations to learn if they are to reach and remain at the top of the competitive environment of business? The answer relates to the use of organizational resources to build a competitive advantage. **Competitive advantage** is the ability of one organization to outperform other organizations because it produces desired goods or services more efficiently and effectively than its competitors. The four building blocks of competitive advantage are superior *efficiency; quality; speed, flexibility,* and *innovation;* and *responsiveness to customers* (see Figure 1.6).

Organizations increase their efficiency when they reduce the quantity of resources (such as people and raw materials) they use to produce goods or services. In today's competitive environment, organizations continually search for new ways to use their resources to improve efficiency. Many organizations are training their workforces in the new skills and techniques needed to operate heavily computerized assembly plants. Similarly, cross-training gives employees the range of skills they need to perform many different tasks; and organizing employees in new ways, such as in self-managed teams, lets them make good use of their skills. These are important steps in the effort to improve productivity. Japanese and German companies invest far more in training employees than do American or Italian companies.

Managers must improve efficiency if their organizations are to compete successfully with companies operating in Mexico, China, Malaysia, and other countries where employees are paid comparatively low wages. New methods must be devised either to increase efficiency or to gain some other competitive advantage—higher-quality goods, for example—if outsourcing and the loss of jobs to low-cost countries are to be prevented.

The challenge from global organizations such as Korean electronics manufacturers, Mexican agricultural producers, and European design and financial companies also has increased pressure on companies to develop the skills and abilities of their workforces in order to improve the quality of their goods and services. One major thrust to improving quality has been to introduce the quality-enhancing techniques known as *total quality management (TQM)*. Employees

competitive advantage The ability of one organization to outperform other organizations because it produces desired goods or services more efficiently and effectively than they do.

Figure 1.6

Building Blocks of Competitive Advantage

involved in TQM are often organized into quality control teams and are responsible for finding new and better ways to perform their jobs; they also must monitor and evaluate the quality of the goods they produce. We discuss ways of managing TQM successfully in Chapter 9.

Today companies can win or lose the competitive race depending on their *speed*—how fast they can bring new products to market—or their *flexibility*—how easily they can change or alter the way they perform their activities to respond to actions of their competitors. Companies that have speed and flexibility are agile competitors: Their managers have superior planning and organizing abilities; they can think ahead, decide what to do, and then speedily mobilize their resources to respond to a changing environment. We examine how managers can build speed and flexibility in their organizations in later chapters. Michael Dell and Tim Cook are working hard to make Dell and Apple agile companies that can react to the technological changes taking place in a digital world—their problem is how to maintain their competitive advantage against Samsung, HP, Nokia, and Google.

innovation The process of creating new or improved goods and services or developing better ways to produce or provide them.

Innovation, the process of creating new or improved goods and services that customers want or developing better ways to produce or provide goods and services, poses a special challenge. Managers must create an organizational setting in which people are encouraged to be innovative. Typically innovation takes place in small groups or teams; management decentralizes control of work activities to team members and creates an organizational culture that rewards risk taking. For example, a team composed of Apple and Nike employees came up with the idea for a new model of iPod that would be able to record and measure the distance its owner had run, among other things, and the companies formed an alliance to make it.[42] Managing innovation and creating a work setting that encourages risk taking are among the most difficult managerial tasks. Innovation is discussed in depth in Chapter 9.

Organizations compete for customers with their products and services, so training employees to be responsive to customers' needs is vital for all organizations, but particularly for service organizations. Retail stores, banks, and hospitals, for example, depend entirely on their employees to perform behaviors that result in high-quality service at a reasonable cost.[43] As many countries (the United States, Canada, and Switzerland are just a few) move toward a more service-based economy (in part because of the loss of manufacturing jobs to China, Malaysia, and other countries with low labor costs), managing behavior in service organizations is becoming increasingly important. Many organizations are empowering their customer service employees and giving them the authority to take the lead in providing high-quality customer service. As noted previously, empowering nonmanagerial employees and creating self-managed teams change the role of first-line managers and lead to more efficient use of organizational resources.

turnaround management The creation of a new vision for a struggling company based on a new approach to planning and organizing to make better use of a company's resources and allow it to survive and prosper.

Sometimes the best efforts of managers to revitalize their organization's fortunes fail; and faced with bankruptcy, the directors of these companies are forced to appoint a new CEO who has a history of success in rebuilding a company. **Turnaround management** is the creation of a new vision for a struggling company using a new approach to planning and organizing to make better use of a company's resources and allow it to survive and eventually prosper—something Apple's Steve Jobs excelled at. It involves developing radical new strategies such as how to reduce the number of products sold or change how they are made and distributed, or close corporate and manufacturing operations to reduce costs. Organizations that appoint turnaround CEOs are generally experiencing a crisis because they have become inefficient or ineffective; sometimes this is because of poor management over a continuing period, and sometimes it occurs because a competitor introduces a new product or technology that makes their own products unattractive to customers. For example, when Apple introduced the iPhone in 2007, sales of the former best-selling Motorola Razr cell phone plummeted because customers demand state-of-the-art products. Motorola has not recovered because it has no smartphone to compete with Apple, although it introduced new phones using Google's Android platform in 2009. Similarly, sales of BlackBerry and Nokia smartphones have plunged while those of Samsung and HTC have increased as these companies introduced Android smartphones that can compete with the iPhone.

Achieving a competitive advantage requires that managers use all their skills and expertise, as well as their companies' other resources, to find new and improved ways to improve efficiency, quality, innovation, and responsiveness to customers. We revisit this theme often as we examine the ways managers plan strategies, organize resources and activities, and lead and control people and groups to increase efficiency and effectiveness.

Maintaining Ethical and Socially Responsible Standards

Managers at all levels, especially after the recent economic crisis, are under considerable pressure to make the best use of resources to increase the level at which their organizations perform.[44] For example, top managers feel pressure from shareholders to increase the performance of the entire organization to boost its stock price, improve profits, or raise dividends. In turn, top managers may pressure middle managers to find new ways to use organizational resources to increase efficiency or quality and thus attract new customers and earn more revenues—and then middle managers hit on their department's supervisors.

Pressure to increase performance can be healthy for an organization because it leads managers to question how the organization is working, and it encourages them to find new and better ways to plan, organize, lead, and control. However, too much pressure to perform can be harmful.[45] It may induce managers to behave unethically, and even illegally, when dealing with people and groups inside and outside the organization.[46]

A purchasing manager for a nationwide retail chain, for example, might buy inferior clothing as a cost-cutting measure or ignore the working conditions under which products are made to obtain low-priced products. These issues faced the managers of companies that make footwear and clothing in the 1990s, when customers learned about the sweatshop conditions in which garment and shoe workers around the world labored. Today companies such as Nike, Walmart, and Apple are trying to stop sweatshop practices and prevent managers abroad from adopting work practices that harm their workers. They now employ hundreds of inspectors who police the factories overseas that make the products they sell and who can terminate contracts with suppliers when they behave in an unethical or illegal way. Nevertheless, in a 2010 report Apple revealed that its investigations showed that sweatshop conditions still existed in some of the factories it used abroad. Apple said that at least 55 of the 102 factories were ignoring Apple's rule that staff cannot work more than 60 hours a week, for example. Apple is continuing its efforts to reduce these abuses.[47]

Similarly, to secure a large foreign contract, a sales manager in a large company, such as in the defense or electronics industry, might offer bribes to foreign officials to obtain lucrative contracts—even though this is against the law. In 2010, for example, German electronic equipment maker Siemens agreed to pay $1.4 billion in fines to settle claims that it paid bribes and kickbacks to organizations around the world between 2001 and 2007. Securities and Exchange Commission (SEC) Chairman Christopher Cox alleged, "Siemens paid staggering amounts of money to circumvent the rules and gain business. Now, they will pay for it with the largest settlement in the history of the Foreign Corrupt Practices Act since it became law in 1977."[48]

The issue of social responsibility, discussed in Chapter 4, centers on deciding what obligations a company has toward the people and groups affected by its activities—such as employees, customers, or the cities in which it operates. Some companies have strong views about social responsibility; their managers believe they should protect the interests of others. But some managers may decide to act in an unethical way and put their own interests first, hurting others in the process. A recent example showing why managers must always keep the need to act in an ethical and socially responsible way at the forefront of their decision making is profiled in the following "Ethics in Action" box.

Ethics in Action

Everything Is *Not* Coming Up Roses

Every year on Valentine's Day tens of millions of roses are delivered to sweethearts and loved ones in the United States, and anyone who has bought roses knows that their price has been falling steadily. One of the main reasons for this is that rose growing is now concentrated in poorer countries in Central and South America. Rose growing has been a boon to poor countries where the extra income women earn

Ecuadorian farm laborers, such as the women pictured here, endure grueling conditions when picking and bundling roses Every time you consider roses for your sweetie, you can choose to either ignore these situations, or you can choose to only buy roses grown and harvested under fair labor practices.

can mean the difference between starvation or not for their families. Ecuador, for example, is the fourth biggest rose grower in the world, and the industry employs over 50,000 women who tend, pick, and package roses for above its national minimum wage. Most of these women are employed by Rosas del Ecuador, the company that controls the rose business in that country.

The hidden side of the global rose-growing business is that poorer countries tend to have lax or unenforced health and safety laws, something that lowers rose-growing costs in these countries. And, critics argue, many rose-growing companies and countries are not considering the well-being of their workers. For example, although the CEO of Rosas del Ecuador, Erwin Pazmino, denies workers are subjected to unsafe conditions, almost 60% of his workers have reported blurred vision, nausea, headaches, asthma, and other symptoms of pesticide poisoning.[49] Workers labor in hot, poorly ventilated greenhouses in which roses have been sprayed with pesticides and herbicides. Safety equipment such as masks and ventilators is scarce and the long hours women work add to chemical overexposure. If workers complain, they may be fired and blacklisted, which makes it hard for them to find other jobs. So, to protect their families' well-being, workers rarely complain and so their health remains at risk.

Clearly, rose buyers worldwide need to be aware of these working conditions when deciding to buy roses, just as buyers of inexpensive clothing and footwear became concerned in the last few decades when they found out about the sweatshop conditions in which garment and shoe workers labored. Companies like Nike and Walmart have made major efforts to stop sweatshop practices, and they now employ hundreds of inspectors who police the factories overseas that make the products they sell. In a similar way, the main buyers and distributors of flowers for the U.S. market also are beginning to consider the well-being of the workers who grow them.

Managing a Diverse Workforce

A major challenge for managers everywhere is to recognize the ethical need and legal requirement to treat human resources fairly and equitably. Today the age, gender, race, ethnicity, religion, sexual preference, and socioeconomic composition of the workforce presents new challenges for managers. To create a highly trained and motivated workforce, as well as to avoid lawsuits, managers must establish human resource management (HRM) procedures and practices that are legal and fair and do not discriminate against any organizational members.[50] Today most organizations understand that to motivate effectively and take advantage of the talents of a diverse workforce, they must make promotion opportunities available to each and every employee.[51] Managers must recognize the performance-enhancing possibilities of a diverse workforce, such as the ability to take advantage of the skills and experiences of different kinds of people.[52] Accenture provides a good example of a company that has utilized the potential of its diverse employees.

Accenture is a global management consulting company that serves the IT needs of thousands of client companies located in over 120 countries around the world. A major driving force behind Accenture's core organizational vision is to manage and promote diversity in order to improve employee performance and client satisfaction. At Accenture, managers at all levels realize consultants bring distinct experiences, talents, and values to their work, and a major management initiative is to take advantage of that diversity to encourage collaboration between consultants to improve the service Accenture provides to each of its clients. Because Accenture's clients are also diverse by country, religion, ethnicity, and so forth, it tries to match its teams of consultants to the attributes of its diverse clients.

Global consulting company Accenture is a first-mover in taking advantage of the diverse skills and knowledge of its consultants to create teams that can provide the customized solutions needed to best satisfy clients such as large overseas companies.

Accenture provides hundreds of diversity management training programs to its consultants each year using its 13 teams of global human capital and diversity experts, who collaborate to create its programs. Accenture also encourages each of its consultants to pursue opportunities to "work across different geographies, workforces, and generations to create agile global leaders."[53] In 2010 one-third of its global workforce was composed of women, who also hold 16% of its management positions at all levels. Accenture chooses to buy from suppliers who can also demonstrate their commitment to diversity, and in 2010 nearly $300 million or 15% of Accenture's purchasing came from small minority- or women-owned suppliers. The firm also provides diversity training programs to its suppliers and prospective suppliers around the world to show them how diversity can increase their efficiency and effectiveness. In all these ways, Accenture uses its expertise in managing diversity to promote individual and organizational performance—one reason it has become the most successful and fast-growing consultancy company in the world.

Managers who value their diverse employees not only invest in developing these employees' skills and capabilities but also succeed best in promoting performance over the long run. Today more organizations are realizing that people are their most important resource and that developing and protecting human resources is the most important challenge for managers in a competitive global environment. Kevin Rollins, a former CEO of Dell, commented, "I've seen firsthand the power of a diverse workforce. Leveraging the similarities and differences of all team members enables Dell to develop the best products, provide a superior customer experience, and contribute in meaningful ways to the communities where we do business."[54] And as Takahiro Moriguchi of Union Bank of California said when accepting a national diversity award for his company when he was its CEO, "By searching for talent from among the disabled, both genders, veterans, gay, all ethnic groups and all nationalities, we gain access to a pool of ideas, energy, and creativity as wide and varied as the human race itself."[55] We discuss the many issues surrounding the management of a diverse workforce in Chapter 5.

Utilizing IT and E-Commerce

As we have discussed, another important challenge for managers is to continually utilize efficient and effective new IT that can link and enable managers and employees to better perform their jobs—whatever their level in the organization. One example of how IT has changed the jobs of people at all organizational levels comes from UPS, where, until 2006, its drivers relied on maps, note cards, and their own experience to plan the fastest way to deliver hundreds of parcels each day. This changed after UPS invested over $600 million to develop a computerized route optimization system that each evening plans each of its 56,000 drivers' routes for the next day in the most efficient way by, for example, minimizing the number of left turns that waste both time and gas. The program has been incredibly successful and has been continuously updated so that by 2010 UPS drivers covered tens of million fewer miles each month while they delivered ever-increasing numbers of packages faster.

Increasingly, new kinds of IT enable not just individual employees but also self-managed teams by giving them important information and allowing virtual interactions around the globe using the Internet. Increased global coordination helps improve quality and increase the pace of innovation. Microsoft, Hitachi, IBM, and most companies now search for new IT that can help them build a competitive advantage. The importance of IT is discussed in detail in Chapters 16 and 18, and throughout the text you will find icons that alert you to examples of how IT is changing the way companies operate.

UPS Dispatch Coordinator Jim McCauley shows driver Muamer Pleh how many stops he will be making in his next delivery run—all made possible by the company's new software that allows each driver to plan the most efficient delivery route each day, which saves the company time and money.

Practicing Global Crisis Management

Today another challenge facing managers and organizations is global crisis management. The causes of global crises or disasters fall into two main categories: natural causes and human causes. Crises that arise because of natural causes include the hurricanes, tsunamis, earthquakes, famines, and diseases that have devastated so many countries in the 2000s; hardly any country has been untouched by their effects. In 2010 both Haiti and Chile experienced severe earthquakes that killed thousands of people and left tens of thousands more homeless. Despite the extensive foreign aid they have received, both these countries will probably need years to recover from these crises and rebuild their economies and infrastructure.

Human-created crises result from factors such as industrial pollution, poor attention to worker and workplace safety, global warming and the destruction of the natural habitat or environment, and geopolitical tensions and terrorism. Human-created crises, such as global warming due to emissions of carbon dioxide and other gases, may intensify the effects of natural disasters. For example, increasing global temperatures and acid rain may have increased the intensity of hurricanes, led to unusually strong rains, and contributed to lengthy droughts. Scientists believe that global warming is responsible for the rapid destruction of coral reefs, forests, animal species, and the natural habitat in many parts of the world. The shrinking polar ice caps are expected to raise the sea level by a few critical inches.

Increasing geopolitical tensions, which are partly the result of the speed of the globalization process itself, have upset the balance of world power as different countries and geographic regions attempt to protect their own economic and political interests. Rising oil prices, for example, have strengthened the bargaining power of oil-supplying countries. This has led the United States to adopt global political strategies, including its war on terrorism, to secure the supply of oil vital to protecting its national interest. In a similar way, countries in Europe have been forming contracts and allying with Russia to obtain its supply of natural gas, and Japan and China have been negotiating with Iran and Saudi Arabia. The rise of global terrorism and terrorist groups is to a large degree the result of changing political, social, and economic conditions that have made it easier for extremists to influence whole countries and cultures.

Finally, industrial pollution and limited concern for the health and safety of workers have become increasingly significant problems for companies and countries. Companies in heavy industries such as coal and steel have polluted millions of acres of land around major cities in eastern Europe and Asia; billion-dollar cleanups are necessary. The 1986 Chernobyl nuclear power plant meltdown released over 1,540 times as much radiation into the air as occurred at Hiroshima; over 50,000 people died as a result, while hundreds of thousands more have been affected. In the area of worker health and safety, one example of a company whose managers paid too little attention to preventing crises is oil refiner British Petroleum, which is discussed in the following "Managing Globally" box.

Managing
Globally

A Concern for Safety Explodes at BP

In 2009 a U.S. judge finally approved British Petroleum's (BP) plea agreement to pay $50 million—the largest U.S. criminal environmental fine ever—after pleading guilty to charges stemming from a 2005 explosion that killed 15 workers and injured 180 workers at BP's Texas City oil refinery, the third largest in the United States, situated 40 miles from Houston. The explosion was the third largest ever in the United States and the fifth largest globally. "We deeply regret the harm that was caused by this terrible tragedy. We take very seriously the commitments we've made as part of the plea agreement," said BP spokesman Daren Beaudo.

An investigation revealed that the 2005 explosion occurred because BP had relaxed safety procedures at its Texas City refinery to reduce operating costs. The U.S.

The remains of BP's Texas City oil refinery after the huge explosion that killed 15 workers and injured hundreds more. BP faces billions in penalties, fines, and punitive damages from this debacle, and its woes continue on in the wake of the April 2010 Gulf of Mexico oil spill.

Occupational Health and Safety Association (OSHA) decided the 2005 explosion was caused by defective pressure relief systems and by poor safety management programs. Consequently, in 1997 OSHA issued its largest fine up to that date, $21 million, against BP for the lapses that led to the refinery explosion because BP sacrificed safety at the refinery to cut costs. The judgment also required the U.S. unit of London-based BP to serve three years on probation while the company tried to solve more than 500 serious safety violations that had been discovered during the investigation.

Beyond the formal fines, however, BP faced hundreds of lawsuits stemming from the explosion from workers and their families and the people and organizations that had been affected by the blast, which was felt miles from the refinery. It is estimated that BP spent over *2 billion* to settle these claims, most of which were settled privately outside the courts. After paying so much in legal costs and fines, and given the bad publicity it experienced globally, you might think a company like BP would immediately move to improve its safety procedures. However, while it paid these costs, it also earned $21 billion in profit during the same year. So how did its top management respond?

Not in a highly responsive way. In 2009 OSHA issued a new record $87 million fine against the oil giant for failing to correct the safety violations identified after the 2005 explosion. The 2007 agreement between BP and OSHA included a detailed list of ways in which BP should improve safety procedures at the plant—something its managers vowed to do. But a six-month inspection revealed hundreds of violations of the 2007 agreement to repair hazards at the refinery, and OSHA decided BP had failed to live up to the terms of its commitment to protect employees and that another catastrophe was possible because BP had a major safety problem in the "culture" of this refinery.

BP responded strongly to these accusations, arguing that it had spent hundreds of millions of dollars to correct the safety problems. BP also said that after it reviewed safety procedures at its four U.S. refineries and found that its Cherry Point refinery had the best process safety culture, the head of that refinery had been promoted to oversee better implementation of process safety across BP's U.S. operations. In 2007, however, another serious incident occurred when 10 workers claimed they were injured when a toxic substance was released at the Texas City plant, which BP denied. (A jury subsequently decided in favor of these workers, who were awarded over $200 million in punitive damages in 2009.)

In any event, in 2007 BP's board of directors decided to move quickly. They fired its CEO and many other top managers and appointed a new CEO, Anthony Hayward, who was instructed to make global refinery safety a key organizational priority. The board also decided to make a substantial portion of the future stock bonuses for the CEO and other top managers dependent on BP's future safety record, and the board committed over $5 billion to improving safety across the company's global operations.

Hayward's efforts seemed to be working, but in April 2010 the Deepwater Horizon oil-drilling platform that BP had leased from its U.S.-based owner Transocean exploded, killing 11 employees; and the fractured oil pipe began to release millions of barrels of oil into the Gulf of Mexico. Despite all of BP's attempts to use its expertise to stop the oil gushing from the pipe, a mile below the sea, oil continued to flow into the gulf. Finally, in late 2010 two relief wells that BP drilled stopped the flow of oil. The damage caused by the spill has been enormous, however, and by 2012 BP had reserved over $20 billion to pay potential fines and compensation that are still being determined as lawsuits between the oil companies, and between the companies and the federal government, continue to be settled.

Management has an important role to play in helping people, organizations, and countries respond to global crises; such crises provide lessons in how to plan, organize, lead, and control the resources needed to both forestall and respond effectively to a crisis. Crisis management involves making important choices about how to (1) create teams to facilitate rapid decision making and communication, (2) establish the organizational chain of command and reporting relationships necessary to mobilize a fast response, (3) recruit and select the right people to lead and work in such teams, and (4) develop bargaining and negotiating strategies to manage the conflicts that arise whenever people and groups have different interests and objectives. How well managers make such decisions determines how quickly an effective response to a crisis can be implemented, and it sometimes can prevent or reduce the severity of the crisis itself.

Summary and Review

LO1-1

WHAT IS MANAGEMENT? A manager is a person responsible for supervising the use of an organization's resources to meet its goals. An organization is a collection of people who work together and coordinate their actions to achieve a wide variety of goals. Management is the process of using organizational resources to achieve organizational goals effectively and efficiently through planning, organizing, leading, and controlling. An efficient organization makes the most productive use of its resources. An effective organization pursues appropriate goals and achieves these goals by using its resources to create goods or services that customers want.

LO1-2 **MANAGERIAL TASKS** The four principal managerial tasks are planning, organizing, leading, and controlling. Managers at all levels of the organization and in all departments perform these tasks. Effective management means managing these activities successfully.

LO1-3, 1-4 **LEVELS AND SKILLS OF MANAGERS** Organizations typically have three levels of management. First-line managers are responsible for the day-to-day supervision of nonmanagerial employees. Middle managers are responsible for developing and utilizing organizational resources efficiently and effectively. Top managers have cross-departmental responsibility. Three main kinds of managerial skills are conceptual, human, and technical. The need to develop and build technical skills leads organizations to divide managers into departments according to their job-specific responsibilities. Top managers must establish appropriate goals for the entire organization and verify that department managers are using resources to achieve those goals.

LO1-5 **RECENT CHANGES IN MANAGEMENT PRACTICES** To increase efficiency and effectiveness, many organizations have altered how they operate. Managers have restructured and downsized operations and outsourced activities to reduce costs. Companies are also empowering their workforces and using self-managed teams to increase efficiency and effectiveness. Managers are increasingly using IT to achieve these objectives.

LO1-6 **CHALLENGES FOR MANAGEMENT IN A GLOBAL ENVIRONMENT** Today's competitive global environment presents many interesting challenges to managers. One of the main challenges is building a competitive advantage by increasing efficiency; quality; speed, flexibility, and innovation; and customer responsiveness. Other challenges include behaving in an ethical and socially responsible way toward people inside and outside the organization, managing a diverse workforce, utilizing new IT, and practicing global crisis management.

Management in Action

Topics for Discussion and Action

Discussion

1. Describe the difference between efficiency and effectiveness, and identify real organizations that you think are, or are not, efficient and effective. **[LO1-1]**

2. In what ways can managers at each of the three levels of management contribute to organizational efficiency and effectiveness? **[LO1-3]**

3. Identify an organization that you believe is high-performing and one that you believe is low-performing. Give five reasons why you think the performance levels of the two organizations differ so much. **[LO1-2, 1-4]**

4. What are the building blocks of competitive advantage? Why is obtaining a competitive advantage important to managers? **[LO1-5]**

5. In what ways do you think managers' jobs have changed the most over the last 10 years? Why have these changes occurred? **[LO1-6]**

Action

6. Choose an organization such as a school or a bank; visit it; then list the different organizational resources it uses. How do managers use these resources to maintain and improve its performance? **[LO1-2, 1-4]**

7. Visit an organization, and talk to first-line, middle, and top managers about their respective management roles in the organization and what they do to help the organization be efficient and effective. **[LO1-3, 1-4]**

8. Ask a middle or top manager, perhaps someone you already know, to give examples of how he or she performs the managerial tasks of planning, organizing, leading, and controlling. How much time does he or she spend in performing each task? **[LO1-3]**

9. Like Mintzberg, try to find a cooperative manager who will allow you to follow him or her around for a day. List the roles the manager plays, and indicate how much time he or she spends performing them. **[LO1-3, 1-4]**

Building Management Skills

Thinking about Managers and Management [LO1-2, 1-3, 1-4]

Think of an organization that has provided you with work experience and the manager to whom you reported (or talk to someone who has had extensive work experience); then answer these questions:

1. Think about your direct supervisor. Of what department is he or she a member, and at what level of management is this person?

2. How do you characterize your supervisor's approach to management? For example, which particular management tasks and roles does this person perform most often? What kinds of management skills does this manager have?

3. Do you think the tasks, roles, and skills of your supervisor are appropriate for the particular job he or she performs? How could this manager improve his or her task performance? How can IT affect this?

4. How did your supervisor's approach to management affect your attitudes and behavior? For example,

how well did you perform as a subordinate, and how motivated were you?

5. Think about the organization and its resources. Do its managers use organizational resources effectively? Which resources contribute most to the organization's performance?

6. Describe how the organization treats its human resources. How does this treatment affect the attitudes and behaviors of the workforce?

7. If you could give your manager one piece of advice or change one management practice in the organization, what would it be?

8. How attuned are the managers in the organization to the need to increase efficiency, quality, innovation, or responsiveness to customers? How well do you think the organization performs its prime goals of providing the goods or services that customers want or need the most?

Managing Ethically [LO1-1, 1-3]

Think about an example of unethical behavior that you observed in the past. The incident could be something you experienced as an employee or a customer or something you observed informally.

Questions

1. Either by yourself or in a group, give three reasons why you think the behavior was unethical.

For example, what rules or norms were broken? Who benefited or was harmed by what took place? What was the outcome for the people involved?

2. What steps might you take to prevent such unethical behavior and encourage people to behave in an ethical way?

Small Group Breakout Exercise [LO1-2, 1-3, 1-4]

Opening a New Restaurant

Form groups of three or four people, and appoint one group member as the spokesperson who will communicate your findings to the entire class when called on by the instructor. Then discuss the following scenario:

You and your partners have decided to open a large full-service restaurant in your local community; it will be open from 7 a.m. to 10 p.m. to serve breakfast, lunch, and dinner. Each of you is investing $50,000 in the venture, and together you have secured a bank loan for $300,000 to begin operations. You and your partners have little experience in managing a restaurant beyond serving meals or eating in restaurants, and you now face the task of deciding how you will manage the restaurant and what your respective roles will be.

1. Decide what each partner's managerial role in the restaurant will be. For example, who will be responsible for the necessary departments and specific activities? Describe your managerial hierarchy.

2. Which building blocks of competitive advantage do you need to establish to help your restaurant succeed? What criteria will you use to evaluate how successfully you are managing the restaurant?

3. Discuss the most important decisions that must be made about (a) planning, (b) organizing, (c) leading, and (d) controlling to allow you and your partners to use organizational resources effectively and build a competitive advantage.

4. For each managerial task, list the issues to solve, and decide which roles will contribute the most to your restaurant's success.

Exploring the World Wide Web [LO1-2]

Go to the General Electric (GE) website at www.ge.com, click on "our company," then "company information," and then "Jeffrey Immelt," GE's CEO. You will see a list of articles that discuss his management style; click on articles such as "GE: Why the Company Still Has Spark, 2010" in *The Guardian* and "How to Build Great Leaders" in *Fortune*.

Search these articles or others for information that describes Immelt's approach to planning, organizing, leading, and controlling GE. What is his approach to managing? What effects has this approach had on GE's performance?

Be the Manager [LO1-2, 1-5]

Problems at Achieva

You have just been called in to help managers at Achieva, a fast-growing Internet software company that specializes

in business-to-business (B2B) network software. Your job is to help Achieva solve some management problems that have arisen because of its rapid growth.

Customer demand to license Achieva's software has boomed so much in just two years that more than 50 new software programmers have been added to help develop a new range of software products. Achieva's growth has been so swift that the company still operates informally, its organizational structure is loose and flexible, and programmers are encouraged to find solutions to problems as they go along. Although this structure worked well in the past, you have been told that problems are arising.

There have been increasing complaints from employees that good performance is not being recognized in the organization and that they do not feel equitably treated.

Moreover, there have been complaints about getting managers to listen to their new ideas and to act on them. A bad atmosphere is developing in the company, and recently several talented employees left. Your job is to help Achieva's managers solve these problems quickly and keep the company on the fast track.

Questions

1. What kinds of organizing and controlling problems is Achieva suffering from?

2. What kinds of management changes need to be made to solve them?

Fortune Case in the News

Bob Iger: Disney's Fun King

The weekly roundtable, at which the heads of Disney's (DIS) business units gather in Burbank, California, is at the core of how Iger runs this conglomerate. The company, which had $40.9 billion in revenue in fiscal 2011, has grown too complex to be run in the autocratic manner of some previous CEOs—it now comprises four divisions, multiple business models, and five key brands (Disney, ESPN, ABC, Marvel, and Pixar). So Iger, 61, does more listening than talking. "I've heard Bob say more than once, 'If I can't trust a person to do that, then I need a different person,'" says Disney EVP and CFO Jay Rasulo. "And so we all are empowered to basically run those business areas. I would say that Bob has a states vs. federal philosophy."

It doesn't always work. Disney's interactive division is losing money. The film division has had some bombs—after the latest, *John Carter,* studio head Richard Ross lost his job. But since Iger took over from Michael Eisner after a messy governance struggle in 2005, he has pulled Disney out of the rut it was stuck in. Iger greatly increased capital spending during the recession as rivals retrenched. Earnings, driven by acquisitions, have nearly doubled, to $4.85 billion in fiscal 2011. The stock price has risen 80% during his tenure. "Bob

is just very effective," says Warren Buffett, who has known Iger for decades. "He's always calm and rational and makes sense, and therefore he gets things done through other people. He runs things without a heavy hand."

"In a strange way," Iger says, "I am the brand manager of Disney." He sees his job as building, in the words of his friend the late Steve Jobs, more "brand deposits" than "brand withdrawals." But it isn't enough to find the right managers and leave them alone; you also have to know when to dive deep, in part because Disney's business is such that a hit show or app or toy, if exploited correctly, can propagate throughout the company and become that sought-after thing, a "franchise." *Pirates of the Caribbean,* the smash film series, began as a ride; *High School Musical* and *Phineas and Ferb* both started as cable TV shows on the Disney Channel; the "Fairies" idea came from Disney's small publishing group, just to name four.

Walking the tightrope between extending Disney's brands and knowing when to leave well enough alone is a tricky challenge—not that we feel so sorry for a guy whose actual day job involves screening movies, riding rides, and schmoozing with athletes. What follows is an exclusive look at how Iger runs one of the best-known

businesses in the world. Iger jokes that if he ever wrote a book about his career, he would title it *I've Been Bought,* referring to the two acquisitions he survived (Cap Cities buying ABC, and Disney buying Cap Cities). But if there is anything that defines his nearly seven years as Disney's CEO, it is what he has bought—especially, iconic brands Pixar and Marvel.

When Iger took over the top job, expectations were tepid. Sure, he had been a star in his years at ABC, where he started in 1974 as an entry-level studio supervisor in New York and moved up through sports and entertainment. At Cap Cities, which bought ABC in 1985, Iger, known for his work ethic and candid style, became the clear successor to CEO Tom Murphy. Then, as Murphy puts it, "We sold the company out from under him" to Disney in 1996.

Iger stayed at Disney as Eisner's long record of success ground to a halt. Iger ran ABC and then became president of Disney in 2000—even though Eisner reportedly told directors that Iger wasn't up to the top job. The board looked at outsiders before giving the CEO post to Iger. Perceptions changed suddenly when Iger showed up at his first board meeting with a plan to buy Pixar, the company that had stolen the mantle of animation away from Disney. Created by former Disney animator John Lasseter, Ed Catmull, and Steve Jobs, Pixar had a successful partnership with Disney until the collaboration frayed in a personality conflict between Eisner and Jobs. Iger called Jobs the day he was named CEO, and the two became friends.

At the board meeting, Iger presented a 20-year look at Disney animation, which had stumbled after successes like *The Lion King* and *The Little Mermaid.* "I said, 'I've got to fix this, and here are the three choices.'" One was to keep the status quo. The second was to find someone new to run the studio. The third was to buy Pixar. Says John Pepper Jr., then Disney's chairman: "It's a meeting I will never forget. He said, 'Ladies and gentlemen, we must have this.'" The room went silent. The problem, Iger continued, was that it would be very expensive, and he didn't know if it was for sale.

As it turned out, Pixar was for sale, and it was very expensive ($7.4 billion). But the discussion wasn't simply about the price. Jobs and his cofounders had no interest in Disneyfication. They wanted guarantees that Pixar would remain in Northern California under its current leadership and would keep its culture. Iger eagerly agreed. The deal, announced in January 2006, changed Disney fundamentally: No longer was the Disney way the only way.

Six years later, it appears that Iger has kept his promise to let Pixar be. Pixar looks and feels like a Silicon Valley company. Not only can you bring your pet or kid to work, but you can also drink at the funky bars that the creatives have set up in their offices. There is plenty of Pixar nostalgia—Lasseter's office is filled with toys, and Buzz Lightyear greets you at the main entrance—but hardly anything to remind you that this is part of the Disney juggernaut. "Practicing a kind of cultural imperialism or autocracy on cultures that have thrived without you is just the wrong thing," Iger says. When the deal closed, he appointed Lasseter and Catmull to run Disney's animation studios as well as Pixar. "What's interesting," Lasseter says, "is that he actually said most of the time the big companies come in and influence little companies when they buy them. He, in fact, wanted the opposite to happen."

Three and a half years later, Iger made his second big acquisition, spending $4.3 billion to buy Marvel Entertainment. The home of characters like Iron Man and Captain America, Marvel helped Disney reach more boys and boost its flagging live-action-movie pipeline. It also provided a new stream of characters for Disney's $3 billion consumer products machine. Like Pixar, Marvel has been largely left to run its own affairs. Its boss, Ike Perlmutter, is a secretive man who has never given an interview—and who was the only top Disney executive not to be made available for this story. So far, based on the $178 million opening weekend for *The Avengers,* the first Marvel/Disney release, it looks as if the deal is paying off.

But Iger's hands-off approach has its limits. The day I visit Walt Disney Studios, March 19, is not a great day for the live-action division, or for its chairman, Rich Ross. As I take a seat in Ross's airy office, news has just crossed the wire that the company is going to take a $200 million write-down on the film *John Carter,* one of the most colossal bombs in movie history. Ross answers questions gamely, but he looks as if he would rather be having a root canal. "What Bob would like us to do," he says, "is follow through and learn lessons to do a better job going forward."

Iger's December 2010 appointment of Ross was controversial from the get-go. Iger sacked longtime studio head Dick Cook to make way for Ross, the Disney Channel superstar responsible for Hannah Montana and other tween hits. Ross exemplified one of Iger's core beliefs—that a really talented executive could work just as well in another job. But the studio business—while responsible for just 16% of Disney's fiscal 2011 revenue and 7% of operating profits—has always been an insider's gig, and Ross had a steep learning curve.

As the *John Carter* debacle unfolds, I ask Iger what it means for Ross and for the company. He makes a show of not pointing fingers, saying the failure belongs to everyone. "The leadership moment for me," he says, echoing Ross, "was making sure that we . . . accepted it for what it was, which was clearly a big disappointment and failure, and that we moved on." But on April 20, Ross is out; Iger insists that Ross's departure "had absolutely zero to do with *John Carter*" and that he was simply the wrong fit—something that had become increasingly clear as time went on. "Once you conclude that person is not right for the long term, you have to move," says Iger. "I take full responsibility for it. I made the decision to put him in."

Jeffrey Katzenberg, CEO of rival DreamWorks Animation (DWA) and a friend of Iger, says, "Bob is someone who is genuinely admired, respected, and incredibly charming. But underneath that is a really very determined executive, and when the killer instinct is required he has got it in a big way."

Last October, Iger announced that he would step down as CEO in March 2015 and stay on as chairman until June 2016. The announcement surprised many Disney watchers. Why make that decision so far in advance? Would it set off a horserace within the company à la GE (GE), and would that be a good thing or a bad thing? Says Warren Buffett: "I would say the only mistake Bob Iger has made is setting his resignation date. If I owned the place, Bob would not be retiring."

Questions for Discussion

1. Use the chapter material to decide what different kinds of management challenges Bob Iger faced as he took control of managing Walt Disney.

2. In what kinds of ways did he respond to these challenges— for example, in his approach to planning, leading, organizing and controlling?

3. Search the web. How are Bob Iger and Disney currently performing?

Source: J. Reingold and M. Adamo, "Bob Iger: Disney's Fun King," *Fortune,* May 21, 2012. © 2012 Time Inc. Used under license.

CHAPTER 2

The Evolution of Management Thought

Learning Objectives

After studying this chapter, you should be able to:

LO2-1 Describe how the need to increase organizational efficiency and effectiveness has guided the evolution of management theory.

LO2-2 Explain the principle of job specialization and division of labor, and tell why the study of person–task relationships is central to the pursuit of increased efficiency.

LO2-3 Identify the principles of administration and organization that underlie effective organizations.

LO2-4 Trace the changes in theories about how managers should behave to motivate and control employees.

LO2-5 Explain the contributions of management science to the efficient use of organizational resources.

LO2-6 Explain why the study of the external environment and its impact on an organization has become a central issue in management thought.

A MANAGER'S CHALLENGE

Finding Better Ways to Make Cars

What is the best way to manage the work process? Car production has changed dramatically over the years as managers have applied different management principles to organize and control work activities. Prior to 1900, small groups of skilled workers cooperated to hand-build cars with parts that often had to be altered and modified to fit together. This system, a type of *small-batch production,* was expensive; assembling just one car took considerable time and effort, and skilled workers could produce only a few cars per day. Although these cars were of high quality, they were too expensive for most customers. Managers needed better methods to increase efficiency, reduce costs, and sell more cars.

Henry Ford revolutionized the car industry. In 1913 Ford opened the Highland Park car plant in Detroit to produce the Model T Ford, and his team of manufacturing managers pioneered the development of *mass-production manufacturing,* which made small-batch car production inefficient. In mass production, moving conveyor belts bring the cars to the workers, and each worker performs a single assigned task along the production line. Ford experimented to discover the most efficient way for each worker to perform an assigned task; and this was that each worker should

Mass automobile production then and now. (a) In 1904 workers in Detroit, Michigan assemble a Ford as a team. (b) In 2008 workers in Chongqing,China assemble fords in a similar manner. Today, leaner product lines and more efficient factories help keep American car manufacturers afloat, while quality control issues continue to raise challenges.

perform one narrow, specialized task, such as bolting on the door or attaching the door handle. As a result, jobs in the Ford car plant became repetitive because they required little use of a worker's skills.[1]

Ford's management approach increased efficiency and reduced costs so much that by 1920 he was able to reduce the price of a car by two-thirds and sold more than 2 million cars a year.[2] Ford became the leading car company in the world, and competitors rushed to adopt its new mass-production techniques.

The next major change in management thinking about car assembly occurred in Japan when Ohno Taiichi, a Toyota production engineer, pioneered the development of *lean manufacturing* in the 1960s after touring the U.S. factories of GM, Ford, and Chrysler. The management philosophy behind lean manufacturing is to continuously find methods to improve the efficiency of the production process to reduce costs, increase quality, and reduce car assembly time. Lean production is based on the idea that if workers have input and can participate in the decision-making process, their knowledge can be used to increase efficiency.

In lean manufacturing, workers work on a moving production line, but they are organized into small teams, each of which is responsible for a particular phase of car assembly, such as installing the car's transmission or electrical wiring system. Each team member is expected to learn the tasks of all members of that team, and each work group is responsible not only for assembling cars but also for finding ways to increase quality and reduce costs. By 1970 Japanese managers had applied the new lean production system so efficiently that

they were producing higher-quality cars at lower prices than U.S. carmakers. By 1980 Japanese carmakers dominated the global market.

To compete, managers of U.S. carmakers visited Japan to learn the new manufacturing principles of lean production. All the Big Three U.S. carmakers spent billions of dollars implementing lean manufacturing; GM established its Saturn car division as a way to experiment with this new way of involving workers. In the 1990s U.S. carmakers also increased the number of robots they used on the assembly line and their use of IT to build and track the quality of cars being produced. Indeed, for a time it seemed that robots rather than employees would be building cars in the future. However, Toyota discovered something interesting at its first fully roboticized car plant. When only robots build cars, efficiency does not continually increase because, unlike people, robots cannot provide input to improve the work process. The optimum manufacturing methods must continuously work to find the right balance between using people, machinery, computers, and IT.

In the 2000s global car companies continued to compete fiercely to improve and perfect ways to make cars. Toyota remained the leader in pioneering new ways to manage its assembly lines to increase quality and efficiency; but other carmakers such as Honda, Nissan, and Hyundai, as well as Ford and GM, also made major strides to close the quality gap with Japanese carmakers. Nevertheless, U.S. carmakers steadily lost ground to their Japanese and European competitors because they could not make cars with the styling, quality, and price their customers demanded. It seemed that the future of all the Big Three

U.S. carmakers was in doubt as they lost billions of dollars throughout the 1990s, and it seemed they might go out of business.

Everything changed in the carmaking business in 2009 after the economic and financial crisis led car sales to plummet, and every carmaker, including Toyota, lost billions of dollars. To stay afloat, most global carmakers had to rely on billions of dollars in assistance from their governments to stay in business because they could not pay their employees or finance their customers. At the same time the crisis showed that U.S. carmakers were essentially bankrupt because outdated contracts with their car dealers, unions, and workers had raised their overhead costs so high they could not compete globally. After borrowing billions from the U.S. government, GM was forced into bankruptcy to reduce its costs; Ford and Chrysler were able to form new contracts to reduce their costs. By 2011 all three U.S. carmakers reported that they were once again making good profits and had repaid the U.S. government a large percentage of the money they had borrowed. How had they managed to do this?

To achieve this, U.S. carmakers had been forced to shut down hundreds of inefficient factories, lay off hundreds of thousands of car workers, and reduce the range of vehicles they produced. To survive, they focused their resources on a new range of vehicles that managers believed would have the greatest appeal to customers. Managers raced to develop the cars customers wanted to buy and to make them reliable and cost-effective.

However, another milestone in carmaking history came in 2010 when Toyota—known as the quality leader—came under intense scrutiny because of claims that some of its cars suffered from uncontrolled acceleration due to brake defects and that it had been late in responding to owner complaints despite many accidents. Other carmakers also admitted defects, and the issue of how to better measure quality and safety to improve performance is currently a leading concern of carmakers. All carmakers are trying to find better ways to use the hundreds of computer sensors inside each vehicle to understand how to make a car more efficiently and effectively, and by 2012 global carmakers had once again significantly increased the quality and reliability of their vehicles.

Overview

As this sketch of the evolution of management thinking in global car manufacturing suggests, changes in management practices occur as managers, theorists, researchers, and customers look for ways to increase how efficiently and effectively cars are made. The driving force behind the evolution of management theory is the search for better ways to use organizational resources to make goods and services. Advances in management thought typically occur as managers and researchers find better ways to perform the principal management tasks: planning, organizing, leading, and controlling human and other organizational resources.

In this chapter we examine how management thought has evolved in modern times and the central concerns that have guided ongoing advances in management theory. First we examine the so-called classical management theories that emerged around the turn of the

20th century. These include scientific management, which focuses on matching people and tasks to maximize efficiency, and administrative management, which focuses on identifying the principles that will lead to the creation of the most efficient system of organization and management. Next we consider behavioral management theories developed both before and after World War II; these focus on how managers should lead and control their workforces to increase performance. Then we discuss management science theory, which developed during World War II and has become increasingly important as researchers have developed rigorous analytical and quantitative techniques to help managers measure and control organizational performance. Finally, we discuss changes in management practices from the middle to the late 1900s and focus on the theories developed to help explain how the external environment affects the way organizations and managers operate.

By the end of this chapter you will understand how management thought and theory have evolved over time. You will also understand how economic, political, and cultural forces have affected the development of these theories and how managers and their organizations have changed their behavior as a result. In Figure 2.1 we summarize the chronology of the management theories discussed in this chapter.

Scientific Management Theory

LO2-1 Describe how the need to increase organizational efficiency and effectiveness has guided the evolution of management theory.

The evolution of modern management began in the closing decades of the 19th century, after the industrial revolution had swept through Europe and America. In the new economic climate, managers of all types of organizations—political, educational, and economic—were trying to find better ways to satisfy customers' needs. Many major economic, technical, and cultural changes were taking place at this time. The introduction of steam power and the development of sophisticated machinery and equipment changed how goods were produced, particularly in the weaving and clothing industries. Small workshops run by skilled workers who produced hand-manufactured products (a system called *crafts production*) were being replaced by large factories in which sophisticated machines controlled by hundreds or even thousands of unskilled or semiskilled workers made products. For example, raw cotton and wool, which in the past had been spun into yarn by families or whole villages working together, were now shipped to factories where workers operated machines that spun and wove large quantities of yarn into cloth.

Owners and managers of the new factories found themselves unprepared for the challenges accompanying the change from small-scale crafts production to large-scale mechanized manufacturing. Moreover, many managers and supervisors in these workshops and factories were engineers who had only a technical orientation. They were unprepared for the social problems that occur when people work together in large groups in a factory or shop system. Managers began to search for new techniques to manage their organizations' resources, and soon they began to focus on ways to increase the efficiency of the worker–task mix.

Figure 2.1

The Evolution of Management Theory

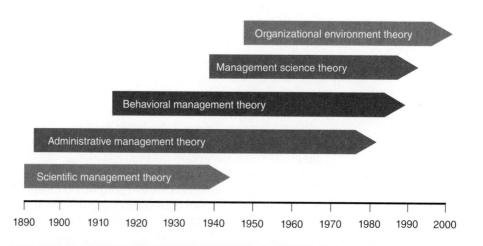

LO2-2 Explain the principle of job specialization and division of labor, and tell why the study of person–task relationships is central to the pursuit of increased efficiency.

Job Specialization and the Division of Labor

Initially management theorists were interested in why the new machine shops and factory system were more efficient and produced greater quantities of goods and services than older crafts-style production operations. Nearly 200 years before, Adam Smith had been one of the first writers to investigate the advantages associated with producing goods and services in factories. A famous economist, Smith journeyed around England in the 1700s studying the effects of the industrial revolution.[3] In a study of factories that produced various pins or nails, Smith identified two different manufacturing methods. The first was similar to crafts-style production, in which each worker was responsible for all the 18 tasks involved in producing a pin. The other had each worker performing only one or a few of these 18 tasks.

Smith found that the performance of the factories in which workers specialized in only one or a few tasks was much greater than the performance of the factory in which each worker performed all 18 pin-making tasks. In fact, Smith found that 10 workers specializing in a particular task could make 48,000 pins a day, whereas those workers who performed all the tasks could make only a few thousand.[4] Smith reasoned that this performance difference occurred because the workers who specialized became much more skilled at their specific tasks and as a group were thus able to produce a product faster than the group of workers who each performed many tasks. Smith concluded that increasing the level of job specialization—the process by which a division of labor occurs as different workers specialize in tasks—improves efficiency and leads to higher organizational performance.[5]

Armed with the insights gained from Adam Smith's observations, other managers and researchers began to investigate how to improve job specialization to increase performance. Management practitioners and theorists focused on how managers should organize and control the work process to maximize the advantages of job specialization and the division of labor.

job specialization The process by which a division of labor occurs as different workers specialize in different tasks over time.

scientific management The systematic study of relationships between people and tasks for the purpose of redesigning the work process to increase efficiency.

F. W. Taylor and Scientific Management

Frederick W. Taylor (1856–1915) is best known for defining the techniques of scientific management, the systematic study of relationships between people and tasks for the purpose of redesigning the work process to increase efficiency. Taylor was a manufacturing manager who eventually became a consultant and taught other managers how to apply his scientific management techniques. Taylor believed that if the amount of time and effort that each worker expends to produce a unit of output (a finished good or service) can be reduced by increasing specialization and the division of labor, the production process will become more efficient. According to Taylor, the way to create the most efficient division of labor could best be determined by scientific management techniques rather than by intuitive or informal rule-of-thumb knowledge. Based on his experiments and observations as a manufacturing manager in a variety of settings, he developed four principles to increase efficiency in the workplace:

- Principle 1: *Study the way workers perform their tasks, gather all the informal job knowledge that workers possess, and experiment with ways of improving how tasks are performed.*

To discover the most efficient method of performing specific tasks, Taylor studied in great detail and measured the ways different workers went about performing their tasks. One of the main tools he used was a time-and-motion study, which involves the careful timing and recording of the actions taken to perform a particular task. Once Taylor understood the existing method of performing a task, he then experimented to increase specialization. He tried different methods of dividing and coordinating the various tasks necessary to produce a finished product. Usually this meant simplifying jobs and having each worker perform fewer, more routine tasks, as at the pin factory or on Ford's car assembly line. Taylor

Frederick W. Taylor, founder of scientific management, and one of the first people to study the behavior and performance of people at work.

also sought to find ways to improve each worker's ability to perform a particular task—for example, by reducing the number of motions workers made to complete the task, by changing the layout of the work area or the type of tools workers used, or by experimenting with tools of different sizes.

- **Principle 2:** *Codify the new methods of performing tasks into written rules and standard operating procedures.*

Once the best method of performing a particular task was determined, Taylor specified that it should be recorded so this procedure could be taught to all workers performing the same task. These new methods further standardized and simplified jobs—essentially making jobs even more routine. In this way efficiency could be increased throughout an organization.

- **Principle 3:** *Carefully select workers who possess skills and abilities that match the needs of the task, and train them to perform the task according to the established rules and procedures.*

To increase specialization, Taylor believed workers had to understand the tasks that were required and be thoroughly trained to perform the tasks at the required level. Workers who could not be trained to this level were to be transferred to a job where they were able to reach the minimum required level of proficiency.[6]

- **Principle 4:** *Establish a fair or acceptable level of performance for a task, and then develop a pay system that rewards performance above the acceptable level.*

To encourage workers to perform at a high level of efficiency, and to give them an incentive to reveal the most efficient techniques for performing a task, Taylor advocated that workers benefit from any gains in performance. They should be paid a bonus and receive some percentage of the performance gains achieved through the more efficient work process.[7]

By 1910 Taylor's system of scientific management had become nationally known and in many instances was faithfully and fully practiced.[8] However, managers in many organizations chose to implement the new principles of scientific management selectively. This decision ultimately resulted in problems. For example, some managers using scientific management obtained increases in performance, but rather than sharing performance gains with workers through bonuses as Taylor had advocated, they simply increased the amount of work that each worker was expected to do. Many workers experiencing the reorganized work system found that as their performance increased, managers required that they do more work for the same pay. Workers also learned that performance increases often meant fewer jobs and a greater threat of layoffs because fewer workers were needed. In addition, the specialized, simplified jobs were often monotonous and repetitive, and many workers became dissatisfied with their jobs.

Scientific management brought many workers more hardship than gain and a distrust of managers who did not seem to care about workers' well-being.[9] These dissatisfied workers resisted attempts to use the new scientific management techniques and at times even withheld their job knowledge from managers to protect their jobs and pay. It is not difficult for workers to conceal the true potential efficiency of a work system to protect their interests. Experienced machine operators, for example, can slow their machines in undetectable ways by adjusting the tension in the belts or by misaligning the gears. Workers sometimes even develop informal work rules that discourage high performance and encourage shirking as work groups attempt to identify an acceptable or fair performance level (a tactic discussed in the next section).

Unable to inspire workers to accept the new scientific management techniques for performing tasks, some organizations increased the mechanization of the work process. For example, one reason why Henry Ford introduced moving

Charlie Chaplin tries to extricate a fellow employee from the machinery of mass production in this scene from *Modern Times*. The complex machinery is meant to represent the power that machinery has over the worker in the new work system.

conveyor belts in his factory was the realization that when a conveyor belt controls the pace of work (instead of workers setting their own pace), workers can be pushed to perform at higher levels—levels that they may have thought were beyond their reach. Charlie Chaplin captured this aspect of mass production in one of the opening scenes of his famous movie *Modern Times* (1936). In the film Chaplin caricatured a new factory employee fighting to work at the machine-imposed pace but losing the battle to the machine. Henry Ford also used the principles of scientific management to identify the tasks that each worker should perform on the production line and thus to determine the most effective division of labor to suit the needs of a mechanized production system.

From a performance perspective, the combination of the two management practices—(1) achieving the right worker–task specialization and (2) linking people and tasks by the speed of the production line—makes sense. It produces the huge cost savings and dramatic output increases that occur in large organized work settings. For example, in 1908 managers at the Franklin Motor Company using scientific management principles redesigned the work process, and the output of cars increased from 100 cars a *month* to 45 cars a *day;* workers' wages, however, increased by only 90%.[10] From other perspectives, however, scientific management practices raise many concerns. The definition of workers' rights, not by the workers themselves but by the owners or managers, raised an ethical issue that we examine in the following "Ethics in Action" box.

Ethics in Action

Fordism in Practice

From 1908 to 1914, through trial and error, Henry Ford's talented team of production managers pioneered the development of the moving conveyor belt and thus changed manufacturing practices forever. Although the technical aspects of the move to mass production were a dramatic financial success for Ford and for the millions of Americans who could now afford cars, for the workers who actually produced the cars many human and social problems resulted.

With simplification of the work process, workers grew to hate the monotony of the moving conveyor belt. By 1914 Ford's car plants were experiencing huge employee turnover—often reaching levels as high as 300% or 400% per year as workers left because they could not handle the work-induced stress.[11] Henry Ford recognized these problems and made an announcement: From that point on, to motivate his workforce, he would reduce the length of the workday from nine hours to eight hours, and the company would *double* the basic wage from $2.50 to $5.00 per day. This was a dramatic increase, similar to an announcement today of an overnight doubling of the minimum wage. Ford became an internationally famous figure, and the word *Fordism* was coined for his new approach.[12]

Ford's apparent generosity, however, was matched by an intense effort to control the resources—both human and material—with which his empire was built. He employed hundreds of inspectors to check up on employees, both inside and outside his factories. In the factory, supervision was close and confining. Employees were not allowed to leave their places at the production line, and they were not permitted to talk to one another. Their job was to concentrate fully on the task at hand. Few employees could adapt to this system, and they developed ways of talking out of the sides of their mouths, like ventriloquists, and invented a form of speech that became known as the "Ford Lisp."[13] Ford's obsession with control brought him into greater and greater conflict with managers, who often were fired when they disagreed with him. As a result, many talented people left Ford to join a growing number of rival car companies.

Outside the workplace, Ford went so far as to establish what he called the "Sociological Department" to check up on how his employees lived and spent their time.

Henry Ford sits in an early model Ford outside a showroom in Detroit, Michigan, shortly after the corporation was formed in 1903. By 1914 Ford's car plants were experiencing huge employee turnover as workers left because they could not handle the work-induced stress.

Inspectors from this department visited the homes of employees and investigated their habits and problems. Employees who exhibited behaviors contrary to Ford's standards (for instance, if they drank too much or were always in debt) were likely to be fired. Clearly Ford's efforts to control his employees led him and his managers to behave in ways that today would be considered unacceptable and unethical and in the long run would impair an organization's ability to prosper.

Despite the problems of worker turnover, absenteeism, and discontent at Ford Motor Company, managers of the other car companies watched Ford reap huge gains in efficiency from the application of the new management principles. They believed their companies would have to imitate Ford if they were to survive. They followed Taylor and used many of his followers as consultants to teach them how to adopt the techniques of scientific management. In addition, Taylor elaborated his principles in several books, including *Shop Management* (1903) and *The Principles of Scientific Management* (1911), which explain in detail how to apply the principles of scientific management to reorganize the work system.[14]

Taylor's work has had an enduring effect on the management of production systems. Managers in every organization, whether it produces goods or services, now carefully analyze the basic tasks that must be performed and try to devise work systems that allow their organizations to operate most efficiently.

The Gilbreths

Two prominent followers of Taylor were Frank Gilbreth (1868–1924) and Lillian Gilbreth (1878–1972), who refined Taylor's analysis of work movements and made many contributions to time-and-motion study.[15] Their aims were to (1) analyze every individual action necessary to perform a particular task and break it into each of its component actions, (2) find better ways to perform each component action, and (3) reorganize each of the component actions so that the action as a whole could be performed more efficiently—at less cost in time and effort.

The Gilbreths often filmed a worker performing a particular task and then separated the task actions, frame by frame, into their component movements. Their goal was to maximize the efficiency with which each individual task was performed so that gains across tasks would add up to enormous savings of time and effort. Their attempts to develop improved management principles were captured—at times quite humorously—in the movie *Cheaper by the Dozen,* a new version of which appeared in 2004, which depicts how the Gilbreths (with their 12 children) tried to live their own lives according to these efficiency principles and apply them to daily actions such as shaving, cooking, and even raising a family.[16]

Eventually the Gilbreths became increasingly interested in the study of fatigue. They studied how physical characteristics of the workplace contribute to job stress that often leads to fatigue and thus poor performance. They isolated factors that result in worker fatigue, such as lighting, heating, the color of walls, and the design of tools and machines. Their pioneering studies paved the way for new advances in management theory.

This scene from *Cheaper by the Dozen* illustrates how "efficient families," such as the Gilbreths, use formal family courts to solve problems of assigning chores to different family members and to solve disputes when they arise.

In workshops and factories, the work of the Gilbreths, Taylor, and many others had a major effect on the practice of management. In comparison with the old crafts system, jobs in the new system were more repetitive, boring, and monotonous as a result of the application of scientific management principles, and workers became increasingly dissatisfied. Frequently the management of work settings became a game between workers and managers: Managers tried to initiate work practices to increase performance, and workers tried to hide the true potential efficiency of the work setting to protect their own well-being.[17] The story of how Andrew Carnegie created the most successful industrial company of his day, Carnegie Steel, illustrates the kind of management thinking that was sweeping through the United States at that time, the looming battles between management and workers, and the growing number of trade unions that were springing up to represent workers' interests (see the accompanying "Manager as a Person" box).

Manager as a Person

Andrew Carnegie, depicted here in later life. His legacy is a complicated one of hard work as an immigrant, a rise to power and wealth through hardnosed management, accusations of monopolistic business practices, and a dedication to philanthropy that caused him to avow that "no one should die rich."

Andrew Carnegie Creates the New Industrial Company

Andrew Carnegie, born in Scotland in 1835, was the son of a master handloom weaver who, at that time, employed four apprentices to weave fine linen tablecloths. His family was well-to-do, yet 10 years later they were living in poverty. Why? Advances in weaving technology had led to the invention of steam-powered weaving looms that could produce large quantities of cotton cloth at a much lower price than was possible through handloom weaving. Handloom weavers could not compete at such low prices, and Carnegie's father was put out of business.

In 1848 Carnegie's family, like hundreds of thousands of other families in Europe at the time, emigrated to the United States to find work and survive. They settled near Pittsburgh, where they had relatives, and Carnegie's father continued to weave tablecloths and sell them door-to-door for around $6 a week. Carnegie found a job as a "bobbin boy," replacing spools of thread on power looms in a textile factory. He took home $1.20 for working a 60-hour week.

After his employer found out he could read and write, a rare skill at that time, Carnegie became a bookkeeper for the factory. In his spare time he became a telegraph messenger and learned telegraphy. He began to deliver telegrams to Tom Scott, a top manager at the Pennsylvania Railroad, who came to appreciate Carnegie's drive and talents. Scott made him his personal telegrapher for an astonishing sum of $35 a week. Carnegie was now 17; seven years later, when he was 24, he was promoted to Scott's job, superintendent of the railroad's western division. At 30 he was offered the top job of superintendent of the *whole* railroad! Carnegie had made his name by continually finding ways to use resources more productively to reduce costs and increase profitability. Under his oversight of the western division, his company's stock price had shot up—which explains why he was offered the railroad's top job. He had also invested cleverly in railroad stock and was now a wealthy man with an income of $48,000 a year, of which only $2,800 came from his railroad salary.

Carnegie had ambitions other than remaining in his top railroad job, however. He had noticed U.S. railroads' growing demand for steel rails as they expanded rapidly across the country. At that time steel was made by the method of small-batch production, a labor-intensive process in which groups of employees worked together to produce small quantities of steel. This method was expensive and the steel produced cost $135 a ton. As he searched for ways to reduce the cost of steel-making, Carnegie was struck by the fact that many different companies performed each of the different operations necessary to convert iron ore into finished steel products. One company smelted iron ore into "pig iron." Another company transported the pig iron to other companies that rolled the pig iron into bars or slabs. Many other companies then bought these bars and slabs and made them into finished products such as steel rails, nails, wire, and so on. Intermediaries that bought the products of one company and then sold them to another connected the activities of these different companies. The many exchanges involved in converting iron ore into finished products greatly increased operating costs. At each stage of the production process, iron and steel had to be shipped to the next company and reheated until they became soft enough to work on. Moreover, these intermediaries were earning large profits for providing this service, which raised the cost of the finished products.

The second thing Carnegie noticed was that the steel produced by British steel mills was of a higher quality than that made in U.S. mills. The British had made major advances in steelmaking technology, and U.S. railroads preferred to buy their steel rails. On one of his frequent trips to Britain Carnegie saw a demonstration of Sir Henry Bessemer's new "hot blasting" method for making steel. Bessemer's famous process made it possible to produce great quantities of higher-quality steel *continuously*—as a process, not in small batches. Carnegie instantly realized the enormous cost-saving potential of the new technology. He rushed to become the first steelmaker in the United States to adopt it.

Carnegie subsequently sold all his railroad stock and used the proceeds to create the Carnegie Steel Company, the first low-cost Bessemer steelmaking plant in the United States. Determined to retain the profit that intermediaries were making in his business, he decided his company would perform *all* the steelmaking operations necessary to convert iron ore into finished products. For example, he constructed rolling mills to make steel rails next to his blast furnace so iron ore could be converted into finished steel products in one continuous process. Carnegie's innovations led to a dramatic fall in steelmaking costs and revolutionized the U.S. steel industry. His new production methods reduced the price of U.S. steel from $135 a ton to $12 a ton! Despite the cheaper price, his company was still enormously profitable, and he plowed back all his profits into building his steel business and constructed many new low-cost steel plants. By 1900 most of his competitors had been driven out of business because of his low prices; his company was the leading U.S. steelmaker, and he was one of the richest men in the world.

Although the story of Carnegie's new approach to management might seem like "business as usual," there is another side to Carnegie's management style. Critics say he increased profitability "on the backs" of his workers. Despite the enormous increase in productivity he achieved by using the new mass-production steelmaking technology, he was continually driven by the need to find every way possible to reduce operating costs. To increase productivity, Carnegie gradually increased the normal workday from an already long 10 hours to 12 hours, six days a week. He also paid his workers the lowest wage rate possible even though their increasing skills in mastering the new technology were contributing to the huge increase in productivity. He paid no attention to improving the safety of his mills, where workers toiled in dangerous conditions and thousands of workers were injured each year by spills of molten steel. Any attempts by workers to improve their work conditions were rejected, and Carnegie routinely crushed any of the workers' attempts to unionize. In implementing new management techniques and creating the modern industrial company, Carnegie also created the need for new administrative management theory—theory that could help managers find better ways of organizing and controlling resources to increase performance, as well as find new strategies for negotiating with and managing the increasingly unionized workforce that modern production methods had brought into being.

Administrative Management Theory

Side by side with scientific managers like Carnegie studying the person–technology mix to increase efficiency, other managers and researchers were focusing on **administrative management**, the study of how to create an organizational structure and control system that leads to high efficiency and effectiveness. *Organizational structure* is the system of task and authority relationships that controls how employees use resources to achieve the organization's goals. Two of the most influential early views regarding the creation of efficient systems of organizational administration were developed in Europe: Max Weber, a German sociology professor, developed one theory; and Henri Fayol, the French manager who developed the model of management introduced in Chapter 1, developed the other.

LO2-3 Identify the principles of administration and organization that underlie effective organizations.

administrative management The study of how to create an organizational structure and control system that leads to high efficiency and effectiveness.

bureaucracy A formal system of organization and administration designed to ensure efficiency and effectiveness.

authority The power to hold people accountable for their actions and to make decisions concerning the use of organizational resources.

The Theory of Bureaucracy

Max Weber (1864–1920) wrote at the turn of the 20th century, when Germany was undergoing its industrial revolution.[18] To help Germany manage its growing industrial enterprises while it was striving to become a world power, Weber developed the principles of **bureaucracy**—a formal system of organization and administration designed to ensure efficiency and effectiveness. A bureaucratic system of administration is based on the five principles summarized in Figure 2.2:

- Principle 1: *In a bureaucracy, a manager's formal authority derives from the position he or she holds in the organization.*

Authority is the power to hold people accountable for their actions and to make decisions concerning the use of organizational resources. Authority gives managers the right to direct and control their subordinates' behavior to achieve organizational goals. In a bureaucratic system of administration, obedience is owed to a manager not because of any personal qualities—such as personality, wealth, or social status—but because the manager occupies a position that is associated with a certain level of authority and responsibility.[19]

- Principle 2: *In a bureaucracy, people should occupy positions because of their performance, not because of their social standing or personal contacts.*

Figure 2.2
Weber's Principles of Bureaucracy

Max Weber developed the principles of bureaucracy during Germany's burgeoning industrial revolution to help organizations increase their efficiency and effectiveness.

This principle was not always followed in Weber's time and is often ignored today. Some organizations and industries are still affected by social networks in which personal contacts and relations, not job-related skills, influence hiring and promotional decisions.

- *Principle 3: The extent of each position's formal authority and task responsibilities, and its relationship to other positions in an organization, should be clearly specified.*

When the tasks and authority associated with various positions in the organization are clearly specified, managers and workers know what is expected of them and what to expect from each other. Moreover, an organization can hold all its employees strictly accountable for their actions when they know their exact responsibilities.

- *Principle 4: Authority can be exercised effectively in an organization when positions are arranged hierarchically, so employees know whom to report to and who reports to them.*[20]

Managers must create an organizational hierarchy of authority that makes it clear who reports to whom and to whom managers and workers should go if conflicts or problems arise. This principle is especially important in the armed forces, FBI, CIA, and other organizations that deal with sensitive issues involving possible major repercussions. It is vital that managers at high levels of the hierarchy be able to hold subordinates accountable for their actions.

- *Principle 5: Managers must create a well-defined system of rules, standard operating procedures, and norms so they can effectively control behavior within an organization.*

rules Formal written instructions that specify actions to be taken under different circumstances to achieve specific goals.

Rules are formal written instructions that specify actions to be taken under different circumstances to achieve specific goals (for example, if A happens, do B). **Standard operating procedures (SOPs)** are specific sets of written instructions about how to perform a certain aspect of a task. A rule might state that at the end of the workday employees are to leave their machines in good order, and a set of SOPs would specify exactly how they should do so, itemizing which machine parts must be oiled or replaced. **Norms** are unwritten, informal codes of conduct that prescribe how people should act in particular situations and are considered important by most members of a group or organization. For example, an organizational norm in a restaurant might be that waiters should help each other if time permits.

standard operating procedures (SOPs) Specific sets of written instructions about how to perform a certain aspect of a task.

Rules, SOPs, and norms provide behavioral guidelines that increase the performance of a bureaucratic system because they specify the best ways to accomplish organizational tasks. Companies such as McDonald's and Walmart have developed extensive rules and procedures to specify the behaviors required of their employees, such as "Always greet the customer with a smile."

norms Unwritten, informal codes of conduct that prescribe how people should act in particular situations and are considered important by most members of a group or organization.

Weber believed organizations that implement all five principles establish a bureaucratic system that improves organizational performance. The specification of positions and the use of rules and SOPs to regulate how tasks are performed make it easier for managers to organize and control the work of subordinates. Similarly, fair and equitable selection and promotion systems improve managers' feelings of security, reduce stress, and encourage organizational members to act ethically and further promote the interests of the organization.[21]

If bureaucracies are not managed well, however, many problems can result. Sometimes managers allow rules and SOPs, "bureaucratic red tape," to become so cumbersome that decision making is slow and inefficient and organizations cannot change. When managers rely too much on rules to solve problems and not enough on their own skills and judgment, their behavior becomes inflexible. A key challenge for managers is to use bureaucratic principles to benefit, rather than harm, an organization.

Fayol's Principles of Management

Henri Fayol (1841–1925) was the CEO of Comambault Mining. Working at the same time as Weber, but independently, Fayol identified 14 principles (summarized in Table 2.1) that he

Table 2.1
Fayol's 14 Principles of Management

Division of labor Job specialization and the division of labor should increase efficiency, especially if managers take steps to lessen workers' boredom.

Authority and responsibility Managers have the right to give orders and the power to exhort subordinates for obedience.

Unity of command An employee should receive orders from only one superior.

Line of authority The length of the chain of command that extends from the top to the bottom of an organization should be limited.

Centralization Authority should not be concentrated at the top of the chain of command.

Unity of direction The organization should have a single plan of action to guide managers and workers.

Equity All organizational members are entitled to be treated with justice and respect.

Order The arrangement of organizational positions should maximize organizational efficiency and provide employees with satisfying career opportunities.

Initiative Managers should allow employees to be innovative and creative.

Discipline Managers need to create a workforce that strives to achieve organizational goals.

Remuneration of personnel The system that managers use to reward employees should be equitable for both employees and the organization.

Stability of tenure of personnel Long-term employees develop skills that can improve organizational efficiency.

Subordination of individual interests to the common interest Employees should understand how their performance affects the performance of the whole organization.

Esprit de corps Managers should encourage the development of shared feelings of comradeship, enthusiasm, or devotion to a common cause.

believed essential to increase the efficiency of the management process.[22] We discuss these principles in detail here because, although they were developed at the turn of the 20th century, they remain the bedrock on which much of recent management theory and research is based. In fact, as the "Management Insight" box following this discussion suggests, modern writers such as well-known management guru Tom Peters continue to extol these principles.

DIVISION OF LABOR A champion of job specialization and the division of labor for reasons already mentioned, Fayol was nevertheless among the first to point out the downside of too much specialization: boredom—a state of mind likely to diminish product quality, worker initiative, and flexibility. As a result, Fayol advocated that workers be given more job duties to perform or be encouraged to assume more responsibility for work outcomes—a principle increasingly applied today in organizations that empower their workers.

AUTHORITY AND RESPONSIBILITY Like Weber, Fayol emphasized the importance of authority and responsibility. Fayol, however, went beyond Weber's formal authority, which derives from a manager's position in the hierarchy, to recognize the *informal* authority that derives from personal expertise, technical knowledge, moral worth, and the ability to lead and to generate commitment from subordinates. (The study of authority is the subject of recent research into leadership, discussed in Chapter 14.)

unity of command A reporting relationship in which an employee receives orders from, and reports to, only one superior.

UNITY OF COMMAND The principle of **unity of command** specifies that an employee should receive orders from, and report to, only one superior. Fayol believed that *dual command,* the reporting relationship that exists when two supervisors give orders to the same subordinate, should be avoided except in exceptional circumstances. Dual command confuses subordinates, undermines order and discipline, and creates havoc within the formal hierarchy of authority. Assessing any manager's authority and responsibility in a system of dual command is difficult, and the manager who is bypassed feels slighted and angry and may be uncooperative in the future.

Henri Fayol, who maintained Weber's principles of formal organization but added recognition of the pivotal role played by informal authority.

line of authority The chain of command extending from the top to the bottom of an organization.

centralization The concentration of authority at the top of the managerial hierarchy.

unity of direction The singleness of purpose that makes possible the creation of one plan of action to guide managers and workers as they use organizational resources.

equity The justice, impartiality, and fairness to which all organizational members are entitled.

LINE OF AUTHORITY The **line of authority** is the chain of command extending from the top to the bottom of an organization. Fayol was one of the first management theorists to point out the importance of limiting the length of the chain of command by controlling the number of levels in the managerial hierarchy. The more levels in the hierarchy, the longer communication takes between managers at the top and bottom and the slower the pace of planning and organizing. Restricting the number of hierarchical levels to lessen these communication problems lets an organization act quickly and flexibly; this is one reason for the recent trend toward restructuring (discussed in Chapter 1).

Fayol also pointed out that when organizations are split into different departments or functions, each with its own hierarchy, it is important to allow middle and first-line managers in each department to interact with managers at similar levels in other departments. This interaction helps speed decision making because managers know each other and know whom to go to when problems arise. For cross-departmental integration to work, Fayol noted the importance of keeping one's superiors informed about what is taking place so that lower-level decisions do not harm activities taking place in other parts of the organization. One alternative to cross-departmental integration is to create cross-departmental teams controlled by a team leader (see Chapter 1).

CENTRALIZATION Fayol also was one of the first management writers to focus on **centralization**, the concentration of authority at the top of the managerial hierarchy. Fayol believed authority should not be concentrated at the top of the chain of command. One of the most significant issues that top managers face is how much authority to centralize at the top of the organization and what authority to decentralize to managers and workers at lower hierarchical levels. This important issue affects the behavior of people at all levels in the organization.

If authority is very centralized, only managers at the top make important decisions and subordinates simply follow orders. This arrangement gives top managers great control over organizational activities and helps ensure that the organization is pursuing its strategy, but it makes it difficult for the people who are closest to problems and issues to respond to them in a timely manner. It also can reduce the motivation of middle and first-line managers and make them less flexible and adaptable because they become reluctant to make decisions on their own, even when doing so is necessary. They get used to passing the buck. As we saw in Chapter 1, the pendulum is now swinging toward decentralization as organizations seek to empower middle managers and create self-managed teams that monitor and control their own activities both to increase organizational flexibility and to reduce operating costs and increase efficiency.

UNITY OF DIRECTION Just as there is a need for unity of command, there is also a need for **unity of direction**, the singleness of purpose that makes possible the creation of one plan of action to guide managers and workers as they use organizational resources. An organization without a single guiding plan becomes inefficient and ineffective; its activities become unfocused, and individuals and groups work at cross-purposes. Successful planning starts with top managers working as a team to craft the organization's strategy, which they communicate to middle managers, who decide how to use organizational resources to implement the strategy.

EQUITY As Fayol wrote, "For personnel to be encouraged to carry out their duties with all the devotion and loyalty of which they are capable, they must be treated with respect for their own sense of integrity, and equity results from the combination of respect and justice."[23] **Equity**—the justice, impartiality, and fairness to which all organizational members are entitled—is receiving much attention today; the desire to treat employees fairly is a primary concern of managers. (Equity theory is discussed in Chapter 13.)

ORDER   Like Taylor and the Gilbreths, Fayol was interested in analyzing jobs, positions, and individuals to ensure that the organization was using resources as efficiently as possible. To Fayol, **order** meant the methodical arrangement of positions to provide the organization with the greatest benefit and to provide employees with career opportunities that satisfy their needs. Thus Fayol recommended the use of organizational charts to show the position and duties of each employee and to indicate which positions an employee might move to or be promoted into in the future. He also advocated that managers engage in extensive career planning to help ensure orderly career paths. Career planning is of primary interest today as organizations increase the resources they are willing to devote to training and developing their workforces.

order The methodical arrangement of positions to provide the organization with the greatest benefit and to provide employees with career opportunities.

INITIATIVE   Although order and equity are important means to fostering commitment and loyalty among employees, Fayol believed managers must also encourage employees to exercise **initiative**, the ability to act on their own without direction from a superior. Used properly, initiative can be a major source of strength for an organization because it leads to creativity and innovation. Managers need skill and tact to achieve the difficult balance between the organization's need for order and employees' desire for initiative. Fayol believed the ability to strike this balance was a key indicator of a superior manager.

initiative The ability to act on one's own without direction from a superior.

DISCIPLINE   In focusing on the importance of **discipline**—obedience, energy, application, and other outward marks of respect for a superior's authority—Fayol was addressing the concern of many early managers: how to create a workforce that was reliable and hardworking and would strive to achieve organizational goals. According to Fayol, discipline results in respectful relations between organizational members and reflects the quality of an organization's leadership and a manager's ability to act fairly and equitably.

discipline Obedience, energy, application, and other outward marks of respect for a superior's authority.

REMUNERATION OF PERSONNEL   Fayol proposed reward systems including bonuses and profit-sharing plans, which are increasingly used today as organizations seek improved ways to motivate employees. Convinced from his own experience that an organization's payment system has important implications for organizational success, Fayol believed effective reward systems should be equitable for both employees and the organization, encourage productivity by rewarding well-directed effort, not be subject to abuse, and be uniformly applied to employees.

STABILITY OF TENURE OF PERSONNEL   Fayol also recognized the importance of long-term employment, and this idea has been echoed by contemporary management gurus such as Tom Peters, Jeff Pfeffer, and William Ouchi. When employees stay with an organization for extended periods, they develop skills that improve the organization's ability to use its resources.

SUBORDINATION OF INDIVIDUAL INTERESTS TO THE COMMON INTEREST
The interests of the organization as a whole must take precedence over the interests of any individual or group if the organization is to survive. Equitable agreements must be established between the organization and its members to ensure that employees are treated fairly and rewarded for their performance and to maintain the disciplined organizational relationships so vital to an efficient system of administration.

ESPRIT DE CORPS   As this discussion of Fayol's ideas suggests, the appropriate design of an organization's hierarchy of authority and the right mix of order and discipline foster cooperation and commitment. Likewise, a key element in a successful organization is the development of **esprit de corps**, a French expression that refers to shared feelings of comradeship, enthusiasm, or devotion to a common cause among members of a group. Esprit de corps can result when managers encourage personal, verbal contact between managers and workers and encourage communication to solve problems and implement solutions. (Today the term *organizational culture* is used to refer to these shared feelings; this concept is discussed at length in Chapter 3.)

esprit de corps Shared feelings of comradeship, enthusiasm, or devotion to a common cause among members of a group.

Some of the principles that Fayol outlined have faded from contemporary management practices, but most have endured. The characteristics of organizations that Tom Peters and Robert Waterman identified as being "excellently managed" in their best-selling book *In Search of Excellence* (1982) are discussed in the following "Management Insight."[24]

Management Insight

Peters and Waterman's Excellent Companies

In the early 1980s Tom Peters and Robert Waterman identified 62 organizations that they considered to be the best-performing organizations in the United States. They asked, "Why do these companies perform better than their rivals?" and discovered that successful organizations are managed according to three sets of related principles. Those principles have a great deal in common with Fayol's principles.

First, Peters and Waterman argued, top managers of successful companies create principles and guidelines that emphasize managerial autonomy and entrepreneurship and encourage risk taking and *initiative.* For example, they allow middle managers to develop new products even though there is no assurance that these products will be winners. In high-performing organizations, top managers are closely involved in the day-to-day operations of the company, provide *unity of command* and *unity of direction,* and do not simply make isolated decisions. Top managers *decentralize authority* to lower-level managers and nonmanagerial employees and give them the freedom to get involved and the motivation to get things done.

The second approach that managers of excellent organizations use to increase performance is to create one central plan that puts organizational goals at center stage. In high-performing organizations, managers focus attention on what the organization does best, and the emphasis is on continuously improving the goods and services the organization provides to its customers. Managers of top-performing companies resist the temptation to get sidetracked into pursuing ventures outside their area of expertise just because they seem to promise a quick return. These managers also focus on customers and establish close relationships with them to learn their needs; responsiveness to customers increases competitive advantage.

The third set of management principles pertains to organizing and controlling the organization. Excellent companies establish a *division of work* and a *division of authority and responsibility* that will motivate employees to *subordinate their individual interests to the common interest.* Inherent in this approach is the belief that high performance derives from individual skills and abilities and that *equity, order, initiative,* and other indications of respect for the individual create the *esprit de corps* that fosters productive behavior. An emphasis on entrepreneurship and respect for every employee leads the best managers to create a structure that gives employees room to exercise *initiative* and motivates them to succeed. Because a simple, streamlined managerial hierarchy is best suited to achieving this outcome, top managers keep the line of *authority* as short as possible. They also decentralize authority to permit employee participation, but they keep enough control to maintain *unity of direction.*

As this insight into contemporary management suggests, the basic concerns that motivated Fayol continue to inspire management theorists.[25] The principles that Fayol and Weber set forth still provide clear and appropriate guidelines that managers can use to create a work setting that efficiently and effectively uses organizational resources. These principles remain the bedrock of modern management theory; recent researchers have refined or developed

LO2-4 Trace the changes in theories about how managers should behave to motivate and control employees.

them to suit modern conditions. For example, Weber's and Fayol's concerns for equity and for establishing appropriate links between performance and reward are central themes in contemporary theories of motivation and leadership.

Behavioral Management Theory

behavioral management The study of how managers should behave to motivate employees and encourage them to perform at high levels and be committed to the achievement of organizational goals.

Because the writings of Weber and Fayol were not translated into English and published in the United States until the late 1940s, American management theorists in the first half of the 20th century were unaware of the contributions of these European pioneers. American management theorists began where Taylor and his followers left off. Although their writings were different, these theorists all espoused a theme that focused on **behavioral management**, the study of how managers should personally behave to motivate employees and encourage them to perform at high levels and be committed to achieving organizational goals.

The Work of Mary Parker Follett

If F. W. Taylor is considered the father of management thought, Mary Parker Follett (1868–1933) serves as its mother.[26] Much of her writing about management and about the way managers should behave toward workers was a response to her concern that Taylor was ignoring the human side of the organization. She pointed out that management often overlooks the multitude of ways in which employees can contribute to the organization when managers allow them to participate and exercise initiative in their everyday work lives.[27] Taylor, for example, never proposed that managers should involve workers in analyzing their jobs to identify better ways to perform tasks or should even ask workers how they felt about their jobs. Instead he used time-and-motion experts to analyze workers' jobs for them. Follett, in contrast, argued that because workers know the most about their jobs, they should be involved in job analysis and managers should allow them to participate in the work development process.

Follett proposed that "authority should go with knowledge . . . whether it is up the line or down." In other words, if workers have the relevant knowledge, then workers, rather than managers, should be in control of the work process itself, and managers should behave as coaches and facilitators—not as monitors and supervisors. In making this statement, Follett anticipated the current interest in self-managed teams and empowerment. She also recognized the importance of having managers in different departments communicate directly with each other to speed decision making. She advocated what she called "cross-functioning": members of different departments working together in cross-departmental teams to accomplish projects—an approach that is increasingly used today.[28]

Fayol also mentioned expertise and knowledge as important sources of managers' authority, but Follett went further. She proposed that knowledge and expertise, and not managers' formal authority deriving from their position in the hierarchy, should decide who will lead at any particular moment. She believed, as do many management theorists today, that power is fluid and should flow to the person who can best help the organization achieve its goals. Follett took a horizontal view of power and authority, in contrast to Fayol, who saw the formal line of authority and vertical chain of command as being most essential to effective management. Follett's behavioral approach to management was very radical for its time.

Mary Parker Follett, an early management thinker who advocated, "Authority should go with knowledge . . . whether it is up the line or down."

The Hawthorne Studies and Human Relations

Probably because of its radical nature, Follett's work was unappreciated by managers and researchers until quite recently. Most continued to follow in the footsteps of Taylor and the Gilbreths. To increase efficiency, they studied

Workers in a telephone manufacturing plant in 1931. Around this time, researchers at the Hawthorne Works of the Western Electric Company began to study the effects of work setting characteristics—such as lighting and rest periods—on productivity. To their surprise, they discovered that workers' productivity was affected more by the attention they received from researchers than by the characteristics of the work setting—a phenomenon that became known as the Hawthorne effect.

ways to improve various characteristics of the work setting, such as job specialization or the kinds of tools workers used. One series of studies was conducted from 1924 to 1932 at the Hawthorne Works of the Western Electric Company.[29] This research, now known as the *Hawthorne studies,* began as an attempt to investigate how characteristics of the work setting—specifically the level of lighting or illumination—affect worker fatigue and performance. The researchers conducted an experiment in which they systematically measured worker productivity at various levels of illumination.

The experiment produced some unexpected results. The researchers found that regardless of whether they raised or lowered the level of illumination, productivity increased. In fact, productivity began to fall only when the level of illumination dropped to the level of moonlight—a level at which workers could presumably no longer see well enough to do their work efficiently.

The researchers found these results puzzling and invited a noted Harvard psychologist, Elton Mayo, to help them. Mayo proposed another series of experiments to solve the mystery. These experiments, known as the *relay assembly test experiments,* were designed to investigate the effects of other aspects of the work context on job performance, such as the effect of the number and length of rest periods and hours of work on fatigue and monotony.[30] The goal was to raise productivity.

During a two-year study of a small group of female workers, the researchers again observed that productivity increased over time, but the increases could not be solely attributed to the effects of changes in the work setting. Gradually the researchers discovered that, to some degree, the results they were obtaining were influenced by the fact that the researchers themselves had become part of the experiment. In other words, the presence of the researchers was affecting the results because the workers enjoyed receiving attention and being the subject of study and were willing to cooperate with the researchers to produce the results they believed the researchers desired.

Hawthorne effect The finding that a manager's behavior or leadership approach can affect workers' level of performance.

human relations movement A management approach that advocates the idea that supervisors should receive behavioral training to manage subordinates in ways that elicit their cooperation and increase their productivity.

Subsequently it was found that many other factors also influence worker behavior, and it was not clear what was actually influencing the Hawthorne workers' behavior. However, this particular effect—which became known as the **Hawthorne effect**—seemed to suggest that workers' attitudes toward their managers affect the level of workers' performance. In particular, the significant finding was that each manager's personal behavior or leadership approach can affect performance. This finding led many researchers to turn their attention to managerial behavior and leadership. If supervisors could be trained to behave in ways that would elicit cooperative behavior from their subordinates, productivity could be increased. From this view emerged the **human relations movement**, which advocates that supervisors be behaviorally trained to manage subordinates in ways that elicit their cooperation and increase their productivity.

The importance of behavioral or human relations training became even clearer to its supporters after another series of experiments—the *bank wiring room experiments.* In a study of workers making telephone switching equipment, researchers Elton Mayo and F. J. Roethlisberger discovered that the workers, as a group, had deliberately adopted a norm of output restriction to protect their jobs. Workers who violated this informal production norm were subjected to sanctions by other group members. Those who violated group performance norms and performed above the norm were called "ratebusters"; those who performed below the norm were called "chiselers."

The experimenters concluded that both types of workers threatened the group as a whole. Ratebusters threatened group members because they revealed to managers how fast the work could be done. Chiselers were looked down on because they were not doing their share of the work. Work group members disciplined both ratebusters and chiselers to create a pace of work that the workers (not the managers) thought was fair. Thus a work group's influence over output can be as great as the supervisors' influence. Because the work group can influence the behavior of its members, some management theorists argue that supervisors should be trained to behave in ways that gain the goodwill and cooperation of workers so that supervisors, not workers, control the level of work group performance.

One implication of the Hawthorne studies was that the behavior of managers and workers in the work setting is as important in explaining the level of performance as the technical aspects of the task. Managers must understand the workings of the **informal organization**, the system of behavioral rules and norms that emerge in a group, when they try to manage or change behavior in organizations. Many studies have found that as time passes, groups often develop elaborate procedures and norms that bond members together, allowing unified action either to cooperate with management to raise performance or to restrict output and thwart the attainment of organizational goals.[31] The Hawthorne studies demonstrated the importance of understanding how the feelings, thoughts, and behavior of work group members and managers affect performance. It was becoming increasingly clear to researchers that understanding behavior in organizations is a complex process that is critical to increasing performance.[32] Indeed, the increasing interest in the area of management known as **organizational behavior**, the study of the factors that have an impact on how individuals and groups respond to and act in organizations, dates from these early studies.

informal organization
The system of behavioral rules and norms that emerge in a group.

organizational behavior The study of the factors that have an impact on how individuals and groups respond to and act in organizations.

Theory X and Theory Y

Several studies after World War II revealed how assumptions about workers' attitudes and behavior affect managers' behavior. Perhaps the most influential approach was developed by Douglas McGregor. He proposed two sets of assumptions about how work attitudes and behaviors not only dominate the way managers think but also affect how they behave in organizations. McGregor named these two contrasting sets of assumptions *Theory X* and *Theory Y* (see Figure 2.3).[33]

THEORY X According to the assumptions of Theory X, the average worker is lazy, dislikes work, and will try to do as little as possible. Moreover, workers have little ambition and wish to avoid responsibility. Thus the manager's task is to counteract workers' natural tendencies to avoid work. To keep workers' performance at a high level, the manager must supervise workers closely and control their behavior by means of "the carrot and stick"—rewards and punishments.

Managers who accept the assumptions of Theory X design and shape the work setting to maximize their control over workers' behaviors and minimize workers' control over the pace of work. These managers believe workers must be made to do what is necessary for the

Theory X A set of negative assumptions about workers that leads to the conclusion that a manager's task is to supervise workers closely and control their behavior.

Figure 2.3
Theory X versus Theory Y

THEORY X	THEORY Y
The average employee is lazy, dislikes work, and will try to do as little as possible.	Employees are not inherently lazy. Given the chance, employees will do what is good for the organization.
To ensure that employees work hard, managers should closely supervise employees.	To allow employees to work in the organization's interest, managers must create a work setting that provides opportunities for workers to exercise initiative and self-direction.
Managers should create strict work rules and implement a well-defined system of rewards and punishments to control employees.	Managers should decentralize authority to employees and make sure employees have the resources necessary to achieve organizational goals.

Source: D. McGregor, *The Human Side of Enterprise,* © 1960. Reprinted with permission of The McGraw–Hill Companies, Inc.

success of the organization, and they focus on developing rules, SOPs, and a well-defined system of rewards and punishments to control behavior. They see little point in giving workers autonomy to solve their own problems because they think the workforce neither expects nor desires cooperation. Theory X managers see their role as closely monitoring workers to ensure that they contribute to the production process and do not threaten product quality. Henry Ford, who closely supervised and managed his workforce, fits McGregor's description of a manager who holds Theory X assumptions.

THEORY Y In contrast, Theory Y assumes that workers are not inherently lazy, do not naturally dislike work, and, if given the opportunity, will do what is good for the organization. According to Theory Y, the characteristics of the work setting determine whether workers consider work to be a source of satisfaction or punishment, and managers do not need to closely control workers' behavior to make them perform at a high level because workers exercise self-control when they are committed to organizational goals. The implication of Theory Y, according to McGregor, is that "the limits of collaboration in the organizational setting are not limits of human nature but of management's ingenuity in discovering how to realize the potential represented by its human resources."[34] It is the manager's task to create a work setting that encourages commitment to organizational goals and provides opportunities for workers to be imaginative and to exercise initiative and self-direction.

> **Theory Y** A set of positive assumptions about workers that leads to the conclusion that a manager's task is to create a work setting that encourages commitment to organizational goals and provides opportunities for workers to be imaginative and to exercise initiative and self-direction.

When managers design the organizational setting to reflect the assumptions about attitudes and behavior suggested by Theory Y, the characteristics of the organization are quite different from those of an organizational setting based on Theory X. Managers who believe workers are motivated to help the organization reach its goals can decentralize authority and give more control over the job to workers, both as individuals and in groups. In this setting, individuals and groups are still accountable for their activities; but the manager's role is not to control employees but to provide support and advice, to make sure employees have the resources they need to perform their jobs, and to evaluate them on their ability to help the organization meet its goals. Henri Fayol's approach to administration more closely reflects the assumptions of Theory Y rather than Theory X.

One company that was founded on the type of management philosophy inherent in Theory Y is the electronics company Hewlett-Packard (HP), which from its founding consistently put into practice principles derived from Theory Y. (Go to the company's website at www.hp.com for additional information.) Founders William Hewlett and David Packard—Bill and Dave, as they are still known throughout the organization—established a philosophy of management known as the "HP Way" that is people-oriented, stresses the importance of treating every person with consideration and respect, and offers recognition for achievements.[35]

The HP Way was based on several guiding principles. One was a policy of long-term employment, and in the past HP went to great lengths not to lay off workers. At times when fewer people were needed, rather than lay off workers, management would cut pay and shorten the workday until demand for HP products picked up. This policy strengthened employees' loyalty to the organization. Another guiding principle in the HP Way concerned how to treat members of the organization so they would feel free to be innovative and creative. HP managers believed that every employee of the company was a member of the HP team. They emphasized the need to increase communication among employees, believing that horizontal communication between peers, not just vertical communication up and down the hierarchy, is essential for creating a positive climate for innovation. To promote communication between employees at different levels of the hierarchy, HP encouraged informality. Managers and workers were on a first-name basis with each other and with the founders, Bill and Dave. In addition, Bill and Dave pioneered the technique known as "managing by wandering around": People were expected to wander around learning what others were doing so they could tap into opportunities to develop new

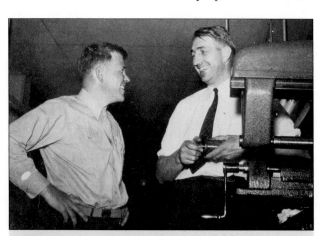

From the time that Dave Packard and Bill Hewlett first set up shop in a garage in 1938, they established a new people-oriented approach to management, known as the "HP Way."

products or find new avenues for cooperation. Bill and Dave also pioneered the principle that employees should spend 15% of their time working on projects of their own choosing, and HP's product design engineers were told to leave their current work out in the open on their desks so anybody could see what they were doing, learn from it, or suggest ways to improve it. Bill and Dave promoted managers because of their ability to engender excitement and enthusiasm for innovation in their subordinates.[36]

HP's practices helped it become one of the leading electronics companies in the world. In the 2000s, however, suffering intense competition from Dell, Sony, and Samsung, HP was forced to abandon the HP Way in order to reduce costs. Major layoffs began to occur as it became clear that HP's very survival was at stake as it battled efficient global competitors, and by 2004 HP had laid off over 40% of its employees and outsourced thousands of jobs abroad to remain competitive. By 2006 HP had turned the corner and by 2008 it was profitable once again and overtook Dell to become the largest global PC maker. Today, companies like 3M, Apple, and Google exemplify those that follow Theory Y and the principles embedded in the HP Way.

Management Science Theory

LO2-5 Explain the contributions of management science to the efficient use of organizational resources.

management science theory An approach to management that uses rigorous quantitative techniques to help managers make maximum use of organizational resources.

Management science theory is a contemporary approach to management that focuses on the use of rigorous quantitative techniques to help managers make maximum use of organizational resources to produce goods and services. In essence, management science theory is a contemporary extension of scientific management, which, as developed by Taylor, also took a quantitative approach to measuring the worker–task mix to raise efficiency. There are many branches of management science; and IT, which is having a significant impact on all kinds of management practices, is affecting the tools managers use to make decisions.[37] Each branch of management science deals with a specific set of concerns:

- *Quantitative management* uses mathematical techniques—such as linear and nonlinear programming, modeling, simulation, queuing theory, and chaos theory—to help managers decide, for example, how much inventory to hold at different times of the year, where to locate a new factory, and how best to invest an organization's financial capital. IT offers managers new and improved ways of handling information so they can make more accurate assessments of the situation and better decisions.

- *Operations management* gives managers a set of techniques they can use to analyze any aspect of an organization's production system to increase efficiency. IT, through the Internet and through growing B2B networks, is transforming how managers acquire inputs and dispose of finished products.

- *Total quality management (TQM)* focuses on analyzing an organization's input, conversion, and output activities to increase product quality.[38] Once again, through sophisticated software packages and computer-controlled production, IT is changing how managers and employees think about the work process and ways of improving it.

- *Management information systems (MISs)* give managers information about events occurring inside the organization as well as in its external environment—information that is vital for effective decision making. Once again, IT gives managers access to more and better information and allows more managers at all levels to participate in the decision-making process.

All these subfields of management science, enhanced by sophisticated IT, provide tools and techniques that managers can use to help improve the quality of their decision making and increase efficiency and effectiveness. We discuss many important developments in management science theory thoroughly in this book. In particular, Chapter 9, "Value Chain Management: Functional Strategies for Competitive Advantage," focuses on how to use operations management and TQM to improve quality, efficiency, and responsiveness to customers. And Chapter 18, "Using Advanced Information Technology to Increase Performance," describes the many ways managers use information systems and technologies to improve their planning, organizing, and controlling functions.

Organizational Environment Theory

An important milestone in the history of management thought occurred when researchers went beyond the study of how managers can influence behavior within organizations to consider how managers control the organization's relationship with its external environment, or **organizational environment**—the set of forces and conditions that operate beyond an organization's boundaries but affect a manager's ability to acquire and utilize resources. Resources in the organizational environment include the raw materials and skilled people that an organization requires to produce goods and services, as well as the support of groups, including customers who buy these goods and services and provide the organization with financial resources. One way of determining the relative success of an organization is to consider how effective its managers are at obtaining scarce and valuable resources.[39] The importance of studying the environment became clear after the development of open-systems theory and contingency theory during the 1960s.

LO2-6 Explain why the study of the external environment and its impact on an organization has become a central issue in management thought.

organizational environment The set of forces and conditions that operate beyond an organization's boundaries but affect a manager's ability to acquire and utilize resources.

open system A system that takes in resources from its external environment and converts them into goods and services that are then sent back to that environment for purchase by customers.

The Open-Systems View

One of the most influential views of how an organization is affected by its external environment was developed by Daniel Katz, Robert Kahn, and James Thompson in the 1960s.[40] These theorists viewed the organization as an **open system**—a system that takes in resources from its external environment and converts or transforms them into goods and services that are sent back to that environment, where they are bought by customers (see Figure 2.4).

At the *input stage* an organization acquires resources such as raw materials, money, and skilled workers to produce goods and services. Once the organization has gathered the necessary resources, conversion begins. At the *conversion stage* the organization's workforce, using appropriate tools, techniques, and machinery, transforms the inputs into outputs of finished goods and services such as cars, hamburgers, or flights to Hawaii. At the *output stage* the organization releases finished goods and services to its external environment, where customers purchase and use them to satisfy their needs. The money the organization obtains from the sales of its outputs allows the organization to acquire more resources so the cycle can begin again.

Figure 2.4

The Organization as an Open System

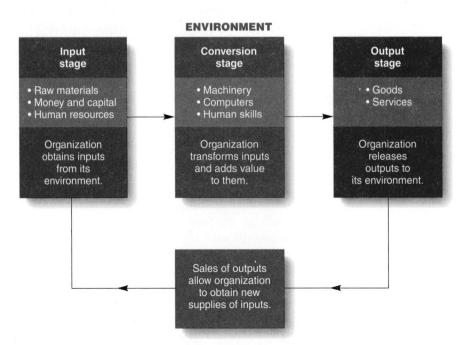

closed system A system that is self-contained and thus not affected by changes occurring in its external environment.

entropy The tendency of a closed system to lose its ability to control itself and thus to dissolve and disintegrate.

synergy Performance gains that result when individuals and departments coordinate their actions.

contingency theory The idea that the organizational structures and control systems managers choose depend on (are contingent on) characteristics of the external environment in which the organization operates.

The system just described is said to be open because the organization draws from and interacts with the external environment in order to survive; in other words, the organization is open to its environment. A **closed system**, in contrast, is a self-contained system that is not affected by changes in its external environment. Organizations that operate as closed systems, that ignore the external environment, and that fail to acquire inputs are likely to experience **entropy**, which is the tendency of a closed system to lose its ability to control itself and thus to dissolve and disintegrate.

Management theorists can model the activities of most organizations by using the open-systems view. Manufacturing companies like Ford and General Electric, for example, buy inputs such as component parts, skilled and semiskilled labor, and robots and computer-controlled manufacturing equipment; then at the conversion stage they use their manufacturing skills to assemble inputs into outputs of cars and appliances. As we discuss in later chapters, competition between organizations for resources is one of several major challenges to managing the organizational environment.

Researchers using the open-systems view are also interested in how the various parts of a system work together to promote efficiency and effectiveness. Systems theorists like to argue that the whole is greater than the sum of its parts; they mean that an organization performs at a higher level when its departments work together rather than separately. **Synergy**, the performance gains that result from the *combined* actions of individuals and departments, is possible only in an organized system. The recent interest in using teams combined or composed of people from different departments reflects systems theorists' interest in designing organizational systems to create synergy and thus increase efficiency and effectiveness.

Contingency Theory

Another milestone in management theory was the development of **contingency theory** in the 1960s by Tom Burns and G. M. Stalker in Britain and Paul Lawrence and Jay Lorsch in the United States.[41] The crucial message of contingency theory is that *there is no one best way to organize:* The organizational structures and the control systems that managers choose depend on (are contingent on) characteristics of the external environment in which the organization operates. According to contingency theory, the characteristics of the environment affect an organization's ability to obtain resources; and to maximize the likelihood of gaining access to resources, managers must allow an organization's departments to organize and control their activities in ways most likely to allow them to obtain resources, given the constraints of the particular environment they face. In other words, how managers design the organizational hierarchy, choose a control system, and lead and motivate their employees is contingent on the characteristics of the organizational environment (see Figure 2.5).

Figure 2.5
Contingency Theory of Organizational Design

Characteristics of the environment… → Determine the design of an organization's structure and control systems.

Organizations in stable environments choose a mechanistic structure (centralized authority, vertical communication flows, control through strict rules and procedures).

Organizations in changing environments choose an organic structure (decentralized authority, horizontal communication flows, cross-departmental cooperation).

There is no one best way to organize; organizational structure depends on the environment in which an organization operates.

An important characteristic of the external environment that affects an organization's ability to obtain resources is the degree to which the environment is changing. Changes in the organizational environment include changes in technology, which can lead to the creation of new products (such as compact discs) and result in the obsolescence of existing products (eight-track tapes); the entry of new competitors (such as foreign organizations that compete for available resources); and unstable economic conditions. In general, the more quickly the organizational environment is changing, the greater are the problems associated with gaining access to resources, and the greater is managers' need to find ways to coordinate the activities of people in different departments to respond to the environment quickly and effectively.

MECHANISTIC AND ORGANIC STRUCTURES   Drawing on Weber's and Fayol's principles of organization and management, Burns and Stalker proposed two basic ways in which managers can organize and control an organization's activities to respond to characteristics of its external environment: They can use a *mechanistic structure* or an *organic structure.*[42] As you will see, a mechanistic structure typically rests on Theory X assumptions, and an organic structure typically rests on Theory Y assumptions.

mechanistic structure An organizational structure in which authority is centralized, tasks and rules are clearly specified, and employees are closely supervised.

When the environment surrounding an organization is stable, managers tend to choose a mechanistic structure to organize and control activities and make employee behavior predictable. In a **mechanistic structure**, authority is centralized at the top of the managerial hierarchy, and the vertical hierarchy of authority is the main means used to control subordinates' behavior. Tasks and roles are clearly specified, subordinates are closely supervised, and the emphasis is on strict discipline and order. Everyone knows his or her place, and there is a place for everyone. A mechanistic structure provides the most efficient way to operate in a stable environment because it allows managers to obtain inputs at the lowest cost, giving an organization the most control over its conversion processes and enabling the most efficient production of goods and services with the smallest expenditure of resources. McDonald's restaurants operate with a mechanistic structure. Supervisors make all important decisions; employees are closely supervised and follow well-defined rules and standard operating procedures.

organic structure An organizational structure in which authority is decentralized to middle and first-line managers and tasks and roles are left ambiguous to encourage employees to cooperate and respond quickly to the unexpected.

In contrast, when the environment is changing rapidly, it is difficult to obtain access to resources, and managers need to organize their activities in a way that allows them to cooperate, to act quickly to acquire resources (such as new types of inputs to produce new kinds of products), and to respond effectively to the unexpected. In an **organic structure**, authority is decentralized to middle and first-line managers to encourage them to take responsibility and act quickly to pursue scarce resources. Departments are encouraged to take a cross-departmental or functional perspective, and cross-functional teams composed of people from different departments are formed. As in Mary Parker Follett's model, the organization operates in an organic way because authority rests with the individuals, departments, and teams best positioned to control the current problems the organization is facing. As a result, managers in an organic structure can react more quickly to a changing environment than can managers in a mechanistic structure. However, an organic structure is generally more expensive to operate because it requires that more managerial time, money, and effort be spent on coordination. So it is used only when needed—when the organizational environment is unstable and rapidly changing.[43] Google, Apple, and IBM are examples of companies that operate with organic structures.

Summary and Review

In this chapter we examined the evolution of management theory and research over the last century. Much of the material in the rest of this book stems from developments and refinements of this work. Indeed, the rest of this book incorporates the results of the extensive research in management that has been conducted since the development of the theories discussed here.

LO2-1, 2-2   SCIENTIFIC MANAGEMENT THEORY   The search for efficiency started with the study of how managers could improve person–task relationships to increase efficiency. The concept of job specialization and division of labor remains the basis for the design of work settings in modern organizations. New developments such as lean production and total quality management are often viewed as advances on the early scientific management principles developed by Taylor and the Gilbreths.

LO2-3   ADMINISTRATIVE MANAGEMENT THEORY   Max Weber and Henri Fayol outlined principles of bureaucracy and administration that are as relevant to managers today as they were when developed at the turn of the 20th century. Much of modern management research refines these principles to suit contemporary conditions. For example, the increasing interest in the use of cross-departmental teams and the empowerment of workers are issues that managers also faced a century ago.

LO2-4   BEHAVIORAL MANAGEMENT THEORY   Researchers have described many different approaches to managerial behavior, including Theories X and Y. Often the managerial behavior that researchers suggest reflects the context of their own historical eras and cultures. Mary Parker Follett advocated managerial behaviors that did not reflect accepted modes of managerial behavior at the time, and her work was largely ignored until conditions changed.

LO2-5   MANAGEMENT SCIENCE THEORY   The various branches of management science theory provide rigorous quantitative techniques that give managers more control over each organization's use of resources to produce goods and services.

LO2-6   ORGANIZATIONAL ENVIRONMENT THEORY   The importance of studying the organization's external environment became clear after the development of open-systems theory and contingency theory during the 1960s. A main focus of contemporary management research is to find methods to help managers improve how they use organizational resources and compete in the global environment. Strategic management and total quality management are two important approaches intended to help managers make better use of organizational resources.

Management in Action

Topics for Discussion and Action

Discussion

1. Choose a fast-food restaurant, a department store, or some other organization with which you are familiar, and describe the division of labor and job specialization it uses to produce goods and services. How might this division of labor be improved? **[LO2-1, 2-2]**

2. Apply Taylor's principles of scientific management to improve the performance of the organization you chose in topic 1. **[LO2-2]**

3. In what ways are Weber's and Fayol's ideas about bureaucracy and administration similar? How do they differ? **[LO2-3]**

4. Which of Weber's and Fayol's principles seem most relevant to the creation of an ethical organization? **[LO2-4, 2-6]**

5. Why was the work of Mary Parker Follett ahead of its time? To what degree do you think it is appropriate today? **[LO2-4, 2-5]**

6. What is contingency theory? What kinds of organizations familiar to you have been successful or unsuccessful in dealing with contingencies from the external environment? **[LO2-6]**

7. Why are mechanistic and organic structures suited to different organizational environments? **[LO2-4, 2-6]**

Action

8. Question a manager about his or her views of the relative importance of Fayol's 14 principles of management. **[LO2-3, 2-4]**

9. Visit at least two organizations in your community, and identify those that seem to operate with a Theory X or a Theory Y approach to management. **[LO2-4]**

Building Management Skills

Managing Your Own Business   [LO2-2, 2-4]

Now that you understand the concerns addressed by management thinkers over the last century, use this exercise to apply your knowledge to developing your management skills.

Imagine that you are the founding entrepreneur of a software company that specializes in developing games for home computers. Customer demand for your games has increased so much that over the last year your company has grown from a busy one-person operation to one with 16 employees. In addition to yourself, you employ six software developers to produce the software, three graphic artists, two computer technicians, two marketing and sales personnel, and two secretaries. In the next year you expect to hire 30 new employees, and you are wondering how best to manage your growing company.

1. Use the principles of Weber and Fayol to decide on the system of organization and management that you think will be most effective for your growing organization. How many levels will the managerial hierarchy of your organization have? How much authority will you decentralize to your subordinates? How will you establish the division of labor between subordinates? Will your subordinates work alone and report to you or work in teams?

2. Which management approach (for example, Theory X or Y) do you propose to use to run your organization? In 50 or fewer words write a statement describing the management approach you believe will motivate and coordinate your subordinates, and tell why you think this style will be best.

Managing Ethically   [LO2-3, 2-4]

How Unethical Behavior Shut Down a Meatpacking Plant

By all appearances the Westland/Hallmark Meat Co. based in Chico, California, was considered to be an efficient and sanitary meatpacking plant. Under the control of its owner and CEO, Steven Mendell, the plant regularly passed inspections by the U.S. Dept. of Agriculture (USDA). Over 200 workers were employed to slaughter cattle and prepare the beef for shipment to fast-food restaurants such as Burger King and Taco Bell. Also, millions of pounds of meat the plant produced yearly were delivered under contract to one of the federal government's most coveted accounts: the National School Lunch Program.[44]

When the Humane Society turned over a videotape (secretly filmed by one of its investigators who had taken a job as a plant employee) to the San Bernardino County District Attorney showing major violations of health procedures, an uproar followed. The videotape showed two workers dragging sick cows up the ramp that led to the slaughterhouse using metal chains and forklifts, and shocking them with electric prods and shooting streams of water in their noses and faces. Not only did the tape show inhumane treatment of animals, but it also provided evidence that the company was flaunting the ban on allowing sick animals to enter the food supply chain—something that federal regulations explicitly outlaw because of fears for human health and safety.

Once the USDA was informed that potentially contaminated beef products had entered the supply chain—especially the one to the nation's schools—it issued a notice for the recall of the 143 million pounds of beef processed in the plant over the last two years, the largest recall in history. In addition, the plant was shut down as the investigation proceeded. CEO Steven Mendell was subpoenaed to appear before the House Panel on Energy and Commerce Committee. He denied that these violations had taken place and that diseased cows had entered the food chain. However, when panel members demanded that he view the videotape that he claimed he had not seen, he was forced to acknowledge that inhumane treatment of animals had occurred.[45] Moreover, federal investigators turned up evidence that as early as 1996 the plant had been cited for overuse of electric prods to speed cattle through the plant and had been cited for other violations since, suggesting that these abuses had been going on for a long period.

Not only were consumers and schoolchildren harmed by these unethical actions, but the plant itself was permanently shut down and all 220 workers lost their jobs. In addition, the employees directly implicated in the video were prosecuted and one, who pleaded guilty to animal abuse, was convicted and sentenced to six months' imprisonment.[46] Clearly, all the people and groups affected by the meatpacking plant have suffered from its unethical and inhumane organizational behaviors and practices.

Questions

1. Use the theories discussed in the chapter to debate the ethical issues involved in the way the Westland/Hallmark Meat Co. business operated.

2. Also use the theories to discuss the ethical issues involved in the way the meatpacking business is being conducted today.

3. Search the web for changes occurring in the meatpacking business.

Small Group Breakout Exercise [LO2-6]

Modeling an Open System

Form groups of three to five people, and appoint one group member as the spokesperson who will communicate your findings to the class when called on by the instructor. Then discuss the following scenario:

Think of an organization with which you are all familiar, such as a local restaurant, store, or bank. After choosing an organization, model it from an open-systems perspective. Identify its input, conversion, and output processes; and identify forces in the external environment that help or hurt the organization's ability to obtain resources and dispose of its goods or services.

Exploring the World Wide Web [LO2-3, 2-6]

Research Ford's website (www.ford.com) and locate and read the material about Ford's history and evolution over time. What have been the significant stages in the company's development? What problems and issues confronted managers at these stages? What challenges face Ford's managers now?

Be the Manager [LO 2-2, 2-4]

How to Manage a Hotel

You have been called in to advise the owners of an exclusive new luxury hotel. For the venture to succeed, hotel employees must focus on providing customers with the highest-quality customer service possible. The challenge is to devise a way of organizing and controlling employees that will promote high-quality service, that will encourage employees to be committed to the hotel, and that will reduce the level of employee turnover and absenteeism—which are typically high in the hotel business.

Questions

1. How do the various management theories discussed in this chapter offer clues for organizing and controlling hotel employees?

2. Which parts would be the most important for an effective system to organize and control employees?

The Wall Street Journal Case in the News [LO 2-3, 2-4]

Mr. Edens Profits from Watching His Workers' Every Move

Control is one of Ron Edens's favorite words. "This is a controlled environment," he says of the blank brick building that houses his company, Electronic Banking System Inc.

Inside, long lines of women sit at spartan desks, slitting envelopes, sorting contents, and filling out "control cards" that record how many letters they have opened and how long it has taken them. Workers here, in "the cage," must process three envelopes a minute. Nearby, other women tap keyboards, keeping pace with a quota that demands 8,500 strokes an hour.

The room is silent. Talking is forbidden. The windows are covered. Coffee mugs, religious pictures, and other adornments are barred from workers' desks.

In his office upstairs, Mr. Edens sits before a TV monitor that flashes images from eight cameras posted throughout the plant. "There's a little bit of Sneaky Pete to it," he says, using a remote control to zoom in on a document atop a worker's desk. "I can basically read that and figure out how someone's day is going."

This day, like most others, is going smoothly, and Mr. Edens's business has boomed as a result. "We maintain a lot of control," he says. "Order and control are everything in this business."

Mr. Edens's business belongs to a small but expanding financial service known as "lockbox processing." Many companies and charities that once did their paperwork in-house now outsource clerical tasks to firms like EBS, which processes donations to groups such as Mothers Against Drunk Driving, the Doris Day Animal League, Greenpeace, and the National Organization for Women.

More broadly, EBS reflects the explosive growth of jobs in which workers perform low-wage and limited tasks in white-collar settings. This has transformed towns like Hagerstown—a blue-collar community hit hard by industrial layoffs in the 1970s—into sites for thousands of jobs in factory-sized offices.

Many of these jobs, though, are part-time, and most pay far less than the manufacturing occupations they replaced. Some workers at EBS start at the minimum wage of $4.25 an hour, and most earn about $6 an hour. The growth of such jobs—which often cluster outside major cities—also completes a curious historic circle. During the industrial revolution, farmers' daughters went to work in textile towns like Lowell, Massachusetts. In postindustrial America, many women of modest means and skills are entering clerical mills where they process paper instead of cloth (coincidentally, EBS occupies a former garment factory).

"The office of the future can look a lot like the factory of the past," says Barbara Garson, author of *The Electronic Sweatshop* and other books on the modern workplace. "Modern tools are being used to bring 19th-century working conditions into the white-collar world."

The time-and-motion philosophies of Frederick Taylor, for instance, have found a 1990s correlate in the phone, computer, and camera, which can be used to monitor workers more closely than a foreman with a stopwatch ever could. Also, the nature of the work often justifies a vigilant eye. In EBS workers handle thousands of dollars in checks and cash, and Mr. Edens says cameras help deter would-be thieves. Tight security also reassures visiting clients. "If you're disorderly, they'll think we're out of control and that things could get lost," says Mr. Edens, who worked as a financial controller for the National Rifle Association before founding EBS in 1983.

But tight observation also helps EBS monitor productivity and weed out workers who don't keep up. "There's multiple uses," Mr. Edens says of surveillance. His desk is covered with computer printouts recording the precise toll of keystrokes tapped by each data entry worker. He also keeps a day-to-day tally of errors. The work floor itself resembles an enormous classroom in the throes of exam period. Desks point toward the front, where a manager keeps watch from a raised platform that workers call "the pedestal" or "the birdhouse." Other supervisors are positioned toward the back of the room. "If you want to watch someone," Mr. Edens explains, "it's easier from behind because they don't know you're watching." There also is a black globe hanging from the ceiling, in which cameras are positioned.

Mr. Edens sees nothing Orwellian about this omniscience. "It's not a Big Brother attitude," he says. "It's more of a calming attitude."

But studies of workplace monitoring suggest otherwise. Experts say that surveillance can create a hostile environment in which workers feel pressured, paranoid, and prone to stress-related illness. Surveillance also can be used punitively, to intimidate workers or to justify their firing.

Following a failed union drive at EBS, the National Labor Relations Board filed a series of complaints against the company, including charges that EBS threatened, interrogated, and spied on workers. As part of an out-of-court settlement, EBS reinstated a fired worker and posted a notice that it would refrain from illegal practices during a second union vote, which also failed.

"It's all noise," Mr. Edens says of the unfair labor charges. As for the pressure that surveillance creates, Mr. Edens sees that simply as "the nature of the beast." He adds, "It's got to add stress when everyone knows their production is being monitored. I don't apologize for that."

Mr. Edens also is unapologetic about the draconian work rules he maintains, including one that forbids all talk unrelated to the completion of each task. "I'm not paying people to chat. I'm paying them to open envelopes," he says. Of the blocked windows, Mr. Edens adds, "I don't want them looking out—it's distracting. They'll make mistakes."

This total focus boosts productivity, but it makes many workers feel lonely and trapped. Some try to circumvent the silence rule, like kids in a school library. "If you don't turn your head and sort of mumble out of the side of your mouth, supervisors won't hear you most of the time," Cindy Kesselring explains during her lunch break. Even so, she feels isolated and often longs for her former job as a waitress. "Work is your social life, particularly if you've got kids," says the 27-year-old mother. "Here it's hard to get to know people because you can't talk."

During lunch, workers crowd in the parking lot outside, chatting nonstop. "Some of us don't eat much because the more you chew the less you can talk," Ms. Kesselring says. There aren't other breaks, and workers aren't allowed to sip coffee or eat at their desks during the long stretches before and after lunch. Hard candy is the only permitted desk snack.

New technology and the breaking down of labor into discrete, repetitive tasks also have effectively stripped jobs such as those at EBS of whatever variety and skills clerical work once possessed. Workers in the cage (an antiquated banking term for a money-handling area) only open envelopes and sort contents; those in the audit department compute figures; and data entry clerks punch in the information that the others have collected. If they make a mistake, the computer buzzes, and a message such as "check digit error" flashes on the screen.

"We don't ask these people to think—the machines think for them," Mr. Edens says. "They don't have to make any decisions." This makes the work simpler but also deepens its monotony. In the cage, Carol Smith says she looks forward to envelopes that contain anything out of the ordinary, such as letters reporting that the donor is deceased. Or she plays mental games. "I think to myself, A goes in this pile, B goes here, and C goes there—sort of like Bingo." She says she sometimes feels "like a machine," particularly when she fills out the "control card" on which she lists "time in" and "time out" for each tray of envelopes. In a slot marked "cage operator" Ms. Smith writes her code number, 3173. "That's me," she says.

Barbara Ann Wiles, a keyboard operator, also plays mind games to break up the boredom. Tapping in the names and addresses of new donors, she tries to imagine the faces behind the names, particularly the odd ones. "Like this one, Mrs. Fittizzi," she chuckles. "I can picture her as a very stout lady with a strong accent, hollering on a street corner." She picks out another: "Doris Angelroth—she's

very sophisticated, a monocle maybe, drinking tea on an overstuffed mohair couch."

It is a world remote from the one Ms. Wiles inhabits. Like most EBS employees, she must juggle her low-paying job with child care. On this Friday, for instance, Ms. Wiles will finish her eight-hour shift at about 4 p.m., go home for a few hours, then return for a second shift from midnight to 8 a.m. Otherwise she would have to come in on Saturday to finish the week's work. "This way I can be home on the weekend to look after my kids," she says.

Others find the work harder to leave behind at the end of the day. In the cage, Ms. Smith says her husband used to complain because she often woke him in the middle of the night. "I'd be shuffling my hands in my sleep," she says, mimicking the motion of opening envelopes.

Her cage colleague, Ms. Kesselring, says her fiancé has a different gripe. "He dodges me for a couple of hours after work because I don't shut up—I need to talk, talk, talk," she says. And there is one household task she can no longer abide.

"I won't pay bills because I can't stand to open another envelope," she says. "I'll leave letters sitting in the mailbox for days."

Questions for Discussion

1. Which of the management theories described in the chapter does Ron Edens make most use of?

2. What do you think are the effects of this approach on (a) workers and (b) supervisors?

3. Do you regard Ron Edens's approach to management as ethical and acceptable or unethical and unacceptable in the 2000s? Why?

Source: T. Horwitz, "Mr. Edens Profits from Watching His Workers' Every Move," *The Wall Street Journal*, December 1, 1994. Copyright © 1994. Reproduced with permission of Dow Jones & Company, Inc. via Copyright Clearance Center.

CHAPTER 3

Values, Attitudes, Emotions, and Culture: The Manager as a Person

Learning Objectives

After studying this chapter, you should be able to:

LO3-1 Describe the various personality traits that affect how managers think, feel, and behave.

LO3-2 Explain what values and attitudes are and describe their impact on managerial action.

LO3-3 Appreciate how moods and emotions influence all members of an organization.

LO3-4 Describe the nature of emotional intelligence and its role in management.

LO3-5 Define organizational culture and explain how managers both create and are influenced by organizational culture.

A MANAGER'S CHALLENGE

Kevin Plank's Determination Pays Off at Under Armour

How can managers succeed against tough odds? When Kevin Plank was a walk-on fullback football player at the University of Maryland in the 1990s, he often became annoyed that his T-shirt was soaked and weighted down with sweat. Always an original thinker, he wondered why athletic apparel couldn't be make out of some kind of polyester blend that would help athletes' and sports aficionados' muscles stay cool while wicking away, and not holding, moisture from sweat.[1] As he was finishing his undergraduate studies at Maryland, he started experimenting with different fabrics, testing their durability, comfort, and water resistance with the help of a local tailor. A prototype of Under Armour's first product—the 0039 compression shirt—was developed.[2]

Upon graduation from the University of Maryland, Plank was offered a position at Prudential Life Insurance. An entrepreneur at heart willing to risk everything to pursue his bold ideas, Plank realized that accepting a secure position with an insurance company would have driven him nuts. Thus, he turned down the Prudential offer and mustered his determination to sell his innovative T-shirt.[3] With little business training or experience, and a lot of perseverance and discipline, Plank pursued the makings of what would become

a major competitor of Nike 16 years later with net revenues over $1.4 billion in 2011.[4] Entering and succeeding in the competitive

No wonder the fabrics perform so well! With an inventor like Kevin Plank, Under Armour's innovative endurance products give larger sporting goods companies a run for their money.

sports apparel industry dominated by huge players like Nike with vast resources and a widely recognized brand would seem like an impossible feat even for a seasoned business person with access to capital. With around $20,000 in the bank and the resolve to turn his idea into a viable venture, Plank succeeded against all odds.[5]

Very outgoing and confident, Plank used his network of athletic contacts from playing on teams in high school, military school, and the University of Maryland to get the word out about the shirt.[6] From the various teams he had played on, he was familiar enough with around 40 NFL players to contact them and tell them about the shirt. Living out of his car with his trunk full of shirts, Plank drove around to training camps and schools to show athletes and managers his new product. Teaming up with two partners, Plank began running his business from the basement of his grandmother's house in Georgetown, Washington D.C., with the help of a $250,000 small-business loan. As business and orders picked up, Under Armour outgrew the basement and set up shop on Sharp Street in Baltimore.[7] The rest has literally been history.

Today, Under Armour provides all sports teams' uniforms and apparel for school stores for 10 Division 1 schools including the University of Maryland, Boston College, and Auburn University. In January of 2011 at the BCS National Championship game when Oregon (which Nike supplies) played Auburn, it was also billed as Nike versus Under Armour. Under Armour is sold by major athletic retail chains such as the Sports Authority and Dick's Sporting Goods and also has its own retail and outlet stores. Around 19% of Under Armour's sales are from Dick's and 9% from the Sports Authority.[8]

Under Armour currently produces and sells apparel, shoes, and accessories for women, men, and youth for athletics, sports, outdoor activities, and fitness.[9] The apparel is focused on regulating body temperature and improving performance under different conditions and is organized into three lines. Each line comes in three styles—tight fit or compression, fitted or athletic fit, and loose fit or relaxed. The HEATGEAR® line is to be worn in hot to warm temperatures singly or under equipment and is made of a microfiber blend that wicks sweat away from the skin, keeping wearers cool and dry. The very first compression T-shirt Plank originally developed and sold was a HEATGEAR® product that remains popular today. COLDGEAR®, which is to be worn in cold temperatures, wicks sweat away from the body and circulates body heat to maintain body temperature so that wearers are both warm and dry in cold weather. ALLSEASONSGEAR®, to be worn in temperatures that change, keeps people warm when it's chilly and cool and dry when it's warm.[10]

As chairman, CEO, and president, Plank has created and maintained a culture at Under Armour that is true to his own personality and values. Just as he and his two partners worked as a team to start Under Armour, a team mentality pervades the culture and the brand. As employee Erin Wendell puts it, "Working here is like being part of a sports team."[11] Accomplishing great feats, taking risks, being active and excited, open minded, ambitious, imaginative, and courageous are important to Plank and part of Under Armour's culture as is a focus on health. So is the hard work, determination, and conviction that got Plank through the early days of driving around to schools and training camps with boxes of T-shirts in the trunk of his car.

Never one to rest on his laurels, Plank has a sign over the doors of Under Armour's product design offices that reads, "WE HAVE NOT YET BUILT OUR DEFINING PRODUCT."[12]

Today, Under Armour is a global company with 5,400 employees, operating in North America, Europe, the Middle East, Africa, Asia, and Latin America though most employees work in the United States. While increases in market share of the U.S. sports apparel market have been relatively flat for key competitors like Nike and the adidas Group, Under Armour's share of this market rose from 0.6% in 2003 to 2.6% in 2010, according to Sporting Goods Intelligence. In contrast, Nike's market share fell from 7.4% to 7% over this time period and adidas's market share rose from 5.3% to 5.5%.[13]

Under Armour is currently headquartered in what used to be the 400,000 square foot Tide Point complex where Procter & Gamble used to manufacture detergent in Baltimore.[14] Some of the original names of the facilities like Joy and Cheer remain and seem aptly fit for a company like Under Armour. Plans are under way to build a 20,000 square foot retail store in Baltimore, and Under Armour opened its first store in China in May of 2011.[15] To Baltimore's depressed economy, Under Armour has made major contributions, employing 2,000 people in the Baltimore area. Clearly, Plank demonstrates that being original, daring, and taking risks while at the same time being highly determined, disciplined, and persevering can help managers and entrepreneurs succeed against tough odds. As he puts it, "There's an entrepreneur right now, scared to death . . . Get out of your garage and go take a chance, and start your business."[16]

Overview

Like people everywhere, Kevin Plank has his own distinctive personality, values, ways of viewing things, and personal challenges and disappointments. In this chapter we focus on the manager as a feeling, thinking human being. We start by describing enduring characteristics that influence how managers manage, as well as how they view other people, their organizations, and the world around them. We also discuss how managers' values, attitudes, and moods play out in organizations, shaping organizational culture. By the end of this chapter, you will appreciate how the personal characteristics of managers influence the process of management in general—and organizational culture in particular.

LO3-1 Describe the various personality traits that affect how managers think, feel, and behave.

Enduring Characteristics: Personality Traits

All people, including managers, have certain enduring characteristics that influence how they think, feel, and behave both on and off the job. These characteristics are **personality traits**: particular tendencies to feel, think, and act in certain ways that can be used to describe the personality of every individual. It is important to understand the personalities of managers because their personalities influence their behavior and their approach to managing people and resources.

Some managers are demanding, difficult to get along with, and highly critical of other people. Other managers may be as concerned about effectiveness and efficiency as highly critical managers but are easier to get along with, are likable, and frequently praise the people around them. Both management styles may produce excellent results, but their effects on employees are quite different. Do managers deliberately decide to

personality traits Enduring tendencies to feel, think, and act in certain ways.

adopt one or the other of these approaches to management? Although they may do so part of the time, in all likelihood their personalities account for their different approaches. Indeed, research suggests that the way people react to different conditions depends, in part, on their personalities.[17]

The Big Five Personality Traits

We can think of an individual's personality as being composed of five general traits or characteristics: extraversion, negative affectivity, agreeableness, conscientiousness, and openness to experience.[18] Researchers often consider these the Big Five personality traits.[19] Each of them can be viewed as a continuum along which every individual or, more specifically, every manager falls (see Figure 3.1).

Some managers may be at the high end of one trait continuum, others at the low end, and still others somewhere in between. An easy way to understand how these traits can affect a person's approach to management is to describe what people are like at the high and low ends of each trait continuum. As will become evident as you read about each trait, no single trait is right or wrong for being an effective manager. Rather, effectiveness is determined by a complex interaction between the characteristics of managers (including personality traits) and the nature of the job and organization in which they are working. Moreover, personality traits that enhance managerial effectiveness in one situation may impair it in another.

extraversion The tendency to experience positive emotions and moods and to feel good about oneself and the rest of the world.

EXTRAVERSION   Extraversion is the tendency to experience positive emotions and moods and feel good about oneself and the rest of the world. Managers who are high on extraversion (often called *extraverts*) tend to be sociable, affectionate, outgoing, and friendly. Managers who are low on extraversion (often called *introverts*) tend to be less inclined toward social interactions and to have a less positive outlook. Being high on extraversion may be an asset for managers whose jobs entail especially high levels of social interaction. Managers who are low on extraversion may nevertheless be highly effective and efficient, especially when their jobs do not require much social interaction. Their quieter approach may enable them to accomplish quite a bit of work in limited time. See Figure 3.2 for an example of a scale that can be used to measure a person's level of extraversion.

Figure 3.1

The Big Five Personality Traits

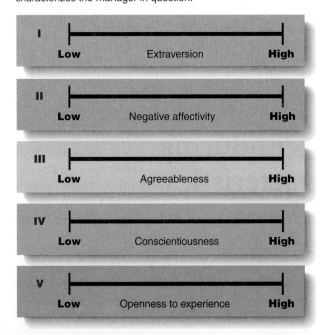

Managers' personalities can be described by determining which point on each of the following dimensions best characterizes the manager in question:

Figure 3.2

Measures of Extraversion, Agreeableness, Conscientiousness, and Openness to Experience

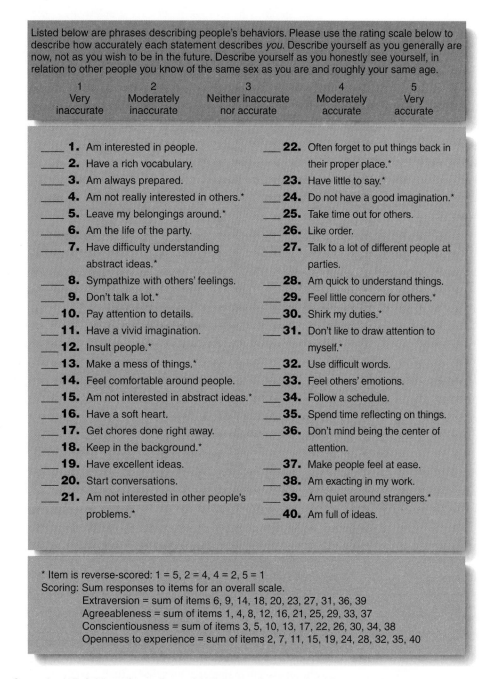

Listed below are phrases describing people's behaviors. Please use the rating scale below to describe how accurately each statement describes *you*. Describe yourself as you generally are now, not as you wish to be in the future. Describe yourself as you honestly see yourself, in relation to other people you know of the same sex as you are and roughly your same age.

1	2	3	4	5
Very inaccurate	Moderately inaccurate	Neither inaccurate nor accurate	Moderately accurate	Very accurate

____ **1.** Am interested in people.

____ **2.** Have a rich vocabulary.

____ **3.** Am always prepared.

____ **4.** Am not really interested in others.*

____ **5.** Leave my belongings around.*

____ **6.** Am the life of the party.

____ **7.** Have difficulty understanding abstract ideas.*

____ **8.** Sympathize with others' feelings.

____ **9.** Don't talk a lot.*

___ **10.** Pay attention to details.

___ **11.** Have a vivid imagination.

___ **12.** Insult people.*

___ **13.** Make a mess of things.*

___ **14.** Feel comfortable around people.

___ **15.** Am not interested in abstract ideas.*

___ **16.** Have a soft heart.

___ **17.** Get chores done right away.

___ **18.** Keep in the background.*

___ **19.** Have excellent ideas.

___ **20.** Start conversations.

___ **21.** Am not interested in other people's problems.*

___ **22.** Often forget to put things back in their proper place.*

___ **23.** Have little to say.*

___ **24.** Do not have a good imagination.*

___ **25.** Take time out for others.

___ **26.** Like order.

___ **27.** Talk to a lot of different people at parties.

___ **28.** Am quick to understand things.

___ **29.** Feel little concern for others.*

___ **30.** Shirk my duties.*

___ **31.** Don't like to draw attention to myself.*

___ **32.** Use difficult words.

___ **33.** Feel others' emotions.

___ **34.** Follow a schedule.

___ **35.** Spend time reflecting on things.

___ **36.** Don't mind being the center of attention.

___ **37.** Make people feel at ease.

___ **38.** Am exacting in my work.

___ **39.** Am quiet around strangers.*

___ **40.** Am full of ideas.

* Item is reverse-scored: 1 = 5, 2 = 4, 4 = 2, 5 = 1
Scoring: Sum responses to items for an overall scale.
       Extraversion = sum of items 6, 9, 14, 18, 20, 23, 27, 31, 36, 39
       Agreeableness = sum of items 1, 4, 8, 12, 16, 21, 25, 29, 33, 37
       Conscientiousness = sum of items 3, 5, 10, 13, 17, 22, 26, 30, 34, 38
       Openness to experience = sum of items 2, 7, 11, 15, 19, 24, 28, 32, 35, 40

Source: Lewis R. Goldberg, Oregon Research Institute, http://ipip.ori.org/ipip/. Reprinted with permission.

negative affectivity The tendency to experience negative emotions and moods, to feel distressed, and to be critical of oneself and others.

NEGATIVE AFFECTIVITY   Negative affectivity is the tendency to experience negative emotions and moods, feel distressed, and be critical of oneself and others. Managers high on this trait may often feel angry and dissatisfied and complain about their own and others' lack of progress. Managers who are low on negative affectivity do not tend to experience many negative emotions and moods and are less pessimistic and critical of themselves and others. On the plus side, the critical approach of a manager high on negative affectivity may sometimes spur both the manager and others to improve their performance. Nevertheless, it is probably more pleasant to work with a manager who is low on negative affectivity; the better working relationships that such a manager is likely to cultivate also can be an important asset. Figure 3.3 is an example of a scale developed to measure a person's level of negative affectivity.

Figure 3.3
A Measure of Negative Affectivity

Instructions: Listed below are a series of statements a person might use to describe her/his attitudes, opinions, interests, and other characteristics. If a statement is true or largely true, put a "T" in the space next to the item. Or if the statement is false or largely false, mark an "F" in the space.

Please answer every statement, even if you are not completely sure of the answer. Read each statement carefully, but don't spend too much time deciding on the answer.

_____ **1.** I worry about things a lot.

_____ **2.** My feelings are often hurt.

_____ **3.** Small problems often irritate me.

_____ **4.** I am often nervous.

_____ **5.** My moods often change.

_____ **6.** Sometimes I feel bad for no apparent reason.

_____ **7.** I often have very strong emotions such as anger or anxiety without really knowing why.

_____ **8.** The unexpected can easily startle me.

_____ **9.** Sometimes, when I am thinking about the day ahead of me, I feel anxious and tense.

_____ **10.** Small setbacks sometimes bother me too much.

_____ **11.** My worries often cause me to lose sleep.

_____ **12.** Some days I seem to be always "on edge."

_____ **13.** I am more sensitive than I should be.

_____ **14.** Sometimes I go from feeling happy to sad, and vice versa, for no good reason.

Scoring: Level of negative affectivity is equal to the number of items answered "True."

Source: Auke Tellegen, *Brief Manual for the Differential Personality Questionnaire,* Copyright © 1982. Paraphrased version reproduced by permission of University of Minnesota Press.

agreeableness
The tendency to get along well with other people.

AGREEABLENESS Agreeableness is the tendency to get along well with others. Managers who are high on the agreeableness continuum are likable, tend to be affectionate, and care about other people. Managers who are low on agreeableness may be somewhat distrustful of others, unsympathetic, uncooperative, and even at times antagonistic. Being high on agreeableness may be especially important for managers whose responsibilities require that they develop good, close relationships with others. Nevertheless, a low level of agreeableness may be an asset in managerial jobs that actually require that managers be antagonistic, such as drill sergeants and some other kinds of military managers. See Figure 3.2 for an example of a scale that measures a person's level of agreeableness.

conscientiousness
The tendency to be careful, scrupulous, and persevering.

CONSCIENTIOUSNESS Conscientiousness is the tendency to be careful, scrupulous, and persevering.[20] Managers who are high on the conscientiousness continuum are organized and self-disciplined; those who are low on this trait might sometimes appear to lack direction and self-discipline. Conscientiousness has been found to be a good predictor of performance in many kinds of jobs, including managerial jobs in a variety of organizations.[21] Entrepreneurs who found their own companies, like Kevin Plank profiled in "A Manager's Challenge," often are high on conscientiousness, and their persistence and determination help them to overcome obstacles and turn their ideas into successful new ventures. Figure 3.2 provides an example of a scale that measures conscientiousness.

openness to experience
The tendency to be original, have broad interests, be open to a wide range of stimuli, be daring, and take risks.

OPENNESS TO EXPERIENCE Openness to experience is the tendency to be original, have broad interests, be open to a wide range of stimuli, be daring, and take risks.[22] Managers who are high on this trait continuum may be especially likely to take risks and be innovative in their planning and decision making. Entrepreneurs who start their own businesses—like Bill Gates of Microsoft, Jeff Bezos of Amazon.com, and Anita Roddick of The Body Shop—are, in all likelihood, high on openness to experience, which has contributed to their success as entrepreneurs and managers. Kevin Plank, discussed in this chapter's "A Manager's Challenge," founded his own company and continues to explore new ways for it to grow—a testament to his high level of openness to experience. Managers who are low on openness to experience may be less prone to take risks and more conservative in their planning and decision making. In certain organizations and positions, this tendency might be an asset. The manager of the fiscal office in a public university, for example, must ensure that all university departments and units follow the university's rules and regulations pertaining to budgets, spending accounts, and reimbursements of expenses. Figure 3.2 provides an example of a measure of openness to experience.

Managers who come up with and implement radically new ideas are often high on openness to experience, as is true of Mike Rowe, creator of the hit Discovery Channel TV show *Dirty Jobs*.

Manager as a Person

Who Would Have Thought *Dirty Jobs* Would Be a Hit?

Mike Rowe is hardly the person you would have thought could have created a hit TV show like the Discovery Channel's *Dirty Jobs*.[23] Not the most ambitious of types, and as an actor for over two decades who never made it big, his work experiences have ranged from performing with the Baltimore Opera to selling fake simulated diamonds on QVC to appearing in Tylenol commercials.[24] While cohosting a local TV show on CBS-5 in San Francisco, Rowe hit on the idea behind *Dirty Jobs*. Rowe did a segment on the show called "Somebody's Gotta Do It," viewers liked it, and it really struck a chord with him personally.[25]

His openness to experience led him to develop a TV show featuring him working as an apprentice to men and women performing the kinds of hard, dirty work we all depend on and no one wants to do (think bat cave scavenger, worm dung farmer, roadkill cleaner, sewer inspector, pig farmer . . .).[26] As he puts it, his show features "men and women who do the kinds of jobs that make civilized life possible for the rest of us."[27] Although he originally had a hard time finding a home for *Dirty Jobs* (the Discovery Channel turned him down twice before agreeing to air a pilot series in 2003), the show has become a hit.[28]

Rowe's openness to experience enables him to get down and dirty with the best of them, try his hand at all sorts of dirty jobs, and thoroughly enjoy it. As would be expected, all sorts of mishaps occur—and that is part of the fun. Rowe has come to appreciate the earnestness of the workers he profiles—"the celebration of work, and the mixing of pain and fun."[29] Interestingly enough, as one who never had embraced the value of too much hard work in the past, Rowe has gleaned from *Dirty Jobs* a healthy respect and admiration for the people who perform all sorts of dirty jobs, work hard at them, and are happy when the work is done.[30]

Mike Rowe's openness to experience has given him a real appreciation of all kinds of work and jobs.

Successful managers occupy a variety of positions on the Big Five personality trait continua. One highly effective manager may be high on extraversion and negative affectivity; another equally effective manager may be low on both these traits; and still another may be somewhere in between. Members of an organization must understand these differences among managers because they can shed light on how managers behave and on their approach to planning, leading, organizing, or controlling. If subordinates realize, for example, that their manager is low on extraversion, they will not feel slighted when their manager seems to be aloof because they will realize that by nature he or she is simply not outgoing.

Managers themselves also need to be aware of their own personality traits and the traits of others, including their subordinates and fellow managers. A manager who knows that he has a tendency to be highly critical of other people might try to tone down his negative approach. Similarly, a manager who realizes that her chronically complaining subordinate tends to be so negative because of his personality may take all his complaints with a grain of salt and realize that things probably are not as bad as this subordinate says they are.

In order for all members of an organization to work well together and with people outside the organization, such as customers and suppliers, they must understand each other. Such understanding comes, in part, from an appreciation of some fundamental ways in which people differ from one another—that is, an appreciation of personality traits.

Other Personality Traits That Affect Managerial Behavior

Many other specific traits in addition to the Big Five describe people's personalities. Here we look at traits that are particularly important for understanding managerial effectiveness: locus of control; self-esteem; and the needs for achievement, affiliation, and power.

internal locus of control The tendency to locate responsibility for one's fate within oneself.

LOCUS OF CONTROL   People differ in their views about how much control they have over what happens to and around them. The locus of control trait captures these beliefs.[31] People with an **internal locus of control** believe they themselves are responsible for their own fate; they see their own actions and behaviors as being major and decisive determinants of important outcomes such as attaining levels of job performance, being promoted, or being turned down for a choice job assignment. Some managers with an internal locus of control see the success of a whole organization resting on their shoulders. One example is Kevin Plank in "A Manager's Challenge." An internal locus of control also helps to ensure ethical behavior and decision making in an organization because people feel accountable and responsible for their own actions.

external locus of control The tendency to locate responsibility for one's fate in outside forces and to believe one's own behavior has little impact on outcomes.

People with an **external locus of control** believe that outside forces are responsible for what happens to and around them; they do not think their own actions make much of a difference. As such, they tend not to intervene to try to change a situation or solve a problem, leaving it to someone else.

Managers need an internal locus of control because they *are* responsible for what happens in organizations; they need to believe they can and do make a difference, as does Kevin Plank at Under Armour. Moreover, managers are responsible for ensuring that organizations and their members behave in an ethical fashion, and for this as well they need an internal locus of control—they need to know and feel they can make a difference.

self-esteem The degree to which individuals feel good about themselves and their capabilities.

SELF-ESTEEM   Self-esteem is the degree to which individuals feel good about themselves and their capabilities. People with high self-esteem believe they are competent, deserving, and capable of handling most situations, as does Kevin Plank. People with low self-esteem have poor opinions of themselves, are unsure about their capabilities, and question their ability to succeed at different endeavors.[32] Research suggests that people tend to choose activities and goals consistent with their levels of self-esteem. High self-esteem is desirable for managers because it facilitates their setting and keeping high standards for themselves, pushes them ahead on difficult projects, and gives them the confidence they need to make and carry out important decisions.

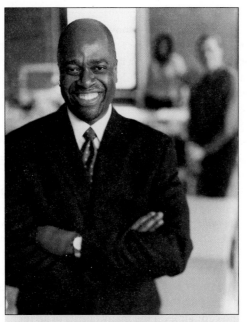

Confidence matters: A manager who takes difficulties in stride and can effectively lead is able to inspire subordinates while getting the job done.

need for achievement The extent to which an individual has a strong desire to perform challenging tasks well and to meet personal standards for excellence.

need for affiliation The extent to which an individual is concerned about establishing and maintaining good interpersonal relations, being liked, and having other people get along.

need for power The extent to which an individual desires to control or influence others.

NEEDS FOR ACHIEVEMENT, AFFILIATION, AND POWER Psychologist David McClelland has extensively researched the needs for achievement, affiliation, and power.[33] The **need for achievement** is the extent to which an individual has a strong desire to perform challenging tasks well and to meet personal standards for excellence. People with a high need for achievement often set clear goals for themselves and like to receive performance feedback. The **need for affiliation** is the extent to which an individual is concerned about establishing and maintaining good interpersonal relations, being liked, and having the people around him or her get along with one another. The **need for power** is the extent to which an individual desires to control or influence others.[34]

Research suggests that high needs for achievement and for power are assets for first-line and middle managers and that a high need for power is especially important for upper-level managers.[35] One study found that U.S. presidents with a relatively high need for power tended to be especially effective during their terms of office.[36] A high need for affiliation may not always be desirable in managers because it might lead them to try too hard to be liked by others (including subordinates) rather than doing all they can to ensure that performance is as high as it can and should be. Although most research on these needs has been done in the United States, some studies suggest that these findings may also apply to people in other countries such as India and New Zealand.[37]

Taken together, these desirable personality traits for managers—an internal locus of control, high self-esteem, and high needs for achievement and power—suggest that managers need to be take-charge people who not only believe their own actions are decisive in determining their own and their organizations' fates but also believe in their own capabilities. Such managers have a personal desire for accomplishment and influence over others.

Values, Attitudes, and Moods and Emotions

What are managers striving to achieve? How do they think they should behave? What do they think about their jobs and organizations? And how do they actually feel at work? We can find some answers to these questions by exploring managers' values, attitudes, and moods.

Values, attitudes, and moods and emotions capture how managers experience their jobs as individuals. *Values* describe what managers are trying to achieve through work and how they think they should behave. *Attitudes* capture their thoughts and feelings about their specific jobs and organizations. *Moods and emotions* encompass how managers actually feel when they are managing. Although these three aspects of managers' work experience are highly personal, they also have important implications for understanding how managers behave, how they treat and respond to others, and how, through their efforts, they help contribute to organizational effectiveness through planning, leading, organizing, and controlling.

LO3-2 Explain what values and attitudes are and describe their impact on managerial action.

Values: Terminal and Instrumental

terminal value A lifelong goal or objective that an individual seeks to achieve.

The two kinds of personal values are *terminal* and *instrumental*. A **terminal value** is a personal conviction about lifelong goals or objectives; an **instrumental value** is a personal conviction about desired modes of conduct or ways of behaving.[38] Terminal values often lead to

instrumental value A mode of conduct that an individual seeks to follow.

norms Unwritten, informal codes of conduct that prescribe how people should act in particular situations and are considered important by most members of a group or organization.

value system The terminal and instrumental values that are guiding principles in an individual's life.

the formation of **norms**, which are unwritten, informal codes of conduct, such as behaving honestly or courteously, that prescribe how people should act in particular situations and are considered important by most members of a group or organization.

Milton Rokeach, a leading researcher in the area of human values, identified 18 terminal values and 18 instrumental values that describe each person's value system (see Figure 3.4).[39] By rank ordering the terminal values from 1 (most important as a guiding principle in one's life) to 18 (least important as a guiding principle in one's life) and then rank ordering the instrumental values from 1 to 18, people can give good pictures of their **value systems**—what they are striving to achieve in life and how they want to behave.[40] (You can gain a good understanding of your own values by rank ordering first the terminal values and then the instrumental values listed in Figure 3.4.)

Several of the terminal values listed in Figure 3.4 seem to be especially important for managers—such as *a sense of accomplishment (a lasting contribution), equality (brotherhood, equal opportunity for all),* and *self-respect (self-esteem).* A manager who thinks a sense of accomplishment is of paramount importance might focus on making a lasting contribution to an organization by developing a new product that can save or prolong lives, as is true of managers at Medtronic (a company that makes medical devices such as cardiac pacemakers), or by opening a new foreign subsidiary. A manager who places equality at the top of his or her list of terminal values may be at the forefront of an organization's efforts to support, provide equal opportunities to, and capitalize on the many talents of an increasingly diverse workforce.

Other values are likely to be considered important by many managers, such *as a comfortable life (a prosperous life), an exciting life (a stimulating, active life), freedom (independence, free choice),* and *social recognition (respect, admiration).* The relative importance that

Figure 3.4
Terminal and Instrumental Values

Terminal Values	Instrumental Values
A comfortable life (a prosperous life)	Ambitious (hardworking, aspiring)
An exciting life (a stimulating, active life)	Broad-minded (open-minded)
A sense of accomplishment (lasting contribution)	Capable (competent, effective)
A world at peace (free of war and conflict)	Cheerful (lighthearted, joyful)
A world of beauty (beauty of nature and the arts)	Clean (neat, tidy)
Equality (brotherhood, equal opportunity for all)	Courageous (standing up for your beliefs)
Family security (taking care of loved ones)	Forgiving (willing to pardon others)
Freedom (independence, free choice)	Helpful (working for the welfare of others)
Happiness (contentedness)	Honest (sincere, truthful)
Inner harmony (freedom from inner conflict)	Imaginative (daring, creative)
Mature love (sexual and spiritual intimacy)	Independent (self-reliant, self-sufficient)
National security (protection from attack)	Intellectual (intelligent, reflective)
Pleasure (an enjoyable, leisurely life)	Logical (consistent, rational)
Salvation (saved, eternal life)	Loving (affectionate, tender)
Self-respect (self-esteem)	Obedient (dutiful, respectful)
Social recognition (respect, admiration)	Polite (courteous, well-mannered)
True friendship (close companionship)	Responsible (dependable, reliable)
Wisdom (a mature understanding of life)	Self-controlled (restrained, self-disciplined)

managers place on each terminal value helps explain what they are striving to achieve in their organizations and what they will focus their efforts on.

Several of the instrumental values listed in Figure 3.4 seem to be important modes of conduct for managers, such as being *ambitious (hardworking, aspiring), broad-minded (open-minded), capable (competent, effective), responsible (dependable, reliable),* and *self-controlled (restrained, self-disciplined).* Moreover, the relative importance a manager places on these and other instrumental values may be a significant determinant of actual behaviors on the job. A manager who considers being *imaginative (daring, creative)* to be highly important, for example, is more likely to be innovative and take risks than is a manager who considers this to be less important (all else being equal). A manager who considers being *honest (sincere, truthful)* to be of paramount importance may be a driving force for taking steps to ensure that all members of a unit or organization behave ethically, as indicated in the following "Ethics in Action" box.

Ethics in Action

Telling the Truth at Gentle Giant Moving

Gentle Giant Moving Company, based in Somerville, Massachusetts, was founded by Larry O'Toole in 1980 and now has over $28 million in revenues and offices in multiple states.[41] Gentle Giant opened its newest office, Great Giant Moving and Storage, in 2011 in San Francisco, California.[42] Although moving is undoubtedly hard work and many people would never think about having a career in this industry, Gentle Giant's unique culture and approach to managing people have not only contributed to the company's success but also provided its employees with satisfying careers. For

At Gentle Giant Moving Company, employees are given leadership training, access to company outings, and the opportunity to advance to management positions.

example, when Ryan Libby was in college, he worked for Gentle Giant during one of his summer vacations to make some extra money. After graduating from college, he was the assistant manager for the Providence, Rhode Island, Gentle Giant Office. Now Libby is branch manager for Providence.[43] As he puts it, "First it was just a paycheck, and it kind of turned into a long-term career."[44]

Libby is just the kind of employee O'Toole seeks to hire—employees who start out driving moving trucks and eventually move into management positions running offices. Whereas some moving companies hire a lot of temporary help in the summer to meet seasonal demand, 60% of Gentle Giant employees are employed full-time.[45] Because the demand for moving services is lower in the winter, Gentle Giant uses this time to give employees training and leadership development activities. Of course new employees receive training in the basics of moving: packing, lifting, and carrying household goods in a safe manner. However, employees looking to advance in the company receive training in a host of other areas ranging from project management, communication, problem solving, and customer relations to leadership. An overarching goal of Gentle Giant's training efforts is inculcating in employees the importance of honesty. According to O'Toole, "We really emphasize that what matters most to us is telling the truth."[46]

Training benefits Gentle Giant's employees, customers, and the company as a whole. About one-third of the company's office and management employees started out driving moving trucks. Customers are satisfied because employees are capable, honest, and professional. And the company has continued to grow, prosper, and receive recognition in the business press as well as awards. For example, Gentle Giant was named one of the 15 Top Small Workplaces by *The Wall Street Journal* in collaboration with Winning Workplaces (a nonprofit organization that focuses on helping small and medium-size companies improve their work environments).[47]

Having fun and getting to know each other as people are also important at Gentle Giant.[48] The company holds parties and arranges outings for employees to sporting events, amusement parks, and other local attractions. Most workdays, O'Toole takes an employee out to lunch. Some college athletes are attracted to work for Gentle Giant because they see moving as a way to keep fit while at the same time having the opportunity to grow and develop on the job and move into a managerial position if they desire.[49]

All in all, managers' value systems signify what managers as individuals are trying to accomplish and become in their personal lives and at work. Thus managers' value systems are fundamental guides to their behavior and efforts at planning, leading, organizing, and controlling.

Attitudes

attitude A collection of feelings and beliefs.

An **attitude** is a collection of feelings and beliefs. Like everyone else, managers have attitudes about their jobs and organizations, and these attitudes affect how they approach their jobs. Two of the most important attitudes in this context are job satisfaction and organizational commitment.

job satisfaction The collection of feelings and beliefs that managers have about their current jobs.

JOB SATISFACTION   Job satisfaction is the collection of feelings and beliefs that managers have about their current jobs.[50] Managers who have high levels of job satisfaction generally like their jobs, feel they are fairly treated, and believe their jobs have many desirable features or characteristics (such as interesting work, good pay and job security, autonomy, or nice coworkers). Figure 3.5 shows sample items from two scales that managers can use to measure job satisfaction. Levels of job satisfaction tend to increase as one moves up the hierarchy in an organization. Upper managers, in general, tend to be more satisfied with their jobs than entry-level employees. Managers' levels of job satisfaction can range from very low to very high.

One might think that in tough economic times when unemployment is high and layoffs are prevalent, people who do have jobs might be relatively satisfied with them. However, this is not necessarily the case. For example, in December 2009 the U.S. unemployment rate was 10%, 85,000 jobs were lost from the economy, and the underemployment rate (which includes people who have given up looking for jobs and those who are working part-time because they can't find a full-time position) was 17.3%.[51] During these recessionary conditions, job satisfaction levels in the United States fell to record lows.[52]

The Conference Board has been tracking levels of U.S. job satisfaction since 1987, when 61.1% of workers surveyed indicated that they were satisfied with their jobs.[53] In 2009 only 45% of workers surveyed indicated that they were satisfied with their jobs, an all-time low for the survey.[54] Some sources of job dissatisfaction include uninteresting work, lack of job security, incomes that have not kept pace with inflation, and having to spend more money on health insurance. For example, three times as many workers in 2009 had to contribute to paying for their health insurance and had rising levels of contributions compared to 1980. Only 43% of workers thought their jobs were secure in 2009 compared to 59% in 1987. In the 2000s, average household incomes adjusted for inflation declined.[55]

Of all age groups, workers under 25 were the most dissatisfied with their jobs. More specifically, approximately 64% of workers in this age group were dissatisfied with their jobs, perhaps due to declining opportunities and relatively low earnings. Around 22% of all respondents didn't think they would still have the same job in a year.[56]

Some organizations have combined a concern about protecting the environment with a concern about preserving workers' jobs and avoiding layoffs, as illustrated in the following "Ethics in Action."

Figure 3.5

Sample Items from Two Measures of Job Satisfaction

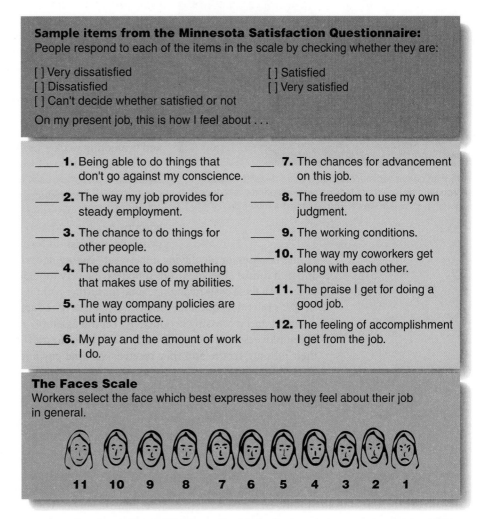

Sample items from the Minnesota Satisfaction Questionnaire:
People respond to each of the items in the scale by checking whether they are:

[ ] Very dissatisfied   [ ] Satisfied
[ ] Dissatisfied   [ ] Very satisfied
[ ] Can't decide whether satisfied or not

On my present job, this is how I feel about . . .

_____ **1.** Being able to do things that don't go against my conscience.

_____ **2.** The way my job provides for steady employment.

_____ **3.** The chance to do things for other people.

_____ **4.** The chance to do something that makes use of my abilities.

_____ **5.** The way company policies are put into practice.

_____ **6.** My pay and the amount of work I do.

_____ **7.** The chances for advancement on this job.

_____ **8.** The freedom to use my own judgment.

_____ **9.** The working conditions.

_____ **10.** The way my coworkers get along with each other.

_____ **11.** The praise I get for doing a good job.

_____ **12.** The feeling of accomplishment I get from the job.

The Faces Scale
Workers select the face which best expresses how they feel about their job in general.

11   10   9   8   7   6   5   4   3   2   1

Source: D. J. Weiss et al., *Manual for the Minnesota Satisfaction Questionnaire.* Copyrighted by the Vocational Psychology Research, University of Minnesota.; Copyright © 1975 by the American Psychological Association. Adapted by permission of Randall B. Dunham and J. B. Brett.

Ethics in
Action

Protecting the Environment and Jobs at Subaru of Indiana Automotive

Subaru of Indiana Automotive (SIA) is located in Lafayette, Indiana; produces the Subaru Legacy, Outback, and Tribeca; and has over 3,000 employees.[57] While the U.S. auto industry has had its share of major problems ranging from massive layoffs to huge bankruptcies, SIA has never laid off employees.[58] In fact, SIA employees receive annual raises, premium-free health care, substantial amounts of overtime work, financial counseling, the option of earning a Purdue University degree at the production facility, and pay for volunteer work. While 46,000 auto jobs have been lost in Indiana and several auto manufacturing plants have shut down in the state, SIA appears to be thriving.[59]

At the same time, SIA has been on an uncompromising mission to protect the environment and save money by eliminating waste. Around 98% of the waste at SIA is recycled or composted with considerable efficiencies and cost savings.[60] An on-site broker manages bids for recycled metals, glass, plastic, and paper. Only about 2% of waste is

More than corn in Indiana? Definitely more benefits for the environment as Subaru of Indiana pioneers efforts to reduce packaging, eliminate waste, and reuse extra materials.

incinerated and this is done locally at an operation that converts waste to fuel. Suppliers are encouraged to minimize packaging, which enables SIA to get better deals from them, and boxes and containers shipping parts and materials back and forth from Japan to Indiana are reused, cutting costs. Scrap from welding is sold in copper auctions. Executive Vice President Tom Easterday estimates that SIA saves over $5 million per year from its efforts to eliminate waste, recycle, and compost.[61]

SIA combines its minimal environmental impact philosophy with a commitment to reducing worker injuries and promoting worker health.[62] For example, rather than inspecting the quality of welds by taking cars apart as was customary, SIA now uses ultrasonic technology to check welds. This change reduced worker injuries from jackhammers and metals waste and results in a process that is more effective, quicker, and less expensive. SIA has a free on-site gym with wellness and weight loss programs.[63] Workers receive bonuses for identifying unnecessary packaging and processes, which can cut costs and be a source of rebates from suppliers, the very top bonus being a brand new Subaru Legacy. All these costs savings are used for further plant investments and overtime pay.[64]

SIA's relentless quest for efficiency in terms of reducing waste/protecting the environment and increasing productivity on the assembly line does put a lot of pressure on employees who are expected to work long hours.[65] Nonetheless, they know that their jobs are secure and they receive overtime pay and premium-free health insurance. When the Japanese earthquake in 2011 forced the plant to slow down because of disruptions in the supply of parts from Japan, SIA continued to pay all its employees their full wages to volunteer in the local community. Thus, it is not surprising that there are about 10 applicants for each open position at SIA. Clearly, SIA has demonstrated it is possible to protect the environment and protect jobs to the benefit of all.[66]

organizational citizenship behaviors (OCBs) Behaviors that are not required of organizational members but that contribute to and are necessary for organizational efficiency, effectiveness, and competitive advantage.

In general, it is desirable for managers to be satisfied with their jobs, for at least two reasons. First, satisfied managers may be more likely to go the extra mile for their organization or perform **organizational citizenship behaviors (OCBs)**—behaviors that are not required of organizational members but that contribute to and are necessary for organizational efficiency, effectiveness, and competitive advantage.[67] Managers who are satisfied with their jobs are more likely to perform these "above and beyond the call of duty" behaviors, which can range from putting in long hours when needed to coming up with truly creative ideas and overcoming obstacles to implement them (even when doing so is not part of the manager's job), or to going out of one's way to help a coworker, subordinate, or superior (even when doing so entails considerable personal sacrifice).[68]

A second reason why it is desirable for managers to be satisfied with their jobs is that satisfied managers may be less likely to quit.[69] A manager who is highly satisfied may never even think about looking for another position; a dissatisfied manager may always be on the lookout for new opportunities. Turnover can hurt an organization because it results in the loss of the experience and knowledge that managers have gained about the company, industry, and business environment.

A growing source of dissatisfaction for many lower- and middle-level managers, as well as for nonmanagerial employees, is the threat of unemployment and increased workloads from organizational downsizings and layoffs. Organizations that try to improve their efficiency through restructuring and layoffs often eliminate a sizable number of first-line and middle management positions. This decision obviously hurts the managers who are laid off, and it also can reduce the job satisfaction levels of managers who remain. They might fear being the next to be let go. In addition, the workloads of remaining employees often are dramatically increased as a result of restructuring, and this can contribute to dissatisfaction.

How managers and organizations handle layoffs is of paramount importance, not only for the layoff victims but also for employees who survive the layoff and keep their jobs.[70] Showing compassion and empathy for layoff victims, giving them as much advance notice as possible about the layoff, providing clear information about severance benefits, and helping layoff victims in their job search efforts are a few of the ways in which managers can humanely manage a layoff.[71] For example, when Ron Thomas, vice president of organizational development for Martha Stewart Living Omnimedia, had to lay off employees as a result of closing the organization's catalog business, he personally called all the catalog businesses he knew to find out about potential positions for laid-off employees.[72] Efforts such as Thomas's to help layoff victims find new jobs can contribute to the job satisfaction of those who survive the layoff. As

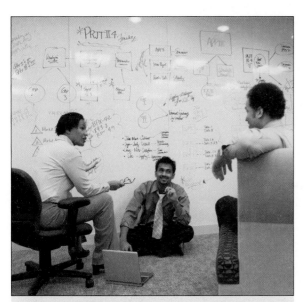

Brainstorming for hours and staying late flow naturally when you know your work is appreciated, your job is secure, and you are valued.

Thomas puts it, "If you handle a restructuring well, the word gets out that you're a good place to work . . . if we post a job opening today, we'll get 1,500 résumés tomorrow."[73]

Unfortunately, when the unemployment rate is high, laid-off employees sometimes find it difficult to find new jobs and can remain jobless for months.[74] For small businesses, the decision to lay off employees and communicating that decision can be especially painful because managers often have developed close personal relationships with the people they have to let go, know their families, and fear what will happen to them with the loss of a steady income.[75] Shelly Polum, vice president for administration at Ram Tool, a small family-owned manufacturing company in Grafton, Wisconsin, broke down in tears in her office after she had to let employees know they were being laid off.[76] When Charlie Thomas, vice president of Shuqualak Lumber in Shuqualak, Mississippi, had to announce layoffs of close to a quarter of his employees, he wrote a speech that he could not get through without stopping and retreating to his office to pull himself together. As he put it, "I couldn't get it out . . . It just killed my soul."[77] As these managers realize, getting laid off during a recession can be devastating for employees and their families because jobs are few and far between.

organizational commitment The collection of feelings and beliefs that managers have about their organization as a whole.

ORGANIZATIONAL COMMITMENT Organizational commitment is the collection of feelings and beliefs that managers have about their organization as a whole.[78] Managers who are committed to their organizations believe in what their organizations are doing, are proud of what these organizations stand for, and feel a high degree of loyalty toward their organizations. Committed managers are more likely to go above and beyond the call of duty to help their company and are less likely to quit.[79] Organizational commitment can be especially strong when employees and managers truly believe in organizational values; it also leads to a strong organizational culture, as found in Under Armour.

Organizational commitment is likely to help managers perform some of their figurehead and spokesperson roles (see Chapter 1). It is much easier for a manager to persuade others both inside and outside the organization of the merits of what the organization has done and is seeking to accomplish if the manager truly believes in and is committed to the organization. Figure 3.6 is an example of a scale that can measure a person's level of organizational commitment.

Do managers in different countries have similar or different attitudes? Differences in the levels of job satisfaction and organizational commitment among managers in different countries are likely because these managers have different kinds of opportunities and rewards and because they face different economic, political, and sociocultural forces in their organizations' general environments. Levels of organizational commitment from one country to another may depend on the extent to which countries have legislation affecting firings and layoffs and the extent to which citizens of a country are geographically mobile.

LO3-3   Appreciate how moods and emotions influence all members of an organization.

Moods and Emotions

Just as you sometimes are in a bad mood and at other times are in a good mood, so too are managers. A **mood** is a feeling or state of mind. When people are in a positive mood, they feel excited, enthusiastic, active, or elated.[80] When people are in a negative mood, they feel

mood A feeling or state of mind.

Figure 3.6
A Measure of Organizational Commitment

People respond to each of the items in the scale by checking whether they:
[ ] Strongly disagree   [ ] Slightly agree
[ ] Moderately disagree   [ ] Moderately agree
[ ] Slightly disagree   [ ] Strongly agree
[ ] Neither disagree nor agree

_____ **1.** I am willing to put in a great deal of effort beyond that normally expected in order to help this organization be successful.

_____ **2.** I talk up this organization to my friends as a great organization to work for.

_____ **3.** I feel very little loyalty to this organization.*

_____ **4.** I would accept almost any type of job assignment in order to keep working for this organization.

_____ **5.** I find that my values and the organization's values are very similar.

_____ **6.** I am proud to tell others that I am part of this organization.

_____ **7.** I could just as well be working for a different organization as long as the type of work was similar.*

_____ **8.** This organization really inspires the very best in me in the way of job performance.

_____ **9.** It would take very little change in my present circumstances to cause me to leave this organization.*

_____ **10.** I am extremely glad that I chose this organization to work for over others I was considering at the time I joined.

_____ **11.** There's not too much to be gained by sticking with this organization indefinitely.*

_____ **12.** Often, I find it difficult to agree with this organization's policies on important matters relating to its employees.*

_____ **13.** I really care about the fate of this organization.

_____ **14.** For me this is the best of all possible organizations for which to work.

_____ **15.** Deciding to work for this organization was a definite mistake on my part.*

Scoring: Responses to items 1, 2, 4, 5, 6, 8, 10, 13, and 14 are scored such that 1 = strongly disagree; 2 = moderately disagree; 3 = slightly disagree; 4 = neither disagree nor agree; 5 = slightly agree; 6 = moderately agree; and 7 = strongly agree. Responses to "*" items 3, 7, 9, 11, 12, and 15 are scored 7 = strongly disagree; 6 = moderately disagree; 5 = slightly disagree; 4 = neither disagree nor agree; 3 = slightly agree; 2 = moderately agree; and 1 = strongly agree. Responses to the 15 items are averaged for an overall score from 1 to 7; the higher the score, the higher the level of organizational commitment.

Source: L. W. Porter and F. J. Smith, "Organizational Commitment Questionnaire," in J. D. Cook, S. J. Hepworth, T. D. Wall, and P. B. Warr, eds., _The Experience of Work: A Compendium and Review of 259 Measures and Their Use_ (New York: Academic Press, 1961), 85–86.

distressed, fearful, scornful, hostile, jittery, or nervous.[81] People who are high on extraversion are especially likely to experience positive moods; people who are high on negative affectivity are especially likely to experience negative moods. People's situations or circumstances also determine their moods; however, receiving a raise is likely to put most people in a good mood regardless of their personality traits. People who are high on negative affectivity are not always in a bad mood, and people who are low on extraversion still experience positive moods.[82]

Emotions are more intense feelings than moods, are often directly linked to whatever caused the emotion, and are more short-lived.[83] However, once whatever has triggered the

emotions Intense, relatively short-lived feelings.

emotion has been dealt with, the feelings may linger in the form of a less intense mood.[84] For example, a manager who gets very angry when a subordinate has engaged in an unethical behavior may find his anger decreasing in intensity once he has decided how to address the problem. Yet he continues to be in a bad mood the rest of the day, even though he is not directly thinking about the unfortunate incident.[85]

Research has found that moods and emotions affect the behavior of managers and all members of an organization. For example, research suggests that the subordinates of managers who experience positive moods at work may perform at somewhat higher levels and be less likely to resign and leave the organization than the subordinates of managers who do not tend to be in a positive mood at work.[86] Other research suggests that under certain conditions creativity might be enhanced by positive moods, whereas under other conditions negative moods might push people to work harder to come up with truly creative ideas.[87] Recognizing that both mood states have the potential to contribute to creativity in different ways, recent research suggests that employees may be especially likely to be creative to the extent that they experience both mood states (at different times) on the job and to the extent that the work environment is supportive of creativity.[88]

Other research suggests that moods and emotions may play an important role in ethical decision making. For example, researchers at Princeton University found that when people are trying to solve difficult personal moral dilemmas, the parts of their brains that are responsible for emotions and moods are especially active.[89]

More generally, emotions and moods give managers and all employees important information and signals about what is going on in the workplace.[90] Positive emotions and moods signal that things are going well and thus can lead to more expansive, and even playful, thinking. Negative emotions and moods signal that there are problems in need of attention and areas for improvement. So when people are in negative moods, they tend to be more detail-oriented and focused on the facts at hand.[91] Some studies suggest that critical thinking and devil's advocacy may be promoted by a negative mood, and sometimes especially accurate judgments may be made by managers in negative moods.[92]

As indicated in the following "Management Insight," emotions can sometimes be the impetus for important changes in an organization.

Management Insight

Emotions as Triggers for Changes in Organizations

In our personal lives, intense emotional experiences can often be triggers for changes for the better. For example, the fear that accompanies a near miss auto accident may prompt a driver to slow down and leave more time to get to destinations. Embarrassment experienced from being underprepared for a major presentation might prompt a student to be more prepared in the future. Anger over being treated poorly can sometimes help people get out of bad personal relationships.

Interestingly enough, some managers and organizations are using emotions to prompt needed changes. For example, the CEO of North American Tool, Curt Lansbery, was dismayed that employees weren't contributing as much as they could to their 401(k) retirement plans because the company had a matched contribution plan whereby it contributed a percentage of an employee's contribution.[93] North American Tool makes industrial cutting machinery and each year has an annual 401(k) enrollment meeting. Lansbery decided to bring a bag full of money to the next meeting that equaled the amount of money employees did not receive the prior year because they did not contribute the maximum to their 401(k) plans. He dumped the money on a table and told the employees that this really should be their money, not the company's.[94] The negative feelings that this invoked in employees—there's a bunch of

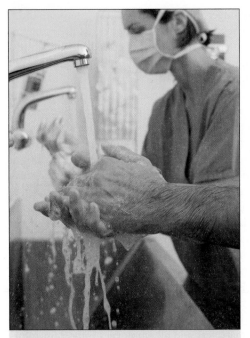

Need to change your culture? Try a tug at the heartstrings—or the gut. A screensaver image of how quickly and how thoroughly medical personnel hands got dirty was the impetus for a turnaround at a hospital with low hand-washing stats.

money that should be ours and is not—prompted many more to maximize their 401(k) contributions for the coming year and reap the benefits of the matched contribution plan.[95]

Dr. Leon Bender and other colleagues at Cedars-Sinai Medical Center were concerned that doctors and nurses weren't washing their hands as often as they should.[96] Repeated hand-washing by medical staff is a key contributor to keeping patients free of secondary bacterial infections; avoiding these kinds of preventable bacterial infections acquired in hospitals can save patients' lives. Despite their efforts to encourage more hand washing in the Center, their compliance rates with standards was around 80%. The Center was due for an inspection during which a minimum compliance rate of 90% was needed.[97]

After lunch one day, a group of around 20 doctors and staff were requested by the Center's epidemiologist to put their hands on an agar plate.[98] After the agar plates were cultured, they showed that the doctors' and administrators' hands were coated with bacteria. Photos of the cultured plates were circulated and one was made into a screen saver for the computers on the hospital's networks. The disgust experienced by everyone who saw the screen saver and the photos was a powerful impetus for change, and compliance with hand-washing protocols increased to close to 100%. It remained at a high level.[99] Hence, emotions can be useful triggers for needed changes in organizations.[100]

Managers and other members of an organization need to realize that how they feel affects how they treat others and how others respond to them, including their subordinates. For example, a subordinate may be more likely to approach a manager with a somewhat unusual but potentially useful idea if the subordinate thinks the manager is in a good mood. Likewise, when managers are in very bad moods, their subordinates might try to avoid them at all costs. Figure 3.7 is an example of a scale that can measure the extent to which a person experiences positive and negative moods at work.

Emotional Intelligence

emotional intelligence
The ability to understand and manage one's own moods and emotions and the moods and emotions of other people.

In understanding the effects of managers' and all employees' moods and emotions, it is important to take into account their levels of emotional intelligence. **Emotional intelligence** is the ability to understand and manage one's own moods and emotions and the moods and emotions of other people.[101] Managers with a high level of emotional intelligence are more likely to understand how they are feeling and why, and they are more able to effectively manage their feelings. When managers are experiencing stressful feelings and emotions such as fear or anxiety, emotional intelligence lets them understand why and manage these feelings so they do not get in the way of effective decision making.[102]

Emotional intelligence also can help managers perform their important roles such as their interpersonal roles (figurehead, leader, and liaison).[103] Understanding how your subordinates feel, why they feel that way, and how to manage these feelings is central to developing strong interpersonal bonds with them.[104] Moreover, emotional intelligence has the potential to contribute to effective leadership in multiple ways[105] and can help managers make lasting contributions to society. For example, Bernard (Bernie) Goldhirsh founded *Inc.* magazine in 1979, a time when entrepreneurs received more notoriety than respect, if they were paid attention at all.[106] Goldhirsh was an entrepreneur himself at the time, with his own publishing company. He recognized the vast contributions entrepreneurs could make to society, creating something out of nothing, and also realized firsthand what a tough task entrepreneurs faced.[107] His emotional intelligence helped him understand the challenges and frustrations entrepreneurs like himself faced and their need for support.

Figure 3.7

A Measure of Positive and Negative Mood at Work

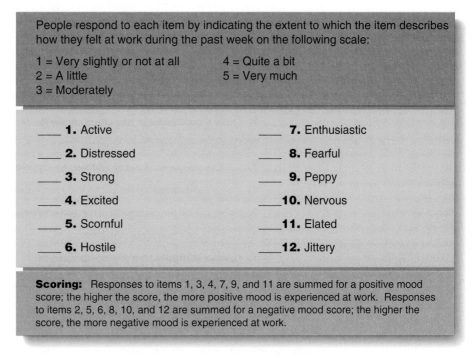

People respond to each item by indicating the extent to which the item describes how they felt at work during the past week on the following scale:

1 = Very slightly or not at all	4 = Quite a bit
2 = A little	5 = Very much
3 = Moderately	

____ **1.** Active   ____ **7.** Enthusiastic

____ **2.** Distressed   ____ **8.** Fearful

____ **3.** Strong   ____ **9.** Peppy

____ **4.** Excited   ____**10.** Nervous

____ **5.** Scornful   ____**11.** Elated

____ **6.** Hostile   ____**12.** Jittery

Scoring: Responses to items 1, 3, 4, 7, 9, and 11 are summed for a positive mood score; the higher the score, the more positive mood is experienced at work. Responses to items 2, 5, 6, 8, 10, and 12 are summed for a negative mood score; the higher the score, the more negative mood is experienced at work.

Source: A. P. Brief, M. J. Burke, J. M. George, B. Robinson, and J. Webster, "Should Negative Affectivity Remain an Unmeasured Variable in the Study of Job Stress?" *Journal of Applied Psychology* 72 (1988), 193–98; M. J. Burke, A. P. Brief, J. M. George, L. Roberson, and J. Webster, "Measuring Affect at Work: Confirmatory Analyses of Competing Mood Structures with Conceptual Linkage in Cortical Regulatory Systems," *Journal of Personality and Social Psychology* 57 (1989), 1091–102.

When Goldhirsh founded *Inc.,* entrepreneurs had few sources to which they could turn for advice, guidance, and solutions to management problems. *Inc.* was born to fill this gap and give entrepreneurs information and support by profiling successful and unsuccessful entrepreneurial ventures, highlighting management techniques that work, and providing firsthand accounts of how successful entrepreneurs developed and managed their businesses.[108]

Goldhirsh's emotional intelligence helped him recognize the many barriers entrepreneurs face and the emotional roller coaster of staking all one has on an idea that may or may not work. Goldhirsh believed that helping society understand the entrepreneurial process through *Inc.* magazine not only helped entrepreneurs but also enlightened bankers, lawmakers, and the public at large about the role these visionaries play, the challenges they face, and the support their ventures depend on.[109]

Emotional intelligence helps managers understand and relate well to other people.[110] It also helps managers maintain their enthusiasm and confidence and energize subordinates to help the organization attain its goals.[111] Recent theorizing and research suggest that emotional intelligence may be especially important in awakening employee creativity.[112] Managers themselves are increasingly recognizing the importance of emotional intelligence. An example of a scale that measures emotional intelligence is provided in Figure 3.8.

LO3-5 Define organizational culture and explain how managers both create and are influenced by organizational culture.

Organizational Culture

Personality is a way of understanding why all managers and employees, as individuals, characteristically think and behave in different ways. However, when people belong to the same organization, they tend to share certain beliefs and values that lead them to act in similar ways.[113]

Organizational culture comprises the shared set of beliefs, expectations, values, norms, and work routines that influence how members of an organization relate

Figure 3.8
A Measure of Emotional Intelligence

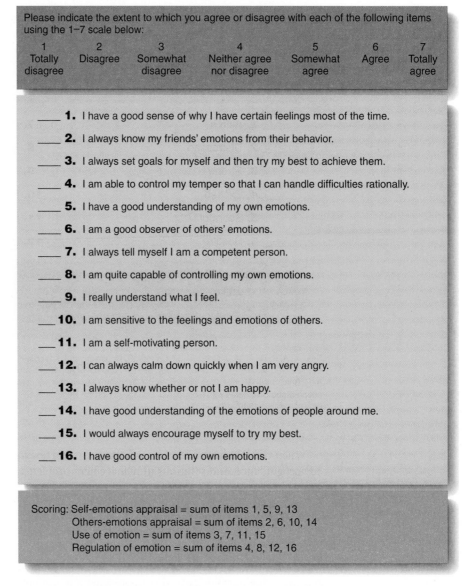

Please indicate the extent to which you agree or disagree with each of the following items using the 1–7 scale below:

1	2	3	4	5	6	7
Totally disagree	Disagree	Somewhat disagree	Neither agree nor disagree	Somewhat agree	Agree	Totally agree

_____ **1.** I have a good sense of why I have certain feelings most of the time.

_____ **2.** I always know my friends' emotions from their behavior.

_____ **3.** I always set goals for myself and then try my best to achieve them.

_____ **4.** I am able to control my temper so that I can handle difficulties rationally.

_____ **5.** I have a good understanding of my own emotions.

_____ **6.** I am a good observer of others' emotions.

_____ **7.** I always tell myself I am a competent person.

_____ **8.** I am quite capable of controlling my own emotions.

_____ **9.** I really understand what I feel.

_____ **10.** I am sensitive to the feelings and emotions of others.

_____ **11.** I am a self-motivating person.

_____ **12.** I can always calm down quickly when I am very angry.

_____ **13.** I always know whether or not I am happy.

_____ **14.** I have good understanding of the emotions of people around me.

_____ **15.** I would always encourage myself to try my best.

_____ **16.** I have good control of my own emotions.

Scoring: Self-emotions appraisal = sum of items 1, 5, 9, 13
Others-emotions appraisal = sum of items 2, 6, 10, 14
Use of emotion = sum of items 3, 7, 11, 15
Regulation of emotion = sum of items 4, 8, 12, 16

Source: K. Law, C. Wong, and L. Song, "The Construct and Criterion Validity of Emotional Intelligence and Its Potential Utility for Management Studies," _Journal of Applied Psychology_ 89, no. 3 (June 2004), 496; C. S. Wong and K. S. Law, "The Effects of Leader and Follower Emotional Intelligence on Performance and Attitude: An Exploratory Study," _Leadership Quarterly_ 13 (2002), 243–74.

organizational culture
The shared set of beliefs, expectations, values, norms, and work routines that influence how individuals, groups, and teams interact with one another and cooperate to achieve organizational goals.

to one another and work together to achieve organizational goals. In essence, organizational culture reflects the distinctive ways in which organizational members perform their jobs and relate to others inside and outside the organization. It may, for example, be how customers in a particular hotel chain are treated from the time they are greeted at check-in until they leave; or it may be the shared work routines that research teams use to guide new product development. When organizational members share an intense commitment to cultural values, beliefs, and routines and use them to achieve their goals, a _strong_ organizational culture exists.[114] When organizational members are not strongly committed to a shared system of values, beliefs, and routines, organizational culture is weak.

The stronger the culture of an organization, the more one can think about it as being the "personality" of an organization because it influences the way its members behave.[115] Organizations that possess strong cultures may differ on a wide variety of dimensions that determine how their members behave toward one another and perform their jobs. For example,

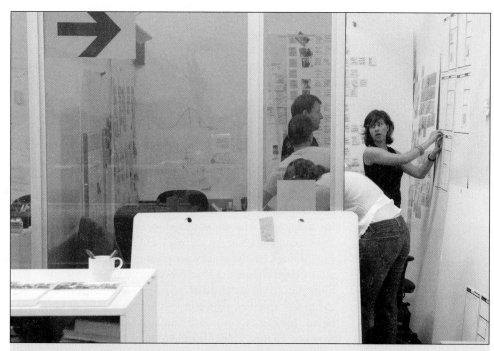

IDEO employees brainstorming—informal communication, casual attire, and flexibility are all hallmarks of this organization.

organizations differ in how members relate to each other (formally or informally), how important decisions are made (top-down or bottom-up), willingness to change (flexible or unyielding), innovation (creative or predictable), and playfulness (serious or serendipitous). In an innovative design firm like IDEO Product Development in Silicon Valley, employees are encouraged to adopt a playful attitude toward their work, look outside the organization to find inspiration, and adopt a flexible approach toward product design that uses multiple perspectives.[116] IDEO's culture is vastly different from that of companies such as Citibank and ExxonMobil, in which employees treat each other in a more formal or deferential way, employees are expected to adopt a serious approach to their work, and decision making is constrained by the hierarchy of authority.

Managers and Organizational Culture

While all members of an organization can contribute to developing and maintaining organizational culture, managers play a particularly important part in influencing organizational culture[117] because of their multiple and important roles (see Chapter 1). How managers create culture is most vividly evident in start-ups of new companies. Entrepreneurs who start their own companies are typically also the start-ups' top managers until the companies grow and become profitable. Often referred to as the firms' founders, these managers literally create their organizations' cultures.

The founders' personal characteristics play an important role in the creation of organizational culture. Benjamin Schneider, a well-known management researcher, developed a model that helps to explain the role that founders' personal characteristics play in determining organizational culture.[118] His model, called the **attraction–selection–attrition (ASA) framework**, posits that when founders hire employees for their new ventures, they tend to be attracted to and choose employees whose personalities are similar to their own.[119] These similar employees are more likely to stay with the organization. Although employees who are dissimilar in personality might be hired, they are more likely to leave the organization over time.[120] As a result of these attraction, selection, and attrition processes, people in the organization tend to have similar personalities, and the typical or dominant personality profile of organizational members determines and shapes organizational culture.[121]

attraction–selection–attrition (ASA) framework A model that explains how personality may influence organizational culture.

For example, when David Kelley became interested in engineering and product design challenges in the late 1970s, he realized that who he was as a person meant he would not be happy working in a typical corporate environment. Kelley is high on openness to experience, driven to go where his interests take him, and not content to follow others' directives. Kelley recognized that he needed to start his own business, and with the help of other Stanford-schooled engineers and design experts, IDEO was born.[122]

From the start, IDEO's culture has embodied Kelley's spirited, freewheeling approach to work and design—from colorful and informal workspaces to an emphasis on networking and communicating with as many people as possible to understand a design problem. No project or problem is too big or too small for IDEO; the company designed the Apple Lisa computer and mouse (the precursor of the Mac) and the Palm as well as the Crest Neat Squeeze toothpaste dispenser and the Racer's Edge water bottle.[123] Kelley hates rules, job titles, big corner offices, and all the other trappings of large traditional organizations that stifle creativity. Employees who are attracted to, selected by, and remain with IDEO value creativity and innovation and embrace one of IDEO's mottos: "Fail often to succeed sooner."[124]

Although ASA processes are most evident in small firms such as IDEO, they also can operate in large companies.[125] According to the ASA model, this is a naturally occurring phenomenon to the extent that managers and new hires are free to make the kinds of choices the model specifies. However, while people tend to get along well with others who are similar to themselves, too much similarity in an organization can impair organizational effectiveness. That is, similar people tend to view conditions and events in similar ways and thus can be resistant to change. Moreover, organizations benefit from a diversity of perspectives rather than similarity in perspectives (see Chapter 5). At IDEO Kelley recognized early on how important it is to take advantage of the diverse talents and perspectives that people with different personalities, backgrounds, experiences, and education can bring to a design team. Hence IDEO's design teams include not only engineers but others who might have a unique insight into a problem, such as anthropologists, communications experts, doctors, and users of a product. When new employees are hired at IDEO, they meet many employees who have different backgrounds and characteristics; the focus is not on hiring someone who will fit in but, rather, on hiring someone who has something to offer and can "wow" different kinds of people with his or her insights.[126]

In addition to personality, other personal characteristics of managers shape organizational culture; these include managers' values, attitudes, moods and emotions, and emotional intelligence.[127] For example, both terminal and instrumental values of managers play a role in determining organizational culture. Managers who highly value freedom and equality, for example, might be likely to stress the importance of autonomy and empowerment in their organizations, as well as fair treatment for all. As another example, managers who highly value being helpful and forgiving might not only tolerate mistakes but also emphasize the importance of organizational members' being kind and helpful to one another.

Managers who are satisfied with their jobs, are committed to their organizations, and experience positive moods and emotions might also encourage these attitudes and feelings in others. The result would be an organizational culture emphasizing positive attitudes and feelings. Research suggests that attitudes like job satisfaction and organizational commitment can be affected by the influence of others. Managers are in a particularly strong position to engage in social influence given their multiple roles. Moreover, research suggests that moods and emotions can be contagious and that spending time with people who are excited and enthusiastic can increase one's own levels of excitement and enthusiasm.

The Role of Values and Norms in Organizational Culture

Shared terminal and instrumental values play a particularly important role in organizational culture. *Terminal values* signify what an organization and its employees are trying to accomplish, and *instrumental values* guide how the organization and its members achieve organizational goals. In addition to values, shared norms also are a key aspect of organizational culture. Recall that norms are unwritten, informal rules or guidelines that prescribe appropriate behavior in particular situations. For example, norms at IDEO include not being critical of others' ideas, coming up with multiple ideas before settling on one, and developing prototypes of new products.[128]

Managers determine and shape organizational culture through the kinds of values and norms they promote in an organization. Some managers, like David Kelley of IDEO, cultivate values and norms that encourage risk taking, creative responses to problems and opportunities, experimentation, tolerance of failure in order to succeed, and autonomy.[129] Top managers at organizations such as Microsoft and Google encourage employees to adopt such values to support their commitment to innovation as a source of competitive advantage.

Other managers, however, might cultivate values and norms that tell employees they should be conservative and cautious in their dealings with others and should consult their superiors before making important decisions or any changes to the status quo. Accountability for actions and decisions is stressed, and detailed records are kept to ensure that policies and procedures are followed. In settings where caution is needed—nuclear power stations, oil refineries, chemical plants, financial institutions, insurance companies—a conservative, cautious approach to making decisions might be appropriate.[130] In a nuclear power plant, for example, the catastrophic consequences of a mistake make a high level of supervision vital. Similarly, in a bank or mutual fund company, the risk of losing investors' money makes a cautious approach to investing appropriate.

Managers of different kinds of organizations deliberately cultivate and develop the organizational values and norms that are best suited to their task and general environments, strategy, or technology. Organizational culture is maintained and transmitted to organizational members through the values of the founder, the process of socialization, ceremonies and rites, and stories and language (see Figure 3.9).

VALUES OF THE FOUNDER From the ASA model just discussed, it is clear that founders of an organization can have profound and long-lasting effects on organizational culture. Founders' values inspire the founders to start their own companies and, in turn, drive the nature of these new companies and their defining characteristics. Thus an organization's founder and his or her terminal and instrumental values have a substantial influence on the values, norms, and standards of behavior that develop over time within the organization.[131] Founders set the scene for the way cultural values and norms develop because their own values guide the building of the company, and they hire other managers and employees who they believe will share these values and help the organization to attain them. Moreover, new managers quickly learn from the founder what values and norms are appropriate in the organization and thus what is desired of them. Subordinates imitate the style of the founder and, in turn, transmit their values and norms to their subordinates. Gradually, over time, the founder's values and norms permeate the organization.[132]

A founder who requires a great display of respect from subordinates and insists on proprieties such as formal job titles and formal dress encourages subordinates to act in this way toward their subordinates. Often a founder's personal values affect an organization's

Figure 3.9

Factors That Maintain and Transmit Organizational Culture

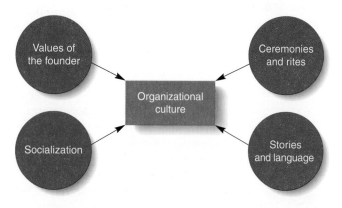

competitive advantage. For example, McDonald's founder Ray Kroc insisted from the beginning on high standards of customer service and cleanliness at McDonald's restaurants; these became core sources of McDonald's competitive advantage. Similarly, Bill Gates, the founder of Microsoft, pioneered certain cultural values in Microsoft. Employees are expected to be creative and to work hard, but they are encouraged to dress informally and to personalize their offices. Gates also established a host of company events such as cookouts, picnics, and sports events to emphasize to employees the importance of being both an individual and a team player.

SOCIALIZATION   Over time, organizational members learn from each other which values are important in an organization and the norms that specify appropriate and inappropriate behaviors. Eventually organizational members behave in accordance with the organization's values and norms—often without realizing they are doing so.

organizational socialization The process by which newcomers learn an organization's values and norms and acquire the work behaviors necessary to perform jobs effectively.

Organizational socialization is the process by which newcomers learn an organization's values and norms and acquire the work behaviors necessary to perform jobs effectively.[133] As a result of their socialization experiences, organizational members internalize an organization's values and norms and behave in accordance with them not only because they think they have to but because they think these values and norms describe the right and proper way to behave.[134]

At Texas A&M University, for example, all new students are encouraged to go to "Fish Camp" to learn how to be an "Aggie" (the traditional nickname of students at the university). They learn about the ceremonies that have developed over time to commemorate significant events or people in A&M's history. In addition, they learn how to behave at football games and in class and what it means to be an Aggie. As a result of this highly organized socialization program, by the time new students arrive on campus and start their first semester, they have been socialized into what a Texas A&M student is supposed to do, and they have relatively few problems adjusting to the college environment.

Most organizations have some kind of socialization program to help new employees learn the ropes—the values, norms, and culture of the organization. The military, for example, is well known for the rigorous socialization process it uses to turn raw recruits into trained soldiers. Organizations such as the Walt Disney Company also put new recruits through a rigorous training program to teach them to perform well in their jobs and play their parts in helping Disneyland visitors have fun in a wholesome theme park. New recruits at Disney are called "cast members" and attend Disney University to learn the Disney culture and their parts in it. Disney's culture emphasizes the values of safety, courtesy, entertainment, and efficiency, and these values are brought to life for newcomers at Disney University. Newcomers also learn about the attraction area they will be joining (such as Adventureland or Fantasyland) at Disney University and then receive on-the-job socialization in the area itself from experienced cast members.[135] Through organizational socialization, founders and managers of an organization transmit to employees the cultural values and norms that shape the behavior of organizational members. Thus the values and norms of founder Walt Disney live on today at Disneyland as newcomers are socialized into the Disney way.

How does Snow White stay so perfectly in character when meeting her littlest fans? Rigorous training through Disney University, a socialization process Disney requires of all its employees.

CEREMONIES AND RITES   Another way in which managers can create or influence organizational culture is by developing organizational ceremonies and rites—formal events that recognize incidents of importance to the organization as a whole and to specific employees.[136] The most common rites that organizations use to transmit cultural norms and values to their members are rites of passage, of integration, and of enhancement (see Table 3.1).[137]

Rites of passage determine how individuals enter, advance within, and leave the organization. The socialization programs developed by military organizations (such as the U.S. Army)

Table 3.1

Organizational Rites

Type of Rite	Example of Rite	Purpose of Rite
Rite of passage	Induction and basic training	Learn and internalize norms and values
Rite of integration	Office Christmas party	Build common norms and values
Rite of enhancement	Presentation of annual award	Motivate commitment to norms and values

or by large accountancy and law firms are rites of passage. Likewise, the ways in which an organization prepares people for promotion or retirement are rites of passage.

Rites of integration, such as shared announcements of organizational successes, office parties, and company cookouts, build and reinforce common bonds among organizational members. IDEO uses many rites of integration to make its employees feel connected to one another and special. In addition to having wild "end-of-year" celebratory bashes, groups of IDEO employees periodically take time off to go to a sporting event, movie, or meal, or sometimes on a long bike ride or for a sail. These kinds of shared activities not only reinforce IDEO's culture but also can be a source of inspiration on the job (for example, IDEO has been involved in making movies such as *The Abyss* and *Free Willy*). One 35-member design studio at IDEO led by Dennis Boyle has bimonthly lunch fests with no set agenda—anything goes. While enjoying great food, jokes, and camaraderie, studio members often end up sharing ideas for their latest great products, and the freely flowing conversation that results often leads to creative insights.[138]

A company's annual meeting also may be used as a ritual of integration, offering an opportunity to communicate organizational values to managers, other employees, and shareholders.[139] Walmart, for example, makes its annual stockholders' meeting an extravagant ceremony that celebrates the company's success. The company often flies thousands of its highest-performing employees to its annual meeting at its Bentonville, Arkansas, headquarters for a huge weekend entertainment festival complete with star musical performances. Walmart believes that rewarding its supporters with entertainment reinforces the company's high-performance values and culture. The proceedings are shown live over closed-circuit television in all Walmart stores so all employees can join in the rites celebrating the company's achievements.[140]

Rites of enhancement, such as awards dinners, newspaper releases, and employee promotions, let organizations publicly recognize and reward employees' contributions and thus strengthen their commitment to organizational values. By bonding members within the organization, rites of enhancement reinforce an organization's values and norms.

Stories and language also communicate organizational culture. Stories (whether fact or fiction) about organizational heroes and villains and their actions provide important clues about values and norms. Such stories can reveal the kinds of behaviors that are valued by the organization and the kinds of practices that are frowned on.[141] At the heart of McDonald's rich culture are hundreds of stories that organizational members tell about founder Ray Kroc. Most of these stories focus on how Kroc established the strict operating values and norms that are at the heart of McDonald's culture. Kroc was dedicated to achieving perfection in McDonald's quality, service, cleanliness, and value for money (QSC&V), and these four central values permeate McDonald's culture. For example, an often retold story describes what happened when Kroc and a group of managers from the Houston region were touring various restaurants. One of the restaurants was having a bad day operationally. Kroc was incensed about the long lines of customers, and he was furious when he realized that the products customers were receiving that day were not up to his high standards. To address the problem, he jumped up and stood on the front counter to get the attention of all customers and operating crew personnel. He introduced himself, apologized for the long wait and cold food, and told the customers they could have freshly cooked food or their money back—whichever they wanted. As a result, the customers left happy; and when Kroc checked on the restaurant later, he found that his message had gotten through to its managers and crew—performance had improved. Other stories describe Kroc scrubbing dirty toilets and picking up litter inside or outside a restaurant. These and similar stories are spread around the organization by McDonald's employees. They are the stories that have helped establish Kroc as McDonald's "hero."

Because spoken language is a principal medium of communication in organizations, the characteristic slang or jargon—that is, organization-specific words or phrases—that people use to frame and describe events provides important clues about norms and values. "McLanguage," for example, is prevalent at all levels of McDonald's. A McDonald's employee described as having "ketchup in his or her blood" is someone who is truly dedicated to the McDonald's way—someone who has been completely socialized to its culture. McDonald's has an extensive training program that teaches new employees "McDonald's speak," and new employees are welcomed into the family with a formal orientation that illustrates Kroc's dedication to QSC&V.

The concept of organizational language encompasses not only spoken language but how people dress, the offices they occupy, the cars they drive, and the degree of formality they use when they address one another. For example, casual dress reflects and reinforces Microsoft's entrepreneurial culture and values. Formal business attire supports the conservative culture found in many banks, which emphasize the importance of conforming to organizational norms such as respect for authority and staying within one's prescribed role. When employees speak and understand the language of their organization's culture, they know how to behave in the organization and what is expected of them.

At IDEO, language, dress, the physical work environment, and extreme informality all underscore a culture that is adventuresome, playful, risk taking, egalitarian, and innovative. For example, at IDEO, employees refer to taking the consumers' perspective when designing products as "being left-handed." Employees dress in T-shirts and jeans, the physical work environment continually evolves and changes depending on how employees wish to personalize their workspace, no one "owns" a fancy office with a window, and rules are nonexistent.[142]

Culture and Managerial Action

While founders and managers play a critical role in developing, maintaining, and communicating organizational culture, this same culture shapes and controls the behavior of all employees, including managers themselves. For example, culture influences how managers perform their four main functions: planning, organizing, leading, and controlling. As we consider these functions, we continue to distinguish between top managers who create organizational values and norms that encourage creative, innovative behavior and top managers who encourage a conservative, cautious approach by their subordinates. We noted earlier that both kinds of values and norms can be appropriate depending on the situation and type of organization.

PLANNING   Top managers in an organization with an innovative culture are likely to encourage lower-level managers to participate in the planning process and develop a flexible approach to planning. They are likely to be willing to listen to new ideas and to take risks involving the development of new products. In contrast, top managers in an organization with conservative values are likely to emphasize formal top-down planning. Suggestions from lower-level managers are likely to be subjected to a formal review process, which can significantly slow decision making. Although this deliberate approach may improve the quality of decision making in a nuclear power plant, it can have unintended consequences. In the past, at conservative IBM, the planning process became so formalized that managers spent most of their time assembling complex slide shows and overheads to defend their current positions rather than thinking about what they should do to keep IBM abreast of the changes taking place in the computer industry. When former CEO Lou Gerstner took over, he used every means at his disposal to abolish this culture, even building a brand-new campus-style headquarters to change managers' mind-sets. IBM's culture underwent further changes initiated by its next CEO, Samuel Palmisano, who is now chairman of the board.[143]

ORGANIZING   What kinds of organizing will managers in innovative and in conservative cultures encourage? Valuing creativity, managers in innovative cultures are likely to try to create an organic structure—one that is flat, with few levels in the hierarchy, and one in which authority is decentralized so employees are encouraged to work together to solve ongoing problems. A product team structure may be suitable for an organization with an innovative culture. In contrast, managers in a conservative culture are likely to create a well-defined hierarchy of authority and establish clear reporting relationships so employees know exactly whom to report to and how to react to any problems that arise.

LEADING   In an innovative culture, managers are likely to lead by example, encouraging employees to take risks and experiment. They are supportive regardless of whether employees succeed or fail. In contrast, managers in a conservative culture are likely to use management by objectives and to constantly monitor subordinates' progress toward goals, overseeing their every move. We examine leadership in detail in Chapter 14 when we consider the leadership styles that managers can adopt to influence and shape employee behavior.

CONTROLLING   The ways in which managers evaluate, and take actions to improve, performance differ depending on whether the organizational culture emphasizes formality and caution or innovation and change. Managers who want to encourage risk taking, creativity, and innovation recognize that there are multiple potential paths to success and that failure must be accepted for creativity to thrive. Thus they are less concerned about employees' performing their jobs in a specific, predetermined manner and in strict adherence to preset goals and more concerned about employees' being flexible and taking the initiative to come up with ideas for improving performance. Managers in innovative cultures are also more concerned about long-term performance than short-term targets because they recognize that real innovation entails much uncertainty that necessitates flexibility. In contrast, managers in cultures that emphasize caution and maintenance of the status quo often set specific, difficult goals for employees, frequently monitor progress toward these goals, and develop a clear set of rules that employees are expected to adhere to.

The values and norms of an organization's culture strongly affect the way managers perform their management functions. The extent to which managers buy into the values and norms of their organization shapes their view of the world and their actions and decisions in particular circumstances. In turn, the actions that managers take can have an impact on the performance of the organization. Thus organizational culture, managerial action, and organizational performance are all linked together.

While our earlier example of IDEO illustrates how organizational culture can give rise to managerial actions that ultimately benefit the organization, this is not always the case. The cultures of some organizations become dysfunctional, encouraging managerial actions that harm the organization and discouraging actions that might improve performance.[144] Corporate scandals at large companies like Enron, Tyco, and WorldCom show how damaging a dysfunctional culture can be to an organization and its members. For example, Enron's arrogant, "success at all costs" culture led to fraudulent behavior on the part of its top managers.[145] Unfortunately hundreds of Enron employees paid a heavy price for the unethical behavior of these top managers and the dysfunctional organizational culture. Not only did these employees lose their jobs, but many also lost their life savings in Enron stock and pension funds, which became worth just a fraction of their former value before the wrongdoing at Enron came to light. We discuss ethics and ethical cultures in depth in the next chapter.

Summary and Review

LO3-1

ENDURING CHARACTERISTICS: PERSONALITY TRAITS   Personality traits are enduring tendencies to feel, think, and act in certain ways. The Big Five general traits are extraversion, negative affectivity, agreeableness, conscientiousness, and openness to experience. Other personality traits that affect managerial behavior are locus of control, self-esteem, and the needs for achievement, affiliation, and power.

LO3-2, 3-3, 3-4   **VALUES, ATTITUDES, AND MOODS AND EMOTIONS**   A terminal value is a personal conviction about lifelong goals or objectives; an instrumental value is a personal conviction about modes of conduct. Terminal and instrumental values have an impact on what managers try to achieve in their organizations and the kinds of behaviors they engage in. An attitude is a collection of feelings and beliefs. Two attitudes important for understanding managerial behaviors include job satisfaction (the collection of feelings and beliefs that managers have about their jobs) and organizational commitment (the collection of feelings and beliefs that managers have about their organizations). A mood is a feeling or state of mind; emotions are intense feelings that are short-lived and directly linked to their causes. Managers' moods and emotions, or how they feel at work on a day-to-day basis, have the potential to impact not only their own behavior and effectiveness but also those of their subordinates. Emotional intelligence is the ability to understand and manage one's own and other people's moods and emotions.

LO3-5   **ORGANIZATIONAL CULTURE**   Organizational culture is the shared set of beliefs, expectations, values, norms, and work routines that influence how members of an organization relate to one another and work together to achieve organizational goals. Founders of new organizations and managers play an important role in creating and maintaining organizational culture. Organizational socialization is the process by which newcomers learn an organization's values and norms and acquire the work behaviors necessary to perform jobs effectively.

Management in Action

Topics for Discussion and Action

Discussion

1. Discuss why managers who have different types of personalities can be equally effective and successful. **[LO3-1]**

2. Can managers be too satisfied with their jobs? Can they be too committed to their organizations? Why or why not? **[LO3-2]**

3. Assume that you are a manager of a restaurant. Describe what it is like to work for you when you are in a negative mood. **[LO3-3]**

4. Why might managers be disadvantaged by low levels of emotional intelligence? **[LO3-4]**

Action

5. Interview a manager in a local organization. Ask the manager to describe situations in which he or she is especially likely to act in accordance with his or her values. Ask the manager to describe situations in which he or she is less likely to act in accordance with his or her values. **[LO3-2]**

6. Watch a popular television show, and as you watch it, try to determine the emotional intelligence levels of the characters the actors in the show portray. Rank the characters from highest to lowest in terms of emotional intelligence. As you watched the show, what factors influenced your assessments of emotional intelligence levels? **[LO3-4]**

7. Go to an upscale clothing store in your neighborhood, and go to a clothing store that is definitely not upscale. Observe the behavior of employees in each store as well as the store's environment. In what ways are the organizational cultures in each store similar? In what ways are they different? **[LO3-5]**

Building Management Skills

Diagnosing Culture [LO3-5]

Think about the culture of the last organization you worked for, your current university, or another organization or club to which you belong. Then answer the following questions:

1. What values are emphasized in this culture?

2. What norms do members of this organization follow?

3. Who seems to have played an important role in creating the culture?

4. In what ways is the organizational culture communicated to organizational members?

Managing Ethically [LO3-1, 3-2]

Some organizations rely on personality and interest inventories to screen potential employees. Other organizations attempt to screen employees by using paper-and-pencil honesty tests.

Questions

1. Either individually or in a group, think about the ethical implications of using personality and interest inventories to screen potential employees. How might this practice be unfair to potential applicants? How might organizational members who are in charge of hiring misuse it?

2. Because of measurement error and validity problems, some relatively trustworthy people may "fail" an honesty test given by an employer. What are the ethical implications of trustworthy people "failing" honesty tests, and what obligations do you think employers should have when relying on honesty tests for screening?

Small Group Breakout Exercise

Making Difficult Decisions in Hard Times [LO3-2, 3-3, 3-4, 3-5]

Form groups of three or four people, and appoint one member as the spokesperson who will communicate your findings to the whole class when called on by the instructor. Then discuss the following scenario:

You are on the top management team of a medium-size company that manufactures cardboard boxes, containers, and other cardboard packaging materials. Your company is facing increasing levels of competition for major corporate customer accounts, and profits have declined significantly. You have tried everything you can to cut costs and remain competitive, with the exception of laying off employees. Your company has had a no-layoff policy for the past 20 years, and you believe it is an important part of the organization's culture. However, you are experiencing mounting pressure to increase your firm's performance, and your no-layoff policy has been questioned by shareholders. Even though you haven't decided whether to lay off employees and thus break with a 20-year

tradition for your company, rumors are rampant in your organization that something is afoot, and employees are worried. You are meeting today to address this problem.

1. Develop a list of options and potential courses of action to address the heightened competition and decline in profitability that your company has been experiencing.

2. Choose your preferred course of action, and justify why you will take this route.

3. Describe how you will communicate your decision to employees.

4. If your preferred option involves a layoff, justify why. If it doesn't involve a layoff, explain why.

Exploring the World Wide Web [LO3-1, 3-2, 3-5]

Go to IDEO's website (www.ideo.com) and read about this company. Try to find indicators of IDEO's culture that are provided on the website. How does the design of the website itself, and the pictures and words it contains,

communicate the nature of IDEO's organizational culture? What kinds of people do you think would be attracted to IDEO? What kinds of people do you think would be likely to be dissatisfied with a job at IDEO?

Be the Manager [LO3-1, 3-2, 3-3, 3-4, 3-5]

You have recently been hired as the vice president for human resources in an advertising agency. One problem that has been brought to your attention is the fact that the creative departments at the agency have dysfunctionally high levels of conflict. You have spoken with members of each of these departments, and in each one it seems that a few members of the department are creating all the

problems. All these individuals are valued contributors who have many creative ad campaigns to their credit. The high levels of conflict are creating problems in the departments, and negative moods and emotions are much more prevalent than positive feelings. What are you going to do to both retain valued employees and alleviate the excessive conflict and negative feelings in these departments?

Fortune Case in the News [LO3-1, 3-2, 3-3, 3-4]

Who Built Build-a-Bear? Interview by Dinah Eng

Maxine Clark, the 63-year-old founder of Build-a-Bear, was always a shopper, even as a kid. So it made sense that she would wind up in retail. Clark eventually made it to the top—as president of Payless Shoe-Source. But the job wasn't enough—the spark was gone, she said—and she left in 1996. Clark then went on a search to find another idea that would rekindle her love for the business. The result: A simple shopping trip with a friend's daughter produced the idea for a single stuffed-animal factory in the St. Louis Galleria mall in 1997. Today Build-a-Bear Workshop operates 425 stores worldwide. (In 2011 it had revenue of $394.4 million but showed a small loss, largely because of a one-time charge.) Here's the chief executive bear's story:

One of my favorite things as a child was to go shopping with my mom, and looking was as good as buying. I always had a curiosity about how people shopped. In 1971, when I graduated from college, I wanted to do anything women weren't doing at the time. So I went to work for Hecht in Washington, D.C., as a retail executive trainee and kept getting promoted up the ladder of May Co., which was later bought by Federated Department Stores (now known as Macy's).

In 1976, I was promoted to the May corporate offices in St. Louis and worked for the CEO on business development, special projects, and acquisitions. In the 1980s, I moved to the discount side of the company, and in 1992, I became president of Payless ShoeSource. When I got to the top, my financial rewards were very high, but my psychic income bank account was nearly empty. I felt the retail world had lost its spark. I wanted to be more creative again, so in 1996, I left the company.

One day, I was shopping with Katie Burkhardt, the daughter of one of my good friends, and her brother Jack, who collected Ty Beanie Babies. When we couldn't find anything new, Katie picked up a Beanie Baby and said we could make one. She meant we could go home and make the small bears, but I heard something different. Her words gave me the idea to create a company that would allow people to create their own customized stuffed animals. I did some research and began putting together a plan.

I'd been a buyer all over the world, so I knew how things were made. I began talking to friends and their kids about this idea. Build-a-Bear Workshop would be like a theme park factory in a mall. Every parent said, Why would you want to make your own stuffed animal when you can buy it at Target? But the kids of my friends were so excited about doing it. There were no formal focus groups, but from the beginning, Build-a-Bear Workshop has had a Cub Advisory Board, which is a group of children who offer their opinions about our products and services. Kids have insights and offer inspiration by looking at the world differently.

In 1997, I withdrew $750,000 from my retirement account to get Build-a-Bear Workshop off the ground. That covered start-up costs and the building of the first prototype store. I also secured a bank line of credit for inventory and working capital, with my house as collateral. I knew I wanted to build a multimillion-dollar business with hundreds of units, and I realized I didn't have the ready cash to fund that growth. I knew I'd have to partner with outside investors.

While we were building our first store, coming soon signs prompted a *St. Louis Business Journal* story about our unique hands-on concept. The article caught the eye of Barney Ebsworth, who owned a private

investment firm, and his partner, Wayne Smith. They bought in for 20% for $4.5 million, so with that, I had enough to go for several years, and we hadn't even opened yet.

The first store opened in the St. Louis Galleria on a Sunday, and there were lines out the door. In the beginning, landlords didn't know the concept, so persuading people to rent us space was hard. In year two, we had malls begging us to come in. Other investors came in 1998 and 1999. We had to turn investors away after that because the business was so successful, we didn't need their money.

We started with just bears and clothes. We added shoes and accessories, then more animals. We licensed products and started carrying costumes from Disney and Major League Baseball teams. We hit a good nerve. At a time when everything was going high tech, high touch and hands-on was a good balance.

We started when the Internet was just getting popular, so we were able to track people in our loyalty program from day one, and continually do customer research. We're constantly creating new product, so there's no niche that needs to be filled. Everything is focused on the customers and giving them a good experience. We want to engage kids beyond selling them something in our store. Every year we look for 10 children around the country who are doing things to help their communities, and we name them our Huggable Heroes. We focus on good price, convenience, and location, and we hope that when you leave, you have a smile on your face. Successful retailers—whether it's Macy's or Apple—do these things.

We began in big cities, and when we got up to store 150, we started opening in smaller markets with good-size family communities and tourist destinations. In 2004 we opened our first overseas store in Japan, and are now in 19 countries. Almost 40% of our store base is outside of the United States, and we are putting the support and infrastructure in place to continue this expansion. We also see e-commerce as a growth opportunity—on our website and through mobile technology.

The recession affected the business substantially. We slowed our growth, cut costs, and mall traffic was down. We strategically closed some stores, opened stores in new locations, and updated existing locations. Now, mall traffic is coming back.

Maxine Clark

Chief executive, Build-a-Bear Workshop

My Advice

Take your employees seriously. Every six weeks we do Chief Chat at headquarters. Employees can ask any questions they want. We get good feedback and understand what matters to our associates. We also do remote conferences with people in the stores by Skype, and I go to the stores all the time.

Write the biggest business plan you can. You can always cut it back. The first purpose of the business plan is to convince yourself that it's an idea you really want to do. If you're not convinced, you'll never be able to convince anyone else.

Understand the value of partnerships. In the beginning, our vendors were willing to make a couple hundred pieces of everything. Normally they wouldn't do such a small amount. But then they benefited from our success. Always ask, What can we do together to get more than our money's worth?

Questions for Discussion

1. What personality traits do you think Maxine Clark is high on?

2. What terminal and instrumental values do you think might be especially important to her?

3. What moods and emotions do you think she is likely to experience?

4. Do you think she is high or low on emotional intelligence? Why do you think this?

CHAPTER 4

Ethics and Social Responsibility

Learning Objectives

After studying this chapter, you should be able to:

LO4-1 Explain the relationship between ethics and the law.

LO4-2 Differentiate between the claims of the different stakeholder groups that are affected by managers and their companies' actions.

LO4-3 Describe four rules that can help companies and their managers act in ethical ways.

LO4-4 Discuss why it is important for managers to behave ethically.

LO4-5 Identify the four main sources of managerial ethics.

LO4-6 Distinguish among the four main approaches toward social responsibility that a company can take.

A MANAGER'S CHALLENGE

Apple and Foxconn Protect Its Products and the Workers Who Make Them

Apple has rules that govern all its functional activities, but consider how it enforces the rules designed to protect the secrets of its innovative new products against the rules about protecting the rights of its employees overseas who make those products. Today, all Apple products are assembled by huge specialist outsourcing companies abroad, such as Foxconn, which operates several huge factories in mainland China that employ over 350,000 workers who assemble Apple's products. Foxconn is a subsidiary of Taiwan's giant outsourcer, Hon Hai Precision Industry, whose secretive multibillionaire CEO Terry Gou is willing to go to great lengths to protect Apple's secrecy and recommend its products.

Apple has long been known for its concern for secrecy; it strives to keep the details of its new products under development hidden until their launch. Steve Jobs's increasing concern to protect its secrets led Apple to sue a college student who published a website that contained details of its future products; it has also brought legal action against many bloggers who reveal details about its new products. Under Jobs's leadership, even in its own U.S. product development subunits, Apple was known for strict rules that prevented engineers from discussing the project they are working on with other engineers to prevent the flow of information across employees and subunits and so protect product secrecy; employees who break these rules could be fired. Apple also developed uncompromising rules that govern how its outsourcers should protect product secrecy.

To keep its business, outsourcers like Foxconn go to extreme lengths to follow Apple's rules and follow stringent security guidelines in their manufacturing plants to protect the details of its new products. For example,

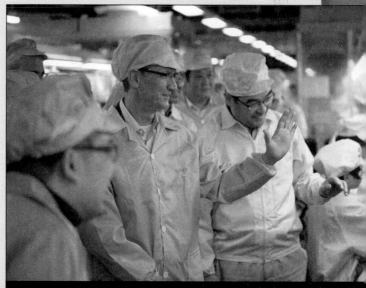

Apple faces scrutiny and criticism after press coverage leaked information on the harsh circumstances of many employees at its production factory in China. Here, CEO Tim Cook visits Foxconn Technology in order to make sure that not just secrecy but also employee welfare make it to the top of the company's priorities.

Apple dictates that the final product should not be assembled until as late as possible to meet its launch date; so while workers learn how to assemble each component, they have no idea what collection of components will go into the final product. Also, outsourcers control their factories to make it easier to enforce such rules. For example, Foxconn's massive plant in Longhua, China, employs more than 350,000 workers who are discouraged from even leaving the factory because it offers them a full array of low-cost services such as canteens, dormitories, and recreational facilities. If employees leave the plant, they are searched and metal detectors are used to ensure they do not take components with them. They are also scanned when they return and so are the truck drivers who bring components to the factory and anyone else who enters it. Apple's contracts include a confidentiality clause with stiff penalties in the event of a security breach, and Apple performs surprise factory inspections to ensure outsourcers follow its rules.

Apple insists its outsourcers create elaborate rules that build "secrecy" walls around their assembly plants. But these same walls make it much more difficult to enforce the extensive and well-publicized rules Apple has developed regarding the fair and ethical treatment of employees who work in these gigantic "sweatshops." For example, in 2010 after reports claimed Foxconn was not following Apple's rules regarding the way employees should be treated at work, Apple audited its factories and found many violations that were never publicly disclosed.[1] Apple was criticized for allowing its products to be made at plants with poor employment practices—despite the fact that it claims to enforce many rules governing how they should be treated. Apple's ethical position came under increased scrutiny in June 2010 when it was widely publicized that 11 workers at Foxconn's plant at Shenzhen had committed suicide and that Foxconn almost doubled workers' wages to try to improve morale. The bottom line is that Apple develops rules to protect the secrecy of its products and rules that protect the rights of the workers who labor in factories to make those products. But which rules does it spend the most time and effort to develop and enforce. And which rules does it regard as being the ones that are most important to consider in its ethical decision making?

After Tim Cook became CEO in 2011, he moved quickly to monitor whether or not Apple's 160 suppliers were following its ethical stance on the treatment of employees. Cook made personal visits to Foxconn plants in China, something that Jobs had never done; the number of supplier audits increased to 230, almost double that of 2010, and Cook announced that "Every year we expand our program, we go deeper in our supply chain, we make it harder to comply. All of this means that workers will be treated better and better with each passing year. It's not something we feel like we have done what we can do; much remains to be done."[2] In a 500-page report issued in 2012, Apple announced that new audits had revealed that child labor had been used in Foxconn's and other Chinese factories that made its iPads and other electronic devices. Apple admitted that sweatshop-like conditions had existed inside these factories, and at least 55 of the 102 factories had ignored its rule that employees should work no more than 60 hours per week. Apple said at least three of its assemblers had repeatedly falsified its records to conceal child labor practices and long employee hours, and it terminated all contracts with that factory.

In a landmark development for the way Western companies do business in China, Apple announced in 2012 it had agreed to work with partner Foxconn to substantially improve wages and working conditions at the factories that produce its wildly popular products. Foxconn will hire tens of thousands of new workers, clamp down on illegal overtime, improve safety protocols and upgrade worker housing and other amenities. Working conditions at many Chinese manufacturers that supply Western companies are considerably inferior to those at Foxconn, and the Apple-Foxconn agreement will raise costs for other manufacturers who contract with these companies, including Dell, HP, Amazon.com, Nokia, and Sony. The agreement will likely result in higher prices, but Cook has now demonstrated that the ethical treatment of workers is at the forefront of Apple's agenda, and all these other global companies will be forced to follow its lead so that working conditions around the globe are likely to steadily improve.

Overview

As the story of Apple and Foxconn suggests, an ethical dimension is always present in management decision making that involves the production and sale of products—whether they are food products, cars, computers, or clothing—because managers' decisions affect people's well-being. But globally, nations, companies, and managers differ enormously in their commitment to these people, or *stakeholders*—various groups of people who may benefit or be harmed by how managers make decisions that affect them. Managers of some companies make the need to behave ethically toward stakeholders their main priority. Managers of other companies pursue their own self-interest at the expense of their stakeholders and do harm to them—such as the harm done to the millions of people around the world who work in dangerous, unsanitary conditions or who work for a pittance.

In this chapter we examine the obligations and responsibilities of managers and the companies they work for toward the people and society that are affected by their actions. First we examine the nature of ethics and the sources of ethical problems. Next we discuss the major stakeholder groups that are affected by how companies operate. We also look at four rules or guidelines managers can use to decide whether a specific business decision is ethical or unethical. Finally we consider the sources of managerial ethics and the reasons why it is important for a company to behave in a socially responsible manner. By the end of this chapter you will understand the central role of ethics in shaping the practice of management and the life of a people, society, and nation.

The Nature of Ethics

Suppose you see a person being mugged. Will you act in some way to help, even though you risk being hurt? Will you walk away? Perhaps you might not intervene but will you call the police? Does how you act depend on whether the person being mugged is a fit male, an elderly person, or a street person? Does it depend on whether other people are around so you can tell yourself, "Oh well, someone else will help or call the police. I don't need to"?

Ethical Dilemmas

The situation just described is an example of an **ethical dilemma**, the quandary people find themselves in when they have to decide if they should act in a way that might help another person or group and is the right thing to do, even though doing so might go against their own self-interest.[3] A dilemma may also arise when a person has to choose between two different courses of action, knowing that whichever course he or she selects will harm one person or group even while it may benefit another. The ethical dilemma here is to decide which course of action is the lesser of two evils.

People often know they are confronting an ethical dilemma when their moral scruples come into play and cause them to hesitate, debate, and reflect upon the rightness or goodness of a course of action. Moral scruples are thoughts and feelings that tell a person what is right or wrong; they are a part of a person's ethics. Ethics are the inner guiding moral principles, values, and beliefs that people use to analyze or interpret a situation and then decide what is the right or appropriate way to behave. Ethics also indicate what is inappropriate behavior and how a person should behave to avoid harming another person.

The essential problem in dealing with ethical issues, and thus solving moral dilemmas, is that no absolute or indisputable rules or principles can be developed to decide whether an action is ethical or unethical. Put simply, different people or groups may dispute which actions are ethical or unethical depending on their personal self-interest and specific attitudes, beliefs, and values—concepts we discussed in Chapter 3. How, therefore, are we and companies and their managers and employees to decide what is ethical and so act appropriately toward other people and groups?

ethics The inner guiding moral principles, values, and beliefs that people use to analyze or interpret a situation and then decide what is the right or appropriate way to behave.

LO4-1 Explain the relationship between ethics and the law.

Ethics and the Law

The first answer to this question is that society as a whole, using the political and legal process, can lobby for and pass laws that specify what people can and cannot do. Many different kinds of laws govern business—for example, laws against fraud and deception and laws governing how companies can treat their employees and customers. Laws also specify what sanctions or punishments will follow if those laws are broken. Different groups in society lobby for which laws should be passed based on their own personal interests and beliefs about right and wrong. The group that can summon the most support can pass laws that align with its interests and beliefs. Once a law is passed, a decision about what the appropriate behavior is with regard to a person or situation is taken from the personally determined ethical realm to the societally determined legal realm. If you do not conform to the law, you can be prosecuted; and if you are found guilty of breaking the law, you can be punished. You have little say in the matter; your fate is in the hands of the court and its lawyers.

In studying the relationship between ethics and law, it is important to understand that *neither laws nor ethics are fixed principles* that do not change over time. Ethical beliefs change as time passes; and as they do so, laws change to reflect the changing ethical beliefs of a society. It was seen as ethical, and it was legal, for example, to acquire and possess slaves in ancient Rome and Greece and in the United States until the late 19th century. Ethical views regarding whether slavery was morally right or appropriate changed, however. Slavery was made illegal in the United States when those in power decided that slavery degraded the meaning of being human. Slavery makes a statement about the value or worth of human beings and about their right to life, liberty, and the pursuit of happiness. And if we deny these rights to other people, how can we claim to have any natural rights to these things?

Moreover, what is to stop any person or group that becomes powerful enough to take control of the political and legal process from enslaving us and denying us the right to be free and to own property? In denying freedom to others, one risks losing it oneself, just as stealing from others opens the door for them to steal from us in return. "Do unto others as you would have them do unto you" is a common ethical or moral rule that people apply in such situations to decide what is the right thing to do.

Changes in Ethics over Time

There are many types of behavior—such as murder, theft, slavery, rape, and driving while intoxicated—that most people currently believe are unacceptable and unethical and should therefore be illegal. However, the ethics of many other actions and behaviors are open to dispute. Some people might believe a particular behavior—for example, smoking tobacco or possessing guns—is unethical and so should be made illegal. Others might argue that it is up to the individual or group to decide if such behaviors are ethical and thus whether a particular behavior should remain legal.

As ethical beliefs change over time, some people may begin to question whether existing laws that make specific behaviors illegal are still appropriate. They might argue that although a specific behavior is deemed illegal, this does not make it unethical and thus the law should be changed. In the United States, for example, it is illegal to possess or use marijuana (cannabis). To justify this law, it is commonly argued that smoking marijuana leads people to try more dangerous drugs. Once the habit of taking drugs has been acquired, people can get hooked on them. More powerful drugs such as murderous heroin and other narcotics are fearfully addictive, and most people cannot stop using them without help. Thus the use of marijuana, because it might lead to further harm, is an unethical practice.

It has been documented medically, however, that marijuana use can help people with certain illnesses. For example, for cancer sufferers who are undergoing chemotherapy and for those with AIDS who are on potent medications, marijuana offers relief from many treatment side effects, such as nausea and lack of appetite. Yet in the United States it is illegal in many states for doctors to prescribe marijuana for these patients, so their suffering continues. Since 1996, however, 15 states have made it legal to prescribe marijuana for medical purposes; nevertheless, the federal government has sought to stop such state legislation. The U.S. Supreme Court ruled in 2005 that only Congress or the states could decide whether medical marijuana use should be made legal, and people in many states are currently lobbying for a relaxation of state laws against its use for medical purposes.[4] In Canada there has been a widespread movement to decriminalize marijuana. While not making the drug legal, decriminalization removes the threat of prosecution even for uses that are not medically related and allows the drug to be taxed. In 2012, for example, initiatives are underway in several states to decriminalize the possession of small amounts of marijuana for personal use as well as to make it more widely available to people legally for medical purposes. A major ethical debate is currently raging over this issue in many states and countries.

The important point to note is that while ethical beliefs lead to the development of laws and regulations to prevent certain behaviors or encourage others, laws themselves change or even disappear as ethical beliefs change. In Britain in 1830 a person could be executed for over 350 different crimes, including sheep stealing. Today the death penalty is no longer legal in Britain. Thus both ethical and legal rules are *relative:* No absolute or unvarying standards exist to determine how we should behave, and people are caught up in moral dilemmas all the time. Because of this we have to make ethical choices.

Coldbath Fields Prison, London, circa 1810. The British criminal justice system around this time was severe: There were over 350 different crimes for which a person could be executed, including sheep stealing. As ethical beliefs change over time, so do laws.

The previous discussion highlights an important issue in understanding the relationship between ethics, law, and business. Throughout the 2010s many scandals plagued major companies such as Guidant, Siemens, Merck, Pfizer, and others. Managers in some of these companies clearly broke the law and used illegal means to defraud investors, market their products to customers, or raise the prices of their products to customers.

In other cases managers took advantage of loopholes in the law to divert hundreds of millions of dollars of company capital into their own personal fortunes. At WorldCom, for example, former CEO Bernie Ebbers used his position to place six personal friends on the 13-member board of directors. Although this is not illegal, obviously these people would vote in his favor at board meetings. As a result of their support, Ebbers received huge stock options and a personal loan of over $150 million from WorldCom. In return, his supporters were well rewarded for being directors; for example, Ebbers allowed them to use WorldCom's corporate jets for a minimal cost, saving them hundreds of thousands of dollars a year.[5] In 2012 a scandal erupted at Chesapeake Energy after it was revealed its CEO Aubrey McClendon had received over $1 billion in loans from the company to fund his personal financial ventures.

In the light of these events some people said, "Well, what these people did was not illegal," implying that because such behavior was not illegal it was also not unethical. However, not being illegal does *not* make behavior ethical; such behavior is clearly unethical.[6] In many cases laws are passed *later* to close loopholes and prevent unethical people, such as Ebbers and McClendon, from taking advantage of them to pursue their own self-interest at the expense of others. Like ordinary people, managers must decide what is appropriate and inappropriate as they use a company's resources to produce goods and services for customers.[7]

Stakeholders and Ethics

Just as people have to work out the right and wrong ways to act, so do companies. When the law does not specify how companies should behave, their managers must decide the right or ethical way to behave toward the people and groups affected by their actions. Who are the people or groups that are affected by a company's business decisions? If a company behaves in an ethical way, how does this benefit people and society? Conversely, how are people harmed by a company's unethical actions?

The people and groups affected by how a company and its managers behave are called its stakeholders. **Stakeholders** supply a company with its productive resources; as a result, they have a claim on and a stake in the company.[8] Because stakeholders can directly benefit or be harmed by its actions, the ethics of a company and its managers are important to them. Who are a company's major stakeholders? What do they contribute to a company, and what do they claim in return? Here we examine the claims of these stakeholders—stockholders; managers; employees; suppliers and distributors; customers; and community, society, and nation-state (Figure 4.1).

stakeholders The people and groups that supply a company with its productive resources and so have a claim on and a stake in the company.

LO4-2 Differentiate between the claims of the different stakeholder groups that are affected by managers and their companies' actions.

Stockholders

Stockholders have a claim on a company because when they buy its stock or shares they become its owners. When the founder of a company decides to publicly incorporate the business to raise capital, shares of the stock of that company are issued. This stock grants its buyers ownership of a certain percentage of the company and the right to receive any future stock dividends. For example, in 2005 Microsoft decided to pay the owners of its 5 billion shares a special dividend payout of $32 billion. Bill Gates received $3.3 billion in dividends based on his stockholding, and he donated this money to the Bill and Melinda Gates Foundation, to which he has reportedly donated over $30 billion to date, with the promise of much more to come; and Warren Buffet committed to donate at least $30 billion to the Gates Foundation over the next decade. The two richest people in the world have decided to give away a large part of their wealth to serve global ethical causes—in particular to address global health concerns such as malnutrition, malaria, tuberculosis, and AIDS.

Stockholders are interested in how a company operates because they want to maximize the return on their investment. Thus they watch the company and its managers closely to ensure

Figure 4.1

Types of Company Stakeholders

that management is working diligently to increase the company's profitability.[9] Stockholders also want to ensure that managers are behaving ethically and not risking investors' capital by engaging in actions that could hurt the company's reputation. Managers of companies such as Chesapeake Energy, Goldman Sachs, and WorldCom pursued their own self-interest at the expense of their stakeholders. As a result of these managers' unethical actions, in 2006 World-Com's ex-CEO Bernie Ebbers was sentenced to a long jail term, in 2012 two Goldman Sachs directors accused of insider trading also received jail sentences, and Aubrey McClendon was forced to resign as CEO and is currently under investigation by the Securities and Exchange Commission.

Managers

Managers are a vital stakeholder group because they are responsible for using a company's financial, capital, and human resources to increase its performance and thus its stock price.[10] Managers have a claim on an organization because they bring to it their skills, expertise, and experience. They have the right to expect a good return or reward by investing their human capital to improve a company's performance. Such rewards include good salaries and benefits, the prospect of promotion and a career, and stock options and bonuses tied to company performance.

Managers are the stakeholder group that bears the responsibility to decide which goals an organization should pursue to most benefit stakeholders and how to make the most efficient use of resources to achieve those goals. In making such decisions, managers are frequently in the position of having to juggle the interests of different stakeholders, including themselves.[11] These sometimes difficult decisions challenge managers to uphold ethical values because some decisions that benefit certain stakeholder groups (managers and stockholders) harm other groups (individual workers and local communities). For example, in economic downturns or when a company experiences performance shortfalls, layoffs may help cut costs (thus benefiting shareholders) at the expense of the employees laid off. Many U.S. managers have recently faced this difficult decision. Until the 2009 financial crisis sent unemployment soaring over 10%, on average about 1.6 million U.S. employees out of a total labor force of 140 million were affected by mass layoffs each year; and over 3 million jobs from the United States, Europe, and Japan have been outsourced to Asia since 2005. Layoff decisions are always difficult: They not only take a heavy toll on workers, their families, and local communities but also mean the loss of the contributions of valued employees to an organization. In 2010, after GM pulled out, Toyota announced it would close down its NUMMI plant in Fremont, California; the resulting loss of jobs would raise total unemployment to 25% in this community. Whenever decisions such as these are made—benefiting some groups at the expense of others—ethics come into play.

As we discussed in Chapter 1, managers must be motivated and given incentives to work hard in the interests of stockholders. Their behavior must also be scrutinized to ensure they do not behave illegally or unethically, pursuing goals that threaten stockholders and the company's interests.[12] Unfortunately we have seen in the 2010s how easy it is for top managers to find ways to ruthlessly pursue their self-interest at the expense of stockholders and employees because laws and regulations are not strong enough to force them to behave ethically.

In a nutshell, the problem has been that in many companies corrupt managers focus not on building the company's

Rajat Kumar Gupta, former Goldman Sachs board member, leaves a Manhattan court after surrendering to federal authorities on October 26, 2011 in New York City. Gupta was charged with conspiracy and securities fraud, stemming from a massive hedge fund insider trading case.

capital and stockholders' wealth but on maximizing their own personal capital and wealth. In an effort to prevent future scandals, the Securities and Exchange Commission (SEC), the government's top business watchdog, has begun to rework the rules governing a company's relationship with its auditor, as well as regulations concerning stock options, and to increase the power of outside directors to scrutinize a CEO. The SEC's goal is to outlaw many actions that were previously classified as merely unethical. For example, companies are now forced to reveal to stockholders the value of the stock options they give their top executives and directors and when they give them these options; this shows how much such payments reduce company profits. Managers and directors can now be prosecuted if they disguise or try to hide these payments. In the 2010s the SEC announced many new rules requiring that companies disclose myriad details of executive compensation packages to investors; already the boards of directors of many companies have stopped giving CEOs perks such as free personal jet travel, membership in exclusive country clubs, and luxury accommodations on "business trips." Also Congress has been considering a major new set of financial regulations that would prevent the many unethical and illegal actions of managers of banks and other financial institutions that led to the 2009 financial crisis; one of these regulations is the "Volcker Rule," which prohibits any "banking entity" from proprietary stock trading and from owning or sponsoring relationships with hedge funds and other private funds.

Indeed, many experts argue that the rewards given to top managers, particularly the CEO and COO, grew out of control in the 2000s. Top managers are today's "aristocrats," and through their ability to influence the board of directors and raise their own pay, they have amassed personal fortunes worth hundreds of millions of dollars. For example, according to a study by the Federal Reserve, U.S. CEOs now get paid about 600 times what the average worker earns, compared to about 40 times in 1980—a staggering increase. In 2011, the average CEO was paid $6.9 million, for example. We noted in Chapter 1 that besides their salaries, top managers often receive tens of millions in stock bonuses and options—even when their companies perform poorly.

Is it ethical for top managers to receive such vast amounts of money from their companies? Do they really earn it? Remember, this money could have gone to shareholders in the form of dividends. It could also have reduced the huge salary gap between those at the top and those at the bottom of the hierarchy. Many people argue that the growing disparity between the rewards given to CEOs and to other employees is unethical and should be regulated. CEO pay has skyrocketed because CEOs are the people who set and control one another's salaries and bonuses; they can do this because they sit on the boards of other companies as outside directors. Others argue that because top managers play an important role in building a company's capital and wealth, they deserve a significant share of its profits. Some recent research has suggested that the companies whose CEO compensation includes a large percentage of stock options tend to experience big share losses more often than big gains, and that on average, company performance improves as stock option use declines.[13] The debate over how much money CEOs and other top managers should be paid is still raging, particularly because the financial crisis beginning in 2009 showed how much money the CEOs of troubled financial companies earned even as their companies' performance and stock prices collapsed. For example, Countrywide Mortgage, which pioneered the subprime business, suffered losses of over $1.7 billion in 2007, and its stock fell 80%; yet its CEO Angelo Mozilo still received $20 million in stock awards and sold stock options worth $121 million before the company's price collapsed.

Ethics and Nonprofit Organizations

The issue of what is fair compensation for top managers is not limited to for-profit companies; it is one of many issues facing nonprofits. The many ethics scandals that have plagued companies in the 2010s might suggest that the issue of ethics is important only for profit-seeking companies, but this would be untrue. There are almost 2 million private nonprofit charitable and philanthropic organizations in the United States, and charges that their managers have acted in unethical and even illegal ways have grown in the 2010s. For example, many states and the federal government are investigating the huge salaries that the top executives of charitable institutions earn.

One impetus for this was the revelation that the NYSE, which is classified as a charitable organization, paid its disgraced top executive Richard A. Grasso over $187 million in pension benefits. It turns out that over 200 nonprofits pay their top executives more than $1 million a year in salary, and the boards of trustees or directors of many of these organizations also enjoy lavish perks and compensation for attendance at board meetings. And unlike for-profit companies, which are required by law to provide detailed reports of their operations to their shareholders, nonprofits do not have shareholders, so the laws governing disclosure are far weaker. As a result, the board and its top managers have considerable latitude to decide how they will spend a nonprofit's resources, and little oversight exists.

To remedy this situation, many states and the federal government are considering new laws that would subject nonprofits to strict Sarbanes-Oxley-type regulations that force the disclosure of issues related to managerial compensation and financial integrity. There are also efforts in progress to strengthen the legal power of the IRS to oversee nonprofits' expenditures so that it has more scope to examine how these organizations spend their resources on managerial and director compensation and perks.

Experts hope that the introduction of new rules and regulations to monitor and oversee how nonprofits spend their funds will result in much more value being created from the funds given by donors. After all, every cent that is spent administering a nonprofit is a cent not being used to help the people or cause for which the money was intended. Major ethical issues are involved because some badly run charities spend 70 cents of every dollar on administration costs. And charges have been leveled against charities such as the Red Cross for mishandling the hundreds of millions of dollars they received in donations after Hurricane Katrina struck. Major changes have been made in the Red Cross to address these issues. Clearly the directors and managers of all organizations need to carefully consider the ethical issues involved in their decision making.

Employees

A company's employees are the hundreds of thousands of people who work in its various departments and functions, such as research, sales, and manufacturing. Employees expect to receive rewards consistent with their performance. One principal way that a company can act ethically toward employees and meet their expectations is by creating an occupational structure that fairly and equitably rewards employees for their contributions. Companies, for example, need to develop recruitment, training, performance appraisal, and reward systems that do not discriminate against employees and that employees believe are fair.

Suppliers and Distributors

No company operates alone. Every company is in a network of relationships with other companies that supply it with the inputs (such as raw materials, components, contract labor, and clients) that it needs to operate. It also depends on intermediaries such as wholesalers and retailers to distribute its products to the final customers. Suppliers expect to be paid fairly and promptly for their inputs; distributors expect to receive quality products at agreed-upon prices. Once again, many ethical issues arise in how companies contract and interact with their suppliers and distributors. Important issues concerning product quality and safety specifications are governed by the contracts a company signs with its suppliers and distributors, for example; however, many problems can arise, as the following "Ethics in Action" suggests.

Ethics
in Action

Unethical Managers Imperil the Supply of Peanut Butter

Peanut Corporation of America's (PCA) president, Stewart Parnell, was fond of telling his friends and clients in his hometown of Lynchburg, Virginia, just how good things were in his commercial peanut butter processing business, which operated three plants in Virginia, Georgia, and Texas. The company produced industrial-sized containers of peanut butter that were included as an ingredient in more than 3,900 products: cakes, candies, cookies, peanut crackers, ice cream, snack mixes, and pet food made by over 200 different companies, including Kellogg's and Nestlé. Also, the peanut butter was shipped to school systems and food outlets around the United States, where it was used to make millions of peanut butter and jelly sandwiches.

Parnell had a reputation as an upstanding businessman and a generous donor to many worthy causes, so it came as a shock to his friends and customers when a major nationwide outbreak of salmonella poisoning was traced by the Food and Drug Administration (FDA) to the peanut butter produced at his plant in Blakely, Georgia. PCA's contaminated peanut butter had caused over 600 illnesses and nine deaths across the United States. The 200 food makers who used or sold Parnell's products were forced to recall more than 1,900 different peanut butter products. This was one of the nation's largest food recalls even though PCA accounted for only 2% of the nation's supply of peanut butter. In the immediate aftermath of the nationwide outbreak, peanut butter sales plummeted 24% across the board, and total industry losses amounted to over $1 billion. How could this tragedy and disaster have occurred?[14]

Stewart Parnell, the erstwhile owner of PCA, was called before Congress to answer for poor safety standards at PCA plants. A full year later, more problems having come to light, PCA's doors are closed for good.

Apparently the major cause of the disaster was the unethical and illegal actions of owner and manager Parnell. The FDA investigation that took place at the PCA Georgia plant in 2009 revealed serious problems with food safety at that plant and inadequate cleaning and sanitary procedures. The investigation also revealed internal company documents that showed at least 12 instances in which the company's own tests of its products in 2007 and 2008 found they were contaminated by salmonella. But PCA managers had taken no steps to clean up operations or protect food safety; in fact Parnell's poor attention to food safety was traced back to 1990, when inspectors found toxic mold in products produced in PCA's Virginia plant.[15]

After interviewing employees, FDA investigators found that this long-term inattention to food safety had arisen inside PCA's processing plants because Parnell was worried about maximizing his profits, especially after the prices of peanut products had fallen. To reduce operating costs, Parnell ordered a plant manager to ship products that had already been identified as contaminated and had pleaded with health inspectors to let him "turn the raw peanuts on our floor into money." Somehow the Georgia plant received information about the dates on which the plant would be inspected—so on those days the plant was scrubbed clean.[16]

After the problems with the Georgia plant were discovered, it was shut down and the other PCA plants were inspected closely and also closed down; for example, PCA's Texas plant was closed after salmonella was discovered along with "dead rodents, rodent excrement, and bird feathers."

After hundreds of lawsuits were filed against the company because of the deaths and illnesses caused by its contaminated products, PCA was forced to seek protection under the U.S. bankruptcy code. The company is now defunct; its unethical and illegal management practices put it out of business, and the bankruptcy court in charge of PCA agreed to a $12 million settlement—the money coming from PCA's insurance policies because the Parnell family lost nearly everything it owned. After being criticized for the length of time it took the FDA to finally close down PCA's operations, FDA officials responded that the agency doesn't have the personnel or funding to regulate the millions of shipments made within the food industry every week. In large part, the FDA and the U.S. public must rely on the basic integrity, ethics, and honesty of food industry managers to make food that is safe to eat.

It is instructive to see how two major firms, Nestlé and Kellogg's, manage their relationships with suppliers to ensure that they act in an ethical way and make safe products. In fact, before the problems at PCA were made public in 2008, Nestlé was in the process of deciding whether to continue to purchase from PCA. Nestlé has a policy of using its own inspectors to investigate potential suppliers' operating facilities. When they found rodent feces and live beetles on two separate occasions while touring PCA's plants, the company decided to find a new peanut supplier—which saved it millions of dollars because it did not suffer from product recalls. On the other hand, Kellogg's does not use its own inspectors but relies on third parties, such as FDA inspectors, to investigate suppliers. As a result, Kellogg's continued to buy PCA's peanuts and lost more than $70 million because it had to recall its peanut products.

Many other issues depend on business ethics. For example, numerous products sold in U.S. stores have been outsourced to countries that do not have U.S.-style regulations and laws to protect the workers who make these products. All companies must take an ethical position on the way they obtain and make the products they sell. Commonly this stance is published on a company's website. Table 4.1 presents part of the Gap's statement about its approach to global ethics (www.gapinc.com).

Table 4.1
Some Principles from the Gap's Code of Vendor Conduct

As a condition of doing business with Gap Inc., each and every factory must comply with this Code of Vendor Conduct. Gap Inc. will continue to develop monitoring systems to assess and ensure compliance. If Gap Inc. determines that any factory has violated this Code, Gap Inc. may either terminate its business relationship or require the factory to implement a corrective action plan. If corrective action is advised but not taken, Gap Inc. will suspend placement of future orders and may terminate current production.

I. General Principles

Factories that produce goods for Gap Inc. shall operate in full compliance with the laws of their respective countries and with all other applicable laws, rules, and regulations.

II. Environment

Factories must comply with all applicable environmental laws and regulations. Where such requirements are less stringent than Gap Inc.'s own, factories are encouraged to meet the standards outlined in Gap Inc.'s statement of environmental principles.

III. Discrimination

Factories shall employ workers on the basis of their ability to do the job, without regard to race, color, gender, nationality, religion, age, maternity, or marital status.

IV. Forced Labor

Factories shall not use any prison, indentured, or forced labor.

V. Child Labor

Factories shall employ only workers who meet the applicable minimum legal age requirement or are at least 14 years of age, whichever is greater. Factories must also comply with all other applicable child labor laws. Factories are encouraged to develop lawful workplace apprenticeship programs for the educational benefit of their workers, provided that all participants meet both Gap Inc.'s minimum age standard of 14 and the minimum legal age requirement.

VI. Wages & Hours

Factories shall set working hours, wages, and overtime pay in compliance with all applicable laws. Workers shall be paid at least the minimum legal wage or a wage that meets local industry standards, whichever is greater. While it is understood that overtime is often required in garment production, factories shall carry out operations in ways that limit overtime to a level that ensures humane and productive working conditions.

Customers

Customers are often regarded as the most critical stakeholder group because if a company cannot attract them to buy its products, it cannot stay in business. Thus managers and employees must work to increase efficiency and effectiveness in order to create loyal customers and attract new ones. They do so by selling customers quality products at a fair price and providing good after-sales service. They can also strive to improve their products over time and provide guarantees to customers about the integrity of their products like Whole Foods Market, profiled in the following "Ethics in Action" box.

Ethics in Action

Whole Foods Market Practices What It Preaches

The Whole Foods Market supermarket chain was founded by two hippies in Austin, Texas, in 1978 as a natural counterculture food store. Today it is the world's leading retailer of natural and organic foods, with over 300 stores in North America and the United Kingdom.[17] Whole Foods specializes in selling chemical- and drug-free meat, poultry, and produce; its products are the "purest" possible, meaning it selects the ones least adulterated by artificial additives, sweeteners, colorings, and preservatives.[18] Despite the high prices it charges for its pure produce, sales per store are growing, and its revenues had grown to over $10 billion by 2012.[19] Why has Whole Foods been so successful? Founder and CEO John Mackey says it is because of the principles he established to manage his company since its beginning—principles founded on the need to behave in an ethical and socially responsible way toward everybody affected by its business. How Whole Foods views its responsibilities to stakeholders and its approach to ethical business are depicted in Figure 4.2.

Mackey says he started his business for three reasons—to have fun, to make money, and to contribute to the well-being of other people.[20] The company's mission is based on its members' collective responsibility to the well-being of the people and groups it affects, its *stakeholders;* in order of priority, at Whole Foods these are customers, team members, investors, suppliers, the community, and the natural environment. Mackey measures his company's success by how well it satisfies the needs of these stakeholders. His ethical stance toward customers is that they are guaranteed that Whole Foods products are 100% organic, hormone-free, or as represented. To help achieve this promise, Whole Foods insists that its suppliers also behave in an ethical way so it knows, for example, that the beef it sells comes from cows pastured on grass, not corn-fed in feed lots, and the chicken it sells is from free-range hens and not from hens that have been confined in tiny cages that prevent movement.

Mackey's management approach toward "team members," as Whole Foods employees are called, is also based on a well-defined ethical position. He says, "We put great emphasis at Whole Foods on the 'Whole People' part of the company mission. We believe in helping support our team members to grow as individuals—to become 'Whole People.' We allow tremendous individual initiative at Whole Foods, and that's why our

Where do your grocery dollars go? Whole Foods Market's goal is to make shopping fun and socially responsible. Customers' money supports an organization that monitors its suppliers, rewards its employees, and seeks to reduce its impact on the environment.

company is so innovative and creative."[21] Mackey claims that each supermarket in the chain is unique because in each one team members are constantly experimenting with new and better ways to serve customers and improve their well-being. As team members learn, they become "self-actualized" or self-fulfilled, and this increase in their well-being translates into a desire to increase the well-being of other stakeholders.

Finally, Mackey's strong views on ethics and social responsibility also serve shareholders. Mackey does not believe the object of being in business is to primarily maximize profits for shareholders; he puts customers first. He believes, however, that companies that behave ethically and strive to satisfy the needs of customers and employees simultaneously satisfy the needs of investors because high profits are the result of loyal customers and committed employees. Indeed, since Whole Foods issued shares to the public in 1992, the value of those shares has increased 25 times in value. Clearly, taking a strong position on ethics and social responsibility has worked so far at Whole Foods.

Many laws protect customers from companies that attempt to provide dangerous or shoddy products. Laws allow customers to sue a company whose product causes them injury or harm, such as a defective tire or vehicle. Other laws force companies to clearly disclose the interest rates they charge on purchases—an important hidden cost that customers frequently do not factor into their purchase decisions. Every year thousands of companies are prosecuted for breaking these laws, so "buyer beware" is an important rule customers must follow when buying goods and services.

Figure 4.2
Whole Foods Market's Stakeholder Approach to Ethical Business

New business paradigm

Community, Society, and Nation

The effects of the decisions made by companies and their managers permeate all aspects of the communities, societies, and nations in which they operate. *Community* refers to physical locations like towns or cities or to social milieus like ethnic neighborhoods in which companies are located. A community provides a company with the physical and social infrastructure that allows it to operate; its utilities and labor force; the homes in which its managers and employees live; the schools, colleges, and hospitals that serve their needs; and so on.

Through the salaries, wages, and taxes it pays, a company contributes to the economy of its town or region and often determines whether the community prospers or declines. Similarly, a company affects the prosperity of a society and a nation and, to the degree that a company is involved in global trade, all the countries it operates in and thus the prosperity of the global economy. We have already discussed the many issues surrounding global outsourcing and the loss of jobs in the United States, for example.

Although the individual effects of the way each McDonald's restaurant operates might be small, for instance, the combined effects of how all McDonald's and other fast-food companies do business are enormous. In the United States alone, over 500,000 people work in the fast-food industry, and many thousands of suppliers like farmers, paper cup manufacturers, builders, and so on depend on it for their livelihood. Small wonder then that the ethics of the fast-food business are scrutinized closely. This industry was the major lobbyer against attempts to raise the national minimum wage (which was raised to $7.25 an hour in 2009 where it remains in 2012, up from $5.15—a figure that had not changed since 1997), for example, because a higher minimum wage would substantially increase its operating costs. However, responding to protests about chickens raised in cages where they cannot move, McDonald's—the largest egg buyer in the United States—issued new ethical guidelines concerning cage size and related matters that its egg suppliers must abide by if they are to retain its business. What ethical rules does McDonald's use to decide its stance toward minimum pay or minimum cage size?

Business ethics are also important because the failure of a company can have catastrophic effects on a community; a general decline in business activity affects a whole nation. The decision of a large company to pull out of a community, for example, can seriously threaten the community's future. Some companies may attempt to improve their profits by engaging in actions that, although not illegal, can hurt communities and nations. One of these actions is pollution. For example, many U.S. companies reduce costs by trucking their waste to Mexico, where it is legal to dump waste in the Rio Grande. The dumping pollutes the river from the Mexican side, but the U.S. side of the river is increasingly experiencing pollution's negative effects.

Rules for Ethical Decision Making

When a stakeholder perspective is taken, questions on company ethics abound.[22] What is the appropriate way to manage the claims of all stakeholders? Company decisions that favor one group of stakeholders, for example, are likely to harm the interests of others.[23] High prices charged to customers may bring high returns to shareholders and high salaries to managers in the short run. If in the long run customers turn to companies that offer lower-cost products, however, the result may be declining sales, laid-off employees, and the decline of the communities that support the high-priced company's business activity.

When companies act ethically, their stakeholders support them. For example, banks are willing to supply them with new capital, they attract highly qualified job applicants, and new customers are drawn to their products. Thus ethical companies grow and expand over time, and all their stakeholders benefit. The results of unethical behavior are loss of reputation and resources, shareholders selling their shares, skilled managers and employees leaving the company, and customers turning to the products of more reputable companies.

When making business decisions, managers must consider the claims of all stakeholders.[24] To help themselves and employees make ethical decisions and behave in ways that benefit their stakeholders, managers can use four ethical rules or principles to analyze the effects of their business decisions on stakeholders: the *utilitarian, moral rights, justice,* and *practical* rules (Figure 4.3).[25] These rules are useful guidelines that help managers decide on the

Figure 4.3
Four Ethical Rules

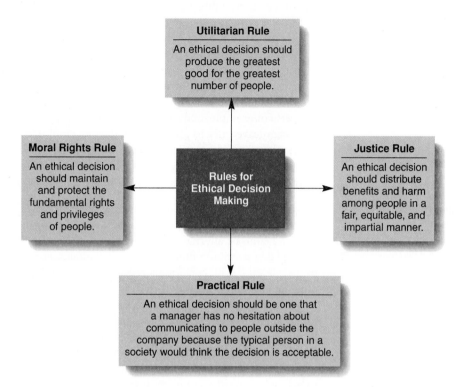

Utilitarian Rule

An ethical decision should produce the greatest good for the greatest number of people.

Moral Rights Rule

An ethical decision should maintain and protect the fundamental rights and privileges of people.

Rules for Ethical Decision Making

Justice Rule

An ethical decision should distribute benefits and harm among people in a fair, equitable, and impartial manner.

Practical Rule

An ethical decision should be one that a manager has no hesitation about communicating to people outside the company because the typical person in a society would think the decision is acceptable.

appropriate way to behave in situations where it is necessary to balance a company's self-interest and the interests of its stakeholders. Remember, the right choices will lead resources to be used where they can create the most value. If all companies make the right choices, all stakeholders will benefit in the long run.[26]

utilitarian rule An ethical decision is a decision that produces the greatest good for the greatest number of people.

UTILITARIAN RULE The **utilitarian rule** is that an ethical decision is a decision that produces the greatest good for the greatest number of people. To decide which is the most ethical course of business action, managers should first consider how different possible courses of business action would benefit or harm different stakeholders. They should then choose the course of action that provides the most benefits, or, conversely, the one that does the least harm, to stakeholders.[27]

The ethical dilemma for managers is this: How do you measure the benefit and harm that will be done to each stakeholder group? Moreover, how do you evaluate the rights of different stakeholder groups, and the relative importance of each group, in coming to a decision? Because stockholders own the company, shouldn't their claims be held above those of employees? For example, managers might face a choice of using global outsourcing to reduce costs and lower prices or continuing with high-cost production at home. A decision to use global outsourcing benefits shareholders and customers but will result in major layoffs that will harm employees and the communities in which they live. Typically, in a capitalist society such as the United States, the interests of shareholders are put above those of employees, so production will move abroad. This is commonly regarded as being an ethical choice because in the long run the alternative, home production, might cause the business to collapse and go bankrupt, in which case greater harm will be done to all stakeholders.

LO4-3 Describe four rules that can help companies and their managers act in ethical ways.

moral rights rule An ethical decision is one that best maintains and protects the fundamental or inalienable rights and privileges of the people affected by it.

MORAL RIGHTS RULE Under the **moral rights rule**, an ethical decision is one that best maintains and protects the fundamental or inalienable rights and privileges of the people affected by it. For example, ethical decisions protect people's rights to freedom, life and safety, property, privacy, free speech, and freedom of conscience. The adage "Do unto others as you would have them do unto you" is a moral rights principle that managers should use to decide which rights to uphold. Customers must also consider the rights of the companies and people who create the products they wish to consume (see the "Ethics in Action" box "Digital Piracy, Ethics, and Napster").

From a moral rights perspective, managers should compare and contrast different courses of business action on the basis of how each course will affect the rights of the company's different stakeholders. Managers should then choose the course of action that best protects and upholds the rights of *all* stakeholders. For example, decisions that might significantly harm the safety or health of employees or customers would clearly be unethical choices.

The ethical dilemma for managers is that decisions that will protect the rights of some stakeholders often will hurt the rights of others. How should they choose which group to protect? For example, in deciding whether it is ethical to snoop on employees, or search them when they leave work to prevent theft, does an employee's right to privacy outweigh an organization's right to protect its property? Suppose a coworker is having personal problems and is coming in late and leaving early, forcing you to pick up the person's workload. Do you tell your boss even though you know this will probably get that person fired?

justice rule An ethical decision distributes benefits and harms among people and groups in a fair, equitable, or impartial way.

JUSTICE RULE   The justice rule is that an ethical decision distributes benefits and harms among people and groups in a fair, equitable, or impartial way. Managers should compare and contrast alternative courses of action based on the degree to which they will fairly or equitably distribute outcomes to stakeholders. For example, employees who are similar in their level of skill, performance, or responsibility should receive similar pay; allocation of outcomes should not be based on differences such as gender, race, or religion.

The ethical dilemma for managers is to determine the fair rules and procedures for distributing outcomes to stakeholders. Managers must not give people they like bigger raises than they give to people they do not like, for example, or bend the rules to help their favorites. On the other hand, if employees want managers to act fairly toward them, then employees need to act fairly toward their companies by working hard and being loyal. Similarly, customers need to act fairly toward a company if they expect it to be fair to them—something people who illegally copy digital media should consider.

practical rule An ethical decision is one that a manager has no reluctance about communicating to people outside the company because the typical person in a society would think it is acceptable.

PRACTICAL RULE   Each of these rules offers a different and complementary way of determining whether a decision or behavior is ethical, and all three rules should be used to sort out the ethics of a particular course of action. Ethical issues, as we just discussed, are seldom clear-cut, however, because the rights, interests, goals, and incentives of different stakeholders often conflict. For this reason many experts on ethics add a fourth rule to determine whether a business decision is ethical: The practical rule is that an ethical decision is one that a manager has no hesitation or reluctance about communicating to people outside the company because the typical person in a society would think it is acceptable. A business decision is probably acceptable on ethical grounds if a manager can answer yes to each of these questions:

1. Does my decision fall within the accepted values or standards that typically apply in business activity today?
2. Am I willing to see the decision communicated to all people and groups affected by it— for example, by having it reported in newspapers or on television?
3. Would the people with whom I have a significant personal relationship, such as family members, friends, or even managers in other organizations, approve of the decision?

Applying the practical rule to analyze a business decision ensures that managers are taking into account the interests of all stakeholders.[28] After applying this rule, managers can judge if they have chosen to act in an ethical or unethical way, and they must abide by the consequences.

LO4-4   Discuss why it is important for managers to behave ethically.

Why Should Managers Behave Ethically?

Why is it so important that managers, and people in general, should act ethically and temper their pursuit of self-interest by considering the effects of their actions on others? The answer is that the relentless pursuit of self-interest can lead to a collective disaster when one or more people start to profit from being unethical because this encourages other people to act in the same way.[29] More and more people jump onto the bandwagon, and soon everybody is trying to manipulate the situation to serve their personal ends with no regard for the effects of their action on others. The situation brought about by Napster is an example of what is called the "tragedy of the commons."

Suppose that in an agricultural community there is common land that everybody has an equal right to use. Pursuing self-interest, each farmer acts to make the maximum use of the free resource by grazing his or her own cattle and sheep. Collectively all the farmers overgraze the land, which quickly becomes worn out. Then a strong wind blows away the exposed top-soil, so the common land is destroyed. The pursuit of individual self-interest with no consideration of societal interests leads to disaster for each individual and for the whole society because scarce resources are destroyed.[30] For example, consider digital piracy; the tragedy that would result if all people were to steal digital media would be the disappearance of music, movie, and book companies as creative people decided there was no point in working hard to produce original songs, stories, and so on.

We can look at the effects of unethical behavior on business activity in another way. Suppose companies and their managers operate in an unethical society, meaning one in which stakeholders routinely try to cheat and defraud one another. If stakeholders expect each other to cheat, how long will it take them to negotiate the purchase and shipment of products? When they do not trust each other, stakeholders will probably spend hours bargaining over fair prices, and this is a largely unproductive activity that reduces efficiency and effectiveness.[31] The time and effort that could be spent improving product quality or customer service are lost to negotiating and bargaining. Thus, unethical behavior ruins business commerce, and society has a lower standard of living because fewer goods and services are produced, as Figure 4.4 illustrates.

Figure 4.4

Some Effects of Ethical and Unethical Behavior

trust The willingness of one person or group to have faith or confidence in the goodwill of another person, even though this puts them at risk.

On the other hand, suppose companies and their managers operate in an ethical society, meaning stakeholders believe they are dealing with others who are basically moral and honest. In this society stakeholders have a greater reason to trust others. **Trust** is the willingness of one person or group to have faith or confidence in the goodwill of another person, even though this puts them at risk (because the other might act in a deceitful way). When trust exists, stakeholders are likely to signal their good intentions by cooperating and providing information that makes it easier to exchange and price goods and services. When one person acts in a trustworthy way, this encourages others to act in the same way. Over time, as greater trust between stakeholders develops, they can work together more efficiently and effectively, which raises company performance (see Figure 4.4). As people see the positive results of acting in an honest way, ethical behavior becomes a valued social norm, and society in general becomes increasingly ethical.

As noted in Chapter 1, a major responsibility of managers is to protect and nurture the resources under their control. Any organizational stakeholders—managers, workers, stockholders, suppliers—who advance their own interests by behaving unethically toward other stakeholders, either by taking resources or by denying resources to others, waste collective resources. If other individuals or groups copy the behavior of the unethical stakeholder, the rate at which collective resources are misused increases, and eventually few resources are available to produce goods and services. Unethical behavior that goes unpunished creates incentives for people to put their unbridled self-interests above the rights of others.[32] When this happens, the benefits that people reap from joining together in organizations disappear quickly.

reputation The esteem or high repute that individuals or organizations gain when they behave ethically.

An important safeguard against unethical behavior is the potential for loss of reputation.[33] **Reputation**, the esteem or high repute that people or organizations gain when they behave ethically, is an important asset. Stakeholders have valuable reputations that they must protect because their ability to earn a living and obtain resources in the long run depends on how they behave.

If a manager misuses resources and other parties regard that behavior as being at odds with acceptable standards, the manager's reputation will suffer. Behaving unethically in the short run can have serious long-term consequences. A manager who has a poor reputation will have difficulty finding employment with other companies. Stockholders who see managers behaving unethically may refuse to invest in their companies, and this will decrease the stock price, undermine the companies' reputations, and ultimately put the managers' jobs at risk.[34]

All stakeholders have reputations to lose. Suppliers who provide shoddy inputs find that organizations learn over time not to deal with them, and eventually, like PCA, they go out of business. Powerful customers who demand ridiculously low prices find that their suppliers become less willing to deal with them, and resources ultimately become harder for them to obtain. Workers who shirk responsibilities on the job find it hard to get new jobs when they are fired. In general, if a manager or company is known for being unethical, other stakeholders are likely to view that individual or organization with suspicion and hostility, creating a poor reputation. But a manager or company known for ethical business practices will develop a good reputation.[35]

In summary, in a complex, diverse society, stakeholders, and people in general, need to recognize they are part of a larger social group. How they make decisions and act not only affects them personally but also affects the lives of many other people. Unfortunately, for some people, the daily struggle to survive and succeed or their total disregard for others' rights can lead them to lose that bigger connection to other people. We can see our relationships to our families and friends, to our school, church, and so on. But we must go further and keep in mind the effects of our actions on other people—people who will be judging our actions and whom we might harm by acting unethically. Our moral scruples are like those "other people" but are inside our heads.

Ethics and Social Responsibility

Some companies, like GlaxoSmithKline, Bristol Myers Squib, Prudential Insurance, Whole Foods, and Blue Cross–Blue Shield, are known for their ethical business practices.[36] Other companies, such as PAC and Enron, which are now out of business, or WorldCom, Tyco, and Siemens, which have been totally restructured, repeatedly engaged in unethical

LO4-5 Identify the four main sources of managerial ethics.

and illegal business activities. What explains such differences between the ethics of these companies and their managers?

There are four main determinants of differences in ethics between people, employees, companies, and countries: *societal* ethics, *occupational* ethics, *individual* ethics, and *organizational* ethics—especially the ethics of a company's top managers.[37] (See Figure 4.5.)

Societal Ethics

societal ethics Standards that govern how members of a society should deal with one another in matters involving issues such as fairness, justice, poverty, and the rights of the individual.

Societal ethics are standards that govern how members of a society should deal with one another in matters involving issues such as fairness, justice, poverty, and the rights of the individual. Societal ethics emanate from a society's laws, customs, and practices and from the unwritten values and norms that influence how people interact with each other. People in a particular country may automatically behave ethically because they have *internalized* (made a part of their morals) certain values, beliefs, and norms that specify how they should behave when confronted with an ethical dilemma.

Societal ethics vary among societies. Countries like Germany, Japan, Sweden, and Switzerland are known as being some of the most ethical countries in the world, with strong values about social order and the need to create a society that protects the welfare of all their citizens. In other countries the situation is different. In many economically poor countries bribery is standard practice to get things done—such as getting a telephone installed or a contract awarded. In the United States and other economically advanced countries, bribery is considered unethical and has been made illegal.

IBM experienced the problem of different ethical standards in its Argentine division; so did Siemens, the German company, in many of its global divisions. At IBM managers became involved in an unethical scheme to secure a $250 million contract for IBM to provide and service the computers of one of Argentina's largest state-owned banks. After $6 million was paid to bribe the bank executives who agreed to give IBM the contract, IBM announced that it had fired the three top managers of its Argentine division. According to IBM, transactions like this, though unethical by IBM's standards, are not necessarily illegal under Argentine law. The Argentine managers were fired, however, for failing to follow IBM's organizational rules, which preclude bribery to obtain contracts in foreign countries. Moreover, bribery violates the U.S. Foreign Corrupt Practices Act, which forbids payment of bribes by U.S. and global companies to secure contracts abroad, makes companies liable for the actions of their foreign managers,

Figure 4.5
Sources of Ethics

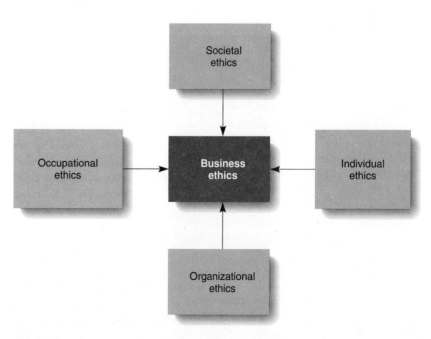

and allows global companies found in violation to be prosecuted in the United States. By firing the managers, IBM signaled that it would not tolerate unethical behavior by any of its employees, and it continues today to take a rigorous stance toward ethical issues; Siemens was fined over $800 million by U.S. government authorities for its global bribery violations.

Countries also differ widely in their beliefs about appropriate treatment for their employees. In general, the poorer a country is, the more likely employees are to be treated with little regard. One issue of particular concern on a global level is whether it is ethical to use child labor, as discussed in the following "Ethics in Action" box.

Ethics in Action

Is It Right to Use Child Labor?

In recent years, the number of U.S. companies that buy their products from low-cost foreign suppliers has been growing, and concern about the ethics associated with employing young children in factories has been increasing. In Pakistan, children as young as 6 years old work long hours in deplorable conditions to make rugs and carpets for export to Western countries. Children in poor countries throughout Africa, Asia, and South America work in similar conditions. Is it ethical to employ children in factories, and should U.S. companies buy and sell products made by these children?

Opinions about the ethics of child labor vary widely. Robert Reich, an economist and secretary of labor in the first Clinton administration, believed that the practice is totally reprehensible and should be outlawed on a global level. Another view, championed by *The Economist* magazine, is that while nobody wants to see children employed in factories, citizens of rich countries need to recognize that in poor countries children are often a family's breadwinners. Thus, denying children employment would cause whole families to suffer, and one wrong (child labor) might produce a greater wrong (poverty). Instead *The Economist* favors regulating the conditions under which children are employed and hopes that over time, as poor countries become richer, the need for child employment will disappear.

Many U.S. retailers buy clothing from low-cost foreign suppliers, and managers in these companies have had to take their own ethical stance on child labor. Managers in Walmart, Target, JCPenney, and Gap Inc. (see Table 4.1) have followed U.S. standards and rules and have policies dictating that their foreign suppliers not employ child labor. They have also vowed to sever ties with any foreign supplier found violating this standard.

Afghan boys weave a rug while their father stands nearby inside their home in Kabul, Afghanistan. Afghan rug makers contract children to make rugs, paying their families roughly $8 per yard. Making one 18-foot rug takes approximately a month, and the children often work in shifts around their schooling or other household duties.

Apparently, however, retailers differ widely in how they enforce such policies. It has been estimated that more than 300,000 children under age 14 are employed in garment factories in Guatemala, a popular low-cost location for clothing manufacturers that supply the U.S. market. These children frequently work more than 60 hours a week and often are paid less than $3 a day—close to the minimum wage in Guatemala. Many U.S. retailers do not check up on their foreign suppliers. Clearly, if U.S. retailers are to be true to their ethical stance on this troubling issue, they cannot ignore the fact that they are buying clothing made by children, and they must do more to regulate the conditions under which these children work.

One recent attempt to do this is through the Fair Factories Clearinghouse, a joint effort launched by companies such as Apple, L.L. Bean, Reebok, and Timberland to pool the information they collect about the work practices of the factories with which they have contracted to make their products. The aim is to create a single set of labor code standards that plants the world over must comply with if they are to be certified as ethical suppliers—or else they will be axed by all reputable companies.[38]

Occupational Ethics

occupational ethics
Standards that govern how members of a profession, trade, or craft should conduct themselves when performing work-related activities.

Occupational ethics are standards that govern how members of a profession, trade, or craft should conduct themselves when performing work-related activities.[39] For example, medical ethics govern how doctors and nurses should treat their patients. Doctors are expected to perform only necessary medical procedures and to act in the patient's interest, not their own self-interest. The ethics of scientific research require that scientists conduct their experiments and present their findings in ways that ensure the validity of their conclusions. Like society at large, most professional groups can impose punishments for violations of ethical standards.[40] Doctors and lawyers can be prevented from practicing their professions if they disregard professional ethics and put their own interests first.

Within an organization, occupational rules and norms often govern how employees such as lawyers, researchers, and accountants should make decisions to further stakeholder interests. Employees internalize the rules and norms of their occupational group (just as they do those of society) and often follow them automatically when deciding how to behave. Because most people tend to follow established rules of behavior, people frequently take ethics for granted. However, when occupational ethics are violated, such as when scientists fabricate data to disguise the harmful effects of products, ethical issues come to the forefront. For example, Merck scientists were accused of playing down evidence that Vioxx, a best-selling drug, increased the risk of heart attacks; the drug was pulled from the market. Top researchers in pharmaceutical companies have been accused of deliberately hiding research evidence that revealed the harmful effects of products such as Merck's Vioxx painkilling drug and Guidant's heart pacemaker, so doctors and patients could not make informed medical treatment decisions. Table 4.2 lists some failures or lapses in professional ethics according to type of functional manager.

Individual Ethics

individual ethics Personal standards and values that determine how people view their responsibilities to others and how they should act in situations when their own self-interests are at stake.

Individual ethics are personal standards and values that determine how people view their responsibilities to other people and groups and thus how they should act in situations when their own self-interests are at stake.[41] Sources of individual ethics include the influence of one's family, peers, and upbringing in general. The experiences gained over a lifetime—through membership in social institutions such as schools and religions, for example—also contribute to the development of the personal standards and values that a person uses to evaluate a situation and decide what is the morally right or wrong way to behave. However, suppose you are the son or daughter of a mobster, and your upbringing and education take place in an organized crime context; this affects how you evaluate a situation. You may come to believe that it is ethical to do anything and perform any act, up to and including murder, if it benefits your family or friends. These are your ethics. They are obviously not the ethics of the wider society and so are subject to sanction. In a similar way, managers and employees in an organization may come to believe that actions they take to promote or protect their organization are more important than any harm these actions may cause other stakeholders. So they behave unethically or illegally, and when this is discovered, they also are sanctioned—as happened to New York's cab drivers.

Check that meter before you pay! Relying on cab driver honesty failed in NYC, finally resulting in tighter regulation of the industry.

Table 4.2

Some Failures in Professional Ethics

For manufacturing and materials management managers:

- Releasing products that are not of a consistent quality because of defective inputs.
- Producing product batches that may be dangerous or defective and harm customers.
- Compromising workplace health and safety to reduce costs (for example, to maximize output, employees are not given adequate training to maintain and service machinery and equipment).

For sales and marketing managers:

- Knowingly making unsubstantiated product claims.
- Engaging in sales campaigns that use covert persuasive or subliminal advertising to create customer need for the product.
- Marketing to target groups such as the elderly, minorities, or children to build demand for a product.
- Having ongoing campaigns of unsolicited junk mail, spam, door-to-door, or telephone selling.

For accounting and finance managers:

- Engaging in misleading financial analysis involving creative accounting or "cooking the books" to hide salient facts.
- Authorizing excessive expenses and perks to managers, customers, and suppliers.
- Hiding the level and amount of top management and director compensation.

For human resource managers:

- Failing to act fairly, objectively, and in a uniform way toward different employees or kinds of employees because of personal factors such as personality and beliefs.
- Excessively encroaching on employee privacy through non-job-related surveillance or personality, ability, and drug testing.
- Failing to respond to employee observations and concerns surrounding health and safety violations, hostile workplace issues, or inappropriate or even illegal behavior by managers or employees.

In 2009 the New York City taxi commission, which regulates cab fares, began an investigation after it found that one cab driver from Brooklyn, Wasim Khalid Cheema, overcharged 574 passengers in just one month. The taxi drivers' scheme, the commission said, involved 1.8 million rides and cost passengers an average of $4 to $5 extra per trip. The drivers pressed a button on the taxi's payment meter that categorized the fare as a Code No. 4, which is charged for trips outside the city to Nassau or Westchester and is twice the rate of Code No. 1, which is charged for rides within New York City limits. Passengers can see which rate is being charged by looking at the meter, but few bother to do so; they rely on the cab driver's honesty.

After the commission discovered the fraud, it used GPS data, collected in every cab, to review millions of trips within New York City and found that in 36,000 cabs the higher rates were improperly activated at least once; in each of about 3,000 cabs it was done more than 100 times; and 35,558 of the city's roughly 48,000 drivers had applied the higher rate. This scheme cost New York City riders more than $8 million plus all the higher tips they paid as a result of the higher charges. The fraud ranks as one of the biggest in the taxi industry's history, and New York City Mayor Michael R. Bloomberg said criminal charges could be brought against cab drivers.

The commission also demanded that in the future a new digital metering system be introduced to alert passengers, who would have to acknowledge that they accepted the higher rate charge. Also, officials said taxi companies would eventually be forced to use meters based on a GPS system that would automatically set the charge based on the location of the cab, and drivers would no longer be able to manually activate the higher rate—and cheat their customers. In 2011, 630 taxi drivers had their licenses revoked.

In general, many decisions or behaviors that one person finds unethical, such as using animals for cosmetics testing, may be acceptable to another person. If decisions or behaviors are not illegal, individuals may agree to disagree about their ethical beliefs, or they may try to impose their own beliefs on other people and make those ethical beliefs the law. In all cases, however, people should develop and follow the ethical criteria described earlier to balance their self-interests against those of others when determining how they should behave in a particular situation.

Organizational Ethics

organizational ethics The guiding practices and beliefs through which a particular company and its managers view their responsibility toward their stakeholders.

Organizational ethics are the guiding practices and beliefs through which a particular company and its managers view their responsibility toward their stakeholders. The individual ethics of a company's founders and top managers are especially important in shaping the organization's code of ethics. Organizations whose founders had a vital role in creating a highly ethical code of organizational behavior include UPS, Procter & Gamble, Johnson & Johnson, and the Prudential Insurance Company. Johnson & Johnson's code of ethics—its credo—reflects a well-developed concern for its stakeholders (see Figure 4.6). Company credos, such

Figure 4.6
Johnson & Johnson's Credo

Our Credo

We believe our first responsibility is to the doctors, nurses and patients,
to mothers and fathers and all others who use our products and services.
In meeting their needs everything we do must be of high quality.
We must constantly strive to reduce our costs
in order to maintain reasonable prices.
Customers' orders must be serviced promptly and accurately.
Our suppliers and distributors must have an opportunity
to make a fair profit.

We are responsible to our employees,
the men and women who work with us throughout the world.
Everyone must be considered as an individual.
We must respect their dignity and recognize their merit.
They must have a sense of security in their jobs.
Compensation must be fair and adequate,
and working conditions clean, orderly and safe.
We must be mindful of ways to help our employees fulfill
their family responsibilities.
Employees must feel free to make suggestions and complaints.
There must be equal opportunity for employment, development
and advancement for those qualified.
We must provide competent management,
and their actions must be just and ethical.

We are responsible to the communities in which we live and work
and to the world community as well.
We must be good citizens—support good works and charities
and bear our fair share of taxes.
We must encourage civic improvements and better health and education.
We must maintain in good order
the property we are privileged to use,
protecting the environment and natural resources.

Our final responsibility is to our stockholders.
Business must make a sound profit.
We must experiment with new ideas.
Research must be carried on, innovative programs developed
and mistakes paid for.
New equipment must be purchased, new facilities provided
and new products launched.
Reserves must be created to provide for adverse times.
When we operate according to these principles,
the stockholders should realize a fair return.

Johnson & Johnson

Source: © Johnson & Johnson. Used with permission.

as that of Johnson & Johnson, are meant to deter self-interested, unethical behavior; to demonstrate to managers and employees that a company will not tolerate people who, because of their own poor ethics, put their personal interests above the interests of other organizational stakeholders and ignore the harm they are inflicting on others; and to demonstrate that those who act unethically will be punished.

Managers or workers may behave unethically if they feel pressured to do so by the situation they are in and by unethical top managers. People typically confront ethical issues when weighing their personal interests against the effects of their actions on others. Suppose a manager knows that promotion to vice president is likely if she can secure a $100 million contract, but getting the contract requires bribing the contract giver with $1 million. The manager reasons that performing this act will ensure her career and future, and what harm would it do anyway? Bribery is common and she knows that, even if she decides not to pay the bribe, someone else surely will. So what to do? Research seems to suggest that people who realize they have the most at stake in a career sense or a monetary sense are the ones most likely to act unethically. And it is exactly in this situation that a strong code of organizational ethics can help people behave in the right or appropriate way. *The New York Times* detailed code of ethics (see nytco.com/corporate_governance/code_of_ethics/business_ethics.html), for example, was crafted by its editors to ensure the integrity and honesty of its journalists as they report sensitive information.

If a company's top managers consistently endorse the ethical principles in its corporate credo, they can prevent employees from going astray. Employees are much more likely to act unethically when a credo does not exist or is disregarded. Arthur Andersen, for example, did not follow its credo at all; its unscrupulous partners ordered middle managers to shred records that showed evidence of their wrongdoing. Although the middle managers knew this was wrong, they followed the orders because they responded to the personal power and status of the partners and not the company's code of ethics. They were afraid they would lose their jobs if they did not behave unethically, but their actions cost them their jobs anyway.

Top managers play a crucial role in determining a company's ethics. It is clearly important, then, that when making appointment decisions, the board of directors should scrutinize the reputations and ethical records of top managers. It is the responsibility of the board to decide whether a prospective CEO has the maturity, experience, and integrity needed to head a company and be entrusted with the capital and wealth of the organization, on which the fate of all its stakeholders depends. Clearly a track record of success is not enough to decide whether a top manager is capable of moral decision making; a manager might have achieved this success through unethical or illegal means. It is important to investigate prospective top managers and examine their credentials. Although the best predictor of future behavior is often past behavior, the board of directors needs to be on guard against unprincipled executives who use unethical means to rise to the top of the organizational hierarchy. For this reason it is necessary that a company's directors continuously monitor the behavior of top executives. In the 2000s this increased scrutiny has led to the dismissal of many top executives for breaking ethical rules concerning issues such as excessive personal loans, stock options, inflated expense accounts, and even sexual misconduct—as the "Ethics in Action" box discusses below.

Ethics in Action

Jonathan Reckford Rebuilds Goodwill at Habitat for Humanity

Habitat for Humanity is the 17th largest U.S. nonprofit, and its mission is to build or renovate cost-effective, modest homes in partnership with families in need, who repay the organization by helping to build their own homes or the homes of others and by

When Habitat for Humanity needed a new CEO, they looked to Jonathan Reckford, a Presbyterian pastor and former executive at Walt Disney and Best Buy. Reckford, pictured here with Habitat spokesperson Jimmy Carter, quickly implemented best-practice techniques in order to help Habitat perform more effectively.

repaying a no-profit mortgage. Founded decades ago by Millard and Linda Fuller, it receives more than $1 billion in donations a year for its work in more than 90 countries around the world. In 2004 a scandal struck the nonprofit when Millard Fuller was accused of sexually harassing a female employee. The board brought in an investigator to review the complaint. As the investigation unfolded, the Fullers' behavior and ongoing comments about the matter were deemed divisive to the organization's work and led to their dismissal.

In the 2000s the efficiency and effectiveness of nonprofits have been questioned, and many analysts believe that nonprofits need to introduce new management techniques to improve their level of performance. Indeed, one study estimated that nonprofits could save $100 billion by using such techniques as total quality management and benchmarking, which involve an organization's imitating a company that excels in performing some functional activity.

So Habitat's board of directors searched for a new CEO who could simultaneously help the organization continue its work and improve its performance. The person they chose was Jonathan Reckford, a former Walt Disney and Best Buy executive and a Presbyterian pastor. Reckford relished the challenge of using his management skills to find better ways to use Habitat's $1 billion in donations and to attract more donors. Quickly Reckford began to introduce best practice techniques. For example, modeling companies like Dell and Walmart that use their huge buying power to lower their input costs, he emphasized the need for volume purchasing of building products. He introduced new kinds of output controls to provide detailed feedback on vital aspects of Habitat's performance, such as the number of new houses it built in different regions and countries and the time and cost of construction involved per house. He also introduced better human resource management practices, including creating a promotion ladder in Habitat and raising salaries to competitive levels found in other nonprofits. He decided to move a portion of Habitat's headquarters from the small city in which it had been founded to Atlanta, Georgia, to make it easier to hire skilled functional managers. Finally, he established a new set of goals and priorities for the company; and given that Reckford took over only a month after Hurricane Katrina struck, one obvious priority was to rebuild homes along the Gulf Coast. Habitat's goal was to begin to construct or complete 1,000 permanent homes by the end of 2007—a feat it achieved by May 2007, upon which Reckford announced that its new goal was to build 1,000 more.[42]

Habitat for Humanity has steadily increased its international focus; for example, it already had 50 employees in place in Haiti in 2010 when the earthquake struck. Reckford, traveling with singer Ricky Martin, toured the earthquake's devastation and announced, "With more than 200,000 houses severely damaged or destroyed and 1.2 million people homeless or displaced, there is a critical need for shelter in Haiti. Based on our responses to the Asian tsunami and Hurricanes Katrina and Rita in the U.S. Gulf Coast, we are confident that we can empower families to improve their housing conditions by giving them the tools and then working alongside them. But Habitat for Humanity is in need of significant financial support so that we can help 50,000 families improve their lives."[43] In total, since its founding in 1976, Habitat has built, rehabilitated, repaired, or improved more than 350,000 houses worldwide that provide simple and affordable shelter to over 1.75 million people.

Approaches to Social Responsibility

LO4-6 Distinguish among the four main approaches toward social responsibility that a company can take.

social responsibility The way a company's managers and employees view their duty or obligation to make decisions that protect, enhance, and promote the welfare and well-being of stakeholders and society as a whole.

A company's ethics are the result of differences in societal, organizational, occupational, and individual ethics. In turn, a company's ethics determine its stance or position on social responsibility. A company's stance on **social responsibility** is the way its managers and employees view their duty or obligation to make decisions that protect, enhance, and promote the welfare and well-being of stakeholders and society as a whole.[44] As we noted earlier, when no laws specify how a company should act toward stakeholders, managers must decide the right, ethical, and socially responsible thing to do. Differences in business ethics can lead companies to diverse positions or views on their responsibility toward stakeholders.

Many kinds of decisions signal a company's beliefs about its obligations to make socially responsible business decisions (see Table 4.3). The decision to spend money on training and educating employees—investing in them—is one such decision; so is the decision to minimize or avoid layoffs whenever possible. The decision to act promptly and warn customers when a batch of defective merchandise has been accidentally sold is another one. Companies that try to hide such problems show little regard for social responsibility. In the past both GM and Ford tried to hide the fact that several of their vehicles had defects that made them dangerous to drive; the companies were penalized with hundreds of millions of dollars in damages for their unethical behavior, and today they move more quickly to recall vehicles to fix problems. In 2010 quality leader Toyota apologized for being slow to announce recalls to fix brake system problems on some of its vehicles, which had caused uncontrolled acceleration; Toyota had to deal with a public relations nightmare as a result. On the other hand, after HP discovered one of its most popular cameras could catch fire if users attempted to recharge ordinary batteries, it quickly announced a software fix for the problem; informing the public was the right thing to do.[45] The way a company announces business problems or admits its mistakes provides strong clues about its stance on social responsibility.

Four Different Approaches

The strength of companies' commitment to social responsibility can range from low to high (see Figure 4.7). At the low end of the range is an **obstructional approach**, in which companies

obstructional approach Companies and their managers choose *not* to behave in a socially responsible way and instead behave unethically and illegally.

Table 4.3

Forms of Socially Responsible Behavior

Managers are being socially responsible and showing their support for their stakeholders when they

- Provide severance payments to help laid-off workers make ends meet until they can find another job.
- Give workers opportunities to enhance their skills and acquire additional education so they can remain productive and do not become obsolete because of changes in technology.
- Allow employees to take time off when they need to and provide health care and pension benefits for employees.
- Contribute to charities or support various civic-minded activities in the cities or towns in which they are located. (Target and Levi Strauss both contribute 5% of their profits to support schools, charities, the arts, and other good works.)
- Decide to keep open a factory whose closure would devastate the local community.
- Decide to keep a company's operations in the United States to protect the jobs of American workers rather than move abroad.
- Decide to spend money to improve a new factory so it will not pollute the environment.
- Decline to invest in countries that have poor human rights records.
- Choose to help poor countries develop an economic base to improve living standards.

Figure 4.7

Four Approaches to Social Responsibility

| Obstructionist approach | Defensive approach | Accommodative approach | Proactive approach |

Low social responsibility   Social Responsibility   High social responsibility

and their managers choose *not* to behave in a socially responsible way. Instead they behave unethically and often illegally and do all they can to prevent knowledge of their behavior from reaching other organizational stakeholders and society at large. Managers at the Manville Corporation adopted this approach when they sought to hide evidence that asbestos causes lung damage; so too did tobacco companies when they sought to hide evidence that cigarette smoking causes lung cancer. In 2010 it was revealed that the managers of Lehman Brothers, whose bankruptcy helped propel the 2008–2009 financial crisis, used loopholes in U.K. law to hide billions of dollars of worthless assets on its balance sheet to disguise its poor financial condition.

Top managers at Enron also acted in an obstructionist way when they prevented employees from selling Enron shares in their pension funds while they sold hundreds of millions of dollars' worth of their own Enron stock. Most employees lost all their retirement savings. Senior partners at Arthur Andersen who instructed their subordinates to shred files chose an obstructionist approach that caused not only a loss of reputation but devastation for the organization and for all stakeholders involved. These companies are no longer in business. The unethical behavior characteristic of the obstructionist approach is exemplified by how PCA's president put his personal interests before customers' health and above the law.

A **defensive approach** indicates at least some commitment to ethical behavior.[46] Defensive companies and managers stay within the law and abide strictly by legal requirements but make no attempt to exercise social responsibility beyond what the law dictates; thus they can and often do act unethically. These are the kinds of companies, like Computer Associates, WorldCom, and Merrill Lynch, that gave their managers large stock options and bonuses even as company performance was declining rapidly. The managers are the kind who sell their stock in advance of other stockholders because they know their company's performance is about to fall. Although acting on inside information is illegal, it is often hard to prove because top managers have wide latitude regarding when they sell their shares. The founders of most dot-com companies took advantage of this legal loophole to sell billions of dollars of their dot-com shares before their stock prices collapsed. When making ethical decisions, such managers put their own interests first and commonly harm other stakeholders.

An **accommodative approach** acknowledges the need to support social responsibility. Accommodative companies and managers agree that organizational members ought to behave legally and ethically, and they try to balance the interests of different stakeholders so the claims of stockholders are seen in relation to the claims of other stakeholders. Managers adopting this approach want to make choices that are reasonable in the eyes of society and want to do the right thing.

This approach is the one taken by the typical large U.S. company, which has the most to lose from unethical or illegal behavior. Generally, the older and more reputable a company, the more likely its managers are to curb attempts by their subordinates to act unethically. Large companies like GM, Intel, DuPont, and Dell seek every way to build their companies' competitive advantage. Nevertheless, they rein in attempts by their managers to behave

defensive approach Companies and their managers behave ethically to the degree that they stay within the law and strictly abide by legal requirements.

accommodative approach Companies and their managers behave legally and ethically and try to balance the interests of different stakeholders as the need arises.

unethically or illegally, knowing the grave consequences such behavior can have on future profitability. Sometimes they fail, however, such as when it was revealed in 2009 that senior executives at Intel and AMD gave inside information to a hedge fund manager and received millions in kickbacks.

proactive approach
Companies and their managers actively embrace socially responsible behavior, going out of their way to learn about the needs of different stakeholder groups and using organizational resources to promote the interests of all stakeholders.

Companies and managers taking a **proactive approach** actively embrace the need to behave in socially responsible ways. They go out of their way to learn about the needs of different stakeholder groups and are willing to use organizational resources to promote the interests not only of stockholders but also of the other stakeholders such as their employees and communities. U.S. steelmaker Nucor is one such company. In 1977 its visionary CEO Ken Iverson announced that throughout its history Nucor had never laid off one employee, and even though a major recession was raging, it did not plan to start now. In 2009 Nucor CEO Daniel R. DiMicco announced that Nucor again would not start layoffs despite the fact its steel mills were operating at only 50% of capacity (compared to 95% just months earlier) because customers had slashed orders due to the recession. While rivals laid off thousands of employees, Nucor remained loyal to its employees. However, even though there were no layoffs, both managers and employees took major cuts in pay and bonuses to weather the storm together, as they always had, and they searched for ways to reduce operating costs so they would all benefit when the economy recovered, and by 2012 their sacrifice paid off: Nucor was doing well again.

Proactive companies are often at the forefront of campaigns for causes such as a pollution-free environment; recycling and conservation of resources; the minimization or elimination of the use of animals in drug and cosmetics testing; and the reduction of crime, illiteracy, and poverty. For example, companies like McDonald's, Google, Green Mountain Coffee, Whole Foods, and Target all have reputations for being proactive in the support of stakeholders such as their suppliers or the communities in which they operate.

Why Be Socially Responsible?

Several advantages result when companies and their managers behave in a socially responsible manner. First, demonstrating its social responsibility helps a company build a good reputation. Reputation is the trust, goodwill, and confidence others have in a company that lead them to want to do business with it. The rewards for a good company reputation are increased business and improved ability to obtain resources from stakeholders.[47] Reputation thus can enhance profitability and build stockholder wealth; and behaving responsibly socially is the economically right thing to do because companies that do so benefit from increasing business and rising profits.

Wanna bike around the office complex in your blue jeans? Google's model of employee social responsibility lets you do whatever floats your boat—so the company's boat floats higher.

A second major reason for companies to act responsibly toward employees, customers, and society is that, in a capitalist system, companies as well as the government, have to bear the costs of protecting their stakeholders, providing health care and income, paying taxes, and so on. So if all companies in a society act responsibly, the quality of life as a whole increases.

Moreover, how companies behave toward their employees determines many of a society's values and norms and the ethics of its citizens, as already noted. It has been suggested that if all organizations adopted a caring approach and agreed that their responsibility is to promote the interests of their employees, a climate of caring would pervade the wider society. Experts point to Japan, Sweden, Germany, the Netherlands, and Switzerland as countries where organizations are highly socially responsible and where, as a result, crime, poverty, and unemployment rates are relatively low, literacy rates are relatively high, and sociocultural values promote harmony between different groups of people. Business activity affects all aspects of people's lives, so how business behaves toward stakeholders affects how stakeholders behave toward business. You "reap what you sow," as the adage goes.

The Role of Organizational Culture

Although an organization's code of ethics guides decision making when ethical questions arise, managers can go one step further by ensuring that important ethical values and norms are key features of an organization's culture. For example, Herb Kelleher and Coleen Barrett created Southwest Airlines' culture in which promoting employee well-being is a main company priority; this translates into organizational values and norms dictating that layoffs should be avoided and employees should share in the profits the company makes.[48] Google, UPS, and Toyota are among the many companies that espouse similar values. When ethical values and norms such as these are part of an organization's culture, they help organizational members resist self-interested action because they recognize that they are part of something bigger than themselves.[49]

Managers' roles in developing ethical values and standards in other employees are important. Employees naturally look to those in authority to provide leadership, just as a country's citizens look to its political leaders, and managers become ethical role models whose behavior is scrutinized by subordinates. If top managers are perceived as being self-interested and not ethical, their subordinates are not likely to behave in an ethical manner. Employees may think that if it's all right for a top manager to engage in dubious behavior, it's all right for them too, and for employees this might mean slacking off, reducing customer support, and not taking supportive kinds of actions to help their company. The actions of top managers such as CEOs and the president of the United States are scrutinized so closely for ethical improprieties because their actions represent the values of their organizations and, in the case of the president, the values of the nation.

ethics ombudsperson
A manager responsible for communicating and teaching ethical standards to all employees and monitoring their conformity to those standards.

Managers can also provide a visible means of support to develop an ethical culture. Increasingly, organizations are creating the role of ethics officer, or **ethics ombudsperson**, to monitor their ethical practices and procedures. The ethics ombudsperson is responsible for communicating ethical standards to all employees, designing systems to monitor employees' conformity to those standards, and teaching managers and employees at all levels of the organization how to respond to ethical dilemmas appropriately.[50] Because the ethics ombudsperson has organizationwide authority, organizational members in any department can communicate instances of unethical behavior by their managers or coworkers without fear of retribution. This arrangement makes it easier for everyone to behave ethically. In addition, ethics ombudspeople can provide guidance when organizational members are uncertain about whether an action is ethical. Some organizations have an organizationwide ethics committee to provide guidance on ethical issues and help write and update the company code of ethics.

Ethical organizational cultures encourage organizational members to behave in a socially responsible manner. One company epitomized in the past as a prime example of an ethical, socially responsible firm was Johnson & Johnson (J&J). The ethical values and norms in Johnson & Johnson's culture, along with its credo (see http://www.jnj.com/connect/about-jnj/jnj-credo/), guided its managers to make the right decision in difficult situations for decades. However, in the 2010s, J&J's corporate reputation has become increasingly tarnished—as discussed in the "Case in the News"—as it managers lost J&J's focus on its stakeholders.

Summary and Review
LO4-1

THE NATURE OF ETHICS   Ethical issues are central to how companies and their managers make decisions, and they affect not only the efficiency and effectiveness of company operations but also the prosperity of the nation. The result of ethical behavior is a general increase in company performance and in a nation's standard of living, well-being, and wealth.

An ethical dilemma is the quandary people find themselves in when they have to decide if they should act in a way that might help another person or group and is the right thing to do, even though it might go against their own self-interest. Ethics are the inner guiding moral principles, values, and beliefs that people use to analyze or interpret a situation and then decide what is the right or appropriate way to behave.

Ethical beliefs alter and change as time passes, and as they do so laws change to reflect the changing ethical beliefs of a society.

LO4-2, 4-4   STAKEHOLDERS AND ETHICS   Stakeholders are people and groups who have a claim on and a stake in a company. The main stakeholder groups are stockholders, managers, employees, suppliers and distributors, customers, and the community, society, and nation. Companies and their managers need to make ethical business decisions that promote the well-being of their stakeholders and avoid doing them harm.

LO4-3, 4-5   To determine whether a business decision is ethical, managers can use four ethical rules to analyze it: the utilitarian, moral rights, justice, and practical rules. Managers should behave ethically because this avoids the tragedy of the commons and results in a general increase in efficiency, effectiveness, and company performance. The main determinants of differences in a manager's, company's, and country's business ethics are societal, occupational, individual, and organizational.

LO4-6   ETHICS AND SOCIAL RESPONSIBILITY   A company's stance on social responsibility is the way its managers and employees view their duty or obligation to make decisions that protect, enhance, and promote the welfare and well-being of stakeholders and society as a whole.

There are four main approaches to social responsibility: obstructionist, defensive, accommodative, and proactive. The rewards from behaving in a socially responsible way are a good reputation, the support of all organizational stakeholders, and thus superior company performance.

Management in Action

Topics for Discussion and Action

Discussion

1. What is the relationship between ethics and the law? **[LO4-1]**

2. Why do the claims and interests of stakeholders sometimes conflict? **[LO4-2]**

3. Why should managers use ethical criteria to guide their decision making? **[LO4-3]**

4. As an employee of a company, what are some of the most unethical business practices that you have encountered in its dealings with stakeholders? **[LO4-4]**

5. What are the main determinants of business ethics? **[LO4-5]**

Action

6. Find a manager and ask about the most important ethical rules he or she uses to make the right decisions. **[LO4-3]**

7. Find an example of (a) a company that has an obstructionist approach to social responsibility and (b) one that has an accommodative approach. **[LO4-6]**

Building Management Skills

Dealing with Ethical Dilemmas [LO4-1, 4-4]

Use the chapter material to decide how you, as a manager, should respond to each of the following ethical dilemmas:

1. You are planning to leave your job to go work for a competitor; your boss invites you to an important meeting where you will learn about new products your company will be bringing out next year. Do you go to the meeting?

2. You're the manager of sales in an expensive sports car dealership. A young executive who has just received a promotion comes in and wants to buy a car that you know is out of her price range. Do you encourage the executive to buy it so you can receive a big commission on the sale?

3. You sign a contract to manage a young rock band, and that group agrees to let you produce their next seven records, for which they will receive royalties of 5%. Their first record is a smash hit and sells millions. Do you increase their royalty rate on future records?

Managing Ethically [LO4-3, 4-5]

Apple Juice or Sugar Water?

In the early 1980s Beech-Nut, a maker of baby foods, was in grave financial trouble as it strove to compete with Gerber Products, the market leader. Threatened with bankruptcy if it could not lower its operating costs, Beech-Nut entered an agreement with a low-cost supplier of apple juice concentrate. The agreement would save the company over $250,000 annually when every dollar counted. Soon one of Beech-Nut's food scientists became concerned about the quality of the concentrate. He believed it was not made from apples alone but contained large quantities of corn syrup and cane sugar. He brought this information to the attention of top managers at Beech-Nut, but they were obsessed with the need to keep costs down and chose to ignore his concerns. The company continued to produce and sell its product as pure apple juice.[51]

Eventually investigators from the U.S. Food and Drug Administration (FDA) confronted Beech-Nut with evidence that the concentrate was adulterated. The top managers issued denials and quickly shipped the remaining stock of apple juice to the market before their inventory could be seized. The scientist who had questioned the purity of the apple juice had resigned from Beech-Nut, but he decided to blow the whistle on the company. He told the FDA that Beech-Nut's top management had known of the problem with the concentrate and had acted to maximize company profits rather than to inform customers about the additives in the apple juice. In 1987 the company pleaded guilty to charges that it had deliberately sold adulterated juice and was fined over $2 million. Its top managers were also found guilty and were sentenced to prison terms. The company's reputation was ruined, and it was eventually sold to Ralston Purina, now owned by Nestlé, which installed a new management team and a new ethical code of values to guide future business decisions.

Questions

1. Why is it that an organization's values and norms can become too strong and lead to unethical behavior?

2. What steps can a company take to prevent this problem—to stop its values and norms from becoming so inwardly focused that managers and employees lose sight of their responsibility to their stakeholders?

Small Group Breakout Exercise

Is Chewing Gum the "Right" Thing to Do? [LO4-1, 4-3]

Form groups of three or four people, and appoint one member as the spokesperson who will communicate your findings to the class when called on by the instructor. Then discuss the following scenario:

In the United States the right to chew gum is taken for granted. Although it is often against the rules to chew gum in a high school classroom, church, and so on, it is legal to do so on the street. If you possess or chew gum on a street in Singapore, you can be arrested. Chewing gum has been made illegal in Singapore because those in power believe it creates a mess on pavements and feel that people cannot be trusted to dispose of their gum properly and thus should have no right to use it.

1. What makes chewing gum acceptable in the United States and unacceptable in Singapore?

2. Why can you chew gum on the street but not in a church?

3. How can you use ethical principles to decide when gum chewing is ethical or unethical and if and when it should be made illegal?

Exploring the World Wide Web [LO4-2, 4-5]

Go to Walmart's website (www.walmart.com) and read the information there about the company's stance on the ethics of global outsourcing and the treatment of workers in countries abroad. Then search the web for some recent stories about Walmart's global purchasing practices and reports on the enforcement of its code of conduct.

1. What ethical principles guide Walmart's approach to global purchasing?

2. Does Walmart appear to be doing a good job of enforcing its global code of conduct?

Be the Manager [LO4-3]

Creating an Ethical Code

You are an entrepreneur who has decided to go into business and open a steak and chicken restaurant. Your business plan requires that you hire at least 20 people as chefs, waiters, and so on. As the owner, you are drawing up a list of ethical principles that each of these people will receive and must agree to when he or she accepts a job offer. These principles outline your view of what is right or acceptable behavior and what will be expected both from you and from your employees.

Create a list of the five main ethical rules or principles you will use to govern how your business operates. Be sure to spell out how these principles relate to your stakeholders; for example, state the rules you intend to follow in dealing with your employees and customers.

Bloomberg Businessweek Case in the News [LO4-1, 4-3, 4-5]

J&J Names Gorsky as New CEO after Product Recalls

Johnson & Johnson (J&J) named Alex Gorsky to succeed Chief Executive Officer William C. Weldon as the world's second biggest health care company tries to rebound from recalls of products ranging from children's Tylenol to artificial hip implants. Gorsky, 51, will take over April 26 as the ninth leader in J&J's 126-year history, the New Brunswick, New Jersey-based company said today in a statement. He emerged after a yearlong competition with Sheri S. McCoy, 53, head of the pharmaceutical unit. Weldon, 63, the departing CEO, will remain board chairman, the company said in the statement.

J&J, maker of everything from Band-Aids to cancer drugs, generated $65 billion in 2011 sales. While Gorsky takes over a company that has seen a revival in its drug business, the device unit he ran faces thousands of lawsuits over recalled artificial hips and vaginal mesh implants that prompted a safety warning last year from U.S. regulators. "It's been a challenging time for devices, but not through any of Alex's doing," said Rick Wise, a Leerink Swann & Co. analyst in New York, by telephone. Gorsky is "a thoughtful, disciplined, capable guy" who should steer J&J well, he said.

Gorsky joined J&J's Janssen Pharmaceutica unit in 1988 as a sales representative, according to a company biography. He then left the company in 2004 to join Basel, Switzerland-based Novartis AG, where he headed North American pharmaceuticals. Four years later, he returned to J&J, and he was named worldwide chairman of the devices and diagnostics group in 2009. Gorsky will be paid $1.2 million as J&J's CEO, the company said in a filing. Weldon, in

an e-mailed statement, described Gorsky as "an experienced, visionary and disciplined leader with more than 20 years of increased and broad-based responsibilities over two separate periods of employment with Johnson & Johnson." J&J sales may rise to $66.4 billion this year, Lawrence Biegelsen, a Wells Fargo Securities analyst in New York, predicted in a January 25 note to clients. That includes $26.2 billion in device revenue, $25 billion from the drug unit, and $15.2 billion from the consumer division. New York-based Pfizer Inc. is the world's biggest seller of medical products.

J&J has struggled with quality control in its consumer health units. On February 17, the company said it was recalling more than half a million bottles of infants' Tylenol, because of complaints with the bottle's SimpleMeasure dosing system. It was the latest of hundreds of millions of packets of Tylenol, Motrin, Benadryl, and other products pulled due to foul odors, adulterated ingredients, and bad labeling over two years. Sales growth in the devices unit headed by Gorsky have also slowed, hurt by unemployment in the United States and European austerity measures, Leerink Swann's Wise said. Those problems may tarnish Weldon's legacy, said Jonas, who has a buy rating on the company's stock. "They really dropped the ball in a pretty egregious way," he said. "His legacy to a certain extent will be impacted by that. But he has done a good job outside of the consumer business."

Weldon, J&J's leader since 2002, pulled off the two biggest deals in company history: the $16.6 billion purchase of Pfizer's consumer products in 2006 and last year's

agreement to buy orthopedics maker Synthes Inc. for $21.3 billion. The latter is pending regulatory reviews. The last three years brought less favorable headlines. J&J was forced to recall dozens of brands, including hundreds of millions of over-the-counter medicines and 93,000 of the faulty hip implants. It also faced a series of lawsuits for its alleged illegal marketing of prescription drugs. Through last week, J&J shares had climbed 2.6% under Weldon, trailing the 14% gain of the S&P's Health Care Index.

Questions for Discussion

1. J&J used to be a company renowned for its focus on supporting the interests of its stakeholders, and its managers went out of their way to control product safety. Using the material in this chapter, what kinds of issues and factors do you think led managers to drop the ball and make the mistakes that have cost the company hundreds of millions of dollars in fines?

2. How can J&J's new CEO Alex Gorsky work to improve the ethical values in J&J's culture to ensure it will not engage in unethical and even illegal actions again? What kind of stance on social responsibility should J&J adopt to restore customer goodwill?

3. Search the web for information about how J&J is working to improve its ethical decision making.

CHAPTER 5

Managing Diverse Employees in a Multicultural Environment

Learning Objectives

After studying this chapter, you should be able to:

LO5-1 Discuss the increasing diversity of the workforce and the organizational environment.

LO5-2 Explain the central role that managers play in the effective management of diversity.

LO5-3 Explain why the effective management of diversity is both an ethical and a business imperative.

LO5-4 Discuss how perception and the use of schemas can result in unfair treatment.

LO5-5 List the steps managers can take to effectively manage diversity.

LO5-6 Identify the two major forms of sexual harassment and how they can be eliminated.

A MANAGER'S CHALLENGE

Sodexo and Principal Financial Group Effectively Manage Diversity in Multiple Ways

What steps can organizations take to effectively manage an increasingly diverse workforce? By all counts, the diversity of the workforce is increasing. Effectively managing diversity is more than just ensuring that diverse members of organizations are treated fairly (itself a challenging task). When diversity is effectively managed, organizations can benefit from the diverse perspectives, points of view, experiences, and knowledge bases of their diverse members to produce better goods and services and be responsive to their increasingly diverse customer bases.

Extolling the benefits of effectively managing diversity is one thing; taking real and tangible steps to ensure that an organization continuously improves in this regard is another. Both organizationwide initiatives and the steps that each individual manager takes to effectively manage diversity have the potential for substantial payoffs in terms of both improved organizational effectiveness and maintaining a satisfied, committed, and motivated workforce.

Consider the steps that Sodexo, Inc., a major food and facilities management company serving over 10 million customers per day in businesses, health care facilities, schools and universities, and government

agencies, takes to ensure that diversity is effectively managed.[1] Sodexo encourages managers like Ron Bond, in his late 50s, to interact with diverse groups to gain a better appreciation and understanding of their experiences. When Bond attended a meeting of the Women's Food Service Forum with some of his female coworkers, he stood out as one of the few men in attendance among 1,500 women. Thinking back on his own experiences when, for example, he started out his career and women were rare in the management ranks, Bond gained a deeper appreciation of what it means to be different

Managers at Sodexo, which supplies and manages cafeterias like this one, have taken numerous steps to effectively manage diversity.

in a group or organization. As he suggests, "That's a profound experience . . . I can begin to feel what it must have felt like to be different."[2]

Sodexo provides employees and managers with extensive diversity training, encourages managers to mentor and coach employees who are different from themselves, and bases 25% of top managers' bonuses on their performance on diversity initiatives, including hiring and training diverse employees.[3] Managers are encouraged to sponsor affinity groups for employees that differ from themselves. For example, Bond sponsored the women's affinity group, which provides a forum for female employees to connect with each other and address their mutual concerns (such as a lactation room so new mothers can pump breast milk). Sponsoring such groups helps managers become aware of and address concerns of some employee groups they might never have thought of otherwise. Bond realized that having a lactation room was "just one of those things I'd never thought about."[4]

Lorna Donatone manages a unit of Sodexo that provides food services for cruise companies. Of Swedish and German ancestry and raised in Nebraska, she sponsored Sodexo's Latino affinity group and discovered a better way to serve her unit's customers. Donatone now relies on more bilingual materials to promote the services she provides to cruise companies and their customers. As senior vice president and global chief diversity officer for Sodexo, Dr. Rohini Anand indicates, "To really engage people, you have to create a series of epiphanies and take leaders through those epiphanies."[5]

Sodexo's effective management of diversity has not gone unnoticed in the business community, and the company and its diverse employees have received numerous awards and recognition for their diversity initiatives.[6] Frequently ranked as a best place to work for diverse employees by magazines such as *DiversityInc., Working Mother,* and *Latina Style,* Sodexo received the Catalyst Award in 2012 for its efforts to provide women with opportunities for advancement.[7] Dr. Anand was named one of the Top 20 Diversity Champions by *Diversity Edge* magazine, and Ivan Gutierrez, who heads up Sodexo's supply management unit, was named one of 28 Young Hispanic Corporate Achievers by the Hispanic Association on Corporate Responsibility.[8]

Principal Financial Group, headquartered in Des Moines, Iowa, operates in a vastly different industry: financial products, services, and insurance.[9] Yet Principal Financial also has been recognized for its effective management of diversity by *Fortune* magazine; Principal earned the second highest rating in the Corporate Equality Index of the Human Rights Campaign.[10] To ensure that opportunities are open for diverse employees, Principal has offered its employees flexible work schedules since 1974—decades before many other companies provided this option. And employees who take advantage of this and other benefits, such as having 12 weeks off work after the birth of a child, do not find their career progress hampered as is sometimes the case at other companies.[11]

Valarie Vest, a regional client service director at Principal, was on her second maternity leave when her supervisors called to offer her a promotion to a position that included more responsibility, more travel, and relocation to a different city. They thought she was the best candidate for the position and let her decide if she wanted to take it. She was delighted to accept the position, which includes managing 10 employees.[12]

Principal seeks to hire diverse employees and then gives them the resources and opportunities to help them reach their potential while helping Principal achieve its goals. These resources and opportunities include, but are not limited to, mentoring programs, multicultural celebrations, on-site child care, development programs, and domestic partner benefits.[13] Additionally, there are a variety of employee resource groups that all employees can join to network, engage in career development activities, and become involved in the community.[14] Thus, it is not surprising that Principal continues to receive rewards and recognition for its effective management of diversity. For example, in 2012, Principal was named a Top 50 Company for Executive Women by the National Association for Female Executives.[15]

All in all, Sodexo and Principal Financial Group are among the growing numbers of companies that are reaping the benefits of an increasingly diverse workforce.

Overview

As indicated in "A Manager's Challenge," effective management of diversity means much more than hiring diverse employees. It means learning to appreciate and respond appropriately to the needs, attitudes, beliefs, and values that diverse people bring to an organization. It also means correcting misconceptions about why and how various kinds of employee groups differ from one another and finding the most effective way to use the skills and talents of diverse employees.

In this chapter we focus on the effective management of diversity in an environment that is becoming increasingly diverse in all respects. Not only is the diversity of the global workforce increasing, but suppliers and customers are also becoming increasingly diverse. Managers need to proactively manage diversity to attract and retain the best employees and effectively compete in a diverse global environment. For example, managers at the audit and consulting firm Deloitte & Touche have instituted a program to encourage minority suppliers to compete for its business, and the firm sponsors schools and colleges that supply a stream of well-trained recruits.[16]

Sometimes well-intentioned managers inadvertently treat one group of employees differently from another group, even though there are no performance-based differences between the two groups. This chapter explores why differential treatment occurs and the steps managers and organizations can take to ensure that diversity, in all respects, is effectively managed for the good of all organizational stakeholders.

LO5-1 Discuss the increasing diversity of the workforce and the organizational environment.

The Increasing Diversity of the Workforce and the Environment

One of the most important management issues to emerge over the last 40 years has been the increasing diversity of the workforce. **Diversity** is dissimilarities—differences—among people due to age, gender, race, ethnicity, religion, sexual orientation, socioeconomic background, education, experience, physical appearance, capabilities/disabilities, and any other characteristic that is used to distinguish between people (see Figure 5.1).

Diversity raises important ethical issues and social responsibility issues (see Chapter 4). It is also a critical issue for organizations, one that if not handled well can bring an organization to its knees, especially in our increasingly global

Figure 5.1

Sources of Diversity in the Workplace

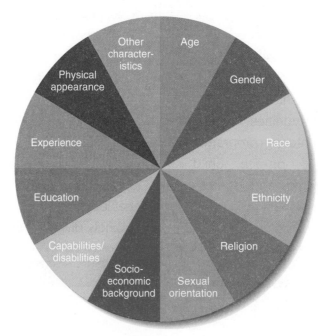

environment. There are several reasons why diversity is such a pressing concern and an issue both in the popular press and for managers and organizations:

- There is a strong ethical imperative in many societies that diverse people must receive equal opportunities and be treated fairly and justly. Unfair treatment is also illegal.

- Effectively managing diversity can improve organizational effectiveness.[17] When managers effectively manage diversity, they not only encourage other managers to treat diverse members of an organization fairly and justly but also realize that diversity is an important organizational resource that can help an organization gain a competitive advantage.

- There is substantial evidence that diverse individuals continue to experience unfair treatment in the workplace as a result of biases, stereotypes, and overt discrimination.[18] In one study, résumés of equally qualified men and women were sent to high-priced Philadelphia restaurants (where potential earnings are high). Though equally qualified, men were more than twice as likely as women to be called for a job interview and more than five times as likely to receive a job offer.[19] Findings from another study suggest that both women and men tend to believe that women will accept lower pay than men; this is a possible explanation for the continuing gap in pay between men and women.[20]

Other kinds of diverse employees may face even greater barriers. For example, the federal Glass Ceiling Commission Report indicated that African Americans have the hardest time being promoted and climbing the corporate ladder, that Asians are often stereotyped into technical jobs, and that Hispanics are assumed to be less well educated than other minority groups.[21] (The term **glass ceiling** alludes to the invisible barriers that prevent minorities and women from being promoted to top corporate positions.)[22]

Before we can discuss the multitude of issues surrounding the effective management of diversity, we must document just how diverse the U.S. workforce is becoming.

glass ceiling A metaphor alluding to the invisible barriers that prevent minorities and women from being promoted to top corporate positions.

Age

According to data from the U.S. Census Bureau and the CIA's World Fact Book, the median age of a person in the United States is the highest it has ever been, 36.9 years.[23] Moreover, by 2030 it is projected that close to 20% of the population will be 65 or over.[24] The Age Discrimination in Employment Act of 1967 prohibits age discrimination.[25] Although we discuss federal employment legislation in more depth in Chapter 12, major equal employment opportunity legislation that prohibits discrimination among diverse groups is summarized in Table 5.1.

The aging of the population suggests managers need to be vigilant to ensure that employees are not discriminated against because of age. Moreover, managers need to ensure that the policies and procedures they have in place treat all workers fairly, regardless of their ages. Additionally, effectively managing diversity means employees of diverse ages are able to learn from each other, work well together, and take advantage of the different perspectives each has to offer.

Gender

Women and men are almost equally represented in the U.S. workforce (approximately 53.3% of the U.S. workforce is male and 46.7% female),[26] yet women's median weekly earnings are esti-

At Loft Studio Marcel Weber, a more experienced architect helps guide a new employee—just one example of how respecting and valuing each person's unique contributions actually benefits your bottom line and your long-term success.

mated to be $688 compared to $843 for men.[27] Thus the gender pay gap appears to be as alive and well as the glass ceiling. According to the nonprofit organization Catalyst, which studies women in business, while women compose about 51.5% of the employees in managerial and professional positions,[28] only around 14.1% of executive officers in the 500 largest U.S. companies (that is, the *Fortune* 500) are women, and only 7.5% of the top earner executive officers are women.[29] These women, such as Virginia Rometty, CEO of IBM, and Indra Nooyi, CEO of PepsiCo, stand out among their male peers and often receive a disparate amount of attention in the media. (We address this issue later, when we discuss the effects of being salient.) Women are also very underrepresented on boards of directors—they currently hold 16.1% of the board seats of *Fortune* 500 companies.[30] However, as Sheila Wellington, former president of Catalyst, indicates, "Women either control or influence nearly all consumer purchases, so it's important to have their perspective represented on boards."[31]

Table 5.1
Major Equal Employment Opportunity Laws Affecting Human Resources Management

Year	Law	Description
1963	Equal Pay Act	Requires that men and women be paid equally if they are performing equal work.
1964	Title VII of the Civil Rights Act	Prohibits discrimination in employment decisions on the basis of race, religion, sex, color, or national origin; covers a wide range of employment decisions, including hiring, firing, pay, promotion, and working conditions.
1967	Age Discrimination in Employment Act	Prohibits discrimination against workers over the age of 40 and restricts mandatory retirement.
1978	Pregnancy Discrimination Act	Prohibits discrimination against women in employment decisions on the basis of pregnancy, childbirth, and related medical decisions.
1990	Americans with Disabilities Act	Prohibits discrimination against disabled individuals in employment decisions and requires that employers make accommodations for disabled workers to enable them to perform their jobs.
1991	Civil Rights Act	Prohibits discrimination (as does Title VII) and allows for the awarding of punitive and compensatory damages, in addition to back pay, in cases of intentional discrimination.
1993	Family and Medical Leave Act	Requires that employers provide 12 weeks of unpaid leave for medical and family reasons, including paternity and illness of a family member.

A female executive enjoying the company plane is not as rare a sight today as it used to be; nevertheless, the glass ceiling remains a very real barrier to women in the business workforce.

Additionally, research conducted by consulting firms suggests that female executives outperform their male colleagues in skills such as motivating others, promoting good communication, turning out high-quality work, and being a good listener.[32] For example, the Hagberg Group performed in-depth evaluations of 425 top executives in a variety of industries, with each executive rated by approximately 25 people. Of the 52 skills assessed, women received higher ratings than men on 42 skills, although at times the differences were small.[33] Results of a study conducted by Catalyst found that organizations with higher proportions of women in top management positions had significantly better financial performance than organizations with lower proportions of female top managers.[34] Another study conducted by Catalyst found that companies with three or more women on their boards of directors performed better in terms of returns on equity, sales, and invested capital than companies with fewer women on their boards or no women.[35] All in all, studies such as these make one wonder why the glass ceiling continues to hamper the progress of women in business (a topic we address later in the chapter).

Race and Ethnicity

The U.S. Census Bureau distinguished between the following races in the 2010 Census: American Indian or Alaska Native, Asian Indian, Black, African American, or Negro, Chinese, Filipino, Japanese, Korean, Vietnamese, Other Asian, Native Hawaiian, Guamanian or Chamorro, Samoan, Other Pacific Islander, White, and other races.[36] Although *ethnicity* refers to a grouping of people based on some shared characteristic such as national origin, language, or culture, the U.S. Census Bureau treats ethnicity in terms of whether a person is Hispanic, Latino, or of Spanish origin or not.[37] Hispanics, also referred to as Latinos, are people whose origins are in Spanish cultures such as those of Cuba, Mexico, Puerto Rico, and South and Central America. Hispanics can be of different races.[38] According to a recent poll, most Hispanics prefer to be identified by their country of origin (such as Mexican, Cuban, or Salvadoran) rather than by the overarching term *Hispanic*.[39]

The racial and ethnic diversity of the U.S. population is increasing at an exponential rate, as is the composition of the workforce.[40] According to the U.S. Census Bureau, approximately one of every three U.S. residents belongs to a minority group (i.e., is not a non-Hispanic White).[41] More specifically, 16.3% of the population is Hispanic or Latino, 83.7% of the population is not Hispanic or Latino, and 63.7% of the population is White alone (i.e., white and not Hispanic or Latino).[42] For those individuals self-identifying one race in the 2010 U.S. Census, approximately 72.4% of the population is White, 12.6% is Black or African American, 0.9% is American Indian or Alaska Native, 4.8% is Asian, 0.2% is Native Hawaiian and Other Pacific Islander, and 6.2% is another race; 2.9% of the population self-identified two or more races.[43] According to projections released by the U.S. Census Bureau, the composition of the U.S. population in 2050 will be quite different from its composition today; in 2050, the U.S. population is projected to be 54% minority.[44]

The increasing racial and ethnic diversity of the workforce and the population as a whole underscores the importance of effectively managing diversity. Statistics compiled by the Bureau of Labor statistics suggest that much needs to be done in terms of ensuring that diverse employees have equal opportunities. For example, median weekly earnings for Black men are approximately 75.8% of median earnings for White men; median weekly earnings for Black women are approximately 84.8% of median earnings for White women.[45] In the remainder of this chapter, we focus on the fair treatment of diverse employees and explore why this is such an important challenge and what managers can do to meet it. We begin by taking a broader perspective and considering how increasing racial and ethnic diversity in an organization's environment (such as customers and suppliers) affects decision making and organizational effectiveness.

At a general level, managers and organizations are increasingly being reminded that stakeholders in the environment are diverse and expect organizational decisions and actions to reflect this diversity. For example, the NAACP (National Association for the Advancement of Colored People) and Children Now (an advocacy group) have lobbied the entertainment industry to increase the diversity in television programming, writing, and producing.[46] The need for such increased diversity is more than apparent. For example, while Hispanics make up 12.5% of the U.S. population (or 35 million potential TV viewers), only about 2% of the characters in prime-time TV shows are Hispanics (of the 2,251 characters in prime-time shows, only 47 are Hispanic), according to a study conducted by Children Now.[47] Moreover, only about 1.3% of the evening network TV news stories are reported by Hispanic correspondents, according to the Center for Media and Public Affairs.[48]

Pressure is mounting on networks to increase diversity for a variety of reasons revolving around the diversity of the population as a whole, TV viewers, and consumers. For example, home and automobile buyers are increasingly diverse, reflecting the increasing diversity of the population as a whole.[49] Moreover, managers have to be especially sensitive to avoid stereotyping different groups when they communicate with potential customers. For example, Toyota Motor Sales USA made a public apology to the Reverend Jesse Jackson and his Rainbow Coalition for using a print advertisement depicting an African-American man with a Toyota RAV4 sport utility image embossed on his gold front tooth.[50]

Religion

Title VII of the Civil Rights Act prohibits discrimination based on religion (as well as based on race/ethnicity, country of origin, and sex; see Table 5.1 and Chapter 12). In addition to enacting Title VII, in 1997 the federal government issued "The White House Guidelines on Religious Exercise and Expression in the Federal Workplace."[51] These guidelines, while technically applicable only in federal offices, also are frequently relied on by large corporations. The guidelines require that employers make reasonable accommodations for religious practices, such as observances of holidays, as long as doing so does not entail major costs or hardships.[52]

A key issue for managers when it comes to religious diversity is recognizing and being aware of different religions and their beliefs, with particular attention being paid to when religious holidays fall. For example, critical meetings should not be scheduled during a holy day for members of a certain faith, and managers should be flexible in allowing people to have time off for religious observances. According to Lobna Ismail, director of a diversity training company in Silver Spring, Maryland, when managers acknowledge, respect, and make even small accommodations for religious diversity, employee loyalty is often enhanced. For example, allowing employees to leave work early on certain days instead of taking a lunch break or posting holidays for different religions on the company calendar can go a long way toward making individuals of diverse religions feel respected and valued as well as enabling them to practice their faith.[53] According to research conducted by the Tanenbaum Center for Interreligious Understanding in New York, while only about 23% of employees who feel they are victims of religious discrimination actually file complaints, about 45% of these employees start looking for other jobs.[54]

Capabilities/Disabilities

The Americans with Disabilities Act (ADA) of 1990 prohibits discrimination against persons with disabilities and also requires that employers make reasonable accommodations to enable these people to effectively perform their jobs. On the surface, few would argue with the intent of this legislation. However, as managers attempt to implement policies and procedures to comply with the ADA, they face a number of interpretation and fairness challenges.

On one hand, some people with real disabilities warranting workplace accommodations are hesitant to reveal their disabilities to their employers and claim the accommodations they deserve.[55] On the other hand, some employees abuse the ADA by seeking unnecessary accommodations for disabilities that may or may not exist.[56] Thus it is perhaps not surprising that the passage of the ADA does not appear to have increased employment rates significantly for those with disabilities.[57] A key challenge for managers is to promote an environment in which employees needing accommodations feel comfortable disclosing their need and, at the same time, to ensure that the accommodations not only enable those with disabilities to effectively perform their jobs but also are perceived to be fair by those not disabled.[58]

In addressing this challenge, often managers must educate both themselves and their employees about the disabilities, as well as the real capabilities, of those who are disabled. For example, during Disability Awareness Week, administrators at the University of Notre Dame sought to increase the public's knowledge of disabilities while also heightening awareness of the abilities of persons who are disabled.[59] The University of Houston conducted a similar program called "Think Ability."[60] According to Cheryl Amoruso, director of the University of Houston's Center for Students with Disabilities, many people are unaware of the prevalence of disabilities as well as misinformed about their consequences. She suggests, for example, that although students may not be able to see, they can still excel in their coursework and have successful careers.[61] Accommodations enabling such students to perform up to their capabilities are covered under the ADA.

The ADA also protects employees with acquired immune deficiency syndrome (AIDS) from being discriminated against in the workplace. AIDS is caused by the human immunodeficiency virus (HIV) and is transmitted through sexual contact, infected needles, and contaminated blood products. HIV is not spread through casual nonsexual contact. Yet out of ignorance, fear, or prejudice, some people wish to avoid all contact with anyone infected with HIV. Infected individuals may not necessarily develop AIDS, and some individuals with HIV are able to remain effective performers of their jobs while not putting others at risk.[62]

AIDS awareness training can help people overcome their fears and also give managers a tool to prevent illegal discrimination against HIV-infected employees. Such training focuses on educating employees about HIV and AIDS, dispelling myths, communicating relevant organizational policies, and emphasizing the rights of HIV-positive employees to privacy and an environment that allows them to be productive.[63] The need for AIDS awareness training is underscored by some of the problems HIV-positive employees experience once others in their workplace become aware of their condition.[64] Moreover, organizations are required to make reasonable accommodations to enable people with AIDS to effectively perform their jobs.

Thus managers have an obligation to educate employees about HIV and AIDS, dispel myths and the stigma of AIDS, and ensure that HIV-related discrimination is not occurring in the workplace. For example, Home Depot has provided HIV training and education to its store managers; such training was sorely needed given that over half of the managers indicated it was the first time they had the opportunity to talk about AIDS.[65] Moreover, advances in medication and treatment mean that more infected individuals are able to continue working or are able to return to work after their condition improves. Thus managers need to ensure that these employees are fairly treated by all members of their organizations.[66] And managers and organizations that do not treat HIV-positive employees in a fair manner, as well as provide reasonable accommodations (such as allowing time off for doctor visits or to take medicine), risk costly lawsuits.

Socioeconomic Background

The term *socioeconomic background* typically refers to a combination of social class and income-related factors. From a management perspective, socioeconomic diversity (and in particular diversity in income levels) requires that managers be sensitive and responsive to the needs and concerns of individuals who might not be as well off as others. U.S. welfare reform in the middle to late 1990s emphasized the need for single mothers and others receiving public assistance to join or return to the workforce. In conjunction with a strong economy, this led to record declines in the number of families, households, and children living below the poverty level, according to the 2000 U.S. census.[67] However, the economic downturns in the early and late 2000s suggest that some past gains, which lifted families out of poverty, have been reversed. In a strong economy, it is much easier for poor people with few skills to find jobs; in a weak economy, when companies lay off employees in hard times, people who need their incomes the most are unfortunately often the first to lose their jobs.[68] And in recessionary times, it is difficult for laid-off employees to find new positions. For example, in December 2009 there was an average of 6.1 unemployed workers for every open position.[69]

According to statistics released by the US Census Bureau in 2011, the official poverty rate in the United States increased to 15.1% or 46.2 million people in 2010; in 2009, the poverty rate was 14.3% or 43.6 million people.[70] The Census Bureau relies on predetermined threshold income figures, based on family size and composition, adjusted annually for inflation, to determine the poverty level. Families whose income falls below the threshold level are considered poor.[71] For example, in 2010 a family of four was considered poor if their annual income fell below $22,314.[72] When workers earn less than $10 or $15 per hour, it is often difficult, if not impossible, for them to meet their families' needs.[73] Moreover, increasing numbers of families are facing the challenge of finding suitable child care arrangements that enable the adults to work long hours and/or through the night to maintain an adequate income level. New information technology has led to more businesses operating 24 hours a day, creating real challenges for workers on the night shift, especially those with children.[74]

Hundreds of thousands of parents across the country are scrambling to find someone to care for their children while they are working the night shift, commuting several hours a day, working weekends and holidays, or putting in long hours on one or more jobs. This has led to the opening of day care facilities that operate around the clock as well as to managers seeking ways to provide such care for children of their employees. For example, the Children's Choice Learning Center in Las Vegas, Nevada, operates around the clock to accommodate employees working nights in neighboring casinos, hospitals, and call centers. Randy Donahue, a security guard who works until midnight, picks his children up from the center when he gets off work; his wife is a nurse on the night shift.[75]

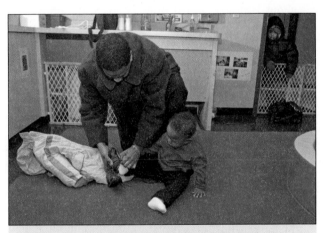

A father drops his children off at a day care facility before going to work. Managers need to be aware that many employees deal with challenging socioeconomic factors such as long commutes and finding suitable child care arrangements.

Judy Harden, who focuses on families and child care issues for the United Workers Union, indicates that the demands families are facing necessitate around-the-clock and odd-hour child care options. Many parents simply do not have the choice of working at hours that allow them to take care of their children at night and/or on weekends, never mind when the children are sick.[76] Some parents and psychologists feel uneasy having children separated from their families for so much time and particularly at night. Most agree that, unfortunately for many families, this is not a choice but a necessity.[77]

Socioeconomic diversity suggests that managers need to be sensitive and responsive to the needs and concerns of workers who may be less fortunate than themselves in terms of income and financial resources, child care and elder care options, housing opportunities, and existence of sources of social and family support. Moreover—and equally important—managers should try to give such individuals opportunities to learn, advance, and make meaningful contributions to their organizations while improving their economic well-being.

Sexual Orientation

According to research conducted by Gary Gates of the Williams Institute at the UCLA School of Law, approximately 3.5% of adults in the United States or 9 million U.S. residents self-identify as lesbian, gay, bisexual, or transgender (LGBT).[78] Although no federal law prohibits discrimination based on sexual orientation, 20 states have such laws, and a 1998 executive order prohibits sexual orientation discrimination in civilian federal offices.[79] Moreover, an increasing number of organizations recognize the minority status of LGBT employees, affirm their rights to fair and equal treatment, and provide benefits to same-sex partners of gay and lesbian employees.[80] For example, a vast majority of *Fortune* 500 companies prohibit discrimination based on sexual orientation, and a majority of the *Fortune* 500 provide domestic partner benefits.[81] As indicated in the following "Focus on Diversity" box, managers can take many steps to ensure that sexual orientation is not used to unfairly discriminate among employees.

Preventing Discrimination Based on Sexual Orientation

Although gays and lesbians have made great strides in attaining fair treatment in the workplace, much more needs to be done. In a study conducted by Harris Interactive Inc. (a research firm) and Witeck Communications Inc. (a marketing firm), over 40% of gay and lesbian employees indicated that they had been unfairly treated, denied a promotion, or pushed to quit their jobs because of their sexual orientation.[82] Given continued harassment and discrimination despite the progress that has been made,[83] many gay and lesbian employees fear disclosing their sexual orientation in the workplace and thus live a life of secrecy. While there are a few openly gay top managers, such as David Geffen, cofounder of DreamWorks SKG, and Allan Gilmour, former vice chairman and CFO of Ford and currently a member of the board of directors of DTE Energy Holding Company, many others choose not to disclose or discuss their personal lives, including long-term partners.[84]

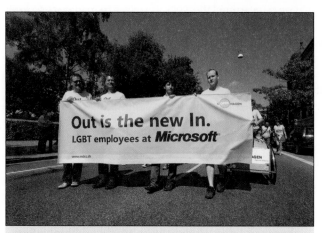

Danish employees of Microsoft raise awareness at Copenhagen's annual Gay Pride Parade. Corporate backing, such as that displayed here, can go a long way towards making sure workplaces are safe and respectful for everyone.

Thus it is not surprising that many managers are taking active steps to educate and train their employees about issues of sexual orientation. S. C. Johnson & Sons, Inc., maker of Raid insecticide and Glade air fresheners in Racine, Wisconsin, provides mandatory training to its plant managers to overturn stereotypes; and Eastman Kodak, Merck & Co., Ernst & Young, and Toronto-Dominion Bank all train managers in how to prevent sexual orientation discrimination.[85] Other organizations such as Lucent Technologies, Microsoft, and Southern California Edison send employees to seminars conducted at prominent business schools. And many companies such as Raytheon, IBM, Eastman Kodak, and Lockheed Martin provide assistance to their gay and lesbian employees through gay and lesbian support groups.[86] Recently, JPMorgan Chase, Goldman Sachs Group, and Bank of America were recognized as Best Places to Work 2012 for gay, lesbian, bisexual, and transgender employees by the Human Rights Campaign, a nonprofit organization that advocates for the civil rights of LGBT people.[87]

The Chubb Group of Insurance Companies, a property and casualty insurance company, provides its managers with a two-hour training session to help create work environments that are safe and welcoming for lesbian, gay, bisexual, and transgender (LGBT) people.[88] The sessions are conducted by two Chubb employees; usually one of the trainers is straight and the other is gay. The sessions focus on issues that affect a manager's ability to lead diverse teams, such as assessing how safe and welcoming the workplace is for LGBT people, how to refer to gay employees' significant others, and how to respond if employees or customers use inappropriate language or behavior. The idea for the program originated from one of Chubb's employee resource groups. Managers rate the program highly and say they are better able to respond to the concerns of their LGBT employees while creating a safe and productive work environment for all.[89] In 2012, the Chubb Group was also recognized as one of the Best Places to Work by the Human Right Campaign.[90]

Other Kinds of Diversity

Other kinds of diversity are important in organizations, are critical for managers to deal with effectively, and also are potential sources of unfair treatment. For example, organizations and teams need members with diverse backgrounds and experiences. This is clearly illustrated by the prevalence of cross-functional teams in organizations whose members might come from various departments such as marketing, production, finance, and sales (teams are covered in depth in Chapter 15). A team responsible for developing and introducing a new product, for example, often needs the expertise of employees not only from R&D and engineering but also from marketing, sales, production, and finance.

Other types of diversity can affect how employees are treated in the workplace. For example, employees differ from each other in how attractive they are (based on the standards of the cultures in which an organization operates) and in body weight. Whether individuals are attractive or unattractive, thin or overweight, in most cases has no bearing on their job performance unless they have jobs in which physical appearance plays a role, such as modeling. Yet sometimes these physical sources of diversity end up influencing advancement rates and salaries. A study published in the *American Journal of Public Health* found that highly educated obese women earned approximately 30% less per year than women who were not obese and men (regardless of whether or not the men were obese).[91] Clearly managers need to ensure that all employees are treated fairly, regardless of their physical appearance.

LO5-2 Explain the central role that managers play in the effective management of diversity.

Managers and the Effective Management of Diversity

The increasing diversity of the environment—which, in turn, increases the diversity of an organization's workforce—increases the challenges managers face in effectively managing diversity. Each of the kinds of diversity just discussed presents a particular set of issues managers need to appreciate before they can respond to them effectively. Understanding these issues is not always a simple matter, as many informed managers have discovered. Research on how different groups are currently treated and the unconscious biases that might adversely affect them is vital because it helps managers become aware of the many subtle and unobtrusive ways in which diverse employee groups can come to be treated unfairly over time. Managers can take many more steps to become sensitive to the ongoing effects of diversity in their organizations, take advantage of all the contributions diverse employees can make, and prevent diverse employees from being unfairly treated.

Critical Managerial Roles

In each of their managerial roles (see Chapter 1), managers can either promote the effective management of diversity or derail such efforts; thus they are critical to this process. For example, in their interpersonal roles, managers can convey that the effective management of diversity is a valued goal and objective (figurehead role), can serve as a role model and institute policies and procedures to ensure that diverse organizational members are treated fairly (leader role), and can enable diverse individuals and groups to coordinate their efforts and cooperate with each other both inside the organization and at the organization's boundaries (liaison role). In Table 5.2 we summarize some ways managers can ensure that diversity is effectively managed as they perform their different roles.

Given the formal authority that managers have in organizations, they typically have more influence than rank-and-file employees. When managers commit to supporting diversity, as was discussed for managers at Sodexo and Principal Financial Group in "A Manager's Challenge," their authority and positions of power and status influence other members of an organization to make a similar commitment.[92] Research on social influence supports such a link: People are likely to be influenced and persuaded by others who have high status.[93]

Table 5.2

Managerial Roles and the Effective Management of Diversity

Type of Role	Specific Role	Example
Interpersonal	Figurehead	Conveys that the effective management of diversity is a valued goal and objective.
	Leader	Serves as a role model and institutes policies and procedures to ensure that diverse members are treated fairly.
	Liaison	Enables diverse individuals to coordinate their efforts and cooperate with one another.
Informational	Monitor	Evaluates the extent to which diverse employees are being treated fairly.
	Disseminator	Informs employees about diversity policies and initiatives and the intolerance of discrimination.
	Spokesperson	Supports diversity initiatives in the wider community and speaks to diverse groups to interest them in career opportunities.
Decisional	Entrepreneur	Commits resources to develop new ways to effectively manage diversity and eliminate biases and discrimination.
	Disturbance handler	Takes quick action to correct inequalities and curtail discriminatory behavior.
	Resource allocator	Allocates resources to support and encourage the effective management of diversity.
	Negotiator	Works with organizations (e.g., suppliers) and groups (e.g., labor unions) to support and encourage the effective management of diversity.

Moreover, when managers commit to diversity, their commitment legitimizes the diversity management efforts of others.[94] In addition, resources are devoted to such efforts, and all members of an organization believe that their diversity-related efforts are supported and valued. Consistent with this reasoning, top management commitment and rewards for the support of diversity are often cited as critical ingredients in the success of diversity management initiatives.[95] Additionally, seeing managers express confidence in the abilities and talents of diverse employees causes other organizational members to be similarly confident and helps reduce any misconceived misgivings they may have as a result of ignorance or stereotypes.[96]

Two other important factors emphasize why managers are so central to the effective management of diversity. The first factor is that women, African Americans, Hispanics, and other minorities often start out at a slight disadvantage due to how they are perceived by others in organizations, particularly in work settings where they are a numerical minority. As Virginia Valian, a psychologist at Hunter College who studies gender, indicates, "In most organizations women begin at a slight disadvantage. A woman does not walk into the room with the same status as an equivalent man, because she is less likely than a man to be viewed as a serious professional."[97]

The second factor is that research suggests that slight differences in treatment can accumulate and result in major disparities over time. Even small differences—such as a very slight favorable bias toward men for promotions—can lead to major differences in the number of male and female managers over time.[98] Thus while women and other minorities are sometimes advised not to make "a mountain out of a molehill" when they perceive they have been unfairly treated, research conducted by Valian and others suggests that molehills (slight differences in treatment based on irrelevant distinctions such as race, gender, or ethnicity) can turn into mountains over time (major disparities in important outcomes such as promotions) if they are ignored.[99] Once again, managers have the obligation, from both an ethical and a business perspective, to prevent any disparities in treatment and outcomes due to irrelevant distinctions such as race or ethnicity.

The Ethical Imperative to Manage Diversity Effectively

Effectively managing diversity not only makes good business sense (which is discussed in the next section) but also is an ethical imperative in U.S. society. Two moral principles guide managers in their efforts to meet this imperative: distributive justice and procedural justice.

distributive justice A moral principle calling for fair distribution of pay, promotions, and other organizational resources based on meaningful contributions that individuals have made and not personal characteristics over which they have no control.

DISTRIBUTIVE JUSTICE   The principle of **distributive justice** dictates fair distribution of pay, promotions, job titles, interesting job assignments, office space, and other organizational resources among members of an organization. These outcomes should be distributed according to the meaningful contributions that individuals have made to the organization (such as time, effort, education, skills, abilities, and performance levels) and not irrelevant personal characteristics over which individuals have no control (such as gender, race, or age).[100] Managers have an obligation to ensure that distributive justice exists in their organizations. This does not mean that all members of an organization receive identical or similar outcomes; rather, it means that members who receive more favorable outcomes than others have made substantially higher or more significant contributions to the organization.

Is distributive justice common in organizations in corporate America? Probably the best way to answer this question is to say things are getting better. Fifty years ago, overt discrimination against women and minorities was common; today organizations are inching closer toward the ideal of distributive justice. Statistics comparing the treatment of women and minorities with the treatment of other employees suggest that most managers need to take a proactive approach to achieve distributive justice in their organizations.[101] For example, across occupations, women consistently earn less than men (see Table 5.3) according to data collected by the U.S. Bureau of Labor Statistics.[102] Even in occupations dominated by women, such as sales and office occupations, men tend to earn more than women.[103]

In many countries, managers have not only an ethical obligation to strive to achieve distributive justice in their organizations but also a legal obligation to treat all employees fairly. They risk being sued by employees who believe they are not being fairly treated. That is precisely what six African-American Texaco employees did when they experienced racial bias and discrimination.[104]

procedural justice A moral principle calling for the use of fair procedures to determine how to distribute outcomes to organizational members.

PROCEDURAL JUSTICE   The principle of **procedural justice** requires that managers use fair procedures to determine how to distribute outcomes to organizational members.[105] This principle applies to typical procedures such as appraising subordinates' performance, deciding who should receive a raise or a promotion, and deciding whom to lay off when an organization is forced to downsize. Procedural justice exists, for example, when managers (1) carefully appraise a subordinate's performance; (2) take into account any environmental obstacles to high performance beyond the subordinate's control, such as lack of supplies,

Table 5.3

Median Weekly Earnings for Full-Time Workers by Sex and Occupation in 2011

Occupation	Men	Women	Women's Earnings as a Percentage of Men's
Management, professional, and related	$1,269	$941	74
Service	551	433	79
Sales and office	738	602	82
Natural resources, construction, and maintenance	740	515	70
Production, transportation, and material moving	651	485	75

Source: "Household Data; Annual Averages; 39. Median Weekly Earnings of Full-Time Wage and Salary Workers by Detailed Occupation and Sex," http://www.bls.gov/cps/cpsaat39.pdf, April 11, 2012.

machine breakdowns, or dwindling customer demand for a product; and (3) ignore irrelevant personal characteristics such as the subordinate's age or ethnicity. Like distributive justice, procedural justice is necessary not only to ensure ethical conduct but also to avoid costly lawsuits.

Effectively Managing Diversity Makes Good Business Sense

Diverse organizational members can be a source of competitive advantage, helping an organization provide customers with better goods and services.[106] The variety of points of view and approaches to problems and opportunities that diverse employees provide can improve managerial decision making. Suppose the Budget Gourmet frozen food company is trying to come up with creative ideas for new frozen meals that will appeal to health-conscious, time-conscious customers tired of the same old frozen fare. Which group do you think is likely to come up with the most creative ideas: a group of white women with marketing degrees from Yale University who grew up in upper-middle-class families in the Northeast or a racially mixed group of men and women who grew up in families with varying income levels in different parts of the country and attended a mix of business schools (New York University, Oklahoma State, University of Michigan, UCLA, Cornell University, Texas A&M University, and Iowa State)? Most people would agree that the diverse group is likely to have a wider range of creative ideas. Although this example is simplistic, it underscores one way in which diversity can lead to a competitive advantage.

Just as the workforce is becoming increasingly diverse, so too are the customers who buy an organization's goods or services. In an attempt to suit local customers' needs and tastes, organizations like Target often vary the selection of products available in stores in different cities and regions.[107]

Diverse members of an organization are likely to be attuned to what goods and services diverse segments of the market want and do not want. Automakers, for example, are increasingly assigning women to their design teams to ensure that the needs and desires of female customers are taken into account in new car design.

For Darden Restaurants, the business case for diversity rests on market share and growth. Darden seeks to satisfy the needs and tastes of diverse customers by providing menus in Spanish in communities with large Hispanic populations.[108] Similarly, market share and growth and the identification of niche markets led Tracey Campbell to cater to travelers with disabilities.[109] She heads InnSeekers, a telephone and online listing resource for bed and breakfasts. Nikki Daruwala works for the Calvert Group in Bethesda, Maryland, a mutual fund that emphasizes social responsibility and diversity. She indicates that profit alone is more than enough of an incentive to effectively manage diversity. As she puts it, "You can look at an automaker. There are more women making decisions about car buying or home buying . . . $3.72 trillion per year are spent by women."[110]

Another way that effective management of diversity can improve profitability is by increasing retention of valued employees, which decreases the costs of hiring replacements for those who quit as well as ensures that all employees are highly motivated. In terms of retention, given the current legal environment, more and more organizations are attuned to the need to emphasize the importance of diversity in hiring. Once hired, if diverse employees think they are being unfairly treated, however, they will be likely to seek opportunities elsewhere. Thus recruiting diverse employees has to be followed up by ongoing effective management of diversity to retain valued organizational members.

If diversity is not effectively managed and turnover rates are higher for members of groups who are not treated fairly, profitability will suffer on several counts. Not only are the future contributions of diverse employees lost when they quit, but the organization also has to bear the costs of hiring replacement workers. According to the Employment Management Association, on average it costs more than $10,000 to hire a new employee; other estimates are significantly higher. For example, Ernst & Young estimates it costs about $1,200,000 to replace 10 professionals, and the diversity consulting firm Hubbard & Hubbard estimates replacement costs average one-and-a-half times an employee's annual salary.[111] Moreover, additional costs from failing to effectively manage diversity stem from time lost due to the barriers diverse members of an organization perceive as thwarting their progress and advancement.[112]

Effectively managing diversity makes good business sense for another reason. More and more, managers and organizations concerned about diversity are insisting that their suppliers also support diversity.[113]

Finally, from both business and ethical perspectives, effective management of diversity is necessary to avoid costly lawsuits such as those settled by Advantica (owner of the Denny's chain) and the Coca-Cola Company. In 2000 Coca-Cola settled a class action suit brought by African-American employees, at a cost of $192 million. The damage such lawsuits cause goes beyond the monetary awards to the injured parties; it can tarnish a company's image. One positive outcome of Coca-Cola's 2000 settlement is the company's recognition of the need to commit additional resources to diversity management initiatives. Coca-Cola is increasing its use of minority suppliers, instituting a formal mentoring program, and instituting days to celebrate diversity with its workforce.[114]

By now it should be clear that effectively managing diversity is a necessity on both ethical and business grounds. This brings us to the question of why diversity presents managers and all of us with so many challenges—a question we address in the next section on perception.

LO5-4 Discuss how perception and the use of schemas can result in unfair treatment.

Perception

Most people tend to think that the decisions managers make in organizations and the actions they take are the result of objective determination of the issues involved and the surrounding situation. However, each manager's interpretation of a situation or even of another person is precisely that—an interpretation. Nowhere are the effects of perception more likely to lead to different interpretations than in the area of diversity. This is because each person's interpretation of a situation, and subsequent response to it, is affected by his or her own age, race, gender, religion, socioeconomic status, capabilities, and sexual orientation. For example, different managers may see the same 21-year-old black male, gay, gifted, and talented subordinate in different ways: One may see a creative maverick with a great future in the organization, while another may see a potential troublemaker who needs to be watched closely.

perception The process through which people select, organize, and interpret what they see, hear, touch, smell, and taste to give meaning and order to the world around them.

Perception is the process through which people select, organize, and interpret sensory input—what they see, hear, touch, smell, and taste—to give meaning and order to the world around them.[115] All decisions and actions of managers are based on their subjective perceptions. When these perceptions are relatively accurate—close to the true nature of what is actually being perceived—good decisions are likely to be made and appropriate actions taken. Managers of fast-food restaurant chains such as McDonald's, Pizza Hut, and Wendy's accurately perceived that their customers were becoming more health-conscious in the 1980s and 1990s and added salad bars and low-fat entries to their menus. Managers at Kentucky Fried Chicken, Jack-in-the-Box, and Burger King took much longer to perceive this change in what customers wanted.

One reason why McDonald's is so successful is that its managers go to great lengths to make sure their perceptions of what customers want are accurate. McDonald's has over 14,880 restaurants outside the United States that generate over $14.1 billion in annual revenues.[116] Key to McDonald's success in these diverse markets are managers' efforts to perceive accurately a country's culture and taste in food and then to act on these perceptions. For instance, McDonald's serves veggie burgers in Holland and black currant shakes in Poland.[117]

When managers' perceptions are relatively inaccurate, managers are likely to make bad decisions and take inappropriate actions, which hurt organizational effectiveness. Bad decisions concerning diversity for reasons of age, ethnicity, or sexual orientation include (1) not hiring qualified people, (2) failing to promote top-performing subordinates, who subsequently may take their skills to competing organizations, and (3) promoting poorly performing managers because they have the same "diversity profile" as the manager or managers making the decision.

Factors That Influence Managerial Perception

Several managers' perceptions of the same person, event, or situation are likely to differ because managers differ in personality, values, attitudes, and moods (see Chapter 3). Each of these factors can influence how someone perceives a person or situation. An older middle manager who is high on openness to experience is likely to perceive the recruitment of able young managers as a positive learning opportunity; a similar middle manager who is low on openness to experience may perceive able younger subordinates as a threat. A manager who has high levels of job satisfaction and organizational commitment may perceive a job transfer to another department or geographic location that has very different employees (age, ethnicity, and so on) as an opportunity to learn and develop new skills. A dissatisfied, uncommitted manager may perceive the same transfer as a demotion.

Managers' and all organizational members' perceptions of one another also are affected by their past experiences with and acquired knowledge about people, events, and situations—information that is organized into preexisting schemas. **Schemas** are abstract knowledge structures stored in memory that allow people to organize and interpret information about a person, an event, or a situation.[118] Once a person develops a schema for a kind of person or event, any newly encountered person or situation that is related to the schema activates it, and information is processed in ways consistent with the information stored in the schema. Thus people tend to perceive others by using the expectations or preconceived notions contained in their schemas.[119] Once again, these expectations are derived from past experience and knowledge.

People tend to pay attention to information that is consistent with their schemas and to ignore or discount inconsistent information. Thus schemas tend to be reinforced and strengthened over time because the information attended to is seen as confirming the schemas. This also results in schemas being resistant to change.[120] This does not mean schemas never change; if that were the case, people could never adapt to changing conditions and learn from their mistakes. Rather, it suggests that schemas are slow to change and that a considerable amount of contradictory information needs to be encountered for people to change their schemas.

Schemas that accurately depict the true nature of a person or situation are functional because they help people make sense of the world around them. People typically confront so much information that it is not possible to make sense of it without relying on schemas. Schemas are dysfunctional when they are inaccurate because they cause managers and all members of an organization to perceive people and situations inaccurately and assume certain things that are not necessarily true.

Psychologist Virginia Valian refers to inaccurate preconceived notions of men and women as gender schemas. **Gender schemas** are a person's preconceived notions about the nature of men and women and their traits, attitudes, behaviors, and preferences.[121] Research suggests that among white middle-class Americans, the following gender schemas are prevalent: Men are action-oriented, assertive, independent, and task-focused; women are expressive, nurturing, and oriented toward and caring of other people.[122] Any schemas such as these—which assume a single visible characteristic such as gender causes a person to possess specific traits and tendencies—are bound to be inaccurate. For example, not all women are alike and not all men are alike, and many women are more independent and task-focused than men. Gender schemas can be learned in childhood and are reinforced in a number of ways in society. For instance, while young girls may be encouraged by their parents to play with toy trucks and tools (stereotypically masculine toys), boys generally are not encouraged, and sometimes are actively discouraged, from playing with dolls (stereotypically feminine toys).[123] As children grow up, they learn that occupations dominated by men have higher status than occupations dominated by women.

Perception as a Determinant of Unfair Treatment

Even though most people would agree that distributive justice and procedural justice are desirable goals, diverse organizational members are sometimes treated unfairly, as previous examples illustrate. Why is this problem occurring? One important overarching reason is inaccurate perceptions. To the extent that managers and other members of an organization rely on inaccurate schemas such as gender schemas to guide their perceptions of each other, unfair treatment is likely to occur.

Gender schemas are a kind of **stereotype**, which is composed of simplistic and often inaccurate beliefs about the typical characteristics of particular groups of people. Stereotypes are usually based on a visible characteristic such as a person's age, gender, or race.[124] Managers who allow stereotypes to influence their perceptions assume erroneously that a person

schema An abstract knowledge structure that is stored in memory and makes possible the interpretation and organization of information about a person, event, or situation.

gender schemas Preconceived beliefs or ideas about the nature of men and women and their traits, attitudes, behaviors, and preferences.

stereotype Simplistic and often inaccurate beliefs about the typical characteristics of particular groups of people.

possesses a whole host of characteristics simply because the person happens to be an Asian woman, a white man, or a lesbian, for example. African-American men are often stereotyped as good athletes; Hispanic women as subservient.[125] Obviously there is no reason to assume that every African-American man is a good athlete or that every Hispanic woman is subservient. Stereotypes, however, lead people to make such erroneous assumptions. A manager who accepts stereotypes might, for example, decide not to promote a highly capable Hispanic woman into a management position because the manager is certain that she will not be assertive enough to supervise others.

A recent study suggests that stereotypes might hamper the progress of mothers in their organizations when they are seeking to advance in positions that are traditionally held by men. According to the study, based on gender stereotypes, people tend to view mothers as less competent in terms of skills and capabilities related to advancing in such positions.[126]

People with disabilities might also be unfairly treated due to stereotypes.[127] Although the ADA requires (as mentioned previously) that organizations provide disabled employees with accommodations, employment rates of people with disabilities have declined in recent years. As profiled in the following "Ethics in Action" box, a number of organizations have not only provided employment opportunities for disabled adults but also have benefited from their valuable contributions.[128]

Ethics in Action

Disabled Employees Make Valuable Contributions

Some large organizations like McDonald's, Walmart, Home Depot, and Walgreens actively recruit disabled employees to work in positions such as cashiers, maintenance workers, greeters, shelf stockers, and floor workers that help customers find items. Home Depot, for example, works with a nonprofit agency called Ken's Krew, Inc., founded by parents of disabled adults, to recruit and place disabled employees in its stores. Thus far, working with Ken's Krew has enabled Home Depot to recruit and place around 100 disabled adults in over 50 of its stores.[129]

Often, when given the opportunity, disabled employees make valuable contributions to their organizations. Walgreens opened an automated distribution center in Anderson, South Carolina, in which more than 40% of its 264 employees are disabled.[130] For disabled employees like 18-year-old Harrison Mullinax, who has autism and checks in merchandise to be distributed to drugstores with a bar code scanner, having a regular job is a godsend. Randy Lewis, senior vice president of distribution and logistics at Walgreens, thought about hiring workers with disabilities when Walgreens was considering using technology to increase automation levels in a distribution center. Lewis, the father of a young adult son who has autism, was aware of how difficult it can be for young adults like his son to find employment. Various accommodations were made, like redesigning workstations and computer displays to suit employees' needs, and employees received appropriate training in how to do their jobs. Some days, disabled employees are actually the most productive in the center. As Lewis puts it, "One thing we found is they can all do the job. . . . What surprised us is the environment that it's created. It's a building where everybody helps each other out."[131]

Working through his training as a greeter, Jamie Heal embraces his job at Walmart with gusto. His new-found independence became a catalyst for life changes (going by the name Cameron was one) as well as a deeper sense of self-respect.

Walgreens is a large organization, but small organizations also have benefited from the valuable contributions of disabled employees. Habitat International, founded by current CEO David Morris and his father Saul over 30 years ago, is a manufacturer and contractor of indoor–outdoor carpet and artificial grass and a supplier to home improvement companies like Lowe's and Home Depot.[132] Habitat's profits have steadily increased over the years, and the factory's defect rate is less than 0.5%.[133]

Morris attributes Habitat's success to its employees, 75% of whom have either a physical or a mental disability or both.[134] Habitat has consistently provided employment opportunities to people with disabilities such as Down syndrome, schizophrenia, or cerebral palsy.[135] The company has also hired the homeless, recovering alcoholics, and non-English-speaking refugees from other countries. And these employees were relied on by plant manager Connie Presnell when she needed to fill a rush order by assigning it to a team of her fastest workers.[136] Habitat pays its employees regionally competitive wages and has low absence and turnover rates. Employees who need accommodations to perform their jobs are provided them, and Habitat has a highly motivated, satisfied, and committed workforce.[137]

While Habitat has actually gained some business from clients who applaud its commitment to diversity, Habitat's ethical values and social responsibility have also led the company to forgo a major account when stereotypes reared their ugly heads. Several years ago CEO Morris dropped the account of a distribution company because its representatives had made derogatory comments about his employees. Although it took Habitat two years to regain the lost revenues from this major account, Morris had no regrets.[138] Habitat's commitment to diversity and fair treatment is a win–win situation; the company is thriving, and so are its employees.[139]

bias The systematic tendency to use information about others in ways that result in inaccurate perceptions.

Inaccurate perceptions leading to unfair treatment of diverse members of an organization also can be due to biases. **Biases** are systematic tendencies to use information about others in ways that result in inaccurate perceptions. Because of the way biases operate, people often are unaware that their perceptions of others are inaccurate. There are several types of biases.

The *similar-to-me effect* is the tendency to perceive others who are similar to ourselves more positively than we perceive people who are different.[140] The similar-to-me effect is summed up by the saying, "Birds of a feather flock together." It can lead to unfair treatment of diverse employees simply because they are different from the managers who are perceiving them, evaluating them, and making decisions that affect their future in the organization.

Managers (particularly top managers) are likely to be white men. Although these managers may endorse the principles of distributive and procedural justice, they may unintentionally fall into the trap of perceiving other white men more positively than they perceive women and minorities. This is the similar-to-me effect. Being aware of this bias as well as using objective information about employees' capabilities and performance as much as possible in decision making about job assignments, pay raises, promotions, and other outcomes can help managers avoid the similar-to-me effect.

Social status—a person's real or perceived position in a society or an organization—can be the source of another bias. The *social status effect* is the tendency to perceive individuals with high social status more positively than we perceive those with low social status. A high-status person may be perceived as smarter and more believable, capable, knowledgeable, and responsible than a low-status person, even in the absence of objective information about either person.

The salience effect focuses extra attention on a person who stands out from the group mold. Part of being a good manager includes being aware of these sorts of tendencies and actively working against them.

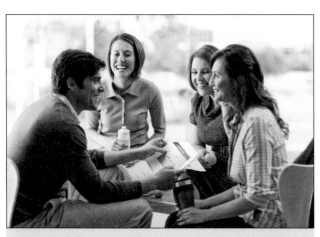

Here, the only guy in a work group basks in the extra attention he's receiving from everyone else. Salience does not always work in one's favor, however—extra scrutiny, higher standards, and disproportionate expectations may result, so check your intentions when you encounter groups like this one.

Imagine being introduced to two people at a company holiday party. Both are white men in their late 30s, and you learn that one is a member of the company's top management team and the other is a supervisor in the mailroom. From this information alone, you might assume that the top manager is smarter, more capable, more responsible, and even more interesting than the mailroom supervisor. Because women and minorities have traditionally had lower social status than white men, the social status effect may lead some people to perceive women and minorities less positively than they perceive white men.

Have you ever stood out in a crowd? Maybe you were the only man in a group of women; or maybe you were dressed formally for a social gathering, and everyone else was in jeans. Salience (that is, conspicuousness) is another source of bias. The *salience effect* is the tendency to focus attention on individuals who are conspicuously different from us. When people are salient, they often feel as though all eyes are watching them, and this perception is not far from the mark. Salient individuals are more often the object of attention than are other members of a work group, for example. A manager who has six white subordinates and one Hispanic subordinate reporting to her may inadvertently pay more attention to the Hispanic in group meetings because of the salience effect. In "A Manager's Challenge," Rod Bond of Sodexo experienced salience firsthand when he attended the Women's Food Service Forum.

Individuals who are salient are often perceived to be primarily responsible for outcomes and operations and are evaluated more extremely in either a positive or a negative direction.[141] Thus when the Hispanic subordinate does a good job on a project, she receives excessive praise, and when she misses a deadline, she is excessively chastised.

Overt Discrimination

overt discrimination
Knowingly and willingly denying diverse individuals access to opportunities and outcomes in an organization.

Inaccurate schemas and perceptual biases can lead well-meaning managers and organizational members to unintentionally discriminate against others. On the other hand, **overt discrimination**, or knowingly and willingly denying diverse individuals access to opportunities and outcomes in an organization, is intentional and deliberate. Overt discrimination is both unethical and illegal. Unfortunately, just as some managers steal from their organizations, others engage in overt discrimination.

Overt discrimination is a clear violation of the principles of distributive and procedural justice. Moreover, when managers are charged with overt discrimination, costly lawsuits can ensue. Organizations ranging from the Adam's Mark chain of luxury hotels, Texaco, and Ford Motor Company to Johnson & Johnson, BellSouth, the National Football League, General Electric, Walmart, and Nike either have settled or face pending lawsuits alleging overt workplace discrimination.[142] Whereas in the past, lawsuits due to overt workplace discrimination focused on unfair treatment of women and minority group members, given the aging of the U.S. workforce, increasing numbers of discrimination cases are being brought by older workers who believe they were unfairly dismissed from their jobs due to their age.[143]

Despite all the advances that have been made, allegations of overt discrimination based on gender, race, age, and other forms of diversity continue to occur in the United States. For example, Nike settled a class action lawsuit filed on behalf of 400 African-American employees of its Chicago Niketown store.[144] Employees claimed that managers used racial slurs when referring to African-American employees and customers, gave African-American employees lower-paying jobs, made unwarranted accusations of theft, and had security personnel monitor employees and customers based on race.[145] Although Nike denied the allegations, as part of the settlement, Nike agreed to pay current and former employees $7.6 million and also agreed to promote effective management of diversity, partly by providing diversity training to all managers and supervisors in the store.[146]

Overt discrimination continues to be a problem in other countries as well. For example, although Japan passed its first Equal Employment Opportunity Law in 1985 and Japanese women are increasingly working in jobs once dominated by men, professional Japanese women have continued to find it difficult to advance in their careers and assume managerial positions.[147] Women make up almost half of the Japanese workforce, but only around 10% of managerial positions in business and government are occupied by women, according to the International Labor Organization agency of the United Nations.[148]

According to the United Nations Development Program's gender empowerment measure, which assesses the participation of women in a country's politics and economy, Japan is the most unequal of the world's wealthy nations when it comes to women.[149] Takako Ariishi has witnessed women's struggle in Japan firsthand. As an employee of a family-owned manufacturing business that supplies parts to Nissan,[150] Ariishi was fired by her own father (who was then president of the company) when she had a son (her father claimed that her son would be his successor as president). Nonetheless, when Ariishi's father died, she took over as company president. Her company is one of 160 Nissan suppliers in Japan, and the heads of these companies meet twice a year; Ariishi is the only woman among the 160 presidents, and the first time the group met, she was asked to wait in a separate room with the secretaries. Miiko Tsuda, an employee of a tutoring company, indicates that she is paid less than her male coworkers, and she is often asked to push elevator buttons and make tea for male coworkers. Only 5 of the company's 300 management employees are women.[151]

Overt discrimination also can be a potential problem when in comes to layoff decisions, as profiled in the following "Focus on Diversity" box.

Focus on Diversity

Layoff Discrimination?

Organizational restructurings, a weak economy, and the recession that began in December 2007[152] led to record numbers of U.S. employees being laid off from 2007 to 2010. Although it is always a challenge for managers to decide who should be let go when layoffs take place, some laid-off employees felt that factors that should be irrelevant to this tough decision played a role in the layoffs at their former employers. And while many workers who believe they were unfairly discriminated against do not pursue legal remedies, some filed lawsuits alleging discrimination in layoff decisions.

Age-related discrimination complaints have been at record highs in recent times.[153] A press release issued in 2012 by the EEOC indicates that "The number of age discrimination charges filed with the Commission increased by 50% since 2000."[154] Although this might be due to the fact that there were more older employees in the workforce than in previous years, David Grinberg, speaking on behalf of the EEOC, suggests that the rise in age discrimination allegations could also be due to the fact that older workers tend to be paid more and have better benefits.[155] For example, Joan Zawacki, in her late 50s, was laid off from her position as a vice president at the Cartus division of Realogy Corp. after having worked at the company for over 30 years. According to Zawacki, senior managers such as herself were told to discreetly talk with older workers in a friendly manner and suggest that they inquire with human resources about early retirement packages while protecting the jobs of younger workers. Zawacki indicates that she was laid off after not having convinced an older employee in her department to retire. A company spokesperson disputed the allegations in Zawacki's age discrimination lawsuit. In addition, over 90 employees at the Lawrence Livermore National Laboratory have filed complaints alleging age discrimination in layoffs. Eddy Stappaerts, a 62-year-old senior scientist who had worked at the lab for 11 years and has a PhD from Stanford University, says, "A week before I was laid off, my boss said my contributions were essential."[156] He alleges that some of the work he did was given to a younger employee.[157]

Some women laid off from their jobs in the financial industry filed lawsuits alleging gender discrimination. Laid-off female executives at Citigroup, Merrill Lynch, Bank of America, and Bank of Tokyo have claimed that gender played a role in their firings.[158] In some cases the women had done very well in their early years with the firms, were transferred to less desirable positions after becoming pregnant and

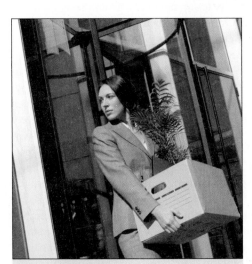

Who gets laid off and why? Discrimination runs across the board of business practices, including the arena of layoffs.

taking maternity leaves, and ultimately were let go. Some of these women suggest that they were laid off even though they were just as (or more) qualified as men who were able to keep their jobs.[159]

Four former human resource managers at Dell filed a class action lawsuit alleging that Dell's massive layoffs discriminated against women and employees over age 40 and that women were unfairly treated in pay and promotions.[160] Dell agreed to settle the lawsuit for $9.1 million while not admitting any wrongdoing.[161] Although many companies charged with discrimination allege that no discrimination took place, clearly these are matters for the courts to decide.[162]

How to Manage Diversity Effectively

Various kinds of barriers arise to managing diversity effectively in organizations. Some barriers originate in the person doing the perceiving; others are based on the information and schemas that have built up over time concerning the person being perceived. To overcome these barriers and effectively manage diversity, managers (and other organizational members) must possess or develop certain attitudes and values and the skills needed to change other people's attitudes and values.

LO5-5 List the steps managers can take to effectively manage diversity.

Steps in Managing Diversity Effectively

Managers can take a number of steps to change attitudes and values and promote the effective management of diversity. Here we describe these steps, some of which we have referred to previously (see Table 5.4).

SECURE TOP MANAGEMENT COMMITMENT As we mentioned earlier in the chapter, top management's commitment to diversity is crucial for the success of any diversity-related initiatives. Top managers need to develop the correct ethical values and performance- or business-oriented attitudes that allow them to make appropriate use of their human resources.

STRIVE TO INCREASE THE ACCURACY OF PERCEPTIONS One aspect of developing the appropriate values and attitudes is to take steps to increase the accuracy of perceptions. Managers should consciously attempt to be open to other points of view and perspectives, seek them out, and encourage their subordinates to do the same.[163] Organizational members who are open to other perspectives put their own beliefs and knowledge to an important reality test and will be more inclined to modify or change them when necessary.

Table 5.4
Promoting the Effective Management of Diversity

- Secure top management commitment.
- Increase the accuracy of perceptions.
- Increase diversity awareness.
- Increase diversity skills.
- Encourage flexibility.
- Pay close attention to how employees are evaluated.
- Consider the numbers.
- Empower employees to challenge discriminatory behaviors, actions, and remarks.
- Reward employees for effectively managing diversity.
- Provide training utilizing a multipronged, ongoing approach.
- Encourage mentoring of diverse employees.

Managers should not be afraid to change their views about a person, issue, or event; moreover, they should encourage their subordinates to be open to changing their views in the light of disconfirming evidence. Additionally, managers and all members of an organization should strive to avoid making snap judgments about people; rather, judgments should be made only when sufficient and relevant information has been gathered.[164]

INCREASE DIVERSITY AWARENESS   It is natural for managers and other members of an organization to view other people from their own perspective because their own feelings, thoughts, attitudes, and experiences guide their perceptions and interactions. The ability to appreciate diversity, however, requires that people become aware of other perspectives and the various attitudes and experiences of others. Many diversity awareness programs in organizations strive to increase managers' and workers' awareness of (1) their own attitudes, biases, and stereotypes and (2) the differing perspectives of diverse managers, subordinates, coworkers, and customers. Diversity awareness programs often have these goals:[165]

- Providing organizational members with accurate information about diversity.
- Uncovering personal biases and stereotypes.
- Assessing personal beliefs, attitudes, and values and learning about other points of view.
- Overturning inaccurate stereotypes and beliefs about different groups.
- Developing an atmosphere in which people feel free to share their differing perspectives and points of view.
- Improving understanding of others who are different from oneself.

Sometimes simply taking the time to interact with someone who is different in some way can increase awareness. When employees and managers are at social functions or just having lunch with a coworker, often the people they interact with are those they feel most comfortable with. If all members of an organization make an effort to interact with people they ordinarily would not, mutual understanding is likely to be enhanced.[166]

In large organizations, top managers are often far removed from entry-level employees—they may lack a real understanding and appreciation for what these employees do day in and day out, the challenges and obstacles they face, and the steps that can be taken to improve effectiveness. Recognizing this fact, some managers have taken concrete steps to improve their understanding of the experiences, attitudes, and perspectives of frontline employees, as indicated in the following "Management Insight" box.

Management Insight

Top Execs Improve Their Understanding of the Front Line

A growing number of organizations are implementing programs whereby top managers spend time performing the jobs of frontline employees to improve their understanding of the challenges these employees face and ways to improve their working conditions.[167] For example, DaVita Inc.,[168] a major provider of kidney dialysis services in the United States, has a program called "Reality 101" through which senior executives who have never worked in a dialysis clinic spend three days working as clinic technicians. Dialysis helps patients whose kidneys are not working properly to eliminate waste from their bloodstream. Treatments last around four hours, and patients often require multiple treatments per week.[169]

Carolyn Kibler, a senior executive at DaVita who oversees 48 clinics and around 750 employees, gained a much better understanding of the challenges technicians face, the nature of their jobs, and how best to manage them as a result of her participation in Reality 101. A former nurse, Kibler was surprised at how physically and emotionally demanding the job was and the high levels of stress it entailed. She also gained a real

"Now how did I do that, again?" Spending time doing frontline work can be immensely beneficial for executives to understand the nuts and bolts of their subordinates' days.

appreciation of the high levels of empathy technicians have for their patients—trying to make them as comfortable as possible, helping them deal with their frustrations, and mourning the loss of those who die as a result of their often multiple medical problems.[170]

Realizing how hard technicians work and how hectic and stressful the clinics can be, Kibler is now more understanding when paperwork is submitted late due to staff shortages, gives positive feedback to those who might have to miss meetings or conference calls to treat patients, tries to avoid giving clinics last-minute requests and deadlines for reports, and is more forthcoming with praise for clinic staff. More fully appreciating how patient care is the top priority and the nature of work on the clinic floor, Kibler is also more sensitive to how her own initiatives might affect these frontline employees and the patients they serve. As she indicates, "I am more conscious of the power of my words and my actions and the impact they have down in the organization."[171]

As part of its "Now Who's Boss Day," senior executives at Loews Hotels perform entry-level jobs one day per year to appreciate and understand the challenges in these jobs and ways to make performing them easier while improving customer service.[172] This program originated when Loews then CEO and current chairman Jonathan Tisch[173] took part in a reality TV show called *Now Who's Boss?* and performed the jobs of pool attendant, housekeeper, and bellman at a Florida hotel. He perspired so much in the polyester uniform people in these jobs were required to wear that he changed the uniform. As a result of another manager's experience in the trenches, handlebars were installed on room service carts so they weren't as difficult to push.[174]

Clearly the jobs frontline employees perform are essential for organizational functioning. When top managers, who are far removed from these jobs, gain a better understanding of these jobs and the employees who perform them, they are in a better position to manage them effectively.

INCREASE DIVERSITY SKILLS Efforts to increase diversity skills focus on improving how managers and their subordinates interact with each other and improving their ability to work with different kinds of people.[175] An important issue here is being able to communicate with diverse employees. Diverse organizational members may have different communication styles, may differ in their language fluency, may use words differently, may differ in the nonverbal signals they send through facial expressions and body language, and may differ in how they perceive and interpret information. Managers and their subordinates must learn to communicate effectively with one another if an organization is to take advantage of the skills and abilities of its diverse workforce. Educating organizational members about differences in ways of communicating is often a good starting point.

Diversity education can help managers and subordinates gain a better understanding of how people may interpret certain kinds of comments. Diversity education also can help employees learn how to resolve misunderstandings. Organizational members should feel comfortable enough to "clear the air" and solve communication difficulties and misunderstandings as they occur rather than letting problems grow and fester without acknowledgment.

ENCOURAGE FLEXIBILITY Managers and their subordinates must learn how to be open to different approaches and ways of doing things. This does not mean organizational members have to suppress their personal styles. Rather, it means they must be open to, and not feel threatened by, different approaches and perspectives and must have the patience and flexibility needed to understand and appreciate diverse perspectives.[176]

To the extent feasible, managers should also be flexible enough to incorporate the differing needs of diverse employees. Earlier we mentioned that religious diversity suggests that people of certain religions might need time off for holidays that are traditionally workdays in the United States; managers need to anticipate and respond to such needs with flexibility (perhaps letting people skip the lunch hour so they can leave work early). Moreover, flexible work hours, the option to work from home, and cafeteria-style benefit plans (see Chapter 12) are just a few of the many ways in which managers can respond to the differing needs of diverse employees while enabling those employees to be effective contributors to an organization.

PAY CLOSE ATTENTION TO HOW ORGANIZATIONAL MEMBERS ARE EVALUATED   Whenever feasible, it is desirable to rely on objective performance indicators (see Chapter 12) because they are less subject to bias. When objective indicators are not available or are inappropriate, managers should ensure that adequate time and attention are focused on the evaluation of employees' performance and that evaluators are held accountable for their evaluations.[177] Vague performance standards should be avoided.[178]

CONSIDER THE NUMBERS   Looking at the numbers of members of different minority groups and women in various positions, at various levels in the hierarchy, in locations that differ in their desirability, and in any other relevant categorizations in an organization can tell managers important information about potential problems and ways to rectify them.[179] If members of certain groups are underrepresented in particular kinds of jobs or units, managers need to understand why this is the case and resolve any problems they might uncover.

EMPOWER EMPLOYEES TO CHALLENGE DISCRIMINATORY BEHAVIORS, ACTIONS, AND REMARKS   When managers or employees witness another organizational member being unfairly treated, they should be encouraged to speak up and rectify the situation. Top managers can make this happen by creating an organizational culture (see Chapter 3) that has zero tolerance for discrimination. As part of such a culture, organizational members should feel empowered to challenge discriminatory behavior, whether the behavior is directed at them or they witness it being directed at another employee.[180]

REWARD EMPLOYEES FOR EFFECTIVELY MANAGING DIVERSITY   If effective management of diversity is a valued organizational objective, then employees should be rewarded for their contributions to this objective, as is true at Sodexo in "A Manager's Challenge."[181] For example, after settling a major race discrimination lawsuit, Coca-Cola Company now ties managers' pay to their achievement of diversity goals. Examples of other organizations that do so include American Express and Bayer Corporation.[182]

PROVIDE TRAINING UTILIZING A MULTIPRONGED, ONGOING APPROACH
Many managers use a multipronged approach to increase diversity awareness and skills in their organizations; they use films and printed materials supplemented by experiential exercises to uncover hidden biases and stereotypes. Sometimes simply providing a forum for people to learn about and discuss their differing attitudes, values, and experiences can be a powerful means of increasing awareness. Also useful are role-plays that enact problems resulting from lack of awareness and show the increased understanding that comes from appreciating others' viewpoints. Accurate information and training experiences can debunk stereotypes. Group exercises, role-plays, and diversity-related experiences can help organizational members develop the skills they need to work effectively with a variety of people. Many organizations hire outside consultants to provide diversity training, in addition to utilizing their own in-house diversity experts.[183]

United Parcel Service (UPS), a package delivery company, developed an innovative community internship program to increase the diversity awareness and skills of its managers and, at the same time, benefit the wider community. Upper and middle managers participating in the program take one month off the job to be community interns.[184] They work in community organizations helping people who in many instances are very different from themselves—such organizations include a detention center in McAllen, Texas, for Mexican immigrants; homeless shelters; AIDS centers; Head Start programs; migrant farmworker assistance groups; and groups aiming to halt the spread of drug abuse in inner cities.

Interacting with and helping diverse people enhances the interns' awareness of diversity because they experience it firsthand. Bill Cox, a UPS division manager who spent a month

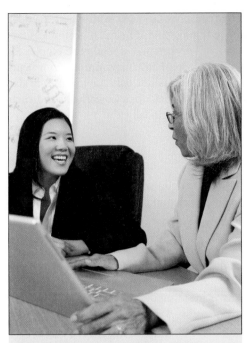

The mentoring process allows a newer employee the chance to gain an edge through informal conversation.

in the McAllen detention center, summed up his experience of diversity: "You've got these [thousands of] migrant workers down in McAllen . . . and they don't want what you have. All they want is an opportunity to earn what you have. That's a fundamental change in understanding that only comes from spending time with these people."[185]

Many managers who complete the UPS community internship program have superior diversity skills as a result of their experiences. During their internships, they learn about different cultures and approaches to work and life; they learn to interact effectively with people whom they ordinarily do not come into contact with; and they are forced to learn flexibility because of the dramatic differences between their roles at the internship sites and their roles as managers at UPS.

ENCOURAGE MENTORING OF DIVERSE EMPLOYEES

Unfortunately African Americans and other minorities continue to be less likely to attain high-level positions in their organizations; and for those who do attain them, the climb up the corporate ladder typically takes longer than it does for white men. David Thomas, a professor at the Harvard Business School, has studied the careers of minorities in corporate America. One of his major conclusions is that mentoring is very important for minorities, most of whom have reached high levels in their organizations by having a solid network of mentors and contacts.[186] **Mentoring** is a process by which an experienced member of an organization (the mentor) provides advice and guidance to a less experienced member (the protégé) and helps the less experienced member learn how to advance in the organization and in his or her career.

mentoring A process by which an experienced member of an organization (the mentor) provides advice and guidance to a less experienced member (the protégé) and helps the less experienced member learn how to advance in the organization and in his or her career.

According to Thomas, effective mentoring is more than providing instruction, offering advice, helping build skills, and sharing technical expertise. Of course these aspects of mentoring are important and necessary. However, equally important is developing a high-quality, close, and supportive relationship with the protégé. Emotional bonds between a mentor and a protégé can enable a protégé, for example, to express fears and concerns, and sometimes even reluctance to follow a mentor's advice. The mentor can help the protégé build his or her confidence and feel comfortable engaging in unfamiliar work behaviors.[187]

Sexual Harassment

LO5-6 Identify the two major forms of sexual harassment and how they can be eliminated.

Sexual harassment seriously damages both the people who are harassed and the reputation of the organization in which it occurs. It also can cost organizations large amounts of money. In 1995, for example, Chevron Corporation agreed to pay $2.2 million to settle a sexual harassment lawsuit filed by four women who worked at the Chevron Information Technology Company in San Ramon, California. One woman involved in the suit said she had received violent pornographic material through the company mail. Another, an electrical engineer, said she had been asked to bring pornographic videos to Chevron workers at an Alaska drill site.[188] More recently, in 2001 TWA settled a lawsuit to the tune of $2.6 million that alleged that female employees were sexually harassed at JFK International Airport in New York. According to the EEOC, not only was sexual harassment tolerated at TWA, but company officials did little to curtail it when it was brought to their attention.[189]

Unfortunately the events at Chevron and TWA are not isolated incidents.[190] In 2011, two lawsuits were filed against American Apparel and its founder and CEO, Dov Charney, alleging sexual harassment.[191] Of the 607 women surveyed by the National Association for Female Executives, 60% indicated that they had experienced some form of sexual harassment.[192] In a survey conducted by the Society for Human Resource Management of 460 companies, 36% of the companies indicated that, within the last 24 months, one or more employees claimed that they had been sexually harassed.[193] Sexual harassment victims can be women or men, and their harassers do not necessarily have to be of the opposite sex.[194] However, women are the most frequent victims of sexual harassment, particularly those in male-dominated occupations or those who occupy positions stereotypically associated with certain gender relationships, such as a female secretary reporting to a male boss. Though it occurs less frequently, men can also be victims of sexual harassment. For instance, several male employees at Jenny Craig filed a lawsuit claiming they were subject to lewd and inappropriate comments from female coworkers and managers.[195] Sexual harassment is not only unethical; it is also illegal. Managers have an ethical obligation to ensure that they, their coworkers, and their subordinates never engage in sexual harassment, even unintentionally.

Forms of Sexual Harassment

There are two basic forms of sexual harassment: quid pro quo sexual harassment and hostile work environment sexual harassment. **Quid pro quo sexual harassment** occurs when a harasser asks or forces an employee to perform sexual favors to keep a job, receive a promotion, receive a raise, obtain some other work-related opportunity, or avoid receiving negative consequences such as demotion or dismissal.[196] This "Sleep with me, honey, or you're fired" form of harassment is the more extreme type and leaves no doubt in anyone's mind that sexual harassment has taken place.[197]

quid pro quo sexual harassment Asking for or forcing an employee to perform sexual favors in exchange for receiving some reward or avoiding negative consequences.

hostile work environment sexual harassment Telling lewd jokes, displaying pornography, making sexually oriented remarks about someone's personal appearance, and other sex-related actions that make the work environment unpleasant.

Hostile work environment sexual harassment is more subtle. It occurs when organizational members face an intimidating, hostile, or offensive work environment because of their sex.[198] Lewd jokes, sexually oriented comments or innuendos, vulgar language, displays of pornography, displays or distribution of sexually oriented objects, and sexually oriented remarks about one's physical appearance are examples of hostile work environment sexual harassment.[199] A hostile work environment interferes with organizational members' ability to perform their jobs effectively and has been deemed illegal by the courts. Managers who engage in hostile work environment harassment or allow others to do so risk costly lawsuits for their organizations. For example, in February 2004 a federal jury awarded Marion Schwab $3.24 million after deliberating on her sexual harassment case against FedEx.[200] Schwab was the only female tractor-trailer driver at the FedEx facility serving the Harrisburg International Airport vicinity in Middletown, Pennsylvania, from 1997 to 2000. During that period she was the target of sexual innuendos, was given inferior work assignments, and was the brunt of derogatory comments about her appearance and the role of women in society. On five occasions the brakes on her truck were tampered with. The federal EEOC sued FedEx, and Schwab was part of the suit.[201]

The courts have recently recognized other forms of hostile work environment harassment, in addition to sexual harassment. For example, in June 2006 a California jury awarded $61 million in punitive and compensatory damages to two FedEx Ground drivers. The drivers, who are of Lebanese descent, indicated that they faced a hostile work environment and high levels of stress because a manager harassed them with racial slurs for two years.[202]

Steps Managers Can Take to Eradicate Sexual Harassment

Managers have an ethical obligation to eradicate sexual harassment in their organizations. There are many ways to accomplish this objective. Here are four initial steps managers can take to deal with the problem:[203]

- *Develop and clearly communicate a sexual harassment policy endorsed by top management.* This policy should include prohibitions against both quid pro quo and hostile work environment sexual harassment. It should contain (1) examples of types of behavior that are unacceptable, (2) a procedure for employees to use to report instances of harassment, (3) a discussion of the disciplinary actions that will be taken when harassment has taken place, and (4) a commitment to educate and train organizational members about sexual harassment.

- *Use a fair complaint procedure to investigate charges of sexual harassment.* Such a procedure should (1) be managed by a neutral third party, (2) ensure that complaints are dealt with promptly and thoroughly, (3) protect and fairly treat victims, and (4) ensure that alleged harassers are fairly treated.

- *When it has been determined that sexual harassment has taken place, take corrective actions as soon as possible.* These actions can vary depending on the severity of the harassment. When harassment is extensive, prolonged, of a quid pro quo nature, or severely objectionable in some other manner, corrective action may include firing the harasser.

- *Provide sexual harassment education and training to all organizational members, including managers.* The majority of *Fortune* 500 firms currently provide this education and training for their employees. Managers at DuPont, for example, developed DuPont's "A Matter of Respect" program to help educate employees about sexual harassment and eliminate its occurrence. The program includes a four-hour workshop in which participants are given information that defines sexual harassment, sets forth the company's policy against it, and explains how to report complaints and access a 24-hour hotline. Participants watch video clips showing actual instances of harassment. One clip shows a saleswoman having dinner with a male client who, after much negotiating, seems about to give her company his business when he suddenly suggests that they continue their conversation in his hotel room. The saleswoman is confused about what to do. Will she be reprimanded if she says no and the deal is lost? After watching a video, participants discuss what they have seen, why the behavior is inappropriate, and what organizations can do to alleviate the problem.[204] Throughout the program, managers stress to employees that they do not have to tolerate sexual harassment or get involved in situations in which harassment is likely to occur.

Barry S. Roberts and Richard A. Mann, experts on business law and authors of several books on the topic, suggest a number of additional factors that managers and all members of an organization need to keep in mind about sexual harassment:[205]

- Every sexual harassment charge should be taken seriously.

- Employees who go along with unwanted sexual attention in the workplace can be sexual harassment victims.

- Employees sometimes wait before they file complaints of sexual harassment.

- An organization's sexual harassment policy should be communicated to each new employee and reviewed with current employees periodically.

- Suppliers and customers need to be familiar with an organization's sexual harassment policy.

- Managers should give employees alternative ways to report incidents of sexual harassment.

- Employees who report sexual harassment must have their rights protected; this includes being protected from any potential retaliation.

- Allegations of sexual harassment should be kept confidential; those accused of harassment should have their rights protected.

- Investigations of harassment charges and any resultant disciplinary actions need to proceed in a timely manner.

- Managers must protect employees from sexual harassment from third parties they may interact with while performing their jobs, such as suppliers or customers.[206]

Summary and Review

THE INCREASING DIVERSITY OF THE WORKFORCE AND THE ENVIRONMENT Diversity is dissimilarity or differences among people. Diversity is a pressing concern for managers and organizations for business and ethical reasons. There are multiple forms of diversity such as age, gender, race and ethnicity, religion, capabilities/disabilities, **LO5-1** socioeconomic background, sexual orientation, and physical appearance.

LO5-2, 5-3 **MANAGERS AND THE EFFECTIVE MANAGEMENT OF DIVERSITY** Both the workforce and the organizational environment are increasingly diverse, and effectively managing this diversity is an essential component of management. In each of their managerial roles, managers can encourage the effective management of diversity, which is both an ethical and a business imperative.

LO5-4 PERCEPTION   Perception is the process through which people select, organize, and interpret sensory input to give meaning and order to the world around them. It is inherently subjective. Schemas guide perception; when schemas are based on a single visible characteristic such as race or gender, they are stereotypes and highly inaccurate, leading to unfair treatment. Unfair treatment also can result from biases and overt discrimination.

LO5-5 HOW TO MANAGE DIVERSITY EFFECTIVELY   Managers can take many steps to effectively manage diversity. Effective management of diversity is an ongoing process that requires frequent monitoring.

LO5-6 SEXUAL HARASSMENT   Two forms of sexual harassment are quid pro quo sexual harassment and hostile work environment sexual harassment. Steps that managers can take to eradicate sexual harassment include development and communication of a sexual harassment policy endorsed by top management, use of fair complaint procedures, prompt corrective action when harassment occurs, and sexual harassment training and education.

Management in Action

Topics for Discussion and Action

Discussion

1. Discuss why violations of the principles of distributive and procedural justice continue to occur in modern organizations. What can managers do to uphold these principles in their organizations? **[LO5-2, 5-3, 5-4, 5-5]**

2. Why do workers who test positive for HIV sometimes get discriminated against? **[LO5-1, 5-4]**

3. Why would some employees resent accommodations made for employees with disabilities that are dictated by the Americans with Disabilities Act? **[LO5-1, 5-4]**

4. Discuss the ways in which schemas can be functional and dysfunctional. **[LO5-4]**

5. Discuss an occasion when you may have been treated unfairly because of stereotypical thinking. What stereotypes were applied to you? How did they result in your being treated unfairly? **[LO5-4]**

6. How does the similar-to-me effect influence your own behavior and decisions? **[LO5-4]**

7. Why is mentoring particularly important for minorities? **[LO5-5]**

8. Why is it important to consider the numbers of different groups of employees at various levels in an organization's hierarchy? **[LO5-5]**

9. Think about a situation in which you would have benefited from mentoring but a mentor was not available. What could you have done to try to get the help of a mentor in this situation? **[LO5-5]**

Action

10. Choose a *Fortune* 500 company not mentioned in the chapter. Conduct research to determine what steps this organization has taken to effectively manage diversity and eliminate sexual harassment. **[LO5-2, 5-5, 5-6]**

Building Management Skills **[LO5-1, 5-2, 5-3, 5-4, 5-5, 5-6]**

Solving Diversity-Related Problems

Think about the last time that you (1) were treated unfairly because you differed from a decision maker on a particular dimension of diversity or (2) observed someone else being treated unfairly because that person differed from a decision maker on a particular dimension of diversity. Then answer these questions:

1. Why do you think the decision maker acted unfairly in this situation?

2. In what ways, if any, were biases, stereotypes, or overt discrimination involved in this situation?

3. Was the decision maker aware that he or she was acting unfairly?

4. What could you or the person who was treated unfairly have done to improve matters and rectify the injustice on the spot?

5. Was any sexual harassment involved in this situation? If so, what kind was it?

6. If you had authority over the decision maker (that is, if you were his or her manager or supervisor), what steps would you take to ensure that the decision maker no longer treated diverse individuals unfairly?

Managing Ethically **[LO5-1, 5-2, 5-3, 5-5]**

Some companies require that their employees work long hours and travel extensively. Employees with young children, employees taking care of elderly relatives, and employees who have interests outside the workplace sometimes find that their careers are jeopardized if they try to work more reasonable hours or limit their work-related travel. Some of these employees feel that it is unethical for their managers to expect so much of them in the workplace and not understand their needs as parents and caregivers.

Questions

1. Either individually or in a group, think about the ethical implications of requiring long hours and extensive amounts of travel for some jobs.

2. What obligations do you think managers and companies have to enable employees to have balanced lives and meet nonwork needs and demands?

Small Group Breakout Exercise [LO5-1, 5-2, 5-3, 5-4, 5-5]

Determining If a Problem Exists

Form groups of three or four people, and appoint one member as the spokesperson who will communicate your findings to the whole class when called on by the instructor. Then discuss the following scenario:

You and your partners own and manage a local chain of restaurants, with moderate to expensive prices, that are open for lunch and dinner during the week and for dinner on weekends. Your staff is diverse, and you believe that you are effectively managing diversity. Yet on visits to the different restaurants you have noticed that your African-American employees tend to congregate together and communicate mainly with each other. The same is true for your Hispanic employees and your white employees. You are meeting with your partners today to discuss this observation.

1. Discuss why the patterns of communication that you observed might be occurring in your restaurants.

2. Discuss whether your observation reflects an underlying problem. If so, why? If not, why not?

3. Discuss whether you should address this issue with your staff and in your restaurants. If so, how and why? If not, why not?

Exploring the World Wide Web [LO5-1, 5-2, 5-3, 5-5, 5-6]

Go to the U.S. government websites that deal with employment issues, diversity, and sexual harassment, such as the websites of the Equal Employment Opportunity Commission (EEOC) and the Bureau of Labor Statistics. After reviewing these websites, develop a list of tips to help managers effectively manage diversity and avoid costly lawsuits.

Be the Manager [LO5-1, 5-2, 5-3, 5-4, 5-5]

You are Maria Herrera and have been recently promoted to the position of director of financial analysis for a medium-sized consumer goods firm. During your first few weeks on the job, you took the time to have lunch with each of your subordinates to try to get to know them better. You have 12 direct reports who are junior and senior financial analysts who support different product lines. Susan Epstein, one of the female financial analysts you had lunch with, made the following statement: "I'm so glad we finally have a woman in charge. Now, hopefully things will get better around here." You pressed Epstein to elaborate, but she clammed up. She indicated that she didn't want to

unnecessarily bias you and that the problems were pretty self-evident. In fact, Epstein was surprised that you didn't know what she was talking about and jokingly mentioned that perhaps you should spend some time undercover, observing her group and their interactions with others.

You spoke with your supervisor and the former director, who had been promoted and had volunteered to be on call if you had any questions. Neither man knew of any diversity-related issues in your group. In fact, your supervisor's response was, "We've got a lot of problems, but fortunately that's not one of them."

What are you going to do to address this issue?

Bloomberg Businessweek Case in the News [LO5-1, LO5-2, LO5-3, LO5-4, LO5-5, LO5-6]

Slamming Natty Light Between Lines of C++

Danilo Stern-Sapad writes code for a living, but don't call him a geek. He wears sunglasses and blasts 2Pac while programming. He enjoys playing *Battle Shots*—like the board game Battleship, but with liquor—at the office. He and his fellow coders at Los Angeles start-up BetterWorks are lavished with attention by tech industry recruiters desperate for engineering talent. "We got invited to a party in Malibu where there were naked women in the hot tub," says Stern-Sapad, 25. "We're the cool programmers."

Tech's latest boom has generated a new, more testosterone-fueled breed of coder. Sure, the job still requires enormous brainpower, but today's engineers are drawn from diverse backgrounds, and many eschew the laboratory intellectualism that prevailed when semiconductors ruled Silicon Valley. "I don't need to wear a pocket protector to be a programmer," says John Manoogian III, a software engineer and entrepreneur.

At some start-ups the pendulum has swung so far in the other direction that it's given rise to a new "title": brogrammer. A portmanteau of the frathouse moniker "bro" and "programmer," the term has become the subject of a Facebook group joined by over 21,000 people; the name of a series of hacker get-togethers in Austin, Texas; the punch line for online ads; and the topic of a humorous discussion on question-and-answer site Quora titled "How does a programmer become a brogrammer?" (One pointer: Drink Red Bull, beer, and "brotein" shakes.) "There's a rising group of developers who are much more sociable and like to go out and have fun, and I think brogramming speaks to that audience," says

Gagan Biyani, cofounder and president of Udemy, a start-up that offers coding lessons on the web.

There's also an audience that feels left out of the joke. Women made up 21% of all programmers in 2010, down from 24% in 2000, according to the U.S. Bureau of Labor Statistics. Anything that encourages the perception of tech as being male-dominated is likely to contribute to this decline, says Sara Chipps, founder of Girl Develop It, a series of software development workshops. "This brogramming thing would definitely turn off a lot of women from working" at start-ups, says Chipps.

A poster recently displayed at a Stanford University career fair by Klout, a social media analytics company, tried to woo computer science graduates by asking: "Want to bro down and crush code? Klout is hiring." Says Chipps: "No. I don't want to bro down. I can't imagine that a girl would see that and say 'I totally want to do that; it sounds awesome.'" Klout CEO Joe Fernandez says the sign was just a joke and "definitely not meant to be an exclusionary thing," and that the company hired a female programmer at the fair. At the University of Pennsylvania, a computer science club had to back down from plans to wear T-shirts saying "Brogrammer" to a school festival when female members objected to it.

In business, the brogramming culture seems to be confined to smaller outfits, says Kamakshi Sivaramakrishnan, the first female engineer at mobile ad start-up AdMob. When the company was bought by Google in 2010, she was surrounded by a more diverse team of programmers. "The frat boy mentality among engineering men is a little more pronounced in the start-up

world than in the more mature organizations," she says.

While a few start-ups like Better-Works (engineer population: 14 men, one woman) may be overrun by bros, at most others the trend is confined to a few. At Santa Monica (California)-based Gravity, engineering director Jim Plush is referred to as the "resident brogrammer" and has affixed his computer monitor to a treadmill so he can exercise two to three hours a day while programming. At Justin. tv, in San Francisco, cofounder Justin Kan rides a motorcycle to work and listens to Swedish dubstep music on his headphones. "It's not like a frat house," says Kan. "My desk is the brogramming lounge."

Questions for Discussion

1. In what ways might a "brogrammer" atmosphere interfere with the effective management of diversity?

2. What are some of the problems with associating certain stereotypes with occupations such as associating programming with stereotypes like "geek," "nerd," or "brogrammer"?

3. How might a "brogrammer" atmosphere make it difficult for firms to attract and retain women?

4. What are some of the potential implications of having a "brogrammer" atmosphere for the incidence of sexual harassment in organizations?

Source: "Slamming Natty Light Between Lines of C++" by Douglas MacMillan. *Bloomberg Businessweek*, March 5–March 11, 2012, pp. 44–45. Bloomberg L. P. Copyright © 2012. All rights reserved.

CHAPTER 6

Managing in the Global Environment

Learning Objectives

After studying this chapter, you should be able to:

LO6-1 Explain why the ability to perceive, interpret, and respond appropriately to the global environment is crucial for managerial success.

LO6-2 Differentiate between the global task and global general environments.

LO6-3 Identify the main forces in the global task and general environments, and describe the challenges that each force presents to managers.

LO6-4 Explain why the global environment is becoming more open and competitive, and identify the forces behind the process of globalization that increase the opportunities, complexities, challenges, and threats managers face.

LO6-5 Discuss why national cultures differ and why it is important that managers be sensitive to the effects of falling trade barriers and regional trade associations on the political and social systems of nations around the world.

A MANAGER'S CHALLENGE

Nokia Flips Its Approach to Managing the Global Environment

Why is managing the global environment so complex today? Nokia has experienced enormous problems in the 2010s because the popularity of smartphones has soared and companies like Apple, BlackBerry, Samsung, and Motorola (now owned by Google) are competing vigorously to offer customers the smartphone that contains the latest features and technology. In fact, in 2012 Samsung took over from Nokia as the world's largest cell phone maker, and Nokia's stock price has plunged in the 2010s as its attempts to fight back continue to fail and it is losing billions of dollars.

To a large degree the reason for Nokia's problems center around the way it has traditionally managed the global environment compared to its cell phone competitors. To keep their costs to a minimum, its competitors have outsourced their cell phone production to Asian companies. Nokia did not because historically a major reason for Nokia's dominance in cell phones was its skills in global supply chain management that allowed it to provide low-cost phones that could be customized to the needs of customers in different world regions. Nokia's global strategy was to make its phones in the world region in which they were sold; Nokia built expensive state-of-the-art factories in Germany, Brazil, China,

and India. In 2008 it opened a new plant in Romania to make phones for the expanding eastern European and Russian market.

A major reason for beginning operations in Romania was its low labor costs. In fact, once Nokia's Romanian factory was up and running, Nokia closed its factory in Bochum, Germany, in 2008 because it was too expensive to operate. Even so, Nokia was hard-headed about how efficiently it expected its Romanian factory to operate because *all* its global factories were required to operate at the same level of efficiency that its *most* efficient global factory has achieved. Nokia's

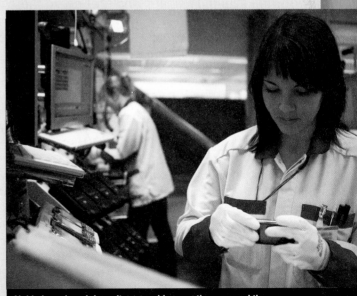

Nokia has closed down its assembly operations around the world, such as this one in Romania, and outsourced all cell phone assembly to companies in China to lower costs.

goal was to continuously improve efficiency over time by encouraging managers to find ways to lower costs and then share this knowledge across the company.

Finally, in 2010, Nokia's CEO Olli-Pekka Kallasvuo realized that Nokia's strategy had failed and that the company needed to recruit a new CEO who understood how to change the way it managed the environment. Stephen Elop became Nokia's CEO in September 2010, the first non-Finn ever to be named to the top position. Elop left Microsoft, where he had been head of its business division, and announced that Nokia would team up with Microsoft to supply its new smartphone software and dump its own Simian platform. In April 2011 Elop announced it would axe 7,000 jobs and outsource its Symbian software development unit to cut $1.2 billion in costs. The move included laying off 4,000 staff and transferring another 3,000 to services firm Accenture—12% of its phone unit workforce.

Then in September 2011 Elop announced the closure of its assembly plant in Romania and in January 2012 the closure of its operations in Finland, Hungary, and Mexico. In the future all smartphone assembly would be outsourced to Asia with the loss of over 15,000 jobs. In addition, Nokia announced it would cut 17,000 more jobs or almost a quarter of its workforce in its Nokia Siemens Network division, a global telecommunications joint venture with Siemens.

Elop was betting Nokia's future on developing its close ties with Microsoft, and in October 2011 Nokia unveiled two sleek new smartphones based on Microsoft Windows in time for Christmas, a major step in its fight back against Apple and Google.[1] These phones did not sell well despite their reasonable pricing, and Nokia's competitive position continued to deteriorate. In June 2012 Elop announced plans to cut another 10,000 jobs globally and warned its second-quarter loss from its cell phone business would be larger than expected. Its stock price continued to plunge and many analysts wondered if Nokia could survive or whether it would become a takeover target. Despite its new approach to managing the global environment Nokia was still losing the battle against Samsung and Apple and its future looks bleak indeed.

Overview

Top managers of a global company like Nokia operate in an environment where they compete with other companies for scarce and valuable resources. Managers of companies large and small have found that to survive and prosper in the 21st century most organizations must become **global organizations** that operate and compete not only domestically, at home, but also globally, in countries around the world. Operating in the global environment is uncertain and unpredictable because it is complex and changes constantly.

If organizations are to adapt successfully to this changing environment, their managers must learn to understand the forces that operate in it and how these forces give rise to opportunities and threats. In this chapter we examine why the environment, both domestically and globally, has become more open, vibrant, and competitive. We examine how forces in the task and general environments affect global organizations and their managers. By the end of this chapter, you will appreciate the changes that are taking place in the environment and understand why it is important for managers to develop a global perspective as they strive to increase organizational efficiency and effectiveness.

global organization An organization that operates and competes in more than one country.

LO6-1 Explain why the ability to perceive, interpret, and respond appropriately to the global environment is crucial for managerial success.

What Is the Global Environment?

The **global environment** is a set of forces and conditions in the world outside an organization's boundary that affect how it operates and shape its behavior.[2] These forces change over time and thus present managers with *opportunities* and *threats*. Some changes in the global environment, such as the development of efficient new production technology, the availability of lower-cost components, or the opening of new global markets, create opportunities for managers to make and sell more products, obtain more resources and capital, and thereby strengthen their organization. In contrast, the rise of new global competitors, a global economic recession, or an oil shortage poses threats that can devastate an organization if managers are unable to sell its products, causing revenues and profits to plunge. The quality of managers' understanding of forces in the global environment and their ability to respond appropriately to those forces, such as Sony's managers' ability to make and sell the electronic products that customers around the world want to buy, are critical factors affecting organizational performance.

In this chapter we explore the nature of these forces and consider how managers can respond to them. To identify opportunities and threats caused by forces in the environment, it is helpful for managers to distinguish between the *task environment* and the more encompassing *general environment* (see Figure 6.1).

The **task environment** is the set of forces and conditions that originates with global suppliers, distributors, customers, and competitors; these forces and conditions affect an organization's ability to obtain inputs and dispose of its outputs. The task environment contains the forces that have the most *immediate* and *direct* effect on managers because they pressure and influence managers daily. When managers turn on the radio or television, arrive at their offices in the morning, open their mail, or look at their computer screens, they are likely to learn about problems facing them because of changing conditions in their organization's task environment.

The **general environment** includes the wide-ranging global, economic, technological, sociocultural, demographic, political, and legal forces that affect the organization and its task environment. For the individual manager, opportunities and threats resulting from changes in the general environment are often more difficult to identify and respond to than are events in the task environment. However, changes in these forces can have major impacts on managers and their organizations.

LO6-2 Differentiate between the global task and global general environments.

global environment The set of global forces and conditions that operates beyond an organization's boundaries but affects a manager's ability to acquire and utilize resources.

task environment The set of forces and conditions that originates with suppliers, distributors, customers, and competitors and affects an organization's ability to obtain inputs and dispose of its outputs because they influence managers daily

general environment The wide-ranging global, economic, technological, sociocultural, demographic, political, and legal forces that affect an organization and its task environment.

The Task Environment

Forces in the task environment result from the actions of suppliers, distributors, customers, and competitors both at home and abroad (see Figure 6.1). These four groups affect a manager's ability to obtain resources and dispose of outputs daily, weekly, and monthly and thus have a significant impact on short-term decision making.

Suppliers

suppliers Individuals and organizations that provide an organization with the input resources it needs to produce goods and services.

Suppliers are the individuals and companies that provide an organization with the input resources (such as raw materials, component parts, or employees) it needs to produce goods and services. In return, the suppliers receive payment for those goods and services. An important aspect of a manager's job is to ensure a reliable supply of input resources.

For example, take Dell Computer, the company we focused on in Chapter 1. Dell has many suppliers of component parts such as microprocessors (Intel and AMD) and disk drives (Quantum and Seagate Technologies). It also has suppliers of preinstalled software, including the operating system and specific applications software (Microsoft and Adobe). Dell's providers of capital, such as banks and financial institutions, are also important suppliers. Cisco Systems and Oracle are important providers of Internet hardware and software for dot-coms.

Dell has several suppliers of labor. One source is the educational institutions that train future Dell employees and therefore provide the company with skilled workers. Another is trade unions, organizations that represent employee interests and can control the supply of

LO6-3 Identify the main forces in the global task and general environments, and describe the challenges that each force presents to managers.

Figure 6.1

Forces in the Global Environment

labor by exercising the right of unionized workers to strike. Unions also can influence the terms and conditions under which labor is employed. Dell's workers are not unionized; when layoffs became necessary because of the financial crisis and recession beginning in 2009, Dell had few problems in laying off workers to reduce costs. In organizations and industries where unions are strong, however, such as the transportation industry, an important part of a manager's job is negotiating and administering agreements with unions and their representatives.

Changes in the nature, number, or type of suppliers produce opportunities and threats to which managers must respond if their organizations are to prosper. For example, a major supplier-related threat that confronts managers arises when suppliers' bargaining position is so strong that they can raise the prices of the inputs they supply to the organization. A supplier's bargaining position is especially strong when (1) the supplier is the sole source of an input and (2) the input is vital to the organization.[3] For example, for 17 years G. D. Searle was the sole supplier of NutraSweet, the artificial sweetener used in most diet soft drinks. Not only was NutraSweet an important ingredient in diet soft drinks, but it also was one for which there was no acceptable substitute (saccharin and other artificial sweeteners raised health concerns). Searle earned its privileged position because it invented and held the patent for NutraSweet, and patents prohibit other organizations from introducing competing products for 17 years. As a result, Searle was able to demand a high price for NutraSweet, charging twice the price of an equivalent amount of sugar; and paying that price raised the costs of soft drink manufacturers such as Coca-Cola and PepsiCo. When Searle's patent expired, many other companies introduced products similar to NutraSweet, and prices fell.[4] In the 2000s, Splenda, which was made by McNeil Nutritionals, owned by Tate & Lyle, a British company, replaced NutraSweet as the artificial sweetener of choice, and NutraSweet's price fell further; Splenda began to command a high price from soft drink companies.[5]

In contrast, when an organization has many suppliers for a particular input, it is in a relatively strong bargaining position with those suppliers and can demand low-cost, high-quality inputs from them. Often an organization can use its power with suppliers to force them to reduce their prices, as Dell frequently does. Dell, for example, is constantly searching for low-cost suppliers abroad to keep its PC prices competitive. At a global level, organizations can buy products from suppliers overseas or become their own suppliers by manufacturing their products abroad.

It is important that managers recognize the opportunities and threats associated with managing the global supply chain. On one hand, gaining access to low-cost products made abroad represents an opportunity for U.S. companies to lower their input costs. On the other hand, managers who fail to use low-cost overseas suppliers create a threat and put their organizations at a competitive disadvantage.[6] Levi Strauss, for example, was slow to realize that it could not compete with the low-priced jeans sold by Walmart and other retailers, and it was eventually forced to close all its U.S. jean factories and outsource manufacturing to low-cost overseas suppliers to cut the price of its jeans to a competitive level. Now it sells its low-priced jeans in Walmart. The downside to global outsourcing is, of course, the loss of millions of U.S. jobs, an issue we have discussed in previous chapters.

A common problem facing managers of large global companies such as Ford, Sony, and Dell is managing the development of a global supplier network that will allow their companies to keep costs down and quality high. For example, Boeing's 777 jet was originally built using many components from over 500 global suppliers; for example, eight Japanese suppliers made parts for the 777 fuselage, doors, and wings.[7] Boeing chose these suppliers because they were the best in the world at performing their particular activities and Boeing's goal was to produce a high-quality final product.[8] Pleased with the outcome, Boeing decided to outsource a greater percentage of components to global suppliers when it designed the new Boeing 787 Dreamliner; however, as we discussed in Chapter 1 many serious problems arose that delayed the introduction of the new aircraft for several years.

The purchasing activities of global companies have become increasingly complicated as a result of the development of a whole range of skills and competencies in different countries around the world. It is clearly in companies' interests to search out the lowest-cost, best-quality suppliers. IT and the Internet are continually making it easier for companies to coordinate complicated long-distance exchanges involving the purchasing of inputs and the disposal of outputs—something Sony has taken advantage of as it trims the number of its suppliers to reduce costs.

global outsourcing The purchase or production of inputs or final products from overseas suppliers to lower costs and improve product quality or design.

Global outsourcing occurs when a company contracts with suppliers in other countries to make the various inputs or components that go into its products or to assemble the final products to reduce costs. For example, Apple contracts with companies in Taiwan and China to make inputs such as the chips, batteries, and LCD displays that power its digital devices; then it contracts with outsourcers such as Foxconn to assemble its final products—such as iPods, iPhones, and iPads. Apple also outsources the distribution of its products around the world by contracting with companies such as FedEx or DHL.

Global outsourcing has grown enormously to take advantage of national differences in the cost and quality of resources such as labor or raw materials that can significantly reduce manufacturing costs or increase product quality or reliability. Today such global exchanges are becoming so complex that some companies specialize in managing other companies' global supply chains. Global companies use the services of overseas intermediaries or brokers, which are located close to potential suppliers, to find the suppliers that can best meet the needs of a particular company. They can design the most efficient supply chain for a company to outsource the component and assembly operations required to produce its final products. Because these suppliers are located in thousands of cities in many countries, finding them is difficult. Li & Fung, based in Hong Kong, is one broker that has helped

The purchasing activities of global companies have become increasingly complicated in recent years. Hundreds of suppliers around the world produce parts for Boeing's new Dreamliner.

hundreds of major U.S. companies to outsource their component or assembly operations to suitable overseas suppliers, especially suppliers in mainland China.[9]

Although outsourcing to take advantage of low labor costs has helped many companies perform better, in the 2010s its risks have also become apparent, especially when issues such as reliability, quality, and speed are important. For example, as noted above, the introduction of Boeing's 787 Dreamliner plane was delayed for several years because the company increased its reliance on companies abroad to make vital components and many of these had problems in meeting Boeing's delivery requirements. Clearly, outsourcing decisions need to be carefully considered given the nature of a company's products.[10] For example, Caterpillar decided to "insource" production of excavators back to the United States because lower U.S. labor costs and increasing global shipping costs had made this the most efficient way to do business. On the other hand, some companies do not outsource manufacturing; they prefer to establish their own assembly operations and factories in countries around the world to protect their proprietary technology. For example, most global automakers own their production operations in China to retain control over their global decision making and keep their operations secret. An interesting example of the supply problems that have developed between Nokia and Microsoft is discussed in the following "Managing Globally" box.

Managing Globally

How Microsoft Became a Powerful Nokia Supplier

As discussed at the beginning of this chapter, when Nokia appointed Stephen Elop as CEO, among his first moves was to dump Nokia's free Symbian cell phone software that was powering millions of new phones every year and to introduce new smartphones based on the Windows 7 software phone platform. The Lumina 900 became Nokia's flagship product and was designed to compete with the Apple iPhone and Samsung Galaxy, but sales never took off and only hundreds of thousands were sold compared to millions of its rivals' phones.

In London, Stephen Elop, chief executive officer of Nokia, gestures as Steve Ballmer, chief executive officer of Microsoft, looks on. Nokia, the world's biggest maker of mobile phones, said it's forming a software partnership with Microsoft Corp., a bet that together the two companies can better challenge Google and Apple.

From the start, analysts wondered if Nokia had been smart to put "all its eggs in one basket" by moving to the Windows 7 platform, which, lacking the thousands of developers needed to develop phone applications, was always one step behind Google's Android and Apple's iOS 5 phone software. Poor Lumina smartphone sales and the layoff of over 40,000 employees seemed to suggest Elop's new global initiatives were not working out, and Nokia experienced a major blow in June 2012 when Microsoft made a surprising announcement.

In order to compete effectively against the Android and iOS 5 platforms, it would introduce new advanced phone software—the Windows 8 platform—in late 2012. However, the problem for Nokia was that its flagship Lumina 900 smartphone could not be upgraded to this new software platform. This was because Windows 7 smartphones run on single-core processors but all smartphone makers were moving to use multicore processors and high-definition screens that support more sophisticated video and gaming applications. And these would only run on the Windows 8 phone platform! This was a disaster for Nokia; it made its current Windows smartphones essentially obsolete despite their low pricing.

Essentially, Microsoft had become a powerful supplier (of software) to Nokia and it was riding roughshod over Nokia in order to protect its own global competitive position and was allowing Nokia to "go to the dogs." Windows Phone 8 brings the operating system into parity with Android and iOS smartphones; for Microsoft it was a possible "game-changing" platform that could attract key smartphone makers such as HTC, Samsung, and LG. In fact, Microsoft announced that Samsung, HTC, and Huawei are working on Windows Phone 8 smartphones—so too is Nokia.

However, analysts recognizing the body blow Nokia had experienced drastically cut their estimates of Nokia's 2013 revenues by over 30% and cut estimates of Nokia's Windows Phone unit sales down to 34 million handsets, 41% lower than they had previously predicted! Nokia downplayed the news, arguing its low pricing would help attract customers because they were getting great value. But most analysts felt that Microsoft had used its power to its own advantage and that customers would wait for the Windows 8 platform that would be available from several smartphone makers, so Nokia had lost its competitive advantage, especially because it had not unveiled any new Windows Phone 8 handsets.

Nokia's new CEO began to attract a lot of criticism from analysts who argued that Elop had made major mistakes and had no global roadmap for the company to follow; it was losing top talent and replacing it with managers from Microsoft. Moreover, his main focus seems to have been on reducing costs, which is still not working, and he has neglected expensive product development in his drive to keep costs low. Analysts became even more convinced Nokia could not survive, and many hoped that Microsoft, which has caused many of its current problems, would take over the company that is worth one-third of what it was just three years ago.

Distributors

distributors Organizations that help other organizations sell their goods or services to customers.

Distributors are organizations that help other organizations sell their goods or services to customers. The decisions managers make about how to distribute products to customers can have important effects on organizational performance. For example, package delivery companies such as Federal Express, UPS, and the U.S. Postal Service have become vital distributors for the millions of items bought online and shipped to customers by dot-com companies both at home and abroad.

The changing nature of distributors and distribution methods can bring opportunities and threats for managers. If distributors become so large and powerful that they can control customers' access to a particular organization's goods and services, they can threaten the organization by demanding that it reduce the prices of its goods and services.[11] For example, the huge retail distributor Walmart controls its suppliers' access to millions of customers and thus can demand that its suppliers reduce their prices to keep its business. If an organization such as Procter & Gamble refuses to reduce its prices, Walmart might respond by buying products only from Procter & Gamble's competitors—companies such as Unilever and Colgate. To reduce costs, Walmart also has used its power as a distributor to demand that all its suppliers adopt a new wireless radio frequency scanning technology to reduce the cost of shipping and stocking products in its stores; otherwise it would stop doing business with them.[12]

It is illegal for distributors to collaborate or collude to keep prices high and thus maintain their power over buyers; however, this frequently happens. In the early 2000s several European drug companies conspired to keep the price of vitamins artificially high. In 2005 the three largest global makers of flash memory, including Samsung, were found guilty of price fixing (they collaborated to keep prices high); in 2010 the major suppliers of LCD screens were also found guilty of conspiring to keep prices high. All these companies paid hundreds of millions of dollars in fines, and many of their top executives were sentenced to jail terms.

Customers

customers Individuals and groups that buy the goods and services an organization produces.

Customers are the individuals and groups that buy the goods and services an organization produces. For example, Dell's customers can be segmented into several distinct groups: (1) individuals who purchase PCs for home use, (2) small companies, (3) large companies, and (4) government agencies and educational institutions. Changes in the number and types of customers or in customers' tastes and needs create opportunities and threats. An organization's success depends on its responsiveness to customers—whether it can satisfy their needs. In the PC industry, customers are demanding thinner computers, better graphics and speed, and increased wireless and Internet connections—and lower prices—and PC makers must respond to the changing types and needs of customers, such as by introducing tablet computers. A school, too, must adapt to the changing needs of its customers. For example, if more Spanish-speaking students enroll, additional classes in English as a second language may need to be scheduled. A manager's ability to identify an organization's main customer groups, and make the products that best satisfy their particular needs, is a crucial factor affecting organizational and managerial success.

The most obvious opportunity associated with expanding into the global environment is the prospect of selling goods and services to millions or billions of new customers, as Amazon.com's CEO Jeff Bezos discovered when he expanded his company's operations in many countries.[13] Similarly, Accenture and Cap Gemini, two large consulting companies, established regional operating centers around the globe, and they recruit and train thousands of overseas consultants to serve the needs of customers in their respective world regions.

Today many products have gained global customer acceptance. This consolidation is occurring both for consumer goods and for business products and has created enormous opportunities for managers. The worldwide acceptance of Coca-Cola, Apple iPods, McDonald's hamburgers, and Samsung smartphones is a sign that the tastes and preferences of customers in different countries may not be so different after all.[14] Likewise, large global markets exist for business products such as telecommunications equipment, electronic components, and computer and financial services. Thus Cisco and Siemens sell their telecommunications equipment; Intel, its microprocessors; and Oracle and SAP, their business systems management software, to customers all over the world.

Competitors

competitors Organizations that produce goods and services that are similar to a particular organization's goods and services.

One of the most important forces an organization confronts in its task environment is competitors. **Competitors** are organizations that produce goods and services that are similar and comparable to a particular organization's goods and services. In other words, competitors are organizations trying to attract the same customers. Dell's competitors include other domestic PC makers (such as Apple and HP) as well as overseas competitors (such as Sony and Toshiba in Japan, Lenovo, the Chinese company that bought IBM's PC division, and Acer, the Taiwanese company that bought Gateway). Similarly, dot-com stockbroker E*Trade has other competitors such as Ameritrade, Scottrade, and Charles Schwab.

Rivalry between competitors is potentially the most threatening force managers must deal with. A high level of rivalry typically results in price competition, and falling prices reduce customer revenues and profits. In the early 2000s competition in the PC industry became intense because Dell was aggressively cutting costs and prices to increase its global market share.[15] IBM had to exit the PC business after it lost billions in its battle against low-cost rivals, and Gateway and HP also suffered losses while Dell's profits soared. By 2006, however, HP's fortunes had recovered because it had found ways to lower its costs and offer stylish new PCs, and Apple was growing rapidly, so Dell's profit margins shrunk. In 2009, HP overtook Dell to become the largest global PC maker, and in 2010 Apple's and Acer's sales were also expanding rapidly. Dell's managers had failed to appreciate how fast its global competitors were catching up and had not developed the right strategies to keep the company at the top.

potential competitors Organizations that presently are not in a task environment but could enter if they so choose.

Although extensive rivalry between existing competitors is a major threat to profitability, so is the potential for new competitors to enter the task environment. **Potential competitors** are organizations that are not presently in a task environment but have the resources to enter if they so choose. In 2010, Amazon.com, for example, was not in the furniture or large appliance business, but it could enter these businesses if its managers decided it could profitably sell such products online—and in 2012 it does sell furniture and large appliances. When new competitors enter an industry, competition increases and prices and profits decrease—as furniture and electronic stores such as Best Buy have discovered as they battle Amazon.com.

barriers to entry Factors that make it difficult and costly for an organization to enter a particular task environment or industry.

BARRIERS TO ENTRY   In general, the potential for new competitors to enter a task environment (and thus increase competition) is a function of barriers to entry.[16] **Barriers to entry**

are factors that make it difficult and costly for a company to enter a particular task environment or industry.[17] In other words, the more difficult and costly it is to enter the task environment, the higher are the barriers to entry. The higher the barriers to entry, the fewer the competitors in an organization's task environment and thus the lower the threat of competition. With fewer competitors, it is easier to obtain customers and keep prices high.

Barriers to entry result from three main sources: economies of scale, brand loyalty, and government regulations that impede entry (see Figure 6.2). **Economies of scale** are the cost advantages associated with large operations. Economies of scale result from factors such as manufacturing products in very large quantities, buying inputs in bulk, or making more effective use of organizational resources than do competitors by fully utilizing employees' skills and knowledge. If organizations already in the task environment are large and enjoy significant economies of scale, their costs are lower than the costs that potential entrants will face, and newcomers will find it expensive to enter the industry. Amazon.com, for example, enjoys significant economies of scale relative to most other dot-com companies because of its highly efficient distribution system.[18]

Brand loyalty is customers' preference for the products of organizations currently in the task environment. If established organizations enjoy significant brand loyalty, a new entrant will find it difficult and costly to obtain a share of the market. Newcomers must bear huge advertising costs to build customer awareness of the goods or services they intend to provide.[19] Today Google, Amazon.com, and eBay enjoy a high level of brand loyalty and have some of the highest website hit rates, which allows them to increase their marketing revenues.

In some cases, *government regulations* function as a barrier to entry at both the industry and the country levels. Many industries that were deregulated, such as air transport, trucking, utilities, and telecommunications, experienced a high level of new entry after deregulation; this forced existing companies in those industries to operate more efficiently or risk being put out of business. At the national and global levels, administrative barriers are government policies that create barriers to entry and limit imports of goods by overseas companies. Japan is well known for the many ways in which it attempts to restrict the entry of overseas competitors or lessen their impact on Japanese firms. Japan has come under intense pressure to relax and abolish regulations such as those governing the import of rice, for example.

The Japanese rice market, like many other Japanese markets, was closed to overseas competitors until 1993 to protect Japan's thousands of high-cost, low-output rice farmers. Rice cultivation is expensive in Japan because of the country's mountainous terrain, and Japanese consumers have always paid high prices for rice. Under overseas pressure, the Japanese government opened the market; but overseas competitors are allowed to export to Japan only 8% of its annual rice consumption to protect its farmers.

economies of scale Cost advantages associated with large operations.

brand loyalty Customers' preference for the products of organizations currently existing in the task environment.

The tyranny of the lower price. A Japanese businessman purchases a frozen U.S.-sourced rice O-bento lunch at a Nippon Tokyo store. Nippon's importing practices have angered Japanese rice farmers.

Figure 6.2
Barriers to Entry and Competition

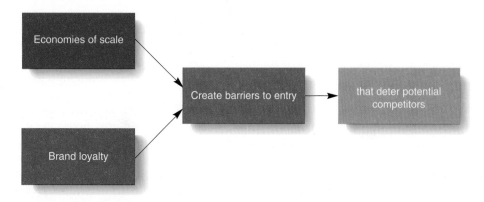

In the 2000s, however, an alliance between organic rice grower Lundberg Family Farms of California and the Nippon Restaurant Enterprise Co. found a new way to break into the Japanese rice market. Because there is no tariff on rice used in processed foods, Nippon converts the U.S. organic rice into "O-bento," an organic hot boxed lunch packed with rice, vegetables, chicken, beef, and salmon, all imported from the United States. The lunches, which cost about $4 compared to a Japanese rice bento that costs about $9, are sold at railway stations and other outlets throughout Japan and have become very popular. A storm of protest from Japanese rice farmers arose because the entry of U.S. rice growers forced them to leave their rice fields idle or grow less profitable crops. Other overseas companies are increasingly forming alliances with Japanese companies to find new ways to break into the high-priced Japanese market, and little by little, Japan's restrictive trade practices are being whittled away.

In summary, intense rivalry among competitors creates a task environment that is highly threatening and makes it increasingly difficult for managers to gain access to the resources an organization needs to make goods and services. Conversely, low rivalry results in a task environment where competitive pressures are more moderate and managers have greater opportunities to acquire the resources they need to make their organizations effective.

The General Environment

Economic, technological, sociocultural, demographic, political, and legal forces in the general environment often have important effects on forces in the task environment that determine an organization's ability to obtain resources—effects that managers may not be aware of. For example, the sudden, dramatic upheavals in the mortgage and banking industry that started in 2007 were brought about by a combination of the development of complex new financial lending instruments called derivatives; a speculative boom in commodities and housing prices; and lax government regulation that allowed unethical bankers and financial managers to exploit the derivatives to make immense short-term profits. These events triggered the economic crisis of 2008–2009 that caused stock markets around the world to plummet, devastating the retirement savings of hundreds of millions of ordinary people, and caused layoffs of millions of employees as companies slashed their workforces because customers reduced their spending.

The implication is clear: Managers must continuously analyze forces in the general environment because these forces affect ongoing decision making and planning. How well managers can perform this task determines how quickly an organization can respond to the changes taking place. Next we discuss the major forces in the general environment and examine their impact on an organization's task environment.

Economic Forces

economic forces Interest rates, inflation, unemployment, economic growth, and other factors that affect the general health and well-being of a nation or the regional economy of an organization.

Economic forces affect the general health and well-being of a country or world region. They include interest rates, inflation, unemployment, and economic growth. Economic forces produce many opportunities and threats for managers. Low levels of unemployment and falling interest rates give people more money to spend, and as a result organizations can sell more goods and services. Good economic times affect the supply of resources that become easier or more inexpensive to acquire, and organizations have an opportunity to flourish. High-tech companies enjoyed this throughout the 1990s when computer and electronics companies like Sony made record profits as the global economy boomed because of advances in IT and growing global trade.

In contrast, worsening macroeconomic conditions, like those in the 2010s, pose a major threat because they reduce managers' ability to gain access to the resources their organizations need to survive and prosper. Profit-seeking organizations such as hotels and retail stores have fewer customers during economic downturns; hotel rates dropped by 14% in 2009 compared to 2008, for example, just as retail sales plunged. Nonprofits such as charities and colleges also saw donations decline by more than 20% because of the economic downturn.

Poor economic conditions make the environment more complex and managers' jobs more difficult and demanding. Companies often need to reduce the number of their managers and employees, streamline their operations, and identify ways to acquire and use resources more efficiently and effectively. Successful managers realize the important effects that economic forces have on their organizations, and they pay close attention to what is occurring in the economy at the national and regional levels to respond appropriately.

Technological Forces

technology The combination of skills and equipment that managers use in designing, producing, and distributing goods and services.

technological forces Outcomes of changes in the technology managers use to design, produce, or distribute goods and services.

Technology is the combination of tools, machines, computers, skills, information, and knowledge that managers use to design, produce, and distribute goods and services; **technological forces** are outcomes of changes in that technology. The overall pace of technological change has accelerated greatly in the last decades because technological advances in microprocessors and computer hardware and software have spurred technological advances in most businesses and industries. The effects of changing technological forces are still increasing in magnitude.[20]

Technological forces can have profound implications for managers and organizations. Technological change can make established products obsolete—for example, cathode-ray tube (CRT) computer monitors and televisions (such as Sony's Trinitron), bound sets of encyclopedias, and newspapers and magazines—forcing managers to find new ways to satisfy customer needs. Although technological change can threaten an organization, it also can create a host of new opportunities for designing, making, or distributing new and better kinds of goods and services. Ever more powerful microprocessors developed by Intel and AMD, which now have 8 or 12 processing cores on each chip, are continuing the IT revolution that has spurred demand for all kinds of new digital computing devices and services and has affected the competitive position of all high-tech companies. Will Google's new suite of software devastate Microsoft, for example, just as Microsoft's devastated IBM in the 1990s? Managers must move quickly to respond to such changes if their organizations are to survive and prosper.

Changes in IT are altering the nature of work itself within organizations, including that of the manager's job. Today telecommuting, videoconferencing, and text messaging are everyday activities that let managers supervise and coordinate geographically dispersed employees. Salespeople in many companies work from home offices and commute electronically to work. They communicate with other employees through companywide electronic communication networks using tablet PCs and smartphones to orchestrate "face-to-face" meetings with coworkers across the country or globe.

Sociocultural Forces

sociocultural forces Pressures emanating from the social structure of a country or society or from the national culture.

social structure The traditional system of relationships established between people and groups in a society.

national culture The set of values that a society considers important and the norms of behavior that are approved or sanctioned in that society.

Sociocultural forces are pressures emanating from the social structure of a country or society or from the national culture, such as the concern for diversity, discussed in the previous chapter. Pressures from both sources can either constrain or facilitate the way organizations operate and managers behave. **Social structure** is the traditional system of relationships established between people and groups in a society. Societies differ substantially in social structure. In societies that have a high degree of social stratification, there are many distinctions among individuals and groups. Caste systems in India and Tibet and the recognition of numerous social classes in Great Britain and France produce a multilayered social structure in each of those countries. In contrast, social stratification is lower in relatively egalitarian New Zealand and in the United States, where the social structure reveals few distinctions among people. Most top managers in France come from the upper classes of French society, but top managers in the United States come from all strata of American society.

Societies also differ in the extent to which they emphasize the individual over the group. Such differences may dictate how managers need to motivate and lead employees.

National culture is the set of values that a society considers important and the norms of behavior that are approved or sanctioned in that society. Societies differ substantially in the values and norms they emphasize. For example, in the United States individualism is highly valued, but in Korea and Japan individuals are expected to conform to group expectations.[21] National culture, discussed at length later in this chapter, also affects how managers motivate and coordinate employees and how organizations do business. Ethics, an important aspect of national culture, were discussed in detail in Chapter 4.

Pick your poison. The American trend towards fitness has prompted traditional soft drink manufacturers to expand their offerings into a staggering array of energy drinks.

Social structure and national culture not only differ across societies but also change within societies over time. In the United States, attitudes toward the roles of women, sex, marriage, and gays and lesbians changed in each past decade. Many people in Asian countries such as Hong Kong, Singapore, Korea, and even China think the younger generation is far more individualistic and "American-like" than previous generations. Currently, throughout much of Eastern Europe, new values that emphasize individualism and entrepreneurship are replacing communist values based on collectivism and obedience to the state. The pace of change is accelerating.

Individual managers and organizations must be responsive to changes in, and differences among, the social structures and national cultures of all the countries in which they operate. In today's increasingly integrated global economy, managers are likely to interact with people from several countries, and many managers live and work abroad. Effective managers are sensitive to differences between societies and adjust their behavior accordingly.

Managers and organizations also must respond to social changes within a society. In the last decades, for example, Americans have become increasingly interested in their personal health and fitness. Managers who recognized this trend early and took advantage of the opportunities that resulted from it were able to reap significant gains for their organizations, such as chains of health clubs. PepsiCo used the opportunity presented by the fitness trend and took market share from archrival Coca-Cola by being the first to introduce diet colas and fruit-based soft drinks. Then Quaker Oats made Gatorade the most popular energy drink, and now others like Red Bull, Monster, and Rockstar are increasing in popularity. The health trend, however, did not offer opportunities to all companies; to some it posed a threat. Tobacco companies came under intense pressure due to consumers' greater awareness of negative health impacts from smoking. The rage for "low-carb" foods in the 2000s increased demand for meat and protein, and bread and doughnut companies such as Kraft and Krispy Kreme suffered—until the ongoing recession boosted the sale of inexpensive products such as macaroni and cheese and hamburger helper.

Demographic Forces

demographic forces Outcomes of changes in, or changing attitudes toward, the characteristics of a population, such as age, gender, ethnic origin, race, sexual orientation, and social class.

Demographic forces are outcomes of changes in, or changing attitudes toward, the characteristics of a population, such as age, gender, ethnic origin, race, sexual orientation, and social class. Like the other forces in the general environment, demographic forces present managers with opportunities and threats and can have major implications for organizations. We examined the nature of these challenges in depth in our discussion of diversity in Chapter 5.

Today most industrialized nations are experiencing the aging of their populations as a consequence of falling birth and death rates and the aging of the baby boom generation. Consequently, the absolute number of older people has increased substantially, which has generated opportunities for organizations that cater to older people, such as the home health care, recreation, and medical industries, which have seen an upswing in demand for their services. The aging of the population also has several implications for the workplace. Most significant are a relative decline in the number of young people joining the workforce and an increase in the number of active employees who are postponing retirement beyond the traditional age of 65. Indeed, the continuing financial crisis in the 2010s has made it impossible for millions of older people to retire because their savings have been decimated. These changes suggest that organizations need to find ways to motivate older employees and use their skills and knowledge—an issue that many Western societies have yet to tackle.

Political and Legal Forces

political and legal forces Outcomes of changes in laws and regulations, such as deregulation of industries, privatization of organizations, and increased emphasis on environmental protection.

Political and legal forces are outcomes of changes in laws and regulations. They result from political and legal developments that take place within a nation, within a world region, or across the world and significantly affect managers and organizations everywhere.

Political processes shape a nation's laws and the international laws that govern the relationships between nations. Laws constrain the operations of organizations and managers and thus create both opportunities and threats.[22] For example, throughout much of the industrialized world there has been a strong trend toward deregulation of industries previously controlled by the state and privatization of organizations once owned by the state such as airlines, railways, and utility companies.

Another important political and legal force affecting managers and organizations is the political integration of countries that has been taking place during the last decades.[23] Increasingly, nations are forming political unions that allow free exchange of resources and capital. The growth of the European Union (EU) is one example: Common laws govern trade and commerce between EU member countries, and the European Court has the right to examine the business of any global organization and to approve any proposed mergers between overseas companies that operate inside the EU. For example, Microsoft's anticompetitive business practices came under scrutiny, and it was fined hundreds of millions for its uncompetitive practice of bundling its Internet Explorer web browser with its software. As part of its agreement with the European Court, Microsoft agreed that, beginning in 2010, it would ship its Windows 7 software with a choice of 10 web browsers (such as Chrome, Safari, and Mozilla). Also, in 2012, after months of delay, the court allowed the merger between Motorola and Google to proceed although the court was also investigating Google for possible anticompetitive online advertising practices. The North American Free Trade Agreement (NAFTA), discussed later in the chapter, has more modest political goals; but like the EU, it has changed the laws that affect international commerce by lowering barriers to the free flow of goods and services between member nations.[24]

Indeed, international agreements to abolish laws and regulations that restrict and reduce trade between countries have been having profound effects on global organizations. The falling legal trade barriers create enormous opportunities for companies to sell goods and services internationally. But by allowing overseas companies to compete in a nation's domestic market for customers, falling trade barriers also pose a serious threat because they increase competition in the task environment. Between 1980 and 2010, for example, Japanese companies increased their share of the U.S. car market from around 20% to 40%; Taiwanese companies' share grew from 2% to 7%. In essence, removing legal restrictions on global trade has the same effect as deregulating industries and removing restrictions against competition: It increases the intensity of competition in the task environment and forces conservative, slow-moving companies—such as GM and Chrysler—to become more efficient, improve product quality, and learn new values and norms to compete in the global environment. To help turn around their performance, GM was forced to declare bankruptcy in 2009 and Chrysler was bought by Fiat, and the performance of both these companies has improved in the 2010s.

LO6-4 Explain why the global environment is becoming more open and competitive, and identify the forces behind the process of globalization that increase the opportunities, complexities, challenges, and threats managers face.

Deregulation, privatization, and the removal of legal barriers to trade are just a few of the many ways in which changing political and legal forces can challenge organizations and managers. Others include increased emphasis on environmental protection and the preservation of endangered species, increased emphasis on workplace safety, and legal constraints against discrimination on the basis of race, gender, or age. Managers face major challenges when they seek to take advantage of the opportunities created by changing political, legal, and economic forces.

The Changing Global Environment

The 21st century has banished the idea that the world is composed of distinct national countries and markets that are separated physically, economically, and culturally. Managers need to recognize that companies compete in a truly global marketplace, which is the source of the opportunities and threats they must respond to. Managers continually confront the challenges of global competition such as establishing operations in a country abroad, obtaining inputs from suppliers abroad, or managing in a different national culture.[25] (See Figure 6.3.)

In essence, as a result of falling trade barriers, managers view the global environment as open—that is, as an environment in which companies are free to buy goods and services from, and sell goods and services to, whichever companies and countries they choose. They also

Figure 6.3
The Global Environment

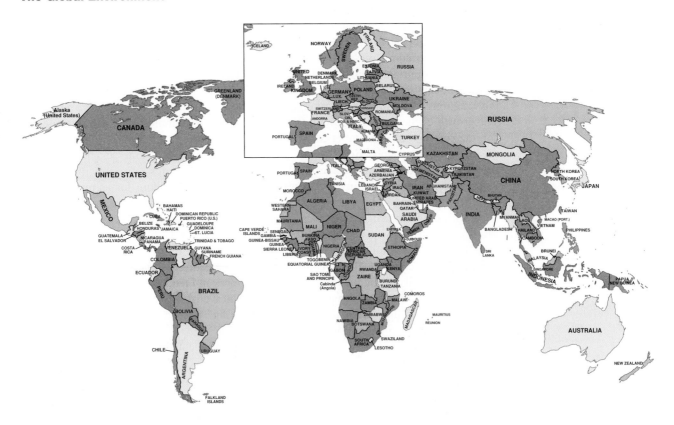

are free to compete against each other to attract customers around the world. All large companies must establish an international network of operations and subsidiaries to build global competitive advantage. Coca-Cola and PepsiCo, for example, have competed aggressively for decades to develop the strongest global soft drink empire, just as Toyota and Honda have built hundreds of car plants around the world to provide the vehicles that global customers like.

In this section we first explain how this open global environment is the result of globalization and the flow of capital around the world. Next we examine how specific economic, political, and legal changes, such as the lowering of barriers to trade and investment, have increased globalization and led to greater interaction and exchanges between organizations and countries. Then we discuss how declining barriers of distance and culture have also increased the pace of globalization, and we consider the specific implications of these changes for managers and organizations. Finally we note that nations still differ widely from each other because they have distinct cultural values and norms and that managers must appreciate these differences to compete successfully across countries.

The Process of Globalization

Perhaps the most important reason why the global environment has become more open and competitive is the increase in globalization. **Globalization** is the set of specific and general forces that work together to integrate and connect economic, political, and social systems *across* countries, cultures, or geographic regions. The result of globalization is that nations and peoples become increasingly *interdependent* because the same forces affect them in similar ways. The fates of peoples in different countries become interlinked as the world's markets and businesses become increasingly interconnected. And as nations become more interdependent, they become more similar to one another in the sense that people develop a similar liking for products as diverse as cell phones, iPods, blue jeans, soft drinks, sports teams, Japanese cars, and foods such as curry, green tea, and Colombian coffee. One outcome of globalization is that the world is becoming a "global village": Products, services, or people

globalization The set of specific and general forces that work together to integrate and connect economic, political, and social systems *across* countries, cultures, or geographical regions so that nations become increasingly interdependent and similar.

can become well known throughout the world—something IKEA, with its range of furniture designed to appeal to customers around the world, is taking advantage of, as the following "Managing Globally" box describes.

Managing
Globally

IKEA Is on Top of the Furniture World

IKEA is the largest furniture chain in the world, and in 2012 the Swedish company operated over 337 stores in 40 countries. In 2011 IKEA sales soared to over $40 billion, or over 23% of the global furniture market; but to its managers and employees this was just the tip of the iceberg. They believed IKEA was poised for massive growth throughout the world in the 2010s because it could provide what the average customer wanted: well-designed and well-made contemporary furniture at an affordable price. IKEA's ability to provide customers with affordable furniture is the result of its approach to globalization, to how it treats its global employees and operates its global store empire. In a nutshell, IKEA's global approach focuses on simplicity, attention to detail, cost-consciousness, and responsiveness in every aspect of its operations and behavior.

IKEA's global approach derives from the personal values and beliefs of its founder, Ingvar Kamprad, about how companies should treat their employees and customers. Kamprad, who is in his 80s (and in 2012 was one of the top 10 richest people in the world), was born in Smaland, a poor Swedish province whose citizens are known for being entrepreneurial, frugal, and hardworking. Kamprad definitely absorbed these values—when he entered the furniture business, he made them the core of his management approach. He teaches store managers and employees his values; his beliefs about the need to operate in a no-frills, cost-conscious way; and his view that they are all in business "together," by which he means that every person who works in his global empire plays an essential role and has an obligation to everyone else.

What does Kamprad's approach mean in practice? All IKEA employees fly coach class on business trips, stay in inexpensive hotels, and keep traveling expenses to a minimum. And IKEA stores operate on the simplest rules and procedures possible, with employees expected to cooperate to solve problems and get the job done. Many famous stories circulate about the frugal Kamprad, such as that he always flies coach class and that when he takes a soda can from the minibar in a hotel room, he replaces it with one bought in a store—despite the fact that he is a multibillionaire.

IKEA's employees see what Kamprad's global approach means as soon as they are recruited to work in a store in one of the many countries in which the company operates. They start learning about IKEA's global corporate culture by performing jobs at the bottom of the ladder, and they are quickly trained to perform all the various jobs involved in store operations. During this process they internalize IKEA's global values and norms, which center on the importance the company attaches to their taking the initiative and responsibility for solving problems and for focusing on customers. Employees are rotated between departments and sometimes stores, and rapid promotion is possible for those who demonstrate the enthusiasm and togetherness that show they have bought into IKEA's global culture.

Most of IKEA's top managers rose from its ranks, and the company holds "breaking the bureaucracy weeks," in which managers are required to work in stores and warehouses for a week each year to make sure they and all employees stay committed to IKEA's global values. No matter which country they operate in, all employees wear informal clothes to work at IKEA—Kamprad has always worn an open-neck

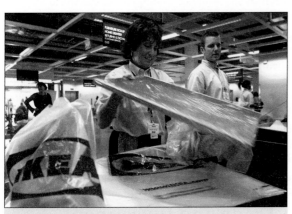

Need a new kitchen table? How about a cute rug to go with it, and while you're at it, a cookie sheet, too? Options await you at any one of the thousands of IKEA stores worldwide.

shirt—and there are no marks of status such as executive dining rooms or private parking places. Employees believe that if they buy into IKEA's work values, behave in ways that keep its growing global operations streamlined and efficient, and focus on being one step ahead of potential problems, they will share in its success. Promotion, training, above-average pay, a generous store bonus system, and the personal well-being that comes from working in a company where people feel valued are some of the rewards that Kamprad pioneered to build and strengthen IKEA's global approach.

Whenever IKEA enters a new country, it sends its most experienced store managers to establish its global approach in its new stores. When IKEA first entered the United States, the attitude of U.S. employees puzzled its managers. Despite their obvious drive to succeed and their good education, employees seemed reluctant to take initiative and assume responsibility. IKEA's managers discovered that their U.S. employees were afraid mistakes would result in the loss of their jobs, so the managers strove to teach employees the "IKEA way." The approach paid off: The United States has become the company's second best country market, and IKEA plans to open many more U.S. stores, as well as stores around the world, over the next decade.[26]

But what drives or spurs globalization? What makes companies like IKEA, Toyota, or Microsoft want to venture into an uncertain global environment? The answer is that the path of globalization is shaped by the ebb and flow of *capital*—valuable wealth-generating assets or resources that people move through companies, countries, and world regions to seek their greatest returns or profits. Managers, employees, and companies like IKEA and Sony are motivated to try to profit or benefit by using their skills to make products customers around the world want to buy. The four principal forms of capital that flow between countries are these:

- *Human capital:* the flow of people around the world through immigration, migration, and emigration.

- *Financial capital:* the flow of money capital across world markets through overseas investment, credit, lending, and aid.

- *Resource capital:* the flow of natural resources, parts, and components between companies and countries, such as metals, minerals, lumber, energy, food products, microprocessors, and auto parts.

- *Political capital:* the flow of power and influence around the world using diplomacy, persuasion, aggression, and force of arms to protect the right or access of a country, world region, or political bloc to the other forms of capital.

Most of the economic advances associated with globalization are the result of these four capital flows and the interactions between them, as nations compete on the world stage to protect and increase their standards of living and to further the political goals and social causes that are espoused by their societies' cultures. The next sections look at the factors that have increased the rate at which capital flows between companies and countries. In a positive sense, the faster the flow, the more capital is being utilized where it can create the most value, such as people moving to where their skills earn them more money, or investors switching to the stocks or bonds that give them higher dividends or interest, or companies finding lower-cost sources of inputs. In a negative sense, however, a fast flow of capital also means that individual countries or world regions can find themselves in trouble when companies and investors move their capital to invest it in more productive ways in other countries or world regions—often those with lower labor costs or rapidly expanding markets. When capital leaves a country, the results are higher unemployment, recession, and a lower standard of living for its people.

Declining Barriers to Trade and Investment

One of the main factors that has speeded globalization by freeing the movement of capital has been the decline in barriers to trade and investment, discussed earlier. During the 1920s and 1930s many countries erected formidable barriers to international trade and investment

tariff A tax that a government imposes on imported or, occasionally, exported goods.

in the belief that this was the best way to promote their economic well-being. Many of these barriers were high tariffs on imports of manufactured goods. A **tariff** is a tax that a government imposes on goods imported into one country from another. The aim of import tariffs is to protect domestic industries and jobs, such as those in the auto or steel industry, from overseas competition by raising the price of these products from abroad. In 2009, for example, the U.S. government increased the tariffs on vehicle tires imported from China to protect U.S. tire makers from unfair competition; in 2012 it imposed a 30% tariff on imports of Chinese solar panels after U.S. solar companies complained that the Chinese government was unfairly subsidizing this industry.

The reason for removing tariffs is that, very often, when one country imposes an import tariff, others follow suit and the result is a series of retaliatory moves as countries progressively raise tariff barriers against each other. In the 1920s this behavior depressed world demand and helped usher in the Great Depression of the 1930s and massive unemployment. Beginning with the 2009 economic crisis, the governments of most countries have worked hard in the 2010s not to fall into the trap of raising tariffs to protect jobs and industries in the short run because they know the long-term consequences of this would be the loss of even more jobs. Governments of countries that resort to raising tariff barriers ultimately reduce employment and undermine the economic growth of their countries because capital and resources will always move to their most highly valued use—wherever that is in the world.[27]

GATT AND THE RISE OF FREE TRADE   After World War II, advanced Western industrial countries, having learned from the Great Depression, committed themselves to the goal of removing barriers to the free flow of resources and capital between countries. This commitment was reinforced by acceptance of the principle that free trade, rather than tariff barriers, was the best way to foster a healthy domestic economy and low unemployment.[28]

free-trade doctrine The idea that if each country specializes in the production of the goods and services that it can produce most efficiently, this will make the best use of global resources.

The **free-trade doctrine** predicts that if each country agrees to specialize in the production of the goods and services that it can produce most efficiently, this will make the best use of global capital resources and will result in lower prices.[29] For example, if Indian companies are highly efficient in the production of textiles and U.S. companies are highly efficient in the production of computer software, then, under a free-trade agreement, capital would move to India and be invested there to produce textiles, while capital from around the world would flow to the United States and be invested in its innovative computer software companies. Consequently, prices of both textiles and software should fall because each product is being produced where it can be made at the lowest cost, benefiting consumers and making the best use of scarce capital. This doctrine is also responsible for the increase in global outsourcing and the loss of millions of U.S. jobs in textiles and manufacturing as capital has been invested in factories in Asian countries such as China and Malaysia. However, millions of U.S. jobs have also been created because of new capital investments in the high-tech, IT, and service sectors, which in theory should offset manufacturing job losses in the long run.

Historically, countries that accepted this free-trade doctrine set as their goal the removal of barriers to the free flow of goods, services, and capital between countries. They attempted to achieve this through an international treaty known as the General Agreement on Tariffs and Trade (GATT). In the half-century since World War II, there have been eight rounds of GATT negotiations aimed at lowering tariff barriers. The last round, the Uruguay Round, involved 117 countries and succeeded in lowering tariffs by over 30% from the previous level. It also led to the dissolving of GATT and its replacement by the World Trade Organization (WTO), which continues the struggle to reduce tariffs and has more power to sanction countries that break global agreements.[30] On average, the tariff barriers among the governments of developed countries declined from over 40% in 1948 to about 3% today, causing a dramatic increase in world trade.[31]

Declining Barriers of Distance and Culture

Historically, barriers of distance and culture also closed the global environment and kept managers focused on their domestic market. The management problems Unilever, the huge British-based soap and detergent maker, experienced at the turn of the 20th century illustrate the effect of these barriers.

Founded in London during the 1880s by William Lever, a Quaker, Unilever had a worldwide reach by the early 1900s and operated subsidiaries in most major countries of the British Empire, including India, Canada, and Australia. Lever had a very hands-on, autocratic management style and found his far-flung business empire difficult to control. The reason for Lever's control problems was that communication over great distances was difficult. It took six weeks to reach India by ship from England, and international telephone and telegraph services were unreliable.

Another problem Unilever encountered was the difficulty of doing business in societies that were separated from Britain by barriers of language and culture. Different countries have different sets of national beliefs, values, and norms, and Lever found that a management approach that worked in Britain did not necessarily work in India or Persia (now Iran). As a result, management practices had to be tailored to suit each unique national culture. After Lever's death in 1925, top management at Unilever lowered or *decentralized* (see Chapter 10) decision-making authority to the managers of the various national subsidiaries so they could develop a management approach that suited the country in which they were operating. One result of this strategy was that the subsidiaries grew distant and remote from one another, which reduced Unilever's performance.[32]

Since the end of World War II, a continuing stream of advances in communications and transportation technology has worked to reduce the barriers of distance and culture that affected Unilever and all global organizations. Over the last decades, global communication has been revolutionized by developments in satellites, digital technology, the Internet and global computer networks, and video teleconferencing that allow transmission of vast amounts of information and make reliable, secure, and instantaneous communication possible between people and companies anywhere in the world.[33] This revolution has made it possible for a global organization—a tiny garment factory in Li & Fung's network or a huge company such as IKEA or Unilever—to do business anywhere, anytime, and to search for customers and suppliers around the world.

One of the most important innovations in transportation technology that has opened the global environment has been the growth of commercial jet travel. New York is now closer in travel time to Tokyo than it was to Philadelphia in the days of the 13 colonies—a fact that makes control of far-flung international businesses much easier today than in William Lever's era. In addition to speeding travel, modern communications and transportation technologies have also helped reduce the cultural distance between countries. The Internet and its millions of websites facilitate the development of global communications networks and media that are helping to create a worldwide culture above and beyond unique national cultures. Moreover, television networks such as CNN, MTV, ESPN, BBC, and HBO can now be received in many countries, and Hollywood films are shown throughout the world.

Effects of Free Trade on Managers

The lowering of barriers to trade and investment and the decline of distance and culture barriers has created enormous opportunities for companies to expand the market for their goods and services through exports and investments in overseas countries. The shift toward a more open global economy has created not only more opportunities to sell goods and services in markets abroad but also the opportunity to buy more from other countries. For example, the success of clothing companies such as Lands' End has been based on its managers' willingness to import low-cost clothing and bedding from overseas manufacturers. Lands' End works closely with manufacturers in Hong Kong, Malaysia, Taiwan, and China to make the clothing that its managers decide has the quality and styling its customers want at a price they will pay.[34] A manager's job is more challenging in a dynamic global environment because of the increased intensity of competition that goes hand in hand with the lowering of barriers to trade and investment.

REGIONAL TRADE AGREEMENTS   The growth of regional trade agreements such as the North American Free Trade Agreement (NAFTA), and more recently the Central American Free Trade Agreement (CAFTA), also presents opportunities and threats for managers and their organizations. In North America, NAFTA, which became effective in 1994, had the aim of abolishing the tariffs on 99% of the goods traded between Mexico, Canada, and the United States by 2004. Although it did not achieve this lofty goal, NAFTA has removed most barriers on the cross-border flow of resources, giving, for example, financial institutions and retail businesses in Canada and the United States unrestricted access to the Mexican marketplace. After NAFTA was signed, there was a flood of investment into Mexico from the United States, as well as many other countries such as Japan. Walmart, Costco, Ford, and many major U.S. retail chains expanded their operations in Mexico; Walmart, for example, is stocking many more products from Mexico in its U.S. stores, and its Mexican store chain is also expanding rapidly.

The establishment of free-trade areas creates an opportunity for manufacturing organizations because it lets them reduce their costs. They can do this either by shifting production to the lowest-cost location within the free-trade area (for example, U.S. auto and textile companies shifting production to Mexico) or by serving the whole region from one location rather than establishing separate operations in each country. Some managers, however, view regional free-trade agreements as a threat because they expose a company based in one member country to increased competition from companies based in the other member countries. NAFTA has had this effect; today Mexican managers in some industries face the threat of head-to-head competition against efficient U.S. and Canadian companies. But the opposite is true as well: U.S. and Canadian managers are experiencing threats in labor-intensive industries, such as the flooring tile, roofing, and textile industries, where Mexican businesses have a cost advantage.

In 2005 the U.S. House of Representatives approved the formation of CAFTA, a regional trade agreement designed to eliminate tariffs on products moving between the United States and all countries in Central America. By 2006 the Dominican Republic, El Salvador, Guatemala, Nicaragua, and Honduras had also approved and implemented the agreement, but Costa Rica still has not. CAFTA is seen as a stepping-stone toward establishing the Free Trade Area of the Americas (FTAA), which is an ambitious attempt to establish a free-trade agreement that would increase economic prosperity throughout the Americas. FTAA would include all South American and Caribbean nations except Cuba, as well as those of North and Central America. However, the economic problems many countries have been experiencing, together with major political and ideological differences—such as the political resistance within the United States because of jobs lost to Mexico and Canada—have slowed the process of integration and globalization. The more competitive environment NAFTA has brought about has increased both the opportunities that managers can take advantage of and the threats they must respond to in performing their jobs effectively.

The Role of National Culture

Despite evidence that countries are becoming more similar because of globalization, and that the world may become "a global village," the cultures of different countries still vary widely because of vital differences in their values, norms, and attitudes. As noted earlier, national culture includes the values, norms, knowledge, beliefs, moral principles, laws, customs, and other practices that unite the citizens of a country.[35] National culture shapes individual behavior by specifying appropriate and inappropriate behavior and interaction with others. People learn national culture in their everyday lives by interacting with those around them. This learning starts at an early age and continues throughout their lives.

Cultural Values and Norms

values Ideas about what a society believes to be good, right, desirable, or beautiful.

The basic building blocks of national culture are values and norms. **Values** are beliefs about what a society considers to be good, right, desirable, or beautiful—or their opposites. They provide the basic underpinnings for notions of individual freedom, democracy, truth, justice, honesty, loyalty, social obligation, collective responsibility, the appropriate roles for men and women, love, sex, marriage, and so on. Values are more than merely abstract concepts; they are invested with considerable emotional significance. People argue, fight, and even die over values such as freedom or dignity.

Although deeply embedded in society, values are not static; they change over time, but change is often the result of a slow and painful process. For example, the value systems of many formerly communist states such as Georgia, Hungary, and Romania have undergone significant changes as those countries move away from values that emphasize state control towards values that emphasizes individual freedom. Social turmoil often results when countries undergo major changes in their values, as is happening today in Asia, South America, and the Middle East.

norms Unwritten, informal codes of conduct that prescribe how people should act in particular situations and are considered important by most members of a group or organization.

Norms are unwritten, informal codes of conduct that prescribe appropriate behavior in particular situations and are considered important by most members of a group or organization. They shape the behavior of people toward one another. Two types of norms play a major role in national culture: mores and folkways. **Mores** are norms that are considered to be of central importance to the functioning of society and to social life. Accordingly, the violation of mores brings serious retribution. Mores include proscriptions against murder, theft, adultery, and incest. In many societies mores have been enacted into law. Thus, all advanced societies have laws against murder and theft. However, there are many differences in mores from one society to another.[36] In the United States, for example, drinking alcohol is widely accepted; but in Saudi Arabia consumption of alcohol is viewed as a serious violation of social mores and is punishable by imprisonment.

mores Norms that are considered to be central to the functioning of society and to social life.

folkways The routine social conventions of everyday life.

Folkways are the routine social conventions of everyday life. They concern customs and practices such as dressing appropriately for particular situations, good social manners, eating with the correct utensils, and neighborly behavior. Although folkways define how people are expected to behave, violation of folkways is not a serious or moral matter. People who violate folkways are often thought to be eccentric or ill-mannered, but they are not usually considered immoral or wicked. In many countries, strangers are usually excused for violating folkways because they are unaccustomed to local behavior; but if they repeat the violation, they are censured because they are expected to learn appropriate behavior. Hence the importance of managers working in countries abroad to gain wide experience.

LO6-5 Discuss why national cultures differ and why it is important that managers be sensitive to the effects of falling trade barriers and regional trade associations on the political and social systems of nations around the world.

Hofstede's Model of National Culture

Researchers have spent considerable time and effort identifying similarities and differences in the values and norms of different countries. One model of national culture was developed by Geert Hofstede.[37] As a psychologist for IBM, Hofstede collected data on employee values and norms from more than 100,000 IBM employees in 64 countries. Based on his research, Hofstede developed five dimensions along which national cultures can be placed (see Figure 6.4).[38]

individualism A worldview that values individual freedom and self-expression and adherence to the principle that people should be judged by their individual achievements rather than by their social background.

INDIVIDUALISM VERSUS COLLECTIVISM   The first dimension, which Hofstede labeled "individualism versus collectivism," has a long history in human thought. **Individualism** is a worldview that values individual freedom and self-expression and adherence to the principle that people should be judged by their individual achievements rather than by their social background. In Western countries, individualism usually includes admiration for personal success, a strong belief in individual rights, and high regard for individual entrepreneurs.[39]

In contrast, **collectivism** is a worldview that values subordination of the individual to the goals of the group and adherence to the principle that people should be judged by their contribution to the group. Collectivism was widespread in communist countries but has become less prevalent since the collapse of communism in most of those countries. Japan is a noncommunist country where collectivism is highly valued.

collectivism A worldview that values subordination of the individual to the goals of the group and adherence to the principle that people should be judged by their contribution to the group.

Collectivism in Japan traces its roots to the fusion of Confucian, Buddhist, and Shinto thought that occurred during the Tokugawa period in Japanese history (1600–1870s).[40] A central value that emerged during this period was strong attachment to the group—whether a village, a work group, or a company. Strong identification with the group is said to create pressures for collective action in Japan, as well as strong pressure for conformity to group norms and a relative lack of individualism.[41]

Managers must realize that organizations and organizational members reflect their national culture's emphasis on individualism or collectivism. Indeed, one of the major reasons why Japanese and American management practices differ is that Japanese culture values collectivism and U.S. culture values individualism.[42]

Figure 6.4
Hofstede's Model of National Culture

Source: G. Hofstede, B. Nevijen, D. D. Ohayv, and G. Sanders, "Measuring Organizational Cultures: A Qualitative and Quantitative Study across Twenty Cases," *Administrative Science Quarterly* 35, no. 2 (June 1990), 286–316. Copyright © 1990 by Cornell University, Johnson Graduate School of Management. Reproduced with permission of Sage Publications, Inc. via Copyright Clearance Center.

power distance The degree to which societies accept the idea that inequalities in the power and well-being of their citizens are due to differences in individuals' physical and intellectual capabilities and heritage.

POWER DISTANCE By power distance Hofstede meant the degree to which societies accept the idea that inequalities in the power and well-being of their citizens are due to differences in individuals' physical and intellectual capabilities and heritage. This concept also encompasses the degree to which societies accept the economic and social differences in wealth, status, and well-being that result from differences in individual capabilities.

Societies in which inequalities are allowed to persist or grow over time have *high power distance.* In high-power-distance societies, workers who are professionally successful amass wealth and pass it on to their children, and, as a result, inequalities may grow over time. In such societies, the gap between rich and poor, with all the attendant political and social consequences, grows very large. In contrast, in societies with *low power distance,* large inequalities between citizens are not allowed to develop. In low-power-distance countries, the government uses taxation and social welfare programs to reduce inequality and improve the welfare of the least fortunate. These societies are more attuned to preventing a large gap between rich and poor and minimizing discord between different classes of citizens.

Advanced Western countries such as the United States, Germany, the Netherlands, and the United Kingdom have relatively low power distance and high individualism. Economically poor Latin American countries such as Guatemala and Panama, and Asian countries such as Malaysia and the Philippines, have high power distance and low individualism.[43] These findings suggest that the cultural values of richer countries emphasize protecting the rights of individuals and, at the same time, provide a fair chance of success to every member of society.

achievement orientation A worldview that values assertiveness, performance, success, and competition.

ACHIEVEMENT VERSUS NURTURING ORIENTATION Societies that have an achievement orientation value assertiveness, performance, success, competition, and results. Societies that have a nurturing orientation value the quality of life, warm personal relationships, and services and care for the weak. Japan and the United States tend to be achievement-oriented; the Netherlands, Sweden, and Denmark are more nurturing-oriented.

nurturing orientation A worldview that values the quality of life, warm personal friendships, and services and care for the weak.

UNCERTAINTY AVOIDANCE Societies as well as individuals differ in their tolerance for uncertainty and risk. Societies low on uncertainty avoidance (such as the United States and Hong Kong) are easygoing, value diversity, and tolerate differences in personal beliefs and actions. Societies high on uncertainty avoidance (such as Japan and France) are more rigid and skeptical about people whose behaviors or beliefs differ from the norm. In these societies, conformity to the values of the social and work groups to which a person belongs is the norm, and structured situations are preferred because they provide a sense of security.

uncertainty avoidance The degree to which societies are willing to tolerate uncertainty and risk.

long-term orientation A worldview that values thrift and persistence in achieving goals.

short-term orientation A worldview that values personal stability or happiness and living for the present.

LONG-TERM VERSUS SHORT-TERM ORIENTATION   The last dimension that Hofstede described is orientation toward life and work.[44] A national culture with a **long-term orientation** rests on values such as thrift (saving) and persistence in achieving goals. A national culture with a **short-term orientation** is concerned with maintaining personal stability or happiness and living for the present. Societies with a long-term orientation include Taiwan and Hong Kong, well known for their high rate of per capita savings. The United States and France have a short-term orientation, and their citizens tend to spend more and save less.

National Culture and Global Management

Differences among national cultures have important implications for managers. First, because of cultural differences, management practices that are effective in one country might be troublesome in another. General Electric's managers learned this while trying to manage Tungsram, a Hungarian lighting products company GE acquired for $150 million. GE was attracted to Tungsram, widely regarded as one of Hungary's best companies, because of Hungary's low wage rates and the possibility of using the company as a base from which to export lighting products to western Europe. GE transferred some of its best managers to Tungsram and hoped it would soon become a leader in Europe. Unfortunately many problems arose.

One problem resulted from major misunderstandings between the American managers and the Hungarian workers. The Americans complained that the Hungarians were lazy; the Hungarians thought the Americans were pushy. The Americans wanted strong sales and marketing functions that would pamper customers. In the prior command economy, sales and marketing activities were unnecessary. In addition, Hungarians expected GE to deliver Western-style wages, but GE came to Hungary to take advantage of the country's low-wage structure.[45] As Tungsram's losses mounted, GE managers had to admit that, because of differences in basic attitudes between countries, they had underestimated the difficulties they would face in turning Tungsram around. Nevertheless, by 2001 these problems had been solved, and the increased efficiency of GE's Hungarian operations made General Electric a major player in the European lighting market, causing it to invest another $1 billion.[46]

Often, management practices must be tailored to suit the cultural contexts within which an organization operates. An approach effective in the United States might not work in Japan, Hungary, or Mexico because of differences in national culture. For example, U.S.-style pay-for-performance systems that emphasize the performance of individuals might not work well in Japan, where individual performance in pursuit of group goals is the value that receives emphasis.

Managers doing business with individuals from another country must be sensitive to the value systems and norms of that country and behave accordingly. For example, Friday is the Islamic Sabbath. Thus it would be impolite and inappropriate for a U.S. manager to schedule a busy day of activities for Saudi Arabian managers on a Friday.

A culturally diverse management team can be a source of strength for an organization participating in the global marketplace. Compared to organizations with culturally homogeneous management teams, organizations that employ managers from a variety of cultures have a better appreciation of how national cultures differ, and they tailor their management systems and behaviors to the differences.[47] Indeed, one advantage that many Western companies have over their Japanese competitors is greater willingness to create global teams composed of employees from different countries around the world who can draw on and share their different cultural experiences and knowledge to provide service that is customized to the needs of companies in different countries. For example, because IT services account for more than half of IBM's $90 billion annual revenues, it has been searching for ways to better use its talented workforce to both lower costs and offer customers unique, specialized kinds of services that its competitors cannot. IBM has developed several kinds of techniques to accomplish this.[48]

In the 2000s, IBM created "competency centers" around the world staffed by employees who share the same specific IT skill.

IT services with an edge: IBM's new competency centers customize teams of workers who can manage their own tasks.

In India, for example, today, IBM employs over 20,000 IT personnel who specialize in providing technical customer support for large U.S. companies. These employees work in self-managed teams and are responsible for managing all aspects of a particular client's specific needs. By using teams, IBM can offer high-quality personalized service at a low price and compete effectively in the global marketplace.

Most of IBM's employees are concentrated in competency centers located in the countries in which IBM has the most clients and does the most business. These employees have a wide variety of skills, developed from their previous work experience, and the challenge facing IBM is to use these experts efficiently. To accomplish this, IBM used its own IT expertise to develop sophisticated software that allows it to create self-managed teams composed of IBM experts who have the optimum mix of skills to solve a client's particular problems. First, IBM programmers analyze the skills and experience of its 80,000 global employees and enter the results into the software program. Then they analyze and code the nature of a client's specific problem and input that information. IBM's program matches each specific client problem to the skills of IBM's experts and identifies a list of "best fit" employees. One of IBM's senior managers narrows this list and decides on the actual composition of the self-managed team. Once selected, team members, from wherever they happen to be in the world, assemble as quickly as possible and go to work analyzing the client's problem. Together, team members use their authority. This new IT lets IBM create an ever-changing set of global self-managed teams that form to develop the software and service package necessary to solve the problems of IBM's global clients. At the same time, IBM's IT also optimizes the use of its whole talented workforce because each employee is placed in his or her "most highly valued use"—that is, in the team where the employee's skills can best increase efficiency and effectiveness. In some cases it is not easy for a company to harmonize the skills, attitudes, values, and experience of employees from different countries as the problems Sony has experienced, discussed in the following "Manager as a Person," suggest.

Manager as
a Person

Kazuo Hirai Replaces Howard Stringer as CEO of Sony

Sony, the Japanese electronics maker, was renowned in the 1990s for using its engineering prowess to develop blockbuster new products such as the Walkman, Trinitron TV, and PlayStation.[49] Sony's engineers were given freedom to pursue their own ideas, and its different product teams pursued their own innovations; but major problems arose with this approach in the 2000s. Companies in Korea and Taiwan (e.g., LG and Samsung) made major innovations in technologies, such as the development of advanced LCD screen displays and flash memory, that made Sony's technologies obsolete. On the product front, companies such as Apple, Samsung, and Nintendo developed new digital devices such as the iPod, smartphones, and the Wii game console that better met customer needs than Sony's old-fashioned and expensive products. Also, all these companies had worked to reduce manufacturing costs and engaged in extensive outsourcing so that Sony lost its competitive advantage in both technology and price and it began to lose billions of dollars.

By 2005 Sony was in serious trouble, and at this crucial point in their company's history, Sony's Japanese top managers turned to a *gaijin,* or non-Japanese, executive to lead their company. Their choice was Sir Howard Stringer, a Welshman, the previous head of Sony's North American operations who had been instrumental in cutting costs and increasing the profits of Sony's U.S. division. Once he became CEO in 2005, Stringer faced the immediate problem of reducing Sony's operating costs that were more than double those of its competitors, even as it was losing its technological leadership. Stringer had to make many radical strategic decisions.

Kazuo Hirai and Sir Howard Stringer are both committed to finding ways to turn around the performance of the flagging multinational.

Japan is a country where large companies traditionally had a policy of lifetime employment, but Stringer made it clear that layoffs were inevitable. Within five years he cut Sony's Japanese workforce by over 25,000 employees and closed 12 factories to reduce costs. Stringer also recognized how widespread power struggles among the top managers of Sony's different product divisions were hurting the company, and he made it clear that these problems had to stop. At Sony, like many other Japanese companies, the top managers of its divisions worked to protect their own divisions' interests—not Sony's. As Sony's performance fell, competition between managers increased, which slowed strategic decision making, made it harder for the company to innovate new products, and increased operating costs as each division fought for the funding necessary to develop new products.

Many top divisional managers, including the manager of Sony's successful PlayStation division, ignored Stringer; he replaced them and worked steadily to downsize Sony's bloated corporate headquarters staff and to change its ineffective culture. In Stringer's own words, the present culture or "business of Sony has been management, not making products." In 2009, to speed change, Stringer announced he would take control of the struggling core electronics division *and* would add the title of president to his existing roles as chairman and CEO to speed the reorganization of Sony's divisions. He also replaced four more top executives with younger managers who had held positions outside Japan and were "familiar with the digital world."

Stringer worked hard to bring the realities of global competition to the forefront and change Sony's managers' values and attitudes; his goal was to cut operating costs by over $10 billion or 40%. To achieve this, he announced Sony would rapidly expand its use of outsourcing and centralize purchasing. By 2010, financial results suggested that Stringer's initiatives were finally paying off—he had stemmed Sony's huge losses and its products were selling better—and he expected Sony to become profitable by 2011. In 2010, Sony announced a major initiative to push into new digital, but so were its competitors such as Apple and Samsung, which were quickly innovating new kinds of mobile devices such as smartphones and tablet computers; global rivalry was intense and Sony had not regained a competitive advantage.

Stringer, who was now in his late 60s, searched for a successor who would continue to pursue cultural change and change its global strategies; he recommended to the board that Kazuo Hirai replace him as president and CEO while he would become chairman. Hirai, Sony's youngest CEO ever, is fluent in English, has extensive overseas experience, and was not part of Sony's old culture. Hirai has an important advantage over Stringer—a work history that allows him to move effortlessly between Sony's U.S. and Japanese operations. Apparently Stringer, who can't speak Japanese, spent years not realizing many of his directives as CEO were being ignored by the managers of its operating divisions.

Stringer announced that "Kaz is a globally focused executive; I believe his tough-mindedness and leadership skills will be of great benefit to the company and its customers in the months and years ahead."[50] Stringer had appointed Hirai to turn around its struggling gaming division; in 2006, he set about simplifying and outsourcing the manufacture of components, rolling out a slim-line version of the console in 2009 and cutting its price by 25%. Hirai pledged to continue to follow Stringer's efforts to streamline costs in all Sony's divisions. Also, he promised to review Sony's businesses that produce more than 2,000 products, to exit those that are uncompetitive, and to focus on a narrower range of advanced digital products.

Summary and Review

LO6-1

WHAT IS THE GLOBAL ENVIRONMENT? The global environment is the set of forces and conditions that operates beyond an organization's boundaries but affects a manager's ability to acquire and use resources. The global environment has two components: the task environment and the general environment.

LO6-2, 6-3 **THE TASK ENVIRONMENT** The task environment is the set of forces and conditions that originates with global suppliers, distributors, customers, and competitors and influences managers daily. The opportunities and threats associated with forces in the task environment become more complex as a company expands globally.

LO6-2, 6-3 **THE GENERAL ENVIRONMENT** The general environment comprises wide-ranging global economic, technological, sociocultural, demographic, political, and legal forces that affect an organization and its task environment.

LO6-4, 6-5 **THE CHANGING GLOBAL ENVIRONMENT** In recent years there has been a marked shift toward a more open global environment in which capital flows more freely as people and companies search for new opportunities to create profit and wealth. This has hastened the process of globalization. Globalization is the set of specific and general forces that work together to integrate and connect economic, political, and social systems across countries, cultures, or geographic regions so that nations become increasingly interdependent and similar. The process of globalization has been furthered by declining barriers to international trade and investment and declining barriers of distance and culture.

Management in Action

Topics for Discussion and Action

Discussion

1. Why is it important for managers to understand the forces in the global environment that are acting on them and their organizations? **[LO6-1]**

2. Which organization is likely to face the most complex task environment—a biotechnology company trying to develop a cure for cancer or a large retailer like The Gap or Macy's? Why? **[LO6-2, 6-3]**

3. The population is aging because of declining birth rates, declining death rates, and the aging of the baby boom generation. What might some of the implications of this demographic trend be for (a) a pharmaceutical company and (b) the home construction industry? **[LO6-1, 6-2, 6-3]**

4. How do political, legal, and economic forces shape national culture? What characteristics of national culture do you think have the most important effect on how successful a country is in doing business abroad? **[LO6-3, 6-5]**

5. After the passage of NAFTA, many U.S. companies shifted production operations to Mexico to take advantage of lower labor costs and lower standards for environmental and worker protection. As a result, they cut their costs and were better able to survive in an increasingly competitive global environment. Was their behavior ethical—that is, did the ends justify the means? **[LO6-4]**

Action

6. Choose an organization and ask a manager in that organization to list the number and strengths of forces in the organization's task environment. Ask the manager to pay particular attention to identifying opportunities and threats that result from pressures and changes in customers, competitors, and suppliers. **[LO6-1, 6-2, 6-3]**

Building Management Skills

Analyzing an Organization's Environment [LO6-1, 6-2, 6-3]

Pick an organization with which you are familiar. It can be an organization in which you have worked or currently work or one that you interact with regularly as a customer (such as the college you are attending). For this organization do the following:

1. Describe the main forces in the global task environment that are affecting the organization.

2. Describe the main forces in the global general environment that are affecting the organization.

3. Explain how environmental forces affect the job of an individual manager within this organization. How do they determine the opportunities and threats that its managers must confront?

Managing Ethically [LO6-4, 6-5]

In recent years the number of U.S. companies that buy their inputs from low-cost overseas suppliers has been growing, and concern about the ethics associated with employing young children in factories has been increasing. In Pakistan and India, children as young as six years old work long hours to make rugs and carpets for export to Western countries or clay bricks for local use. In countries like Malaysia and in Central America, children and teenagers routinely work long hours in factories and sweatshops to produce the clothing that is found in most U.S. discount and department stores.

Questions

1. Either by yourself or in a group, discuss whether it is ethical to employ children in factories and whether U.S. companies should buy and sell products made by these children. What are some arguments for and against child labor?

2. If child labor is an economic necessity, what methods could be employed to make it as ethical a practice as possible? Or is it simply unethical?

Small Group Breakout Exercise

How to Enter the Copying Business [LO6-1, 6-2]

Form groups of three to five people, and appoint one group member as the spokesperson who will communicate your findings to the whole class when called on by the instructor. Then discuss the following scenario:

You and your partners have decided to open a small printing and copying business in a college town of 100,000 people. Your business will compete with companies like FedEx Kinko's. You know that over 50% of small businesses fail in their first year, so to increase your chances of success, you have decided to perform a detailed analysis of the task environment of the copying business to discover what opportunities and threats you will encounter.

1. Decide what you must know about (a) your future customers, (b) your future competitors, and (c) other critical forces in the task environment if you are to be successful.

2. Evaluate the main barriers to entry into the copying business.

3. Based on this analysis, list some steps you would take to help your new copying business succeed.

Exploring the World Wide Web [LO6-2, 6-3, 6-4]

Go to Fuji Films' website (www.fujifilm.com), click on "About Us," "History," and then "Corporate History," and consider how Fuji's global activities have expanded over time.

1. How would you characterize the way Fuji manages the global environment? For example, how has Fuji responded to the needs of customers in different countries?

2. How have increasing global competition and declining barriers of distance and culture affected Fuji's global operations?

Be the Manager [LO6-1, 6-2]

The Changing Environment of Retailing

You are the new manager of a major clothing store that is facing a crisis. This clothing store has been the leader in its market for the last 15 years. In the last three years, however, two other major clothing store chains have opened, and they have steadily been attracting customers away from your store—your sales are down 30%. To find out why, your store surveyed former customers and learned that they perceive your store as not keeping up with changing fashion trends and new forms of customer service. In examining how the store operates, you found out that the 10 purchasing managers who buy the clothing and accessories for the store have been buying from the same clothing suppliers and have become reluctant to try new ones. Moreover, salespeople rarely, if ever, make suggestions for changing how the store operates, and they don't respond to customer requests; the culture of the store has become conservative and risk-averse.

Questions

1. Analyze the major forces in the task environment of a retail clothing store.

2. Devise a program that will help other managers and employees to better understand and respond to their store's task environment.

Fortune Case in the News [LO6-1, 6-4, 6-5]

Akio Toyoda: Toyota's Comeback Kid

When the final tally was made for 2011, Toyota Motor (TM), formerly the world's largest automaker, slipped to third place in production behind General Motors (GM) and Volkswagen. It's not surprising: Toyota has endured a string of calamities over the past three years—natural and man-made—that would make even the company's famous paranoia seem like sunny optimism. The latest is *endaka,* the strong yen that causes everything that Toyota manufactures in Japan to be more expensive and undermines its profitability. A November issue of *Automotive News* predicted "more misery" for Toyota as "sales slip, floods delay, shoppers stray."

At the head of the company all this time has been a young president who was effectively born into the job and has little experience in crisis management: Akio Toyoda, the grandson of the company's founder. For a decade, while the automaker was being run by professional managers, Akio rose up the corporate ladder without making much of a mark. (For the sake of clarity, we'll use his first name, pronounced a-KEY-o, in this story.) Thrust into the presidency in 2009, he immediately had to cope with a global recession, massive recalls, and a deadly tsunami. Auto production plummeted and at the same time Toyota lost its most important competitive advantage: its reputation for exceptional quality. Americans saw Akio apologizing before Congress and later tearing up in a YouTube video. U.S. market share tumbled. After reaching 18.3% at the end of 2009, it fell all the way to 12.9% for 2011. Emboldened by the recall crisis, competitors spread word that Toyota, once considered the unstoppable force of the automotive world, had been reduced to the status of also-ran.

But I had been hearing different things—that Toyota had coped remarkably well with the tsunami and that the recall crisis had served as a wake-up call for a company grown complacent. With a big boost from its new president, who took an intensely personal interest in its products, it was connecting with customers again.

Toyota's Big Product Offensive

The Toyoda scion was traveling to the U.S. more frequently to fire up dealers and had taken charge personally of the sagging Lexus brand. Independent studies were beginning to show that Toyota cars were regaining their reputation for quality and value. With 19 new or redesigned models coming in calendar 2012—an exceptionally large number—including a big expansion of the Prius hybrid line, the Toyota steamroller seemed ready to regain its old momentum.

One of Toyota's guiding principles in times of crisis is *genchi genbutsu,* or "go and see." So to find out for myself what the changes meant for a company I had been covering for more than 20 years, I interviewed Toyota executives in California and New York and then flew to Japan.

Of all the woes Toyota has suffered, none has stung like the recall crisis of 2009–10. Ignited by reports of horrific accidents, some fatal, caused by cars that ran out of control and couldn't be braked to a stop, it eventually involved the recall [of] more than 8 million Toyotas and Lexuses—equivalent to a year's production. Independent investigations turned up no mechanical or electronic defects—only some misplaced floor mats and sticky accelerator pedals to go along with driver error—but exposed major flaws in the corporate culture. Toyota, it turned out, was still being managed the way it had been in the 1950s: Every decision was tightly controlled in Japan; the U.S. was treated like a vassal state. When American managers found defects in vehicles, they had to follow a tortuous bureaucratic process to register their complaints in Japan, where they were often met with skepticism and defensiveness. As it had long feared, Toyota had succumbed to "big-company disease."

Consumer confidence in its cars plummeted and Toyota's higher-ups were shaken. "We learned we are not so ahead of competitors as we might have thought," Yoshimi Inaba, who heads sales and administration in the U.S., told me. "We were a little complacent." Toyota began to develop quicker reflexes. When a defect was identified in a Lexus SUV, Toyota organized a recall in just eight days. But it balked at delegating more executive authority to America. Rather than designate one person to head all of its North American operations, it maintained its traditional silo structure. Its giant sales operation in Southern California, and its equally large manufacturing complex headquartered in Kentucky, continued reporting to different executives in Japan.

Just as it was trying to put the recall crisis behind it, the new management was tested again in March, when an earthquake and massive tidal wave disrupted production. The tsunami damaged plants in the north of Japan, disrupting the supply of over 500 parts, and Toyota couldn't find replacements. Its first-tier just-in-time suppliers near Toyota City were not directly affected, but up north were second- and third-tier suppliers that Toyota did not know much about.

Akio assembled general managers of departments such as body engineering and powertrain in Japan and took the unusual step of instructing them to restore production and not waste time reporting upward. They sent two-man teams of engineers to visit each supplier plant and to identify and locate backup parts until the suppliers were running again. By April, unavailable parts were down to 150, and by May, according to Liker's count, all but 30 of the 500 parts were available. Toyota solved the problems in half the time expected, but Liker figures the company still lost 800,000 production units—10% of its annual output. Plans to make up most of the shortfall through overtime work were pushed back by October floods in Thailand that affected about 100 suppliers. As a result, inventories in North America won't be completely replenished until March.

As I fidgeted through a 14-hour flight, I wondered about how committed this ponderous and bureaucratic company was to change. After overnighting in Tokyo, I moved on to Nagoya, Japan's third-largest city, and met with executive vice president Yukitoshi Funo, one of Akio's key advisers. Funo, who holds an MBA from Columbia and formerly oversaw U.S. sales, told me there had been an upheaval at Toyota. "[Akio] has dramatically changed the way the company is managed," he said through an interpreter. "There are two major pillars to how he manages: First, be fast; and second, be flexible. Usually Japanese companies are based on a 'bottom up' management style, which slows down the pace of decision making. In looking at other companies, we realized the need for a certain level of 'top down' to move quickly."

Akio shrank the board of directors by half and took out layers of management. Funo revealed a more significant development: Akio has begun meeting informally with his five top advisers every Tuesday morning to review the company's operations. They work so closely together that Funo called it "pit work" management. No agendas or written reports are allowed, and decisions are made on the spot. "Basically, the six people have a very strong personal bond. So it's not a very emotional or heated debate as we have a very good understanding among each other." They can move quickly. After Akio visited Tesla Motors in California in 2010, the Tuesday morning meeting signed off on a $50 million investment in the electric-car maker. Subsequently Toyota agreed to buy $60 million worth of Tesla batteries to power its all-electric RAV 4 crossover.

Funo said Akio has made another fundamental change in the way Toyota is managed. Traditionally, Toyota has rotated its top executives, so a sales specialist could be assigned to purchasing, or a product engineer to manufacturing. Now they stay within their specialties so that they can leverage their experience. "It's very American," said Funo. The next day I made the 40-minute car ride to Toyota City to meet with Takeshi Uchiyamada, Toyota's top engineer and another participant in the Tuesday morning meetings. In 1993, Uchiyamada accepted the challenge of Toyota's elders to develop a car with 50%-better fuel economy; today he's known as the father of the Prius. More than 3 million of the hybrids have been sold since 1997, and it has been expanded into a subbrand with additional models.

Akio is pushing Toyota to make "always better cars," and Uchiyamada is the point man. For years enthusiasts have complained that Toyota treats cars like transportation appliances and allows companies such as Hyundai to seize design leadership. Uchiyamada says the critics were right. He told me: "Basically, Toyota's growth had been underpinned by QDR [quality, dependability, reliability] that was very high compared with competitors'. Compared with past practices, we need to make products that are even more attractive. We have stepped up our efforts emphasizing design, high quality of the interiors."

Questions for Discussion

1. How has Akio Toyoda changed the way Toyota is managing the global environment?

2. What kinds of factors in the global environment most impact the way a global carmaker like Toyota operates? For example, in what ways are the needs of global customers changing?

3. Search the web to see how Toyota is currently performing—is it the number one global carmaker again?

Source: Alex Taylor III, "Akio Toyoda: Toyota's Comeback Kid," *Fortune,* February 27, 2012. © 2012 Time Inc. Used under license.

CHAPTER 7

Decision Making, Learning, Creativity, and Entrepreneurship

Learning Objectives

After studying this chapter, you should be able to:

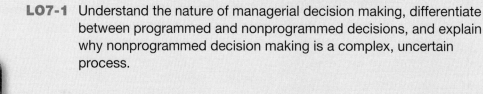

LO7-1 Understand the nature of managerial decision making, differentiate between programmed and nonprogrammed decisions, and explain why nonprogrammed decision making is a complex, uncertain process.

LO7-2 Describe the six steps managers should take to make the best decisions, and explain how cognitive biases can lead managers to make poor decisions.

LO7-3 Identify the advantages and disadvantages of group decision making, and describe techniques that can improve it.

LO7-4 Explain the role that organizational learning and creativity play in helping managers to improve their decisions.

LO7-5 Describe how managers can encourage and promote entrepreneurship to create a learning organization, and differentiate between entrepreneurs and intrapreneurs.

A MANAGER'S CHALLENGE

Decision Making and Learning Are the Keys to Entrepreneurial Success

Why are decision making and learning an ongoing challenge for managers of businesses large and small? All managers must make decisions day in and day out under considerable uncertainty. And sometimes those decisions come back to haunt them if they turn out poorly. Sometimes, even highly effective managers make bad decisions. Other times, factors beyond a manager's control, such as unforeseen changes in the environment, cause a good decision to result in unexpected negative consequences. Effective managers recognize the critical importance of making decisions on an ongoing basis as well as learning from prior decisions.

Decision making has been an ongoing challenge for Marc Shuman, founder and president of GarageTek, headquartered in Syosset, New York.[1] Since founding his company less than 15 years ago,[2] he has met this challenge time and time again, recognizing when decisions need to be made and learning from feedback about prior decisions.

Shuman was working with his father in a small business, designing and building interiors of department stores, when he created and installed a series of wall panels with flexible shelving for a store to display its merchandise. When he realized that some of his employees were using the same concept in their own homes to organize the clutter in their basements and garages, he recognized that he had a potential opportunity to start a new business, GarageTek, designing and installing custom garage systems to organize and maximize storage capacities and uses for home garage space.[3] A strong housing market at the time, the popularity of closet organizing systems, and the recognition that many people's lives were getting busier and more complicated led him to believe that homeowners would be glad to pay someone to design and install a system that would help them gain control over some of the clutter in their lives.[4]

Garage Tek Express, Shuman's latest innovation, allows franchisees to set up and sell his organizing and shelving systems right out of their homes.

Schuman decided to franchise his idea because he feared that other entrepreneurs were probably having similar thoughts and competition could be around the corner.[5] Within three years GarageTek had 57 franchises in 33 states, contributing revenues to the home office of around $12 million. While this would seem to be an enviable track record of success, Shuman recognized that although many of the franchises were succeeding, some were having serious problems. With the help of a consulting company, Shuman and home office managers set about trying to figure out why some franchises were failing. They gathered detailed information about each franchise: the market served, pricing strategies, costs, managerial talent, and franchisee investment. From this information, Shuman learned that the struggling franchises tended either to have lower levels of capital investment behind them or to be managed by nonowners.[6]

Shuman learned from this experience. He now has improved decision criteria for accepting new franchisees to help ensure that their investments of time and money lead to a successful franchise.[7] Shuman also decided to give new franchisees much more training and support than he had in the past. New franchisees now receive two weeks of training at the home office that culminates in their preparing a one-year marketing and business plan;[8] on-site assistance in sales, marketing, and operations; a multivolume training manual; a sales and marketing kit; and access to databases and GarageTek's intranet. Franchisees learn from each other through monthly conference calls and regional and national meetings.[9]

Recently Shuman decided that his "one size fits all" approach to franchising might need to be modified.[10] That is, while he used to require that all franchisees have roughly the same minimal amount of capital invested in their businesses and pay the same fees, he realized that some markets are bigger, require a greater investment, and have higher operating costs than others and also that some potential franchisees might want to invest more capital in their businesses than others.[11] Thus, he decided to have two different kinds of franchises.

The more traditional kind of franchise operates in a top 50 market based on the demographics of homeowners in the area and has the highest potential returns for franchisees' investments. Franchisees initially invest between $198, 000 and $246,000 in their business, which includes a $50,000 franchise fee. During the first year of operations, their marketing and royalty fees are lowered.[12] The newer kind of franchise, GarageTek Express, can be operated out of a franchisee's home, is located in a top 51–100 market based on homeowner demographics, requires an initial investment of between $75,000 and $127,000 and also has lowered marketing and royalty fees for the first year.[13] While GarageTek was founded in New York and initially operated only in the United States, Shuman decided to offer licensing agreements to entrepreneurs interested in distributing GarageTek solutions in other countries.[14]

By 2012, GarageTek had franchises covering 60 markets in the United States and also had expanded overseas into the United Kingdom, Australia, New Zealand, South Africa, and Russia.[15] And Shuman continues to make decisions day in and day out; in his words, "We're not, by any stretch, done."[16]

Overview

"A Manager's Challenge" illustrates how decision making and learning from prior decisions are an ongoing challenge for managers that can have a profound influence on organizational effectiveness. Shuman's decision to seize an opportunity and start GarageTek and his subsequent decisions along the way have had a profound effect on his business. The decisions managers make at all levels in companies large and small can have a dramatic impact on the growth and prosperity of these companies and the well-being of their employees, customers, and other stakeholders. Yet such decisions can be difficult to make because they are fraught with uncertainty.

In this chapter we examine how managers make decisions, and we explore how individual, group, and organizational factors affect the quality of the decisions they make and ultimately determine organizational performance. We discuss the nature of managerial decision making and examine some models of the decision-making process that help reveal the complexities of successful decision making. Then we outline the main steps of the decision-making process; in addition, we explore the biases that may cause capable managers to make poor decisions both as individuals and as members of a group. Next we examine how managers can promote organizational learning and creativity and improve the quality of decision making throughout an organization. Finally we discuss the important role of entrepreneurship in promoting organizational creativity, and we differentiate between entrepreneurs and intrapreneurs. By the end of this chapter you will appreciate the critical role of management decision making in creating a high-performing organization.

LO7-1 Understand the nature of managerial decision making, differentiate between programmed and nonprogrammed decisions, and explain why nonprogrammed decision making is a complex, uncertain process.

The Nature of Managerial Decision Making

Every time managers act to plan, organize, direct, or control organizational activities, they make a stream of decisions. In opening a new restaurant, for example, managers have to decide where to locate it, what kinds of food to provide, which people to employ, and so on. Decision making is a basic part of every task managers perform. In this chapter we study how these decisions are made.

As we discussed in the last three chapters, one of the main tasks facing a manager is to manage the organizational environment. Forces in the external environment give rise to many opportunities and threats for managers and their organizations. In addition, inside an organization managers must address many opportunities and threats that may arise as organizational resources are used. To deal with these opportunities and threats, managers must make decisions—that is, they must select one solution from a set of alternatives. **Decision making** is the process by which managers respond to opportunities and threats by analyzing the options and making determinations, or *decisions,* about specific organizational goals and courses of action. Good decisions result in the selection of appropriate goals and courses of action that increase organizational performance; bad decisions lower performance.

Decision making in response to opportunities occurs when managers search for ways to improve organizational performance to benefit customers, employees, and other stakeholder groups. In "A Manager's Challenge," Marc Shuman seized the opportunities to start his own business, offer two kinds of franchises with different levels of investment, and expand internationally. *Decision making in response to threats* occurs when events inside or outside the organization adversely affect organizational performance and managers search for ways to increase performance.[17] When his company was in its early years, Shuman realized that some of his franchisees were having problems and he made a series of decisions to rectify matters.[18] Decision making is central to being a manager, and whenever managers engage in planning, organizing, leading, and controlling—their four principal tasks—they are constantly making decisions.

Managers are always searching for ways to make better decisions to improve organizational performance. At the same time they do their best to avoid costly mistakes that will hurt organizational performance. Examples of spectacularly good decisions include Martin Cooper's decision to develop the first cell phone at Motorola and Apple's decision to develop the iPod.[19] Examples of spectacularly bad decisions include the decision by managers at NASA and Morton Thiokol to launch the *Challenger* space shuttle—a decision that killed six astronauts in 1986—and the decision by NASA to launch the *Columbia* space shuttle in 2003, which killed seven astronauts.

decision making The process by which managers respond to opportunities and threats by analyzing options and making determinations about specific organizational goals and courses of action.

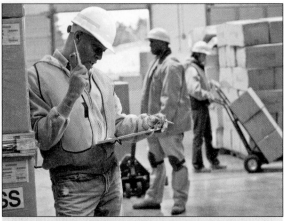

Programmed decisions allow warehouse supervisors such as this one to develop simple rubrics so the job is done consistently and with less error.

Programmed and Nonprogrammed Decision Making

Regardless of the specific decisions a manager makes, the decision-making process is either programmed or nonprogrammed.[20]

PROGRAMMED DECISION MAKING Programmed **decision making** is a *routine*, virtually automatic process. Programmed decisions are decisions that have been made so many times in the past that managers have developed rules or guidelines to be applied when certain situations inevitably occur. Programmed decision making takes place when a school principal asks the school board to hire a new teacher whenever student enrollment increases by 40 students; when a manufacturing supervisor hires new workers whenever existing workers' overtime increases by more than 10%; and when an office manager orders basic office supplies, such as paper and pens, whenever the inventory of supplies drops below a certain level. Furthermore, in the last example, the office manager probably orders the same amount of supplies each time.

programmed decision making Routine, virtually automatic decision making that follows established rules or guidelines.

This decision making is called *programmed* because office managers, for example, do not need to repeatedly make new judgments about what should be done. They can rely on long-established decision rules such as these:

- *Rule 1:* When the storage shelves are three-quarters empty, order more copy paper.
- *Rule 2:* When ordering paper, order enough to fill the shelves.

Managers can develop rules and guidelines to regulate all routine organizational activities. For example, rules can specify how a worker should perform a certain task, and rules can specify the quality standards that raw materials must meet to be acceptable. Most decision making that relates to the day-to-day running of an organization is programmed decision making. Examples include deciding how much inventory to hold, when to pay bills, when to bill customers, and when to order materials and supplies. Programmed decision making occurs when managers have the information they need to create rules that will guide decision making. There is little ambiguity involved in assessing when the stockroom is empty or counting the number of new students in class.

As profiled in the following "Focus on Diversity," effectively training new employees is essential to reap the benefits of programmed decision making.

Focus on Diversity

Programmed Decision Making at UPS

UPS is unrivaled in its use of programmed decision making. Practically all the motions, behaviors, and actions that its drivers perform each day have been carefully honed to maximize efficiency and minimize strain and injuries while delivering high-quality customer service. For example, a 12-step process prescribes how drivers should park their trucks, locate the package they are about to deliver, and step off the truck in 15.5 seconds (a process called "selection" at UPS).[21] Rules and routines such as these are carefully detailed in UPS's "340 Methods" manual (UPS actually has far more than 340 methods). Programmed decision making dictates where drivers should stop to get gas, how they should hold their keys in their hands, and how to lift and lower packages.[22]

When programmed decision making is so heavily relied on, ensuring that new employees learn tried-and-true routines is essential. UPS has traditionally taught new employees with a two-week period of lectures followed by practice.[23] In the 2000s,

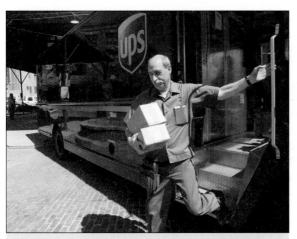

UPS driver training enforces productivity and safety by teaching new employees a variety of programmed decisions.

however, managers began to wonder if they needed to alter their training methods to suit their new Generation Y trainees (Generation Y typically refers to people born after 1980), who were not so keen on memorization and drills.[24] Generation Y trainees seemed to require more training time to become effective drivers (90–180 days compared to a typical average of 30–45 days), and quit rates for new drivers had increased.[25]

Given the fundamental importance of performance programs for UPS operations, managers decided to try to alter the training new hires receive so it would be better received by Generation Y trainees. In the late 2000s, UPS opened an innovative Landover, Maryland, training center called UPS Integrad, which has over 11,000 square feet and cost over $30 million to build and equip. Integrad was developed over a three-year period through a collaborative effort of over 170 people, including UPS top managers (many of whom started their careers with UPS as drivers), teams from Virginia Tech and MIT, animators from the Indian company Brainvisa, and forecasters from the Institute for the Future with the support of a grant from the Department of Labor for $1.8 million.[26] Results thus far suggest that Integrad training results in greater driver proficiency and fewer first-year accidents and injuries.[27]

Training at Integrad emphasizes hands-on learning.[28] For example, at Integrad a UPS truck with transparent sides is used to teach trainees selection so they can actually see the instructor performing the steps and then practice the steps themselves rather than trying to absorb the material in a lecture. Trainees can try different movements and see, with the help of computer diagrams and simulations, how following UPS routines will help protect them from injury and how debilitating work as a driver can be if they do not follow routines. Video recorders track and document what trainees do correctly and incorrectly so they can see it for themselves rather than relying on feedback from an instructor, which they might question. As Stephen Jones, who is in charge of training for UPS and manages Integrad, indicates, "Tell them what they did incorrectly, and they'll tell you, 'I didn't do that. You saw wrong.' This way we've got it on tape and they can see it for themselves."[29]

At Integrad, trainees get practice driving in a pseudo town that has been constructed in a parking lot.[30] They also watch animated demonstrations on computer screens, participate in simulations, take electronic quizzes, and receive scores on various components that are retained in a database to track learning and performance. Recognizing that Generation Y trainees have a lot of respect for expertise and reputation, older employees also are brought in to facilitate learning at Integrad. For example, long-time UPS employee Don Petersik, who is about to retire, trains facilitators at Integrad and shares stories with them to reinforce the UPS culture—such as the time he was just starting out as a preloader and, unknown to him, the founder of UPS, Jim Casey, approached him and said, "Hi, I'm Jim. I work for UPS."[31] As Petersik indicates, "What's new about the company now is that our teaching style matches your learning styles."[32] Clearly, when learning programmed decision making is of utmost importance, as it is at UPS, it is essential to take into account diversity in learning styles and approaches.

nonprogrammed decision making Nonroutine decision making that occurs in response to unusual, unpredictable opportunities and threats.

NONPROGRAMMED DECISION MAKING Suppose, however, managers are not certain that a course of action will lead to a desired outcome. Or in even more ambiguous terms, suppose managers are not even sure what they are trying to achieve. Obviously rules cannot be developed to predict uncertain events.

Nonprogrammed decision making is required for these *nonroutine* decisions. Nonprogrammed decisions are made in response to unusual or novel opportunities and threats.

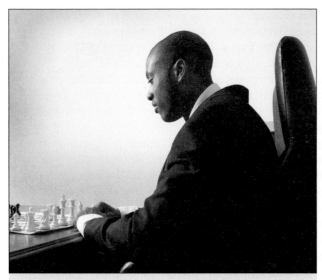

Nonprogrammed decision making covers areas with no previous benchmarks or rubrics, such as seen in this photo.

intuition Feelings, beliefs, and hunches that come readily to mind, require little effort and information gathering, and result in on-the-spot decisions.

reasoned judgment A decision that requires time and effort and results from careful information gathering, generation of alternatives, and evaluation of alternatives.

Nonprogrammed decision making occurs when there are no ready-made decision rules that managers can apply to a situation. Rules do not exist because the situation is unexpected or uncertain and managers lack the information they would need to develop rules to cover it. Examples of nonprogrammed decision making include decisions to invest in a new technology, develop a new kind of product, launch a new promotional campaign, enter a new market, expand internationally, or start a new business as did Marc Shuman in "A Manager's Challenge."

How do managers make decisions in the absence of decision rules? They may rely on their **intuition**—feelings, beliefs, and hunches that come readily to mind, require little effort and information gathering, and result in on-the-spot decisions.[33] Or they may make **reasoned judgments**— decisions that require time and effort and result from careful information gathering, generation of alternatives, and evaluation of alternatives. "Exercising" one's judgment is a more rational process than "going with" one's intuition. For reasons that we examine later in this chapter, both intuition and judgment often are flawed and can result in poor decision making. Thus the likelihood of error is much greater in nonprogrammed decision making than in programmed decision making.[34] In the remainder of this chapter, when we talk about decision making, we are referring to *nonprogrammed* decision making because it causes the most problems for managers and is inherently challenging.

Sometimes managers have to make rapid decisions and don't have time to carefully consider the issues involved. They must rely on their intuition to quickly respond to a pressing concern. For example, when fire chiefs, captains, and lieutenants manage firefighters battling dangerous, out-of-control fires, they often need to rely on their expert intuition to make on-the-spot decisions that will protect the lives of the firefighters and save the lives of others, contain the fires, and preserve property—decisions made in emergency situations entailing high uncertainty, high risk, and rapidly changing conditions.[35] In other cases managers do have time to make reasoned judgments, but there are no established rules to guide their decisions, such as when deciding whether to proceed with a proposed merger.

Regardless of the circumstances, making nonprogrammed decisions can result in effective or ineffective decision making. As indicated in the following "Manager as a Person," managers have to be on their guard to avoid being overconfident in decisions that result from either intuition or reasoned judgment.

The classical and administrative decision-making models reveal many of the assumptions, complexities, and pitfalls that affect decision making. These models help reveal the factors that managers and other decision makers must be aware of to improve the quality of

Manager as
a Person

Curbing Overconfidence

Should managers be confident in their intuition and reasoned judgments?[36] Decades of research by Nobel Prize winner Daniel Kahneman, his longtime collaborator the late Amos Tversky, and other researchers suggests that managers (like all people) tend to be overconfident in the decisions they make, whether based on intuition or reasoned judgment.[37] And with overconfidence comes failure to evaluate and rethink the wisdom of the decisions one makes and failure to learn from mistakes.[38]

Kahneman distinguishes between the intuition of managers who are truly expert in the content domain of a decision and the intuition of managers who have some knowledge and experience but are not true experts.[39] Although the intuition of both types can be faulty, that of experts is less likely to be flawed. This is why fire captains can make good decisions and why expert chess players can make good moves, in both cases without spending much time or deliberating carefully on what, for non-experts, is a complicated set of circumstances. What distinguishes expert managers from those with limited expertise is that the experts have extensive experience under conditions in which they receive quick and clear feedback about the outcomes of their decisions.[40]

Unfortunately managers who have some experience in a content area but are not true experts tend to be overly confident in their intuition and their judgments.[41] As Kahneman puts it, "People jump to statistical conclusions on the basis of very weak evidence. We form powerful intuitions about trends and about the replicability of results on the basis of information that is truly inadequate."[42] Not only do managers, and all people, tend to be overconfident about their intuition and judgments, but they also tend not to learn from mistakes. Compounding this undue optimism is the human tendency to be overconfident in one's own abilities and influence over unpredictable events. Surveys have found that the majority of people think they are above average, make better decisions, and are less prone to making bad decisions than others (of course it is impossible for most people to be above average on any dimension).[43]

Examples of managerial overconfidence abound. Research has consistently found that mergers tend to turn out poorly—postmerger profitability declines, stock prices drop, and so forth. For example, Chrysler had the biggest profits of the three largest automakers in the United States when it merged with Daimler; the merger was a failure and both Chrysler and Daimler would have been better off if it never had happened.[44] One would imagine that top executives and boards of directors would learn from this research and from articles in the business press about the woes of merged companies (such as the AOL–Time Warner merger and the Hewlett-Packard–Compaq merger).[45] Evidently not. Top managers seem to overconfidently believe that they can succeed where others have failed.[46] Similarly, whereas fewer than 35% of new small ventures succeed as viable businesses for more than five years, entrepreneurs, on average, tend to think that they have a 6 out of 10 chance of being successful.[47]

Jeffrey Pfeffer, a professor at Stanford University's Graduate School of Business, suggests that managers can avoid the perils of overconfidence by critically evaluating the decisions they have made and the outcomes of those decisions. They should admit to themselves when they have made a mistake and really learn from their mistakes (rather than dismissing them as flukes or situations out of their control). In addition, managers should be leery of too much agreement at the top. As Pfeffer puts it, "If two people agree all the time, one of them is redundant."[48]

their decision making. Keep in mind, however, that the classical and administrative models are just guides that can help managers understand the decision-making process. In real life the process is typically not cut-and-dried, but these models can help guide a manager through it.

The Classical Model

classical decision-making model A prescriptive approach to decision making based on the assumption that the decision maker can identify and evaluate all possible alternatives and their consequences and rationally choose the most appropriate course of action.

One of the earliest models of decision making, the **classical model**, is *prescriptive,* which means it specifies how decisions *should* be made. Managers using the classical model make a series of simplifying assumptions about the nature of the decision-making process (see Figure 7.1). The premise of the classical model is that once managers recognize the need to make a decision, they should be able to generate a complete list of *all* alternatives and consequences and make the best choice. In other words, the classical model assumes managers have access to *all* the

Figure 7.1
The Classical Model of Decision Making

optimum decision The most appropriate decision in light of what managers believe to be the most desirable consequences for the organization.

information they need to make the **optimum decision**, which is the most appropriate decision possible in light of what they believe to be the most desirable consequences for the organization. Furthermore, the classical model assumes managers can easily list their own preferences for each alternative and rank them from least to most preferred to make the optimum decision.

The Administrative Model

James March and Herbert Simon disagreed with the underlying assumptions of the classical model of decision making. In contrast, they proposed that managers in the real world do *not* have access to all the information they need to make a decision. Moreover, they pointed out that even if all information were readily available, many managers would lack the mental or psychological ability to absorb and evaluate it correctly. As a result, March and Simon developed the **administrative model** of decision making to explain why decision making is always an inherently uncertain and risky process—and why managers can rarely make decisions in the manner prescribed by the classical model. The administrative model is based on three important concepts: *bounded rationality, incomplete information,* and *satisficing.*

administrative model An approach to decision making that explains why decision making is inherently uncertain and risky and why managers usually make satisfactory rather than optimum decisions.

BOUNDED RATIONALITY   March and Simon pointed out that human decision-making capabilities are bounded by people's cognitive limitations—that is, limitations in their ability to interpret, process, and act on information.[49] They argued that the limitations of human intelligence constrain the ability of decision makers to determine the optimum decision. March and Simon coined the term **bounded rationality** to describe the situation in which the number of alternatives a manager must identify is so great and the amount of information so vast that it is difficult for the manager to even come close to evaluating it all before making a decision.[50]

INCOMPLETE INFORMATION   Even if managers had unlimited ability to evaluate information, they still would not be able to arrive at the optimum decision because they would have incomplete information. Information is incomplete because the full range of decision-making alternatives is unknowable in most situations, and the consequences associated with known alternatives are uncertain.[51] In other words, information is incomplete because of risk and uncertainty, ambiguity, and time constraints (see Figure 7.2).

bounded rationality Cognitive limitations that constrain one's ability to interpret, process, and act on information.

risk The degree of probability that the possible outcomes of a particular course of action will occur.

RISK AND UNCERTAINTY   As we saw in Chapter 6, forces in the organizational environment are constantly changing. **Risk** is present when managers know the possible outcomes of a particular course of action and can assign probabilities to them. For example, managers in the biotechnology industry know that new drugs have a 10% probability of successfully passing advanced clinical trials and a 90% probability of failing. These probabilities reflect the experiences of thousands of drugs that have gone through advanced clinical trials. Thus when

Figure 7.2

Why Information Is Incomplete

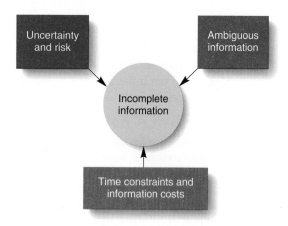

managers in the biotechnology industry decide to submit a drug for testing, they know that there is only a 10% chance that the drug will succeed, but at least they have some information on which to base their decision.

uncertainty Unpredictability.

When **uncertainty** exists, the probabilities of alternative outcomes *cannot* be determined and future outcomes are *unknown*. Managers are working blind. Because the probability of a given outcome occurring is not known, managers have little information to use in making a decision. For example, in 1993, when Apple Computer introduced the Newton, its personal digital assistant (PDA), managers had no idea what the probability of a successful product launch for a PDA might be. Because Apple was the first to market this totally new product, there was no body of well-known data that Apple's managers could draw on to calculate the probability of a successful launch. Uncertainty plagues most managerial decision making.[52] Although Apple's initial launch of its PDA was a disaster due to technical problems, an improved version was more successful.

ambiguous information
Information that can be interpreted in multiple and often conflicting ways.

AMBIGUOUS INFORMATION   A second reason why information is incomplete is that much of the information managers have at their disposal is **ambiguous information**. Its meaning is not clear—it can be interpreted in multiple and often conflicting ways.[53] Take a look at Figure 7.3. Do you see a young woman or an old woman? In a similar fashion, managers often interpret the same piece of information differently and make decisions based on their own interpretations.

Figure 7.3

Ambiguous Information: Young Woman or Old Woman?

TIME CONSTRAINTS AND INFORMATION COSTS   The third reason why information is incomplete is that managers have neither the time nor the money to search for all possible alternative solutions and evaluate all the potential consequences of those alternatives. Consider the situation confronting a Ford Motor Company purchasing manager who has one month to choose a supplier for a small engine part. There are 20,000 potential suppliers for this part in the United States alone. Given the time available, the purchasing manager cannot contact all potential suppliers and ask each for its terms (price, delivery schedules, and so on). Moreover, even if the time were available, the costs of obtaining the information, including the manager's own time, would be prohibitive.

SATISFICING.   March and Simon argued that managers do not attempt to discover every alternative when faced with bounded rationality, an uncertain future, unquantifiable risks, considerable ambiguity, time constraints, and high information costs. Rather, they use a strategy known as **satisficing**, which is exploring a limited sample of all potential alternatives.[54] When managers satisfice, they search for and choose acceptable, or satisfactory, ways to respond to problems and opportunities rather than trying to make the optimal decision.[55] In the case of the Ford purchasing manager's search, for example, satisficing may involve asking a limited number of suppliers for their terms, trusting that they are representative of suppliers in general, and making a choice from that set. Although this course of action is reasonable from the perspective of the purchasing manager, it may mean that a potentially superior supplier is overlooked.

> **satisficing** Searching for and choosing an acceptable, or satisfactory, response to problems and opportunities, rather than trying to make the best decision.

March and Simon pointed out that managerial decision making is often more art than science. In the real world, managers must rely on their intuition and judgment to make what seems to them to be the best decision in the face of uncertainty and ambiguity.[56] Moreover, managerial decision making is often fast-paced; managers use their experience and judgment to make crucial decisions under conditions of incomplete information. Although there is nothing wrong with this approach, decision makers should be aware that human judgment is often flawed. As a result, even the best managers sometimes make poor decisions.[57]

Steps in the Decision-Making Process

Using the work of March and Simon as a basis, researchers have developed a step-by-step model of the decision-making process and the issues and problems that managers confront at each step. Perhaps the best way to introduce this model is to examine the real-world nonprogrammed decision making of Scott McNealy at a crucial point in Sun Microsystems' history. McNealy was a founder of Sun Microsystems and was the chairman of the board of directors until Sun was acquired by Oracle in 2010.[58]

In early August 1985, Scott McNealy, then CEO of Sun Microsystems[59] (a hardware and software computer workstation manufacturer focused on network solutions), had to decide whether to go ahead with the launch of the new Carrera workstation computer, scheduled for September 10. Sun's managers had chosen the date nine months earlier when the development plan for the Carrera was first proposed. McNealy knew it would take at least a month to prepare for the September 10 launch, and the decision could not be put off.

> **LO7-2**   Describe the six steps managers should take to make the best decisions, and explain how cognitive biases can lead managers to make poor decisions.

Customers were waiting for the new machine, and McNealy wanted to be the first to provide a workstation that took advantage of Motorola's powerful 16-megahertz 68020 microprocessor. Capitalizing on this opportunity would give Sun a significant edge over Apollo, its main competitor in the workstation market. McNealy knew, however, that committing to the September 10 launch date was risky. Motorola was having production problems with the 16-megahertz 68020 microprocessor and could not guarantee Sun a steady supply of these chips. Moreover, the operating system software was not completely free of bugs.

If Sun launched the Carrera on September 10, the company might have to ship some machines with software that was not fully operational, was likely to crash the system, and utilized Motorola's less powerful 12-megahertz 68020 microprocessor instead of the 16-megahertz version.[60] Of course Sun could later upgrade the microprocessor and operating system software in any machines purchased by early customers, but the company's reputation would suffer. If Sun did not go ahead with the September launch, the company would miss an important opportunity.[61] Rumors were circulating in the industry that Apollo would be launching a new machine of its own in December.

McNealy clearly had a difficult decision to make. He had to decide quickly whether to launch the Carrera, but he did not have all the facts. He did not know, for example, whether the microprocessor or operating system problems could be resolved by September 10; nor did he know whether Apollo was going to launch a competing machine in December. But he could not wait to find these things out—he had to make a decision. We'll see what he decided later in the chapter.

Many managers who must make important decisions with incomplete information face dilemmas similar to McNealy's. Managers should consciously follow six steps to make a good decision (see Figure 7.4).[62] We review these steps in the remainder of this section.

Recognize the Need for a Decision

The first step in the decision-making process is to recognize the need for a decision. Scott McNealy recognized this need, and he realized a decision had to be made quickly.

Some stimuli usually spark the realization that a decision must be made. These stimuli often become apparent because changes in the organizational environment result in new kinds of opportunities and threats. This happened at Sun Microsystems. The September 10 launch date had been set when it seemed that Motorola chips would be readily available. Later, with the supply of chips in doubt and bugs remaining in the system software, Sun was in danger of failing to meet its launch date.

The stimuli that spark decision making are as likely to result from the actions of managers inside an organization as they are from changes in the external environment.[63] An organization possesses a set of skills, competencies, and resources in its employees and in departments such as marketing, manufacturing, and research and development. Managers who actively pursue opportunities to use these competencies create the need to make decisions. Managers thus can be proactive or reactive in recognizing the need to make a decision, but the important issue is that they must recognize this need and respond in a timely and appropriate way.[64]

Generate Alternatives

Having recognized the need to make a decision, a manager must generate a set of feasible alternative courses of action to take in response to the opportunity or threat. Management experts cite failure to properly generate and consider different alternatives as one reason why

Figure 7.4

Six Steps in Decision Making

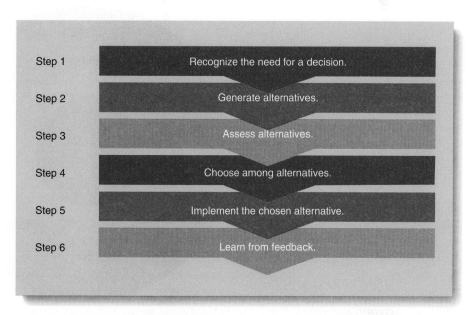

Step 1	Recognize the need for a decision.
Step 2	Generate alternatives.
Step 3	Assess alternatives.
Step 4	Choose among alternatives.
Step 5	Implement the chosen alternative.
Step 6	Learn from feedback.

managers sometimes make bad decisions.[65] In the Sun Microsystems decision, the alternatives seemed clear: to go ahead with the September 10 launch or to delay the launch until the Carrera was 100% ready for market introduction. Often, however, the alternatives are not so obvious or so clearly specified.

One major problem is that managers may find it difficult to come up with creative alternative solutions to specific problems. Perhaps some of them are used to seeing the world from a single perspective—they have a certain "managerial mind-set." Many managers find it difficult to view problems from a fresh perspective. According to best-selling management author Peter Senge, we all are trapped within our personal mental models of the world—our ideas about what is important and how the world works.[66] Generating creative alternatives to solve problems and take advantage of opportunities may require that we abandon our existing mind-sets and develop new ones—something that usually is difficult to do.

The importance of getting managers to set aside their mental models of the world and generate creative alternatives is reflected in the growth of interest in the work of authors such as Peter Senge and Edward de Bono, who have popularized techniques for stimulating problem solving and creative thinking among managers.[67] Later in this chapter, we discuss the important issues of organizational learning and creativity in detail.

Assess Alternatives

Once managers have generated a set of alternatives, they must evaluate the advantages and disadvantages of each one.[68] The key to a good assessment of the alternatives is to define the opportunity or threat exactly and then specify the criteria that *should* influence the selection of alternatives for responding to the problem or opportunity. One reason for bad decisions is that managers often fail to specify the criteria that are important in reaching a decision.[69] In general, successful managers use four criteria to evaluate the pros and cons of alternative courses of action (see Figure 7.5):

1. *Legality:* Managers must ensure that a possible course of action will not violate any domestic or international laws or government regulations.
2. *Ethicalness:* Managers must ensure that a possible course of action is ethical and will not unnecessarily harm any stakeholder group. Many decisions managers make may help

Figure 7.5

General Criteria for Evaluating Possible Courses of Action

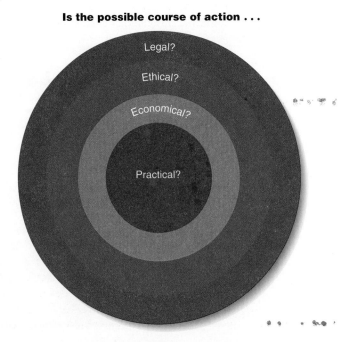

Is the possible course of action . . .

Legal?

Ethical?

Economical?

Practical?

some organizational stakeholders and harm others (see Chapter 4). When examining alternative courses of action, managers need to be clear about the potential effects of their decisions.

3. *Economic feasibility:* Managers must decide whether the alternatives are economically feasible—that is, whether they can be accomplished given the organization's performance goals. Typically managers perform a cost–benefit analysis of the various alternatives to determine which one will have the best net financial payoff.

4. *Practicality:* Managers must decide whether they have the capabilities and resources required to implement the alternative, and they must be sure the alternative will not threaten the attainment of other organizational goals. At first glance an alternative might seem economically superior to other alternatives; but if managers realize it is likely to threaten other important projects, they might decide it is not practical after all.

Often a manager must consider these four criteria simultaneously. Scott McNealy framed the problem at hand at Sun Microsystems quite well. The key question was whether to go ahead with the September 10 launch date. Two main criteria were influencing McNealy's choice: the need to ship a machine that was as "complete" as possible (the *practicality* criterion) and the need to beat Apollo to market with a new workstation (the *economic feasibility* criterion). These two criteria conflicted. The first suggested that the launch should be delayed; the second, that the launch should go ahead. McNealy's actual choice was based on the relative importance that he assigned to these two criteria. In fact, Sun Microsystems went ahead with the September 10 launch, which suggests that McNealy thought the need to beat Apollo to market was the more important criterion.

Some of the worst managerial decisions can be traced to poor assessment of the alternatives, such as the decision to launch the *Challenger* space shuttle, mentioned earlier. In that case, the desire of NASA and Morton Thiokol managers to demonstrate to the public the success of the U.S. space program in order to ensure future funding (*economic feasibility*) conflicted with the need to ensure the safety of the astronauts (*ethicalness*). Managers deemed the economic criterion more important and decided to launch the space shuttle even though there were unanswered questions about safety. Tragically, some of the same decision-making problems that resulted in the *Challenger* tragedy led to the demise of the *Columbia* space shuttle 17 years later, killing all seven astronauts on board.[70] In both the *Challenger* and the *Columbia* disasters, safety questions were raised before the shuttles were launched; safety concerns took second place to budgets, economic feasibility, and schedules; top decision makers seemed to ignore or downplay the inputs of those with relevant technical expertise; and speaking up was discouraged.[71] Rather than making safety a top priority, decision makers seemed overly concerned with keeping on schedule and within budget.[72]

As indicated in the following "Ethics in Action," in order to help ensure that decisions meet the *ethicalness* criteria, some organizations have created the position of chief sustainability officer.

Ethics in Action

Helping to Ensure Decisions Contribute to Sustainability

Some large organizations have added the position of chief sustainability officer to their ranks of top managers reporting to the chief executive officer or chief operating officer. Chief sustainability officers are typically concerned with helping to ensure that decisions that are made in organizations conserve energy and protect the environment.[73] For example, Scott Wicker is the first chief sustainability officer for UPS.[74] Wicker leads a team that presides over a sustainability directors committee and a sustainability working committee focused on developing performance indicators and goals pertaining to sustainability to guide decision making.[75]

Linda Fisher, shown above, directs DuPont's efforts to ease its impact on the environment, juggling questions of plant waste, carcinogen release, worker safely, and consumer wellness every day.

Linda Fisher is the vice president of DuPont Safety, Health & Environment and chief sustainability officer at DuPont. Before she joined DuPont, she held a variety of positions related to sustainability, including the position of deputy administrator of the Environmental Protection Agency.[76] Fisher leads efforts at DuPont to make decisions that help to reduce energy consumption, toxins and carcinogens in the air, and greenhouse gas emissions and help DuPont's customers reduce their environmental footprints. Protecting both the environment and human safety is a priority for Fisher and DuPont.[77]

Beatriz Perez is the chief sustainability officer for Coca-Cola, leading a global office of sustainability.[78] While Coca-Cola has 500 different brands yielding 3,500 products, sustainability is a companywide initiative centered around major goals and initiatives.[79] These goals include water conservation and returning to the environment the water that Coca-Cola consumes in making its products, reducing packaging waste and increasing recycling, and protecting the environment from pollution by, for example, using hybrid trucks, having energy efficient manufacturing facilities, and improving the sustainability of refrigeration methods.[80] Clearly, ensuring that decisions contribute to sustainability means much more than simply complying with legal requirements. Having chief sustainability officers with dedicated teams and offices focused on sustainability might be a step in the right direction.

Choose among Alternatives

Once the set of alternative solutions has been carefully evaluated, the next task is to rank the various alternatives (using the criteria discussed in the previous section) and make a decision. When ranking alternatives, managers must be sure *all* the information available is brought to bear on the problem or issue at hand. As the Sun Microsystems case indicates, however, identifying all *relevant* information for a decision does not mean the manager has *complete* information; in most instances, information is incomplete.

Perhaps more serious than the existence of incomplete information is the often-documented tendency of managers to ignore critical information, even when it is available. We discuss this tendency in detail later when we examine the operation of cognitive biases and groupthink.

Implement the Chosen Alternative

Once a decision has been made and an alternative has been selected, it must be implemented, and many subsequent and related decisions must be made. After a course of action has been decided—say, to develop a new line of women's clothing—thousands of subsequent decisions are necessary to implement it. These decisions would involve recruiting dress designers, obtaining fabrics, finding high-quality manufacturers, and signing contracts with clothing stores to sell the new line.

Although the need to make subsequent decisions to implement the chosen course of action may seem obvious, many managers make a decision and then fail to act on it. This is the same as not making a decision at all. To ensure that a decision is implemented, top managers must assign to middle managers the responsibility for making the follow-up decisions necessary to achieve the goal. They must give middle managers sufficient resources to achieve the goal, and they must hold the middle managers accountable for their performance. If the middle managers succeed in implementing the decision, they should be rewarded; if they fail, they should be subject to sanctions.

Learn from Feedback

The final step in the decision-making process is learning from feedback. Effective managers always conduct a retrospective analysis to see what they can learn from past successes or failures. Managers who do not evaluate the results of their decisions do not learn from experience; instead they stagnate and are likely to make the same mistakes again and again.[81] To avoid this problem, managers must establish a formal procedure with which they can learn from the results of past decisions. The procedure should include these steps:

1. Compare what actually happened to what was expected to happen as a result of the decision.
2. Explore why any expectations for the decision were not met.
3. Derive guidelines that will help in future decision making.

Managers who always strive to learn from past mistakes and successes are likely to continuously improve the decisions they make. A significant amount of learning can take place when the outcomes of decisions are evaluated, and this assessment can produce enormous benefits. Learning from feedback is particularly important for entrepreneurs who start their own businesses, as illustrated in "A Manager's Challenge."

Cognitive Biases and Decision Making

In the 1970s psychologists Daniel Kahneman and Amos Tversky suggested that because all decision makers are subject to bounded rationality, they tend to use **heuristics**, which are rules of thumb that simplify the process of making decisions.[82] Kahneman and Tversky argued that rules of thumb are often useful because they help decision makers make sense of complex, uncertain, and ambiguous information. Sometimes, however, the use of heuristics can lead to systematic errors in the way decision makers process information about alternatives and make decisions. **Systematic errors** are errors that people make over and over and that result in poor decision making. Because of cognitive biases, which are caused by systematic errors, otherwise capable managers may end up making bad decisions.[83] Four sources of bias that can adversely affect the way managers make decisions are prior hypotheses, representativeness, the illusion of control, and escalating commitment (see Figure 7.6).

heuristics Rules of thumb that simplify decision making.

systematic errors Errors that people make over and over and that result in poor decision making.

Prior-Hypothesis Bias

Decision makers who have strong prior beliefs about the relationship between two variables tend to make decisions based on those beliefs *even when presented with evidence that their beliefs are wrong*. In doing so, they fall victim to **prior-hypothesis bias**. Moreover, decision makers tend to seek and use information that is consistent with their prior beliefs and to ignore information that contradicts those beliefs.

prior-hypothesis bias A cognitive bias resulting from the tendency to base decisions on strong prior beliefs even if evidence shows that those beliefs are wrong.

Representativeness Bias

Many decision makers inappropriately generalize from a small sample or even from a single vivid case or episode; these are instances of the **representativeness bias**. Consider the case of a bookstore manager in the southeast United States who decided to partner with a local independent school for a "Book Day": Students and parents from the school would be encouraged to buy books at the bookstore as a fund-raiser for the school, and the bookstore would share a small portion of proceeds from these sales with the school. After quite a bit of planning, the Book Day generated lackluster sales and publicity for the store. When other public and

representativeness bias A cognitive bias resulting from the tendency to generalize inappropriately from a small sample or from a single vivid event or episode.

Figure 7.6

Sources of Cognitive Bias at the Individual and Group Levels

independent schools approached the manager with similar proposals for fund-raising and Book Days, the manager declined based on her initial bad experience. As a result, she lost real opportunities to expand sales and gain word-of-mouth advertising and publicity for her store; her initial bad experience was the result of an inadvertent scheduling snafu at the school, whereby a key lacrosse game was scheduled the same day as the Book Day.

Illusion of Control

illusion of control A source of cognitive bias resulting from the tendency to overestimate one's own ability to control activities and events.

Other errors in decision making result from the **illusion of control**, which is the tendency of decision makers to overestimate their ability to control activities and events. Top managers seem particularly prone to this bias. Having worked their way to the top of an organization, they tend to have an exaggerated sense of their own worth and are overconfident about their ability to succeed and to control events.[84] The illusion of control causes managers to overestimate the odds of a favorable outcome and, consequently, to make inappropriate decisions. As mentioned earlier, most mergers turn out unfavorably; yet time and time again, top managers overestimate their abilities to combine companies with vastly different cultures in a successful merger.[85]

Escalating Commitment

escalating commitment A source of cognitive bias resulting from the tendency to commit additional resources to a project even if evidence shows that the project is failing.

Having already committed significant resources to a course of action, some managers commit more resources to the project *even if they receive feedback that the project is failing.*[86] Feelings of personal responsibility for a project apparently bias the analysis of decision makers and lead to this **escalating commitment**. The managers decide to increase their investment of time and money in a course of action and even ignore evidence that it is illegal, unethical, uneconomical, or impractical (see Figure 7.5). Often the more appropriate decision would be to cut their losses and run.

Consider the case of Mark Gracin, who owns a landscape company in the southwest United States. Gracin had a profitable business doing general landscape work (such as mowing grass, picking up leaves, and fertilizing) for homeowners in a large city. To expand his business into landscape design, he hired a landscape designer, advertised landscape design services in local newspapers, and gave his existing customers free design proposals for their front and back yards. After a few months, Gracin had no landscape design customers. Still convinced that landscape design was a great way to expand his business despite this negative feedback, he decided he needed to do more. He rented a small office for his landscape designer (who used to work from her own home office) to work from and meet with clients, hired an assistant for the designer, had a public relations firm create promotional materials, and started advertising on local TV. These efforts also did not generate sufficient interest in his landscape design services to offset their costs. Yet Gracin's escalating commitment caused him to continue to pour money into trying to drum up business in landscape design. In fact, Gracin reluctantly decided to abandon his landscape design services only when he realized he could no longer afford their mounting costs.

Be Aware of Your Biases

How can managers avoid the negative effects of cognitive biases and improve their decision-making and problem-solving abilities? Managers must become aware of biases and their effects, and they must identify their own personal style of making decisions.[87] One useful way for managers to analyze their decision-making style is to review two decisions that they made recently—one decision that turned out well and one that turned out poorly. Problem-solving experts recommend that managers start by determining how much time to spend on each of the decision-making steps, such as gathering information to identify the pros and cons of alternatives or ranking the alternatives, to make sure they spend sufficient time on each step.[88]

Another recommended technique for examining decision-making style is for managers to list the criteria they typically use to assess and evaluate alternatives—the heuristics (rules of thumb) they typically employ, their personal biases, and so on—and then critically evaluate the appropriateness of these different factors.

Many individual managers are likely to have difficulty identifying their own biases, so it is often advisable for managers to scrutinize their own assumptions by working with other managers to help expose weaknesses in their decision-making style. In this context, the issue of group decision making becomes important.

Group Decision Making

Many (or perhaps most) important organizational decisions are made by groups or teams of managers rather than by individuals. Group decision making is superior to individual decision making in several respects. When managers work as a team to make decisions and solve problems, their choices of alternatives are less likely to fall victim to the biases and errors discussed previously. They are able to draw on the combined skills, competencies, and accumulated knowledge of group members and thereby improve their ability to generate feasible alternatives and make good decisions. Group decision making also allows managers to process more information and to correct one another's errors. And in the implementation phase, all managers affected by the decisions agree to cooperate. When a group of managers makes a decision (as opposed to one top manager making a decision and imposing it on subordinate managers), the probability that the decision will be implemented successfully increases. (We discuss how to encourage employee participation in decision making in Chapter 14.)

Some potential disadvantages are associated with group decision making. Groups often take much longer than individuals to make decisions. Getting two or more managers to agree to the same solution can be difficult because managers' interests and preferences are often different. In addition, just like decision making by individual managers, group decision making can be undermined by biases. A major source of group bias is *groupthink*.

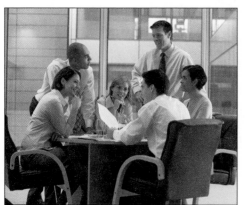

When everyone agrees right off the bat, the lack of conflict could be indicative of groupthink.

groupthink A pattern of faulty and biased decision making that occurs in groups whose members strive for agreement among themselves at the expense of accurately assessing information relevant to a decision.

The Perils of Groupthink

Groupthink is a pattern of faulty and biased decision making that occurs in groups whose members strive for agreement among themselves at the expense of accurately assessing information relevant to a decision.[89] When managers are subject to groupthink, they collectively embark on a course of action without developing appropriate criteria to evaluate alternatives. Typically a group rallies around one central manager, such as the CEO, and the course of action that manager supports. Group members become blindly committed to that course of action without evaluating its merits. Commitment is often based on an emotional, rather than an objective, assessment of the optimal course of action.

The decision President Kennedy and his advisers made to launch the unfortunate Bay of Pigs invasion in Cuba in 1962, the decisions made by President Johnson and his advisers from 1964 to 1967 to escalate the war in Vietnam, the decision made by President Nixon and his advisers in 1972 to cover up the Watergate break-in, and the decision made by NASA and Morton Thiokol in 1986 to launch the ill-fated *Challenger* shuttle—all were likely influenced by groupthink. After the fact, decision makers such as these who may fall victim to groupthink are often surprised that their decision-making process and outcomes were so flawed.

When groupthink occurs, pressures for agreement and harmony within a group have the unintended effect of discouraging individuals from raising issues that run counter to majority opinion. For example, when managers at NASA and Morton Thiokol fell victim to groupthink, they convinced each other that all was well and that there was no need to delay the launch of the *Challenger* space shuttle.

Devil's Advocacy and Dialectical Inquiry

The existence of cognitive biases and groupthink raises the question of how to improve the quality of group and individual decision making so managers make decisions that are realistic and are based on thorough evaluation of alternatives. Two techniques known to counteract groupthink and cognitive biases are devil's advocacy and dialectic inquiry (see Figure 7.7).[90]

Figure 7.7
Devil's Advocacy and Dialectical Inquiry

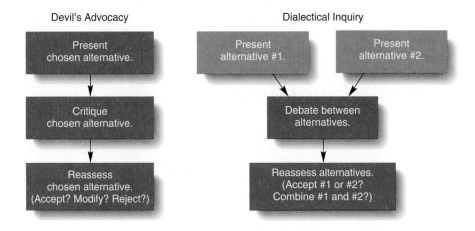

devil's advocacy Critical analysis of a preferred alternative, made in response to challenges raised by a group member who, playing the role of devil's advocate, defends unpopular or opposing alternatives for the sake of argument.

dialectical inquiry Critical analysis of two preferred alternatives in order to find an even better alternative for the organization to adopt.

organizational learning The process through which managers seek to improve employees' desire and ability to understand and manage the organization and its task environment.

learning organization An organization in which managers try to maximize the ability of individuals and groups to think and behave creatively and thus maximize the potential for organizational learning to take place.

LO7-4 Explain the role that organizational learning and creativity play in helping managers to improve their decisions.

Devil's advocacy is a critical analysis of a preferred alternative to ascertain its strengths and weaknesses before it is implemented.[91] Typically one member of the decision-making group plays the role of devil's advocate. The devil's advocate critiques and challenges the way the group evaluated alternatives and chose one over the others. The purpose of devil's advocacy is to identify all the reasons that might make the preferred alternative unacceptable after all. In this way, decision makers can be made aware of the possible perils of recommended courses of action.

Dialectical inquiry goes one step further. Two groups of managers are assigned to a problem, and each group is responsible for evaluating alternatives and selecting one of them.[92] Top managers hear each group present its preferred alternative, and then each group critiques the other's position. During this debate, top managers challenge both groups' positions to uncover potential problems and perils associated with their solutions. The goal is to find an even better alternative course of action for the organization to adopt.

Both devil's advocacy and dialectical inquiry can help counter the effects of cognitive biases and groupthink.[93] In practice, devil's advocacy is probably easier to implement because it involves less managerial time and effort than does dialectical inquiry.

Diversity among Decision Makers

Another way to improve group decision making is to promote diversity in decision-making groups (see Chapter 5).[94] Bringing together managers of both genders from various ethnic, national, and functional backgrounds broadens the range of life experiences and opinions that group members can draw on as they generate, assess, and choose among alternatives. Moreover, diverse groups are sometimes less prone to groupthink because group members already differ from each other and thus are less subject to pressures for uniformity.

Organizational Learning and Creativity

The quality of managerial decision making ultimately depends on innovative responses to opportunities and threats. How can managers increase their ability to make nonprogrammed decisions that will allow them to adapt to, modify, and even drastically alter their task environments so they can continually increase organizational performance? The answer is by encouraging organizational learning.[95]

Organizational learning is the process through which managers seek to improve employees' desire and ability to understand and manage the organization and its task environment so employees can make decisions that continuously raise organizational effectiveness.[96] A **learning organization** is one in which managers do everything possible to

creativity A decision maker's ability to discover original and novel ideas that lead to feasible alternative courses of action.

maximize the ability of individuals and groups to think and behave creatively and thus maximize the potential for organizational learning to take place. At the heart of organizational learning is **creativity**, which is the ability of a decision maker to discover original and novel ideas that lead to feasible alternative courses of action. Encouraging creativity among managers is such a pressing organizational concern that many organizations hire outside experts to help them develop programs to train their managers in the art of creative thinking and problem solving.

Creating a Learning Organization

How do managers go about creating a learning organization? Learning theorist Peter Senge identified five principles for creating a learning organization (see Figure 7.8):[97]

1. For organizational learning to occur, top managers must allow every person in the organization to develop a sense of *personal mastery*. Managers must empower employees and allow them to experiment, create, and explore what they want.

2. As part of attaining personal mastery, organizations need to encourage employees to develop and use *complex mental models*—sophisticated ways of thinking that challenge them to find new or better ways of performing a task—to deepen their understanding of what is involved in a particular activity. Here Senge argued that managers must encourage employees to develop a taste for experimenting and risk taking.[98]

3. Managers must do everything they can to promote group creativity. Senge thought that *team learning* (learning that takes place in a group or team) is more important than individual learning in increasing organizational learning. He pointed out that most important decisions are made in subunits such as groups, functions, and divisions.

4. Managers must emphasize the importance of *building a shared vision*—a common mental model that all organizational members use to frame problems or opportunities.

5. Managers must encourage *systems thinking* (a concept drawn from systems theory, discussed in Chapter 2). Senge emphasized that to create a learning organization, managers must recognize the effects of one level of learning on another. Thus, for example, there is little point in creating teams to facilitate team learning if managers do not also take steps to give employees the freedom to develop a sense of personal mastery.

Building a learning organization requires that managers change their management assumptions radically. Developing a learning organization is neither a quick nor an easy process. Senge worked with Ford Motor Company to help managers make Ford a learning organization. Why would Ford want this? Top management believed that to compete successfully Ford must improve its members' ability to be creative and make the right decisions.

Increasingly, managers are being called on to promote global organizational learning. For example, managers at Walmart have used the lessons derived from its failures and successes in one country to promote global organizational learning across the many countries in which it now operates. For instance, when Walmart entered Malaysia, it was convinced customers there would respond to its one-stop shopping format. It found, however, that Malaysians

Figure 7.8

Senge's Principles for Creating a Learning Organization

enjoy the social experience of shopping in a lively market or bazaar and thus did not like the impersonal efficiency of the typical Walmart store. As a result, Walmart learned the importance of designing store layouts to appeal specifically to the customers of each country in which it operates.

When purchasing and operating a chain of stores in another country, such as the British ASDA chain, Walmart now strives to retain what customers value in the local market while taking advantage of its own accumulated organizational learning. For example, Walmart improved ASDA's information technology used for inventory and sales tracking in stores and enrolled ASDA in Walmart's global purchasing operations, which has enabled the chain to pay less for certain products, sell them for less, and, overall, significantly increase sales. At the same time Walmart empowered local ASDA managers to run the stores; as the president of ASDA indicates, "This is still essentially a British business in the way it's run day to day."[99] Clearly global organizational learning is essential for companies such as Walmart that have significant operations in multiple countries.

Promoting Individual Creativity

Research suggests that when certain conditions are met, managers are more likely to be creative. People must be given the opportunity and freedom to generate new ideas.[100] Creativity declines when managers look over the shoulders of talented employees and try to "hurry up" a creative solution. How would you feel if your boss said you had one week to come up with a new product idea to beat the competition? Creativity results when employees have an opportunity to experiment, to take risks, and to make mistakes and learn from them. And employees must not fear that they will be looked down on or penalized for ideas that might at first seem outlandish; sometimes those ideas yield truly innovative products and services.[101] Highly innovative companies such as Google, Apple, and Facebook are well known for the wide degree of freedom they give their managers and employees to experiment and develop innovative goods and services.[102]

Once managers have generated alternatives, creativity can be fostered by giving them constructive feedback so they know how well they are doing. Ideas that seem to be going nowhere can be eliminated and creative energies refocused in other directions. Ideas that seem promising can be promoted, and help from other managers can be obtained.[103]

Top managers must stress the importance of looking for alternative solutions and should visibly reward employees who come up with creative ideas. Being creative can be demanding and stressful. Employees who believe they are working on important, vital issues are motivated to put forth the high levels of effort that creativity demands. Creative people like to receive the acclaim of others, and innovative organizations have many kinds of ceremonies and rewards to recognize creative employees.

Employees on the front line are often in a good position to come up with creative ideas for improvements but may be reluctant to speak up or share their ideas. In order to encourage frontline employees to come up with creative ideas and share them, some managers have used contests and rewards.[104] Contests and rewards signal the importance of coming up with creative ideas and encourage employees to share them. Examples of companies that have benefited from contests and rewards for creativity include Hammond's Candies in Denver, Colorado; Borrego Solar Systems in San Diego, California; and Infosurv in Atlanta, Georgia.

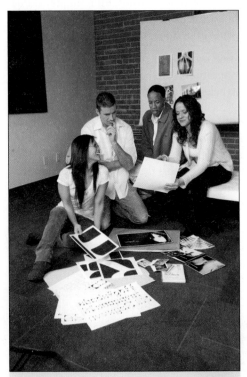

Get off e-mail and lose the desk! Giving yourself and your employees the time and space to know that contributions off the beaten track are valued increases the ability to think outside the box.

Promoting Group Creativity

To encourage creativity at the group level, organizations can use group problem-solving techniques that promote creative ideas and innovative solutions. These techniques can also prevent groupthink and help managers uncover biases. Here we look at three group decision-making techniques: *brainstorming,* the *nominal group technique,* and the *Delphi technique.*

BRAINSTORMING *Brainstorming* is a group problem-solving technique in which managers meet face-to-face to generate and debate a wide variety of alternatives from which to make a decision.[105] Generally from 5 to 15 managers meet in a closed-door session and proceed like this:

- One manager describes in broad outline the problem the group is to address.

- Group members share their ideas and generate alternative courses of action.

- As each alternative is described, group members are not allowed to criticize it; everyone withholds judgment until all alternatives have been heard. One member of the group records the alternatives on a flip chart.

- Group members are encouraged to be as innovative and radical as possible. Anything goes; and the greater the number of ideas put forth, the better. Moreover, group members are encouraged to "piggyback" or build on each other's suggestions.

- When all alternatives have been generated, group members debate the pros and cons of each and develop a short list of the best alternatives.

Brainstorming is very useful in some problem-solving situations—for example, when managers are trying to find a name for a new perfume or car model. But sometimes individuals working alone can generate more alternatives. The main reason for the loss of productivity in brainstorming appears to be **production blocking**, which occurs because group members cannot always simultaneously make sense of all the alternatives being generated, think up additional alternatives, and remember what they were thinking.[106]

NOMINAL GROUP TECHNIQUE To avoid production blocking, the **nominal group technique** is often used. It provides a more structured way of generating alternatives in writing and gives each manager more time and opportunity to come up with potential solutions. The nominal group technique is especially useful when an issue is controversial and when different managers might be expected to champion different courses of action. Generally a small group of managers meets in a closed-door session and adopts the following procedures:

- One manager outlines the problem to be addressed, and 30 or 40 minutes are allocated for group members, working individually, to write down their ideas and solutions. Group members are encouraged to be innovative.

- Managers take turns reading their suggestions to the group. One manager writes all the alternatives on a flip chart. No criticism or evaluation of alternatives is allowed until all alternatives have been read.

- The alternatives are then discussed, one by one, in the sequence in which they were proposed. Group members can ask for clarifying information and critique each alternative to identify its pros and cons.

- When all alternatives have been discussed, each group member ranks all the alternatives from most preferred to least preferred, and the alternative that receives the highest ranking is chosen.[107]

DELPHI TECHNIQUE Both the nominal group technique and brainstorming require that managers meet to generate creative ideas and engage in joint problem solving. What happens if managers are in different cities or in different parts of the world and cannot meet face-to-face? Videoconferencing is one way to bring distant managers together to brainstorm. Another way is to use the **Delphi technique**, which is a written approach to creative problem solving.[108] The Delphi technique works like this:

- The group leader writes a statement of the problem and a series of questions to which participating managers are to respond.

- The questionnaire is sent to the managers and departmental experts who are most knowledgeable about the problem. They are asked to generate solutions and mail the questionnaire back to the group leader.

production blocking A loss of productivity in brainstorming sessions due to the unstructured nature of brainstorming.

nominal group technique A decision-making technique in which group members write down ideas and solutions, read their suggestions to the whole group, and discuss and then rank the alternatives.

delphi technique A decision-making technique in which group members do not meet face-to-face but respond in writing to questions posed by the group leader.

LO7-5 Describe how managers can encourage and promote entrepreneurship to create a learning organization, and differentiate between entrepreneurs and intrapreneurs.

- A team of top managers records and summarizes the responses. The results are then sent back to the participants, with additional questions to be answered before a decision can be made.

- The process is repeated until a consensus is reached and the most suitable course of action is apparent.

Entrepreneurship and Creativity

entrepreneur An individual who notices opportunities and decides how to mobilize the resources necessary to produce new and improved goods and services.

social entrepreneur An individual who pursues initiatives and opportunities and mobilizes resources to address social problems and needs in order to improve society and well-being through creative solutions.

Entrepreneurs are individuals who notice opportunities and decide how to mobilize the resources necessary to produce new and improved goods and services. Entrepreneurs make all of the planning, organizing, leading, and controlling decisions necessary to start new business ventures. Thus entrepreneurs are an important source of creativity in the organizational world. These people, such as David Filo and Jerry Yang (founders of Yahoo!), make vast fortunes when their businesses succeed. Or they are among the millions of people who start new business ventures only to lose their money when they fail. Despite the fact that many small businesses fail in the first three to five years, a good portion of men and women in today's workforce want to start their own companies.[109]

Social entrepreneurs are individuals who pursue initiatives and opportunities to address social problems and needs in order to improve society and well-being, such as reducing poverty, increasing literacy, protecting the natural environment, or reducing substance abuse.[110] Social entrepreneurs seek to mobilize resources to solve social problems through creative solutions.[111]

As indicated in the following "Ethics in Action" box, although social entrepreneurs often face challenges in raising funds to support their initiatives, their options are increasing.

Ethics in Action

Finding Funding to Do Good

Typically venture capitalists who provide funding for entrepreneurs to start their businesses are concerned with getting a good return on their investment and not having to wait a long time to do so; and banks expect entrepreneurs to have a prior track record of success. For social entrepreneurs, this can make raising funds to support their new ventures a real challenge. Fortunately an increasing number of social venture funds seek to invest in companies that are focused on social goals.[112]

World of Good, Inc., was founded by UC Berkeley MBA graduates Priya Haji and Siddharth Sanghvi with the mission to create opportunities for thousands of producers and artisans in the developing world by bringing their products to the mainstream consumer market.[113] This organization seeks to create a global network of entrepreneurs in the informal sector, uplifted by their direct access to large-scale markets and empowered through the use of ethical wage standards. World of Good has helped more than 40,000 artisans in 70 countries receive fair wages for their artisan work.[114]

When Priya Haji, the company's cofounder and former CEO, initially sought funding for her venture, she had to look beyond traditional banks, which weren't interested because she didn't have a three-year track record.[115] "For them, it didn't make sense," Haji says. "There is a consumer driven demand for this kind of ethical consumption, but the debt markets don't understand that." Instead Haji turned to social lenders and she reached a deal with three of them: RSF Social Finance, Root Capital, and Shared Interest, each of which insists that portfolio companies maintain their social missions as they grow.[116] Their investment paid off: The company has been both very successful and true to its mission. In fact, a few years ago eBay

Priya Haji, founder of World of Good, Inc.

acquired World of Good, Inc., as part of its sustainability portfolio, and the company is now called WorldofGood.com by eBay.[117]

When Charlie Crystle sought funding for Mission Research, the social enterprise he cofounded to provide nonprofits with fund-raising software, traditional investors questioned some of Mission's practices—such as giving the software away to nonprofits with annual budgets of less than $25,000—and even the fact that he was starting a business focused on selling to nonprofits.[118] Crystle was able to secure $300,000 in funding from Underdog Ventures in return for a 5% share in the company. Unlike other venture capital firms that aim to sell their stake in new ventures within five to seven years, Underdog is willing to wait seven to eight years and also requires that companies it invests in get prior approval from Underdog if they want to change their social mission.[119]

World of Good and Mission Research have both been very successful since receiving funding from social investors.[120] Of equal importance, they also are achieving their social goals, which is a prime reason they were founded.

Many managers, scientists, and researchers employed by companies engage in entrepreneurial activity, and they are an important source of organizational creativity. They are involved in innovation, developing new and improved products and ways to make them, which we describe in detail in Chapter 9. Such employees notice opportunities for either quantum or incremental product improvements and are responsible for managing the product development process. These individuals are known as **intrapreneurs** to distinguish them from entrepreneurs who start their own businesses. But in general, entrepreneurship involves creative decision making that gives customers new or improved goods and services.

There is an interesting relationship between entrepreneurs and intrapreneurs. Many managers with intrapreneurial talents become dissatisfied if their superiors decide neither to support nor to fund new product ideas and development efforts that the managers think will succeed. What do intrapreneurial managers who feel they are getting nowhere do? Often they decide to leave their current organizations and start their own companies to take advantage of their new product ideas! In other words, intrapreneurs become entrepreneurs and found companies that often compete with the companies they left. To avoid losing these individuals, top managers must find ways to facilitate the entrepreneurial spirit of their most creative employees. In the remainder of this section we consider issues involved in promoting successful entrepreneurship in both new and existing organizations.

intrapreneur A manager, scientist, or researcher who works inside an organization and notices opportunities to develop new or improved products and better ways to make them.

Entrepreneurship and New Ventures

The fact that a significant number of entrepreneurs were frustrated intrapreneurs provides a clue about the personal characteristics of people who are likely to start a new venture and bear all the uncertainty and risk associated with being an entrepreneur.

CHARACTERISTICS OF ENTREPRENEURS   Entrepreneurs are likely to possess a particular set of the personality characteristics we discussed in Chapter 3. First, they are likely to be high on the personality trait of *openness to experience,* meaning they are predisposed to be original, to be open to a wide range of stimuli, to be daring, and to take risks. Entrepreneurs also are likely to have an *internal locus of control,* believing that they are responsible for what happens to them and that their own actions determine important outcomes such as the success or failure of a new business. People with an external locus of control, in contrast, would be unlikely to leave a secure job in an organization and assume the risk associated with a new venture.

Entrepreneurs are likely to have a high level of *self-esteem* and feel competent and capable of handling most situations—including the stress and uncertainty surrounding a plunge into a risky new venture. Entrepreneurs are also likely to have a high *need for achievement* and have a strong desire to perform challenging tasks and meet high personal standards of excellence.

ENTREPRENEURSHIP AND MANAGEMENT   Given that entrepreneurs are predisposed to activities that are somewhat adventurous and risky, in what ways can people become involved in entrepreneurial ventures? One way is to start a business from scratch. Taking advantage of modern IT, some people start solo ventures or partnerships.

When people who go it alone succeed, they frequently need to hire other people to help them run the business. Michael Dell, for example, began his computer business as a college student and within weeks had hired several people to help him assemble computers from the components he bought from suppliers. From his solo venture grew Dell Computer.

Some entrepreneurs who start a new business have difficulty deciding how to manage the organization as it grows; **entrepreneurship** is *not* the same as management. Management encompasses all the decisions involved in planning, organizing, leading, and controlling resources. Entrepreneurship is noticing an opportunity to satisfy a customer need and then deciding how to find and use resources to make a product that satisfies that need. When an entrepreneur has produced something customers want, entrepreneurship gives way to management because the pressing need becomes providing the product both efficiently and effectively. Frequently a founding entrepreneur lacks the skills, patience, and experience to engage in the difficult and challenging work of management. Some entrepreneurs find it hard to delegate authority because they are afraid to risk their company by letting others manage it. As a result they become overloaded and the quality of their decision making declines. Other entrepreneurs lack the detailed knowledge necessary to establish state-of-the-art information systems and technology or to create the operations management procedures that are vital to increase the efficiency of their organizations' production systems. Thus, to succeed, it is necessary to do more than create a new product; an entrepreneur must hire managers who can create an operating system that will let a new venture survive and prosper.

> **entrepreneurship** The mobilization of resources to take advantage of an opportunity to provide customers with new or improved goods and services.

> **product champion** A manager who takes "ownership" of a project and provides the leadership and vision that take a product from the idea stage to the final customer.

Intrapreneurship and Organizational Learning

The intensity of competition today, particularly from agile small companies, has made it increasingly important for large established organizations to promote and encourage intrapreneurship to raise their level of innovation and organizational learning. As we discussed earlier, a learning organization encourages all employees to identify opportunities and solve problems, thus enabling the organization to continuously experiment, improve, and increase its ability to provide customers with new and improved goods and services. The higher the level of intrapreneurship, the higher will be the level of learning and innovation. How can organizations promote organizational learning and intrapreneurship?

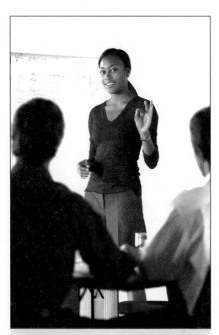

Intrapreneurs face unique challenges in balancing their championing of new ideas with the company's overall need for stability.

PRODUCT CHAMPIONS   One way to promote intrapreneurship is to encourage individuals to assume the role of **product champion**, a manager who takes "ownership" of a project and provides the leadership and vision that take a product from the idea stage to the final customer. 3M, a company well known for its attempts to promote intrapreneurship, encourages all its managers to become product champions and identify new product ideas. A product champion becomes responsible for developing a business plan for the product. Armed with this business plan, the champion appears before 3M's product development committee, a team of senior 3M managers who probe the strengths and weaknesses of the plan to decide whether it should be funded. If the plan is accepted, the product champion assumes responsibility for product development.

SKUNKWORKS The idea behind the product champion role is that employees who feel ownership for a project are inclined to act like outside entrepreneurs and go to great lengths to make the project succeed. Using skunkworks and new venture divisions can also strengthen this feeling of ownership. A **skunkworks** is a group of intrapreneurs who are deliberately separated from the normal operation of an organization—for example, from the normal chain of command—to encourage them to devote all their attention to developing new products. The idea is that if these people are isolated, they will become so intensely involved in a project that development time will be relatively brief and the quality of the final product will be enhanced. The term *skunkworks* was coined at the Lockheed Corporation, which formed a team of design engineers to develop special aircraft such as the U2 spy plane. The secrecy with which this unit functioned and speculation about its goals led others to refer to it as "the skunkworks."

skunkworks A group of intrapreneurs who are deliberately separated from the normal operation of an organization to encourage them to devote all their attention to developing new products.

REWARDS FOR INNOVATION To encourage managers to bear the uncertainty and risk associated with the hard work of entrepreneurship, it is necessary to link performance to rewards. Increasingly companies are rewarding intrapreneurs on the basis of the outcome of the product development process. Intrapreneurs are paid large bonuses if their projects succeed, or they are granted stock options that can make them millionaires if their products sell well. Both Microsoft and Google, for example, have made hundreds of their employees multimillionaires as a result of the stock options they were granted as part of their reward packages. In addition to receiving money, successful intrapreneurs can expect to receive promotion to the ranks of top management. Most of 3M's top managers, for example, reached the executive suite because they had a track record of successful entrepreneurship. Organizations must reward intrapreneurs equitably if they wish to prevent them from leaving and becoming outside entrepreneurs who might form a competitive new venture. Nevertheless, intrapreneurs frequently do so.

Summary and Review

LO7-1

THE NATURE OF MANAGERIAL DECISION MAKING Programmed decisions are routine decisions made so often that managers have developed decision rules to be followed automatically. Nonprogrammed decisions are made in response to situations that are unusual or novel; they are nonroutine decisions. The classical model of decision making assumes that decision makers have complete information; are able to process that information in an objective, rational manner; and make optimum decisions. March and Simon argued that managers exhibit bounded rationality, rarely have access to all the information they need to make optimum decisions, and consequently satisfice and rely on their intuition and judgment when making decisions.

LO7-2 **STEPS IN THE DECISION-MAKING PROCESS** When making decisions, managers should take these six steps: recognize the need for a decision, generate alternatives, assess alternatives, choose among alternatives, implement the chosen alternative, and learn from feedback.

LO7-2 **COGNITIVE BIASES AND DECISION MAKING** Most of the time managers are fairly good decision makers. On occasion, however, problems can result because human judgment can be adversely affected by the operation of cognitive biases that result in poor decisions. Cognitive biases are caused by systematic errors in the way decision makers process information and make decisions. Sources of these errors include prior hypotheses, representativeness, the illusion of control, and escalating commitment. Managers should undertake a personal decision audit to become aware of their biases and thus improve their decision making.

LO7-3   **GROUP DECISION MAKING**   Many advantages are associated with group decision making, but there are also several disadvantages. One major source of poor decision making is groupthink. Afflicted decision makers collectively embark on a dubious course of action without questioning the assumptions that underlie their decision. Managers can improve the quality of group decision making by using techniques such as devil's advocacy and dialectical inquiry and by increasing diversity in the decision-making group.

LO7-4   **ORGANIZATIONAL LEARNING AND CREATIVITY**   Organizational learning is the process through which managers seek to improve employees' desire and ability to understand and manage the organization and its task environment so employees can make decisions that continuously raise organizational effectiveness. Managers must take steps to promote organizational learning and creativity at the individual and group levels to improve the quality of decision making.

LO7-5   **ENTREPRENEURSHIP**   Entrepreneurship is the mobilization of resources to take advantage of an opportunity to provide customers with new or improved goods and services. Entrepreneurs find new ventures of their own. Intrapreneurs work inside organizations and manage the product development process. Organizations need to encourage intrapreneurship because it leads to organizational learning and innovation.

Management in Action

Topics for Discussion and Action

Discussion

1. What are the main differences between programmed decision making and nonprogrammed decision making? [LO7-1]

2. In what ways do the classical and administrative models of decision making help managers appreciate the complexities of real-world decision making? [LO7-1]

3. Why do capable managers sometimes make bad decisions? What can individual managers do to improve their decision-making skills? [LO7-1, 7-2]

4. In what kinds of groups is groupthink most likely to be a problem? When is it least likely to be a problem? What steps can group members take to ward off groupthink? [LO7-3]

5. What is organizational learning, and how can managers promote it? [LO7-4]

6. What is the difference between entrepreneurship and intrapreneurship? [LO7-5]

Action

7. Ask a manager to recall the best and the worst decisions he or she ever made. Try to determine why these decisions were so good or so bad. [LO7-1, 7-2, 7-3]

8. Think about an organization in your local community or your university, or an organization that you are familiar with, that is doing poorly. Now think of questions managers in the organization should ask stakeholders to elicit creative ideas for turning around the organization's fortunes. [LO7-4]

Building Management Skills

How Do You Make Decisions? [LO7-1, 7-2, 7-4]

Pick a decision you made recently that has had important consequences for you. It may be your decision about which college to attend, which major to select, whether to take a part-time job, or which part-time job to take. Using the material in this chapter, analyze how you made the decision:

1. Identify the criteria you used, either consciously or unconsciously, to guide your decision making.

2. List the alternatives you considered. Were they all possible alternatives? Did you unconsciously (or consciously) ignore some important alternatives?

3. How much information did you have about each alternative? Were you making the decision on the basis of complete or incomplete information?

4. Try to remember how you reached the decision. Did you sit down and consciously think through the implications of each alternative, or did you make the decision on the basis of intuition? Did you use any rules of thumb to help you make the decision?

5. In retrospect, do you think your choice of alternative was shaped by any of the cognitive biases discussed in this chapter?

6. Having answered the previous five questions, do you think in retrospect that you made a reasonable decision? What, if anything, might you do to improve your ability to make good decisions in the future?

Managing Ethically [LO7-3]

Sometimes groups make extreme decisions—decisions that are either more risky or more conservative than they would have been if individuals acting alone had made them. One explanation for the tendency of groups to make extreme decisions is diffusion of responsibility.

In a group, responsibility for the outcomes of a decision is spread among group members, so each person feels less than fully accountable. The group's decision is extreme because no individual has taken full responsibility for it.

Questions

1. Either alone or in a group, think about the ethical implications of extreme decision making by groups.

2. When group decision making takes place, should members of a group each feel fully accountable for outcomes of the decision? Why or why not?

Small Group Breakout Exercise

Brainstorming [LO7-3, 7-4]

Form groups of three or four people, and appoint one member as the spokesperson who will communicate your findings to the class when called on by the instructor. Then discuss the following scenario:

You and your partners are trying to decide which kind of restaurant to open in a centrally located shopping center that has just been built in your city. The problem confronting you is that the city already has many restaurants that provide different kinds of food at all price ranges. You have the resources to open any type of restaurant. Your challenge is to decide which type is most likely to succeed.

Use brainstorming to decide which type of restaurant to open. Follow these steps:

1. As a group, spend 5 or 10 minutes generating ideas about the alternative restaurants that the members think will be most likely to succeed. Each group member should be as innovative and creative as possible, and no suggestions should be criticized.

2. Appoint one group member to write down the alternatives as they are identified.

3. Spend the next 10 or 15 minutes debating the pros and cons of the alternatives. As a group, try to reach a consensus on which alternative is most likely to succeed.

After making your decision, discuss the pros and cons of the brainstorming method, and decide whether any production blocking occurred.

When called on by the instructor, the spokesperson should be prepared to share your group's decision with the class, as well as the reasons for the group's decision.

Exploring the World Wide Web [LO7-4]

Go to www.brainstorming.co.uk. This website contains "Training on Creative Techniques" and "Creativity Puzzles." Spend at least 30 minutes on the training and/or puzzles. Think about what you have learned. Come up with specific ways in which you can be more creative in your thinking and decision making based on what you have learned.

Be the Manager [LO7-1, 7-2, 7-3, 7-4, 7-5]

You are a top manager who was recently hired by an oil field services company in Oklahoma to help it respond more quickly and proactively to potential opportunities in its market. You report to the chief operating officer (COO), who reports to the CEO, and you have been on the job for eight months. Thus far you have come up with three initiatives you carefully studied, thought were noteworthy, and proposed and justified to the COO. The COO seemed cautiously interested when you presented the proposals, and each time he indicated he would think about them and discuss them with the CEO because considerable resources were involved. Each time you never heard back from the COO, and after a few weeks elapsed, you casually asked the COO if there was any news on the proposal in question. For the first proposal, the COO said, "We think it's a good idea, but the timing is off. Let's shelve it for the time being and reconsider it next year." For the second proposal, the COO said, "Mike [the CEO] reminded me that we tried that two years ago and it wasn't well received in the market. I am surprised I didn't remember it myself when you first described the proposal, but it came right back to me once Mike mentioned it." For the third proposal, the COO simply said, "We're not convinced it will work."

You believe your three proposed initiatives are viable ways to seize opportunities in the marketplace, yet you cannot proceed with any of them. Moreover, for each proposal, you invested considerable time and even worked to bring others on board to support the proposal, only to have it shot down by the CEO. When you interviewed for the position, both the COO and the CEO claimed they wanted "an outsider to help them step out of the box and innovate." Yet your experience to date has been just the opposite. What are you going to do?

The Wall Street Journal Case in the News [LO7-1, LO7-2, LO7-4, LO7-5]

"Super Size Me" Generation Takes Over at McDonald's

When Travis Heriaud decided to spend $40,000 on the grand opening of a new McDonald's here—sponsoring a book giveaway for local children and hosting a parade of zoo animals—his father, Lee, balked.

Lee Heriaud, a 59-year-old owner of 12 McDonald's restaurants, warned that the event risked erasing cash flow for a full year. "You've gone overboard here," he told his son.

Travis, 30, pressed ahead—and busted the budget for the grand-opening spending by adding even more new-store promotions. However, first-year revenue at the restaurant is now on track to beat McDonald's projections by 50%. And other McDonald's in the area are adopting his tactics.

The results surprised the elder Mr. Heriaud: "It was difficult to get my head around the price tag," he says. "I just didn't think it would pay off."

McDonald's Corp. may seem like just another giant corporation, but its secret sauce has always been its small-business franchisees—and now that network is undergoing one of its biggest generational transformations in decades as the children of owners start taking over from their parents.

As with any entrepreneurial venture, the transition is fraught with challenges. McDonald's prides itself on carefully selecting its franchisees, so it is loath to encourage raw nepotism. The sons and daughters of McDonald's franchisees aren't automatically entitled to become franchisees and they can't inherit their parents' restaurants. Rather, they have to undergo a one- to five-year process of proving themselves capable of running strong restaurants before they can be approved franchisees. "The next gens don't have a birthright to be an owner operator; they earn it," says John Kujawa, vice president of franchising for McDonald's USA.

So far, the results are mixed, say McDonald's executives and franchisees. Having grown up in an era of "Fast Food Nation" and "Super Size Me," the next generation is moving quickly to address criticism of the fast-food industry. The younger franchisees are proposing everything from healthier foods—including gluten-free hamburger buns and organic produce—to more corporate responsibility on issues like recycling and providing community services like books for low-income kids. The group also promotes use of more technology, such as installing Wi-Fi in restaurants and building McDonald's Facebook pages.

The changes aren't always welcome to the older franchisees, some of whom have resisted new ideas as benign as credit cards. The Oak Brook, Illinois, corporate headquarters has passed on some ideas, preferring to wait and see if they have broad appeal before they are adopted.

Still, this group of young owners is likely to have a growing impact on the nation's largest fast food chain by revenue: Next-generation McDonald's franchise owners, whose parents or grandparents owned restaurants, currently make up the largest percentage of franchisees ever, 30% of the U.S. base—up from 18% in 2001. The company expects the figure to reach 37% in the next five years.

In Oak Brook, McDonald's management credits next generation franchisees with proposing some of the company's most popular products and services, says Jim Johannesen, McDonald's USA chief operating officer.

Among their changes: a line of upscale burgers with thicker patties called Angus burgers that have contributed to sales growth; free Wi-Fi, which has helped keep McDonald's competitive with Starbucks Corp.; a picture-based ordering system that shaves precious seconds from customer wait times; and payment by credit card, which boosted the value of transactions, since people tend to order more when they charge it.

The credit-card option worried Houston franchisee Nelly Quijano, 66, who says she had made some computer accounting mistakes over the years. She feared she would make similar mistakes with the credit-card machines and lose track of sales. "I wasn't against it; I was scared," she said.

But her daughter, Mariselle Quijano, 30, who now owns six McDonald's, urged her mother to switch to cashless payment. "Today, hardly anyone carries cash," she told her mother. After installing the machines, sales immediately improved at their restaurants.

Another seemingly simple idea, Mr. Johannesen said, was to keep

McDonald's open later into the evening, which has helped the company wring more sales out of existing restaurants. Today, nearly 40% of its U.S. outlets are open around the clock, up from about 30% seven years ago. "Our young people helped us understand that there's a lot more going on when the rest of us are sleeping than we would have known," Mr. Johannesen says.

But the company isn't gung ho about every idea.

Brittaney Kerby, of Austin, Texas, recently stopped working at her father's McDonald's restaurants and took out a loan to open her own so she could make her own decisions.

Ms. Kerby, 32, has been pushing McDonald's executives during regional meetings to start a recycling program for employees' soda cans and restaurant products like cardboard boxes. Partly because of her efforts, McDonald's agreed to test the program on a regional basis, in Austin, beginning in April.

Ms. Kerby has been less successful in convincing corporate management on some of her other ideas, such as composting and installing rooftop gardens in restaurants. She asked the company's menu management team to discuss broadening offerings to include organic produce and items for people with food allergies—like gluten-free hamburger buns. But so far, to no avail.

"It's always an open dialogue," she says. "You don't hear a straight-up 'No.'"

McDonald's spokeswoman Dayna Proud says new ideas need to be appropriate for all 14,000 restaurants in the United States. "Not to say it couldn't happen or that we're not looking at things like gluten-free buns and organic produce," Ms. Proud said. "But with a system the size of ours it has to be something that has an appeal to the masses."

Indeed, it isn't the first time McDonald's headquarters has resisted new ideas. A longtime franchisee in the South recalls the company's reticence to adopt a fish sandwich back in

the early 1960s. Proposed by a Cincinnati franchisee, because his mostly Catholic patrons didn't eat meat on Fridays, the idea was considered radical at the time, he said. It took five years of testing and development for the Filet-O-Fish to be included on McDonald's national menu.

"It's very difficult to get any changes through at McDonald's whether you're a younger or an older franchisee," he said.

Ms. Proud, who confirmed the fish story, said that when the company makes a change "it needs to be right for our customers, our restaurants, our franchisees and our suppliers and so that process and the discussions that occur take time."

Still, corporate managers emphasize that they are relying on the young franchisees for fresh ideas to sustain their multiyear growth tear.

McDonald's shares have nearly quadrupled since the end of 2003, when it adopted a plan to slow new-store openings in the United States and improve restaurant operations. But some investors are wondering how much more room there is to grow.

After the company posted another strong quarter in January, its shares dropped as investors questioned how much upside is left. Thursday, McDonald's is expected to announce another month of strong same-store sales for February.

Some younger franchisees are taking a different approach to criticism than their parents' generation. For example, Brandon O'Rourke, a 39-year-old franchisee, decided to proactively approach what he calls the "haters," or people who dislike McDonald's.

Mr. O'Rourke, who until recently owned two McDonald's in Denver and is now opening five in Phoenix, has visited McDonald's citrus growers in Florida, chicken farmers in Arkansas, potato fields in Idaho, and beef processing plants in Oklahoma. He says what he has seen has given him confidence in the quality of McDonald's food and ammunition to fend off critics.

More than a year ago, he invited some mothers who were blogging about whether to let their kids eat fast food for a tour of a kitchen at one of his restaurants. Some of them had thought the eggs in the Egg McMuffin were cut from a giant log of processed egg and were surprised to see that McDonald's actually cracks eggs in the restaurant, he says. The moms later blogged about what they saw.

Recently, he fielded questions from 7th and 8th graders at his daughter's school after a teacher showed the documentary "Super Size Me." One kid, he recalls, thought McDonald's killed chickens by putting them in a blender. "I could answer all their questions because I had seen it for myself," Mr. O'Rourke says.

Some smaller changes are helping individual franchisees at a time when restaurants are fighting for market share and even tiny details can influence which restaurant a person chooses.

Adrian Smith, a 39-year-old franchisee in North Carolina, persuaded his dad to add more electrical outlets to his restaurants to make it easier for people to plug in their laptops. "I think we've got to stay relevant and fresh for our customers. We need to be a destination," he says.

Travis Heriaud, the Arizona franchisee, says that with years of experience under his belt, his dad sometimes has a better feel for customer psychology than he does. In January, when McDonald's offered a free small coffee giveaway in some parts of the country for two weeks, the younger Mr. Heriaud wanted to discount medium and large coffees, too. His father said they would be leaving money on the table and argued to leave medium and large prices unchanged.

To see who was right, they agreed to test both strategies in a few of their stores. It turned out the elder Mr. Heriaud was right: While people were happy to get a free small coffee, those who wanted a bigger size were willing to pay full price and didn't expect a discount.

When it came to his community-outreach plan, though, the younger Mr. Heriaud's instincts proved correct.

Tolleson, west of Phoenix, was once a strong agricultural community; the smell of dairy farms can still be powerful in the right wind. In studying the market, the younger Mr. Heriaud learned that manufacturing and food-service distribution had overtaken agriculture, that local schools were short of funds and the local library was struggling to get kids to participate in its summer reading program.

He argued to his father that, since they were already spending $1.7 million to build a restaurant, it made sense to invest another $40,000 to try to demonstrate that their restaurant aimed to be part of the community. "We have a responsibility to be good corporate citizens," the younger man said.

He decided to hold community events year-round, rather than stop after the grand opening last March. To encourage participation in the library summer reading program, Mr. Heriaud handed out free books and had Ronald McDonald do readings.

In the fall, he held a back-to-school fair and handed out free backpacks; more than 100 families waited in line for an hour for freebies. As Christmas drew near, he held a toy drive, brought in the local high-school choir to sing carols, and invited kids to pose for photos with Santa.

The plan ended up costing $50,000. Sales this year are expected to total more than $3 million, which is far higher than the $2 million the company projected the store to ring up and higher than the $2.5 million McDonald's restaurants around the country average annually. The Heriauds say they will more than recoup their $50,000 investment.

When Travis Heriaud shared his results with other Phoenix franchisees, all 220 restaurants in the area started adopting parts of his strategy.

This month, the restaurants plan to offer free breakfast to kids before taking standardized tests. In September, they have pledged to hand out new backpacks to kids and provide information on how to get afterschool tutoring.

Ana Cruz, a 27-year-old mother of two, was eating lunch at the Tolleson McDonald's recently while her three-year-old son clambered around on some playground equipment. She said the restaurant's efforts—including donations to her daughter's school—eased her mind about eating there.

At first, "I wasn't thrilled that it was McDonald's that was donating to my daughter's school," Ms. Cruz says, "because it's not too healthy." But she says that, over time, she appreciated the various efforts. "They don't come off like they're only about getting people to come in," Ms. Cruz says.

Questions for Discussion

1. To what extent do McDonald's franchisees and managers at headquarters make nonprogrammed decisions?

2. To what extent are the decisions they make characterized by risk and uncertainty?

3. What are some of the ways in which franchisees and managers recognize the need to make a decision? To what extent do they learn from feedback?

4. To what extent do you think franchisees and managers satisfice when they make decisions? Why do you think this is the case?

Source: Julie Jargon, "'Super Size Me' Generation Takes Over at McDonald's," *The Wall Street Journal,* March 8, 2012, pp. A1, A14. Copyright © 2012. Reproduced with permission of Dow Jones & Company, Inc. Republished with permission of Copyright Clearance Center.

CHAPTER 8

The Manager as a Planner and Strategist

Learning Objectives

After studying this chapter, you should be able to:

LO8-1 Identify the three main steps of the planning process and explain the relationship between planning and strategy.

LO8-2 Describe some techniques managers can use to improve the planning process so they can better predict the future and mobilize organizational resources to meet future contingencies.

LO8-3 Differentiate between the main types of business-level strategies and explain how they give an organization a competitive advantage that may lead to superior performance.

LO8-4 Differentiate between the main types of corporate-level strategies and explain how they are used to strengthen a company's business-level strategy and competitive advantage.

LO8-5 Describe the vital role managers play in implementing strategies to achieve an organization's mission and goals.

A MANAGER'S CHALLENGE

Groupon's Strategy to Become the Leader in the Online Coupon Market

What makes it hard to compete in an industry? In 2010, Google offered to buy Groupon, the online "daily deal" coupon start-up company for $6 billion—an astonishingly high offer many analysts said—but Groupon rejected Google's offer, leaving analysts surprised. Why? Groupon's founders decided that they could make much more money from their new company if they could develop strategies to allow the company to stay ahead of potential competitors (such as Google and Amazon), and establish it as the dominant company in this segment of the online advertising market. Facebook had refused early takeover offers from companies such as Microsoft and Google, and Facebook's initial public offering was expected to value the company at over $1 billion (in fact, Facebook raised over $1.6 billion when it went public in 2012 at $38 a share, valuing the company at more than $100 billion!). If Facebook's value could increase so much in a short period of time then so could Groupon's.

Groupon was originally a website called "The Point" founded by Andrew Mason in 2007, which was designed to allow a critical mass of people to connect online and participate together as members in a joint endeavor. When enough people joined, a "tipping point" was reached that allowed them to act as a *group,* and to take advantages of buying opportunities that could not be obtained by any single person acting alone. As Mason stated in a letter to prospective investors in 2011: "I started The Point to empower the little guy and solve the world's unsolvable problems."[1] A big idea— it quickly became clear to Mason that Internet users really liked the opportunity to act together and get great deals on location-specific goods and services; online coupons that changed day-by-day brought people together.

Mason transformed The Point into "Groupon," and quickly began hiring software

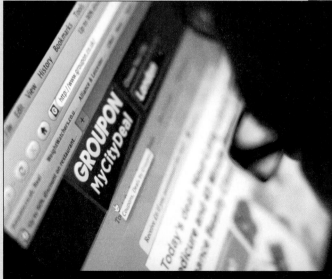

Groupon's initial splash appears to have subsided into a ripple. How would you advise them to innovate ahead of their new competitors?

engineers and salespeople who shared his vision: people acting together to increase their buying power. As Mason wrote: "[A]s an antidote to a common ailment for us city-dwellers there's so much cool stuff to do, but the choice can be overwhelming. With so many options, sometimes the easiest thing is to go to a familiar restaurant, or just stay at home and watch a movie. As a result, we miss out on trying all the cool things our cities have to offer."[2] In 2009, Groupon's online coupon service was launched in major cities around the United States, and its strategy was to focus on providing one specific coupon that offered big discounts on a particular good or service each day, in a specific geographic location. Groupon's strategy was thus based on leveraging its members' collective buying power to obtain great deals from companies that online customers found hard to resist. However, to achieve this it needed to expand its user base. To accomplish this Groupon had to attract companies that were anxious to capture the attention of new customers by offering them good deals and samples of their goods and services, such as restaurant meals or recreational experiences. To increase Groupon's customer-base and encourage buyers to purchase its online coupons it had to offer them protection; so Groupon promises that if users feel disappointed in a transaction they can call it to obtain a refund. Groupon's website states that nothing is more important than treating customers well; and the companies offering discount coupons know they must also work hard to attract and keep Groupon users—their customers.

Groupon's revenues increased 15 times between 2009 and 2011 as its user base grew to 50 million spearheaded by Mason's vision and business-level strategy. While global sales were nonexistent in March 2010, they were 53% of Groupon's revenues by March 2011, just one year later. Its explosive growth led Google to realize the potential of Groupon to leverage its own competences in Internet advertising in new ways and build its online advertising market share.

However, when Groupon refused Google's offer, it took on a major risk: It was pursuing a *focused differentiation strategy* based on becoming the leader in the online coupon sales segment of the online advertising market. If it succeeded, it would become a major online differentiator potentially worth tens of billions of dollars. However, the risk for Groupon is, What barriers to entry exist to stop any other leading Internet differentiator—such as Google, Amazon.com, or Facebook (which has over 750,000 million active users)—from imitating Groupon's approach to offering online coupons and stealing its customers?

Groupon cannot patent its online coupon idea, so how is this young company going to attract and retain the growing number of web users who are attracted to the online coupon market, which is the only way it can increase its market share and become the established leader? Mason's strategy included soliciting tens of millions of dollars from private investors and then pursuing an initial stock offering to raise the funding necessary to launch an aggressive global expansion plan to stay ahead of competitors. Groupon went public in November 2011 at $20 a share, which valued the company at $13 billion, and its stock price rose to a high of $25.[3]

Being the "first-mover" in a new market is a major strategic advantage, so pouring money into sales and marketing and software development to improve its online storefront and allow Groupon to remain the global leader is worth it. Amazon.com and eBay, for example, grew in this same way—they spent billions to become the online retail portals of choice and now reap the benefits of their innovative strategies.

By 2012, however, Groupon faced the prospect of cutthroat competition from Internet giants. For example, Google announced the launch of an online coupon service that offered discounts from restaurants and other merchants if enough people agree to buy the coupons. This service, called Living Social, is similar to the daily deals offered by Groupon. Google has continued to test and improve its service as it seeks to become a major competitor and has rapidly expanded its offerings in major U.S. cities. Google also unveiled a new mobile payment service that allows users to pay for products directly through their smartphones. Similarly, Amazon .com launched a daily deal service and other Internet companies are rushing to enter this market.

Only time will tell if Groupon can maintain its leadership over this niche of the online advertising market or whether competitors will crush it. Will Groupon's refusal to take Google's $6 billion buyout offer in 2010 seem like a gigantic mistake? Its stock price fell to less than $5 a share in September 2012, down 50% from its initial offering price, which values Groupon at around $3 billion.

Overview

As competition in the growing online coupon market suggests, in a fast-changing competitive environment managers must continually evaluate how well their products are meeting customer needs, and they must engage in thorough, systematic planning to find new strategies to tailor their products to better meet those needs. This chapter explores the manager's role both as planner and as strategist. First, we discuss the nature and importance of planning, the kinds of plans managers develop, and the levels at which planning takes place. Second, we discuss the three major steps in the planning process: (1) determining an organization's mission and major goals, (2) choosing or formulating strategies to realize the mission and goals, and (3) selecting the most effective ways to implement and put these strategies into action. We also examine several techniques, such as scenario planning and SWOT analysis, that can help managers improve the quality of their planning; and we discuss a range of strategies managers can use to give their companies a competitive advantage over their rivals. By the end of this chapter, you will understand the vital role managers carry out when they plan, develop, and implement strategies to create a high-performing organization.

LO8-1 Identify the three main steps of the planning process and explain the relationship between planning and strategy.

planning Identifying and selecting appropriate goals and courses of action; one of the four principal tasks of management.

strategy A cluster of decisions about what goals to pursue, what actions to take, and how to use resources to achieve goals.

Planning and Strategy

mission statement A broad declaration of an organization's purpose that identifies the organization's products and customers and distinguishes the organization from its competitors.

Planning, as we noted in Chapter 1, is a process managers use to identify and select appropriate goals and courses of action for an organization.[4] The organizational plan that results from the planning process details the goals of the organization and the specific strategies managers will implement to attain those goals. Recall from Chapter 1 that a strategy is a cluster of related managerial decisions and actions to help an organization attain one of its goals. Thus planning is both a goal-making and a strategy-making process.

In most organizations, planning is a three-step activity (see Figure 8.1). The first step is determining the organization's mission and goals. A mission statement is a broad declaration of an organization's overriding purpose, what it is seeking to achieve from its activities; this statement also identifies what is *unique or important* about its products to its employees

Figure 8.1
Three Steps in Planning

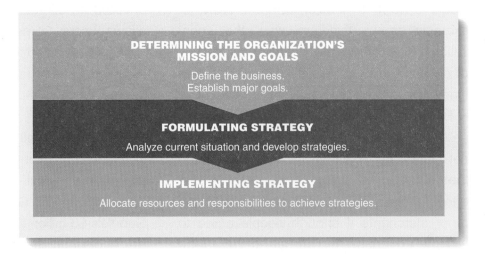

DETERMINING THE ORGANIZATION'S
MISSION AND GOALS

Define the business.
Establish major goals.

FORMULATING STRATEGY

Analyze current situation and develop strategies.

IMPLEMENTING STRATEGY

Allocate resources and responsibilities to achieve strategies.

and customers; finally it *distinguishes or differentiates* the organization in some ways from its competitors. (Three examples of mission statements, those created by Cisco Systems, Walmart, and AT&T, are illustrated later in Figure 8.4.)

The second step is formulating strategy. Managers analyze the organization's current situation and then conceive and develop the strategies necessary to attain the organization's mission and goals. The third step is implementing strategy. Managers decide how to allocate the resources and responsibilities required to implement the strategies among people and groups within the organization.[5] In subsequent sections of this chapter we look in detail at the specifics of these steps. But first we examine the general nature and purpose of planning.

The Nature of the Planning Process

Essentially, to perform the planning task, managers (1) establish and discover where an organization is at the *present time;* (2) determine where it should be in the future, its *desired future state;* and (3) decide how to *move it forward* to reach that future state. When managers plan, they must forecast what may happen in the future to decide what to do in the present. The better their predictions, the more effective will be the strategies they formulate to take advantage of future opportunities and counter emerging competitive threats in the environment. As previous chapters noted, however, the external environment is uncertain and complex, and managers typically must deal with incomplete information and bounded rationality. This is why planning and strategy making are so difficult and risky; and if managers' predictions are wrong and strategies fail, organizational performance falls.

Why Planning Is Important

Almost all managers participate in some kind of planning because they must try to predict future opportunities and threats and develop a plan and strategies that will result in a high-performing organization. Moreover, the absence of a plan often results in hesitations, false steps, and mistaken changes of direction that can hurt an organization or even lead to disaster. Planning is important for four main reasons:

1. *Planning is necessary to give the organization a sense of direction and purpose.*[6] A plan states what goals an organization is trying to achieve and what strategies it intends to use to achieve them. Without the sense of direction and purpose that a formal plan provides, managers may interpret their own specific tasks and jobs in ways that best suit themselves. The result will be an organization that is pursuing multiple and often conflicting

goals and a set of managers who do not cooperate and work well together. By stating which organizational goals and strategies are important, a plan keeps managers on track so they use the resources under their control efficiently and effectively.

2. *Planning is a useful way of getting managers to participate in decision making about the appropriate goals and strategies for an organization.* Effective planning gives all managers the opportunity to participate in decision making. At Intel, for example, top managers, as part of their annual planning process, regularly request input from lower-level managers to determine what the organization's goals and strategies should be.

3. *A plan helps coordinate managers of the different functions and divisions of an organization to ensure that they all pull in the same direction and work to achieve its desired future state.* Without a well-thought-out plan, for example, it is possible that the manufacturing function will make more products than the sales function can sell, resulting in a mass of unsold inventory. In fact, this happened in the natural gas and auto industries in 2011–2012 when a glut of natural gas and cars forced companies to discount prices to attract customers and sell their surplus inventory.

4. *A plan can be used as a device for controlling managers within an organization.* A good plan specifies not only which goals and strategies the organization is committed to but also *who* bears the responsibility for putting the strategies into action to attain the goals. When managers know they will be held accountable for attaining a goal, they are motivated to do their best to make sure the goal is achieved.

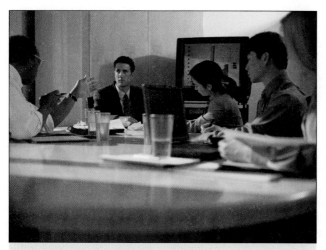

A group of managers meets to plot their company's strategy. Their ability to assess opportunities and challenges and to forecast the future doesn't just depend on brilliance. Such tools as SWOT analysis can significantly bolster the accuracy of their predictions.

Henri Fayol, the originator of the model of management we discussed in Chapter 1, said that effective plans should have four qualities: unity, continuity, accuracy, and flexibility.[7] *Unity* means that at any time only one central, guiding plan is put into operation to achieve an organizational goal; more than one plan to achieve a goal would cause confusion and disorder. *Continuity* means that planning is an ongoing process in which managers build and refine previous plans and continually modify plans at all levels—corporate, business, and functional—so they fit together into one broad framework. *Accuracy* means that managers need to make every attempt to collect and use all available information in the planning process. Of course managers must recognize that uncertainty exists and that information is almost always incomplete (for reasons we discussed in Chapter 7). Despite the need for continuity and accuracy, however, Fayol emphasized that the planning process should be *flexible* enough so plans can be altered and changed if the situation changes; managers must not be bound to a static plan.

Levels of Planning

In large organizations planning usually takes place at three levels of management: corporate, business or division, and department or functional. Consider how General Electric (GE) operates. One of the world's largest global organizations, GE competes in over 150 different businesses or industries.[8] GE has three main levels of management: corporate level, business or divisional level, and functional level (see Figure 8.2). At the corporate level are CEO and Chairman Jeffrey Immelt, his top management team, and their corporate support staff. Together they are responsible for planning and strategy making for the organization as a whole.

Below the corporate level is the business level. At the business level are the different *divisions* or *business units* of the company that compete in distinct industries; GE has over 150 divisions, including GE Aircraft Engines, GE Financial Services, GE Lighting, GE Motors, and GE Plastics. Each division or business unit has its own set of *divisional managers* who control planning and strategy for their particular division or unit. So, for example, GE Lighting's divisional managers plan how to operate globally to reduce costs while meeting the needs of customers in different countries.

Figure 8.2
Levels of Planning at General Electric

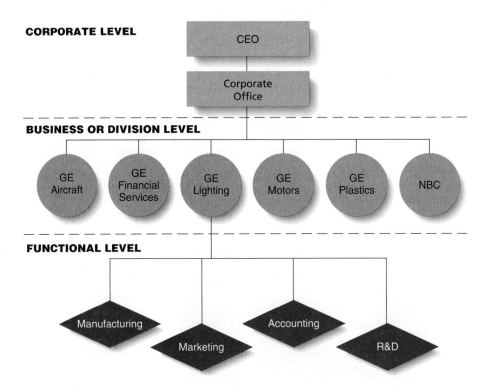

Going down one more level, each division has its own set of *functions* or *departments,* such as manufacturing, marketing, human resource management (HRM), and research and development (R&D). For example, GE Aircraft has its own marketing function, as do GE Lighting and GE Motors. Each division's *functional managers* are responsible for the planning and strategy making necessary to increase the efficiency and effectiveness of their particular function. So, for example, GE Lighting's marketing managers are responsible for increasing the effectiveness of its advertising and sales campaigns in different countries to improve lightbulb sales.

Levels and Types of Planning

As just discussed, planning at GE, as at all other large organizations, takes place at each level. Figure 8.3 shows the link between these three levels and the three steps in the planning and strategy-making process illustrated in Figure 8.1.

corporate-level plan Top management's decisions pertaining to the organization's mission, overall strategy, and structure.

The **corporate-level plan** contains top management's decisions concerning the organization's mission and goals, overall (corporate-level) strategy, and structure (see Figure 8.3). **Corporate-level strategy** specifies in which industries and national markets an organization intends to compete and why. One of the goals stated in GE's corporate-level plan is that GE should be first or second in market share in every industry in which it competes. A division that cannot attain this goal may be sold to another company. GE Medical Systems was sold to Thompson of France for this reason. Another GE goal is to acquire other companies that can help a division build its market share to reach its corporate goal of being first or second in an industry.

corporate-level strategy A plan that indicates in which industries and national markets an organization intends to compete.

In general, corporate-level planning and strategy are the primary responsibility of top or corporate managers.[9] The corporate-level goal of GE is to be the first or second leading company in every industry in which it competes. Jeffrey Immelt and his top management team decide which industries GE should compete in to achieve this goal. The corporate-level plan provides the framework within which divisional managers create their business-level plans. At the business level, the managers of each division create a **business-level plan** that details

business-level plan Divisional managers' decisions pertaining to divisions' long-term goals, overall strategy, and structure.

Figure 8.3
Levels and Types of Planning

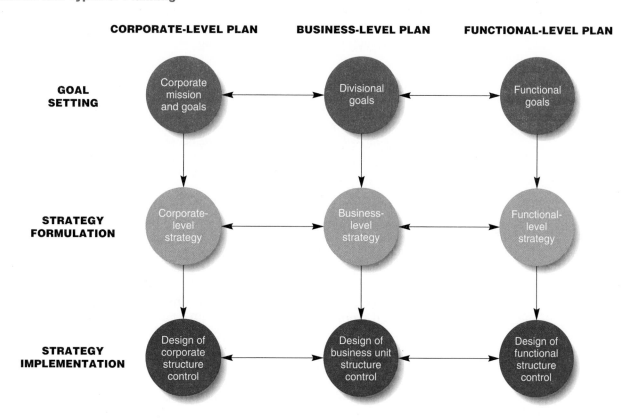

CORPORATE-LEVEL PLAN BUSINESS-LEVEL PLAN FUNCTIONAL-LEVEL PLAN

GOAL SETTING — Corporate mission and goals ⟷ Divisional goals ⟷ Functional goals

STRATEGY FORMULATION — Corporate-level strategy ⟷ Business-level strategy ⟷ Functional-level strategy

STRATEGY IMPLEMENTATION — Design of corporate structure control ⟷ Design of business unit structure control ⟷ Design of functional structure control

business-level strategy A plan that indicates how a division intends to compete against its rivals in an industry.

(1) the long-term divisional goals that will allow the division to meet corporate goals and (2) the division's business-level strategy and structure necessary to achieve divisional goals. **Business-level strategy** outlines the specific methods a division, business unit, or organization will use to compete effectively against its rivals in an industry. Managers at GE's lighting division (currently number two in the global lighting industry, behind the Dutch company Philips NV) develop strategies designed to help their division take over the number one spot and better contribute to GE's corporate goals. The lighting division's specific strategies might focus on ways to reduce costs in all departments to lower prices and so gain market share from Philips. For example, GE has expanded its European lighting operations in Hungary, which is a low-cost location.[10]

functional-level plan Functional managers' decisions pertaining to the goals that they propose to pursue to help the division attain its business-level goals.

At the functional level, the business-level plan provides the framework within which functional managers devise their plans. A **functional-level plan** states the goals that the managers of each function will pursue to help their division attain its business-level goals, which, in turn, will allow the entire company to achieve its corporate goals. **Functional-level strategy** is a plan of action that managers of individual functions (such as manufacturing or marketing) can follow to improve the ability of each function to perform its task-specific activities in ways that add value to an organization's goods and services and thereby increase the value customers receive. Thus, for example, consistent with the lighting division's strategy of driving down costs, its manufacturing function might adopt the goal "To reduce production costs by 20% over the next three years," and functional strategies to achieve this goal might include (1) investing in state-of-the-art European production facilities and (2) developing an electronic global business-to-business network to reduce the costs of inputs and inventory holding. The many ways in which managers can use functional-level strategy to strengthen business-level strategy are discussed in detail in Chapter 9.

functional-level strategy A plan of action to improve the ability of each of an organization's functions to perform its task-specific activities in ways that add value to an organization's goods and services.

In the planning process, it is important to ensure that planning across the three different levels is *consistent*—functional goals and strategies should be consistent with divisional goals and strategies, which, in turn, should be consistent with corporate goals and strategies, and vice versa. When consistency is achieved, the whole company operates in harmony; activities at one level reinforce and strengthen those at the other levels, increasing efficiency and effectiveness. To help accomplish this, each function's plan is linked to its division's business-level plan, which, in turn, is linked to the corporate plan. Although few organizations are as large and complex as GE, most plan in the same way as GE and have written plans, which are frequently updated, to guide managerial decision making.

Time Horizons of Plans

time horizon The intended duration of a plan.

Plans differ in their **time horizons,** the periods of time over which they are intended to apply or endure. Managers usually distinguish among *long-term plans,* with a time horizon of five years or more; *intermediate-term plans,* with a horizon between one and five years; and *short-term plans,* with a horizon of one year or less.[11] Typically corporate- and business-level goals and strategies require long- and intermediate-term plans, and functional-level goals and strategies require intermediate- and short-term plans.

Although most companies operate with planning horizons of five years or more, this does not mean that managers undertake major planning exercises only once every five years and then "lock in" a specific set of goals and strategies for that period. Most organizations have an annual planning cycle that is usually linked to the annual financial budget (although a major planning effort may be undertaken only every few years). So a corporate- or business-level plan that extends over several years is typically treated as a *rolling plan*—a plan that is updated and amended every year to take account of changing conditions in the external environment. Thus the time horizon for an organization's 2012 corporate-level plan might be 2017; for the 2013 plan it might be 2018; and so on. The use of rolling plans is essential because of the high rate of change in the environment and the difficulty of predicting competitive conditions five years in the future. Rolling plans enable managers to make midcourse corrections if environmental changes warrant or to change the thrust of the plan altogether if it no longer seems appropriate. The use of rolling plans allows managers to plan flexibly without losing sight of the need to plan for the long term.

Standing Plans and Single-Use Plans

Another distinction often made between plans is whether they are standing plans or single-use plans. Managers create standing and single-use plans to help achieve an organization's specific goals. *Standing plans* are used in situations in which programmed decision making is appropriate. When the same situations occur repeatedly, managers develop policies, rules, and standard operating procedures (SOPs) to control the way employees perform their tasks. A policy is a general guide to action; a rule is a formal, written guide to action; and a standing operating procedure is a written instruction describing the exact series of actions that should be followed in a specific situation. For example, an organization may have a standing plan about ethical behavior by employees. This plan includes a policy that all employees are expected to behave ethically in their dealings with suppliers and customers; a rule that requires any employee who receives from a supplier or customer a gift worth more than $20 to report the gift; and an SOP that obliges the recipient of the gift to make the disclosure in writing within 30 days.

LO8-2 Describe some techniques managers can use to improve the planning process so they can better predict the future and mobilize organizational resources to meet future contingencies.

In contrast, *single-use plans* are developed to handle nonprogrammed decision making in unusual or one-of-a-kind situations. Examples of single-use plans include *programs,* which are integrated sets of plans for achieving certain goals, and *projects,* which are specific action plans created to complete various aspects of a program. One of NASA's major programs was to reach the moon, and one project in this program was to develop a lunar module capable of landing on the moon and returning to the earth.

Scenario Planning

scenario planning The generation of multiple forecasts of future conditions followed by an analysis of how to respond effectively to each of those conditions.

Earlier we noted that effective plans have four qualities: unity, continuity, accuracy, and flexibility. One of the most widely used planning methods or techniques that can help managers create plans that have these qualities is scenario planning. **Scenario planning** (also known as *contingency planning*) is the generation of multiple forecasts of future conditions followed by an analysis of how to respond effectively to each of those conditions.

As we know all too well, oil and gas prices are unpredictable. Oil industry managers therefore sometimes use scenario planning to deal with this chaotic market.

As noted previously, planning is about trying to forecast and predict the future in order to be able to anticipate future opportunities and threats. The future, however, is inherently unpredictable. How can managers best deal with this unpredictability? This question preoccupied managers at Royal Dutch Shell, the third largest global oil company, in the 1980s. In 1984 oil was $30 a barrel, and most analysts and managers, including Shell's, believed it would hit $50 per barrel by 1990. Although these high prices guaranteed high profits, Shell's top managers decided to conduct a scenario-planning exercise. Shell's corporate and divisional managers were told to use scenario planning to generate different future scenarios of conditions in the oil market and then to develop a set of plans that detailed how they would respond to these opportunities and threats if any such scenario occurred.

One scenario assumed that oil prices would fall to $15 per barrel, and managers had to decide what they should do to remain profitable in such a case. Managers went to work with the goal of creating a plan consisting of a series of recommendations. The final plan included proposals to cut oil exploration costs by investing in new technologies, to accelerate investments in cost-efficient oil-refining facilities, and to weed out unprofitable gas stations.[12] In reviewing these proposals, top management came to the conclusion that even if oil prices continued to rise, all of these actions would benefit Shell and increase its profit margin. So they decided to put the cost-cutting plan into action. As it happened, in the mid-1980s oil prices did not rise; they collapsed to $15 a barrel, but Shell, unlike its competitors, had already taken steps to be profitable in a low-oil-price world. Consequently, by 1990 the company was twice as profitable as its major competitors.

As this example suggests, because the future is unpredictable—the $30-a-barrel oil level was not reached again until the early 2000s, for example—the best way to improve planning is first to generate "multiple futures," or scenarios of the future, based on different assumptions about conditions that *might prevail* in the future and then to develop different plans that detail what a company should do if one of these scenarios occurs. Scenario planning is a learning tool that raises the quality of the planning process and can bring real benefits to an organization.[13] Shell's success with scenario planning influenced many other companies to adopt similar systems. By 2000 more than 60% of *Fortune* 500 companies were using some version of scenario planning, and the number has increased since then. A major advantage of scenario planning is its ability not only to anticipate the challenges of an uncertain future but also to educate managers to think about the future—*to think strategically.*[14]

Determining the Organization's Mission and Goals

As we discussed earlier, determining the organization's mission and goals is the first step of the planning process. Once the mission and goals are agreed upon and formally stated in the corporate plan, they guide the next steps by defining which strategies are appropriate.[15] Figure 8.4 presents the missions and goals of three companies: Cisco, Walmart, and AT&T.

Defining the Business

To determine an organization's *mission*—the overriding reason it exists to provide customers with goods or services they value—managers must first *define its business* so they can

Figure 8.4

Three Mission Statements

COMPANY	MISSION STATEMENT
Cisco	Cisco solutions provide competitive advantage to our customers through more efficient and timely exchange of information, which in turn leads to cost savings, process efficiencies, and closer relationships with our customers, prospects, business partners, suppliers, and employees.
Walmart	We work for you. We think of ourselves as buyers for our customers, and we apply our considerable strengths to get the best value for you. We've built Walmart by acting on behalf of our customers, and that concept continues to propel us. We're working hard to make our customers' shopping easy.
AT&T	We are dedicated to being the world's best at bringing people together—giving them easy access to each other and to the information and services they want and need—anytime, anywhere.

identify what kind of value customers are receiving. To define the business, managers must ask three related questions about a company's products: (1) *Who* are our customers? (2) *What* customer needs are being satisfied? (3) *How* are we satisfying customer needs?[16] Managers ask these questions to identify the customer needs that the organization satisfies and how the organization satisfies those needs. Answering these questions helps managers identify not only the customer needs they are satisfying now but also the needs they should try to satisfy in the future and who their true competitors are. All this information helps managers plan and establish appropriate goals.

Establishing Major Goals

Once the business is defined, managers must establish a set of primary goals to which the organization is committed. Developing these goals gives the organization a sense of direction or purpose. In most organizations, articulating major goals is the job of the CEO, although other managers have input into the process. Thus, at GE, CEO Immelt's primary goal is still to be one of the two best performers in every industry in which the company competes, even though this is highly challenging. However, the best statements of organizational goals are ambitious—that is, they *stretch* the organization and require that each of its members work to improve company performance.[17] The role of **strategic leadership**, the ability of the CEO and top managers to convey a compelling vision of what they want to achieve to their subordinates, is important here. If subordinates buy into the vision and model their behaviors on their leaders, they develop a willingness to undertake the hard, stressful work that is necessary for creative, risk-taking strategy making.[18] Many popular books such as *Built to Last* provide lucid accounts of strategic leaders establishing "big, hairy, audacious goals (BHAGs)" that serve as rallying points to unite their subordinates.[19]

Although goals should be challenging, they should also be realistic. Challenging goals give managers at all levels an incentive to look for ways to improve organizational performance, but a goal that is clearly unrealistic and impossible to attain may prompt managers to give up.[20] Jeff Immelt has to be careful not to set unrealistic sales targets for GE's divisions that might discourage their top managers, for example.

Finally, the time period in which a goal is expected to be achieved should be stated. Time constraints are important because they emphasize that a goal must be attained within a reasonable period; they inject a sense of urgency into goal attainment and act as a motivator. GE's managers committed themselves to reviving the fortunes of its appliance division in the 2010s and to significantly increase sales; the division is once again profitable and is no longer for sale.[21]

strategic leadership The ability of the CEO and top managers to convey a compelling vision of what they want the organization to achieve to their subordinates.

Formulating Strategy

In **strategy formulation** managers work to develop the set of strategies (corporate, divisional, and functional) that will allow an organization to accomplish its mission and achieve its goals.[22] Strategy formulation begins with managers' systematically analyzing the factors or forces inside an organization and outside in the global environment that affect the organization's ability to meet its goals now and in the future. SWOT analysis and the five forces model are two handy techniques managers can use to analyze these factors.

strategy formulation The development of a set of corporate, business, and functional strategies that allow an organization to accomplish its mission and achieve its goals.

SWOT analysis A planning exercise in which managers identify organizational strengths (S) and weaknesses (W) and environmental opportunities (O) and threats (T).

SWOT Analysis

SWOT analysis is a planning exercise in which managers identify *internal* organizational strengths (S) and weaknesses (W) and *external* environmental opportunities (O) and threats (T). Based on a SWOT analysis, managers at the different levels of the organization select the corporate, business, and functional strategies to best position the organization to achieve its mission and goals (see Figure 8.5). In Chapter 6 we discussed forces in the task and general environments that have the potential to affect an organization. We noted that changes in these forces can produce opportunities that an organization might take advantage of and threats that may harm its current situation.

The first step in SWOT analysis is to identify an organization's strengths and weaknesses. Table 8.1 lists many important strengths (such as high-quality skills in marketing and in research and development) and weaknesses (such as rising manufacturing costs and outdated technology). The task facing managers is to identify the strengths and weaknesses that characterize the present state of their organization.

The second step in SWOT analysis begins when managers embark on a full-scale SWOT planning exercise to identify potential opportunities and threats in the environment that affect the organization now or may affect it in the future. Examples of possible opportunities and threats that must be anticipated (many of which were discussed in Chapter 6) are listed in Table 8.1. Scenario planning is often used to strengthen this analysis.

With the SWOT analysis completed, and strengths, weaknesses, opportunities, and threats identified, managers can continue the planning process and determine specific strategies for achieving the organization's mission and goals. The resulting strategies should enable the organization to attain its goals by taking advantage of opportunities, countering threats, building strengths, and correcting organizational weaknesses. To appreciate how managers use SWOT analysis to formulate strategy, consider how Douglas Conant, CEO of Campbell Soup since 2001, has used it to find strategies to turn around the performance of the troubled food products maker. In fact, his self-described mission was to take a "bad" company and lift its performance to "extraordinary" by the end of 2011—something he has achieved compared to its competitors.[23]

Figure 8.5

Planning and Strategy Formulation

SWOT Analysis
A planning exercise to identify strengths and weaknesses inside an organization and opportunities and threats in the environment

Corporate-Level Strategy
A plan of action to manage the growth and development of an organization so as to maximize its long-run ability to create value

Business-Level Strategy
A plan of action to take advantage of favorable opportunities and find ways to counter threats so as to compete effectively in an industry

Functional-Level Strategy
A plan of action to improve the ability of an organization's departments to create value

Table 8.1

Questions for SWOT Analysis

Potential Strengths	Potential Opportunities	Potential Weaknesses	Potential Threats
Well-developed strategy?	Expand core business(es)?	Poorly developed strategy?	Attacks on core business(es)?
Strong product lines?	Exploit new market segments?	Obsolete, narrow product lines?	Increase in domestic competition?
Broad market coverage?	Widen product range?	Rising manufacturing costs?	Increase in foreign competition?
Manufacturing competence?	Extend cost or differentiation advantage?	Decline in R&D innovations?	Change in consumer tastes?
Good marketing skills?	Diversify into new growth businesses?	Poor marketing plan?	Fall in barriers to entry?
Good materials management systems?	Expand into foreign markets?	Poor materials management systems?	Rise in new or substitute products?
R&D skills and leadership?	Apply R&D skills in new areas?	Loss of customer goodwill?	Increase in industry rivalry?
Human resource competencies?	Enter new related businesses?	Inadequate human resources?	New forms of industry competition?
Brand-name reputation?	Vertically integrate forward?	Loss of brand name?	Potential for takeover?
Cost of differentiation advantage?	Vertically integrate backward?	Growth without direction?	Changes in demographic factors?
Appropriate management style?	Overcome barriers to entry?	Loss of corporate direction?	Changes in economic factors?
Appropriate organizational structure?	Reduce rivalry among competitors?	Infighting among divisions?	Downturn in economy?
Appropriate control systems?	Apply brand-name capital in new areas?	Loss of corporate control?	Rising labor costs?
Ability to manage strategic change?	Seek fast market growth?	Inappropriate organizational structure and control systems?	Slower market growth?
Others?	Others?	High conflict and politics?	Others?
		Others?	

Manager as
a Person

Douglas Conant Keeps Campbell Soup Hot

Campbell Soup Co., one of the oldest and best-known global food companies, saw demand for its major product, condensed soup, plummet by 30% between 1998 and 2004 as customers switched from high-salt, processed soups to more healthful low-fat, low-salt varieties. Campbell's profits and stock price plunged as its condensed soup business collapsed, and in 2001 its directors brought in a new CEO, Douglas Conant, to help the troubled company. Conant decided it was necessary to develop a three-year turnaround plan to help the company strengthen its market position against aggressive competitors such as General Mills, whose Progresso Soup division had attracted away many Campbell customers with its innovative new lines of healthful soup.

One of Conant's first actions was to initiate a thorough SWOT planning exercise. *External analysis* of the environment identified the growth of the organic and

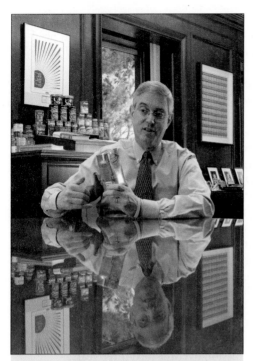

Douglas Conant, CEO of Campbell's, has revitalized the company through SWOT analysis. From SWOT analysis he has learned how to innovate successful new food products, and Campbell's has emerged as a leader in the low-carb, health-conscious, and luxury-food market segments.

health food segment of the food market and the increasing number of other kinds of convenience foods as a threat to Campbell's core soup business. It also revealed three growth opportunities: (1) the growing market for health and sports drinks, in which Campbell already was a competitor with its V8 juice; (2) the growing market for quality bread and cookies, in which Campbell competed with its Pepperidge Farm brand; and (3) chocolate products, where Campbell's Godiva brand had enjoyed increasing sales throughout the 1990s.

With the analysis of the environment complete, Conant turned his attention to his organization's resources and capabilities. His *internal analysis* of Campbell identified a number of major weaknesses. These included staffing levels that were too high relative to its competitors and high costs associated with manufacturing its soups because of the use of outdated machinery.

Also, Conant noted that Campbell had a conservative culture in which people seemed to be afraid to take risks—something that was a real problem in an industry where customer tastes are always changing and new products must be developed constantly. At the same time, the SWOT analysis identified an enormous strength: Campbell enjoyed huge economies of scale because of the enormous quantity of food products that it makes, and it also had a first-rate R&D division capable of developing exciting new food products.

Using the information from this SWOT analysis, Conant and his managers decided that Campbell needed to use its product development skills to revitalize its core products and modify or reinvent them in ways that would appeal to increasingly health-conscious and busy consumers. Conant stressed convenience with microwaveable soups and cans that open with a pull. The recipes became more healthful for its soups, V8 drinks, and Pepperidge Farm snacks because Conant needed to expand Campbell's share of the health, sports, snack, and luxury food market segments. Also, to increase sales, Campbell needed to tap into new food outlets, such as corporate cafeterias, college dining halls, and other mass eateries, to expand consumers' access to its foods. Finally, Conant decided to decentralize authority to managers at lower levels in the organization and make them responsible for developing new soup, bread, and chocolate products that met customers' changing needs. In this way he hoped to revitalize Campbell's slow-moving culture and speed the flow of improved and new products to the market.

Conant put his new plan into action, sales of new soup products increased, and he began to put more emphasis on sales of soup at outlets such as 7-11 and Subway and less on supermarket sales.[24] By 2005 analysts felt that he had made a significant difference in Campbell's performance but that there was still a lot to do—Campbell's operating margins were still shrinking. Carrying on the SWOT analysis, Conant decided Campbell should produce more products to meet the needs of the "low-carb diet," such as new kinds of low-carb bread and cookies. He also decided to shrink the company's operations to lower costs. His goal was to raise profit margins to the level of his major competitors Kraft and General Mills by 2007 using a new three-year plan based on this SWOT analysis.[25]

By 2007 Conant had substantially achieved his goals: Sales of soup had recovered, and the Pepperidge Farm and Godiva divisions were earning record sales and profits.[26] (Sales of Goldfish crackers had increased by 100%!) Campbell's stock price soared, and Conant and employees at all levels received bonuses that rewarded their intense efforts to turn around the company. However, Conant immediately set in motion a new round of SWOT analysis to find fresh opportunities for developing new products.[27]

On the threat side, it was clear that customers wanted more nutritious food and snack products; so Conant set into motion research to make Campbell's food products more appealing to health-conscious customers. One major opportunity was to reformulate a number of its soups to reduce sodium content, and it introduced new kinds of low-salt soup in 2007. Another opportunity was to develop nutritious luxury soups that would command premium prices.[28] Both these initiatives worked well. On the other hand, pursuing his new goal of making Campbell's foods more nutritious led Conant to question if its highly profitable Godiva chocolate brand was still a good fit for the company. He decided it had become a weakness, and in 2008 he sold it for $850 million.[29] He used some of the proceeds of this sale to build new company strengths. For example, he invested in R&D to develop the skills needed to customize Campbell's brands to the needs of customers in countries such as India and China—a move that spearheaded global expansion into major soup-eating nations.

Under Conant, Campbell's profits and stock price have increased each year during the 2000s; and with a culture of innovation permeating the organization, in 2012 its future looks even brighter. Thanks to his leadership, employees are more engaged and involved, sales are up, and many new leaders and managers have been promoted to change the company's culture and stretch its employees. How does Conant himself encourage employees to perform at a high level? Obviously he rewards good performance, but he also sends around 20 daily "thank-you" e-mail messages to employees at every level of the organization to show he understands how everyone can contribute to help the company meet its goals and mission over the next three years.

The Five Forces Model

A well-known model that helps managers focus on the five most important competitive forces, or potential threats, in the external environment is Michael Porter's five forces model. We discussed the first four forces in the following list in Chapter 6. Porter identified these five factors as major threats because they affect how much profit organizations competing within the same industry can expect to make:

- *The level of rivalry among organizations in an industry:* The more that companies compete against one another for customers—for example, by lowering the prices of their products or by increasing advertising—the lower is the level of industry profits (low prices mean less profit).

- *The potential for entry into an industry:* The easier it is for companies to enter an industry—because, for example, barriers to entry, such as brand loyalty, are low—the more likely it is for industry prices and therefore industry profits to be low.

- *The power of large suppliers:* If there are only a few large suppliers of an important input, then suppliers can drive up the price of that input, and expensive inputs result in lower profits for companies in an industry.

- *The power of large customers:* If only a few large customers are available to buy an industry's output, they can bargain to drive down the price of that output. As a result, industry producers make lower profits.

- *The threat of substitute products:* Often the output of one industry is a substitute for the output of another industry (plastic may be a substitute for steel in some applications, for example; similarly, bottled water is a substitute for cola). When a substitute for their product exists, companies cannot demand high prices for it or customers will switch to the substitute, and this constraint keeps their profits low.

Porter argued that when managers analyze opportunities and threats, they should pay particular attention to these five forces because they are the major threats an organization will encounter. It is the job of managers at the corporate, business, and functional levels to formulate strategies to counter these threats so an organization can manage its task and general environments, perform at a high level, and generate high profits. At Campbell, Conant performed such analysis to identify the opportunities and threats stemming from the actions of food industry rivals. For example, as noted earlier, General Mills' Progresso Soups division developed more healthful kinds of soups, and this increased rivalry and lowered Campbell's sales and profits until it successfully developed new lines of healthful soups. Both companies have been affected by the threat of rising global food prices as the costs of wheat, corn, rice, and dairy products have increased. Both companies are striving to reduce operating costs to limit food price increases because the company with the lowest prices will attract the most customers and gain a competitive advantage—especially during the recent recession.

Today competition is tough in most industries, whether companies make cars, soup, computers, or dolls. The term **hypercompetition** applies to industries that are characterized by permanent, ongoing, intense competition brought about by advancing technology or changing customer tastes and fads and fashions.[30] Clearly, planning and strategy formulation are much more difficult and risky when hypercompetition prevails in an industry.

hypercompetition Permanent, ongoing, intense competition brought about in an industry by advancing technology or changing customer tastes.

Formulating Business-Level Strategies

Michael Porter, the researcher who developed the five forces model, also developed a theory of how managers can select a business-level strategy—a plan to gain a competitive advantage in a particular market or industry.[31] Porter argued that business-level strategy creates a competitive advantage because it allows an organization (or a division of a company) to *counter and reduce* the threat of the five industry forces. That is, successful business-level strategy reduces rivalry, prevents new competitors from entering the industry, reduces the power of suppliers or buyers, and lowers the threat of substitutes—and this raises prices and profits.

According to Porter, to obtain these higher profits managers must choose between two basic ways of increasing the value of an organization's products: *differentiating the product* to increase its value to customers or *lowering the costs* of making the product. Porter also argues that managers must choose between serving the whole market or serving just one segment or part of a market. Based on those choices, managers choose to pursue one of four business-level strategies: low cost, differentiation, focused low cost, or focused differentiation (see Table 8.2).

LO8-3 Differentiate between the main types of business-level strategies and explain how they give an organization a competitive advantage that may lead to superior performance.

Low-Cost Strategy

low-cost strategy Driving the organization's costs down below the costs of its rivals.

With a **low-cost strategy**, managers try to gain a competitive advantage by focusing the energy of all the organization's departments or functions on driving the company's costs down below the costs of its industry rivals. This strategy, for example, would require that manufacturing managers search for new ways to reduce production costs, R&D managers focus on developing new products that can be manufactured more cheaply, and marketing managers find ways to lower the costs of attracting customers. According to Porter, companies pursuing a low-cost strategy can sell a product for less than their rivals sell it and yet still make a good profit because of their lower costs. Thus such organizations enjoy a competitive advantage based on their low prices. For example, BIC pursues a low-cost strategy: It offers

Table 8.2
Porter's Business-Level Strategies

Strategy	Number of Market Segments Served	
	Many	Few
Low cost	√	
Focused low cost		√
Differentiation	√	
Focused differentiation		√

customers razor blades priced lower than Gillette's and ballpoint pens less expensive than those offered by Cross or Waterman. Also, when existing companies have low costs and can charge low prices, it is difficult for new companies to enter the industry because entering is always an expensive process.

Differentiation Strategy

differentiation strategy
Distinguishing an organization's products from the products of competitors on dimensions such as product design, quality, or after-sales service.

With a **differentiation strategy**, managers try to gain a competitive advantage by focusing all the energies of the organization's departments or functions on *distinguishing* the organization's products from those of competitors on one or more important dimensions, such as product design, quality, or after-sales service and support. Often the process of making products unique and different is expensive. This strategy, for example, frequently requires that managers increase spending on product design or R&D to differentiate products, and costs rise as a result. Organizations that successfully pursue a differentiation strategy may be able to charge a *premium price* for their products; the premium price lets organizations pursuing a differentiation strategy recoup their higher costs. Coca-Cola, PepsiCo, and Procter & Gamble are some of the many well-known companies that pursue a strategy of differentiation. They spend enormous amounts of money on advertising to differentiate, and create a unique image for, their products. Also, differentiation makes industry entry difficult because new companies have no brand name to help them compete and customers don't perceive other products to be close substitutes, so this also allows premium pricing and results in high profits.

"Stuck in the Middle"

According to Porter's theory, managers cannot simultaneously pursue both a low-cost strategy and a differentiation strategy. Porter identified a simple correlation: Differentiation raises costs and thus necessitates premium pricing to recoup those high costs. For example, if BIC suddenly began to advertise heavily to try to build a strong global brand image for its products, BIC's costs would rise. BIC then could no longer make a profit simply by pricing its blades or pens lower than Gillette or Cross. According to Porter, managers must choose between a low-cost strategy and a differentiation strategy. He refers to managers and organizations that have not made this choice as being "stuck in the middle."

Organizations stuck in the middle tend to have lower levels of performance than do those that pursue a low-cost or a differentiation strategy. To avoid being stuck in the middle, top managers must instruct departmental managers to take actions that will result in either low cost or differentiation.

However, exceptions to this rule can be found. In many organizations managers have been able to drive costs below those of rivals and simultaneously differentiate their products from those offered by rivals.[32] For example, Toyota's production system is the most efficient—and still one of the most reliable—of any global carmaker, as we discuss in the next chapter. This efficiency gives Toyota a low-cost advantage over its rivals in the global car industry. At the same time, Toyota has differentiated its cars from those of rivals on the basis of superior design and quality. This superiority allows the company to charge a premium price for many of its popular models.[33] Thus Toyota seems to be simultaneously pursuing both a low-cost and a differentiated business-level strategy. This example suggests that although Porter's ideas may be valid in most cases, very well managed companies such as Cisco, Campbell, Toyota, and McDonald's may have both low costs and differentiated products—and so make the highest profits of any company in an industry.

Focused Low-Cost and Focused Differentiation Strategies

focused low-cost strategy Serving only one segment of the overall market and trying to be the lowest-cost organization serving that segment.

Both the differentiation strategy and the low-cost strategy are aimed at serving many or most segments of a particular market, such as for cars, toys, foods, or computers. Porter identified two other business-level strategies that aim to serve the needs of customers in only one or a few market segments.[34] Managers pursuing a **focused low-cost strategy** serve one or a few

focused differentiation strategy Serving only one segment of the overall market and trying to be the most differentiated organization serving that segment.

segments of the overall market and aim to make their organization the lowest-cost company serving that segment. By contrast, managers pursuing a **focused differentiation strategy** serve just one or a few segments of the market and aim to make their organization the most differentiated company serving that segment.

Companies pursuing either of these strategies have chosen to *specialize* in some way by directing their efforts at a particular kind of customer (such as serving the needs of babies or affluent customers) or even the needs of customers in a specific geographic region (customers on the East or West Coast). BMW, for example, pursues a focused differentiation strategy, producing cars exclusively for higher-income customers. By contrast, Toyota pursues a differentiation strategy and produces cars that appeal to consumers in almost all segments of the car market, from basic transportation (Toyota Corolla) through the middle of the market (Toyota Camry) to the high-income end of the market (Lexus). An interesting example of how a company pursuing a focused low-cost strategy, by specializing in one market segment, can compete with powerful differentiators is profiled in the following "Management Insight" box.

Management Insight

Different Ways to Compete in the Soft Drink Business

"Coke" and "Pepsi" are household names worldwide. Together Coca-Cola and PepsiCo control over 70% of the global soft drink market and over 75% of the U.S. soft drink market. Their success can be attributed to the differentiation strategies they developed to produce and promote their products—strategies that have made them two of the most profitable global organizations. There are several parts to their differentiation strategies. First, both companies built global brands by manufacturing the soft drink concentrate that gives cola its flavor but then selling the concentrate in a syrup form to bottlers throughout the world. The bottlers are responsible for producing and distributing the actual cola. They add carbonated water to the syrup, package the resulting drinks, and distribute them to vending machines, supermarkets, restaurants, and other retail outlets. The bottlers must also sign an exclusive agreement that prohibits them from bottling or distributing the products of competing soft drink companies. This creates a barrier to entry that helps prevent new companies from entering the industry.

Second, Coca-Cola and PepsiCo charge the bottlers a premium price for the syrup; they then invest a large part of the profits in advertising to build and maintain brand awareness. The hundreds of millions they spend on advertising to develop a global brand name help Coca-Cola and PepsiCo differentiate their products so consumers are more likely to buy a Coke or a Pepsi than a less well-known cola. Moreover, brand loyalty allows both companies to charge a premium or comparatively high price for what is, after all, merely colored water and flavoring.

In the last decade the global soft drink environment has undergone a major change, however, because of Gerald Pencer, a Canadian entrepreneur who came up with a new strategy for competing against these

"I'll have a Coke" may not be as easy a decision for much longer, as Cott and other competitors wedge lower-cost sodas into the big retail chains.

powerful differentiators. Pencer's strategy was to produce a high-quality, low-priced cola, manufactured and bottled by the Cott Corporation, of which he was CEO at the time, but to sell it as the private-label house brand of major retail stores such as Walmart (Sam's Cola brand) and supermarket chains such as Kroger's (Big K brand), thus bypassing the bottlers. Pencer could implement his focused low-cost strategy and charge a low price for his soft drinks because he did not need to spend on advertising (the retail stores did that) and because Cott's soft drinks are distributed by the store chains and retailers using their efficient national distribution systems, such as the nationwide trucking system developed by giant retailer Walmart. Retailers are willing to do this because Cott's low-cost soft drinks allow them to make much more profit than they receive from selling Coke or Pepsi. At the same time, the products build their store brand image.

Pencer implemented this plan first in Canada and then quickly expanded into the United States as retailers' demand for his products grew. He went on to supply the international market by offering to sell soft drink concentrate to global retailers at prices lower than Coca-Cola and PepsiCo. By 2004 Cott was the world's largest supplier of retailer-branded carbonated soft drinks.[35] It has manufacturing facilities in Canada, the United States, and the United Kingdom, and a syrup concentrate production plant in Columbus, Georgia, that supply most of the private-label grocery store, drugstore, mass merchandising, and convenience store chains in these countries. However, note that while Cott is the leading supplier of retailer-branded sodas, it is still focusing on its low-cost strategy. It makes no attempt to compete with Coke and Pepsi, which pursue differentiation strategies and whose brand-name sodas dominate the global soda market. Indeed, in the 2010s both these companies announced plans to buy back their bottlers at a cost of billions of dollars because this would increase their long-term profits—a strategy known as vertical integration, discussed later in the chapter.[36] But Cott is its own bottler; it knows the value of this strategy.

Increasingly, smaller companies are finding it easier to pursue a focused strategy and compete successfully against large, powerful, low-cost and differentiated companies because of advances in IT that lower costs and enable them to reach and attract customers—such as Groupon, discussed in "A Manager's Challenge" box. By establishing a storefront on the web, thousands of small, specialized companies have been able to carve out a profitable niche against large bricks-and-mortar and virtual competitors. Zara, a Spanish manufacturer of fashionable clothing whose sales have soared in recent years, provides an excellent example of the way even a small bricks-and-mortar company can use IT to pursue a focused strategy and compete globally.[37] Zara has managed to position itself as the low-price, low-cost leader in the fashion segment of the clothing market, against differentiators like Gucci, Dior, and Armani, because it has applied IT to its specific needs. Zara has created IT that allows it to manage its design and manufacturing process in a way that minimizes the inventory it has to carry—the major cost borne by a clothing retailer. However, its IT also gives its designers instantaneous feedback on which clothes are selling well and in which countries, and this gives Zara a competitive advantage from differentiation. Specifically, Zara can manufacture more of a particular kind of dress or suit to meet high customer demand, decide which clothing should be sold in its rapidly expanding network of global stores, and constantly change the mix of clothes it offers customers to keep up with fashion—at low cost.

Zara's IT also lets it efficiently manage the interface between its design and manufacturing operations. Zara takes only five weeks to design a new collection and then a week to make it. Fashion houses like Chanel and Armani, by contrast, can take six or more months to design a collection and then three more months to make it available in stores.[38] This short time to market gives Zara great flexibility and allows the company to respond quickly to the rapidly changing fashion market, in which fashions can change several times a year. Because of the quick manufacturing-to-sales cycle and just-in-time fashion, Zara offers its clothes collections at relatively low prices and still makes profits that are the envy of the fashion clothing industry.[39]

Zara models an incredibly successful strategy in jumping on trends and turning out new fashion lines in record time, while its smart store layout allows shoppers to quickly find which styles appeal to them.

Zara has been able to pursue a focused strategy that is simultaneously low-cost and differentiated because it has developed many strengths in functions such as clothing design, marketing, and IT that have given it a competitive advantage. Developing functional-level strategies that strengthen business-level strategy and increase competitive advantage is a vital managerial task. Discussion of this important issue is left until the next chapter. First, we need to go up one planning level and examine how corporate strategy helps an organization achieve its mission and goals.

Formulating Corporate-Level Strategies

Once managers have formulated the business-level strategies that will best position a company, or a division of a company, to compete in an industry and outperform its rivals, they must look to the future. If their planning has been successful, the company will be generating high profits, and their task now is to plan how to invest these profits to increase performance over time.

Recall that *corporate-level strategy* is a plan of action that involves choosing in which industries and countries a company should invest its resources to achieve its mission and goals. In choosing a corporate-level strategy, managers ask, How should the growth and development of our company be managed to increase its ability to create value for customers (and thus increase its performance) over the long run? Managers of effective organizations actively seek new opportunities to use a company's resources to create new and improved goods and services for customers. Examples of organizations whose product lines are growing rapidly are Google, Intel, Apple, and Toyota, whose managers pursue any feasible opportunity to use their companies' skills to provide customers with new products.

In addition, some managers must help their organizations respond to threats due to changing forces in the task or general environment that have made their business-level strategies less effective and reduced profits. For example, customers may no longer be buying the kinds of goods and services a company is producing (high-salt soup, bulky CRT televisions, or gas-guzzling SUVs), or other organizations may have entered the market and attracted away customers (this happened to Sony in the 2000s after Apple and Samsung began to produce better mp3 players, laptops, and smartphones). Top managers aim to find corporate strategies that can help the organization strengthen its business-level strategies and thus respond to these changes and improve performance.

The principal corporate-level strategies that managers use to help a company grow and keep it at the top of its industry, or to help it retrench and reorganize to stop its decline, are (1) concentration on a single industry, (2) vertical integration, (3) diversification, and (4) international expansion. An organization will benefit from pursuing any of these strategies only when the strategy helps further increase the value of the organization's goods and services so that more customers buy them. Specifically, to increase the value of goods and services, a corporate-level strategy must help a company, or one of its divisions, either (1) lower the costs of developing and making products or (2) increase product differentiation so that more customers want to buy the products even at high or premium prices. Both of these outcomes strengthen a company's competitive advantage and increase its performance.

Concentration on a Single Industry

concentration on a single industry Reinvesting a company's profits to strengthen its competitive position in its current industry.

Most growing companies reinvest their profits to strengthen their competitive position in the industry in which they are currently operating; in doing so, they pursue the corporate-level strategy of **concentration on a single industry**. Most commonly, an organization uses its functional skills to develop new kinds of products, or it expands the number of locations in which it uses those skills. For example, Apple continuously introduces improved mobile wireless digital devices such as the iPhone and iPad, whereas McDonald's, which began as one restaurant in California, focused all its efforts on using its resources to quickly expand across the globe to become the biggest and most profitable U.S. fast-food company. The way in which Krispy Kreme focuses all its efforts on the doughnut business is discussed in the following "Management Insight" box.

Management Insight

Krispy Kreme Doughnuts Are Hot Again

Founded in 1937 in Newington, Connecticut, Krispy Kreme is a leading specialty retailer of premium-quality yeast-raised doughnuts; it had over 635 stores operating in 2012. Krispy Kreme's doughnuts have a broad customer following and command a premium price because of their unique taste and quality. The way it has developed competences to increase its operating efficiency and responsiveness to customers is instructive. Krispy Kreme calls its store production operations "doughnut theater" because its physical layout is designed so that customers can see and smell the doughnuts being made by its impressive company-built doughnut-making machines.

What are elements of its production competency? The story starts with the 70-year-old company's secret doughnut recipe that it keeps locked up in a vault. None of its franchisees know the recipe for making its dough, and Krispy Kreme sells the ready-made dough and other ingredients to its stores. Even the machines used to make the doughnuts are company designed and produced, so no doughnut maker can imitate its unique cooking methods and thus create a similar competing product. The doughnut-making machines are designed to produce a wide variety of different kinds of doughnuts in small quantities, and each store makes and sells between 4,000 and 10,000 dozen doughnuts per day.

Krispy Kreme constantly refines its production system to improve the efficiency of its small-batch operations. For example, it redesigned its doughnut machine to include a high-tech extruder that uses air pressure to force doughnut dough into row after row of rings or shells. Employees used to have to adjust air pressure manually as the dough load lightened. Now this is all done automatically. A redesigned doughnut icer dips finished pastries into a puddle of chocolate frosting; employees had to dunk the doughnuts two at a time by hand before the machine was invented. Although the effect of these innovations may seem small, its 635 stores worldwide make billions of doughnuts and they add up to significant gains in productivity—and more satisfied customers. Clearly, Krispy Kreme has developed a niche in the fast-food industry where its superior products command a premium price; it is pursuing a focused strategy that in the 2010s resulted in a soaring stock price.

On the other hand, when organizations are performing effectively, they often decide to enter *new industries* in which they can use their growing profits to establish new operating divisions to create and make a wider range of more valuable products. Thus they begin to pursue vertical integration or diversification—such as Coca-Cola, PepsiCo, and Campbell's Soup, discussed earlier.

Vertical Integration

When an organization is performing well in its industry, managers often see new opportunities to create value either by producing the inputs it uses to make its products or by distributing and selling its products to customers. Managers at E. & J. Gallo Winery, for example, realized they could lower Gallo's costs if the company produced its own wine bottles rather than buying bottles from a glass company that was earning good profits from its bottle sales to Gallo. So Gallo established a new division to produce glass bottles more cheaply than buying them; it quickly found it could also produce bottles in new shapes to help differentiate its wines. **Vertical integration** is a corporate-level strategy in which a company expands its business operations either backward into a new industry that produces inputs for the company's products (*backward vertical integration*) or forward into a new industry that uses, distributes, or sells the company's products (*forward vertical integration*).[40] A steel company that buys iron ore mines and enters the raw materials industry to supply the ore needed to make steel is engaging in backward vertical integration. A PC maker that decides to enter the retail industry and open a chain of company-owned retail outlets to sell its PCs is engaging in forward integration. For example, Apple entered the retail industry when it set up a chain of Apple stores to sell its computers and other electronic devices.

Figure 8.6 illustrates the four main stages in a typical raw material to customer value chain; value is added to the product at each stage by the activities involved in each industry. For a company based in the assembly stage, backward integration would involve establishing a new division in the intermediate manufacturing or raw material production industries; and forward integration would involve establishing a new division to distribute its products to wholesalers or a retail division to sell directly to customers. A division at one stage or one industry receives the product produced by the division in the previous stage or industry, transforms it in some way—adding value—and then transfers the output at a higher price to the division at the next stage in the chain.

As an example of how this industry value chain works, consider the cola segment of the soft drink industry. In the raw material industry, suppliers include sugar companies and manufacturers of artificial sweeteners such as NutraSweet and Splenda, which are used in diet colas. These companies sell their products to companies in the soft drink industry that make concentrate—such as Coca-Cola and PepsiCo, which mix these inputs with others to produce the cola concentrate. In the process, they add value to these inputs. The concentrate producers then sell the concentrate to companies in the bottling and distribution industry, which add carbonated water to the concentrate and package the resulting drinks—again adding value to the concentrate. Next the bottlers distribute and sell the soft drinks to retailers, including stores such as Costco and Walmart and fast-food chains such as McDonald's. Companies in the retail industry add value by making the product accessible to customers, and they profit from direct sales to customers. Thus, value and profit are added by companies at each stage in the raw material to consumer chain.

The reason managers pursue vertical integration is that it allows them either to add value to their products by making them special or unique or to lower the costs of making and selling them. An example of using forward vertical integration to increase differentiation is Apple's decision to open its own stores to make its unique products more accessible to customers who

vertical integration
Expanding a company's operations either backward into an industry that produces inputs for its products or forward into an industry that uses, distributes, or sells its products.

Figure 8.6

Stages in a Vertical Value Chain

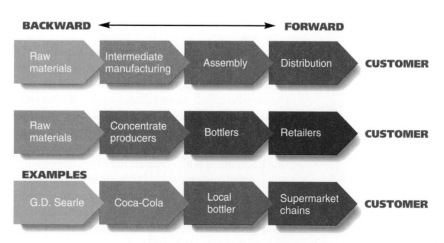

could try them out before they bought them. An example of using forward vertical integration to lower costs is Matsushita's decision to open company-owned stores to sell its Panasonic and JVC products and thus keep the profit that otherwise would be earned by independent retailers.[41] So too is Coca-Cola's and PepsiCo's decision to buy their bottlers so they can better differentiate their products and lower costs in the future.

Although vertical integration can strengthen an organization's competitive advantage and increase its performance, it can also reduce an organization's flexibility to respond to changing environmental conditions and create threats that must be countered by changing the organization's strategy. For example, IBM used to produce most of the components of its mainframe computers. Although this made sense in the past when IBM enjoyed a major competitive advantage, it became a major handicap for the company in the 1990s when the increasing use of organizationwide networks of PCs cut demand for mainframes. IBM had lost its competitive advantage and found itself with an excess capacity problem in its component operations. Closing down this capacity by exiting the computer components industry cost IBM over $5 billion.[42]

Thus, when considering vertical integration as a strategy to add value, managers must be careful because sometimes it may *reduce* a company's ability to create value when the environment changes. This is why so many companies now outsource the production of component parts to other companies and, like IBM, have exited the components industry—by vertically *disintegrating* backward. IBM, however, found a profitable new opportunity for forward vertical integration in the 2000s: It entered the IT consulting services industry to provide advice to large companies about how to install and manage their computer hardware and software, which has become the major source of IBM's profitability in the 2000s.[43]

Diversification

diversification Expanding a company's business operations into a new industry in order to produce new kinds of valuable goods or services.

Diversification is the corporate-level strategy of expanding a company's business operations into a new industry in order to produce new kinds of valuable goods or services.[44] Examples include PepsiCo's diversification into the snack food business with the purchase of Frito Lay, and Cisco's diversification into consumer electronics when it purchased Linksys. There are two main kinds of diversification: related and unrelated.

related diversification Entering a new business or industry to create a competitive advantage in one or more of an organization's existing divisions or businesses.

RELATED DIVERSIFICATION **Related diversification** is the strategy of entering a new business or industry to create a competitive advantage in one or more of an organization's existing divisions or businesses. Related diversification can add value to an organization's products if managers can find ways for its various divisions or business units to share their valuable skills or resources so that synergy is created.[45] **Synergy** is obtained when the value created by two divisions cooperating is greater than the value that would be created if the two divisions operated separately and independently. For example, suppose two or more divisions of a diversified company can use the same manufacturing facilities, distribution channels, or advertising campaigns—that is, share functional activities. Each division has to invest fewer resources in a shared functional activity than it would have to invest if it performed the functional activity by itself. Related diversification can be a major source of cost savings when divisions share the costs of performing a functional activity.[46] Similarly, if one division's R&D skills can improve another division's products and increase their differentiated appeal, this synergy can give the second division an important competitive advantage over its industry rivals—so the company as a whole benefits from diversification.

synergy Performance gains that result when individuals and departments coordinate their actions.

The way Procter & Gamble's disposable diaper and paper towel divisions cooperate is a good example of the successful production of synergies. These divisions share the costs of procuring inputs such as paper and packaging; a joint sales force sells both products to retail outlets; and both products are shipped using the same distribution system. This resource sharing has enabled both divisions to reduce their costs, and as a result, they can charge lower prices than their competitors and so attract more customers.[47] In addition, the divisions can share the research costs of developing new and improved products, such as finding more absorbent material, that increase both products' differentiated appeal. This is something that is also at the heart of 3M's corporate strategy.[48] From the beginning, 3M has pursued related

How did we ever survive without Post-it Notes? 3M's intense focus on solving customer problems results in new products that sell well, including countless variations of the original sticky note.

diversification and created new businesses by leveraging its skills in research and development. Today the company is composed of more than 40 separate divisions positioned in six major business groups: transportation, health care, industrial, consumer and office, electronics and communications, and specialty materials. The company currently operates with the goal of producing 40% of sales revenues from products introduced within the previous four years.[49]

How does 3M do it? First, the company is a science-based enterprise with a strong tradition of innovation and risk taking. Risk taking is encouraged and failure is not punished but is seen as a natural part of the process of creating new products and business.[50] Second, 3M's management is relentlessly focused on the company's customers and the problems they face. Many of 3M's products have come from helping customers to solve difficult problems. Third, managers set stretch goals that require the company to create new products and businesses at a rapid rate. Fourth, employees are given considerable autonomy to pursue their own ideas; indeed, 15% of employees' time can be spent working on projects of their own choosing without management approval. Many products have resulted from this autonomy, including the ubiquitous Post-it Notes. Fifth, while products belong to business units and business units are responsible for generating profits, the technologies belong to every unit within the company. Anyone at 3M is free to try to develop new applications for a technology developed by its business units. Finally, 3M organizes many companywide meetings where researchers from its different divisions are brought together to share the results of their work. An example of a company that acquired another company to realize the benefits of related diversification is discussed in the following "Management Insight" box.

Management Insight

VF Corp. Acquires Timberland to Realize the Benefits from Related Diversification

In June 2011, U.S.-based VF Corp., the global apparel and clothing maker, announced that it would acquire Timberland, the U.S.-based global footwear maker, for $2 billion.[51] VF is the maker of such established clothing brands as Lee and Wrangler Jeans, Nautica, Kipling, and outdoor apparel makers such as The North Face, JanSport, and Eagle Creek. Timberland is well known for its tough waterproof leather footwear, such as its best-selling hiking boots and its classic boat shoes; it also licenses the right to make clothing and accessories under its brand name. Why would a clothing maker purchase a footwear company that primarily competes in a different industry?

The reason, according to VF's CEO Eric Wiseman, is that the Timberland deal would be a "transformative" acquisition that would add footwear to VF's fastest-growing division, the outdoor and action sports business, which contributed $3.2 billion of VF's total revenues of $7.7 billion.[52] By combining the products of the clothing and footwear division, Wiseman claimed that VF could almost double Timberland's profitability by increasing its global sales by at least 15%. At the same time, the addition of the Timberland brand would increase the sales of VF's outdoor brands such as The North Face by 10%. The result would be a major increase in VF's revenues and profitability.

Why would this merger of two very different companies result in so much more value being created? The first reason is that it would allow the company to offer an extended range of outdoor products—clothing, shoes, backpacks, and accessories—that could all

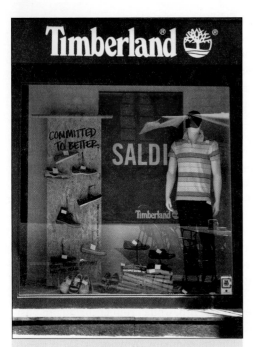

Don't forget the shoes: VF's acquistion of Timberland allows them to package their other outdoor clothing goods with the tried-and-true footwear, boosting sales no matter which brand the market knows.

be packaged together, distributed to retailers, and marketed and sold to customers. The result would be substantial cost savings because purchasing, distribution, and marketing costs would now be shared between the different brands or product lines in VF's expanded portfolio. In addition, VF would be able to increasingly differentiate its outdoor products by, for example, linking its brand The North Face with the Timberland brand so that customers purchasing outdoor clothing would be more likely to purchase Timberland hiking boots and related accessories such as backpacks offered by VF's other outdoor brands.

In addition, although Timberland is a well-known popular brand in the United States, it generates more than 50% of its revenues from global sales (especially in high-growth markets like China) and it has a niche presence in many countries such as the U.K. and Japan.[53] VF generates only 30% of its revenues from global sales; by taking advantage of the commonalities between its outdoor brands, VF argued that purchasing Timberland would increase its sales in overseas markets, and also increase the brand recognition and sales of its other primary brands such as Wrangler Jeans and Nautica. Thus, the acquisition would allow VF to increase the global differentiated appeal of all its brands, resulting in lower costs. VF would also be able to negotiate better deals with specialist outsourcing companies abroad, and economies of scale would result from reduced global shipping and distribution costs.[54] In a conference call to analysts, Wiseman said, "Timberland has been our Number 1 acquisition priority. It knits together two powerful companies into a new global player in the outdoor and action sports space."

In sum, to pursue related diversification successfully, managers search for new businesses where they can use the existing skills and resources in their departments and divisions to create synergies, add value to new products and businesses, and improve their competitive position and that of the entire company. In addition, managers may try to acquire a company in a new industry because they believe it possesses skills and resources that will improve the performance of one or more of their existing divisions. If successful, such skill transfers can help an organization to lower its costs or better differentiate its products because they create synergies between divisions.

unrelated diversification
Entering a new industry or buying a company in a new industry that is not related in any way to an organization's current businesses or industries.

UNRELATED DIVERSIFICATION   Managers pursue **unrelated diversification** when they establish divisions or buy companies in new industries that are *not* linked in any way to their current businesses or industries. One main reason for pursuing unrelated diversification is that sometimes managers can buy a poorly performing company, transfer their management skills to that company, turn around its business, and increase its performance—all of which create value.

Another reason for pursuing unrelated diversification is that purchasing businesses in different industries lets managers engage in *portfolio strategy,* which is apportioning financial resources among divisions to increase financial returns or spread risks among different businesses, much as individual investors do with their own portfolios. For example, managers may transfer funds from a rich division (a "cash cow") to a new and promising division (a "star") and, by appropriately allocating money between divisions, create value. Though used as a popular explanation in the 1980s for unrelated diversification, portfolio strategy ran into increasing criticism in the 1990s because it simply does not work.[55] Why? As managers expand the scope of their organization's operations and enter more and more industries, it becomes increasingly difficult for top managers to be knowledgeable about all of the organization's diverse businesses. Managers do not have the time to process all of the information required to adequately assess the strategy and performance of each division, and so the performance of the entire company often falls.

This problem has occurred at GE, as its then CEO Reg Jones commented: "I tried to review each business unit plan in great detail. This effort took untold hours and placed a tremendous burden on the corporate executive office. After a while I began to realize that no matter how hard we would work, we could not achieve the necessary in-depth understanding of the 40-odd business unit plans."[56] Unable to handle so much information, top managers are overwhelmed and eventually make important resource allocation decisions on the basis of only a superficial analysis of the competitive position of each division. This usually results in value being lost rather than created.[57]

Thus, although unrelated diversification can potentially create value for a company, research evidence suggests that *too much* diversification can cause managers to lose control of their organization's core business. As a result, diversification can reduce value rather than create it.[58] Because of this, during the last decade there has been an increasing trend for diversified companies to divest many of their unrelated, and sometimes related, divisions. Managers in companies like Tyco, Dial, and Textron have sold off many or most of their divisions and focused on increasing the performance of the core division that remained—in other words, they went back to a strategy of concentrating on a single industry.[59] For example, in 2007 Tyco split into three different companies when it spun off its health care and electronics businesses and focused its activities on engineered and fire and security products, such as its ADT home security business.[60] By 2009 each of the different companies was performing at a higher level under its own team of top managers; by 2012 each division's performance had improved even further.[61]

International Expansion

As if planning whether to vertically integrate, diversify, or concentrate on the core business were not a difficult enough task, corporate-level managers also must decide on the appropriate way to compete internationally. A basic question confronts the managers of any organization that needs to sell its products abroad and compete in more than one national market: To what extent should the organization customize features of its products and marketing campaign to different national conditions?[62]

global strategy Selling the same standardized product and using the same basic marketing approach in each national market.

If managers decide that their organization should sell the same standardized product in each national market in which it competes, and use the same basic marketing approach, they adopt a **global strategy**.[63] Such companies undertake little, if any, customization to suit the specific needs of customers in different countries. But if managers decide to customize products and marketing strategies to specific national conditions, they adopt a **multidomestic strategy**. Matsushita, with its Panasonic and JVC brands, has traditionally pursued a global strategy, selling the same basic TVs, camcorders, and DVD and MP3 players in every country in which it does business and often using the same basic marketing approach. Unilever, the European food and household products company, has pursued a multidomestic strategy. Thus, to appeal to German customers, Unilever's German division sells a different range of food products and uses a different marketing approach than its North American division.

multidomestic strategy Customizing products and marketing strategies to specific national conditions.

Both global and multidomestic strategies have advantages and disadvantages. The major advantage of a global strategy is the significant cost savings associated with not having to customize products and marketing approaches to different national conditions. For example, Rolex watches, Ralph Lauren or Tommy Hilfiger clothing, Chanel or Armani clothing or accessories or perfume, Dell computers, Chinese-made plastic toys and buckets, and U.S.-grown rice and wheat are all products that can be sold using the same marketing across many countries by simply changing the language. Thus, companies can save a significant amount of money. The major disadvantage of pursuing a global strategy is that by ignoring national differences, managers may leave themselves vulnerable to local competitors that differentiate their products to suit local tastes.

Global food makers Kellogg's and Nestlé learned this when they entered the Indian processed food market, which is worth over $100 billion a year. These companies did not understand how to customize their products to the tastes of the Indian market and initially suffered large losses. When Kellogg's launched its breakfast cereals in India, for example, it failed to understand that most Indians eat cooked breakfasts because milk is normally not pasteurized. Today, with the growing availability of pasteurized or canned milk, it offers exotic cereals made from basmati rice and flavored with mango to appeal to customers. Similarly, Nestlé's Maggi noodles failed to please Indian customers until it gave them a "marsala" or mixed curry spice flavor; today its noodles have become a staple in Indian school lunches.

The advantages and disadvantages of a multidomestic strategy are the opposite of those of a global strategy. The major advantage of a multidomestic strategy is that by customizing product offerings and marketing approaches to local conditions, managers may be able to gain market share or charge higher prices for their products. The major disadvantage is that customization raises production costs and puts the multidomestic company at a price disadvantage because it often has to charge prices higher than the prices charged by competitors pursuing a global strategy. Obviously the choice between these two strategies calls for trade-offs.

Managers at Gillette, the well-known razor blade maker that is now part of Procter & Gamble (P&G), created a strategy that combined the best features of both international strategies. Like P&G, Gillette has always been a global organization because its managers quickly saw the advantages of selling its core product, razor blades, in as many countries as possible. Gillette's strategy over the years has been pretty constant: Find a new country with a growing market for razor blades, form a strategic alliance with a local razor blade company and take a majority stake in it, invest in a large marketing campaign, and then build a modern factory to make razor blades and other products for the local market. For example, when Gillette entered Russia after the breakup of the Soviet Union, it saw a huge opportunity to increase sales. It formed a joint venture with a local company called Leninets Concern, which made a razor known as the Sputnik, and then with this base began to import its own brands into Russia. When sales grew sharply, Gillette decided to offer more products in the market and built a new plant in St. Petersburg.[64]

In establishing factories in countries where labor and other costs are low and then distributing and marketing its products to countries in that region of the world, Gillette pursued a global strategy. However, all of Gillette's research and development and design activities are located in the United States. As it develops new kinds of razors, it equips its foreign factories to manufacture them when it decides that local customers are ready to trade up to the new product. So, for example, Gillette's latest razor may be introduced in a country abroad years later than in the United States. Thus Gillette customizes its products to the needs of different countries and so also pursues a multidomestic strategy.

By pursuing this kind of international strategy, Gillette achieves low costs and still differentiates and customizes its product range to suit the needs of each country or world region.[65] P&G pursues a similar international strategy, and the merger between them to create the world's largest consumer products company came about because of the value that could be realized by pursuing related diversification at a global level. For example, P&G's corporate managers realized that substantial global synergies could be obtained by combining their global manufacturing, distribution, and sales operations across countries and world regions. These synergies have saved billions of dollars.[66] At the same time, by pooling their knowledge of the needs of customers in different countries, the combined companies can better differentiate and position products throughout the world. P&G's strategy is working; its principal competitors Colgate and Unilever have not performed well in the 2010s, and P&G has developed a commanding global position.

A study in contrasts. Matsushita, with its Panasonic brand (shown on the left), has largely pursued a global strategy, selling the same basic TVs and DVD players in every market and using a similar marketing message. Unilever, on the other hand, has pursued a multidomestic strategy, tailoring its product line and marketing approach to specific locations. On the right, the CEO of Hindustan Unilever, Keki Dadiseth, holds a box of Surf detergent designed for local customers.

CHOOSING A WAY TO EXPAND INTERNATIONALLY As we have discussed, a more competitive global environment has proved to be both an opportunity and a threat for organizations and managers. The opportunity is that organizations that expand globally can open new markets, reach more customers, and gain access to new sources of raw materials and to low-cost suppliers of inputs. The threat is that organizations that expand globally are likely to encounter new competitors in the foreign countries they enter and must respond to new political, economic, and cultural conditions.

Before setting up foreign operations, managers of companies such as Amazon.com, Lands' End, GE, P&G, and Boeing needed to analyze the forces in the environment of a particular country (such as Korea or Brazil) to choose the right method to expand and respond to those forces in the most appropriate way. In general, four basic ways to operate in the global environment are importing and exporting, licensing and franchising, strategic alliances, and wholly owned foreign subsidiaries, Gillette's preferred approach. We briefly discuss each one, moving from the lowest level of foreign involvement and investment required of a global organization and its managers, and the least amount of risk, to the high end of the spectrum (see Figure 8.7).[67]

IMPORTING AND EXPORTING The least complex global operations are exporting and importing. A company engaged in **exporting** makes products at home and sells them abroad. An organization might sell its own products abroad or allow a local organization in the foreign country to distribute its products. Few risks are associated with exporting because a company does not have to invest in developing manufacturing facilities abroad. It can further reduce its investment abroad if it allows a local company to distribute its products.

exporting Making products at home and selling them abroad.

importing Selling products at home that are made abroad.

A company engaged in **importing** sells products at home that are made abroad (products it makes itself or buys from other companies). For example, most of the products that Pier 1 Imports and The Limited sell to their customers are made abroad. In many cases the appeal of a product—Irish crystal, French wine, Italian furniture, or Indian silk—is that it is made abroad. The Internet has made it much easier for companies to tell potential foreign buyers about their products; detailed product specifications and features are available online, and informed buyers can communicate easily with prospective sellers.

licensing Allowing a foreign organization to take charge of manufacturing and distributing a product in its country or world region in return for a negotiated fee.

LICENSING AND FRANCHISING In **licensing**, a company (the licenser) allows a foreign organization (the licensee) to take charge of both manufacturing and distributing one or more of its products in the licensee's country or world region in return for a negotiated fee. Chemical maker DuPont might license a local factory in India to produce nylon or Teflon. The advantage of licensing is that the licenser does not have to bear the development costs associated with opening up in a foreign country; the licensee bears the costs. The risks associated with this strategy are that the company granting the license has to give its foreign partner access to its technological know-how and so risks losing control of its secrets.

franchising Selling to a foreign organization the rights to use a brand name and operating know-how in return for a lump-sum payment and a share of the profits.

Whereas licensing is pursued primarily by manufacturing companies, franchising is pursued primarily by service organizations. In **franchising**, a company (the franchiser) sells to a foreign organization (the franchisee) the rights to use its brand name and operating know-how in return for a lump-sum payment and share of the franchiser's profits. Hilton Hotels might sell a franchise to a local company in Chile to operate hotels under the Hilton name in return for a franchise payment. The advantage of franchising is that the franchiser does not have to bear the development costs of overseas expansion and

Figure 8.7

Four Ways to Expand Internationally

Level of foreign involvement and investment
and degree of risk

avoids the many problems associated with setting up foreign operations. The downside is that the organization that grants the franchise may lose control over how the franchisee operates, and product quality may fall. In this way franchisers, such as Hilton, Avis, and McDonald's, risk losing their good names. American customers who buy McDonald's hamburgers in Korea may reasonably expect those burgers to be as good as the ones they get at home. If they are not, McDonald's reputation will suffer over time. Once again, the Internet facilitates communication between partners and allows them to better meet each other's expectations.

STRATEGIC ALLIANCES   One way to overcome the loss-of-control problems associated with exporting, licensing, and franchising is to expand globally by means of a strategic alliance. In a **strategic alliance**, managers pool or share their organization's resources and know-how with those of a foreign company, and the two organizations share the rewards or risks of starting a new venture in a foreign country. Sharing resources allows a U.S. company, for example, to take advantage of the high-quality skills of foreign manufacturers and the specialized knowledge of foreign managers about the needs of local customers and to reduce the risks involved in a venture. At the same time, the terms of the alliance give the U.S. company more control over how the good or service is produced or sold in the foreign country than it would have as a franchiser or licenser.

A strategic alliance can take the form of a written contract between two or more companies to exchange resources, or it can result in the creation of a new organization. A **joint venture** is a strategic alliance among two or more companies that agree to jointly establish and share the ownership of a new business.[68] An organization's level of involvement abroad increases in a joint venture because the alliance normally involves a capital investment in production facilities abroad in order to produce goods or services outside the home country. Risk, however, is reduced. The Internet and global teleconferencing provide the increased communication and coordination necessary for global partners to work together. For example, Coca-Cola and Nestlé formed a joint venture to market their teas, coffees, and health-oriented beverages in more than 50 countries.[69] Similarly, BP Amoco and Italy's ENI formed a joint venture to build a $2.5 billion gas liquefaction plant in Egypt.[70]

WHOLLY OWNED FOREIGN SUBSIDIARIES   When managers decide to establish a **wholly owned foreign subsidiary**, they invest in establishing production operations in a foreign country independent of any local direct involvement. Many Japanese car component companies, for example, have established their own operations in the United States to supply U.S.-based Japanese carmakers such as Toyota and Honda with high-quality car components.

Operating alone, without any direct involvement from foreign companies, an organization receives all of the rewards and bears all of the risks associated with operating abroad.[71] This method of international expansion is much more expensive than the others because it requires a higher level of foreign investment and presents managers with many more threats. However, investment in a foreign subsidiary or division offers significant advantages: It gives an organization high potential returns because the organization does not have to share its profits with a foreign organization, and it reduces the level of risk because the organization's managers have full control over all aspects of their foreign subsidiary's operations. Moreover, this type of investment allows managers to protect their technology and know-how from foreign organizations. Large well-known companies like DuPont, GM, and P&G, which have plenty of resources, make extensive use of wholly owned subsidiaries.

Obviously, global companies can use many of these different corporate strategies simultaneously to create the most value and strengthen their competitive position. We discussed earlier how P&G pursues related diversification at the global level while it pursues an international strategy that is a mixture of global and multidomestic. P&G also pursues vertical integration: It operates factories that make many of the specialized chemicals used in its products; it operates in the container industry and makes the thousands of different glass and plastic bottles and jars that contain its products; it prints its own product labels; and it distributes its products using its own fleet of trucks. Although P&G is highly diversified, it still puts the focus on its core individual product lines because it is famous for pursuing brand management—it concentrates resources around each brand, which in effect is managed as a "separate company." So P&G is trying to add value in every way it can from its corporate and business strategies. At

---

strategic alliance An agreement in which managers pool or share their organization's resources and know-how with a foreign company, and the two organizations share the rewards and risks of starting a new venture.

joint venture A strategic alliance among two or more companies that agree to jointly establish and share the ownership of a new business.

wholly owned foreign subsidiary Production operations established in a foreign country independent of any local direct involvement.

the business level, for example, P&G aggressively pursues differentiation and charges premium prices for its products. However, it also strives to lower its costs and pursues the corporate-level strategies just discussed to achieve this. The way in which Samsung, the second largest global electronics company (discussed in the following "Managing Globally" box), chose to expand globally also illustrates the complex issues surrounding developing the right strategies to expand globally.

Managing Globally

How Samsung Became a Global Technology Leader

In the 2000s Samsung Electronics, based in Seoul, Korea, became the second most profitable global technology company after Microsoft. Samsung accomplished this when its CEO Lee Kun Hee decided to develop and build competencies first in low-cost manufacturing, and second in R&D, and then use them to make new and improved products for customers the world over.

Samsung's core industry is the consumer electronics industry; in the 1990s its engineers studied how companies such as Sony, Panasonic, Motorola, and Nokia had innovated products such as the Walkman, home video recorders, high-quality televisions, and cell phones. Then they imitated this technology but used Samsung's low-cost advantage to make lower-priced versions of these products that they could sell at lower prices. For example, Samsung decided to enter the cell phone industry and to make lower-cost phones than companies such as Nokia and Motorola. Samsung also entered the semiconductor industry in which it worked to make the lowest-cost memory chips; soon it became the global cost leader. It also entered markets for other digital products such as cameras, printers, and storage devices.

Samsung was pursuing the corporate-level strategy of related diversification; its goal was to increase its profitability by using and developing its core competencies in product development and manufacturing to enter new industries and produce attractive new products for global customers. Samsung's strategy was successful and profitable, but it was not playing in the same league as Sony or Nokia, for example. CEO Hee decided to adopt new strategies that would allow his company to compete head-to-head with leading global electronics companies to make it a global technology leader. Now Samsung's goal was not to imitate technology innovated by Sony, Nokia, and so on, but for its engineers to develop the R&D skills necessary to develop leading-edge technologies, such as LCD displays, to create products more advanced than those of its competitors.[72]

As this Samsung employee demonstrates, the invention of color screens hit a sweet spot in the digital phone market; now we can't live without carrying around detailed photos of our dogs, friends, and workplaces.

Within a decade, SE became the leading supplier of advanced flash memory chips and LCD screens—premium-priced products that it sold to other global electronics makers, including Japanese flat screen TV makers such as Sony. Samsung also developed a new core competence in global marketing. For example, in the early 2000s Samsung was first to realize customers wanted color screens for their cell phones to play games and built-in cameras to send photographs to their friends. Both of these incremental advances allowed Samsung to increase its share of the cell phone market and it has become the largest cell phone maker.[73]

Today Samsung has become one of the most innovative global electronics makers; however, like most other electronics companies it has been forced to find ways to reduce costs because of the global recession. In 2009 Samsung's new CEO Lee Yoon Woo announced a major restructuring that would consolidate its four global divisions into two to reduce costs but still speed product development. Samsung's semiconductor and LCD display businesses are now combined into a new Device Solutions Division, and its television, mobile phone, and consumer electronics products such as printers and computers are in the Digital Media and Communications Division. Because all of Samsung's products use in-house chips and LCD displays, this means that while SE is pursuing related diversification, it is also using its low-cost skills to benefit from vertical integration as it continues its rapid global expansion in the 2010s.

Planning and Implementing Strategy

After identifying appropriate business and corporate strategies to attain an organization's mission and goals, managers confront the challenge of putting those strategies into action. Strategy implementation is a five-step process:

1. Allocating responsibility for implementation to the appropriate individuals or groups.
2. Drafting detailed action plans that specify how a strategy is to be implemented.
3. Establishing a timetable for implementation that includes precise, measurable goals linked to the attainment of the action plan.
4. Allocating appropriate resources to the responsible individuals or groups.
5. Holding specific individuals or groups responsible for the attainment of corporate, divisional, and functional goals.

LO8-5 Describe the vital role managers play in implementing strategies to achieve an organization's mission and goals.

The planning process goes beyond just identifying effective strategies; it also includes plans to ensure that these strategies are put into action. Normally the plan for implementing a new strategy requires the development of new functional strategies, the redesign of an organization's structure, and the development of new control systems; it might also require a new program to change an organization's culture. These are issues we address in the next three chapters.

Summary and Review

PLANNING Planning is a three-step process: (1) determining an organization's mission and goals; (2) formulating strategy; and (3) implementing strategy. Managers use planning to identify and select appropriate goals and courses of action for an organization and to decide how to allocate the resources they need to attain those goals and carry out those actions. A good plan builds commitment for the organization's goals, gives the organization a sense of direction and purpose, coordinates the different functions and divisions of the organization, and controls managers by making them accountable for specific goals. In large organizations planning takes place at three levels: corporate, business or divisional, and functional or departmental. Long-term plans have a time horizon of five years or more; intermediate-term plans, between one and five years; and short-term plans, one year or less.

LO8-1, 8-2

LO8-1, 8-2, 8-3, 8-4 **DETERMINING MISSION AND GOALS AND FORMULATING STRATEGY** Determining the organization's mission requires that managers define the business of the organization and establish major goals. Strategy formulation requires that managers perform a SWOT analysis and then choose appropriate strategies at the corporate, business, and functional levels. At the business level, managers are responsible for developing a successful low-cost and/ or differentiation strategy, either for the whole market or a particular segment of it. At the functional level, departmental managers develop strategies to help the organization either add value to its products by differentiating them or lower the costs of value creation. At the corporate level, organizations use strategies such as concentration on a single industry, vertical integration, related and unrelated diversification, and international expansion to strengthen their competitive advantage by increasing the value of the goods and services provided to customers.

LO8-5 **IMPLEMENTING STRATEGY** Strategy implementation requires that managers allocate responsibilities to appropriate individuals or groups; draft detailed action plans that specify how a strategy is to be implemented; establish a timetable for implementation that includes precise, measurable goals linked to the attainment of the action plan; allocate appropriate resources to the responsible individuals or groups; and hold individuals or groups accountable for the attainment of goals.

Management in Action

Topics for Discussion and Action

Discussion

1. Describe the three steps of planning. Explain how they are related. [LO8-1]

2. How can scenario planning help managers predict the future? [LO8-2]

3. What is the relationship among corporate-, business-, and functional-level strategies, and how do they create value for an organization? [LO8-3, 8-4]

4. Pick an industry and identify four companies in the industry that pursue one of the four main business-level strategies (low-cost, focused low-cost, and so on). [LO8-2, 8-3]

5. What is the difference between vertical integration and related diversification? [LO8-4]

Action

6. Ask a manager about the kinds of planning exercises he or she regularly uses. What are the purposes of these exercises, and what are their advantages or disadvantages? [LO8-1, 8-2]

7. Ask a manager to identify the corporate- and business-level strategies used by his or her organization. [LO8-3, 8-4]

Building Management Skills

How to Analyze a Company's Strategy [LO8-3, 8-4]

Pick a well-known business organization that has received recent press coverage and that provides annual reports at its website. From the information in the articles and annual reports, answer these questions:

1. What is (are) the main industry(ies) in which the company competes?

2. What business-level strategy does the company seem to be pursuing in this industry? Why?

3. What corporate-level strategies is the company pursuing? Why?

4. Have there been any major changes in its strategy recently? Why?

Managing Ethically [LO8-2, 8-5]

A few years ago, IBM announced that it had fired the three top managers of its Argentine division because of their involvement in a scheme to secure a $250 million contract for IBM to provide and service the computers of one of Argentina's largest state-owned banks. The three executives paid $14 million of the contract money to a third company, CCR, which paid nearly $6 million to phantom companies. This $6 million was then used to bribe the bank executives who agreed to give IBM the contract.

These bribes are not necessarily illegal under Argentine law. Moreover, the three managers argued that all companies have to pay bribes to get new business contracts, and they were not doing anything that managers in other companies were not.

Questions

1. Either by yourself or in a group decide if the business practice of paying bribes is ethical or unethical.

2. Should IBM allow its foreign divisions to pay bribes if all other companies are doing so?

3. If bribery is common in a particular country, what effect would this likely have on the nation's economy and culture?

Small Group Breakout Exercise

Low Cost or Differentiation? [LO8-2, 8-3]

Form groups of three or four people, and appoint one member as the spokesperson who will communicate your findings to the class when called on by the instructor. Then discuss the following scenario:

You are a team of managers of a major national clothing chain, and you have been charged with finding a way to restore your organization's competitive advantage. Recently your organization has been experiencing increasing competition from two sources. First, discount stores such as Walmart and Target have been undercutting your prices because they buy their clothes from low-cost foreign manufacturers, whereas you buy most of yours from high-quality domestic suppliers. Discount stores have been attracting your customers who buy at the low end of the price range. Second, small boutiques opening in malls provide high-price designer clothing and are attracting your customers at the high end of the market. Your company has become

stuck in the middle, and you have to decide what to do: Should you start to buy abroad so you can lower your prices and pursue a low-cost strategy? Should you focus on the high end of the market and become more of a differentiator? Or should you try to pursue both a low-cost strategy and a differentiation strategy?

1. Using scenario planning, analyze the pros and cons of each alternative.

2. Think about the various clothing retailers in your local malls and city, and analyze the choices they have made about how to compete along the low-cost and differentiation dimensions.

Exploring the World Wide Web [LO8-1, 8-3, 8-4]

Go to Google (www.google.com) and click on "About Google"; then click on "Corporate Info" and explore this web page. For example, click on "Technology," "Business, Culture," "Milestones," and the "Ten Things" that guide Google's corporate philosophy.

1. How would you describe Google's mission and goals?

2. What business-level strategies is Google pursuing? Why?

3. What corporate-level strategies is Google pursuing? Why?

Be the Manager [LO8-2, 8-3]

A group of investors in your city is considering opening a new upscale supermarket to compete with the major supermarket chains that are currently dominating the city's marketplace. They have called you in to help them determine what kind of upscale supermarket they should open. In other words, how can they best develop a competitive advantage against existing supermarket chains?

Questions

1. List the supermarket chains in your city, and identify their strengths and weaknesses.

2. What business-level strategies are these supermarkets currently pursuing?

3. What kind of supermarket would do best against the competition? What kind of business-level strategy should it pursue?

Bloomberg Businessweek Case in the News [LO8-1, 8-2, 8-3]

KFC's Big Game of Chicken

Even at nightfall, it's easy to spot signs of Ghana's growing wealth in downtown Accra—from the Toyota (TM) Land Cruisers scattered among honking taxis to the ripples of laughter that emanate from a packed rooftop lounge. There's the young man window-shopping for electronics as he talks on his cell phone, while, nearby, three Chinese executives climb into a sedan. But nothing beats the massive illuminated red-and-white bucket perched atop a 20-foot pole, emblazoned with a grinning, goateed Colonel Harland Sanders. For Americans, Sanders may be the faded icon who founded Kentucky Fried Chicken (now KFC) 60 years ago. For Ghanaians, the Colonel, who just arrived in September, is a symbol that their small West African country is now on the map.

This KFC is housed in a three-story building with floor-to-ceiling windows, semicircular booths, and flat-screen televisions. "This is how middle-class people want to eat," says surveyor B. B. Acquah, as he pulls apart a piece of Extra Crispy Chicken. "I came around out of curiosity, and I'd have to say this is better than what we have." Indeed, the chain's launch last fall was even covered on national TV.

More than 5,000 miles away in New York, "greasy" is the word used by a 27-year-old sales associate named Melinda Chan. She's in a KFC near Times Square, staring at the box on her tray, which contains a battered thigh, a drumstick, some potato wedges, and a Diet Pepsi. "This must be, like, 1,000 calories," says Chan. (She's not far off, according to calorie counts posted on the menu board.) Chan is seated downstairs in a cramped store that also sells pizzas under the Pizza Hut banner. The dining room is nearly empty; a few tables away, a disheveled-looking man is working his way through a tray of food that someone left behind. "I almost never eat here," says Chan, looking a little embarrassed as she eyes her surroundings and reminisces about a "cute" KFC she once saw in Paris. "Can you believe this is Times Square?"

Brands rise and brands fall, though they don't often do both at the same time, and under the same leadership. Yet that's exactly what has happened at KFC. The fried-chicken chain is part of Yum! Brands, which also owns Pizza Hut and Taco Bell, and represents almost half of the roughly 37,000 restaurants the company operates in 120 countries. KFC has the added distinction of being both the best performer and the biggest headache in the family. In emerging markets such as China, India, and Africa, it's a muscular player bursting with optimism, innovation, and growth potential. China was home to 3,701 KFC outlets at the end of last year; McDonald's had 1,464. In Africa, KFC plans to enter seven new countries this year (including Uganda, Zimbabwe, and the Democratic Republic of the Congo) and expects to generate $2 billion in sales from 1,200 KFCs across the continent by 2014. In the United States, which is still KFC's largest market with 4,780 units, it has closed restaurants and lost share to rivals such as Chick-fil-A and Popeyes. The goal there has been less to rebuild than to "refranchise," reducing the percentage of company-owned KFCs from 35% about a decade ago to 5% by the end of this year.

For years, investors have endorsed Yum's strategy of selling ever more fried chicken in China while reducing investment at home. This has allowed the fast-food giant to increase earnings per share by 13% for 10 straight years—a record it expects to maintain until at least 2020—and led to a quadrupling of the stock price. But failing on the home front carries other costs, from frustrated franchisees who are skeptical about a promised turnaround, to consumers who are choosing to eat chicken elsewhere. And it's all happening with a brand Ghanaians and millions of others worldwide are supposed to associate with high-end American-style chicken. Even fans of the stock, such as UBS analyst David Palmer, have wondered: "How did such a stale fast-food concept become such a juggernaut overseas?"

The man behind the Colonel is David Novak, 59, who has led Yum since it was spun off from PepsiCo in 1997, first as president, then as CEO in 2000. In that time Novak has accumulated about $400 million in compensation, stocks, and options. While Novak has fueled Yum's expansion abroad, U.S. franchisees have languished. The franchisees are restless, and not only because same-store sales dropped 4.3% last year, according to market research firm Technomic. Of more than a dozen franchisees contacted, most declined to speak on the record about management in Louisville, likely because there's no upside to alienating the company that controls their restaurants. Most do say they have yet to feel much love from management and few display much enthusiasm for its vision of global expansion. Tales of closures or franchisees selling off assets are common. A bankrupt Kazi Foods agreed to sell off 113 KFC units, mostly in the Northeast for $56.2 million. While owner Zubair Kazi didn't return calls for comment, an executive close to the company says the man who was once the country's second-largest franchisee is "in a state of shock" and blames Yum for disjointed marketing.

Tensions between Yum and franchisees worsened after the company's nationwide "Unthink KFC" ad campaign in 2009. Franchisees felt a slogan aimed at promoting grilled chicken undermined the brand, and they sued Yum for marketing control. A judge ruled last year that the two sides had to compromise and get along, and Novak is again talking about a new unity of purpose. He admits that "we're not as reliable as we should be," but he also projects the aura of a man who feels he has been dealt a bum hand. Not only is Novak stuck with a patchwork of cramped, aging outlets in second-tier locations, but he also has to deal with franchise owners whose interests may be at odds with his own. Some have long-standing rural outlets that rarely stray beyond fried chicken; others are urban outlets that bear the legacy of a failed cobranding exercise that Novak launched several years ago, combining Taco Bells, Pizza Huts, and KFCs into one fast-food joint.

It's not that Americans don't enjoy chicken. Per capita consumption, according to the U.S. Department of Agriculture, rose more than 10% from 2001 to 2011. "The idea that Americans no longer want fried chicken is a myth," says Cheryl Bachelder, CEO of AFC Enterprises and president of the Popeyes Louisiana Kitchen brand. "They just want it in a range of forms that taste good, and they want to know what they're getting when they walk through your door." Bachelder has increased market share, profits, and the number of stores across the United States to 1,627 last year. From 2001 to 2003, she worked alongside Novak as president of KFC's U.S. operations. While she declines to comment on Novak directly, she's taken potshots at KFC through ads and taste tests and contends that any brand that's shrinking just isn't trying.

On earnings calls, Novak barely speaks of KFC's U.S. business. Some believe he would like to boost the U.S. operation to sell it off and exit the market. "It all comes down to one thing: winning," he says. "You go where you can get results." While Novak acknowledges that things

aren't where he wants them to be in the United States, he thinks 2012 will be a better year. "That's what we're trying to work on: We want to go after all this explosive global growth and grow KFC in the U.S." Novak, however, seems determined that what is working now will continue to work. "If you have the capability to be a global company, you should be a global company," he says. "That's a choice we've made, and I feel pretty good about how we've built the business."

Questions for Discussion

1. What is the principal strategy the CEO of KFC is pursuing? What are its advantages?

2. What are some potential disadvantages of pursuing this strategy? How might this hurt the company's competitive advantage in the future?

3. Search the web to find how well KFC is currently performing.

Source: Diane Brady, "KFC's Big Game of Chicken," *Bloomberg Businessweek,* March 29, 2012. Bloomberg L.P. Copyright © 2012. All rights reserved.

CHAPTER 9

Value Chain Management: Functional Strategies for Competitive Advantage

Learning Objectives

After studying this chapter, you should be able to:

LO9-1 Explain the role of functional strategy and value chain management in achieving superior quality, efficiency, innovation, and responsiveness to customers.

LO9-2 Describe what customers want, and explain why it is so important for managers to be responsive to their needs.

LO9-3 Explain why achieving superior quality is so important, and understand the challenges facing managers and organizations that seek to implement total quality management.

LO9-4 Explain why achieving superior efficiency is so important, and understand the different kinds of techniques that need to be employed to increase efficiency.

LO9-5 Differentiate between two forms of innovation, and explain why innovation and product development are crucial components of the search for competitive advantage.

A MANAGER'S CHALLENGE

Zynga Develops New Functional Strategies to Create Value in Online Social Gaming

How can managers increase operating performance? Zynga Inc., based near Marina del Rey, California, is the most popular maker of online social games—a rapidly growing and highly competitive segment of the game software and content industry. Every month, 1 out of 10 users of the WWW play one or more of Zynga's 55 games, which include Farmville, Cityville, Zynga Poker, and Mafia Wars. About four-fifths of the U.S. population, around 250 million people, play its games each month.

In 2011, Zynga rolled out a new online game, Empires & Allies, which took the company into the "action and strategy" gaming arena, one that has been dominated by leading game developer, Electronic Arts (EA), some of whose blockbuster games include Crysis 2, Star Wars, The Sims, and Portal 2. Also, Microsoft, Nintendo, and Sony are major developers of action games that can be played on their proprietary gaming consoles—the Xbox, Wii, and PlayStation, respectively. Today, many of the games these companies make can also be purchased in versions that can be played on desktop PCs, laptops, and mobile computing devices such as smartphones and tablets.

The strategy of leading game developers like EA and Sony is to innovate blockbuster

Moving fast—some might say, too fast to gain lasting traction—and staying light on personnel has pushed Zynga into the arena of online gaming competition. But can they successfully transition to other platforms than Facebook? Your clicks will determine their future.

games that may each sell millions of copies at a price of $50 to $75 each, so they generate billions of dollars in revenues and profits. Each of these games is the result of the creativity and skills of hundreds of developers who work together for two or more years to create a new game before it is released for sale. The popularity of the games they innovate determines their companies' success; customers are responding to their strategy of innovating a unique game that can be sold at a premium price.

How did Zynga manage to enter and compete successfully in the highly competitive social gaming industry against giants such as EA and Nintendo? Because its principal founder, Mark Pincus, armed with only $29 million in venture capital raised from investors, decided to pursue a strategy to develop its games using an approach that was unique in the software gaming industry. Pincus's approach was to start small, and a score or more of game developers worked interactively in small teams to continuously innovate, develop, and then perfect a new game such as Farmville that better met customer needs. As each new game was launched and revenue from online users started to come in, Pincus could recruit new game developers, and by 2011 Zynga employed over 1,200 game developers and designers who worked to innovate a variety of games in a relaxed, campus-like environment.

Mark Skaggs, Zynga's senior vice president of product design, describes the company's strategy towards game making as "fast, light, and right."[1] Zynga's games take only a few weeks or months to design because its teams of developers work in self-managed groups that have around 30 members. All the ongoing work of each team member, and the way they continuously make changes

to a game, is immediately obvious to other team members because they are connected through interactive real-time software that allows them to evaluate how the changes being made will affect the overall nature of the game. Team members can continuously approve, disapprove, or find ways to improve the way a game works, modify its objectives, and add new features over time to help increase the appeal of the game to Zynga's hundreds of millions of online users when it is released.

However, the other aspect of its strategy that works so well for Zynga lies in its competency to continue to customize and change every game it develops to better appeal to the likes and dislikes of its users—even *after* the game has been released online. Unlike the leading game makers who cannot change their games after they have been released, much of the game development at Zynga takes place *after* a Zynga game is released. Its designers work round the clock to add content, correct errors, test new features, and constantly adjust a new game based upon real-time feedback about how game players are "interacting" with it; and this feedback allows developers to discover what users enjoy the most.

One of Zynga's unique competencies is its ability to track the performance of each feature and design element of a game by what it calls A/B testing. Zynga creates two different groups of online players—A and B—who act as guinea pigs as their responses to a game that has been modified or improved with new features are monitored. By counting how many players click on the new feature, Zynga knows if players like it and what they want—so its developers can continuously change the dynamics of the game to make it more satisfying to users. The result is that its online games get better and better over time in the sense that they become more appealing to users. As Greg Black, Empires & Allies' lead game designer, says, "We can mine our users and see in real time what they like to do."[2] So, for example, while the first thousands of players of Empires & Allies were trying to work out how to play the game and conquer their rivals on their computer screens, the game's developers were watching their efforts and using their experiences to continually craft and improve the way the game is played to make it more exciting.

This amazing interactive approach to online game development is quite different from the approach of the industry leaders and so is the way it monetizes or obtains revenues from its games. All Zynga's online games are provided free of charge to hundreds of millions of online users—but to be able to use each game's advanced features, users have to pay for them or agree to participate in some form of online marketing exercise. The popularity of online social games is based on the number of daily active users, which in Zynga's case is 50 to 60 million a day (it has an audience of 240 million players on Facebook alone). So if only 2% to 5% of its players spend money on the extra game features that can be bought cheaply—often for nickels or dimes—with 50 million users a day, Zynga is already obtaining revenues of over $200 million a year. And the more games that Zynga can encourage users to play, the more money it earns! When the company announced a public offering of its shares in December 2011 at $10 a share, all the shares were sold valuing the company at $10 billion and the stock rose to $14 in March 2012.

However, investors' enthusiasm quickly soured in April 2012 when it became clear how dependent Zynga was on obtaining revenues from Facebook users, and they also began to worry about the lasting appeal of Zynga's games when the company announced a decline in its user base by 8%. Did Zynga have the competencies to allow it to continue to create value for its customers in the future? Zynga's stock price plunged to $5 by June 2012 as analysts questioned how strong its functional competencies really are, and if they could be sustained. But Zynga responded by announcing a variety of new games that it would introduce in 2012, including three new "ville" games, and a major push to make its games available on all kinds of mobile digital devices, not just on Facebook. This will be its biggest push in five years to attract millions of new users, but only time will tell if Zynga will be able to maintain its competitive advantage. Indeed, after Zynga failed to meet revenue and profit targets in July 2012 its stock plunged by 35% to a record low.[3]

Overview As "A Manager's Challenge" suggests, the companies that dominate an industry can never take their leading position for granted. A new competitor can emerge with novel or superior functional-level strategies that can change the nature of industry competition. By 2011 gaming industry leaders like EA, Sony, and Nintendo were experiencing major problems because of the increasing use of mobile computing devices such as smartphones and laptops in the online social gaming market.

In this chapter we focus on the functional-level strategies managers can use to achieve superior efficiency, quality, innovation, and responsiveness to customers and so build competitive advantage. We also examine the nature of an organization's value chain and discuss how the combined or cooperative efforts of managers across the value chain are required if an organization is to achieve its mission and goal of maximizing the amount of value its products provide customers. By the end of this chapter, you will understand the vital role value chain management plays in creating competitive advantage and a high-performing organization.

Functional Strategies, the Value Chain, and Competitive Advantage

As we noted in Chapter 8, managers can use two basic business-level strategies to add value to an organization's products and achieve a competitive advantage over industry rivals. First, managers can pursue a *low-cost strategy* and lower the costs of creating value to attract customers by keeping product prices as low as or lower than competitors' prices. Second, managers can pursue a *differentiation strategy* and add value to a product by finding ways to make it superior in some way to the products of other companies. If they are successful and customers see greater value in the product, then like Apple they can charge a premium or higher price for the product. The four specific ways in which managers can lower costs and/or increase differentiation to obtain a competitive advantage were mentioned in Chapter 1 and are reviewed here; how organizations seek to achieve them is the topic of this chapter. (See Figure 9.1.)

LO9-1 Explain the role of functional strategy and value chain management in achieving superior quality, efficiency, innovation, and responsiveness to customers.

1. *Achieve superior efficiency.* Efficiency is a measure of the amount of inputs required to produce a given amount of outputs. The fewer the inputs required to produce a given output, the higher is efficiency and the lower the cost of outputs. For example, in the 1990s Dell was the leader in global supply chain management and had a major cost advantage over its rivals, but in the 2000s its rivals adopted more efficient supply chain and manufacturing techniques, significantly reducing their costs, and Dell lost its competitive advantage.

2. *Achieve superior quality.* Quality means producing goods and services that have attributes—such as design, styling, performance, and reliability—that customers perceive as being superior to those found in competing products.[4] Providing high-quality products creates a brand-name reputation for an organization's products, and this enhanced reputation allows it to charge higher prices. In the car industry, for example, Toyota's reputation for making reliable vehicles allowed it to outperform rival carmakers and gives it a competitive advantage.

3. *Achieve superior innovation, speed, and flexibility.* Anything new or better about the way an organization operates or the goods and services it produces is the result of innovation. Successful innovation gives an organization something *unique* or different about its products that rivals lack—more attractive, useful, sophisticated products or superior

Figure 9.1

Four Ways to Create a Competitive Advantage

production processes that strengthen its competitive advantage. Innovation adds value to products and allows the organization to further differentiate itself from rivals and attract customers who are often willing to pay a premium price for unique products. Today Nintendo's and Sony's competitive advantage in gaming has been eroded because companies like Zynga make some of the most innovative new mobile online games.

4. *Attain superior responsiveness to customers.* An organization that is responsive to customers tries to satisfy their needs and give them *exactly* what they want. An organization that treats customers better than its rivals do also provides a valuable service some customers may be willing to pay a higher price for. Managers can increase responsiveness by providing excellent after-sales service and support and by working to provide improved products or services to customers in the future. Today smartphone companies such as Samsung, Apple, and Nokia are searching for ways to better satisfy changing customer needs for higher-quality video, sound, and Internet connection speed.

Functional Strategies and Value Chain Management

functional-level strategy
A plan of action to improve the ability of each of an organization's functions to perform its task-specific activities in ways that add value to an organization's goods and services.

Functional-level strategy is a plan of action to improve the ability of each of an organization's functions or departments (such as manufacturing or marketing) to perform its task-specific activities in ways that add value to an organization's goods and services. A company's **value chain** is the coordinated series or sequence of functional activities necessary to transform inputs such as new product concepts, raw materials, component parts, or professional skills into the finished goods or services customers value and want to buy (see Figure 9.2). Each functional activity along the chain *adds value* to the product when it lowers costs or gives the product differentiated qualities that increase the price a company can charge for it.

value chain The coordinated series or sequence of functional activities necessary to transform inputs such as new product concepts, raw materials, component parts, or professional skills into the finished goods or services customers value and want to buy.

Value chain management is the development of a set of functional-level strategies that support a company's business-level strategy and strengthen its competitive advantage. Functional managers develop the strategies that increase efficiency, quality, innovation, and/or responsiveness to customers and thus strengthen an organization's competitive advantage. So the better the fit between functional- and business-level strategies, the greater will be the organization's competitive advantage, and the better able the organization is to achieve its mission and goal of maximizing the amount of value it gives customers. Each function along the value chain has an important role to play in value creation.

value chain management
The development of a set of functional-level strategies that support a company's business-level strategy and strengthen its competitive advantage.

As Figure 9.2 suggests, the starting point of the value chain is often the search for new and improved products that will better appeal to customers, so the activities of the product development and marketing functions become important. *Product development* is the engineering and scientific research activities involved in innovating new or improved products that add value to a product. For example, Apple has been a leader in developing new kinds of mobile digital devices that have become so popular among buyers that its products are rapidly

Figure 9.2
Functional Activities and the Value Chain

imitated by its competitors. Once a new product has been developed, the *marketing function's* task is to persuade customers that the product meets their needs and convince them to buy it. Marketing can help create value through brand positioning and advertising that increase customer perceptions of the utility of a company's product. For example, the French company Perrier persuaded U.S. customers that carbonated bottled water is worth $2 per liter—much more than the 75 cents it costs to purchase a gallon of spring water. Perrier's marketing function developed strategies that made customers want to buy the product, and major U.S. companies such as Coca-Cola and PepsiCo rushed to bring out their own bottled water labels to capitalize on customers' growing appetite for "differentiated" bottled water.

Even the best-designed product can fail if the marketing function hasn't devised a careful plan to persuade people to buy it and try it out—or to make sure customers really want it. For this reason, marketing often conducts consumer research to discover unmet customer product needs and to find better ways to tailor existing products to satisfy customer needs. Marketing then presents its suggestions to product development, which performs its own research to discover how best to design and make the new or improved products.

At the next stage of the value chain, the *materials management function* controls the movement of physical materials from the procurement of inputs through production and to distribution and delivery to the customer. The efficiency with which this is carried out can significantly lower costs and create more value. Walmart has the most efficient materials management function in the retail industry. By tightly controlling the flow of goods from its suppliers through its stores and into the hands of customers, Walmart has eliminated the need to hold large inventories of goods. Lower inventories mean lower costs and hence greater value creation.

The *production function* is responsible for creating, assembling, or providing a good or service—for transforming inputs into outputs. For physical products, when we talk about production, we generally mean manufacturing and assembly. For services such as banking or retailing, production takes place when the service is actually provided or delivered to the customer (for example, when a bank originates a loan for a customer, it is engaged in "production" of the loan). By performing its activities efficiently, the production function helps to lower costs. For example, the efficient production operations of Honda and Toyota have made them more profitable than competitors such as Renault, Volkswagen, and Chrysler. The production function can also perform its activities in a way that is consistent with high product quality, which leads to differentiation (and higher value) and to lower costs.

At the next stage in the value chain, the *sales function* plays a crucial role in locating customers and then informing and persuading them to buy the company's products. Personal selling—that is, direct face-to-face communication by salespeople with existing and potential customers to promote a company's products—is a crucial value chain activity. Which products retailers choose to stock, for example, or which drugs doctors choose to prescribe often depends on the salesperson's ability to inform and persuade customers that his or her company's product is superior and thus the best choice.

Finally, the role of the *customer service function* is to provide after-sales service and support. This function can create a perception of superior value in the minds of customers by solving customer problems and supporting customers after they have purchased the product. For example, FedEx can get its customers' parcels to any point in the world within 24 hours, thereby lowering the cost of its own value creation activities. Finally, customer service controls the electronic systems for tracking sales and inventory, pricing products, selling products, dealing with customer inquiries, and so on, all of which can greatly increase responsiveness to customers. Indeed, an important activity of sales and customer service is to tell product development and marketing why a product is meeting or not meeting customers' needs so the product can be redesigned or improved. Hence a feedback loop links the end of the value chain to its beginning (see Figure 9.2).

In the rest of this chapter, we examine the functional strategies used to manage the value chain to improve quality, efficiency, innovation, and responsiveness to customers. Notice, however, that achieving superior quality, efficiency, and innovation is *part* of attaining superior responsiveness to customers. Customers want value for their money, and managers who develop functional strategies that result in a value chain capable of creating innovative, high-quality, low-cost products best deliver this value to customers. For this reason, we begin by discussing how functional managers can increase responsiveness to customers.

Improving Responsiveness to Customers

All organizations produce outputs—goods or services—that are consumed by customers, who, in buying these products, provide the monetary resources most organizations need to survive. Because customers are vital to organizational survival, managers must correctly identify their customers and pursue strategies that result in products that best meet their needs. This is why the marketing function plays such an important part in the value chain, and good value chain management requires that marketing managers focus on defining their company's business in terms of the customer *needs* it is satisfying and not by the *type of products* it makes—or the result can be disaster.[5] For example, Kodak's managers said "no thanks" when the company was offered the rights to "instant photography," which was later marketed by Polaroid. Why did they make this mistake? Because the managers adopted a product-oriented approach to their business that didn't put the needs of customers first. Kodak's managers believed their job was to sell high-quality glossy photographs to people. Why would they want to become involved in instant photography, which results in inferior-quality photographs? In reality, Kodak was not satisfying people's needs for high-quality photographs; it was satisfying the need customers had to *capture and record the images of their lives*—their birthday parties, weddings, graduations, and so on. And people wanted those images quickly so they could share them right away with other people—which is why today digital photography has taken off and Kodak filed for bankruptcy in 2012.

What Do Customers Want?

Given that satisfying customer demand is central to the survival of an organization, an important question is "What do customers want?" Although specifying *exactly* what customers want is not possible because their needs vary from product to product, it is possible to identify some general product attributes or qualities that most customers prefer:

1. A lower price to a higher price.
2. High-quality products to low-quality products.
3. Quick service and good after-sales service to slow service and poor after-sales support.
4. Products with many useful or valuable features to products with few features.
5. Products that are, as far as possible, customized or tailored to their unique needs.

Managers know that the more desired product attributes a company's value chain builds into its products, the higher the price that must be charged to cover the costs of developing and making the product. So what do managers of a customer-responsive organization do? They try to develop functional strategies that allow the organization's value chain to deliver to customers either *more* desired product attributes for the *same price* or the *same* product attributes for a *lower price*.[6] For example, Walmart's "price rollbacks" or reductions are possible because it constantly searches for lower-cost suppliers or more efficient ways to manage its product inventory and deliver it to stores. It told its suppliers, for example, that if they did not put on their products new radio frequency tags (RFTs) that allow inventory to be monitored electronically as it is distributed globally, it would cease to buy from them.[7] In general, new IT has allowed many organizations to offer new models of products with more attributes at a price similar to or even lower than that of earlier models, and so in the last decade customers have been able to choose from a wider variety of higher-quality products and receive quicker customer service.

Managing the Value Chain to Increase Responsiveness to Customers

Because satisfying customers is so important, managers try to design and improve the way their value chains operate so they can supply products that have the desired attributes—quality, cost, and features. For example, the need to respond to customer demand for competitively priced, quality cars drove U.S. carmakers like Ford and GM to imitate Japanese companies and copy how Toyota and Honda perform

Kodak fell behind in the digital camera market by focusing more on products than on customers.

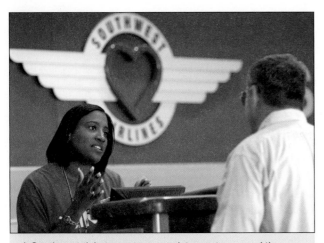

A Southwest ticket agent may assist a customer and then turn around to load her or his baggage as part of the organization's emphasis on cross-training workers for multiple tasks. Southwest's operating system is geared toward satisfying customer demand for low-priced, reliable, and convenient air travel, making it one of the most consistently successful airlines in recent years.

their value chain activities. Today the imperative of satisfying customer needs shapes the activities of U.S. carmakers' materials management and manufacturing functions. As an example of the link between responsiveness to customers and an organization's value chain, consider how Southwest Airlines, the most profitable U.S. airline, operates.[8]

The major reason for Southwest's success is that it has pursued functional strategies that improve how its value chain operates to give customers what they want. Southwest commands high customer loyalty precisely because it can deliver products, such as flights from Houston to Dallas, that have all the desired attributes: reliability, convenience, and low price. In each of its functions, Southwest's strategies revolve around finding ways to lower costs. For example, Southwest offers a no-frills approach to in-flight customer service; no meals are served onboard, and there are no first-class seats. Southwest does not subscribe to the big reservation computers used by travel agents because the booking fees are too costly. Also, the airline flies only one aircraft, the fuel-efficient Boeing 737, which keeps training and maintenance costs down. All this translates into low prices for customers.

Southwest's reliability derives from the fact that it has the quickest aircraft turnaround time in the industry. A Southwest ground crew needs only 15 minutes to turn around an incoming aircraft and prepare it for departure. This speedy operation helps keep flights on time. Southwest has such a quick turnaround because it has a flexible workforce that has been cross-trained to perform multiple tasks. Thus the person who checks tickets might also help with baggage loading if time is short.

Southwest's convenience comes from its scheduling multiple flights every day between its popular locations, such as Dallas and Houston, and its use of airports that are close to downtown areas (Hobby at Houston and Love Field at Dallas) instead of using more distant major airports.[9] In sum, Southwest's excellent value chain management has given it a competitive advantage in the airline industry. Another company that has found a way to be responsive to customers by offering them faster service is First Global Xpress, which is profiled in the following "Management Insight" box.

Management Insight

First Global Xpress Delivers Packages Faster, Cheaper, and Greener

First Global Xpress (FGX) is a small $10 million global package shipping company that claims it can ship packages from the 12 largest U.S. cities on the East Coast anywhere around the globe 24 hours faster and more reliably (its package loss rate is 1% compared to the industry average of over 8%) than large competitors such as FedEx and UPS. Also, FGX claims it can ship its over 400 customers' packages at a 20% lower cost than its large rivals and in a "greener way" because it uses less fuel oil with a 30% savings in CO_2 emissions.[10] How has it created the value chain strategies to achieve this?

First, large shipping companies like FedEx and DHL rely on a "hub-and-spoke" package distribution system so that no matter where a package is collected or its destination, it has to go through a central hub first, where packages from all over the United States are sorted for shipment to their final destination. This means that a customer's shipment, say from New York to London, has to take two different flights—one to get to a hub, such as FedEx's hub in Memphis, Tennessee, and then another to get to England. FGX does not own aircraft; it has been rapidly forming alliances with over 100 different global airlines

Can upstart company FGX successfully compete with FedEx and others? Direct shipping routes and alliances with major airlines are two of the ways FGX believes it can become a major player in the industry.

that can ship its customers' packages directly from city to city—from New York to London, for example, which saves time and money. Of course commercial airlines charge a fee for this service, but when demand for global air travel is declining and fuel costs are rising, forming an alliance with FGX is profitable for their bottom lines. As a result, airlines such as Continental, Virgin Atlantic, and Air France are willing to work closely with FGX to ensure that its packages are shipped directly and reliably to their destination cities. Because its flights are direct, FGX can also claim that it is providing this service "in a more socially responsible, greener way."

FGX hopes to grow quickly and offer its service from other large U.S. cities such as Chicago, Houston, and Los Angeles. And its CEO claims, "Over the next five years FGX plans to keep growing, replicating its model for clients worldwide. Every day, FGX offers you the chance to save money, cut time off of your deliveries, and reduce your carbon footprint—all through the simple solution of shipping direct." The challenge facing its managers is to keep its value chain operations lean and efficient—just as Southwest does in the passenger segment of the airline business.[11]

Although managers must seek to improve their responsiveness to customers by improving how the value chain operates, they should not offer a level of responsiveness to customers that results in costs becoming *too high*—something that threatens an organization's future performance and survival. For example, a company that customizes every product to the unique demands of individual customers is likely to see its costs grow out of control.

Customer Relationship Management

customer relationship management (CRM) A technique that uses IT to develop an ongoing relationship with customers to maximize the value an organization can deliver to them over time.

One functional strategy managers can use to get close to customers and understand their needs is **customer relationship management (CRM)**. CRM is a technique that uses IT to develop an ongoing relationship with customers to maximize the value an organization can deliver to them over time. By the 2000s most large companies had installed sophisticated CRM IT to track customers' changing demands for a company's products; this became a vital tool to maximize responsiveness to customers. CRM IT monitors, controls, and links each of the functional activities involved in marketing, selling, and delivering products to customers, such as monitoring the delivery of products through the distribution channel, monitoring salespeople's selling activities, setting product pricing, and coordinating after-sales service. CRM systems have three interconnected components: sales and selling, after-sales service and support, and marketing.

Suppose a sales manager has access only to sales data that show the total sales revenue each salesperson generated in the last 30 days. This information does not break down how much revenue came from sales to existing customers versus sales to new customers. What important knowledge is being lost? First, if most revenues are earned from sales to existing customers, this suggests that the money being spent by a company to advertise and promote its products is not attracting new customers and so is being wasted. Second, important dimensions involved in sales are pricing, financing, and order processing. In many companies, to close a deal, a salesperson has to send the paperwork to a central sales office that handles matters such as approving the customer for special financing and determining specific shipping and delivery dates. In some companies, different departments handle these activities, and it can take a long time to get a response from them; this keeps customers waiting—something that often leads to lost sales. Until CRM systems were introduced, these kinds of problems were widespread and resulted in missed sales and higher operating costs. Today the sales and selling CRM software contains *best sales practices* that analyze this information and then recommend ways to improve how the sales process operates.

One company that has improved its sales and after-sales practices by implementing CRM is Empire HealthChoice Inc., the largest health insurance provider in New York, which sells its policies through 1,800 sales agents. For years these agents were responsible for collecting all the customer-specific information needed to determine the price of each policy. Once they had collected the necessary information, the agents called Empire to get price quotes. After waiting days for these quotes, the agents relayed them back to customers, who often then modified their requests to reduce the cost of their policies. When this occurred, the agents had to telephone Empire again to get revised price quotes. Because this frequently happened several times with each transaction, it often took more than 20 days to close a sale and another 10 days for customers to get their insurance cards.[12]

Recognizing that these delays were causing lost sales, Empire decided to examine how a CRM system could improve the sales process. Its managers chose a web-based system so agents themselves could calculate the insurance quotes online. Once an agent enters a customer's data, a quote is generated in just a few seconds. The agent can continually modify a policy while sitting face-to-face with the customer until the policy and price are agreed upon. As a result, the sales process can now be completed in a few hours, and customers receive their insurance cards in 2 to 3 days rather than 10.[13]

When a company implements after-sales service and support CRM software, salespeople are required to input detailed information about their follow-up visits to customers. Because the system tracks and documents every customer's case history, salespeople have instant access to a record of everything that occurred during previous phone calls or visits. They are in a much better position to respond to customers' needs and build customer loyalty, so a company's after-sales service improves. Cell phone companies like T-Mobile and Sprint, for example, require that telephone sales reps collect information about all customers' inquiries, complaints, and requests, and this is recorded electronically in customer logs. The CRM module can analyze the information in these logs to evaluate whether the customer service reps are meeting or exceeding the company's required service standards.

A CRM system can also identify the top 10 reasons for customer complaints. Sales managers can then work to eliminate the sources of these problems and improve after-sales support procedures. The CRM system also identifies the top 10 best service and support practices, which can then be taught to all sales reps.

Finally, as a CRM system processes information about changing customer needs, this improves marketing in many ways. Marketing managers, for example, have access to detailed customer profiles, including data about purchases and the reasons why individuals were or were not attracted to a company's products. Armed with this knowledge, marketing can better identify customers and the specific product attributes they desire. It may become clear, for example, that a targeted customer group has a specific need that is not satisfied by a product—such as a need for a cell phone containing a 20-megapixel video camera and a GPS system. With real-time information, marketing can work with product development to redesign the product to better meet customer needs. In sum, a CRM system is a comprehensive method of gathering crucial information about how customers respond to a company's products. It is a powerful functional strategy used to align a company's products with customer needs.

Improving Quality

LO9-3 Explain why achieving superior quality is so important, and understand the challenges facing managers and organizations that seek to implement total quality management.

As noted earlier, high-quality products possess attributes such as superior design, features, reliability, and after-sales support; these products are designed to better meet customer requirements.[14] Quality is a concept that can be applied to the products of both manufacturing and service organizations—goods such as an Apple computer or services such as Southwest Airlines flight service or customer service in a Citibank branch. Why do managers seek to control and improve the quality of their organizations' products?[15] There are two reasons (see Figure 9.3).

First, customers usually prefer a higher-quality product to a lower-quality product. So an organization able to provide, *for the same price,* a product of higher quality than a competitor's

Figure 9.3

The Impact of Increased Quality on Organizational Performance

product is serving its customers better—it is being more responsive to its customers. Often, providing high-quality products creates a brand-name reputation for an organization's products. This enhanced reputation may allow the organization to charge more for its products than its competitors can charge, and thus it makes greater profits. For example, in 2011 Lexus was ranked number one, as it has been for over a decade, on the J. D. Power list of the 10 most reliable carmakers.[16] The high quality of Lexus vehicles enables the company to charge higher prices for its cars than the prices charged by rival carmakers.

The second reason for trying to boost product quality is that higher product quality can increase efficiency and thereby lower operating costs and boost profits. Achieving high product quality lowers operating costs because of the effect of quality on employee productivity: Higher product quality means less employee time is wasted in making defective products that must be discarded or in providing substandard services, and thus less time has to be spent fixing mistakes. This translates into higher employee productivity, which also means lower costs. The way each manager can have an impact on quality and cost is discussed in the following "Manager as a Person" box.

Manager as a
Person

Female Manufacturing Plant Managers Help Increase Product Quality

Building cars remains primarily a male occupation. In 2012 roughly three out of four automotive manufacturing jobs are held by men, and women still number less than 20% of automotive manufacturing managers. Today, however, more women than men are buying new vehicles, and that shift, together with an increasing concern for diversity, has prompted major carmakers to promote more women into key management positions.[17] However, few women enroll in automotive and mechanical engineering programs because assembly plants have a reputation of being unpleasant, dirty, noisy, places to work.

At Ford Motors, however, two of its female plant managers, Gloria Georger and Jan Allman, provide good examples of women who accepted the challenge of entering the manufacturing world. They embraced the opportunities such a job offers and developed the leadership skills that have allowed them to rise to become plant managers responsible for overseeing vehicle quality and operating costs in multibillion dollar manufacturing plants that employ thousands of employees.

Gloria Georger had no plans to pursue a manufacturing job and majored in accounting, but one recruiter commented on her outgoing personality and suggested she consider manufacturing where her interpersonal skills might be valuable—and manufacturing paid better than accounting. She took a job at U.S. Steel's plant in Gary, Indiana, and sure enough, her ability to motivate and work smoothly with employees led her to be promoted to production supervisor. Moreover, she claims the job helped develop her capability to manage unexpected challenges that always arise. She moved to Ford in 1986 when few women worked in manufacturing, but she quickly demonstrated the willingness to learn the cultural values and norms of its manufacturing operations, and she had a personality that allowed her to embrace and succeed in handling challenges from her mainly male colleagues and subordinates. Once again, she came to be regarded as a competent team leader and steadily worked her way up the hierarchy of Ford's manufacturing function in different Ford plants until being promoted to her current position as the head of Ford's stamping plant in Chicago Heights, Illinois.[18]

Jan Allman is in charge of Ford's Torrence Avenue assembly plant where, in 2011, two shifts of 2,500 assembly line workers will produce the Ford Taurus, Lincoln MKS, and the next-generation Explorer SUV. The parts produced by Georger's plant are assembled into the final vehicle at the Torrence Avenue plant, so close cooperation between the two plant managers is essential. Allman joined Ford in 1986 as a line engineer of an engine plant after receiving an engineering degree; she was one of two women out of 100 engineers Ford selected as interns to evaluate their performance before making hiring decisions. Allman rose to become the manufacturing engineering manager in charge of the engine plant, a position rarely held by a woman. Her hands-on leadership style under difficult conditions impressed her colleagues, who could see the attention she paid to every detail of the assembly process and the agreeable way in which she treated, and was treated by, employees. Hence, she was promoted to manager of one of Ford's major assembly plants.

Both Allman and Georger agree that the growing number of women Ford has recruited into manufacturing over time has helped change the values and norms of its manufacturing culture.[19] Not only has it reduced the level of conflict between managers and workers, but it has promoted cooperation and helped to promote Ford's focus on increasing product quality, which is one of its major competitive advantages in the tough game of car making today.

Total Quality Management

total quality management (TQM) A management technique that focuses on improving the quality of an organization's products and services.

At the forefront of the drive to improve product quality is a functional strategy known as total quality management.[20] **Total quality management (TQM)** focuses on improving the quality of an organization's products and stresses that *all* of an organization's value chain activities should be directed toward this goal. TQM requires the cooperation of managers in every function of an organization and across functions.[21] To show how TQM works, we next describe the way that Citibank used the technique. Then, using Citibank as an example, we look at the 10 steps that are necessary for managers to implement a successful TQM program.

In the 2000s Citibank's top managers decided the bank could retain and expand its customer base only if it could increase customer loyalty, so they decided to implement a TQM program to better satisfy customer needs. As the first step in its TQM effort, Citibank identified the factors that dissatisfy its customers. When analyzing the complaints, it found that most concerned the time it took to complete a customer's request, such as responding to an account problem or getting a loan. So Citibank's managers began to examine how they handled each kind of customer request. For each distinct request, they formed a cross-functional team that broke down the request into the steps required, between people and departments, to complete the response. In analyzing the steps, teams found that many of them were unnecessary and could be replaced by using the right information systems. They also found that delays often occurred because employees did not know how to handle a request. They were not being given the right kind of training, and when they couldn't handle a request, they simply put it aside until a supervisor could deal with it.

Citibank's second step to increase its responsiveness was to implement an organization-wide TQM program. Managers and supervisors were charged with reducing the complexity of the work process and finding the most effective way to process each particular request, such as a request for a loan. Managers were also charged with training employees to answer each specific request. The results were remarkable. For example, in the loan department the TQM program reduced by 75% the number of handoffs necessary to process a request. The department's average response time dropped from several hours to 30 minutes. What are the 10 steps in TQM that made this possible?

1. *Build organizational commitment to quality.* TQM will do little to improve the performance of an organization unless all employees embrace it, and this often requires a change in an organization's culture.[22] At Citibank the process of changing culture began at the top. First a group of top managers, including the CEO, received training in TQM from consultants from Motorola. Each member of the top management group was then given the responsibility of training a group at the next level in the hierarchy, and so on down through the organization until all 100,000 employees had received basic TQM training.

2. *Focus on the customer.* TQM practitioners see a focus on the customer as the starting point.[23] According to TQM philosophy, the customer, not managers in quality control or engineering, defines what quality is. The challenge is fourfold: (1) to identify what customers want from the good or service that the company provides; (2) to identify what the company actually provides to customers; (3) to identify any gap between what customers want and what they actually get (the quality gap); and (4) to formulate a plan for closing the quality gap. The efforts of Citibank managers to increase responsiveness to customers illustrate this aspect of TQM well.

3. *Find ways to measure quality.* Another crucial element of TQM is the development of a measuring system that managers can use to evaluate quality. Devising appropriate measures is relatively easy in manufacturing companies, where quality can be measured by criteria such as defects per million parts. It is more difficult in service companies, where outputs are less tangible. However, with a little creativity, suitable quality measures can be devised as they were by managers at Citibank. Similarly, at L.L.Bean, the mail-order retailer, managers use the percentage of orders that are correctly filled as one of their quality measures.

4. *Set goals and create incentives.* Once a measure has been devised, managers' next step is to set a challenging quality goal and to create incentives for reaching that goal. At Citibank the CEO set an initial goal of reducing customer complaints by 50%. One way of creating incentives to attain a goal is to link rewards, such as bonus pay and promotional opportunities, to the goal.

5. *Solicit input from employees.* Employees are a major source of information about the causes of poor quality, so it is important that managers establish a system for soliciting employee suggestions about improvements that can be made. At most companies, like Citibank, this is an ongoing endeavor—the process never stops.

6. *Identify defects and trace them to their source.* A major source of product defects is the production system; a major source of service defects is poor customer service procedures. TQM preaches the need for managers to identify defects in the work process, trace those defects back to their source, find out why they occurred, and make corrections so they do not occur again. Today IT makes quality measurement much easier.

inventory The stock of raw materials, inputs, and component parts that an organization has on hand at a particular time.

7. *Introduce just-in-time inventory systems.* **Inventory** is the stock of raw materials, inputs, and component parts that an organization has on hand at a particular time. When the materials management function designs a **just-in-time (JIT) inventory system**, parts or supplies arrive at the organization when they are needed, not before. Also, under a JIT inventory system, defective parts enter an organization's operating system immediately; they are not warehoused for months before use. This means defective inputs can be quickly spotted. JIT is discussed more later in the chapter.

just-in-time (JIT) inventory system A system in which parts or supplies arrive at an organization when they are needed, not before.

8. *Work closely with suppliers.* A major cause of poor-quality finished goods is poor-quality component parts. To decrease product defects, materials managers must work closely with suppliers to improve the quality of the parts they supply. Managers at Xerox worked closely with suppliers to get them to adopt TQM programs, and the result was a huge reduction in the defect rate of component parts. Managers also need to work closely with suppliers to get them to adopt a JIT inventory system, also required for high quality.

9. *Design for ease of production.* The more steps required to assemble a product or provide a service, the more opportunities there are for making a mistake. It follows that designing products that have fewer parts or finding ways to simplify providing a service should be linked to fewer defects or customer complaints. For example, Apple continually redesigns the way it assembles its mobile digital devices to reduce the number of assembly steps required, and it constantly searches for new ways to reduce the number of components that have to be linked together. The consequence of these redesign efforts was a continuous fall in assembly costs and marked improvement in product quality during the 2000s.

10. *Break down barriers between functions.* Successful implementation of TQM requires substantial cooperation between the different value chain functions. Materials managers have to cooperate with manufacturing managers to find high-quality inputs that reduce manufacturing costs; marketing managers have to cooperate with manufacturing so that customer problems identified by marketing can be acted on; information systems have to cooperate with all other functions of the company to devise suitable IT training programs; and so on.

In essence, to increase quality, all functional managers need to cooperate to develop goals and spell out exactly how they will be achieved. Managers should embrace the philosophy that mistakes, defects, and poor-quality materials are not acceptable and should be eliminated. Functional managers should spend more time working with employees and providing them with the tools they need to do the job. Managers should create an environment in which employees will not be afraid to report problems or recommend improvements. Output goals and targets need to include not only numbers or quotas but also some indicators of quality to promote the production of defect-free output. Functional managers also need to train employees in new skills to keep pace with changes in the workplace. Finally, achieving better quality requires that managers develop organizational values and norms centered on improving quality.

Six Sigma A technique used to improve quality by systematically improving how value chain activities are performed and then using statistical methods to measure the improvement.

SIX SIGMA   One TQM technique called **Six Sigma** has gained increasing popularity in the last decade, particularly because of the well-publicized success GE enjoyed as a result of implementing it across its operating divisions. The goal of Six Sigma is to improve a company's quality to only three defects per million by systematically altering the way all the processes involved in value chain activities are performed, and then carefully measuring how much improvement has been made using statistical methods. Six Sigma shares with TQM its focus on improving value chain processes to increase quality; but it differs because TQM emphasizes top-down organizationwide employee involvement, whereas the Six Sigma approach is to create teams of expert change agents, known as "green belts and black belts," to take control of the problem-finding and problem-solving process and then to train other employees in implementing solutions. The following "Management Insight" box shows how Six Sigma works at the Starwood hotel chain.

Management
Insight

How Starwood Uses Six Sigma to Improve Hotel Performance

Starwood Hotels & Resorts, based in White Plains, New York, is one of the largest global hotel chains and one of the most profitable—its profit margins are nearly 15% higher than rivals such as Hilton and Marriott. Why? Starwood attributes a significant part of its high performance to its use of Six Sigma, which it began to use in 2001 to improve the quality of service it provides its guests.[24]

   The company's Six Sigma group is led by Brian Mayer, the vice president of "Six Sigma Operations Management & Room Support," whose father and grandfather both worked in the hospitality industry. Mayer, a Six Sigma expert, helped by a small group

Guests and a bellhop share a laugh at a Starwood resort. The Starwood company remains one of the most highly profitable in the entire industry based on its rigorous Six Sigma program, listening ear toward customers, and attention to employee needs.

of other experts he recruited, implemented the program in 2001. Since then they have trained 150 Starwood employees as "black belts" and another 2,700 as "green belts" in the practices of Six Sigma. Black belts are the lead change agents in Starwood hotels who take responsibility for managing the change process to meet its main objectives—increasing quality customer service and responsiveness.[25] Green belts are the employees trained by Mayer's experts and each hotel's black belt to become the Six Sigma team in each hotel who work together to develop new ideas or programs that will improve customer responsiveness, and to find the work procedures and processes that will implement the new programs most effectively to improve customer service quality.

Almost all the new initiatives that have permeated the thousands of individual hotels in the Starwood chain come from these Six Sigma teams—whose work has improved the company's performance by hundreds of millions of dollars. For example, the "Unwind Program" was an initiative developed to cater to the interests of the 34% of hotel guests that a study found felt lonely and isolated in overnight hotel stays. Its purpose was to make guests feel at home so they would become return customers. The chain's Six Sigma teams began brainstorming ideas for new kinds of activities and services that would encourage nightly guests to leave their rooms and gather in the lobby, where they could meet and mingle with other guests and so feel more at home. They came up with hundreds of potential new programs. An initial concept was to offer guests short complimentary massages in the lobby, hoping to encourage them to book massage sessions that would boost hotel revenues. Teams at each hotel then dreamed up other programs that they felt would best meet guest needs. These ranged from fire dancing in hotels in Fiji to Chinese watercolor painting in hotels in Beijing.[26] These ideas are shared across all the hotels in the chain using Starwood's proprietary "E-Tool," which contains thousands of successful projects that have worked—and the specific work procedures needed to perform them successfully.

In another major project, Starwood's managers were concerned about the number of injuries hotel employees sustained during their work, such as back strain injuries common among the housekeepers who cleaned rooms. The black and green belt teams studied how housekeepers worked in the various hotels and, pooling their knowledge, realized several changes could reduce injuries. For example, they found that a large number of back strains occurred early in housekeepers' shifts because they were not "warmed up," so one central coordinating team developed a series of job-related stretching exercises. This team also looked at the cleaning tools used, and after experimenting with different sizes and types found that curved, longer-handled tools, which required less bending and stretching, could significantly reduce injuries. To date the program has reduced the accident rate from 12 to 2 for every 200,000 work hours—a major achievement.

As Starwood has found, having teams of Six Sigma specialists trained to always be alert for opportunities to improve the tens of thousands of different work procedures that help create high-quality customer service pays off. For guests and employees, the result is greater satisfaction and loyalty to the hotel chain in the form of both repeat guest visits and reduced employee turnover.

Improving Efficiency

The third goal of value chain management is to increase the efficiency of the various functional activities. The fewer the input resources required to produce a given volume of output, the higher will be the efficiency of the operating system. So efficiency is a useful measure of how well an organization uses all its resources—such as labor, capital, materials, or energy—to produce its outputs, or goods and services. Developing functional strategies to improve efficiency is an extremely important issue for managers because increased efficiency lowers production costs, which lets an organization make a greater profit or attract more customers by lowering its price. Several important functional strategies are discussed here.

LO9-4 Explain why achieving superior efficiency is so important, and understand the different kinds of techniques that need to be employed to increase efficiency.

Facilities Layout, Flexible Manufacturing, and Efficiency

The strategies managers use to lay out or design an organization's physical work facilities also determine its efficiency. First, the way in which machines and workers are organized or grouped together into workstations affects the efficiency of the operating system. Second, a major determinant of efficiency is the cost associated with setting up the equipment needed to make a particular product. **Facilities layout** is the strategy of designing the machine–worker interface to increase operating system efficiency. **Flexible manufacturing** is a strategy based on the use of IT to reduce the costs associated with the product assembly process or the way services are delivered to customers. For example, this might be how computers are made on a production line or how patients are routed through a hospital.

facilities layout The strategy of designing the machine–worker interface to increase operating system efficiency.

flexible manufacturing The set of techniques that attempt to reduce the costs associated with the product assembly process or the way services are delivered to customers.

FACILITIES LAYOUT The way in which machines, robots, and people are grouped together affects how productive they can be. Figure 9.4 shows three basic ways of arranging workstations: product layout, process layout, and fixed-position layout.

In a *product layout,* machines are organized so that each operation needed to manufacture a product or process a patient is performed at workstations arranged in a fixed sequence. In manufacturing, workers are stationary in this arrangement, and a moving conveyor belt takes the product being worked on to the next workstation so that it is progressively assembled. Mass production is the familiar name for this layout; car assembly lines are probably the best-known example. It used to be that product layout was efficient only when products were created in large quantities; however, the introduction of modular assembly lines controlled by computers is making it efficient to make products in small batches.

In a *process layout,* workstations are not organized in a fixed sequence. Rather, each workstation is relatively self-contained, and a product goes to whichever workstation is needed to perform the next operation to complete the product. Process layout is often suited to manufacturing settings that produce a variety of custom-made products, each tailored to the needs of a different kind of customer. For example, a custom furniture manufacturer might use a process layout so different teams of workers can produce different styles of chairs or tables made from different kinds of woods and finishes. Such a layout also describes how a patient

Figure 9.4
Three Facilities Layouts

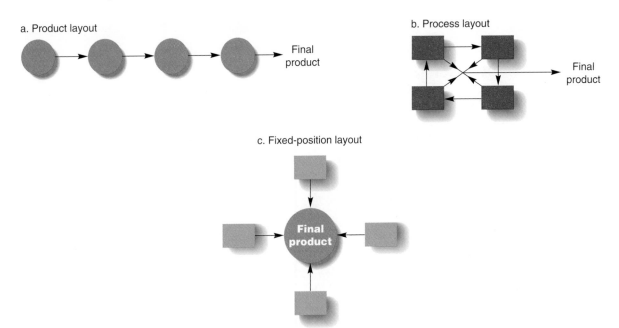

a. Product layout

Final product

b. Process layout

Final product

c. Fixed-position layout

Final product

might go through a hospital from emergency room to X-ray room, to operating room, and so on. A process layout provides the flexibility needed to change a product, whether it is a PC or a patient's treatment. Such flexibility, however, often reduces efficiency because it is expensive.

In a *fixed-position layout,* the product stays in a fixed position. Its component parts are produced in remote workstations and brought to the production area for final assembly. Increasingly, self-managed teams are using fixed-position layouts. Different teams assemble each component part and then send the parts to the final assembly team, which makes the final product. A fixed-position layout is commonly used for products such as jet airliners, mainframe computers, and gas turbines—products that are complex and difficult to assemble or so large that moving them from one workstation to another would be difficult. The effects of moving from one facilities layout to another can be dramatic, as the following "Manager as a Person" box suggests.

Manager as a Person

Paddy Hopkirk Improves Facilities Layout

Paddy Hopkirk established his car accessories business in Bedfordshire, England, shortly after he had shot to car-racing fame by winning the famous Monte Carlo Rally. Sales of Hopkirk's accessories, such as bicycle racks and axle stands, were always brisk; but Hopkirk was the first to admit that his operating system left a lot to be desired, so he invited consultants to help reorganize the system.

After analyzing his factory's operating system, the consultants realized that the source of the problem was the facilities layout Hopkirk had established. Over time, as sales grew, Hopkirk simply added new workstations to the operating system as they were needed. The result was a process layout in which the product being assembled moved in the irregular sequences shown in the "Before Change" half of Figure 9.5. The consultants suggested that to save time and effort, the workstations should be reorganized into the sequential product layout shown in the "After Change" illustration.

Figure 9.5
Changing a Facilities Layout[27]

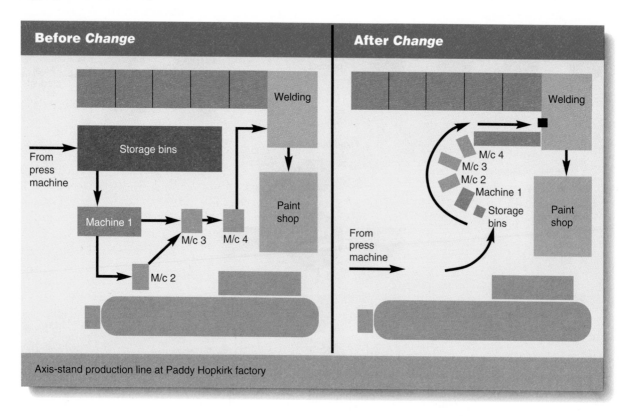

Axis-stand production line at Paddy Hopkirk factory

Once this change was made, the results were dramatic. One morning the factory was an untidy sprawl of workstations surrounded by piles of crates holding semi-finished components. Two days later, when the 170-person workforce came back to work, the machines had been brought together into tightly grouped workstations arranged in the fixed sequence shown in the illustration. The piles of components had disappeared, and the newly cleared floor space was neatly marked with color-coded lines mapping out the new flow of materials between workstations.

In the first full day of production, efficiency increased by as much as 30%. The space needed for some operations had been cut in half, and work in progress had been cut considerably. Moreover, the improved layout allowed some jobs to be combined, freeing operators for deployment elsewhere in the factory. An amazed Hopkirk exclaimed, "I was expecting a change but nothing as dramatic as this . . . it is fantastic."[28]

FLEXIBLE MANUFACTURING   In a manufacturing company, a major source of costs is setting up the equipment needed to make a particular product. One of these costs is that of production forgone because nothing is produced while the equipment is being set up. For example, components manufacturers often need as much as half a day to set up automated production equipment when switching from production of one component part (such as a washer ring for the steering column of a car) to another (such as a washer ring for the steering column of a truck). During this half-day, a manufacturing plant is not producing anything, but employees are paid for this "nonproductive" time.

It follows that if setup times for complex production equipment can be reduced, so can setup costs, and efficiency will rise; that is, the time that plant and employees spend in actually producing something will increase. This simple insight has been the driving force behind the development of flexible manufacturing techniques.

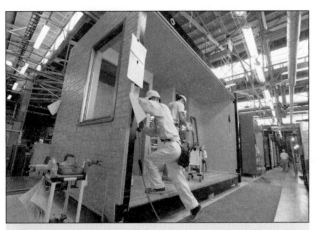

Housing units move on the production line as employees of Toyota Motor Corporation work during the installation process at the company's Kasugai Housing Works, one of the plants of Toyota home-brand houses on Kasugai, Aichi Prefecture, Japan. Toyota entered the housing industry 30 years ago where it applies the plant technology and experience it gained through producing cars.

Flexible manufacturing aims to reduce the time required to set up production equipment.[29] By redesigning the manufacturing process so production equipment geared for manufacturing one product can be quickly replaced with equipment geared to make another product, setup times and costs can be reduced dramatically. Another favorable outcome from flexible manufacturing is that a company can produce many more varieties of a product than before in the same amount of time. Thus flexible manufacturing increases a company's ability to be responsive to its customers.

Increasingly, organizations are experimenting with new designs for operating systems that not only allow workers to be more productive but also make the work process more flexible, thus reducing setup costs. Some Japanese companies are experimenting with facilities layouts arranged as a spiral, as the letter Y, and as the number 6, to see how these configurations affect setup costs and worker productivity.[30]An interesting example of a company that built a new factory to obtain the benefits from flexible manufacturing is the German company Igus Inc. Igus makes over 28,000 polymer bearings and energy supply cable products used in applications the world over. Increasing global competition led Igus managers to realize they needed to build a new factory that could handle the company's rapidly growing product line. At Igus new products are often introduced daily, so flexibility is the company's prime requirement. Moreover, because many of its products are highly customized, the specific and changing needs of its customers drive new product development.

Igus's new factory was designed for flexibility. As big as three football fields, the factory has nothing tied down or bolted to the floor. All the machines, computers, and equipment can be moved and repositioned to suit changing product requirements. Moreover, all Igus employees are trained to be flexible and can perform many of the necessary production tasks. For example, when one new product line proved popular with customers, its employees and production operations were relocated four times as it grew into larger spaces. Igus can change its operating system at a moment's notice and with minimal disruption; and because the company operates seven days a week, 24 hours a day, these changes are constant. Igus's decision to create a flexible factory of the future has paid off as its global sales more than tripled in the 2000s.

Just-in-Time Inventory and Efficiency

As noted earlier, a just-in-time inventory system gets components to the assembly line just as they are needed and thus drives down costs. In a JIT inventory system, component parts travel from suppliers to the assembly line in a small wheeled container known as a *kanban*. Assembly-line workers empty the kanbans, which are sent back to the suppliers as the signal to produce another small batch of component parts, and so the process repeats itself. This system can be contrasted with a just-in-case view of inventory, which leads an organization to stockpile excess inputs in a warehouse in case it needs them to meet sudden upturns in demand.

JIT inventory systems have major implications for efficiency. Great cost savings can result from increasing inventory turnover and reducing inventory holding costs, such as warehousing and storage costs and the cost of capital tied up in inventory. Although companies that manufacture and assemble products can obviously use JIT to great advantage, so can service organizations.[31] Walmart, the biggest retailer in the United States, uses JIT systems to replenish the stock in its stores at least twice a week. Many Walmart stores receive daily deliveries. Walmart's main competitors typically restock every two weeks. Walmart can maintain the same service levels as these competitors but at one-fourth the inventory holding cost. Faster inventory turnover has helped Walmart achieve an efficiency-based competitive advantage in the retailing industry.[32]

United Electric's kanban system involves suppliers in automatic checking and restocking, shortening production time and lowering costs.

Even a small company can benefit from a kanban, as the experience of United Electric Controls, headquartered in Watertown, Massachusetts, suggests. United Electric is the market leader in the application of threshold detection and switching technology. At one time the company simply warehoused its inputs and dispensed them as needed. Then it decided to reduce costs by storing these inputs at their point of use in the production system. However, this also caused problems because inventories of some inputs started to increase while other inputs were used up without anyone knowing which input stopped production.

So managers decided to experiment with a supplier kanban system even though United Electric had fewer than 40 suppliers and they were up to date with its input requirements. Managers decided to store a three-week supply of parts in a central storeroom—a supply large enough to avoid unexpected shortages.[33] They began by asking their casting supplier to deliver inputs in kanbans and bins. Once a week, this supplier checks the bins to determine how much stock needs to be delivered the following week. Other suppliers were then asked to participate in this system, and now more than 35 major suppliers operate some form of the kanban system.

By all measures of performance, the kanban system has succeeded. Inventory holding costs have fallen sharply. Products are delivered to all customers on time. And new products' design-to-production cycles have dropped by 50% because suppliers are now involved much earlier in the design process so they can supply new inputs as needed.

Self-Managed Work Teams and Efficiency

Another functional strategy to increase efficiency is the use of self-managed work teams.[34] A typical self-managed team consists of 5 to 15 employees who produce an entire product instead of just parts of it.[35] Team members learn all team tasks and move from job to job. The result is a flexible workforce because team members can fill in for absent coworkers. The members of each team also assume responsibility for scheduling work and vacations, ordering materials, and hiring new members—previously all responsibilities of first-line managers. Because people often respond well to greater autonomy and responsibility, the use of empowered self-managed teams can increase productivity and efficiency. Moreover, cost savings arise from eliminating supervisors and creating a flatter organizational hierarchy, which further increase efficiency.

The effect of introducing self-managed teams is often an increase in efficiency of 30% or sometimes much more. After the introduction of flexible manufacturing technology and self-managed teams, a GE plant in Salisbury, North Carolina, increased efficiency by 250% compared with other GE plants producing the same products.[36]

Process Reengineering and Efficiency

process reengineering
The fundamental rethinking and radical redesign of business processes to achieve dramatic improvement in critical measures of performance such as cost, quality, service, and speed.

The value chain is a collection of functional activities or business processes that transforms one or more kinds of inputs to create an output that is of value to the customer.[37] **Process reengineering** involves the fundamental rethinking and radical redesign of business processes (and thus the *value chain*) to achieve dramatic improvements in critical measures of performance such as cost, quality, service, and speed.[38] Order fulfillment, for example, can be thought of as a business process: When a customer's order is received (the input), many different functional tasks must be performed as necessary to process the order, and then the ordered goods are delivered to the customer (the output). Process reengineering boosts efficiency when it reduces the number of order fulfillment tasks that must be performed, or reduces the time they take, and so reduces operating costs.

For an example of process reengineering in practice, consider how Ford used it. One day a manager from Ford was working at its Japanese partner Mazda and discovered that Mazda had only five people in its accounts payable department. The Ford manager was shocked because Ford's U.S. operation had 500 employees in accounts payable. He reported his discovery to Ford's U.S. managers, who decided to form a task force to study this difference.

Ford managers discovered that procurement began when the purchasing department sent a purchase order to a supplier and sent a copy of the purchase order to Ford's accounts payable department. When the supplier shipped the goods and they arrived at Ford, a clerk at the receiving dock completed a form describing the goods and sent the form to accounts payable. The supplier, meanwhile, sent accounts payable an invoice. Thus accounts payable received three documents relating to these goods: a copy of the original purchase order, the receiving document, and the invoice. If the information in all three was in agreement (most of the time it was), a clerk in accounts payable issued payment. Occasionally, however, all three documents did not agree. And Ford discovered that accounts payable clerks spent most of their time straightening out the 1% of instances in which the purchase order, receiving document, and invoice contained conflicting information.[39]

Ford managers decided to reengineer the procurement process to simplify it. Now when a buyer in the purchasing department issues a purchase order to a supplier, that buyer also enters the order into an online database. As before, suppliers send goods to the receiving dock. When the goods arrive, the clerk at the receiving dock checks a computer terminal to see whether the received shipment matches the description on the purchase order. If it does, the clerk accepts the goods and pushes a button on the terminal keyboard that tells the database the goods have arrived. Receipt of the goods is recorded in the database, and a computer automatically issues and sends a check to the supplier. If the goods do not correspond to the description on the purchase order in the database, the clerk at the dock refuses the shipment and sends it back to the supplier.

Payment authorization, which used to be performed by accounts payable, is now accomplished at the receiving dock. The new process has come close to eliminating the need for an accounts payable department. In some parts of Ford, the size of the accounts payable department has been cut by 95%. By reducing the head count in accounts payable, the reengineering effort reduced the amount of time wasted on unproductive activities, thereby increasing the efficiency of the total organization.

Information Systems, the Internet, and Efficiency

With the rapid spread of computers, the explosive growth of the Internet and corporate intranets, and high-speed digital Internet technology, the information systems function is moving to center stage in the quest for operating efficiencies and a lower cost structure. The impact of information systems on productivity is wide-ranging and potentially affects all other activities of a company. For example, Cisco Systems has been able to realize significant cost savings by moving its ordering and customer service functions online. The company has just 300 service agents handling all its customer accounts, compared to the 900 it would need if sales were not handled online. The difference represents an annual savings of $30 million a year. Moreover, without automated customer service functions, Cisco calculates that it would need at least 1,000 additional service engineers, which would cost around $100 million.

All large companies today use the Internet to manage the value chain, feeding real-time information about order flow to suppliers, which use this information to schedule their own production to provide components on a just-in-time basis. This approach reduces the costs of coordination both between the company and its customers and between the company and its suppliers. Using the Internet to automate customer and supplier interactions substantially reduces the number of employees required to manage these interfaces, which significantly reduces costs. This trend extends beyond high-tech companies. Banks and financial service companies are finding that they can substantially reduce costs by moving customer accounts and support functions online. Such a move reduces the need for customer service representatives, bank tellers, stockbrokers, insurance agents, and others. For example, it costs about $1 when a customer executes a transaction at a bank, such as shifting money from one account to another; over the Internet the same transaction costs about $0.01.

Improving Innovation

As discussed in Chapter 6, *technology* comprises the skills, know-how, experience, body of scientific knowledge, tools, machines, computers, and equipment used in the design, production, and distribution of goods and services. Technology is involved in all functional activities, and the rapid advance of technology today is a significant factor in managers' attempts to improve how their value chains innovate new kinds of goods and services or ways to provide them.

Two Kinds of Innovation

Two principal kinds of innovation can be identified based on the nature of the technological change that brings them about. **Quantum product innovation** results in the development of new, often radically different, kinds of goods and services because of fundamental shifts in technology brought about by pioneering discoveries. Examples are the creation of the Internet and the World Wide Web that have revolutionized the computer, cell phone, and media/music industries, and biotechnology, which has transformed the treatment of illness by creating new, genetically engineered medicines. McDonald's development of the principles behind the provision of fast food also qualifies as a quantum product innovation.

Incremental product innovation results in gradual improvements and refinements of existing products over time as existing technologies are perfected and functional managers, like those at Apple, Toyota, and McDonald's, learn how to perform value chain activities in better ways—ways that add more value to products. For example, since their debut, Google's staffers have made thousands of incremental improvements to the company's search engine, Chrome Internet browser, and Android operating system—changes that have enhanced their capabilities enormously such as giving them the ability to work on all kinds of mobile devices and making them available in many different languages.

Quantum product innovations are relatively rare; most managers' activities focus on incremental product innovations that result from ongoing technological advances. For example, every time Dell or HP puts a new, faster Intel or AMD chip into a PC, or Google improves its search engine's capability, the company is making incremental product innovations. Similarly, every time car engineers redesign a car model, and every time McDonald's managers work to improve the flavor and texture of burgers, fries, and salads, their product development efforts are intended to lead to incremental product innovations. Incremental innovation is frequently as important as—or even more important than—quantum innovation in raising a company's performance. Indeed, as discussed next, it is often managers' ability to successfully manage incremental product development that results in success or failure in an industry—as Dell found out to its cost.

The need to speed innovation and quickly develop new and improved products becomes especially important when the technology behind the product is advancing rapidly. This is because the first companies in an industry to adopt the new technology will be able to develop products that better meet customer needs and gain a "first-mover" advantage over their rivals. Indeed, managers who do not quickly adopt and apply new technologies to innovate products may soon find they have no customers for their products—and destroy their organizations. In sum, the greater the rate of technological change in an industry, the more important it is for managers to innovate.

Strategies to Promote Innovation and Speed Product Development

There are several ways in which managers can promote innovation and encourage the development of new products. **Product development** is the management of the value chain activities involved in bringing new or improved goods and services to the market. The steps that Monte Peterson, former CEO of Thermos, took to develop a new barbecue grill show how good product development should proceed. Peterson had no doubt about how to increase Thermos's sales of barbecue grills: Motivate Thermos's functional managers to create new and improved models. So Peterson assembled a cross-functional product development team of five functional managers (from marketing, engineering, manufacturing, sales, and finance)

LO9-5 Differentiate between two forms of innovation, and explain why innovation and product development are crucial components of the search for competitive advantage.

quantum product innovation The development of new, often radically different, kinds of goods and services because of fundamental shifts in technology brought about by pioneering discoveries.

incremental product innovation The gradual improvement and refinement of existing products that occur over time as existing technologies are perfected.

product development The management of the value chain activities involved in bringing new or improved goods and services to the market.

and told them to develop a new barbecue grill within 18 months. To ensure that they were not spread too thin, he assigned them to this team only. Peterson also arranged for leadership of the team to rotate. Initially, to focus on what customers wanted, the marketing manager would take the lead; then, when technical developments became the main consideration, leadership would switch to engineering; and so on.

Team members christened the group the "lifestyle team." To find out what people really wanted in a grill, the marketing manager and nine subordinates spent a month on the road, visiting customers. What they found surprised them. The stereotype of Dad slaving over a smoky barbecue grill was wrong—more women were barbecuing. Many cooks were tired of messy charcoal, and many homeowners did not like rusty grills that spoiled the appearance of their decks. Moreover, environmental and safety issues were increasing in importance. In California charcoal starter fluid is considered a pollutant and is banned; in New Jersey the use of charcoal and gas grills on the balconies of condos and apartments has been prohibited to avoid fires. Based on these findings, the team decided Thermos had to produce a barbecue grill that not only made the food taste good but also looked attractive, used no pollutants, and was safe for balcony use (which meant it had to be electric).

Within one year the basic attributes of the product were defined, and leadership of the team moved to engineering. The critical task for engineering was to design a grill that gave food the cookout taste that conventional electric grills could not provide because they did not get hot enough. To raise the cooking temperature, Thermos's engineers designed a domed vacuum top that trapped heat inside the grill, and they built electric heat rods directly into the surface of the grill. These features made the grill hot enough to sear meat and give it brown barbecue lines and a barbecue taste.

Manufacturing had been active from the early days of the development process, making sure any proposed design could be produced economically. Because manufacturing was involved from the beginning, the team avoided some costly mistakes. At one critical team meeting the engineers said they wanted tapered legs on the grill. Manufacturing explained that tapered legs would have to be custom-made—and would raise manufacturing costs—and persuaded the team to go with straight legs.

When the new grill was introduced on schedule, it was an immediate success. The study of many product development successes, such as that of Thermos's lifestyle team, suggests three strategies managers can implement to increase the likelihood that their product development efforts will result in innovative and successful new products.

INVOLVE BOTH CUSTOMERS AND SUPPLIERS Many new products fail when they reach the marketplace because they were designed with scant attention to customer needs. Successful product development requires inputs from more than just an organization's members; also needed are inputs from customers and suppliers. Thermos team members spent a month on the road, visiting customers to identify their needs. The revolutionary electric barbecue grill was a direct result of this process. In other cases companies have found it worthwhile to include customer representatives as peripheral members of their product development teams. Boeing, for example, has included its customers, the major airlines, in the design of its most recent commercial jet aircraft, the 787 Dreamliner. Boeing builds a mockup of the aircraft's cabin and then, over a period of months, allows each airline's representatives to experiment with repositioning the galleys, seating, aisles, and bathrooms to best meet the needs of their particular airline. Boeing has learned a great deal from this process.

ESTABLISH A STAGE–GATE DEVELOPMENT FUNNEL One of the most common mistakes managers make in product development is trying to fund too many new projects at any one time. This approach spreads the activities of the different value chain functions too thinly over too many different projects. As a consequence, no single project is given the functional resources and attention required.

One strategy for solving this problem is for managers to develop a structured process for evaluating product development proposals and deciding which to support and which to reject. A common solution is to establish a

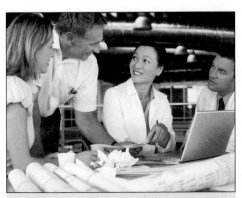

Cross-functionality at its best. Here, two research scientists, an executive, and a marketing manager put their heads together to figure out what's next.

stage–gate development funnel A planning model that forces managers to choose among competing projects so organizational resources are not spread thinly over too many projects.

stage–gate development funnel, a technique that forces managers to choose among competing projects so functional resources are not spread thinly over too many projects. The funnel gives functional managers control over product development and allows them to intervene and take corrective action quickly and appropriately (see Figure 9.6).

At stage 1 the development funnel has a wide mouth, so top managers initially can encourage employees to come up with as many new product ideas as possible. Managers can create incentives for employees to come up with ideas. Many organizations run "bright-idea programs" that reward employees whose ideas eventually make it through the development process. Other organizations allow research scientists to devote a certain amount of work time to their own projects. Top managers at 3M, for example, have a 15% rule: They expect a research scientist to spend 15% of the workweek working on a project of his or her own choosing. Ideas may be submitted by individuals or by groups. Brainstorming (see Chapter 7) is a technique that managers frequently use to encourage new ideas.

New product ideas are written up as brief proposals. The proposals are submitted to a cross-functional team of managers, who evaluate each proposal at gate 1. The cross-functional team considers a proposal's fit with the organization's strategy and its technical feasibility. Proposals that are consistent with the strategy of the organization and are judged technically feasible pass through gate 1 and into stage 2. Other proposals are turned down (although the door is often left open for reconsidering a proposal later).

product development plan A plan that specifies all of the relevant information that managers need in order to decide whether to proceed with a full-blown product development effort.

The primary goal in stage 2 is to draft a detailed product development plan. The **product development plan** specifies all of the relevant information that managers need to decide whether to go ahead with a full-blown product development effort. The product development plan should include strategic and financial objectives, an analysis of the product's market potential, a list of desired product features, a list of technological requirements, a list of financial and human resource requirements, a detailed development budget, and a time line that contains specific milestones (for example, dates for prototype completion and final launch).

A cross-functional team of managers normally drafts this plan. Good planning requires a good strategic analysis (see Chapter 8), and team members must be prepared to spend considerable time in the field with customers, trying to understand their needs. Drafting a product development plan generally takes about three months. Once completed, the plan is reviewed by a senior management committee at gate 2 (see Figure 9.6). These managers focus on the details of the plan to see whether the proposal is attractive (given its market potential) and viable (given the technological, financial, and human resources that would be needed to develop the product). Senior managers making this review keep in mind all other product development efforts currently being undertaken by the organization. One goal at this point is to ensure that limited organizational resources are used to their maximum effect.

At gate 2 projects are rejected, sent back for revision, or allowed to pass through to stage 3, the development phase. Product development starts with the formation of a cross-functional team that is given primary responsibility for developing the product. In some companies, at

Figure 9.6

A Stage–Gate Development Funnel

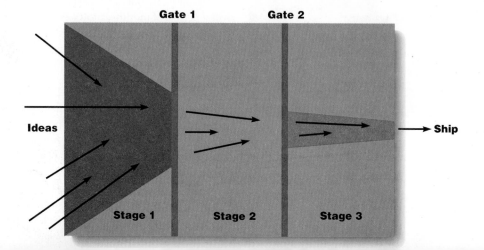

contract book A written agreement that details product development factors such as responsibilities, resource commitments, budgets, time lines, and development milestones.

the beginning of stage 3 top managers and cross-functional team members sign a **contract book**, a written agreement that details factors such as responsibilities, resource commitments, budgets, time lines, and development milestones. Signing the contract book is viewed as the symbolic launch of a product development effort. The contract book is also a document against which actual development progress can be measured. At 3M, for example, team members and top management negotiate a contract and sign a contract book at the launch of a development effort, thereby signaling their commitment to the objectives contained in the contract.

The stage 3 development effort can last anywhere from six months to 10 years, depending on the industry and type of product. Some electronics products have development cycles of 6 months, but it takes from three to five years to develop a new car, about five years to develop a new jet aircraft, and as long as 10 years to develop a new medical drug.

ESTABLISH CROSS-FUNCTIONAL TEAMS A smooth-running cross-functional team also seems to be a critical component of successful product development, as the experience of Thermos suggests. Marketing, engineering, and manufacturing personnel are **core members** of a successful product development team—the people who have primary responsibility for the product development effort. Other people besides core members work on the project when the need arises, but the core members (generally from three to six individuals) stay with the project from inception to completion of the development effort (see Figure 9.7).

core members The members of a team who bear primary responsibility for the success of a project and who stay with a project from inception to completion.

The reason for using a cross-functional team is to ensure a high level of coordination and communication among managers in different functions. Input from both marketing and manufacturing members of Thermos's lifestyle team determined the characteristics of the barbecue that the engineers on the team ended up designing.

If a cross-functional team is to succeed, it must have the right kind of leadership and it must be managed effectively. To be successful, a product development team needs a team leader who can rise above a functional background and take a cross-functional view. In addition to having effective leadership, successful cross-functional product development teams have several other key characteristics. Often core members of successful teams are located close to one another, in the same office space, to foster a sense of shared mission and commitment to a development program. Successful teams develop a clear sense of their objectives and how they will be achieved, the purpose again being to create a sense of shared mission. The way in which Google uses many of these strategies to promote innovation is discussed in the following "Management Insight" box.

Figure 9.7

Members of a Cross-Functional Product Development Team

Innovation and Product Development
Are Google's Major Imperatives

The history of Google, the Internet search engine company, began in 1995 when two Stanford graduate computer science students, Sergey Brin and Larry Page, decided to collaborate to develop a new kind of search engine technology.[40] They understood the limitations of existing search engines, and by 1998 they had developed a superior engine that they felt was ready to go online. They raised $1 million from family, friends, and risk-taking "angel" investors to buy the hardware necessary to connect Google to the Internet.

At first Google answered 10,000 inquiries a day, but in a few months it was answering 500,000. By fall 1999 it was handling 3 million; by fall 2000, 60 million; and by spring 2001, 100 million per day. In the 2000s Google became the dominant search engine, handling around 75% of inquiries by 2010; it is one of the top five most used Internet companies, and rivals like Microsoft are working hard to catch up and beat Google at its own game.

Google's explosive growth is largely due to the culture of innovation its founders cultivated from the start. Although by 2012 Google had grown to 35,000 employees worldwide, its founders claim that Google still maintains a small-company feel because its culture empowers its employees, who are called staffers or "Googlers," to create the best software possible. Brin and Page created Google's innovative culture in several ways.

From the beginning, lacking space and seeking to keep operating costs low, Google staffers worked in "high-density clusters." Three or four employees, each equipped with a high-powered Linux workstation, shared a desk, couch, and chairs that were large rubber balls, working together to improve the company's technology. Even when Google moved into more spacious surroundings at its "Googleplex" headquarters building, staffers continued to work in shared spaces. Google designed the building so staffers constantly meet one another in its funky lobby; in its Google Café, where everyone eats together; in its state-of-the-art recreational facilities; and in its "snack rooms," equipped with bins packed with cereals, gummi bears, yogurt, carrots, and make-your-own cappuccino. Google also created many social gatherings of employees, such as a TGIF open meetings and a twice weekly outdoor roller hockey game where staffers are encouraged to bring down the founders.[41]

All this attention to creating what might be the "grooviest" company headquarters in the world did not come about by chance. Brin and Page knew that Google's most important strength would be its ability to attract the best software engineers in the world and then motivate them to perform well. Common offices, lobbies, cafés, and so on bring staffers into close contact with one another, develop collegiality, and encourage them to share new ideas with their colleagues and to constantly improve Google's search engine technology and find new ways to expand the company. The freedom Google gives its staffers to pursue new ideas is a clear indication of its founders' desire to empower them to be innovative and to look off the beaten path for new ideas. Finally, recognizing that staffers who innovate important new software applications should be rewarded for their achievements, Google's founders give them stock in the company, effectively making staffers its owners as well.

Their focus on innovation did not blind Brin and Page to the need to build a viable competitive strategy so Google could compete effectively in the cutthroat search engine market. They recognized, however, that they lacked business experience; they had never had to craft strategies to

From the beginning, Google employees have worked in "high-density clusters," which contributes to their camaraderie and cooperative innovations—whether they're sitting on therapeutic bouncy balls or ergonomic office chairs.

compete with giants like Microsoft and Yahoo. Moreover, they also had never been responsible for building a strong set of value chain functions. So they recruited a team of talented and experienced functional managers to help them manage their company. Brin and Page's understanding that successful product development requires building a strong organizational architecture has paid off. It has become one of the most successful and profitable global companies and hardly a day goes by without some news story about some new innovation in one of its product groups.

Google prospers because of its founders' ability to create a culture that encourages staffers to be innovative and because of their willingness to delegate authority for product development to managers and staffers. Managing innovation is an increasingly important aspect of a manager's job in an era of dramatic changes in advanced IT. Promoting successful new product development is difficult and challenging, and some product development efforts are much more successful than others. In sum, managers need to recognize that successful innovation and product development cut across roles and functions and require a high level of cooperation. They should recognize the importance of common values and norms in promoting the high levels of cooperation and cohesiveness necessary to build a culture for innovation. They also should reward successful innovators and make heroes of the employees and teams who develop successful new products. Finally, managers should fully utilize the product development techniques just discussed to guide the process.

Summary and Review

LO9-1

VALUE CHAIN MANAGEMENT AND COMPETITIVE ADVANTAGE To achieve high performance, managers try to improve their responsiveness to customers, the quality of their products, and the efficiency of their organization. To achieve these goals, managers can use a number of value chain management techniques to improve the way an organization operates.

LO9-2 IMPROVING RESPONSIVENESS TO CUSTOMERS To achieve high performance in a competitive environment, it is imperative that the organization's value chain be managed to produce outputs that have the attributes customers desire. A central task of value chain management is to develop new and improved operating systems that enhance the ability of the organization to economically deliver more of the product attributes that customers desire for the same price. Techniques such as CRM and TQM, JIT, flexible manufacturing, and process reengineering are popular because they promise to do this. As important as responsiveness to customers is, however, managers need to recognize that there are limits to how responsive an organization can be and still cover its costs.

LO9-3 IMPROVING QUALITY Managers seek to improve the quality of their organization's output because doing so enables them to better serve customers, to raise prices, and to lower production costs. Total quality management focuses on improving the quality of an organization's products and services and stresses that all of an organization's operations should be directed toward this goal. Putting TQM into practice requires having an organizationwide commitment to TQM, having a strong customer focus, finding ways to measure quality, setting quality improvement goals, soliciting input from employees about how to improve product quality, identifying defects and tracing them to their source, introducing just-in-time inventory systems, getting suppliers to adopt TQM practices, designing products for ease of manufacture, and breaking down barriers between functional departments.

LO9-4 IMPROVING EFFICIENCY Improving efficiency requires one or more of the following: the introduction of a TQM program, the adoption of flexible manufacturing technologies, the introduction of just-in-time inventory systems, the establishment of self-managed work teams, and the application of process reengineering. Top management is responsible for setting the context within which efficiency improvements can take place by, for example, emphasizing the need for continuous improvement. Functional-level managers bear prime responsibility for identifying and implementing efficiency-enhancing improvements in operating systems.

LO9-5   IMPROVING PRODUCT INNOVATION   When technology is changing, managers must quickly innovate new and improved products to protect their competitive advantage. Some value chain strategies managers can use to achieve this are (1) involving both customers and suppliers in the development process; (2) establishing a stage–gate development funnel for evaluating and controlling different product development efforts; and (3) establishing cross-functional teams composed of individuals from different functional departments, and giving each team a leader who can rise above his or her functional background.

Management in Action

Topics for Discussion and Action

Discussion

1. What is CRM, and how can it help improve responsiveness to customers? **[LO9-2]**

2. What are the main challenges in implementing a successful total quality management program? **[LO9-3]**

3. What is efficiency, and what are some strategies managers can use to increase it? **[LO9-4]**

4. Why is it important for managers to pay close attention to value chain management if they wish to be responsive to their customers? **[LO9-1, 9-2]**

5. What is innovation, and what are some strategies managers can use to develop successful new products? **[LO9-5]**

Action

6. Ask a manager how responsiveness to customers, quality, efficiency, and innovation are defined and measured in his or her organization. **[LO9-1, 9-2]**

7. Go to a local store, restaurant, or supermarket; observe how customers are treated; and list the ways in which you think the organization is being responsive or unresponsive to the needs of its customers. How could this business improve its responsiveness to customers? **[LO9-1, 9-2]**

Building Management Skills

Managing the Value Chain [LO9-1, 9-2]

Choose an organization with which you are familiar—one that you have worked in or patronized or one that has received extensive coverage in the popular press. The organization should be involved in only one industry or business. Answer these questions about the organization:

1. What is the output of the organization?

2. Describe the value chain activities that the organization uses to produce this output.

3. What product attributes do customers of the organization desire?

4. Try to identify improvements that might be made to the organization's value chain to boost its responsiveness to customers, quality, efficiency, and innovation.

Managing Ethically [LO9-1, 9-4]

After implementing efficiency-improving techniques, many companies commonly lay off hundreds or thousands of employees whose services are no longer required. And frequently remaining employees must perform more tasks more quickly—a situation that can generate employee stress and other work-related problems. Also, these employees may experience guilt because they stayed while many of their colleagues and friends were fired.

Questions

1. Either by yourself or in a group, think through the ethical implications of using a new functional strategy to improve organizational performance.

2. What criteria would you use to decide which kind of strategy is ethical to adopt and how far to push employees to raise the level of their performance?

3. How big a layoff, if any, is acceptable? If layoffs are acceptable, what could be done to reduce their harm to employees?

Small Group Breakout Exercise

How to Compete in the Sandwich Business [LO9-1, 9-2]

Form groups of three or four people, and appoint one member as the spokesperson who will communicate your findings to the class when called on by the instructor. Then discuss the following scenario:

You and your partners are thinking about opening a new kind of sandwich shop that will compete head-to-head with Subway and Thundercloud Subs. Because these chains have good brand-name recognition, it is vital that you find some source of competitive advantage for your new sandwich shop, and you are meeting to brainstorm ways of obtaining one.

1. Identify the product attributes that a typical sandwich shop customer wants the most.

2. In what ways do you think you will be able to improve on the operations and processes of existing sandwich shops and increase responsiveness to customers through better product quality, efficiency, or innovation?

Exploring the World Wide Web [LO9-3, 9-4]

In the 2010s Toyota was accused of allowing its desire for rapid global growth to undermine its commitment to quality and safety in the design of its vehicles, creating problems such as the design failure of the acceleration and braking systems in some of its vehicles. Search the web for articles about the way Toyota has responded to these problems.

1. How have the recalls that Toyota announced affected current public opinion about the company's record for quality and reliability?

2. How has Toyota changed its strategies toward value chain management as a result of these quality and safety problems?

Be the Manager [LO9-1, 9-3, 9-4, 9-5]

How to Build Flatscreen Displays

You are the top manager of a start-up company that will produce innovative new flatscreen displays for PC makers like Apple and HP. The flatscreen display market is highly competitive, so there is considerable pressure to reduce costs. Also, PC makers are demanding ever-higher quality and better features to please customers. In addition, they demand that delivery of your product meets their production schedule needs. Functional managers want your advice on how to best meet these requirements, especially because they are in the process of recruiting new workers and building a production facility.

Questions

1. What kinds of techniques discussed in the chapter can help your functional managers to increase efficiency?

2. In what ways can these managers develop a program to increase quality and innovation?

3. What critical lessons do these managers need to learn about value chain management?

Bloomberg Businessweek Case in the News [LO9-1, 9-2]

Home Depot's Fix-It Lady: Chief Financial Officer Carol Tomé Has a Shot at CEO, If She Can Solve the Retailer's Technology Problems

Carol B. Tomé, the chief financial officer at Home Depot and a leading contender to be the retailer's next chief executive, has caught the technology bug. "I can't wait until the day when I have my credit card loaded up on my smartphone, and I don't even have to carry my wallet—just walk around with my phone," she says, gesturing toward the orange-and-beige Store No. 121, visible from her 22nd-floor conference room in Atlanta. "It's tap and go. It's going to happen. It's all ages, all generations."

It is September 2010 and Home Depot is weeks away from unveiling a mobile app allowing consumers to order merchandise via their iPhone or iPad. "We're already there," Tomé says, visibly pleased that the home-improvement chain would beat its smaller but faster-growing rival, Lowe's, in the race to introduce such a feature. Lowe's still hasn't introduced its iPhone app, yet Home Depot's small victory is misleading. The world's largest retailer of potting soil and two-by-fours has actually lagged in technology. Until last year, employees stocked shelves as they had for 15 years, using computers powered by motorboat batteries and rolled around stores on bulky carts. The retailer still doesn't offer customers the option to order online and pick up merchandise in stores, as Lowe's (LOW) does. Above all, the company must attract younger consumers accustomed to shopping online, often with devices they carry in a pocket or handbag.

During 2010 Tomé oversaw tech spending of $350 million, or a third of all capital expenditures. Several former top Home Depot executives say Tomé would be the logical internal choice to succeed CEO Frank Blake, 61, when he retires. Her chances of becoming the fifth CEO in Home Depot's 33-year existence may depend on whether she succeeds at improving the chain's in-store technology as well as boosting online transactions, which amounted to less than $1 billion, or 1.5% of its 2010 sales.

Home Depot's tech troubles provide some sobering lessons for other brick-and-mortar retailers as they try to capture mobile-device sales. When processing special orders for customers, Home Depot employees are now forced to use "prehistoric" technology, hurting both service and sales, Marvin Ellison, the company's executive vice president for U.S. stores, said at a Goldman Sachs conference in New York. Home Depot also needs to improve its website to lure the 7 in 10 customers who first browse online, Blake said at the conference.

For more than a decade, the company neglected the tech revolution, preferring to open stores—more than 100 a year through 2005. Today there are 2,244 in all. Tomé was in the thick of the real estate binge. She still heads the corporate committee that oversaw that expansion, though in 2008 it became clear that demand for big-box home-improvement stores had reached the saturation point. Now it is up to her to approve the big-ticket tech spending needed to move Home Depot online.

In 15 years at the company, Tomé is the only senior executive to work for all four of its CEOs. She has advanced, colleagues say, by combining sharp intelligence with a zeal to learn the business from the hammers and nails on up. A coat rack in her office bears more than 90 orange aprons decorated by employees of stores she has visited. Tomé tours at least one outlet a week, talking to customers and quizzing workers. "Carol can mix paint," says Cara Kinzey, a senior vice president for information technology, recalling a particularly detailed grilling by the CFO over the 2009 purchase of new paint-blending equipment and other improvements. "We always have to pay for these projects with results."

Getting Home Depot up to speed on technology became a key test for Tomé. Under her leadership in 2010 the company laid out $60 million to buy 40,000 handheld devices to replace the in-store computers from the early 1990s. In October it launched a blogging site at homedepot.com where managers and employees can make suggestions about ways to improve store performance. As part of a broader upgrade of checkout systems, the company's U.S. stores have lately installed contact-less scanners for reading credit-card information on smartphones. They're not in use yet, says Dwaine Kimmet, treasurer and vice president for financial services. "We did it for the future, to keep our options open. We were very much like that Kevin Costner movie: Build a store, and they will come," Tomé explains. "That's no longer the case. We need to look at what we're doing inside the company to grow. Our economic engine will be driven by productivity and efficiency."

Questions for Discussion

1. Why is it so important that Home Depot improve its operating systems?

2. In what ways can updating its IT help Home depot improve its (a) responsiveness to customers, (b) quality, and (c) efficiency?

3. What is the most effective way that a home improvement company such as Home Depot or Lowe's can improve your shopping experience?

Source: Chris Burritt, "Home Depot's Fix-It Lady," *Bloomberg Businessweek*, January 13, 2011. Bloomberg L.P. Copyright © 2012. All rights reserved.

CHAPTER 10

Managing Organizational Structure and Culture

Learning Objectives

After studying this chapter, you should be able to:

LO10-1 Identify the factors that influence managers' choice of an organizational structure.

LO10-2 Explain how managers group tasks into jobs that are motivating and satisfying for employees.

LO10-3 Describe the types of organizational structures managers can design, and explain why they choose one structure over another.

LO10-4 Explain why managers must coordinate jobs, functions, and divisions using the hierarchy of authority and integrating mechanisms.

LO10-5 List the four sources of organizational culture, and explain why and how a company's culture can lead to competitive advantage.

A MANAGER'S CHALLENGE

UPS and Walmart Know How to Build Persuasive Cultures

How should managers organize to improve performance? United Parcel Service (UPS) was founded as a bicycle messenger service in 1907 by James E. Casey. Today it controls more than three-fourths of the U.S. ground and air parcel service, delivering over 10 million packages a day in its fleet of 150,000 trucks. It is also the most profitable company in its industry and employs over 250,000 people globally. Walmart, the largest retailer in the world, was founded by Sam Walton; today it employs over a million people and is the most profitable company in its industry. What do these companies have in common? They were both founded by managers who wanted their employees to take a hands-on approach to their jobs and be completely committed to their mission—total customer satisfaction. And to achieve this both these founders created strong values and norms about how employees should behave and in the process created performance-enhancing organizational cultures

At UPS, from the beginning Casey made efficiency and economy the company's driving values and loyalty, humility, discipline, dependability, and intense effort the key norms its employees should adopt. UPS has always gone to extraordinary lengths to develop and maintain these values and norms

in its workforce.[1] First, its control systems from the top of the company down to its trucking operations are the subject of intense scrutiny by the company's 3,000 industrial engineers, who continually search for ways to measure outputs and behaviors to improve efficiency. They time every part of an employee's job. Truck drivers, for example, are told in extraordinary detail how to perform their tasks: They must step from their truck with their right foot first, fold their money face-up, carry packages under their left arm, walk at a pace of 3 feet per second, and slip the key ring holding

The 10-foot greeting expectation, the sundown rule, and the Walmart Cheer, shown here, are all parts of Walmart's effective enculturation process. Employees trained into these standards soon learn to pass them along to others, while tales of superior examples work their way into company legends.

their truck keys over their third finger. Employees are not allowed to have beards, must be carefully groomed, and are instructed in how to deal with customers. Drivers who perform below average receive visits from training supervisors who accompany them on their delivery routes and teach how to raise their performance level. Not surprisingly, because of this intensive training and close behavior control, UPS employees internalize the company's strong norms about the appropriate ways to behave to help the organization achieve its values of economy and efficiency. In fact, today UPS offers a consulting service to other companies in global supply chain management to teach them how to recreate its values and norms of efficiency and economy that the company has pursued for the last hundred years because these were the values of its founder.

In a similar way, to involve employees (called "associates") at all levels and encourage them to develop work behaviors focused on providing quality customer service, Walton established strong cultural values and norms for Walmart. One of the norms that associates are expected to follow is the "10-foot attitude." This norm encourages associates, in Walton's words, to "promise that whenever you come within 10 feet of a customer, you will look him in the eye, greet him, and ask him if you can help him." The "sundown rule" states that employees should strive to answer customer requests by sundown of the day they are made. The Walmart cheer ("Give me a W; give me an A," and so on) is used in all its stores.[2]

The strong customer-oriented values that Walton created are exemplified in the stories Walmart members tell one another about associates' concern for customers. They include stories like the one about Sheila, who risked her own safety when she jumped in front of a car to prevent a little boy from being struck; about Phyllis, who administered CPR to a customer who had suffered a heart attack in her store; and about Annette, who gave up the Power Ranger she had on layaway for her own son to fulfill the birthday wish of a customer's son. The strong Walmart culture helps control and motivate employees to achieve the stringent output and financial targets the company has set for itself.

Although both founders are long gone, their companies still seem governed by the values and norms they established. Their new managers take seriously their charge to provide efficient service to customers, and in any delivery by a UPS employee or visit to a Walmart store, it is possible to observe how employees still buy into these values and are rewarded for doing so. Both these companies have taken their values and norms and established them in their overseas divisions around the world so that they have truly global cultures that allow managers and employees to better communicate and work together as they manage their global supply chains to protect their competitive advantage.

Overview

As the examples of UPS and Walmart suggest, the values and norms of an organizational culture are a powerful influence on employee motivation and behavior. How an organization's structure is designed also affects employees' behavior and how well an organization operates, so in a quickly changing global environment it is important for managers to identify the best way to organize people and resources to increase efficiency and effectiveness.

In Part 4 of this book, we examine how managers can organize and control human and other resources to create high-performing organizations. To organize and control (two of the four tasks of management identified in Chapter 1), managers must design an organizational architecture that makes the best use of resources to produce the goods and services customers want. **Organizational architecture** is the combination of organizational structure, culture, control systems, and human resource management (HRM) systems that together determine how efficiently and effectively organizational resources are used.

By the end of this chapter, you will be familiar not only with various forms of organizational structures and cultures but also with various factors that determine the organizational design choices that managers make. Then, in Chapters 11 and 12, we examine issues surrounding the design of an organization's control systems and HRM systems.

organizational architecture The organizational structure, control systems, culture, and human resource management systems that together determine how efficiently and effectively organizational resources are used.

Designing Organizational Structure

LO10-1 Identify the factors that influence managers' choice of an organizational structure.

Organizing is the process by which managers establish the structure of working relationships among employees to allow them to achieve organizational goals efficiently and effectively. **Organizational structure** is the formal system of task and job reporting relationships that determines how employees use resources to achieve organizational goals.[3] *Organizational culture,* discussed in Chapter 3, is the shared set of beliefs, values, and norms that influence how people and groups work together to achieve organizational goals. **Organizational design** is the process by which managers create a specific type of organizational structure and culture so a company can operate in the most efficient and effective way.[4]

Once a company decides what kind of work attitudes and behaviors it wants from its employees, managers create a particular arrangement of task and authority relationships, and promote specific cultural values and norms, to obtain these desired attitudes and behaviors. The challenge facing all companies is to design a structure and a culture that (1) *motivate* managers and employees to work hard and to develop supportive job behaviors and attitudes and (2) *coordinate* the actions of employees, groups, functions, and divisions to ensure they work together efficiently and effectively.

As noted in Chapter 2, according to contingency theory, managers design organizational structures to fit the factors or circumstances that are affecting the company the most and causing the most uncertainty.[5] Thus there is no one best way to design an organization: Design reflects each organization's specific situation, and researchers have argued that in some situations stable, mechanistic structures may be most appropriate while in others flexible, organic structures might be the most effective. Four factors are important determinants of the type of organizational structure or culture managers select: the nature of the organizational environment, the type of strategy the organization pursues, the technology (and particularly information technology) the organization uses, and the characteristics of the organization's human resources (see Figure 10.1).[6]

organizational structure A formal system of task and reporting relationships that coordinates and motivates organizational members so they work together to achieve organizational goals.

organizational design The process by which managers make specific organizing choices that result in a particular kind of organizational structure.

The Organizational Environment

In general, the more quickly the external environment is changing and the greater the uncertainty within it, the greater are the problems managers face in trying to gain access to scarce resources. In this situation, to speed decision making and communication and make it easier to obtain resources, managers typically make organizing choices that result in more flexible structures and entrepreneurial cultures.[7] They are likely to decentralize authority, empower lower-level employees to make important operating decisions, and encourage values and norms that emphasize change and innovation—a more organic form of organizing.

In contrast, if the external environment is stable, resources are readily available, and uncertainty is low, then less coordination and communication among people and functions are needed to obtain resources. Managers can make organizing choices that bring more stability or formality to the organizational structure and can establish values and norms that emphasize obedience and being a team player. Managers in this situation prefer to make decisions within a clearly defined hierarchy of authority and to use detailed rules, standard operating procedures (SOPs), and restrictive norms to guide and govern employees' activities—a more mechanistic form of organizing.

Figure 10.1

Factors Affecting Organizational Structure

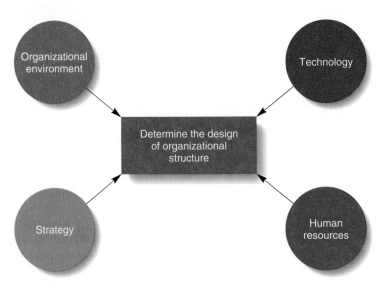

As we discussed in Chapter 6, change is rapid in today's marketplace, and increasing competition both at home and abroad is putting greater pressure on managers to attract customers and increase efficiency and effectiveness. Consequently, interest in finding ways to structure organizations—such as through empowerment and self-managed teams—to allow people and departments to behave flexibly has been increasing.

Strategy

Chapter 8 suggests that once managers decide on a strategy, they must choose the right means to implement it. Different strategies often call for the use of different organizational structures and cultures. For example, a differentiation strategy aimed at increasing the value customers perceive in an organization's goods and services usually succeeds best in a flexible structure with a culture that values innovation; flexibility facilitates a differentiation strategy because managers can develop new or innovative products quickly—an activity that requires extensive cooperation among functions or departments. In contrast, a low-cost strategy that is aimed at driving down costs in all functions usually fares best in a more formal structure with more conservative norms, which gives managers greater control over the activities of an organization's various departments.[8]

In addition, at the corporate level, when managers decide to expand the scope of organizational activities by vertical integration or diversification, for example, they need to design a flexible structure to provide sufficient coordination among the different business divisions.[9] As discussed in Chapter 8, many companies have been divesting businesses because managers have been unable to create a competitive advantage to keep them up to speed in fast-changing industries. By moving to a more flexible structure, managers gain more control over their different businesses. Finally, expanding internationally and operating in many different countries challenges managers to create organizational structures that allow organizations to be flexible on a global level.[10] As we discuss later, managers can group their departments or divisions in several ways to allow them to effectively pursue an international strategy.

Technology

Recall that technology is the combination of skills, knowledge, machines, and computers that are used to design, make, and distribute goods and services. As a rule, the more complicated the technology that an organization uses, the more difficult it is to regulate or control it because more unexpected events can arise. Thus the more complicated the technology, the greater is the need for a flexible structure and progressive culture to enhance managers' ability to respond to unexpected situations—and give them the freedom and desire to work out new solutions to the problems they encounter. In contrast, the more routine the technology, the more appropriate is a formal structure because tasks are simple and the steps needed to produce goods and services have been worked out in advance.

What makes a technology routine or complicated? One researcher who investigated this issue, Charles Perrow, argued that two factors determine how complicated or nonroutine technology is: task variety and task analyzability.[11] *Task variety* is the number of new or unexpected problems or situations that a person or function encounters in performing tasks or jobs. *Task analyzability* is the degree to which programmed solutions are available to people or functions to solve the problems they encounter. Nonroutine or complicated technologies are characterized by high task variety and low task analyzability; this means many varied problems occur and solving these problems requires significant nonprogrammed decision making. In contrast, routine technologies are characterized by low task variety and high task analyzability; this means the problems encountered do not vary much and are easily resolved through programmed decision making.

Examples of nonroutine technology are found in the work of scientists in an R&D laboratory who develop new products or discover new drugs, and they are seen in the planning exercises an organization's top management team uses to chart the organization's future strategy. Examples of routine technology include typical mass-production or assembly operations, where workers perform the same task repeatedly and where managers have already identified the programmed solutions necessary to perform a task efficiently. Similarly, in service organizations such as fast-food restaurants, the tasks that crew members perform in making and serving fast food are routine.

LO10-2 Explain how managers group tasks into jobs that are motivating and satisfying for employees.

Human Resources

A final important factor affecting an organization's choice of structure and culture is the characteristics of the human resources it employs. In general, the more highly skilled its workforce, and the greater the number of employees who work together in groups or teams, the more likely an organization is to use a flexible, decentralized structure and a professional culture based on values and norms that foster employee autonomy and self-control. Highly skilled employees, or employees who have internalized strong professional values and norms of behavior as part of their training, usually desire greater freedom and autonomy and dislike close supervision.

Flexible structures, characterized by decentralized authority and empowered employees, are well suited to the needs of highly skilled people. Similarly, when people work in teams, they must be allowed to interact freely and develop norms to guide their own work interactions, which also is possible in a flexible organizational structure. Thus, when designing organizational structure and culture, managers must pay close attention to the needs of the workforce and to the complexity and kind of work employees perform.

In summary, an organization's external environment, strategy, technology, and human resources are the factors to be considered by managers seeking to design the best structure and culture for an organization. The greater the level of uncertainty in the organization's environment, the more complex its strategy and technologies, and the more highly qualified and skilled its workforce, the more likely managers are to design a structure and a culture that are flexible, can change quickly, and allow employees to be innovative in their responses to problems, customer needs, and so on. The more stable the organization's environment, the less complex and more well understood its strategy or technology, and the less skilled its workforce, the more likely managers are to design an organizational structure that is formal and controlling and a culture whose values and norms prescribe how employees should act in particular situations.

Later in the chapter we discuss how managers can create different kinds of organizational cultures. First, however, we discuss how managers can design flexible or formal organizational structures. The way an organization's structure works depends on the organizing choices managers make about three issues:

- How to group tasks into individual jobs.
- How to group jobs into functions and divisions.
- How to allocate authority and coordinate or integrate functions and divisions.

Grouping Tasks into Jobs: Job Design

job design The process by which managers decide how to divide tasks into specific jobs.

The first step in organizational design is **job design**, the process by which managers decide how to divide into specific jobs the tasks that have to be performed to provide customers with goods and services. Managers at McDonald's, for example, have decided how best to divide the tasks required to provide customers with fast, cheap food in each McDonald's restaurant. After experimenting with different job arrangements, McDonald's managers decided on a basic division of labor among chefs and food servers. Managers allocated all the tasks involved in actually cooking the food (putting oil in the fat fryers, opening packages of frozen french fries, putting beef patties on the grill, making salads, and so on) to the job of chef. They allocated all the tasks involved in giving the food to customers (such as greeting customers, taking orders, putting fries and burgers into bags, adding salt, pepper, and napkins, and taking money) to food servers. In addition, they created other jobs—the job of dealing with drive-through customers, the job of keeping the restaurant clean, and the job of overseeing employees and responding to unexpected events. The result of the job design process is a *division of labor* among employees, one that McDonald's managers have discovered through experience is most efficient.

At Subway, the roles of chef and server are combined into one, making the job "larger" than the jobs of McDonald's more specialized food servers. The idea behind job enlargement is that increasing the range of tasks performed by the worker will reduce boredom.

Establishing an appropriate division of labor among employees is a critical part of the organizing process, one that is vital to increasing efficiency and effectiveness. At McDonald's, the tasks associated with chef and food server were split into different jobs because managers found that, for the kind of food McDonald's serves, this approach was most efficient. It is efficient because when each employee is given fewer tasks to perform (so that each job becomes more specialized), employees become more productive at performing the tasks that constitute each job.

At Subway sandwich shops, however, managers chose a different kind of job design. At Subway there is no division of labor among the people who make the sandwiches, wrap the sandwiches, give them to customers, and take the money. The roles of chef and food server are combined into one. This different division of tasks and jobs is efficient for Subway and not for McDonald's because Subway serves a limited menu of mostly submarine-style sandwiches that are prepared to order. Subway's production system is far simpler than McDonald's; McDonald's menu is much more varied, and its chefs must cook many different kinds of foods. In 2010, however, Subway announced that it would start its own breakfast menu to increase its product sales.

job simplification The process of reducing the number of tasks that each worker performs.

Managers of every organization must analyze the range of tasks to be performed and then create jobs that best allow the organization to give customers the goods and services they want. In deciding how to assign tasks to individual jobs, however, managers must be careful not to take **job simplification**, the process of reducing the number of tasks that each worker performs, too far.[12] Too much job simplification may reduce efficiency rather than increase it if workers find their simplified jobs boring and monotonous, become demotivated and unhappy, and, as a result, perform at a low level.

Job Enlargement and Job Enrichment

In an attempt to create a division of labor and design individual jobs to encourage workers to perform at a higher level and be more satisfied with their work, several researchers have proposed ways other than job simplification to group tasks into jobs: job enlargement and job enrichment.

job enlargement Increasing the number of different tasks in a given job by changing the division of labor.

Job enlargement is increasing the number of different tasks in a given job by changing the division of labor.[13] For example, because Subway food servers make the food as well as serve it, their jobs are "larger" than the jobs of McDonald's food servers. The idea behind job enlargement is that increasing the range of tasks performed by a worker will reduce boredom and fatigue and may increase motivation to perform at a high level—increasing both the quantity and the quality of goods and services provided, as the following "Management Insight" box suggests.

Dick's Drive-In Restaurants

Dick's Drive-In Restaurants are a five-store family-owned hamburger chain based in Seattle, Washington. Founded in 1954, its owners have pursued an innovative approach to retaining hard-working employees in the fast-food industry—an industry known for its high level of employee turnover rates.[14] From the beginning, Dick's decided to pay its employees well above the industry average and offer them many benefits, too. Dick's pays its 150 part-time employees $11 an hour, covers 100% of the cost of employees' health insurance and if they work at Dick's for more than six months up to $10,000 toward the cost of their four-year college tuition!

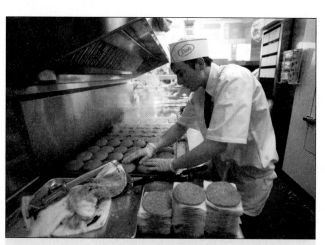

Serving up extraordinary employee benefits along with the burgers, Dick's Drive-In sets the bar high against its larger competitors and proves that looking after one's own pays off!

Dick's competitors, on the other hand—national hamburger chains like Wendy's and McDonald's—pay their part-time employees at the minimum wage of $7.25 an hour and offer them no health insurance or benefits—certainly nothing that can compare to Dick's. When asked why Dick's adopts this approach, Jim Spady, its vice president, answered, "We've been around since 1954 and one thing we've always believed is that there is nothing more important than finding and training and keeping the best people you possibly can."[15] The way to do this is by creating a work structure and culture that motivate and encourage employees to perform at a high level.

Dick's approach to managing its culture begins when it recruits new hires straight from high school. Its managers emphasize that they are looking for hard work and long-term commitment from employees. They stress further that in return Dick's will help and support employees by providing them with above-average pay, health care insurance, and tuition money while they work their way through school. Dick's expects its employees to perform to the best of their abilities to get its burgers, and its customers, out the door as fast as they can. Work-wise employees are expected to perform all of the various tasks involved in the burger restaurant such as taking orders, cooking the food, and cleaning up the premises. When performing their work, Dick's employees don't wait to be asked to do something; they know what to do to provide customers with the freshest burger Seattle has to offer.

Dick's approach to organizing leads to high performance and low turnover that keep operating costs low. Furthermore, Dick's managers have discovered that if employees stay for at least six months, its lower operating costs more than compensate for the extra pay and benefits employees receive. Dick's approach has therefore created a *win-win* situation for the company and its employees. If a person has to work their way through college, then Dick's seems to be a good place to do it.[16]

job enrichment Increasing the degree of responsibility a worker has over his or her job.

Job enrichment is increasing the degree of responsibility a worker has over a job by, for example, (1) empowering workers to experiment to find new or better ways of doing the job, (2) encouraging workers to develop new skills, (3) allowing workers to decide how to do the work and giving them the responsibility for deciding how to respond to unexpected situations, and (4) allowing workers to monitor and measure their own performance.[17] The idea behind job enrichment is that increasing workers' responsibility increases their involvement in their jobs and thus improves their interest in the quality of the goods they make or the services they provide—an approach that Dick's restaurant managers follow.

301

In general, managers who make design choices that increase job enrichment and job enlargement are likely to increase the degree to which people behave flexibly rather than rigidly or mechanically. Narrow, specialized jobs are likely to lead people to behave in predictable ways; workers who perform a variety of tasks and who are allowed and encouraged to discover new and better ways to perform their jobs are likely to act flexibly and creatively. Thus managers who enlarge and enrich jobs create a flexible organizational structure, and those who simplify jobs create a more formal structure. If workers are grouped into self-managed work teams, the organization is likely to be flexible because team members provide support for each other and can learn from one another.

LO10-3 Describe the types of organizational structures managers can design, and explain why they choose one structure over another.

The Job Characteristics Model

J. R. Hackman and G. R. Oldham's job characteristics model is an influential model of job design that explains in detail how managers can make jobs more interesting and motivating.[18] Hackman and Oldham's model (see Figure 10.2) also describes the likely personal and organizational outcomes that will result from enriched and enlarged jobs.

According to Hackman and Oldham, every job has five characteristics that determine how motivating the job is. These characteristics determine how employees react to their work and lead to outcomes such as high performance and satisfaction and low absenteeism and turnover:

- *Skill variety:* The extent to which a job requires that an employee use a wide range of different skills, abilities, or knowledge. Example: The skill variety required by the job of a research scientist is higher than that called for by the job of a McDonald's food server.

- *Task identity:* The extent to which a job requires that a worker perform all the tasks necessary to complete the job, from the beginning to the end of the production process. Example: A craftsworker who takes a piece of wood and transforms it into a custom-made desk has higher task identity than does a worker who performs only one of the numerous operations required to assemble a flat-screen TV.

- *Task significance:* The degree to which a worker feels his or her job is meaningful because of its effect on people inside the organization, such as coworkers, or on people outside the organization, such as customers. Example: A teacher who sees the effect of his or her efforts in a well-educated and well-adjusted student enjoys high task significance compared to a dishwasher who monotonously washes dishes as they come to the kitchen.

- *Autonomy:* The degree to which a job gives an employee the freedom and discretion needed to schedule different tasks and decide how to carry them out. Example: Salespeople who have to plan their schedules and decide how to allocate their time among

Figure 10.2

The Job Characteristics Model

Source: J. Richard Hackman and Greg R. Oldham, *Work Redesign,* 1st edition, © 1980. Reproduced by permission of Pearson Education, Inc., Upper Saddle River, New Jersey.

different customers have relatively high autonomy compared to assembly-line workers, whose actions are determined by the speed of the production line.

* *Feedback:* The extent to which actually doing a job provides a worker with clear and direct information about how well he or she has performed the job. Example: An air traffic controller whose mistakes may result in a midair collision receives immediate feedback on job performance; a person who compiles statistics for a business magazine often has little idea of when he or she makes a mistake or does a particularly good job.

Hackman and Oldham argue that these five job characteristics affect an employee's motivation because they affect three critical psychological states (see Figure 10.2). The more employees feel that their work is *meaningful* and that they are *responsible for work outcomes and responsible for knowing how those outcomes affect others,* the more motivating work becomes and the more likely employees are to be satisfied and to perform at a high level. Moreover, employees who have jobs that are highly motivating are called on to use their skills more and to perform more tasks, and they are given more responsibility for doing the job. All of the foregoing are characteristic of jobs and employees in flexible structures where authority is decentralized and where employees commonly work with others and must learn new skills to complete the range of tasks for which their group is responsible.

Grouping Jobs into Functions and Divisions: Designing Organizational Structure

Once managers have decided which tasks to allocate to which jobs, they face the next organizing decision: how to group jobs together to best match the needs of the organization's environment, strategy, technology, and human resources. Typically managers first decide to group jobs into departments and then design a *functional structure* to use organizational resources effectively. As an organization grows and becomes more difficult to control, managers must choose a more complex organizational design, such as a divisional structure or a matrix or product team structure. The different way in which managers can design organizational structure are discussed next. Selecting and designing an organizational structure to increase efficiency and effectiveness is a significant challenge. As noted in Chapter 8, managers reap the rewards of a well-thought-out strategy only if they choose the right type of structure to implement the strategy. The ability to make the right kinds of organizing choices is often what differentiates effective from ineffective managers and creates a high-performing organization.

Functional Structure

A *function* is a group of people, working together, who possess similar skills or use the same kind of knowledge, tools, or techniques to perform their jobs. Manufacturing, sales, and research and development are often organized into functional departments. A **functional structure** is an organizational structure composed of all the departments that an organization requires to produce its goods or services. Figure 10.3 shows the functional structure that Pier 1 Imports, the home furnishings company, uses to supply its customers with a range of goods from around the world to satisfy their desires for new and innovative products.

Pier 1's main functions are finance and administration, merchandising (purchasing the goods), stores (managing the retail outlets), planning and allocations (managing marketing, credit, and product distribution), and human resources. Each job inside a function exists because it helps the function perform the activities necessary for high organizational performance. Thus within the planning and allocations function are all the jobs necessary to efficiently advertise Pier 1's products to increase their appeal to customers (such as promotion, photography, and visual communication) and then to distribute and transport the products to stores.

There are several advantages to grouping jobs according to function. First, when people who perform similar jobs are grouped together, they can learn from observing one another and thus become more specialized and can perform at a higher level. The tasks associated with

functional structure An organizational structure composed of all the departments that an organization requires to produce its goods or services.

Figure 10.3
The Functional Structure of Pier 1 Imports

one job often are related to the tasks associated with another job, which encourages cooperation within a function. In Pier 1's planning department, for example, the person designing the photography program for an ad campaign works closely with the person responsible for designing store layouts and with visual communication experts. As a result, Pier 1 is able to develop a strong, focused marketing campaign to differentiate its products.

Second, when people who perform similar jobs are grouped together, it is easier for managers to monitor and evaluate their performance.[19] Imagine if marketing experts, purchasing experts, and real estate experts were grouped together in one function and supervised by a manager from merchandising. Obviously the merchandising manager would not have the expertise to evaluate all these different people appropriately. A functional structure allows workers to evaluate how well coworkers are performing their jobs, and if some workers are performing poorly, more experienced workers can help them develop new skills.

Finally, managers appreciate functional structure because it lets them create the set of functions they need to scan and monitor the competitive environment and obtain information about how it is changing.[20] With the right set of functions in place, managers are in a good position to develop a strategy that allows the organization to respond to its changing situation. Employees in the marketing group can specialize in monitoring new marketing developments that will allow Pier 1 to better target its customers. Employees in merchandising can monitor all potential suppliers of home furnishings both at home and abroad to find the goods most likely to appeal to Pier 1's customers and manage Pier 1's global supply chain.

Pier 1 organizes its operations by function, which means that employees can more easily learn from one another and improve the service they provide to its customers.

As an organization grows, and particularly as its task environment and strategy change because it is beginning to produce a wider range of goods and services for different kinds of customers, several problems can make a functional structure less efficient and effective.[21] First, managers in different functions may find it more difficult to communicate and coordinate with one another when they are responsible for several different kinds of products, especially as the organization grows both domestically and internationally. Second, functional managers may become so preoccupied with supervising their own specific departments and achieving their departmental goals that they lose sight of organizational goals. If that happens, organizational effectiveness will suffer because managers will be viewing issues and problems facing the organization only from their own, relatively narrow, departmental perspectives.[22] Both of these problems can reduce efficiency and effectiveness.

Divisional Structures: Product, Market, and Geographic

divisional structure An organizational structure composed of separate business units within which are the functions that work together to produce a specific product for a specific customer.

As the problems associated with growth and diversification increase over time, managers must search for new ways to organize their activities to overcome the problems associated with a functional structure. Most managers of large organizations choose a **divisional structure** and create a series of business units to produce a specific kind of product for a specific kind of customer. Each *division* is a collection of functions or departments that work together to produce the product. The goal behind the change to a divisional structure is to create smaller, more manageable units within the organization. There are three forms of divisional structure (see Figure 10.4).[23] When managers organize divisions according to the *type of good or service* they provide, they adopt a product structure. When managers organize divisions according to the *area of the country or world* they operate in, they adopt a geographic structure. When managers organize divisions according to *the type of customer* they focus on, they adopt a market structure.

PRODUCT STRUCTURE   Imagine the problems that managers at Pier 1 would encounter if they decided to diversify into producing and selling cars, fast food, and health insurance—in addition to home furnishings—and tried to use their existing set of functional managers to

Figure 10.4
Product, Market, and Geographic Structures

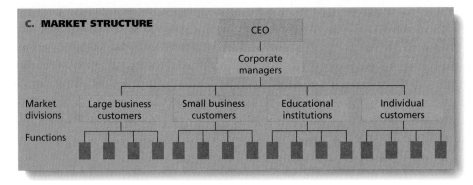

oversee the production of all four kinds of products. No manager would have the necessary skills or abilities to oversee those four products. No individual marketing manager, for example, could effectively market cars, fast food, health insurance, and home furnishings at the same time. To perform a functional activity successfully, managers must have experience in specific markets or industries. Consequently, if managers decide to diversify into new industries or to expand their range of products, they commonly design a product structure to organize their operations (see Figure 10.4a).

product structure An organizational structure in which each product line or business is handled by a self-contained division.

Using a **product structure**, managers place each distinct product line or business in its own self-contained division and give divisional managers the responsibility for devising an appropriate business-level strategy to allow the division to compete effectively in its industry or market.[24] Each division is self-contained because it has a complete set of all the functions—marketing, R&D, finance, and so on—that it needs to produce or provide goods or services efficiently and effectively. Functional managers report to divisional managers, and divisional managers report to top or corporate managers.

Grouping functions into divisions focused on particular products has several advantages for managers at all levels in the organization. First, a product structure allows functional managers to specialize in only one product area, so they can build expertise and fine-tune their skills in this particular area. Second, each division's managers can become experts in their industry; this expertise helps them choose and develop a business-level strategy to differentiate

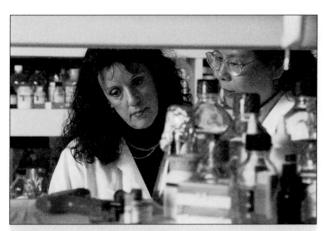

When Glaxo Wellcome and SmithKline Beecham merged, managers resolved the problem of how to coordinate the activities of thousands of research scientists by organizing them into product divisions focusing on clusters of diseases.

their products or lower their costs while meeting the needs of customers. Third, a product structure frees corporate managers from the need to supervise directly each division's day-to-day operations; this latitude lets corporate managers create the best corporate-level strategy to maximize the organization's future growth and ability to create value. Corporate managers are likely to make fewer mistakes about which businesses to diversify into or how to best expand internationally, for example, because they can take an organization-wide view.[25] Corporate managers also are likely to evaluate better how well divisional managers are doing, and they can intervene and take corrective action as needed.

The extra layer of management, the divisional management layer, can improve the use of organizational resources. Moreover, a product structure puts divisional managers close to their customers and lets them respond quickly and appropriately to the changing task environment. One pharmaceutical company that successfully adopted a new product structure to better organize its activities is GlaxoSmithKline.

The need to innovate new kinds of prescription drugs to boost performance is a continual battle for pharmaceutical companies. In the 2000s many of these companies have been merging to try to increase their research productivity, and one of them, GlaxoSmithKline, was created from the merger between Glaxo Wellcome and SmithKline Beecham.[26] Prior to the merger, both companies experienced a steep decline in the number of new prescription drugs their scientists were able to invent. The problem facing the new company's top managers was how to best use and combine the talents of the scientists and researchers from both of the former companies to allow them to quickly innovate exciting new drugs.

Top managers realized that after the merger there would be enormous problems associated with coordinating the activities of the thousands of research scientists who were working on hundreds of different kinds of drug research programs. Understanding the problems associated with large size, the top managers decided to group the researchers into eight product divisions to allow them to focus on particular clusters of diseases such as heart disease or viral infections. The members of each product division were told they would be rewarded based on the number of new prescription drugs they were able to invent and the speed with which they could bring these new drugs to the market. GlaxoSmithKline's new product structure worked well; its research productivity doubled after the reorganization, and a record number of new drugs moved into clinical trials.[27]

GEOGRAPHIC STRUCTURE   When organizations expand rapidly both at home and abroad, functional structures can create special problems because managers in one central location may find it increasingly difficult to deal with the different problems and issues that may arise in each region of a country or area of the world. In these cases, a **geographic structure**, in which divisions are broken down by geographic location, is often chosen (see Figure 10.4b). To achieve the corporate mission of providing next-day mail service, Fred Smith, CEO of FedEx, chose a geographic structure and divided up operations by creating a division in each region. Large retailers such as Macy's, Neiman Marcus, and Brooks Brothers also use a geographic structure. Because the needs of retail customers differ by region—for example, shorts in California and down parkas in the Midwest—a geographic structure gives retail regional managers the flexibility they need to choose the range of products that best meets the needs of regional customers.

geographic structure An organizational structure in which each region of a country or area of the world is served by a self-contained division.

In adopting a *global geographic structure,* such as shown in Figure 10.5a, managers locate different divisions in each of the world regions where the organization operates. Managers are most likely to do this when they pursue a multidomestic strategy because customer needs vary widely by country or world region. For example, if products that appeal to U.S. customers do not sell in Europe, the Pacific Rim, or South America, managers must customize the products to meet the needs of customers in those different world regions; a global geographic structure with global divisions will allow them to do this. For example, food and beverage companies need to customize the taste of their products to closely match the desires of customers in different countries and world regions. Although this approach sometimes works well, it can also result in a disaster, as the following "Managing Globally" box discusses.

Managing Globally

Avon's Global Geographic Structure Results in a Disaster

After a decade of profitable growth, Avon suddenly began to experience falling global sales in the mid-2000s both in developing markets in Central Europe, Russia, and China, a major source of its rising sales, and in the United States and Mexico. Avon's stock price plunged in 2007 and its CEO Andrea Jung was shocked by this turn of events.[28] After several months jetting around the globe to visit the managers of its different global divisions, Jung came to a surprising conclusion: Avon's rapid global expansion had given these managers too much autonomy. They had gained so much authority to control operations in their respective geographic regions or countries that they now made decisions to benefit their own divisions—and these decisions had hurt the performance of the whole company.

Avon's country-level managers from Poland to Mexico ran their own factories, made their own product development decisions, and developed their own advertising campaigns. And these decisions were often based on poor marketing knowledge and with little concern for operating costs; their goal was to increase sales as fast as possible. Also, when too much authority is decentralized to managers lower in an organization's hierarchy, these managers often recruit more managers to help them build their country "empires." The result was that Avon's global organizational hierarchy had exploded—it had risen from 7 levels to 15 levels of managers in a decade as tens of thousands of extra managers were hired around the globe.[29]

Sherilyn McCoy, Avon's new CEO, inherited more than just her title from her predecessor Andrea Jung. Continuing Jung's cuts of managerial positions and needless products while fending off takeover attempts gives McCoy's position a fresh challenge each day.

Jung realized she had to lay off thousands of Avon's global managers and restructure its organizational hierarchy to reduce costs and increase profitability. She embarked on a program to take away the authority of Avon's country-level managers and transfer authority to managers in charge of global product divisions who were located at corporate headquarters to streamline decision making and reduce costs. She cut out seven levels of management and laid off 25% of Avon's global managers in its 114 worldwide markets. Then, using teams of expert product group managers from corporate headquarters, she examined the way Avon operated to find out how Avon's operating costs could be slashed. In Mexico one team found that country managers' desire to expand their empires led to the development of a staggering 13,000 different products! Not only had this led product development costs to soar; it had also caused major marketing problems—how could Avon's Mexican sales reps learn about the differences between so many products to help customers choose the right ones for them? In Avon's new structure, the goal is to centralize all major new product development.

Jung and all her managers were focused on making operational decisions in the best interests of the whole company, but their continuing efforts to streamline the company's organizational structure failed and losses continued to increase. Continuing efforts to restructure and downsize the company and realign its global value chain operations were not enough to turn the company around. In 2012, after rising shareholder protests, Jung was replaced as CEO by Sherilyn S. McCoy, formerly head of consumer products at Johnson & Johnson.[30] However, its stock price had fallen so low it became a takeover target and perfume maker Coty offered $10.7 billion to buy Avon, which had been valued at $45 billion in 2008! Clearly, losing control of a company's structure can be disastrous.

In contrast, to the degree that customers abroad are willing to buy the same kind of product or slight variations thereof, managers are more likely to pursue a global strategy. In this case they are more likely to use a global product structure. In a *global product structure,* each product division, not the country and regional managers, takes responsibility for deciding where to manufacture its products and how to market them in countries worldwide (see Figure 10.5b). Product division managers manage their own global value chains and decide where to establish foreign subsidiaries to distribute and sell their products to customers in foreign countries.

MARKET STRUCTURE Sometimes the pressing issue facing managers is to group functions according to the type of customer buying the product in order to tailor the products the organization offers to each customer's unique demands. A PC maker such as Dell, for example, has several kinds of customers, including large businesses (which might demand networks of computers linked to a mainframe computer), small companies (which may need just a few PCs linked together), educational users in schools and universities (which might want thousands of independent PCs for their students), and individual users (who may want a high-quality multimedia PC so they can play the latest video games).

market structure An organizational structure in which each kind of customer is served by a self-contained division; also called *customer structure.*

To satisfy the needs of diverse customers, a company might adopt a **market structure**, which groups divisions according to the particular kinds of customers they serve (see Figure 10.4c). A market structure lets managers be responsive to the needs of their customers and allows them to act flexibly in making decisions in response to customers' changing needs. To spearhead its turnaround, for example, Dell created four streamlined market divisions that each focus on being responsive to one particular type of customer: individual consumers, small businesses, large companies, and government and state agencies. All kinds of organizations need to continually evaluate their structures, as is suggested in the following "Management Insight" box that examines how a major school district increased its performance.

Figure 10.5

Global Geographic and Global Product Structures

Management
Insight

A School District Moves from
a Geographic to a Market Structure

Like all organizations, state and city government agencies such as school districts may become too tall and bureaucratic over time and, as they grow, develop ineffective and inefficient organizational structures. This happened to the Houston Independent School District (HISD) when the explosive growth of the city during the last decades added over a million new students to school rolls. As Houston expanded many miles in every direction to become the fourth largest U.S. city, successive HISD superintendents adopted a geographic structure to coordinate and control all the teaching functions involved in creating high-performing elementary, middle, and high schools. The HISD eventually created five different geographic regions or regional school districts. And over time each regional district sought to control more of its own functional activities and became increasingly critical of HISD's central administration. The result was a slowdown in decision making, infighting between districts, an increasingly ineffectual team of district administrators, and falling student academic test scores across the city.

In 2010 a new HISD superintendent was appointed who, working on the suggestions of HISD's top managers, decided to reorganize HISD into a market structure. HISD's new organizational structure is now grouped by the needs of its customers— its students—and three "chief officers" oversee all of Houston's high schools, middle schools, and elementary schools, respectively. The focus will now be on the needs of its three types of students, not on the needs of the former five regional managers. Over 270 positions were eliminated in this restructuring, saving over $8 million per year, and many observers hope to see more cost savings ahead.

Many important support functions were recentralized to HISD's headquarters office to eliminate redundancies and reduce costs, including teacher professional development. Also, a new support function called school improvement was formed with managers charged to share ideas and information between schools and oversee their performance on many dimensions to improve service and student performance. HISD administrators also hope that eliminating the regional geographic structure will encourage schools to share best practices and cooperate so that student education and test scores will improve over time.

Matrix and Product Team Designs

Moving to a product, market, or geographic divisional structure allows managers to respond more quickly and flexibly to the particular circumstances they confront. However, when information technology or customer needs are changing rapidly and the environment is uncertain, even a divisional structure may not give managers enough flexibility to respond to the environment quickly. To operate effectively under these conditions, managers must design the most flexible kind of organizational structure available: a matrix structure or a product team structure (see Figure 10.6).

matrix structure An organizational structure that simultaneously groups people and resources by function and by product.

MATRIX STRUCTURE In a **matrix structure**, managers group people and resources in two ways simultaneously: by function and by product.[31] Employees are grouped by *functions* to allow them to learn from one another and become more skilled and productive. In addition, employees are grouped into *product teams* in which members of different functions work together to develop a specific product. The result is a complex network of reporting relationships among product teams and functions that makes the matrix structure very flexible (see Figure 10.6a). Each person in a product team reports to two managers: (1) a functional boss, who assigns individuals to a team and evaluates their performance from a functional perspective, and (2) the boss of the product team, who evaluates their performance on the team. Thus team members are known as *two-boss employees*. The functional employees

Figure 10.6

Matrix and Product Team Structures

assigned to product teams change over time as the specific skills that the team needs change. At the beginning of the product development process, for example, engineers and R&D specialists are assigned to a product team because their skills are needed to develop new products. When a provisional design has been established, marketing experts are assigned to the team to gauge how customers will respond to the new product. Manufacturing personnel join when it is time to find the most efficient way to produce the product. As their specific jobs are completed, team members leave and are reassigned to new teams. In this way the matrix structure makes the most use of human resources.

To keep the matrix structure flexible, product teams are empowered and team members are responsible for making most of the important decisions involved in product development.[32] The product team manager acts as a facilitator, controlling the financial resources and trying to keep the project on time and within budget. The functional managers try to ensure that the product is the best it can be to maximize its differentiated appeal.

High-tech companies that operate in environments where new product development takes place monthly or yearly have used matrix structures successfully for many years, and the need to innovate quickly is vital to the organization's survival. The flexibility afforded by a matrix structure lets managers keep pace with a changing and increasingly complex environment.[33]

PRODUCT TEAM STRUCTURE The dual reporting relationships that are at the heart of a matrix structure have always been difficult for managers and employees to deal with. Often the functional boss and the product boss make conflicting demands on team members, who do not know which boss to satisfy first. Also, functional and product team bosses may come into conflict over precisely who is in charge of which team members and for how long. To avoid these problems, managers have devised a way of organizing people and resources that still allows an organization to be flexible but makes its structure easier to operate: a product team structure.

The **product team structure** differs from a matrix structure in two ways: (1) It does away with dual reporting relationships and two-boss employees, and (2) functional employees are permanently assigned to a cross-functional team that is empowered to bring a new or redesigned product to market. A **cross-functional team** is a group of managers brought together from different departments to perform organizational tasks. When managers are grouped into cross-functional teams, the artificial boundaries between departments disappear, and a narrow focus on departmental goals is replaced with a general interest in working together to achieve organizational goals. The results of such changes have been dramatic: Ford can introduce a new model of car in two years, down from four; Black & Decker can innovate new products in months, not years; and Hallmark Cards can respond to changing customer demands for types of cards in weeks, not months.

Members of a cross-functional team report only to the product team manager or to one of his or her direct subordinates. The heads of the functions have only an informal advisory relationship with members of the product teams—the role of functional managers is only to counsel and help team members, share knowledge among teams, and provide new technological developments that can help improve each team's performance (see Figure 10.6b).[34]

Increasingly, organizations are making empowered cross-functional teams an essential part of their organizational architecture to help them gain a competitive advantage in fast-changing organizational environments. For example, Newell Rubbermaid, the well-known maker of more than 5,000 household products, moved to a product team structure because its managers wanted to speed up the rate of product innovation. Managers created 20 cross-functional teams composed of five to seven people from marketing, manufacturing, R&D, and other functions.[35] Each team focuses its energies on a particular product line, such as garden products, bathroom products, or kitchen products. These teams develop more than 365 new products a year.

product team structure An organizational structure in which employees are permanently assigned to a cross-functional team and report only to the product team manager or to one of his or her direct subordinates.

cross-functional team A group of managers brought together from different departments to perform organizational tasks.

A committee looks over an artist's work during a meeting at Hallmark in Kansas City. At Hallmark, cross-functional teams like this one can respond quickly to changing customer needs.

Coordinating Functions and Divisions

The more complex the structure a company uses to group its activities, the greater are the problems of *linking and coordinating* its different functions and divisions. Coordination becomes a problem because each function or division develops a different orientation toward the other groups that affects how it interacts with them. Each function or division comes to view the problems facing the company from its own perspective; for example, they may develop different views about the major goals, problems, or issues facing a company.

At the functional level, the manufacturing function typically has a short-term view; its major goal is to keep costs under control and get the product out the factory door on time. By contrast, the product development function has a long-term viewpoint because developing a new product is a relatively slow process and high product quality is seen as more important than low costs. Such differences in viewpoint may make manufacturing and product development managers reluctant to cooperate and coordinate their activities to meet company goals. At the divisional level, in a company with a product structure, employees may become concerned more with making *their* division's products a success than with the profitability of the entire company. They may refuse, or simply not see, the need to cooperate and share information or knowledge with other divisions.

The problem of linking and coordinating the activities of different functions and divisions becomes more acute as the number of functions and divisions increases. We look first at how managers design the hierarchy of authority to coordinate functions and divisions so that they work together effectively. Then we focus on integration and examine the different integrating mechanisms managers can use to coordinate functions and divisions.

Allocating Authority

As organizations grow and produce a wider range of goods and services, the size and number of their functions and divisions increase. To coordinate the activities of people, functions, and divisions and to allow them to work together effectively, managers must develop a clear hierarchy of authority.[36] **Authority** is the power vested in a manager to make decisions and use resources to achieve organizational goals by virtue of his or her position in an organization. The **hierarchy of authority** is an organization's *chain of command*—the relative authority that each manager has—extending from the CEO at the top, down through the middle managers and first-line managers, to the nonmanagerial employees who actually make goods or provide services. Every manager, at every level of the hierarchy, supervises one or more subordinates. The term **span of control** refers to the number of subordinates who report directly to a manager.

Figure 10.7 shows a simplified picture of the hierarchy of authority and the span of control of managers in McDonald's in 2012. At the top of the hierarchy is Jim Skinner, CEO and vice chairman of McDonald's board of directors, who took control in 2004.[37] Skinner is the manager who has ultimate responsibility for McDonald's performance, and he has the authority to decide how to use organizational resources to benefit McDonald's stakeholders.[38] Don Thompson, next in line, is president and COO and is responsible for overseeing all of McDonald's global restaurant operations. Thompson reports directly to Skinner, as does chief financial officer Peter Bensen. Unlike the other managers, Bensen is not a **line manager**, someone in the direct line or chain of command who has formal authority over people and resources. Rather, Bensen is a **staff manager**, responsible for one of McDonald's specialist functions, finance. Worldwide chief operations officer Jeff Stratton is responsible for overseeing all functional aspects of McDonald's overseas operations, which are headed by the presidents of world regions: Europe; Canada and Latin America; and Asia/Pacific, Middle East, and Africa. Jan Fields is president of McDonald's U.S. operations and reports to Thompson.

Managers at each level of the hierarchy confer on managers at the next level down the authority to decide how to use organizational resources. Accepting this authority, those lower-level managers are accountable for how well they make those decisions. Managers who make the right decisions are typically promoted, and organizations motivate managers with the prospects of promotion and increased responsibility within the chain of command.

Below Fields are the other main levels or layers in the McDonald's domestic chain of command—executive vice presidents of its West, Central, and East regions, zone managers, regional managers, and supervisors. A hierarchy is also evident in each company-owned McDonald's restaurant. At the top is the store manager; at lower levels are the first assistant, shift managers, and crew personnel. McDonald's managers have decided that this hierarchy of authority best allows the company to pursue its business-level strategy of providing fast food at reasonable prices—and its stock price has exploded in the 2000s as its performance has increased.

TALL AND FLAT ORGANIZATIONS As an organization grows in size (normally measured by the number of its managers and employees), its hierarchy of authority normally lengthens, making the organizational structure taller.

authority The power to hold people accountable for their actions and to make decisions concerning the use of organizational resources.

hierarchy of authority An organization's chain of command, specifying the relative authority of each manager.

span of control The number of subordinates who report directly to a manager.

line manager Someone in the direct line or chain of command who has formal authority over people and resources at lower levels.

staff manager Someone responsible for managing a specialist function, such as finance or marketing.

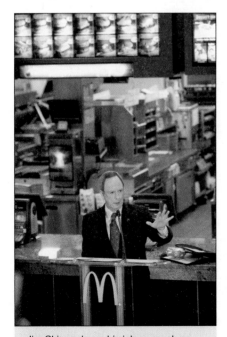

Jim Skinner loves his job as much as his customers love that secret sauce. In charge of a tall company hierarchy, he's got his eye on each Big Mac—but he's also enjoying the benefits of high stock prices as his well-oiled machine continues to dominate the fast-food industry.

Figure 10.7

The Hierarchy of Authority and Span of Control at McDonald's Corporation

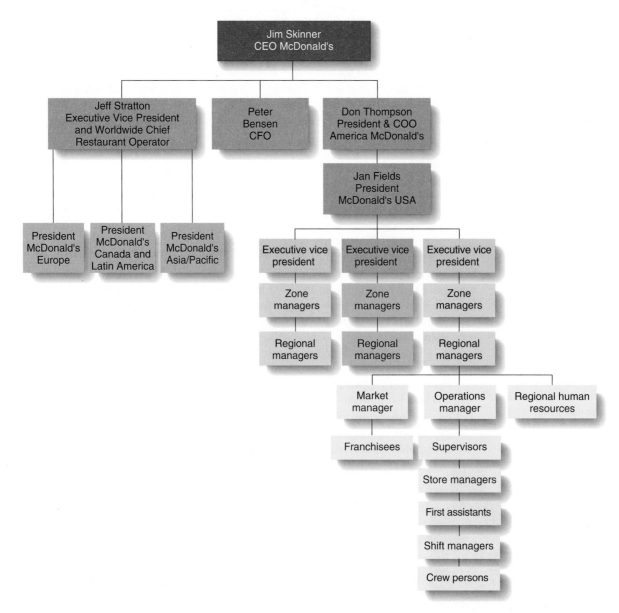

A *tall* organization has many levels of authority relative to company size; a *flat* organization has fewer levels relative to company size (see Figure 10.8).[39] As a hierarchy becomes taller, problems that make the organization's structure less flexible and slow managers' response to changes in the organizational environment may result.

Communication problems may arise when an organization has many levels in the hierarchy. It can take a long time for the decisions and orders of upper-level managers to reach managers further down in the hierarchy, and it can take a long time for top managers to learn how well their decisions worked. Feeling out of touch, top managers may want to verify that lower-level managers are following orders and may require written confirmation from them. Middle managers, who know they will be held strictly accountable for their actions, start devoting too much time to the process of making decisions to improve their chances of being right. They might even try to avoid responsibility by making top managers decide what actions to take.

Another communication problem that can result is the distortion of commands and messages being transmitted up and down the hierarchy, which causes managers at different levels to interpret what is happening differently. Distortion of orders and messages can be accidental, occurring because different managers interpret messages from their own narrow functional

Figure 10.8

Tall and Flat Organizations

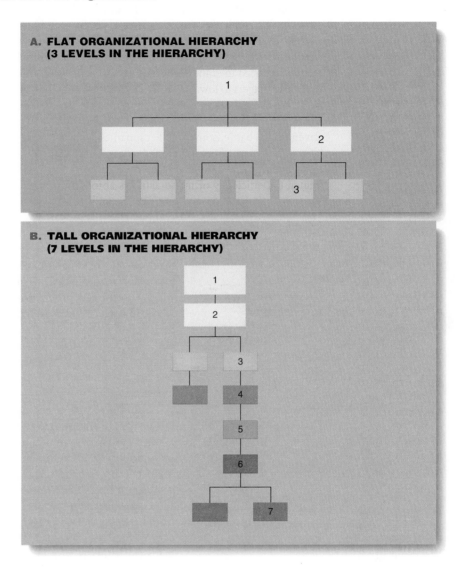

A. FLAT ORGANIZATIONAL HIERARCHY (3 LEVELS IN THE HIERARCHY)

B. TALL ORGANIZATIONAL HIERARCHY (7 LEVELS IN THE HIERARCHY)

perspectives. Or distortion can be intentional, occurring because managers low in the hierarchy decide to interpret information in a way that increases their own personal advantage.

Another problem with tall hierarchies is that they usually indicate that an organization is employing many managers, and managers are expensive. Managerial salaries, benefits, offices, and secretaries are a huge expense for organizations. Large companies such as IBM and GM pay their managers millions of dollars a year. During the current recession hundreds of thousands of managers were laid off as companies restructured and downsized their workforces to reduce costs, and they were still doing this in 2012.

THE MINIMUM CHAIN OF COMMAND   To ward off the problems that result when an organization becomes too tall and employs too many managers, top managers need to ascertain whether they are employing the right number of middle and first-line managers and whether they can redesign their organizational architecture to reduce the number of managers. Top managers might well follow a basic organizing principle—the principle of the minimum chain of command—which states that top managers should always construct a hierarchy with the fewest levels of authority necessary to efficiently and effectively use organizational resources.

Effective managers constantly scrutinize their hierarchies to see whether the number of levels can be reduced—for example, by eliminating one level and giving the responsibilities of managers at that level to managers above and by empowering employees below. One manager who constantly worked to empower employees and keep the hierarchy flat is Colleen C. Barrett, the highest-ranking woman in the airline industry until she stepped down to become its "president emeritus" in 2008.[40] At Southwest she was well known for continually reaffirming Southwest's message that employees should feel free to go above and beyond their prescribed roles to provide better customer service. Her central message was that Southwest values, trusts, and empowers its employees, who should not look to supervisors for guidance but find their own ways to do the job better. The need to empower workers is increasing as companies work to reduce the number of middle managers to lower costs and to compete with low-cost overseas competitors.

In the United States over 5 million manufacturing jobs have been lost to factories in low-cost countries abroad in the 2000s. While many large U.S. manufacturing companies have given up the battle, some small companies such as electronics maker Plexus Corp. have been able to find ways of organizing that allow them to survive and prosper in a low-cost manufacturing world. They have done this by creating empowered work teams. U.S. companies cannot match the efficiency of manufacturers abroad in producing high volumes of a single product, such as millions of a particular circuit board used in a laptop computer. So Plexus's managers decided to focus their efforts on developing a manufacturing technology called "low–high" that could efficiently produce low volumes of many different kinds of products. Plexus's managers formed a team to design an organizational structure based on creating four "focused factories" in which control over production decisions is given to the workers, whose managers cross-trained them so that they can perform all the operations involved in making a product in their "factory." Now, when work slows down at any point in the production of a particular product, a worker further along the production process can move back to help solve the problem that has arisen at the earlier stage.[41]

These two employees monitoring the progress of a circuit board production line embody cross-functional empowerment. If problems occur, they have the authority and expertise to make any changes necessary to keep the production line at full speed.

Furthermore, managers organized workers into self-managed teams that are empowered to make all the decisions necessary to make a particular product in one of the four factories. Because each product is different, the ability of the teams to make rapid decisions and respond to unexpected contingencies is vital on a production line, where time is money. At Plexus, managers, by allowing teams to experiment, have reduced changeover time from hours to as little as 30 minutes so the line is making products over 80% of the time.[42] The flexibility brought about by self-managed teams is why Plexus is so efficient and can compete against low-cost manufacturers abroad.

CENTRALIZATION AND DECENTRALIZATION OF AUTHORITY Another way in which managers can keep the organizational hierarchy flat is by **decentralizing authority**—that is, by giving lower-level managers and nonmanagerial employees the right to make important decisions about how to use organizational resources.[43] If managers at higher levels give lower-level employees the responsibility of making important decisions and only *manage by exception,* then the problems of slow and distorted communication noted previously are kept to a minimum. Moreover, fewer managers are needed because their role is not to make decisions but to act as coach and facilitator and to help other employees make the best decisions. In addition, when decision-making authority is low in the organization and near the customer, employees are better able to recognize and respond to customer needs.

decentralizing authority
Giving lower-level managers and nonmanagerial employees the right to make important decisions about how to use organizational resources.

Decentralizing authority allows an organization and its employees to behave in a flexible way even as the organization grows and becomes taller. This is why managers are so interested in empowering employees, creating self-managed work teams, establishing cross-functional teams, and even moving to a product team structure. These design innovations help keep the organizational architecture flexible and responsive to complex task and general environments, complex technologies, and complex strategies.

Although more and more organizations are taking steps to decentralize authority, *too much* decentralization has certain disadvantages. If divisions, functions, or teams are given too much decision-making authority, they may begin to pursue their own goals at the expense of organizational goals. Managers in engineering design or R&D, for example, may become so focused on making the best possible product that they fail to realize that the best product may be so expensive few people are willing or able to buy it. Also, too much decentralization can cause lack of communication among functions or divisions; this prevents the synergies of cooperation from ever materializing, and organizational performance suffers.

Top managers must seek the balance between centralization and decentralization of authority that best meets the four major contingencies an organization faces (see Figure 10.1). If managers are in a stable environment, are using well-understood technology, and are producing stable kinds of products (such as cereal, canned soup, or books), there is no pressing need to decentralize authority, and managers at the top can maintain control of much of organizational decision making.[44] However, in uncertain, changing environments where high-tech companies are producing state-of-the-art products, top managers must often empower employees and allow teams to make important strategic decisions so the organization can keep up with the changes taking place. No matter what its environment, a company that fails to control the balance between centralization and decentralization will find its performance suffering, as the example of the companies profiled in the following "Management Insight" box suggests.

Management Insight

To Decentralize and Centralize: Union Pacific and Yahoo!

Union Pacific (UP), one of the biggest railroad freight carriers in the United States, faced a crisis when an economic boom in the early 2000s led to a record increase in the amount of freight the railroad had to transport—but at the same time the railroad was experiencing record delays in moving this freight. UP's customers complained bitterly about the problem, and the delays cost the company tens of millions of dollars in penalty payments. Why the problem? UP's top managers decided to centralize authority high in the organization and to standardize operations to cut operating costs. All scheduling and route planning were handled centrally at headquarters to increase efficiency. The job of regional managers was largely to ensure the smooth flow of freight through their regions.

Recognizing that efficiency had to be balanced by the need to be responsive to customers, UP announced a sweeping reorganization. Regional managers would have the authority to make everyday operational decisions; they could alter scheduling and routing to accommodate customer requests even if it raised costs. UP's goal was to "return to excellent performance by simplifying our processes and becoming easier to deal with." In deciding to decentralize authority, UP was following the lead of its competitors that had already decentralized their operations. Its managers would continue to "decentralize decision making into the field, while fostering improved customer responsiveness, operational excellence, and personal accountability." The result has been continued success for the company; in fact, in 2010 Union Pacific was recognized as the top railroad in on-time service performance and customer service by several large companies.

Yahoo! has been forced by circumstances to pursue a different approach to decentralization. In 2009, after Microsoft failed to take over Yahoo! because of the resistance of Jerry Wang, a company founder, the company's stock price plunged. Wang, who had come under intense criticism for preventing the merger, resigned as CEO and was replaced by Carol Bartz, who had a long history of success in managing online companies. Bartz moved quickly to find ways to reduce Yahoo!'s cost structure and simplify its operations to maintain its strong online brand identity. Intense competition from the growing popularity of online companies such as Google, Facebook, and Twitter also threatened its popularity.

Bartz decided the best way to restructure Yahoo! was to recentralize authority. To gain more control over its different business units and reduce operating costs, she decided to centralize functions that had previously been performed by Yahoo!'s different business units, such as product development and marketing activities. For example, all the company's publishing and advertising functions were centralized and put under the control of a single executive. Yahoo!'s European, Asian, and emerging markets divisions were centralized, and another top executive took control. Bartz's goal was to find out how she could make the company's resources perform better. While she was centralizing authority, she was also holding many "town hall" meetings asking Yahoo! employees from all functions, "What would you do if you were me?" Even as she centralized authority to help Yahoo! recover its dominant industry position, she was looking for the input of employees at every level in the hierarchy.

Nevertheless, shareholders decided that Bartz was not moving fast enough to find ways to restructure the company. In 2011 she was replaced as CEO and a new round of massive layoffs and restructuring took place to try to focus the company on markets in which it could compete against other dot-coms that had more resources, and in 2012 the company was still in major trouble.

LO10-4 Explain why managers must coordinate jobs, functions, and divisions using the hierarchy of authority and integrating mechanisms.

Integrating and Coordinating Mechanisms

Much coordination takes place through the hierarchy of authority. However, several problems are associated with establishing contact among managers in different functions or divisions. As discussed earlier, managers from different functions and divisions may have different views about what must be done to achieve organizational goals. But if the managers have equal authority (as functional managers typically do), the only manager who can tell them what to do is the CEO, who has the ultimate authority to resolve conflicts. The need to solve everyday conflicts, however, wastes top management time and slows strategic decision making; indeed, one sign of a poorly performing structure is the number of problems sent up the hierarchy for top managers to solve.

To increase communication and coordination among functions or between divisions and to prevent these problems from emerging, top managers incorporate various **integrating mechanisms** into their organizational architecture. The greater the complexity of an organization's structure, the greater is the need for coordination among people, functions, and divisions to make the organizational structure work efficiently and effectively.[45] Thus when managers adopt a divisional, matrix, or product team structure, they must use complex integrating mechanisms to achieve organizational goals. Several integrating mechanisms are available to managers to increase communication and coordination.[46] Figure 10.9 lists these mechanisms, as well as examples of the individuals or groups who might use them.

integrating mechanisms Organizing tools that managers can use to increase communication and coordination among functions and divisions.

LIAISON ROLES   Managers can increase coordination among functions and divisions by establishing liaison roles. When the volume of contacts between two functions increases, one way to improve coordination is to give one manager in each function or division the responsibility for coordinating with the other. These managers may meet daily, weekly, monthly, or as needed. A liaison role is illustrated in Figure 10.9; the small dot represents the person within a function who has responsibility for coordinating with the other function. Coordinating is part of the liaison's full-time job, and usually an informal relationship develops between the people involved, greatly easing strains between functions. Furthermore, liaison roles provide a way of transmitting information across an organization, which is important in large organizations whose employees may know no one outside their immediate function or division.

TASK FORCES   When more than two functions or divisions share many common problems, direct contact and liaison roles may not provide sufficient coordination. In these cases, a more complex integrating mechanism, a **task force**, may be appropriate (see Figure 10.9). One manager from each relevant function or division is assigned to a task force that meets to solve a specific, mutual problem; members are responsible for reporting to their departments on the issues addressed and the solutions recommended. Task forces are often called *ad hoc committees* because they are temporary; they may meet on a regular basis or only a few times. When the problem or issue is solved, the task force is no longer needed; members return to their normal roles in their departments or are assigned to other task forces. Typically task force members also perform many of their normal duties while serving on the task force.

task force A committee of managers from various functions or divisions who meet to solve a specific, mutual problem; also called *ad hoc committee.*

Figure 10.9

Types and Examples of Integrating Mechanisms

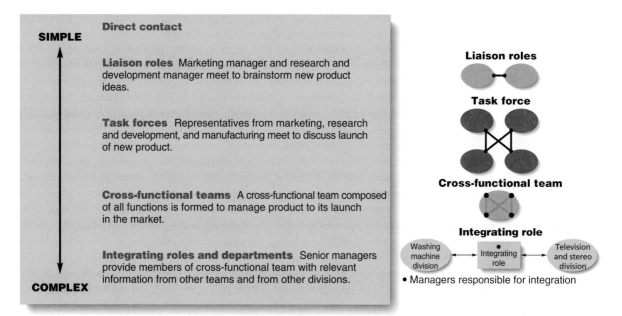

CROSS-FUNCTIONAL TEAMS   In many cases the issues addressed by a task force are recurring problems, such as the need to develop new products or find new kinds of customers. To address recurring problems effectively, managers are increasingly using permanent integrating mechanisms such as cross-functional teams. An example of a cross-functional team is a new product development committee that is responsible for the choice, design, manufacturing, and marketing of a new product. Such an activity obviously requires a great deal of integration among functions if new products are to be successfully introduced, and using a complex integrating mechanism such as a cross-functional team accomplishes this. As discussed earlier, in a product team structure people and resources are grouped into permanent cross-functional teams to speed products to market. These teams assume long-term responsibility for all aspects of development and making the product.

INTEGRATING ROLES   An integrating role is a role whose only function is to increase coordination and integration among functions or divisions to achieve performance gains from synergies. Usually managers who perform integrating roles are experienced senior managers who can envisage how to use the resources of the functions or divisions to obtain new synergies. One study found that DuPont, the giant chemical company, had created 160 integrating roles to coordinate the different divisions of the company and improve corporate performance.[47] The more complex an organization and the greater the number of its divisions, the more important integrating roles are.

In summary, to keep an organization responsive to changes in its task and general environments as it grows and becomes more complex, managers must increase coordination among functions and divisions by using complex integrating mechanisms. Managers must decide on the best way to organize their structures—that is, choose the structure that allows them to make the best use of organizational resources.

Organizational Culture

The second principal issue in organizational design is to create, develop, and maintain an organization's culture. As we discussed in Chapter 3, **organizational culture** is the shared set of beliefs, expectations, values, and norms that influence how members of an organization relate to one another and cooperate to achieve organizational goals. Culture influences the work behaviors and attitudes of individuals and groups in an organization because its members adhere

organizational culture
The shared set of beliefs, expectations, values, and norms that influence how members of an organization relate to one another and cooperate to achieve organizational goals.

to shared values, norms, and expected standards of behavior. Employees *internalize* organizational values and norms and then let these values and norms guide their decisions and actions.[48]

A company's culture is a result of its pivotal or guiding values and norms. A company's *values* are the shared standards that its members use to evaluate whether they have helped the company achieve its vision and goals. The values a company might adopt include any or all of the following standards: excellence, stability, predictability, profitability, economy, creativity, morality, and usefulness. A company's *norms* specify or prescribe the kinds of shared beliefs, attitudes, and behaviors that its members should observe and follow. Norms are informal, but powerful, rules about how employees should behave or conduct themselves in a company if they are to be accepted and help it to achieve its goals. Norms can be equally as constraining as the formal written rules contained in a company's handbook. Companies might encourage workers to adopt norms such as working hard, respecting traditions and authority, and being courteous to others; being conservative, cautious, and a "team player"; being creative and courageous and taking risks; or being honest and frugal and maintaining high personal standards. Norms may also prescribe certain specific behaviors such as keeping one's desk tidy, cleaning up at the end of the day, taking one's turn to bring doughnuts, and even wearing jeans on Fridays.

Ideally a company's norms help the company achieve its values. For example, a new computer company whose culture is based on values of excellence and innovation may try to attain this high standard by encouraging workers to adopt norms about being creative, taking risks, and working hard now and looking long-term for rewards (this combination of values and norms leads to an *entrepreneurial* culture in a company). On the other hand, a bank or insurance company that has values of stability and predictability may emphasize norms of cautiousness and obedience to authority (the result of adopting these values and norms would be a *stable, conservative* culture in a company).

Over time, members of a company learn from one another how to perceive and interpret various events that happen in the work setting and to respond to them in ways that reflect the company's guiding values and norms. This is why organizational culture is so important: When a strong and cohesive set of organizational values and norms is in place, employees focus on what is best for the organization in the long run—all their decisions and actions become oriented toward helping the organization perform well. For example, a teacher spends personal time after school coaching and counseling students; an R&D scientist works 80 hours a week, evenings, and weekends to help speed up a late project; or a salesclerk at a department store runs after a customer who left a credit card at the cash register. An interesting example of a manager who has been working hard to change a company's dysfunctional culture is profiled in the following "Manager as a Person" box.

Manager as a Person

Alan Mulally Transforms Ford's Culture

After a loss of more than $13 billion in 2006, William Ford III, who had been Ford Motor's CEO for five years, decided he was not the right person to turn around the company's performance.[49] In fact, it became apparent that he was a part of Ford's problems because he and other Ford top managers tried to build and protect their own corporate empires, and none would ever admit that mistakes had occurred over the years. As a result the whole company's performance had suffered; its future was in doubt. Finally, Ford's board of directors realized they needed an outsider to change Ford's culture and the way it operated, and they recruited Alan Mulally from Boeing to become Ford's new CEO.

After arriving at Ford, Mulally attended hundreds of executive meetings with his new managers; and at one meeting he became confused why one top division manager, who obviously did not know the answer to one of Mulally's questions concerning the performance of his car division, had rambled on for several minutes trying to disguise his ignorance. Mulally turned to his second-in-command, Mark Fields, and asked him why the

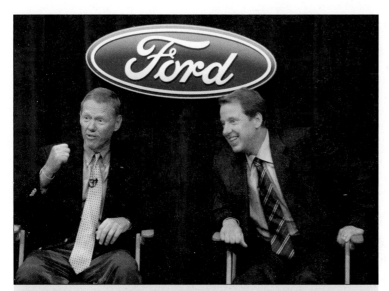

Ford CEO Alan Mulally (left), with former CEO Bill Ford (right), who realized the company needed an outsider at the helm to change Ford's insular, self-protective culture.

manager had done that. Fields explained that "at Ford you never admit when you don't know something." He also told Mulally that when he arrived as a middle manager at Ford and wanted to ask his boss to lunch to gain information about divisional operations, he was told, "What rank are you at Ford? Don't you know that a subordinate never asks a superior to lunch?"[50]

It turned out that over the years Ford had develop a tall hierarchy composed of managers whose main goal was to protect their turf and avoid any direct blame for its plunging car sales. When asked why car sales were falling, they did not admit to bad design and poor quality issues in their divisions; instead they hid in the details. They brought thick notebooks and binders to meetings, listing the high prices of components and labor costs to explain why their own particular car models were not selling well—or even why they had to be sold at a loss. Why, Mulally wondered, did Ford's top executives have this inward-looking, destructive mind-set?

Mulally soon realized the problem was the values and norms in Ford's culture that had created a situation in which the managers of its different divisions and functions thought the best way to maintain their jobs, salaries, and status was to hoard, rather than share, information. Thus values and norms of secrecy and ambiguity, and of emphasizing status and rank, to protect their information had developed. The reason only the boss could ask a subordinate to lunch was to allow superiors to protect their information and positions. Ford's culture allowed managers to hide their problems and poor performance. What could Mulally do? He issued a direct order that the managers of every division should share with every other Ford division a detailed statement of the costs they incurred to build each of its vehicles. He insisted that each of Ford's divisional presidents should attend a weekly (rather than a monthly) meeting to share and discuss openly the problems all the company's divisions faced. He also told them they should bring a different subordinate with them to each meeting so every manager in the hierarchy would learn of the problems that had been kept hidden.[51]

Essentially, Mulally's goal was to demolish the dysfunctional values and norms of Ford's culture that focused managers' attention on their own empires at the expense of the whole company. No longer would they be allowed to protect their own careers at the expense of customers. Mulally's goal was to create new values and norms that it was fine to admit mistakes, share information about all aspects of model design and costs, and of course find ways to speed development and reduce costs. He also wanted to emphasize norms of cooperation within and across divisions to improve performance.

How could this situation have gone unchanged in a major car company that has been experiencing increased competition since the mid-1970s? The answer is that the norms and values of an organization's culture are difficult to change; and despite Ford's major problems, no CEO had been able to change the mind-set of the top managers in the company. Ford had become more hierarchical and bureaucratic over time as its problems increased because poor performance led managers to become more defensive and concerned with defending their empires.

By 2010 it was clear that Mulally had changed Ford's values and norms; the company finally reported a profit in the spring of 2010 and has been profitable ever since; in 2012 it was the highest performing U.S. carmaker. The managers who could not or would not conform to Ford's new culture were gone; the others had internalized the need to work towards strengthening Ford's new culture that was now focused on satisfying the needs of customers, not the needs of its top managers.

Where Does Organizational Culture Come From?

In managing organizational architecture, some important questions that arise are these: Where does organizational culture come from? Why do different companies have different cultures? Why might a culture that for many years helped an organization achieve its goals suddenly harm the organization?

Organizational culture is shaped by the interaction of four main factors: the personal and professional characteristics of people within the organization, organizational ethics, the nature of the employment relationship, and the design of its organizational structure (see Figure 10.10). These factors work together to produce different cultures in different organizations and cause changes in culture over time.

CHARACTERISTICS OF ORGANIZATIONAL MEMBERS   The ultimate source of organizational culture is the people who make up the organization. If you want to know why organizational cultures differ, look at how the characteristics of their members differ. Organizations A, B, and C develop distinctly different cultures because they attract, select, and retain people who have different values, personalities, and ethics.[52] Recall the attraction–selection–attrition model from Chapter 3. People may be attracted to an organization whose values match theirs; similarly, an organization selects people who share its values. Over time, people who do not fit in leave. The result is that people inside the organization become more similar, the values of the organization become more pronounced and clear-cut, and the culture becomes distinct from those of similar organizations.[53]

The fact that an organization's members become similar over time and come to share the same values may actually hinder their ability to adapt and respond to changes in the environment.[54] This happens when the organization's values and norms become so strong and promote so much cohesiveness in members' attitudes that the members begin to misperceive the environment, as did Ford's top managers.[55] Companies such as Ford, Google, Apple, and Microsoft need a strong set of values that emphasize innovation and hard work; they also need to be careful their success doesn't lead members to believe their company is the best

Figure 10.10
Sources of an Organization's Culture

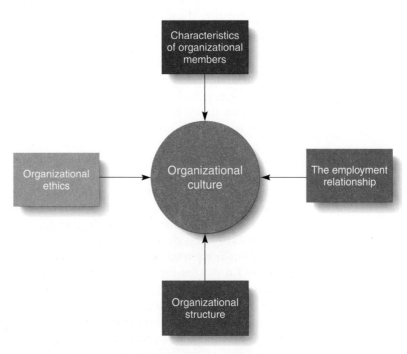

in the business. Companies frequently make this mistake. One famous example is the CEO of Digital Equipment, who in the 1990s laughed off the potential threat posed by PCs to his powerful minicomputers, claiming, "Personal computers are just toys." This company no longer exists.

ORGANIZATIONAL ETHICS The managers of an organization can set out purposefully to develop specific cultural values and norms to control how its members behave. One important class of values in this category stems from **organizational ethics**, which are the moral values, beliefs, and rules that establish the appropriate way for an organization and its members to deal with each other and with people outside the organization. Recall from Chapter 4 that ethical values rest on principles stressing the importance of treating organizational stakeholders fairly and equitably. Managers and employees are constantly making choices about the right, or ethical, thing to do; and to help them make ethical decisions, top managers purposefully implant ethical values into an organization's culture.[56] Consequently ethical values, and the rules and norms that embody them, become an integral part of an organization's culture and determine how its members will manage situations and make decisions.

organizational ethics The moral values, beliefs, and rules that establish the appropriate way for an organization and its members to deal with each other and with people outside the organization.

THE EMPLOYMENT RELATIONSHIP A third factor shaping organizational culture is the nature of the employment relationship a company establishes with its employees via its human resource policies and practices. Recall from Chapter 1 our discussion of the changing relationship between organizations and their employees due to the growth of outsourcing and employment of contingent workers. Like a company's hiring, promotion, and layoff policies, human resource policies, along with pay and benefits, can influence how hard employees will work to achieve the organization's goals, how attached they will be to the organization, and whether they will buy into its values and norms.[57] As we discuss in Chapter 12, an organization's human resource policies are a good indicator of the values in its culture concerning its responsibilities to employees. Consider the effects of a company's promotion policy, for example: A company with a policy of promoting from within will fill higher-level positions with employees who already work for the organization. On the other hand, a company with a policy of promotion from without will fill its open positions with qualified outsiders. What does this say about each organization's culture?

Promoting from within will bolster strong values and norms that build loyalty, align employees' goals with the organization, and encourage employees to work hard to advance within the organization. If employees see no prospect of being promoted from within, they are likely to look for better opportunities elsewhere, cultural values and norms result in self-interested behavior, and cooperation and cohesiveness fall. The tech sector has gone through great turmoil in recent years, and over 2 million U.S. tech employees lost their jobs during the 2000s because of outsourcing and the recession. Apple, HP, and IBM—known for their strong employee-oriented values that emphasized long-term employment and respect for employees—were among the many companies forced to lay off employees, and their cultures have changed as a result. To rebuild their cultures and make their remaining employees feel like "owners," many companies have HRM pay policies that reward superior performance with bonuses and stock options.[58] For example, Southwest Airlines and Google established companywide stock option systems that encourage their employees to be innovative and responsive to customers.

ORGANIZATIONAL STRUCTURE We have seen how the values and norms that shape employee work attitudes and behaviors derive from an organization's people, ethics, and HRM policies. A fourth source of cultural values comes from the organization's structure. *Different kinds of structure give rise to different kinds of culture;* so to create a certain culture, managers often need to design a particular type of structure. Tall and highly centralized structures give rise to totally different sets of norms, rules, and cultural values than do structures that are flat and decentralized. In a tall, centralized organization people have little personal autonomy, and norms that focus on being cautious, obeying authority, and respecting traditions emerge because predictability and stability are desired goals. In a flat, decentralized structure people have more freedom to choose and control their own activities, and norms that focus on being creative and courageous and taking risks appear, giving rise to a culture in which innovation and flexibility are desired goals.

Whether a company is centralized or decentralized also leads to the development of different kinds of cultural values. By decentralizing authority and empowering employees, an organization can establish values that encourage and reward creativity or innovation. In doing this, an organization signals employees that it's okay to be innovative and do things their own way—as long as their actions are consistent with the good of the organization. Conversely, in some organizations it is important that employees do not make decisions on their own and that their actions be open to the scrutiny of superiors. In cases like this, centralization can be used to create cultural values that reinforce obedience and accountability. For example, in nuclear power plants, values that promote stability, predictability, and obedience to authority are deliberately fostered to prevent disasters.[59] Through norms and rules, employees are taught the importance of behaving consistently and honestly, and they learn that sharing information with supervisors, especially information about mistakes or errors, is the only acceptable form of behavior.[60]

An organization that seeks to manage and change its culture must take a hard look at all four factors that shape culture: the characteristics of its members, its ethical values, its human resource policies, and its organizational structure. However, changing a culture can be difficult because of the way these factors interact and affect one another.[61] Often a major reorganization is necessary for a cultural change to occur, as we discuss in the next chapter.

Strong, Adaptive Cultures versus Weak, Inert Cultures

Many researchers and managers believe that employees of some organizations go out of their way to help the organization because it has a strong and cohesive organizational culture—an adaptive culture that controls employee attitudes and behaviors. *Adaptive cultures* are those whose values and norms help an organization to build momentum and to grow and change as needed to achieve its goals and be effective. By contrast, *inert cultures* are those whose values and norms fail to motivate or inspire employees; they lead to stagnation and, often, failure over time. What leads to a strong adaptive culture or one that is inert and hard to change?

Researchers have found that organizations with strong adaptive cultures, like 3M, UPS, Microsoft, and IBM, invest in their employees. They demonstrate their commitment to their members by, for example, emphasizing the long-term nature of the employment relationship and trying to avoid layoffs. These companies develop long-term career paths for their employees and spend a lot of money on training and development to increase employees' value to the organization. In these ways, terminal and instrumental values pertaining to the worth of human resources encourage the development of supportive work attitudes and behaviors.

In adaptive cultures employees often receive rewards linked directly to their performance and to the performance of the company as a whole. Sometimes employee stock ownership plans (ESOPs) are developed in which workers as a group are allowed to buy a significant percentage of their company's stock. Workers who are owners of the company have additional incentive to develop skills that allow them to perform highly and search actively for ways to improve quality, efficiency, and performance.

Some organizations, however, develop cultures with values that do not include protecting and increasing the worth of their human resources as a major goal. Their employment practices are based on short-term employment according to the needs of the organization and on minimal investment in employees who perform simple, routine tasks. Moreover, employees are not often rewarded on the basis of their performance and thus have little incentive to improve their skills or otherwise invest in the organization to help it achieve goals. If a company has an inert culture, poor working relationships frequently develop between the organization and its employees, and instrumental values of noncooperation, laziness, and loafing and work norms of output restriction are common.

Moreover, an adaptive culture develops an emphasis on entrepreneurship and respect for the employee and allows the use of organizational structures, such as the cross-functional team structure, that empower employees to make decisions and motivate them to succeed. By contrast, in an inert culture, employees are content to be told what to do and have little incentive or motivation to perform beyond minimum work requirements. As you might expect, the emphasis is on close supervision and hierarchical authority, which result in a culture that makes it difficult to adapt to a changing environment.

Google, discussed earlier, is a good example of a company in which managers strive to create an adaptive culture that is based on values that emphasize creativity and innovation and where decision making is pushed right down to the bottom line to teams of employees who take up the challenge of developing the advanced software and hardware for which the company is known. Bureaucracy is kept to a minimum at Google; its adaptive culture is based on informal and personal relationships and norms of cooperation and teamwork. To help strengthen its culture, Google built a futuristic open-plan campus in which its engineers can work together to innovate ever more advanced products such as its new Nexus tablet that it announced in 2012.[62] Google's cultural values and norms can't be written down but are present in the work routines that cement people together and in the language and stories its members use to orient themselves to the company.

Another company with an adaptive culture is GlaxoSmithKline, the prescription drug maker discussed earlier in the chapter. Much of GSK's success can be attributed to its ability to recruit the best research scientists because its adaptive culture nurtures scientists and emphasizes values and norms of innovation. Scientists are given great freedom to pursue intriguing ideas even if the commercial payoff is questionable. Moreover, researchers are inspired to think of their work as a quest to alleviate human disease and suffering worldwide, and GSK has a reputation as an ethical company whose values put people above profits.

Although the experience of Google and GSK suggests that organizational culture can give rise to managerial actions that ultimately benefit the organization, this is not always the case. The cultures of some organizations become dysfunctional, encouraging managerial actions that harm the organization and discouraging actions that might improve performance.[63] For example, Sunflower Electric Power, an electricity generation and transmission cooperative, almost went bankrupt in the early 2000s. A committee of inquiry set up to find the source of the problem put the blame on Sunflower's CEO and decided he had created an abusive culture based on fear and blame that encouraged managers to fight over and protect their turf—an inert culture. The CEO was fired and a new CEO was appointed to change the cooperative's culture, which he found hard to do because his top managers were so used to the old values and norms. With the help of consultants, he changed values and norms to emphasize cooperation, teamwork, and respect for others—which involved firing many top managers. Clearly, managers can influence how their organizational culture develops over time.

Summary and Review

LO10-1

DESIGNING ORGANIZATIONAL STRUCTURE   The four main determinants of organizational structure are the external environment, strategy, technology, and human resources. In general, the higher the level of uncertainty associated with these factors, the more appropriate is a flexible, adaptable structure as opposed to a formal, rigid one.

LO10-2   **GROUPING TASKS INTO JOBS**   Job design is the process by which managers group tasks into jobs. To create more interesting jobs, and to get workers to act flexibly, managers can enlarge and enrich jobs. The job characteristics model is a tool that managers can use to measure how motivating or satisfying a particular job is.

LO10-3   **ORGANIZATIONAL STRUCTURE: GROUPING JOBS INTO FUNCTIONS AND DIVISIONS**   Managers can choose from many kinds of organizational structures to make the best use of organizational resources. Depending on the specific organizing problems they face, managers can choose from functional, product, geographic, market, matrix, product team, and hybrid structures.

LO10-4   **COORDINATING FUNCTIONS AND DIVISIONS**   No matter which structure managers choose, they must decide how to distribute authority in the organization, how many levels to have in the hierarchy of authority, and what balance to strike between centralization and decentralization to keep the number of levels in the hierarchy to a minimum. As organizations grow, managers must increase integration and coordination among functions and divisions. Four integrating mechanisms that facilitate this are liaison roles, task forces, cross-functional teams, and integrating roles.

LO10-5   **ORGANIZATIONAL CULTURE**   Organizational culture is the set of values, norms, and standards of behavior that control how individuals and groups in an organization interact with one another and work to achieve organizational goals. The four main sources of organizational culture are member characteristics, organizational ethics, the nature of the employment relationship, and the design of organizational structure. How managers work to influence these four factors determines whether an organization's culture is strong and adaptive or inert and difficult to change.

Management in Action

Topics for Discussion and Action

Discussion

1. Would a flexible or a more formal structure be appropriate for these organizations? (a) A large department store, (b) a Big Five accounting firm, (c) a biotechnology company. Explain your reasoning. **[LO10-1, 10-2]**

2. Using the job characteristics model as a guide, discuss how a manager can enrich or enlarge subordinates' jobs. **[LO10-2]**

3. How might a salesperson's job or a secretary's job be enlarged or enriched to make it more motivating? **[LO10-2, 10-3]**

4. When and under what conditions might managers change from a functional to (a) a product, (b) a geographic, or (c) a market structure? **[LO10-1, 10-3]**

5. How do matrix structure and product team structure differ? Why is product team structure more widely used? **[LO10-1, 10-3, 10-4]**

6. What is organizational culture, and how does it affect the way employees behave? **[LO10-5]**

Action

7. Find and interview a manager and identify the kind of organizational structure that his or her organization uses to coordinate its people and resources. Why is the organization using that structure? Do you think a different structure would be more appropriate? Which one? **[LO10-1, 10-3, 10-4]**

8. With the same or another manager, discuss the distribution of authority in the organization. Does the manager think that decentralizing authority and empowering employees are appropriate? **[LO10-1, 10-3]**

9. Interview some employees of an organization and ask them about the organization's values and norms, the typical characteristics of employees, and the organization's ethical values and socialization practices. Using this information, try to describe the organization's culture and the way it affects how people and groups behave. **[LO10-1, 10-5]**

Building Management Skills

Understanding Organizing [LO10-1, 10-2, 10-3]

Think of an organization with which you are familiar, perhaps one you have worked for—such as a store, restaurant, office, church, or school. Then answer the following questions:

1. Which contingencies are most important in explaining how the organization is organized? Do you think it is organized in the best way?

2. Using the job characteristics model, how motivating do you think the job of a typical employee is in this organization?

3. Can you think of any ways in which a typical job could be enlarged or enriched?

4. What kind of organizational structure does the organization use? If it is part of a chain, what kind of structure does the entire organization use? What other structures discussed in the chapter might allow the organization to operate more effectively? For

example, would the move to a product team structure lead to greater efficiency or effectiveness? Why or why not?

5. How many levels are there in the organization's hierarchy? Is authority centralized or decentralized? Describe the span of control of the top manager and of middle or first-line managers.

6. Is the distribution of authority appropriate for the organization and its activities? Would it be possible to flatten the hierarchy by decentralizing authority and empowering employees?

7. What are the principal integrating mechanisms used in the organization? Do they provide sufficient coordination among individuals and functions? How might they be improved?

8. Now that you have analyzed the way this organization is structured, what advice would you give its managers to help them improve how it operates?

Managing Ethically [LO10-1, 10-3, 10-5]

Suppose an organization is downsizing and laying off many of its middle managers. Some top managers charged with deciding whom to terminate might decide to keep the subordinates they like, and who are obedient to them, rather than the ones who are difficult or the best performers. They might also decide to lay off the most highly paid subordinates even if they are high performers. Think of the ethical issues involved in designing a hierarchy, and discuss the following issues.

Questions

1. What ethical rules (see Chapter 4) should managers use to decide which employees to terminate when redesigning their hierarchy?

2. Some people argue that employees who have worked for an organization for many years have a claim on the organization at least as strong as that of its shareholders. What do you think of the ethics of this position—can employees claim to "own" their jobs if they have contributed significantly to the organization's past success? How does a socially responsible organization behave in this situation?

Small Group Breakout Exercise

Bob's Appliances [LO10-1, 10-3]

Form groups of three or four people, and appoint one member as the spokesperson who will communicate your findings to the class when called on by the instructor. Then discuss the following scenario:

Bob's Appliances sells and services household appliances such as washing machines, dishwashers, ranges, and refrigerators. Over the years, the company has developed a good reputation for the quality of its customer service, and many local builders patronize the store. However, large retailers such as Best Buy, Walmart, and Costco are also providing an increasing range of appliances. Moreover, to attract more customers these stores also carry a complete range of consumer electronics products—LCD TVs, computers, and digital devices. Bob Lange, the owner of Bob's Appliances, has decided that if he is to stay in business, he must widen his product range and compete directly with the chains.

In 2007 he decided to build a 20,000-square-foot store and service center, and he is now hiring new employees to sell and service the new line of consumer electronics. Because of his company's increased size, Lange is not sure of the best way to organize the employees. Currently he uses a functional structure; employees are divided into sales, purchasing and accounting, and repair. Bob is wondering whether selling and servicing consumer electronics is so different from selling and servicing appliances that he should move to a product structure (see the accompanying figure) and create separate sets of functions for each of his two lines of business.[64]

You are a team of local consultants whom Bob has called in to advise him as he makes this crucial choice. Which structure do you recommend? Why?

FUNCTIONAL STRUCTURE

PRODUCT STRUCTURE

Exploring the World Wide Web [LO10-3]

Go to the website of Kraft, the food services company (www.kraft.com). Click on "Corporate Information" and then explore its brands.

1. Given the way it describes its brands, what kind of divisional structure do you think Kraft uses? Why do you think it uses this structure?

2. Click on featured brands and look at products like its Oreo cookies. How is Kraft managing its different brands to increase global sales? What do you think are the main challenges Kraft faces in managing its global food business to improve performance?

3. Why did Kraft decide to split up into two different companies in 2011?

Be the Manager [LO10-1, 10-3, 10-5]

Speeding Up Website Design

You have been hired by a website design, production, and hosting company whose new animated website designs are attracting a lot of attention and many customers. Currently, employees are organized into different functions such as hardware, software design, graphic art, and website hosting, as well as functions such as marketing and human resources. Each function takes its turn to work on a new project from initial customer request to final online website hosting.

The problem the company is experiencing is that it typically takes one year from the initial idea stage to the time a website is up and running; the company wants to shorten this time by half to protect and expand its market niche. In talking to other managers, you discover that they believe the company's current functional structure is the source

of the problem—it is not allowing employees to develop websites fast enough to satisfy customers' demands. They want you to design a better structure.

Questions

1. Discuss how you can improve the way the current functional structure operates so it speeds website development.

2. Discuss the pros and cons of moving to a (a) multidivisional, (b) matrix, and (c) product team structure to reduce website development time.

3. Which of these structures do you think is most appropriate, and why?

4. What kind of culture would you help create to make the company's structure work more effectively?

Bloomberg Businessweek Case in the News [LO10-3, 10-4]

Larry Page's Google 3.0: The company co-founder and his star deputies are trying to root out bureaucracy and rediscover the nimble moves of youth.

Every Monday afternoon at the Googleplex in Mountain View, Calif., more than a dozen of Google's top executives gather in the company's boardroom. The weekly meeting, known as Execute, was launched last summer with a specific mission: to get the near-sovereign leaders of Google's far-flung product groups into a single room and harmonize their disparate initiatives. Google cofounder Sergey Brin runs the meeting, along with new Chief Executive Officer Larry Page and soon-to-be-former CEO Eric Schmidt. The unstated goal is to save the search giant from the ossification that can paralyze large corporations.

It won't be easy, because Google is a tech conglomerate, an assemblage of parts that sometimes work at cross-purposes. Among the most important barons at the meeting: Andy Rubin, who oversees the Android operating system for mobile phones; Salar Kamangar, who runs the video-sharing site YouTube; and Vic Gundotra, who heads up Google's secret project to combat the social network Facebook. "We needed to get these different product leaders together to find time to talk through all the integration points," says Page during a telephone interview with *Bloomberg BusinessWeek* minutes before a late-January Execute session. "Every time we increase the size of the company, we need to keep things going to make sure we keep our speed, pace, and passion."

The new weekly ritual—like the surprise announcement on Jan. 20 that Page will take over from Schmidt in April—marks a significant shift in strategy at the world's most famous Internet company. Welcome to Google 3.0. In the 1.0 era, which ran from 1996 to 2001, Page and Brin incubated the company at Stanford University and in a Menlo Park (Calif.) garage. In 2001 they ushered in the triumphant 2.0 era by hiring Schmidt, a tech industry grown-up who'd been CEO of Novell. Now comes the third phase, led by Page and dedicated to rooting out bureaucracy and rediscovering the nimble moves of youth.

Although Google recently reported that fourth-quarter profits jumped 29% over the previous year, its stock rose only 13.7% over the past 12 months and perhaps the most serious rap against the company: that its loosely organized structure is growing unwieldy and counterproductive. The creative chaos inside Google's halls—a decentralized jungle of innovation, as one prominent venture capitalist puts it—once empowered employees to make bold moves, such as creating Gmail, the search-based e-mail system. Other than Android, the culture has recently produced a string of flops, such as Google Buzz, a Twitter clone, and Google Wave, a wonky service that let people collaborate online.

Page doesn't explicitly blame those missteps on the company's loosely knit management or the famous troika at the top. Yet he concedes, "We do pay a price for [shared decision making], in terms of speed and people not necessarily knowing where they go to ask questions." His elevation to CEO, he says, "is really a clarification of our roles. I think it will help with our speed."

Former Google employees are encouraged. "Larry is a visionary, the kind of person that inspires people to do more, be better, reach farther," says Douglas Merrill, Google's chief information officer until 2008. "He would walk around the engineering department and, with just a word or two, guide or redirect projects and leave the developers feeling great about the coaching." Page says one of his goals is to take the decisive leadership style they have shown within their product groups, spread it across the company, and apply it to major decisions. "We've been inspired by a lot of the people who have been operating with more autonomy and clear decision-making authority," he says.

For example, Andy Rubin is as adept at creating mechanical marvels in his home as he is writing the software that runs tablets and mobile phones. His latest invention, produced with several Google colleagues, is "Java the Bot," a wheeled two-armed robot that can roll up to an espresso machine and perform all the steps needed to make a decent cup of coffee. (It's still in development.) Since Google acquired his eight-person start-up, Android, in 2005, Rubin has expended most of his entrepreneurial energy within the Googleplex. His Android platform has pulled off arguably the fastest land grab in tech history, jumping from also-ran to market leader with 26% of the smartphone market, vs. 25% for iPhone (BlackBerry was first, with 33%, but is losing ground). Android's success has made Rubin a model inside Google for how executives can run units autonomously. "We need even more of those," Page says of Android.

Because Rubin's mission to create a mobile operating system was so distinct from the rest of Google's goals, he was given unique leeway in managing his division. He can hire his own team and even controls the landscaping around his office building, which he decorates with super-sized ornaments of the desserts (éclair, cupcake) that give versions of Android their name. Google "did a very good job of giving us autonomy," Rubin says. "We can move really, really quickly." Page, Brin, and Schmidt deserve much of the credit for Google's success—but not all of it. "The key to making Google viable was the people they hired in the early days, many of whom are still there and are super-rich," says Steven Levy, author of the forthcoming book *In the Plex: How Google Thinks, Works, and Shapes Our Lives.* "They are part of the inner circle that makes the big decisions."

Over the past few years, Google has lost a stream of executives to startups, venture capital firms, and, most embarrassingly, Facebook. Sundar Pichai bucked the trend. A vice president for product management in charge of the Chrome browser, Pichai, 38, was recently courted by Twitter, the hot microblogging startup. Pichai won't say whether Google sweetened his compensation, but he confirms that he's not leaving. "I'm staying. I'm happy here," he says. "I look at this as a life journey that I've been on for a long time."

How social media will and won't change Google's world is an ongoing conversation at Google's weekly Execute meetings—and it underscores Larry Page's biggest problem as Google's new CEO. Page values strong, idiosyncratic leaders who know their domains and have their own aggressive agendas. All these rising stars have to work together. The mobile team has to coordinate with the nascent local and e-commerce groups. Rubin's app-based Android vision of the future has to square with Pichai's push for the wide-open Web of Chrome OS; and Singhal's search division has to find common ground with Vic Gundotra and the new czars of social. Can they integrate their plans while satisfying Larry Page's need for speed? At some point, Page may have to dispense with the philosophical discussions, put some limits on the open atmosphere of geeky experimentation, and make some tough decisions. It's not very "Googley." But it's the central challenge of Google 3.0.

Questions for Discussion

1. How would you describe how Google's organizational structure has developed since its founding?

2. What are some of the problems that Google has run into recently as a result of its organizational structure?

3. In what ways do you think Larry page needs to change Google's structure to make it work more effectively?

Source: B. Stone, "Larry Page's Google 3.0: The Company Co-Founder and His Star Deputies Are Trying to Root Out Bureaucracy and Rediscover the Nimble Moves of Youth," by *Bloomberg BusinessWeek,* January 26, 2011. Bloomberg L.P. Copyright © 2012. All rights reserved.

CHAPTER 11

Organizational Control and Change

Learning Objectives

After studying this chapter, you should be able to:

LO11.1 Define organizational control and explain how it increases organizational effectiveness.

LO11.2 Describe the four steps in the control process and the way it operates over time.

LO11.3 Identify the main output controls, and discuss their advantages and disadvantages as means of coordinating and motivating employees.

LO11.4 Identify the main behavior controls, and discuss their advantages and disadvantages as a means of coordinating and motivating employees.

LO11.5 Discuss the relationship between organizational control and change, and explain why managing change is a vital management task.

A MANAGER'S CHALLENGE

United Technologies Has an "ACE" Up Its Sleeve

What is the best way to control people and resources? United Technologies Corporation (UTC), based in Hartford, Connecticut, is a company that owns a wide variety of other companies that operate in different businesses and industries. Some of the companies in UTC's portfolio are better known than UTC itself, such as Sikorsky Aircraft Corporation; Pratt & Whitney, the aircraft engine and component maker; Otis Elevator Company; Carrier air conditioning; and Chubb, the security and lock maker. Today, investors frown upon companies like UTC that own and operate companies in widely different industries. There is a growing perception that managers can better run a company when it operates as an independent or stand-alone entity. How can UTC justify owning and operating all these companies under the control of a powerful team of corporate managers? UTC's CEO George David claims that he created a unique and sophisticated corporate control system that adds value *across* UTC's diverse businesses.

David joined Otis Elevator as an assistant to its CEO in 1975, but within one year Otis was acquired by UTC, which sent David to manage its South American operations and later gave him responsibility for its Japanese operations. Otis had formed an alliance with Matsushita to develop an elevator for the Japanese market, and the resulting "Elevonic 401," after being installed widely in Japanese buildings, proved to be a disaster. It broke down much more often than elevators made by other Japanese companies, and customers were concerned about its reliability and safety. Matsushita was extremely embarrassed about the elevator's failure and assigned one of its leading total quality management (TQM) experts, Yuzuru Ito, to head a team of Otis engineers to find out why it performed so poorly.

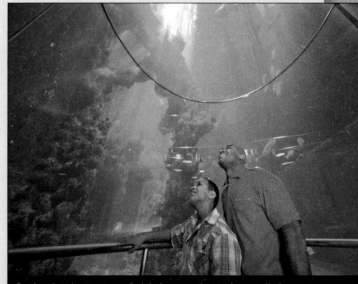

Getting the elevator to work right is not such mundane stuff after all! Here, Otis' innovations allow a father and son to enjoy a ride in an elevator that takes folks for an inside view of **The Deep,** a spectacular aquarium in Yorkshire, England.

Under Ito's direction all the employees—managers, designers, and production workers—who had produced the elevator analyzed why the elevators were malfunctioning. This intensive study led to a total redesign of the elevator, and when their new and improved elevator was launched worldwide, it met with great success. Otis's share of the global elevator market increased dramatically, and one result was that David was named president of UTC in 1992. He was given the responsibility to cut costs across the entire corporation, including its important Pratt & Whitney division, and his success in reducing UTC's operating costs led to his appointment as CEO in 1994. Responsible for all of UTC's diverse companies, David decided that the best way to increase UTC's performance, which had been falling, was to find ways to improve efficiency and quality in all its constituent companies. He convinced Ito to move to Hartford and take responsibility for championing the kinds of improvements that had by now transformed the Otis division, and Ito began to develop UTC's control system, which is known as Achieving Competitive Excellence, or ACE.

ACE is a set of tasks and procedures used by employees from the shop floor to top managers to analyze all aspects of the way a product is made. The goal is to find ways to improve quality and reliability, to lower the costs of making the product, and especially to find ways to make the next generation of a particular product perform better—in other words, to encourage technological innovation. David makes every employee in every function and at every level take responsibility for achieving the incremental, step-by-step gains that can result in innovative and efficient products that enable a company to dominate its industry.

David named these ACE techniques "process disciplines," and they are used to increase the performance of all UTC's different companies. Through these techniques he created the extra value for UTC's shareholders that justifies UTC's owning and operating such a diverse set of businesses. David and his managers believed that the gains that can be achieved from UTC's process disciplines are never-ending because its own R&D—in which it invests over $2.5 billion a year—is constantly producing product innovations that can help all its businesses. Indeed, recognizing that its skills in creating process improvements are specific to manufacturing companies, UTC's strategy is to acquire only companies that make products that can benefit from the use of its ACE program—hence, for example, its Chubb acquisition. At the same time, David only bought companies that had the potential to remain or become the leading companies in their industries. Thus while UTC uses its ACE control system to strengthen the competencies of the companies it acquires, it also ensures these acquisitions have valuable skills that can strengthen the competencies of UTC's existing businesses. David's successes can be seen in the performance that UTC achieved in the years he was in control: Its sales and profits soared and UTC is one of the top performers of the companies that make up the Dow Jones industrial average.[1]

Overview

As we discussed in Chapter 10, the first task facing managers is to establish a structure of task and job reporting relationships that allows organizational members to use resources most efficiently and effectively. Structure alone, however, does not provide the incentive or motivation for people to behave in ways that help achieve organizational goals. When managers choose how to influence, shape, and regulate the activities of organizational divisions, functions, and employees to achieve the organization's mission and goals, they establish the second foundation of organizational architecture: organizational control. An organization's structure provides the organization with a skeleton, but its control systems give it the muscles, sinews, nerves, and sensations that allow managers to regulate and govern its activities. The control systems also give managers specific feedback on how well the organization and its members are performing. The managerial functions of organizing and controlling are inseparable, and effective managers must learn to make them work together in a harmonious way.

In this chapter, we look in detail at the nature of organizational control and describe the main steps in the control process. We also discuss the different types of control systems that are available to managers to shape and influence organizational activities—*output control, behavior control,* and *clan control.*[2] Finally, we discuss the important issue of organizational change, which is possible only when managers have put in place a control system that allows them to adjust the way people and groups behave and alter or transform the way the organization operates. Control is the essential ingredient that is needed to bring about and manage organizational change efficiently and effectively. By the end of this chapter, you will appreciate the different forms of control available to managers and understand why developing an appropriate control system is vital to increasing organizational performance.

What Is Organizational Control?

As noted in Chapter 1, *controlling* is the process whereby managers monitor and regulate how efficiently and effectively an organization and its members are performing the activities necessary to achieve organizational goals. As discussed in previous chapters, when planning and organizing, managers develop the organizational strategy and structure that they hope will allow the organization to use resources most effectively to create value for customers. In controlling, managers monitor and evaluate whether the organization's strategy and structure are working as intended, how they could be improved, and how they might be changed if they are not working.

LO11-1 Define organizational control and explain how it increases organizational effectiveness.

Control, however, does not mean just reacting to events after they have occurred. It also means keeping an organization on track, anticipating events that might occur, and then changing the organization to respond to whatever opportunities or threats have been identified. Control is concerned with keeping employees motivated, focused on the important problems confronting the organization, and working together to make the changes that will help an organization improve its performance over time.

The Importance of Organizational Control

To understand the importance of organizational control, consider how it helps managers obtain superior efficiency, quality, responsiveness to customers, and innovation—the four building blocks of competitive advantage.

To determine how efficiently they are using their resources, managers must be able to accurately measure how many units of inputs (raw materials, human resources, and so on) are being used to produce a unit of output, such as a Toyota vehicle. Managers also must be able to measure how many units of outputs (goods and services) are being produced. A control system contains the measures or yardsticks that let managers assess how efficiently the organization is producing goods and services. Moreover, if managers experiment with changing how the organization produces goods and services to find a more efficient way of producing them, these measures tell managers how successful they have been. For example, when managers at UTC decided to adopt ACE process disciplines to increase quality and efficiency, they used measures such as time taken to make one unit of a product and cost savings per unit produced to evaluate how well ACE worked. Without a control system in place, managers have no idea how well their organization is performing and how its performance can be improved—information that is becoming increasingly important in today's highly competitive environment.

Today much of the competition among organizations centers on increasing the quality of goods and services. In the car industry, for example, cars within each price range compete in features, design, and reliability. Thus whether a customer buys a Ford Taurus, GM Malibu, Chrysler 300, Toyota Camry, or Honda Accord depends significantly on the design and quality of each car. Organizational control is important in determining the quality of goods and services because it gives managers feedback on product quality. If the managers of carmakers consistently measure the number of customer complaints and the number of new cars returned for repairs, or if school principals measure how many students drop out of school or how achievement scores on nationally based tests vary over time, they have a good indication of how much quality they have built into their product—whether it is an educated student or a car that does not break down. Effective managers create a control system that consistently monitors the quality of goods and services so they can continuously improve quality—an approach to change that gives them a competitive advantage. This is not always easy, even for companies that have traditionally been acknowledged as global quality leaders, as the following "Management Insight" box suggests.

Management Insight

Toyota Makes Major Improvements to Its Quality Control System

Toyota has long been known as a company that strives to improve its car design and production systems to enhance efficiency, quality, innovation, and customer responsiveness. It pioneered the system of "lean production" that changed how cars are assembled and has been imitated by all global carmakers because it dramatically improves vehicle reliability. Also, Toyota pursues total quality management that makes production-line employees responsible for continuously finding incremental improvements to work procedures that drive down costs and drive up quality. In the 2000s, under the leadership of Toyota's president, Katsuaki Watanabe, the company developed new control systems to further improve efficiency and quality and to strengthen its competitive advantage over rivals such as Volkswagen, Ford, and Mazda. For example, it implemented an advanced TQM program to improve control over various functions as its global operations grew rapidly. One new TQM manufacturing strategy was "pokayoke," or mistake-proofing, an initiative that focuses on the assembly process stages that produce the most quality problems; employees double- and triple-check operating procedures at a particular stage to discover defective parts or fix improper assembly operations that might lead to subsequent customer complaints. Another strategy was "CCC21," which involves working with suppliers to jointly develop control systems that would lower the cost of Toyota's car components by 30%; this program has saved billions of dollars in the last decade. Toyota also implemented a new manufacturing process called GBL that allowed it to build factories that can assemble several different car models on the same production line with no loss in efficiency or quality—a major competitive advantage.

Does Toyota's pokayoke process actually work? Sales of their automobiles have rebounded somewhat since the horror stories of the 2010 recalls, but only time will tell if their manufacturing controls are back on track.

Although Toyota is a world leader in developing control systems that improve value chain management, it would be a mistake to believe that its record is perfect. Over the years it made many mistakes and errors as it searched for new ways to increase innovation, quality, and efficiency. On the quality front, for example, it made mistakes when its engineers designed parts such as air-conditioning systems and airbags that proved defective and many vehicle recalls were necessary to correct them. On the efficiency front, vehicles became more difficult to assemble in the 2000s because both components and work processes became increasingly complex. And during the 2000s Toyota's managers increasingly failed to realize the need to train employees to improve their work performance and so prevent vehicle recalls. One reason was Toyota's rapid expansion around the globe.[3] In the 2000s, for example, Toyota recalled over 10 million vehicles in the United States and Japan—almost three times its previous rate. Its president, Katsuaki Watanabe, publicly apologized for these increasing errors but affirmed that Toyota was now back on the right track with many new global quality and manufacturing initiatives in place.

So it came as a tremendous shock to Toyota when in 2010 increasing reports of uncontrolled acceleration in some of its vehicles, particularly the Prius hybrid, were publicized in the global media. Stories said hundreds of drivers of Toyota vehicles had experienced this problem, and several deaths were attributed to this problem. Toyota was forced to recall more than 6 million U.S. vehicles because of problems with accelerator pedals and braking. At first the problems were attributed to floor mats becoming stuck under accelerator pedals; however, within weeks it was discovered that the design of the accelerator pedals was also faulty. By March 2010 Toyota dealers had repaired over 2 million recalled U.S. cars and trucks (50,000 a day) by shaving and adding metal shims to accelerator pedals to prevent their sticking.

The current president of Toyota, Akio Toyoda, a member of the founding family, who took up his post in 1999, publicly apologized to Toyota customers in the United States and around the world, admitting that the company had been slow to respond to the braking problems that it had been aware of for months—and which it had been working to solve. Toyoda vowed to revamp Toyota's sprawling organizational structure to improve its ability to control vital issues such as quality and safety—although these product development problems had supposedly been fixed three years earlier under the quality push by former president Watanabe.

President Toyoda admitted that Toyota's control problems have proved difficult to solve because its push to become the world's largest carmaker (it overtook GM as the global leader in 2008) had let it drift away from its core value of focusing on the customer. And Toyoda announced a new companywide control system to improve quality and reliability. Toyota would increase the number of its technology centers in North America to seven from one, as well as around the world, and recruit hundreds of new engineers to uncover potential problems with vehicle quality. Also Toyota said it would decentralize control to engineers at the front line to speed decision making so it can react more quickly to emerging quality problems.[4]

Although its quality problems led to plunging car sales in 2010, by 2011 sales had recovered. Clearly, customers believe that Toyota has learned from its mistakes and that its improved systems of output and bureaucratic control will help to reduce or prevent such design quality problems in the future.

Effective organizational control can also increase responsiveness to customers. Managers can help make their organizations more responsive to customers, for example, if they develop a control system, such as a CRM system, that allows them to evaluate how well customer contact employees perform their jobs. Monitoring employee behavior can help managers find ways to increase employees' performance levels, perhaps by revealing areas in which skill training can help employees or in which new procedures can allow employees to perform their jobs better—as UTC and carmakers such as Toyota have discovered. Also, when employees know their behaviors are being monitored, they have more incentive to be helpful and consistent in how they act toward customers. To improve customer service, for example,

Toyota regularly surveys customers about their experiences with particular Toyota dealers. If a dealership receives too many customer complaints, Toyota's managers investigate the dealership to uncover the sources of the problems and suggest solutions; if necessary, they might even threaten to reduce the number of cars a dealership receives to force the dealer to improve the quality of its customer service.

Finally, controlling can raise the level of innovation in an organization—one of the main goals of UTC's ACE system and Toyota's quality techniques. Successful innovation takes place when managers create an organizational setting in which employees feel empowered to be creative and in which authority is decentralized to employees so they feel free to experiment and take control of their work activities. Deciding on the appropriate control systems to encourage risk taking is an important management challenge; organizational culture is vital in this regard. To encourage work teams at UTC to perform at a high level, top managers monitored the performance of each team, for example, by examining how each team reduced costs or increased quality—and used a bonus system related to performance to reward each team. The team manager then evaluated each team member's individual performance, and the most innovative employees received promotions and rewards based on their superior performance.

Control Systems and IT

control systems Formal target-setting, monitoring, evaluation, and feedback systems that provide managers with information about how well the organization's strategy and structure are working.

Control systems are formal target-setting, monitoring, evaluation, and feedback systems that provide managers with information about whether the organization's strategy and structure are working efficiently and effectively.[5] Effective control systems alert managers when something is going wrong and give them time to respond to opportunities and threats. An effective control system has three characteristics: It is flexible enough to allow managers to respond as necessary to unexpected events; it provides accurate information about organizational performance; and it gives managers information in a timely manner because making decisions on the basis of outdated information is a recipe for failure.

New forms of IT have revolutionized control systems because they facilitate the flow of accurate and timely information up and down the organizational hierarchy and between functions and divisions. Today employees at all levels of the organization routinely feed information into a company's information system or network and start the chain of events that affect decision making in some other part of the organization. This could be the department store clerk whose scanning of purchased clothing tells merchandise managers what kinds of clothing need to be reordered or the salesperson in the field who feeds into a tablet computer the CRM information necessary to inform marketing about customers' changing needs.

feedforward control
Control that allows managers to anticipate problems before they arise.

Control and information systems are developed to measure performance at each stage in the process of transforming inputs into finished goods and services (see Figure 11.1). At the input stage, managers use **feedforward control** to anticipate problems before they arise so problems do not occur later during the conversion process.[6] For example, by giving stringent

Figure 11.1
Three Types of Control

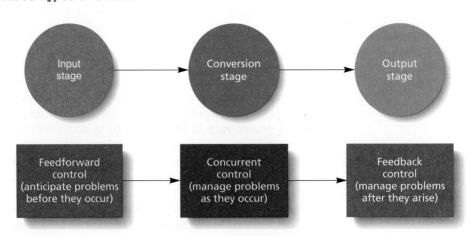

product specifications to suppliers in advance (a form of performance target), an organization can control the quality of the inputs it receives from its suppliers and thus avoid potential problems during the conversion process. Also, IT can be used to keep in contact with suppliers and to monitor their progress. Similarly, by screening job applicants, often by viewing their résumés electronically and using several interviews to select the most highly skilled people, managers can lessen the chance that they will hire people who lack the necessary skills or experience to perform effectively. In general, the development of management information systems promotes feedforward control that gives managers timely information about changes in the task and general environments that may impact their organization later on. Effective managers always monitor trends and changes in the external environment to try to anticipate problems. (We discuss management information systems in detail in Chapter 18.)

concurrent control Control that gives managers immediate feedback on how efficiently inputs are being transformed into outputs so managers can correct problems as they arise.

At the conversion stage, **concurrent control** gives managers immediate feedback on how efficiently inputs are being transformed into outputs so managers can correct problems as they arise. Concurrent control through IT alerts managers to the need to react quickly to whatever is the source of the problem, whether it is a defective batch of inputs, a machine that is out of alignment, or a worker who lacks the skills necessary to perform a task efficiently. Concurrent control is at the heart of total quality management programs (discussed in Chapter 9), in which workers are expected to constantly monitor the quality of the goods or services they provide at every step of the production process and inform managers as soon as they discover problems. One of the strengths of UTC's ACE system, for example, is that all its employees are involved in identifying and solving design and quality problems and finding better ways to assemble its products to increase quality and reduce costs. When problems are corrected on an ongoing basis, the result is finished products that are more valuable to customers and command higher prices.

feedback control Control that gives managers information about customers' reactions to goods and services so corrective action can be taken if necessary.

At the output stage, managers use **feedback control** to provide information about customers' reactions to goods and services so corrective action can be taken if necessary. For example, a feedback control system that monitors the number of customer returns alerts managers when defective products are being produced, and a management information system (MIS) that measures increases or decreases in relative sales of different products alerts managers to changes in customer tastes so they can increase or reduce the production of specific products.

The Control Process

LO11-2 Describe the four steps in the control process and the way it operates over time.

The control process, whether at the input, conversion, or output stage, can be broken down into four steps: establishing standards of performance and then measuring, comparing, and evaluating actual performance (see Figure 11.2).[7]

- Step 1: *Establish the standards of performance, goals, or targets against which performance is to be evaluated.*

At step 1 in the control process managers decide on the standards of performance, goals, or targets that they will use in the future to evaluate the performance of the entire organization or part of it (such as a division, a function, or an individual). The standards of performance that managers select measure efficiency, quality, responsiveness to customers, and innovation.[8] If managers decide to pursue a low-cost strategy, for example, they need to measure efficiency at all levels in the organization.

At the corporate level, a standard of performance that measures efficiency is operating costs, the actual costs associated with producing goods and services, including all employee-related costs. Top managers might set a corporate goal of "reducing operating costs by 10% for the next three years" to increase efficiency. Corporate managers might then evaluate divisional managers for their ability to reduce operating costs within their respective divisions, and divisional managers might set cost-saving targets for functional managers. Thus performance standards selected at one level affect those at the other levels, and ultimately the performance of individual managers is evaluated in terms of their ability to reduce costs.

The number of standards or indicators of performance that an organization's managers use to evaluate efficiency, quality, and so on can run into the thousands or hundreds of thousands. Managers at each level are responsible for selecting standards that will best allow them to evaluate how well the part of the organization they are responsible for is performing.[9] Managers must be careful to choose standards of performance that let them assess how well

Figure 11.2

Four Steps in Organizational Control

Step 1	Establish the standards of performance, goals, or targets against which performance is to be evaluated.
Step 2	Measure actual performance.
Step 3	Compare actual performance against chosen standards of performance.
Step 4	Evaluate the result and initiate corrective action if the standard is not being achieved.

they are doing with all four building blocks of competitive advantage. If managers focus on just one standard (such as efficiency) and ignore others (such as determining what customers really want and innovating a new line of products to satisfy them), managers may end up hurting their organization's performance.

- Step 2: *Measure actual performance.*

Once managers have decided which standards or targets they will use to evaluate performance, the next step in the control process is to measure actual performance. In practice, managers can measure or evaluate two things: (1) the actual *outputs* that result from the behavior of their members and (2) the *behaviors* themselves (hence the terms *output control* and *behavior control* used in this chapter).[10]

Sometimes both outputs and behaviors can be easily measured. Measuring outputs and evaluating behavior is relatively easy in a fast-food restaurant, for example, because employees are performing routine tasks. Managers at Home Depot are rigorous in using output control to measure how fast inventory flows through stores. Similarly, managers of a fast-food restaurant can easily measure outputs by counting how many customers their employees serve, the time each transaction takes, and how much money each customer spends. Managers can easily observe each employee's behavior and quickly take action to solve any problems that may arise.

When an organization and its members perform complex, nonroutine activities that are intrinsically hard to measure, it is more challenging for managers to measure outputs or behavior.[11] It is difficult, for example, for managers in charge of R&D departments at Intel or AMD, or at Microsoft or Google, to measure performance or to evaluate the performance of individual members because it can take several years to determine whether the new products that engineers and scientists are developing will be profitable. Moreover, it is impossible for a manager to measure how creative an engineer or scientist is by watching his or her actions.

In general, the more nonroutine or complex organizational activities are, the harder it is for managers to measure outputs or behaviors.[12] Outputs, however, are usually easier to measure than behaviors because they are more tangible and objective. Therefore, the first kind of performance measures that managers tend to use is those that measure outputs. Then managers develop performance measures or standards that allow them to evaluate behaviors to determine whether employees at all levels are working toward organizational goals. Some simple behavior measures are (1) whether employees come to work on time and (2) whether employees consistently follow the established rules for greeting and serving customers. The various types of output and behavior control and how they are used at the different organizational levels—corporate, divisional, functional, and individual—are discussed in detail subsequently.

- Step 3: *Compare actual performance against chosen standards of performance.*

During step 3, managers evaluate whether—and to what extent—performance deviates from the standards of performance chosen in step 1. If performance is higher than expected, managers might decide they set performance standards too low and may raise them for the next period to challenge their subordinates.[13] Managers at successful companies are well known for the way they try to improve performance in manufacturing settings by constantly raising performance standards to motivate managers and workers to find new ways to reduce costs or increase quality.

However, if performance is too low and standards were not reached, or if standards were set so high that employees could not achieve them, managers must decide whether to take corrective action.[14] It is easy to take corrective action when the reasons for poor performance can be identified—for instance, high labor costs. To reduce costs, managers can search for low-cost overseas suppliers, invest more in technology, or implement cross-functional teams. More often, however, the reasons for poor performance are hard to identify. Changes in the environment, such as the emergence of a new global competitor, a recession, or an increase in interest rates, might be the source of the problem. Within an organization, perhaps the R&D function underestimated the problems it would encounter in developing a new product or the extra costs of doing unforeseen research or perhaps the faulty design of just one component in thousands slipped through the cracks. If managers are to take any form of corrective action, step 4 is necessary.

- Step 4: *Evaluate the result and initiate corrective action (that is, make changes) if the standard is not being achieved.*

The final step in the control process is to evaluate the results and bring about change as appropriate. Whether or not performance standards have been met, managers can learn a great deal during this step. If managers decide the level of performance is unacceptable, they must try to change how work activities are performed to solve the problem. Sometimes performance problems occur because the work standard was too high—for example, a sales target was too optimistic and impossible to achieve. In this case, adopting more realistic standards can reduce the gap between actual performance and desired performance.

However, if managers determine that something in the situation is causing the problem, then to raise performance they will need to change how resources are being utilized or shared.[15] Perhaps the latest technology is not being used; perhaps workers lack the advanced training needed to perform at a higher level; perhaps the organization needs to buy its inputs or assemble its products abroad to compete against low-cost rivals; perhaps it needs to restructure itself or reengineer its work processes using Six Sigma to increase efficiency. Or perhaps it needs to change its monitoring and reward systems as suggested by the experience of eBay in the following "Management Insight" box.

Management Insight

Control Problems Arise between eBay and Its Sellers

Since its founding in 1995, eBay has always cultivated good relationships with the millions of sellers that advertise their goods for sale on its website. Over time, however, to increase its revenues and profits, eBay has steadily increased the fees it charges sellers to list their products on its sites, to insert photographs, to use its PayPal online payment service, and so on. Although this caused some grumbling among sellers because it reduced their profit margins, eBay increasingly engaged in extensive advertising that attracted millions more buyers to use its website so that sellers received better prices and their total profits also increased. As a result, they remained largely satisfied with eBay's fee structure.

This all changed when a new CEO, John Donahoe, took over from eBay's long-time CEO, Meg Whitman, who had built the company into a dot.com giant. By the late 2000s, eBay's revenues and profits had not increased fast enough to keep its investors happy, and its stock price plunged. One of Donahoe's first moves to increase performance was

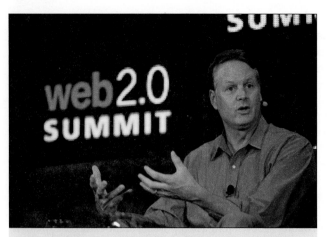

John Donahoe new CEO of eBay, learned the hard way that gleaning feedback from a wide range of stakeholders remains absolutely essential when making major changes in organizational control.

to announce a major overhaul of eBay's fee structure and feedback policy.[16] eBay's new fee structure would reduce upfront listing costs but increase back-end commissions on completed sales and payments. For its small sellers that already had thin profit margins, these fee hikes were painful. In addition, in the future eBay announced it would block sellers from leaving negative feedback about buyers—feedback such as buyers didn't pay for the goods they purchased or took too long to do so. The feedback system that eBay had originally developed has been a major source of its success because it allows buyers to know they are dealing with reputable sellers and vice versa. All sellers and buyers have feedback scores that provide them with a reputation as good—or bad—people to do business with, and these scores reduce the risks involved in online transactions. Donahoe claimed this change was to improve the buyer's experience because many buyers had complained that if they left negative feedback for a seller—the seller would then leave negative feedback for the buyer!

Together, however, these changes resulted in a blaze of conflict between eBay and its millions of sellers who perceived they were being harmed by these changes, that they had lost their prestige and standing at eBay, and their bad feelings resulted in a revolt. Blogs and forums across the Internet were filled with messages claiming that eBay had abandoned its smaller sellers and was pushing them out of business in favor of high-volume "powersellers" who contributed more to eBay's profits. eBay and Donahoe received millions of hostile e-mails and sellers threatened they would move their business elsewhere, such as onto Amazon.com and Yahoo!, which were both trying to break into eBay's market. Sellers even organized a one-week boycott of eBay during which they would list no items with the company to express their dismay and hostility. Many sellers did shut down their eBay online storefronts and moved to Amazon.com, which by 2010 claimed that its network of sites had overtaken eBay in monthly unique viewers or "hits" for the first time.

The bottom line was that the level of conflict between eBay and its buyers had dramatically escalated and eBay's reputation with sellers was suffering; one survey found that while over 50% of buyers thought Amazon.com was an excellent sales channel, only 23% regarded eBay as excellent. In essence, the bitter feelings produced by the changes eBay had made were likely to result in increasing long-run conflict that would hurt its future performance. Realizing his changes had backfired, Donahoe reversed course in 2009 and eliminated several of eBay's fee increases and revamped its feedback system so that buyers and sellers can now respond to one another's comments in a fairer way.

These moves did improve and smooth over the bad feeling between sellers and eBay, but the old "community relationship" it had enjoyed with buyers in its early years largely disappeared. As this example suggests, finding ways to avoid conflict—such as by testing the waters in advance and asking sellers for their reactions to fee and feedback changes—could have avoided many of the problems that arose. Nevertheless, in the 2010s, eBay's turnaround plan has shown signs of success and its revenues and profits have steadily increased—as has its stock price.

The simplest example of a control system is the thermostat in a home. By setting the thermostat, you establish the standard of performance with which actual temperature is to be compared. The thermostat contains a sensing or monitoring device, which measures the actual temperature against the desired temperature. Whenever there is a difference between them, the furnace or air-conditioning unit is activated to bring the temperature back to the standard. In other words, corrective action is initiated. This is a simple control system: It is entirely self-contained and the target (temperature) is easy to measure.

Figure 11.3

Three Organizational Control Systems

Type of control	Mechanisms of control
Output control	Financial measures of performance Organizational goals Operating budgets
Behavior control	Direct supervision Management by objectives Rules and standard operating procedures
Clan control	Values Norms Socialization

Establishing targets and designing measurement systems are much more difficult for managers because the high level of uncertainty in the organizational environment means managers rarely know what might happen in the future. Thus it is vital for managers to design control systems to alert them to problems quickly so they can be dealt with before they become threatening. Obviously Toyota was too slow to react to its accelerator pedal problem, which has cost it billions of dollars in vehicle recalls, lawsuits, and lost business. Another issue is that managers are not just concerned about bringing the organization's performance up to some predetermined standard; they want to push that standard forward to encourage employees at all levels to find new ways to raise performance. This is something that Toyota has traditionally excelled at, which is why customers are not afraid to buy its vehicles.

In the following sections, we consider three important types of control systems that managers use to coordinate and motivate employees to ensure that they pursue superior efficiency, quality, innovation, and responsiveness to customers: output control, behavior control, and clan control (see Figure 11.3). Managers use all three to shape, regulate, and govern organizational activities, no matter what specific organizational structure is in place. However, as Figure 11.3 suggests, an important element of control is embedded in organizational culture, which is discussed later.

Output Control

All managers develop a system of output control for their organizations. First they choose the goals or output performance standards or targets that they think will best measure efficiency, quality, innovation, and responsiveness to customers. Then they measure to see whether the performance goals and standards are being achieved at the corporate, divisional, functional, and individual employee levels of the organization. The three main mechanisms that managers use to assess output or performance are financial measures, organizational goals, and operating budgets.

LO11-3 Identify the main output controls, and discuss their advantages and disadvantages as means of coordinating and motivating employees.

Financial Measures of Performance

Top managers are most concerned with overall organizational performance and use various financial measures to evaluate it. The most common are profit ratios, liquidity ratios, leverage ratios, and activity ratios. They are discussed here and summarized in Table 11.1.[17]

- *Profit ratios* measure how efficiently managers are using the organization's resources to generate profits. *Return on investment (ROI),* an organization's net income before taxes divided by its total assets, is the most commonly used financial performance measure because it allows managers of one organization to compare performance with that of other organizations. ROI lets managers assess an organization's competitive advantage. *Operating margin* is calculated by dividing a company's operating profit (the amount

Table 11.1

Four Measures of Financial Performance

Profit Ratios

Return on investment $=$	$\dfrac{\text{Net profit before taxes}}{\text{Total assets}}$	Measures how well managers are using the organization's resources to generate profits.
Operating margin $=$	$\dfrac{\text{Total operating profit}}{\text{Sales revenues}}$	A measure of how much percentage profit a company is earning on sales; the higher the percentage, the better a company is using its resources to make and sell the product.

Liquidity Ratios

Current ratio $=$	$\dfrac{\text{Current assets}}{\text{Current liabilities}}$	Do managers have resources available to meet claims of short-term creditors?
Quick ratio $=$	$\dfrac{\text{Current assets} - \text{Inventory}}{\text{Current liabilities}}$	Can managers pay off claims of short-term creditors without selling inventory?

Leverage Ratios

Debt-to-assets ratio $=$	$\dfrac{\text{Total debt}}{\text{Total assets}}$	To what extent have managers used borrowed funds to finance investments?
Times-covered ratio $=$	$\dfrac{\text{Profit before interest and taxes}}{\text{Total interest charges}}$	Measures how far profits can decline before managers cannot meet interest charges. If this ratio declines to less than 1, the organization is technically insolvent.

Activity Ratios

Inventory turnover $=$	$\dfrac{\text{Cost of good sold}}{\text{Inventory}}$	Measures how efficiently managers are turning inventory over so that excess inventory is not carried.
Days sales outstanding $=$	$\dfrac{\text{Current accounts receivable}}{\text{Sales for period divided by days in period}}$	Measures how efficiently managers are collecting revenues from customers to pay expenses.

---

it has left after all the costs of making the product and running the business have been deducted) by sales revenues. This measure tells managers how efficiently an organization is using its resources; every successful attempt to reduce costs will be reflected in increased operating profit, for example. Also, operating margin is a means of comparing one year's performance to another; for example, if managers discover operating margin has improved by 5% from one year to the next, they know their organization is building a competitive advantage.

- *Liquidity ratios* measure how well managers have protected organizational resources to be able to meet short-term obligations. The *current ratio* (current assets divided by current liabilities) tells managers whether they have the resources available to meet the claims of short-term creditors. The *quick ratio* shows whether they can pay these claims without selling inventory.

- *Leverage ratios,* such as the *debt-to-assets ratio* and the *times-covered ratio,* measure the degree to which managers use debt (borrow money) or equity (issue new shares) to finance ongoing operations. An organization is highly leveraged if it uses more debt than equity. Debt can be risky when net income or profit fails to cover the interest on the debt—as some people learn too late when their paychecks do not allow them to pay off their credit cards.

- *Activity ratios* show how well managers are creating value from organizational assets. *Inventory turnover* measures how efficiently managers are turning inventory over so excess inventory is not carried. *Days sales outstanding* reveals how efficiently managers are collecting revenue from customers to pay expenses.

The objectivity of financial measures of performance is the reason why so many managers use them to assess the efficiency and effectiveness of their organizations. When an organization fails to meet performance standards such as ROI, revenue, or stock price targets, managers know they must take corrective action. Thus financial controls tell managers when a corporate reorganization might be necessary, when they should sell off divisions and exit businesses, or when they should rethink their corporate-level strategies.[18] Today financial controls are taught to all organizational employees, as the following "Management Insight" box describes.

Management Insight

Making the Financial Figures Come Alive

You might think financial control is the province of top managers and employees lower in the organization don't need to worry about the numbers or about how their specific activities affect those numbers. However, some top managers make a point of showing employees exactly how their activities affect financial ratios, and they do so because employees' activities directly affect a company's costs and its sales revenues. One of those managers is Michael Dell.

Dell goes to enormous lengths to convince employees that they need to watch every dime spent in making the PCs that have made his company so prosperous, as well as in saying every word or making every phone call or service call that is needed to sell or repair them. Dell believes all his managers need to have at their fingertips detailed information about Dell's cost structure, including assembly costs, selling costs, and after-sales costs, in order to squeeze out every cent of operating costs. One good reason for this is that Dell puts a heavy emphasis on the operating margin financial ratio in measuring his company's performance. Dell doesn't care about how much profits or sales are growing individually; he cares about how these two figures work together because only if profits are growing faster than sales is the company increasing its long-run profitability by operating more efficiently and effectively.

So he insists that his managers search for every way possible to reduce costs or make customers happier and then help employees learn the new procedures to achieve these goals. At Dell's boot camp for new employees in Austin, Texas, he has been known to bring financial charts that show employees how each minute spent on performing some job activity such as dealing with suppliers or customers affects bottom-line profitability. In the 2010s all kinds of companies are training employees at all levels in how their specific job activities, and the way their functions operate, affect the financial ratios used to judge how well an organization is performing.

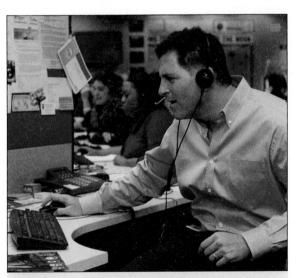

Michael Dell prepares to work the phone lines at Dell's U.S. customer service call center. Dell's emphasis on productivity everywhere means he has no qualms about sitting in an entry-level position for a day both to learn what his employees face and to better teach them.

Although financial information is an important output control, financial information by itself does not tell managers all they need to know about the four building blocks of competitive advantage. Financial results inform managers about the results of decisions they have already made; they do not tell managers how to find new opportunities to build competitive advantage in the future. To encourage a future-oriented approach, top managers must establish organizational goals that encourage middle and first-line managers to achieve superior efficiency, quality, innovation, and responsiveness to customers.

Organizational Goals

Once top managers consult with lower-level managers and set the organization's overall goals, they establish performance standards for the divisions and functions. These standards specify for divisional and functional managers the level at which their units must perform if the organization is to achieve its overall goals.[19] Each division is given a set of specific goals to achieve (see Figure 11.4). We saw in Chapter 8, for example, that Jeffrey Immelt, CEO of GE, has established the goal of having each GE division be first or second in its industry in profit. Divisional managers then develop a business-level strategy (based on achieving superior efficiency or innovation) that they hope will allow them to achieve that goal.[20] In consultation with functional managers, they specify the functional goals that the managers of different functions need to achieve to allow the division to achieve its goals. For example, sales managers might be evaluated for their ability to increase sales; materials management managers, for their ability to increase the quality of inputs or lower their costs; R&D managers, for the number of products they innovate or the number of patents they receive. In turn, functional managers establish goals that first-line managers and nonmanagerial employees need to achieve to allow the function to achieve its goals.

Output control is used at every level of the organization, and it is vital that the goals set at each level harmonize with the goals set at other levels so managers and other employees throughout the organization work together to attain the corporate goals that top managers have set.[21] It is also important that goals be set appropriately so managers are motivated to accomplish them. If goals are set at an impossibly high level, managers might work only halfheartedly to achieve them because they are certain they will fail. In contrast, if goals are set so low that they are too easy to achieve, managers will not be motivated to use all their resources as efficiently and effectively as possible. Research suggests that the best goals are specific, difficult goals—goals that challenge and stretch managers' ability but are not out of reach and do not require an impossibly high expenditure of managerial time and energy. Such goals are often called *stretch goals*.

Deciding what is a specific difficult goal and what is a goal that is too difficult or too easy is a skill that managers must develop. Based on their own judgment and work experience, managers at all levels must assess how difficult a certain task is, and they must assess the ability of a particular subordinate manager to achieve the goal. If they do so successfully, challenging, interrelated goals—goals that reinforce one another and focus on achieving overall corporate objectives—will energize the organization.

Operating Budgets

operating budget A budget that states how managers intend to use organizational resources to achieve organizational goals.

Once managers at each level have been given a goal or target to achieve, the next step in developing an output control system is to establish operating budgets that regulate how managers and workers attain their goals. An **operating budget** is a blueprint that states how managers intend to use organizational resources to achieve organizational goals efficiently. Typically managers at one level allocate to subordinate managers a specific amount of resources to

Figure 11.4
Organizationwide Goal Setting

Corporate-level managers set goals for individual divisions that will allow the organization to achieve corporate goals.

Divisional managers set goals for each function that will allow the division to achieve its goals.

Functional managers set goals for each individual worker that will allow the function to achieve its goals.

produce goods and services. Once they have been given a budget, these lower-level managers must decide how to allocate money for different organizational activities. They are then evaluated for their ability to stay within the budget and to make the best use of available resources. For example, managers at GE's washing machine division might have a budget of $50 million to spend on developing and selling a new line of washing machines. They must decide how much money to allocate to the various functions such as R&D, engineering, and sales so the division generates the most customer revenue and makes the biggest profit.

Large organizations often treat each division as a singular or stand-alone responsibility center. Corporate managers then evaluate each division's contribution to corporate performance. Managers of a division may be given a fixed budget for resources and be evaluated on the amount of goods or services they can produce using those resources (this is a cost or expense budget approach). Alternatively, managers may be asked to maximize the revenues from the sales of goods and services produced (a revenue budget approach). Or managers may be evaluated on the difference between the revenues generated by the sales of goods and services and the budgeted cost of making those goods and services (a profit budget approach). Japanese companies' use of operating budgets and challenging goals to increase efficiency is instructive in this context.

In summary, three components—objective financial measures, challenging goals and performance standards, and appropriate operating budgets—are the essence of effective output control. Most organizations develop sophisticated output control systems to allow managers at all levels to keep accurate account of the organization so they can move quickly to take corrective action as needed.[22] Output control is an essential part of management.

Problems with Output Control

When designing an output control system, managers must be careful to avoid some pitfalls. For example, they must be sure the output standards they create motivate managers at all levels and do not cause managers to behave in inappropriate ways to achieve organizational goals.

Suppose top managers give divisional managers the goal of doubling profits over a three-year period. This goal seems challenging and reachable when it is jointly agreed upon, and in the first two years profits go up by 70%. In the third year, however, an economic recession hits and sales plummet. Divisional managers think it is increasingly unlikely that they will meet their profit goal. Failure will mean losing the substantial monetary bonus tied to achieving the goal. How might managers behave to try to preserve their bonuses?

Perhaps they might find ways to reduce costs because profit can be increased either by raising sales revenues or reducing costs. Thus divisional managers might cut back on expensive research activities, delay machinery maintenance, reduce marketing expenditures, and lay off middle managers and workers to reduce costs so that at the end of the year they will make their target of doubling profits and receive their bonuses. This tactic might help them achieve a short-run goal—doubling profits—but such actions could hurt long-term profitability or ROI (because a cutback in R&D can reduce the rate of product innovation, a cutback in marketing will lead to the loss of customers, and so on).

The message is clear: Although output control is a useful tool for keeping managers and employees at all levels motivated and the organization on track, it is only a guide to appropriate action. Managers must be sensitive in how they use output control and must constantly monitor its effects at all levels in the organization—and on customers and other stakeholders.

LO11-4 Identify the main behavior controls, and discuss their advantages and disadvantages as a means of coordinating and motivating employees.

Behavior Control

Organizational structure by itself does not provide any mechanism that motivates managers and nonmanagerial employees to behave in ways that make the structure work—or even improve how it works; hence the need for control. Put another way, managers can develop an organizational structure that has the right grouping of divisions and functions, and an effective chain of command, but it will work as designed *only* if managers also establish control systems that motivate and shape employee behavior in ways that *match* this structure.[23] Output control is one method of motivating employees; behavior control is another method. This section examines three mechanisms of behavior control that managers can use to keep subordinates on track and make organizational structures work as they are designed to work: direct supervision, management by objectives, and rules and standard operating procedures (see Figure 11.3).

Direct Supervision

The most immediate and potent form of behavior control is direct supervision by managers who actively monitor and observe the behavior of their subordinates, teach subordinates the behaviors that are appropriate and inappropriate, and intervene to take corrective action as needed. Moreover, when managers personally supervise subordinates, they lead by example and in this way can help subordinates develop and increase their own skill levels. (Leadership is the subject of Chapter 14.)

Direct supervision allows managers at all levels to become personally involved with their subordinates and allows them to mentor subordinates and develop their management skills. Thus control through personal supervision can be an effective way of motivating employees and promoting behaviors that increase efficiency and effectiveness.[24]

Nevertheless, certain problems are associated with direct supervision. First, it is expensive because a manager can personally manage only a relatively small number of subordinates effectively. Therefore, if direct supervision is the main kind of control being used in an organization, a lot of managers will be needed and costs will increase. For this reason, output control is usually preferred to behavior control; indeed, output control tends to be the first type of control that managers at all levels use to evaluate performance. Second, direct supervision can *demotivate* subordinates. This occurs if employees feel they are under such close scrutiny that they are not free to make their own decisions or if they feel they are not being evaluated in an accurate and impartial way. Team members and other employees may start to pass the buck, avoid responsibility, and cease to cooperate with other team members if they feel their manager is not accurately evaluating their performance and is favoring some people over others.

Third, as noted previously, for many jobs personal control through direct supervision is simply not feasible. The more complex a job is, the more difficult it is for a manager to evaluate how well a subordinate is performing. The performance of divisional and functional managers, for example, can be evaluated only over relatively long periods (this is why an output control system is developed), so it makes little sense for top managers to continually monitor their performance. However, managers can still communicate the organization's mission and goals to their subordinates and reinforce the values and norms in the organization's culture through their own personal style.

Management by Objectives

management by objectives (MBO) A goal-setting process in which a manager and each of his or her subordinates negotiate specific goals and objectives for the subordinate to achieve and then periodically evaluate the extent to which the subordinate is achieving those goals.

To provide a framework within which to evaluate subordinates' behavior and, in particular, to allow managers to monitor progress toward achieving goals, many organizations implement some version of management by objectives. **Management by objectives (MBO)** is a formal system of evaluating subordinates on their ability to achieve specific organizational goals or performance standards and to meet operating budgets.[25] Most organizations use some form of MBO system because it is pointless to establish goals and then fail to evaluate whether they are being achieved. Management by objectives involves three specific steps:

- Step 1: *Specific goals and objectives are established at each level of the organization.*

MBO starts when top managers establish overall organizational objectives, such as specific financial performance goals or targets. Then objective setting cascades down throughout the organization as managers at the divisional and functional levels set their goals to achieve corporate objectives.[26] Finally first-level managers and employees jointly set goals that will contribute to achieving functional objectives.

- Step 2: *Managers and their subordinates together determine the subordinates' goals.*

An important characteristic of management by objectives is its participatory nature. Managers at every level sit down with each of the subordinate managers who report directly to them, and together they determine appropriate and feasible goals for the subordinate and bargain over the budget that the subordinate will need to achieve his or her goals. The participation of subordinates in the objective-setting process is a way of strengthening their commitment to achieving their goals and meeting their budgets.[27] Another reason why it is so important for subordinates (both individuals and teams) to participate in goal setting is that doing so enables them to tell managers what they think they can realistically achieve.[28]

- Step 3: *Managers and their subordinates periodically review the subordinates' progress toward meeting goals.*

Once specific objectives have been agreed on for managers at each level, managers are accountable for meeting those objectives. Periodically they sit down with their subordinates to evaluate their progress. Normally salary raises and promotions are linked to the goal-setting process, and managers who achieve their goals receive greater rewards than those who fall short. (The issue of how to design reward systems to motivate managers and other organizational employees is discussed in Chapter 13.)

In the companies that have decentralized responsibility for the production of goods and services to empowered teams and cross-functional teams, management by objectives works somewhat differently. Managers ask each team to develop a set of goals and performance targets that the team hopes to achieve—goals that are consistent with organizational objectives. Managers then negotiate with each team to establish its final goals and the budget the team will need to achieve them. The reward system is linked to team performance, not to the performance of any one team member.

Cypress Semiconductor offers an interesting example of how IT can be used to manage the MBO process quickly and effectively. In the fast-moving semiconductor business, a premium is placed on organizational adaptability. At Cypress, CEO T. J. Rodgers was facing a problem: How could he control his growing 1,500-employee organization without developing a bureaucratic management hierarchy? Rodgers believed that a tall hierarchy hinders the ability of an organization to adapt to changing conditions. He was committed to maintaining a flat and decentralized organizational structure with a minimum of management layers. At the same time, he needed to control his employees to ensure that they performed in a manner consistent with the goals of the company.[29] How could he achieve this without resorting to direct supervision and the lengthy management hierarchy that it implies?

To solve this problem, Rodgers implemented an online information system through which he can monitor what every employee and team is doing in his fast-moving and decentralized organization. Each employee maintains a list of 10 to 15 goals, such as "Meet with marketing for new product launch" or "Make sure to check with customer X." Noted next to each goal are when it was agreed upon, when it is due to be finished, and whether it has been finished. All this information is stored on a central computer. Rodgers claims that he can review the goals of all employees in about four hours and that he does so each week.[30] How is this possible? He *manages by exception* and looks only for employees who are falling behind. He then calls them, not to scold but to ask whether there is anything he can do to help them get the job done. It takes only about half an hour each week for employees to review and update their lists. This system allows Rodgers to exercise control over his organization without resorting to the expensive layers of a management hierarchy and direct supervision.

MBO does not always work out as planned, however. Managers and their subordinates at all levels must believe that performance evaluations are accurate and fair. Any suggestion that personal biases and political objectives play a part in the evaluation process can lower or even destroy MBO's effectiveness as a control system. This is why many organizations work so hard to protect the integrity of their systems.

Also, when people work in teams, each member's contribution to the team and each team's contribution to the goals of the organization must be fairly evaluated. This is not easy to do. It depends on managers' ability to create an organizational control system that measures performance accurately and fairly and links performance evaluations to rewards so that employees stay motivated and coordinate their activities to achieve the organization's mission and goals. Microsoft's problem was that the changes it made to its control system (new performance evaluation measures) as the company grew hurt its ability to motivate its employees.

Table 11.2
Team Rules of Conduct

1. All employees must call their supervisor or leader before 5:55 a.m. to notify of absence or tardiness.

2. Disciplinary action will be issued to any employee who abuses sick leave policy.

3. Disciplinary action will be issued to any employee whose assigned area is not up to custodial standards.

4. If a door is locked when you go in to clean an office, it's your responsibility to lock it back up.

5. Name tags and uniforms must be worn daily.

6. Each employee is responsible for buffing hallways and offices. Hallways must be buffed weekly, offices periodically.

7. All equipment must be put in closets during 9:00 a.m. and 11 a.m. breaks.

8. Do not use the elevator to move trash or equipment from 8:50 to 9:05, 9:50 to 10:05, 11:50 to 12:05, or 1:50 to 2:05 to avoid breaks between classes.

9. Try to mop hallways when students are in classrooms, or mop floors as you go down to each office.

10. Closets must be kept clean and all equipment must be clean and operative.

11. Each employee is expected to greet building occupants with "Good morning."

12. Always knock before entering offices and conference rooms.

13. Loud talking, profanity, and horseplay will not be tolerated inside buildings.

14. All custodial carts must be kept uniform and cleaned daily.

15. You must have excellent "public relations" with occupants at all times.

Bureaucratic Control

bureaucratic control
Control of behavior by means of a comprehensive system of rules and standard operating procedures.

When direct supervision is too expensive and management by objectives is inappropriate, managers might turn to another mechanism to shape and motivate employee behavior: bureaucratic control. **Bureaucratic control** is control by means of a comprehensive system of rules and standard operating procedures (SOPs) that shapes and regulates the behavior of divisions, functions, and individuals. In Chapter 2 we discussed Weber's theory of bureaucracy and noted that all organizations use bureaucratic rules and procedures but some use them more than others.[31] Recall that rules and SOPs are formal, written instructions that specify a series of actions that employees should follow to achieve a given end; in other words, if *A* happens, then do *B* and *C*. For example, a simple set of rules developed by the supervisor of some custodial workers (Crew G) at a Texas A&M University building clearly established task responsibilities and clarified expectations (see Table 11.2).

Rules and SOPs guide behavior and specify what employees are to do when they confront a problem that needs a solution. It is the responsibility of a manager to develop rules that allow employees to perform their activities efficiently and effectively. Rules and SOPs also clarify people's expectations about one another and prevent misunderstandings over responsibility or the use of power. Such guidelines can prevent a supervisor from arbitrarily increasing a subordinate's workload and prevent a subordinate from ignoring tasks that are a legitimate part of the job.

When employees follow the rules that managers have developed, their behavior is *standardized*—actions are performed the same way time and time again—and the outcomes of their work are predictable. And to the degree that managers can make employees' behavior predictable, there is no need to monitor the outputs of behavior because *standardized behavior leads to standardized outputs,* such as goods and services of the same uniform quality. Suppose a worker at Toyota comes up with a way to attach exhaust pipes that reduces the number of steps in the assembly process and increases efficiency. Always on the lookout for ways to standardize and improve procedures, managers make this idea the basis of a new rule that says,

"From now on, the procedure for attaching the exhaust pipe to the car is as follows." If all workers follow the rule to the letter, every car will come off the assembly line with its exhaust pipe attached in the new way, and there will be no need to check exhaust pipes at the end of the line.

In practice, mistakes and lapses of attention happen, so output control is used at the end of the line, and each car's exhaust system is given a routine inspection. However, the number of quality problems with the exhaust system is minimized because the rule (bureaucratic control) is being followed. Service organizations such as retail stores, fast-food restaurants, and home improvement stores also attempt to standardize employee behavior, such as customer service quality, by instructing employees in the correct way to greet customers or the appropriate way to serve and bag food. Employees are trained to follow the rules that have proved to be most effective in a particular situation, and the better trained the employees are, the more standardized is their behavior and the more trust managers can have that outputs (such as food quality) will be consistent. An interesting example of how creating the wrong rules can reduce performance occurred at Gateway (now part of PC maker Acer), which saw its customer satisfaction rating plummet as a result of its new rules. Managers at Gateway discovered that the reason for rising customer dissatisfaction was the new rules they had created to reduce the increasing costs of after-sales service. When customers installed additional software on their new Gateway computers, this often caused problems with the software already installed on the PC. It often took customer reps considerable time to iron out the problems, and Gateway was spending millions of dollars in employee time to solve these problems. To reduce costs, managers told its service reps to inform customers that if they installed any other software on their machines, this would invalidate Gateway's warranty. This infuriated customers who obviously had the right to install other software. Gateway also began to reward customer reps based on how quickly they handled customer calls; the more calls they handled in an hour or day, the higher their bonuses. The effect of these changes was to motivate customer reps to keep service calls short. Customers resented this treatment, and when Gateway's managers realized what was happening, they went back to the old system and customer satisfaction soared. To prevent unexpected problems, it is necessary to carefully choose and evaluate the rules and policies used to control employees' behavior.

In contrast to the situation at Gateway, Dave Lilly, an ex-nuclear submarine commander, chose the right rules for siteROCK, whose business is hosting and managing other companies' websites to keep them running and error-free. A customer's website that goes down or runs haywire is the enemy. To maximize his employees' performance and increase their ability to respond to unexpected online events, Lilly decided they needed a comprehensive set of rules and SOPs to cover the main known problems.[32] Lilly insisted that every problem-solving procedure should be written down and recorded. siteROCK's employees developed over 30 thick binders that list all the processes and checklists they need to follow when an unexpected event happens. Moreover, again drawing from his military experience, Lilly instituted a "two-person rule": Whenever the unexpected happens, each employee must immediately tell a coworker and the two together should attempt to solve the problem. The goal is simple: Use the rules to achieve a quick resolution of a complex issue. If the existing rules don't work, employees must experiment; and when they find a solution, it is turned into a new rule to be included in the procedures book to aid the future decision making of all employees in the organization.

Problems with Bureaucratic Control

Like all organizations, UTC, Dell, and siteROCK make extensive use of bureaucratic control because rules and SOPs effectively control routine organizational activities. With a bureaucratic control system in place, managers can manage by exception and intervene and take corrective action only when necessary. However, managers need to be aware of a number of problems associated with bureaucratic control because such problems can reduce organizational effectiveness.[33]

First, establishing rules is always easier than discarding them. Organizations tend to become overly bureaucratic over time as managers do everything according to the rule book. If the amount of red tape becomes too great, decision making slows and managers react sluggishly to changing conditions. This can imperil an organization's survival if agile new competitors emerge. Once a siteROCK employee has found a better rule, the old one is discarded.

Looks like even Mickey Mouse approves! Bob Iger's redesign of Disney's methods of innovation and planning lets employees get moving faster on new ideas.

Second, because rules constrain and standardize behavior and lead people to behave in predictable ways, people might become so used to automatically following rules that they stop thinking for themselves. Thus too much standardization can actually *reduce* the level of learning taking place in an organization and get the organization off track if managers and workers focus on the wrong issues. An organization thrives when its members are constantly thinking of new ways to increase efficiency, quality, and customer responsiveness. By definition, new ideas do not come from blindly following standardized procedures. Similarly, the pursuit of innovation implies a commitment by managers to discover new ways of doing things; innovation, however, is incompatible with extensive bureaucratic control.

Consider, for example, what happened at Walt Disney when Bob Iger became CEO of the troubled company. Bob Iger had been COO of Disney under CEO Michael Eisner, and he had noticed that Disney was plagued by slow decision making that had led to many mistakes in putting its new strategies into action. Its Disney stores were losing money; its Internet properties were flops; and even its theme parks seemed to have lost their luster as few new rides or attractions were introduced. Iger believed one of the main reasons for Disney's declining performance was that it had become too tall and bureaucratic and its top managers were following financial rules that did not lead to innovative strategies.

One of Iger's first moves to turn around the performance of the poorly performing company was to dismantle Disney's central strategic planning office. In this office several levels of managers were responsible for sifting through all the new ideas and innovations sent up by Disney's different business divisions, such as theme parks, movies, and gaming, and then deciding which ones to present to the CEO. Iger saw the strategic planning office as a bureaucratic bottleneck that reduced the number of ideas coming from below. So he dissolved the office and reassigned its managers back to the different business units.[34] The result of cutting an unnecessary layer in Disney's hierarchy has been that more new ideas are generated by its different business units. The level of innovation has increased because managers are more willing to speak out and champion their ideas when they know they are dealing directly with the CEO and a top management team searching for innovative ways to improve performance—rather than a layer of strategic planning bureaucrats concerned only with the bottom line.[35]

Managers must always be sensitive about the way they use bureaucratic control. It is most useful when organizational activities are routine and well understood and when employees are making programmed decisions—for example, in mass-production settings such as Ford or in routine service settings such as stores like Target or Midas Muffler. Bureaucratic control is much less useful in situations where nonprogrammed decisions have to be made and managers have to react quickly to changes in the task environment. There are also ethical issues involved in the way managers can create, use, and enforce bureaucratic rules and SOPs to their own advantage and harm others as the following "Ethics in Action" box suggests.

Ethics in Action

How Dishonest Top Managers Can Develop Rules That Can Corrupt Any Organization—Even a Court

Court judges at the federal, state, or county level are expected to possess the highest ethical standards and abide by the rule of law; they are the top managers who organize and control the legal system and the courts. Why should ordinary citizens believe they are protected by the legal system and their individual rights will be upheld fairly and objectively if they cannot trust their judges? Then imagine the shock citizens of Luzerne County in the heart of Pennsylvania's struggling coal country experienced in 2009 when an FBI investigation revealed that two respected county judges, Mark Ciavarella and Michael Conahan, had conspired to use the managerial power of their office to profit financially by sending thousands of teenagers to jail.

How these managers controlled the county's judicial organization for this unethical and illegal purpose was revealed when investigators found that the number of youths entering detention in Luzerne County was two to three times higher than in similar counties—and these teens were being jailed for trivial violations. A boy who shoplifted a $4 bottle of nutmeg was jailed, for example, and so was the boy with him, who was charged with conspiracy to shoplift because he was physically present. A girl who created a MySpace page that taunted her school administrator was also incarcerated.

Judges Ciavarella and Conahan's plan to subvert the court's organization and control system worked as follows. At that time Conahan controlled the county court and its budget, and Ciavarella controlled sentencing in the juvenile court, that is, many of their rules and SOPs. As the top managers of the court system, they were largely unsupervised. Over time they worked together to shut down the old county-run juvenile detention center by refusing to send teens there and cutting off its funding. Meanwhile they created their own organization, a privately owned detention center built by the judges' corrupt associates, to replace the facility. Then the judges contracted with the county to pay $58 million to use their detention center for 10 years. The judges admitted they took "at least" $2.6 million in payoffs from their private youth detention center and tried to hide this dishonest income by creating false income tax records.

Most of the teens sentenced were on trial for minor first offenses, and their time in court to defend themselves often lasted for only minutes. Most were unrepresented because their parents were told it was "unnecessary to have a lawyer"; as a consequence, one boy remained locked up for over two years. The Pennsylvania Supreme Court has expunged the records of over 2,000 youths who were sent into detention by Ciavarella because of his unethical behavior. "They sold their oath of offices to the highest bidders and engaged in ongoing schemes to defraud the public of honest services that were expected from them," said Deron Roberts, chief of the FBI's Scranton office.[36]

In 2009 these corrupt ex-justices agreed to a plea bargain stating that they would spend seven years in jail and pay back millions of dollars. This plea bargain collapsed in October 2009 when the presiding judge decided it was too lenient, and in 2010 they faced charges that could lead them to spend decades in jail.[37] In fact, in August 2011, Ciavarella received a 28-year sentence; unethical managers eventually face the consequences of their unsavory actions.

Pictured are disgraced former judges Mark Ciavarella and Michael Conahan as they leave the courtroom building during their trial, which accused them of giving thousands of teenagers illegal jail terms in order to benefit financially.

To use output control and behavior control, managers must be able to identify the outcomes they want to achieve and the behaviors they want employees to perform to achieve those outcomes. For many of the most important and significant organizational activities, however, output control and behavior control are inappropriate for several reasons:

- A manager cannot evaluate the performance of workers such as doctors, research scientists, or engineers by observing their daily behavior.

- Rules and SOPs are of little use in telling a doctor how to respond to an emergency situation or a scientist how to discover something new.

- Output controls such as the amount of time a surgeon takes for each operation or the costs of making a discovery are crude measures of the quality of performance.

How can managers attempt to control and regulate the behavior of their subordinates when personal supervision is of little use, when rules cannot be developed to tell employees what to do, and when outputs and goals cannot be measured at all or can be measured usefully only over long periods?

Clan Control

clan control The control exerted on individuals and groups in an organization by shared values, norms, standards of behavior, and expectations.

One source of control increasingly being used by organizations is **clan control**, which takes advantage of the power of internalized values and norms to guide and constrain employee attitudes and behavior in ways that increase organizational performance.[38] The first function of a control system is to shape the behavior of organizational members to ensure that they are working toward organizational goals and to take corrective action if those goals are not being met. The second function of control, however, is to keep organizational members focused on thinking about what is best for their organization in the future and to keep them looking for new opportunities to use organizational resources to create value. Clan control serves this dual function of keeping organizational members goal-directed while open to new opportunities because it takes advantage of the power of organizational culture, discussed in the previous chapter.

Organizational culture functions as a kind of control system because managers can deliberately try to influence the kind of values and norms that develop in an organization—values and norms that specify appropriate and inappropriate behaviors and so determine the way its members behave.[39] We discussed the sources of organizational culture and the way managers can help create different kinds of cultures in Chapter 10, so there is no need to repeat this discussion here. Instead, the following "Management Insight" box describes how Google's founders created a specific kind of company culture that still flourishes today.

Management Insight

How Google's Founders Created a Groovy Culture

Google, whose fast-growing product line includes a continuously improving search engine, web-browser, e-mail, chat has a mission, "to organize the world's information and make it universally accessible and useful." The company was started in 1995 when two computer science Stanford graduates, Sergey Brin and Larry Page, collaborated to develop a new kind of search engine technology. They understood the shortcomings of existing search engines and by 1998 they had developed a superior search engine they felt was ready to go online. They raised $1 million from family, friends, and risk-taking "angel" investors to buy the hardware necessary to connect Google's software to the Internet.

At first, Google answered only 10,000 inquiries a day—its plain home page is hardly welcoming—but within a few months it was answering 500,000 inquiries; by the end of 1999, 3 million inquiries, and by the spring of 2001 it reached 100 million inquiries per day! In 2010 Google is the most widely used global search engine, it has over a 65% market share and it is one of the top five most-used Internet websites. Google's rise has been so rapid that rivals like Yahoo! and Microsoft are struggling to compete and prevent Google from providing all the other services they offer—and doing it better and for free (Google makes billions of dollars of revenues by selling the advertising space used on all kinds of websites).

Google's explosive growth is largely due to the culture or entrepreneurship and innovation its founders cultivated from the start. Although by 2010 Google has grown to over 20,000 employees worldwide, its founders claim that it still maintains a small company feel because its culture empowers employees, whom it calls staffers or "Googlers," to create the best software possible. Brin and Page created Google's entrepreneurial culture in several ways.

From the start, lacking office space and desperate to keep costs low, Google staffers worked in "high-density clusters," that encouraged intensive team interactions. Three or four staffers, each equipped with a powerful server PC, worked at a common desk or on couches or rubber ball chairs to improve its technology. Even when Google moved into more spacious surroundings at its modernistic "Googleplex"headquarters building in Mountain View, California, staffers continued to work in shared spaces so its team atmosphere or culture became normal.

Google also designed its building so staffers could continually meet each other; in places such as Google's funky lobby, the Google Café where everyone eats together, in its state-of-the-art recreational facilities, and in its "snack rooms" equipped with bins packed with cereals, gummi bears, yogurt, carrots, and, of course make-your-own cappuccinos. They also created opportunities for employees to gather together at informal events such as a TGIF open meeting and a twice-weekly outdoor roller-hockey game.

All this attention to creating what just might be the "grooviest" company headquarters in the world did not come about by chance. Brin and Page knew that Google's most important strength would be its ability to attract the best software engineers in the world and motivate them to perform well. Common offices, lobbies, cafes, and so on bring all staffers into close contact with each other, which develops collegiality, encourages them to share their new ideas, and to continually work to improve Google's online applications and develop new products (click the Google Labs tab on its website) to grow the company.

The freedom Google gives its staffers to pursue new ideas is a clear signal of its founders' desire to empower them to be innovative and work hard to make Google the software power-house of the future. But to motivate staffers to innovate important new software applications Google's founders reward their achievements by giving them stock in the company, which makes staffers owners as well and over a thousand Google staffers have already become millionaires as a result.

Organizational Change

organizational change The movement of an organization away from its present state and toward some preferred future state to increase its efficiency and effectiveness.

LO11-5 Discuss the relationship between organizational control and change, and explain why managing change is a vital management task.

As we have discussed, many problems can arise if an organization's control systems are not designed correctly. One of these problems is that an organization cannot change or adapt in response to a changing environment unless it has effective control over its activities. Companies can lose this control over time, as happened to Toyota, discussed in the earlier "Management Insight" box; or they can change in ways that make them more effective, as happened to UPS and Walmart. **Organizational change** is the movement of an organization away from its present state toward some preferred future state to increase its efficiency and effectiveness.

Interestingly enough, there is a fundamental tension or need to balance two opposing forces in the control process that influences how organizations change. As just noted, organizations and their managers need to be able to control their activities and make their operations routine and predictable. At the same time, however, organizations have to be responsive to the need to change, and managers and employees have to "think on their feet" and realize when they need to depart from routines to be responsive to unpredictable events. In other words, even though adopting the right set of output and behavior controls is essential for improving efficiency, because the environment is dynamic and uncertain, employees also need to feel that they have the autonomy to depart from routines as necessary to increase effectiveness. (See Figure 11.5.)

For this reason many researchers believe that the highest-performing organizations are those that are constantly changing—and thus become experienced at doing so—in their search to become more efficient and effective. Companies like UPS, Toyota, and Walmart are constantly changing the mix of their activities to move forward even as they seek to make their existing operations more efficient. For example, UPS entered the air express parcel market, bought a chain of mailbox stores, and began offering a consulting service. At the same time it has been increasing the efficiency of its ground and global air transport network.

Figure 11.5

Organizational Control and Change

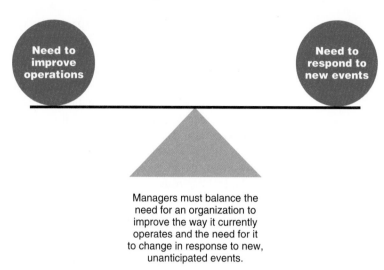

Managers must balance the need for an organization to improve the way it currently operates and the need for it to change in response to new, unanticipated events.

Lewin's Force-Field Theory of Change

Researcher Kurt Lewin developed a theory about organizational change. According to his *force-field theory,* a wide variety of forces arise from the way an organization operates—from its structure, culture, and control systems—that make organizations resistant to change. At the same time a wide variety of forces arise from changing task and general environments that push organizations toward change. These two sets of forces are always in opposition in an organization.[40] When the forces are evenly balanced, the organization is in a state of inertia and does not change. To get an organization to change, managers must find a way to *increase* the forces for change, *reduce* resistance to change, or do *both* simultaneously. Any of these strategies will overcome inertia and cause an organization to change.

Figure 11.6 illustrates Lewin's theory. An organization at performance level P1 is in balance: Forces for change and resistance to change are equal. Management, however, decides that the organization should strive to achieve performance level P2. To get to level P2, managers must *increase* the forces for change (the increase is represented by the lengthening of the up arrows), *reduce* resistance to change (the reduction is represented by the shortening of the down arrows), or both. If managers pursue any of the three strategies successfully, the organization will change and reach performance level P2. Before we look in more detail at the techniques managers can use to overcome resistance and facilitate change, we need to look at the types of change they can implement to increase organizational effectiveness.

Evolutionary and Revolutionary Change

Managers continually face choices about how best to respond to the forces for change. There are several types of change that managers can adopt to help their organizations achieve desired future states.[41] In general, types of change fall into two broad categories: evolutionary change and revolutionary change.[42]

evolutionary change Change that is gradual, incremental, and narrowly focused.

Evolutionary change is gradual, incremental, and narrowly focused. Evolutionary change is not drastic or sudden but, rather, is a constant attempt to improve, adapt, and adjust strategy and structure incrementally to accommodate changes taking place in the environment.[43] Sociotechnical systems theory and total quality management, or kaizen, are two instruments of evolutionary change. Such improvements might entail using technology in a better way or reorganizing the work process.

Some organizations, however, need to make major changes quickly. Faced with drastic, unexpected changes in the environment (for example, a new technological breakthrough) or with an impending disaster resulting from mismanagement, an organization might need to act quickly and decisively. In this case, revolutionary change is called for.

Figure 11.6
Lewin's Force-Field Model of Change

The figure shows axes labeled "Level of performance" (vertical) and "Time" (horizontal), with "Resistance to change" forces pointing down and "Forces for change" pointing up, at levels P1 and P2, connected by "Change."

revolutionary change Change that is rapid, dramatic, and broadly focused.

Revolutionary change is rapid, dramatic, and broadly focused. Revolutionary change involves a bold attempt to quickly find new ways to be effective. It is likely to result in a radical shift in ways of doing things, new goals, and a new structure for the organization. The process has repercussions at all levels in the organization—corporate, divisional, functional, group, and individual. Reengineering, restructuring, and innovation are three important instruments of revolutionary change.

Managing Change

The need to constantly search for ways to improve efficiency and effectiveness makes it vital that managers develop the skills necessary to manage change effectively. Several experts have proposed a model of change that managers can follow to implement change successfully— that is, to move an organization away from its present state and toward some desired future state to increase its efficiency and effectiveness.[44] Figure 11.7 outlines the steps in this process. In the rest of this section we examine each one.

ASSESSING THE NEED FOR CHANGE   Organizational change can affect practically all aspects of organizational functioning, including organizational structure, culture, strategies, control systems, and groups and teams, as well as the human resource management system and critical organizational processes such as communication, motivation, and leadership. Organizational change can alter how managers carry out the critical tasks of planning, organizing, leading, and controlling and the ways they perform their managerial roles.

Deciding how to change an organization is a complex matter because change disrupts the status quo and poses a threat, prompting employees to resist attempts to alter work relationships and procedures. Organizational learning—the process through which managers try to increase organizational members' abilities to understand and appropriately respond to changing conditions—can be an important impetus for change and can help all members of an organization, including managers, effectively make decisions about needed changes.

Assessing the need for change calls for two important activities: recognizing that there is a problem and identifying its source. Sometimes the need for change is obvious, such as when an organization's performance is suffering. Often, however, managers have trouble determining that something is going wrong because problems develop gradually; organizational performance may slip for a number of years before a problem becomes obvious. Thus during the first step in the change process, managers need to recognize that there is a problem that requires change.

Often the problems that managers detect have produced a gap between desired performance and actual performance. To detect such a gap, managers need to look at performance

Figure 11.7

Four Steps in the Organizational Change Process

measures—such as falling market share or profits, rising costs, or employees' failure to meet their established goals or stay within budgets—that indicate whether change is needed. These measures are provided by organizational control systems, discussed earlier in the chapter.

To discover the source of the problem, managers need to look both inside and outside the organization. Outside the organization, they must examine how changing environmental forces may be creating opportunities and threats that are affecting internal work relationships. Perhaps the emergence of low-cost competitors abroad has led to conflict among different departments that are trying to find new ways to gain a competitive advantage. Managers also need to look within the organization to see whether its structure is causing problems between departments. Perhaps a company does not have integrating mechanisms in place to allow different departments to respond to low-cost competition.

DECIDING ON THE CHANGE TO MAKE Once managers have identified the source of the problem, they must decide what they think the organization's ideal future state would be. In other words, they must decide where they would like their organization to be in the future—what kinds of goods and services it should be making, what its business-level strategy should be, how the organizational structure should be changed, and so on. During this step, managers also must plan how to attain the organization's ideal future state.

This step in the change process also includes identifying obstacles or sources of resistance to change. Managers must analyze the factors that may prevent the company from reaching its ideal future state. Obstacles to change are found at the corporate, divisional, departmental, and individual levels of the organization.

Corporate-level changes in an organization's strategy or structure, even seemingly trivial changes, may significantly affect how divisional and departmental managers behave. Suppose that to compete with low-cost foreign competitors, top managers decide to increase the resources spent on state-of-the-art machinery and reduce the resources spent on marketing or R&D. The power of manufacturing managers would increase, and the power of marketing and R&D managers would fall. This decision would alter the balance of power among departments and might increase conflict as departments fight to retain their status in the organization. An organization's present strategy and structure are powerful obstacles to change.

Whether a company's culture is adaptive or inert facilitates or obstructs change. Organizations with entrepreneurial, flexible cultures, such as high-tech companies, are much easier to change than are organizations with more rigid cultures, such as those sometimes found in large, bureaucratic organizations like the military or GM.

The same obstacles to change exist at the divisional and departmental levels. Division managers may differ in their attitudes toward the changes that top managers propose and, if their interests and power seem threatened, will resist those changes. Managers at all levels usually fight to protect their power and control over resources. Because departments have different goals and time horizons, they may also react differently to the changes other managers propose. When top managers are trying to reduce costs, for example, sales managers may resist attempts to cut back on sales expenditures if they believe that problems stem from manufacturing managers' inefficiencies.

At the individual level, too, people often resist change because it brings uncertainty and stress. For example, individuals may resist the introduction of a new technology because they are uncertain about their abilities to learn it and effectively use it.

These obstacles make organizational change a slow process. Managers must recognize the potential obstacles to change and take them into consideration. Some obstacles can be overcome by improving communication so all organizational members are aware of the need for change and of the nature of the changes being made. Empowering employees and inviting them to participate in planning for change also can help overcome resistance and allay employees' fears. In addition, managers can sometimes overcome resistance by emphasizing group or shared goals such as increased organizational efficiency and effectiveness. The larger and more complex an organization is, the more complex is the change process.

top-down change A fast, revolutionary approach to change in which top managers identify what needs to be changed and then move quickly to implement the changes throughout the organization.

bottom-up change A gradual or evolutionary approach to change in which managers at all levels work together to develop a detailed plan for change.

IMPLEMENTING THE CHANGE   Generally, managers implement—that is, introduce and manage—change from the top down or from the bottom up.[45] **Top-down change** is implemented quickly: Top managers identify the need for change, decide what to do, and then move quickly to implement the changes throughout the organization. For example, top managers may decide to restructure and downsize the organization and then give divisional and departmental managers specific goals to achieve. With top-down change, the emphasis is on making the changes quickly and dealing with problems as they arise; it is revolutionary in nature.

Bottom-up change is typically more gradual or evolutionary. Top managers consult with middle and first-line managers about the need for change. Then, over time, managers at all levels work to develop a detailed plan for change. A major advantage of bottom-up change is that it can co-opt resistance to change from employees. Because the emphasis in bottom-up change is on participation and on keeping people informed about what is going on, uncertainty and resistance are minimized. Pfizer's new chief of research did not have the luxury of adopting an evolutionary approach; he had to take swift action to turn around the company, as the following "Manager as a Person" box describes.

Manager as
a Person

Pfizer's Big Push to Create Blockbuster Drugs

Pfizer is the largest global pharmaceuticals company with sales of almost $68 billion in 2011.[46] In the past Pfizer's researchers have innovated some of the most successful and profitable drugs in the market, such as its leading cholesterol reducer Lipitor, which earns $13 billion a year. In the 2010s, however, it has run into major roadblocks in innovating new blockbuster drugs. Although many of the drugs in its new product development seemed to be winners, when Pfizer's scientists tested them on groups of people, they failed to work as planned; this was a major crisis for Pfizer. With no new drugs in its pipeline, and with blockbusters like Lipitor due to lose their patent protection in a few years, Pfizer desperately needed to find ways to make its product development pipeline work. And one manager, Martin Mackay, believed he knew how to do it.

When Pfizer's longtime R&D chief retired, Mackay, his deputy, made it clear to CEO Jeffrey Kindler that he wanted the job. Kindler made it equally clear he thought the company could use some fresh ideas, and he began to bring in outsiders to interview for the job. So Mackay quickly created a detailed plan for changing Pfizer's organizational structure and culture as he believed the company needed. Kindler reviewed the plan and was so impressed that he promoted Mackay to the top R&D position in 2008. What was Mackay's plan?

Mackay had watched how Pfizer's organizational structure had become taller and taller over time as a result of huge mergers with pharmaceutical companies Warner Lambert and Pharmacia. After every merger, with more managers and levels in the hierarchy, there was a much greater need for committees to integrate across all

Something to smile about: Martin Mackay's overhaul of Pfizer's structure cuts out superfluous processes and allows researchers to spend more time doing what they love! The company has a ways to go in rejuvenating its profits but Mackay can rest easy knowing he's put it on the right track for profitability

their activities. Mackay felt that too many managers and committees had resulted in Pfizer's R&D function developing a bureaucratic culture, in which scientists had to follow more and more rules and procedures to perform and report on their work. His plan was to change this situation.

Mackay slashed the number of management layers between top managers and scientists from 14 to 7. He abolished the scores of product development committees that he felt hampered, not helped, the process of transforming innovative ideas into blockbuster drugs. After streamlining the hierarchy of authority, he focused his efforts on reducing the number of bureaucratic rules scientists had to follow, many of which he thought unnecessary. He and his team examined all the types of reports in which scientists were supposed to report the results of their work for evaluation. He then eliminated every kind of report that he considered superfluous and that merely slowed down the innovation process. For example, scientists had been in the habit of submitting quarterly and monthly reports to executives explaining each drug's progress; Mackay told them to pick which one they wanted to keep and the other would be eliminated.

Mackay's goal was to move the company to more of an organic structure, which (as you recall from Chapter 2) is flat and decentralized, and in which teams of scientists can develop the norms and values that encourage a culture of innovation and entrepreneurship. Certainly Pfizer's scientists reported that they felt "liberated" by the new structure, and in 2008 drugs were moving faster along the pipeline. However, new drugs can take seven to eight years from idea stage to market, so only time will tell. Meanwhile Mackay looked outside the company and formed alliances with small drug start-up companies to bring in new outside talent and open up the R&D function to new ideas and approaches. Often companies like Pfizer end up taking over these start-ups and integrating them into their structure, so this is one more avenue he is using to help create a new culture of innovation at the company.

---

benchmarking The process of comparing one company's performance on specific dimensions with the performance of other high-performing organizations.

EVALUATING THE CHANGE   The last step in the change process is to evaluate how successful the change effort has been in improving organizational performance.[47] Using measures such as changes in market share, in profits, or in Pfizer's case the ability of its scientists to innovate new drugs, managers compare how well an organization is performing after the change with how well it was performing before. Managers also can use **benchmarking**, comparing their performance on specific dimensions with the performance of high-performing organizations to decide how successful a change effort has been. For example, when Xerox was performing poorly in the 1980s, it benchmarked the efficiency of its distribution operations against that of L.L.Bean, the efficiency of its central computer operations against that of John Deere, and the efficiency of its marketing abilities against that of Procter & Gamble. Those three companies are renowned for their skills in these different areas, and by studying how they performed, Xerox was able to dramatically increase its own performance. Benchmarking is a key tool in total quality management, an important change program discussed in Chapter 9.

In summary, organizational control and change are closely linked because organizations operate in environments that are constantly changing; so managers must be alert to the need to change their strategies and structures. Managers of high-performing organizations are attuned to the need to continually modify the way they operate, and they adopt techniques like empowered work groups and teams, benchmarking, and global outsourcing to remain competitive in a global world.

Summary and Review

LO11-1, 11-2

WHAT IS ORGANIZATIONAL CONTROL?   Controlling is the process whereby managers monitor and regulate how efficiently and effectively an organization and its members are performing the activities necessary to achieve organizational goals. Controlling is a four-step process: (1) establishing performance standards, (2) measuring actual performance, (3) comparing actual performance against performance standards, and (4) evaluating the results and initiating corrective action if needed.

LO11-3   **OUTPUT CONTROL**   To monitor output or performance, managers choose goals or performance standards that they think will best measure efficiency, quality, innovation, and responsiveness to customers at the corporate, divisional, departmental or functional, and individual levels. The main mechanisms that managers use to monitor output are financial measures of performance, organizational goals, and operating budgets.

LO11-4   **BEHAVIOR CONTROL**   In an attempt to shape behavior and induce employees to work toward achieving organizational goals, managers use direct supervision, management by objectives, and bureaucratic control by means of rules and standard operating procedures.

CLAN CONTROL   Clan control is the control exerted on individuals and groups by shared values, norms, and prescribed standards of behavior. An organization's culture is deliberately fashioned to emphasize the values and norms top managers believe will lead to high performance.

LO11-5   **ORGANIZATIONAL CHANGE**   There is a need to balance two opposing forces in the control process that influences the way organizations change. On one hand, managers need to be able to control organizational activities and make their operations routine and predictable. On the other hand, organizations have to be responsive to the need to change, and managers must understand when they need to depart from routines to be responsive to unpredictable events. The four steps in managing change are (1) assessing the need for change, (2) deciding on the changes to make, (3) implementing change, and (4) evaluating the results of change.

Management in Action

Topics for Discussion and Action

Discussion

1. What is the relationship between organizing and controlling? [LO11-1]

2. How do output control and behavior control differ? [LO11-2, 11-3]

3. Why is it important for managers to involve subordinates in the control process? [LO11-3, 11-4]

4. What kind of controls would you expect to find most used in (a) a hospital, (b) the Navy, and (c) a city police force? Why? [LO11-2, 11-3, 11-4]

5. What are the main obstacles to organizational change? What techniques can managers use to overcome these obstacles? [LO11-1, 11-5]

Action

6. Ask a manager to list the main performance measures that he or she uses to evaluate how well the organization is achieving its goals. [LO11-1, 11-3, 11-4]

7. Ask the same or a different manager to list the main forms of output control and behavior control that he or she uses to monitor and evaluate employee behavior. [LO11-3, 11-4]

Building Management Skills

Understanding Controlling [LO11-1, 11-3, 11-4]

For this exercise you will analyze the control systems used by a real organization such as a department store, restaurant, hospital, police department, or small business. It can be the organization that you investigated in Chapter 10 or a different one. Your objective is to uncover all the different ways in which managers monitor and evaluate the performance of the organization and employees.

1. At what levels does control take place in this organization?

2. Which output performance standards (such as financial measures and organizational goals) do managers use most often to evaluate performance at each level?

3. Does the organization have a management by objectives system in place? If it does, describe it. If it does not, speculate about why not.

4. How important is behavior control in this organization? For example, how much of managers' time is spent directly supervising employees? How formalized is the organization? Do employees receive a book of rules to teach them how to perform their jobs?

5. What kind of culture does the organization have? What are the values and norms? What effect does the organizational culture have on the way employees behave or treat customers?

6. Based on this analysis, do you think there is a fit between the organization's control systems and its culture? What is the nature of this fit? How could it be improved?

Managing Ethically [LO11-1, 11-5]

Some managers and organizations go to great lengths to monitor their employees' behavior, and they keep extensive records about employees' behavior and performance. Some organizations also seem to possess norms and values that cause their employees to behave in certain ways.

Questions

1. Either by yourself or in a group, think about the ethical implications of organizations' monitoring and collecting information about their employees.

What kinds of information is it ethical or unethical to collect? Why? Should managers and organizations tell subordinates they are collecting such information?

2. Similarly, some organizations' cultures seem to develop norms and values that cause their members to behave in unethical ways. When and why does a strong norm that encourages high performance become one that can cause people to act unethically? How can organizations keep their values and norms from becoming "too strong"?

Small Group Breakout Exercise

How Best to Control the Sales Force? [LO11-1, 11-3, 11-5]

Form groups of three or four people, and appoint one member as the spokesperson who will communicate your findings to the class when called on by the instructor. Then discuss the following scenario:

You are the regional sales managers of an organization that supplies high-quality windows and doors to building supply centers nationwide. Over the last three years, the rate of sales growth has slackened. There is increasing evidence that, to make their jobs easier, salespeople are primarily servicing large customer accounts and ignoring small accounts. In addition, the salespeople are not dealing promptly with customer questions and complaints, and this inattention has resulted in poor after-sales service. You have talked about these problems, and you are meeting to design a control system to increase both the amount of sales and the quality of customer service.

1. Design a control system that you think will best motivate salespeople to achieve these goals.

2. What relative importance do you put on (a) output control, (b) behavior control, and (c) organizational culture in this design?

Exploring the World Wide Web [LO11-1, 11-5]

Go to the website of Google. Look at pages such as "Jobs at Google," "Life at Google," "Company Overview," and "Our Culture."

1. How would you expect Google's values and norms to affect its employees' behavior?

2. How does Google design its organizational structure and workspace to shape its culture?

Be the Manager

You have been asked by your company's CEO to find a way to improve the performance of its teams of web design and web hosting specialists and programmers. Each team works on a different aspect of website production; and while each is responsible for the quality of its own performance, its performance also depends on how well the other teams perform. Your task is to create a control system that will help to increase the performance of each team separately and facilitate cooperation among the teams. This is necessary because the various projects are interlinked and affect one another just as the different parts of a car must fit together. Because competition in the website production market is intense, it is imperative that each website is up and running as quickly as possible and incorporates all the latest advances in website software technology.

Questions

1. What kind of output controls will best facilitate positive interactions both within the teams and among the teams?

2. What kind of behavior controls will best facilitate positive interactions both within the teams and among the teams?

3. How would you help managers develop a culture to promote high team performance?

Time Case in the News [LO11-1, 11-2, 11-4]

 TIME

Can Google Star Marissa Mayer Save Yahoo?

Marissa Mayer, formerly vice president for search products and user experience at Google Inc., was Google's 20th employee; a 37-year-old self-proclaimed "geek," she was already one of the most respected executives in Silicon Valley. But her appointment as the new CEO of Internet giant Yahoo instantly propels her to a whole new level: Mayer is now one of the most prominent female chief executives in the world. It's an inspired—and inspiring—choice for Yahoo, which desperately needs an injection of fresh energy after a series of failed CEOs and eroding esprit de corps.

Industry observers greeted news of Mayer's hiring warmly. But once the euphoria wears off, she'll face a steep challenge: reversing a years-long slide that has seen the onetime Internet pioneer eclipsed by Google, its erstwhile search rival, as well as newer upstarts like Facebook and Twitter. Yahoo's turnaround will come into sharp relief on Tuesday, July 17 2012, when the company reports second quarter earnings after the close of the stock market.

Mayer's appointment is a high water-mark in what was already a distinguished career. A Wausau, Wisconsin native, Mayer joined Google in 1999 after earning a B.S. in Symbolic Systems and an M.S. in Computer Science at Stanford University, where she specialized in artificial intelligence. She was Google's first female engineer and the company's 20th employee overall. She quickly took the helm of the company's user interface team, where she was instrumental in developing Google's iconic, minimalist search box layout. Mayer would eventually become responsible for many of Google's most successful consumer-facing products, including Gmail, Google News, and Google Maps. At the search giant, she developed a reputation for her laser-like focus on the user experience and became a compelling spokesperson for a company that for many years was ambivalent—to put it mildly—about public relations. In a statement, Google CEO Larry Page called Mayer "a tireless champion of our users," and said, "We will miss her talents at Google."

At Google, Mayer's intensity was legendary, even at a company filled with brilliant engineers, according to Douglas Edwards, an early Google employee who served as brand manager at the company from 1999 to 2005. "If everyone else at Google was a hundred-watt bulb illuminating a single corner of the company, Marissa was a flashing neon sign, casting light and shadow in all colors across the entire Googleplex," Edwards wrote in his 2011 book *I'm Feeling Lucky: The Confessions of Google Employee Number 59.*

Mayer became a trusted adviser to Google founders Page and Sergey Brin, and eventually joined the company's elite operating committee, responsible for overall management of the search giant. But in recent years, Mayer's ascent within Google appeared to have stalled, especially after Page shook up the company's management ranks upon succeeding Eric Schmidt as CEO last year. For the ambitious Mayer, the chance to assume command at one of the most well-known Internet companies in the world seems to have been too good to pass up.

"I am honored and delighted to lead Yahoo, one of the Internet's premier destinations for more than 700 million users," Mayer said in a statement Monday. "I look forward to working with the company's dedicated employees to bring innovative products, content, and personalized experiences to users and advertisers all around the world." Mayer's first day on the job is Tuesday July 17—she delivered her resignation to Google by phone Monday—but it's unclear if she will join Yahoo's earnings call after the stock market closes. Late Monday, Mayer disclosed that she's pregnant with her first child with husband Zachary Bogue, a Bay Area lawyer.

Yahoo is clearly hoping that Mayer's appointment represents a clean break from the tumult of the last few years. The situation reached a nadir earlier this year during a bizarre episode involving former CEO Scott Thompson, who admitted he didn't possess the computer science degree he listed on his resumé when he got the Yahoo job. Thompson, who had replaced the outspoken Carol Bartz as CEO, was soon jettisoned. Veteran media executive Ross Levinsohn was named interim CEO, and although many observers speculated that he might be tapped for the permanent job, Yahoo's board clearly felt that more drastic change was needed. "Marissa is a well-known visionary leader in user experience and product design and one of Silicon Valley's most exciting strategists in technology development," Yahoo cofounder David Filo said in a statement.

By picking Mayer, an accomplished engineer with a keen eye for design, Yahoo is signaling that it intends to make technology and user experience top priorities. For Yahoo's long-suffering engineers, that should be good news. Still, the company faces a steep climb to return to its former glory. In recent years, Yahoo has been adrift, lacking a clear vision and strategy as it's been eclipsed by Google as well as social media upstarts like Facebook and Twitter. Yahoo still has a massive audience, but it no longer commands the respect it once did.

Yahoo's stock has been down 40% over the last five years, and has stagnated since 2010, but rose 2% in after-hours trading on news of Mayer's hiring.

Wall Street analysts offered cautious praise. "We believe Mayer's background as one of Google's earliest engineers and her experience overseeing key products suggests the company will refocus on the user experience and pace of innovation," JPMorgan analyst Doug Anmuth wrote in a note to clients: "Importantly, we believe Mayer may also be able to attract more high-quality engineering talent to Yahoo!, which we think is needed after several years of strategic and leadership flux." Citigroup's Mark Mahaney called the hire "bold" and said he has "high regards for Ms. Mayer's organizational skills, consumer Internet industry knowledge and her ability to focus efforts of a large team of engineers on product innovation."

Mayer's first job will be inspiring her troops to believe in Yahoo once again. She'll have to develop a vision of where she wants to take the company, and then map out a plan to execute on that vision. This turnaround won't happen overnight; it will be a long road. But for now, Yahoo employees, shareholders, and Silicon Valley at-large should savor Mayer's appointment. It's the most inspired decision the purple-hued Internet portal has taken in many years.

Questions for Discussion

1. Why is it so important for Yahoo to improve its IT systems and website products/services?

2. In what ways can Mayer use her IT expertise to help improve Yahoo's (a) responsiveness to online users, and (b) the quality and innovativeness of its website products/services?

3. What are the most effective ways in which an online portal such as Yahoo or any Internet portal can improve its users' online experience?

Source: S. Gustin, *Time* (Business Online), July 17, 2012. © 2012 Time Inc. Used under license.

CHAPTER 12

Human Resource Management

Learning Objectives

After studying this chapter, you should be able to:

LO12-1 Explain why strategic human resource management can help an organization gain a competitive advantage.

LO12-2 Describe the steps managers take to recruit and select organizational members.

LO12-3 Discuss the training and development options that ensure organizational members can effectively perform their jobs.

LO12-4 Explain why performance appraisal and feedback are such crucial activities, and list the choices managers must make in designing effective performance appraisal and feedback procedures.

LO12-5 Explain the issues managers face in determining levels of pay and benefits.

LO12-6 Understand the role that labor relations play in the effective management of human resources.

A MANAGER'S CHALLENGE

Happy Employees Provide Exceptional Service at Zappos

How can managers ensure that employees will provide excellent service and be happy doing so? Nothing is conventional about the online retailer Zappos, headquartered in Henderson, Nevada.[1] Think accountants running Pinewood Derby car races during the workday, a conference room that a team decorated to simulate a log cabin, employees ringing cowbells and blowing horns during visitor tours, costume parades, and managers spending 10–20% of their time socializing with their subordinates.[2] And the list could go on. Yet Zappos, founded in 1999 as a struggling online shoe shop, rode out the dot-com bust to earn over $1.6 billion in annual revenues in 2010 and be ranked 11th on *Fortune* magazine's list of the One Hundred Best Companies to Work For in 2012.[3] In 2009 Amazon.com purchased Zappos for shares worth $1.2 billion.[4] As a wholly owned subsidiary of Amazon, Zappos continues to be led by its long-standing CEO Tony Hsieh; Hsieh was the initial primary investor who kept Zappos afloat as a start-up and became its CEO in 2000.[5]

Key to Zappos's success is a focus on people—having happy employees provide exceptional service to customers.[6] In fact, Hsieh's own experiences helped him realize the importance of employees being happy and having fun at work. Hsieh, who has a computer science degree from Harvard, started his first company, LinkExchange, when he was in his early 20s. This company enabled small web publishers to trade advertising on each other's sites and also sold advertising. When he was 24, Hsieh sold LinkExchange to Microsoft for $265 million. Despite this phenomenal early success, Hsieh felt uneasy because he no longer much enjoyed going to work, and the people around him seemed more interested in cashing out than building something long-term.[7]

Hsieh decided to build something long-lasting and a workplace in which happy

Mission: Create fun and a little weirdness—accomplished! If you'd like to work in a T-shirt surrounded by your favorite plants, a plastic skull, and personalized balloons while getting the chance to develop your business savvy, check out Zappos's job openings.

employees wanted to come to work each day. Zappos was one of 27 start-ups that Hsieh invested in along with his partner and former classmate, Alfred Lin, through their venture capital fund Venture Frogs. Although some of these succeeded (such as Ask.com and OpenTable), many did not live through the dot-com bust. When Zappos was struggling, Hsieh stepped in with more funds and became involved in running the company.[8]

Zappos has expanded from selling shoes to selling a wide range of products ranging from clothing and handbags to housewares, watches, and jewelry.[9] What is distinctive about Zappos is not so much the products it sells but rather the exceptional service it provides customers.[10] Customers receive free shipping on products both ways (for purchases and returns), and Zappos has a 365-day return policy. Its website prominently displays a toll-free telephone number that customers can call to speak to a member of the Customer Loyalty Team (CLT) 24 hours a day, seven days a week.[11] CLT members have great autonomy to keep customers happy the way they think is best. Their call times are not monitored, and they do not read from scripts. They make decisions on their own, such as providing refunds for defective goods or sending flowers to a customer who had a death in the family, without having to consult a manager. And they strive to make personal connections with their customers. Some calls last for hours, and team members regularly send personal notes to customers.[12] Providing exceptional service that leads to repeat business from happy customers and good word-of-mouth advertising is central to Zappos's approach to business.[13]

Unfortunately, Zappos had to temporarily shut down its phones in January of 2012 when hackers accessed data pertaining to customers from one of Zappos's servers in Kentucky. As a security precaution, Zappos expired customers' passwords and instructed them on how to create new passwords via an e-mail message from Hsieh, who also encouraged them to change passwords for other sites that might have been the same as their Zappos's passwords.[14] Hsieh explained the need to temporarily respond to customers' inquiries via e-mail given the high volume of calls expected from Zappos's more than 24 million customers.[15]

Central to the guiding philosophy at Zappos is having a happy workforce of satisfied employees who actually want to come to work each day and have fun on and off the job.[16] Thus Hsieh and other managers at Zappos go to great lengths to ensure that the Zappos core values and unique culture are maintained and strengthened. The core values of Zappos are these: "1. Deliver WOW through Service; 2. Embrace and Drive Change; 3. Create Fun and a Little Weirdness; 4. Be Adventurous, Creative, and Open-Minded; 5. Pursue Growth and Learning; 6. Build Open and Honest Relationships with Communication; 7. Build a Positive Team and Family Spirit; 8. Do More with Less; 9. Be Passionate and Determined; 10. Be Humble."[17]

Because of the importance of having happy employees, Zappos goes to great lengths to effectively manage human resources. Potential new hires are interviewed by human resources, to make sure they will work well in Zappos's culture and support its values, as well as by the department doing the hiring, to determine their suitability for the position they are interviewing for. If human resources and the hiring manager disagree in their assessments of an applicant, Hsieh interviews the applicant himself and makes the final decision.[18]

Newly hired employees receive extensive training. For example, the CLT new hires who answer calls have two weeks of classroom training followed by two weeks of training in answering calls. Once the training is completed, they are given the opportunity to receive $2,000 and pay for the time they spent in training if they want to quit.[19] This way only new hires who want to stay with the company remain.

Experienced employees are encouraged to continue to grow and develop on the job. For example, employees who have worked at Zappos for two or fewer years have over 200 hours of classroom training and development during their work hours and are required to read nine books about business. More experienced employees receive training and development in such areas as financial planning and speaking in public. Zappos has a company library well stocked with multiple copies of business books and books about personal growth and development for employees to borrow and read. As Hsieh indicates, "The vision is that three years from now, almost all our hires will be entry-level people. . . . We'll provide them with training and mentorship, so that within five to seven years, they can become senior leaders within the company."[20]

Although pay for entry-level employees is not high, Zappos pays for all their health care; and upon announcing that Zappos would become a subsidiary of Amazon.com, employees were told they would each receive a retention bonus equivalent to 40% of their yearly salary and a Kindle.[21] In any case, Zappos's phenomenal growth in revenues and being ranked 11th among the 100 Best Companies to Work For in 2012 suggest that human resources are being effectively managed to promote happiness among customers and employees alike.[22]

Overview

Managers are responsible for acquiring, developing, protecting, and utilizing the resources an organization needs to be efficient and effective. One of the most important resources in all organizations is human resources—the people involved in producing and distributing goods and services. Human resources include all members of an organization, ranging from top managers to entry-level employees. Effective managers like Tony Hsieh in "A Manager's Challenge" realize how valuable human resources are and take active steps to make sure their organizations build and fully utilize their human resources to gain a competitive advantage.

This chapter examines how managers can tailor their human resource management system to their organization's strategy and structure. We discuss in particular the major components of human resource management: recruitment and selection, training and development, performance appraisal, pay and benefits, and labor relations. By the end of this chapter you will understand the central role human resource management plays in creating a high-performing organization.

LO12-1 Explain why strategic human resource management can help an organization gain a competitive advantage.

human resource management (HRM) Activities that managers engage in to attract and retain employees and to ensure that they perform at a high level and contribute to the accomplishment of organizational goals.

Strategic Human Resource Management

Organizational architecture (see Chapter 10) is the combination of organizational structure, control systems, culture, and a human resource management system that managers develop to use resources efficiently and effectively. **Human resource management (HRM)** includes all the activities managers engage in to attract and retain employees and to ensure that they perform at a high level and contribute to the accomplishment of organizational goals. These activities make up an organization's human resource management system, which has five major components:

Figure 12-1

Components of a Human Resource Management System

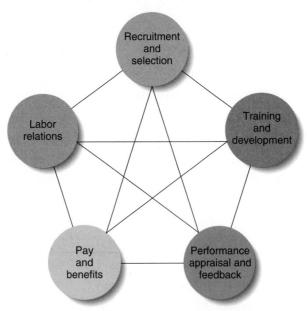

Each component of an HRM system influences
the others, and all five must fit together.

recruitment and selection, training and development, performance appraisal and feedback, pay and benefits, and labor relations (see Figure 12.1).

strategic human resource management The process by which managers design the components of an HRM system to be consistent with each other, with other elements of organizational architecture, and with the organization's strategy and goals.

Strategic human resource management is the process by which managers design the components of an HRM system to be consistent with each other, with other elements of organizational architecture, and with the organization's strategy and goals.[23] The objective of strategic HRM is the development of an HRM system that enhances an organization's efficiency, quality, innovation, and responsiveness to customers—the four building blocks of competitive advantage. At Zappos in "A Manager's Challenge," HRM practices ensure that all employees provide excellent customer service.

As part of strategic human resource management, some managers have adopted "Six Sigma" quality improvement plans. These plans ensure that an organization's products and services are as free of errors or defects as possible through a variety of human resource–related initiatives. Jack Welch, former CEO of General Electric Company, has indicated that these initiatives saved his company millions of dollars; and other companies, such as Whirlpool and Motorola, also have implemented Six Sigma initiatives. For such initiatives to be effective, however, top managers have to be committed to Six Sigma, employees must be motivated, and there must be demand for the products or services of the organization in the first place. David Fitzpatrick, head of Deloitte Consulting's Lean Enterprise Practice, estimates that most Six Sigma plans are not effective because the conditions for effective Six Sigma are not in place. For example, if top managers are not committed to the quality initiative, they may not devote the necessary time and resources to make it work and may lose interest in it prematurely.[24]

Overview of the Components of HRM

Managers use *recruitment and selection,* the first component of an HRM system, to attract and hire new employees who have the abilities, skills, and experiences that will help an organization achieve its goals. Microsoft Corporation, for example, has the goal of remaining the premier computer software company in the world. To achieve this goal, managers at Microsoft realize the importance of hiring only the best software designers: Hundreds of highly qualified candidates are interviewed and rigorously tested. This careful attention to selection has contributed to Microsoft's competitive advantage. Microsoft has little trouble recruiting top programmers because candidates know they will be at the forefront of the industry if they work for Microsoft.[25]

After recruiting and selecting employees, managers use the second component, *training and development,* to ensure that organizational members develop the skills and abilities that will enable them to perform their jobs effectively in the present and the future. Training and development compose an ongoing process; changes in technology and the environment, as well as in an organization's goals and strategies, often require that organizational members learn new techniques and ways of working. At Microsoft, newly hired program designers receive on-the-job training by joining small teams that include experienced employees who serve as mentors or advisers. New recruits learn firsthand from team members how to go about developing computer systems that are responsive to customers' programming needs.[26]

The third component, *performance appraisal and feedback,* serves two different purposes in HRM. First, performance appraisal can give managers the information they need to make good human resources decisions—decisions about how to train, motivate, and reward organizational members.[27] Thus the performance appraisal and feedback component is a kind of *control system* that can be used with management by objectives (discussed in Chapter 11). Second, feedback from performance appraisal serves a developmental purpose for members of an organization. When managers regularly evaluate their subordinates' performance, they can provide employees with valuable information about their strengths and weaknesses and the areas in which they need to concentrate.

On the basis of performance appraisals, managers distribute *pay* to employees, which is part of the fourth component of an HRM system. By rewarding high-performing organizational members with pay raises, bonuses, and the like, managers increase the likelihood that an organization's most valued human resources will be motivated to continue their high levels of contribution to the organization. Moreover, if pay is linked to performance, high-performing employees are more likely to stay with the organization, and managers are more likely to fill positions that become open with highly talented individuals. *Benefits* such as health insurance are important outcomes that employees receive by virtue of their membership in an organization.

Last, but not least, *labor relations* encompass the steps that managers take to develop and maintain good working relationships with the labor unions that may represent their employees' interests. For example, an organization's labor relations component can help managers establish safe working conditions and fair labor practices in their offices and plants.

Managers must ensure that all five of these components fit together and complement their company's structure and control systems.[28] For example, if managers decide to decentralize authority and empower employees, they need to invest in training and development to ensure that lower-level employees have the knowledge and expertise they need to make the decisions that top managers would make in a more centralized structure.

Each of the five components of HRM influences the others (see Figure 12.1).[29] The kinds of people that the organization attracts and hires through recruitment and selection, for example, determine (1) the kinds of training and development that are necessary, (2) the way performance is appraised, and (3) the appropriate levels of pay and benefits. Managers at Microsoft ensure that their organization has highly qualified program designers by (1) recruiting and selecting the best candidates, (2) guiding new hires with experienced team members, (3) appraising program designers' performance in terms of their individual contributions and their teams' performance, and (4) basing programmers' pay on individual and team performance.

Effectively managing human resources helps ensure that both customers and employees are satisfied and loyal, as illustrated in the following "Managing Globally" box.

**Managing
Globally**

Managing Human Resources at Semco

Ricardo Semler was 21 years old (and one of the youngest graduates from the Harvard Business School MBA program) when he took his father's place as head of the family business, Semco, based in São Paolo, Brazil, in 1984.[30] His father Antonio had founded Semco in 1954 as a machine shop; the company went on to become a manufacturer of marine pumps for the shipbuilding industry, with $4 million a year in

Ricardo Semler recognizes that Semco's success hinges on its employees.

revenues when Ricardo Semler took over. Today Semco's revenues are over $200 million a year from a diverse set of businesses ranging from the development and manufacture of industrial mixing and refrigeration equipment to the provision of systems to manage communication, correspondence, and goods exchanges between an organization and its suppliers, customers, and partners.[31] Semco prides itself on being a premier provider of goods and services in its markets and has loyal customers.[32]

Semler is the first to admit that Semco's track record of success is due to its human resources—its employees. In fact, Semler so firmly believes in Semco's employees that he and the other top managers are reluctant to tell employees what to do. Semco has no rules, regulations, or organizational charts; hierarchy is eschewed; and workplace democracy rules the day. Employees have levels of autonomy unheard of in other companies, and flexibility and trust are built into every aspect of human resource management at Semco.[33]

Human resource practices at Semco revolve around maximizing the contributions employees make to the company, and this begins by hiring individuals who want to, can, and will contribute. Semco strives to ensure that all selection decisions are based on relevant and complete information. Job candidates are first interviewed as a group; the candidates meet many employees, receive a tour of the company, and interact with potential coworkers. This gives Semco a chance to size up candidates in ways more likely to reveal their true natures, and it gives the candidates a chance to learn about Semco. When finalists are identified from the pool, multiple Semco employees interview each one five or six more times to choose the best person(s) to be hired. The result is that both Semco and new hires make informed decisions and are mutually committed to making the relation a success.[34]

Once hired, entry-level employees participate in the Lost in Space program, in which they rotate through different positions and units of their own choosing for about a year.[35] In this way, the new hires learn about their options and can decide where their interests lie, and the units they work in learn about the new hires. At the end of the year, the new employees may be offered a job in one of the units in which they worked, or they may seek a position elsewhere in Semco. Seasoned Semco employees are also encouraged to rotate positions and work in different parts of the company to keep them fresh, energized, and motivated and to give them the opportunity to contribute in new ways as their interests change.[36]

Performance is appraised at Semco in terms of results; all employees and managers must demonstrate that they are making valuable contributions and deserve to be "rehired." For example, each manager's performance is anonymously appraised by all the employees who report to him or her, and the appraisals are made publicly available in Semco. Employees also can choose how they are paid from a combination of 11 different compensation options, ranging from fixed salaries, bonuses, and profit sharing to royalties on sales or profits and arrangements based on meeting annual self-set goals. Flexibility in compensation promotes risk taking and innovation, according to Semler, and maximizes returns to employees in terms of their pay and to the company in terms of revenues and profitability.[37] Flexibility, autonomy, the ability to change jobs often, and control of working hours and even compensation are some of the ways by which Semler strives to ensure that employees are loyal and involved in their work because they *want* to be; turnover at Semco is less than 1% annually.[38] And with human resource practices geared toward maximizing contributions and performance, Semco is well poised to continue to provide value to its customers.

The Legal Environment of HRM

In the rest of this chapter we focus in detail on the choices managers must make in strategically managing human resources to attain organizational goals and gain a competitive advantage. Effectively managing human resources is a complex undertaking for managers, and we provide an overview of some major issues they face. First, however, we need to look at how the legal environment affects human resource management.

The local, state, and national laws and regulations that managers and organizations must abide by add to the complexity of HRM. For example, the U.S. government's commitment to **equal employment opportunity (EEO)** has resulted in the creation and enforcement of a number of laws that managers must abide by. The goal of EEO is to ensure that all citizens have an equal opportunity to obtain employment regardless of their gender, race, country of origin, religion, age, or disabilities. Table 12.1 summarizes some of the major EEO laws affecting HRM. Other laws, such as the Occupational Safety and Health Act of 1970, require that managers ensure that employees are protected from workplace hazards and safety standards are met.

In Chapter 5 we explained how effectively managing diversity is an ethical and business imperative, and we discussed the many issues surrounding diversity. EEO laws and their enforcement make the effective management of diversity a legal imperative as well. The Equal Employment Opportunity Commission (EEOC) is the division of the Department of Justice that enforces most EEO laws and handles discrimination complaints. In addition, the EEOC issues guidelines for managers to follow to ensure that they are abiding by EEO laws. For example, the Uniform Guidelines on Employee Selection Procedures issued by the EEOC (in conjunction with the Departments of Labor and Justice and the Civil Service Commission) guide managers on how to ensure that the recruitment and selection component of human resource management complies with Title VII of the Civil Rights Act (which prohibits discrimination based on gender, race, color, religion, and national origin).[39]

Contemporary challenges that managers face related to the legal environment include how to eliminate sexual harassment (see Chapter 5 for an in-depth discussion of sexual harassment), how to accommodate employees with disabilities, how to deal with employees who have substance abuse problems, and how to manage HIV-positive employees and employees

equal employment opportunity (EEO) The equal right of all citizens to the opportunity to obtain employment regardless of their gender, age, race, country of origin, religion, or disabilities.

Table 12.1
Major Equal Employment Opportunity Laws Affecting HRM

Year	Law	Description
1963	Equal Pay Act	Requires that men and women be paid equally if they are performing equal work.
1964	Title VII of the Civil Rights Act	Prohibits employment discrimination on the basis of race, religion, sex, color, or national origin; covers a wide range of employment decisions, including hiring, firing, pay, promotion, and working conditions.
1967	Age Discrimination in Employment Act	Prohibits discrimination against workers over the age of 40 and restricts mandatory retirement.
1978	Pregnancy Discrimination Act	Prohibits employment discrimination against women on the basis of pregnancy, childbirth, and related medical decisions.
1990	Americans with Disabilities Act	Prohibits employment discrimination against individuals with disabilities and requires that employers make accommodations for such workers to enable them to perform their jobs.
1991	Civil Rights Act	Prohibits discrimination (as does Title VII) and allows the awarding of punitive and compensatory damages, in addition to back pay, in cases of intentional discrimination.
1993	Family and Medical Leave Act	Requires that employers provide 12 weeks of unpaid leave for medical and family reasons, including paternity and illness of a family member.

with AIDS.[40] HIV-positive employees are infected with the virus that causes AIDS but may show no AIDS symptoms and may not develop AIDS in the near future. Often such employees are able to perform their jobs effectively, and managers must take steps to ensure that they are allowed to do so and are not discriminated against in the workplace.[41] Employees with AIDS may or may not be able to perform their jobs effectively, and, once again, managers need to ensure that they are not unfairly discriminated against.[42] Many organizations have instituted AIDS awareness training programs to educate organizational members about HIV and AIDS, dispel myths about how HIV is spread, and ensure that individuals infected with the HIV virus are treated fairly and are able to be productive as long as they can be while not putting others at risk.[43]

LO12-2 Describe the steps managers take to recruit and select organizational members.

Recruitment and Selection

recruitment Activities that managers engage in to develop a pool of qualified candidates for open positions.

selection The process that managers use to determine the relative qualifications of job applicants and their potential for performing well in a particular job.

human resource planning Activities that managers engage in to forecast their current and future needs for human resources.

outsource To use outside suppliers and manufacturers to produce goods and services.

Recruitment includes all the activities managers engage in to develop a pool of qualified candidates for open positions.[44] **Selection** is the process by which managers determine the relative qualifications of job applicants and their potential for performing well in a particular job. Before actually recruiting and selecting employees, managers need to engage in two important activities: human resource planning and job analysis (Figure 12.2).

Human Resource Planning

Human resource planning includes all the activities managers engage in to forecast their current and future human resource needs. Current human resources are the employees an organization needs today to provide high-quality goods and services to customers. Future human resource needs are the employees the organization will need at some later date to achieve its longer-term goals.

As part of human resource planning, managers must make both demand forecasts and supply forecasts. *Demand forecasts* estimate the qualifications and numbers of employees an organization will need given its goals and strategies. *Supply forecasts* estimate the availability and qualifications of current employees now and in the future, as well as the supply of qualified workers in the external labor market.

As a result of their human resource planning, managers sometimes decide to **outsource** to fill some of their human resource needs. Instead of recruiting and selecting employees to produce goods and services, managers contract with people who are not members of their organization to produce goods and services. Managers in publishing companies, for example, frequently contract with freelance editors to copyedit books that they intend to publish. Kelly Services is an organization that provides the services of technical and professional employees to managers who want to use outsourcing to fill some of their human resource requirements in these areas.[45]

Two reasons why human resource planning sometimes leads managers to outsource are flexibility and cost. First, outsourcing can give managers increased flexibility, especially when accurately forecasting human resource needs is difficult, human resource needs fluctuate over time, or finding skilled workers in a particular area is difficult. Second, outsourcing can sometimes allow managers to use human resources at a lower cost. When work is outsourced, costs can be lower for a number of reasons: The organization does not have to provide benefits to workers; managers can contract for work only when the work is needed; and managers do

Figure 12.2
The Recruitment and Selection System

not have to invest in training. Outsourcing can be used for functional activities such as after-sales service on appliances and equipment, legal work, and the management of information systems.[46]

Outsourcing has disadvantages, however.[47] When work is outsourced, managers may lose some control over the quality of goods and services. Also, individuals performing outsourced work may have less knowledge of organizational practices, procedures, and goals and less commitment to an organization than regular employees. In addition, unions resist outsourcing because it has the potential to eliminate some of their members. To gain some of the flexibility and cost savings of outsourcing and avoid some of its disadvantages, a number of organizations, such as Microsoft and IBM, rely on a pool of temporary employees to, for example, debug programs.

A major trend reflecting the increasing globalization of business is the outsourcing of office work, computer programming, and technical jobs from the United States and countries in western Europe, with high labor costs, to countries like India and China, with low labor costs.[48] For example, computer programmers in India and China earn a fraction of what their U.S. counterparts earn. Outsourcing (or *offshoring,* as it is also called when work is outsourced to other countries) has also expanded into knowledge-intensive work such as engineering, research and development, and the development of computer software. According to a study conducted by The Conference Board and Duke University's Offshoring Research Network, more than half of U.S. companies surveyed have some kind of offshoring strategy related to knowledge-intensive work and innovation.[49] Why are so many companies engaged in offshoring, and why are companies that already offshore work planning to increase the extent of offshoring? While cost savings continue to be a major motivation for offshoring, managers also want to take advantage of an increasingly talented global workforce and be closer to the growing global marketplace for goods and services.[50]

Major U.S. companies often earn a substantial portion of their revenues overseas. For example, Hewlett-Packard, Caterpillar, and IBM earn over 60% of their revenues from overseas markets. And many large companies employ thousands of workers overseas. For example, IBM employs close to 100,000 workers in India and Hewlett-Packard, over 25,000.[51] Managers at some smaller companies have offshored work to Sri Lanka, Russia, and Egypt.[52] Key challenges for managers who offshore are retaining sufficient managerial control over activities and employee turnover.[53] In recent times, there have been some interesting developments in outsourcing to other countries as profiled in the following "Managing Globally."

Managing
Globally

Recent Trends in Outsourcing

Countries in Latin America and Eastern Europe are becoming increasingly popular outsourcing destinations for skilled professional workers in the areas of finance, accounting, research, and procurement. For example, São Paulo, Brazil has a sizable population of engineering and business school graduates who speak English and can perform a diverse set of tasks ranging from financial analysis to video game development.[54] A Brazilian trade group for technology, Brasscom, indicates that there are more Java programmers in Brazil than in any other country and Brazil has the second highest number of COBOL programmers. Thus, perhaps it is not surprising that IBM's ninth research center is located in São Paulo.[55]

It typically costs more to outsource work to Latin American countries than to India. For example, outsourcing an entry-level accounting job to India costs around 51% less than hiring a worker in the United States; outsourcing the same job to Argentina costs about 13% less than hiring a U.S. worker.[56] However, if the Argentinian has a better understanding of business and is more skilled at interacting with clients, bearing the added costs might make sense. Additionally, if client interaction levels are high, it is advantageous for outsourcing countries and home countries to be

Indian office workers face a downswing in the amount of outsourced jobs from the United States. Argentina offers stiff competition with skilled workers whose hours are more closely aligned to the U.S. time zones but who can still be paid less than their U.S. counterparts.

in similar time zones. The time difference between New York and Argentina, for example, is much smaller than the time difference between New York and India.[57]

Copal Partners, which is an outsourcing company in Gurgaon, India, that provides research services on investments, recently opened an office in Buenos Aires, in part because of the benefits of being in a closer time zone with clients. As Rishi Khosla, the CEO of Copal puts it, "If you're working with a hedge fund manager where you have to interact 10 to 15 times a day, having someone in about the same time zone is important."[58] Tata Consultancy Services, the Indian outsourcing giant, has over 8,000 employees in South American countries, including Peru and Paraguay.[59]

Countries in Eastern Europe are also seeing surges in outsourcing. For example, Microsoft, Ernst & Young, and IBM have all opened outsourcing facilities in Wroclaw, Poland. Ernst & Young actually has six outsourcing centers in cities in Poland that together have around 1,300 employees.[60] Young people in Poland are more likely to be college educated than in India and they tend to be very multilingual. Jacek Levernes, who manages outsourcing to Europe, Africa, and the Middle East for Hewlett-Packard's Wroclaw, Poland, facility indicates that having 26 different languages spoken in the center is very advantageous for interacting with clients in different countries in these regions. Guatemala is also an outsourcing destination for companies like Capgemini Consulting and Coco-Cola enterprises. Evidently the trend toward "near-shoring" to countries closer to home certainly has its advantages.[61]

Job Analysis

job analysis Identifying the tasks, duties, and responsibilities that make up a job and the knowledge, skills, and abilities needed to perform the job.

Job analysis is a second important activity that managers need to undertake prior to recruitment and selection.[62] **Job analysis** is the process of identifying (1) the tasks, duties, and responsibilities that make up a job (the *job description*) and (2) the knowledge, skills, and abilities needed to perform the job (the *job specifications*).[63] For each job in an organization, a job analysis needs to be done.

Job analysis can be done in a number of ways, including observing current employees as they perform the job or interviewing them. Often managers rely on questionnaires compiled by jobholders and their managers. The questionnaires ask about the skills and abilities needed to perform the job, job tasks and the amount of time spent on them, responsibilities, supervisory activities, equipment used, reports prepared, and decisions made.[64] The Position Analysis Questionnaire (PAQ) is a comprehensive standardized questionnaire that many managers rely on to conduct job analyses.[65] It focuses on behaviors jobholders perform, working conditions, and job characteristics and can be used for a variety of jobs.[66] The PAQ contains 194 items organized into six divisions: (1) information input (where and how the jobholder acquires information to perform the job), (2) mental processes (reasoning, decision making, planning, and information processing activities that are part of the job), (3) work output (physical activities performed on the job and machines and devices used), (4) relationships with others (interactions with other people that are necessary to perform the job), (5) job context (the physical and social environment of the job), and (6) other job characteristics (such as work pace).[67] A trend, in some organizations, is toward more flexible jobs in which tasks and responsibilities change and cannot be clearly specified in advance. For these kinds of jobs, job analysis focuses more on determining the skills and knowledge workers need to be effective and less on specific duties.

After managers have completed human resource planning and job analyses for all jobs in an organization, they will know their human resource needs and the jobs they need to fill. They will also know what knowledge, skills, and abilities potential employees need to perform those jobs. At this point, recruitment and selection can begin.

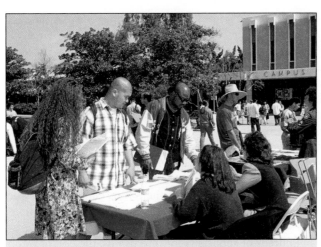

Many colleges and universities hold job fairs to connect employers with students looking for jobs.

External and Internal Recruitment

As noted earlier, recruitment is what managers do to develop a pool of qualified candidates for open positions.[68] They traditionally have used two main types of recruiting, external and internal, which are now supplemented by recruiting over the Internet.

EXTERNAL RECRUITING   When managers recruit externally to fill open positions, they look outside the organization for people who have not worked for the organization previously. There are multiple means through which managers can recruit externally: advertisements in newspapers and magazines, open houses for students and career counselors at high schools and colleges or on-site at the organization, career fairs at colleges, and recruitment meetings with groups in the local community.

Many large organizations send teams of interviewers to college campuses to recruit new employees. External recruitment can also take place through informal networks, as occurs when current employees inform friends about open positions in their companies or recommend people they know to fill vacant spots. Some organizations use employment agencies for external recruitment, and some external recruitment takes place simply through walk-ins—job hunters coming to an organization and inquiring about employment possibilities.

With all the downsizing and corporate layoffs that have taken place in recent years, you might think external recruiting would be a relatively easy task for managers. However, it often is not, because even though many people may be looking for jobs, many jobs that are open require skills and abilities that these job hunters do not have. Managers needing to fill vacant positions and job hunters seeking employment opportunities are increasingly relying on the Internet to connect with each other through employment websites such as Monster.com[69] and JobLine International.[70] Major corporations such as Coca-Cola, Cisco, Ernst & Young, Canon, and Telia have relied on JobLine to fill global positions.[71]

External recruiting has both advantages and disadvantages for managers. Advantages include having access to a potentially large applicant pool, being able to attract people who have the skills, knowledge, and abilities that an organization needs to achieve its goals, and being able to bring in newcomers who may have a fresh approach to problems and be up to date on the latest technology. These advantages have to be weighed against the disadvantages, including the relatively high costs of external recruitment. Employees recruited externally also lack knowledge about the inner workings of the organization and may need to receive more training than those recruited internally. Finally, when employees are recruited externally, there is always uncertainty concerning whether they will actually be good performers. Nonetheless, there are steps managers can take to reduce some of the uncertainty surrounding external recruitment, as profiled in the following "Information Technology Byte" box.

Information Technology Byte

Fog Creek Software's Approach to Recruiting

Fog Creek Software is a small, privately owned software company founded in 2000 by Joel Spolsky and Michael Pryor in a renovated loft in the Fashion District of New York City.[72] Fog Creek has earned a profit each year since its founding.[73] Hiring great computer software developers is essential for a company like Fog Creek; according to Spolsky, the top 1% of software developers outperform average developers by a ratio of around

Fog Creek Software uses paid summer internships to help identify and attract promising software developers.

10:1. And the top 1% are the inventive types who can successfully develop new products while also being highly efficient.[74]

Finding, never mind recruiting, the top 1% is a real challenge for a small company like Fog Creek because many of these people already have great jobs and are not looking to switch employers. Realizing that the top 1% of developers might rarely apply for positions with Fog Creek (or any other company), Fog Creek uses paid summer internships to recruit over 50% of its developers while they are still in college; they are hired full-time after graduation.[75]

In the fall of every year, Fog Creek sends personalized letters to computer science majors across the country who have the potential to be top developers in the future, contacts professors at leading computer science programs for recommendations, and also seeks applications through their website.[76] This process yields hundreds of applicants for internships, the best of whom are then given a phone interview. During the interview, the candidates describe themselves and their classes, are asked how they would go about solving a software development problem or challenge, and then can ask anything they want about the company or living in New York City.[77]

Those who do well in the phone interview are flown to New York for an all-expense paid visit to Fog Creek—they are met at the airport in a limousine, stay in a hip hotel, receive welcoming gifts in their rooms, have a full day of interviews at Fog Creek, and then are given the option of staying two extra nights (at no cost to themselves) to get a feel for New York City. Typically only one out of every three recruits who has an on-site visit receives an internship offer.[78]

Interns perform real software development work—several summers ago, a team of four interns developed a new successful technology support product called Fog Creek Copilot.[79] This both motivates the interns and helps managers decide which interns they would like to hire. The interns are treated well—in addition to being paid, they receive free housing and are invited to outings, parties, and cultural events in New York City. At the conclusion of the internships, managers have a good sense of which interns are great programmers. These top programmers are offered jobs upon graduation with generous salaries, excellent working conditions, and great benefits. Although Fog Creek's approach to external recruitment is lengthy and expensive, it more than pays for itself by identifying and attracting top programmers. As Spolsky indicates, "An internship program creates a pipeline for great employees. It's a pretty long pipeline, so you need to have a long-term perspective, but it pays off in spades."[80]

INTERNAL RECRUITING   When recruiting is internal, managers turn to existing employees to fill open positions. Employees recruited internally are either seeking **lateral moves** (job changes that entail no major changes in responsibility or authority levels) or promotions. Internal recruiting has several advantages. First, internal applicants are already familiar with the organization (including its goals, structure, culture, rules, and norms). Second, managers already know the candidates; they have considerable information about their skills and abilities and actual behavior on the job. Third, internal recruiting can help boost levels of employee motivation and morale, both for the employee who gets the job and for other workers. Those who are not seeking a promotion or who may not be ready for one can see that promotion is a possibility in the future; or a lateral move can alleviate boredom once a job has been fully mastered and can also be a useful way to learn new skills. Finally, internal recruiting is normally less time-consuming and expensive than external recruiting.

Given the advantages of internal recruiting, why do managers rely on external recruiting as much as they do? The answer lies in the disadvantages of internal recruiting—among them, a limited pool of candidates and a tendency among those candidates to be set in the organization's ways. Often the organization simply does not have suitable internal candidates. Sometimes, even when suitable internal applicants are available, managers may rely on external recruiting to find the very best candidate or to help bring new ideas and approaches into their

lateral move A job change that entails no major changes in responsibility or authority levels.

organization. When organizations are in trouble and performing poorly, external recruiting is often relied on to bring in managerial talent with a fresh approach.

HONESTY IN RECRUITING   At times, when trying to recruit the most qualified applicants, managers may be tempted to paint rosy pictures of both the open positions and the organization as a whole. They may worry that if they are honest about advantages and disadvantages, they either will not be able to fill positions or will have fewer or less qualified applicants. A manager trying to fill a secretarial position, for example, may emphasize the high level of pay and benefits the job offers and fail to mention the fact that the position is usually a dead-end job offering few opportunities for promotion.

Research suggests that painting a rosy picture of a job and the organization is not a wise recruiting strategy. Recruitment is more likely to be effective when managers give potential applicants an honest assessment of both the advantages and the disadvantages of the job and organization. Such an assessment is called a **realistic job preview (RJP)**.[81] RJPs can reduce the number of new hires who quit when their jobs and organizations fail to meet their unrealistic expectations, and they help applicants decide for themselves whether a job is right for them.

Take the earlier example of the manager trying to recruit a secretary. The manager who paints a rosy picture of the job might have an easy time filling it but might hire a secretary who expects to be promoted quickly to an administrative assistant position. After a few weeks on the job, the secretary may realize that a promotion is unlikely no matter how good his or her performance, become dissatisfied, and look for and accept another job. The manager then has to recruit, select, and train another new secretary. The manager could have avoided this waste of valuable organizational resources by using a realistic job preview. The RJP would have increased the likelihood of hiring a secretary who was comfortable with few promotional opportunities and subsequently would have been satisfied to remain on the job.

realistic job preview (RJP) An honest assessment of the advantages and disadvantages of a job and organization.

The Selection Process

Once managers develop a pool of applicants for open positions through the recruitment process, they need to find out whether each applicant is qualified for the position and likely to be a good performer. If more than one applicant meets these two conditions, managers must further determine which applicants are likely to be better performers than others. They have several selection tools to help them sort out the relative qualifications of job applicants and appraise their potential for being good performers in a particular job. These tools include background information, interviews, paper-and-pencil tests, physical ability tests, performance tests, and references (see Figure 12.3).[82]

Figure 12.3
Selection Tools

BACKGROUND INFORMATION   To aid in the selection process, managers obtain background information from job applications and from résumés. Such information might include the highest levels of education obtained, college majors and minors, type of college or university attended, years and type of work experience, and mastery of foreign languages. Background information can be helpful both to screen out applicants who are lacking key qualifications (such as a college degree) and to determine which qualified applicants are more promising than others. For example, applicants with a BS may be acceptable, but those who also have an MBA may be preferable.

Increasing numbers of organizations are performing background checks to verify the background information prospective employees provide (and also to uncover any negative information such as crime convictions).[83] According to Automatic Data Processing, Inc. (ADP), an outsourcing company that performs payroll and human resource functions for organizations, more and more companies are performing background checks on prospective employees and are uncovering inaccuracies, inconsistencies, and negative information not reported on applications.[84] According to ADP, about 30% of applicants provide some form of false information with regards to their employment history.[85] And in some cases, background checks reveal prior convictions.[86]

INTERVIEWS   Virtually all organizations use interviews during the selection process, as is true at Zappos in "A Manager's Challenge." Interviews may be structured or unstructured. In a *structured interview,* managers ask each applicant the same standard questions (such as "What are your unique qualifications for this position?" and "What characteristics of a job are most important to you?"). Particularly informative questions may be those that prompt an interviewee to demonstrate skills and abilities needed for the job by answering the question. Sometimes called *situational interview questions,* these often present interviewees with a scenario they would likely encounter on the job and ask them to indicate how they would handle it.[87] For example, applicants for a sales job may be asked to indicate how they would respond to a customer who complains about waiting too long for service, a customer who is indecisive, and a customer whose order is lost.

An *unstructured interview* proceeds more like an ordinary conversation. The interviewer feels free to ask probing questions to discover what the applicant is like and does not ask a fixed set of questions determined in advance. In general, structured interviews are superior to unstructured interviews because they are more likely to yield information that will help identify qualified candidates, are less subjective, and may be less influenced by the interviewer's biases.

Even when structured interviews are used, however, the potential exists for the interviewer's biases to influence his or her judgment. Recall from Chapter 5 how the similar-to-me effect can cause people to perceive others who are similar to themselves more positively than those who are different and how stereotypes can result in inaccurate perceptions. Interviewers must be trained to avoid these biases and sources of inaccurate perceptions as much as possible. Many of the approaches to increasing diversity awareness and diversity skills described in Chapter 5 are used to train interviewers to avoid the effects of biases and stereotypes. In addition, using multiple interviewers can be advantageous because their individual biases and idiosyncrasies may cancel one another out.[88]

When conducting interviews, managers cannot ask questions that are irrelevant to the job in question; otherwise their organizations run the risk of costly lawsuits. It is inappropriate and illegal, for example, to inquire about an interviewee's spouse or to ask questions about whether an interviewee plans to have children. Because questions such as these are irrelevant to job performance, they are discriminatory and violate EEO laws (see Table 12.1). Thus interviewers need to be instructed in EEO laws and informed about questions that may violate those laws.

Managers can use interviews at various stages in the selection process. Some use interviews as initial screening devices; others use them as a final hurdle that applicants must jump.

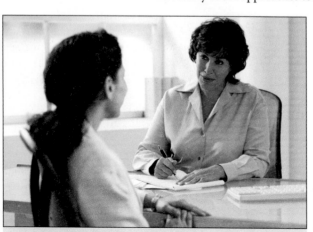

Practically all organizations use some kind of interview during the selection process.

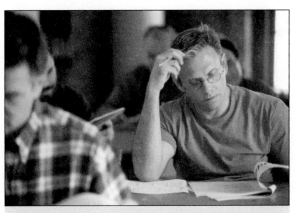

Yes, it still exists! Employees struggle to get in the doors by completing, on paper, an ability and personality exam.

Regardless of when they are used, managers typically use other selection tools in conjunction with interviews because of the potential for bias and for inaccurate assessments of interviewees. Even though training and structured interviews can eliminate the effects of some biases, interviewers can still come to erroneous conclusions about interviewees' qualifications. Interviewees, for example, who make a bad initial impression or are overly nervous in the first minute or two of an interview tend to be judged more harshly than less nervous candidates, even if the rest of the interview goes well.

PAPER-AND-PENCIL TESTS The two main kinds of paper-and-pencil tests used for selection purposes are ability tests and personality tests; both kinds of tests can be administered in hard copy or electronic form. *Ability tests* assess the extent to which applicants possess the skills necessary for job performance, such as verbal comprehension or numerical skills. Autoworkers hired by General Motors, Chrysler, and Ford, for example, are typically tested for their ability to read and to do mathematics.[89]

Personality tests measure personality traits and characteristics relevant to job performance. Some retail organizations, for example, give job applicants honesty tests to determine how trustworthy they are. The use of personality tests (including honesty tests) for hiring purposes is controversial. Some critics maintain that honesty tests do not really measure honesty (that is, they are not valid) and can be faked by job applicants. Before using any paper-and-pencil tests for selection purposes, managers must have sound evidence that the tests are actually good predictors of performance on the job in question. Managers who use tests without such evidence may be subject to costly discrimination lawsuits.

PHYSICAL ABILITY TESTS For jobs requiring physical abilities, such as firefighting, garbage collecting, and package delivery, managers use physical ability tests that measure physical strength and stamina as selection tools. Autoworkers are typically tested for mechanical dexterity because this physical ability is an important skill for high job performance in many auto plants.[90]

PERFORMANCE TESTS *Performance tests* measure job applicants' performance on actual job tasks. Applicants for secretarial positions, for example, typically are required to complete a keyboarding test that measures how quickly and accurately they type. Applicants for middle and top management positions are sometimes given short-term projects to complete—projects that mirror the kinds of situations that arise in the job being filled—to assess their knowledge and problem-solving capabilities.[91]

Assessment centers, first used by AT&T, take performance tests one step further. In a typical assessment center, about 10 to 15 candidates for managerial positions participate in a variety of activities over a few days. During this time they are assessed for the skills an effective manager needs—problem-solving, organizational, communication, and conflict resolution skills. Some of the activities are performed individually; others are performed in groups. Throughout the process, current managers observe the candidates' behavior and measure performance. Summary evaluations are then used as a selection tool.

REFERENCES Applicants for many jobs are required to provide references from former employers or other knowledgeable sources (such as a college instructor or adviser) who know the applicants' skills, abilities, and other personal characteristics. These individuals are asked to provide candid information about the applicant. References are often used at the end of the selection process to confirm a decision to hire. Yet the fact that many former employers are reluctant to provide negative information in references sometimes makes it difficult to interpret what a reference is really saying about an applicant.

In fact, several recent lawsuits filed by applicants who felt that they were unfairly denigrated or had their privacy invaded by unfavorable references from former employers have caused managers to be increasingly wary of providing any negative information in a reference, even if it is accurate. For jobs in which the jobholder is responsible for the safety and

reliability The degree to which a tool or test measures the same thing each time it is used.

validity The degree to which a tool or test measures what it purports to measure.

training Teaching organizational members how to perform their current jobs and helping them acquire the knowledge and skills they need to be effective performers.

development Building the knowledge and skills of organizational members so they are prepared to take on new responsibilities and challenges.

needs assessment An assessment of which employees need training or development and what type of skills or knowledge they need to acquire.

lives of other people, however, failing to provide accurate negative information in a reference does not just mean that the wrong person might get hired; it may also mean that other people's lives will be at stake.

THE IMPORTANCE OF RELIABILITY AND VALIDITY Whatever selection tools a manager uses need to be both reliable and valid. **Reliability** is the degree to which a tool or test measures the same thing each time it is administered. Scores on a selection test should be similar if the same person is assessed with the same tool on two different days; if there is quite a bit of variability, the tool is unreliable. For interviews, determining reliability is more complex because the dynamic is personal interpretation. That is why the reliability of interviews can be increased if two or more different qualified interviewers interview the same candidate. If the interviews are reliable, the interviewers should come to similar conclusions about the interviewee's qualifications.

Validity is the degree to which a tool measures what it purports to measure—for selection tools, it is the degree to which the test predicts performance on the tasks or job in question. Does a physical ability test used to select firefighters, for example, actually predict on-the-job performance? Do assessment center ratings actually predict managerial performance? Do keyboarding tests predict secretarial performance? These are all questions of validity. Honesty tests, for example, are controversial because it is not clear that they validly predict honesty in such jobs as retailing and banking.

Managers have an ethical and legal obligation to use reliable and valid selection tools. Yet reliability and validity are matters of degree rather than all-or-nothing characteristics. Thus managers should strive to use selection tools in such a way that they can achieve the greatest degree of reliability and validity. For ability tests of a particular skill, managers should keep up to date on the latest advances in the development of valid paper-and-pencil tests and use the test with the highest reliability and validity ratings for their purposes. Regarding interviews, managers can improve reliability by having more than one person interview job candidates.

Training and Development

Training and development help to ensure that organizational members have the knowledge and skills needed to perform jobs effectively, take on new responsibilities, and adapt to changing conditions. **Training** focuses primarily on teaching organizational members how to perform their current jobs and helping them acquire the knowledge and skills they need to be effective performers. **Development** focuses on building the knowledge and skills of organizational members so they are prepared to take on new responsibilities and challenges. Training tends to be used more frequently at lower levels of an organization; development tends to be used more frequently with professionals and managers.

Before creating training and development programs, managers should perform a **needs assessment** to determine which employees need training or development and what type of skills or knowledge they need to acquire (see Figure 12.4).[92]

Types of Training

There are two types of training: classroom instruction and on-the-job training.

CLASSROOM INSTRUCTION Through classroom instruction, employees acquire knowledge and skills in a classroom setting. This instruction may take place within the organization or outside it, such as through courses at local colleges and universities. Many organizations establish their own formal instructional divisions—some are even called "colleges"—to provide needed classroom instruction. For example, at Disney, classroom instruction and other forms of training and developing are provided to employees at Disney University.[93]

All in this together! New employees gathered in a small room listen to their instructor going over the basics before they complete an on-screen assessment of what they have learned.

Figure 12.4
Training and Development

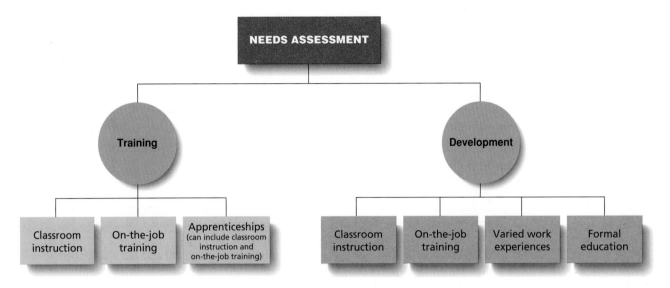

Classroom instruction frequently uses videos and role playing in addition to traditional written materials, lectures, and group discussions. *Videos* can demonstrate appropriate and inappropriate job behaviors. For example, by watching an experienced salesperson effectively deal with a loud and angry customer, inexperienced salespeople can develop skills in handling similar situations. During *role playing,* trainees either directly participate in or watch others perform actual job activities in a simulated setting. At McDonald's Hamburger University, for example, role playing helps franchisees acquire the knowledge and skills they need to manage their restaurants.

Simulations also can be part of classroom instruction, particularly for complicated jobs that require an extensive amount of learning and in which errors carry a high cost. In a simulation, key aspects of the work situation and job tasks are duplicated as closely as possible in an artificial setting. For example, air traffic controllers are trained by simulations because of the complicated nature of the work, the extensive amount of learning involved, and the very high costs of air traffic control errors.

on-the-job training
Training that takes place in the work setting as employees perform their job tasks.

ON-THE-JOB TRAINING In **on-the-job training,** learning occurs in the work setting as employees perform their job tasks. On-the-job training can be provided by coworkers or supervisors or can occur simply as jobholders gain experience and knowledge from doing the work. Newly hired waiters and waitresses in chains such as Red Lobster or the Olive Garden often receive on-the-job training from experienced employees. The supervisor of a new bus driver for a campus bus system may ride the bus for a week to ensure that the driver has learned the routes and follows safety procedures. Chefs learn to create new and innovative dishes by experimenting with different combinations of ingredients and cooking techniques. For all on-the-job training, employees learn by doing.

Managers often use on-the-job training on a continuing basis to ensure that their subordinates keep up to date with changes in goals, technology, products, or customer needs and desires. For example, sales representatives at Mary Kay Cosmetics Inc. receive ongoing training so they not only know about new cosmetic products and currently popular colors but also are reminded of Mary Kay's guiding principles. Mary Kay's expansion into Russia has succeeded in part because of the ongoing training that Mary Kay's Russian salespeople receive.[94]

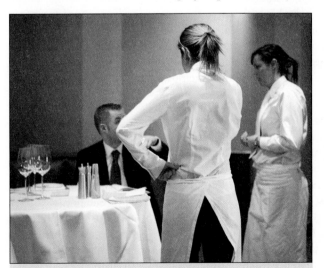

At many restaurants, new employees receive on-the-job training by shadowing more experienced waiters and waitresses as they go about their work.

Types of Development

Although both classroom instruction and on-the-job training can be used for development as well as training, development often includes additional activities such as varied work experiences and formal education.

VARIED WORK EXPERIENCES   Top managers need to develop an understanding of, and expertise in, a variety of functions, products and services, and markets. To develop executives who will have this expertise, managers frequently make sure that employees with high potential have a wide variety of different job experiences, some in line positions and some in staff positions. Varied work experiences broaden employees' horizons and help them think about the big picture. For example, one- to three-year stints overseas are being used increasingly to provide managers with international work experiences. With organizations becoming more global, managers need to understand the different values, beliefs, cultures, regions, and ways of doing business in different countries.

Another development approach is mentoring. (Recall from Chapter 5 that a *mentor* is an experienced member of an organization who provides advice and guidance to a less experienced member, called a *protégé*.) Having a mentor can help managers seek out work experiences and assignments that will contribute to their development and can enable them to gain the most possible from varied work experiences.[95] Although some mentors and protégés hook up informally, organizations have found that formal mentoring programs can be valuable ways to contribute to the development of managers and all employees.

Formal mentoring programs ensure that mentoring takes place in an organization, structure the process, and make sure diverse organizational members have equal access to mentors. Participants receive training, efforts are focused on matching mentors and protégés so meaningful developmental relationships ensue, and organizations can track reactions and assess the potential benefits of mentoring. Formal mentoring programs can also ensure that diverse members of an organization receive the benefits of mentoring. A study conducted by David A. Thomas, a professor at the Harvard Business School, found that members of racial minority groups at three large corporations who were very successful in their careers had the benefit of mentors. Formal mentoring programs help organizations make this valuable development tool available to all employees.[96]

When diverse members of an organization lack mentors, their progress in the organization and advancement to high-level positions can be hampered. Ida Abott, a lawyer and consultant on work-related issues, presented a paper to the Minority Corporate Counsel Association in which she concluded, "The lack of adequate mentoring has held women and minority lawyers back from achieving professional success and has led to high rates of career dissatisfaction and attrition."[97]

Mentoring can benefit all kinds of employees in all kinds of work.[98] John Washko, a manager at the Four Seasons hotel chain, benefited from the mentoring he received from Stan Bromley on interpersonal relations and how to deal with employees; mentor Bromley, in turn, found that participating in the Four Seasons' mentoring program helped him develop his own management style.[99] More generally, development is an ongoing process for all managers, and mentors often find that mentoring contributes to their own personal development.

FORMAL EDUCATION   Many large corporations reimburse employees for tuition expenses they incur while taking college courses and obtaining advanced degrees. This is not just benevolence on the part of the employer or even a simple reward given to the employee; it is an effective way to develop employees who can take on new responsibilities and more challenging positions. For similar reasons, corporations spend thousands of dollars sending managers to executive development programs such as executive MBA programs. In these programs, experts teach managers the latest in business and management techniques and practices.

To save time and travel costs, some managers rely on *long-distance learning* to formally educate and develop employees. Using videoconferencing technologies, business schools such as the Harvard Business School, the University of Michigan, and Babson College teach courses on video screens in corporate conference rooms. Business schools also customize courses and degrees to fit the development needs of employees in a particular company and/or a particular geographic region.[100]

Transfer of Training and Development

Whenever training and development take place off the job or in a classroom setting, it is vital for managers to promote the transfer of the knowledge and skills acquired *to the actual work situation*. Trainees should be encouraged and expected to use their newfound expertise on the job.

Performance Appraisal and Feedback

performance appraisal
The evaluation of employees' job performance and contributions to their organization.

performance feedback
The process through which managers share performance appraisal information with subordinates, give subordinates an opportunity to reflect on their own performance, and develop, with subordinates, plans for the future.

The recruitment/selection and training/development components of a human resource management system ensure that employees have the knowledge and skills needed to be effective now and in the future. Performance appraisal and feedback complement recruitment, selection, training, and development. **Performance appraisal** is the evaluation of employees' job performance and contributions to the organization. **Performance feedback** is the process through which managers share performance appraisal information with their subordinates, give subordinates an opportunity to reflect on their own performance, and develop, with subordinates, plans for the future. Before performance feedback, performance appraisal must take place. Performance appraisal could take place without providing performance feedback, but wise managers are careful to provide feedback because it can contribute to employee motivation and performance.

Performance appraisal and feedback contribute to the effective management of human resources in several ways. Performance appraisal gives managers important information on which to base human resource decisions.[101] Decisions about pay raises, bonuses, promotions, and job moves all hinge on the accurate appraisal of performance. Performance appraisal can also help managers determine which workers are candidates for training and development and in what areas. Performance feedback encourages high levels of employee motivation and performance. It lets good performers know that their efforts are valued and appreciated. It also lets poor performers know that their lackluster performance needs improvement. Performance feedback can give both good and poor performers insight on their strengths and weaknesses and ways in which they can improve their performance in the future.

Types of Performance Appraisal

Performance appraisal focuses on the evaluation of traits, behaviors, and results.[102]

TRAIT APPRAISALS When trait appraisals are used, managers assess subordinates on personal characteristics that are relevant to job performance, such as skills, abilities, or personality. A factory worker, for example, may be evaluated based on her ability to use computerized equipment and perform numerical calculations. A social worker may be appraised based on his empathy and communication skills.

Three disadvantages of trait appraisals often lead managers to rely on other appraisal methods. First, possessing a certain personal characteristic does not ensure that the personal characteristic will actually be used on the job and result in high performance. For example, a factory worker may possess superior computer and numerical skills but be a poor performer due to low motivation. The second disadvantage of trait appraisals is linked to the first. Because traits do not always show a direct association with performance, workers and courts of law may view them as unfair and potentially discriminatory. The third disadvantage of trait appraisals is that they often do not enable managers to give employees feedback they can use to improve performance. Because trait appraisals focus on relatively enduring human characteristics that change only over the long term, employees can do little to change their behavior in response to performance feedback from a trait appraisal. Telling a social worker that he lacks empathy says little about how he can improve his interactions with clients, for example. These disadvantages suggest that managers should use trait appraisals only when they can demonstrate that the assessed traits are accurate and important indicators of job performance.

BEHAVIOR APPRAISALS   Through behavior appraisals, managers assess how workers perform their jobs—the actual actions and behaviors that workers exhibit on the job. Whereas trait appraisals assess what workers *are like,* behavior appraisals assess what workers *do.* For example, with a behavior appraisal, a manager might evaluate a social worker on the extent to which he looks clients in the eye when talking with them, expresses sympathy when they are upset, and refers them to community counseling and support groups geared toward the specific problems they are encountering. Behavior appraisals are especially useful when *how* workers perform their jobs is important. In educational organizations such as high schools, for example, the numbers of classes and students taught are important, but also important is how they are taught or the methods teachers use to ensure that learning takes place.

Behavior appraisals have the advantage of giving employees clear information about what they are doing right and wrong and how they can improve their performance. And because behaviors are much easier for employees to change than traits, performance feedback from behavior appraisals is more likely to lead to improved performance.

RESULTS APPRAISALS   For some jobs, *how* people perform the job is not as important as *what* they accomplish or the results they obtain. With results appraisals, managers appraise performance by the results or the actual outcomes of work behaviors. Take the case of two new car salespeople. One salesperson strives to develop personal relationships with her customers. She spends hours talking to them and frequently calls them to see how their decision-making process is going. The other salesperson has a much more hands-off approach. He is very knowledgeable, answers customers' questions, and then waits for them to come to him. Both salespersons sell, on average, the same number of cars, and the customers of both are satisfied with the service they receive, according to postcards the dealership mails to customers asking for an assessment of their satisfaction. The manager of the dealership appropriately uses results appraisals (sales and customer satisfaction) to evaluate the salespeople's performance because it does not matter which behavior salespeople use to sell cars as long as they sell the desired number and satisfy customers. If one salesperson sells too few cars, however, the manager can give that person performance feedback about his or her low sales.

OBJECTIVE AND SUBJECTIVE APPRAISALS   Whether managers appraise performance in terms of traits, behaviors, or results, the information they assess is either *objective* or *subjective.* **Objective appraisals** are based on facts and are likely to be numerical—the number of cars sold, the number of meals prepared, the number of times late, the number of audits completed. Managers often use objective appraisals when results are being appraised because results tend to be easier to quantify than traits or behaviors. When *how* workers perform their jobs is important, however, subjective behavior appraisals are more appropriate than results appraisals.

Subjective appraisals are based on managers' perceptions of traits, behaviors, or results. Because subjective appraisals rest on managers' perceptions, there is always the chance that they are inaccurate (see Chapter 5). This is why both researchers and managers have spent considerable time and effort on determining the best way to develop reliable and valid subjective measures of performance.

Some of the more popular subjective measures such as the graphic rating scale, the behaviorally anchored rating scale (BARS), and the behavior observation scale (BOS) are illustrated in Figure 12.5.[103] When graphic rating scales are used, performance is assessed along a continuum with specified intervals. With a BARS, performance is assessed along a scale with clearly defined scale points containing examples of specific behaviors. A BOS assesses performance by how often specific behaviors are performed. Many managers may use both objective and subjective appraisals. For example, a salesperson may be appraised both on the dollar value of sales (objective) and the quality of customer service (subjective).

In addition to subjective appraisals, some organizations employ *forced rankings* whereby supervisors must rank their subordinates and assign them to different categories according to their performance (which is subjectively appraised). For example, at Lending Tree, managers and employees are ranked by their superiors as a "1" (top 15% based on individual performance and goals), "2" (middle 75%), or "3" (bottom 10%).[104] While the forced ranking system was originally adopted at Lending Tree to reward high performers and make it less likely that they would seek positions elsewhere, in tough times when housing and mortgage sales are down, the

objective appraisal An appraisal that is based on facts and is likely to be numerical.

subjective appraisal An appraisal that is based on perceptions of traits, behaviors, or results.

Figure 12.5

Subjective Measures of Performance

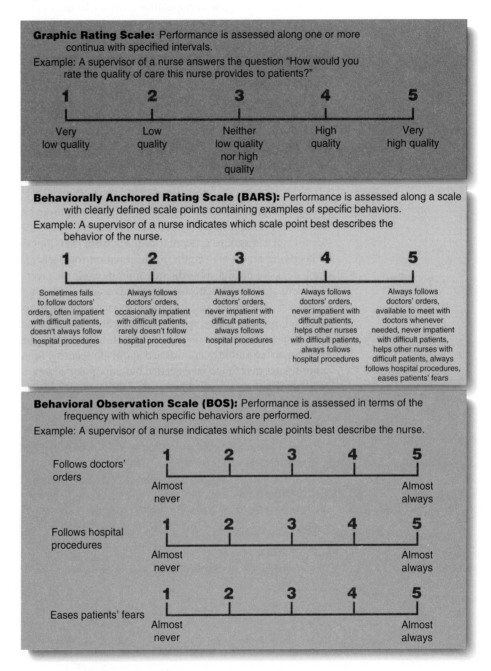

"3's" are the ones mostly likely to be laid off if layoffs take place.[105] While some managers are proponents of forced rankings, others are strongly opposed to the practice. Proponents believe that forced rankings help ensure that human resource decisions are made based on merit, top performers are recognized, and all employees know where they stand relative to others. Opponents of forced ranking believe that forced rankings can be demoralizing, lead to a competitive environment unsupportive of cooperation and teamwork, and also result in favoritism. And forced rankings schemes that force managers to group percentages of employees in certain predetermined categories might not make sense if the predetermined categories do not match the distribution of performance across the employees. For example, a forced ranking system might require a manager to "force" 20% of his or her subordinates into the bottom ranking designation when in fact most of the subordinates' performance is average or above average and only 5 to 10% of employees are poor performers. When forced rankings are applied on a regional basis, they can cause conflict and political maneuvering among managers, each of whom wants to ensure that his or her subordinates are ranked in the better categories. Interestingly enough, while forced rankings were popularized, in part, by their use at General Electric under the leadership of Jack Welch, GE no longer uses a forced ranking system.

Who Appraises Performance?

We have been assuming that managers or the supervisors of employees evaluate performance. This is a reasonable assumption: Supervisors are the most common appraisers of performance.[106] Performance appraisal is an important part of most managers' job duties. Managers are responsible for not only motivating their subordinates to perform at a high level but also making many decisions hinging on performance appraisals, such as pay raises or promotions. Appraisals by managers can be usefully augmented by appraisals from other sources (see Figure 12.6).

SELF, PEERS, SUBORDINATES, AND CLIENTS   When self-appraisals are used, managers supplement their evaluations with an employee's assessment of his or her own performance. Peer appraisals are provided by an employee's coworkers. Especially when subordinates work in groups or teams, feedback from peer appraisals can motivate team members while giving managers important information for decision making. A growing number of companies are having subordinates appraise their managers' performance and leadership as well. And sometimes customers or clients assess employee performance in terms of responsiveness to customers and quality of service. Although appraisals from these sources can be useful, managers need to be aware of potential issues that may arise when they are used. Subordinates sometimes may be inclined to inflate self-appraisals, especially if organizations are downsizing and they are worried about job security. Managers who are appraised by their subordinates may fail to take needed but unpopular actions out of fear that their subordinates will appraise them negatively. Some of these potential issues can be mitigated to the extent that there are high levels of trust in an organization.

360-degree appraisal A performance appraisal by peers, subordinates, superiors, and sometimes clients who are in a position to evaluate a manager's performance.

360-DEGREE PERFORMANCE APPRAISALS   To improve motivation and performance, some organizations include 360-degree appraisals and feedback in their performance appraisal systems, especially for managers. In a **360-degree appraisal** a variety of people, beginning with the manager and including peers or coworkers, subordinates, superiors, and sometimes even customers or clients, appraise a manager's performance. The manager receives feedback based on evaluations from these multiple sources.

Figure 12.6
Who Appraises Performance?

How am I doing? Sitting down for an honest and open performance appraisal with your immediate supervisor can help keep you on track.

Companies in a variety of industries rely on 360-degree appraisals and feedback.[107] For 360-degree appraisals and feedback to be effective, there has to be trust throughout an organization. More generally, trust is a critical ingredient in any performance appraisal and feedback procedure. In addition, research suggests that 360-degree appraisals should focus on behaviors rather than traits or results and that managers need to carefully select appropriate raters. Moreover, appraisals tend to be more honest when made anonymously and when raters have been trained in how to use 360-degree appraisal forms.[108] Additionally, managers need to think carefully about the extent to which 360-degree appraisals are appropriate for certain jobs and be willing to modify any appraisal system they implement if they become aware of unintended problems it creates.[109]

Even when 360-degree appraisals are used, it is sometimes difficult to design an effective process by which subordinates' feedback can be communicated to their managers; but advances in information technology can solve this problem. For example, ImproveNow.com has online questionnaires that subordinates fill out to evaluate the performance of their managers and give the managers feedback. Each subordinate of a particular manager completes the questionnaire independently, all responses are tabulated, and the manager is given specific feedback on behaviors in a variety of areas, such as rewarding good performance, looking out for subordinates' best interests and being supportive, and having a vision for the future.[110]

Effective Performance Feedback

For the appraisal and feedback component of a human resource management system to encourage and motivate high performance, managers must give their subordinates feedback. To generate useful information to feed back to their subordinates, managers can use both formal and informal appraisals. **Formal appraisals** are conducted at set times during the year and are based on performance dimensions and measures that have been specified in advance. A salesperson, for example, may be evaluated by his or her manager twice a year on the performance dimensions of sales and customer service, sales being objectively measured from sales reports, and customer service being measured with a BARS (see Figure 12.5).

Managers in most large organizations use formal performance appraisals on a fixed schedule dictated by company policy, such as every six months or every year. An integral part of a formal appraisal is a meeting between the manager and the subordinate in which the subordinate is given feedback on performance. Performance feedback lets subordinates know which areas they are excelling in and which areas need improvement; it should also tell them *how* they can improve their performance. Realizing the value of formal appraisals, managers in many large corporations have committed substantial resources to updating their performance appraisal procedures and training low-level managers in how to use them and provide accurate feedback to employees.[111]

Formal performance appraisals supply both managers and subordinates with valuable information; but subordinates often want more frequent feedback, and managers often want to motivate subordinates as the need arises. For these reasons many companies supplement formal performance appraisal with frequent **informal appraisals**, for which managers and their subordinates meet as the need arises to discuss ongoing progress and areas for improvement. Moreover, when job duties, assignments, or goals change, informal appraisals can give workers timely feedback concerning how they are handling their new responsibilities.

Managers often dislike providing performance feedback, especially when the feedback is negative, but doing so is an important managerial activity.[112] Here are some guidelines for giving effective performance feedback that contributes to employee motivation and performance:

- *Be specific and focus on behaviors or outcomes that are correctable and within a worker's ability to improve.* Example: Telling a salesperson that he is too shy when interacting with customers is likely to lower his self-confidence and prompt him to become defensive. A more effective approach would be to give the salesperson feedback about specific behaviors to engage in—greeting customers as soon as they enter the department, asking customers whether they need help, and volunteering to help customers find items.

formal appraisal An appraisal conducted at a set time during the year and based on performance dimensions and measures that were specified in advance.

informal appraisal An unscheduled appraisal of ongoing progress and areas for improvement.

- *Approach performance appraisal as an exercise in problem solving and solution finding, not criticizing.* Example: Rather than criticizing a financial analyst for turning in reports late, the manager helps the analyst determine why the reports are late and identify ways to better manage her time.

- *Express confidence in a subordinate's ability to improve.* Example: Instead of being skeptical, a first-level manager tells a subordinate that he is confident that the subordinate can increase quality levels.

- *Provide performance feedback both formally and informally.* Example: The staff of a preschool receives feedback from formal performance appraisals twice a year. The school director also provides frequent informal feedback such as complimenting staff members on creative ideas for special projects, noticing when they do a particularly good job handling a difficult child, and pointing out when they provide inadequate supervision.

- *Praise instances of high performance and areas of a job in which a worker excels.* Example: Rather than focusing on just the negative, a manager discusses the areas her subordinate excels in as well as the areas in need of improvement.

- *Avoid personal criticisms and treat subordinates with respect.* Example: An engineering manager acknowledges her subordinates' expertise and treats them as professionals. Even when the manager points out performance problems to subordinates, she refrains from criticizing them personally.

- *Agree to a timetable for performance improvements.* Example: A first-level manager and his subordinate decide to meet again in one month to determine whether quality levels have improved.

In following these guidelines, managers need to remember *why* they are giving performance feedback: to encourage high levels of motivation and performance. Moreover, the information that managers gather through performance appraisal and feedback helps them determine how to distribute pay raises and bonuses.

Pay and Benefits

Pay includes employees' base salaries, pay raises, and bonuses and is determined by a number of factors such as characteristics of the organization and the job and levels of performance. Employee *benefits* are based on membership in an organization (and not necessarily on the particular job held) and include sick days, vacation days, and medical and life insurance. In Chapter 13 we discuss how pay can motivate organizational members to perform at a high level, as well as the different kinds of pay plans managers can use to help an organization achieve its goals and gain a competitive advantage. As you will learn, it is important to link pay to behaviors or results that contribute to organizational effectiveness. Next we focus on establishing an organization's pay level and pay structure.

LO12-5 Explain the issues managers face in determining levels of pay and benefits.

Pay Level

pay level The relative position of an organization's pay incentives in comparison with those of other organizations in the same industry employing similar kinds of workers.

Pay level is a broad comparative concept that refers to how an organization's pay incentives compare, in general, to those of other organizations in the same industry employing similar kinds of workers. Managers must decide if they want to offer relatively high wages, average wages, or relatively low wages. High wages help ensure that an organization is going to be able to recruit, select, and retain high performers, but high wages also raise costs. Low wages give an organization a cost advantage but may undermine the organization's ability to select and recruit high performers and to motivate current employees to perform at a high level. Either of these situations may lead to inferior quality or inadequate customer service.

In determining pay levels, managers should take into account their organization's strategy. A high pay level may prohibit managers from effectively pursuing a low-cost strategy. But a high pay level may be worth the added costs in an organization whose competitive advantage lies in superior quality and excellent customer service. As one might expect, hotel and motel chains with a low-cost strategy, such as Days Inn and Hampton Inns, have lower pay levels than chains striving to provide high-quality rooms and services, such as the Four Seasons. In fact, the Four Seasons treats and pays its employees very well, as profiled in the following "Management Insight" box.

Management Insight

Treating Employees Well Leads to Satisfied Customers

Four Seasons Hotels and Resorts is one of only around a dozen companies to be ranked one of the "100 Best Companies to Work For" every year since *Fortune* magazine started this annual ranking of companies.[113] And the Four Seasons often receives other awards and recognition such as being named the "Best Hotel Group Worldwide" by *Gallivanter's Guide* and dominating *Travel + Leisure*'s World's Best Awards Readers' Poll and Condé Nast *Traveler*'s Readers' Choice Awards based on customers' responses.[114] In an industry in which annual turnover rates are relatively high, the Four Seasons' voluntary turnover rate is 10%.[115] Evidently employees and customers alike are satisfied with how they are treated at the Four Seasons. Understanding that the two are causally linked is perhaps the key to the Four Seasons' success. As the Four Seasons' founder, chairman of the board, and CEO Isadore Sharp[116] suggests, "How you treat your employees is how you expect them to treat the customer."[117]

The Four Seasons was founded by Sharp in 1961 when he opened his first hotel called the Four Seasons Motor Hotel in a less-than-desirable area outside downtown Toronto. Whereas his first hotel had 125 inexpensively priced rooms appealing to the individual traveler, his fourth hotel was built to appeal to business travelers and conventions with 1,600 rooms, conference facilities, several restaurants, banquet halls, and shops in an arcade. Both these hotels were successful, but Sharp decided he could provide customers with a different kind of hotel experience by combining the best features of both kinds of hotel experiences—the sense of closeness and personal attention that a small hotel brings with the amenities of a big hotel to suit the needs of business travelers.[118]

At the Four Seasons, treating employees well leads to satisfied customers. Everyone wins!

Sharp sought to provide the kind of personal service that would really help business travelers on the road—giving them the amenities they have at home and in the office and miss when traveling on business. Thus the Four Seasons was the first hotel chain to provide bathrobes, shampoo, round-the-clock room service, laundry and dry cleaning services, large desks in every room, two-line phones, and round-the-clock secretarial assistance.[119] While these are relatively concrete ways of personalizing the hotel experience, Sharp realized that how employees treat customers is just as, or perhaps even more, important. When employees view each customer as an individual with his or her own needs and desires, and empathetically try to meet these needs and desires and help customers both overcome any problems or challenges they face and truly enjoy their hotel experience, a hotel can indeed serve the purposes of a home away from home (and an office away from office), and customers are likely to be both loyal and highly satisfied.[120]

Sharp has always realized that for employees to treat customers well, the Four Seasons needs to treat its employees well. Salaries are relatively high at the Four Seasons by industry standards (between the 75th and 90th percentiles); employees participate in a profit sharing plan; and the company contributes to their 401(k) plans. Four Seasons pays 78% of employees' health insurance premiums and provides free dental insurance.[121]

All employees get free meals in the hotel cafeteria, have access to staff showers and a locker room, and receive an additional highly attractive benefit—once a new employee has worked for the Four Seasons for six months, he or she can stay for three nights free at any Four Seasons hotel or resort in the world. After a year of employment, this benefit increases to six free nights, and it continues to grow as tenure with the company increases. Employees like waitress Michelle De Rochemont love this benefit. As she indicates, "You're never treated like just an employee. You're a guest. . . . You come back from those trips on fire. You want to do so much for the guest."[122]

The Four Seasons also tends to promote from within.[123] For example, while recent college graduates may start out as assistant managers, those who do well and have high aspirations could potentially become general managers in less than 15 years. This helps to ensure that managers have empathy and respect for those in lower-level positions as well as the ingrained ethos of treating others (employees, subordinates, coworkers, and customers) as they would like to be treated. All in all, treating employees well leads to satisfied customers at the Four Seasons.[124]

Pay Structure

pay structure The arrangement of jobs into categories reflecting their relative importance to the organization and its goals, levels of skill required, and other characteristics.

After deciding on a pay level, managers have to establish a pay structure for the different jobs in the organization. A **pay structure** clusters jobs into categories reflecting their relative importance to the organization and its goals, levels of skill required, and other characteristics managers consider important. Pay ranges are established for each job category. Individual jobholders' pay within job categories is then determined by factors such as performance, seniority, and skill levels.

There are some interesting global differences in pay structures. Large corporations based in the United States tend to pay their CEOs and top managers higher salaries than do their European or Japanese counterparts. Also, the pay differential between employees at the bottom of the corporate hierarchy and those higher up is much greater in U.S. companies than in European or Japanese companies.[125]

Concerns have been raised over whether it is equitable or fair for CEOs of large companies in the United States to be making millions of dollars in years when their companies are restructuring and laying off a large portion of their workforces.[126] Additionally, the average CEO in the United States typically earns over 360 times what the average hourly worker earns.[127] Is a pay structure with such a huge pay differential ethical? Shareholders and the public are increasingly asking this very question and asking large corporations to rethink their pay structures.[128] Also troubling are the millions of dollars in severance packages that some CEOs receive when they leave their organizations. When many workers are struggling to find and keep jobs and make ends meet, more and more people are questioning whether it is ethical for some top managers to be making so much money.[129]

Benefits

Organizations are legally required to provide certain benefits to their employees, including workers' compensation, Social Security, and unemployment insurance. Workers' compensation helps employees financially if they become unable to work due to a work-related injury or illness. Social Security provides financial assistance to retirees and disabled former employees. Unemployment insurance provides financial assistance to workers who lose their jobs due to no fault of their own. The legal system in the United States views these three benefits as ethical requirements for organizations and thus mandates that they be provided.

Other benefits such as health insurance, dental insurance, vacation time, pension plans, life insurance, flexible working hours, company-provided day care, and employee assistance and wellness programs have traditionally been provided at the option of employers. The Health Care Reform Bill signed by President Barack Obama in March 2010 contains provisions whereby, starting in 2014, employers with 50 or more employees may face fines if they don't provide their employees with health insurance coverage.[130] Recall that an attractive benefit at Zappos in "A Manager's Challenge" is that Zappos pays for all health care costs. Benefits enabling workers to balance the demands of their jobs and of their lives away from the office or factory are of growing importance for many workers who have competing demands on their scarce time and energy.

In some organizations, top managers determine which benefits might best suit the employees and organization and offer the same benefit package to all employees. Other organizations, realizing that employees' needs and desires might differ, offer **cafeteria-style benefit plans** that let employees themselves choose the benefits they want. Cafeteria-style benefit plans sometimes help managers deal with employees who feel unfairly treated because they are unable to take advantage of certain benefits available to other employees who, for example, have children. Some organizations have success with cafeteria-style benefit plans; others find them difficult to manage.

As health care costs escalate and overstretched employees find it hard to take time to exercise and take care of their health, more companies are providing benefits and incentives to promote employee wellness. AstraZeneca International offers its employees on-site counseling with a nutritionist and pays employees $125 for voluntarily taking a health risk assessment that covers wellness-related factors such as weight and nutrition.[131] Dole Food Company rewards employees with points toward gift certificates for participating in wellness activities provided on-site, such as yoga classes.[132]

For working parents, family-friendly benefits are especially attractive, as profiled in the following "Focus on Diversity" box.

cafeteria-style benefit plan A plan from which employees can choose the benefits they want.

Focus on Diversity

Family-Friendly Benefits at Guerra DeBerry Coody

Guerra DeBerry Coody is a small public relations and advertising firm based in San Antonio, Texas.[133] Founded in 1995,[134] the firm has fewer than 100 employees and over $50 million in annual revenues. Guerra DeBerry Coody was named a "Top Small Workplace" by *The Wall Street Journal* and Winning Workplaces, a nonprofit organization. Employees at Guerra DeBerry Coody nominated their employer for this award, and given the family-friendly benefits this firm provides, it is easy to understand why.[135]

Guerra DeBerry Coody provides on-site employee child care until employees' children enter kindergarten, with the firm covering 85% of the cost and employees paying $20 per day per child.[136] Employees can spend time with their children during the workday—employees often eat with their children, play with them, and settle them down for naps. The on-site child care center has a ratio of 1 child care worker for every 2 children enrolled, and around 11 children are currently enrolled. Employees with older children can bring their children to work after school if they wish. Senior account supervisor Patti Tanner sometimes has her two young teenage children come to the office after school. She indicates, "I don't even have any angst about having them here because I know it's completely and totally accepted."[137]

Guerra DeBerry Coody provides other benefits that help employees deal with the multiple demands and obligations in their lives. For example, employees can apply for interest-free loans from the company.

Guerra DeBerry Coody offers family-friendly benefits such as child care.

Employees also have the options of working from home, telecommuting, and adopting flexible work schedules. Guerra DeBerry Coody provides free health insurance for all its employees, and those with dependents needing coverage can purchase it for around $125–$200 per month. The company also contributes to a 401(k) retirement plan for its employees.[138] As Frank Guerra, one of the founding partners of Guerra DeBerry Coody, indicated upon the firm being named a "Top Small Workplace," "With or without this recognition we are so proud that we have the ability to offer our employees a family-friendly work environment where everyone has a vested interest in each other and in the business, caring for one another like family."[139]

LO12-6 Understand the role that labor relations play in the effective management of human resources.

Same-sex domestic partner benefits are also being used to attract and retain valued employees. Gay and lesbian workers are reluctant to work for companies that do not provide the same kinds of benefits for their partners as those provided for partners of the opposite sex.[140]

Labor Relations

labor relations The activities managers engage in to ensure that they have effective working relationships with the labor unions that represent their employees' interests.

Labor relations are the activities managers engage in to ensure that they have effective working relationships with the labor unions that represent their employees' interests. Although the U.S. government has responded to the potential for unethical and unfair treatment of workers by creating and enforcing laws regulating employment (including the EEO laws listed in Table 12.1), some workers believe a union will ensure that their interests are fairly represented in their organizations.

Before we describe unions in more detail, let's take a look at some examples of important employment legislation. In 1938 the government passed the Fair Labor Standards Act, which prohibited child labor and provided for minimum wages, overtime pay, and maximum working hours to protect workers' rights. In 1963 the Equal Pay Act mandated that men and women performing equal work (work requiring the same levels of skill, responsibility, and effort performed in the same kind of working conditions) receive equal pay (see Table 12.1). In 1970 the Occupational Safety and Health Act mandated procedures for managers to follow to ensure workplace safety. These are just a few of the U.S. government's efforts to protect workers' rights. State legislatures also have been active in promoting safe, ethical, and fair workplaces.

Unions

Unions exist to represent workers' interests in organizations. Given that managers have more power than rank-and-file workers and that organizations have multiple stakeholders, there is always the potential that managers might take steps that benefit one set of stakeholders such as shareholders while hurting another such as employees. For example, managers may decide to speed up a production line to lower costs and increase production in the hopes of increasing returns to shareholders. Speeding up the line, however, could hurt employees forced to work at a rapid pace and may increase the risk of injuries. Also, employees receive no additional pay for the extra work they are performing. Unions would represent workers' interests in a scenario such as this one.

Congress acknowledged the role that unions could play in ensuring safe and fair workplaces when it passed the National Labor Relations Act of 1935. This act made it legal for workers to organize into unions to protect their rights and interests and declared certain unfair or unethical organizational practices to be illegal. The act also established the National Labor Relations Board (NLRB) to oversee union activity. Currently the NLRB conducts certification elections, which are held among the employees of an organization to determine whether they want a union to represent their interests. The NLRB also makes judgments concerning unfair labor practices and specifies practices that managers must refrain from.

Employees might vote to have a union represent them for any number of reasons.[141] They may think their wages and working conditions need improvement. They may believe managers are not treating them with respect. They may think their working hours are unfair or they need more job security or a safer work environment. Or they may be dissatisfied with management and find it difficult to communicate their concerns to their bosses. Regardless of the specific reason, one overriding reason is power: A united group inevitably wields more power than an individual, and this type of power may be especially helpful to employees in some organizations.

Although these would seem to be potent forces for unionization, some workers are reluctant to join unions. Sometimes this reluctance is due to the perception that union leaders are corrupt. Some workers may simply believe that belonging to a union might not do them much good or may actually cause more harm than good while costing them money in membership dues. Employees also might not want to be forced into doing something they do not want to, such as striking because the union thinks it is in their best interest. Moreover, although unions can be a positive force in organizations, sometimes they also can be a negative force, impairing organizational effectiveness. For example, when union leaders resist needed changes in an organization or are corrupt, organizational performance can suffer.

The percentage of U.S. workers represented by unions today is smaller than it was in the 1950s, an era when unions were especially strong.[142] In the 1950s, around 35% of U.S. workers were union members; in 2011, 11.8% of workers were members of unions.[143] The American Federation of Labor–Congress of Industrial Organizations (AFL-CIO) includes 56 voluntary member unions representing over 12 million workers.[144] Overall, approximately 14.8 million workers in the United States belong to unions.[145] Union influence in manufacturing and heavy industries has been on the decline; more generally, approximately 6.9% of private sectors workers are union members.[146] However, around 37% of government workers belong to unions.[147] Unions have made inroads in other segments of the workforce, particularly the low-wage end. Garbage collectors in New Jersey, poultry plant workers in North Carolina, and janitors in Baltimore are among the growing numbers of low-paid workers who are currently finding union membership attractive. North Carolina poultry workers voted in a union partly because they thought it was unfair that they had to buy their own gloves and hairnets used on the job and had to ask their supervisors' permission to go to the restroom.[148]

Union membership and leadership, traditionally dominated by white men, are becoming increasingly diverse. For example, Linda Chavez-Thompson was the executive vice president of the AFL-CIO from 1995 to 2007 and was the first woman and Hispanic to hold a top management position in the federation.[149] Labor officials in Washington, D.C., also are becoming increasingly diverse. Elaine L. Chao, the 24th U.S. Secretary of Labor,[150] was the first Asian-American woman to hold an appointment in a U.S. president's cabinet.[151] In terms of union membership, women now make up over 45% of unionized workers.[152]

Collective Bargaining

collective bargaining
Negotiations between labor unions and managers to resolve conflicts and disputes about issues such as working hours, wages, benefits, working conditions, and job security.

Collective bargaining is negotiation between labor unions and managers to resolve conflicts and disputes about important issues such as working hours, wages, working conditions, and job security. Before sitting down with management to negotiate, union members sometimes go on strike to drive home their concerns to managers. Once an agreement that union members support has been reached (sometimes with the help of a neutral third party called a *mediator*), union leaders and managers sign a contract spelling out the terms of the collective bargaining agreement. We discuss conflict and negotiation in depth in Chapter 17, but some brief observations are in order here because collective bargaining is an ongoing consideration in labor relations.

The signing of a contract, for example, does not finish the collective bargaining process. Disagreement and conflicts can arise over the interpretation of the contract. In such cases, a neutral third party called an *arbitrator* is usually called in to resolve the conflict. An important component of a collective bargaining agreement is a *grievance procedure* through which workers who believe they are not being fairly treated are allowed to voice their concerns and have their interests represented by the union. Workers who think they were unjustly fired in violation of a union contract, for example, may file a grievance, have the union represent them, and get their jobs back if an arbitrator agrees with them. Union members sometimes go on strike when managers make decisions that the members think will hurt them and are not in their best interests.

Summary and Review

LO12-1

STRATEGIC HUMAN RESOURCE MANAGEMENT Human resource management (HRM) includes all the activities managers engage in to ensure that their organizations can attract, retain, and effectively use human resources. Strategic HRM is the process by which managers design the components of a human resource management system to be consistent with each other, with other elements of organizational architecture, and with the organization's strategies and goals.

LO12-2 RECRUITMENT AND SELECTION Before recruiting and selecting employees, managers must engage in human resource planning and job analysis. Human resource planning includes all the activities managers engage in to forecast their current and future needs for human resources. Job analysis is the process of identifying (1) the tasks, duties, and responsibilities that make up a job and (2) the knowledge, skills, and abilities needed to perform the job. Recruitment includes all the activities managers engage in to develop a pool of qualified applicants for open positions. Selection is the process by which managers determine the relative qualifications of job applicants and their potential for performing well in a particular job.

LO12-3 TRAINING AND DEVELOPMENT Training focuses on teaching organizational members how to perform effectively in their current jobs. Development focuses on broadening organizational members' knowledge and skills so they are prepared to take on new responsibilities and challenges.

LO12-4 PERFORMANCE APPRAISAL AND FEEDBACK Performance appraisal is the evaluation of employees' job performance and contributions to the organization. Performance feedback is the process through which managers share performance appraisal information with their subordinates, give them an opportunity to reflect on their own performance, and develop with them plans for the future. Performance appraisal gives managers useful information for decision making. Performance feedback can encourage high levels of motivation and performance.

LO12-5 PAY AND BENEFITS Pay level is the relative position of an organization's pay incentives in comparison with those of other organizations in the same industry employing similar workers. A pay structure clusters jobs into categories according to their relative importance to the organization and its goals, the levels of skill required, and other characteristics. Pay ranges are then established for each job category. Organizations are legally required to provide certain benefits to their employees; other benefits are provided at the discretion of employers.

LO12-6 LABOR RELATIONS Labor relations include all the activities managers engage in to ensure that they have effective working relationships with the labor unions that represent their employees' interests. The National Labor Relations Board oversees union activity. Collective bargaining is the process through which labor unions and managers resolve conflicts and disputes and negotiate agreements.

Management in Action

Topics for Discussion and Action

Discussion

1. Discuss why it is important for human resource management systems to be in sync with an organization's strategy and goals and with each other. [LO12-1]

2. Discuss why training and development are ongoing activities for all organizations. [LO12-3]

3. Describe the type of development activities you think middle managers are most in need of. [LO12-3]

4. Evaluate the pros and cons of 360-degree performance appraisals and feedback. Would you like your performance to be appraised in this manner? Why or why not? [LO12-4]

5. Discuss why two restaurants in the same community might have different pay levels. [LO12-5]

6. Explain why union membership is becoming more diverse. [LO12-6]

Action

7. Interview a manager in a local organization to determine how that organization recruits and selects employees. [LO12-2]

Building Management Skills

Analyzing Human Resource Management Systems [LO12-1, 12-2, 12-3, 12-4, 12-5]

Think about your current job or a job you have had in the past. If you have never had a job, interview a friend or family member who is currently working. Answer the following questions about the job you have chosen:

1. How are people recruited and selected for this job? Are the recruitment and selection procedures the organization uses effective or ineffective? Why?

2. What training and development do people who hold this job receive? Are the training and development appropriate? Why or why not?

3. How is performance of this job appraised? Does performance feedback contribute to motivation and high performance on this job?

4. What levels of pay and benefits are provided on this job? Are these levels appropriate? Why or why not?

Managing Ethically [LO12-4, 12-5]

Some managers do not want to become overly friendly with their subordinates because they are afraid that if they do so their objectivity when conducting performance appraisals and making decisions about pay raises and promotions will be impaired. Some subordinates resent it when they see one or more of their coworkers being very friendly with the boss; they are concerned about the potential for favoritism. Their reasoning runs something like this: If two subordinates are equally qualified for a promotion and one is a good friend of the boss and the other is a mere acquaintance, who is more likely to receive the promotion?

Questions

1. Either individually or in a group, think about the ethical implications of managers' becoming friendly with their subordinates.

2. Do you think managers should feel free to socialize and become good friends with their subordinates outside the workplace if they so desire? Why or why not?

Small Group Breakout Exercise

Building a Human Resource Management System [LO12-1, 12-2, 12-3, 12-4, 12-5]

Form groups of three or four people, and appoint one group member as the spokesperson who will communicate your findings to the class when called on by the instructor. Then discuss the following scenario:

You and your three partners are engineers who minored in business at college and have decided to start a consulting business. Your goal is to provide manufacturing process engineering and other engineering services to large and small organizations. You forecast that there will be an increased use of outsourcing for these activities. You discussed with managers in several large organizations the services you plan to offer, and they expressed considerable interest. You have secured funding to start your business and now are building the HRM system. Your human resource planning suggests that you need to hire between five and eight experienced engineers with good communication skills, two clerical/secretarial workers, and two MBAs who between them have financial, accounting, and human resource skills. You

are striving to develop your human resources in a way that will enable your new business to prosper.

1. Describe the steps you will take to recruit and select (a) the engineers, (b) the clerical/secretarial workers, and (c) the MBAs.

2. Describe the training and development the engineers, the clerical/secretarial workers, and the MBAs will receive.

3. Describe how you will appraise the performance of each group of employees and how you will provide feedback.

4. Describe the pay level and pay structure of your consulting firm.

Exploring the World Wide Web [LO12-2]

Go to www.net-temps.com, a website geared toward temporary employment. Imagine that you have to take a year off from college and are seeking a one-year position. Guided by your own interests, use this website to learn about your options and possible employment opportunities.

1. What are the potential advantages of online job searching and recruiting? What are the potential disadvantages?

2. Would you ever rely on a website like this to help you find a position? Why or why not?

Be the Manager [LO12-4]

You are Walter Michaels and have just received some disturbing feedback. You are the director of human resources for Maxi Vision Inc., a medium-size window and glass door manufacturer. You recently initiated a 360-degree performance appraisal system for all middle and upper managers at Maxi Vision, including yourself, but excluding the most senior executives and the top management team.

You were eagerly awaiting the feedback you would receive from the managers who report to you; you had recently implemented several important initiatives that affected them and their subordinates, including a complete overhaul of the organization's performance appraisal system. While the managers who report to you were evaluated based on 360-degree appraisals, their subordinates were evaluated using a 20-question BARS scale you recently created that focuses on behaviors. Conducted annually,

appraisals are an important input into pay raise and bonus decisions.

You were so convinced that the new performance appraisal procedures were highly effective that you hoped your own subordinates would mention them in their feedback to you. And boy did they! You were amazed to learn that the managers *and* their subordinates thought the new BARS scales were unfair, inappropriate, and a waste of time. In fact, the managers' feedback to you was that their own performance was suffering, based on the 360-degree appraisals they received, because their subordinates hated the new appraisal system and partially blamed their bosses, who were part of management. Some managers even admitted giving all their subordinates approximately the same scores on the scales so their pay raises and bonuses would not be affected by their performance appraisals.

CHAPTER 13

Motivation and Performance

Learning Objectives

After studying this chapter, you should be able to:

LO13-1 Explain what motivation is and why managers need to be concerned about it.

LO13-2 Describe from the perspectives of expectancy theory and equity theory what managers should do to have a highly motivated workforce.

LO13-3 Explain how goals and needs motivate people and what kinds of goals are especially likely to result in high performance.

LO13-4 Identify the motivation lessons that managers can learn from operant conditioning theory and social learning theory.

LO13-5 Explain why and how managers can use pay as a major motivation tool.

A MANAGER'S CHALLENGE

How Enterprise Rent-A-Car Motivates Employees

How can managers motivate employees to provide excellent customer service? Enterprise Rent-A-Car was founded by Jack Taylor in 1957 in St. Louis, Missouri, as a very small auto leasing business.[1] Today, Enterprise Holdings, which owns and operates Enterprise Rent-A-Car, is the biggest car rental company in the world with over $14 billion in revenues and over 70,000 employees. Enterprise has over 7,700 locations in the United States, Canada, the United Kingdom, Ireland, and Germany.[2] One of the biggest employers of new college graduates in the United States, Enterprise typically hires over 8,000 college graduates each year.[3] While starting salaries tend to be on the low end and the work can be hard (e.g., four assistant managers once sued the company claiming that they should receive overtime pay), Enterprise has been ranked among the top 50 best companies for new college graduates to launch their careers by *Bloomberg Businessweek* magazine.[4]

A privately held company, Enterprise is very much a family business. In its entire history, Enterprise has had only two CEOs, founder Jack Taylor, who is now retired but still involved in the company, and his son Andrew Taylor, who became president in 1980 and CEO in 1991. Jack Taylor's daughter, Jo Ann

Taylor Kindle (Andrew's sister), manages much of Enterprise's and the Taylor family's philanthropic activities. Chrissy Taylor, Andrew's daughter, and Carolyn Kindle Payne, Jo Ann's daughter, are both managers at Enterprise who started out as management trainees (Andrew started out washing and moving around cars when he was 16 years old prior to obtaining his bachelor's degree in business and becoming a management trainee).[5] Nonetheless, Enterprise's policy of promoting from within ensures that all employees who perform well have the opportunity to advance in the company.[6]

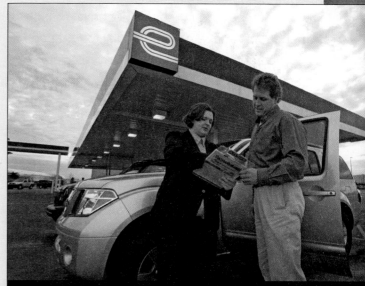

Customer service with a difference: this employee exhibits the high levels of motivation typical of Enterprise's workers because she knows that everyone in Enterprise cuts their teeth on the same positions, follows the same promotion path, and enjoys the same type of benefits tied to the performance of their specific area.

One of the keys to Enterprise's success is the way it motivates its employees to provide excellent customer service.[7] Practically all entry-level hires participate in Enterprise's Management Training Program.[8] As part of the program, new hires learn all aspects of the company business, and how to provide excellent customer service. Management trainees first have a four-day training session focused primarily on Enterprise's culture. They are then assigned to a branch office for around 8 to 12 months where they learn all aspects of the business, from negotiating with body shops to helping customers to washing cars. As part of this training, they learn how important high-quality customer service is to Enterprise and how they can personally provide great service, increasing their confidence levels.[9]

All those who do well in the program are promoted after about a year to the position of management assistant. Management assistants who do well are promoted to become assistant branch managers with responsibility for mentoring and supervising employees. Assistant managers who do well can be promoted to become branch managers who are responsible for managing a branch's employees and provision of customer service, rental car fleet, and financial performance. Branch managers with about five years of experience in the position often move on to take up management positions at headquarters or assume the position of area manager overseeing all the branches in a certain geographic region.[10] By training all new hires in all aspects of the business including the provision of excellent customer service, by providing them with valuable experience with increasing levels of responsibility and empowerment, and by providing all new hires who perform well with the opportunity to advance in the company, Enterprise has developed a highly motivated workforce. As Patrick Farrell, vice president of corporate communications indicated, "What's unique about our company is that everyone came up through the same system, from the CEOs on down . . . 100% of our operations personnel started as management trainees."[11]

In addition to motivating high performance and excellent customer service through training and promotional opportunities, Enterprise also uses financial incentives to motivate employees. Essentially, each branch is considered a profit center and the managers overseeing the branch and in charge of all aspects of its functioning have the autonomy and responsibility for the branch's profitability almost as if the branch was their own small business or franchise.[12] All branch employees at the rank of assistant manager and higher earn incentive compensation whereby their monthly pay depends upon the profitability of their branch. Managers at higher levels, such as area managers, have their monthly pay linked to the profitability of the region they oversee. Thus, managers at all levels know that their pay is linked to the profitability of the parts of Enterprise for which they are responsible. And they have the autonomy to make decisions ranging from buying and selling cars to opening new branches.[13]

Providing high-quality customer service is essential at Enterprise.[14] One of the trademarks of this service is Enterprise's long-standing practice of picking up customers who need to rent cars from their homes or workplaces and then dropping them off where they need to go once they return their rental cars. To continuously keep track of how well branches are doing in providing high-quality customer service, Enterprise developed the Enterprise Service Quality index (ESQi).[15] The ESQi is based on phone calls that are made to 1 out of every 15 customers to follow up on their experience renting a car from Enterprise. Basically, customers are asked how satisfied they were with the experience and if they would rent a car from Enterprise again. Based on satisfaction scores, managers at each branch and unit of the company can see how well they are doing compared to the overall average for the company and take steps, when needed, to improve the quality of the service they provide.[16]

Another way in which Enterprise motivates its employees is through its philanthropic activities and initiatives to protect the natural environment.[17] For example, the Enterprise Rent-A-Car Foundation has committed $50 million to plant 50 million trees over a 50-year period in public forests.[18] The foundation also focuses on supporting and giving back to the communities in which Enterprise operates, whether it is donating $3,000 to an outreach center for troubled teens in Syracuse, New York, or donating $30 million to fund plant research around the world sponsored by the Missouri Botanical Garden.[19] In 2012, Enterprise joined the 100,000 Jobs Mission, a group of 41 companies focused on together hiring a minimum of 100,000 veterans by 2020.[20] Of all rental car companies, Enterprise has the biggest fleet of fuel-efficient cars, over 7,000 hybrid gas/electric cars, and over 70,000 cars that can use fuel that is composed of 15% gasoline and 85% ethanol (E85).[21] As Andrew Taylor suggests, "We're not going to be able to save the world . . . but we think we can have an effect on the space where we play every day as a business. And we think that's what our customers and especially our employees want us to do."[22] All in all, the multiple ways in which Enterprise motivates its employees and satisfies its customers have contributed to its ongoing success story.[23]

Overview

Even with the best strategy in place and an appropriate organizational architecture, an organization will be effective only if its members are motivated to perform at a high level. Jack and Andrew Taylor in "A Manager's Challenge" clearly realize this. One reason why leading is such an important managerial activity is that it entails ensuring that each member of an organization is motivated to perform highly and help the organization achieve its goals. When managers are effective, the outcome of the leading process is a highly motivated workforce. A key challenge for managers of organizations both large and small is to encourage employees to perform at a high level.

In this chapter we describe what motivation is, where it comes from, and why managers need to promote high levels of it for an organization to be effective and achieve its goals. We examine important theories of motivation: expectancy theory, need theories, equity theory, goal-setting theory, and learning theories. Each gives managers important insights about how to motivate organizational members. The theories are complementary in that each focuses on a different aspect of motivation. Considering all the theories together helps managers gain a rich understanding of the many issues and problems involved in encouraging high levels of motivation throughout an organization. Last, we consider the use of pay as a motivation tool. By the end of this chapter you will understand what it takes to have a highly motivated workforce.

The Nature of Motivation

motivation Psychological forces that determine the direction of a person's behavior in an organization, a person's level of effort, and a person's level of persistence.

intrinsically motivated behavior Behavior that is performed for its own sake.

Motivation may be defined as psychological forces that determine the direction of a person's behavior in an organization, a person's level of effort, and a person's level of persistence in the face of obstacles.[24] The *direction of a person's behavior* refers to the many possible behaviors a person could engage in. For example, employees at Enterprise Rent-A-Car know that they should do whatever is required to provide high-quality customer service such as giving customers rides to pick up and drop off rental cars. *Effort* refers to how hard people work. Employees at Enterprise exert high levels of effort to provide superior customer service. *Persistence* refers to whether, when faced with roadblocks and obstacles, people keep trying or give up. Branch managers at Enterprise Rent-A-Car persistently seek to improve the profitability of their branches while maintaining very high levels of customer service.

Motivation is central to management because it explains *why* people behave the way they do in organizations[25]—why employees at Enterprise Rent-A-Car provide excellent customer service. Motivation also explains why a waiter is polite or rude and why a kindergarten teacher really tries to get children to enjoy learning or just goes through the motions. It explains why some managers truly put their organizations' best interests first, whereas others are more concerned with maximizing their salaries and why—more generally—some workers put forth twice as much effort as others.

Motivation can come from *intrinsic* or *extrinsic* sources. **Intrinsically motivated behavior** is behavior that is performed for its own sake; the source of motivation is actually performing the behavior, and motivation comes from doing the work itself. Many managers are intrinsically motivated; they derive a sense of accomplishment and achievement from helping the organization achieve its goals and gain competitive advantages. Jobs that are interesting and challenging or high on the five characteristics described by the job characteristics model (see Chapter 10) are more likely to lead to intrinsic motivation than are jobs that are boring or do not use a person's skills and abilities. An elementary school teacher who really enjoys teaching children, a computer programmer who loves solving programming problems, and a commercial photographer who relishes taking creative photographs are all intrinsically motivated. For these individuals, motivation comes from performing their jobs—teaching children, finding bugs in computer programs, and taking pictures.

A lack of intrinsic motivation at work sometimes propels people to make major changes in their lives, as illustrated in the following "Managing Globally" box.

Managing Globally

Seeking Intrinsic Motivation in Far Flung Places

Dom Jackman and Rob Symington, then in their late 20s, were doing financial consulting work for Ernst & Young in London when they were both struck by how lacking their jobs felt in terms of intrinsic motivation. As Symington put it, "It felt like the work we did, crunching spreadsheets, just didn't matter to anyone, including to our customers or employers."[26] Realizing that they were probably not the only young workers in the finance field who didn't enjoy the work they were doing, Jackman and Symington decided to do something about it. They quit their jobs and created Escape the City, a website devoted to assisting bankers and finance professionals find interesting and exciting work in far-flung places.[27] By the way, "The City" refers to the financial district in London and hence Escape the City is a fitting name for a website oriented toward "escaping unfulfilling corporate jobs."[28]

Employers pay to list positions on the site that entail initiative and adventure while job seekers can sign up for free.[29] Weekly e-mails inform job seekers of interesting opportunities they might want to pursue, ranging from African charity work and employment with venture capital firms in Mongolia to microfinance work in India and

Escape the City's founders offer a previously untapped motivation to bored young office workers the world over: enjoy meaningful work where they want!

surf camps in Morocco. Escape the City earned profits its first year in operation and has expanded to the United States with a New York office led my Mike Howe, who used to work for Merrill Lynch.[30]

Asia Pacific Investment Partners hired an operations manager and a communications manager from posting listings on the site.[31] Will Tindall landed the latter position and as chief communications officer for Asia Pacific he works out of Hong Kong, Ulan Bator, and London. Harry Minter found a position as the manager of Guludo Beach Lodge in Mozambique—he used to work in the hedge fund field at Headstart Advisers.[32] Of course, not all professionals in finance and the corporate world find their work to be uninteresting and demotivating. Indeed, some are very intrinsically motivated by the work they do. Nonetheless, for those who are not motivated and desire more exciting, interesting, and meaningful work, Escape the City certainly expands the set of options they might want to consider.

---

extrinsically motivated behavior Behavior that is performed to acquire material or social rewards or to avoid punishment.

Extrinsically motivated behavior is behavior that is performed to acquire material or social rewards or to avoid punishment; the source of motivation is the consequences of the behavior, not the behavior itself. A car salesperson who is motivated by receiving a commission on all cars sold, a lawyer who is motivated by the high salary and status that go along with the job, and a factory worker who is motivated by the opportunity to earn a secure income are all extrinsically motivated. Their motivation comes from the consequences they receive as a result of their work behaviors.

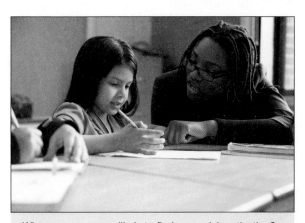

Where are you more likely to find prosocial motivation? Here in the classroom as a teacher walks her student through that tricky math problem. Getting companies to foster this type of motivation is a bit trickier!

People can be intrinsically motivated, extrinsically motivated, or both intrinsically and extrinsically motivated.[33] A top manager who derives a sense of accomplishment and achievement from managing a large corporation and strives to reach year-end targets to obtain a hefty bonus is both intrinsically and extrinsically motivated. Similarly, a nurse who enjoys helping and taking care of patients and is motivated by having a secure job with good benefits is both intrinsically and extrinsically motivated. At Enterprise Rent-A-Car, employees are both extrinsically motivated, because of opportunities for promotions and having their pay linked to the performance of their branches or units, and intrinsically motivated because they get a sense of satisfaction out of serving customers and learning new things. Whether workers are intrinsically motivated, extrinsically motivated, or both depends on a wide variety of factors: (1) workers' own personal characteristics (such as their personalities, abilities, values, attitudes, and needs), (2) the nature of their jobs (such as whether they have been enriched or where they are on the five core characteristics of the job characteristics model), and (3) the nature of the organization (such as its structure, its culture, its control systems, its human resource management system, and the ways in which rewards such as pay are distributed to employees).

prosocially motivated behavior Behavior that is performed to benefit or help others.

In addition to being intrinsically or extrinsically motivated, some people are prosocially motivated by their work.[34] **Prosocially motivated behavior** is behavior that is performed to benefit or help others.[35] Behavior can be prosocially motivated in addition to being extrinsically and/or intrinsically motivated. An elementary school teacher who not only enjoys the process of teaching young children (has high intrinsic motivation) but also has a strong desire to give children the best learning experience possible and help those with learning disabilities overcome their challenges, and who keeps up with the latest research on child development and teaching methods in an effort to continually improve the effectiveness of his teaching, has high prosocial motivation in addition to high intrinsic motivation. A surgeon who specializes in organ transplants, enjoys the challenge of performing complex operations, has a strong desire to help her patients regain their health and extend their lives through successful organ transplants, and is also motivated by the relatively high income she earns has high intrinsic, prosocial, and extrinsic motivation. Recent preliminary research suggests that when workers have high prosocial motivation, also having high intrinsic motivation can be especially beneficial for job performance.[36]

Regardless of whether people are intrinsically, extrinsically, or prosocially motivated, they join and are motivated to work in organizations to obtain certain outcomes. An **outcome** is anything a person gets from a job or organization. Some outcomes, such as autonomy, responsibility, a feeling of accomplishment, and the pleasure of doing interesting or enjoyable work, result in intrinsically motivated behavior. Outcomes, such as improving the lives or well-being of other people and doing good by helping others, result in prosocially motivated behavior. Other outcomes, such as pay, job security, benefits, and vacation time, result in extrinsically motivated behavior.

Organizations hire people to obtain important inputs. An **input** is anything a person contributes to the job or organization, such as time, effort, education, experience, skills, knowledge, and actual work behaviors. Inputs such as these are necessary for an organization to achieve its goals. Managers strive to motivate members of an organization to contribute inputs—through their behavior, effort, and persistence—that help the organization achieve its goals. How do managers do this? They ensure that members of an organization obtain the outcomes they desire when they make valuable contributions to the organization. Managers use outcomes to motivate people to contribute their inputs to the organization. Giving people outcomes when they contribute inputs and perform well aligns the interests of employees with the goals of the organization as a whole because when employees do what is good for the organization, they personally benefit.

This alignment between employees and organizational goals as a whole can be described by the motivation equation depicted in Figure 13.1. Managers seek to ensure that people are motivated to contribute important inputs to the organization, that these inputs are put to good use or focused in the direction of high performance, and that high performance results in workers' obtaining the outcomes they desire.

Each of the theories of motivation discussed in this chapter focuses on one or more aspects of this equation. Each theory focuses on a different set of issues that managers need to address to have a highly motivated workforce. Together, the theories provide a comprehensive set of guidelines for managers to follow to promote high levels of employee

outcome Anything a person gets from a job or organization.

input Anything a person contributes to his or her job or organization.

Figure 13.1
The Motivation Equation

motivation. Effective managers, such as Andrew Taylor in "A Manager's Challenge," tend to follow many of these guidelines, whereas ineffective managers often fail to follow them and seem to have trouble motivating organizational members.

Expectancy Theory

Expectancy theory, formulated by Victor H. Vroom in the 1960s, posits that motivation is high when workers believe that high levels of effort lead to high performance and high performance leads to the attainment of desired outcomes. Expectancy theory is one of the most popular theories of work motivation because it focuses on all three parts of the motivation equation: inputs, performance, and outcomes. Expectancy theory identifies three major factors that determine a person's motivation: *expectancy, instrumentality,* and *valence* (see Figure 13.2).[37]

Expectancy

Expectancy is a person's perception about the extent to which effort (an input) results in a certain level of performance. A person's level of expectancy determines whether he or she believes that a high level of effort results in a high level of performance. People are motivated to put forth a lot of effort on their jobs only if they think that their effort will pay off in high performance—that is, if they have high expectancy. Think about how motivated you would be to study for a test if you thought that no matter how hard you tried, you would get a D. Think about how motivated a marketing manager would be who thought that no matter how hard he or she worked, there was no way to increase sales of an unpopular product. In these cases, expectancy is low, so overall motivation is also low.

Members of an organization are motivated to put forth a high level of effort only if they think that doing so leads to high performance.[38] In other words, in order for people's motivation to be high, expectancy must be high. Thus, in attempting to influence motivation, managers need to make sure their subordinates believe that if they do try hard, they can actually succeed. One way managers can boost expectancies is through expressing confidence in their subordinates' capabilities. Managers at The Container Store, for example, express high levels of confidence in their subordinates. As Container Store cofounder Garrett Boone put it, "Everybody we hire, we hire as a leader. Anybody in our store can take an action that you might think of typically being a manager's action."[39]

Figure 13.2

Expectancy, Instrumentality, and Valence

| Effort (an important input) | Performance | Outcomes |

Expectancy
A person's perception about the extent to which his or her effort will result in a certain level of performance.

Instrumentality
A person's perception about the extent to which performance at a certain level will result in the attainment of outcomes.

Valence
How desirable each of the outcomes available from a job or organization is to a person.

In addition to expressing confidence in subordinates, other ways for managers to boost subordinates' expectancy levels and motivation are by providing training so people have the expertise needed for high performance and increasing their levels of autonomy and responsibility as they gain experience so they have the freedom to do what it takes to perform at a high level. For example, the Best Buy chain of stores selling electronics, computers, music and movies, and gadgets of all sorts boosts salespeople's expectancies by giving them extensive training in on-site meetings and online. Electronic learning terminals in each department not only help salespeople learn how different systems work and can be sold as an integrated package but also enable them to keep up to date with the latest advances in technology and products. Salespeople also receive extensive training in how to determine customers' needs.[40] At Enterprise Rent-A-Car in "A Manager's Challenge," the Management Training Program helps new hires develop high levels of expectancy and these high levels of expectancy are maintained as experienced employees are given more responsibility and autonomy to ensure that their branches are profitable and provide excellent customer service.

Instrumentality

instrumentality In expectancy theory, a perception about the extent to which performance results in the attainment of outcomes.

Expectancy captures a person's perceptions about the relationship between effort and performance. **Instrumentality**, the second major concept in expectancy theory, is a person's perception about the extent to which performance at a certain level results in the attainment of outcomes (see Figure 13.2). According to expectancy theory, employees are motivated to perform at a high level only if they think high performance will lead to (or is *instrumental* for attaining) outcomes such as pay, job security, interesting job assignments, bonuses, or a feeling of accomplishment. In other words, instrumentalities must be high for motivation to be high—people must perceive that because of their high performance they will receive outcomes.[41]

Managers promote high levels of instrumentality when they link performance to desired outcomes. In addition, managers must clearly communicate this linkage to subordinates. By making sure that outcomes available in an organization are distributed to organizational members on the basis of their performance, managers promote high instrumentality and motivation. When outcomes are linked to performance in this way, high performers receive more outcomes than low performers. In "A Manager's Challenge," Andrew Taylor raises levels of instrumentality and motivation for Enterprise Rent-A-Car employees by linking opportunities for promotion and pay to performance.

Another example of high instrumentality contributing to high motivation can be found in the Cambodian immigrants who own, manage, and work in more than 80% of the doughnut shops in California.[42] These immigrants see high performance as leading to many important outcomes such as income, a comfortable existence, family security, and the autonomy provided by working in a small business. Their high instrumentality contributes to their high motivation to succeed.

Valence

valence In expectancy theory, how desirable each of the outcomes available from a job or organization is to a person.

Although all members of an organization must have high expectancies and instrumentalities, expectancy theory acknowledges that people differ in their preferences for outcomes. For many people, pay is the most important outcome of working. For others, a feeling of accomplishment or enjoying one's work is more important than pay. The term **valence** refers to how desirable each of the outcomes available from a job or organization is to a person. To motivate organizational members, managers need to determine which outcomes have high valence for them—are highly desired—and make sure that those outcomes are provided when members perform at a high level.

From "A Manager's Challenge," it appears that not only pay but also autonomy, responsibility, and opportunities from promotions are highly valent outcomes for many employees at Enterprise Rent-A-Car.

Providing employees with highly valent outcomes not only can contribute to high levels of motivation but also has the potential to reduce turnover, as indicated in the following "Management Insight" box.

Management Insight

Motivating and Retaining Employees at The Container Store

Kip Tindell and Garrett Boone founded The Container Store in Dallas, Texas, in 1978, and Tindell currently serves as CEO and chairman (Boone is chairman emeritus).[43] When they opened their first store, they were out on the floor trying to sell customers their storage and organization products that would economize on space and time and make purchasers' lives a little less complicated. The Container Store has grown to include 58 stores in 23 U.S. markets from coast to coast; although the original store in Dallas had only 1,600 square feet, the stores today average around 25,000 square feet.[44] The phenomenal growth in the size of the stores has been matched by impressive growth rates in sales and profits.[45] Surprisingly enough, Tindell can still be found on the shop floor tidying shelves and helping customers carry out their purchases.[46] And that, perhaps, is an important clue to the secret of their success. The Container Store has been consistently ranked among *Fortune* magazine's "100 Best Companies to Work For" for 13 years running.[47] In 2012, The Container Store was 22nd on this list.[48]

Early on, Tindell and Boone recognized that people are The Container Store's most valuable asset and that after hiring great people, one of the most important managerial tasks is motivating them. One would think motivating employees might be especially challenging in the retail industry, which has an average annual turnover rate of 100% or more.[49] At The Container Store annual turnover is less than 10%, a testament to Tindell's ability to motivate.[50]

The Container Store's motivational approach means that each employee works as a leader—and that those in managerial positions still walk the floor to tidy displays. Results are extremely positive, with the retail chain boasting significantly lower turnover rates than other chains in the industry.

Tindell and Boone have long recognized the importance of rewarding employees for a job well done with highly valent outcomes. For example, starting salaries for salespeople are around $40,000, which is significantly higher than retail averages; and employees receive merit pay increases for superior sales performance. To encourage high individual performance as well as teamwork and cooperation, both individual and team-based rewards are given at The Container Store. Some high-performing salespeople earn more than their store managers, which suits the store managers fine as long as equitable procedures are used and rewards are distributed fairly.[51]

Professional development is another valent outcome employees obtain from working at The Container Store. Full-time salespeople receive over 240 hours of training their first year, and all employees have ongoing opportunities for additional training and development.[52] Employees also have flexible work options and flexible benefits; medical, dental, and 401(k) retirement plans; job security; a casual dress code; and access to a variety of wellness programs ranging from yoga classes and chair massages to a personalized web-based nutrition and exercise planner.[53] Another valent outcome is the opportunity to work with other highly motivated individuals in an environment that exudes enthusiasm and excitement. Not only are The Container Store's employees motivated, but they also look forward to coming to work and feel as if their coworkers and managers are part of their family. Employees feel pride in what they do—helping customers organize their lives, save space and time, and have a better sense of well-being. Hence they not only personally benefit from high performance by receiving highly valent outcomes but also feel good about the products they sell and the help they give customers.[54] Tindell evidently has never lost sight of the importance of motivation for both organizations and their members.

Figure 13.3
Expectancy Theory

Bringing It All Together

According to expectancy theory, high motivation results from high levels of expectancy, instrumentality, and valence (see Figure 13.3). If any one of these factors is low, motivation is likely to be low. No matter how tightly desired outcomes are linked to performance, if a person thinks it is practically impossible to perform at a high level, motivation to perform at a high level will be exceedingly low. Similarly, if a person does not think outcomes are linked to high performance, or if a person does not desire the outcomes that are linked to high performance, motivation to perform at a high level will be low. Effective managers realize the importance of high levels of expectancy, instrumentality, and valence and take concrete steps to ensure that their employees are highly motivated.

Need Theories

A **need** is a requirement or necessity for survival and well-being. The basic premise of **need theories** is that people are motivated to obtain outcomes at work that will satisfy their needs. Need theory complements expectancy theory by exploring in depth which outcomes motivate people to perform at a high level. Need theories suggest that to motivate a person to contribute valuable inputs to a job and perform at a high level, a manager must determine what needs the person is trying to satisfy at work and ensure that the person receives outcomes that help to satisfy those needs when the person performs at a high level and helps the organization achieve its goals.

There are several need theories. Here we discuss Abraham Maslow's hierarchy of needs, Clayton Alderfer's ERG theory, Frederick Herzberg's motivator-hygiene theory, and David McClelland's needs for achievement, affiliation, and power. These theories describe needs that people try to satisfy at work. In doing so, they give managers insights about what outcomes motivate members of an organization to perform at a high level and contribute inputs to help the organization achieve its goals.

LO13-3 Explain how goals and needs motivate people and what kinds of goals are especially likely to result in high performance.

need A requirement or necessity for survival and well-being.

need theories Theories of motivation that focus on what needs people are trying to satisfy at work and what outcomes will satisfy those needs.

Maslow's hierarchy of needs An arrangement of five basic needs that, according to Maslow, motivate behavior. Maslow proposed that the lowest level of unmet needs is the prime motivator and that only one level of needs is motivational at a time.

Maslow's Hierarchy of Needs

Psychologist Abraham Maslow proposed that all people seek to satisfy five basic kinds of needs: physiological needs, safety needs, belongingness needs, esteem needs, and self-actualization needs (see Table 13.1).[55] He suggested that these needs constitute a **hierarchy of needs**, with the most basic or compelling needs—physiological and safety needs—at the bottom. Maslow argued that these lowest-level needs must be met before a person strives to satisfy needs higher up in the hierarchy, such as self-esteem needs. Once a need is satisfied, Maslow proposed, it ceases to operate as a source of motivation. The lowest level of *unmet*

Table 13.1

Maslow's Hierarchy of Needs

	Needs	Description	Examples of How Managers Can Help People Satisfy These Needs at Work
Highest-level needs	**Self-actualization needs**	The needs to realize one's full potential as a human being.	By giving people the opportunity to use their skills and abilities to the fullest extent possible.
	Esteem needs	The needs to feel good about one-self and one's capabilities, to be respected by others, and to receive recognition and appreciation.	By granting promotions and recognizing accomplishments.
	Belongingness needs	Needs for social interaction, friendship, affection, and love.	By promoting good interpersonal relations and organizing social functions such as company picnics and holiday parties.
	Safety needs	Needs for security, stability, and a safe environment.	By providing job security, adequate medical benefits, and safe working conditions.
Lowest-level needs (most basic or compelling)	**Physiological needs**	Basic needs for things such as food, water, and shelter that must be met in order for a person to survive.	By providing a level of pay that enables a person to buy food and clothing and have adequate housing.

The lowest level of unsatisfied needs motivates behavior; once this level of needs is satisfied, a person tries to satisfy the needs at the next level.

No one pumps their fist over their laptop unless it's for a good reason! Clearly, whipping an obnoxious spreadsheet into shape and sending out a calmly worded press release makes for satisfied self-actualization needs.

needs in the hierarchy is the prime motivator of behavior; if and when this level is satisfied, needs at the next highest level in the hierarchy motivate behavior.

Although this theory identifies needs that are likely to be important sources of motivation for many people, research does not support Maslow's contention that there is a need hierarchy or his notion that only one level of needs is motivational at a time.[56] Nevertheless, a key conclusion can be drawn from Maslow's theory: People try to satisfy different needs at work. To have a motivated workforce, managers must determine which needs employees are trying to satisfy in organizations and then make sure that individuals receive outcomes that satisfy their needs when they perform at a high level and contribute to organizational effectiveness. By doing this, managers align the interests of individual members with the interests of the organization as a whole. By doing what is good for the organization (that is, performing at a high level), employees receive outcomes that satisfy their needs.

In our increasingly global economy, managers must realize that citizens of different countries might differ in the needs they seek to satisfy through work.[57] Some research suggests, for example, that people in Greece and Japan are especially motivated by safety needs and that people in Sweden, Norway, and Denmark are motivated by belongingness needs.[58] In less developed countries with low standards of living, physiological and safety needs are likely to be the prime motivators of behavior. As countries become wealthier and have higher standards of living, needs related to personal growth and accomplishment (such as esteem and self-actualization) become important motivators of behavior.

Table 13.2
Alderfer's ERG Theory

	Needs	Description	Examples of How Managers Can Help People Satisfy These Needs at Work
Highest-level needs	**Growth needs**	The needs for self-development and creative and productive work.	By allowing people to continually improve their skills and abilities and engage in meaningful work.
	Relatedness needs	The needs to have good interpersonal relations, to share thoughts and feelings, and to have open two-way communication.	By promoting good interpersonal relations and by providing accurate feedback.
Lowest-level needs	**Existence needs**	Basic needs for food, water, clothing, shelter, and a secure and safe environment.	By promoting enough pay to provide for the basic necessities of life and safe working conditions.

As lower-level needs are satisfied, a person is motivated to satisfy higher-level needs. When a person is unable to satisfy higher-level needs (or is frustrated), motivation to satisfy lower-level needs increases.

Alderfer's ERG Theory

Alderfer's ERG theory The theory that three universal needs—for existence, relatedness, and growth—constitute a hierarchy of needs and motivate behavior. Alderfer proposed that needs at more than one level can be motivational at the same time.

Clayton **Alderfer's ERG theory** collapsed the five categories of needs in Maslow's hierarchy into three universal categories—existence, relatedness, and growth—also arranged in a hierarchy (see Table 13.2). Alderfer agreed with Maslow that as lower-level needs become satisfied, a person seeks to satisfy higher-level needs. Unlike Maslow, however, Alderfer believed that a person can be motivated by needs at more than one level at the same time. A cashier in a supermarket, for example, may be motivated by both existence needs and relatedness needs. The existence needs motivate the cashier to come to work regularly and not make mistakes so his job will be secure and he will be able to pay his rent and buy food. The relatedness needs motivate the cashier to become friends with some of the other cashiers and have a good relationship with the store manager. Alderfer also suggested that when people experience *need frustration* or are unable to satisfy needs at a certain level, they will focus more intently on satisfying the needs at the next lowest level in the hierarchy.[59]

As with Maslow's theory, research does not support some of the specific ideas outlined in ERG theory, such as the existence of the three-level need hierarchy that Alderfer proposed.[60] However, for managers, the important message from ERG theory is the same as that from Maslow's theory: Determine what needs your subordinates are trying to satisfy at work, and make sure they receive outcomes that satisfy these needs when they perform at a high level to help the organization achieve its goals.

Herzberg's Motivator-Hygiene Theory

Herzberg's motivator-hygiene theory A need theory that distinguishes between motivator needs (related to the nature of the work itself) and hygiene needs (related to the physical and psychological context in which the work is performed) and proposes that motivator needs must be met for motivation and job satisfaction to be high.

Adopting an approach different from Maslow's and Alderfer's, Frederick Herzberg focused on two factors: (1) outcomes that can lead to high levels of motivation and job satisfaction and (2) outcomes that can prevent people from being dissatisfied. According to **Herzberg's motivator-hygiene theory**, people have two sets of needs or requirements: motivator needs and hygiene needs.[61] *Motivator needs* are related to the nature of the work itself and how challenging it is. Outcomes such as interesting work, autonomy, responsibility, being able to grow and develop on the job, and a sense of accomplishment and achievement help to satisfy motivator needs. To have a highly motivated and satisfied workforce, Herzberg suggested, managers should take steps to ensure that employees' motivator needs are being met.

Hygiene needs are related to the physical and psychological context in which the work is performed. Hygiene needs are satisfied by outcomes such as pleasant and comfortable working conditions, pay, job security, good relationships with coworkers, and effective supervision. According to Herzberg, when hygiene needs are not met, workers are dissatisfied, and when hygiene needs are met, workers are not dissatisfied. Satisfying hygiene needs, however, does not result in high levels of motivation or even high levels of job satisfaction. For motivation and job satisfaction to be high, motivator needs must be met.

Many research studies have tested Herzberg's propositions, and, by and large, the theory fails to receive support.[62] Nevertheless, Herzberg's formulations have contributed to our understanding of motivation in at least two ways. First, Herzberg helped to focus researchers' and managers' attention on the important distinction between intrinsic motivation (related to motivator needs) and extrinsic motivation (related to hygiene needs), covered earlier in the chapter. Second, his theory prompted researchers and managers to study how jobs could be designed or redesigned so they are intrinsically motivating.

McClelland's Needs for Achievement, Affiliation, and Power

need for achievement The extent to which an individual has a strong desire to perform challenging tasks well and to meet personal standards for excellence.

Psychologist David McClelland extensively researched the needs for achievement, affiliation, and power.[63] The **need for achievement** is the extent to which an individual has a strong desire to perform challenging tasks well and to meet personal standards for excellence. People with a high need for achievement often set clear goals for themselves and like to receive performance feedback. The **need for affiliation** is the extent to which an individual is concerned about establishing and maintaining good interpersonal relations, being liked, and having the people around him or her get along with each other. The **need for power** is the extent to which an individual desires to control or influence others.[64]

need for affiliation The extent to which an individual is concerned about establishing and maintaining good interpersonal relations, being liked, and having the people around him or her get along with each other.

Although each of these needs is present in each of us to some degree, their importance in the workplace depends on the position one occupies. For example, research suggests that high needs for achievement and for power are assets for first-line and middle managers and that a high need for power is especially important for upper managers.[65] One study found that U.S. presidents with a relatively high need for power tended to be especially effective during their terms of office.[66] A high need for affiliation may not always be desirable in managers and other leaders because it might lead them to try too hard to be liked by others (including subordinates) rather than doing all they can to ensure that performance is as high as it can and should be. Although most research on these needs has been done in the United States, some studies suggest that the findings may be applicable to people in other countries as well, such as India and New Zealand.[67]

need for power The extent to which an individual desires to control or influence others.

Other Needs

Clearly, more needs motivate workers than the needs described by these four theories. For example, more and more workers are feeling the need for work–life balance and time to take care of their loved ones while simultaneously being highly motivated at work. Thus, for example, not being required to work excessive hours and being able to take time off when needed can help meet needs for work–life balance. Interestingly enough, recent research suggests that being exposed to nature (even just being able to see some trees from an office window) has many salutary effects, and a lack of such exposure can impair well-being and performance.[68] Thus having some time during the day when one can at least see nature may be another important need.

Managers of successful companies often strive to ensure that as many of their valued employees' needs as possible are satisfied in the workplace. This is illustrated by the following "Information Technology Byte" box on the SAS Institute.

Information Technology Byte

High Motivation at the SAS Institute

The SAS Institute is in the enviable position of being listed on *Fortune* magazine's annual ranking of the "100 Best Companies to Work For" for 15 years in a row; in 2012 the SAS Institute was ranked third.[69] The SAS Institute is the world's largest privately owned software company, with over 11,900 employees worldwide and approximately $2.4 billion in revenues.[70] Every indicator suggests that SAS employees are highly motivated and perform well while also working 35-hour weeks. How do managers at SAS do it? In large part, by ensuring that employees are highly motivated and the variety of needs they bring to the workplace are satisfied by doing a good job at SAS.[71]

Satisfying the need for intrinsically motivating work has been a key priority at SAS. Managers strive to make sure that each employee is motivated by the work he or she performs, and employees are encouraged to change jobs to prevent becoming bored with their work (even if the job changes require that SAS provide additional training). Moreover, in contrast to the approach at some of the company's competitors, all new product development work at SAS is performed in-house, so employees have the opportunity to experience the excitement of developing a new product and seeing it succeed.[72]

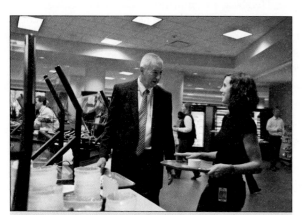

Running into your boss's boss in the cafeteria isn't quite so daunting when the food is good, your pay is reasonable, and you know your kids are happily playing in the awesome day care just up the road! SAS knows how to keep its employees engaged in their work by recognizing a broad range of worker needs.

The SAS Institute satisfies employees' needs for economic security by paying them fairly and providing them with secure jobs. Employees have their own offices, and the work environment is rich in pleasant vistas, whether there are artwork on the walls or views of the rolling hills of Cary, North Carolina, at company headquarters. Managers at SAS realize that needs for work–life balance are a top priority for many of their employees and seek to satisfy these needs in a variety of ways, including 35-hour workweeks, on-site day care and medical care, unlimited sick days, and high chairs in the company cafeteria so that employees can dine with their kids. Moreover, employees and their families are encouraged to use the 200 acres that surround company headquarters for family walks and picnics.[73]

Since the company was founded, CEO James Goodnight has been committed to motivating employees to develop creative and high-quality products that meet customers' needs. Today, over 50,000 customer sites utilize SAS software products for a wide variety of purposes including risk management, monitoring and measuring performance, managing relations with suppliers and customers, and detecting fraud.[74] SAS also provides educational software for schools and teachers through SAS in School.[75] Clearly, motivating employees and helping to satisfy their needs is a win-win situation for SAS.

Equity Theory

Equity theory is a theory of motivation that concentrates on people's perceptions of the fairness of their work *outcomes* relative to, or in proportion to, their work *inputs*. Equity theory complements expectancy and need theories by focusing on how people perceive the relationship between the outcomes they receive from their jobs and organizations and the inputs they contribute. Equity theory was formulated in the 1960s by J. Stacy Adams, who stressed that what is important in determining motivation is the *relative* rather than the *absolute* levels of outcomes a person receives and inputs a person contributes. Specifically, motivation is influenced by the comparison of one's own outcome–input ratio with the outcome–input ratio of a referent.[76] The *referent* could be another person or a group of people who are perceived to be similar to oneself; the referent also could be oneself in a previous job or one's expectations about what outcome–input ratios should be. In a comparison of one's own outcome–input ratio to a referent's ratio, one's *perceptions* of outcomes and inputs (not any objective indicator of them) are key.

LO13-2 Describe from the perspectives of expectancy theory and equity theory what managers should do to have a highly motivated workforce.

equity theory A theory of motivation that focuses on people's perceptions of the fairness of their work outcomes relative to their work inputs.

equity The justice, impartiality, and fairness to which all organizational members are entitled.

Equity

Equity exists when a person perceives his or her own outcome–input ratio to be equal to a referent's outcome–input ratio. Under conditions of equity (see Table 13.3), if a referent receives more outcomes than you receive, the referent contributes proportionally more inputs to the organization, so his or her outcome–input ratio still equals your ratio. Maria Sanchez and Claudia King, for example, both work in a shoe store in a large mall. Sanchez is paid more per hour than King but also contributes more inputs, including being responsible for some of the store's bookkeeping, closing the store, and periodically depositing cash in the bank. When King compares her outcome–input ratio to Sanchez's (her referent's), she perceives the ratios

Table 13.3
Equity Theory

Condition	Person		Referent	Example
Equity	$\dfrac{\text{Outcomes}}{\text{Inputs}}$	=	$\dfrac{\text{Outcomes}}{\text{Inputs}}$	An engineer perceives that he contributes more inputs (time and effort) and receives proportionally more outcomes (a higher salary and choice job assignments) than his referent.
Underpayment inequity	$\dfrac{\text{Outcomes}}{\text{Inputs}}$	 < (less than)	$\dfrac{\text{Outcomes}}{\text{Inputs}}$	An engineer perceives that he contributes more inputs but receives the same outcomes as his referent.
Overpayment inequity	$\dfrac{\text{Outcomes}}{\text{Inputs}}$	 > (greater than)	$\dfrac{\text{Outcomes}}{\text{Inputs}}$	An engineer perceives that he contributes the same inputs but receives more outcomes than his referent.

to be equitable because Sanchez's higher level of pay (an outcome) is proportional to her higher level of inputs (bookkeeping, closing the store, and going to the bank).

Similarly, under conditions of equity, if you receive more outcomes than a referent, your inputs are perceived to be proportionally higher. Continuing with our example, when Sanchez compares her outcome–input ratio to King's (her referent's) ratio, she perceives them to be equitable because her higher level of pay is proportional to her higher level of inputs.

When equity exists, people are motivated to continue contributing their current levels of inputs to their organizations to receive their current levels of outcomes. If people wish to increase their outcomes under conditions of equity, they are motivated to increase their inputs.

Inequity

inequity Lack of fairness.

Inequity, or lack of fairness, exists when a person's outcome–input ratio is not perceived to be equal to a referent's. Inequity creates pressure or tension inside people and motivates them to restore equity by bringing the two ratios back into balance.

There are two types of inequity: underpayment inequity and overpayment inequity (see Table 13.3). **Underpayment inequity** exists when a person's own outcome–input ratio is perceived to be *less* than that of a referent. In comparing yourself to a referent, you think you are *not* receiving the outcomes you should be, given your inputs. **Overpayment inequity** exists when a person perceives that his or her own outcome–input ratio is *greater* than that of a referent. In comparing yourself to a referent, you think you are receiving *more* outcomes than you should be, given your inputs.

underpayment inequity
The inequity that exists when a person perceives that his or her own outcome–input ratio is less than the ratio of a referent.

overpayment inequity
The inequity that exists when a person perceives that his or her own outcome–input ratio is greater than the ratio of a referent.

Ways to Restore Equity

According to equity theory, both underpayment inequity and overpayment inequity create tension that motivates most people to restore equity by bringing the ratios back into balance.[77] When people experience *underpayment* inequity, they may be motivated to lower their inputs by reducing their working hours, putting forth less effort on the job, or being absent; or they may be motivated to increase their outcomes by asking for a raise or a promotion. Susan Richie, a financial analyst at a large corporation, noticed that she was working longer hours and getting more work accomplished than a coworker who had the same position, yet they both received the exact same pay and other outcomes. To restore equity, Richie decided to stop coming in early and staying late. Alternatively, she could have tried to restore equity by trying to increase her outcomes, perhaps by asking her boss for a raise.

When people experience underpayment inequity and other means of equity restoration fail, they can change their perceptions of their own or the referent's inputs or outcomes. For example, they may realize that their referent is really working on more difficult projects than they are or that they really take more time off from work than their referent does. Alternatively, if people who feel they are underpaid have other employment options, they may leave the organization. As an example, John Steinberg, an assistant principal in a high school, experienced underpayment inequity when he realized all the other assistant principals of high schools in his school district had received promotions to the position of principal even though they had been in their jobs for a shorter time than he had. Steinberg's performance had always been appraised as being high, so after his repeated requests for a promotion went unheeded, he found a job as a principal in a different school district.

When people experience *overpayment* inequity, they may try to restore equity by changing their perceptions of their own or their referent's inputs or outcomes. Equity can be restored when people realize they are contributing more inputs than they originally thought. Equity also can be restored by perceiving the referent's inputs to be lower or the referent's outcomes to be higher than one originally thought. When equity is restored in this way, actual inputs and outcomes are unchanged, and the person being overpaid takes no real action. What is changed is how people think about or view their or the referent's inputs and outcomes. For instance, Mary McMann experienced overpayment inequity when she realized she was being paid $2 an hour more than a coworker who had the same job as she did in a health food store and who contributed the same amount of inputs. McMann restored equity by changing her perceptions of her inputs. She realized she worked harder than her coworker and solved more problems that came up in the store.

Experiencing either overpayment or underpayment inequity, you might decide that your referent is not appropriate because, for example, the referent is too different from yourself. Choosing a more appropriate referent may bring the ratios back into balance. Angela Martinez, a middle manager in the engineering department of a chemical company, experienced overpayment inequity when she realized she was being paid quite a bit more than her friend, who was a middle manager in the marketing department of the same company. After thinking about the discrepancy for a while, Martinez decided that engineering and marketing were so different that she should not be comparing her job to her friend's job even though they were both middle managers. Martinez restored equity by changing her referent; she picked a middle manager in the engineering department as a new referent.

Motivation is highest when as many people as possible in an organization perceive that they are being equitably treated—their outcomes and inputs are in balance. Top contributors and performers are motivated to continue contributing a high level of inputs because they are receiving the outcomes they deserve. Mediocre contributors and performers realize that if they want to increase their outcomes, they have to increase their inputs. Managers of effective organizations, like Andrew Taylor at Enterprise Rent-A-Car, realize the importance of equity for motivation and performance and continually strive to ensure that employees believe they are being equitably treated.

The dot-com boom, its subsequent bust, and two recessions, along with increased global competition, have resulted in some workers putting in longer and longer working hours (increasing their inputs) without any increase in their outcomes. For those whose referents are not experiencing a similar change, perceptions of inequity are likely. According to Jill Andresky Fraser, author of *White Collar Sweatshop*, over 25 million U.S. workers work more than 49 hours per week in the office, almost 11 million work more than 60 hours per week in the office, and many also put in additional work hours at home. Moreover, advances in information technology, such as e-mail and cell phones, have resulted in work intruding on home time, vacation time, and even special occasions.[78]

LO13-3 Explain how goals and needs motivate people and what kinds of goals are especially likely to result in high performance.

Goal-Setting Theory

Goal-setting theory focuses on motivating workers to contribute their inputs to their jobs and organizations; in this way it is similar to expectancy theory and equity theory. But goal-setting theory takes this focus a step further by considering as well how managers can ensure that organizational members focus their inputs in the direction of high performance and the achievement of organizational goals.

goal-setting theory A theory that focuses on identifying the types of goals that are most effective in producing high levels of motivation and performance and explaining why goals have these effects.

Ed Locke and Gary Latham, the leading researchers for goal-setting theory, suggested that the goals organizational members strive to attain are prime determinants of their motivation and subsequent performance. A *goal* is what a person is trying to accomplish through his or her efforts and behaviors.[79] Just as you may have a goal to get a good grade in this course, so do members of an organization have goals they strive to meet. For example, salespeople at Neiman Marcus strive to meet sales goals, while top managers pursue market share and profitability goals.

Goal-setting theory suggests that to stimulate high motivation and performance, goals must be *specific* and *difficult*.[80] Specific goals are often quantitative—a salesperson's goal to

Specific, difficult goals can encourage people to exert high levels of effort and to focus efforts in the right direction.

sell $500 worth of merchandise per day, a scientist's goal to finish a project in one year, a CEO's goal to reduce debt by 40% and increase revenues by 20%, a restaurant manager's goal to serve 150 customers per evening. In contrast to specific goals, vague goals such as "doing your best" or "selling as much as you can" do not have much motivational impact.

Difficult goals are hard but not impossible to attain. In contrast to difficult goals, easy goals are those that practically everyone can attain, and moderate goals are goals that about one-half of the people can attain. Both easy and moderate goals have less motivational power than difficult goals.

Regardless of whether specific, difficult goals are set by managers, workers, or teams of managers and workers, they lead to high levels of motivation and performance. When managers set goals for their subordinates, their subordinates must accept the goals or agree to work toward them; also, they should be committed to them or really want to attain them. Some managers find that having subordinates participate in the actual setting of goals boosts their acceptance of and commitment to the goals. In addition, organizational members need to receive *feedback* about how they are doing; feedback can often be provided by the performance appraisal and feedback component of an organization's human resource management system (see Chapter 12). More generally, goals and feedback are integral components of performance management systems such as management by objectives (see Chapter 11).

Specific, difficult goals affect motivation in two ways. First, they motivate people to contribute more inputs to their jobs. Specific, difficult goals cause people to put forth high levels of effort, for example. Just as you would study harder if you were trying to get an A in a course instead of a C, so too will a salesperson work harder to reach a $500 sales goal instead of a $200 sales goal. Specific, difficult goals also cause people to be more persistent than easy, moderate, or vague goals when they run into difficulties. Salespeople who are told to sell as much as possible might stop trying on a slow day, whereas having a specific, difficult goal to reach causes them to keep trying.

A second way in which specific, difficult goals affect motivation is by helping people focus their inputs in the right direction. These goals let people know what they should be focusing their attention on, whether it is increasing the quality of customer service or sales or lowering new product development times. The fact that the goals are specific and difficult also frequently causes people to develop *action plans* for reaching them.[81] Action plans can include the strategies to attain the goals and timetables or schedules for the completion of different activities crucial to goal attainment. Like the goals themselves, action plans also help ensure that efforts are focused in the right direction and that people do not get sidetracked along the way.

Although specific, difficult goals have been found to increase motivation and performance in a wide variety of jobs and organizations both in the United States and abroad, recent research suggests that they may detract from performance under certain conditions. When people are performing complicated and challenging tasks that require them to focus on a considerable amount of learning, specific, difficult goals may actually impair performance.[82] Striving to reach such goals may direct some of a person's attention away from learning about the task and toward trying to figure out how to achieve the goal. Once a person has learned the task and it no longer seems complicated or difficult, then the assignment of specific, difficult goals is likely to have its usual effects. Additionally, for work that is very creative and uncertain, specific, difficult goals may be detrimental.

LO13-4 Identify the motivation lessons that managers can learn from operant conditioning theory and social learning theory.

learning theories Theories that focus on increasing employee motivation and performance by linking the outcomes that employees receive to the performance of desired behaviors and the attainment of goals.

Learning Theories

The basic premise of **learning theories** as applied to organizations is that managers can increase employee motivation and performance by how they link the outcomes that employees receive to the performance of desired behaviors and the attainment of goals. Thus learning theory focuses on the linkage between performance and outcomes in the motivation equation (see Figure 13.1).

learning A relatively permanent change in knowledge or behavior that results from practice or experience.

Learning can be defined as a relatively permanent change in a person's knowledge or behavior that results from practice or experience.[83] Learning takes place in organizations when people learn to perform certain behaviors to receive certain outcomes. For example, a person learns to perform at a higher level than in the past or to come to work earlier because he or she is motivated to obtain the outcomes that result from these behaviors, such as a pay raise or praise from a supervisor. In "A Manager's Challenge," Enterprise Rent-A-Car's emphasis on training ensures that new hires learn how to provide excellent customer service and perform all the tasks necessary for successful branch operations.

Training can spur learning in all kinds of jobs and organizations, even ones where a good portion of the workforce is working freelance-style, at home, and part-time, as indicated in the following "Management Insight" box.

Management Insight

Training Spurs Learning at Stella & Dot

Stella & Dot, based in San Francisco, is a social selling company that sells jewelry and accessories exclusively through independent stylists who host trunk shows in their homes and online. Founded by Jessica Herrin, who started the firm by designing jewelry, is its current CEO, and was a cofounder of the WeddingChannel.com, Stella & Dot has grown to have over $200 million in sales.[84] Stella & Dot has approximately 10,000 stylists who work out of their homes, many of them part-time. According to Herrin, one of the keys to their success is the training they provide to stylists.[85]

Jessica Herrin knows how important on-the-job training remains for all employees. Her early failure with Stella & Dot taught her that the company could only succeed if it remained nimble, flexible, and was able to foster strong communication among employees to keep the ideas flowing.

The company has its own online learning center, called Stella & Dot University, where stylists have access to interactive videos, guidebooks, tutorials, and audio training. Online quizzes ensure that learning takes place and stylists receive immediate feedback when they master a content area. Weekly phone calls with headquarters also focus on coaching and training stylists to learn how best to market and sell products.[86] Herrin herself makes it a point to send personal e-mails, and she phones a minimum of 10 stylists a day to see how they are doing and to congratulate them when things go well.[87]

There are also many opportunities for stylists to learn from each other. High-performing stylists relate the keys to their own success in webcams in their homes, how they managed the process, and the obstacles they were able to overcome.[88] A national annual conference also enables stylists to learn from each other by providing networking opportunities and training sessions led by high-performing stylists. Training also is provided on a regional basis by local high-performing stylists.[89] In all of its training efforts, Stella & Dot emphasizes treating stylists with respect as the professionals that they are and celebrating successes.[90] All in all, facilitating learning through training has certainly paid off for Stella & Dot.

Of the different learning theories, operant conditioning theory and social learning theory provide the most guidance to managers in their efforts to have a highly motivated workforce.

Operant Conditioning Theory

operant conditioning theory The theory that people learn to perform behaviors that lead to desired consequences and learn not to perform behaviors that lead to undesired consequences.

According to **operant conditioning theory**, developed by psychologist B. F. Skinner, people learn to perform behaviors that lead to desired consequences and learn not to perform behaviors that lead to undesired consequences.[91] Translated into motivation terms, Skinner's theory means that people will be motivated to perform at a high level and attain their work goals to the extent that high performance and goal attainment allow them to obtain outcomes they desire. Similarly, people avoid performing behaviors that lead to outcomes they do not desire. By linking the performance of *specific behaviors* to the attainment of *specific outcomes,* managers can motivate organizational members to perform in ways that help an organization achieve its goals.

Operant conditioning theory provides four tools that managers can use to motivate high performance and prevent workers from engaging in absenteeism and other behaviors that detract from organizational effectiveness. These tools are positive reinforcement, negative reinforcement, extinction, and punishment.[92]

positive reinforcement
Giving people outcomes they desire when they perform organizationally functional behaviors.

POSITIVE REINFORCEMENT   Positive reinforcement gives people outcomes they desire when they perform organizationally functional behaviors. These desired outcomes, called *positive reinforcers,* include any outcomes that a person desires, such as pay, praise, or a promotion. Organizationally functional behaviors are behaviors that contribute to organizational effectiveness; they can include producing high-quality goods and services, providing high-quality customer service, and meeting deadlines. By linking positive reinforcers to the performance of functional behaviors, managers motivate people to perform the desired behaviors.

negative reinforcement
Eliminating or removing undesired outcomes when people perform organizationally functional behaviors.

NEGATIVE REINFORCEMENT   Negative reinforcement also can encourage members of an organization to perform desired or organizationally functional behaviors. Managers using negative reinforcement actually eliminate or remove undesired outcomes once the functional behavior is performed. These undesired outcomes, called *negative reinforcers,* can range from a manager's constant nagging or criticism to unpleasant assignments or the ever-present threat of losing one's job. When negative reinforcement is used, people are motivated to perform behaviors because they want to stop receiving or avoid undesired outcomes. Managers who try to encourage salespeople to sell more by threatening them with being fired are using negative reinforcement. In this case, the negative reinforcer is the threat of job loss, which is removed once the functional behavior is performed.

Whenever possible, managers should try to use positive reinforcement. Negative reinforcement can create a very unpleasant work environment and even a negative culture in an organization. No one likes to be nagged, threatened, or exposed to other kinds of negative outcomes. The use of negative reinforcement sometimes causes subordinates to resent managers and try to get back at them.

IDENTIFYING THE RIGHT BEHAVIORS FOR REINFORCEMENT   Even managers who use positive reinforcement (and refrain from using negative reinforcement) can get into trouble if they are not careful to identify the right behaviors to reinforce—behaviors that are truly functional for the organization. Doing this is not always as straightforward as it might seem. First, it is crucial for managers to choose behaviors over which subordinates have control; in other words, subordinates must have the freedom and opportunity to perform the behaviors that are being reinforced. Second, it is crucial that these behaviors contribute to organizational effectiveness.

extinction Curtailing the performance of dysfunctional behaviors by eliminating whatever is reinforcing them.

EXTINCTION   Sometimes members of an organization are motivated to perform behaviors that detract from organizational effectiveness. According to operant conditioning theory, all behavior is controlled or determined by its consequences; one way for managers to curtail the performance of dysfunctional behaviors is to eliminate whatever is reinforcing the behaviors. This process is called extinction.

Suppose a manager has a subordinate who frequently stops by his office to chat—sometimes about work-related matters but at other times about various topics ranging from politics to last night's football game. The manager and the subordinate share certain interests and views, so these conversations can get quite involved, and both seem to enjoy them. The manager, however, realizes that these frequent and sometimes lengthy conversations are causing him to stay at work later in the evenings to make up for the time he loses during the day. The manager also realizes that he is reinforcing his subordinate's behavior by acting interested in the topics the subordinate brings up and responding at length to them. To extinguish this behavior, the manager stops acting interested in these non-work-related conversations and keeps his responses polite and friendly but brief. No longer being reinforced with a pleasurable conversation, the subordinate eventually ceases to be motivated to interrupt the manager during working hours to discuss non-work-related issues.

punishment Administering an undesired or negative consequence when dysfunctional behavior occurs.

PUNISHMENT   Sometimes managers cannot rely on extinction to eliminate dysfunctional behaviors because they do not have control over whatever is reinforcing the behavior or because they cannot afford the time needed for extinction to work. When employees are performing dangerous behaviors or behaviors that are illegal or unethical, the behavior needs to be eliminated immediately. Sexual harassment, for example, is an organizationally dysfunctional behavior that cannot be tolerated. In such cases managers often rely on **punishment**, which is administering an undesired or negative consequence to subordinates when they perform the dysfunctional behavior. Punishments used by organizations range from verbal reprimands to pay cuts, temporary suspensions, demotions, and firings. Punishment, however, can have some unintended side effects—resentment, loss of self-respect, a desire for retaliation—and should be used only when necessary.

To avoid the unintended side effects of punishment, managers should keep in mind these guidelines:

- Downplay the emotional element involved in punishment. Make it clear that you are punishing a person's performance of a dysfunctional behavior, not the person himself or herself.

- Try to punish dysfunctional behaviors as soon as possible after they occur and make sure the negative consequence is a source of punishment for the individuals involved. Be certain that organizational members know exactly why they are being punished.

- Try to avoid punishing someone in front of others because this can hurt a person's self-respect and lower esteem in the eyes of coworkers as well as make coworkers feel uncomfortable.[93] Even so, making organizational members aware that an individual who has committed a serious infraction has been punished can sometimes be effective in preventing future infractions and teaching all members of the organization that certain behaviors are unacceptable. For example, when organizational members are informed that a manager who has sexually harassed subordinates has been punished, they learn or are reminded of the fact that sexual harassment is not tolerated in the organization.

Managers and students alike often confuse negative reinforcement and punishment. To avoid such confusion, keep in mind the two major differences between them. First, negative reinforcement is used to promote the performance of functional behaviors in organizations; punishment is used to stop the performance of dysfunctional behaviors. Second, negative reinforcement entails the *removal* of a negative consequence when functional behaviors are performed; punishment entails the *administration* of negative consequences when dysfunctional behaviors are performed.

organizational behavior modification (OB MOD) The systematic application of operant conditioning techniques to promote the performance of organizationally functional behaviors and discourage the performance of dysfunctional behaviors.

ORGANIZATIONAL BEHAVIOR MODIFICATION   When managers systematically apply operant conditioning techniques to promote the performance of organizationally functional behaviors and discourage the performance of dysfunctional behaviors, they are engaging in **organizational behavior modification (OB MOD)**.[94] OB MOD has been successfully used to improve productivity, efficiency, attendance, punctuality, safe work practices, customer service, and other important behaviors in a wide variety of organizations such as banks, department stores, factories, hospitals, and construction sites.[95] The five basic steps in OB MOD are described in Figure 13.4.

OB MOD works best for behaviors that are specific, objective, and countable, such as attendance and punctuality, making sales, or putting telephones together, all of which lend themselves to careful scrutiny and control. OB MOD may be questioned because of its lack of relevance to certain work behaviors (for example, the many work behaviors that are not specific, objective, and countable). Some people also have questioned it on ethical grounds. Critics of OB MOD suggest that it is overly controlling and robs workers of their dignity, individuality, freedom of choice, and even creativity. Supporters counter that OB MOD is a highly effective means of promoting organizational efficiency. There is some merit to both sides of this argument. What is clear, however, is that when used appropriately, OB MOD gives managers a technique to motivate the performance of at least some organizationally functional behaviors.[96]

Figure 13.4

Five Steps in OB MOD

STEPS

- Managers identify an important behavior.
- Managers measure the frequency with which the behavior is occurring.
- Managers determine if people know whether they should be performing the behavior and what consequences they receive when they do perform it.
- Managers develop and apply a strategy entailing the use of positive reinforcement, negative reinforcement, punishment, or extinction.
- Managers measure the frequency of the behavior.
- Managers determine if the problem is solved.
  - No
  - Yes
- Managers maintain the behavior by continuing to use the strategy.

EXAMPLE

- Assembling computer printers.
- Each worker assembles, on average, 10 printers per day.
- Workers know that they should assemble as many printers as they can per day while maintaining high quality; however, they receive the same hourly wage regardless of the number of printers they assemble.
- Positively reinforce workers such that they receive $5 for each defect-free printer they assemble instead of an hourly wage.
- Each worker assembles, on average, 14 printers per day.
- Problem solved.
- Maintain positive reinforcement.

Source: Adapted from *Organizational Behavior Modification and Beyond* by F. Luthans and R. Kreitner (Scott, Foresman, 1985). With permission of the authors.

Social Learning Theory

social learning theory A theory that takes into account how learning and motivation are influenced by people's thoughts and beliefs and their observations of other people's behavior.

Social learning theory proposes that motivation results not only from direct experience of rewards and punishments but also from a person's thoughts and beliefs. Social learning theory extends operant conditioning's contribution to managers' understanding of motivation by explaining (1) how people can be motivated by observing other people performing a behavior and being reinforced for doing so (*vicarious learning*), (2) how people can be motivated to control their behavior themselves (*self-reinforcement*), and (3) how people's beliefs about their ability to successfully perform a behavior affect motivation (*self-efficacy*).[97] We look briefly at each of these motivators.

vicarious learning Learning that occurs when the learner becomes motivated to perform a behavior by watching another person performing it and being reinforced for doing so; also called *observational learning.*

VICARIOUS LEARNING Vicarious learning, often called *observational learning,* occurs when a person (the learner) becomes motivated to perform a behavior by watching another person (the model) performing the behavior and being positively reinforced for doing so. Vicarious learning is a powerful source of motivation on many jobs in which people learn to perform functional behaviors by watching others. Salespeople learn how to help customers, medical school students learn how to treat patients, law clerks learn how to practice law, and nonmanagers learn how to be managers, in part, by observing experienced members of an organization perform these behaviors properly and be reinforced for them. In general,

How do you treat that? When medical students enter residency, they learn vicariously by shadowing a full physician on his or her rounds.

people are more likely to be motivated to imitate the behavior of models who are highly competent, are (to some extent) experts in the behavior, have high status, receive attractive reinforcers, and are friendly or approachable.[98]

To promote vicarious learning, managers should strive to have the learner meet the following conditions:

- The learner observes the model performing the behavior.

- The learner accurately perceives the model's behavior.

- The learner remembers the behavior.

- The learner has the skills and abilities needed to perform the behavior.

- The learner sees or knows that the model is positively reinforced for the behavior.[99]

self-reinforcer Any desired or attractive outcome or reward that a person gives to himself or herself for good performance.

SELF-REINFORCEMENT   Although managers are often the providers of reinforcement in organizations, sometimes people motivate themselves through self-reinforcement. People can control their own behavior by setting goals for themselves and then reinforcing themselves when they achieve the goals.[100] *Self-reinforcers* are any desired or attractive outcomes or rewards that people can give to themselves for good performance, such as a feeling of accomplishment, going to a movie, having dinner out, buying a new CD, or taking time out for a golf game. When members of an organization control their own behavior through self-reinforcement, managers do not need to spend as much time as they ordinarily would trying to motivate and control behavior through the administration of consequences because subordinates are controlling and motivating themselves. In fact, this self-control is often referred to as the *self-management of behavior.*

When employees are highly skilled and are responsible for creating new goods and services, managers typically rely on self-control and self-management of behavior, as is the case at Google. Employees at Google are given the flexibility and autonomy to experiment, take risks, and sometimes fail as they work on new projects. They are encouraged to learn from their failures and apply what they learn to subsequent projects.[101] Google's engineers are given one day a week to work on their own projects that they are highly involved with, and new products such as Google News often emerge from these projects.[102]

self-efficacy A person's belief about his or her ability to perform a behavior successfully.

SELF-EFFICACY   Self-efficacy is a person's belief about his or her ability to perform a behavior successfully.[103] Even with all the most attractive consequences or reinforcers hinging on high performance, people are not going to be motivated if they do not think they can actually perform at a high level. Similarly, when people control their own behavior, they are likely to set for themselves difficult goals that will lead to outstanding accomplishments only if they think they can reach those goals. Thus self-efficacy influences motivation both when managers provide reinforcement and when workers themselves provide it.[104] The greater the self-efficacy, the greater is the motivation and performance. In "A Manager's Challenge," managers at Enterprise Rent-A-Car boost self-efficacy by providing employees with training, increasing their levels of autonomy and responsibility as they gain experience with the company, and expressing confidence in their ability to manage their units. Such verbal persuasion, as well as a person's own past performance and accomplishments and the accomplishments of other people, plays a role in determining a person's self-efficacy.

LO13-5 Explain why and how managers can use pay as a major motivation tool.

Pay and Motivation

In Chapter 12 we discussed how managers establish a pay level and structure for an organization as a whole. Here we focus on how, once a pay level and structure are in place, managers can use pay to motivate employees to perform at a high level and attain their work goals. Pay is used to motivate entry-level workers, first-line and middle managers, and even top managers such as CEOs. Pay can be used to motivate people to perform behaviors that help an organization achieve its goals, and it can be used to motivate people to join and remain with an organization.

Each of the theories described in this chapter alludes to the importance of pay and suggests that pay should be based on performance:

- *Expectancy theory:* Instrumentality, the association between performance and outcomes such as pay, must be high for motivation to be high. In addition, pay is an outcome that has high valence for many people.

- *Need theories:* People should be able to satisfy their needs by performing at a high level; pay can be used to satisfy several different kinds of needs.

- *Equity theory:* Outcomes such as pay should be distributed in proportion to inputs (including performance levels).

- *Goal-setting theory:* Outcomes such as pay should be linked to the attainment of goals.

- *Learning theories:* The distribution of outcomes such as pay should be contingent on the performance of organizationally functional behaviors.

As these theories suggest, to promote high motivation, managers should base the distribution of pay to organizational members on performance levels so that high performers receive more pay than low performers (other things being equal).[105] A compensation plan basing pay on performance is often called a **merit pay plan**.

merit pay plan A compensation plan that bases pay on performance.

In tough economic times, when organizations lay off employees and pay levels and benefits of those who are at least able to keep their jobs may be cut while their responsibilities are often increased,[106] managers are often limited in the extent to which they can use merit pay, if at all.[107] Nonetheless, in such times, managers can still try to recognize top performers. Jenny Miller, manager of 170 engineers in the commercial systems engineering department at Rockwell Collins, an aerospace electronics company in Cedar Rapids, Iowa, experienced firsthand the challenge of not being able to recognize top performers with merit pay during tough economic times.[108] Rockwell Collins laid off 8% of its workforce, and the workloads for the engineers Miller managed increased by about 15%. The engineers were working longer hours without receiving any additional pay; there was a salary freeze, so they knew raises were not in store. With a deadline approaching for flight deck software for a customer, she needed some engineers to work over the Thanksgiving holiday and so sent out an e-mail request for volunteers. Approximately 20 employees volunteered. In recognition of their contributions, Miller gave them each a $100 gift card.[109]

A $100 gift card might not seem like much for an employee who is already working long hours to come to work over the Thanksgiving holiday for no additional pay or time off. Yet Steve Nieuwsma, division vice president at Rockwell Collins, indicates that the gift cards at least signaled that managers recognized and appreciated employees' efforts and sought to thank them for it. Not being able to give his employees raises at that time, Nieuwsma also gave gift cards to recognize contributions and top performers in amounts varying between $25 and $500.[110]

Once managers have decided to use a merit pay plan, they face two important choices: whether to base pay on individual, group, or organizational performance and whether to use salary increases or bonuses.

Basing Merit Pay on Individual, Group, or Organizational Performance

Managers can base merit pay on individual, group, or organizational performance. When individual performance (such as the dollar value of merchandise a salesperson sells, the number of loudspeakers a factory worker assembles, and a lawyer's billable hours) can be accurately determined, individual motivation is likely to be highest when pay is based on individual performance.[111] When members of an organization work closely together and individual performance cannot be accurately determined (as in a team of computer programmers developing a single software package), pay cannot be based on individual performance, and a group- or organization-based plan must be used. When the attainment of organizational goals hinges on members' working closely together and cooperating with each other (as in a small construction company that builds custom homes), group- or organization-based plans may be more appropriate than individual-based plans.[112]

It is possible to combine elements of an individual-based plan with a group- or organization-based plan to motivate each individual to perform highly and, at the same time, motivate all individuals to work well together, cooperate with one another, and help one another as needed. Lincoln Electric, a very successful company and a leading manufacturer of welding machines, uses a combination individual- and organization-based plan.[113] Pay is based on individual performance. In addition, each year the size of a bonus fund depends on organizational performance. Money from the bonus fund is distributed to people on the basis of their contributions to the organization, attendance, levels of cooperation, and other indications of performance. Employees of Lincoln Electric are motivated to cooperate and help one another because when the firm as a whole performs well, everybody benefits by having a larger bonus fund. Employees also are motivated to contribute their inputs to the organization because their contributions determine their share of the bonus fund.

Salary Increase or Bonus?

Managers can distribute merit pay to people in the form of a salary increase or a bonus on top of regular salaries. Although the dollar amount of a salary increase or bonus might be identical, bonuses tend to have more motivational impact for at least three reasons. First, salary levels are typically based on performance levels, cost-of-living increases, and so forth, from the day people start working in an organization, which means the absolute level of the salary is based largely on factors unrelated to *current* performance. A 5% merit increase in salary, for example, may seem relatively small in comparison to one's total salary. Second, a current salary increase may be affected by other factors in addition to performance, such as cost-of-living increases or across-the-board market adjustments. Third, because organizations rarely reduce salaries, salary levels tend to vary less than performance levels do. Related to this point is the fact that bonuses give managers more flexibility in distributing outcomes. If an organization is doing well, bonuses can be relatively high to reward employees for their contributions. However, unlike salary increases, bonus levels can be reduced when an organization's performance lags. All in all, bonus plans have more motivational impact than salary increases because the amount of the bonus can be directly and exclusively based on performance.[114]

Consistent with the lessons from motivation theories, bonuses can be linked directly to performance and vary from year to year and employee to employee, as at Gradient Corporation, a Cambridge, Massachusetts, environmental consulting firm.[115] Another organization that successfully uses bonuses is Nucor Corporation. Steelworkers at Nucor tend to be much more productive than steelworkers in other companies—probably because they can receive bonuses tied to performance and quality that can range from 130% to 150% of their regular base pay.[116] During the economic downturn in 2007–2009, Nucor struggled as did many other companies, and bonus pay for steelworkers dropped considerably. However, managers at Nucor avoided having to lay off employees by finding ways to cut costs and having employees work on maintenance activities and safety manuals, along with taking on tasks that used to be performed by independent contractors, such as producing specialty parts and mowing the grass.[117]

employee stock option A financial instrument that entitles the bearer to buy shares of an organization's stock at a certain price during a certain period or under certain conditions.

In addition to receiving pay raises and bonuses, high-level managers and executives are sometimes granted employee stock options. **Employee stock options** are financial instruments that entitle the bearer to buy shares of an organization's stock at a certain price during a certain period or under certain conditions.[118] For example, in addition to salaries, stock options are sometimes used to attract high-level managers. The exercise price is the stock price at which the bearer can buy the stock, and the vesting conditions specify when the bearer can actually buy the stock at the exercise price. The option's exercise price is generally set equal to the market price of the stock on the date it is granted, and the vesting conditions might specify that the manager has to have worked at the organization for 12 months or perhaps met some performance target (perhaps an increase in profits) before being able to exercise the option. In high-technology firms and start-ups, options are sometimes used in a similar fashion for employees at various levels in the organization.[119]

From a motivation standpoint, stock options are used not so much to reward past individual performance but, rather, to motivate employees to work in the future for the good of the company as a whole. This is true because stock options issued at current stock prices have value in the future only if an organization does well and its stock price appreciates; thus giving employees stock options should encourage them to help the organization improve its performance over time.[120] At high-technology start-ups and dot-coms, stock options have often motivated potential employees to leave promising jobs in larger companies and work for the start-ups. In the late 1990s and early 2000s, many dot-commers were devastated to learn not only that their stock options were worthless, because their companies went out of business or were doing poorly, but also that they were unemployed. Unfortunately stock options have also led to unethical behavior; for example, sometimes individuals seek to artificially inflate the value of a company's stock to increase the value of stock options.

Examples of Merit Pay Plans

Managers can choose among several merit pay plans, depending on the work that employees perform and other considerations. Using *piece-rate pay,* an individual-based merit plan, managers base employees' pay on the number of units each employee produces, whether televisions, computer components, or welded auto parts. Managers at Lincoln Electric use piece-rate pay to determine individual pay levels. Advances in information technology have dramatically simplified the administration of piece-rate pay in a variety of industries.

Using *commission pay,* another individual-based merit pay plan, managers base pay on a percentage of sales. Managers at the successful real estate company Re/Max International Inc. use commission pay for their agents, who are paid a percentage of their sales. Some department stores, such as Neiman Marcus, use commission pay for their salespeople.

Examples of organizational-based merit pay plans include the Scanlon plan and profit sharing. The *Scanlon plan* (developed by Joseph Scanlon, a union leader in a steel and tin plant in the 1920s) focuses on reducing expenses or cutting costs; members of an organization are motivated to propose and implement cost-cutting strategies because a percentage of the cost savings achieved during a specified time is distributed to the employees.[121] Under *profit sharing,* employees receive a share of an organization's profits. Regardless of the specific kind of plan that is used, managers should always strive to link pay to the performance of behaviors that help an organization achieve its goals.

Japanese managers in large corporations have long shunned merit pay plans in favor of plans that reward seniority. However, more and more Japanese companies are adopting merit-based pay due to its motivational benefits; among such companies are SiteDesign,[122] Tokio Marine and Fire Insurance, and Hissho Iwai, a trading organization.[123]

Summary and Review

THE NATURE OF MOTIVATION   Motivation encompasses the psychological forces within a person that determine the direction of the person's behavior in an organization, the person's level of effort, and the person's level of persistence in the face of obstacles. Managers strive to motivate people to contribute their inputs to an organization, to focus

LO13-1   these inputs in the direction of high performance, and to ensure that people receive the outcomes they desire when they perform at a high level.

LO13-2   **EXPECTANCY THEORY**   According to expectancy theory, managers can promote high levels of motivation in their organizations by taking steps to ensure that expectancy is high (people think that if they try, they can perform at a high level), instrumentality is high (people think that if they perform at a high level, they will receive certain outcomes), and valence is high (people desire these outcomes).

LO13-3   **NEED THEORIES**   Need theories suggest that to motivate their workforces, managers should determine what needs people are trying to satisfy in organizations and then ensure that people receive outcomes that satisfy these needs when they perform at a high level and contribute to organizational effectiveness.

LO13-2   EQUITY THEORY   According to equity theory, managers can promote high levels of motivation by ensuring that people perceive that there is equity in the organization or that outcomes are distributed in proportion to inputs. Equity exists when a person perceives that his or her own outcome–input ratio equals the outcome–input ratio of a referent. Inequity motivates people to try to restore equity.

LO13-3   GOAL-SETTING THEORY   Goal-setting theory suggests that managers can promote high motivation and performance by ensuring that people are striving to achieve specific, difficult goals. It is important for people to accept the goals, be committed to them, and receive feedback about how they are doing.

LO13-4   LEARNING THEORIES   Operant conditioning theory suggests that managers can motivate people to perform highly by using positive reinforcement or negative reinforcement (positive reinforcement being the preferred strategy). Managers can motivate people to avoid performing dysfunctional behaviors by using extinction or punishment. Social learning theory suggests that people can also be motivated by observing how others perform behaviors and receive rewards, by engaging in self-reinforcement, and by having high levels of self-efficacy.

LO13-5   PAY AND MOTIVATION   Each of the motivation theories discussed in this chapter alludes to the importance of pay and suggests that pay should be based on performance. Merit pay plans can be individual-, group-, or organization-based and can entail the use of salary increases or bonuses.

Management in Action

Topics for Discussion and Action

Discussion

1. Discuss why two people with similar abilities may have very different expectancies for performing at a high level. [LO13-2]

2. Describe why some people have low instrumentalities even when their managers distribute outcomes based on performance. [LO13-2]

3. Analyze how professors try to promote equity to motivate students. [LO13-2]

4. Describe three techniques or procedures that managers can use to determine whether a goal is difficult. [LO13-3]

5. Discuss why managers should always try to use positive reinforcement instead of negative reinforcement. [LO13-4]

Action

6. Interview three people who have the same kind of job (such as salesperson, waiter/waitress, or teacher), and determine what kinds of needs each is trying to satisfy at work. [LO13-3]

7. Interview a manager in an organization in your community to determine the extent to which the manager takes advantage of vicarious learning to promote high motivation among subordinates. [LO13-3]

Building Management Skills

Diagnosing Motivation [LO13-1, 13-2, 13-3, 13-4]

Think about the ideal job that you would like to obtain upon graduation. Describe this job, the kind of manager you would like to report to, and the kind of organization you would be working in. Then answer the following questions:

1. What would be your levels of expectancy and instrumentality on this job? Which outcomes would have high valence for you on this job? What steps would your manager take to influence your levels of expectancy, instrumentality, and valence?

2. Whom would you choose as a referent on this job? What steps would your manager take to make you feel that you were being equitably treated? What would you do if, after a year on the job, you experienced underpayment inequity?

3. What goals would you strive to achieve on this job? Why? What role would your manager play in determining your goals?

4. What needs would you strive to satisfy on this job? Why? What role would your manager play in helping you satisfy these needs?

5. What behaviors would your manager positively reinforce on this job? Why? What positive reinforcers would your manager use?

6. Would there be any vicarious learning on this job? Why or why not?

7. To what extent would you be motivated by self-control on this job? Why?

8. What would be your level of self-efficacy on this job? Why would your self-efficacy be at this level? Should your manager take steps to boost your self-efficacy? If not, why not? If so, what would these steps be?

Managing Ethically [LO13-5]

Sometimes pay is so contingent upon performance that it creates stress for employees. Imagine a salesperson who knows that if sales targets are not met, she or he will not be able to make a house mortgage payment or pay the rent.

Questions

1. Either individually or in a group, think about the ethical implications of closely linking pay to performance.

2. Under what conditions might contingent pay be most stressful, and what steps can managers take to try to help their subordinates perform effectively and not experience excessive amounts of stress?

Small Group Breakout Exercise

Increasing Motivation [LO13-1, 13-2, 13-3, 13-4, 13-5]

Form groups of three or four people, and appoint one member as the spokesperson who will communicate your findings to the class when called on by the instructor. Then discuss the following scenario:

You and your partners own a chain of 15 dry-cleaning stores in a medium-size town. All of you are concerned about a problem in customer service that has surfaced recently. When any one of you spends the day, or even part of the day, in a particular store, clerks seem to provide excellent customer service, spotters make sure all stains are removed from garments, and pressers do a good job of pressing difficult items such as silk blouses. Yet during those same visits customers complain to you about such things as stains not being removed and items being poorly pressed in some of their previous orders; indeed, several customers have brought garments in to be redone. Customers also sometimes comment on having waited too long for service on previous visits. You and your partners are meeting today to address this problem.

1. Discuss the extent to which you believe that you have a motivation problem in your stores.

2. Given what you have learned in this chapter, design a plan to increase the motivation of clerks to provide prompt service to customers even when they are not being watched by a partner.

3. Design a plan to increase the motivation of spotters to remove as many stains as possible even when they are not being watched by a partner.

4. Design a plan to increase the motivation of pressers to do a top-notch job on all clothes they press, no matter how difficult.

Exploring the World Wide Web [LO13-1, 13-2, 13-3, 13-4, 13-5]

If you had the chance to choose which well-known corporation you would work for, which would it be? Now go to the website of that company and find out as much as you can about how it motivates employees. Also, using Google and other search engines, try to find articles in the news about this company. Based on what you have learned, would this company still be your top choice? Why or why not?

Be the Manager [LO13-1, 13-2, 13-3, 13-4, 13-5]

You supervise a team of marketing analysts who work on different snack products in a large food products company. The marketing analysts have recently received undergraduate degrees in business or liberal arts and have been on the job between one and three years. Their responsibilities include analyzing the market for their respective products, including competitors; tracking current marketing initiatives; and planning future marketing campaigns. They also need to prepare quarterly sales and expense reports for their products and estimated budgets for the next three quarters; to prepare these reports, they need to obtain data from financial and accounting analysts assigned to their products.

When they first started on the job, you took each marketing analyst through the reporting cycle, explaining what needs to be done and how to accomplish it and emphasizing the need for timely reports. Although preparing the reports can be tedious, you think the task is pretty straightforward and easily accomplished if the analysts plan ahead and allocate sufficient time for it. When reporting time approaches, you remind the analysts through e-mail messages and emphasize the need for accurate and timely reports in team meetings.

You believe this element of the analysts' jobs couldn't be more straightforward. However, at the end of each quarter, the majority of the analysts submit their reports a day or two late, and, worse yet, your own supervisor (to whom the reports are eventually given) has indicated that information is often missing and sometimes the reports contain errors. Once you started getting flak from your supervisor about this problem, you decided you had better fix things quickly. You met with the marketing analysts, explained the problem, told them to submit the reports to you a day or two early so you could look them over, and more generally emphasized that they really needed to get their act together. Unfortunately, things have not improved much and you are spending more and more of your own time doing the reports. What are you going to do?

Co-Workers Change Places

Employers are mixing it up. Jobs, that is.

Some U.S. businesses are giving employees the chance to complete a stint in a different department or temporarily swap places with a colleague overseas.

Companies have long provided job rotations for higher level executives to give them a sense of how different departments operate, but now they are discovering that short- to medium-term moves for rank-and-file employees help workers sharpen their skills, stay motivated, and identify new roles they might aim for in the future. Moreover, they help address a challenge that many companies are facing: how to better foster collaboration across different specialties and regions.

"In organizations today there is more emphasis on adaptability, teamwork and learning agility. Companies have to be flexible about creating opportunities for employees to opt into projects," says Caroline Paxman, president of the Americas for SHL, a talent-measurement firm.

A 2011 survey by the Society for Human Resource Management found that 43% of employers offer cross-training of some kind to help workers develop proficiencies not related to their current jobs.

At Intel Corp., employees can find temporary assignments by searching an internal database with hundreds of listings. These assignments allow workers "to test-drive a job or make connections in different departments," says Amreen Madhani, who oversees the program which launched last March.

In 11 months, 1,300 positions lasting a few weeks to a year—in areas like HR, finance, strategy, marketing and product development—have been filled.

Not that such swaps are friction-free. "I felt like a deer in the headlights," says Elizabeth Wright Korytkowski,

a 38-year-old benefits specialist who took a four-month assignment with Intel's software-services group.

Still, the rotation provided Ms. Korytkowski an opportunity to interact directly with employees and gain familiarity with new software and HR tools. Since that assignment, she has received a promotion and completed a second special project outside her usual job duties.

These arrangements are increasingly valuable in retaining a restless work force that is accustomed to fast-paced change and innovation, says John Sullivan, a management professor at San Francisco State University.

At Virgin America, a handful of flight attendants recently traded places with colleagues at Virgin Blue (now Virgin Australia) as part of a one-year exchange.

All this movement can come at a price for companies since participants learn on a steep curve at first. Often there is lost productivity and resources.

Generally, skills-based rotations are more valuable than swaps that are purely geographic, says Alec Levenson, a research scientist at the University of Southern California's Center for Effective Organizations. While a program like Virgin's offers employees some short-term benefits, it may have less impact on a company's overall effectiveness, he says.

Still, global exchanges can be a valuable retention tool for multinational companies even when they don't involve a great deal of cross-training.

At PricewaterhouseCoopers LLP, managers nominate six junior staffers who have been at the firm for three to six years to participate in a three-month swap between the U.S. and Australia. The program pairs employees with similar job duties so they can ramp up quickly, says Eliza Scherrer, U.S. global mobility leader for PwC.

The program also builds morale and takes employees "out of their comfort zone," adds Ms. Scherrer.

Terri Lodwick, president of All American Window, a 22-person home-improvement company in Germantown, Wis., says that the long-running job-swap program at her company paid dividends by improving employee retention, customer service, and operations. It also helps ease the potential disruptions during maternity and sick leaves.

At the firm, every employee completes 32 to 40 hours of swaps annually, scheduled in four-hour increments. A receptionist might learn to be an order-taker, while installers and service technicians might cross-train.

Workers "get to see how they fit into the entire organization, not just their little cubicle," Ms. Lodwick says.

Questions for Discussion

1. In what ways might job rotations enhance the motivation and performance of rank-and-file employees?

2. In what ways might job rotations detract from the motivation and performance of rank-and-file employees?

3. In what ways might job rotations for rank-and-file employees contribute to organizational effectiveness?

4. In what ways might job rotations for rank-and-file employees detract from organizational effectiveness?

CHAPTER 14

Leadership

Learning Objectives

After studying this chapter, you should be able to:

LO14-1 Explain what leadership is, when leaders are effective and ineffective, and the sources of power that enable managers to be effective leaders.

LO14-2 Identify the traits that show the strongest relationship to leadership, the behaviors leaders engage in, and the limitations of the trait and behavior models of leadership.

LO14-3 Explain how contingency models of leadership enhance our understanding of effective leadership and management in organizations.

LO14-4 Describe what transformational leadership is, and explain how managers can engage in it.

LO14-5 Characterize the relationship between gender and leadership and explain how emotional intelligence may contribute to leadership effectiveness.

A MANAGER'S CHALLENGE

Doreen Lorenzo Leads Frog Design

How can a manager continuously transform an innovative company in a rapidly changing environment? As president of Frog Design and executive vice president and general manager of its parent company, Aricent Group, Doreen Lorenzo is very accustomed to change.[1] In fact, the mission of Frog Design is "to change the world"; this is also part of Lorenzo's vision for the company as is doing all that can be done to keep employees passionate about this vision and mission.[2] Frog Design assists organizations with the design, engineering, and marketing of innovative services and products in a wide variety of industries ranging from personal electronics, entertainment, media, fashion, and retail to energy, telecommunications, health care, finance, and education. When Lorenzo first joined Frog, the company had around 50 employees.[3] Today, Frog Design employs over 1,000 designers, software engineers, and strategists.[4] Headquartered in San Francisco, California, Frog has offices in the United States in Austin, Boston, New York, and Seattle and overseas offices in Amsterdam, Bangalore, Johannesburg, Kiev, Milan, Munich, Shanghai, and Vinnitsa. Disney, MTV, Intel, Microsoft, Hewlett-Packard, General Electric, and Qualcomm are just a few of Frog's many clients. Frog has innovated throughout

Leapfrogs: Doreen Lorenzo knows how to empower her highly skilled employees to continually achieve more. With respect, listening, and the willingness to make changes based on feedback, Lorenzo enables Frog Design to keep its innovations one jump ahead of everyone else.

its history from helping Apple bring the Apple IIc to fruition in the early 1980s to designing the e-commerce site that generated the most revenues in 2000 (Dell.com) to developing the Roku digital video player.[5] And new clients continue to partner with Frog for help in creating innovative products and services to meet a wide variety of needs.[6]

Leading highly creative professionals, ensuring that Frog Design continues to transform itself, and engaging in continuous innovation to help clients solve problems and better serve their own customers and clients would seem to be a daunting leadership task. Yet Lorenzo certainly is up to the challenge. One key aspect of Lorenzo's personal leadership style is the ways she empowers employees at Frog. Frog strives to hire very creative and passionate designers, engineers, and strategists and Lorenzo recognizes the importance of giving them the autonomy to pursue big ideas. Employees often work in teams and these teams enjoy the challenge of working on difficult and interesting projects that end up going to market; they appreciate having their ideas listened to and heard.[7]

In addition to being empowered to work on projects for clients, employees at Frog are also empowered to make changes internally. For example, a few years back Frog relied on a software package for its own performance appraisal reviews. Employees griped about the package, complaining that the software was cumbersome and it took too much time to enter information into the system.[8] When employees complain about something like this at Frog, managers really listen. In the case of the performance appraisal software, Lorenzo let employees know that if they thought the program that was being used was problematic, perhaps someone could develop a better one. A Frog designer took to the task and designed new performance appraisal software. As Lorenzo puts it, "Organizations of all sizes can encourage everyone, from C-level leaders to junior hires, to pursue their convictions."[9]

Lorenzo also emphasizes the importance of communicating with and listening to employees and being genuinely concerned about their well-being. Through company-wide phone chats, town hall meetings, and visits to the studios, Lorenzo lets employees know how the company is doing and finds out what is on employees' minds. She strives to meet with employees individually so they will feel free to speak their minds and not defer to someone who might be more outgoing in a group setting. She seeks to really learn about her employees, including changes they might like to see in the workplace and about their personal lives. For example, after chatting individually with employees, she realized that many of them were having children and/or had young families. Thus, Frog has incorporated more family-oriented activities into studio life such as some studios having "kid days" when employees can bring their children to the studio for arts and crafts.[10]

For Lorenzo, being in close contact with employees is very important as is listening to and responding to their concerns. She gives the example of an employee with a young family and considerable financial obligations and responsibilities; this employee might need reassurance that Frog is doing well as a company and that his or her job is secure.[11]

While Lorenzo empowers employees, she also recognizes that she needs to provide them with the tools they need to best serve their clients. A firm believer in being honest (to both employees and clients), Lorenzo and other managers at Frog emphasize that you cannot communicate too much information to a client.[12] Clients should know everything there is to know about their projects and should never be surprised; each client has a project website dedicated to their project that they can access anytime and anywhere. Employees receive training in the best ways to present to clients and pitch their ideas. Lorenzo also encourages designers to have a curious mind, be willing to take risks, and have opinions that they are able to communicate and justify.[13]

A very outgoing person by nature, Lorenzo realizes how building in opportunities for people to get together during the workday in a relaxed fashion is important. Each day each Frog studio has coffee time at 4 p.m. when everyone stops working for a while and socializes.[14] In some studios they play games like ping pong, foosball, or pool. Other studios use the time differently. As Lorenzo indicates, "These are intense people. This is a time for them to take a break, talk to people they might not work with, and to listen to things."[15] At 10 a.m. meetings on Mondays at each studio, employees get together to celebrate birthdays and anniversaries as well as talk about projects and what's going on at other studios. Studios are also encouraged to develop their own rituals to enhance well-being, foster good communication, and keep passion and creativity alive. For example, employees at some studios take regular field trips while another studio has sketching sessions on Tuesdays at 12 p.m. during which employees practice sketching together.[16]

All in all, Doreen Lorenzo's approach to leadership has helped Frog Design grow and continue to change and innovate while providing a stimulating and supportive environment for creative types to flourish.[17]

Overview

Doreen Lorenzo exemplifies the many facets of effective leadership. In Chapter 1 we explained that one of the four primary tasks of managers is leading. Thus it should come as no surprise that leadership is a key ingredient in effective management. When leaders are effective, their subordinates or followers are highly motivated, committed, and high-performing. When leaders are ineffective, chances are good that their subordinates do not perform up to their capabilities, are demotivated, and may be dissatisfied as well. Doreen Lorenzo is a leader at the very top of an organization, but leadership is an important ingredient for managerial success at all levels of organizations: top management, middle management, and first-line management. Moreover, leadership is a key ingredient of managerial success for organizations large and small.

In this chapter we describe what leadership is and examine the major leadership models that shed light on the factors that contribute to a manager's being an effective leader. We look at trait and behavior models, which focus on what leaders are like and what they do, and contingency models—Fiedler's contingency model, path–goal theory, and the leader substitutes model—each of which takes into account the complexity surrounding leadership and the role of the situation in leader effectiveness. We also describe how managers can use transformational leadership to dramatically affect their organizations. By the end of this chapter, you will appreciate the many factors and issues that managers face in their quest to be effective leaders.

The Nature of Leadership

leadership The process by which an individual exerts influence over other people and inspires, motivates, and directs their activities to help achieve group or organizational goals.

leader An individual who is able to exert influence over other people to help achieve group or organizational goals.

Leadership is the process by which a person exerts influence over other people and inspires, motivates, and directs their activities to help achieve group or organizational goals.[18] The person who exerts such influence is a **leader**. When leaders are effective, the influence they exert over others helps a group or organization achieve its performance goals. When leaders are ineffective, their influence does not contribute to, and often detracts from, goal attainment. As "A Manager's Challenge" makes clear, Doreen Lorenzo is taking multiple steps to inspire and motivate Frog's employees so they help Frog Design achieve its goals.

Beyond facilitating the attainment of performance goals, effective leadership increases an organization's ability to meet all the contemporary challenges discussed throughout this book, including the need to obtain a competitive advantage, the need to foster ethical behavior, and the need to manage a diverse workforce fairly and equitably. Leaders who exert influence over organizational members to help meet these goals increase their organizations' chances of success.

In considering the nature of leadership, we first look at leadership styles and how they affect managerial tasks and at the influence of culture on leadership styles. We then focus on the key to leadership, *power*, which can come from a variety of sources. Finally we consider the contemporary dynamic of empowerment and how it relates to effective leadership.

Personal Leadership Style and Managerial Tasks

A manager's *personal leadership style*—that is, the specific ways in which a manager chooses to influence other people—shapes how that manager approaches planning, organizing, and controlling (the other principal tasks of managing). Consider Doreen Lorenzo's personal leadership style in "A Manager's Challenge": She empowers employees, emphasizes being open and honest with employees and clients alike, fosters open two-way communication, and really cares about the well-being of employees and fostering their creativity and passion.

Managers at all levels and in all kinds of organizations have their own personal leadership styles that determine not only how they lead their subordinates but also how they perform the other management tasks. Michael Kraus, owner and manager of a dry cleaning store in the northeastern United States, for example, takes a hands-on approach to leadership. He has the sole authority for determining work schedules and job assignments for the 15 employees in his store (an organizing task), makes all important decisions by himself (a planning task), and closely monitors his employees' performance and rewards top performers with pay increases (a control task). Kraus's personal leadership style is effective in his organization. His employees generally are motivated, perform highly, and are satisfied; and his store is highly profitable.

Developing an effective personal leadership style often is a challenge for managers at all levels in an organization. This challenge is often exacerbated when times are tough, due, for example, to an economic downturn or a decline in customer demand. The recession in the late 2000s provided many managers with just such a challenge.

Although leading is one of the four principal tasks of managing, a distinction is often made between managers and leaders. When this distinction is made, managers are thought of as those organizational members who establish and implement procedures and processes to ensure smooth functioning and are accountable for goal accomplishment.[19] Leaders look to the future, chart the course for the organization, and attract, retain, motivate, inspire, and develop relationships with employees based on trust and mutual respect.[20] Leaders provide meaning and purpose, seek innovation rather than stability, and impassion employees to work together to achieve the leaders' vision.[21]

servant leader A leader who has a strong desire to serve and work for the benefit of others.

As part of their personal leadership style, some leaders strive to truly serve others. Robert Greenleaf, who was director of management research at AT&T and upon his retirement in 1964 embarked on a second career focused on writing, speaking, and consulting, came up with the term *servant leadership* to describe these leaders.[22] **Servant leaders**, above all else, have a strong desire to serve and work for the benefit of others.[23] Servant leaders share power with followers and strive to ensure that followers' most important needs are met, they are able to develop as individuals, and their well-being is enhanced, and that attention is paid to those who are least well-off in a society.[24] Greenleaf founded a nonprofit organization called the Greenleaf Center for Servant Leadership (formerly called the Center for Applied Ethics) to foster leadership focused on service to others, power sharing, and a sense of community between organizations and their multiple stakeholders.[25] Some entrepreneurs strive to incorporate servant leadership into their personal leadership styles, as profiled in the following "Ethics in Action" box.

Ethics in Action

Servant Leadership at Zingerman's

Ari Weinzweig and Paul Saginaw founded Zingerman's Delicatessen in Ann Arbor, Michigan, in 1982.[26] Food lovers at heart, Weinzweig and Saginaw delighted in finding both traditional and exotic foods from around the world, making delicious sandwiches to order, and having extensive selections of food items ranging from olives, oils, and vinegars to cheeses, smoked fish, and salami. As their business grew, and to maintain an intimate atmosphere with excellent customer service, Weinzweig and Saginaw expanded from their original deli into a community of related businesses called Zingerman's Community of Businesses. In addition to the original deli, Zingerman's Community of Businesses now includes a mail-order business, a bakery, a catering business, a creamery, a restaurant, a wholesale coffee business, and a training business and has combined annual revenues of over $30 million.[27] From the start, Weinzweig and Saginaw have been devoted to excellent customer service, great food, and a commitment to people and community.[28]

As part of their commitment to people and community, Weinzweig and Saginaw have incorporated servant leadership into their personal leadership styles. As their business has grown and prospered, they have realized that increasing success means greater responsibility to serve others. They strive to treat their employees as well as they treat their customers and give their employees opportunities for growth and development on the job. They have also realized that when their own needs or desires differ from what is best for their company, they should do what is best for the company.[29]

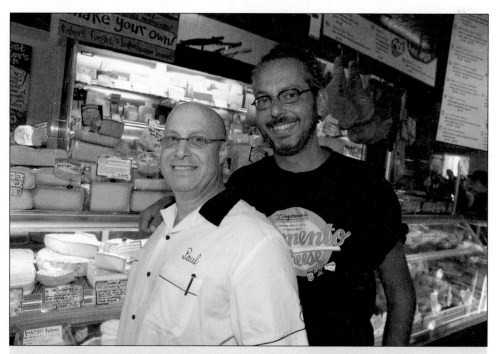

Paul Saginaw (left) and Ari Weinzweig have incorporated servant leadership into their personal leadership styles at Zingerman's.

To this day, the cofounders encourage their employees to let them know how they can help them and what they can do for them. And given Zingerman's culture of mutual respect and trust, employees do not hesitate to communicate how their leaders can serve them in many and varied ways. For example, when Weinzweig visits the Zingerman's Roadhouse restaurant and the staff is very busy, they may ask him to help out by serving customers or cleaning off tables. As he indicates, "People give me assignments all the time. Sometimes I'm the note-taker. Sometimes I'm the cleaner-upper. . . . Sometimes I'm on my hands and knees wiping up what people spilled."[30]

Weinzweig and Saginaw also have a strong sense of commitment to serving the local community; Zingerman's founded the nonprofit organization Food Gatherers to eliminate hunger and distribute food to the needy, and Food Gatherers is now an independent nonprofit responsible for the Washtenaw County Food Bank with over 5,000 volunteers and a 22-member staff.[31] On Zingerman's 20th anniversary, 13 nonprofit community organizations in Ann Arbor erected a plaque next to Zingerman's Delicatessen with a dedication that read, "Thank you for feeding, sheltering, educating, uplifting, and inspiring an entire community."[32] Clearly, for Weinzweig and Saginaw, leadership entails being of service to others.[33]

Leadership Styles across Cultures

Some evidence suggests that leadership styles vary not only among individuals but also among countries or cultures. Some research indicates that European managers tend to be more humanistic or people-oriented than both Japanese and American managers. The collectivistic culture in Japan places prime emphasis on the group rather than the individual, so the importance of individuals' own personalities, needs, and desires is minimized. Organizations in the United States tend to be very profit-oriented and thus tend to downplay the importance of individual employees' needs and desires. Many countries in Europe have a more individualistic perspective than Japan and a more humanistic perspective than the United States, and this may result in some European managers' being more people-oriented than their Japanese or American counterparts. European managers, for example, tend to be reluctant to lay off employees, and when a layoff is absolutely necessary, they take careful steps to make it as painless as possible.[34]

Another cross-cultural difference occurs in time horizons. While managers in any one country often differ in their time horizons, there are also national differences. For example, U.S. organizations tend to have a short-term profit orientation, and thus U.S. managers' personal leadership styles emphasize short-term performance. Japanese organizations tend to have a long-term growth orientation, so Japanese managers' personal leadership styles emphasize long-term performance. Justus Mische, a personnel manager at the European organization Hoechst, suggests that "Europe, at least the big international firms in Europe, have a philosophy between the Japanese, long term, and the United States, short term."[35] Research on these and other global aspects of leadership is in its infancy; as it continues, more cultural differences in managers' personal leadership styles may be discovered.

Power: The Key to Leadership

No matter what one's leadership style, a key component of effective leadership is found in the *power* the leader has to affect other people's behavior and get them to act in certain ways.[36] There are several types of power: legitimate, reward, coercive, expert, and referent power (see Figure 14.1).[37] Effective leaders take steps to ensure that they have sufficient levels of each type and that they use the power they have in beneficial ways.

legitimate power The authority that a manager has by virtue of his or her position in an organization's hierarchy.

LEGITIMATE POWER   Legitimate power is the authority a manager has by virtue of his or her position in an organization's hierarchy. Personal leadership style often influences how a manager exercises legitimate power. Take the case of Carol Loray, who is a first-line manager in a greeting card company and leads a group of 15 artists and designers. Loray has

Figure 14.1
Source of Managerial Power

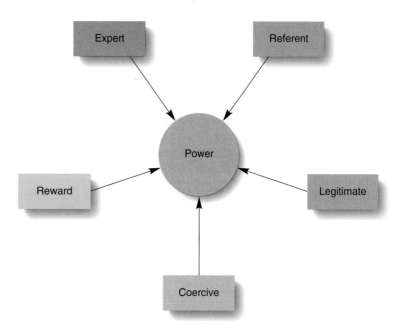

the legitimate power to hire new employees, assign projects to the artists and designers, monitor their work, and appraise their performance. She uses this power effectively. She always makes sure her project assignments match the interests of her subordinates as much as possible so they will enjoy their work. She monitors their work to make sure they are on track but does not engage in close supervision, which can hamper creativity. She makes sure her performance appraisals are developmental, providing concrete advice for areas where improvements could be made. Recently Loray negotiated with her manager to increase her legitimate power so she can now initiate and develop proposals for new card lines.

reward power The ability of a manager to give or withhold tangible and intangible rewards.

REWARD POWER   Reward power is the ability of a manager to give or withhold tangible rewards (pay raises, bonuses, choice job assignments) and intangible rewards (verbal praise, a pat on the back, respect). As you learned in Chapter 13, members of an organization are motivated to perform at a high level by a variety of rewards. Being able to give or withhold rewards based on performance is a major source of power that allows managers to have a highly motivated workforce. Managers of salespeople in retail organizations like Neiman Marcus, Nordstrom, and Macy's[38] and in car dealerships such as Mazda, Ford, and Volvo often use their reward power to motivate their subordinates. Subordinates in organizations such as these often receive commissions on whatever they sell and rewards for the quality of their customer service, which motivate them to do the best they can.

Effective managers use their reward power to show appreciation for subordinates' good work and efforts. Ineffective managers use rewards in a more controlling manner (wielding the "stick" instead of offering the "carrot") that signals to subordinates that the manager has the upper hand. Managers also can take steps to increase their reward power. Carol Loray had the legitimate power to appraise her subordinates' performance, but she lacked the reward power to distribute raises and end-of-year bonuses until she discussed with her own manager why this would be a valuable motivational tool for her to use. Loray now receives a pool of money each year for salary increases and bonuses and has the reward power to distribute them as she sees fit.

coercive power The ability of a manager to punish others.

COERCIVE POWER   Coercive power is the ability of a manager to punish others. Punishment can range from verbal reprimands to reductions in pay or working hours to actual dismissal. In the previous chapter we discussed how punishment can have negative side effects, such as resentment and retaliation, and should be used only when necessary (for example, to curtail a dangerous behavior). Managers who rely heavily on coercive power tend to be ineffective as leaders and sometimes even get fired themselves. William J. Fife is one example; he was fired from his position as CEO of Giddings and Lewis Inc., a manufacturer of factory equipment, because of his overreliance on coercive power. In meetings Fife often verbally criticized, attacked, and embarrassed top managers. Realizing how destructive Fife's use of punishment was for them and the company, these managers complained to the board of directors, who, after a careful consideration of the issues, asked Fife to resign.[39]

Excessive use of coercive power seldom produces high performance and is questionable ethically. Sometimes it amounts to a form of mental abuse, robbing workers of their dignity and causing excessive levels of stress. Overuse of coercive power can even result in dangerous working conditions. Better results and, importantly, an ethical workplace that respects employee dignity can be obtained by using reward power.

expert power Power that is based on the special knowledge, skills, and expertise that a leader possesses.

EXPERT POWER   **Expert power** is based on the special knowledge, skills, and expertise that a leader possesses. The nature of expert power varies, depending on the leader's level in the hierarchy. First-level and middle managers often have technical expertise relevant to the tasks their subordinates perform. Their expert power gives them considerable influence over subordinates. Carol Loray has expert power: She is an artist herself and has drawn and designed some of her company's top-selling greeting cards. Doreen Lorenzo in "A Manager's Challenge" has expert power from being an effective leader at Frog Design for over 14 years. As indicated in the following "Manager as a Person" box, managers with expert power nonetheless need to recognize that they are not always right and seek and encourage input from others.

Manager as a Person

Gregory Maffei and Expert Power

Gregory Maffei is the president and chief executive officer of Liberty Media Corporation, which has operations in the communications, e-commerce, media, technology, and entertainment industries.[40] Liberty owns or has interests in a variety of companies in these industries, such as SiriusXM, Live Nation, True Position, Inc., Expedia, QVC, HSN, Starz, Red Envelope, Evite, ProFlowers, backcountry.com, Barnes & Noble, bodybuilding.com, and the Atlanta National League Baseball Club, Inc.[41]

Judging from his background and experience, Maffei would certainly appear to possess considerable amounts of expert power. With a bachelor's degree from Dartmouth College and an MBA from the Harvard Business School, Maffei held a number of important leadership positions before joining Liberty.[42] For example, he worked with Bill Gates as the chief financial officer of Microsoft and was the chairman of Expedia, the chairman and CEO of 360networks, and the president and chief financial officer for Oracle.[43] He is active in terms of serving on boards of directors and also in the community. For example, he was the president of the Seattle Public Library and currently heads up the budget task force for the governor of Colorado.[44]

Interestingly enough, Maffei is the first to admit that he often doesn't have all the answers.[45] In fact, when he worked with Bill Gates, he realized that Gates often sought input from others and never thought that his ideas were necessarily the right ideas just because he had them.[46] Rather, Gates would ask other

Polling the experts gives Gregory Maffei the extra information and know-how to succeed. Rather than assuming his experience and knowledge guarantee being right, Maffei asks for help to make sure no stone is left unturned.

managers what they thought about his ideas. Maffei realizes the value of getting multiple inputs on ideas and having two-way conversations in which everyone feels free to speak their minds and ask probing questions, even if it is of the CEO. The first manager Maffei promoted at Liberty was a colleague who would consistently question and sometimes critique his ideas; having valuable insights, Maffei recognized how constructive the exchanges of ideas were with this manager. And he strives to have all employees feel comfortable asking him questions and having a two-way conversation with him.[47] While expert power has certainly helped Maffei as CEO of Liberty, so too has his recognition that he is not always right just because he is CEO.[48]

Some top managers derive expert power from their technical expertise. Craig Barrett, chairman of the board of directors of Intel from 2005 to 2009, has a PhD in materials science from Stanford University and is very knowledgeable about the ins and outs of Intel's business—producing semiconductors and microprocessors.[49] Similarly, Bill Gates, chairman of Microsoft, and CEO Steve Ballmer have expertise in software design; and Tachi Yamada, former president of the Bill and Melinda Gates Foundation's Global Health Program and former chairman of research and development at GlaxoSmithKline, has an MD.[50] Many top-level managers, however, lack technical expertise and derive their expert power from their abilities as decision makers, planners, and strategists. Jack Welch, the former well-known leader and CEO of General Electric, summed it up this way: "The basic thing that we at the top of the company know is that we don't know the business. What we have, I hope, is the ability to allocate resources, people, and dollars."[51]

Effective leaders take steps to ensure that they have an adequate amount of expert power to perform their leadership roles. They may obtain additional training or education in their fields, make sure they keep up with the latest developments and changes in technology, stay abreast of changes in their fields through involvement in professional associations, and read widely to be aware of momentous changes in the organization's task and general environments. Expert power tends to be best used in a guiding or coaching manner rather than in an arrogant, high-handed manner.

referent power Power that comes from subordinates' and coworkers' respect, admiration, and loyalty.

REFERENT POWER Referent power is more informal than the other kinds of power. Referent power is a function of the personal characteristics of a leader; it is the power that comes from subordinates' and coworkers' respect, admiration, and loyalty. Leaders who are likable and whom subordinates wish to use as a role model are especially likely to possess referent power, as is true of Doreen Lorenzo in "A Manager's Challenge."

In addition to being a valuable asset for top managers like Lorenzo, referent power can help first-line and middle managers be effective leaders as well. Sally Carruthers, for example, is the first-level manager of a group of secretaries in the finance department of a large state university. Carruthers's secretaries are known to be among the best in the university. Much of their willingness to go above and beyond the call of duty has been attributed to Carruthers's warm and caring nature, which makes each of them feel important and valued. Managers can take steps to increase their referent power, such as taking time to get to know their subordinates and showing interest in and concern for them.

Empowerment: An Ingredient in Modern Management

empowerment The expansion of employees' knowledge, tasks, and decision-making responsibilities.

More and more managers today are incorporating into their personal leadership styles an aspect that at first glance seems to be the opposite of being a leader. In Chapter 1 we described how **empowerment**—the process of giving employees at all levels the authority to make decisions, be responsible for their outcomes, improve quality, and cut costs—is becoming increasingly popular in organizations. When leaders empower their subordinates, the subordinates typically take over some responsibilities and authority that used to reside with the leader or

An empowered employee, like this auto assembly line worker, can halt the production process to correct an error rather than wasting time and money by waiting for a supervisor.

manager, such as the right to reject parts that do not meet quality standards, the right to check one's own work, and the right to schedule work activities. Empowered subordinates are given the power to make some decisions that their leaders or supervisors used to make.

Empowerment might seem to be the opposite of effective leadership because managers are allowing subordinates to take a more active role in leading themselves. In actuality, however, empowerment can contribute to effective leadership for several reasons:

- Empowerment increases a manager's ability to get things done because the manager has the support and help of subordinates who may have special knowledge of work tasks.

- Empowerment often increases workers' involvement, motivation, and commitment; and this helps ensure that they are working toward organizational goals.

- Empowerment gives managers more time to concentrate on their pressing concerns because they spend less time on day-to-day supervision.

Effective managers like Doreen Lorenzo realize the benefits of empowerment. The personal leadership style of managers who empower subordinates often entails developing subordinates' ability to make good decisions as well as being their guide, coach, and source of inspiration. Empowerment is a popular trend in the United States and is a part of servant leadership. Empowerment is also taking off around the world.[52] For instance, companies in South Korea (such as Samsung, Hyundai, and Daewoo), in which decision making typically was centralized with the founding families, are now empowering managers at lower levels to make decisions.[53]

Trait and Behavior Models of Leadership

Leading is such an important process in all organizations—nonprofit organizations, government agencies, and schools, as well as for-profit corporations—that it has been researched for decades. Early approaches to leadership, called the *trait model* and the *behavior model,* sought to determine what effective leaders are like as people and what they do that makes them so effective.

LO14-2 Identify the traits that show the strongest relationship to leadership, the behaviors leaders engage in, and the limitations of the trait and behavior models of leadership.

The Trait Model

The trait model of leadership focused on identifying the personal characteristics that cause effective leadership. Researchers thought effective leaders must have certain personal qualities that set them apart from ineffective leaders and from people who never become leaders. Decades of research (beginning in the 1930s) and hundreds of studies indicate that certain personal characteristics do appear to be associated with effective leadership. (See Table 14.1 for a list of these.)[54] Notice that although this model is called the "trait" model, some of the personal characteristics that it identifies are not personality traits per se but, rather, are concerned with a leader's skills, abilities, knowledge, and expertise. As "A Manager's Challenge" shows, Doreen Lorenzo certainly appears to possess many of these characteristics (such as intelligence, knowledge and expertise, self-confidence, high energy, and integrity and honesty). Leaders who do not possess these traits may be ineffective.

Traits alone are not the key to understanding leader effectiveness, however. Some effective leaders do not possess all these traits, and some leaders who possess them are not effective in their leadership roles. This lack of a consistent relationship between leader traits and leader effectiveness led researchers to shift their attention away from traits and to search for new explanations for effective leadership. Rather than focusing on what leaders are like (the traits they possess), researchers began looking at what effective leaders actually do—in other words, at the behaviors that allow effective leaders to influence their subordinates to achieve group and organizational goals.

Table 14.1

Traits and Personal Characteristics Related to Effective Leadership

Trait	Description
Intelligence	Helps managers understand complex issues and solve problems.
Knowledge and expertise	Help managers make good decisions and discover ways to increase efficiency and effectiveness.
Dominance	Helps managers influence their subordinates to achieve organizational goals.
Self-confidence	Contributes to managers' effectively influencing subordinates and persisting when faced with obstacles or difficulties.
High energy	Helps managers deal with the many demands they face.
Tolerance for stress	Helps managers deal with uncertainty and make difficult decisions.
Integrity and honesty	Help managers behave ethically and earn their subordinates' trust and confidence.
Maturity	Helps managers avoid acting selfishly, control their feelings, and admit when they have made a mistake.

The Behavior Model

After extensive study in the 1940s and 1950s, researchers at The Ohio State University identified two basic kinds of leader behaviors that many leaders in the United States, Germany, and other countries engaged in to influence their subordinates: *consideration* and *initiating structure*.[55]

consideration Behavior indicating that a manager trusts, respects, and cares about subordinates.

CONSIDERATION   Leaders engage in **consideration** when they show their subordinates that they trust, respect, and care about them. Managers who truly look out for the well-being of their subordinates, and do what they can to help subordinates feel good and enjoy their work, perform consideration behaviors. In "A Manager's Challenge," Doreen Lorenzo engages in consideration when she communicates with and listens to employees and ensures that their concerns are being addressed and that they have opportunities to socialize and relax.

At Costco Wholesale Corporation, cofounder and director Jim Senegal believes that consideration not only is an ethical imperative but also makes good business sense,[56] as indicated in the following "Ethics in Action" box.

Ethics
in Action

Consideration at Costco

Managers at Costco, including cofounder and director Jim Senegal and CEO Craig Jelinek, believe consideration is so important that one of the principles in Costco's code of ethics is "Take Care of Our Employees."[57] Costco Wholesale Corporation is the third largest retailer and the top warehouse retailer in the United States.[58] Wages at Costco are an average of $17 per hour—over 40% higher than the average hourly wage at Walmart, Costco's major competitor.[59] Costco pays the majority of health insurance costs for its employees (employees pay around 8% of health insurance costs compared to an industry average of around 25%), and part-time employees receive

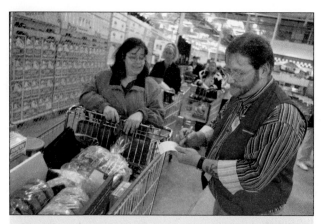

Loyal Costco customers like these know that their bargains don't come at the expense of employees' paychecks and benefits.

health insurance after they have been with the company six months. Overall, about 85% of Costco employees are covered by health insurance, compared with fewer than 45% of employees at Target and Walmart.[60]

Jim Senegal and Craig Jelinek believe that caring about the well-being of employees is a win–win proposition because Costco's employees are satisfied, committed, loyal, and motivated. Additionally, turnover and employee theft rates at Costco are much lower than industry averages.[61] In the retail industry, turnover tends to be high and costly because for every employee who quits, a new hire needs to be recruited, tested, interviewed, and trained. Even though pay and benefits are higher at Costco than at rival Walmart, Costco actually has lower labor costs as a percentage of sales and higher sales per square foot of store space than Walmart.[62]

Additionally, treating employees well helps build customer loyalty at Costco. Surely customers enjoy the bargains and low prices that come from shopping in a warehouse store, the relatively high quality of the goods Costco stocks, and Costco's policy of not marking up prices by more than 14% or 15% (relatively low markups for retail) even if the goods would sell with higher markups. However, customers are also loyal to Costco because they know the company treats its employees well and their bargains are not coming at the expense of employees' paychecks and benefits.[63]

Costco started out as a single warehouse store in Seattle, Washington, in 1983. Now the company has 602 stores (including stores in South Korea, Taiwan, Japan, Australia, Mexico, Canada, and Britain) and tens of millions of members who pay an annual fee to shop at Costco stores.[64] Costco's growth and financial performance are enviable.[65] For example, annual revenues for the 2011 fiscal year were $88.9 billion.[66] Clearly consideration has paid off for Costco and for its employees.[67]

True to caring for the well-being of employees, Costco did not lay off any employees during the recession in the late 2000s.[68] However, some female employees have filed a class action lawsuit alleging gender discrimination at Costco.[69] Costco denies that discrimination has taken place, and in an interview Jim Senegal indicated that Costco has had relatively few lawsuits for an organization of its size.[70] Determining whether discrimination took place at Costco will be a matter for the courts to decide.

initiating structure

Behavior that managers engage in to ensure that work gets done, subordinates perform their jobs acceptably, and the organization is efficient and effective.

INITIATING STRUCTURE   Leaders engage in **initiating structure** when they take steps to make sure that work gets done, subordinates perform their jobs acceptably, and the organization is efficient and effective. Assigning tasks to individuals or work groups, letting subordinates know what is expected of them, deciding how work should be done, making schedules, encouraging adherence to rules and regulations, and motivating subordinates to do a good job are all examples of initiating structure.[71]

Michael Teckel, the manager of an upscale store selling imported men's and women's shoes in a midwestern city, engages in initiating structure when he establishes weekly work, lunch, and break schedules to ensure that the store has enough salespeople on the floor. Teckel also initiates structure when he discusses the latest shoe designs with his subordinates so they are knowledgeable with customers, when he encourages adherence to the store's refund and exchange policies, and when he encourages his staff to provide high-quality customer service and to avoid a hard-sell approach.

Initiating structure and consideration are independent leader behaviors. Leaders can be high on both, low on both, or high on one and low on the other. Many effective leaders, like Doreen Lorenzo of Frog Design, engage in both of these behaviors.

Leadership researchers have identified leader behaviors similar to consideration and initiating structure. Researchers at the University of Michigan, for example, identified two categories of leadership behaviors, *employee-centered behaviors* and *job-oriented behaviors,* that correspond roughly to consideration and initiating structure, respectively.[72] Models of leadership popular with consultants also tend to zero in on these two kinds of behaviors. For example, Robert Blake and Jane Mouton's Managerial Grid focuses on *concern for people* (similar to consideration) and *concern for production* (similar to initiating structure). Blake and Mouton advise that effective leadership often requires both a high level of concern for people and a high level of concern for production.[73] As another example, Paul Hersey and Kenneth Blanchard's model focuses on *supportive behaviors* (similar to consideration) and *task-oriented behaviors* (similar to initiating structure). According to Hersey and Blanchard, leaders need to consider the nature of their subordinates when trying to determine the extent to which they should perform these two behaviors.[74]

You might expect that effective leaders and managers would perform both kinds of behaviors, but research has found that this is not necessarily the case. The relationship between performance of consideration and initiating-structure behaviors and leader effectiveness is not clear-cut. Some leaders are effective even when they do not perform consideration or initiating-structure behaviors, and some leaders are ineffective even when they perform both kinds of behaviors. Like the trait model of leadership, the behavior model alone cannot explain leader effectiveness. Realizing this, researchers began building more complicated models of leadership, focused not only on the leader and what he or she does but also on the situation or context in which leadership occurs.

Contingency Models of Leadership

LO14-3 Explain how contingency models of leadership enhance our understanding of effective leadership and management in organizations.

Simply possessing certain traits or performing certain behaviors does not ensure that a manager will be an effective leader in all situations calling for leadership. Some managers who seem to possess the right traits and perform the right behaviors turn out to be ineffective leaders. Managers lead in a wide variety of situations and organizations and have various kinds of subordinates performing diverse tasks in a multiplicity of environmental contexts. Given the wide variety of situations in which leadership occurs, what makes a manager an effective leader in one situation (such as certain traits or behaviors) is not necessarily what that manager needs to be equally effective in a different situation. An effective army general might not be an effective university president; an effective restaurant manager might not be an effective clothing store manager; an effective football team coach might not be an effective fitness center manager; and an effective first-line manager in a manufacturing company might not be an effective middle manager. The traits or behaviors that may contribute to a manager's being an effective leader in one situation might actually result in the same manager being an ineffective leader in another situation.

Contingency models of leadership take into account the situation or context within which leadership occurs. According to contingency models, whether or not a manager is an effective leader is the result of the interplay between what the manager is like, what he or she does, and the situation in which leadership takes place. Contingency models propose that whether a leader who possesses certain traits or performs certain behaviors is effective depends on, or is contingent on, the situation or context. In this section we discuss three prominent contingency models developed to shed light on what makes managers effective leaders: Fred Fiedler's contingency model, Robert House's path–goal theory, and the leader substitutes model. As you will see, these leadership models are complementary; each focuses on a somewhat different aspect of effective leadership in organizations.

Fiedler's Contingency Model

Fred E. Fiedler was among the first leadership researchers to acknowledge that effective leadership is contingent on, or depends on, the characteristics of the leader *and* of the situation. Fiedler's contingency model helps explain why a manager may be an effective leader in one situation and ineffective in another; it also suggests which kinds of managers are likely to be most effective in which situations.[75]

LEADER STYLE   As with the trait approach, Fiedler hypothesized that personal characteristics can influence leader effectiveness. He used the term *leader style* to refer to a manager's characteristic approach to leadership and identified two basic leader styles: *relationship-oriented* and *task-oriented.* All managers can be described as having one style or the other.

Relationship-oriented leaders are primarily concerned with developing good relationships with their subordinates and being liked by them. Relationship-oriented managers focus on having high-quality interpersonal relationships with subordinates. This does not mean, however, that the job does not get done when such leaders are at the helm. But it does mean that the quality of interpersonal relationships with subordinates is a prime concern for relationship-oriented leaders.

Task-oriented leaders are primarily concerned with ensuring that subordinates perform at a high level and focus on task accomplishment. While task-oriented leaders also may be concerned about having good interpersonal relationships with their subordinates, task accomplishment is their prime concern.

In his research, Fiedler measured leader style by asking leaders to rate the coworker with whom they have had the most difficulty working (called the least preferred coworker or LPC) on a number of dimensions, such as whether the person is boring or interesting, gloomy or cheerful, enthusiastic or unenthusiastic, cooperative or uncooperative. Relationship-oriented leaders tend to describe the LPC in relatively positive terms; their concern for good relationships leads them to think well of others. Task-oriented leaders tend to describe the LPC in negative terms; their concern for task accomplishment causes them to think badly about others who make getting the job done difficult. Thus relationship-oriented and task-oriented leaders are sometimes referred to as high-LPC and low-LPC leaders, respectively.

SITUATIONAL CHARACTERISTICS   According to Fiedler, leadership style is an enduring characteristic; managers cannot change their style, nor can they adopt different styles in different kinds of situations. With this in mind, Fiedler identified three situational characteristics that are important determinants of how favorable a situation is for leading: leader–member relations, task structure, and position power. When a situation is favorable for leading, it is relatively easy for a manager to influence subordinates so they perform at a high level and contribute to organizational efficiency and effectiveness. In a situation unfavorable for leading, it is much more difficult for a manager to exert influence.

LEADER–MEMBER RELATIONS   The first situational characteristic Fiedler described, leader–member relations, is the extent to which followers like, trust, and are loyal to their leader. Situations are more favorable for leading when leader–member relations are good.

TASK STRUCTURE   The second situational characteristic Fiedler described, task structure, is the extent to which the work to be performed is clear-cut so that a leader's subordinates know what needs to be accomplished and how to go about doing it. When task structure is high, the situation is favorable for leading. When task structure is low, goals may be vague, subordinates may be unsure of what they should be doing or how they should do it, and the situation is unfavorable for leading.

Task structure was low for Geraldine Laybourne when she was a top manager at Nickelodeon, the children's television network. It was never precisely clear what would appeal to her young viewers, whose tastes can change dramatically, or how to motivate her subordinates to come up with creative and novel ideas.[76] In contrast, Herman Mashaba, founder of Black Like Me, a hair care products company based in South Africa, seemed to have relatively high task structure when he started his company. His company's goals were to produce and sell inexpensive hair care products to native Africans, and managers accomplished these goals by using simple yet appealing packaging and distributing the products through neighborhood beauty salons.[77]

POSITION POWER   The third situational characteristic Fiedler described, position power, is the amount of legitimate, reward, and coercive power a leader has by virtue of his or her position in an organization. Leadership situations are more favorable for leading when position power is strong.

COMBINING LEADER STYLE AND THE SITUATION   By considering all possible combinations of good and poor leader–member relations, high and low task structure, and strong and weak position power, Fiedler identified eight leadership situations, which vary in their favorability for leading (see Figure 14.2). After extensive research, he determined that

---

relationship-oriented leaders Leaders whose primary concern is to develop good relationships with their subordinates and to be liked by them.

task-oriented leaders Leaders whose primary concern is to ensure that subordinates perform at a high level.

leader–member relations The extent to which followers like, trust, and are loyal to their leader; a determinant of how favorable a situation is for leading.

task structure The extent to which the work to be performed is clear-cut so that a leader's subordinates know what needs to be accomplished and how to go about doing it; a determinant of how favorable a situation is for leading.

position power The amount of legitimate, reward, and coercive power that a leader has by virtue of his or her position in an organization; a determinant of how favorable a situation is for leading.

Figure 14.2

Fiedler's Contingency Theory of Leadership

Relationship-oriented leaders are most effective in moderately favorable situations for leading (IV, V, VI, VII).
Task-oriented leaders are most effective in very favorable situations (I, II, III) or very unfavorable situations (VIII) for leading.

relationship-oriented leaders are most effective in moderately favorable situations (IV, V, VI, and VII in Figure 14.2) and task-oriented leaders are most effective in situations that are either very favorable (I, II, and III) or very unfavorable (VIII).

PUTTING THE CONTINGENCY MODEL INTO PRACTICE Recall that, according to Fiedler, leader style is an enduring characteristic that managers cannot change. This suggests that for managers to be effective, either managers need to be placed in leadership situations that fit their style or situations need to be changed to suit the managers. Situations can be changed, for example, by giving a manager more position power or taking steps to increase task structure, such as by clarifying goals.

Take the case of Mark Compton, a relationship-oriented leader employed by a small construction company, who was in a very unfavorable situation and was having a rough time leading his construction crew. His subordinates did not trust him to look out for their well-being (poor leader–member relations); the construction jobs he supervised tended to be novel and complex (low task structure); and he had no control over the rewards and disciplinary actions his subordinates received (weak position power). Recognizing the need to improve matters, Compton's supervisor gave him the power to reward crew members with bonuses and overtime work as he saw fit and to discipline crew members for poor-quality work and unsafe on-the-job behavior. As his leadership situation improved to moderately favorable, so too did Compton's effectiveness as a leader and the performance of his crew.

Research studies tend to support some aspects of Fiedler's model but also suggest that, like most theories, it needs some modifications.[78] Some researchers have questioned what the LPC scale really measures. Others find fault with the model's premise that leaders cannot alter their styles. That is, it is likely that at least some leaders can diagnose the situation they are in and, when their style is inappropriate for the situation, modify their style so that it is more in line with what the leadership situation calls for.

House's Path–Goal Theory

path–goal theory A contingency model of leadership proposing that leaders can motivate subordinates by identifying their desired outcomes, rewarding them for high performance and the attainment of work goals with these desired outcomes, and clarifying for them the paths leading to the attainment of work goals.

In what he called **path–goal theory**, leadership researcher Robert House focused on what leaders can do to motivate their subordinates to achieve group and organizational goals.[79] The premise of path–goal theory is that effective leaders motivate subordinates to achieve goals by (1) clearly identifying the outcomes that subordinates are trying to obtain from the workplace, (2) rewarding subordinates with these outcomes for high performance and the attainment of work goals, and (3) clarifying for subordinates the *paths* leading to the attainment of work *goals*. Path–goal theory is a contingency model because it proposes that the steps managers should take to motivate subordinates depend on both the nature of the subordinates and the type of work they do.

Based on the expectancy theory of motivation (see Chapter 13), path–goal theory gives managers three guidelines to being effective leaders:

1. *Find out what outcomes your subordinates are trying to obtain from their jobs and the organization.* These outcomes can range from satisfactory pay and job security to reasonable working hours and interesting and challenging job assignments. After identifying these outcomes, the manager should have the *reward power* needed to distribute or withhold the outcomes. Mark Crane, for example, is the vice principal of a large elementary school. Crane determined that the teachers he leads are trying to obtain the following outcomes from their jobs: pay raises, autonomy in the classroom, and the choice of which grades they teach. Crane had reward power for the latter two outcomes, but the school's principal determined how the pool of money for raises was to be distributed each year. Because Crane was the first-line manager who led the teachers and was most familiar with their performance, he asked the principal (his boss) to give him some say in determining pay raises. Realizing that this made a lot of sense, his principal gave Crane full power to distribute raises and requested only that Crane review his decisions with him before informing the teachers about them.

2. *Reward subordinates for high performance and goal attainment with the outcomes they desire.* The teachers and administrators at Crane's school considered several dimensions of teacher performance to be critical to achieving their goal of providing high-quality education: excellent in-class instruction, special programs to enhance student interest and learning (such as science and computer projects), and availability for meetings with parents to discuss their children's progress and special needs. Crane distributed pay raises to the teachers based on the extent to which they performed highly on each of these dimensions. The top-performing teachers were given first choice of grade assignments and also had practically complete autonomy in their classrooms.

3. *Clarify the paths to goal attainment for subordinates, remove any obstacles to high performance, and express confidence in subordinates' capabilities.* This does not mean that a manager needs to tell subordinates what to do. Rather, it means that a manager needs to make sure subordinates are clear about what they should be trying to accomplish and have the capabilities, resources, and confidence levels needed to be successful. Crane made sure all the teachers understood the importance of the three targeted goals and asked them whether, to reach them, they needed any special resources or supplies for their classes. Crane also gave additional coaching and guidance to teachers who seemed to be struggling. For example, Patrick Conolly, in his first year of teaching after graduate school, was unsure how to use special projects in a third grade class and how to react to parents who were critical. Conolly's teaching was excellent, but he felt insecure about how he was doing on this dimension. To help build Conolly's confidence, Crane told Conolly that he thought he could be one of the school's top teachers (which was true). He gave Conolly some ideas about special projects that worked particularly well with the third grade, such as a writing project. Crane also role-played teacher–parent interactions with Conolly. Conolly played the role of a particularly dissatisfied or troubled parent, while Crane played the role of a teacher trying to solve the underlying problem while making the parent feel that his or her child's needs were being met. Crane's efforts to clarify the paths to goal attainment for Conolly paid off: Within two years the local PTS voted Conolly teacher of the year.

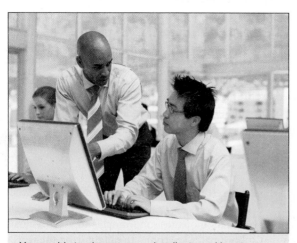

You could stand over your subordinate and berate him or you could empower him to find the solution by working to see where the issue developed. Supportive managers make a world of difference in retaining and motivating employees.

Path–goal theory identifies four kinds of leadership behaviors that motivate subordinates:

- *Directive behaviors* are similar to initiating structure and include setting goals, assigning tasks, showing subordinates how to complete tasks, and taking concrete steps to improve performance.

- *Supportive behaviors* are similar to consideration and include expressing concern for subordinates and looking out for their best interests.

- *Participative behaviors* give subordinates a say in matters and decisions that affect them.

- *Achievement-oriented behaviors* motivate subordinates to perform at the highest level possible by, for example, setting challenging goals, expecting that they be met, and believing in subordinates' capabilities.

Which of these behaviors should managers use to lead effectively? The answer to this question depends, or is contingent on, the nature of the subordinates and the kind of work they do.

Directive behaviors may be beneficial when subordinates are having difficulty completing assigned tasks, but they might be detrimental when subordinates are independent thinkers who work best when left alone. *Supportive* behaviors are often advisable when subordinates are experiencing high levels of stress. *Participative* behaviors can be particularly effective when subordinates' support of a decision is required. *Achievement-oriented* behaviors may increase motivation levels of highly capable subordinates who are bored from having too few challenges, but they might backfire if used with subordinates who are already pushed to their limit.

The Leader Substitutes Model

leadership substitute A characteristic of a subordinate or of a situation or context that acts in place of the influence of a leader and makes leadership unnecessary.

The leader substitutes model suggests that leadership is sometimes unnecessary because substitutes for leadership are present. A **leadership substitute** is something that acts in place of the influence of a leader and makes leadership unnecessary. This model suggests that under certain conditions managers do not have to play a leadership role—members of an organization sometimes can perform at a high level without a manager exerting influence over them.[80] The leader substitutes model is a contingency model because it suggests that in some situations leadership is unnecessary.

Take the case of David Cotsonas, who teaches English at a foreign language school in Cyprus, an island in the Mediterranean Sea. Cotsonas is fluent in Greek, English, and French; is an excellent teacher; and is highly motivated. Many of his students are businesspeople who have some rudimentary English skills and wish to increase their fluency to be able to conduct more of their business in English. He enjoys not only teaching them English but also learning about the work they do, and he often keeps in touch with his students after they finish his classes. Cotsonas meets with the director of the school twice a year to discuss semiannual class schedules and enrollments.

With practically no influence from a leader, Cotsonas is a highly motivated top performer at the school. In his situation, leadership is unnecessary because substitutes for leadership are present. Cotsonas's teaching expertise, his motivation, and his enjoyment of his work are substitutes for the influence of a leader—in this case the school's director. If the school's director were to try to influence how Cotsonas performs his job, Cotsonas would probably resent this infringement on his autonomy, and it is unlikely that his performance would improve because he is already one of the school's best teachers.

As in Cotsonas's case, *characteristics of subordinates*—such as their skills, abilities, experience, knowledge, and motivation—can be substitutes for leadership.[81] *Characteristics of the situation or context*—such as the extent to which the work is interesting and enjoyable—also can be substitutes. When work is interesting and enjoyable, as it is for Cotsonas, jobholders do not need to be coaxed into performing because performing is rewarding in its own right. Similarly, when managers *empower* their subordinates or use *self-managed work teams* (discussed in detail in Chapter 15), the need for leadership influence from a manager is decreased because team members manage themselves.

Substitutes for leadership can increase organizational efficiency and effectiveness because they free up some of managers' valuable time and allow managers to focus their efforts on discovering new ways to improve organizational effectiveness. The director of the language school, for example, was able to spend much of his time making arrangements to open a second school in Rhodes, an island in the Aegean Sea, because of the presence of leadership substitutes, not only for Cotsonas but for most other teachers at the school as well.

Table 14.2

Contingency Models of Leadership

Model	Focus	Key Contingencies
Fiedler's contingency model	Describes two leader styles, relationship-oriented and task-oriented, and the kinds of situations in which each kind of leader will be most effective.	Whether a relationship-oriented or a task-oriented leader is effective is contingent on the situation.
House's path–goal theory	Describes how effective leaders motivate their followers.	The behaviors that managers should engage in to be effective leaders are contingent on the nature of the subordinates and the work they do.
Leader substitutes model	Describes when leadership is unnecessary.	Whether leadership is necessary for subordinates to perform highly is contingent on characteristics of the subordinates and the situation.

Bringing It All Together

Effective leadership in organizations occurs when managers take steps to lead in a way that is appropriate for the situation or context in which leadership occurs and for the subordinates who are being led. The three contingency models of leadership just discussed help managers focus on the necessary ingredients for effective leadership. They are complementary in that each one looks at the leadership question from a different angle. Fiedler's contingency model explores how a manager's leadership style needs to be matched to that person's leadership situation for maximum effectiveness. House's path–goal theory focuses on how managers should motivate subordinates and describes the specific kinds of behaviors managers can engage in to have a highly motivated workforce. The leadership substitutes model alerts managers to the fact that sometimes they do not need to exert influence over subordinates and thus can free up their time for other important activities. Table 14.2 recaps these three contingency models of leadership.

LO14-4 Describe what transformational leadership is, and explain how managers can engage in it.

Transformational Leadership

Time and time again, throughout business history, certain leaders seem to literally transform their organizations, making sweeping changes to revitalize and renew operations. For example, when Sue Nokes became senior vice president of sales and customer service at T-Mobile USA in 2002, the quality of T-Mobile's customer service was lower than that of its major competitors; on average, 12% of employees were absent on any day; and annual employee turnover was over 100%.[82] T-Mobile USA is a subsidiary of Deutsche Telekom; has 36,000 employees; and provides wireless voice, messaging, and data services.[83] When Nokes arrived at T-Mobile, valuable employees were quitting their jobs and customers weren't receiving high-quality service; neither employees nor customers were satisfied with their experience with the company.[84] However, by the late 2000s T-Mobile was regularly receiving highest rankings for customer care and satisfaction in the wireless category by J. D. Power and Associates, absence and turnover rates substantially declined, and around 80% of employees indicated that they were satisfied with their jobs.[85] In fact, when Nokes visited call centers, it was not uncommon for employees to greet her with cheers and accolades.[86]

Nokes transformed T-Mobile into a company in which satisfied employees provide excellent service to customers.[87]

Sue Nokes exhibited transformational leadership at T-Mobile.

transformational leadership Leadership that makes subordinates aware of the importance of their jobs and performance to the organization and aware of their own needs for personal growth and that motivates subordinates to work for the good of the organization.

When managers have such dramatic effects on their subordinates and on an organization as a whole, they are engaging in transformational leadership. **Transformational leadership** occurs when managers change (or transform) their subordinates in three important ways:[88]

1. *Transformational managers make subordinates aware of how important their jobs are for the organization and how necessary it is for them to perform those jobs as best they can so the organization can attain its goals.* At T-Mobile, Nokes visited call centers, conducted focus groups, and had town hall meetings to find out what employees and customers were unhappy with and what steps she could take to improve matters.[89] Her philosophy was that when employees are satisfied with their jobs and view their work as important, they are much more likely to provide high-quality customer service. She made employees aware of how important their jobs were by the many steps she took to improve their working conditions, ranging from providing them with their own workspaces to substantially raising their salaries.[90] She emphasized the importance of providing excellent customer service by periodically asking employees what was working well and what was not working well, asking them what steps could be taken to improve problem areas, and taking actions to ensure that employees were able to provide excellent customer service. Nokes also instituted a performance measurement system to track performance in key areas such as quality of service and speed of problem resolution.[91] She sincerely told employees, "You are No. 1, and the customer is why."[92]

2. *Transformational managers make their subordinates aware of the subordinates' own needs for personal growth, development, and accomplishment.* Nokes made T-Mobile's employees aware of their own needs in this regard by transforming training and development at T-Mobile and increasing opportunities for promotions to more responsible positions. Employees now spend over 130 hours per year in training and development programs and team meetings. Nokes also instituted a promote-from-within policy, and around 80% of promotions are given to current employees.[93]

3. *Transformational managers motivate their subordinates to work for the good of the organization as a whole, not just for their own personal gain or benefit.* Nokes emphasized that employees should focus on what matters to customers, coworkers, and T-Mobile as a whole. She let employees know that when they were unnecessarily absent from their jobs, they were not doing right by their coworkers. And she emphasized the need to try to resolve customer problems in a single phone call so customers can get on with their busy lives.[94]

When managers transform their subordinates in these three ways, subordinates trust the managers, are highly motivated, and help the organization achieve its goals. How do managers such as Nokes transform subordinates and produce dramatic effects in their organizations? There are at least three ways in which transformational leaders can influence their followers: by being a charismatic leader, by intellectually stimulating subordinates, and by engaging in developmental consideration (see Table 14.3).

Table 14.3
Transformational Leadership

Transformational managers

- Are charismatic.
- Intellectually stimulate subordinates.
- Engage in developmental consideration.

Subordinates of transformational managers

- Have increased awareness of the importance of their jobs and high performance.
- Are aware of their own needs for growth, development, and accomplishment.
- Work for the good of the organization and not just their own personal benefit.

Being a Charismatic Leader

charismatic leader An enthusiastic, self-confident leader who is able to clearly communicate his or her vision of how good things could be.

Transformational managers such as Nokes are **charismatic leaders**. They have a vision of how good things could be in their work groups and organizations that is in contrast with the status quo. Their vision usually entails dramatic improvements in group and organizational performance as a result of changes in the organization's structure, culture, strategy, decision making, and other critical processes and factors. This vision paves the way for gaining a competitive advantage. From "A Manager's Challenge," it is clear that part of Doreen Lorenzo's vision for Frog Design is to help Frog change the world.

Charismatic leaders are excited and enthusiastic about their vision and clearly communicate it to their subordinates, as does Doreen Lorenzo. The excitement, enthusiasm, and self-confidence of a charismatic leader contribute to the leader's being able to inspire followers to enthusiastically support his or her vision.[95] People often think of charismatic leaders or managers as being "larger than life." The essence of charisma, however, is having a vision and enthusiastically communicating it to others. Thus managers who appear to be quiet and earnest can also be charismatic.

Stimulating Subordinates Intellectually

intellectual stimulation Behavior a leader engages in to make followers aware of problems and view these problems in new ways, consistent with the leader's vision.

Transformational managers openly share information with their subordinates so they are aware of problems and the need for change. The manager causes subordinates to view problems in their groups and throughout the organization from a different perspective, consistent with the manager's vision. Whereas in the past subordinates might not have been aware of some problems, may have viewed problems as a "management issue" beyond their concern, or may have viewed problems as insurmountable, the transformational manager's **intellectual stimulation** leads subordinates to view problems as challenges that they can and will meet and conquer. The manager engages and empowers subordinates to take personal responsibility for helping to solve problems, as did Nokes at T-Mobile.[96]

Engaging in Developmental Consideration

developmental consideration Behavior a leader engages in to support and encourage followers and help them develop and grow on the job.

When managers engage in **developmental consideration**, they not only perform the consideration behaviors described earlier, such as demonstrating true concern for the well-being of subordinates, but go one step further. The manager goes out of his or her way to support and encourage subordinates, giving them opportunities to enhance their skills and capabilities and to grow and excel on the job.[97] As mentioned earlier, Nokes did this in numerous ways. In fact, after she first met with employees in a call center in Albuquerque, New Mexico, Karen Viola, the manager of the call center, said, "Everyone came out crying. The people said that they had never felt so inspired in their lives, and that they had never met with any leader at that level who [they felt] cared."[98]

All organizations, no matter how large or small, successful or unsuccessful, can benefit when their managers engage in transformational leadership. Moreover, while the benefits of transformational leadership are often most apparent when an organization is in trouble, transformational leadership can be an enduring approach to leadership, leading to long-term organizational effectiveness.

The Distinction between Transformational and Transactional Leadership

transactional leadership Leadership that motivates subordinates by rewarding them for high performance and reprimanding them for low performance.

Transformational leadership is often contrasted with transactional leadership. In **transactional leadership**, managers use their reward and coercive powers to encourage high performance. When managers reward high performers, reprimand or otherwise punish low performers, and motivate subordinates by reinforcing desired behaviors and extinguishing or punishing undesired ones, they are engaging in transactional leadership.[99] Managers who effectively influence their subordinates to achieve goals, yet do not seem to be making the kind of dramatic changes that are part of transformational leadership, are engaging in transactional leadership.

Many transformational leaders engage in transactional leadership. They reward subordinates for a job well done and notice and respond to substandard performance. But they also have their eyes on the bigger picture of how much better things could be in their organizations, how much more their subordinates are capable of achieving, and how important it is to treat their subordinates with respect and help them reach their full potential.

Research has found that when leaders engage in transformational leadership, their subordinates tend to have higher levels of job satisfaction and performance.[100] Additionally, subordinates of transformational leaders may be more likely to trust their leaders and their organizations and feel that they are being fairly treated, and this, in turn, may positively influence their work motivation (see Chapter 13).[101]

Gender and Leadership

LO14-5 Characterize the relationship between gender and leadership and explain how emotional intelligence may contribute to leadership effectiveness.

The increasing number of women entering the ranks of management, as well as the problems some women face in their efforts to be hired as managers or promoted into management positions, has prompted researchers to explore the relationship between gender and leadership. Although there are relatively more women in management positions today than there were 10 years ago, there are still relatively few women in top management and, in some organizations, even in middle management.

When women do advance to top management positions, special attention often is focused on them and the fact that they are women. For example, women CEOs of large companies are still rare; those who make it to the top post, such as Indra Nooyi of PepsiCo[102] and Meg Whitman of Hewlett-Packard, are salient. As business writer Linda Tischler puts it, "In a workplace where women CEOs of major companies are so scarce . . . they can be identified, like rock stars, by first name only."[103] Although women have certainly made inroads into leadership positions in organizations, they continue to be underrepresented in top leadership posts. For example, as was indicated in Chapter 5, while around 51.5% of the employees in managerial and professional jobs in the United States are women, only about 14.1% of corporate officers in the *Fortune* 500 are women, and only 7.5% of the top earners are women.[104]

A widespread stereotype of women is that they are nurturing, supportive, and concerned with interpersonal relations. Men are stereotypically viewed as being directive and focused on task accomplishment. Such stereotypes suggest that women tend to be more relationship-oriented as managers and engage in more consideration behaviors, whereas men are more task-oriented and engage in more initiating-structure behaviors. Does the behavior of actual male and female managers bear out these stereotypes? Do women managers lead in different ways than men do? Are male or female managers more effective as leaders?

Research suggests that male and female managers who have leadership positions in organizations behave in similar ways.[105] Women do not engage in more consideration than men, and men do not engage in more initiating structure than women. Research does suggest, however, that leadership style may vary between women and men. Women tend to be somewhat more participative as leaders than are men, involving subordinates in decision making and seeking their input.[106] Male managers tend to be less participative than are female managers, making more decisions on their own and wanting to do things their own way. Moreover, research suggests that men tend to be harsher when they punish their subordinates than do women.[107]

There are at least two reasons why female managers may be more participative as leaders than are male managers.[108] First, subordinates may try to resist the influence of female managers more than they do the influence of male managers. Some subordinates may never have reported to a woman before; some may incorrectly see a management role as being more appropriate for a man than for a woman; and some may just resist being led by a woman. To overcome this resistance and encourage subordinates' trust and respect, women managers may adopt a participative approach.

A second reason why female managers may be more participative is that they sometimes have better interpersonal skills than male managers.[109] A participative approach to leadership requires high levels of interaction and involvement between a manager and his or her subordinates, sensitivity to subordinates' feelings, and the ability to make decisions that may be unpopular with subordinates but necessary for goal attainment. Good interpersonal skills may help female managers have the effective interactions with their subordinates that are crucial to a participative approach.[110] To the extent that male managers have more difficulty managing interpersonal relationships, they may shy away from the high levels of interaction with subordinates necessary for true participation.

The key finding from research on leader behaviors, however, is that male and female managers do *not* differ significantly in their propensities to perform different leader behaviors. Even though they may be more participative, female managers do not engage in more consideration or less initiating structure than male managers.

Perhaps a question even more important than whether male and female managers differ in the leadership behaviors they perform is whether they differ in effectiveness. Consistent with the findings for leader behaviors, research suggests that across different kinds of organizational settings, male and female managers tend to be *equally effective* as leaders.[111] Thus there is no logical basis for stereotypes favoring male managers and leaders or for the existence of the "glass ceiling" (an invisible barrier that seems to prevent women from advancing as far as they should in some organizations). Because women and men are equally effective as leaders, the increasing number of women in the workforce should result in a larger pool of highly qualified candidates for management positions in organizations, ultimately enhancing organizational effectiveness.[112]

Emotional Intelligence and Leadership

Do the moods and emotions leaders experience on the job influence their behavior and effectiveness as leaders? Research suggests this is likely to be the case. For example, one study found that when store managers experienced positive moods at work, salespeople in their stores provided high-quality customer service and were less likely to quit.[113] Another study found that groups whose leaders experienced positive moods had better coordination, whereas groups whose leaders experienced negative moods exerted more effort; members of groups with leaders in positive moods also tended to experience more positive moods themselves; and members of groups with leaders in negative moods tended to experience more negative moods.[114]

A leader's level of emotional intelligence (see Chapter 3) may play a particularly important role in leadership effectiveness.[115] For example, emotional intelligence may help leaders develop a vision for their organizations, motivate their subordinates to commit to this vision, and energize them to enthusiastically work to achieve this vision. Moreover, emotional intelligence may enable leaders to develop a significant identity for their organization and instill high levels of trust and cooperation throughout the organization while maintaining the flexibility needed to respond to changing conditions.[116]

Emotional intelligence also plays a crucial role in how leaders relate to and deal with their followers, particularly when it comes to encouraging followers to be creative.[117] Creativity in organizations is an emotion-laden process; it often entails challenging the status quo, being willing to take risks and accept and learn from failures, and doing much hard work to bring creative ideas to fruition in terms of new products, services, or procedures and processes when uncertainty is bound to be high.[118] Leaders who are high on emotional intelligence are more likely to understand all the emotions surrounding creative endeavors, to be able to awaken and support the creative pursuits of their followers, and to provide the kind of support that enables creativity to flourish in organizations.[119]

Leaders, like people everywhere, sometimes make mistakes. Emotional intelligence may also help leaders respond appropriately when they realize they have made a mistake. Recognizing, admitting, and learning from mistakes can be especially important for entrepreneurs who start their own businesses, as profiled in the following "Focus on Diversity" box.

Management in Action

Topics for Discussion and Action

Discussion

1. Describe the steps managers can take to increase their power and ability to be effective leaders. [LO14-1]

2. Think of specific situations in which it might be especially important for a manager to engage in consideration and in initiating structure. [LO14-2]

3. For your current job or for a future job you expect to hold, describe what your supervisor could do to strongly motivate you to be a top performer. [LO14-3]

4. Discuss why managers might want to change the behaviors they engage in, given their situation, their subordinates, and the nature of the work being done. Do you think managers can readily change their leadership behaviors? Why or why not? [LO14-3]

5. Discuss why substitutes for leadership can contribute to organizational effectiveness. [LO14-3]

6. Describe what transformational leadership is, and explain how managers can engage in it. [LO14-4]

7. Discuss why some people still think men make better managers than women even though research indicates that men and women are equally effective as managers and leaders. [LO14-5]

8. Imagine that you are working in an organization in an entry-level position after graduation and have come up with what you think is a great idea for improving a critical process in the organization that relates to your job. In what ways might your supervisor encourage you to implement your idea? How might your supervisor discourage you from even sharing your idea with others? [LO14-4, 14-5]

Action

9. Interview a manager to find out how the three situational characteristics that Fiedler identified affect his or her ability to provide leadership. [LO14-3]

10. Find a company that has dramatically turned around its fortunes and improved its performance. Determine whether a transformational manager was behind the turnaround and, if one was, what this manager did. [LO14-4]

Building Management Skills

Analyzing Failures of Leadership [LO14-1, 14-2, 14-3, 14-4]

Think about a situation you are familiar with in which a leader was very ineffective. Then answer the following questions:

1. What sources of power did this leader have? Did the leader have enough power to influence his or her followers?

2. What kinds of behaviors did this leader engage in? Were they appropriate for the situation? Why or why not?

3. From what you know, do you think this leader was a task-oriented leader or a relationship-oriented leader? How favorable was this leader's situation for leading?

4. What steps did this leader take to motivate his or her followers? Were these steps appropriate or inappropriate? Why?

5. What signs, if any, did this leader show of being a transformational leader?

Managing Ethically [LO14-1]

Managers who verbally criticize their subordinates, put them down in front of their coworkers, or use the threat of job loss to influence behavior are exercising coercive power. Some employees subject to coercive power believe that using it is unethical.

Questions

1. Either alone or in a group, think about the ethical implications of the use of coercive power.

2. To what extent do managers and organizations have an ethical obligation to put limits on the amount of coercive power that is exercised?

Small Group Breakout Exercise

Improving Leadership Effectiveness [LO14-1, 14-2, 14-3, 14-4]

Form groups of three to five people, and appoint one member as the spokesperson who will communicate your findings and conclusions to the class when called on by the instructor. Then discuss the following scenario:

You are a team of human resource consultants who have been hired by Carla Caruso, an entrepreneur who has started her own interior decorating business. A highly competent and creative interior decorator, Caruso has established a working relationship with most of the major home builders in her community. At first she worked on her own as an independent contractor. Then because of a dramatic increase in the number of new homes being built, she became swamped with requests for her services and decided to start her own company.

She hired a secretary–bookkeeper and four interior decorators, all of whom are highly competent. Caruso still does decorating jobs herself and has adopted a hands-off approach to leading the four decorators who report to her because she feels that interior design is a very personal, creative endeavor. Rather than pay the decorators on some kind of commission basis (such as a percentage of their customers' total billings), she pays them a premium salary, higher than average, so they are motivated to do what's best for a customer's needs and not what will result in higher billings and commissions.

Caruso thought everything was going smoothly until customer complaints started coming in. The complaints ranged from the decorators' being hard to reach, promising unrealistic delivery times, and being late for or failing to keep appointments to their being impatient and rude when customers had trouble making up their minds. Caruso knows her decorators are competent and is concerned that she is not effectively leading and managing them. She wonders, in particular, if her hands-off approach is to blame and if she should change the manner in which she rewards or pays her decorators. She has asked for your advice.

1. Analyze the sources of power that Caruso has available to her to influence the decorators. What advice can you give her to either increase her power base or use her existing power more effectively?

2. Given what you have learned in this chapter (for example, from the behavior model and path–goal theory), does Caruso seem to be performing appropriate leader behaviors in this situation? What advice can you give her about the kinds of behaviors she should perform?

3. What steps would you advise Caruso to take to increase the decorators' motivation to deliver high-quality customer service?

4. Would you advise Caruso to try to engage in transformational leadership in this situation? If not, why not? If so, what steps would you advise her to take?

Exploring the World Wide Web [LO14-1, 14-2, 14-3, 14-4, 14-5]

Go to the website of the Center for Creative Leadership (www.ccl.org). Spend some time browsing through the site to learn more about this organization, which specializes in leadership. Then click on "Customized Services" and then "Coaching Services." Read about the different coaching programs and options the center provides. How do you think leaders might benefit from coaching? What kinds of leaders/managers may find coaching especially beneficial? Do you think coaching services such as those provided by the Center for Creative Leadership can help leaders become more effective? Why or why not?

Be the Manager [LO14-1, 14-2, 14-3, 14-4, 14-5]

You are the CEO of a medium-size company that makes window coverings similar to Hunter Douglas blinds and Duettes. Your company has a real cost advantage in terms of being able to make custom window coverings at costs that are relatively low in the industry. However, the performance of your company has been lackluster. To make needed changes and improve performance, you met with the eight other top managers in your company and charged them with identifying problems and missed opportunities in each of their areas and coming up with an action plan to address the problems and take advantage of opportunities.

Once you gave the managers the okay, they were charged with implementing their action plans in a timely fashion and monitoring the effects of their initiatives monthly for the next 8 to 12 months.

You approved each of the managers' action plans, and a year later most of the managers were reporting that their initiatives had been successful in addressing the problems and opportunities they had identified a year ago. However, overall company performance continues to be lackluster and shows no signs of improvement. You are confused and starting to question your leadership capabilities and approach to change. What are you going to do to improve the performance and effectiveness of your company?

Bloomberg Businessweek Case in the News

[LO14-1, 14-2, 14-3, 14-4]

Years of Chaos and Fail Whales Didn't Stop Twitter. Now the Company that Couldn't Kill Itself May Be About to Take Flight.

Life inside successful Web startups—especially the really successful ones—can be nasty, brutish, and short. As companies grow exponentially, egos clash, investors jockey for control, and business complexities rapidly exceed the managerial abilities of the founders.

Venture capitalist Peter Fenton calls this phenomenon "the violence of a startup." And nowhere has the violence been fiercer, or more public, than at a company Fenton invested in and has helped to guide: Twitter.

Throughout its first five years of existence, Twitter always seemed on the verge of committing some excruciating form of startup *seppuku*. There were constant service outages (epitomized by the ubiquitous "fail whale" cartoon message), an embarrassing security breach in 2009 that released a torrent of internal documents, and nonstop departures of key employees. The *pièce de résistance* was the turmoil at the top: Twitter had three chief executive officers in as many years. That drama culminated with the promotion of serial entrepreneur and former Google executive Dick Costolo as CEO in 2010 and the return last year of one of Twitter's founders, Jack Dorsey, as executive chairman and product chief.

Now something freakish is happening in San Francisco. Twitter, which for years treated the responsibility of earning money as an annoying distraction, may be turning into a viable business. The company has added seasoned executives, pushed its unique symbology like the hashtag (#) and at-symbol handle (@) into the mainstream, and rolled out new advertising products to the delight of big brands such as General Motors and Budweiser, which advertised heavily on the microblog service during this year's Super Bowl. Twitter is on pace for revenue of $260 million in 2012, according to research firm eMarketer. That may be an insignificant fleck on the windshield of rivals Google and Facebook, but it's a sign that Twitter is becoming a plausible contender for the online budgets of the world's top advertisers. "Our ad business is only about 18 months old," says Satya Patel, Twitter's product vice president and, like about 90 of its colleagues, a former Googler. "2011 was the year we began scaling it. And 2012 is the year when we demonstrate that it's a juggernaut."

In the past, Twitter's too-cool-for-revenue attitude enhanced its Silicon Valley mystique. The company still tries to maintain that ethos—its stated mission is "to instantly connect people everywhere to what is most meaningful to them." But really it's jumping headlong into competition for advertisers' Internet budgets. Twitter has also aligned itself closely with Apple, thanks in part to the connections of its chief financial officer, Ali Rowghani, a former CFO of Pixar Animation Studios, the late Steve Jobs's other company. Apple has coded quick access to Twitter into the operating system of the iPhone, iPad, and soon, its desktop PCs and laptops. This will make it far easier for users of Apple devices to join Twitter and reflexively contribute to the service.

Then there's Twitter's management of the hashtag, which is increasingly trumping the clunkier Web URL and even the Facebook profile page as a short, handy identifier for companies and politicians. Before the State of the Union address in January, the White House released a transcript of the speech annotated with hashtags for different subjects. During this year's Super Bowl, 8 out of 42 TV advertisers included a Twitter hashtag in their commercials. Last year only one, Audi, did so.

Brands are using the hashtag in part because it links them directly to an intense and nonstop online conversation. Although still relatively small with 100 million active users (compared with Facebook's 800 million-plus members), Twitter has become the pulse of a planetwide news organism, hosting the dialogue about everything from the Arab Spring to celebrity deaths.

Costolo, 48, is as responsible as anyone for Twitter's maturation. He expanded headcount from 45 to nearly 900 and helped his team develop an irony-free—or at least less ironic—sense of mission. Asked for the millionth time about Twitter's plan to increase revenue, Costolo says he will "probably continue to be more patient than people would expect me to be," adding that he has no immediate plans for an initial public offering. A former member of a Chicago improvisational troupe, he's also known for his self-deprecating sense of humor. Talking about the challenges Twitter faces in blocking spammers who might scare off business, he says, "We can learn from those who came before us and the kinds of things that they went through. I think that will ameliorate some of the concerns that advertisers have." He pauses for a moment. "That was a good use of the word 'ameliorate,' by the way. Don't you think? Right? Someone has to give me credit!"

After joining Twitter in late 2009 as chief operating officer, Costolo's first move was to go on a hiring binge, poaching talent from Google, News Corp., and Oracle. He later collaborated with Fenton and Bill Campbell, a famous Silicon Valley executive coach and Apple board member, to lure Dorsey back into an active role guiding product decisions. Having Dorsey, Costolo says, "clears away a lot of the contentious discussion you might have about whether you should zig or zag in respect to product decisions." Costolo also devised a six-hour leadership course, which he administers to senior executives four times a year, and directed one of the company's first engineers, Alissa Huskey, to lead a team to define Twitter's core values. The entire company eventually joined in and came up with a list of 10 principles, including "Grow our business in a way that makes us proud" and "Innovate through experimentation." That may sound like the worst kind of corporate offsite banality, but Costolo says it helped. "If you don't know where you're going, it seems like any road will take you there," he says.

Before Costolo became CEO, Twitter defined its business model more by what it did not want to do than what it did. In early 2009, it rejected an entreaty by Microsoft to put ads alongside results from searches on the service because it had not decided on a course of action to make money. It also considered and rejected selling data to corporate users about their Twitter activity and who was following them, and shelved a short-lived effort to tweet Groupon-style discounts, concluding those were not big enough businesses.

Twitter still makes money with licensing deals—Microsoft pays to get a real-time feed of tweets for its search engine, Bing. But Costolo firmly established the company's primary identity as a communications tool that lets advertisers contribute content along with other users free of charge—and then pay extra to make their messages more prominent. The centerpiece of Twitter's plans, what Costolo calls "the atomic unit of our ad strategy," is the "promoted tweet," a message from an advertiser that appears near the top of a user's feed. Advertisers pay only when a user "engages" with the tweet—retweets it, say, or clicks on a link. The more people click on an ad, the more the ad appears. Twitter executives trumpet an engagement rate of 3% to 5%, compared with less than 0.5% for normal banner ads.

Costolo credits Ashish Goel, a Stanford University computer science professor and part-time Twitter consultant, with helping the company realize that tweets could double as ads. Goel had an important insight: Everyone on Twitter is a marketer who wants to promote a link, a piece of news, or a personal update. Twitter's strongest appeal to advertisers was to allow them to pay to add more heft to a standard message. Ads could then flow not only to the central Twitter website but to all of the various Twitter software programs on the Web and on mobile phones, some of which are administered by third-party companies.

After formulating its system, Twitter moved cautiously to roll it out. In 2010 it monitored how many ads it could show users before they became frustrated. It later dabbled by opening advertising to Starbucks, Virgin America, Best Buy, and a few other big companies. For Walt Disney, then about to premiere *Toy Story 3*, Twitter developed the "promoted trend," which sits atop the list of popular topics on the main Twitter page for a full day and currently sells for about $120,000 in the U.S. It also started selling "promoted accounts" to advertisers that wanted to pay to have their Twitter names featured to users, a surefire way to add followers.

In summer 2010, Costolo recruited Adam Bain, an easygoing News Corp. sales executive, to run Twitter's ad efforts. Bain was an unlikely choice; he hailed from Fox Interactive Media, whose banner ads on Myspace.com tended to be gaudy, disruptive, and annoying to users. (Remember those infamous "punch the monkey" ads?) Bain describes his decision to move to Twitter as a "Jerry Maguire moment," a workplace epiphany where he discovered a fundamentally better form of Web advertising. Banner ads, he realized, "forced bad incentives and bad behavior by marketers" because blinky, brash ads were the only ones that grabbed users' attention and elicited their clicks. Twitter had "cracked the code on a new form of advertising," where ads are treated like every other kind of content on the site.

Bain spent his first few months at Twitter outside the office, meeting with ad agencies and advertisers and listening to what they wanted from Twitter. He visited 140 chief marketing officers in 140 days, sometimes with Costolo in tow. (Get it? Tweets max out at 140 characters.) One of Bain's slides showed the path not taken: a clean Twitter website under assault from banner ads hawking lotion, handbags, and cell phones, which descend onto the page amid dramatic clouds of virtual smoke.

The message—Twitter was taking a more nuanced, user-friendly approach—resonated with ad executives. It also left them with questions. CEO Tom Bedecarre of AKQA, a San Francisco-based digital marketing firm, calls himself an admirer of Bain

460

and Costolo and a "drunk-the-Kool-Aid Twitter believer." But he also says Twitter will need to work hard to persuade the rest of the industry to learn how to exploit this new communications medium—right after they were forced to school themselves on the art of Facebook and Google. "Every time there is a new platform, there is a new thing you are measuring," Bedecarre says. "What's the value of a 'like' on Facebook? What's the value of a 'retweet'? I do think that's a challenge for advertisers."

While the New York Giants were beating the New England Patriots in this year's Super Bowl, a different kind of battle erupted on Twitter. General Motors, one of the game's largest advertisers, accompanied its five TV commercials with a wave of simultaneous promotions on Twitter, spending hundreds of thousands of dollars to get its tweets, with links to its TV spots, in front of users of the service. One of those ads, which depicted Chevy Silverado drivers who survive an apocalypse but mourn their absent friend, a Ford owner, set off a minor conflagration. Executives at Ford and GM, along with truck aficionados, waged a war of 140-character tweets over the relative doomsday-surviving attributes of the companies' respective full-size pickups. "At one point it was like the Hatfields and the McCoys online," says Joel Ewanick, GM's chief marketing officer, who gleefully monitored the action from a social media "war room" in GM's Detroit headquarters. "That was our intent. We wanted to give people something to talk about, and Twitter helped us do that."

Over the past six months, Twitter has tried to give advertisers such as GM a variety of new ways to spend money on the service. Last September it began allowing advertisers to send promoted tweets to targeted subsets of people even if they are not following those brands on the service. That same month it began accepting political ads from candidates and political action committees and designating them with a distinctive purple check mark. On Feb. 28, Twitter announced it would also start sending promoted tweets to mobile phones, beating Facebook in the race to make money from exploding mobile Internet use. Later this month, Twitter will open the doors of its ad network to corner bakeries, taco trucks, and other small businesses, which will be able to funnel ads onto the service by submitting bids at Twitter.com without having to talk to a salesperson.

Silicon Valley is watching these plans closely to see whether Twitter can justify the $8 billion valuation it got last summer after an investment by Russian venture capital firm DST Global. There are plenty of reasons for skepticism. Its users are accustomed to selecting whom they follow and what they want to see, and an influx of ads from companies could turn them off, a reaction Twitter engineers internally call "fatigue." The coming tools for small businesses could also pose a problem; such self-service systems tend to attract mischief makers who try to drive traffic to spam- or malware-laden websites. When Google rolled out similar tools for its system, AdWords, early last decade, spammers found cheap search keywords and put links to their websites next to results. Then they stocked those Web pages with worthless ads. Facebook has suffered from similar mischief. In January, Twitter acquired a security company, Dasient, to guard against such manipulation.

For now, many major advertisers are sampling Twitter with budgets far smaller than what they spend on Google or Facebook. In January, Nike sponsored a tweet inviting users to "make it count," a promotion foreshadowing the launch of its body-monitoring bracelet, FuelBand. In February, Walt Disney unveiled a campaign for the new Pixar film, *Brave,* with a promoted trend that invited users to recount their own stories of courage. Verizon Wireless, Subway, and Delta Air Lines have been active as well. "We want to be where our customers are," says John Harrobin, Verizon vice president of digital media and marketing, who nevertheless notes that Facebook ads more often result in sales. Twitter users, he says, are more likely to click on ads and engage with the company's message, "so it's often the first place we use to dispense information."

In January, McDonald's demonstrated one of the risks of Twitter advertising. It rolled out a campaign with the innocuous hashtag #McDStories as part of an effort to promote tales about the farmers who supply the restaurant chain's produce. Critics of the company immediately co-opted the hashtag with stories of food poisoning, weight gain, and poor employee hygiene. Rick Wion, McDonald's social media director, says he's pleased with Twitter's ad tools and will continue to use them despite the potential for blowback. "We know that at times promoted trends can be used by critics to take potshots, but in every case where we've used them, the positive conversations and tweets from our customers far outweigh the negative."

Earlier this year, Newt Gingrich set up a petition on Facebook to reduce the price of gas to $2.50 a gallon by supporting expanded North American oil drilling and the Keystone XL pipeline. His campaign then hawked links to the petition on Twitter. At the start of the Feb. 22 GOP debate in Arizona, the Gingrich campaign paid Twitter to ensure that a tweet with the petition's link appeared each time a user searched for "Newt Gingrich" and also for "Mitt Romney." With Twitter's ads, Gingrich at least momentarily pulled off a feat—eclipsing Romney's message—that political analysts concluded he failed to do in the debate.

Vincent Harris, an outside social media consultant to the Gingrich campaign, says he's spending about four times as much money on Facebook as on Twitter simply because he can reach more voters there. It's math: Facebook reaches 44.6% of the U.S. population and Twitter 9.1% according to eMarketer. Yet it's Twitter, Harris says, that's become an invaluable tool for shaping the opinion of party insiders and pundits. "The beauty of Twitter's ad unit is that it's the best rapid-response tool that exists in politics right now," he says.

None of these advertisers are the unreserved evangelists Twitter might hope them to be. GM's Ewanick says his Twitter ads during the Super Bowl nearly doubled the carmaker's number of followers, to more than 80,000. He also says that maintaining a Twitter presence and supporting a Twitter ad campaign is more resource-intensive than running old-fashioned TV and print ads. All that engagement and authentic-seeming messaging can be exhausting. A company tweet "can't look like it came from some corporate thing," he says. Verizon's Harrobin says the wireless carrier may have overwhelmed its followers with promoted messages from time to time.

Another common gripe is that advertisers can't target segments of users on Twitter in quite the same way as on Facebook, which typically knows a member's age, work and education history, and hometown. People don't volunteer the same data to Twitter, and its targeting tools are not as refined. Costolo says he's not concerned because there's so much promise in targeting users based on an "interest graph"—the set of characteristics that can be gleaned from users' followers and what they click on. He gets animated talking about a treasure trove of data

that's both revealing and noninvasive. "These accounts I follow paint a very compelling picture of the kind of person I am, even if it doesn't paint a picture of exactly which uniquely identifiable individual in the world I am," he says. "I think that allows us to deliver powerful value to advertisers, and powerful value to those who want to speak freely."

He pauses again. "I killed that answer, I absolutely nailed that answer," he says. He gestures at a public-relations colleague. "He's so disappointed in me! 'Why the post-modern ironic references?' "

A few days later, Costolo, done joking around, discusses the company's new headquarters, where most of Twitter's 900 employees will move this summer. Last year, Twitter finalized a lease for a 75-year-old former wholesale furniture market, a building that squats amid an economically depressed area on San Francisco's Market Street filled with panhandlers, dollar stores, and litter-strewn empty lots. It's an unusual location for an Internet phenom, but Twitter, which received tax breaks from the city, is making the space its own. Workers are installing modern elevators and 21st century Web company accoutrements such as coffee bars and two-person conference rooms. They're also turning the roof into a covered deck and cafeteria with towering views of the imperial rotunda

of nearby City Hall. The building is full of art deco details the company plans to keep—a marble lobby and exposed mail chutes, those bygone purveyors of the analog tweet. "We're trying to build a lasting company, a company that will change the world in interesting and beneficial ways," says Costolo. "The new space, in this incredibly historic building, lends gravitas to the mission of the company and the future ahead of it. I think it's consistent with the way we are building the company, as a lasting part of the media world."

Questions for Discussion

1. How would you describe the personal leadership style of Dick Costolo?

2. What are Costolo's sources of power?

3. What behaviors does Costolo appear to engage in?

4. Do you think Costolo is a transformational leader? If so, in what ways has he been a transformational leader? If not, why not?

Source: Brad Stone, "Years of Chaos and Fail Whales Didn't Stop Twitter. Now the Company that Couldn't Kill Itself May Be About to Take Flight." *Bloomberg Businessweek,* March 5–March 11, 2012, 62–67. Bloomberg L.P. Copyright © 2012. All rights reserved.

CHAPTER 15

Effective Groups and Teams

Learning Objectives

After studying this chapter, you should be able to:

LO15-1 Explain why groups and teams are key contributors to organizational effectiveness.

LO15-2 Identify the different types of groups and teams that help managers and organizations achieve their goals.

LO15-3 Explain how different elements of group dynamics influence the functioning and effectiveness of groups and teams.

LO15-4 Explain why it is important for groups and teams to have a balance of conformity and deviance and a moderate level of cohesiveness.

LO15-5 Describe how managers can motivate group members to achieve organizational goals and reduce social loafing in groups and teams.

A MANAGER'S CHALLENGE

Teams Innovate at Boeing

How can managers promote innovation while cutting costs and increasing efficiency? Managers at Boeing have increased their reliance on using teams of employees to promote innovation while cutting costs and improving efficiency.[1] Boeing's 737 is a top-selling jetliner and, faced with high demand, managers at Boeing charged teams with innovating to cut costs, increase efficiency, and increase the number of 737s that could be produced each month in Boeing's Renton, Washington, manufacturing facility. As Eric Lindblad, vice president in charge of manufacturing 737s, put it, "How do you produce more aircraft without expanding the building? . . . Space is the forcing function that means you've got to be creative."[2]

Self-managing, cross-functional teams of around 7 to 10 members typically concentrate on a particular segment of the plane such as the galley, where food and drinks are prepared and stored. Team members have diverse backgrounds and experiences, and thus it is not uncommon for mechanics to be working alongside engineers on the same team. Teams meet as often as their members think it is called for with some teams meeting as frequently as once per week. Some team projects are completed in a relatively short

time period, whereas others can take years with missteps along the way. For example, it

Talk about hands-on inspiration! Here, Boeing's team system seats the group responsible for the plane nose right under a "work in progress" in order to better make decisions.

took a team about five years to develop and design a new, more efficient way to install the hydraulic tubes in the 737 landing gear wheel well area. In the past, four mechanics were crowded into the wheel well, assembling over 600 tubes for a one-day shift and also a segment of the night shift for a single jet. Boeing employees working on other assembly tasks had to navigate around the mechanics installing the tubes. The team trying to improve this process figured out that around 25 clusters of tubes could be put together at another Boeing plant so that mechanics would be installing 25 larger assemblies and less than 100 individual tubes. The new process, while still being improved upon, resulted in around 30 hours less mechanics' time being taken up by tube installation per plane and fewer leaks in the hydraulic system when planes were operational.[3]

Engineer Jay Dorhrmann worked on a team trying to solve a persistent problem—when planes moved along the assembly line, metal parts and fasteners scattered about the plant's floor would occasionally puncture a tire on a plane.[4] The team's first solution to the problem was to install sweepers on the planes' landing gear so that as the plane was moved along the line, the metal parts would be swept out of the way of the tires. Unfortunately, the sweepers didn't work very well and bolts and other metal parts were still puncturing tires. When Dorhrmann was watching a motorcycle race on his day off, he noticed that race crews put covers on tires before races so that they would warm up and have better traction during the race. This gave him an idea for the problem his team had been struggling with—canvas wheel covers that would encircle the four major landing gear tires on the planes as they were moved along the line. This innovation resulted in cost savings of around $10,000 per punctured tire, resulting in about $250,000 per year cost savings as well as savings resulting from mechanics not having to stop their work and take the time to change out a punctured tire. Team members like Dorhrmann get a real sense of accomplishment when their teams' succeed. As Dorhrmann indicates, "It's a good feeling . . . You hated to see these airplanes jacked at the end of the line and people pulling off tires."[5]

Another team came up with the idea to rearrange the work area where engines where prepared for eventual connection to the wings of the 737.[6] Three engines used to be prepared at one time; by reconfiguring the work area, now four engines can be prepared at the same time. Employees in the paint shop figured out how to take less time to complete painting jobs. Some time ago, a team suggested that hay loaders (used for putting bales of hay on trucks in farming) be used to put passenger seats on planes for installation. Boeing still uses the hay loaders for this purpose.[7]

Across all commercial jet programs, Boeing has approximately 1,300 teams focused on innovation, cutting costs, and improving efficiency.[8] Mechanics, engineers, and other Boeing employees who work on the jets on a day-to-day basis, or work on designing new models, are often in a good position to figure out ways to improve the design and assembly process. A big drive behind these efforts is to decrease the amount of time it takes to build a jet and increase the number of jets Boeing can build each month.[9]

With a backlog of orders for around 3,700 jetliners, of which about 2,300 are 737s, it is understandable why managers at Boeing are using teams to spur innovation and increase efficiency while cutting costs.[10] And teams certainly seem to be helping Boeing do just that. At the Renton plant, Boeing used to make 31.5 737 jetliners per month; now the plant is making 35 737s per month. The goal is to increase this number to 42 by 2014. Thus, it is not surprising that Boeing has been hiring additional workers to help fuel the increase in production of jetliners.[11] All in all, teams certainly seem to be contributing to innovation and efficiency at Boeing.[12]

Overview

Boeing is not alone in using groups and teams to improve organizational effectiveness. Managers in companies large and small are using groups and teams to enhance performance, increase responsiveness to customers, spur innovation, and motivate employees. In this chapter we look in detail at how groups and teams can contribute to organizational effectiveness and the types of groups and teams used in organizations. We discuss how different elements of group dynamics influence the functioning and effectiveness of groups, and we describe how managers can motivate group members to achieve organizational goals and reduce social loafing in groups and teams. By the end of this chapter you will appreciate why the effective management of groups and teams is a key ingredient for organizational performance and effectiveness.

Groups, Teams, and Organizational Effectiveness

LO15-1 Explain why groups and teams are key contributors to organizational effectiveness.

group Two or more people who interact with each other to accomplish certain goals or meet certain needs.

team A group whose members work intensely with one another to achieve a specific common goal or objective.

synergy Performance gains that result when individuals and departments coordinate their actions.

A **group** may be defined as two or more people who interact with each other to accomplish certain goals or meet certain needs.[13] A **team** is a group whose members work *intensely* with one another to achieve a specific common goal or objective. As these definitions imply, all teams are groups, but not all groups are teams. The two characteristics that distinguish teams from groups are the *intensity* with which team members work together and the presence of a *specific, overriding team goal or objective.*

Recall from "A Manager's Challenge" how the teams at Boeing had the goal of improving the manufacturing process for a particular part of the 737 jetliner. In contrast, the accountants who work in a small CPA firm are a group: They may interact with one another to achieve goals such as keeping up-to-date on the latest changes in accounting rules and regulations, maintaining a smoothly functioning office, satisfying clients, and attracting new clients. But they are not a team because they do not work intensely with one another. Each accountant concentrates on serving the needs of his or her own clients.

Because all teams are also groups, whenever we use the term *group* in this chapter, we are referring to both groups *and* teams. As you might imagine, because members of teams work intensely together, teams can sometimes be difficult to form, and it may take time for members to learn how to effectively work together. Groups and teams can help an organization gain a competitive advantage because they can (1) enhance its performance, (2) increase its responsiveness to customers, (3) increase innovation, and (4) increase employees' motivation and satisfaction (see Figure 15.1). In this section we look at each of these contributions in turn.

Groups and Teams as Performance Enhancers

One of the main advantages of using groups is the opportunity to obtain a type of **synergy**: People working in a group can produce more or higher-quality outputs than would have been produced if each person had worked separately and all their individual efforts were later combined. The essence of synergy is captured in the saying "The whole is more than the sum of its parts." Factors that can contribute to synergy in groups include the ability of group members to

Figure 15.1

Groups' and Teams' Contributions to Organizational Effectiveness

bounce ideas off one another, to correct one another's mistakes, to solve problems immediately as they arise, to bring a diverse knowledge base to bear on a problem or goal, and to accomplish work that is too vast or all-encompassing for any individual to achieve on his or her own.

To take advantage of the potential for synergy in groups, managers need to make sure that groups are composed of members who have complementary skills and knowledge relevant to the group's work. For example, at Hallmark Cards, synergies are created by bringing together all the different functions needed to create and produce a greeting card in a cross-functional team (a team composed of members from different departments or functions; see Chapter 10). For instance, artists, writers, designers, and marketing experts work together as team members to develop new cards.[14]

Getting multiple perspectives and departmental inputs on a project can enhance performance.

At Hallmark the skills and expertise of the artists complement the contributions of the writers and vice versa. Managers also need to give groups enough autonomy so that the groups, rather than the manager, are solving problems and determining how to achieve goals and objectives, as is true in the cross-functional teams at Hallmark and the teams at Boeing in "A Manager's Challenge." To promote synergy, managers need to empower their subordinates and to be coaches, guides, and resources for groups while refraining from playing a more directive or supervisory role. The potential for synergy in groups may be why more and more managers are incorporating empowerment into their personal leadership styles (see Chapter 14).

When tasks are complex and involve highly sophisticated and rapidly changing technologies, achieving synergies in teams often hinges on having the appropriate mix of backgrounds and areas of expertise represented on the team. In large organizations with operations in many states and countries, managers can rely on databases and software applications to determine which employees might have the expertise needed on a particular team or for a certain project.

Groups, Teams, and Responsiveness to Customers

Being responsive to customers is not always easy. In manufacturing organizations, for example, customers' needs and desires for new and improved products have to be balanced against engineering constraints, production costs and feasibilities, government safety regulations, and marketing challenges. In service organizations such as health maintenance organizations (HMOs), being responsive to patients' needs and desires for prompt, high-quality medical care and treatment has to be balanced against meeting physicians' needs and desires and keeping health care costs under control. Being responsive to customers often requires the wide variety of skills and expertise found in different departments and at different levels in an organization's hierarchy. Sometimes, for example, employees at lower levels in an organization's hierarchy, such as sales representatives for a computer company, are closest to its customers and the most attuned to their needs. However, lower-level employees like salespeople often lack the technical expertise needed for new product ideas; such expertise is found in the research and development department. Bringing salespeople, research and development experts, and members of other departments together in a group or cross-functional team can enhance responsiveness to customers. Consequently, when managers form a team, they must make sure the diversity of expertise and knowledge needed to be responsive to customers exists within the team; this is why cross-functional teams are so popular.

In a cross-functional team, the expertise and knowledge in different organizational departments are brought together in the skills and knowledge of the team members. Managers of high-performing organizations are careful to determine which types of expertise and knowledge are required for teams to be responsive to customers, and they use this information in forming teams.

Teams and Innovation

Innovation—the creative development of new products, new technologies, new services, or even new organizational structures—is a topic we introduced in Chapter 1. Often an individual working alone does not possess the extensive and diverse skills, knowledge, and expertise required for successful innovation. Managers can better encourage innovation by creating teams of diverse individuals who together have the knowledge relevant to a particular type of innovation, as has been the case at Boeing, rather than by relying on individuals working alone.

Using teams to innovate has other advantages. First, team members can often uncover one another's errors or false assumptions; an individual acting alone would not be able to do this. Second, team members can critique one another's approaches and build off one another's strengths while compensating for weaknesses—an advantage of devil's advocacy and dialectical inquiry, discussed in Chapter 7.

To further promote innovation, managers can empower teams and make their members fully responsible and accountable for the innovation process. The manager's role is to provide guidance, assistance, coaching, and the resources that team members need and *not* to closely direct or supervise their activities. To speed innovation, managers also need to form teams in which each member brings some unique resource to the team, such as engineering prowess, knowledge of production, marketing expertise, or financial savvy. Successful innovation sometimes requires that managers form teams with members from different countries and cultures.

Amazon uses teams to spur innovation, and many of the unique features on its website that enable it to be responsive to customers and meet their needs have been developed by teams, as indicated in the following "Information Technology Byte" box.

Information Technology Byte

Pizza Teams Innovate at Amazon

Jeff Bezos, founder, CEO, and chairman of the board of Amazon, is a firm believer in the power of teams to spur innovation.[15] At Amazon, teams have considerable autonomy to develop their ideas and experiment without interference from managers or other groups. And teams are kept deliberately small. According to Bezos, no team should need more than two pizzas to feed its members.[16] If more than two pizzas are needed to nourish a

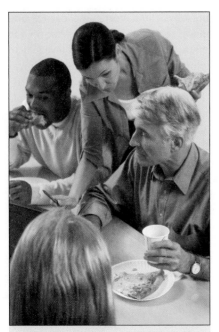

Pepperoni or plain cheese? At Amazon, pizza teams are small enough to need just one of each.

team, the team is too large. Thus teams at Amazon typically have no more than about five to seven members.[17]

"Pizza teams" have come up with unique and popular innovations that individuals working alone might never have thought of. A team developed the "Gold Box" icon that customers can click on to receive special offers that expire within an hour of opening the treasure chest. Another team developed "Search Inside This Book," which allows customers to search and read content from over 100,000 books.[18] And a team developed the Amazon Kindle, a wireless reader that weighs less than 10 ounces, can hold over thousands of titles, can receive automatic delivery of major newspapers and blogs, and has a high-resolution screen that looks like and can be read like paper.[19]

While Bezos gives teams autonomy to develop and run with their ideas, he also believes in careful analysis and testing of ideas. A great advocate of the power of facts, data, and analysis, Bezos feels that whenever an idea can be tested through analysis, analysis should rule the day. When an undertaking is just too large or too uncertain or when data are lacking, Bezos and other experienced top managers make the final call.[20] But to make such judgment calls about implementing new ideas (either by data analysis or expert judgment), truly creative ideas are needed. To date, teams have played a very important role in generating ideas that have helped Amazon to be responsive to its customers, to have a widely known Internet brand name, and to be the highly successful and innovative company it is today.[21]

Groups and Teams as Motivators

Managers often form groups and teams to accomplish organizational goals and then find that using groups and teams brings additional benefits. Members of groups, and especially members of teams (because of the higher intensity of interaction in teams), are likely to be more satisfied than they would have been if they were working on their own. The experience of working alongside other highly charged and motivated people can be stimulating and motivating: Team members can see how their efforts and expertise directly contribute to the achievement of team and organizational goals, and they feel personally responsible for the outcomes or results of their work. This has been the case at Hallmark Cards.

The increased motivation and satisfaction that can accompany the use of teams can also lead to other outcomes, such as lower turnover. This has been Frank B. Day's experience as founder and chairman of the board of Rock Bottom Restaurants Inc.[22] To provide high-quality customer service, Day has organized the restaurants' employees into waitstaff teams, whose members work together to refill beers, take orders, bring hot chicken enchiladas to the tables, or clear off the tables. Team members share the burden of undesirable activities and unpopular shift times, and customers no longer have to wait until a particular waitress or waiter is available. Motivation and satisfaction levels in Rock Bottom restaurants seem to be higher than in other restaurants, and turnover is about half that experienced in other U.S. restaurant chains.[23]

Working in a group or team can also satisfy organizational members' needs for engaging in social interaction and feeling connected to other people. For workers who perform highly stressful jobs, such as hospital emergency and operating room staff, group membership can be an important source of social support and motivation. Family members or friends may not be able to fully understand or appreciate some sources of work stress that these group members experience firsthand. Moreover, group members may cope better with work stressors when they can share them with other members of their group. In addition, groups often devise techniques to relieve stress, such as the telling of jokes among hospital operating room staff.

Why do managers in all kinds of organizations rely so heavily on groups and teams? Effectively managed groups and teams can help managers in their quest for high performance, responsiveness to customers, and employee motivation. Before explaining how managers can effectively manage groups, however, we will describe the types of groups that are formed in organizations.

Types of Groups and Teams

LO15-2 Identify the different types of groups and teams that help managers and organizations achieve their goals.

formal group A group that managers establish to achieve organizational goals.

informal group A group that managers or nonmanagerial employees form to help achieve their own goals or meet their own needs.

top management team A group composed of the CEO, the president, and the heads of the most important departments.

research and development team A team whose members have the expertise and experience needed to develop new products.

To achieve their goals of high performance, responsiveness to customers, innovation, and employee motivation, managers can form various types of groups and teams (see Figure 15.2). **Formal groups** are those that managers establish to achieve organizational goals. The formal work groups are *cross-functional* teams composed of members from different departments, such as those at Hallmark Cards, and *cross-cultural* teams composed of members from different cultures or countries, such as the teams at global carmakers. As you will see, some of the groups discussed in this section also can be considered to be cross-functional (if they are composed of members from different departments) or cross-cultural (if they are composed of members from different countries or cultures).

Sometimes organizational members, managers or nonmanagers, form groups because they feel that groups will help them achieve their own goals or meet their own needs (for example, the need for social interaction). Groups formed in this way are **informal groups**. Four nurses who work in a hospital and have lunch together twice a week constitute an informal group.

The Top Management Team

A central concern of the CEO and president of a company is to form a **top management team** to help the organization achieve its mission and goals. Top management teams are responsible for developing the strategies that result in an organization's competitive advantage; most have between five and seven members. In forming their top management teams, CEOs are well advised to stress diversity in expertise, skills, knowledge, and experience. Thus many top management teams are also cross-functional teams: They are composed of members from different departments, such as finance, marketing, production, and engineering. Diversity helps ensure that the top management team will have all the background and resources it needs to make good decisions. Diversity also helps guard against *groupthink*—faulty group decision making that results when group members strive for agreement at the expense of an accurate assessment of the situation (see Chapter 7).

Research and Development Teams

Managers in pharmaceuticals, computers, electronics, electronic imaging, and other high-tech industries often create **research and development teams** to develop new products.

Figure 15.2
Types of Groups and Teams in Organizations

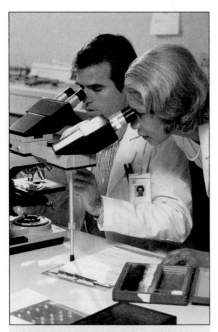

Figuring out if the new pharmaceutical drug is a go takes a strong R&D team made up of medical experts who know the science as well as the market needs.

Managers select R&D team members on the basis of their expertise and experience in a certain area. Sometimes R&D teams are cross-functional teams with members from departments such as engineering, marketing, and production in addition to members from the research and development department.

Command Groups

Subordinates who report to the same supervisor compose a **command group**. When top managers design an organization's structure and establish reporting relationships and a chain of command, they are essentially creating command groups. Command groups, often called *departments* or *units,* perform a significant amount of the work in many organizations. In order to have command groups that help an organization gain a competitive advantage, managers not only need to motivate group members to perform at a high level but also need to be effective leaders. Examples of command groups include the salespeople in a large department store in New York who report to the same supervisor, the employees of a small swimming pool sales and maintenance company in Florida who report to a general manager, the telephone operators at the MetLife insurance company who report to the same supervisor, and workers on an automobile assembly line in the Ford Motor Company who report to the same first-line manager.

Task Forces

Managers form **task forces** to accomplish specific goals or solve problems in a certain time period; task forces are sometimes called *ad hoc committees.* For example, Michael Rider, owner and top manager of a chain of six gyms and fitness centers in the Midwest, created a task force composed of the general managers of the six gyms to determine whether the fitness centers should institute a separate fee schedule for customers who wanted to use the centers only for aerobics classes (and not use other facilities such as weights, steps, tracks, and swimming pools). The task force was given three months to prepare a report summarizing the pros and cons of the proposed change in fee schedules. After the task force completed its report and reached the conclusion that the change in fee structure probably would reduce revenues rather than increase them and thus should not be implemented, it was disbanded. As in Rider's case, task forces can be a valuable tool for busy managers who do not have the time to personally explore an important issue in depth.

Sometimes managers need to form task forces whose work, so to speak, is never done. The task force may be addressing a long-term or enduring problem or issue facing an organization, such as how to most usefully contribute to the local community or how to make sure the organization provides opportunities for potential employees with disabilities. Task forces that are relatively permanent are often referred to as *standing committees.* Membership in standing committees changes over time. Members may have, for example, a two- or three-year term on the committee, and memberships expire at varying times so there are always some members with experience on the committee. Managers often form and maintain standing committees to make sure important issues continue to be addressed.

Self-Managed Work Teams

Self-managed work teams are teams in which members are empowered and have the responsibility and autonomy to complete identifiable pieces of work. On a day-to-day basis, team members decide what the team will do, how it will do it, and which members will perform which specific tasks.[24] Managers assign self-managed work teams' overall goals (such as assembling defect-free computer keyboards) but let team members decide how to meet those goals. Managers usually form self-managed work teams to improve quality, increase motivation and satisfaction, and lower costs. Often, by creating self-managed work teams, they combine tasks that individuals working separately used to perform, so the team is responsible for the whole set of tasks that yields an identifiable output or end product.

command group A group composed of subordinates who report to the same supervisor; also called *department* or *unit.*

task force A committee of managers or nonmanagerial employees from various departments or divisions who meet to solve a specific, mutual problem; also called *ad hoc committee.*

self-managed work team A group of employees who supervise their own activities and monitor the quality of the goods and services they provide.

Managers can take a number of steps to ensure that self-managed work teams are effective and help an organization achieve its goals:[25]

- Give teams enough responsibility and autonomy to be truly self-managing. Refrain from telling team members what to do or solving problems for them even if you (as a manager) know what should be done.

- Make sure a team's work is sufficiently complex so that it entails a number of different steps or procedures that must be performed and results in some kind of finished end product.

- Carefully select members of self-managed work teams. Team members should have the diversity of skills needed to complete the team's work, have the ability to work with others, and want to be part of a team.

- As a manager, realize that your role vis-à-vis self-managed work teams calls for guidance, coaching, and supporting, not supervising. You are a resource for teams to turn to when needed.

- Analyze what type of training team members need and provide it. Working in a self-managed work team often requires that employees have more extensive technical and interpersonal skills.

Managers in a wide variety of organizations have found that self-managed work teams help the organization achieve its goals,[26] as profiled in the following "Management Insight" box.

Management Insight

Self-Managed Teams at Louis Vuitton and Nucor Corporation

Managers at Louis Vuitton, the most valuable luxury brand in the world, and managers at Nucor Corporation, the largest producer of steel and biggest recycler in the United States, have succeeded in effectively using self-managed teams to produce luxury accessories and steel, respectively. Self-managed teams at both companies not only are effective but truly excel and have helped make the companies leaders in their respective industries.[27]

Teams with between 20 and 30 members make Vuitton handbags and accessories. The teams work on only one product at a time; a team with 24 members might produce about 120 handbags per day. Team members are empowered to take ownership of the goods they produce, are encouraged to suggest improvements, and are kept up-to-date on key facts such as products' selling prices and popularity. As Thierry Nogues, a team leader at a Vuitton factory in Ducey, France, puts it, "Our goal is to make everyone as multiskilled and autonomous as possible."[28]

Production workers at Nucor are organized into teams ranging in size from 8 to 40 members based on the kind of work the team is responsible for, such as rolling steel or operating a furnace. Team members have considerable autonomy to make decisions and creatively respond to problems and opportunities, and there are relatively

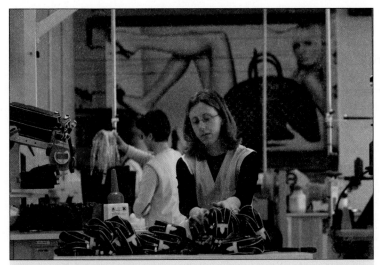

A team member assembles classic Louis Vuitton bags at the company's fine leather goods factory in the Normandy town of Ducey in France.

few layers in the corporate hierarchy, supporting the empowerment of teams.[29] Teams develop their own informal rules for behavior and make their own decisions. As long as team members follow organizational rules and policies (such as those for safety) and meet quality standards, they are free to govern themselves. Managers act as coaches or advisers rather than supervisors, helping teams when needed.[30]

To ensure that production teams are motivated to help Nucor achieve its goals, team members are eligible for weekly bonuses based on the team's performance. Essentially, these production workers receive base pay that does not vary and are eligible to receive weekly bonus pay that can average from 80% to 150% of their regular pay.[31] The bonus rate is predetermined by the work a team performs and the capabilities of the machinery they use. Given the immediacy of the bonus and its potential magnitude, team members are motivated to perform at a high level, develop informal rules that support high performance, and strive to help Nucor reach its goals. Moreover, because all members of a team receive the same amount of weekly bonus money, they are motivated to do their best for the team, cooperate, and help one another out.[32] Of course, in tough economic times such as the recession in the late 2000s, Nucor's production workers' bonuses fall as demand for Nucor's products drops. Nonetheless, Nucor has been able to avoid laying off employees (unlike a lot of other large corporations).[33]

Crafting a luxury handbag and making steel joists couldn't be more different from each other in certain ways. Yet the highly effective self-managed teams at Louis Vuitton and Nucor share some fundamental qualities. These teams really do take ownership of their work and are highly motivated to perform effectively. Team members have the skills and knowledge they need to be effective, they are empowered to make decisions about their work, and they know their teams are making vital contributions to their organizations.[34]

Sometimes employees have individual jobs but also are part of a self-managed team that is formed to accomplish a specific goal or work on an important project. Employees need to perform their own individual job tasks and also actively contribute to the self-managed team so that the team achieves its goal.

Sometimes self-managed work teams can run into trouble. Members may be reluctant to discipline one another by withholding bonuses from members who are not performing up to par or by firing members.[35] Buster Jarrell, a manager who oversaw self-managed work teams in AES Corporation's Houston plant, found that although the self-managed work teams were highly effective, they had a difficult time firing team members who were performing poorly.[36]

The Dallas office of the New York Life Insurance Co. experimented with having members of self-managed teams evaluate one another's performance and determine pay levels. Team members did not feel comfortable assuming this role, however, and managers ended up handling these tasks.[37] One reason for team members' discomfort may be the close personal relationships they sometimes develop with one another. In addition, members of self-managed work teams may sometimes take longer to accomplish tasks, such as when team members have difficulties coordinating their efforts.

Virtual Teams

virtual team A team whose members rarely or never meet face-to-face but, rather, interact by using various forms of information technology such as e-mail, computer networks, telephone, fax, and videoconferences.

Virtual teams are teams whose members rarely or never meet face-to-face but, rather, interact by using various forms of information technology such as e-mail, text messaging, computer networks, telephone, fax, and videoconferences. As organizations become increasingly global, and as the need for specialized knowledge increases due to advances in technology, managers can create virtual teams to solve problems or explore opportunities without being limited by team members needing to work in the same geographic location.[38]

Take the case of an organization that has manufacturing facilities in Australia, Canada, the United States, and Mexico and is encountering a quality problem in a complex manufacturing process. Each of its facilities has a quality control team headed by a quality control manager. The vice president for production does not try to solve the problem by forming and leading a team at one of the four manufacturing facilities; instead she forms and leads a virtual team composed of the quality control managers of the four plants and the plants' general managers. When these team members communicate via e-mail, the company's networking site, and videoconferencing, a wide array of knowledge and experience is brought to solve the problem.

The principal advantage of virtual teams is that they enable managers to disregard geographic distances and form teams whose members have the knowledge, expertise, and experience to tackle a particular problem or take advantage of a specific opportunity.[39] Virtual teams also can include members who are not actually employees of the organization itself; a virtual team might include members of a company that is used for outsourcing. More and more companies, including BP PLC, Nokia Corporation, and Ogilvy & Mather, are using virtual teams.[40]

Members of virtual teams rely on two forms of information technology: synchronous technologies and asynchronous technologies.[41] *Synchronous technologies* let virtual team members communicate and interact with one another in real time simultaneously and include videoconferencing, teleconferencing, and electronic meetings. *Asynchronous technologies* delay communication and include e-mail, electronic bulletin boards, and Internet websites. Many virtual teams use both kinds of technology depending on what projects they are working on.

Increasing globalization is likely to result in more organizations relying on virtual teams to a greater extent.[42] One challenge members of virtual teams face is building a sense of camaraderie and trust among team members who rarely, if ever, meet face-to-face. To address this challenge, some organizations schedule recreational activities, such as ski trips, so virtual team members can get together. Other organizations make sure virtual team members have a chance to meet in person soon after the team is formed and then schedule periodic face-to-face meetings to promote trust, understanding, and cooperation in the teams.[43] The need for such meetings is underscored by research suggesting that while some virtual teams can be as effective as teams that meet face-to-face, virtual team members might be less satisfied with teamwork efforts and have fewer feelings of camaraderie or cohesion. (Group cohesiveness is discussed in more detail later in the chapter.)[44]

Research also suggests that it is important for managers to keep track of virtual teams and intervene when necessary by, for example, encouraging members of teams who do not communicate often enough to monitor their team's progress and making sure team members actually have the time, and are recognized for, their virtual teamwork.[45] Additionally, when virtual teams are experiencing downtime or rough spots, managers might try to schedule face-to-face team time to bring team members together and help them focus on their goals.[46]

Researchers at the London Business School, including Professor Lynda Gratton, recently studied global virtual teams to try to identify factors that might help such teams be effective.[47] Based on their research, Gratton suggests that when forming virtual teams, it is helpful to include a few members who already know each other, other members who are well connected to people outside the team, and when possible, members who have volunteered to be a part of the team.[48] It is also advantageous for companies to have some kind of online site where team members can learn more about each other and the kinds of work they are engaged in, and in particular, a shared online workspace that team members can access around the clock.[49] Frequent communication is beneficial. Additionally, virtual team projects should be perceived as meaningful, interesting, and important by their members to promote and sustain their motivation.[50]

friendship group An informal group composed of employees who enjoy one another's company and socialize with one another.

A recycling interest group organizes like-minded colleagues to help pick up the slack where the formal organization may be lacking.

Friendship Groups

The groups described so far are formal groups created by managers. **Friendship groups** are informal groups composed of employees who enjoy one another's company and socialize with one another. Members of friendship groups may have lunch together, take breaks together, or meet after work for meals, sports, or other activities. Friendship groups help satisfy employees' needs for interpersonal interaction, can provide needed social support in times of stress, and can contribute to people's feeling good at work and being satisfied with their jobs. Managers themselves often form friendship groups. The informal relationships that managers build in friendship groups can often help them solve work-related problems because members of these groups typically discuss work-related matters and offer advice.

Interest Groups

interest group An informal group composed of employees seeking to achieve a common goal related to their membership in an organization.

Employees form informal **interest groups** when they seek to achieve a common goal related to their membership in an organization. Employees may form interest groups, for example, to encourage managers to consider instituting flexible working hours, providing on-site child care, improving working conditions, or more proactively supporting environmental protection. Interest groups can give managers valuable insights into the issues and concerns that are foremost in employees' minds. They also can signal the need for change.

Group Dynamics

How groups function and, ultimately, their effectiveness hinge on group characteristics and processes known collectively as *group dynamics*. In this section we discuss five key elements of group dynamics: group size, tasks, and roles; group leadership; group development; group norms; and group cohesiveness.

Group Size, Tasks, and Roles

LO15-3 Explain how different elements of group dynamics influence the functioning and effectiveness of groups and teams.

Managers need to take group size, group tasks, and group roles into account as they create and maintain high-performing groups and teams.

GROUP SIZE   The number of members in a group can be an important determinant of members' motivation and commitment and group performance. There are several advantages to keeping a group relatively small—between two and nine members. Compared with members of large groups, members of small groups tend to (1) interact more with each other and find it easier to coordinate their efforts, (2) be more motivated, satisfied, and committed, (3) find it easier to share information, and (4) be better able to see the importance of their personal contributions for group success. A disadvantage of small rather than large groups is that members of small groups have fewer resources available to accomplish their goals.

Large groups—with 10 or more members—also offer some advantages. They have more resources at their disposal to achieve group goals than small groups do. These resources include the knowledge, experience, skills, and abilities of group members as well as their actual time and effort. Large groups also let managers obtain the advantages stemming from the **division of labor**—splitting the work to be performed into particular tasks and assigning tasks to individual workers. Workers who specialize in particular tasks are likely to become skilled at performing those tasks and contribute significantly to high group performance.

division of labor Splitting the work to be performed into particular tasks and assigning tasks to individual workers.

The disadvantages of large groups include the problems of communication and coordination and the lower levels of motivation, satisfaction, and commitment that members of large groups sometimes experience. It is clearly more difficult to share information with, and coordinate the activities of, 16 people rather than 8 people. Moreover, members of large groups might not think their efforts are really needed and sometimes might not even feel a part of the group.

In deciding on the appropriate size for any group, managers attempt to gain the advantages of small group size and, at the same time, form groups with sufficient resources to accomplish their goals and have a well-developed division of labor. As a general rule of thumb, groups should have no more members than necessary to achieve a division of labor and provide the resources needed to achieve group goals. In R&D teams, for example, group size is too large when (1) members spend more time communicating what they know to others than applying what they know to solve problems and create new products, (2) individual productivity decreases, and (3) group performance suffers.[51]

task interdependence The degree to which the work performed by one member of a group influences the work performed by other members.

GROUP TASKS   The appropriate size of a high-performing group is affected by the kind of tasks the group is to perform. An important characteristic of group tasks that affects performance is **task interdependence**—the degree to which the work performed by one member

Figure 15.3
Types of Task Interdependence

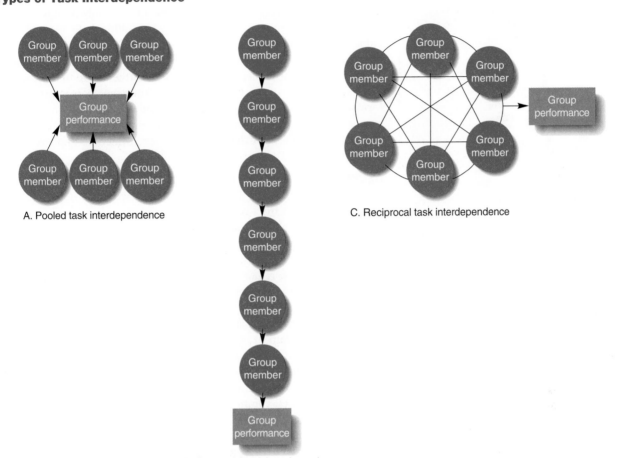

A. Pooled task interdependence

B. Sequential task interdependence

C. Reciprocal task interdependence

of a group influences the work performed by other members.[52] As task interdependence increases, group members need to interact more frequently and intensely with one another, and their efforts have to be more closely coordinated if they are to perform at a high level. Management expert James D. Thompson identified three types of task interdependence: pooled, sequential, and reciprocal (see Figure 15.3).[53]

pooled task interdependence The task interdependence that exists when group members make separate and independent contributions to group performance.

POOLED TASK INTERDEPENDENCE   Pooled task interdependence exists when group members make separate and independent contributions to group performance; overall group performance is the sum of the performance of the individual members (see Figure 15.3a). Examples of groups that have pooled task interdependence include a group of teachers in an elementary school, a group of salespeople in a department store, a group of secretaries in an office, and a group of custodians in an office building. In these examples, group performance, whether it is the number of children who are taught and the quality of their education, the dollar value of sales, the amount of secretarial work completed, or the number of offices cleaned, is determined by summing the individual contributions of group members.

For groups with pooled interdependence, managers should determine the appropriate group size primarily from the amount of work to be accomplished. Large groups can be effective because group members work independently and do not have to interact frequently with one another. Motivation in groups with pooled interdependence will be highest when managers reward group members based on individual performance.

sequential task interdependence The task interdependence that exists when group members must perform specific tasks in a predetermined order.

SEQUENTIAL TASK INTERDEPENDENCE   Sequential task interdependence exists when group members must perform specific tasks in a predetermined order; certain tasks have to be performed before others, and what one worker does affects the work of others (see Figure 15.3b). Assembly lines and mass-production processes are characterized by sequential task interdependence.

First the steak, then the green beans, then the carefully drizzled béarnaise; gourmet kitchens where the presentation is an integral part of the experience exemplify sequential task interdependence.

When group members are sequentially interdependent, group size is usually dictated by the needs of the production process—for example, the number of steps needed in an assembly line to efficiently produce a DVD player. With sequential interdependence, it is difficult to identify individual performance because one group member's performance depends on how well others perform their tasks. A slow worker at the start of an assembly line, for example, causes all workers further down to work slowly. Thus managers are often advised to reward group members for group performance. Group members will be motivated to perform at a high level because if the group performs well, each member will benefit. In addition, group members may put pressure on poor performers to improve so that group performance and rewards do not suffer.

RECIPROCAL TASK INTERDEPENDENCE Reciprocal task interdependence exists when the work performed by each group member is fully dependent on the work performed by other group members; group members have to share information, intensely interact with one another, and coordinate their efforts in order for the group to achieve its goals (see Figure 15.3c). In general, reciprocal task interdependence characterizes the operation of teams, rather than other kinds of groups. The task interdependence of R&D teams, top management teams, and many self-managed work teams is reciprocal.

When group members are reciprocally interdependent, managers are advised to keep group size relatively small because of the necessity of coordinating team members' activities. Communication difficulties can arise in teams with reciprocally interdependent tasks because team members need to interact frequently with one another and be available when needed. As group size increases, communication difficulties increase and can impair team performance.

When a group's members are reciprocally interdependent, managers also are advised to reward group members on the basis of group performance. Individual levels of performance are often difficult for managers to identify, and group-based rewards help ensure that group members will be motivated to perform at a high level and make valuable contributions to the group. Of course, if a manager can identify instances of individual performance in such groups, they too can be rewarded to maintain high levels of motivation. Microsoft and many other companies reward group members for their individual performance as well as for the performance of their group.

reciprocal task interdependence The task interdependence that exists when the work performed by each group member is fully dependent on the work performed by other group members.

group role A set of behaviors and tasks that a member of a group is expected to perform because of his or her position in the group.

GROUP ROLES A **group role** is a set of behaviors and tasks that a member of a group is expected to perform because of his or her position in the group. Members of cross-functional teams, for example, are expected to perform roles relevant to their special areas of expertise. In our earlier example of cross-functional teams at Hallmark Cards, it is the role of writers on the teams to create verses for new cards, the role of artists to draw illustrations, and the role of designers to put verse and artwork together in an attractive and appealing card design. The roles of members of top management teams are shaped primarily by their areas of expertise—production, marketing, finance, research and development—but members of top management teams also typically draw on their broad expertise as planners and strategists.

In forming groups and teams, managers need to clearly communicate to group members the expectations for their roles in the group, what is required of them, and how the different roles in the group fit together to accomplish group goals. Managers also need to realize that group roles often change and evolve as a group's tasks and goals change and as group members gain experience and knowledge. Thus, to get the performance gains that come from experience or "learning by doing," managers should encourage group members to take the initiative to assume additional responsibilities as they see fit and modify their assigned roles. This process, called **role making**, can enhance individual and group performance.

role making Taking the initiative to modify an assigned role by assuming additional responsibilities.

In self-managed work teams and some other groups, group members themselves are responsible for creating and assigning roles. Many self-managed work teams also pick their own team leaders. When group members create their own roles, managers should be available to group members in an advisory capacity, helping them effectively settle conflicts and disagreements. At Johnsonville Foods, for example, the position titles of first-line managers were changed to "advisory coach" to reflect the managers' role vis-à-vis the self-managed work teams they oversaw.[54]

Group Leadership

All groups and teams need leadership. Indeed, as we discussed in detail in Chapter 14, effective leadership is a key ingredient for high-performing groups, teams, and organizations. Sometimes managers assume the leadership role in groups and teams, as is the case in many command groups and top management teams. Or a manager may appoint a member of a group who is not a manager to be group leader or chairperson, as is the case in a task force or standing committee. In other cases, group or team members may choose their own leaders, or a leader may emerge naturally as group members work together to achieve group goals. When managers empower members of self-managed work teams, they often let group members choose their own leaders. Some self-managed work teams find it effective to rotate the leadership role among their members. Whether or not leaders of groups and teams are managers, and whether they are appointed by managers (often referred to as *formal leaders*) or emerge naturally in a group (often referred to as *informal leaders*), they play an important role in ensuring that groups and teams perform up to their potential.

When teams do not live up to their promise, sometimes the problem is a lack of team leadership, as illustrated in the following "Ethics in Action" box.

Ethics in Action

Leadership in Teams at ICU Medical

Dr. George Lopez, an internal medicine physician, founded ICU Medical in San Clemente, California, in 1984 after a patient of his accidentally died when an intravenous (IV) line became inadvertently disconnected.[55] Lopez thought there must be a better way to design components of IV lines so that these kinds of tragic accidents don't happen. He developed a product called the Click Lock, which has both a locking mechanism for IV systems and also a protected needle so that health care workers are protected from accidental needle pricks.[56] Today ICU Medical has over 2,100 employees, and in 2011 revenues were over $302 million.[57] Lopez is CEO of the company, which made *Forbes* magazine's list of "The 200 Best Small Companies."[58] ICU Medical continues to focus on the development and manufacture of products that improve the functioning of IV lines and systems while protecting health care workers from accidental needle pricks.[59] For example, the CLAVE NeedleFree Connector for IV lines is one of ICU Medical's top-selling products.[60]

In the early 1990s, Lopez experienced something not uncommon to successful entrepreneurs as their businesses grow. As the entrepreneur–CEO, he continued to make the majority of important decisions himself; yet he had close to 100 employees, demand for the CLAVE was very high, and he was starting to feel overloaded to the point where he would often sleep at nights in the office.[61] After watching one of his son's hockey games, he realized that a well-functioning team could work wonders; in the case of the hockey game, although the opposing team had an outstanding player, his son's team really pulled together as a team and was able to win the game despite the rival team's outstanding member. Lopez decided to empower employees to form teams to work on a pressing goal for ICU Medical: increasing production.[62] While

Self-managed teams with strong leaders and carefully thought-out guidelines for how to evaluate group decisions make all the difference for such companies as ICU Medical.

employees did form teams and spent a lot of time in team interactions, the teams did not seem to come up with any real tangible results, perhaps because there were no team leaders in place and the teams had no guidelines to help them accomplish their goals.[63]

In an effort to improve team effectiveness, Lopez told employees that teams should elect team leaders. And together with Jim Reitz, ICU Medical's director of human resources, Lopez came up with rules or guidelines teams should follow, such as "challenge the issue, not the person" and "stand up for your position, but never argue against the facts."[64] ICU Medical also started to reward team members for their team's contributions to organizational effectiveness. With these changes, Reitz and Lopez were striving to ensure that teams had leaders, had some guidelines for team member behavior, and were rewarded for their contributions to organizational effectiveness but, at the same time, were not bogged down by unnecessary constraints and structures and were truly self-managing.[65]

With these changes in place, teams at ICU Medical began to live up to their promise. Today any ICU Medical employee can create a team to address a problem, seize an opportunity, or work on a project ranging from developing a new product to making improvements in the physical work environment.[66] The teams have leaders and are self-managing.

Recognizing that self-managed teams still need rules, guidelines, leadership, and structure, a team of employees developed a 25-page guidebook for effective team functioning. And to ensure that teams learn from each other as well as get feedback, teams are required to put up notes from each of their meetings on ICU Medical's intranet, and any employee can provide feedback to any of the teams.[67] All in all, effectively led teams have helped ICU Medical prosper in its efforts to develop and manufacture products that protect the safety of both patients and health care workers.

Group Development over Time

As many managers overseeing self-managed teams have learned, it sometimes takes a self-managed work team two or three years to perform up to its true capabilities.[68] As their experience suggests, what a group is capable of achieving depends in part on its stage of development. Knowing that it takes considerable time for self-managed work teams to get up and running has helped managers have realistic expectations for new teams and know that they need to give new team members considerable training and guidance.

Although every group's development over time is unique, researchers have identified five stages of group development that many groups seem to pass through (see Figure 15.4).[69] In the first stage, *forming,* members try to get to know one another and reach a common understanding of what the group is trying to accomplish and how group members should behave. During this stage, managers should strive to make each member feel that he or she is a valued part of the group.

In the second stage, *storming,* group members experience conflict and disagreements because some members do not wish to submit to the demands of other group members. Disputes may arise over who should lead the group. Self-managed work teams can be particularly vulnerable during the storming stage. Managers need to keep an eye on groups at this stage to make sure conflict does not get out of hand.

During the third stage, *norming,* close ties between group members develop, and feelings of friendship and camaraderie emerge. Group members arrive at a consensus about what goals

Figure 15.4

Five Stages of Group Development

they should seek to achieve and how group members should behave toward one another. In the fourth stage, *performing,* the real work of the group gets accomplished. Depending on the type of group in question, managers need to take different steps at this stage to help ensure that groups are effective. Managers of command groups need to make sure that group members are motivated and that they are effectively leading group members. Managers overseeing self-managed work teams have to empower team members and make sure teams are given enough responsibility and autonomy at the performing stage.

The last stage, *adjourning,* applies only to groups that eventually are disbanded, such as task forces. During adjourning a group is dispersed. Sometimes adjourning takes place when a group completes a finished product, such as when a task force evaluating the pros and cons of providing on-site child care produces a report supporting its recommendation.

Managers should have a flexible approach to group development and should keep attuned to the different needs and requirements of groups at the various stages.[70] Above all else, and regardless of the stage of development, managers need to think of themselves as *resources* for groups. Thus managers always should strive to find ways to help groups and teams function more effectively.

Group Norms

LO15-4 Explain why it is important for groups and teams to have a balance of conformity and deviance and a moderate level of cohesiveness.

group norms Shared guidelines or rules for behavior that most group members follow.

All groups, whether top management teams, self-managed work teams, or command groups, need to control their members' behaviors to ensure that the group performs at a high level and meets its goals. Assigning roles to each group member is one way to control behavior in groups. Another important way in which groups influence members' behavior is through the development and enforcement of group norms.[71] **Group norms** are shared guidelines or rules for behavior that most group members follow. Groups develop norms concerning a wide variety of behaviors, including working hours, the sharing of information among group members, how certain group tasks should be performed, and even how members of a group should dress.

Managers should encourage members of a group to develop norms that contribute to group performance and the attainment of group goals. For example, group norms dictating that each member of a cross-functional team should always be available for the rest of the team when his or her input is needed, return phone calls as soon as possible, inform other team members of travel plans, and give team members a phone number at which he or she can be reached when traveling on business help to ensure that the team is efficient, performs at a high level, and achieves its goals. A norm in a command group of secretaries that dictates that secretaries who happen to have a light workload in any given week should help out secretaries with heavier workloads helps to ensure that the group completes all assignments in a timely and efficient manner. And a norm in a top management team that dictates that team members should always consult with one another before making major decisions helps to ensure that good decisions are made with a minimum of errors.

CONFORMITY AND DEVIANCE Group members conform to norms for three reasons: (1) They want to obtain rewards and avoid punishments. (2) They want to imitate group members whom they like and admire. (3) They have internalized the norm and believe it is the right and proper way to behave.[72] Consider the case of Robert King, who conformed to his department's norm of attending a fund-raiser for a community food bank. King's conformity could be due to (1) his desire to be a member of the group in good standing and to have friendly relationships with other group members (rewards), (2) his copying the behavior of other members of the department whom he respects and who always attend the fund-raiser (imitating other group members), or (3) his belief in the merits of supporting the activities of the food bank (believing that is the right and proper way to behave).

Failure to conform, or deviance, occurs when a member of a group violates a group norm. Deviance signals that a group is not controlling one of its member's behaviors. Groups generally respond to members who behave defiantly in one of three ways:[73]

1. The group might try to get the member to change his or her deviant ways and conform to the norm. Group members might try to convince the member of the need to conform, or they might ignore or even punish the deviant. For example, in a Jacksonville Foods plant, Liz Senkbiel, a member of a self-managed work team responsible for weighing sausages, failed to conform to a group norm dictating that group members should periodically clean up an untidy interview room. Because Senkbiel refused to take part in the team's cleanup efforts, team members reduced her monthly bonus by about $225 for a two-month period.[74] Senkbiel clearly learned the costs of deviant behavior in her team.

2. The group might expel the member.

3. The group might change the norm to be consistent with the member's behavior.

This last alternative suggests that some deviant behavior can be functional for groups. Deviance is functional for a group when it causes group members to evaluate norms that may be dysfunctional but are taken for granted by the group. Often group members do not think about why they behave in a certain way or why they follow certain norms. Deviance can cause group members to reflect on their norms and change them when appropriate.

Consider a group of receptionists in a beauty salon who followed the norm that all appointments would be handwritten in an appointment book and, at the end of each day, the receptionist on duty would enter the appointments into the salon's computer system, which printed out the hairdressers' daily schedules. One day a receptionist decided to enter appointments directly into the computer system when they were being made, bypassing the appointment book. This deviant behavior caused the other receptionists to think about why they were using the appointment book at all. After consulting with the owner of the salon, the group changed its norm. Now appointments are entered directly into the computer, which saves time and reduces scheduling errors.

ENCOURAGING A BALANCE OF CONFORMITY AND DEVIANCE To effectively help an organization gain a competitive advantage, groups and teams need the right balance of conformity and deviance (see Figure 15.5). A group needs a certain level of conformity to ensure that it can control members' behavior and channel it in the direction of high

Figure 15.5

Balancing Conformity and Deviance in Groups

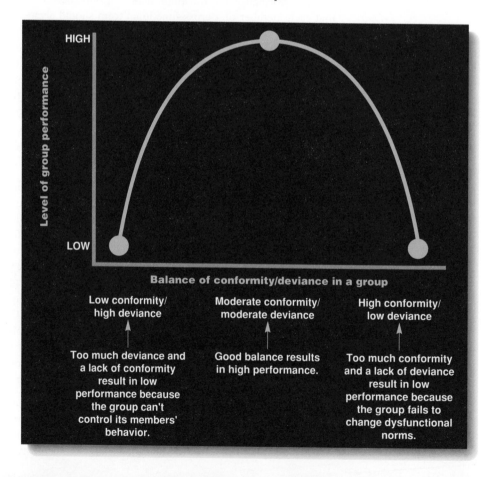

performance and group goal accomplishment. A group also needs a certain level of deviance to ensure that dysfunctional norms are discarded and replaced with functional ones. Balancing conformity and deviance is a pressing concern for all groups, whether they are top management teams, R&D teams, command groups, or self-managed work teams.

The extent of conformity and reactions to deviance within groups are determined by group members themselves. The three bases for conformity just described are powerful forces that more often than not result in group members' conforming to norms. Sometimes these forces are so strong that deviance rarely occurs in groups, and when it does, it is stamped out.

Managers can take several steps to ensure adequate tolerance of deviance in groups so that group members are willing to deviate from dysfunctional norms and, when deviance occurs in their group, reflect on the appropriateness of the violated norm and change the norm if necessary. First, managers can be role models for the groups and teams they oversee. When managers encourage and accept employees' suggestions for changes in procedures, do not rigidly insist that tasks be accomplished in a certain way, and admit when a norm they once supported is no longer functional, they signal to group members that conformity should not come at the expense of needed changes and improvements. Second, managers should let employees know that there are always ways to improve group processes and performance levels and thus opportunities to replace existing norms with norms that will better enable a group to achieve its goals and perform at a high level. Third, managers should encourage members of groups and teams to periodically assess the appropriateness of their norms.

Managers in the innovative design firm IDEO, based in Palo Alto, California (IDEO's culture is described in Chapter 3), have excelled at ensuring that design teams have the right mix of conformity and deviance, resulting in IDEO's designing products in fields ranging from medicine to space travel to computing and personal hygiene, as indicated in the following "Management Insight" box.

Management Insight

Teams Benefit from Deviance and Conformity at IDEO

IDEO has designed many products we now take for granted: the first Apple mouse, stand-up toothpaste containers, flexible shelving for offices, self-sealing drink bottles for sports, blood analyzers, and even equipment used in space travel.[75] Managers and designers at IDEO take pride in being experts at the process of innovation in general, rather than in any particular domain. Of course the company has technical design experts, such as mechanical and electrical engineers, who work on products requiring specialized knowledge; but on the same teams with the engineers might be an anthropologist, a biologist, and a social scientist.[76]

A guiding principle at IDEO is that innovation comes in many shapes and sizes, and it is only through diversity in thought that people can recognize opportunities for innovation. To promote such diversity in thought, new product development at IDEO is a team effort.[77] Moreover, both conformity and deviance are encouraged on IDEO teams.

Deviance, thinking differently, and not conforming to expected ways of doing things and mind-sets are encouraged at IDEO. In fact, innovative ideas often flow when designers try to see things as they really are and are not blinded by thoughts of what is appropriate, what is possible, or how things should be. Often constraints on new product design are created by designers themselves conforming to a certain mind-set about the nature of a product

Deviance, or the capacity to think differently from the status quo, is promoted by IDEO's diverse employee teams, which might include artists, biologists, and anthropologists.

or what a product can or should do and look like. IDEO designers are encouraged to actively break down these constraints in their design teams.[78]

Managers at IDEO realize the need for a certain amount of conformity so members of design teams can work effectively together and achieve their goals. Thus conformity to a few central norms is emphasized in IDEO teams. These norms include understanding what the team is working on (the product, market, or client need), observing real people in their natural environments, visualizing how new products might work and be used, evaluating and refining product prototypes, encouraging wild ideas, and never rejecting an idea simply because it sounds too crazy.[79] As long as these norms are followed, diversity of thought and even deviance promote innovation at IDEO. In fact, another norm at IDEO is to study "rule breakers"—people who don't follow instructions for products, for example, or who try to put products to different uses—because these individuals might help designers identify problems with existing products and unmet consumer needs.[80] All in all, IDEO's focus on encouraging both deviance and conformity in design teams has benefited all of us—we use IDEO-designed products that seem so familiar we take them for granted. We forget these products did not exist until a design team at IDEO was called on by a client to develop a new product or improve an existing one.[81]

Group Cohesiveness

group cohesiveness The degree to which members are attracted to or loyal to their group.

Another important element of group dynamics that affects group performance and effectiveness is **group cohesiveness**, which is the degree to which members are attracted to or loyal to their group or team.[82] When group cohesiveness is high, individuals strongly value their group membership, find the group appealing, and have strong desires to remain a part of the group. When group cohesiveness is low, group members do not find their group particularly appealing and have little desire to retain their group membership. Research suggests that managers should strive to have a moderate level of cohesiveness in the groups and teams they manage because that is most likely to contribute to an organization's competitive advantage.

CONSEQUENCES OF GROUP COHESIVENESS   There are three major consequences of group cohesiveness: level of participation within a group, level of conformity to group norms, and emphasis on group goal accomplishment (see Figure 15.6).[83]

LEVEL OF PARTICIPATION WITHIN A GROUP   As group cohesiveness increases, the extent of group members' participation within the group increases. Participation contributes to group

Figure 15.6

Sources and Consequences of Group Cohesiveness

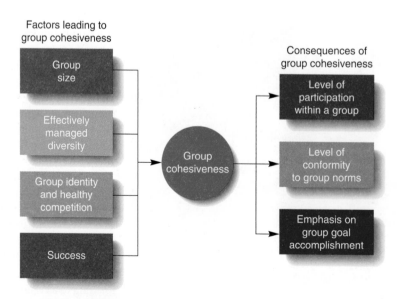

effectiveness because group members are actively involved in the group, ensure that group tasks get accomplished, readily share information with each other, and have frequent and open communication (the important topic of communication is covered in depth in Chapter 16).

A moderate level of group cohesiveness helps ensure that group members actively participate in the group and communicate effectively with one another. The reason why managers may not want to encourage high levels of cohesiveness is illustrated by the example of two cross-functional teams responsible for developing new toys. Members of the highly cohesive Team Alpha often have lengthy meetings that usually start with nonwork-related conversations and jokes, meet more often than most of the other cross-functional teams in the company, and spend a good portion of their time communicating the ins and outs of their department's contribution to toy development to other team members. Members of the moderately cohesive Team Beta generally have efficient meetings in which ideas are communicated and discussed as needed, do not meet more often than necessary, and share the ins and outs of their expertise with one another to the extent needed for the development process. Teams Alpha and Beta have both developed some top-selling toys. However, it generally takes Team Alpha 30% longer to do so than Team Beta. This is why too much cohesiveness can be too much of a good thing.

LEVEL OF CONFORMITY TO GROUP NORMS   Increasing levels of group cohesiveness result in increasing levels of conformity to group norms, and when cohesiveness becomes high, there may be so little deviance in groups that group members conform to norms even when they are dysfunctional. In contrast, low cohesiveness can result in too much deviance and undermine the ability of a group to control its members' behaviors to get things done.

Teams Alpha and Beta in the toy company both had the same norm for toy development. It dictated that members of each team would discuss potential ideas for new toys, decide on a line of toys to pursue, and then have the team member from R&D design a prototype. Recently a new animated movie featuring a family of rabbits produced by a small film company was an unexpected hit, and major toy companies were scrambling to reach licensing agreements to produce toy lines featuring the rabbits. The top management team in the toy company assigned Teams Alpha and Beta to develop the new toy lines quickly to beat the competition.

Members of Team Alpha followed their usual toy development norm even though the marketing expert on the team believed the process could have been streamlined to save time. The marketing expert on Team Beta urged the team to deviate from its toy development norm. She suggested that the team not have R&D develop prototypes but, instead, modify top-selling toys the company already made to feature rabbits and then reach a licensing agreement with the film company based on the high sales potential (given the company's prior success). Once the licensing agreement was signed, the company could take the time needed to develop innovative and unique rabbit toys with more input from R&D.

As a result of the willingness of the marketing expert on Team Beta to deviate from the norm for toy development, the toy company obtained an exclusive licensing agreement with the film company and had its first rabbit toys on the shelves of stores in a record three months. Groups need a balance of conformity and deviance, so a moderate level of cohesiveness often yields the best outcome, as it did in the case of Team Beta.

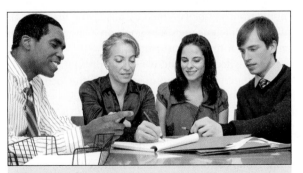

How much cohesiveness is too much? You can answer that question when you evaluate whether a group actually gets something done in its meetings or whether most of the conversation drifting out of the room consists of jokes, life experiences, or comparisons of the last company dinner's entrees.

EMPHASIS ON GROUP GOAL ACCOMPLISHMENT   As group cohesiveness increases, the emphasis placed on group goal accomplishment also increases within a group. A strong emphasis on group goal accomplishment, however, does not always lead to organizational effectiveness. For an organization to be effective and gain a competitive advantage, the different groups and teams in the organization must cooperate with one another and be motivated to achieve *organizational goals,* even if doing so sometimes comes at the expense of the achievement of group goals. A moderate level of cohesiveness motivates group members to accomplish both group and organizational goals. High levels of cohesiveness can cause group members to be so focused on group goal accomplishment that they may strive to achieve group goals no matter what—even when doing so jeopardizes organizational performance.

At the toy company, the major goal of the cross-functional teams was to develop new toy lines that were truly innovative, utilized the latest in technology, and were in some way fundamentally distinct from other toys on the market. When it came to the rabbit project, Team Alpha's high level of cohesiveness contributed to its continued emphasis on its group goal of developing an innovative line of toys; thus the team stuck with its usual design process. Team Beta, in contrast, realized that developing the new line of toys quickly was an important organizational goal that should take precedence over the group's goal of developing groundbreaking new toys, at least in the short term. Team Beta's moderate level of cohesiveness contributed to team members' doing what was best for the toy company in this case.

FACTORS LEADING TO GROUP COHESIVENESS   Four factors contribute to the level of group cohesiveness (see Figure 15.6).[84] By influencing these *determinants of group cohesiveness,* managers can raise or lower the level of cohesiveness to promote moderate levels of cohesiveness in groups and teams.

GROUP SIZE   As we mentioned earlier, members of small groups tend to be more motivated and committed than members of large groups. Thus to promote cohesiveness in groups, when feasible, managers should form groups that are small to medium in size (about 2 to 15 members). If a group is low in cohesiveness and large in size, managers might want to consider dividing the group in half and assigning different tasks and goals to the two newly formed groups.

EFFECTIVELY MANAGED DIVERSITY   In general, people tend to like and get along with others who are similar to themselves. It is easier to communicate with someone, for example, who shares your values, has a similar background, and has had similar experiences. However, as discussed in Chapter 5, diversity in groups, teams, and organizations can help an organization gain a competitive advantage. Diverse groups often come up with more innovative and creative ideas. One reason why cross-functional teams are so popular in organizations like Hallmark Cards is that the diverse expertise represented in the teams results in higher levels of team performance.

In forming groups and teams, managers need to make sure the diversity in knowledge, experience, expertise, and other characteristics necessary for group goal accomplishment is represented in the new groups. Managers then have to make sure this diversity in group membership is effectively managed so groups will be cohesive (see Chapter 5).

GROUP IDENTITY AND HEALTHY COMPETITION   When group cohesiveness is low, managers can often increase it by encouraging groups to develop their own identities or personalities and engage in healthy competition. This is precisely what managers at Eaton Corporation's manufacturing facility in Lincoln, Illinois, did. Eaton's employees manufacture products such as engine valves, gears, truck axles, and circuit breakers. Managers at Eaton created self-managed work teams to cut costs and improve performance. They realized, however, that the teams would have to be cohesive to ensure that they would strive to achieve their goals. Managers promoted group identity by having the teams give themselves names such as "The Hoods," "The Worms," and "Scrap Attack" (a team striving to reduce costly scrap metal waste by 50%). Healthy competition among groups was promoted by displaying measures of each team's performance and the extent to which teams met their goals on a large TV screen in the cafeteria and by rewarding team members for team performance.[85]

If groups are too cohesive, managers can try to decrease cohesiveness by promoting organizational (rather than group) identity and making the organization as a whole the focus of the group's efforts. Organizational identity can be promoted by making group members feel that they are valued members of the organization and by stressing cooperation across groups to promote the achievement of organizational goals. Excessive levels of cohesiveness also can be reduced by reducing or eliminating competition among groups and rewarding cooperation.

SUCCESS   When it comes to promoting group cohesiveness, there is more than a grain of truth to the saying "Nothing succeeds like success." As groups become more successful, they become increasingly attractive to their members, and their cohesiveness tends to increase. When cohesiveness is low, managers can increase cohesiveness by making sure a group can achieve some noticeable and visible successes.

Consider a group of salespeople in the housewares department of a medium-size department store. The housewares department was recently moved to a corner of the store's basement. Its remote location resulted in low sales because of infrequent customer traffic in that part of the store. The salespeople, who were generally evaluated favorably by their supervisors and were valued members of the store, tried various initiatives to boost sales, but to no avail. As a result of this lack of success and the poor performance of their department, their cohesiveness started to plummet. To increase and preserve the cohesiveness of the group, the store manager implemented a group-based incentive across the store. In any month, members of the group with the best attendance and punctuality records would have their names and pictures posted on a bulletin board in the cafeteria and would each receive a $50 gift certificate. The housewares group frequently had the best records, and their success on this dimension helped to build and maintain their cohesiveness. Moreover, this initiative boosted attendance and discouraged lateness throughout the store.

Managing Groups and Teams for High Performance

Now that you understand why groups and teams are so important for organizations, the types of groups managers create, and group dynamics, we consider some additional steps managers can take to make sure groups and teams perform at a high level and contribute to organizational effectiveness. Managers striving to have top-performing groups and teams need to (1) motivate group members to work toward the achievement of organizational goals, (2) reduce social loafing, and (3) help groups manage conflict effectively.

LO15-5 Describe how managers can motivate group members to achieve organizational goals and reduce social loafing in groups and teams.

Motivating Group Members to Achieve Organizational Goals

When work is difficult, tedious, or requires a high level of commitment and energy, managers cannot assume group members will always be motivated to work toward the achievement of organizational goals. Consider a group of house painters who paint the interiors and exteriors of new homes for a construction company and are paid on an hourly basis. Why should they strive to complete painting jobs quickly and efficiently if doing so will just make them feel more tired at the end of the day and they will not receive any tangible benefits? It makes more sense for the painters to adopt a relaxed approach, to take frequent breaks, and to work at a leisurely pace. This relaxed approach, however, impairs the construction company's ability to gain a competitive advantage because it raises costs and increases the time needed to complete a new home.

Managers can motivate members of groups and teams to achieve organizational goals by making sure the members themselves benefit when the group or team performs highly. For example, if members of a self-managed work team know they will receive a weekly bonus based on team performance, they will be motivated to perform at a high level.

Managers often rely on some combination of individual and group-based incentives to motivate members of groups and teams to work toward the achievement of organizational goals. When individual performance within a group can be assessed, pay is often determined by individual performance or by both individual and group performance. When individual performance within a group cannot be accurately assessed, group performance should be the key determinant of pay levels. Many companies that use self-managed work teams base team members' pay in part on team performance.[86] A major challenge for managers is to develop a fair pay system that will lead to both high individual motivation and high group or team performance.

Other benefits managers can make available to high-performance group members—in addition to monetary rewards—include extra resources such as equipment and computer software, awards and other forms of recognition, and choice of future work assignments. For example, members of self-managed work teams that develop new software at companies such as Microsoft often value working on interesting and important projects; members of teams that have performed at a high level are rewarded by being assigned to interesting and important new projects.

At IDEO (profiled earlier in a "Management Insight" box), managers motivate team members by making them feel important. As Tom Kelley, IDEO's general manager, puts it, "When people feel special, they'll perform beyond your wildest dreams."[87] To make IDEO team members feel special, IDEO managers plan unique and fun year-end parties, give teams the opportunity to take time off if they feel they need or want to, encourage teams to take field trips, and see pranks as a way to incorporate fun into the workplace.[88]

Valero Energy motivates groups and teams to achieve organizational goals by valuing its employees, looking out for their well-being, and standing by them in crisis situations.[89] For example, employees with medical emergencies can use Valero's corporate jet if they need to, and Valero covers the complete cost of employee's health insurance premiums.[90] In turn, group members put forth high levels of effort to help Valero achieve its goals. As former Valero CEO and chairman Bill Greehey put it, "The more you do for your employees, the more they do for shareholders and the more they do for the community."[91]

When Hurricane Katrina hit the Louisiana coastline in 2005, the way Valero stood by employees in its St. Charles oil refinery near New Orleans, and the way employees stood by each other and the company, brought plant manager Jonathan Stuart to tears as he was briefing Greehey and other top managers a few days after the hurricane hit.[92] Stuart led a 50-person crew that rode out the hurricane in the shut-down refinery. The day before the storm hit, a supervisor used his personal credit card to buy supplies and stayed up all night preparing meals for the crew. Crew members worked round the clock, putting up new power poles, repairing power lines, and replacing motors. The refinery was up and running within eight days (while a Shell refinery close by was still shut down), and the crew had located all of the plant's 570 employees.[93]

Valero's headquarters had supplies delivered to employees whose homes were damaged; trucks brought in food, water, generators, chain saws, refrigerators, shovels, and Nextel phones (the only cell phone system that was still working). Sixty mobile homes were brought in for employees whose houses were unlivable. Employees and law enforcement personnel were given free fuel, and employees were given up to $10,000 in aide from Valero's SAFE fund. Valero continued issuing paychecks to its employees while other affected refineries did not.[94]

Reducing Social Loafing in Groups

We have been focusing on the steps managers can take to encourage high levels of performance in groups. Managers, however, need to be aware of an important downside to group and team work: the potential for social loafing, which reduces group performance. **Social loafing** is the tendency of individuals to put forth less effort when they work in groups than when they work alone.[95] Have you ever worked on a group project in which one or two group members never seemed to be pulling their weight? Have you ever worked in a student club or committee in which some members always seemed to be missing meetings and never volunteered for activities? Have you ever had a job in which one or two of your coworkers seemed to be slacking off because they knew you or other members of your work group would make up for their low levels of effort? If so, you have witnessed social loafing in action.

Social loafing can occur in all kinds of groups and teams and in all kinds of organizations. It can result in lower group performance and may even prevent a group from attaining its goals. Fortunately managers can take steps to reduce social loafing and sometimes completely eliminate it; we will look at three (see Figure 15.7):

1. *Make individual contributions to a group identifiable.* Some people may engage in social loafing when they work in groups because they think they can hide in the crowd—no one will notice if they put forth less effort than they should. Other people may think if they put forth high levels of effort and make substantial contributions to the group, their contributions will not be noticed and they will receive no rewards for their work—so why bother.[96]

One way that managers can effectively eliminate social loafing is by making individual contributions to a group identifiable so that group members perceive that low and high levels of effort will be noticed and individual contributions evaluated.[97] Managers can accomplish this by assigning specific tasks to group members and holding them accountable for their

social loafing The tendency of individuals to put forth less effort when they work in groups than when they work alone.

Figure 15.7
Three Ways to Reduce Social Loafing

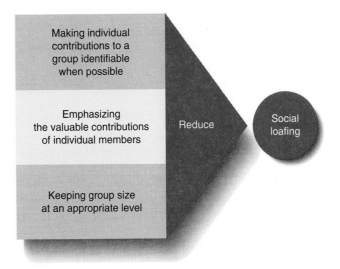

completion. Take the case of a group of eight employees responsible for reshelving returned books in a large public library in New York. The head librarian was concerned that there was always a backlog of seven or eight carts of books to be reshelved, even though the employees never seemed to be particularly busy and some even found time to sit down and read newspapers and magazines. The librarian decided to try to eliminate the apparent social loafing by assigning each employee sole responsibility for reshelving a particular section of the library. Because the library's front desk employees sorted the books by section on the carts as they were returned, holding the shelvers responsible for particular sections was easily accomplished. Once the shelvers knew the librarian could identify their effort or lack thereof, there were rarely any backlogs of books to be reshelved.

Sometimes the members of a group can cooperate to eliminate social loafing by making individual contributions identifiable. For example, in a small security company, members of a self-managed work team who assemble control boxes for home alarm systems start each day by deciding who will perform which tasks that day and how much work each member and the group as a whole should strive to accomplish. Each team member knows that, at the end of the day, the other team members will know exactly how much he or she has accomplished. With this system in place, social loafing never occurs in the team. Remember, however, that in some teams, individual contributions cannot be made identifiable, as in teams whose members are reciprocally interdependent.

2. *Emphasize the valuable contributions of individual members.* Another reason why social loafing may occur is that people sometimes think their efforts are unnecessary or unimportant when they work in a group. They feel the group will accomplish its goals and perform at an acceptable level whether or not they personally perform at a high level. To counteract this belief, when managers form groups, they should assign individuals to a group on the basis of the valuable contributions that *each* person can make to the group as a whole. Clearly communicating to group members why each person's contributions are valuable to the group is an effective means by which managers and group members themselves can reduce or eliminate social loafing.[98] This is most clearly illustrated in cross-functional teams, where each member's valuable contribution to the team derives from a personal area of expertise. By emphasizing why each member's skills are important, managers can reduce social loafing in such teams.

3. *Keep group size at an appropriate level.* Group size is related to the causes of social loafing we just described. As size increases, identifying individual contributions becomes increasingly difficult, and members are increasingly likely to think their individual contributions are not important. To overcome this, managers should form groups with no more members than are needed to accomplish group goals and perform at a high level.[99]

Helping Groups to Manage Conflict Effectively

At some point or other, practically all groups experience conflict either within the group (*intragroup* conflict) or with other groups (*intergroup* conflict). In Chapter 17 we discuss conflict in depth and explore ways to manage it effectively. As you will learn, managers can take several steps to help groups manage conflict and disagreements.

Summary and Review

LO15-1

GROUPS, TEAMS, AND ORGANIZATIONAL EFFECTIVENESS A group is two or more people who interact with each other to accomplish certain goals or meet certain needs. A team is a group whose members work intensely with one another to achieve a specific common goal or objective. Groups and teams can contribute to organizational effectiveness by enhancing performance, increasing responsiveness to customers, increasing innovation, and being a source of motivation for their members.

LO15-2 **TYPES OF GROUPS AND TEAMS** Formal groups are groups that managers establish to achieve organizational goals; they include cross-functional teams, cross-cultural teams, top management teams, research and development teams, command groups, task forces, self-managed work teams, and virtual teams. Informal groups are groups that employees form because they believe the groups will help them achieve their own goals or meet their needs; they include friendship groups and interest groups.

LO15-3 **GROUP DYNAMICS** Key elements of group dynamics are group size, tasks, and roles; group leadership; group development; group norms; and group cohesiveness. The advantages and disadvantages of large and small groups suggest that managers should form groups with no more members than are needed to provide the group with the human resources it needs to achieve its goals and use a division of labor. The type of task interdependence that characterizes a group's work gives managers a clue about the appropriate size of the group. A group role is a set of behaviors and tasks that a member of a group is expected to perform because of his or her position in the group. All groups and teams need leadership.

LO15-3, 15-4 Five stages of development that many groups pass through are forming, storming, norming, performing, and adjourning. Group norms are shared rules for behavior that most group members follow. To be effective, groups need a balance of conformity and deviance. Conformity allows a group to control its members' behavior to achieve group goals; deviance provides the impetus for needed change.

LO15-4 Group cohesiveness is the attractiveness of a group or team to its members. As group cohesiveness increases, so do the level of participation and communication within a group, the level of conformity to group norms, and the emphasis on group goal accomplishment. Managers should strive to achieve a moderate level of group cohesiveness in the groups and teams they manage.

LO15-5 **MANAGING GROUPS AND TEAMS FOR HIGH PERFORMANCE** To make sure groups and teams perform at a high level, managers need to motivate group members to work toward the achievement of organizational goals, reduce social loafing, and help groups to effectively manage conflict. Managers can motivate members of groups and teams to work toward the achievement of organizational goals by making sure members personally benefit when the group or team performs at a high level.

Management in Action

Topics for Discussion and Action

Discussion

1. Why do all organizations need to rely on groups and teams to achieve their goals and gain a competitive advantage? **[LO15-1]**

2. What kinds of employees would prefer to work in a virtual team? What kinds of employees would prefer to work in a team that meets face-to-face? **[LO15-2]**

3. Think about a group that you are a member of, and describe that group's current stage of development. Does the development of this group seem to be following the forming, storming, norming, performing, and adjourning stages described in the chapter? **[LO15-3]**

4. Think about a group of employees who work in a McDonald's restaurant. What type of task interdependence characterizes this group? What potential problems in the group should the restaurant manager be aware of and take steps to avoid? **[LO15-3]**

5. Discuss the reasons why too much conformity can hurt groups and their organizations. **[LO15-4]**

6. Why do some groups have very low levels of cohesiveness? **[LO15-4]**

7. Imagine that you are the manager of a hotel. What steps will you take to reduce social loafing by members of the cleaning staff who are responsible for keeping all common areas and guest rooms spotless? **[LO15-5]**

Action

8. Interview one or more managers in an organization in your local community to identify the types of groups and teams that the organization uses to achieve its goals. What challenges do these groups and teams face? **[LO15-2]**

Building Management Skills

Diagnosing Group Failures [LO15-1, 15-2, 15-3, 15-4, 15-5]

Think about the last dissatisfying or discouraging experience you had as a member of a group or team. Perhaps the group did not accomplish its goals, perhaps group members could agree about nothing, or perhaps there was too much social loafing. Now answer the following questions:

1. What type of group was this?

2. Were group members motivated to achieve group goals? Why or why not?

3. How large was the group, what type of task interdependence existed in the group, and what group roles did members play?

4. What were the group's norms? How much conformity and deviance existed in the group?

5. How cohesive was the group? Why do you think the group's cohesiveness was at this level? What consequences did this level of group cohesiveness have for the group and its members?

6. Was social loafing a problem in this group? Why or why not?

7. What could the group's leader or manager have done differently to increase group effectiveness?

8. What could group members have done differently to increase group effectiveness?

Managing Ethically [LO15-1, 15-2, 15-3, 15-4, 15-5]

Some self-managed teams encounter a vexing problem: One or more members engage in social loafing, and other members are reluctant to try to rectify the situation. Social loafing can be especially troubling if team members' pay is based on team performance and social loafing reduces the team's performance and thus the pay of all members (even the highest performers). Even if managers are aware of the problem, they may be reluctant to take action because the team is supposedly self-managing.

Questions

1. Either individually or in a group, think about the ethical implications of social loafing in a self-managed team.

2. Do managers have an ethical obligation to step in when they are aware of social loafing in a self-managed team? Why or why not? Do other team members have an obligation to try to curtail the social loafing? Why or why not?

Small Group Breakout Exercise

Creating a Cross-Functional Team [LO15-1, 15-2, 15-3, 15-4, 15-5]

Form groups of three or four people, and appoint one member as the spokesperson who will communicate your findings to the class when called on by the instructor. Then discuss the following scenario:

You are a group of managers in charge of food services for a large state university in the Midwest. Recently a survey of students, faculty, and staff was conducted to evaluate customer satisfaction with the food services provided by the university's eight cafeterias. The results were disappointing, to put it mildly. Complaints ranged from dissatisfaction with the type and range of meals and snacks provided, operating hours, and food temperature to frustration about unresponsiveness to current concerns about healthful diets and the needs of vegetarians. You have decided to form a cross-functional team that will further evaluate reactions to the food services and will develop a proposal for changes to be made to increase customer satisfaction.

1. Indicate who should be on this important cross-functional team, and explain why.

2. Describe the goals the team should strive to achieve.

3. Describe the different roles that will need to be performed on this team.

4. Describe the steps you will take to help ensure that the team has a good balance between conformity and deviance and has a moderate level of cohesiveness.

Exploring the World Wide Web [LO15-1, 15-2, 15-3, 15-4, 15-5]

Many consultants and organizations provide team-building services to organizations. Although some managers and teams have found these services to be helpful, others have found them to be a waste of time and money—another consulting fad that provides no real performance benefits. Search online for team-building services, and examine the websites of a few consultants/companies. Based on what you have read, what might be some advantages and disadvantages of team-building services? For what kinds of problems/issues might these services be beneficial, and when might they have little benefit or perhaps even do more harm than good?

Be the Manager [LO15-1, 15-2, 15-3, 15-4, 15-5]

You were recently hired in a boundary-spanning role for the global unit of an educational and professional publishing company. The company is headquartered in New York (where you work) and has divisions in multiple countries. Each division is responsible for translating, manufacturing, marketing, and selling a set of books in its country. Your responsibilities include interfacing with managers in each of the divisions in your region (Central and South America), overseeing their budgeting and financial reporting to headquarters, and leading a virtual team consisting of the top managers in charge of each of the divisions in your region. The virtual team's mission is to promote global learning, explore new potential opportunities and markets, and address ongoing problems. You communicate directly with division managers via telephone and e-mail, as well as written reports, memos, and faxes. When virtual team meetings are convened, videoconferencing is often used.

After your first few virtual team meetings, you noticed that the managers seemed to be reticent about speaking up. Interestingly enough, when each manager communicates with you individually, primarily in telephone conversations and e-mails, she or he tends to be forthcoming and frank, and you feel you have a good rapport with each of them. However, getting the managers to communicate with one another as a virtual team has been a real challenge. At the last meeting you tried to prompt some of the managers to raise issues relevant to the agenda that you knew were on their minds from your individual conversations with them. Surprisingly, the managers skillfully avoided informing their teammates about the heart of the issues in question. You are confused and troubled. Although you feel your other responsibilities are going well, you know your virtual team is not operating like a team at all; and no matter what you try, discussions in virtual team meetings are forced and generally unproductive. What are you going to do to address this problem?

New York Times Case in the News

[LO15-1, 15-2, 15-3, 15-4, 15-5]

The Rise of the New Groupthink

Solitude is out of fashion. Our companies, our schools and our culture are in thrall to an idea I call the New Groupthink, which holds that creativity and achievement come from an oddly gregarious place. Most of us now work in teams, in offices without walls, for managers who prize people skills above all. Lone geniuses are out. Collaboration is in.

But there's a problem with this view. Research strongly suggests that people are more creative when they enjoy privacy and freedom from interruption. And the most spectacularly creative people in many fields are often introverted, according to studies by the psychologists Mihaly Csikszentmihalyi and Gregory Feist. They're extroverted enough to exchange and advance ideas, but see themselves as independent and individualistic. They're not joiners by nature.

One explanation for these findings is that introverts are comfortable working alone—and solitude is a catalyst to innovation. As the influential psychologist Hans Eysenck observed, introversion fosters creativity by "concentrating the mind on the tasks in hand, and preventing the dissipation of energy on social and sexual matters unrelated to work." In other words, a person sitting quietly under a tree in the backyard, while everyone else is clinking glasses on the patio, is more likely to have an apple land on his head. (Newton was one of the world's great introverts: William Wordsworth described him as "A mind for ever/Voyaging through strange seas of Thought, alone.")

Solitude has long been associated with creativity and transcendence. "Without great solitude, no serious work is possible," Picasso said. A central narrative of many religions is the seeker—Moses, Jesus, Buddha—who goes off by himself and brings profound insights back to the community.

Culturally, we're often so dazzled by charisma that we overlook the quiet part of the creative process. Consider Apple. In the wake of Steve Jobs's death, we've seen a profusion of myths about the company's success. Most focus on Mr. Jobs's supernatural magnetism and tend to ignore the other crucial figure in Apple's creation: a kindly, introverted engineering wizard, Steve Wozniak, who toiled alone on a beloved invention, the personal computer.

Rewind to March 1975: Mr. Wozniak believes the world would be a better place if everyone had a user-friendly computer. This seems a distant dream—most computers are still the size of minivans, and many times as pricey. But Mr. Wozniak meets a simpatico band of engineers that call themselves the Homebrew Computer Club. The Homebrewers are excited about a primitive new machine called the Altair 8800. Mr. Wozniak is inspired, and immediately begins work on his own magical version of a computer. Three months later, he unveils his amazing creation for his friend, Steve Jobs. Mr. Wozniak wants to give his invention away free, but Mr. Jobs persuades him to co-found Apple Computer.

The story of Apple's origin speaks to the power of collaboration. Mr. Wozniak wouldn't have been catalyzed by the Altair but for the kindred spirits of Homebrew. And he'd never have started Apple without Mr. Jobs.

But it's also a story of solo spirit. If you look at how Mr. Wozniak got the work done—the sheer hard work of creating something from nothing—he did it alone. Late at night, all by himself.

Intentionally so. In his memoir, Mr. Wozniak offers this guidance to aspiring inventors:

"Most inventors and engineers I've met are like me . . . they live in their heads. They're almost like artists. In fact, the very best of them are artists. And artists work best alone . . . I'm going to give you some advice that might be hard to take. That advice is: Work alone . . . Not on a committee. Not on a team."

And yet. The New Groupthink has overtaken our workplaces, our schools and our religious institutions. Anyone who has ever needed noise-canceling headphones in her own office or marked an online calendar with a fake meeting in order to escape yet another real one knows what I'm talking about. Virtually all American workers now spend time on teams and some 70% inhabit open-plan offices, in which no one has "a room of one's own." During the last decades, the average amount of space allotted to each employee shrank 300 square feet, from 500 square feet in the 1970s to 200 square feet in 2010.

Our schools have also been transformed by the New Groupthink. Today, elementary school classrooms are commonly arranged in pods of desks, the better to foster group learning. Even subjects like math and creative writing are often taught as committee projects. In one fourth-grade classroom I visited in New York City, students engaged in group work were forbidden to ask a question unless every member of the group had the very same question.

The New Groupthink also shapes some of our most influential religious institutions. Many mega-churches feature extracurricular groups organized around every conceivable activity, from parenting to skateboarding to real estate, and expect worshipers to join in. They also emphasize a theatrical style of worship—loving Jesus out loud, for all the congregation to see. "Often the role of a pastor seems closer to that of church cruise director than to the traditional roles of spiritual friend and counselor," said Adam McHugh, an evangelical pastor and author of "Introverts in the Church."

Some teamwork is fine and offers a fun, stimulating, useful way to exchange ideas, manage information and build trust.

But it's one thing to associate with a group in which each member works autonomously on his piece of the puzzle; it's another to be corralled into endless meetings or conference calls conducted in offices that afford no respite from the noise and gaze of co-workers. Studies show that open-plan offices make workers hostile, insecure and distracted. They're also more likely to suffer from high blood pressure, stress, the flu and exhaustion. And people whose work is interrupted make 50% more mistakes and take twice as long to finish it.

Many introverts seem to know this instinctively, and resist being herded together. Backbone Entertainment, a video game development company in Emeryville, Calif., initially used an open-plan office, but found that its game developers, many of whom were introverts, were unhappy. "It was one big warehouse space, with just tables, no walls, and everyone could see each other," recalled Mike Mika, the former creative director. "We switched over to cubicles and were worried about it—you'd think in a creative environment that people would hate that. But it turns out they prefer having nooks and crannies they can hide away in and just be away from everybody."

Privacy also makes us productive. In a fascinating study known as the Coding War Games, consultants Tom DeMarco and Timothy Lister compared the work of more than 600 computer programmers at 92 companies. They found that people from the same companies performed at roughly the same level—but that there was an enormous performance gap between organizations. What distinguished programmers at the top-performing companies wasn't greater experience or better

pay. It was how much privacy, personal workspace and freedom from interruption they enjoyed. 62% of the best performers said their workspace was sufficiently private compared with only 19% of the worst performers. 76% of the worst programmers but only 38% of the best said that they were often interrupted needlessly.

Solitude can even help us learn. According to research on expert performance by the psychologist Anders Ericsson, the best way to master a field is to work on the task that's most demanding for you personally. And often the best way to do this is alone. Only then, Mr. Ericsson told me, can you "go directly to the part that's challenging to you. If you want to improve, you have to be the one who generates the move. Imagine a group class— you're the one generating the move only a small percentage of the time."

Conversely, brainstorming sessions are one of the worst possible ways to stimulate creativity. The brainchild of a charismatic advertising executive named Alex Osborn who believed that groups produced better ideas than individuals, workplace brainstorming sessions came into vogue in the 1950s. "The quantitative results of group brainstorming are beyond question," Mr. Osborn wrote. "One group produced 45 suggestions for a home-appliance promotion, 56 ideas for a money-raising campaign, 124 ideas on how to sell more blankets."

But decades of research show that individuals almost always perform better than groups in both quality and quantity, and group performance gets worse as group size increases. The "evidence from science suggests that business people must be insane to use brainstorming groups," wrote the organizational psychologist Adrian Furnham. "If you have talented and motivated people, they should be encouraged to work alone when creativity or efficiency is the highest priority."

The reasons brainstorming fails are instructive for other forms of group work, too. People in groups tend to sit back and let others do the work; they instinctively mimic others'

opinions and lose sight of their own; and often succumb to peer pressure. The Emory University neuroscientist Gregory Berns found that when we take a stance different from the group's, we activate the amygdala, a small organ in the brain associated with the fear of rejection. Professor Berns calls this "the pain of independence."

The one important exception to this dismal record is electronic brainstorming, where large groups outperform individuals; and the larger the group the better. The protection of the screen mitigates many problems of group work. This is why the Internet has yielded such wondrous collective creations. Marcel Proust called reading a "miracle of communication in the midst of solitude," and that's what the Internet is, too. It's a place where we can be alone together—and this is precisely what gives it power.

My point is not that man is an island. Life is meaningless without love, trust and friendship.

And I'm not suggesting that we abolish teamwork. Indeed, recent studies suggest that influential academic work is increasingly conducted by teams rather than by individuals. (Although teams whose members collaborate remotely, from separate universities, appear to be the most influential of all.) The problems we face in science, economics and many other fields are more complex than ever before, and we'll need to stand on one another's shoulders if we can possibly hope to solve them.

But even if the problems are different, human nature remains the same. And most humans have two contradictory impulses: we love and need one another, yet we crave privacy and autonomy.

To harness the energy that fuels both these drives, we need to move beyond the New Groupthink and embrace a more nuanced approach to creativity and learning. Our offices should encourage casual, cafe-style interactions, but allow people to disappear into personalized, private spaces when they want to be alone.

Our schools should teach children to work with others, but also to work on their own for sustained periods of time. And we must recognize that introverts like Steve Wozniak need extra quiet and privacy to do their best work.

Before Mr. Wozniak started Apple, he designed calculators at Hewlett-Packard, a job he loved partly because HP made it easy to chat with his colleagues. Every day at 10 a.m. and 2 p.m., management wheeled in doughnuts and coffee, and people could socialize and swap ideas. What distinguished these interactions was how low-key they were. For Mr. Wozniak, collaboration meant the ability to share a doughnut and a brainwave with his laid-back, poorly dressed colleagues—who minded not a whit when he disappeared into his cubicle to get the real work done.

Questions for Discussion

1. What are the potential benefits of high levels of teamwork?

2. What are the potential drawbacks of high levels of teamwork?

3. Do you think it is important for workers to have a good balance between time spent working alone and time spent working together in groups or teams? Why or why not?

4. Do you think organizations should provide two kinds of work areas for employees—places to collaborate with others in teams and places to work quietly on one's own with little in the way of interruptions? If so, why? If not, why not?

CHAPTER 16

Promoting Effective Communication

Learning Objectives

After studying this chapter, you should be able to:

LO16-1 Explain why effective communication helps an organization gain a competitive advantage.

LO16-2 Describe the communication process, and explain the role of perception in communication.

LO16-3 Define information richness, and describe the information richness of communication media available to managers.

LO16-4 Describe the communication networks that exist in groups and teams.

LO16-5 Explain how advances in technology have given managers new options for managing communication.

LO16-6 Describe important communication skills that managers need as senders and as receivers of messages and why it is important to understand differences in linguistic styles.

A MANAGER'S CHALLENGE

Fostering Effective Communication and Collaboration at Salesforce.com

How can managers foster effective communication and collaboration? Marc Benioff, cofounder, chairman of the board of directors, and chief executive officer of Salesforce.com, not only fosters effective communication and collaboration in his company, but his company provides its customers with the tools to promote effective communication in their own organizations and with their own customers. An effective communicator himself, Benioff well knows the importance of building a common understanding, trust, and a collaborative atmosphere for effective communication.[1]

Salesforce.com was founded in 1999 and provides its subscribing companies with customer relationship management software and applications via cloud computing—cloud computing entails the delivery of software, services, data management, and storage over the Internet.[2] Thus, through cloud computing, Salesforce.com provides companies with the tools they need to effectively manage sales and relations with their own customers, accounting and data management and storage, and communications within their companies. Salesforce.com has over 100,000 subscribers ranging from Dell, Cisco, and Google to NBCUniversal, Bank of America, and the Japanese government.[3] Rather than subscribers having to purchase, install, upgrade, and maintain software to

Takes one to know one! Marc Benioff's dedication to effective communication within Salesforce.com equips the company's products and processes, enabling Salesforce.com to grow leaps and bounds beyond competitors simply by being the best in their arena.

manage communications and business activities, Salesforce.com enables them to access software, communication tools, and data management and storage over the Internet through cloud computing. Salesforce.com's growth trajectory has been remarkable.[4] As Benioff was quoted in a recent press release, "Last year we became the first enterprise cloud computing company to achieve $2 billion in revenue, and we're now poised to deliver the first ever $3 billion year in fiscal 2013."[5]

With over 7,000 employees and more than 100,000 customers, Salesforce.com is a leader in the move toward social enterprises that use mobile, social, and cloud technology to better serve customers.[6] Salesforce.com offers its subscribers (or customers) access to different kinds of social networks to facilitate the sharing of information, communication, and coordination both internally among employees and externally with customers. For example, Salesforce.com's Chatter is a social networking application (or "app")[7] similar to Facebook for internal use by a company's employees. On computers and mobile devices like smartphones and tablets, and in news feeds and groups open to all employees, employees can communicate with each other, work on drafts, collaborate, get feedback on new ideas, and perform data analyses in real time. Inside Salesforce.com, some groups bring together employees from different functions and hierarchical ranks to share thoughts and ideas about their own work experiences such as the groups named Airing of Grievances and Tribal Knowledge.[8]

Each day, employees at Salesforce.com post approximately 3,000 entries on Chatter, with their identities known to all.[9] Thus, while posts cannot get out of hand, this open forum for real-time communication certainly seems to facilitate collaboration and shared understandings. After Salesforce.com developed and adopted Chatter, managers found that around 30% fewer internal e-mails were being sent among employees. Chatter seems to keep both employees and managers more informed about what is going on in the company. Benioff himself indicated that "I learned more about my company in a few months through using Chatter than I had in the last three years."[10] Chatter is used by the vast majority of Salesforce.com customers without any extra charge.[11]

While Saleforce.com excels in the arena of electronic communication and social networking, Benioff, a consummate salesman, nonetheless recognizes the importance of face-to-face communication as well. As a case in point, consider how he managed the acquisition of Rypple, a Canadian start-up that develops human resources applications.[12] Rypple was founded by Daniel Debow and David Stein, who were speaking at the same conference as Benioff in New York City. Even though Benioff already had had several discussions with the pair about Salesforce.com's potentially acquiring Rypple, the night before the meeting, Benioff took Debow and Stein to one of his favorite Italian restaurants in midtown Manhattan. The next day after the conference events were finished, Benioff took Debow (Stein had a flight back home to catch) to the 2nd Avenue Deli for a tasty deli spread at the counter. Rather than talk business, the two just had a casual conversation. Building a good sense of rapport and a common understanding with the CEO of the company that was going to acquire their company evidently meant a lot to Debow and Stein. Even though they had a better offer to acquire their company from one of Salesforce.com's competitors, they decided to accept Salesforce.com's $60 million bid for Rypple. As Debow puts it, "It wasn't only about deal terms, but corporate culture . . . We barely met the other CEO . . . we entrepreneurs could be part of their family. Nobody can keep up the artifice over a couple of hours of sharing pickles."[13]

Importantly, Benioff is also concerned about giving back to the community and doing volunteer work. Salesforce.com originated the "1/1/1" system of philanthropy that other companies like Google are modeling their approaches after.[14] Essentially, Salesforce.com donates 1% of its employees' paid workdays to volunteer work (six work days per year per employee) and also donates 1% of its services to small nonprofits. Moreover, when Salesforce.com became a public company, it set aside 1% of its stock for the Salesforce Foundation. The foundation focuses on giving grants to programs and initiatives oriented around poverty, education, young people, innovation, and other

arenas in which employees are interested in volunteering. The foundation also helps large nonprofits and institutions of higher education improve their communication efforts by selling them Salesforce.com subscriptions at an 80% discount with the foundation keeping the proceeds from the subscriptions.[15] Interestingly enough, when employees volunteer for projects, they not only have a sense of fulfillment from doing something worthwhile, but they also increase their sense of camaraderie and collaboration with their coworkers. As Julie Trell, who works at the foundation puts it, "You bring your whole self to work . . . Employees bring in their causes, others join in, and it teaches team building."[16] All in all, Salesforce.com appears to be helping many people and organizations be better communicators.[17]

Overview

Even with all the advances in information technology provided by companies like Salesforce.com that are available to managers, ineffective communication continues to take place in organizations. Ineffective communication is detrimental for managers, employees, and organizations; it can lead to poor performance, strained interpersonal relations, poor service, and dissatisfied customers. For an organization to be effective and gain a competitive advantage, managers at all levels need to be good communicators.

communication The sharing of information between two or more individuals or groups to reach a common understanding.

In this chapter we describe the nature of communication and the communication process and explain why all managers and their subordinates need to be effective communicators. We describe the communication media available to managers and the factors they need to consider in selecting a communication medium for each message they send. We consider the communication networks organizational members rely on, and we explore how advances in information technology have expanded managers' range of communication options. We describe the communication skills that help managers to be effective senders and receivers of messages. By the end of this chapter, you will appreciate the nature of communication and the steps managers can take to ensure that they are effective communicators.

LO16-1 Explain why effective communication helps an organization gain a competitive advantage.

Communication and Management

Communication is the sharing of information between two or more individuals or groups to reach a common understanding.[18] First and foremost, no matter how electronically based, communication is a human endeavor and involves individuals and groups. Second, communication does not take place unless a common understanding is reached. Thus, when you call a business to speak to a person in customer service or billing and are bounced between endless automated messages and menu options and eventually hang up in frustration, communication has not taken place.

The Importance of Good Communication

In Chapter 1 we described how an organization can gain a competitive advantage when managers strive to increase efficiency, quality, responsiveness to customers, and innovation. Good communication is essential for attaining each of these four goals and thus is a necessity for gaining a competitive advantage.

Managers can *increase efficiency* by updating the production process to take advantage of new and more efficient technologies and by training workers to operate the new technologies and to expand their skills. Good communication is necessary for managers to learn about new technologies, implement them in their organizations, and train workers in how to use them. Similarly, *improving quality* hinges on effective communication. Managers need to communicate to all members of an organization the meaning and importance of high quality and the routes to attaining it. Subordinates need to communicate quality problems and suggestions for increasing quality to their superiors, and members of self-managed work teams need to share their ideas on improving quality with one another.

Good communication can also help increase *responsiveness to customers.* When the organizational members who are closest to customers, such as department store salespeople and bank tellers, are empowered to communicate customers' needs and desires to managers, managers can better respond to these needs. Managers, in turn, must communicate with other organizational members to determine how best to respond to changing customer preferences.

Innovation, which often takes place in cross-functional teams, also requires effective communication. Members of a cross-functional team developing a new electronic game, for example, must effectively communicate with one another to develop a game that customers will want to play; that will be engaging, interesting, and fun; and that can potentially lead to sequels. Members of the team also must communicate with managers to secure the resources they need for developing the game and to keep managers informed of progress on the project. Innovation in organizations is increasingly taking place on a global level, making effective communication all the more important, as illustrated in the following "Managing Globally" box.

Managing
Globally

Global Communication for Global Innovation

GE Healthcare (headquartered in the United Kingdom) is a provider of medical technology and services and makes medical imaging, diagnostic, and monitoring systems such as CT scanners. With over 46,000 employees around the world, GE Healthcare has approximately $17 billion in revenues.[19] To make the best scanners that meet the needs of doctors and patients around the world with next-generation technology, new product development and manufacture are truly global endeavors at GE Healthcare Technologies. Consider the development of the LightSpeed VCT scanner series (*VCT* stands for "volume controlled tomography") which can perform a full-body scan in under 10 seconds and yields a three-dimensional picture of patients' hearts within five heartbeats.[20]

The LightSpeed was developed through global collaboration. GE managers not only spoke with doctors (including cardiologists and radiologists) around the world to find out what their needs were and what kinds of tests they would perform with the LightSpeed but also gathered information about differences among patients in various countries. Engineers in Hino (Japan), Buc (France), and Waukesha, Wisconsin, developed the electronics for the LightSpeed. Other parts, such as the automated table that patients lie on, are made in Beijing (China) and Hino. Software for the LightSpeed was written in Haifa (Israel), Bangalore (India), Buc, and Waukesha.[21]

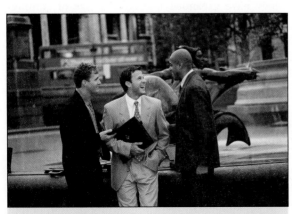

As GE Healthcare learned, conference calls and e-mails are beneficial, but nothing replaces getting managers together for face-to-face conversations and problem solving.

Effective global communication was a challenge and a necessity to successfully develop the LightSpeed series. As Brian Duchinsky, GE's general manager for global CT, put it, "If we sat around in this cornfield west of Milwaukee, we wouldn't come up with the same breadth of good ideas. But yet, getting six countries on the phone to make a decision can be a pain."[22]

GE managers facilitated effective communication in a number of ways—participating in daily conference calls, making sure teams in different countries depended on one another, developing an internal website devoted to the LightSpeed, encouraging teams to ask one another for help, and holding face-to-face meetings in different locations. Although much communication took place electronically, such as through conference calls, face-to-face meetings were also important. As Bob Armstrong, GE's general manager for engineering, indicated, "You need to get your people together in one place if you want them to really appreciate how good everyone is, and how good you are as a team."[23]

Effective communication is necessary for managers and all members of an organization to increase efficiency, quality, responsiveness to customers, and innovation and thus gain a competitive advantage for the organization. Managers therefore must understand the communication process well if they are to perform effectively.

The Communication Process

LO16-2 Describe the communication process, and explain the role of perception in communication.

The communication process consists of two phases. In the *transmission phase,* information is shared between two or more individuals or groups. In the *feedback phase,* a common understanding is ensured. In both phases, a number of distinct stages must occur for communication to take place (see Figure 16.1).[24]

Starting the transmission phase, the **sender,** the person or group wishing to share information with some other person or group, decides on the **message,** what information to communicate. Then the sender translates the message into symbols or language, a process called **encoding;** often messages are encoded into words. **Noise** is a general term that refers to anything that hampers any stage of the communication process.

Once encoded, a message is transmitted through a medium to the **receiver,** the person or group for which the message is intended. A **medium** is simply the pathway, such as a phone call, a letter, a memo, or face-to-face communication in a meeting, through which an encoded message is transmitted to a receiver. At the next stage, the receiver interprets and tries to make sense of the message, a process called **decoding.** This is a critical point in communication.

The feedback phase is initiated by the receiver (who becomes a sender). The receiver decides what message to send to the original sender (who becomes a receiver), encodes it, and transmits it through a chosen medium (see Figure 16.1). The message might contain a confirmation that the original message was received and understood or a restatement of the original message to make sure it has been correctly interpreted, or it might include a request for more information. The original sender decodes the message and makes sure a common understanding has been reached. If the original sender determines that a common understanding has not been reached,

sender The person or group wishing to share information.

message The information that a sender wants to share.

encoding Translating a message into understandable symbols or language.

noise Anything that hampers any stage of the communication process.

receiver The person or group for which a message is intended.

medium The pathway through which an encoded message is transmitted to a receiver.

decoding Interpreting and trying to make sense of a message.

Figure 16.1

The Communication Process

Transmission phase

Message → Encoding → Medium → Decoding by receiver

Sender

Noise

Receiver (now sender)

Decoding by sender (now receiver) ← Medium ← Encoding ← Message

Feedback phase

If a picture is worth a thousand words, so too is nonverbal communication; facial expressions, body language, posture, and eye contact all send powerful messages.

verbal communication
The encoding of messages into words, either written or spoken.

nonverbal communication
The encoding of messages by means of facial expressions, body language, and styles of dress.

sender and receiver cycle through the whole process as many times as needed to reach a common understanding. Feedback eliminates misunderstandings, ensures that messages are correctly interpreted, and enables senders and receivers to reach a common understanding.

The encoding of messages into words, written or spoken, is **verbal communication**. We can also encode messages without using written or spoken language.

Nonverbal communication shares information by means of facial expressions (smiling, raising an eyebrow, frowning, dropping one's jaw), body language (posture, gestures, nods, and shrugs), and even style of dress (casual, formal, conservative, trendy). The trend toward increasing empowerment of the workforce has led some managers to dress informally to communicate that all employees of an organization are team members, working together to create value for customers.

Nonverbal communication can be used to back up or reinforce verbal communication. Just as a warm and genuine smile can back up words of appreciation for a job well done, a concerned facial expression can back up words of sympathy for a personal problem. In such cases, the congruence between the verbal and the nonverbal communication helps to ensure that a common understanding is reached.

Sometimes when members of an organization decide not to express a message verbally, they inadvertently do so nonverbally. People tend to have less control over nonverbal communication, and often a verbal message that is withheld gets expressed through body language or facial expressions. A manager who agrees to a proposal that she or he actually does not like may unintentionally communicate her or his disfavor by grimacing.

Sometimes nonverbal communication is used to send messages that cannot be sent through verbal channels. Many lawyers are well aware of this communication tactic. Lawyers are often schooled in techniques of nonverbal communication, such as choosing where to stand in the courtroom for maximum effect and using eye contact during different stages of a trial. Lawyers sometimes get into trouble for using inappropriate nonverbal communication in an attempt to influence juries. In a Louisiana court, prosecuting attorney Thomas Pirtle was admonished and fined $2,500 by Judge Yada Magee for shaking his head in an expression of doubt, waving his arms indicating disfavor, and chuckling when the attorneys for the defense were stating their case.[25]

The Role of Perception in Communication

Perception plays a central role in communication and affects both transmission and feedback. In Chapter 5 we defined *perception* as the process through which people select, organize, and interpret sensory input to give meaning and order to the world around them. We mentioned that perception is inherently subjective and is influenced by people's personalities, values, attitudes, and moods as well as by their experience and knowledge. When senders and receivers communicate with each other, they are doing so based on their own subjective perceptions. The encoding and decoding of messages and even the choice of a medium hinge on the perceptions of senders and receivers.

In addition, perceptual biases can hamper effective communication. Recall from Chapter 5 that *biases* are systematic tendencies to use information about others in ways that result in inaccurate perceptions. In Chapter 5 we described a number of biases that can cause unfair treatment of diverse members of an organization. The same biases also can lead to ineffective communication. For example, *stereotypes*—simplified and often inaccurate beliefs about the characteristics of particular groups of people—can interfere with the encoding and decoding of messages.

Suppose a manager stereotypes older workers as being fearful of change. When this manager encodes a message to an older worker about an upcoming change in the organization, she may downplay the extent of the change so as not to make the older worker feel stressed. The older worker, however, fears change no more than do his younger colleagues and thus decodes the message to mean that only a minor change is going to be made. The older worker fails to adequately prepare for the change, and his performance subsequently suffers because of his lack of preparation for the change. Clearly this ineffective communication was due to the manager's inaccurate assumptions about older workers. Instead of relying on stereotypes, effective managers strive to perceive other people accurately by focusing on their actual behaviors, knowledge, skills, and abilities. Accurate perceptions, in turn, contribute to effective communication.

The Dangers of Ineffective Communication

Because managers must communicate with others to perform their various roles and tasks, managers spend most of their time communicating, whether in meetings, in telephone conversations, through e-mail, or in face-to-face interactions. Indeed, some experts estimate that managers spend approximately 85% of their time engaged in some form of communication.[26]

Effective communication is so important that managers cannot just be concerned that they themselves are effective communicators; they also have to help their subordinates be effective communicators. When all members of an organization can communicate effectively with one another and with people outside the organization, the organization is much more likely to perform highly and gain a competitive advantage.

When managers and other members of an organization are ineffective communicators, organizational performance suffers and any competitive advantage the organization might have is likely to be lost. Moreover, poor communication sometimes can be downright dangerous and even lead to tragic and unnecessary loss of human life. For example, researchers from Harvard University studied the causes of mistakes, such as a patient receiving the wrong medication, in two large hospitals in the Boston area. They discovered that some mistakes in hospitals occur because of communication problems—physicians not having the information they need to correctly order medications for their patients or nurses not having the information they need to correctly administer medications. The researchers concluded that some of the responsibility for these mistakes lies with hospital management, which has not taken active steps to improve communication.[27]

Communication problems in airplane cockpits and between flying crews and air traffic controllers are unfortunately all too common, sometimes with deadly consequences. In the late 1970s two jets collided in Tenerife (one of the Canary Islands) because of miscommunication between a pilot and the control tower, and 600 people were killed. The tower radioed to the pilot, "Clipper 1736 report clear of runway." The pilot mistakenly interpreted this message to mean that he was cleared for takeoff.[28] Unfortunately, communication problems persist in the airline industry. In 2009 a Northwest Airlines Airbus A320 flew 150 miles past its Minneapolis destination while the crew of the airplane was out of contact with air traffic controllers for over an hour.[29] A safety group at NASA tracked more than 6,000 unsafe flying incidents and found that communication difficulties caused approximately 529 of them.[30] And NASA has its own communication difficulties.[31] In 2004 NASA released a report detailing communication problems at the International Space Station jointly managed and staffed by NASA and the Russian space agency; the problems included inadequate record keeping, missing information, and failure to keep data current.[32]

LO16-3 Define information richness, and describe the information richness of communication media available to managers.

Information Richness and Communication Media

To be effective communicators, managers (and other members of an organization) need to select an appropriate communication medium for each message they send. Should a change in procedures be communicated to subordinates in a memo sent through e-mail? Should a congratulatory message about a major accomplishment be communicated in a letter, in a phone call, or over lunch? Should a layoff announcement be made in a memo or at a plant meeting? Should the members of a purchasing team travel to Europe to cement a major agreement with a new supplier, or should they do so through conference calls and e-mails? Managers deal with these questions day in and day out.

There is no one best communication medium for managers to rely on. In choosing a communication medium for any message, managers need to consider three factors. The first and most important is the level of information richness that is needed. **Information richness** is the amount of information a communication medium can carry and the extent to which the medium enables the sender and receiver to reach a common understanding.[33] The communication media that managers use vary in their information richness (see Figure 16.2).[34] Media high in information richness can carry an extensive amount of information and generally enable receivers and senders to come to a common understanding.

The second factor that managers need to take into account in selecting a communication medium is the *time* needed for communication because managers' and other organizational

information richness The amount of information that a communication medium can carry and the extent to which the medium enables the sender and receiver to reach a common understanding.

Figure 16.2
The Information Richness of Communication Media

members' time is valuable. Managers at United Parcel Service, for example, dramatically reduced the amount of time they spent on communicating by using videoconferences instead of face-to-face communication, which required that managers travel overseas.[35]

The third factor that affects the choice of a communication medium is the *need for a paper or electronic trail* or some kind of written documentation that a message was sent and received. A manager may wish to document in writing, for example, that a subordinate was given a formal warning about excessive lateness.

In the remainder of this section we examine four types of communication media that vary along these three dimensions (information richness, time, and paper or electronic trail).[36]

Face-to-Face Communication

Face-to-face communication is the medium that is highest in information richness. When managers communicate face-to-face, they not only can take advantage of verbal communication but also can interpret each other's nonverbal signals such as facial expressions and body language. A look of concern or puzzlement can sometimes say more than a thousand words, and managers can respond to such nonverbal signals on the spot. Face-to-face communication also enables managers to receive instant feedback. Points of confusion, ambiguity, or misunderstanding can be resolved, and managers can cycle through the communication process as many times as needed to reach a common understanding.

With the growing proliferation of electronic forms of communication, such as e-mail, some managers fear that face-to-face communication is being shortchanged to the detriment of building common understandings and rapport.[37] Moreover, some messages that really should be communicated face-to-face or at least in a phone conversation, and messages that are more efficiently communicated in this manner, are nonetheless sent electronically.[38] As indicated in the following "Management Insight" box, managers need to carefully consider whether face-to-face communication is being shortchanged in their organizations and, if it is, take steps to rectify the situation.

When Face-to-Face Communication Is Called For

Management Insight

Anyone who has participated in one of those frustrating e-mail exchanges where messages shoot back and forth and it seems to take forever to resolve a problem or reach a common understanding knows there must be a better way. In such cases a face-to-face conversation

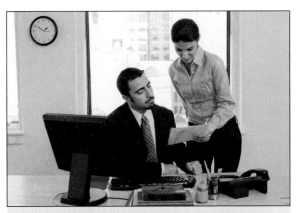

"No E-mail Friday" bolsters in-person conversations and strengthens employee ties.

(or if that is not possible, a phone conversation) often will lead to better outcomes all around.

According to Ron McMillan, a consultant to managers at all ranks and coauthor of best-selling books on communication, e-mail should not be relied on to communicate information that is complex, important, or sensitive.[39] In such cases face-to-face communication (or even a phone conversation) can convey more information than e-mail can, and it is much more effective at generating a common understanding. Research conducted by Professor Albert Mehrabian at UCLA suggests that more meaning is conveyed by nonverbal communication from facial expressions and body language and from tone of voice and vocal inflection than is conveyed by the actual words that are used when communicating.[40] And of course nonverbal communication, tone of voice, and vocal inflection are all missing when e-mail is used. JoAnne Yates, a professor at the Sloan School of Management at MIT, suggests that e-mail is best for simple information that will be readily understood.[41]

Sara Roberts, founder and chief executive officer of Roberts Golden Consulting in San Francisco, recognizes the value of face-to-face communication.[42] Although consultants in her firm regularly communicate with each other, clients, and suppliers via e-mail and this is often efficient and effective, Roberts believes rapport and collaboration can suffer when e-mail is used extensively. So she instituted "No E-mail Fridays" at her firm; on Fridays employees are not to use e-mail unless it is clearly necessary (such as to reply to a client who wants an urgent e-mail response).[43] As Roberts puts it, "No E-mail Friday helps us to remember we really could go over to that person sitting right over there and collaborate more."[44] In fact a growing number of organizations are experimenting with "no e-mail Fridays" to encourage more face-to-face communication and phone conversations.[45]

Allowing opportunities for face-to-face communication can be especially important when trying to effectively communicate with employees located in other countries. For example, Greg Caltabiano, CEO of Teknovus Inc., which is based in Petaluma, California, and has offices in Asia, arranges for U.S. employees to go to Asia and Asian employees to come to the United States to engage in face-to-face communication to build mutual understanding.[46]

management by wandering around A face-to-face communication technique in which a manager walks around a work area and talks informally with employees about issues and concerns.

Management by wandering around is a face-to-face communication technique that is effective for many managers at all levels in an organization.[47] Rather than scheduling formal meetings with subordinates, managers walk around work areas and talk informally with employees about issues and concerns that both employees and managers may have. These informal conversations give managers and subordinates important information and at the same time foster the development of positive relationships. William Hewlett and David Packard, founders and former top managers of Hewlett-Packard, found management by wandering around to be a highly effective way of communicating with their employees.

Because face-to-face communication is highest in information richness, you might think it should always be the medium of choice for managers. This is not the case, however, because of the amount of time it can take and the lack of a paper or electronic trail resulting from it. For messages that are important, personal, or likely to be misunderstood, it is often well worth managers' time to use face-to-face communication and, if need be, supplement it with some form of written communication documenting the message.

Advances in information technology are giving managers new communication media that are close substitutes for face-to-face communication. Many organizations, such as American Greetings Corp. and Hewlett-Packard, are using *videoconferences* to capture some of the advantages of face-to-face communication (such as access to facial expressions) while saving time and money because managers in different locations do not have to travel to meet with

Videoconferencing allows these remotely based teams to see each other around the conference table, the next best thing to actually being in the same office space.

one another. During a videoconference, managers in two or more locations communicate with each other over large TV or video screens; they not only hear each other but also see each other throughout the meeting.

In addition to saving travel costs, videoconferences sometimes have other advantages. Managers at American Greetings have found that decisions get made more quickly when videoconferences are used because more managers can be involved in the decision-making process and therefore fewer managers have to be consulted outside the meeting itself. Managers at Hewlett-Packard have found that videoconferences have shortened new product development time by 30% for similar reasons. Videoconferences also seem to lead to more efficient meetings. Some managers have found that their meetings are 20% to 30% shorter when videoconferences are used instead of face-to-face meetings.[48]

Taking videoconferences a leap forward, Cisco Systems has developed its TelePresence line of products, enabling individuals and teams in different locations to communicate live and in real time over the Internet with high-definition life-size video and excellent audio that make it feel like all participants, no matter where they are, are in the same room.[49] One morning Cisco CEO John Chambers was able to participate in meetings with employees and teams in India, Japan, Cleveland, and London in less than four hours by using TelePresence.[50] Other companies, such as HP, have developed similar products. What distinguishes these products from older videoconferencing systems is the lack of transmission delay and the sharp, clear, life-size video quality.[51]

Spoken Communication Electronically Transmitted

After face-to-face communication, spoken communication electronically transmitted over phone lines (and the World Wide Web and the Internet) is second highest in information richness (see Figure 16.2). Although managers communicating over the telephone do not have access to body language and facial expressions, they do have access to the tone of voice in which a message is delivered, the parts of the message the sender emphasizes, and the general manner in which the message is spoken, in addition to the actual words themselves. Thus telephone conversations can convey extensive amounts of information. Managers can ensure that mutual understanding is reached because they can get quick feedback over the phone and answer questions. When Greg Caltabiano, CEO of Teknovus Inc., wanted to improve communication between engineers in California who design semiconductors for fiber optic networks and employees and customers in Asia, he encouraged the engineers to communicate via the telephone instead of by e-mail.[52]

Skype enables people to communicate using voice and video over the Internet.[53] Thus, Skype enables access to nonverbal forms of communication and video conferences and interviews can be conducted over the Internet with Skype. For example, some business schools who interview top applicants for their PhD programs require an in-person interview prior to making admission decisions. Given the high costs of airline tickets for top overseas candidates, some schools arrange for interviews with these applicants to be conducted via Skype.

Voice mail systems and answering machines also allow managers to send and receive verbal electronic messages over telephone lines. Voice mail systems are companywide systems that let senders record messages for members of an organization who are away from their desks and allow receivers to access their messages even when hundreds of miles away from the office. Such systems are obviously a necessity when managers are frequently out of the office, and managers on the road are well advised to periodically check their voice mail.

Personally Addressed Written Communication

Lower in information richness than electronically transmitted verbal communication is personally addressed written communication (see Figure 16.2). One advantage of face-to-face communication and electronically transmitted verbal communication is that they both tend to demand attention, which helps ensure that receivers pay attention. Personally addressed written communications, such as memos and letters, also have this advantage. Because they are addressed to a particular person, the chances are good that the person will actually pay attention to (and read) them. Moreover, the sender can write the message in a way that the receiver is most likely to understand. Like voice mail, written communication does not enable a receiver to have his or her questions answered immediately; but when messages are clearly written and feedback is provided, common understandings can still be reached.

Even if managers use face-to-face communication, sending a follow-up in writing is often necessary for messages that are important or complicated and need to be referred to later on. This is precisely what Karen Stracker, a hospital administrator, did when she needed to tell one of her subordinates about an important change in how the hospital would be handling denials of insurance benefits. Stracker met with the subordinate and described the changes face-to-face. Once she was sure the subordinate understood them, she handed her a sheet of instructions to follow, which essentially summarized the information they had discussed.

E-mail also fits into this category of communication media because senders and receivers are communicating through personally addressed written words. The words, however, appear on their computer screens rather than on paper. E-mail is so widespread in the business world that some managers find they have to deliberately take time out from managing their e-mail to get their work done, think about pressing concerns, and come up with new and innovative ideas.[54] According to the Radacati Group, an independent market research firm, the average e-mail account in corporations today receives about 18 megabytes of e-mail and attachments per workday; the volume of e-mail is expected to increase over time.[55] To help their employees effectively manage e-mail, a growing number of organizations are instituting training programs to help employees learn how to more effectively use e-mail by sending clearer messages, avoiding e-mail copies to multiple parties who do not really need to see it, and writing clear and informative subject lines.[56] For example, Capital One trains employees to (1) write clear subject lines so recipients know why they are receiving a message and can easily search for it and retrieve it later, and (2) convey information clearly and effectively in the e-mail body.[57]

Ultimately, for messages that are sensitive or potentially misunderstood, or that require the give-and-take of a face-to-face or telephone conversation, relying on e-mail can take considerably more time to reach a common understanding.[58] Additionally, given the lack of nonverbal cues, tone of voice, and intonation in e-mail, senders need to be aware of the potential for misunderstandings.[59] For example, Kristin Byron, a professor of management at Syracuse University, suggests that recipients may have a tendency to perceive some of the e-mail they receive as more negative than the senders intended, based on her research.[60] Senders who are rushed, for example, may send short, curt messages lacking greeting and closing lines because they are so busy.[61] Recipients, however, might read something more negative into messages like these.[62]

The growing popularity of e-mail has also enabled many workers and managers to become *telecommuters*—people who are employed by organizations and work out of offices in their own homes. It is estimated that there are over 34 million telecommuters in the United States.[63] Many telecommuters indicate that the flexibility of working at home lets them be more productive and, at the same time, be closer to their families and not waste time traveling to and from the office.[64] In a study conducted by Georgetown University, 75% of the telecommuters surveyed said their productivity increased, and 83% said their home life improved once they started telecommuting.[65]

Unfortunately the widespread use of e-mail has been accompanied by growing abuse of e-mail. There have been cases of employees sexually harassing coworkers through e-mail, sending pornographic content via e-mail, and sending messages that disparage certain employees or groups.[66] To counter disparaging remarks making their way to employees' in-boxes (and being copied to coworkers), Mark Stevens, CEO of MSCO, a 40-person marketing firm in Purchase, New York, instituted a policy that forbade employees from using e-mail or BlackBerrys to communicate messages that criticized someone else.[67]

Managers need to develop a clear, written policy specifying what company e-mail can and should be used for and what is out of bounds. Managers also should clearly communicate this policy to all members of the organization, as well as tell them what procedures will be used when e-mail abuse is suspected and what consequences will result if the abuse is confirmed. According to a survey conducted by the ePolicy Institute, of the 79% of companies that have an e-mail policy, only about 54% actually give employees training and education to ensure that they understand it.[68] Training and education are important to ensure that employees know not only what the policy is but also what it means for their own e-mail use.

Additionally, e-mail policies should specify how much personal e-mail is appropriate and when the bounds of appropriateness have been overstepped. Just as employees make personal phone calls while on the job (and sometimes have to), so too do they send and receive personal e-mail. In fact, according to Waterford Technologies, a provider of e-mail management and archive services based in Irvine, California, about one-third of e-mail to and from companies is personal or not work-related.[69] Clearly, banning all personal e-mail is impractical and likely to have negative consequences for employees and their organizations (such as lower levels of job satisfaction and increased personal phone conversations). Some companies limit personal e-mail to certain times of the day or a certain amount of time per day; others have employees create lists of contacts from whom they want to receive e-mail at work (family members, children, baby-sitters); still others want personal e-mail to be sent and received through web-based systems like Gmail and Hotmail rather than the corporate e-mail system.[70]

According to the American Management Association, while the majority of organizations have a written policy about e-mail use, some do not have written guidelines for instant messaging.[71] *Instant messaging* allows people who are online and linked through a buddy or contact list to send instant messages back and forth through a small window on their computer screens without having to go through the steps of sending and receiving e-mail.[72]

What about surfing the Internet on company time? According to a study conducted by Websense, approximately half of the employees surveyed indicated that they surfed the web at work, averaging about two hours per week.[73] Most visited news and travel sites, but about 22% of the male respondents and 12% of the female respondents indicated that they visited pornographic websites.[74] Of all those surveyed, 56% said they sent personal e-mail at work. The majority of those surveyed felt that sending personal e-mail and surfing the web had no effect on their performance, and 27% thought that doing so improved their productivity.[75] Other statistics suggest that while overall there is more Internet use at home than at work, individuals who use the Internet at work spend more time on it and visit more sites than do those who use it at home.[76] As indicated in the following "Ethics in Action" box, personal e-mail and Internet surfing at work present managers with some challenging ethical dilemmas.

Ethics in
Action

Monitoring E-mail and Internet Use

A growing number of companies provide managers and organizations with tools to track the websites their employees visit and the e-mail and instant messages they send.[77] For example, network forensic software enables managers to record and replay everything that takes place on employees' computer monitors and can also track keystrokes.[78] Currently a majority of large corporations in the United States monitor their employees' e-mail and Internet usage; the percentage is higher among organizations in certain industries.[79] Most of the organizations that monitor e-mail tell their employees about the monitoring.[80] However, the means by which they let employees know are not necessarily effective. For example, putting information about e-mail monitoring in an employee handbook might be ineffective if most employees do not read the handbook.[81]

Monitoring employees raises concerns about privacy.[82] Most employees would not like to have their bosses listening to their phone conversations; similarly, some believe that monitoring e-mail and tracking Internet use are an invasion of privacy.[83]

Figure 16.3
Communication Networks in Groups and Teams

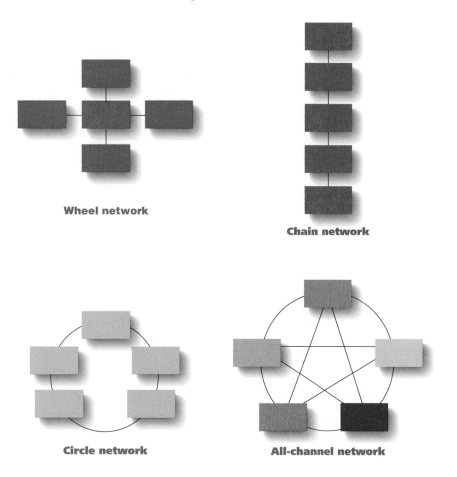

Wheel network

Chain network

Circle network

All-channel network

CIRCLE NETWORK   In a circle network, group members communicate with others who are similar to them in experiences, beliefs, areas of expertise, background, office location, or even where they sit when the group meets. Members of task forces and standing committees, for example, tend to communicate with others who have similar experiences or backgrounds. People also tend to communicate with people whose offices are next to their own. Like wheel and chain networks, circle networks are most often found in groups that are not teams.

ALL-CHANNEL NETWORK   An all-channel network is found in teams. It is characterized by high levels of communication: Every team member communicates with every other team member. Top management teams, cross-functional teams, and self-managed work teams frequently have all-channel networks. The reciprocal task interdependence often found in such teams requires information flows in all directions. Computer software specially designed for use by work groups can help maintain effective communication in teams with all-channel networks because it gives team members an efficient way to share information.

Organizational Communication Networks

An organization chart may seem to be a good summary of an organization's communication network, but often it is not. An organization chart summarizes the *formal* reporting relationships in an organization and the formal pathways along which communication takes place. Often, however, communication is *informal* and flows around issues, goals, projects, and ideas instead

In all-channel networks, like this team, every team member communicates with every other team member.

Formal and Informal Communication Networks in an Organization

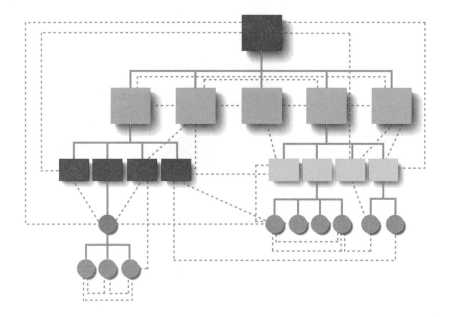

———— Formal pathways of communication summarized in an organization chart.

- - - - - Informal pathways along which a great deal of communication takes place.

of moving up and down the organizational hierarchy in an orderly fashion. Thus an organization's communication network includes not only the formal communication pathways summarized in an organization chart but also informal communication pathways along which a great deal of communication takes place (see Figure 16.4).

Communication can and should occur across departments and groups as well as within them and up and down and sideways in the corporate hierarchy. Communication up and down the corporate hierarchy is often called *vertical* communication. Communication among employees at the same level in the hierarchy, or sideways, is called *horizontal* communication. Managers obviously cannot determine in advance what an organization's communication network will be, nor should they try to. Instead, to accomplish goals and perform at a high level, organizational members should be free to communicate with whomever they need to contact. Because organizational goals change over time, so too do organizational communication networks. Informal communication networks can contribute to an organization's competitive advantage because they help ensure that organizational members have the information they need when they need it to accomplish their goals.

The **grapevine** is an informal organizational communication network along which unofficial information flows quickly, if not always accurately.[100] People in an organization who seem to know everything about everyone are prominent in the grapevine. Information spread over the grapevine can be about issues of either a business nature (an impending takeover) or a personal nature (the CEO's separation from his wife).

grapevine An informal communication network along which unofficial information flows.

External Networks

In addition to participating in networks within an organization, managers, professional employees, and those with work-related ties outside their employing organization often are part of external networks whose members span a variety of companies. For example, scientists working in universities and in corporations often communicate in networks formed around common underlying interests in a particular topic or subfield. As another example, physicians working throughout the country belong to specialty professional associations that help them keep up-to-date on the latest advances in their fields. For some managers and professionals, participation in such interest-oriented networks is as important as, or even more important than, participation in internal company networks. Networks of contacts who are working in the same discipline or field or who have similar expertise and knowledge can be very helpful, for example, when an individual wants to change jobs or find a job after a layoff. Unfortunately, as a result of discrimination and stereotypes, some of these networks are off-limits to certain individuals due to gender or race. For example, the term *old boys' network* alludes to the fact that networks of contacts for job leads, government contracts, or venture capital funding have sometimes been dominated by men and less welcoming of women.[101]

Information Technology and Communication

Advances in information technology have dramatically increased managers' abilities to communicate with others as well as to quickly access information to make decisions. Advances that are having major impacts on managerial communication include the Internet, intranets, groupware, and collaboration software. However, managers must not forget that communication is essentially a human endeavor, no matter how much it may be facilitated by information technology.

LO16-5 Explain how advances in technology have given managers new options for managing communication.

Internet A global system of computer networks.

The Internet

The **Internet** is a global system of computer networks that is easy to join and is used by employees of organizations around the world to communicate inside and outside their companies. Over 245 million people in the United States alone use the Internet, and the use of broadband connections (in place of dial-up service) has dramatically increased.[102] Table 16.1 lists the 20 countries with the most Internet users.[103]

On the Internet, the World Wide Web is the "business district" with multimedia capabilities. Companies' home pages on the web are like offices that potential customers can visit. In

Table 16.1

Top 20 Countries in Internet Usage as of March 31, 2012

Country	Internet Users
China	513,100,000
United States	245,203,319
India	121,000,000
Japan	101,228,736
Brazil	81,798,000
Germany	67,364,898
Russia	61,472,011
Indonesia	55,000,000
United Kingdom	52,731,209
France	50,290,226
Nigeria	45,039,711
Mexico	42,000,000
Korea	40,329,660
Iran	36,500,000
Turkey	36,455,000
Italy	35,800,000
Philippines	33,600,000
Vietnam	30,858,742
Spain	30,654,678
Pakistan	29,128,970

Source: "Top 20 Countries—With the Highest Number of Internet Users," Internet World Stats Usage and Population Statistics, www.internetworldstats.com/top20.htm, June 6, 2012. Used by permission.

attractive graphic displays on home pages, managers communicate information about the goods and services they offer, why customers should want to purchase them, how to purchase them, and where to purchase them. By surfing the web and visiting competitors' home pages, managers can see what their competitors are doing.[104] Each day hundreds of new companies add themselves to the growing number of organizations on the World Wide Web.[105] According to one study, the six "web-savviest" nations (taking into account use of broadband connections) in descending order are Denmark, Great Britain, Sweden, Norway, Finland, and the United States.[106] By all counts, use of the Internet for communication is burgeoning.

Intranets

intranet A companywide system of computer networks.

Growing numbers of managers are finding that the technology on which the World Wide Web and the Internet are based has enabled them to improve communication within their own companies. These managers use this technology to share information within their own companies through company networks called **intranets**. Intranets are being used at many companies including Chevron, Goodyear, Levi Strauss, IBM, Pfizer, Chrysler, Motorola, and Ford.[107]

Intranets allow employees to have many kinds of information at their fingertips. Directories, manuals, inventory figures, product specifications, information about customers, biographies of top managers and the board of directors, global sales figures, meeting minutes, annual reports, delivery schedules, and up-to-the-minute revenue, cost, and profit figures are just a few examples of the information that can be shared through intranets. Intranets can be accessed with different kinds of computers so that all members of an organization can be linked together. Intranets are protected from unwanted intrusions, by hackers or by competitors, by firewall security systems that ask users to provide passwords and other identification before they are allowed access.[108]

The advantage of intranets lies in their versatility as a communication medium. They can be used for a number of different purposes by people who may have little expertise in computer software and programming. While some managers complain that the Internet is too crowded and the World Wide Web too glitzy, informed managers are realizing that using the Internet's technology to create their own computer networks may be one of the Internet's biggest contributions to organizational effectiveness.

Groupware and Collaboration Software

groupware Computer software that enables members of groups and teams to share information with one another.

Groupware is computer software that enables members of groups and teams to share information with one another to improve their communication and performance. In some organizations, such as the Bank of Montreal, managers have had success in introducing groupware into the organization; in other organizations, such as the advertising agency Young & Rubicam, managers have encountered considerable resistance to groupware.[109] Even in companies where the introduction of groupware has been successful, some employees resist using it. Some clerical and secretarial workers at the Bank of Montreal, for example, were dismayed to find that their neat and accurate files were being consolidated into computer files that would be accessible to many of their coworkers.

Managers are most likely to be able to successfully use groupware as a communication medium in their organizations when certain conditions are met:[110]

1. The work is group- or team-based, and members are rewarded, at least in part, for group performance.
2. Groupware has the full support of top management.
3. The culture of the organization stresses flexibility and knowledge sharing, and the organization does not have a rigid hierarchy of authority.
4. Groupware is used for a specific purpose and is viewed as a tool that enables group or team members to work more effectively together, not as a personal source of power or advantage.
5. Employees receive adequate training in the use of computers and groupware.[111]

Employees are likely to resist using groupware and managers are likely to have a difficult time implementing it when people are working primarily on their own and are rewarded for individual performance.[112] Under these circumstances, information is often viewed as a source of power, and people are reluctant to share information with others by means of groupware.

Consider three salespeople who sell insurance policies in the same geographic area; each is paid based on the number of policies he or she sells and on his or her retention of customers. Their supervisor invested in groupware and encouraged them to use it to share information about their sales, sales tactics, customers, insurance providers, and claim histories. The supervisor told the salespeople that having all this information at their fingertips would allow them to be more efficient as well as sell more policies and provide better service to customers.

Even though they received extensive training in how to use the groupware, the salespeople never got around to using it. Why? They all were afraid that giving away their secrets to their coworkers might reduce their own commissions. In this situation, the salespeople were essentially competing with one another and thus had no incentive to share information. Under such circumstances, a groupware system may not be a wise choice of communication medium. Conversely, had the salespeople been working as a team and had they received bonuses based on team performance, groupware might have been an effective communication medium.

For an organization to gain a competitive advantage, managers need to keep up-to-date on advances in information technology such as groupware. But managers should not adopt these or other advances without first considering carefully how the advance in question might improve communication and performance in their particular groups, teams, or whole organization. Moreover, managers need to keep in mind that all of these advances in IT are tools for people to use to facilitate effective communication; they are not replacements for face-to-face communication.

collaboration software
Groupware that promotes and facilitates collaborative, highly interdependent interactions and provides an electronic meeting site for communication among team members.

Collaboration software is groupware that aims to promote collaborative, highly interdependent interactions among members of a team and to provide the team with an electronic meeting site for communication.[113] Collaboration software gives members of a team an online work site where they can post, share, and save data, reports, sketches, and other documents; keep calendars; have team-based online conferences; and send and receive messages. The software can also keep and update progress reports, survey team members about different issues, forward documents to managers, and let users know which of their team members are also online and at the site.[114] Having an integrated online work area can help organize and centralize the work of a team, help ensure that information is readily available as needed, and also help team members make sure important information is not overlooked. Collaboration software can be much more efficient than e-mail or instant messaging for managing ongoing team collaboration and interaction that is not face-to-face. Moreover, when a team does meet face-to-face, all documents the team might need in the meeting are just a click away.[115]

For work that is truly team-based entails a number of highly interdependent yet distinct components, and involves team members with distinct areas of expertise who need to closely coordinate their efforts, collaboration software can be a powerful communication tool. The New York–based public relations company Ketchum Inc. uses collaboration software for some of its projects. For example, Ketchum managed public relations, marketing, and advertising for a new charitable program that Fireman's Fund Insurance Co. undertook. By using the eRoom software provided by Documentum (a part of EMC Corporation), Ketchum employees working on the project at six different locations, employee representatives from Fireman's, and a graphics company that was designing a website for the program were able to share plans, documents, graphic designs, and calendars at an online work site.[116] Members of the Ketchum–Fireman team got e-mail alerts when something had been modified or added to the site. As Ketchum's chief information officer Andy Roach puts it, "The fact that everyone has access to the same document means Ketchum isn't going to waste time on the logistics and can focus on the creative side."[117]

Another company taking advantage of collaboration software is Honeywell International Inc. Managers at Honeywell decided to use the SharePoint collaboration software provided by Microsoft, in part because it can be integrated with other Microsoft software such as Outlook.[118] For example, if a team using SharePoint makes a change to the team's calendar, that change will be automatically made in team members' Outlook calendars.[119] Clearly, collaboration software has the potential to enhance communication efficiency and effectiveness in teams.

Wikis, a result of the open-source software movement, are a free or very low-cost form of collaboration software that a growing number of organizations are using. Wikis enable the organizations not only to promote collaboration and better communication but also to cut back on the use of e-mail,[120] as indicated in the following "Information Technology Byte" box.

Collaborating with Wikis

According to Postini Inc., an e-mail filtering company in Redwood, California, approximately 10% of all e-mail sent and received is legitimate.[121] And while many organizations have invested in filtering software to keep spam from flooding employees' in-boxes, according to the Gartner Group (an Internet research firm), 60% of messages that make their way into employees' in-boxes are spam.[122] Darren Lennard, a managing director at Dresdner Kleinwort Wasserstein, an investment bank in London, was receiving approximately 250 e-mail messages a day, of which only 15% were relevant to his job. Every day Lennard's first and last activities were to clear out his in-box on his BlackBerry—until frustration got the better of him, after a long and grueling workday, and he smashed his BlackBerry on the kitchen countertop in his home.[123]

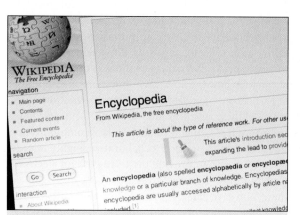

Wikis allow a wide range of people from multiple locations to contribute their specific skills and knowledge to the same task, resulting in a truly collaborative process.

Lennard is not alone in his frustration. J. P. Rangaswani, global chief information officer at Dresdner, who particularly dislikes use of copies on e-mail, wants to reduce the reliance on e-mail communication at the bank. He is taking steps to implement the use of collaboration software and other electronic forms of communication such as instant messaging and RSS (really simple syndication, which enables users to subscribe for information they require). In fact many organizations such as Yahoo!, Eastman Kodak, Walt Disney, and the U.S. government are trying to reduce their reliance on e-mail by turning to other software tools that promote effective communication and collaboration.[124] While e-mail is likely to continue to be extensively used for one-on-one communication, for communication that involves collaboration within and between groups and teams, the use of other more efficient and effective software tools is likely to dramatically increase in the coming years.[125]

In particular, wikis (in Hawaiian, the word *wiki* means "fast"), which are relatively easy to use and low-cost or free, are becoming increasingly popular as collaborative communication tools.[126] A wiki uses server software to enable users to create and revise web pages quickly on a company intranet or through a hosted Internet site. Users who are authorized to access a wiki can log on to it and edit and update data, as well as see what other authorized users have contributed. Wikis enable collaboration in real time, and they keep a history so that users can see what changes were made, for example, to a spreadsheet or a proposal.[127] Some web-based collaboration software providers such as Basecamp provide customers with a wiki as part of their services.[128]

Soar Technology Inc., an artificial intelligence company in Ann Arbor, Michigan, that does work for the U.S. Office of Naval Research, has found that relying on wikis for collaboration has reduced the time it takes to complete projects by 50%.[129] According to Jacob Crossman, an engineer at Soar, wikis save time because they do away with the need for multiple e-mail messages with attachments and eliminate the typical confusion that surrounds multiple iterations of the same document.[130] Dresdner has found that e-mail pertaining to projects that use wikis has been reduced by about 75%, and even meeting times have been significantly lowered.[131] Lennard recently created a wiki to figure out how to increase profits on a certain kind of trade. In the past he would send e-mail with attachments to multiple colleagues, have to integrate and make sense of all the responses he received back from them, and then perhaps follow up with subsequent e-mail. Instead, on the wiki page he created, colleagues contributed ideas, commented on each others' ideas, and revised and edited in real time. Lennard estimates that what would have taken about two weeks to accomplish through e-mail took about two days using a wiki.[132]

Even though IBM has its own collaboration software, Lotus Notes, IBM employees rely on wikis for collaboration to such a great extent that IBM created Wiki Central to manage the wikis. Wiki Central manages over 20,000 IBM wikis and has over 100,000 users.[133] For example, some teams use wikis to coordinate the development of computer software. Wiki Central also gives employees tools to improve and enhance the functioning of their wikis, such as the "polling widget" (used for electronic voting) and the "rating widget" (used to evaluate proposals).[134] Clearly, managers have multiple options to ensure efficient, effective, and collaborative communication.[135]

Communication Skills for Managers

LO16-6 Describe important communication skills that managers need as senders and as receivers of messages and why it is important to understand differences in linguistic styles.

Some of the barriers to effective communication in organizations have their origins in senders. When messages are unclear, incomplete, or difficult to understand, when they are sent over an inappropriate medium, or when no provision for feedback is made, communication suffers. Other communication barriers have their origins in receivers. When receivers pay no attention to or do not listen to messages or when they make no effort to understand the meaning of a message, communication is likely to be ineffective. Sometimes advanced information technology, such as automated phone systems, can hamper effective communication to the extent that the human element is missing.

To overcome these barriers and effectively communicate with others, managers (as well as other organizational members) must possess or develop certain communication skills. Some of these skills are particularly important when managers *send* messages; others are critical when managers *receive* messages. These skills help ensure that managers will be able to share information, will have the information they need to make good decisions and take action, and will be able to reach a common understanding with others.

Communication Skills for Managers as Senders

Organizational effectiveness depends on the ability of managers (as well as other organizational members) to effectively send messages to people both inside and outside the organization. Table 16.2 summarizes seven communication skills that help ensure that when managers send messages, they are properly understood and the transmission phase of the communication process is effective. Let's see what each skill entails.

SEND CLEAR AND COMPLETE MESSAGES Managers need to learn how to send a message that is clear and complete. A message is clear when it is easy for the receiver to understand and interpret, and it is complete when it contains all the information that the sender and receiver need to reach a common understanding. In striving to send messages that are both clear and complete, managers must learn to anticipate how receivers will interpret messages and must adjust messages to eliminate sources of misunderstanding or confusion.

ENCODE MESSAGES IN SYMBOLS THE RECEIVER UNDERSTANDS Managers need to appreciate that when they encode messages, they should use symbols or language that the receiver understands. When sending messages in English to receivers whose native language is not English, for example, it is important to use common vocabulary and to avoid using clichés that, when translated, may make little sense and sometimes are either comical or insulting. **Jargon**, specialized language that members of an occupation, group, or organization develop to facilitate communication among themselves, should never be used when communicating with people outside the occupation, group, or organization.

jargon Specialized language that members of an occupation, group, or organization develop to facilitate communication among themselves.

Table 16.2
Seven Communication Skills for Managers as Senders of Messages

- Send messages that are clear and complete.
- Encode messages in symbols that the receiver understands.
- Select a medium that is appropriate for the message.
- Select a medium that the receiver monitors.
- Avoid filtering and information distortion.
- Ensure that a feedback mechanism is built into messages.
- Provide accurate information to ensure that misleading rumors are not spread.

SELECT A MEDIUM APPROPRIATE FOR THE MESSAGE   As you have learned, when relying on verbal communication, managers can choose from a variety of communication media, including face-to-face communication in person, written letters, memos, newsletters, phone conversations, e-mail, voice mail, faxes, and videoconferences. When choosing among these media, managers need to take into account the level of information richness required, time constraints, and the need for a paper or electronic trail. A primary concern in choosing an appropriate medium is the nature of the message. Is it personal, important, nonroutine, and likely to be misunderstood and in need of further clarification? If it is, face-to-face communication is likely to be in order.

SELECT A MEDIUM THE RECEIVER MONITORS   Another factor that managers need to take into account when selecting a communication medium is whether the medium is one that the receiver monitors. Managers differ in the communication media they pay attention to. Many managers simply select the medium that they themselves use the most and are most comfortable with, but doing this can often lead to ineffective communication. Managers who dislike telephone conversations and too many face-to-face interactions may prefer to use e-mail, send many e-mail messages per day, and check their own e-mail often. Managers who prefer to communicate with people in person or over the phone may have e-mail addresses but may be less likely to respond to e-mail messages. No matter how much a manager likes e-mail, sending e-mail to someone who does not respond to e-mail may be futile. Learning which managers like things in writing and which prefer face-to-face interactions and then using the appropriate medium enhances the chance that receivers will actually receive and pay attention to messages.

A related consideration is whether receivers have disabilities that hamper their ability to decode certain messages. A blind receiver, for example, cannot read a written message. Managers should ensure that employees with disabilities have resources available to communicate effectively with others. For example, deaf employees can effectively communicate over the telephone by using text-typewriters that have a screen and a keyboard on which senders can type messages. The message travels along the phone lines to special operators called *communication assistants,* who translate the typed message into words that the receiver can listen to. The receiver's spoken replies are translated into typewritten text by the communication assistants and appear on the sender's screen. The communication assistants relay messages back and forth to each sender and receiver.[136] Additionally, use of fax and e-mail instead of phone conversations can aid deaf employees.

filtering Withholding part of a message because of the mistaken belief that the receiver does not need or will not want the information.

AVOID FILTERING AND INFORMATION DISTORTION   Filtering occurs when senders withhold part of a message because they (mistakenly) think the receiver does not need the information or will not want to receive it. Filtering can occur at all levels in an organization and in both vertical and horizontal communication. Rank-and-file workers may filter messages they send to first-line managers, first-line managers may filter messages to middle managers, and middle managers may filter messages to top managers. Such filtering is most likely to take place when messages contain bad news or problems that subordinates are afraid they will be blamed for. Managers need to hear bad news and be aware of problems as soon as they occur so they can take swift steps to rectify the problem and limit the damage it may have caused.

Some filtering takes place because of internal competition in organizations or because organizational members fear their power and influence will be diminished if others have access to some of their specialized knowledge. By increasing levels of trust in an organization, taking steps to motivate all employees (and the groups and teams they belong to) to work together to achieve organizational goals, and ensuring that employees realize that when the organization reaches its goals and performs effectively, they too will benefit, this kind of filtering can be reduced.

information distortion Changes in the meaning of a message as the message passes through a series of senders and receivers.

Information distortion occurs when the meaning of a message changes as the message passes through a series of senders and receivers. Some information distortion is accidental—due to faulty encoding and decoding or to a lack of feedback. Other information distortion is deliberate. Senders may alter a message to make themselves or their groups look good and to receive special treatment.

Managers themselves should avoid filtering and distorting information. But how can they eliminate these barriers to effective communication throughout their organization? They need to establish trust throughout the organization. Subordinates who trust their managers believe they will not be blamed for things beyond their control and will be treated fairly. Managers who trust their subordinates give them clear and complete information and do not hold things back.

INCLUDE A FEEDBACK MECHANISM IN MESSAGES Because feedback is essential for effective communication, managers should build a feedback mechanism into the messages they send. They either should include a request for feedback or indicate when and how they will follow up on the message to make sure it was received and understood. When managers write letters and memos or send faxes, they can request that the receiver respond with comments and suggestions in a letter, memo, or fax; schedule a meeting to discuss the issue; or follow up with a phone call. By building feedback mechanisms such as these into their messages, managers ensure that they get heard and are understood.

PROVIDE ACCURATE INFORMATION **Rumors** are unofficial pieces of information of interest to organizational members but with no identifiable source. Rumors spread quickly once they are started, and usually they concern topics that organizational members think are important, interesting, or amusing. Rumors, however, can be misleading and can harm individual employees and their organizations when they are false, malicious, or unfounded. Managers can halt the spread of misleading rumors by giving organizational members accurate information about matters that concern them.

Providing accurate information is especially important in tough economic times like the recession in the late 2000s.[137] During a recession, employees are sometimes laid off or find their working hours or pay levels cut back and often experience high levels of stress. When managers give employees accurate information, this can help reduce their stress levels as well as motivate them to find ways to help their companies weather the tough times.[138] Moreover, when the economy does turn around, employees who received accurate information from their bosses may be more likely to remain with their organizations rather than pursue other opportunities.

rumors Unofficial pieces of information of interest to organizational members but with no identifiable source.

Communication Skills for Managers as Receivers

Managers receive as many messages as they send. Thus managers must possess or develop communication skills that allow them to be effective receivers of messages. Table 16.3 summarizes three of these important skills, which we examine here in greater detail.

PAY ATTENTION Because of their multiple roles and tasks, managers often are overloaded and forced to think about several things at once. Pulled in many different directions, they sometimes do not pay sufficient attention to the messages they receive. To be effective, however, managers should always pay attention to messages they receive, no matter how busy they are. When discussing a project with a subordinate, an effective manager focuses on the project and not on an upcoming meeting with his or her own boss. Similarly, when managers are reading written communication, they should focus on understanding what they are reading; they should not be sidetracked into thinking about other issues.

BE A GOOD LISTENER Managers (and all other members of an organization) can do several things to be good listeners. First, managers should refrain from interrupting senders in the middle of a message so that senders do not lose their train of thought and managers do not jump to erroneous conclusions based on incomplete information. Second, managers should maintain eye contact with senders so that senders feel their listeners are paying attention; doing this also helps managers focus on what they are hearing. Third, after receiving a message, managers should ask questions to clarify points of ambiguity or confusion. Fourth, managers should paraphrase, or restate in their own words, points senders make that are important, complex, or open to alternative interpretations; this is the feedback component so critical to successful communication.

Table 16.3

Three Communication Skills for Managers as Receivers of Messages

- Pay attention.
- Be a good listener.
- Be empathetic.

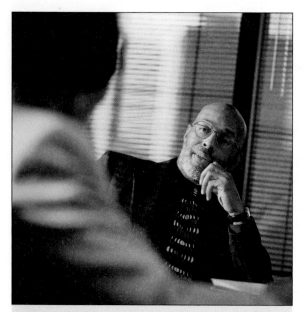

This manager demonstrates that he is paying attention to what his employee is asking for with his eye contact, engaged posture, and focus.

Managers, like most people, often like to hear themselves talk rather than listen to others. Part of being a good communicator, however, is being a good listener—an essential communication skill for managers as receivers of messages transmitted face-to-face and over the telephone.

BE EMPATHETIC   Receivers are empathetic when they try to understand how the sender feels and try to interpret a message from the sender's perspective, rather than viewing the message from only their own point of view. Marcia Mazulo, the chief psychologist in a public school system in the Northwest, recently learned this lesson after interacting with Karen Sanchez, a new psychologist on her staff. Sanchez was distraught after meeting with the parent of a child she had been working with extensively. The parent was difficult to talk to and argumentative and was not supportive of her own child. Sanchez told Mazulo how upset she was, and Mazulo responded by reminding Sanchez that she was a professional and that dealing with such a situation was part of her job. This feedback upset Sanchez further and caused her to storm out of the room.

In hindsight, Mazulo realized that her response had been inappropriate. She had failed to empathize with Sanchez, who had spent so much time with the child and was deeply concerned about the child's well-being. Rather than dismissing Sanchez's concerns, Mazulo realized, she should have tried to understand how Sanchez felt and given her some support and advice for dealing positively with the situation.

Understanding Linguistic Styles

Consider the following scenarios:

- A manager from New York is having a conversation with a manager from Iowa City. The Iowa City manager never seems to get a chance to talk. He keeps waiting for a pause to signal his turn to talk, but the New York manager never pauses long enough. The New York manager wonders why the Iowa City manager does not say much. He feels uncomfortable when he pauses and the Iowa City manager says nothing, so he starts talking again.

- Elizabeth compliments Bob on his presentation to upper management and asks Bob what he thought of her presentation. Bob launches into a lengthy critique of Elizabeth's presentation and describes how he would have handled it differently. This is hardly the response Elizabeth expected.

- Catherine shares with co-members of a self-managed work team a new way to cut costs. Michael, another team member, thinks her idea is a good one and encourages the rest of the team to support it. Catherine is quietly pleased by Michael's support. The group implements "Michael's" suggestion, and it is written up as such in the company newsletter.

- Robert was recently promoted and transferred from his company's Oklahoma office to its headquarters in New Jersey. Robert is perplexed because he never seems to get a chance to talk in management meetings; someone else always seems to get the floor. Robert's new boss wonders whether Robert's new responsibilities are too much for him, although Robert's supervisor in Oklahoma rated him highly and said he is a real "go-getter." Robert is timid in management meetings and rarely says a word.

What do these scenarios have in common? Essentially, they all describe situations in which a misunderstanding of linguistic styles leads to a breakdown in communication. The scenarios are based on the research of linguist Deborah Tannen, who describes **linguistic style** as a person's characteristic way of speaking. Elements of linguistic style include tone of voice, speed, volume, use of pauses, directness or indirectness, choice of words, credit taking, and use of questions, jokes, and other manners of speech.[139] When people's linguistic styles differ and these differences are not understood, ineffective communication is likely.

linguistic style A person's characteristic way of speaking.

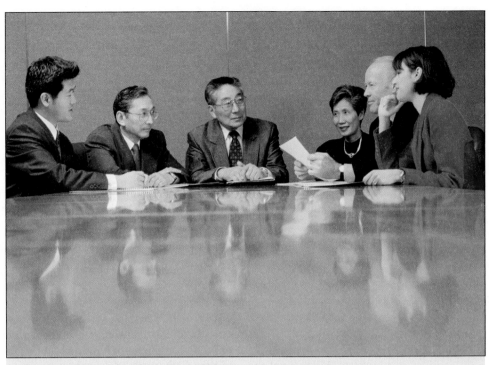

Cross-cultural differences in linguistic style can lead to misunderstandings.

The first and last scenarios illustrate regional differences in linguistic style.[140] The Iowa City manager and Robert from Oklahoma expect the pauses that signal turn taking in conversations to be longer than the pauses made by their colleagues in New York and New Jersey. This difference causes communication problems. The Iowan and transplanted Oklahoman think their Eastern colleagues never let them get a word in edgewise, and the Easterners cannot figure out why their colleagues from the Midwest and South do not get more actively involved in conversations.

Differences in linguistic style can be a particularly insidious source of communication problems because linguistic style is often taken for granted. People rarely think about their own linguistic styles and often are unaware of how linguistic styles can differ. In the example here, Robert did not realize that when dealing with his New Jersey colleagues, he could and should jump into conversations more quickly than he used to do in Oklahoma, and his boss never realized that Robert felt he was not being given a chance to speak in meetings.

The aspect of linguistic style just described, length of pauses, differs by region in the United States. Much more dramatic differences in linguistic style occur cross-culturally.

CROSS-CULTURAL DIFFERENCES Managers from Japan tend to be more formal in their conversations and more deferential toward upper-level managers and people with high status than are managers from the United States. Japanese managers do not mind extensive pauses in conversations when they are thinking things through or when they think further conversation might be detrimental. In contrast, U.S. managers (even managers from regions of the United States where pauses tend to be long) find lengthy pauses disconcerting and feel obligated to talk to fill the silence.[141]

Another cross-cultural difference in linguistic style concerns the appropriate physical distance separating speakers and listeners in business-oriented conversations.[142] The distance between speakers and listeners is greater in the United States, for example, than it is in Brazil or Saudi Arabia. Citizens of different countries also vary in how direct or indirect they are in conversations and the extent to which they take individual credit for accomplishments. Japanese culture, with its collectivist or group orientation, tends to encourage linguistic styles in which group rather than individual accomplishments are emphasized. The opposite tends to be true in the United States.

These and other cross-cultural differences in linguistic style can and often do lead to misunderstandings. For example, when a team of American managers presented a proposal for a joint venture to Japanese managers, the Japanese managers were silent as they thought about the implications of what they had just heard. The American managers took this silence as a sign that the Japanese managers wanted more information, so they went into more detail about the proposal. When they finished, the Japanese were silent again, not only frustrating the Americans but also making them wonder whether the Japanese were interested in the project. The American managers suggested that if the Japanese already had decided they did not want to pursue the project, there was no reason for the meeting to continue. The Japanese were bewildered. They were trying to carefully think out the proposal, yet the Americans thought they were not interested!

Communication misunderstandings and problems like this can be overcome if managers learn about cross-cultural differences in linguistic styles. If the American managers and the Japanese managers had realized that periods of silence are viewed differently in Japan and in the United States, their different linguistic styles might have been less troublesome barriers to communication. Before managers communicate with people from abroad, they should try to find out as much as they can about the aspects of linguistic style that are specific to the country or culture in question. Expatriate managers who have lived in the country in question for an extended time can be good sources of information about linguistic styles because they are likely to have experienced firsthand some of the differences that citizens of a country are not aware of. Finding out as much as possible about cultural differences also can help managers learn about differences in linguistic styles because the two are often closely linked.

GENDER DIFFERENCES   Referring again to the four scenarios that open this section, you may be wondering why Bob launched into a lengthy critique of Elizabeth's presentation after she paid him a routine compliment on his presentation, or you may be wondering why Michael got the credit for Catherine's idea in the self-managed work team. Research conducted by Tannen and other linguists has found that the linguistic styles of men and women differ in practically every culture or language.[143] Men and women take their own linguistic styles for granted and thus do not realize when they are talking with someone of a different gender that differences in their styles may lead to ineffective communication.

In the United States, women tend to downplay differences between people, are not overly concerned about receiving credit for their own accomplishments, and want to make everyone feel more or less on an equal footing so that even poor performers or low-status individuals feel valued. Men, in contrast, tend to emphasize their own superiority and are not reluctant to acknowledge differences in status. These differences in linguistic style led Elizabeth to routinely compliment Bob on his presentation even though she thought he had not done a particularly good job. She asked him how her presentation was so he could reciprocate and give her a routine compliment, putting them on an equal footing. Bob took Elizabeth's compliment and question about her own presentation as an opportunity to confirm his superiority, never realizing that all she was expecting was a routine compliment. Similarly, Michael's enthusiastic support for Catherine's cost-cutting idea and her apparent surrender of ownership of the idea after she described it led team members to assume incorrectly that the idea was Michael's.[144]

Do some women try to prove they are better than everyone else, and are some men unconcerned about taking credit for ideas and accomplishments? Of course. The gender differences in linguistic style that Tannen and other linguists have uncovered are general tendencies evident in *many* women and men, not in *all* women and men.

Where do gender differences in linguistic style come from? Tannen suggests they begin developing in early childhood. Girls and boys tend to play with children of their own gender, and the ways in which girls and boys play are quite different. Girls play in small groups, engage in a lot of close conversation, emphasize how similar they are to one another, and view boastfulness negatively. Boys play in large groups, emphasize status differences, expect leaders to emerge who boss others around, and give one another challenges to try to meet. These differences in styles of play and interaction result in different linguistic styles when boys and girls grow up and communicate as adults. The ways in which men communicate emphasize status differences and play up relative strengths; the ways in which women communicate emphasize similarities and downplay individual strengths.[145]

Interestingly, gender differences are also turning up in how women and men use e-mail and electronic forms of communication. For example, Susan Herring, a researcher at Indiana University, has found that in public electronic forums such as message boards and chat rooms, men tend to make stronger assertions, be more sarcastic, and be more likely to use insults and profanity than women, whereas women are more likely to be supportive, agreeable, and polite.[146] David Silver, a researcher at the University of Washington, has found that women are more expressive electronic communicators and encourage others to express their thoughts and feelings, while men are briefer and more to the point.[147] Interestingly enough, some men find e-mail to be a welcome way to express their feelings to people they care about. For example, real estate broker Mike Murname finds it easier to communicate with, and express his love for, his grown children via e-mail.[148]

MANAGING DIFFERENCES IN LINGUISTIC STYLES Managers should not expect to change people's linguistic styles and should not try to. To be effective, managers need to understand differences in linguistic styles. Knowing, for example, that some women are reluctant to speak up in meetings, not because they have nothing to contribute but because of their linguistic style, should lead managers to ensure that these women have a chance to talk. And a manager who knows certain people are reluctant to take credit for ideas can be careful to give credit where it is deserved. As Tannen points out, "Talk is the lifeblood of managerial work, and understanding that different people have different ways of saying what they mean will make it possible to take advantage of the talents of people with a broad range of linguistic styles."[149]

Summary and Review

LO16-1, 16-2

COMMUNICATION AND MANAGEMENT Communication is the sharing of information between two or more individuals or groups to reach a common understanding. Good communication is necessary for an organization to gain a competitive advantage. Communication occurs in a cyclical process that entails two phases, transmission and feedback.

LO16-3 **INFORMATION RICHNESS AND COMMUNICATION MEDIA** Information richness is the amount of information a communication medium can carry and the extent to which the medium enables the sender and receiver to reach a common understanding. Four categories of communication media, in descending order of information richness, are face-to-face communication (includes videoconferences), electronically transmitted spoken communication (includes voice mail), personally addressed written communication (includes e-mail), and impersonal written communication.

LO16-4 **COMMUNICATION NETWORKS** Communication networks are the pathways along which information flows in an organization. Four communication networks found in groups and teams are the wheel, the chain, the circle, and the all-channel network. An organization chart summarizes formal pathways of communication, but communication in organizations is often informal, as is true of communication through the grapevine.

LO16-5 **INFORMATION TECHNOLOGY AND COMMUNICATION** The Internet is a global system of computer networks that managers around the world use to communicate within and outside their companies. The World Wide Web is the multimedia business district on the Internet. Intranets are internal communication networks that managers can create to improve communication, performance, and customer service. Intranets use the same technology that the Internet and World Wide Web are based on. Groupware is computer software that enables members of groups and teams to share information with one another to improve their communication and performance.

LO16-6 **COMMUNICATION SKILLS FOR MANAGERS** There are various barriers to effective communication in organizations. To overcome these barriers and effectively communicate with others, managers must possess or develop certain communication skills. As senders of messages, managers should send messages that are clear and complete, encode messages in symbols the receiver understands, choose a medium appropriate for the message and monitored by the receiver, avoid filtering and information distortion, include a feedback mechanism in the message, and provide accurate information to ensure that misleading rumors are not spread. Communication skills for managers as receivers of messages include paying attention, being a good listener, and being empathetic. Understanding linguistic styles is also an essential communication skill for managers. Linguistic styles can vary by geographic region, gender, and country or culture. When these differences are not understood, ineffective communication can occur.

Management in Action

Topics for Discussion and Action

Discussion

1. Which medium (or media) do you think would be appropriate for each of the following kinds of messages that a subordinate could receive from his or her boss: (a) a raise, (b) not receiving a promotion, (c) an error in a report prepared by the subordinate, (d) additional job responsibilities, and (e) the schedule for company holidays for the upcoming year? Explain your choices. **[LO16-3]**

2. Discuss the pros and cons of using the Internet and World Wide Web for communication within and between organizations. **[LO16-1, 16-2, 16-3, 16-5]**

3. Why do some organizational members resist using groupware? **[LO16-5]**

4. Why do some managers find it difficult to be good listeners? **[LO16-6]**

5. Explain why subordinates might filter and distort information about problems and performance shortfalls when communicating with their bosses. What steps can managers take to eliminate filtering and information distortion? **[LO16-6]**

6. Explain why differences in linguistic style, when not understood by senders and receivers of messages, can lead to ineffective communication. **[LO16-6]**

Action

7. Interview a manager in an organization in your community to determine with whom he or she communicates on a typical day, what communication media he or she uses, and which typical communication problems the manager experiences. **[LO16-1, 16-2, 16-3, 16-4, 16-5, 16-6]**

Building Management Skills

Diagnosing Ineffective Communication [LO16-1, 16-2, 16-3, 16-4, 16-5, 16-6]

Think about the last time you experienced very ineffective communication with another person—someone you work with, a classmate, a friend, a member of your family. Describe the incident. Then answer the following questions:

1. Why was your communication ineffective in this incident?

2. What stages of the communication process were particularly problematic and why?

3. Describe any filtering or information distortion that occurred.

4. Do you think differences in linguistic styles adversely affected the communication that took place? Why or why not?

5. How could you have handled this situation differently so communication would have been effective?

Managing Ethically [LO16-3, 16-5]

Many employees use their company's Internet connections and e-mail systems to visit websites and send personal e-mail and instant messages.

Questions

1. Either individually or in a group, explore the ethics of using an organization's Internet connection and e-mail system for personal purposes at work and while away from the office. Should employees have some rights to use this resource? When does their behavior become unethical?

2. Some companies track how their employees use the company's Internet connection and e-mail system. Is it ethical for managers to read employees' personal e-mail or to record websites that employees visit? Why or why not?

Small Group Breakout Exercise

Reducing Resistance to Advances in Information Technology [LO16-5]

Form groups of three or four people, and appoint one member as the spokesperson who will communicate your findings to the class when called on by the instructor. Then discuss the following scenario:

You are a team of managers in charge of information and communication in a large consumer products corporation. Your company has already implemented many advances in information technology. Managers and workers have access to e-mail, the Internet, your company's own intranet, groupware, and collaboration software.

Many employees use the technology, but the resistance of some is causing communication problems. A case in point is the use of groupware and collaboration software. Many teams in your organization have access to groupware and are encouraged to use it. While some teams welcome this communication tool and actually have made suggestions for improvements, others are highly resistant to sharing documents in their teams' online workspaces.

Although you do not want to force people to use the technology, you want them to at least try it and give it a chance. You are meeting today to develop strategies for reducing resistance to the new technologies.

1. One resistant group of employees is made up of top managers. Some of them seem computer-phobic and are highly resistant to sharing information online, even with sophisticated security precautions in place. What steps will you take to get these managers to have more confidence in electronic communication?

2. A second group of resistant employees consists of middle managers. Some middle managers resist using your company's intranet. Although these managers do not resist the technology per se and do use electronic communication for multiple purposes, they seem to distrust the intranet as a viable way to communicate and get things done. What steps will you take to get these managers to take advantage of the intranet?

3. A third group of resistant employees is made up of members of groups and teams who do not want to use the groupware that has been provided to them. You think the groupware could improve their communication and performance, but they seem to think otherwise. What steps will you take to get these members of groups and teams to start using groupware?

Exploring the World Wide Web [LO16-5]

Atos Origin is a global information technology company that provides IT services to major corporations to improve, facilitate, integrate, and manage operations, information, and communication across multiple locations. Visit Atos Origin's website at http://www.atos.net/en-us/ and read about this company and the services it provides to improve communication. How can companies like Atos Origin help managers improve communication effectiveness in their organizations? What kinds of organizations and groups are most likely to benefit from services provided by Atos Origin? Why is it beneficial for some organizations to contract with firms like Atos Origin for their IT and communication needs rather than meet these needs internally with their own employees?

Be the Manager [LO16-1, 16-2, 16-3, 16-6]

You supervise support staff for an Internet merchandising organization that sells furniture over the Internet. You always thought that you needed to expand your staff, and just when you were about to approach your boss with such a request, business slowed. Thus your plan to try to add new employees to your staff is on hold.

However, you have noticed a troubling pattern of communication with your staff. Ordinarily, when you want a staff member to work on a task, you e-mail that subordinate the pertinent information. For the last few months, your e-mail requests have gone unheeded, and your subordinates seem to respond to your requests only after you visit them in person and give them a specific deadline. Each time they apologize for not getting to the task sooner but say they are so overloaded with requests that they sometimes even stop answering their phones. Unless someone asks for something more than once, your staff seems to feel the request is not that urgent and can be put on hold. You think this state of affairs is dysfunctional and could lead to serious problems down the road. Also, you are starting to realize that your subordinates seem to have no way of prioritizing tasks—hence some very important projects you asked them to complete were put on hold until you followed up with them about the tasks. Knowing you cannot add employees to your staff in the short term, what are you going to do to improve communication with your overloaded staff?

The Wall Street Journal Case in the News

Doodling for Dollars

Put down that smartphone; pick up that crayon.

Employees at a range of businesses are being encouraged by their companies to doodle their ideas and draw diagrams to explain complicated concepts to colleagues.

While whiteboards long have been staples in conference rooms, companies such as Facebook Inc. are incorporating whiteboards, chalkboards and writable glass on all sorts of surfaces to spark creativity.

Firms are holding training sessions to teach employees the basics of what's known as visual note taking. Others, like vacation-rental company HomeAway Inc. and retailer Zappos, are hiring graphic recorders, consultants who sketch what is discussed at meetings and conferences, cartoon-style, to keep employees engaged.

Doodling proponents say it can help generate ideas, fuel collaboration and simplify communication. It can be especially helpful among global colleagues who don't share a common first language. Putting pen to paper also is seen as an antidote to the pervasiveness of digital culture, getting workers to look up from their devices. And studies show it can help workers retain more information.

Even with advanced gadgets such as smartphones and tablets, "the hand is the easiest way to get something down," says Everett Katigbak, a communication designer at Facebook. Most of the walls at the company's offices around the country have been coated with dry-erase or chalkboard paint or a treatment for glass to allow employees to sketch ideas whenever they arise. The company's offices are filled with jottings, from mathematical equations to doodles of cats and dollar signs.

IdeaPaint Inc., which makes a paint that turns a surface into a whiteboard, says its sales have doubled annually since the product was introduced in 2008. The Ashland, Mass., company says more than half of its business is in the workplace.

Taking notes and drawing may help workers stay more focused, too.

A 2009 study published in the journal *Applied Cognitive Psychology* found that doodlers retained more than nondoodlers when remembering information that had been presented in a boring context, such as a meeting or conference call. The logic, according to Jackie Andrade, a psychology professor at the University of Plymouth in England, is that doodling takes up just enough cognitive energy to prevent the mind from daydreaming.

Last summer, software maker Citrix Systems Inc. opened a "design collaboration" workspace at its Santa Clara, Calif., headquarters. The facility was designed to encourage the company's gadget-obsessed engineers and other employees to let loose and sketch ideas, says Catherine Courage, the company's vice president of product design.

Whiteboards cover almost every wall and table. Markers, sticky notes and construction paper are readily available. There are also pipe cleaners and foam balls for 3-D models, and employees make props like hats and glasses to help them act out concepts.

To loosen up employees, meetings sometimes begin with participants sketching self-portraits. Although some engineers are skeptical and say they can't draw, "it gets them in the mood," Ms. Courage says.

Audra Kalfass, a Citrix software-development engineer, says when she meets with her team and there is a technical issue, "it's natural to start drawing stuff." Since nearly every surface in design meeting rooms can be written on—even the tables are made of whiteboards—"you just grab a marker and you start drawing," she says.

Ms. Kalfass says she is a "horrible" artist. Nevertheless, "it doesn't take much artistic ability to communicate visually. You don't have to be amazing artists . . . It's mostly boxes and lines and stuff like that to get your point across."

At Spectrum Health System, a Grand Rapids, Mich., health-care provider and insurer, technology managers took a workshop with Dan Roam, a San Francisco "visual problem solving" consultant, on using images like stick figures and arrows to explain the complexities of the health-care industry to Spectrum employees.

After the workshop, Chief Information Officer Patrick O'Hare helped create a presentation featuring cartoonlike sketches for the chief executive. In one, the company's three business branches—health insurance, hospitals and physician clinics—were depicted as a body, representing the consumer, divided into three parts.

Mr. O'Hare says he isn't a good artist but the workshop taught him it was "OK to stand up in front of a group and draw stick figures. It doesn't have to be so pristine."

HomeAway, an Austin, Texas, vacation-rental company, hired a graphic facilitator to help train a dozen employees—including senior managers and training and human-resources staff—to use visual shorthand and sketching to help guide meetings, says Lori Knowlton, the company's vice president of human resources. The aim was to better "capture ideas using images," she says. Plus, it is more fun than "being surrounded by spreadsheets and e-mails."

The company also brought in graphic recorder Sunni Brown to help sketch, in real time, what was discussed at a large company meeting on HomeAway's strategy. The resulting cartoonlike image, which serves as the meeting's minutes, hangs framed at the company's headquarters.

At Turner Broadcasting System Inc. in Atlanta, a strategy-development team recently drew tree branches and placed sticky notes on the branches to explore ways to extend the Turner Classic Movies brand, says Jennifer Dorian, a senior vice president.

The exercise yielded more than 200 promising ideas, some of which are in development, says Amy Zehfuss, vice president of network strategy for the Time Warner Inc. unit. "Seeing all the stickies on the tree is a really powerful visual," she says.

Even PowerPoint software developers do their share of doodling.

Jeffrey Murray, principal test manager for the Microsoft Corp. unit, says his team often starts with whiteboard sketches and cartoonlike storyboards when considering new product features.

Sketches help "get everyone on the same page and can convey the emotion and experience of the user," he says. Eventually, the images are transferred to PowerPoint decks, he says. Inevitably, developers sketch and scribble over the deck's whiteboard projections.

Questions for Discussion

1. Under what conditions might sketching and/or doodling contribute to effective communication in organizations?

2. When may sketching and/or doodling detract from effective communication in organizations?

3. Why might some people need training in the use of sketching and doodling to facilitate effective communication?

4. Why might people differ in terms of the extent to which they want to use sketching and/or doodling to communicate in the workplace?

CHAPTER 17

Managing Conflict, Politics, and Negotiation

Learning Objectives

After studying this chapter, you should be able to:

LO17-1 Explain why conflict arises, and identify the types and sources of conflict in organizations.

LO17-2 Describe conflict management strategies that managers can use to resolve conflict effectively.

LO17-3 Understand the nature of negotiation and why integrative bargaining is more effective than distributive negotiation.

LO17-4 Describe ways in which managers can promote integrative bargaining in organizations.

LO17-5 Explain why managers need to be attuned to organizational politics, and describe the political strategies that managers can use to become politically skilled.

A MANAGER'S CHALLENGE

Collaborating and Building Alliances at the Nature Conservancy

How can managers collaborate and build alliances with individuals, groups, and organizations that have seemingly conflicting goals? A large chemical company, a small logging company, or individual fishermen would seem to have not that much in common with a large conservation organization devoted to protecting nature, land, forests, and dwindling fish populations.[1] In fact, it is not difficult to imagine that the conservation organization would be in conflict with such individuals and groups, and some conservation organizations have had heated conflicts with groups and organizations that they felt were threatening the natural environment.

This is definitely not the case, though, with the Nature Conservancy. The Nature Conservancy is the biggest conservation organization in the world.[2] A nonprofit organization, the conservancy has chapters in over 30 countries and every state within the United States. With over 1 million members and assets valued at more than $5 billion, the conservancy's annual income is around $1 billion.[3] The conservancy has either purchased or received as a donation over 177 million acres of land with environmental value. Government agencies often buy this land from the conservancy for the creation of natural preserves and parks. While continuing with this legacy of acquiring

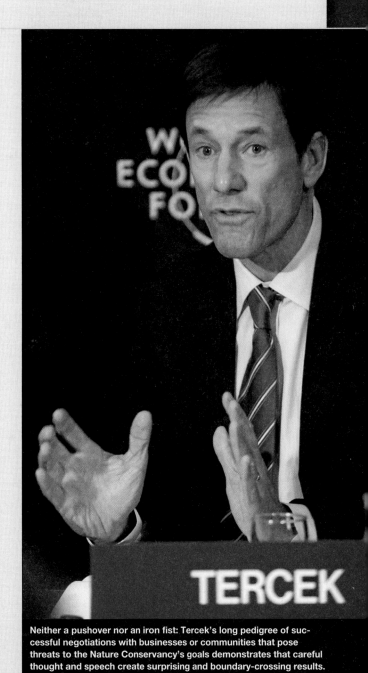

Neither a pushover nor an iron fist: Tercek's long pedigree of successful negotiations with businesses or communities that pose threats to the Nature Conservancy's goals demonstrates that careful thought and speech create surprising and boundary-crossing results.

lands at risk and ensuring that they are preserved, the conservancy has branched out to collaborate with groups and organizations to conserve and protect nature for people and the groups and organizations that provide them with goods and services.[4]

Leading these efforts is a dedicated group of scientists, managers, and leaders at the conservancy. Mark Tercek is the president and chief executive officer of the Nature Conservancy.[5] With a BA in English from Williams College and an MBA from Harvard, Tercek previously worked as the director of the Environmental Strategy Group at Goldman Sachs. Importantly, the initiatives and efforts that Tercek leads to protect nature and the environment at the conservancy are informed by a strong appreciation for ecology and conservation science and research. Peter Kareiva, chief scientist on the Nature Conservancy Leadership Team, leads some 600 scientists who work at the conservancy and is always involved in major decisions that Tercek makes. In fact, Tercek refers to Kareiva as his "closest intellectual advisor."[6] With an MS in environmental biology from the University of California at Irvine and a PhD in ecology and evolutionary biology from Cornell, Kareiva has worked as a professor, taught at eight universities, directed the Northwest Fisheries Science Center Conservation Biology Division of the National Oceanic and Atmospheric Administration, has published over 100 scientific articles, and was elected to the prestigious American Academy of Arts and Sciences.[7]

While one would think that a chemical company and a conservation organization would never be able to partner together, Tercek, Kareiva, and other leaders and scientists at the Nature Conservancy are in the midst of a five-year alliance with Dow Chemical.[8] Dow, with $60 billion in annual sales, makes 5,000 different products at 197 manufacturing facilities in over 35 countries and has periodically faced pollution allegations. For instance, citizens in Saginaw County, Michigan, filed suits against Dow, claiming that Dow polluted a river with dioxin. Why, then, would the Nature Conservancy engage in an alliance with Dow? Part of the reason is to assist Dow with inventorying and valuing its vast land and water resources around the globe. By assessing these natural resources and their "natural capital" value, Dow may be better equipped to figure out how to protect and improve the natural resources it controls.[9]

As part of the alliance, 20 scientists from the conservancy will be allowed admittance to Dow's facilities, including Dow's large complex in Freeport, Texas, which includes 5,000 acres of land and adjacent coastal marshes and wetlands.[10] The scientists will help Dow to figure out how to protect natural resources such as these. For example, it might be the case that Dow can protect its facility in Texas from hurricanes by enhancing the marshland rather than building concrete flood barriers through it. While it is still too early to tell if this will be a viable option, the scientists are using engineering and modeling techniques to help Dow explore its options. Dow has given the conservancy $10 million to defray the costs of its research and will let the scientists publish annual progress reports and submit results of the research to peer-refereed academic journals for consideration for publication.[11]

Nonetheless, critics argue that a conservation organization should not be receiving funding from a huge corporation like Dow. For example, Anne Rolfes, a founding director of the Louisiana Bucket Brigade,[12] which has had run-ins with Dow over alleged pollution, suggests that ". . . Dow is awful . . . We would never take money from them or partner with them."[13] The Bucket Brigade is a nonprofit organization in Louisiana that helps neighborhoods bordering chemical plants and oil refineries keep their lands pollution-free.[14] Kareiva acknowledges that while things might not always go smoothly or as planned, on a global level, the alliance has the potential to yield a net benefit for the environment and conservancy. As Tercek puts it, "I know there's a lot of skepticism about these corporate initiatives, but for Dow to agree with us philosophically that it relies on nature for business reasons and to begin to put a business value on its natural assets, that's huge."[15]

The Nature Conservancy has also formed alliances with fishermen, resulting in the fishermen being able to sustain their livelihoods while meeting more stringent government regulations to protect shrinking fish populations and endangered habitats.[16] The conservancy's approach here and on other initiatives is both to protect nature and the environment and also forge alliances with the people who are dependent upon the environment for their living and well-being—helping those individuals protect the very resource that sustains them.

Other initiatives involved alliances with communities. On the Gulf Coast of the United States, the conservancy created a mile and a half long oyster reef.[17] Instead of locating the reef where it made the most ecological sense, managers and scientists at the conservancy also took into account the income levels of the local communities that would be affected by the presence of the reef. That is, oyster reefs can protect communities from storm surges and citizens of low income neighborhoods suffer the most when their towns are damaged during a storm. Thus, the reef went to a low-income community along the coast.[18]

The Nature Conservancy has also formed alliances with Latin American countries to protect their water supplies. For example, rather than creating water treatment plants, the conservancy helped Columbia to buy land near Bogota's watershed and pay soda plants and sugar farmers to run their businesses in a sustainable fashion.[19] Relying on research and science, Tercek, Kareiva, and other managers and leaders at the Nature Conservancy focus on building alliances with many different kinds of groups and organizations for mutual benefit.[20]

Overview Successful leaders such as Mark Tercek and Peter Kareiva in "A Manager's Challenge" can effectively use their power to influence others and to manage conflict to achieve win–win solutions. In Chapter 14 we described how managers, as leaders, influence other people to achieve group and organizational goals and how managers' sources of power enable them to exert such influence. In this chapter we describe why managers need to develop the skills necessary to manage organizational conflict, politics, and negotiation if they are going to be effective and achieve their goals.

We describe conflict and the strategies managers can use to resolve it effectively. We discuss one major conflict resolution technique, negotiation, in detail, outlining the steps managers can take to be good negotiators. Then we discuss the nature of organizational politics and the political strategies managers can use to maintain and expand their power and use it effectively. By the end of this chapter, you will appreciate why managers must develop the skills necessary to manage these important organizational processes if they are to be effective and achieve organizational goals.

Organizational Conflict

LO17-1 Explain why conflict arises, and identify the types and sources of conflict in organizations.

organizational conflict
The discord that arises when the goals, interests, or values of different individuals or groups are incompatible and those individuals or groups block or thwart one another's attempts to achieve their objectives.

Organizational conflict is the discord that arises when the goals, interests, or values of different individuals or groups are incompatible and those individuals or groups block or thwart one another's attempts to achieve their objectives.[21] Conflict is an inevitable part of organizational life because the goals of different stakeholders such as managers and workers are often incompatible. Organizational conflict also can exist between departments and divisions that compete for resources or even between managers who may be competing for promotion to the next level in the organizational hierarchy.

It is important for managers to develop the skills necessary to manage conflict effectively. In addition, the level of conflict present in an organization has important implications for organizational performance. Figure 17.1 illustrates the relationship between organizational conflict and performance. At point A there is little or no conflict, and organizational performance suffers. Lack of conflict in an organization often signals that managers emphasize conformity at the expense of new ideas, resist change, and strive for agreement rather than effective decision making. As the level of conflict increases from point A to point B, organizational effectiveness is likely to increase. When an organization has an optimum level of conflict, managers are likely to be open to, and encourage, a variety of perspectives; look for ways to improve organizational functioning and effectiveness; and view debates and disagreements as a necessary ingredient of effective decision making and innovation. As the level of conflict increases from point B to point C, conflict escalates to the point where organizational performance suffers. When an organization has a dysfunctionally high level of conflict, managers are likely to waste organizational resources to achieve their own ends,

Figure 17.1

The Effect of Conflict on Organizational Performance

Inappropriately handling legitimate conflict can create lasting damage within one's work group.

to be more concerned about winning political battles than about doing what will lead to a competitive advantage for their organization, and to try to get even with their opponents rather than make good decisions.

Conflict is a force that needs to be managed rather than eliminated.[22] Managers should never try to eliminate all conflict but, rather, should try to keep conflict at a moderate and functional level to promote change efforts that benefit the organization. Additionally, managers should strive to keep conflict focused on substantive, task-based issues and minimize conflict based on personal disagreements and animosities. To manage conflict,[23] managers must understand the types and sources of conflict and be familiar with strategies that can be effective in dealing with it.

Types of Conflict

There are several types of conflict in organizations: interpersonal, intragroup, intergroup, and interorganizational (see Figure 17.2).[24] Understanding how these types differ can help managers deal with conflict.

INTERPERSONAL CONFLICT   Interpersonal conflict is conflict between individual members of an organization, occurring because of differences in their goals or values. Two managers may experience interpersonal conflict when their values concerning protection of the environment differ. One manager may argue that the organization should do only what is required by law. The other manager may counter that the organization should invest in equipment to reduce emissions even though the organization's current level of emissions is below the legal limit.

INTRAGROUP CONFLICT   Intragroup conflict arises within a group, team, or department. When members of the marketing department in a clothing company disagree about how they should spend budgeted advertising dollars for a new line of men's designer jeans, they are experiencing intragroup conflict. Some of the members want to spend all the money on advertisements in magazines. Others want to devote half of the money to billboards and ads in city buses and subways.

INTERGROUP CONFLICT   Intergroup conflict occurs between groups, teams, or departments. R&D departments, for example, sometimes experience intergroup conflict with production departments. Members of the R&D department may develop a new product that they think production can make inexpensively by using existing manufacturing capabilities. Members of the production department, however, may disagree and believe that the costs of making the product will be much higher. Managers of departments usually play a key role in managing intergroup conflicts such as this.

Figure 17.2

Types of Conflict in Organizations

INTERORGANIZATIONAL CONFLICT Interorganizational conflict arises across organizations. Sometimes interorganizational conflict occurs when managers in one organization feel that another organization is not behaving ethically and is threatening the well-being of certain stakeholder groups. Interorganizational conflict also can occur between government agencies and corporations, as illustrated in the following "Ethics in Action" box.

Ethics in Action

The U.S. Labor Department and Big Home Builders Clash

In 2011, the U.S. Labor Department sent letters to big home building companies, including PulteGroup, Inc., D. R. Horton Inc., KB Home, and Lennar Corp., asking them to provide information regarding the names, social security numbers, addresses, hours worked, and pay rates for all their employees for the past two years and also the names of all their contractors.[25] The investigation falls under the rubrics of the Fair Labor Standards Act, which pertains to the federal minimum wage, overtime pay, and youth employment.[26]

And in 2012, the Labor Department petitioned the Federal District Court in Michigan to require PulteGroup, based in Bloomfield Hills, Michigan,[27] to give the department thousands of documents pertaining to its employees and subcontractors.[28] It appears that Pulte did provide the department with records for its own employees. However, Pulte has told the court that it thinks the request for payroll records for building projects from late 2009 to early 2012 in eight states is too all encompassing.[29]

Apparently part of the conflict arises from the fact that, although large building companies like Pulte buy land for homes and market them, they ordinarily rely on contractors to actually build the houses rather than doing it themselves.[30] Unions and other labor groups have griped that the big home builders have lowered wages in the industry by relying on subcontractors who don't pay employees the minimum wage, don't pay overtime pay, and/or don't provide benefits such as health care. In this current case, it appears that the Labor Department wants to make sure that carpenters, roofers, bricklayers, laborers, and other subcontractors are receiving the federal minimum wage, overtime pay, and benefits stipulated by the Fair Labor Standards Act.[31]

Managers at Pulte think that the Labor Department is requiring too much from them in the investigation and subpoena.[32] Some of the other information the department requested were records pertaining to contracts it has with suppliers and contractors for the subsequent 12-month period. James Zeumer, vice president for Investor Communications,[33] indicated that "while the skilled labor crews building our homes are not Pulte employees, our vendor agreements state that contractors are required to comply with all applicable labor laws and wage practices."[34] With the Labor Department and Pulte engaged in conflict, this is one for the courts to decide.

Conflict management hits a wall: Pulte Group's stand-off with the Labor Department's request for comprehensive records of its subcontractors' practices, like how much this worker gets paid, embodies a negotiation failure.

Figure 17.3
Sources of Conflict in Organizations

Sources of Conflict

Conflict in organizations springs from a variety of sources. The ones we examine here are different goals and time horizons, overlapping authority, task interdependencies, different evaluation or reward systems, scarce resources, and status inconsistencies (see Figure 17.3).[35]

DIFFERENT GOALS AND TIME HORIZONS   Recall from Chapter 10 that an important managerial activity is organizing people and tasks into departments and divisions to accomplish an organization's goals. Almost inevitably this grouping creates departments and divisions that have different goals and time horizons, and the result can be conflict. Production managers, for example, usually concentrate on efficiency and cost cutting; they have a relatively short time horizon and focus on producing quality goods or services in a timely and efficient manner. In contrast, marketing managers focus on sales and responsiveness to customers. Their time horizon is longer than that of production because they are trying to be responsive not only to customers' needs today but also to their changing needs in the future to build long-term customer loyalty. These fundamental differences between marketing and production often breed conflict.

Suppose production is behind schedule in its plan to produce a specialized product for a key customer. The marketing manager believes the delay will reduce sales of the product and therefore insists that the product be delivered on time even if saving the production schedule means increasing costs by paying production workers overtime. The production manager says that she will happily schedule overtime if marketing will pay for it. Both managers' positions are reasonable from the perspective of their own departments, and conflict is likely.

OVERLAPPING AUTHORITY   When two or more managers, departments, or functions claim authority for the same activities or tasks, conflict is likely.[36] This is precisely what happened when heirs of the Forman liquor distribution company, based in Washington, D.C., inherited the company from their parents. One of the heirs, Barry Forman, wanted to control the company and was reluctant to share power with the other heirs. Several of the heirs felt they had authority over certain tasks crucial to Forman's success (such as maintaining good relationships with the top managers of liquor companies). What emerged was a battle of wills and considerable conflict, which escalated to the point of being dysfunctional, requiring that the family hire a consulting firm to help resolve it.[37]

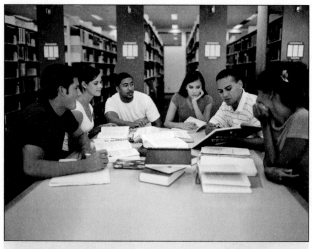

Whenever groups or teams are interdependent, the potential for conflict exists.

TASK INTERDEPENDENCIES   Have you ever been assigned a group project for one of your classes and had one group member who consistently failed to get things done on time? This probably created some conflict in your group because other group members were dependent on the late member's contributions to complete the project. Whenever individuals, groups, teams, or departments are interdependent, the potential for conflict exists.[38] With differing goals and time horizons, the managers of marketing and production come into conflict precisely because the departments are interdependent. Marketing is dependent on production for the goods it markets and sells, and production is dependent on marketing to create demand for the things it makes.

DIFFERENT EVALUATION OR REWARD SYSTEMS   How interdependent groups, teams, or departments are evaluated and rewarded can be another source of conflict.[39] Production managers, for example, are evaluated and rewarded for their success in staying within budget or lowering costs while maintaining quality. So they are reluctant to take any steps that will increase costs, such as paying workers high overtime rates to finish a late order for an important customer. Marketing managers, in contrast, are evaluated and rewarded for their success in generating sales and satisfying customers. So they often think overtime pay is a small price to pay for responsiveness to customers. Thus conflict between production and marketing is rarely unexpected.

SCARCE RESOURCES   Management is the process of acquiring, developing, protecting, and using the resources that allow an organization to be efficient and effective (see Chapter 1). When resources are scarce, management is more difficult and conflict is likely.[40] For example, divisional managers may be in conflict over who has access to financial capital, and organizational members at all levels may be in conflict over who gets raises and promotions.

STATUS INCONSISTENCIES   The fact that some individuals, groups, teams, or departments within an organization are more highly regarded than others in the organization can also create conflict. In some restaurants, for example, the chefs have relatively higher status than the people who wait on tables. Nevertheless, the chefs receive customers' orders from the waitstaff, and the waitstaff can return to the chefs food that their customers or they think is not acceptable. This status inconsistency—high-status chefs taking orders from low-status waitstaff—can be the source of considerable conflict between chefs and the waitstaff. For this reason, some restaurants require that the waitstaff put orders on a spindle, thereby reducing the amount of direct order giving from the waitstaff to the chefs.[41]

LO17-2 Describe conflict management strategies that managers can use to resolve conflict effectively.

compromise A way of managing conflict in which each party is concerned about not only its own goal accomplishment but also the goal accomplishment of the other party and is willing to engage in a give-and-take exchange and make concessions.

collaboration A way of managing conflict in which both parties try to satisfy their goals by coming up with an approach that leaves them better off and does not require concessions on issues that are important to either party.

Conflict Management Strategies

If an organization is to achieve its goals, managers must be able to resolve conflicts in a functional manner. *Functional conflict resolution* means the conflict is settled by compromise or by collaboration between the parties in conflict (later in the chapter we discuss other typically less functional ways in which conflicts are sometimes resolved).[42] **Compromise** is possible when each party is concerned about not only its own goal accomplishment but also the goal accomplishment of the other party and is willing to engage in a give-and-take exchange and to make concessions until a reasonable resolution of the conflict is reached. **Collaboration** is a way of handling conflict in which the parties try to satisfy their goals without making any concessions but, instead, come up with a way to resolve their differences that leaves them both better off.[43] Ravi Kant, vice chairman of the Board of Directors at Tata Motors Ltd.,[44] excelled at using collaboration to resolve conflicts when he was a top manager at Tata, as profiled in the following "Managing Globally" box.

Managing
Globally

Ravi Kant Excels at Collaboration

Ravi Kant, currently vice chairman of the Board of Directors of Tata Motors Ltd.,[45] used collaboration to address a conflict he faced as executive director of Tata Motors' commercial vehicles unit.[46] The commercial vehicles unit of Tata Motors, the biggest automobile manufacturer in India, was interested in acquiring Daewoo's truck division based in Gunsan, South Korea, to increase its capabilities.[47] The Korean truck division was doing poorly, and an auction was being held in Korea to sell off the unit.

When Kant traveled to Korea, he realized that there was resistance among some managers and employees at the Daewoo truck division to being potentially taken over by Tata Motors; they were concerned about what such a takeover would mean for the future of their company.[48]

Kant arranged for Tata managers who were trying to negotiate the deal to take lessons in the Korean language so they could better communicate with the Koreans.[49] He had brochures and other documents about Tata translated into Korean. Tata managers made presentations to multiple parties involved in the auction, including Daewoo managers and employees, the head of the local auto association, Gunsun's mayor, and government decision makers in Seoul, Korea, including the prime minister. In these presentations, Tata managers indicated that if Tata were to win the auction, Daewoo employees would be able to keep their jobs, and efforts would focus on building the Daewoo truck unit into a key exporter while integrating it into Tata Motors (and the larger Tata Group of which it is a part). Kant and Tata's efforts paid off; Tata purchased Daewoo's truck division for $102 million.[50] As Kwang-Ok Chae, CEO of Tata Daewoo,[51] indicated, "Tata had done its homework in everything needed to do business here."[52]

Ravi Kant lowered cross-cultural tensions in the Tata Motors' acquisition of Daewoo's truck division by meeting the Korean company's employees on their own turf.

Throughout the process, Tata managers showed respect for Daewoo employees and managers.[53] At Tata Daewoo a joint board of directors was created, and Kwang-Ok Chae retained his top management position as CEO of the company.[54] When Kant requested that two Tata top managers advise him, Chae made them a part of his top management team. Together Indian and Korean managers focused on ways to increase Tata Daewoo's product line and exports. Although Daewoo had focused on the Korean market, today Tata Daewoo is a major exporter of heavy trucks, and its revenues have increased substantially since the acquisition.[55] Tata Daewoo is the second biggest manufacturer of heavy-duty trucks in Korea and now exports trucks to over 60 countries, including countries in the Middle East, South Africa, Eastern Europe, and Southeast Asia.[56]

Clearly, the process of acquiring a company can be fraught with the potential for conflict, which if not effectively managed can harm both the acquiring company and the company being acquired. The collaborative way in which the acquisition that created Tata Daewoo was handled made both parties better off. Tata Daewoo is now a successful company, employees' and managers' jobs are secure, and the Tata Group as a whole is better off as a result of the acquisition. As Choi Jai Choon, a South Korean labor union leader, indicated, "It's turned out to be a win–win situation."[57]

accommodation An ineffective conflict-handling approach in which one party, typically with weaker power, gives in to the demands of the other, typically more powerful, party.

In addition to compromise and collaboration, there are three other ways in which conflicts are sometimes handled: accommodation, avoidance, and competition.[58] When **accommodation** takes place, one party to the conflict simply gives in to the demands of the other party. Accommodation typically takes place when one party has more power than the other and can pursue its goal attainment at the expense of the weaker party. From an organizational perspective, accommodation is often ineffective: The two parties are not cooperating with each other, they are unlikely to want to cooperate in the future, and the weaker party who gives in or accommodates the more powerful party might look for ways to get back at the stronger party in the future.

avoidance An ineffective conflict-handling approach in which the parties try to ignore the problem and do nothing to resolve their differences.

When conflicts are handled by **avoidance**, the parties to a conflict try to ignore the problem and do nothing to resolve the disagreement. Avoidance is often ineffective because the real source of the disagreement has not been addressed, conflict is likely to continue, and communication and cooperation are hindered.

competition An ineffective conflict-handling approach in which each party tries to maximize its own gain and has little interest in understanding the other party's position and arriving at a solution that will allow both parties to achieve their goals.

Competition occurs when each party to a conflict tries to maximize its own gain and has little interest in understanding the other party's position and arriving at a solution that will allow both parties to achieve their goals. Competition can actually escalate levels of conflict as each party tries to outmaneuver the other. As a way of handling conflict, competition is ineffective for the organization because the two sides to a conflict are more concerned about winning the battle than cooperating to arrive at a solution that is best for the organization and acceptable to both sides. Handling conflicts through accommodation, avoidance, or competition is ineffective from an organizational point of view because the parties do not cooperate with each other and work toward a mutually acceptable solution to their differences.

When the parties to a conflict are willing to cooperate with each other and, through compromise or collaboration, devise a solution that each finds acceptable, an organization is more likely to achieve its goals.[59] Conflict management strategies that managers can use to ensure that conflicts are resolved in a functional manner focus on individuals and on the organization as a whole. Next we describe four strategies that focus on individuals: increasing awareness of the sources of conflict, increasing diversity awareness and skills, practicing job rotation or temporary assignments, and using permanent transfers or dismissals when necessary. We also describe two strategies that focus on the organization as a whole: changing an organization's structure or culture and directly altering the source of conflict.

STRATEGIES FOCUSED ON INDIVIDUALS

INCREASING AWARENESS OF THE SOURCES OF CONFLICT   Sometimes conflict arises because of communication problems and interpersonal misunderstandings. For example, different linguistic styles (see Chapter 16) may lead some men in work teams to talk more and take more credit for ideas than women in those teams. These communication differences can cause conflict when the men incorrectly assume that the women are uninterested or less capable because they participate less and the women incorrectly assume that the men are bossy and are not interested in their ideas because they seem to do all the talking. By increasing people's awareness of this source of conflict, managers can help resolve conflict functionally. Once men and women realize that the source of their conflict is different linguistic styles, they can take steps to interact with each other more effectively. The men can give the women more chances to provide input, and the women can be more proactive in providing this input.

Sometimes personalities clash in an organization. In these situations, too, managers can help resolve conflicts functionally by increasing organizational members' awareness of the source of their difficulties. For example, some people who are not inclined to take risks may come into conflict with those who are prone to taking risks. The non-risk takers might complain that those who welcome risk propose outlandish ideas without justification, whereas the risk takers might complain that their innovative ideas are always getting shot down. When both types of people are made aware that their conflicts are due to fundamental differences in their ways of approaching problems, they will likely be better able to cooperate in coming up with innovative ideas that entail only moderate levels of risk.

INCREASING DIVERSITY AWARENESS AND SKILLS   Interpersonal conflicts also can arise because of diversity. Older workers may feel uncomfortable or resentful about reporting to a younger supervisor, a Hispanic may feel singled out in a group of non-Hispanic workers, or a female top manager may feel that members of her predominantly male top management team band together whenever one of them disagrees with one of her proposals. Whether or not these feelings are justified, they are likely to cause recurring conflicts. Many of the techniques we described in Chapter 5 for increasing diversity awareness and skills can help managers effectively manage diversity and resolve conflicts that originate in differences among organizational members.

Increasing diversity awareness and skills can be especially important when interacting with people, groups, and organizations in other countries, as indicated in the following "Managing Globally" box.

Managing Globally

Think they're outdated? Think again: the business card, the fancier the better, continues to reign in triumph in China. Best to brush up those paper squares when headed there on business, just as it is wise to check out local customs anywhere you go.

Understanding Other Cultures

When interacting with people, groups, and organizations from other cultures, it is particularly important to try to gain an appreciation of their culture to avoid potential misunderstandings and effectively manage conflict. For example, decades ago when Scott McKain, who often travels abroad on business, was at a welcome dinner for a trade delegation to Brazil with the mayor of a local community, the mayor asked McKain how he liked his first Brazilian dinner.[60] Since his mouth was full, McKain gave the mayor an okay gesture with this index finger and thumb. The mayor was shocked—the okay gesture in Brazil has a similar connotation to putting up a middle finger in the United States. McKain was young and inexperienced at the time, but other more experienced members of the trade delegation were able to smooth things over with the mayor.[61]

In China, business cards remain an important part of business etiquette. Business cards should always be professionally made, and when a person receives a business card, it is important to be impressed with it.[62] More generally, the Chinese are very attuned to and respectful of status differences and positions in networks. For instance, a lower status person such as a subordinate should always reach first to shake the hand of a higher status person such as a superior. Brian Su, CEO of a global consulting firm called Artisan Business Group, indicates that "a high-ranking person in the company should never, ever initiate a handshake."[63]

When communicating in a group in China, it is important to maintain harmony, even if this harmony is superficial.[64] Rather than strongly expressing an emotion, it is better to be indirect. Exuberant praise can embarrass a group member because this may elevate his or her status and disturb harmony in the group. Complaints and criticisms should be handled with care, and expressions of negative emotions should be avoided if possible, with messages being expressed in a more indirect manner.[65] For example, Neng Zhao, a Chinese senior associate at private equity company Blue Oak Capital in Beijing, China, once had an American boss and she felt mortified by his directness. Zhao indicated that "I remember I was so embarrassed when my American boss told me he didn't like something I was doing, right in front of me . . . The Chinese way would have been much more indirect."[66]

Before brand consultant Karen Post when to Jeddah, Saudi Arabia, to deliver a lecture on branding to around 400 managers and employees in marketing at Saudi Arabian Airlines, she bought an abaya, a long black robe/dress that some Muslim women wear.[67] Post indicated that on the Saudi Airline flight to Jeddah from New York's Kennedy Airport, some women were wearing the clothes they normally would wear in New York City. However, once the plane was about an hour away from landing and was in Saudi airspace, the women changes into abayas in the restrooms on the planes. Saudi Arabia has many restrictions on what women can and cannot do and U.S. State Department Guidelines indicate that the religious police can compel women to wear abayas.[68] All in all, when working and traveling in other countries, it is important to have a good understanding of the local culture.

PRACTICING JOB ROTATION OR TEMPORARY ASSIGNMENTS Sometimes conflicts arise because individual organizational members simply do not understand the work activities and demands that others in an organization face. A financial analyst, for example, may be required to submit monthly reports to a member of the accounting department. These reports have a low priority for the analyst, who typically turns them in a couple of days late. On each due date the accountant calls the financial analyst, and conflict ensues as the accountant describes in detail why she must have the reports on time and the financial analyst describes everything else he needs to do. In situations such as this, job rotation or temporary assignments, which expand organizational members' knowledge base and appreciation of other departments, can be a useful way of resolving the conflict. If the financial analyst spends some time working in the accounting department, he may appreciate better the need for timely reports. Similarly, a temporary assignment in the finance department may help the accountant realize the demands a financial analyst faces and the need to streamline unnecessary aspects of reporting.

USING PERMANENT TRANSFERS OR DISMISSALS WHEN NECESSARY   Sometimes when other conflict resolution strategies do not work, managers may need to take more drastic steps, including permanent transfers or dismissals.

Suppose two first-line managers who work in the same department are always at each other's throats; frequent bitter conflicts arise between them even though they both seem to get along well with other employees. No matter what their supervisor does to increase their understanding of each other, the conflicts keep occurring. In this case the supervisor may want to transfer one or both managers so they do not have to interact as frequently.

When dysfunctionally high levels of conflict occur among top managers who cannot resolve their differences and understand each other, it may be necessary for one of them to leave the company. This is how Gerald Levin managed such conflict among top managers when he was chairman of Time Warner. Robert Daly and Terry Semel, one of the most respected management teams in Hollywood at the time and top managers in the Warner Brothers film company, had been in conflict with Michael Fuchs, a long-time veteran of Time Warner and head of the music division, for two years. As Semel described it, the company "was running like a dysfunctional family, and it needed one management team to run it."[69] Levin realized that Time Warner's future success rested on resolving this conflict, that it was unlikely that Fuchs would ever be able to work effectively with Daly and Semel, and that he risked losing Daly and Semel to another company if he did not resolve the conflict. Faced with that scenario, Levin asked Fuchs to resign.[70]

STRATEGIES FOCUSED ON THE WHOLE ORGANIZATION

CHANGING AN ORGANIZATION'S STRUCTURE OR CULTURE   Conflict can signal the need for changes in an organization's structure or culture. Sometimes managers can effectively resolve conflict by changing the organizational structure they use to group people and tasks.[71] As an organization grows, for example, the *functional structure* (composed of departments such as marketing, finance, and production) that was effective when the organization was small may cease to be effective, and a shift to a *product structure* might effectively resolve conflicts (see Chapter 10).

Managers also can effectively resolve conflicts by increasing levels of integration in an organization. Recall from Chapter 15 that Hallmark Cards increased integration by using cross-functional teams to produce new cards. The use of cross-functional teams sped new card development and helped resolve conflicts between different departments. Now when a writer and an artist have a conflict over the appropriateness of the artist's illustrations, they do not pass criticisms back and forth from one department to another because they are on the same team and can directly resolve the issue on the spot.

Sometimes managers may need to take steps to change an organization's culture to resolve conflict (see Chapter 3). Norms and values in an organizational culture might inadvertently promote dysfunctionally high levels of conflict that are difficult to resolve. For instance, norms that stress respect for formal authority may create conflict that is difficult to resolve when an organization creates self-managed work teams and managers' roles and the structure of authority in the organization change. Values stressing individual competition may make it difficult to resolve conflicts when organizational members need to put others' interests ahead of their own. In circumstances such as these, taking steps to change norms and values can be an effective conflict resolution strategy.

ALTERING THE SOURCE OF CONFLICT   When the source of conflict is overlapping authority, different evaluation or reward systems, or status inconsistencies, managers can

LO17-3 Understand the nature of negotiation and why integrative bargaining is more effective than distributive negotiation.

sometimes effectively resolve the conflict by directly altering its source. For example, managers can clarify the chain of command and reassign tasks and responsibilities to resolve conflicts due to overlapping authority.

Negotiation

negotiation A method of conflict resolution in which the parties consider various alternative ways to allocate resources to come up with a solution acceptable to all of them.

third-party negotiator An impartial individual with expertise in handling conflicts and negotiations who helps parties in conflict reach an acceptable solution.

mediator A third-party negotiator who facilitates negotiations but has no authority to impose a solution.

arbitrator A third-party negotiator who can impose what he or she thinks is a fair solution to a conflict that both parties are obligated to abide by.

distributive negotiation Adversarial negotiation in which the parties in conflict compete to win the most resources while conceding as little as possible.

integrative bargaining Cooperative negotiation in which the parties in conflict work together to achieve a resolution that is good for them both.

Negotiation is a particularly important conflict resolution technique for managers and other organizational members in situations where the parties to a conflict have approximately equal levels of power. During **negotiation** the parties to a conflict try to come up with a solution acceptable to themselves by considering various alternative ways to allocate resources to each other.[72] Sometimes the sides involved in a conflict negotiate directly with each other. Other times a **third-party negotiator** is relied on. Third-party negotiators are impartial individuals who are not directly involved in the conflict and have special expertise in handling conflicts and negotiations;[73] they are relied on to help the two negotiating parties reach an acceptable resolution of their conflict.[74] When a third-party negotiator acts as a **mediator**, his or her role in the negotiation process is to facilitate an effective negotiation between the two parties; mediators do not force either party to make concessions, nor can they force an agreement to resolve a conflict. **Arbitrators**, on the other hand, are third-party negotiators who can impose what they believe is a fair solution to a dispute that both parties are obligated to abide by.[75]

Distributive Negotiation and Integrative Bargaining

There are two major types of negotiation—distributive negotiation and integrative bargaining.[76] In **distributive negotiation**, the two parties perceive that they have a "fixed pie" of resources that they need to divide.[77] They take a competitive, adversarial stance. Each party realizes that he or she must concede something but is out to get the lion's share of the resources.[78] The parties see no need to interact with each other in the future and do not care if their interpersonal relationship is damaged or destroyed by their competitive negotiation.[79] In distributive negotiations, conflicts are handled by competition.

In **integrative bargaining**, the parties perceive that they might be able to increase the resource pie by trying to come up with a creative solution to the conflict. They do not view the conflict competitively as a win-or-lose situation; instead they view it cooperatively, as a win–win situation in which both parties can gain. Trust, information sharing, and the desire of both parties to achieve a good resolution of the conflict characterize integrative bargaining.[80] In integrative bargaining, conflicts are handled through collaboration and/or compromise.

Consider how Adrian Hofbeck and Joseph Steinberg, partners in a successful German restaurant in the Midwest, resolved their recent conflict. Hofbeck and Steinberg founded the restaurant 15 years ago, share management responsibilities, and share equally in the restaurant's profits. Hofbeck recently decided that he wanted to retire and sell the restaurant, but retirement was the last thing Steinberg had in mind; he wanted to continue to own and manage the restaurant. Distributive negotiation was out of the question, for Hofbeck and Steinberg were close friends and valued their friendship; neither wanted to do something that would hurt the other or their continuing relationship. So they opted for integrative bargaining, which they thought would help them resolve their conflict so both could achieve their goals and maintain their friendship.

Integrative bargaining brings all parties to the table in order to create a solution based on an honest assessment of the problem and a willingness to honor others' interests and values.

Table 17.1

Negotiation Strategies for Integrative Bargaining

- Emphasize superordinate goals.
- Focus on the problem, not the people.
- Focus on interests, not demands.
- Create new options for joint gain.
- Focus on what is fair.

LO17-4 Describe ways in which managers can promote integrative bargaining in organizations.

Strategies to Encourage Integrative Bargaining

Managers in all kinds of organizations can rely on five strategies to facilitate integrative bargaining and avoid distributive negotiation: emphasizing superordinate goals; focusing on the problem, not the people; focusing on interests, not demands; creating new options for joint gain; and focusing on what is fair (see Table 17.1).[81] Hofbeck and Steinberg used each of these strategies to resolve their conflict.

EMPHASIZING SUPERORDINATE GOALS   *Superordinate goals* are goals that both parties agree to regardless of the source of their conflict. Increasing organizational effectiveness, increasing responsiveness to customers, and gaining a competitive advantage are just a few of the many superordinate goals that members of an organization can emphasize during integrative bargaining. Superordinate goals help parties in conflict to keep in mind the big picture and the fact that they are working together for a larger purpose or goal despite their disagreements. Hofbeck and Steinberg emphasized three superordinate goals during their bargaining: ensuring that the restaurant continued to survive and prosper, allowing Hofbeck to retire, and allowing Steinberg to remain an owner and manager as long as he wished.

FOCUSING ON THE PROBLEM, NOT THE PEOPLE   People who are in conflict may not be able to resist the temptation to focus on the other party's shortcomings and weaknesses, thereby personalizing the conflict. Instead of attacking the problem, the parties to the conflict attack each other. This approach is inconsistent with integrative bargaining and can easily lead both parties into a distributive negotiation mode. All parties to a conflict need to keep focused on the problem or on the source of the conflict and avoid the temptation to discredit one another.

Given their strong friendship, this was not much of an issue for Hofbeck and Steinberg, but they still had to be on their guard to avoid personalizing the conflict. Steinberg recalls that when they were having a hard time coming up with a solution, he started thinking that Hofbeck, a healthy 57-year-old, was lazy to want to retire so young: "If only he wasn't so lazy, we would never be in the mess we're in right now." Steinberg never mentioned these thoughts to Hofbeck (who later admitted that sometimes he was annoyed with Steinberg for being such a workaholic) because he realized that doing so would hurt their chances for reaching an integrative solution.

FOCUSING ON INTERESTS, NOT DEMANDS   Demands are *what* a person wants; interests are *why* the person wants them. When two people are in conflict, it is unlikely that the demands of both can be met. Their underlying interests, however, can be met, and meeting them is what integrative bargaining is all about.

Hofbeck's demand was that they sell the restaurant and split the proceeds. Steinberg's demand was that they keep the restaurant and maintain the status quo. Obviously both demands could not be met, but perhaps their interests could be. Hofbeck wanted to be able to retire, invest his share of the money from the restaurant, and live off the returns on the investment. Steinberg wanted to continue managing, owning, and deriving income from the restaurant.

CREATING NEW OPTIONS FOR JOINT GAIN   Once two parties to a conflict focus on their interests, they are on the road to achieving creative solutions to the conflict that will benefit them both. This win–win scenario means that rather than having a fixed set of alternatives from which to choose, the two parties can come up with new alternatives that might even expand the resource pie.

Hofbeck and Steinberg came up with three such alternatives. First, even though Steinberg did not have the capital, he could buy out Hofbeck's share of the restaurant. Hofbeck would provide the financing for the purchase, and in return Steinberg would pay him a reasonable return on his investment (the same kind of return he could have obtained had he taken his money out of the restaurant and invested it). Second, the partners could seek to sell Hofbeck's share in the restaurant to a third party under the stipulation that Steinberg would continue to manage the restaurant and receive income for his services. Third, the partners could continue to jointly own the restaurant. Steinberg would manage it and receive a proportionally greater share of its profits than Hofbeck, who would be an absentee owner not involved in day-to-day operations but would still receive a return on his investment in the restaurant.

FOCUSING ON WHAT IS FAIR   Focusing on what is fair is consistent with the principle of distributive justice, which emphasizes the fair distribution of outcomes based on the meaningful contributions that people make to organizations (see Chapter 5). It is likely that two parties in conflict will disagree on certain points and prefer different alternatives that each party believes may better serve his or her own interests or maximize his or her own outcomes. Emphasizing fairness and distributive justice will help the two parties come to a mutual agreement about what the best solution is to the problem.

Steinberg and Hofbeck agreed that Hofbeck should be able to cut his ties with the restaurant if he chose to do so. They thus decided to pursue the second alternative described and seek a suitable buyer for Hofbeck's share. They were successful in finding an investor who was willing to buy out Hofbeck's share and let Steinberg continue managing the restaurant. And they remained good friends.

When managers pursue these five strategies and encourage other organizational members to do so, they are more likely to be able to effectively resolve their conflicts through integrative bargaining. In addition, throughout the negotiation process, managers and other organizational members need to be aware of, and on their guard against, the biases that can lead to faulty decision making (see Chapter 7).[82]

Organizational Politics

Managers must develop the skills necessary to manage organizational conflict for an organization to be effective. Suppose, however, that top managers are in conflict over the best strategy for an organization to pursue or the best structure to adopt to use organizational resources efficiently. In such situations resolving conflict is often difficult, and the parties to the conflict resort to organizational politics and political strategies to try to resolve the conflict in their favor.

Organizational politics are the activities that managers (and other members of an organization) engage in to increase their power and to use power effectively to achieve their goals and overcome resistance or opposition.[83] Managers often engage in organizational politics to resolve conflicts in their favor.

Political strategies are the specific tactics that managers (and other members of an organization) use to increase their power and to use power effectively to influence and gain the support of other people while overcoming resistance or opposition. Political strategies are especially important when managers are planning and implementing major changes in an organization: Managers need not only to gain support for their change initiatives and influence organizational members to behave in new ways but also to overcome often strong opposition from people who feel threatened by the change and prefer the status quo. By increasing their power, managers are better able to make needed changes. In addition to increasing their power, managers also must make sure they use their power in a way that actually enables them to influence others.

LO17-5 Explain why managers need to be attuned to organizational politics, and describe the political strategies that managers can use to become politically skilled.

organizational politics Activities that managers engage in to increase their power and to use power effectively to achieve their goals and overcome resistance or opposition.

political strategies Tactics that managers use to increase their power and to use power effectively to influence and gain the support of other people while overcoming resistance or opposition.

The Importance of Organizational Politics

The term *politics* has a negative connotation for many people. Some may think that managers who are political have risen to the top not because of their own merit and capabilities but because of whom they know. Or people may think that political managers are self-interested and wield power to benefit themselves, not their organization. There is a grain of truth to this negative connotation. Some managers do appear to misuse their power for personal benefit at the expense of their organization's effectiveness.

Nevertheless, organizational politics are often a positive force. Managers striving to make needed changes often encounter resistance from individuals and groups who feel threatened and wish to preserve the status quo. Effective managers engage in politics to gain support for and implement needed changes. Similarly, managers often face resistance from other managers who disagree with their goals for a group or for the organization and with what they are trying to accomplish. Engaging in organizational politics can help managers overcome this resistance and achieve their goals.

Indeed, managers cannot afford to ignore organizational politics. Everyone engages in politics to a degree—other managers, coworkers, and subordinates, as well as people outside an organization, such as suppliers. Those who try to ignore politics might as well bury their heads in the sand because in all likelihood they will be unable to gain support for their initiatives and goals.

Political Strategies for Gaining and Maintaining Power

Managers who use political strategies to increase and maintain their power are better able to influence others to work toward the achievement of group and organizational goals. (Recall from Chapter 14 that legitimate, reward, coercive, expert, and referent powers help managers influence others as leaders.) By controlling uncertainty, making themselves irreplaceable, being in a central position, generating resources, and building alliances, managers can increase their power (see Figure 17.4).[84] We next look at each of these strategies.

Figure 17.4

Political Strategies for Increasing Power

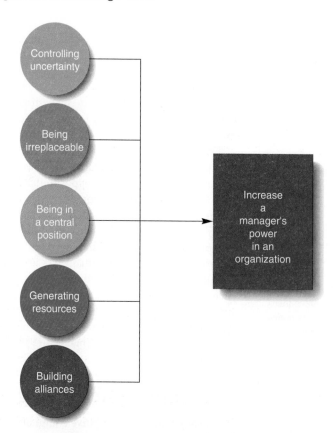

CONTROLLING UNCERTAINTY   Uncertainty is a threat for individuals, groups, and whole organizations and can interfere with effective performance and goal attainment. For example, uncertainty about job security is threatening for many workers and may cause top performers (who have the best chance of finding another job) to quit and take a more secure position with another organization. When an R&D department faces uncertainty about customer preferences, its members may waste valuable resources to develop a product, such as smokeless cigarettes, that customers do not want. When top managers face uncertainty about global demand, they may fail to export products to countries that want them and thus may lose a source of competitive advantage.

Managers who can control and reduce uncertainty for other managers, teams, departments, and the organization as a whole are likely to see their power increase.[85] Managers of labor unions gain power when they can eliminate uncertainty over job security for workers. Marketing and sales managers gain power when they can eliminate uncertainty for other departments such as R&D by accurately forecasting customers' changing preferences. Top managers gain power when they are knowledgeable about global demand for an organization's products. Managers who can control uncertainty are likely to be in demand and be sought after by other organizations.

MAKING ONESELF IRREPLACEABLE   Managers gain power when they have valuable knowledge and expertise that allow them to perform activities no one else can handle. This is the essence of being irreplaceable.[86] The more central these activities are to organizational effectiveness, the more power managers gain from being irreplaceable.

BEING IN A CENTRAL POSITION   Managers in central positions are responsible for activities that are directly connected to an organization's goals and sources of competitive advantage and often are located in central positions in important communication networks in an organization.[87] Managers in key positions have control over crucial organizational activities and initiatives and have access to important information. Other organizational members depend on them for their knowledge, expertise, advice, and support, and the success of the organization as a whole is seen as riding on these managers. These consequences of being in a central position are likely to increase managers' power.

Managers who are outstanding performers, have a wide knowledge base, and have made important and visible contributions to their organizations are likely to be offered central positions that will increase their power.

GENERATING RESOURCES   Organizations need three kinds of resources to be effective: (1) input resources such as raw materials, skilled workers, and financial capital; (2) technical resources such as machinery and computers; and (3) knowledge resources such as marketing, information technology, or engineering expertise. To the extent that a manager can generate one or more of these kinds of resources for an organization, that manager's power is likely to increase.[88] In universities, for example, professors who win large grants to fund their research, from associations such as the National Science Foundation and the Army Research Institute, gain power because of the financial resources they generate for their departments and the university as a whole.

BUILDING ALLIANCES   When managers build alliances, they develop mutually beneficial relationships with people both inside and outside the organization as do Mark Tercek and Peter Kareiva in "A Manager's Challenge." The parties to an alliance support one another because doing so is in their best interests, and all parties benefit from the alliance. Alliances give managers power because they provide the managers with support for their initiatives. Partners to alliances provide support because they know the managers will reciprocate when their partners need support. Alliances can help managers achieve their goals and implement needed changes in organizations because they increase managers' levels of power.

Many powerful top managers focus on building alliances not only inside their organizations but also with individuals, groups, and organizations in the task and general environments on which their organizations depend for resources. These individuals, groups, and organizations enter alliances with managers because doing so is in their best interests and they know they can count on the managers' support when they need it. When managers build alliances, they need to be on their guard to ensure that everything is aboveboard, ethical, and legal.

Political Strategies for Exercising Power

Politically skilled managers not only understand, and can use, the five strategies to increase their power; they also appreciate strategies for exercising their power. These strategies generally focus on how managers can use their power *unobtrusively.*[89] When managers exercise power unobtrusively, other members of an organization may not be aware that the managers are using their power to influence them. They may think they support these managers for a variety of reasons: because they believe it is the rational or logical thing to do, because they believe doing so is in their own best interests, or because they believe the position or decision the managers are advocating is legitimate or appropriate.

The unobtrusive use of power may sound devious, but managers typically use this strategy to bring about change and achieve organizational goals. Political strategies for exercising power to gain the support and concurrence of others include relying on objective information, bringing in an outside expert, controlling the agenda, and making everyone a winner (see Figure 17.5).[90]

RELYING ON OBJECTIVE INFORMATION   Managers require the support of others to achieve their goals, implement changes, and overcome opposition. One way for a manager to gain this support and overcome opposition is to rely on objective information that supports the manager's initiatives. Reliance on objective information leads others to support the manager because of the facts; objective information causes others to believe that what the manager is proposing is the proper course of action. By relying on objective information, politically skilled managers unobtrusively exercise their power to influence others.

Take the case of Mary Callahan, vice president of Better Built Cabinets, a small cabinet company in the Southeast. Callahan is extremely influential in the company; practically every new initiative that she proposes to the president and owner of the company is implemented. Why is Callahan able to use her power in the company so effectively? Whenever she has an idea for a new initiative that she thinks the company might pursue, she and her subordinates begin by collecting objective information supporting the initiative. Recently Callahan decided that Better Built should develop a line of high-priced European-style kitchen cabinets. Before presenting her proposal to Better Built's president, she compiled objective information showing that (1) there was strong unmet demand for these kinds of cabinets, (2) Better Built could manufacture them in its existing production facilities, and (3) the new line had the potential

Figure 17.5

Political Strategies for Exercising Power

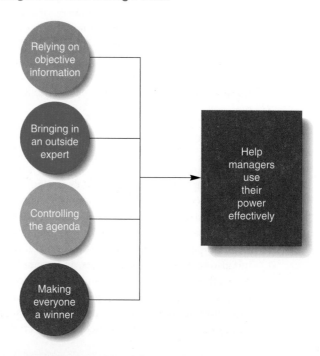

to increase Better Built's sales by 20% while not detracting from sales of the company's other cabinets. Presented with this information, the president agreed to Callahan's proposal. Moreover, the president and other members of Better Built whose cooperation was needed to implement the proposal supported it because they thought it would help Better Built gain a competitive advantage. Using objective information to support her position enabled Callahan to unobtrusively exercise her power and influence others to support her proposal.

BRINGING IN AN OUTSIDE EXPERT   Bringing in an outside expert to support a proposal or decision can, at times, provide managers with some of the same benefits that the use of objective information does. It lends credibility to a manager's initiatives and causes others to believe that what the manager is proposing is the appropriate or rational thing to do. Suppose Callahan had hired a consultant to evaluate whether her idea was a good one. The consultant reports back to the president that the new European-style cabinets are likely to fulfill Callahan's promises and increase Better Built's sales and profits. As with objective information, this information provided by an objective expert can lend a sense of legitimacy to Callahan's proposal and allow her to unobtrusively exercise power to influence others.

Although you might think consultants and other outside experts are neutral or objective, they sometimes are hired by managers who want them to support a certain position or decision in an organization. For instance, when managers face strong opposition from others who fear that a decision will harm their interests, the managers may bring in an outside expert. They hope this expert will be perceived as a neutral observer to lend credibility and "objectivity" to their point of view. The support of an outside expert may cause others to believe that a decision is indeed the right one. Of course sometimes consultants and other outside experts actually are brought into organizations *to be* objective and guide managers on the appropriate course of action.

CONTROLLING THE AGENDA   Managers also can exercise power unobtrusively by controlling the agenda—influencing which alternatives are considered or even whether a decision is made.[91] When managers influence the alternatives that are considered, they can make sure that each considered alternative is acceptable to them and that undesirable alternatives are not in the feasible set. In a hiring context, for example, managers can exert their power unobtrusively by ensuring that job candidates whom they do not find acceptable do not make their way onto the list of finalists for an open position. They do this by making sure that these candidates' drawbacks or deficiencies are communicated to everyone involved in making the hiring decision. When three finalists for an open position are discussed and evaluated in a hiring meeting, a manager may seem to exert little power or influence and just go along with what the rest of the group wants. However, the manager may have exerted power in the hiring process unobtrusively by controlling which candidates made it to the final stage.

Sometimes managers can prevent a decision from being made. A manager in charge of a community relations committee, for example, may not favor a proposal for the organization to become more involved in local youth groups such as the Boy Scouts and the Girl Scouts. The manager can exert influence in this situation by not including the proposal on the agenda for the committee's next meeting. Alternatively, the manager could place the proposal at the end of the agenda for the meeting and feel confident that the committee will run out of time and not get to the last items on the agenda because that is what always happens. Either approach enables the manager to unobtrusively exercise power. Committee members do not perceive this manager as trying to influence them to turn down the proposal. Rather, the manager has made the proposal into a nonissue that is not even considered.

MAKING EVERYONE A WINNER   Often, politically skilled managers can exercise their power unobtrusively because they make sure that everyone whose support they need benefits personally from providing that support. By making everyone a winner, a manager can influence other organizational members because these members see supporting the manager as being in their best interest.

When top managers turn around troubled companies, some organizational members and parts of the organization are bound to suffer due to restructurings that often entail painful layoffs. However, the power of the turnaround CEO often accelerates as it becomes clear that the future of the company is on surer footing and the organization and its stakeholders are winners as a result of the change effort.

Making everyone a winner not only is an effective way of exercising power but, when used consistently and forthrightly, can increase managers' power and influence over time. That is, when a manager actually does make everyone a winner, all stakeholders will see it as in their best interests to support the manager and his or her initiatives. When managers who make everyone a winner have strong ethical values, everyone really is a winner, as profiled in the following "Ethics in Action" box.

Ethics in Action

El Faro Estate Coffee Benefits Multiple Stakeholders

When Estuardo Porras was taking business classes at Pepperdine University in Malibu, California, in the 1990s, he was surprised to see the high prices that Starbucks charged for coffee.[92] In his native country of Guatemala, coffee used to be the major export until prices declined in the 1980s due to a large influx of low-cost coffee beans coming on the market from countries like Vietnam. Porras had a vision of returning to Guatemala, resurrecting an old coffee plantation, and operating it in a socially responsible way that protected the natural environment, looked out for and contributed to the well-being of the workers who operated it and the local community, and produced high-quality coffee beans that a socially responsible organization like Starbucks would be interested in purchasing.[93]

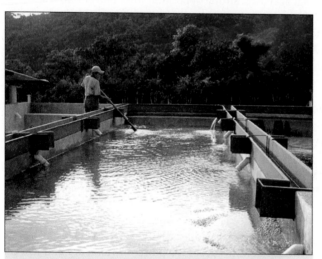

Fermenting coffee beans in recycled water is just one of the many areas in which Estuardo Porras has transformed El Faro into a productive, environmentally responsible enterprise.

Porras returned to Guatemala, borrowed $1.25 million from his father, who had recently sold a Coca-Cola bottling company, and transformed an abandoned plantation called El Faro into a marvel of environmental sustainability, social responsibility, and effectiveness.[94] El Faro Estate Coffee protects the natural environment, helps a poor community, and produces high-quality arabica coffee used by specialty coffee companies like Starbucks. And because of Starbucks' commitment to purchasing coffee beans from growers that abide by ethical, social, and environmental values, El Faro can sell all the coffee beans it grows that meet Starbucks' standards for more than the beans would sell for on the general commodity export market.[95]

El Faro is located near a volcano, and the ash from the volcano provides excellent soil for growing coffee. Coffee beans are fermented in recycled water, and the casings from the beans are eaten by earthworms, yielding an organic fertilizer. Much of the work on the plantation is done by hand.[96] El Faro supports a free elementary school for children in the local community and buses older children to a high school in the vicinity. Employees receive free health care after they have been with El Faro for three months; the care is provided in the plantation's medical office, staffed by a part-time doctor and full-time nurse. They also receive 15 days of paid vacation annually. Many of El Faro's full-time employees and their families live on the plantation; El Faro also has part-time employees.[97]

Porras initially sold El Faro's coffee beans on the commodity export market while persistently trying to make inroads at Starbucks by sending letters and coffee samples to no avail. Eventually an exporter who bought beans from El Faro persuaded two coffee buyers from Starbucks to visit the plantation. After a tour and coffee tasting, the buyers were so delighted with what they saw and tasted that they ordered coffee from El Faro that day and gave Porras the opportunity to participate in a program that gives long-term contracts to growers who are socially responsible.[98]

Today El Faro Estate Coffee is sold exclusively to Starbucks, and Finca El Faro is a Starbucks' C.A.F.E. Practices supplier.[99] Clearly Porras has made everyone a winner and, in the process, has created a sustainable and thriving business.[100]

Summary and Review

LO17-1, 17-2

ORGANIZATIONAL CONFLICT   Organizational conflict is the discord that arises when the goals, interests, or values of different individuals or groups are incompatible and those individuals or groups block or thwart each other's attempts to achieve their objectives. Four types of conflict arising in organizations are interpersonal conflict, intragroup conflict, intergroup conflict, and interorganizational conflict. Sources of conflict in organizations include different goals and time horizons, overlapping authority, task interdependencies, different evaluation or reward systems, scarce resources, and status inconsistencies. Conflict management strategies focused on individuals include increasing awareness of the sources of conflict, increasing diversity awareness and skills, practicing job rotation or temporary assignments, and using permanent transfers or dismissals when necessary. Strategies focused on the whole organization include changing an organization's structure or culture and altering the source of conflict.

LO17-3, 17-4

NEGOTIATION   Negotiation is a conflict resolution technique used when parties to a conflict have approximately equal levels of power and try to come up with an acceptable way to allocate resources to each other. In distributive negotiation, the parties perceive that there is a fixed level of resources for them to allocate, and they compete to receive as much as possible at the expense of the other party, not caring about their relationship in the future. In integrative bargaining, both parties perceive that they may be able to increase the resource pie by coming up with a creative solution to the conflict, trusting each other, and cooperating with each other to achieve a win–win resolution. Five strategies that managers can use to facilitate integrative bargaining are to emphasize superordinate goals; focus on the problem, not the people; focus on interests, not demands; create new options for joint gain; and focus on what is fair.

LO17-5

ORGANIZATIONAL POLITICS   Organizational politics are the activities that managers (and other members of an organization) engage in to increase their power and to use power effectively to achieve their goals and overcome resistance or opposition. Effective managers realize that politics can be a positive force that enables them to make needed changes in an organization. Five important political strategies for gaining and maintaining power are controlling uncertainty, making oneself irreplaceable, being in a central position, generating resources, and building alliances. Political strategies for effectively exercising power focus on how to use power unobtrusively and include relying on objective information, bringing in an outside expert, controlling the agenda, and making everyone a winner.

Management in Action

Topics for Discussion and Action

Discussion

1. Discuss why too little conflict in an organization can be just as detrimental as too much conflict. [LO17-1]

2. Why are compromise and collaboration more effective ways of handling conflict than accommodation, avoidance, and competition? [LO17-2]

3. Why should managers promote integrative bargaining rather than distributive negotiation? [LO17-3]

4. How can managers promote integrative bargaining? [LO17-4]

5. Why do organizational politics affect practically every organization? [LO17-5]

6. Why do effective managers need good political skills? [LO17-5]

7. What steps can managers take to ensure that organizational politics are a positive force leading to a competitive advantage, not a negative force leading to personal advantage at the expense of organizational goal attainment? [LO17-5]

8. Think of a member of an organization whom you know and who is particularly powerful. What political strategies does this person use to increase his or her power? [LO17-5]

9. Why is it best to use power unobtrusively? How are people likely to react to power that is exercised obtrusively? [LO17-5]

Action

10. Interview a manager in a local organization to determine the kinds of conflicts that occur in his or her organization and the strategies that are used to manage them. [LO17-1, 17-2]

Building Management Skills

Effective and Ineffective Conflict Resolution [LO17-1, 17-2]

Think about two recent conflicts that you had with other people—one conflict that you felt was effectively resolved (C1) and one that you felt was ineffectively resolved (C2). The other people involved could be coworkers, students, family members, friends, or members of an organization that you are a member of. Answer the following questions:

1. Briefly describe C1 and C2. What type of conflict was involved in each of these incidents?

2. What was the source of the conflict in C1 and in C2?

3. What conflict management strategies were used in C1 and in C2?

4. What could you have done differently to more effectively manage conflict in C2?

5. How was the conflict resolved in C1 and in C2?

Managing Ethically [LO17-5]

One political strategy managers can engage in is controlling the agenda by subtly influencing which alternatives are considered or even whether a decision is up for discussion. Some employees believe this can be unethical and can prevent important issues from being raised and points of view from being expressed.

Questions

1. Either individually or in a group, think about the ethical implications of controlling the agenda as a political strategy.

2. What steps can managers and organizations take to ensure that this strategy does not result in important issues and differing points of view being suppressed in an organization?

Small Group Breakout Exercise [LO17-3, 17-4]

Negotiating a Solution

Form groups of three or four people. One member of your group will play the role of Jane Rister, one member will play the role of Michael Schwartz, and one or two members will be observer(s) and spokesperson(s) for your group.

Jane Rister and Michael Schwartz are assistant managers in a large department store. They report directly to the store manager. Today they are meeting to discuss some important problems they need to solve but about which they disagree.

The first problem hinges on the fact that either Rister or Schwartz needs to be on duty whenever the store is open. For the last six months, Rister has taken most of the least desirable hours (nights and weekends). They are planning their schedules for the next six months. Rister thought Schwartz would take more of the undesirable times, but Schwartz has informed Rister that his wife has just gotten a nursing job that requires her to work weekends, so he needs to stay home weekends to take care of their infant daughter.

The second problem concerns a department manager who has had a hard time retaining salespeople in his department. The turnover rate in his department is twice that in the other store departments. Rister thinks the manager is ineffective and wants to fire him. Schwartz thinks the high turnover is just a fluke and the manager is effective.

The last problem concerns Rister's and Schwartz's vacation schedules. Both managers want to take off the week of July 4, but one of them needs to be in the store whenever it is open.

1. The group members playing Rister and Schwartz assume their roles and negotiate a solution to these three problems.

2. Observers take notes on how Rister and Schwartz negotiate solutions to their problems.

3. Observers determine the extent to which Rister and Schwartz use distributive negotiation or integrative bargaining to resolve their conflicts.

4. When called on by the instructor, observers communicate to the rest of the class how Rister and Schwartz resolved their conflicts, whether they used distributive negotiation or integrative bargaining, and their actual solutions.

Exploring the World Wide Web [LO17-1, 17-2]

Think of a major conflict in the business world that you have read about in the past few weeks. Then search on the web for magazine and newspaper articles presenting differing viewpoints and perspectives on the conflict.

Based on what you have read, how are the parties to this conflict handling it? Is their approach functional or dysfunctional, and why?

Be the Manager [LO17-1, 17-2, 17-3, 17-4, 17-5]

You are a middle manager in a large corporation, and lately you feel that you are caught between a rock and a hard place. Times are tough; your unit has experienced layoffs; your surviving subordinates are overworked and demoralized; and you feel that you have no meaningful rewards, such as the chance for a pay raise, bonus, or promotion, to motivate them with. Your boss keeps increasing the demands on your unit as well as the unit's

responsibilities. Moreover, you believe that you and your subordinates are being unfairly blamed for certain problems beyond your control. You believe that you have the expertise and skills to perform your job effectively and also that your subordinates are capable and effective in their jobs. Yet you feel that you are on shaky ground and powerless given the current state of affairs. What are you going to do?

Fortune Case in the News [LO17-1, 17-2, 17-3, 17-4]

Is Pinterest the Next Facebook?: An Exclusive Look Inside CEO Ben Silbermann's Social Media Sensation

Ben Silbermann can't stop staring at the refrigerators. The Pinterest co-founder and CEO and I are standing in the break room of his company's garage-size Palo Alto office. He's just flown back from Austin's SXSW interactive festival, and a redesign of his website is two days away. It's all a little overwhelming. But at this moment his full attention is focused on three glowing refrigerators. Sometime during his brief absence, a service has delivered them fully stocked and branded with the company logo. They're wedged into the tiny back-room behind the foosball table that three employees—roughly 15% of his workforce—are using for a conference. "I've been gone for one day, and it's so upscale," he says. "We used to just run to Costco all the time."

That was before. Before Mitt Romney's wife, Ann, began organizing family photos on Pinterest. Before Reese Witherspoon gushed to Conan O'Brien that it was "a collection of the most amazing, wonderful craftiness on the earth!" Before the U.S. Army issued a guide for how to use it, and before Pinterest emerged as the fastest-growing website of all time. In March the site registered 17.8 million users, according to Comscore, a 52% jump in just one month— and it isn't even open to everyone (would-be "pinners" must still request an invitation to join).

Pinterest, for the uninitiated, is a deceptively simple-sounding, insanely addictive social media site that lets users collect and share images on digital pinboards. Most social-networking sites have first become popular among tech's early adopters along the country's coasts. But Pinterest found its most passionate users among the Midwestern scrapbooking set—a mostly female group—who

have turned to it to plan weddings, save recipes, and post ideas for kitchen renovations.

This growth has thrust Silbermann, 29, into the spotlight as investors and businesses alike try to figure out how they can get in on the action. Brands—from large companies like Gap (GPS) and West Elm to online boutiques—are tripping over themselves to establish a presence on it, and some are starting to reap the rewards of being "pinned," a de facto referral that prompts followers to click on product pictures to learn more. In February Pinterest drove more traffic to websites than Twitter, Google+, LinkedIn (LNKD), and YouTube combined. Meanwhile, the same (mostly male) investors who initially passed on Pinterest are kicking themselves. The company in October raised $27 million from venture capital firm Andreessen Horowitz in a deal that valued Pinterest at a reported $200 million. Marc Andreessen himself readily admits he didn't get it until a female researcher on staff urged him to reconsider. Says Andreessen: "Our industry historically . . . do we produce products initially aimed primarily at men or women? You'd have to say men."

Amid all the noise, Silbermann must now build out a company that can keep up with Pinterest's user explosion. This type of hypergrowth has been a challenge for companies to manage—remember the "fail whale" that signaled Twitter was suffering under the weight of its own popularity? In recent weeks Silbermann and his team have held a Monday meeting—usually in the form of a coffee run to Bistro Maxine—to figure out how to keep the site running on Thursday. (Writing a check to Amazon's web service unit usually does the trick.) Oh, and Silbermann must figure out how to make money. To that end, *Fortune*

has learned, Pinterest just hired Tim Kendall, who spent many years as Facebook's director of monetization, to build out the business.

Silbermann seems to be maintaining an almost eerily level head about Pinterest's success as well as the stress of running Silicon Valley's current "it" company. He talks so quietly that during our conversation I felt compelled to drop my own volume to match his. His eye is always on the wall-mounted flat screen that displays real-time data about how pinners are using the service. He takes a regular turn at answering customer-support e-mails, a mundane task that, he says, helps him make Pinterest even better. And while Pinterest's Palo Alto digs feature a poster with the words MOVE FAST AND BREAK THINGS, a mantra at Facebook, Silbermann talks about Pinterest the way one talks about a fragile heirloom. "When you open Pinterest, it should feel like someone has hand-made a book for you," he explains. "Every item should feel like it's handpicked for you by a person you care about."

Silbermann took a somewhat circuitous path to Internet stardom. The son of doctors from West Des Moines, Iowa, he collected things— stamps, leaves, insects—as a child. His sisters became doctors, and he was premed at Yale and majored in political science. Upon his 2003 graduation, he moved to Washington, D.C., where he took a "cube job" running data for a consultancy. That was right around the birth of Web 2.0, and he became hooked on tech blogs. He remembers the first time he stumbled across TechCrunch. Something was happening in Silicon Valley. He wasn't a coder, but he was a huge history buff, and he fell in love with the romantic notion that the Internet defined his generation. "It felt like this was the story of my time, and I just wanted to be close to it," he says. He and his girlfriend (now his wife) moved across the country to Palo Alto, where she became a recruiter at Facebook and he got a job working in customer support and sales at Google.

Silbermann credits Google with helping him dream big—here was a company that decided to take a photograph of every street in the world—but without an engineering degree, he was never going to gain credibility there. And everyone around him was trying to start a tech company. "This is a really strange place," he explains of Silicon Valley. "They love technology here like people I grew up with love sports." So in 2008, even as the economy crashed, Silbermann left Google and hooked up with a college buddy, Paul Sciarra, to try out some startup ideas. Silbermann had held on to his obsessive love for collecting things. So they looped in Evan Sharp, a designer friend who was studying at Columbia's architecture school, to help create a site for people to build collections. Silbermann's wife came up with the name over Thanksgiving dinner.

By January 2010, Silbermann and his co-founders were e-mailing friends and family to invite them to try the service. It was slow going. For one thing, they were hard up for cash, and no one wanted to invest in a startup with three nontechnical founders. (Upon graduation, Sharp took a job as a designer at Facebook, where he worked until last spring, to pay the bills.) What's more, in 2008 most startups were focused on curating real-time information, particularly for mobile platforms. By contrast, Pinterest was all about helping people save things for later—and the bigger the screen, the better the experience. Also, none of the investors who reviewed Pinterest could understand why anyone would want to spend so much time collecting things. Four months in, Pinterest had just a few hundred users.

But then the site began to catch on among friends back in Iowa. Early on,

Silbermann traveled to a Utah design conference, and that group began to use it. A home-schooling parent kept and shared boards of lesson-plan ideas. It was more than a game or some form of entertainment for his core audience. Says Silbermann: "I realized that people were using it for projects that were important in their real lives." Once Pinterest began growing, it didn't stop. Since inception, the site has added an estimated 40% to 50% more subscribers each month.

Last summer Omaha Steaks president Todd Simon and his wife were building a new home near Omaha. A friend recommended Pinterest. Soon they were pinning and "liking" decorating concepts. "For the previous year, we'd been flipping through design magazines, cutting pictures and pinning them to the wall," he said. "This was the equivalent."

Simon took the idea to work, only to discover that his marketing team was one step ahead of him. They'd been noticing customers pinning photographs of their mail-order steaks and other products to digital pinboards for months. In December Omaha Steaks built its own profile and began pinning photos of its delicacies on boards with names like "Delicious discoveries" and "Recipes we want to share." While it's too early to say, the company believes it's having a direct and positive impact on sales.

Essentially, Pinterest excels at something that's very hard to do on the web—help people discover new things. If you can name what you want, after all, Amazon (AMZN) and Google are pretty good tools for helping you find it. But what if you don't know what you want? Social-networking sites have helped businesses influence people, but they are imperfect. People use Facebook and Twitter to talk to each other, not necessarily to discuss things they might want to buy. In contrast, Pinterest users are more often in a shopping mindset when they are using the

service. If you're keeping a pinboard called "Spring handbags I'm considering," there's a good chance you'll click through and make a purchase.

Over time, Pinterest has the potential to translate more quickly to sales dollars than other social-networking sites. Katia Beauchamp, CEO of Birchbox, has already seen that. Pinterest is among the top 10 traffic drivers to the site, which sells beauty products as well as sample-sale subscriptions. It doesn't yet drive as much traffic as, say, Facebook, Beauchamp says, but it results in more direct sales. At this point, businesses can't spend money marketing on Pinterest even if they want to; Silbermann is not ready to talk about how he plans to make money off it. Targeted ads seem like a no-brainer, and new hire Kendall is sure to have some ideas for how to help companies better reach consumers on the site. But Pinterest also could become a platform for would-be entrepreneurs seeking to cash in on their hobbies, much the way eBay (EBAY) unleashed a new class of mom-and-pop vendors.

Pinterest's rise hasn't been all corporate love and celebrity mash letters. Lawyer and photographer Kristin Kowalski sparked a firestorm last month when she blogged about her concerns that Pinterest was letting its users publish other people's content without explicit permission. The terms of service indemnify the company from its users' copyright violations, but the service itself, critics say, encourages users to violate copyrights.

When Silbermann read Kowalski's blogged concerns, he called her up. They spoke for more than an hour. The company will shortly update its terms of service, though Silbermann notes they follow the Digital Millennium Copyright Act. Pinterest also has introduced an opt-out code web publishers can embed in their sites—Yahoo's Flickr has done so too—to prevent pinners from republishing material. Eventually publishers may decide to make more material available if the site becomes a major destination.

Silbermann's handling of the potentially volatile situation shows how his good manners can be an asset. After Kowalski spoke to him, she wrote a lengthy follow-up praising the young CEO. "He didn't yell at me. He didn't accuse me of being a hater," she wrote. "I also truly believe that he is going to work his young, brilliant little butt off to address [my concerns] and remedy the quirks to the best of his and his legal team's ability." She now calls herself a Pinterest cheerleader.

In mid-March Pinterest unveiled a redesigned profile page. During our visit Silbermann and co-founder Sharp walk me through the highlights. "The idea is to help you discover other people," says Silbermann, pointing to a box that now shows the people and brands that pinners repin the most. Click on their handles to see who they follow, and you jump on an endless train of interesting images.

It's clear from the new user page that the Facebook ethos has rubbed off on Pinterest. Each user can upload a profile photo, and there's a stream of continually updating pinboards, not unlike the information on Facebook. Pinterest uses Facebook Connect to let Facebook members log on to Pinterest and opt to publish their activity to their Facebook newsfeed. But as Pinterest gains traction, it becomes a potential threat to the social media giant. Facebook has pretty much captured the U.S. market for subscribers, so its growth is likely to come from engagement—keeping users on the site longer. As more people spend more time pinning— and revealing to marketers the kinds of hobbies and objects they covet— it may cut into the time they have to spend on Facebook.

But this flash popularity does not guarantee success, not for today's web upstarts. More people are connected— one-seventh of the world's population has a Facebook profile—and most of them are mobile. And with such a low barrier to entry, new social services pop up all the time. Pinterest must continue to be better than its competitors if it's going to thrive. Silbermann is already working on the next set of product improvements.

So what does it feel like to be a social site on the verge? "There should be a word for it," says Sharp, shifting to face his co-founder.

Says Silbermann: "It's the intersection of the Venn diagram of fear and joy."

Questions for Discussion

1. What were the sources of the conflict between Kristin Kowalski and Ben Silbermann?

2. How did he handle the conflict?

3. How is he trying to promote collaboration at Pinterest?

4. In what ways might he try to make everyone a winner?

Source: J. Hempel, "Is Pinterest the Next Facebook?: An Exclusive Look Inside CEO Ben Silbermann's Social Media Sensation," *Fortune,* April 9, 2012, 109–114. © 2012 Time Inc. used under license.

CHAPTER 18

Using Advanced Information Technology to Increase Performance

Learning Objectives

After studying this chapter, you should be able to:

LO18-1 Differentiate between data and information, and explain how the attributes of useful information allow managers to make better decisions.

LO18-2 Describe three reasons why managers must have access to information to perform their tasks and roles effectively.

LO18-3 Describe the computer hardware and software innovations that created the IT revolution and changed the way managers behave.

LO18-4 Differentiate among seven performance-enhancing kinds of management information systems.

LO18-5 Explain how IT is helping managers build strategic alliances and network structures to increase efficiency and effectiveness.

A MANAGER'S CHALLENGE

Microsoft: High Tech Giants Also Need the Latest IT

How can managers create competitive advantage through IT? Today, advances in IT are so rapid that even leading IT providers such as software giant Microsoft are often taken by surprise by the sudden popularity of new IT applications or services in areas such as cloud computing, tablet computers, and social networking. These new applications change customers' needs for specific types of computer software and hardware, and, if a company cannot supply customers with the new IT, then they are put at a competitive disadvantage that can quickly lead to lower performance and even business failure.

In 2012 Microsoft was facing challenges in all three of these IT areas and was rushing to fill the gaps in its product line to allow it to protect its Windows operating system and important applications such as its Office software suite that provide most of the company's revenues and profits. During the 2010s, for example, Microsoft acquired several small cloud computing companies to add this software service to its suite of Windows Office software. In 2012 it also announced it had developed a new advanced "surface" tablet computer that would compete against the iPad in the business and commercial or enterprise software segment of the market. Then, in June 2012 it

announced a major new acquisition to speed its entry into the business social networking software segment when it bought Yammer for $1.2 billion.

Basically, Yammer is a Facebook-type social networking software service designed to meet the needs of companies and their employees in the workplace. Social networking for companies' intranets has become a hot commodity in the 2010s, and Microsoft had no software expertise in providing a secure, private, social network for businesses. It was in the same boat as competitors such as Oracle, which bought enterprise

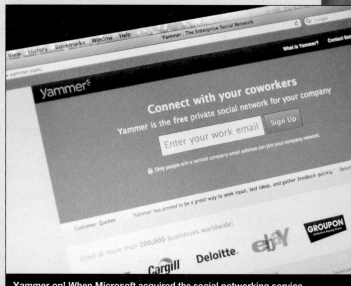

Yammer on! When Microsoft acquired the social networking service for companies, it significantly expanded its ability to offer customers one-stop computing whether the employee is in the office, the field, or working from home.

social networking company Vitrue to fill this gap in its software suite, and Salesforce.com, which bought Buddy Media. Microsoft bought Yammer because it was desperate to provide a secure enterprise networking service to the users of its Office suite of software.

There are several reasons why companies large and small are moving to adopt an enterprise social networking service in order to maintain and improve their competitive advantage. First, today's employees are used to using social networking services such as Facebook and Twitter and understand the many kinds of communication and information sharing advantages that these services provide. Thus when they join an organization or search for ways to interact with their work colleagues, they expect to find such a service on their companies' secure intranet that gives them access to the information they need on a real-time basis. Yammer provides such a secure advanced networking service that goes way beyond the kinds of traditional services that software giants have offered in the past, such as Lotus notes and shared calendars, bulletin boards, or instant messaging.

Moreover, Yammer provides Office with a major social dimension because it offers integration with Microsoft's SharePoint, Microsoft Dynamics, People Card, and Skype services. Using Yammer in Office, employees can stay connected and follow people, teams, documents, and sites in SharePoint. They can also view and embed pictures, videos, and Office content into their networking activity feeds to stay current and update colleagues through Dynamics. Using People Card employees are provided with an integrated view of their contacts everywhere in Office, including status updates, contact information, and activity feeds from Facebook and LinkedIn accounts. Finally, they can utilize Skype's messaging, voice, and teleconferencing services from within their secure Yammer account that acts as a firewall in keeping a company's social network private.

Second, Yammer's secure networking also extends to mobile computing and links employees' smartphones and tablet computers to a company's intranet, making business-critical information available anywhere, anytime to employees in the field. Moreover, once a user signs into Office, the user's personalized settings, including most recently used files, templates, and customer dictionary become available through these mobile devices. Third, the Yammer acquisition strengthened Microsoft's "Office in the Cloud" software application: that is, its Sky-Drive cloud-based computing initiative. Office saves documents created at desk-based PCs or with mobile devices to SkyDrive so users' real-time documents are always available using tablet, PC, and smartphone. With Office on Demand users can access Office even when away from a PC by streaming full-featured applications to a Windows-based PC.

In sum, social networking may have originated as a consumer-based application allowing individual users to share their personal information and build social interest groups, but today it is a vital component of business or enterprise software applications. Companies need a secure way to connect employees to their internal intranets, whether they are working in the office or in the field. And today high-tech rivals like Microsoft, Google, Apple, IBM, and Oracle are all striving to provide businesses with these "software as a service" subscription-based cloud-computing services in order to keep their suites of business software current and relevant to their users' needs. In the 2010s, for example, Google has moved quickly to provide a suite of cloud-based business applications that compete directly with those of Microsoft's Office and has the declared goal of replacing it as the leading provider of business applications software. Given that the size of the global enterprise software market is valued at $280 billion, this will clearly be a major battleground for high-tech companies in the years ahead as they and their customers seek to build and protect their competitive advantage.

Overview

In a world in which business activities of all kinds are increasingly conducted through the Internet, the challenge facing managers is to continually update and improve their use of advancing IT to increase organizational performance. Managers must utilize the most effective IT solutions such as social networking and cloud computing to assist their employees and customers or risk being surpassed by more effective rivals who have developed superior IT competencies. Google and Apple have become two of the most valuable companies in the world because they provide advanced IT solutions that increase people's ability to access, search, and use the potential of the WWW and communicate with others. The most successful B&M and online companies, such as Walmart, Best Buy, Amazon.com, and eBay, excel in developing improved company-specific IT solutions. The implication is clear: There are enormous opportunities for managers of all kinds of organizations to find new ways to use IT to use organizational resources more efficiently and effectively.

In this chapter we begin by looking at the relationship between information and the manager's job and then examine the ongoing IT revolution. Then we discuss six types of management information systems, each of which is based on a different sort of IT, which can help managers perform their jobs more efficiently and effectively. Next we examine the impact of rapidly evolving IT on managers' jobs and on an organization's competitive advantage. By the end of this chapter, you will understand how new developments in IT are profoundly shaping managers' tasks and roles and the way organizations operate.

Information and the Manager's Job

Managers cannot plan, organize, lead, and control effectively unless they have access to information. Information is the source of the knowledge and intelligence they need to make the right decisions. Information, however, is not the same as data.[1] **Data** are raw, unsummarized, and unanalyzed facts such as volume of sales, level of costs, or number of customers. **Information** is data that are organized in a meaningful fashion, such as in a graph showing the changes in sales volume or costs over time. Data alone do not tell managers anything; information, in contrast, can communicate a great deal of useful knowledge to the person who receives it—such as a manager who sees sales falling or costs rising. The distinction between data and information is important because one purpose of IT is to help managers transform data into information to make better managerial decisions.

data Raw, unsummarized, and unanalyzed facts.

information Data that are organized in a meaningful fashion.

To further clarify the difference between data and information, consider a supermarket manager who must decide how much shelf space to allocate to two breakfast cereal brands: Dentist's Delight and Sugar Supreme. Most supermarkets use checkout scanners to record individual sales and store the data on a computer. Accessing this computer, the manager might find that Dentist's Delight sells 50 boxes per day and Sugar Supreme sells 25 boxes per day.

These raw data, however, are of little value in helping the manager decide how to allocate shelf space. The manager also needs to know how much shelf space each cereal currently occupies and how much profit each cereal generates for the supermarket.

Suppose the manager discovers that Dentist's Delight occupies 10 feet of shelf space and Sugar Supreme occupies 4 feet and that Dentist's Delight generates 20 cents of profit a box while Sugar Supreme generates 40 cents of profit a box. By putting these three bits of data together (number of boxes sold, amount of shelf space, and profit per box), the manager gets some useful information on which to base a decision: Dentist's Delight generates $1 of profit per foot of shelf space per day [(50 boxes × $.20)/10 feet], and Sugar Supreme generates $2.50 of profit per foot of shelf space per day [(25 boxes × $.40)/4 feet]. Armed with this information, the manager might decide to allocate less shelf space to Dentist's Delight and more to Sugar Supreme.

Attributes of Useful Information

LO18-1 Differentiate between data and information, and explain how the attributes of useful information allow managers to make better decisions.

Four factors determine the usefulness of information to a manager: quality, timeliness, completeness, and relevance (see Figure 18.1).

QUALITY   Accuracy and reliability determine the quality of information.[2] The greater its accuracy and reliability, the higher is the quality of information. Modern IT gives managers access to high-quality real-time information that they can use to improve long-term decision making and alter short-term operating decisions, such as how much of a particular product to make daily or monthly. Supermarket managers, for example, use handheld bar code readers linked to a server to monitor and record how demand for particular products such as milk, chicken, or bread changes daily so they know how to restock their shelves to ensure the products are always available.

TIMELINESS   Information that is timely is available when it is required to allow managers to make the optimal decision—not after the decision has been made. In today's rapidly changing world, the need for timely information often means information must be available on a real-time basis—hence the enormous growth in the demand for PDAs such as smartphones.[3] **Real-time information** is information that reflects current changes in business conditions. In an industry that experiences rapid changes, real-time information may need to be updated frequently.

real-time information
Frequently updated information that reflects current conditions.

Airlines use real-time information about the number of flight bookings and competitors' prices to adjust their prices hourly to maximize their revenues. Thus, for example, the fare

Figure 18.1
Factors Affecting the Usefulness of Information

for flights from New York to Seattle might change from one hour to the next as fares are reduced to fill empty seats and raised when most seats have been sold. Airlines use real-time information about reservations to adjust fares at the last possible moment to fill planes and maximize revenues. U.S. airlines make more than 100,000 fare changes each day.[4] Obviously the managers who make such pricing decisions need real-time information about current market demand.

COMPLETENESS   Information that is complete gives managers all the information they need to exercise control, achieve coordination, or make an effective decision. Recall from Chapter 7, however, that managers rarely have access to complete information. Instead, because of uncertainty, ambiguity, and bounded rationality, they have to make do with incomplete information.[5] One function of IT is to increase the completeness of managers' information.

RELEVANCE   Information that is relevant is useful and suits a manager's particular needs and circumstances. Irrelevant information is useless and may actually hurt the performance of a busy manager who has to spend valuable time determining whether information is relevant. Given the massive amounts of information that managers are now exposed to and their limited information-processing capabilities, a company's information systems designers need to ensure that managers receive only relevant information.

LO18-2 Describe three reasons why managers must have access to information to perform their tasks and roles effectively.

information technology The set of methods or techniques for acquiring, organizing, storing, manipulating, and transmitting information.

management information system (MIS) A specific form of IT that managers utilize to generate the specific, detailed information they need to perform their roles effectively.

What Is Information Technology?

Information technology (IT) is the set of methods or techniques for acquiring, organizing, storing, manipulating, and transmitting information.[6] A **management information system (MIS)** is a specific form of IT that managers select and use to generate the specific, detailed information they need to perform their roles effectively. Management information systems have existed for as long as there have been organizations, which is a long time indeed—merchants in ancient Egypt used clay tablets to record their transactions. Before the computing age, most systems were paper-based: Clerks recorded important information on paper documents (often in duplicate or triplicate) in words and numbers; sent copies of the documents to superiors, customers, or suppliers; and stored other copies in filing cabinets for future reference.

Rapid advances in the power of IT—specifically the development of ever more powerful and sophisticated computer hardware and software—have had a fundamental impact on organizations and managers, as suggested by the developments in the server data center storage business discussed in "A Manager's Challenge."[7] Some recent IT developments, such as inventory management and customer relationship management (CRM) systems, contribute so much to performance that organizations that do *not* adopt it, or that implement it ineffectively, become uncompetitive compared with organizations that do adopt it.[8] In the 2000s much of the increasing productivity and efficiency of business in general has been attributed to the way organizations and their employees use advancing IT to improve their performance.

Managers need information for three reasons: to make effective decisions, to control the activities of the organization, and to coordinate the activities of the organization. Next we examine these uses of information in detail.

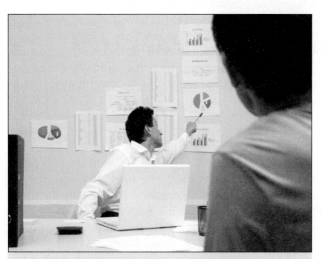

Charts and graphs may be the clichéd centerpieces of managerial meetings, but the data they represent are key for making informed decisions.

Information and Decisions

Much of management (planning, organizing, leading, and controlling) is about making decisions. For example, the marketing manager must decide what price to charge for a product, what distribution channels to use, and what promotional messages to emphasize to maximize sales. The manufacturing manager must decide how much of a product to make and how to make it. The purchasing manager must decide from whom to purchase inputs and what inventory of inputs to hold. The human relations manager must decide how much employees should be paid, how they should be trained, and what benefits they should be given. The engineering manager must make decisions about new product design. Top managers must decide how to allocate scarce financial resources among competing projects, how best to structure and control the organization, and what business-level strategy the organization should be pursuing. And regardless of their functional orientation, all managers have to make decisions about matters such as what performance evaluation to give to a subordinate.

To make effective decisions, managers need information both from inside the organization and from external stakeholders. When deciding how to price a product, for example, marketing managers need information about how consumers will react to different prices. They need information about unit costs because they do not want to set the price below the cost of production. And they need information about competitive strategy because pricing strategy should be consistent with an organization's competitive strategy. Some of this information will come from outside the organization (for example, from consumer surveys) and some from inside the organization (information about production costs comes from manufacturing). As this example suggests, managers' ability to make effective decisions rests on their ability to acquire and process information.

Information and Control

As discussed in Chapter 11, controlling is the process through which managers regulate how efficiently and effectively an organization and its members perform the activities necessary to achieve its stated goals.[9] Managers achieve control over organizational activities by taking four steps (see Figure 11.2 on page 340): (1) They establish measurable standards of performance or goals; (2) they measure actual performance; (3) they compare actual performance against established goals; and (4) they evaluate the results and take corrective action if necessary.[10] The package delivery company UPS, for example, has a delivery goal: to deliver 95% of the overnight packages it picks up by noon the next day.[11] UPS has thousands of U.S. ground stations (branch offices that coordinate the pickup and delivery of packages in a particular area) that are responsible for the physical pickup and delivery of packages. UPS managers monitor the delivery performance of these stations regularly; if they find that the 95% goal is not being attained, they determine why and take corrective action if necessary.

To achieve control over any organizational activity, managers must have information. To control ground station activities, a UPS manager might need to know what percentage of packages each station delivers by noon. To obtain this information the manager uses UPS's own IT; UPS is also a leader in developing proprietary in-house IT. All packages to be shipped to the stations have been scanned with handheld scanners by the UPS drivers who pick them up; then all this information is sent wirelessly through UPS servers to its headquarters' mainframe computer. When the packages are scanned again at delivery, this information is also transmitted through its computer network. Managers can access this information to quickly discover what percentage of packages were delivered by noon of the day after they were picked up, and also how this information breaks down station by station so they can take corrective action if necessary.

Management information systems are used to control all divisional and functional operations. In accounting, for example, information systems are used to monitor expenditures and compare them against budgets.[12] To track expenditures against budgets, managers need information about current expenditures, broken down by relevant organizational units; accounting IT is designed to give managers this information. An example of IT used to monitor and control the daily activities of employees is the online MBO information system used by T. J. Rodgers at Cypress Semiconductor, discussed in Chapter 11. Rodgers implemented IT that allows him to review the goals of all his employees in about four hours.[13] At first glance it might seem that advances in IT would have a limited impact on the business of an office furniture maker; however, this assumption would be incorrect, as the following "Management Insight" box suggests.

Herman Miller's Office of the Future

Managers at Herman Miller have been finding countless ways to use IT and the Internet to give their company a competitive advantage over rival office furniture makers (OFMs) such as Steelcase and Hon.[14] Early on, Miller's managers saw the potential of the Internet for selling its furniture to business customers. Other furniture companies' websites were simply online advertisements for their products, services, and other marketing information. But Miller's managers quickly realized the true potential of using both the company's intranet and the Internet to reach customers to gain competitive advantage.

First Miller's managers developed IT that linked all the company's dealers and salespeople to its manufacturing hub so that sales orders could be coordinated with the custom design department and with manufacturing, enabling customers to receive pricing and scheduling information promptly. Then, with this customer delivery system in place, Miller developed IT to link its manufacturing operations with its network of suppliers so its input supply chain would be coordinated with its customer needs.

When Miller's managers noticed that competitors were imitating its IT, they searched for new ways to maintain their competitive advantage. Soon they realized IT could transform the office furniture business itself. When they began to define Herman Miller as a digital enterprise infused with e-business, they realized IT could not only improve efficiency but also change how the customer experienced Herman Miller and increase value for the customer. A major web initiative was the establishment of an e-learning tool, Uknowit.com, which became Herman Miller's online university. Via the web thousands of Miller's employees and dealers are currently enrolled in Uknowit.com, where they choose from 85 courses covering technology, products and services, product applications, selling skills, and industry competitive knowledge. The benefits to Miller and its dealers and customers from this IT initiative are improved speed to market and ability to respond to competitors' tactics. Salespeople and dealers now have the information and tools they need to better compete for and keep customers.

Moreover, the office furniture business offers highly customized solutions to its customers. A main source of competitive advantage is the ability to give customers exactly what they want at the right price. Using its new IT, Miller's salespeople give design and manufacturing more accurate and timely information, which has reduced specification errors during the selling process. Also, with the new systems, time to market has been reduced and Miller is committed to being able to offer customers highly customized furniture in 10 or fewer business days.

Of course all these IT initiatives have been costly to Herman Miller. Thousands of hours of management time have been spent developing the IT and providing content, such as information about competitors, for the company's online classes. Herman Miller's managers are looking at the long term; they believe they have created a real source of competitive advantage for their company that will sustain it in the years ahead. And the company was voted as one of the most admired companies by *Fortune* because its managers try to keep their IT one step ahead of its competitors.[15]

Herman Miller's custom-made ergonomic office furniture arrives on time due to the company's use of IT that links its dealers with its manufacturing hub.

Information and Coordination

Coordinating department and divisional activities to achieve organizational goals is another basic task of management. As an example of the size of the coordination task that managers face, consider the coordination effort necessary to build Boeing's 787 Dreamliner jet aircraft, which is assembled from over 3 million individual parts.[16] Managers at Boeing have to coordinate the production and delivery of all these parts so that every part arrives at Boeing's Everett, Washington, facility exactly when it is needed (for example, the wings should arrive before the engines). To achieve this high level of coordination, managers need information about which global supplier is producing what part, and when it will be produced. To meet this need, managers at Boeing created global IT that links Boeing to all its suppliers and can track the flow of 3 million components through the production process around the world in real time—an immense task. Indeed, as we noted in earlier chapters, Boeing's IT system could not match the enormous complexity of the task, and the launch of its new airliner was delayed until 2011 because of IT glitches that affected communication with suppliers.

Managers face increasing coordination problems in managing their global supply chains to take advantage of national differences in production costs. As a result, managers must adopt ever more sophisticated IT that helps them coordinate the flow of materials, semifinished goods, and finished products throughout the world. Consider, for example, how Bose, which manufactures some of the world's highest-quality speakers, manages its global supply chain. Bose purchases almost all the components for its speakers, and about half of these components come from overseas suppliers, mainly in Asia. The challenge for managers is to coordinate this global supply chain to minimize Bose's inventory and transportation costs, which is achieved when components arrive at Bose's assembly plant just in time to enter the production process. Bose also has to remain responsive to customer demands, which means its suppliers have to be able to respond quickly to changes in Bose's demand for specific kinds of components and increase or decrease production as needed.

The responsibility for coordinating the supply chain to simultaneously minimize inventory and transportation costs and respond quickly to changing customer demands belongs to Bose's logistics managers. They contracted with W. N. Procter, a Boston-based supply chain manager, to use its proprietary logistics IT, ProcterLink, to give Bose the real-time information it needs to track components parts as they move through the global supply chain.[17] When a shipment leaves a supplier, it is logged into ProcterLink, and from this point on Bose can track the supplies as they move around the globe toward Massachusetts, which allows Bose to fine-tune its production scheduling so components enter the assembly process exactly when they are needed.

How well this system works was illustrated when one Japanese customer unexpectedly doubled its order for Bose speakers. Bose had to gear up its manufacturing in a hurry, but many of its components were stretched out across long distances. By using ProcterLink, Bose was able to locate the needed parts in its supply chain. It broke them out of the normal delivery chain and moved them by air freight to get them to the assembly line in time to meet the accelerated schedule so that Bose could meet the needs of its customer.

The IT Revolution

Advances in IT have enabled managers to make gigantic leaps in the way they can collect more timely, complete, relevant, and high-quality information and use it in more effective ways. To better understand the ongoing revolution in IT that has transformed companies such as Herman Miller and Bose, allowing them to improve their responsiveness to customers, minimize costs, and improve their competitive position, we need to examine several key aspects of advanced IT.

LO18-3 Describe the computer hardware and software innovations that created the IT revolution and changed the way managers behave.

The Effects of Advancing IT

The IT revolution began with the development of the first computers—the hardware of IT—in the 1950s. The language of computers is a digital language of zeros and ones. Words, numbers, images, and sound can all be expressed in zeros and ones. Each letter in the alphabet has its own unique code of zeros and ones, as does each number, each color, and each sound. For example, the digital code for the number 20 is 10100. In the language of computers it takes a lot of zeros and ones to express even a simple sentence, to say nothing of complex color graphics or moving video images. Nevertheless, modern computers can read, process, and store trillions of instructions per second (an *instruction* is a line of software code) and thus vast amounts of zeros and ones. This awesome number-crunching power forms the foundation of the ongoing IT revolution.

The products and services that result from advancing IT are all around us—ever more powerful microprocessors and PCs, high-bandwidth wireless smartphones, sophisticated word-processing software, ever-expanding computer networks, inexpensive digital cameras and camcorders, and more and more useful online information and retailing services that did not exist a generation ago. These products are commonplace and are being continuously improved. Many managers and companies that helped develop the new IT have reaped enormous gains.

However, while many companies have benefited from advancing IT, others have been threatened. Traditional landline telephone companies such as AT&T, Verizon, and other long-distance companies the world over have seen their market dominance threatened by new companies offering Internet, broadband, and wireless telephone technology. They have been forced to respond by buying wireless cell phone companies, building their own high-powered broadband networks, and forming alliances with companies such as Apple to make smartphones that will work on their networks. So advancing IT is both an opportunity and a threat, and managers have to move quickly to protect their companies and maintain their competitive advantage.[18]

On one hand, IT helps create new product opportunities that managers and their organizations can take advantage of—such as online travel and vacation booking. On the other hand, IT creates new and improved products that reduce or destroy demand for older, established products—such as the services provided by bricks-and-mortar travel agents. Walmart, by developing its own sophisticated proprietary IT, has been able to reduce retailing costs so much that it has put hundreds of thousands of small and medium-size stores out of business. Similarly, thousands of small, specialized U.S. bookstores have closed in the last decade as a result of advances in IT that made online bookselling possible.

IT and the Product Life Cycle

product life cycle The way demand for a product changes in a predictable pattern over time.

When IT is advancing, organizational survival requires that managers quickly adopt and apply it. One reason for this is how IT affects the length of the **product life cycle**, which is the way demand for a product changes in a predictable pattern over time.[19] In general, the product life cycle consists of four stages: the embryonic, growth, maturity, and decline stages (see Figure 18.2). In the *embryonic stage* a product has yet to gain widespread acceptance;

Figure 18.2
A Product Life Cycle

Technology advances make phones and tablets prone to particularly short life cycles... so your spiffy new offering can beat out the others in the field, but only for a limited time.

customers are unsure what a product, such as a new smartphone, has to offer, and demand for it is minimal. As a product, like Apple's iPad, becomes accepted by customers (although many products do *not,* like Blackberry's tablet), demand takes off and the product enters its growth stage. In the *growth stage* many consumers are entering the market and buying the product for the first time, and demand increases rapidly. This is the stage Apple iPhones and iPads were in by 2012. In 2012 Google also announced its own Nexus tablet and how fast demand grows for this product will depend on the value customers see in the collection of IT features applications the Nexus offers them.

The growth stage ends and the *maturity stage* begins when market demand peaks because most customers have already bought the product (there are relatively few first-time buyers left). At this stage, demand is typically replacement demand. In the PC market, for example, people who already have a PC trade up to a more powerful model. The iPod is currently in this stage; its users decide whether or not to trade up to a more powerful version that offers greater capabilities. Products such as desktops and laptops and services such as Internet broadband and digital TV services are currently in this stage; for example, AT&T, Comcast, and Direct TV are battling to increase their market share.

Once demand for a product starts to fall, the *decline stage* begins; this typically occurs when advancing IT leads to the development of a more advanced product, making the old one obsolete, such as when the iPod destroyed Sony's Walkman franchise. In general, demand for every generation of a digital device such as a PC, smartphone, or MP3 music player falls off when the current leaders' technology is superseded by new products that incorporate the most recent IT advances. For example, products such as the latest 4G smartphones and tablet computers permit superfast web browsing and downloading of videos, books, and all kinds of digital media. Thus, one reason the IT revolution has been so important for managers is that advances in IT are one of the most significant determinants of the length of a product's life cycle, and therefore of competition in an industry.[20] In more and more industries, advances in IT are shortening product life cycles as customers jump on the latest fad or fashion—such as the Google Nexus tablet in 2012. Google's technology will hurt sales of Amazon.com's Kindle book reader, which was the leader in book downloading and reading in 2011, and Amazon was racing in 2012 to develop the next generation Kindle that can compete with the Nexus. In the clothing industry, which also has a short product life cycle because of quickly changing customer tastes, IT makes it possible to introduce new fashions much more quickly—or dispose of outdated clothing, as the following "Information Technology Byte" feature discusses.

Information Technology Byte

eBay Uses IT to Develop New Ways to Sell Out-of-Fashion Clothing

eBay Inc. is the world's largest online clothing seller; every year it sells millions of articles of new and used clothing in all shapes and sizes—it sold $7.1 billion worth of clothing in 2009 to over 10 million buyers. Until now the merchandise provided by its sellers has determined the choice of clothing it can offer its customers. And with an average of 20 million listings in the clothing category, eBay's site can be hard to navigate and search, which makes it difficult for customers to find what they want. Recognizing its growing problems in 2010, eBay announced a major new initiative to drive up its online clothing sales.

eBay planned to launch a new fashion "microsite," Fashion.ebay.com, and work with the major fashion brands and clothing makers to sell their overstocked merchandise.

eBay's Fashion Vault website is just one of the IT initiatives the company is rolling out in order to compete with other online fashion retailers.

It has already worked out contracts with companies such as Hugo Boss, Donna Karan, and Lord & Taylor to act as sellers in what essentially will be an online outlet mall, and eBay hopes to encourage all major clothing brands to join its initiative. Currently, to dispose of their excess inventory, clothing makers set up their own bricks-and-mortar stores in outlet malls or sell to discount retail stores such as T. J. Maxx and Marshalls.

eBay's new microsite will offer several new ways of selling to customers online. It has developed "flash sales," which are sales of a small selection of fashion merchandise for only short periods to encourage buyers to purchase quickly. In 2010 it also launched "Fashion Vault," which is a fashion service that allows it to compete with online private sales companies such as Gilt.com and Ruelala.com to sell trendy clothing and accessories at deep discounts. Fashion.ebay.com uses a selling format that employs gallery-style photographs and a better search engine that will make it easier for customers to search for specific styles of fashion. For example, its new IT features an improved search engine to allow shoppers to better find brands, fashion trends, and prices; its gallery photographs let buyers see the items they are interested in—but also offer them photographs of similar competing products to improve their buying experience. "We're really transforming the experience," said Lorrie Norrington, president of eBay marketplaces, which also include such e-commerce sites as Shopping.com and Kijiji and accounted for 61% of the company's revenue of $8.7 billion last year. "We're playing to our strengths" in clothing, she said.[21] In 2010 fixed-price selling accounted for over half of eBay's revenues, up from 35% in 2008; in 2012 it was expected to grow to over 55% and Norrington expects it eventually to hit 70%.

eBay's new approach to online fashion retailing will put it in direct competition with Amazon.com and traditional retailers like Macy's and Target. The company plans to transfer all the IT innovations it has made to develop and launch its fashion microsite into other product categories, including home and garden, technology, and media, to increase sales. So far, early signs from its big push into fashion have been positive. According to eBay managers, many clothing makers have expressed interest in its new outlet mall because they see the site as a more efficient way to get rid of excess inventory in the clothing market—where the life cycles of fashions are very short, often only months, so that cost savings from fast inventory turnaround are substantial.

The message for managers is clear: The shorter a product's life cycle because of advancing IT, the more important it is to innovate products quickly and continuously. A PC company that cannot develop a new and improved product line every three to six months will soon find itself in trouble. Increasingly managers are trying to outdo their rivals by being the first to market with a product that incorporates some advance in IT, such as advanced stability or steering control that prevents vehicle wrecks.[22] In sum, the tumbling price of information brought about by advances in IT is at the heart of the IT revolution. So how can managers use all this computing power to their advantage?

The Network of Computing Power

The tumbling price of computing power and applications has allowed all kinds of organizations, large and small, to invest more to develop networks of computer servers that are customized with the mix of hardware and software applications that best meets the needs of their current value chain management as described in the following "Management Insight" box.

Management Insight

Cloud Computing, Bricks and Mortar, and Mobile Container Data Center Storage Solutions

Server computers (servers) are designed to provide powerful information-intensive computing solutions that in the past could have been executed only on huge, expensive mainframe computers. Servers also link networks of desktop and laptop PCs, and they link to wireless personal digital assistants (PDAs) such as netbooks, tablet computers, and smartphones. Using this array of computing devices, a company's employees can access its installed software applications and databases to obtain the real-time information they need to manage ongoing activities. Today servers can process staggering amounts of data to execute highly complex software applications, and they can access and store amazing amounts of information. Server sales have increased greatly over time (the server market was $30 billion in 2011) because of their ever-increasing computing power and low cost compared to mainframes—although most large companies still use a single mainframe as the "brain" that stores the most essential, secret, and important operating routines and to coordinate the company-wide computing network.

Blackbox server racks, such as this one created by Sun Microsystems, now part of Oracle, offer a significant safeguard to companies looking for cost- and space-conscious ways to back up their information.

As large companies began to buy hundreds and then thousands of servers to meet their increasing need to process and store information, server makers such as HP, Dell, and IBM designed *rack servers* that link individual servers together to increase their joint power. For example, a rack server links an individual server into a rack of 10 connected servers; then 10 racks create a network of 100 servers; 100 racks create a network of a thousand servers, and so on. Using software from specialized companies such as IBM and Oracle to link the operations of these server racks, large companies developed "server farms," which are bricks and mortar (B&M) operating facilities that are remote and physically separate from company headquarters. Server farms are database centers composed of thousands of networked server racks that are constantly monitored, maintained, and upgraded by a company's IT engineers (or specialized outsourcers such as IBM) to protect a company's information and databases. Should a company lose such information, it would be helpless; it would have no record of its transactions with its employees, customers, suppliers, and so on. IT storage and database storage are the lifeblood of a global company, which cannot function without them. But a growing concern of managers today is how to reduce the costs of database storage, which are hundreds of millions of dollars for large companies.

In the late 2000s a new way to offer companies a quick, efficient way to enlarge and upgrade their database center capabilities to respond to the vast increase in Internet use was to house these server racks in standard-size storage containers—the same kind of containers hauled on trucks or stacked on cargo ships. The first U.S. server maker to offer such a mobile database solution was Sun (now part of Oracle), which launched its "Blackbox" data center containing its proprietary Solaris rack servers in a 20-foot shipping container. Each Blackbox contained a mobile data center that could deliver the computing capability of a 9,000-square-foot physical data center but would cost only about one-fifth as much. Another company called SGI quickly announced its own new "Concentro" mobile server container—the first self-contained data center based on custom-designed, high-density server racks and data storage housed in a larger 40 × 20-foot shipping container.[23] Because SGI's space-saving rack servers are half as deep as standard servers, it could cram in twice as many individual servers into a 40-foot container as could its competitors. The immense processing power of SGI's Concentro containers, equivalent to a 30,000-square-foot B&M data center, allowed companies to rethink their need for high-cost bricks-and-mortar data centers, especially given the relatively low operating costs of SGI containers compared to physical data centers. Mobile data centers offered companies a low-cost solution and were snapped up by companies such as Google, Yahoo!, and Amazon.

Also in the late 2000s the term *cloud computing* was popularized by companies like IBM, Microsoft, and Google to refer to a new way to offer companies computing and data storage service similar to how they used and paid for utilities like water or electricity. The strategy behind cloud computing was to create (1) a cost-effective Internet-based global platform of hardware and software provided by (2) a network of thousands of interlinked IT companies that had (3) the capability to provide a full range of on-demand software applications, computing services, and database storage to millions of companies and individuals around the world. The advantage of cloud-based web services was that the cost of running applications or storing data through the Internet was much less than the cost of purchasing hardware and installing software on in-house servers. Cloud computing was like an alliance in which IT companies pooled their resources to share processing power and applications that let them offer better prices to customers. For example, installing and managing the software and hardware to operate a specialized software application might cost $50,000 a year; in cloud computing the same service could be rented for $500 a month—this is why Amazon, Google, and Microsoft pushed cloud computing so vigorously.

In sum, cloud computing offered outsourced, pay-as-you-go, on-demand Internet software capabilities to companies for a fee. Of course a major concern of users is information reliability and security. If cloud computing expands, even the largest companies may cease to operate their own database centers and outsource all their information and computing operations to web-based IT providers because they can perform these IT activities at a significantly lower cost than any particular company. The problem facing managers is to choose the most efficient and effective method to manage their company-wide computing networks and database storage operations to reduce operating costs by millions or billions of dollars a year.

network Interlinked computers that exchange information.

As the "Management Insight" box discusses, the typical organizationwide computing network that has emerged over time is a four-tier network solution that consists of "external" PDAs such as netbooks, smartphones, and tablet computers, connected to desktops and laptops, and then through "internal" rack servers to a company's mainframe (see Figure 18.3). Through wireless and wired communication an employee with the necessary permissions can hook into a company's IT system from any location—in the office, at home, on a boat, on the beach, in the air—anywhere a wireless or wired link can be established.

The internal network is composed of "client" desktop and laptop PCs connected by Ethernet to the company's system of rack servers. The client computers that are linked directly to a server constitute a *local area network* (LAN), and most companies have many LANs—for example, one in every division and function. Large companies that need immense processing power have a mainframe computer at the center or hub of the network that can quickly process vast amounts of information, issue commands, and coordinate computing devices at the other levels. The mainframe can also handle electronic communications between servers and PCs situated in different LANs, and the mainframe can connect to the mainframes of other companies. The mainframe is the master computer that controls the operations of all the other types of computers and digital devices as needed and can link them into one integrated system. It also provides the connection to the *external* IT networks outside the organization; for example, it gives a user access to an organization's cloud computing services—but with high security and reliability and only from recognized and protected computing devices. For instance, a manager with a PDA or PC hooked into a four-tier system can access data and

Figure 18.3

A Four-Tier Information System with Cloud Computing

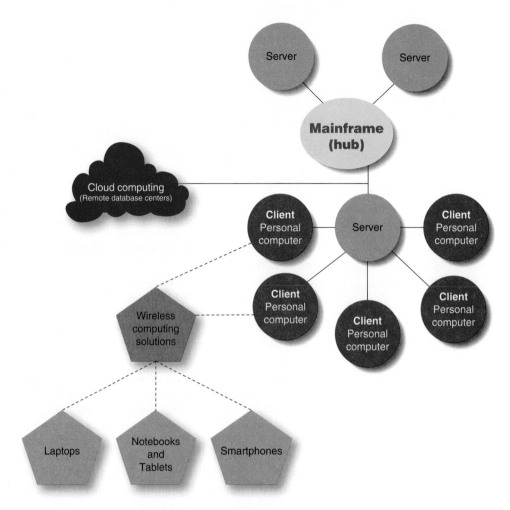

software stored in the local server, in the mainframe, or through the Internet to a cloud-based computing solution hosted by an outsourcer whose B&M database might be located anywhere in the world.

Just as computer hardware has been advancing rapidly, so has computer software. *Operating system software* tells the computer hardware how to run. *Applications software,* such as programs for word processing, spreadsheets, graphics, and database management, is developed for a specific task or use. The increase in the power of computer hardware has allowed software developers to write increasingly powerful programs that are also increasingly user-friendly. By harnessing the rapidly growing power of microprocessors, applications software has vastly increased the ability of managers to acquire, organize, and transmit information. In doing so, it also has improved the ability of managers to coordinate and control the activities of their organization and to make better decisions, as discussed earlier.

LO18-4 Differentiate among seven performance-enhancing kinds of management information systems.

Types of Management Information Systems

Advances in IT have continuously increased managers' ability to obtain the information they need to make better decisions and coordinate and control organizational resources. Next we discuss six types of management information systems (MIS) that have been particularly helpful to managers as they perform their management tasks: transaction-processing systems, operations information systems, decision support systems, expert systems, enterprise resource planning systems, and e-commerce systems (see Figure 18.4). These MIS systems are arranged along a

Figure 18.4

Six Computer-Based Management Information Systems

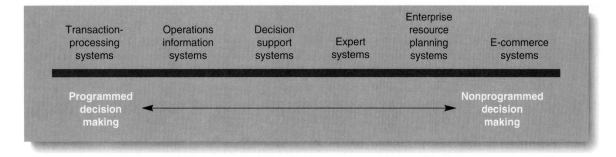

continuum according to the sophistication of the IT they are based on—IT that determines their ability to give managers the information they need to make nonprogrammed decisions. (Recall from Chapter 7 that nonprogrammed decision making occurs in response to unusual, unpredictable opportunities and threats.) We examine each of these systems after focusing on the management information system that preceded them all: the organizational hierarchy.

The Organizational Hierarchy: The Traditional Information System

Traditionally managers have used the organizational hierarchy as the main way to gather the information necessary to make decisions and coordinate and control organizational activities (see Chapter 10 for a detailed discussion of organizational structure and hierarchy). According to business historian Alfred Chandler, the use of the hierarchy as an information network was perfected by U.S. railroad companies in the 1850s.[24] At that time railroads were among the largest U.S. companies, and because of the size of their geographic footprint they faced unique problems of coordination and control. Railroad companies started to solve these problems by designing hierarchical management structures that gave top managers the information they needed to coordinate and control their nationwide operations.

Daniel McCallum, superintendent of the Erie Railroad, realized that the lines of authority and responsibility that defined Erie's management hierarchy also were channels of communication along which information traveled. McCallum established what was perhaps the first modern management information system when he ordered that regular daily and monthly reports should be sent up the hierarchy to top managers so that they could make the best decisions about, for example, controlling costs and setting freight rates. Decisions were then sent back down the hierarchy to be carried out by lower-level managers. When the performance gains from this system were publicized, many organizations imitated the railroads by using their hierarchies to collect, channel, and process information.

Although hierarchy is a useful information system, it has several drawbacks, as we noted in Chapter 10. First, when too many layers of managers exist, it takes a long time for information and requests to travel up the hierarchy and for decisions and answers to travel back down. The slow communication can reduce the timeliness and usefulness of the information and prevent a quick response to changing market conditions.[25] Second, information can be distorted as it moves from one layer of management to another, and information distortion reduces the quality of information.[26] Third, managers have only a limited span of control; so as an organization grows larger and its hierarchy lengthens, more managers must be hired, and this makes the hierarchy an expensive information system. The popular idea that companies with tall management hierarchies are bureaucratic and unresponsive to the needs of their customers arises from the inability of tall hierarchies to effectively process data and give managers timely, complete, relevant, and high-quality information. The management hierarchy is still the best information system available today—the one that results in the best decisions—*if* managers have access to the other kinds of MIS systems discussed next.

Transaction-Processing Systems

A **transaction-processing system** is an MIS designed to handle large volumes of routine recurring transactions (see Figure 18.4). Transaction-processing systems began to appear in the early 1960s with the advent of commercially available mainframe computers. They were the first type of computer-based IT adopted by many organizations, and today they are commonplace. Bank managers use a transaction-processing system to record deposits into, and payments out of, bank accounts. Supermarket managers use a transaction-processing system to record the sale of items and to track inventory levels. More generally, most managers in large organizations use a transaction-processing system to handle tasks such as payroll preparation and payment, customer billing, and payment of suppliers.

Operations Information Systems

Many types of MIS followed hard on the heels of transaction-processing systems in the 1960s as companies like IBM advanced IT. An **operations information system** is an MIS that gathers comprehensive data, organizes them, and summarizes them in a form that is of value to managers. Whereas a transaction-processing system processes routine transactions, an operations information system gives managers information they can use in their nonroutine coordinating, controlling, and decision-making tasks. Most operations information systems are coupled with a transaction-processing system. An operations information system typically accesses data gathered by a transaction-processing system, processes those data into useful information, and organizes that information into a form accessible to managers. Managers often use an operations information system to get sales, inventory, accounting, and other performance-related information. For example, the information that T. J. Rodgers at Cypress Semiconductors gets about individual employee goals and performance is provided by an operations information system.

UPS uses an operations information system to track the performance of its thousands of ground stations. Each ground station is evaluated according to four criteria: delivery (to deliver 95% of all packages within the agreed upon time period), productivity (measured by the number of packages shipped per employee-hour), cost control and efficiency, and station profitability. Each ground station also has specific delivery, efficiency, cost, and profitability targets that it must attain. Every month UPS's operations information system gathers information about these four criteria and summarizes it for top managers, who can then compare the performance of each station against its previously established targets. The system quickly alerts senior managers to underperforming ground stations so they can intervene selectively to help solve any problems that may have given rise to the poor performance.

Decision Support Systems

A **decision support system** provides computer-built models that help managers make better nonprogrammed decisions.[27] Recall from Chapter 7 that nonprogrammed decisions are those that are relatively unusual or novel, such as decisions to invest in new productive capacity, develop a new product, launch a new promotional campaign, enter a new market, or expand internationally. Whereas an operations information system organizes important information for managers, a decision support system gives managers model-building capability and the chance to manipulate information in a variety of ways. Managers might use a decision support system to help them decide whether to cut prices for a product. The decision support system might contain models of how customers and competitors would respond to a price cut. Managers could run these models and use the results as an *aid* to decision making.

The stress on the word *aid* is important—in the final analysis a decision support system is not meant to make decisions for managers. Rather, its function is to give managers valuable information they can use to improve the quality of their decisions. A good example of a sophisticated decision support system is one developed by Judy Lewent for Merck, one of the world's largest makers of pharmaceuticals.[28] The company spends over $3 billion a year on R&D to develop new drugs—an expensive and difficult process that is fraught with risks—and most new drug ideas fail to make it through the development process.

Judy Lewent's Research Planning Model has allowed Merck to more strategically develop promising new drugs while avoiding pitfalls, thus sharpening the company's focus and allowing it to roll out such programs as an HIV/AIDS prevention initiative in China, pictured here.

Given the costs, risks, and uncertainties involved in the new drug development process, Judy Lewent, a financial analysis expert, decided to develop a decision support system to help managers make more effective R&D investment decisions. Her aim was to give Merck's top managers the information they needed to evaluate proposed R&D projects on a case-by-case basis. At the heart of this decision support system is a sophisticated model known as the "Research Planning Model" in Merck.[29] The input variables to the model include data on R&D spending, manufacturing costs, selling costs, and demand conditions. The relationships among the input variables are modeled by several equations that factor in the probability of a drug's making it through the development process and to market. The outputs of this modeling process are the revenues, cash flows, and profits that a project might generate. Merck uses Lewent's decision support system to evaluate all its proposed R&D investment decisions, and Lewent's reward for her innovation was promotion to become Merck's chief financial officer.

Most decision support systems are geared toward aiding middle managers in the decision-making process. For example, a loan manager at a bank might use a decision support system to evaluate the credit risk involved in lending money to a particular client. Rarely does a top manager use a decision support system. One reason for this is that most electronic management information systems have not yet become sophisticated enough to handle effectively the ambiguous types of problems facing top managers. To improve this situation, IT experts have been developing a variant of the decision support system: an executive support system.

executive support system A sophisticated version of a decision support system that is designed to meet the needs of top managers.

An **executive support system** is a sophisticated version of a decision support system that is designed to meet the needs of top managers. One defining characteristic of executive support systems is user-friendliness. Many of them include simple pull-down menus to take a manager through a decision analysis problem. Moreover, they may contain stunning graphics and other visual and interactive features to encourage top managers to use them.[30] Increasingly, executive support systems are used to link top managers virtually so they can function as a team; this type of executive support system is called a **group decision support system**.

group decision support system An executive support system that links top managers so they can function as a team.

Ultimately top managers' intuition, judgment, and integrity will always be needed to decide whether to pursue the course of action suggested by an MIS. There are always many different issues to be factored into a decision, not least of which are its ethical implications.

Artificial Intelligence and Expert Systems

artificial intelligence Behavior performed by a machine that, if performed by a human being, would be called "intelligent."

Artificial intelligence has been defined as behavior by a machine that, if performed by a human being, would be called "intelligent."[31] Artificial intelligence has already made it possible to write programs that can solve problems and perform simple tasks. For example, software programs variously called *software agents, softbots,* or *knowbots* can be used to perform simple managerial tasks such as sorting through reams of data or incoming e-mail messages to look for important ones. The interesting feature of these programs is that from "watching" a manager sort through such data they can "learn" what his or her preferences are. Having done this, they can take over some of this work from the manager, freeing time for the manager to work on other tasks. Most of these programs are still in the development stage, but they may be commonplace within a decade.[32]

expert system A management information system that employs human knowledge, embedded in a computer, to solve problems that ordinarily require human expertise.

Expert systems, the most advanced management information systems available, incorporate artificial intelligence in their design.[33] An **expert system** is a system that employs human

Just making extra sure… roving security detectors like this one rely on artificial intelligence in order to add an extra layer to airport and flight safety.

knowledge, embedded in computer software, to solve problems that ordinarily require human expertise.[34] Mimicking human expertise (and intelligence) requires IT that can at a minimum (1) recognize, formulate, and solve a problem; (2) explain the solution; and (3) learn from experience.

Recent developments in artificial intelligence that go by names such as "fuzzy logic" and "neural networks" have resulted in computer programs that, in a primitive way, try to mimic human thought processes. Although artificial intelligence is still at an early stage of development, an increasing number of business applications are beginning to emerge in the form of expert systems.

Enterprise Resource Planning Systems

To achieve high performance, it is not sufficient just to develop an MIS inside each of a company's functions or divisions to provide better information and knowledge. It is also vital that managers in the different functions and divisions have access to information about the activities of managers in other functions and divisions. The greater the flow of information and knowledge among functions and divisions, the more learning can take place, and this builds a company's stock of knowledge and expertise. This knowledge and expertise are the source of its competitive advantage and profitability.

In the last 25 years, another revolution has taken place in IT as software companies have worked to develop enterprise resource planning systems, which essentially incorporate most MIS aspects just discussed, as well as much more. **Enterprise resource planning (ERP) systems** are multimodule application software packages that allow a company to link and coordinate the entire set of functional activities and operations necessary to move products from the initial design stage to the final customer stage. Essentially ERP systems (1) help each individual function improve its functional-level skills and (2) improve integration among all functions so they work together to build a competitive advantage for the company. Today choosing and designing an ERP system to improve how a company operates is the biggest challenge facing the IT function inside a company. To understand why almost every large global company has installed an ERP system in the last few decades, it is necessary to return to the concept of the value chain, introduced in Chapter 8.

Recall that a company's value chain is composed of the sequence of functional activities that are necessary to make and sell a product. The value chain idea focuses attention on the fact that each function, in sequence, performs its activities to add or contribute value to a product. After one function has made its contribution, it hands the product over to the next function, which makes its own contribution, and so on down the line.

The primary activity of marketing, for example, is to uncover new or changing customer needs or new groups of customers and then decide what kinds of products should be developed to appeal to those customers. It shares or "hands off" its information to product development, where engineers and scientists work to develop and design the new products. In turn, manufacturing and materials management work to find ways to make the new products as efficiently as possible. Then sales is responsible for finding the best way to convince customers to buy these products.

The value chain is useful in demonstrating the sequence of activities necessary to bring products to the market successfully. In an IT context, however, it suggests the enormous amount of information and communication that needs to link and coordinate the activities of all the various functions. Installing an ERP system for a large company can cost tens of millions of dollars. The following "Information Technology Byte" feature discusses the ERP system designed and sold by the German IT company SAP.

enterprise resource planning (ERP) systems Multimodule application software packages that coordinate the functional activities necessary to move products from the design stage to the final customer stage.

Information Technology Byte

SAP's ERP System

SAP, the world's leading supplier of ERP software, introduced the world's first ERP system in 1973. So great was the demand for its software that it had to train thousands of consultants from companies like IBM, HP, Accenture, and Cap Gemini to install and customize its software to meet the needs of companies in different industries throughout the world. Why?

SAP's ERP was demanded by companies because it can manage all the stages of the value chain and strengthen them both individually and jointly when they work together. SAP's software has modules specifically devoted to each of a company's core functional activities. Each module contains a set of "best practices," the optimum way to perform a specific functional activity that increases efficiency, quality, innovation, and responsiveness to customers. SAP's ERP is therefore "the expert system of expert systems." SAP claims that when a company reconfigures its IT system to make SAP's software work, it can achieve productivity gains of 30% to 50%, which amounts to many billions of dollars of savings for large companies.[35]

For each function in the value chain, SAP installs its software module on a function's LAN. Each function then inputs its data into that module in the way specified by SAP. For example, the sales function inputs all the information about customer needs required by SAP's sales module, and the materials management function inputs information about the product specifications it requires from suppliers into SAP's materials management module. These modules give functional managers real-time feedback on ongoing developments in their particular functional activity, such as daily changes in sales of leading products. Each SAP module functions as an expert system that can reason through the information functional employees continually input into it through their laptops or other computers. It recommends new strategies that managers can use to improve functional operations. However, the magic of ERP does not stop there.

SAP's ERP software also connects across functions. Managers in all functions have access to other functions' expert systems, and SAP's software is designed to alert managers when their functional activities will be affected by changes taking place in another function. Thus SAP's ERP system lets managers across the organization better coordinate their activities—a major source of competitive advantage. Moreover, SAP software on corporate mainframe computers takes the information from all the different functional and divisional expert systems and creates a companywide ERP system that shows top managers an overview of the operations of the whole company.

In sum, SAP's ERP system creates a sophisticated top-level expert system that can reason through the huge volume of information provided by the company's functions. It can recognize and diagnose common problems and issues in that information and develop and recommend organizationwide solutions for those problems. Using this information, top managers can improve the fit between their strategies and the changing environment.

As an example of how an ERP system works, let's examine how SAP's software helps managers coordinate their activities to speed product development. Suppose marketing has discovered some new unmet customer need, has suggested what kind of product needs to be developed, and forecasts that the demand for the product will be 40,000 units a year. With SAP's IT, engineers in product development use their expert system to work out how to design the new product in a way that builds in quality at the lowest possible cost. Manufacturing managers, watching product development's progress, work simultaneously to find the best way to make the product and thus use their expert system to find out how to keep operating costs at a minimum.

Remember that SAP's IT gives all the other functions access to this information; they can tap into what is going on between marketing and manufacturing in real time. So materials management managers watching manufacturing make its plans can simultaneously plan how to order supplies of inputs or components from global suppliers or how and when to ship the final product to customers to keep costs at a minimum. At the same time, HRM is tied into the ERP system and uses its expert system to forecast the type and cost of the labor that will be required to carry out the activities in the other functions—for example, the number of manufacturing employees who will be required to make the product or the number of salespeople who will be needed to sell the product to achieve the 40,000 sales forecast.

How does this build competitive advantage and profitability? First, it speeds up product development; companies can bring products to market much more quickly, thereby generating higher sales revenues. Second, SAP's IT focuses on how to drive down operating costs while keeping quality high. Third, SAP's IT is oriented toward the final customer; its CRM module watches how customers respond to the new product and then feeds back this information quickly to the other functions.

To see what this means in practice, let's jump ahead three months and suppose that the CRM component of SAP's ERP software reports that actual sales are 20% below target. Further, the software has reasoned that the problem is occurring because the product lacks a crucial feature that customers want. The product is a smartphone, for example, and customers demand a built-in digital camera. Sales decides this issue deserves major priority and alerts managers in all the other functions about the problem. Now managers can begin to decide how to manage this unexpected situation.

Engineers in product development, for example, use their expert system to work out how much it would cost, and how long it would take, to modify the product so that it includes the missing feature, the digital camera, that customers require. Managers in other functions watch the engineers' progress through the ERP system and can make suggestions for improvement. In the meantime, manufacturing managers know about the slow sales and have already cut back on production to avoid a buildup of the unsold product in the company's warehouse. They are also planning how to phase out this product and introduce the next version, with the digital camera, to keep costs as low as possible. Similarly, materials management managers are contacting digital camera makers to find out how much such a camera will cost and when it can be supplied. Meanwhile marketing managers are researching how they missed this crucial product feature and are developing new sales forecasts to estimate demand for the modified product. They announce a revised sales forecast of 75,000 units of the modified product.

It takes the engineers one month to modify the product; but because SAP's IT has been providing information about the modified product to managers in manufacturing and materials management, the product reaches the market only two months later. Within weeks, the sales function reports that early sales figures for the product have greatly exceeded even marketing's revised forecast. The company knows it has a winning product, and top managers give the go-ahead for manufacturing to build a second production line to double production of the product. All the other functions are expecting this decision; in fact, they have already been experimenting with their SAP modules to find out how long it will take them to respond to such a move. Each function gives the others its latest information so they can all adjust their functional activities accordingly.

This quick and responsive action is possible because of the ERP system that gives a company better control of its manufacturing and materials management activities. Quality is increased because a greater flow of information between functions allows a better-designed product. Innovation is speeded because a company can rapidly change its products to suit the needs of customers. Finally, responsiveness to customers improves because, using its CRM software module, sales can better manage and react to customers' changing needs and provide better service and support to back up the sales of the product. ERP's ability to promote competitive advantage is the reason why managers in so many companies, large and small, are moving to find the best ERP solution for their particular companies.

E-Commerce Systems

e-commerce Trade that takes place between companies, and between companies and individual customers, using IT and the Internet.

business-to-business (B2B) commerce Trade that takes place between companies using IT and the Internet to link and coordinate the value chains of different companies.

E-commerce is trade that takes place between companies, and between companies and individual customers, using IT and the Internet. **Business-to-business (B2B) commerce** is trade that takes place between companies using IT and the Internet to link and coordinate the value chains of different companies. (See Figure 18.5.) The goal of B2B commerce is to increase the

Figure 18.5
Types of E-Commerce

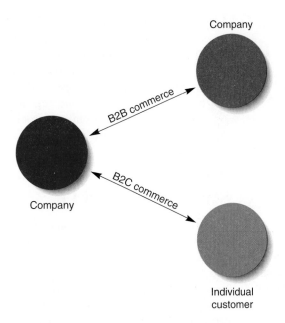

profitability of making and selling goods and services. B2B commerce increases profitability because it lets companies reduce operating costs and may improve product quality. A principal B2B software application is **B2B marketplaces**, which are Internet-based trading platforms that have been set up in many industries to connect buyers and sellers. To participate in a B2B marketplace, companies adopt a common software standard that allows them to search for and share information with one another. Then companies can work together over time to find ways to reduce costs or improve quality.

B2B marketplace An Internet-based trading platform set up to connect buyers and sellers in an industry.

business-to-customer (B2C) commerce Trade that takes place between a company and individual customers using IT and the Internet.

Business-to-customer (B2C) commerce is trade that takes place between a company and individual customers using IT and the Internet. Using IT to connect directly to the customer means companies can avoid having to use intermediaries, such as wholesalers and retailers, who capture a significant part of the profit in the value chain. The use of websites and online stores also lets companies give their customers much more information about the value of their products. This often allows them to attract more customers and thus generate higher sales revenues.

In the 2010s, computer software makers, including Microsoft, Oracle, SAP, and IBM, have rushed to use cloud computing to make their products work seamlessly with the Internet and thus respond to global companies' growing demand for e-commerce software. Previously their software was configured to work only on a particular company's intranet; today their software must be able to network a company's IT systems to other companies, such as their suppliers and distributors. At the same time, as we discussed earlier, companies also need to use social networking software to establish a secure platform their employees can use to share information inside their organizations.

The challenge facing managers now is to select e-commerce software that allows seamless exchange of information between companies anywhere in the world. The stakes are high because global competitive advantage goes to the company first with a major new technological advance. For example, SAP rushed to update its ERP modules to allow transactions over the Internet, and today all its modules have full cloud computing capability. However, Oracle, IBM, and many small specialist companies have also developed ways to provide advanced cloud computing and Internet applications at a lower price, so SAP faces increased global competition.

In summary, by using advanced types of MIS, managers have more control over a company's activities and operations and can work to improve its competitive advantage and profitability. Today the IT function is becoming increasingly important because IT managers select which kind of hardware and software a company will use and then train other functional managers and employees how to use it.

The Impact and Limitations of Information Technology

Advances in IT and management information systems are having important effects on managers and organizations. By improving the ability of managers to coordinate and control the activities of the organization and by helping managers make more effective decisions, modern IT has become a central component of any organization's structure. And evidence that IT can be a source of competitive advantage is growing; organizations that do not adopt leading-edge IT are likely to be at a competitive disadvantage. In this section we examine how the rapid advances in IT are affecting organizational structure and competitive advantage. We also examine problems associated with implementing management information systems effectively, as well as the limitations of MIS.

LO18-5 Explain how IT is helping managers build strategic alliances and network structures to increase efficiency and effectiveness.

strategic alliance An agreement in which managers pool or share their organization's resources and know-how with a foreign company, and the two organizations share the rewards and risks of starting a new venture.

B2B network structure A series of global strategic alliances that an organization creates with suppliers, manufacturers, and distributors to produce and market a product.

Strategic Alliances, B2B Network Structures, and IT

Recently, increasing globalization and the use of new IT have brought about two innovations that are sweeping through U.S. and European companies: electronically managed strategic alliances and B2B network structures. A **strategic alliance** is a formal agreement that commits two or more companies to exchange or share their resources in order to produce and market a product.[36] Most commonly, strategic alliances are formed because the companies share similar interests and believe they can benefit from cooperating. For example, global carmakers such as Honda and GM have formed many strategic alliances with particular suppliers of inputs such as car axles, gearboxes, and air-conditioning systems. Over time these car companies work closely with their suppliers to improve the efficiency and effectiveness of the inputs so that the final product—the car produced—is of higher quality and often can be produced at lower cost. Honda and GM have also established alliances with many different global suppliers because both companies now make several car models that are assembled and sold in many countries around the world.

Throughout the 2000s, the growing sophistication of IT using global intranets, cloud computing, and teleconferencing made it much easier to manage strategic alliances and allow managers to share information and cooperate. One outcome of this has been the growth of strategic alliances into an IT-based network structure. A **B2B network structure** is a formal series of global strategic alliances that one or several organizations create with suppliers, manufacturers, and distributors to produce and market a product. Network structures allow an organization to manage its global value chain in order to find new ways to reduce costs and increase the quality of products—without incurring the high costs of operating a complex organizational structure (such as the costs of employing many managers). More and more U.S. and European companies are relying on global network structures to gain access to low-cost foreign sources of inputs, as discussed in Chapter 6. Shoemakers such as Nike and Adidas are two companies that have used this approach extensively.

Nike is the largest and most profitable sports shoe manufacturer in the world. The key to Nike's success is the network structure that Nike founder and CEO Philip Knight created to allow his company to produce and market shoes. As noted in Chapter 8, the most successful companies today are trying to pursue simultaneously a low-cost and a differentiation strategy. Knight decided early that to do this at Nike he needed to focus his company's efforts on the most important functional activities, such as product design and engineering, and leave the others, such as manufacturing, to other organizations.

By far the largest function at Nike's Oregon headquarters is the design and engineering function, whose members pioneered innovations in sports shoe design such as the air pump and Air Jordans that Nike introduced so successfully. Designers use computer-aided design (CAD) to design Nike shoes, and they electronically store all new product information, including manufacturing instructions. When the designers have finished their work, they electronically transmit the blueprints for the new products to a network of Southeast Asian suppliers and manufacturers with which Nike has formed strategic alliances.[37] Instructions for the design of a new sole may be sent to a supplier in Taiwan; instructions for the leather uppers, to a supplier in Malaysia. The suppliers produce the shoe parts and send them for final assembly to a manufacturer in China with which Nike has established another strategic alliance. From

China the shoes are shipped to distributors throughout the world. 99% of the over 100 million pairs of shoes that Nike makes each year are made in Southeast Asia.

This network structure gives Nike two important advantages. First, Nike can quickly respond to changes in sports shoe fashion. Using its global IT system, Nike literally can change the instructions it gives each of its suppliers overnight, so that within a few weeks its foreign manufacturers are producing new kinds of shoes.[38] Any alliance partners that fail to perform up to Nike's standards are replaced with new partners through the regular B2B marketplace.

Second, Nike's costs are low because wages in Southeast Asia are a fraction of what they are in the United States, and this difference gives Nike a low-cost advantage. Also, Nike's ability to outsource and use foreign manufacturers to produce all its shoes abroad allows Knight to keep the organization's U.S. structure flat and flexible. Nike can use a relatively inexpensive functional structure to organize its activities.

The use of network structures is increasing rapidly as organizations recognize the many opportunities they offer to reduce costs and increase organizational flexibility. U.S. companies spent $300 billion on global supply chain management each year in the 2000s. The push to lower costs has led to the development of B2B marketplaces in which most or all of the companies in an industry (for example, carmakers) use the same software platform to link to each other and establish industry specifications and standards. Then these companies jointly list the quantity and specifications of the inputs they require and invite bids from the thousands of potential suppliers around the world. Suppliers also use the same software platform, so electronic bidding, auctions, and transactions are possible between buyers and sellers around the world. The idea is that high-volume standardized transactions can help drive down costs at the industry level. Also, quality will increase as these relationships become more stable as a B2B network structure develops.

Flatter Structures and Horizontal Information Flows

Rapid advances in IT have been associated with a "delayering" (flattening) of the organizational hierarchy, a move toward greater decentralization and horizontal information flows within organizations, and the concept of the boundaryless organization.[39] By electronically giving managers high-quality, timely, relevant, and relatively complete information, modern management information systems have reduced the need for tall management hierarchies.

Modern IT has reduced the need for a hierarchy to function as a means of coordinating and controlling organizational activities. Also, by reducing the need for hierarchy, modern IT can directly increase an organization's efficiency because fewer employees are required to perform organizational activities. At one time, for example, 13 layers of management separated Kodak's general manager of manufacturing and factory workers; with IT the number of layers has been cut to four. Similarly, Intel found that by increasing the sophistication of its own MIS, it could cut the number of hierarchical layers in the organization from 10 to 5.[40]

The ability of IT to flatten structure and facilitate the flow of horizontal information between employees has led many researchers and consultants to popularize the idea of a **boundaryless organization**. Such an organization is composed of people linked by IT—computers, faxes, computer-aided design systems, and video teleconferencing—who may rarely, if ever, see one another face-to-face. People are utilized when their services are needed, but they are not formal members of an organization; they are functional experts who form an alliance with an organization, fulfill their contractual obligations, and then move on to the next project.

Large consulting companies, such as Accenture, IBM, and McKinsey & Co., use their global consultants in this way. Consultants are connected by laptops to an organization's **knowledge management system**—its company-specific virtual information system that systematizes the knowledge of its employees and facilitates the sharing and integrating of expertise within and between functions and divisions through real-time interconnected IT. Knowledge management systems let employees share their knowledge and expertise and give them virtual access to other employees who have the expertise to solve the problems they encounter as they perform their jobs.

Some organizations, especially those that provide complex services and employ highly trained workers, have gone one step further and created what has been called a virtual organization. A **virtual organization** is one in which employees are linked to an organization's centralized databases by computers, faxes, and videoconferencing and rarely see one another

boundaryless organization An organization whose members are linked by computers, faxes, computer-aided design systems, and video teleconferencing and who rarely, if ever, see one another face-to-face.

knowledge management system A company-specific virtual information system that systematizes the knowledge of its employees and facilitates the sharing and integrating of their expertise.

virtual organization A company in which employees are linked to an organization's centralized databases by computers, faxes, and videoconferencing and rarely meet face-to-face.

face-to-face, if ever.[41] These employees might only infrequently visit the physical premises of their companies; they receive their assignments electronically, report back to their superiors electronically, and operate autonomously.[42] Almost all their employees are out in the field, working anywhere around the globe with clients to solve their problems. Large consultancy companies like IBM and Accenture operate in this fashion as the following "Information Technology Byte" box illustrates. It provides an interesting example of how IT, by decentralizing authority to employees and teams, promotes flexibility and allows a company to better respond to the needs of its global customers.

Information Technology Byte

IBM and Accenture Create "Virtual" Organizations

Accenture, a global management consulting company, has been one of the pioneers in using IT to revolutionize its organizational structure. Its managing partners realized that since only its consultants in the field could diagnose and solve clients' problems, the company should design a structure that facilitated creative, on-the-spot decision making. To accomplish this, Accenture decided to replace its tall hierarchy of authority with a sophisticated IT system to create a virtual organization.[43] First, it flattened the organizational hierarchy, eliminating many managerial levels and set up a shared organization-wide IT system that provides each of Accenture's consultants with the information that he or she needs to solve a client's problem. If the consultant still lacks the specific knowledge needed to solve a client's problem, they can use the system to request expert help from Accenture's thousands of consultants around the globe.[44]

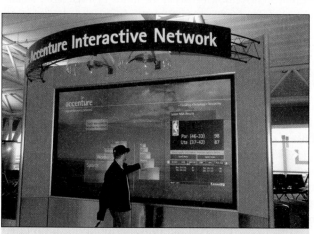

The ultimate flat organization: Accenture's new virtual structure allows point-to-point connections for general information, troubleshooting, and directions to expert advice. The best part? All that IT powers this touch-screen portal so you can double check stats for work, as well as for your NBA team, while walking to your next flight.

To implement the change, Accenture equipped all its consultants with state-of-the-art laptops and smartphones that can connect to its sophisticated corporate intranet and tap into Accenture's large information databases that contain volumes of potentially relevant information. The consultants can also communicate directly using their smartphones and use teleconferencing to help speed problem solving.[45] For example, if a project involves installing a particular kind of IT system, a consultant has quick access to consultants around the globe who have installed the system. Accenture has found that its virtual organization has increased the creativity of its consultants and enhanced their performance. By providing employees with more information and enabling them to easily confer with other people, electronic communication has made consultants more autonomous and willing to make their own decisions, which has led to high performance and made Accenture one of the best-known of all global consulting companies.[46]

Similarly, IBM, which has been experiencing tough competition in the 2000s, has been searching for ways to better utilize its talented workforce to lower costs and offer customers specialized kinds of services that its competitors cannot. IBM has also used IT to develop virtual teams of consultants to accomplish this.

IBM has created "competency centers" around the globe that are staffed by consultants who share the same specific IT skill; its competency centers are located in the countries in which IBM has the most clients and does the most business. To use its consultants most effectively, IBM used its own IT expertise to develop sophisticated software that allows it to create self-managed teams composed of IBM consultants who have the optimum mix of skills to solve a client's particular problems. From these teams, IBM's software engineers first analyze the skills and experience of its consultants and input the results into the software program. Then they analyze and code the nature of a client's specific problem and, using this information, IBM's program then matches each specific client problem to the skills of IBM's consultants and identifies a list of "best fit" employees. One of IBM's senior managers then narrows down this list and selects the actual consultants who will form the self-managed team. Once selected, team members assemble as quickly as possible in the client's home country and go to work to develop the software necessary to solve and manage the client's problem. This new IT allows IBM to create an ever-changing set of global self-managed teams that form to solve the problems of IBM's global clients. In addition, because each team inputs knowledge about its activities into IBM's intranet, then, as at Accenture, consultants and teams can learn from one another so that their problem-solving skills increase over time.

Despite their usefulness, IT, in general, and management information systems, in particular, have some limitations. A serious potential problem is that in all the enthusiasm for MIS, communication via computer networks might lose the vital human element of communication. There is a strong argument that electronic communication should support face-to-face communication rather than replacing it. For example, it would be wrong to make a judgment about an individual's performance merely by "reading the numbers" provided by an MIS. Instead the numbers should be used to alert managers to individuals who may have a performance problem. The nature of this problem should then be explored in a face-to-face meeting, during which more detailed information can be gathered. One drawback of using IT, such as e-mail and teleconferencing, is that employees may spend too much time watching their computer screens and communicating electronically—and little time interacting directly with other employees.[47] If this occurs, important and relevant information may not be obtained because of the lack of face-to-face contact, and the quality of decision making may fall.

Summary and Review

LO18-1, 18-2 **INFORMATION AND THE MANAGER'S JOB**   Computer-based IT is central to the operation of most organizations. By giving managers high-quality, timely, relevant, and relatively complete information, properly implemented IT can improve managers' ability to coordinate and control the operations of an organization and to make effective decisions. Moreover, IT can help the organization attain a competitive advantage through its beneficial impact on productivity, quality, innovation, and responsiveness to customers. Thus modern IT is an indispensable management tool.

LO18-3 **THE IT REVOLUTION**   Over the last 30 years there have been rapid advances in the power and rapid declines in the cost of IT. Falling prices, wireless communication, computer networks, and software developments have all radically improved the power and efficacy of computer-based IT.

LO18-4 **TYPES OF MANAGEMENT INFORMATION SYSTEMS**   Traditionally managers used the organizational hierarchy as the main system for gathering the information they needed to coordinate and control the organization and to make effective decisions. Today managers use six main types of computer-based information systems. Listed in ascending order of sophistication, they are transaction-processing systems, operations information systems, decision support systems, expert systems, enterprise resource planning systems, and e-commerce systems.

LO18-5 **THE IMPACT AND LIMITATIONS OF IT**   Modern IT has changed organizational structure in many ways. Using IT, managers can create electronic strategic alliances and form a B2B network structure. A network structure, based on some shared form of IT, can be formed around one company, or a number of companies can join together to create an industry B2B network. Modern IT also makes organizations flatter and encourages more horizontal cross-functional communication. As this increasingly happens across the organizational boundary, the term *boundaryless organizations* has been coined to refer to virtual organizations whose members are linked electronically.

Management in Action

Topics for Discussion and Action

Discussion

1. To be useful, information must be of high quality, be timely, be relevant, and be as complete as possible. Why does a tall management hierarchy, when used as a management information system, have negative effects on these desirable attributes? [LO18-1]

2. What is the relationship between IT and competitive advantage? [LO18-2]

3. Because of the growth of high-powered, low-cost wireless communications and IT such as videoconferencing, many managers soon may not need to come into the office to do their jobs. They will be able to work at home. What are the pros and cons of such an arrangement? [LO18-3, 18-4]

4. Many companies have reported that it is difficult to implement advanced management information systems such as ERP systems. Why do you think this is so? How might the roadblocks to implementation be removed? [LO18-4]

5. How can IT help in the new product development process? [LO18-4]

6. Why is face-to-face communication between managers still important in an organization? [LO18-4, 18-5]

Action

7. Ask a manager to describe the main kinds of IT that he or she uses on a routine basis at work. [LO18-1, 18-4]

8. Compare the pros and cons of using a network structure to perform organizational activities versus performing all activities in-house or within one organizational hierarchy. [LO18-3, 18-4, 18-5]

9. What are the advantages and disadvantages of business-to-business networks? [LO18-5]

Building Management Skills

Analyzing Management Information Systems [LO18-3, 18-4]

Pick an organization about which you have some direct knowledge. It may be an organization you worked for in the past or are in contact with now (such as the college or school you attend). For this organization, answer the following questions:

1. Describe the management information systems that are used to coordinate and control organizational activities and to help make decisions.

2. Do you think that the organization's existing MIS gives managers high-quality, timely, relevant, and relatively complete information? Why or why not?

3. How might advanced IT improve the competitive position of this organization? In particular, try to identify the impact that a new MIS might have on the organization's efficiency, quality, innovation, and responsiveness to customers.

Managing Ethically [LO18-1, 18-2]

The use of management information systems, such as ERPs, often gives employees access to confidential information from all functions and levels of an organization. Employees can see important information about the company's products that is of great value to competitors. As a result, many companies monitor employees' use of the intranet and Internet to prevent an employee from acting unethically, such as by selling this information to competitors. On the other hand, with access to this information employees might discover that their company has been engaging in unethical or even illegal practices.

Questions

1. Ethically speaking, how far should a company go to protect its proprietary information, given that it also needs to protect the privacy of its employees? What steps can it take?

2. When is it ethical for employees to give information about a company's unethical or illegal practices to a third party, such as a newspaper or government agency?

Small Group Breakout Exercise

Using New Management Information Systems [LO18-2, 18-4]

Form groups of three or four people, and appoint one member as the spokesperson who will communicate your findings to the class when called on by the instructor. Then discuss the following scenario:

You are a team of managing partners of a large management consulting company. You are responsible for auditing your firm's MIS to determine whether it is appropriate and up to date. To your surprise, you find that although your organization has a wireless e-mail system in place and consultants are connected into a powerful local area network (LAN) at all times, most of the consultants (including partners) are not using this technology. It seems that most important decision making still takes place through the organizational hierarchy.

Given this situation, you are concerned that your organization is not exploiting the opportunities offered by new IT to obtain a competitive advantage. You have discussed this issue and are meeting to develop an action plan to get consultants to appreciate the need to learn about and use the new IT.

1. What advantages can you tell consultants they will obtain when they use the new IT?

2. What problems do you think you may encounter in convincing consultants to use the new IT?

3. What steps might you take to motivate consultants to learn to use the new technology?

Exploring the World Wide Web [LO18-2, 18-5]

Go to UPS's website (the specific page is http://www.ups-scs.com/solutions/case_consumer.html). Scroll through the featured case studies including Adidas, Crown premiums, and so on. Read about how UPS used its IT and logistic systems to help these companies, and answer the following questions:

1. What are the main ways in which UPS can use its IT and logistics skills to help its clients?

2. In what specific ways does UPS's IT help these companies improve their efficiency, quality, innovation, and responsiveness to customers, and performance?

Be the Manager [LO18-4]

You are one of the managers of a small specialty maker of custom tables, chairs, and cabinets. You have been charged with finding ways to use IT and the Internet to identify new business opportunities that can improve your company's competitive advantage, such as ways to reduce costs or attract customers.

2. What kinds of IT or MIS can help the company better manage these forces?

3. In what ways can the Internet help this organization improve its competitive position?

Questions

1. What are the various forces in a specialty furniture maker's task environment that have the most effect on its performance?

General Motors Will Slash Outsourcing in IT Overhaul

As Randy Mott, the new CIO of General Motors, goes about his workday, he carries with him a well-worn calculator. It sits in front of him in the place of prominence that most people reserve for a smartphone. Mott, who has been CIO at Walmart, Dell, and Hewlett-Packard and joined GM in February, believes in numbers. And as he tries to transform GM's IT operations, he plans to flip one set of numbers on a scale that no CIO has ever done before.

Today, about 90% of GM's IT services, from running data centers to writing applications, are provided by outsourcing companies such as HP/EDS, IBM, Capgemini, and Wipro, and only 10% are done by GM employees. Mott plans to flip those percentages in about three years—to 90% GM staff, 10% outsourcers. Insourcing IT on that scale will require GM to go on a hiring binge for software developers, project managers, database experts, business analysts, and other IT pros over the next three years. As part of that effort, it plans to create three new software development centers, all of them in the U.S. IT outsourcers, including GM's one-time captive provider, EDS, face the loss of contracts once valued at up to $3 billion a year.

This dramatic move away from outsourcing is just one piece of the "IT transformation" Mott is leading, which includes consolidating data centers and applications, centralizing IT planning and execution, and getting a better grip on GM's customer and production data. GM's IT transformation doesn't emphasize budget cuts but instead centers on delivering more value from IT, much faster. In many ways, the foundation Mott is laying is similar to the one Ford started laying four or five years ago as part of its One Ford/One IT initiative.

The overhaul Mott envisions puts the everyday operations of GM at risk during a time when the world's No. 2 automaker (Toyota is now No. 1) is still climbing out of bankruptcy protection and a $50 billion government bailout. GM's factories, supply chains, and financial reporting rely on the IT organization to keep information flowing in near real time on a global scale. The fact that Mott's boss, CEO Dan Akerson, would bless this level of IT change and accept this level of risk at a still-fragile stage of GM's recovery shows how essential the best data and technology are to the company's future. Akerson "was looking to make changes in the speed and cadence of the company," Mott says. "Whether it was with me or someone else, Dan Akerson was going to do an IT transformation here."

Mott's philosophy on outsourcing at GM, as it was at HP, Dell, and Walmart, is that the company needs more creative, business-changing ideas from IT, and IT teams need to deliver those innovative projects faster. Mott doesn't think GM can be creative or fast enough with outsourced IT. "When the business says 'go,' then that means we start working on a contract; we don't start working on a project," Mott says of the current outsourced model.

The shift away from outsourcing is only the most dramatic element of Mott's IT "transformation." The plan, approved by Akerson and the rest of the executive operating committee, comes straight out of the playbook Mott has developed over a three-decade career in the retail, high-tech, and now automotive industries. Mott's plan for GM is nearly identical to the one he led at HP between 2005 and 2008 under CEO Mark Hurd, before Hurd and then Mott got bounced in an executive shake-up.

Sweeping Transformation

Besides the move away from IT outsourcing, the key elements of Mott's plan include:

>> **Data center consolidation:** GM plans to go from 23 sizable data centers worldwide to just two, both in Michigan. In the process, GM will replace servers, storage, and networking with today's more efficient gear, in hopes of reducing costs and using more automation so that fewer of GM's IT pros are involved in "run the business" kinds of IT operations and more are involved in new development and innovation.

>> **Application consolidation:** Mott estimates that GM can cut 40% or more of the company's 4,000-plus applications that have sprung up in various regions and divisions by moving to standardized, global applications for everything from financials to factory-level processes.

>> **Hiring:** Mott plans to dramatically increase the IT organization's hiring of new college grads and will look to top computer science schools beyond the universities with which it now has recruiting ties. Most of GM's development will be done in the U.S., even though the company's growth is very much tied to China, Brazil, and other countries. Mott does plan to hire internationally to bulk up an "IT planning community" that can gather the requirements needed for GM to build global apps.

>> **Three new software development centers:** One will be in the Detroit area, with

the other two in U.S. locations still to be determined. They'll be chosen based on the kind of development talent the company can attract there, including their proximity to key universities. Dispersing IT development will be a cultural change for the still Detroit-centric GM.

6 Steps for GM

1. **Insourcing** Flipping from 90% outsourced IT to 90% of work done by internal staff. Lots of hiring ahead.

2. **Data center consolidation** From 23 data centers to two new ones, with the latest hardware and more automation.

3. **Application consolidation** 40% or more of GM's apps could go, by moving to standardized, global applications.

4. **Software development centers** Likely three in U.S. sites to be determined, based on the local development talent.

5. **Portfolio management** Every IT project will require a cost-benefit analysis and a priority set by business units.

6. **Data warehouse consolidation** GM has about 200 data marts today and plans to move to one data architecture, so data's easier to access and use.

>> **Portfolio management:** As he did at HP, Mott will require that a cost-benefit analysis be done on every IT project, spelling out the project's benefits in ways that the business unit, finance team, and IT agree to. The results of those CBAs produce a metric Mott calls the "revenue of IT," measuring the value IT projects generate, not just how much they cost. Likewise, Mott will insist that business managers prioritize the various projects they have planned.

>> **Data warehouse consolidation:** GM has about 200 data marts today, and Mott wants to move all of them to one architecture. The goal is to make data easier to access and use, and to integrate it better across groups and divisions to reveal more insights. CEO Akerson told *Fortune* in a May interview, "We're looking at our IT systems real hard. Data warehousing of customer information was not a strength in the company. Maybe it wasn't even existent, but it will be in the future."

Mott's ambitious transformation plan won't be universally popular. End users will complain: You're taking away the application that I love for the greater good of cost savings? Business unit managers will complain: You're making me do a cost-benefit analysis for my little upgrade? Isn't this the kind of bureaucracy a nimble GM needs to avoid? Even Mott's IT team will grumble: You're messing with the fiefdom of IT contractors I manage? Mott's critics at HP complained that he cut too fast and deep, leaving business units vulnerable, or that he spent precious resources on internal bean counting.

There's one additional, controversial piece of Mott's plan: It all happens at once, over the next three years. Mott described it in the past as "choosing is losing." For example, if you move to an insourced IT staff and away from outsourcers, but you don't modernize the data center to increase IT automation, then you won't get the benefit from those new staffers working on new projects instead of maintenance and support work.

It fits Mott's general philosophy that many IT projects fail because they just take too long. It's why he favors putting more staff on a project for a shorter period—doing fewer projects at a time, but faster. "Every month that goes by, every quarter that goes by, the ROI goes down," he says. The clock has started ticking. Mott launched this IT transformation plan internally in late June on a town hall webcast with GM's 1,500 IT employees worldwide. The world will be watching: If Mott and his team botch any of this IT transformation, it could put the company's historic turnaround in jeopardy.

Questions for Discussion

1. In what ways can insourcing IT help GM improve its performance?

2. How will Mott's IT strategy affect the four functions of management?

3. Which kinds of IT systems discussed in the chapter are most likely to help Mott and GM develop new ways to attract customers and increase sales?

Source: C. Murphy, "General Motors Will Slash Outsourcing In IT Overhaul," *InformationWeek*, July 9, 2012. Copyright © 2012 UBM TechWeb. Reprinted with permission.

CREDITS

Notes

Chapter 1

1. H. Dalton, "Apple Chief Tim Cook Opts Out of $75 Million Dividend," www.guardian.co.uk, 25 May 2012.

2. www.apple.com, 2012.

3. G. R. Jones, *Organizational Theory, Design, and Change* (Upper Saddle River, NJ: Pearson, 2011).

4. J. P. Campbell, "On the Nature of Organizational Effectiveness," in P. S. Goodman, J. M. Pennings, et al., *New Perspectives on Organizational Effectiveness* (San Francisco: Jossey-Bass, 1977).

5. M. J. Provitera, "What Management Is: How It Works and Why It's Everyone's Business," *Academy of Management Executive* 17 (August 2003), 152–54.

6. J. McGuire and E. Matta, "CEO Stock Options: The Silent Dimension of Ownership," *Academy of Management Journal* 46 (April 2003), 255–66.

7. www.apple.com, press releases, 2000, 2001, 2003, 2006, 2008, 2009, 2010, 2012.

8. www2.goldmansachs.com, 2010, 2012; www.jpmorganchase.com, 2010, 2012.

9. J. G. Combs and M. S. Skill, "Managerialist and Human Capital Explanations for Key Executive Pay Premium: A Contingency Perspective," *Academy of Management Journal* 46 (February 2003), 63–74.

10. H. Fayol, *General and Industrial Management* (New York: IEEE Press, 1984). Fayol actually identified five different managerial tasks, but most scholars today believe these four capture the essence of Fayol's ideas.

11. P. F. Drucker, *Management Tasks, Responsibilities, and Practices* (New York: Harper & Row, 1974).

12. www.apple.com, press release, 2003.

13. G. McWilliams, "Lean Machine—How Dell Fine-Tunes Its PC Pricing to Gain Edge in a Slow Market," *The Wall Street Journal,* June 8, 2001, A1.

14. R. H. Guest, "Of Time and the Foreman," *Personnel* 32 (1955), 478–86.

15. L. Hill, *Becoming a Manager: Mastery of a New Identity* (Boston: Harvard Business School Press, 1992).

16. Ibid.

17. H. Mintzberg, "The Manager's Job: Folklore and Fact," *Harvard Business Review,* July–August 1975, 56–62.

18. H. Mintzberg, *The Nature of Managerial Work* (New York: Harper & Row, 1973).

19. J. Kotter, *The General Managers* (New York: Free Press, 1992).

20. C. P. Hales, "What Do Managers Do? A Critical Review of the Evidence," *Journal of Management Studies,* January 1986, 88–115; A. I. Kraul, P. R. Pedigo, D. D. McKenna, and M. D. Dunnette, "The Role of the Manager: What's Really Important in Different Management Jobs," *Academy of Management Executive,* November 1989, 286–93.

21. A. K. Gupta, "Contingency Perspectives on Strategic Leadership," in D. C. Hambrick, ed., *The Executive Effect: Concepts and Methods for Studying Top Managers* (Greenwich, CT: JAI Press, 1988), 147–78.

22. D. G. Ancona, "Top Management Teams: Preparing for the Revolution," in J. S. Carroll, ed., *Applied Social Psychology and Organizational Settings* (Hillsdale, NJ: Erlbaum, 1990); D.C. Hambrick and P. A. Mason, "Upper Echelons: The Organization as a Reflection of Its Top Managers," *Academy of Management Journal* 9 (1984), 193–206.

23. T. A. Mahony, T. H. Jerdee, and S. J. Carroll, "The Jobs of Management," *Industrial Relations* 4 (1965), 97–110; L. Gomez-Mejia, J. McCann, and R. C. Page, "The Structure of Managerial Behaviors and Rewards," *Industrial Relations* 24 (1985), 147–54.

24. W. R. Nord and M. J. Waller, "The Human Organization of Time: Temporal Realities and Experiences," *Academy of Management Review* 29 (January 2004), 137–40.

25. R. L. Katz, "Skills of an Effective Administrator," *Harvard Business Review,* September–October 1974, 90–102.

26. Ibid.

27. P. Tharenou, "Going Up? Do Traits and Informal Social Processes Predict Advancing in Management," *Academy of Management Journal* 44 (October 2001), 1005–18.

28. C. J. Collins and K. D. Clark, "Strategic Human Resource Practices, Top Management Team Social Networks, and Firm Performance: The Role of Human Resource Practices in Creating Organizational Competitive Advantage," *Academy of Management Journal* 46 (December 2003), 740–52.

29. R. Stewart, "Middle Managers: Their Jobs and Behaviors," in J. W. Lorsch, ed., *Handbook of Organizational Behavior* (Englewood Cliffs, NJ: Prentice-Hall, 1987), 385–91.

30. S. C. de Janasz, S. E. Sullivan, and V. Whiting, "Mentor Networks and Career Success: Lessons for Turbulent Times," *Academy of Management Executive* 17 (November 2003), 78–92.

31. K. Labich, "Making Over Middle Managers," *Fortune,* May 8, 1989, 58–64.

32. B. Wysocki, "Some Companies Cut Costs Too Far, Suffer from Corporate Anorexia," *The Wall Street Journal,* July 5, 1995, A1.

33. www.dell.com, 2008, 2010, 2012.

34. K. Peterson, "Boeing 787 Delays Cast Hard Light on Outsourcing," www.reuters.com, April 11, 2011.

35. www.boeing.com, press release, 2011, 2012.

36. K. Maher and B. Tita, "Caterpillar Joins 'Onshoring' Trend," www.yahoo.com, March 12, 2010

37. V. U. Druskat and J. V. Wheeler, "Managing from the Boundary: The Effective Leadership of Self-Managing Work Teams," *Academy of Management Journal* 46 (August 2003), 435–58.

38. S. R. Parker, T. D. Wall, and P. R. Jackson, "That's Not My Job: Developing Flexible Work Orientations," *Academy of Management Journal* 40 (1997), 899–929.

39. B. Dumaine, "The New Non-Manager," *Fortune,* February 22, 1993, 80–84.

40. H. G. Baum, A. C. Joel, and E. A. Mannix, "Management Challenges in a New Time," *Academy of Management Journal* 45 (October 2002), 916–31.

41. A. Shama, "Management under Fire: The Transformation of Management in the Soviet Union and Eastern Europe," *Academy of Management Executive* 10 (1993), 22–35.

42. www.apple.com, 2010; www.nike.com, 2010.

43. K. Seiders and L. L. Berry, "Service Fairness: What It Is and Why It Matters," *Academy of Management Executive* 12 (1998), 8–20.

44. T. Donaldson, "Editor's Comments: Taking Ethics Seriously—A Mission Now More Possible," *Academy of Management Review* 28 (July 2003), 363–67.

45. C. Anderson, "Values-Based Management," *Academy of Management Executive* 11 (1997), 25–46.

46. W. H. Shaw and V. Barry, *Moral Issues in Business,* 6th ed. (Belmont, CA: Wadsworth, 1995); T. Donaldson, *Corporations and Morality* (Englewood Cliffs, NJ: Prentice-Hall, 1982).

47. www.apple.com, press release, 2010. 2012.

48. www.sec.gov, 2010, 2012.

49. www.rosasdelecuador.com, 2012; Bohr, J. "Deadly Roses," *The Battalion* February 13 (2006): 3.

50. S. Jackson et al., *Diversity in the Workplace: Human Resource Initiatives* (New York: Guilford Press, 1992).

51. G. Robinson and C. S. Daus, "Building a Case for Diversity," *Academy of Management Executive* 3 (1997), 21–31; S. J. Bunderson and K. M. Sutcliffe, "Comparing Alternative Conceptualizations of Functional Diversity in Management Teams: Process and Performance Effects," *Academy of Management Journal* 45 (October 2002), 875–94.

52. D. Jamieson and J. O'Mara, *Managing Workforce 2000: Gaining a Diversity Advantage* (San Francisco: Jossey-Bass, 1991).

53. http://digital.virtualmarketingpartners.com/vmp/accenture/diversity-inclusion/index.php, 2010.

54. Press release, "Dell CEO Kevin Rollins Cites Workforce Diversity as Key to Gaining Competitive Advantages in Business," www.dell.com, March 6, 2006.

55. "Union Bank of California Honored by U.S. Labor Department for Employment Practices," press release, September 11, 2000.

Chapter 2

1. H. Ford, "Progressive Manufacture," *Encyclopedia Britannica,* 13th ed. (New York: Encyclopedia Co., 1926).

2. R. Edwards, *Contested Terrain: The Transformation of the Workplace in the Twentieth Century* (New York: Basic Books, 1979).

3. A. Smith, *The Wealth of Nations* (London: Penguin, 1982).

4. Ibid., 110.

5. J. G. March and H. A. Simon, *Organizations* (New York: Wiley, 1958).

6. L. W. Fry, "The Maligned F. W. Taylor: A Reply to His Many Critics," *Academy of Management Review* 1 (1976), 124–29.

7. F. W. Taylor, *Shop Management* (New York: Harper, 1903); F. W. Taylor, *The Principles of Scientific Management* (New York: Harper, 1911).

8. J. A. Litterer, *The Emergence of Systematic Management as Shown by the Literature from 1870–1900* (New York: Garland, 1986).

9. H. R. Pollard, *Developments in Management Thought* (New York: Crane, 1974).

10. D. Wren, *The Evolution of Management Thought* (New York: Wiley, 1994), 134.

11. Edwards, *Contested Terrain.*

12. J. M. Staudenmaier Jr., "Henry Ford's Big Flaw," *Invention and Technology* 10 (1994), 34–44.

13. H. Beynon, *Working for Ford* (London: Penguin, 1975).

14. Taylor, *The Principles of Scientific Management.*

15. F. B. Gilbreth, *Primer of Scientific Management* (New York: Van Nostrand Reinhold, 1912).

16. F. B. Gilbreth Jr. and E. G. Gilbreth, *Cheaper by the Dozen* (New York: Crowell, 1948).

17. D. Roy, "Efficiency and the Fix: Informal Intergroup Relations in a Piece Work Setting," *American Journal of Sociology* 60 (1954), 255–66.

18. M. Weber, *From Max Weber: Essays in Sociology,* ed. H. H. Gerth and C. W. Mills (New York: Oxford University Press, 1946); M. Weber, *Economy and Society,* ed. G. Roth and C. Wittich (Berkeley: University of California Press, 1978).

19. C. Perrow, *Complex Organizations,* 2nd ed. (Glenview, IL: Scott, Foresman, 1979).

20. Weber, *From Max Weber,* 331.

21. See Perrow, *Complex Organizations,* chap. 1, for a detailed discussion of these issues.

22. H. Fayol, *General and Industrial Management* (New York: IEEE Press, 1984).

23. Ibid., 79.

24. T. J. Peters and R. H. Waterman Jr., *In Search of Excellence: Lessons from America's Best-Run Companies* (New York: Harper & Row, 1982).

25. R. E. Eccles and N. Nohira, *Beyond the Hype: Rediscovering the Essence of Management* (Boston: Harvard Business School Press, 1992).

26. L. D. Parker, "Control in Organizational Life: The Contribution of Mary Parker Follett," *Academy of Management Review* 9 (1984), 736–45.

27. P. Graham, *M. P. Follett—Prophet of Management: A Celebration of Writings from the 1920s* (Boston: Harvard Business School Press, 1995).

28. M. P. Follett, *Creative Experience* (London: Longmans, 1924).

29. E. Mayo, *The Human Problems of Industrial Civilization* (New York: Macmillan, 1933); F. J. Roethlisberger and W. J. Dickson, *Management and the Worker* (Cambridge: Harvard University Press, 1947).

30. D. W. Organ, "Review of *Management and the Worker,* by F. J. Roethlisberger and W. J. Dickson," *Academy of Management Review* 13 (1986), 460–64.

31. D. Roy, "Banana Time: Job Satisfaction and Informal Interaction," *Human Organization* 18 (1960), 158–61.

32. For an analysis of the problems in distinguishing cause from effect in the Hawthorne studies and in social settings in general, see A. Carey, "The Hawthorne Studies: A Radical Criticism," *American Sociological Review* 33 (1967), 403–16.

33. D. McGregor, *The Human Side of Enterprise* (New York: McGraw-Hill, 1960).

34. Ibid., 48.

35. Peters and Waterman, *In Search of Excellence.*

36. J. Pitta, "It Had to Be Done and We Did It," *Forbes,* April 26, 1993, 148–52.

37. T. Dewett and G. R. Jones, "The Role of Information Technology in the Organization: A Review, Model, and Assessment," *Journal of Management* 27 (2001), 313–46.

38. W. E. Deming, *Out of the Crisis* (Cambridge: MIT Press, 1986).

39. J. D. Thompson, *Organizations in Action* (New York: McGraw-Hill, 1967).

40. D. Katz and R. L. Kahn, *The Social Psychology of Organizations* (New York: Wiley, 1966); Thompson, *Organizations in Action.*

41. T. Burns and G. M. Stalker, *The Management of Innovation* (London: Tavistock, 1961); P. R. Lawrence and J. R. Lorsch, *Organization and Environment* (Boston: Graduate School of Business Administration, Harvard University, 1967).

42. Burns and Stalker, *The Management of Innovation.*

43. C. W. L. Hill and G. R. Jones, *Strategic Management: An Integrated Approach,* 8th ed. (Florence, KY: Cengage, 2010).

44. E. Werner, "Slaughterhouse Owner Acknowledges Abuse," www.pasadenastarnews.com, March 13, 2008.

45. D. Bunis and N. Luna, "Sick Cows Never Made Food Supply, Meat Plant Owner Says," www.ocregister.com, March 12, 2008.

46. "Worker Sentenced in Slaughterhouse Abuse," www.yahoo.com, March 22, 2008.

Chapter 3

1. D. Roberts, "Under Armour Gets Serious," *Fortune,* November 7, 2011, 152–62; K. Plank, As told to Mark Hyman, "How I Did It: Kevin Plank: For the Founder of Apparel-Maker Under Armour, Entrepreneurship Is 99% Perspiration and 1% Polyester," *Inc.,* http://www.inc.com/magazine/20031201/howididit_Printer_Friendly.html, March 26, 2012.

2. Roberts, "Under Armour Gets Serious"; Plank, As told to Mark Hyman, "How I Did It" ; "Under Armour's Kevin Plank: Creating the Biggest, Baddest Brand on the Planet," Knowledge@Wharton, January 5, 2011, http://knowledge.wharton.upenn.edu/printer_friendly.

cfm?articleid=2665, March 26, 2012; "2011 Under Armour Annual Report," Under Armour, Inc. —Annual Report & Proxy, http://investor.underarmour.com/annuals.cfm?sh_print=yes&, March 30, 2012.

3. Roberts, "Under Armour Gets Serious."

4. "2011 Under Armour Annual Report."

5. Roberts, "Under Armour Gets Serious"; "Creating the Biggest, Baddest Brand on the Planet."

6. Roberts, "Under Armour Gets Serious."

7. Ibid.

8. "2011 Under Armour Annual Report."

9. Ibid.

10. "2011 Under Armour Annual Report."

11. Roberts, "Under Armour Gets Serious."

12. Ibid.

13. "2011 Under Armour Annual Report."

14. Roberts, "Under Armour Gets Serious."

15. Roberts, "Under Armour Gets Serious"; "Creating the Biggest, Baddest Brand on the Planet."

16. Roberts, "Under Armour Gets Serious."

17. S. Carpenter, "Different Dispositions, Different Brains," *Monitor on Psychology,* February 2001, 66-68.

18. J. M. Digman, "Personality Structure: Emergence of the Five-Factor Model," *Annual Review of Psychology* 41 (1990), 417–40; R. R. McCrae and P. T. Costa, "Validation of the Five-Factor Model of Personality across Instruments and Observers," *Journal of Personality and Social Psychology* 52 (1987), 81–90; R. R. McCrae and P. T. Costa, "Discriminant Validity of NEO-PIR Facet Scales," *Educational and Psychological Measurement* 52 (1992), 229–37.

19. Digman, "Personality Structure"; McCrae and Costa, "Validation of the Five-Factor Model"; McCrae and Costa, "Discriminant Validity"; R. P. Tett and D. D. Burnett, "A Personality Trait-Based Interactionist Model of Job Performance," *Journal of Applied Psychology* 88, no. 3 (2003), 500–17; J. M. George, "Personality, Five-Factor Model," in S. Clegg and J. R. Bailey, eds., *International Encyclopedia of Organization Studies* (Thousand Oaks, CA: Sage, 2007).

20. L. A. Witt and G. R. Ferris, "Social Skills as Moderator of Conscientiousness–Performance Relationship: Convergent Results across Four Studies," *Journal of Applied Psychology* 88, no. 5 (2003), 809–20; M. J. Simmering, J. A. Colquitt, R. A. Noe, and C. O. L. H. Porter, "Conscientiousness, Autonomy Fit, and Development: A Longitudinal Study," *Journal of Applied Psychology* 88, no. 5 (2003), 954–63.

21. M. R. Barrick and M. K. Mount, "The Big Five Personality Dimensions and Job Performance: A Meta-Analysis," *Personnel Psychology* 44 (1991), 1–26; S. Komar, D. J. Brown, J. A. Komar, and C. Robie, "Faking and the Validity of Conscientiousness: A Monte Carlo Investigation," *Journal of Applied Psychology* 93 (2008), 140–54.

22. Digman, "Personality Structure"; McCrae and Costa, "Validation of the Five-Factor Model"; McCrae and Costa, "Discriminant Validity."

23. E. McGirt, "The Dirtiest Mind in Business: How Filth Met Opportunity and Created a Franchise," *Fast Company* 122 (February 2008), 64, www.fastcompany.com/magazine/122/the-dirtiest-mind-in-business_Printer_Friendl . . . , January 23, 2008; Dirty Jobs: About the Show; Discovery Channel, "Get Down and Dirty," http://dsc.discovery.com/fansites/dirtyjobs/about/about-print.html, February 3, 2010.

24. "Mike Rowe's World: Mike's Bio: Discovery Channel," http://dsc.discovery.com/fansites/dirtyjobs/bio/bio-print.html, January 23, 2008; Dirty Jobs: Discovery Channel, http://dsc.discovery.com/tv/dirty-jobs/, March 30, 2012.

25. McGirt, "The Dirtiest Mind in Business."

26. "Dirty Jobs: Season 1 DVD Set— Discovery Channel Store—754317," http://shopping.discovery.com/product-60948.html?jzid=40588004-66-0, January 25, 2008; "Mike Rowe's World."

27. McGirt, "The Dirtiest Mind in Business."

28. McGirt, "The Dirtiest Mind in Business"; Dirty Jobs: About the Show; Discovery Channel, "Get Down and Dirty," http://dsc.discovery.com/fansites/dirtyjobs/about/about-print.html, February 3, 2010.

29. McGirt, "The Dirtiest Mind in Business;" Dirty Jobs: Discovery Channel, March 30, 2012.

30. McGirt, "The Dirtiest Mind in Business"; M. Rowe, "Seven Dirty Habits of Highly Effluent People: Mike Rose's Seven Rules for Job Satisfaction," *Fast Company* 122 (February 2008), 69, www.fastcompany.com/magazine/122/seven-dirty-habits-of-highly-effluent-people_ . . . , January 23, 2008.

31. J. B. Rotter, "Generalized Expectancies for Internal versus External Control of Reinforcement," *Psychological Monographs* 80 (1966), 1–28; P. Spector, "Behaviors in Organizations as a Function of Employees' Locus of Control," *Psychological Bulletin* 91 (1982), 482–97; Dirty Jobs, March 30, 2012.

32. J. Brockner, *Self-Esteem at Work* (Lexington, MA: Lexington Books, 1988).

33. D. C. McClelland, *Human Motivation* (Glenview, IL: Scott, Foresman, 1985); D. C. McClelland, "How Motives, Skills, and Values Determine What People Do," *American Psychologist* 40 (1985), 812–25; D. C. McClelland, "Managing Motivation to Expand Human Freedom," *American Psychologist* 33 (1978), 201–10.

34. D. G. Winter, *The Power Motive* (New York: Free Press 1973).

35. M. J. Stahl, "Achievement, Power, and Managerial Motivation: Selecting Managerial Talent with the Job Choice Exercise," *Personnel Psychology* 36 (1983), 775–89; D. C. McClelland and D. H. Burnham, "Power Is the Great Motivator," *Harvard Business Review* 54 (1976), 100–10.

36. R. J. House, W. D. Spangler, and J. Woycke, "Personality and Charisma in the U.S. Presidency: A Psychological Theory of Leader Effectiveness," *Administrative Science Quarterly* 36 (1991), 364–96.

37. G. H. Hines, "Achievement, Motivation, Occupations and Labor Turnover in New Zealand," *Journal of Applied Psychology* 58 (1973), 313–17; P. S. Hundal, "A Study of Entrepreneurial Motivation: Comparison of Fast- and Slow-Progressing Small Scale Industrial Entrepreneurs in Punjab, India," *Journal of Applied Psychology* 55 (1971), 317–23.

38. M. Rokeach, *The Nature of Human Values* (New York: Free Press 1973).

39. Ibid.

40. Ibid.

41. K. K. Spors, "Top Small Workplaces 2007: Gentle Giant Moving," *The Wall Street Journal,* October 1, 2007, R4–R5; "Gentle Giant Sees Revenue Boost, *Boston Business Journal,* January 15, 2008, www.gentlegiant.com/news-011508-1.htm, February 5, 2008; Company History: Gentle Giant Moving Company, "Company History," http://www.gentlegiant.com/history.php, February 3, 2010; "Massachusetts Moving Company Gentle Giant Moving Company Celebrates 30 Years in Operation," January 25, 2010, http://www.gentlegiant.com/press/press20100125.php, February 3, 2010.

42. Spors, "Top Small Workplaces 2007."

43. Full Service Moving Company—Gentle Giant History, http://www.gentlegiant.com/moving-companies/full-service-moving.aspx, March 30, 2012.

44. Ryan Libby, Branch manager, Providence, RI, Moving Services and Moving Tips from Gentle Giant Moving Company, http://www.gentlegiant.com/moving-companies/furniture-movers/ryan-libby.aspx.

45. Spors, "Top Small Workplaces 2007."

46. Ibid.

47. Spors, "Top Small Workplaces 2007"; "Gentle Giant Receives Top Small Workplace Award," www.gentlegiant.com/topsmallworkplace.htm, January 5, 2008; "Corporate Overview," http://www.gentlegiant.com/company.php, February 3, 2010.

48. Spors, "Top Small Workplaces 2007."

49. Ibid.

50. A. P. Brief, *Attitudes In and Around Organizations* (Thousand Oaks, CA: Sage, 1998).

51. P. S. Goodman, "U.S. Job Losses in December Dim Hopes for Quick Upswing," *The New York Times,* http://www.nytimes.com/2010/01/09/business/economy/09jobs.html?pagewanted=print, February 3, 2010; U.S. Bureau of Labor Statistics, Economic News Release Employment Situations Summary, http://data.bls.gov/cgi-bin/print.pl/news.release/empsit.nr0.htm, February 3, 2010; B. Steverman, "Layoffs: Short-Term Profits, Long-Term Problems," *BusinessWeek,* http://www.businessweek.com/print/investor/content/jan2010/pi20100113_133780.htm, February 3, 2010.

52. J. Aversa, "Americans' Job Satisfaction Falls to Record Low," http://news.yahoo.com/s/ap/20100105/ap_on_bi_ge/us_unhappy_workers/print, February 3, 2010.

53. The Conference Board, Press Release/News, "U.S. Job Satisfaction at Lowest Level in Two Decades," January 5, 2010, http://www.conference-board.org/utilities/pressPrinterFriendly.cfm?press_ID=3820, February 3, 2010.

54. Aversa, "Americans' Job Satisfaction"; Conference Board, Press Release/News, "U.S. Job Satisfaction."

55. Aversa, "Americans' Job Satisfaction"; Conference Board, Press Release/News, "U.S. Job Satisfaction."

56. Aversa, "Americans' Job Satisfaction"; Conference Board, Press Release/News, "U.S. Job Satisfaction."

57. "Subaru of Indiana Automotive Welcomes New President," Press Release, March 26, 2012, Subaru of Indiana Automotive, Inc., (SIA), http://www.subaru-sia.com/news/release/okawaraPR.pdf, April 2, 2012; "Outline of Production Facility," March 1, 2011, Subaru of Indiana Automotive, Inc., (SIA), http://www.subaru-sia.com/company/sia.outline.english.pdf, April 12, 2012.

58. R. Farzad, "The Scrappiest Car Manufacturer in America," *Bloomberg Businessweek,* June 6, 12, 2011, 68–74.

59. Ibid.

60. Ibid.

61. Ibid.

62. Ibid.

63. Farzad, "Scrappiest Car Manufacturer"; "SIA and Wellfit Reward Weight-Loss Winners," Press Release, November 29, 2011, Subaru of Indiana Automotive, Inc., (SIA), http://www.subaru-sia.com/news/release/20111129.pdf, April 1, 2012.

64. Farzad, "Scrappiest Car Manufacturer."

65. Ibid.

66. Ibid.

67. D. W. Organ, *Organizational Citizenship Behavior: The Good Soldier Syndrome* (Lexington, MA: Lexington Books, 1988).

68. J. M. George and A. P. Brief, "Feeling Good—Doing Good: A Conceptual Analysis of the Mood at Work—Organizational Spontaneity Relationship," *Psychological Bulletin* 112 (1992), 310–29.

69. W. H. Mobley, "Intermediate Linkages in the Relationship between Job Satisfaction and Employee Turnover," *Journal of Applied Psychology* 62 (1977), 237–40.

70. C. Hymowitz, "Though Now Routine, Bosses Still Stumble during Layoff Process," *The Wall Street Journal,* June 25, 2007, B1; J. Brockner, "The Effects of Work Layoffs on Survivors: Research, Theory and Practice," in B. M. Staw and L. L. Cummings, eds., *Research in Organizational Behavior,* vol. 10 (Greenwich, CT: JAI Press, 1988), 213–55.

71. Hymowitz, "Though Now Routine."

72. Ibid.

73. Ibid.

74. Goodman, "U.S. Job Losses in December Dim Hopes for Quick Upswing."

75. M. Luo, "For Small Employers, Rounds of Shedding Workers and Tears," *The New York Times,* May 7, 2009, A1, A3.

76. Luo, "Rounds of Shedding Workers and Tears."

77. Ibid.

78. N. Solinger, W. van Olffen, and R. A. Roe, "Beyond the Three-Component Model of Organizational Commitment," *Journal of Applied Psychology* 93 (2008), 70–83.

79. J. E. Mathieu and D. M. Zajac, "A Review and Meta-Analysis of the Antecedents, Correlates, and Consequences of Organizational Commitment," *Psychological Bulletin* 108 (1990), 171–94.

80. D. Watson and A. Tellegen, "Toward a Consensual Structure of Mood," *Psychological Bulletin* 98 (1985), 219–35.

81. Watson and Tellegen, "Toward a Consensual Structure of Mood."

82. J. M. George, "The Role of Personality in Organizational Life: Issues and Evidence," *Journal of Management* 18 (1992), 185–213.

83. H. A. Elfenbein, "Emotion in Organizations: A Review and Theoretical Integration," in J. P. Walsh and A. P. Brief, eds., *The Academy of Management Annals,* vol. 1 (New York: Lawrence Erlbaum Associates, 2008), 315–86.

84. J. P. Forgas, "Affect in Social Judgments and Decisions: A Multi-Process Model," in M. Zanna, ed., *Advances in Experimental and Social Psychology,* vol. 25 (San Diego, CA: Academic Press, 1992), 227–75; J. P. Forgas and J. M. George, "Affective Influences on Judgments and Behavior in Organizations: An Information Processing Perspective," *Organizational Behavior and Human Decision Processes* 86 (2001), 3–34; J. M. George, "Emotions and Leadership: The Role of Emotional Intelligence," *Human Relations* 53 (2000), 1027–55; W. N. Morris, Mood: *The Frame of Mind* (New York: Springer-Verlag, 1989).

85. George, "Emotions and Leadership."

86. J. M. George and K. Bettenhausen, "Understanding Prosocial Behavior, Sales Performance, and Turnover: A Group Level Analysis in a Service Context," *Journal of Applied Psychology* 75 (1990), 698–709.

87. George and Brief, "Feeling Good—Doing Good"; J. M. George and J. Zhou, "Understanding When Bad Moods Foster Creativity and Good Ones Don't: The Role of Context and Clarity of Feelings," paper presented at the Academy of Management Annual Meeting, 2001; A. M. Isen and R. A. Baron, "Positive Affect as a Factor in Organizational Behavior," in B. M. Staw and L. L. Cummings, eds., *Research in Organizational Behavior,* vol. 13 (Greenwich, CT: JAI Press, 1991), 1–53.

88. J. M. George and J. Zhou, "Dual Tuning in a Supportive Context: Joint Contributions of Positive Mood, Negative Mood, and Supervisory Behaviors to Employee Creativity," *Academy of Management Journal* 50 (2007), 605–22; J. M. George, "Creativity in Organizations," in J. P. Walsh and A. P. Brief, eds., *The Academy of Management Annals,* vol. 1 (New York: Lawrence Erlbaum Associates, 2008), 439–77.

89. J. D. Greene, R. B. Sommerville, L. E. Nystrom, J. M. Darley, and J. D. Cohen, "An FMRI Investigation of Emotional Engagement in Moral Judgment," *Science,* September 14, 2001, 2105–08; L. Neergaard, "Brain Scans Show Emotions Key to Resolving Ethical Dilemmas," *Houston Chronicle,* September 14, 2001, 13A.

90. George and Zhou, "Dual Tuning in a Supportive Context."

91. George and Zhou, "Dual Tuning in a Supportive Context;" J. M. George, "Dual Tuning: A Minimum Condition for Understanding Affect in Organizations?" *Organizational Psychology Review,* no. 2 (2011), 147–64.

92. R. C. Sinclair, "Mood, Categorization Breadth, and Performance Appraisal: The Effects of Order of Information Acquisition and Affective State on Halo, Accuracy, Informational Retrieval, and Evaluations," *Organizational Behavior and Human Decision Processes* 42 (1988), 22–46.

93. D. Heath and C. Heath, "Passion Provokes Action," *Fast Company,* February 2011, 28–30; "Our Management Team," Our Management Team—North American Tool Corporation, North American Tool, http://www.natool.com/staff/our-management-team, April 3, 2012.

94. Heath and Heath, "Passion Provokes Action."

95. Ibid.

96. Heath and Heath, "Passion Provokes Action"; "About Us," About Us, http://cedars-sinai.edu/About-Us/, April 3, 2012.

97. Heath and Heath, "Passion Provokes Action."

98. Ibid.

99. Ibid.

100. Ibid.

101. D. Goleman, *Emotional Intelligence* (New York: Bantam Books, 1994); J. D. Mayer and P. Salovey, "The Intelligence of Emotional Intelligence," *Intelligence* 17 (1993), 433–42; J. D. Mayer and P. Salovey, "What Is Emotional Intelligence?" in P. Salovey and D. Sluyter, eds., *Emotional Development and Emotional Intelligence: Implications for Education* (New York: Basic Books, 1997); P. Salovey and J. D. Mayer, "Emotional Intelligence," *Imagination, Cognition, and Personality* 9 (1989–1990), 185–211.

102. S. Epstein, *Constructive Thinking* (Westport, CT: Praeger, 1998).

103. "Leading by Feel," *Inside the Mind of the Leader,* January 2004, 27–37.

104. P. C. Early and R. S. Peterson, "The Elusive Cultural Chameleon: Cultural Intelligence as a New Approach to Intercultural Training for the Global Manager," *Academy of Management Learning and Education* 3, no. 1 (2004), 100–15.

105. George, "Emotions and Leadership"; S. Begley, "The Boss Feels Your Pain," *Newsweek,* October 12, 1998, 74; D. Goleman, *Working with Emotional Intelligence* (New York: Bantam Books, 1998).

106. J. Bercovici, "Remembering Bernie Goldhirsh," www.medialifemagazine.com/news2003/jun03/jun30/4_thurs/news1thursday.html, April 15, 2004.

107. B. Burlingham, "Legacy: The Creative Spirit," *Inc.,* September 2003, 11–12.

108. Burlingham, "Legacy: The Creative Spirit"; "Inc. magazine," www.inc.com/magazine, May 28, 2006.

109. Burlingham, "Legacy: The Creative Spirit"; "Inc. magazine"; www.inc.com, February 5, 2008.

110. "Leading by Feel," *Inside the Mind of the Leader,* January 2004, 27–37.

111. George, "Emotions and Leadership."

112. J. Zhou and J. M. George, "Awakening Employee Creativity: The Role of Leader Emotional Intelligence," *Leadership Quarterly* 14 (2003), 545–68.

113. H. M. Trice and J. M. Beyer, *The Cultures of Work Organizations* (Englewood Cliffs, NJ: Prentice-Hall, 1993).

114. J. B. Sørensen, "The Strength of Corporate Culture and the Reliability of Firm Performance," *Administrative Science Quarterly* 47 (2002), 70–91.

115. "Personality and Organizational Culture," in B. Schneider and D. B. Smith, eds., *Personality and Organizations* (Mahway, NJ: Lawrence Erlbaum, 2004), 347–69; J. E. Slaughter, M. J. Zickar, S. Highhouse, and D. C. Mohr, "Personality Trait Inferences about Organizations: Development of a Measure and Assessment of Construct Validity," *Journal of Applied Psychology* 89, no. 1 (2004), 85–103.

116. T. Kelley, *The Art of Innovation: Lessons in Creativity from IDEO, America's Leading Design Firm* (New York: Random House, 2001).

117. "Personality and Organizational Culture."

118. B. Schneider, "The People Make the Place," *Personnel Psychology* 40 (1987), 437–53.

119. "Personality and Organizational Culture."

120. Ibid.

121. B. Schneider, H. B. Goldstein, and D. B. Smith, "The ASA Framework: An Update," *Personnel Psychology* 48 (1995), 747–73; J. Schaubroeck, D. C. Ganster, and J. R. Jones, "Organizational and Occupational Influences in the Attraction–Selection–Attrition Process," *Journal of Applied Psychology* 83 (1998), 869–91.

122. Kelley, *The Art of Innovation.*

123. www.ideo.com, February 5, 2008.

124. Kelley, *The Art of Innovation.*

125. "Personality and Organizational Culture."

126. Kelley, *The Art of Innovation.*

127. George, "Emotions and Leadership."

128. Kelley, *The Art of Innovation.*

129. Ibid.

130. D. C. Feldman, "The Development and Enforcement of Group Norms," *Academy of Management Review* 9 (1984), 47–53.

131. G. R. Jones, *Organizational Theory, Design, and Change* (Upper Saddle River, NJ: Prentice-Hall, 2003).

132. H. Schein, "The Role of the Founder in Creating Organizational Culture," *Organizational Dynamics* 12 (1983), 13–28.

133. J. M. George, "Personality, Affect, and Behavior in Groups," *Journal of Applied Psychology* 75 (1990), 107–116.

134. J. Van Maanen, "Police Socialization: A Longitudinal Examination of Job Attitudes in an Urban Police Department," *Administrative Science Quarterly* 20 (1975), 207–28.

135. www.intercotwest.com/Disney; M. N. Martinez, "Disney Training Works Magic," *HRMagazine,* May 1992, 53–57.

136. P. L. Berger and T. Luckman, *The Social Construction of Reality* (Garden City, NY: Anchor Books, 1967).

137. H. M. Trice and J. M. Beyer, "Studying Organizational Culture through Rites and Ceremonials," *Academy of Management Review* 9 (1984), 653–69.

138. Kelley, *The Art of Innovation.*

139. H. M. Trice and J. M. Beyer, *The Cultures of Work Organizations* (Englewood Cliffs, NJ: Prentice-Hall, 1993).

140. B. Ortega, "Wal-Mart's Meeting Is a Reason to Party," *The Wall Street Journal,* June 3, 1994, A1.

141. H. M. Trice and J. M. Beyer, "Studying Organizational Culture through Rites and Ceremonies," *Academy of Management Review* 9 (1984), 653-69.

142. Kelley, *The Art of Innovation.*

143. www.ibm.com; IBM Investor Relations—Corporate Governance, Executive Officers, "Executive Officers," http://www.ibm.com/investor/governance/executive-officers.wss, February 5, 2010; "Board of Directors," IBM Annual Report 2011—Board of Directors and Senior Leadership, http://www.ibm.com/annualreport/2011/board-of-directors.html, April 4, 2012.

144. K. E. Weick, *The Social Psychology of Organization* (Reading, MA: Addison Wesley, 1979).

145. B. McLean and P. Elkind, *The Smartest Guys in the Room: The Amazing Rise and Scandalous Fall of Enron* (New York: Penguin Books, 2003); R. Smith and J. R. Emshwiller, *24 Days: How Two Wall Street Journal Reporters Uncovered the Lies That Destroyed Faith in Corporate America* (New York: HarperCollins, 2003); M. Swartz and S. Watkins, *Power Failure: The Inside Story of the Collapse of ENRON* (New York: Doubleday, 2003).

Chapter 4

1. www.apple.com, press release, 2010, 2011.

2. www.apple.com, press release, 2012.

3. Ibid.

4. D. Kravets, "Supreme Court to Hear Case on Medical Pot," www.yahoo.com, June 29, 2004; C. Lane, "A Defeat for Users of Medical Marihuana," www.washingtonpost.com, June 7, 2005.

5. www.yahoo.com,2003;www.mci.com,2004.

6. J. Child, "The International Crisis of Confidence in Corporations," *Academy of Management Executive* 16 (August 2002), 145–48.

7. T. Donaldson, "Editor's Comments: Taking Ethics Seriously—A Mission Now More Possible," *Academy of Management Review* 28 (July 2003), 463–67.

8. R. E. Freeman, *Strategic Management: A Stakeholder Approach* (Marshfield, MA: Pitman, 1984).

9. J. A. Pearce, "The Company Mission as a Strategic Tool," *Sloan Management Review,* Spring 1982, 15–24.

10. C. I. Barnard, *The Functions of the Executive* (Cambridge, MA: Harvard University Press, 1948).

11. Freeman, *Strategic Management.*

12. P. S. Adler, "Corporate Scandals: It's Time for Reflection in Business Schools," *Academy of Management Executive* 16 (August 2002), 148–50.

13. W. G. Sanders and D. C. Hambrick, "Swinging for the Fences: The Effects of CEO Stock Options on Company Risk Taking and Performance," *Academy of Management Journal* 53, no. 5 (2007), 1055–78.

14. www.fda.org, press release, 2009.

15. Ibid.

16. B. J. Blackledge and S. Lindsey, "Peanut Plant Owner Becomes Recluse after Outbreak," ap.com, February 19, 2009.

17. www.wholefoodsmarket.com, 2012.

18. "The Green Machine," *Newsweek,* March 21, 2005, E8–E10.

19. www.wholefoodsmarket.com, 2012.

20. "John Mackey's Blog: 20 Questions with Sunni's Salon," www.wholefoodsmarket.com, 2006.

21. Ibid.

22. T. L. Beauchamp and N. E. Bowie, eds., *Ethical Theory and Business* (Englewood Cliffs, NJ: Prentice-Hall, 1979); A. MacIntyre, *After Virtue* (South Bend, IN: University of Notre Dame Press, 1981).

23. R. E. Goodin, "How to Determine Who Should Get What," *Ethics,* July 1975, 310–21.

24. E. P. Kelly, "A Better Way to Think about Business" (book review), *Academy of Management Executive* 14 (May 2000), 127–29.

25. T. M. Jones, "Ethical Decision Making by Individuals in Organizations: An Issue Contingent Model," *Academy of Management Journal* 16 (1991), 366–95; G. F. Cavanaugh, D. J. Moberg, and M. Velasquez, "The Ethics of Organizational Politics," *Academy of Management Review* 6 (1981), 363–74.

26. L. K. Trevino, "Ethical Decision Making in Organizations: A Person–Situation Interactionist Model," *Academy of Management Review* 11 (1986), 601–17; W. H. Shaw and V. Barry, *Moral Issues in Business,* 6th ed. (Belmont, CA: Wadsworth, 1995).

27. T. M. Jones, "Instrumental Stakeholder Theory: A Synthesis of Ethics and Economics," *Academy of Management Review* 20 (1995), 404–37.

28. B. Victor and J. B. Cullen, "The Organizational Bases of Ethical Work Climates," *Administrative Science Quarterly* 33 (1988), 101–25.

29. D. Collins, "Organizational Harm, Legal Consequences and Stakeholder Retaliation," *Journal of Business Ethics* 8 (1988), 1–13.

30. R. C. Soloman, *Ethics and Excellence* (New York: Oxford University Press, 1992).

31. T. E. Becker, "Integrity in Organizations: Beyond Honesty and Conscientiousness," *Academy of Management Review* 23 (January 1998), 154–62.

32. S. W. Gellerman, "Why Good Managers Make Bad Decisions," in K. R. Andrews, ed., *Ethics in Practice: Managing the Moral Corporation* (Boston: Harvard Business School Press, 1989).

33. J. Dobson, "Corporate Reputation: A Free Market Solution to Unethical Behavior," *Business and Society* 28 (1989), 1–5.

34. M. S. Baucus and J. P. Near, "Can Illegal Corporate Behavior Be Predicted? An Event History Analysis," *Academy of Management Journal* 34 (1991), 9–36.

35. Trevino, "Ethical Decision Making."

36. "GSK, Merck, and Bristol Myers Squibb Are the World's Most Ethical Companies, across All Sectors, Swiss Study," www.medicalnewstoday.com, January 8, 2006.

37. A. S. Waterman, "On the Uses of Psychological Theory and Research in the Process of Ethical Inquiry," *Psychological Bulletin* 103, no. 3 (1988), 283–98.

38. P. Engardio and R. Dexter, "How to Make Factories Play Fair," www.businessweek.com, November 27, 2006.

39. M. S. Frankel, "Professional Codes: Why, How, and with What Impact?" *Ethics* 8 (1989), 109–15.

40. J. Van Maanen and S. R. Barley, "Occupational Communities: Culture and Control in Organizations," in B. Staw and L. Cummings, eds., *Research in Organizational Behavior,* vol. 6 (Greenwich, CT: JAI Press, 1984), 287–365.

41. Jones, "Ethical Decision Making."

42. A. Soke, "Jimmy Carter Helps Build 1000th and 1001st Home," www.typepad.com, May 22, 2007.

43. www.habitat.org, press release, March 2010.

44. E. Gatewood and A. B. Carroll, "The Anatomy of Corporate Social Response," *Business Horizons,* September–October 1981, 9–16.

45. www.yahoo.com, June 7, 2006.

46. M. Friedman, "A Friedman Doctrine: The Social Responsibility of Business Is to Increase Its Profits," *New York Times Magazine,* September 13, 1970, 33.

47. P. Engardio and M. Arndt, "What Price Reputation?" www.businessweek.com, July 9, 2007.

48. M. Conlin, "Where Layoffs Are a Last Resort," www.businessweek.com, October 8, 2001; Southwest Airlines Fact Sheet, www.southwest.com, 2004.

49. G. R. Jones, *Organizational Theory: Text and Cases* (Englewood Cliffs, NJ: Prentice-Hall, 2008).

50. P. E. Murphy, "Creating Ethical Corporate Structure," *Sloan Management Review,* Winter 1989, 81–87.

51. R. Johnson, "Ralston to Buy Beechnut, Gambling It Can Overcome Apple Juice Scandal," *The Wall Street Journal,* September 18, 1989, B11.

Chapter 5

1. P. Dvorak, "Firms Push New Methods to Promote Diversity," *The Wall Street Journal,* December 18, 2006, B3; www.sodexousa.com/, February 7, 2008, About Us, http://www.sodexousa.com/usen/aboutus/aboutus.asp; February 8, 2010; "Catalyst Honors Initiatives at Sodexo and Commonwealth Bank of Australia with the 2012 Catalyst Award," January 24, 2012, http://www.sodexousa.com/usen/newsroom/press/press12/sodexo_catalyst_award.asp, April 5, 2012.

2. Dvorak, "Firms Push New Methods."

3. Ibid.

4. Ibid.

5. Dvorak, "Firms Push New Methods"; "Sodexo Executive Dr. Rohini Anand Honored with Mosaic Woman Leadership Award," November 17, 2011, http://www.sodexousa.com/usen/newsroom/press/press11/rohinianandmosaicaward.asp, April 5, 2012.

6. "Sodexho Named Large Employer of the Year by Pike Area (Alabama) Committee," www.sodexousa.com/press-releases/pr110907_2.asp, February 6, 2008; No. 6 Sodexo—DiversityInc.com, http://www.diversityinc.com/content/1757/article/5454/?No_6_Sodexo, February 9, 2010; Sodexo Tops 2009 HACR List of Most Inclusive Companies for Hispanics, http://www.sodexousa.com/usen/newsroom/press/press10/hacrcorporateinclusion.asp, February 8, 2010.

7. "Corporate Diversity," www.sodexousa.com/press-factsheets/press_fact_corporate.asp, February 6, 2008; "Sodexho Named to Atlanta Tribune's Top Companies for Minorities," www.sodexousa.com/-press-releases/pr111207_1.asp, February 6, 2008; "Sodexho Recognized as Leader in Corporate Social Responsibility by Montgomery County Chamber of Commerce," www.sodexousa.com/press-releases/pr111507.asp, February 6, 2008; "Catalyst Honors Initiatives at Sodexo and Commonwealth Bank of Australia with the 2012 Catalyst Award," January 24, 2012, http://www.sodexousa.com/usen/newsroom/press/press12/sodexo_catalyst_award.asp, April 5, 2012.

8. "Sodexho Chief Diversity Officer Named among Top 20 Diversity Champions,"

www.sodexhousa.com/press-releases/ pr110907_3.asp, February 6, 2008; "Sodexho Receives Texas DiversityFirst Leadership Award," www.sodexousa. com/press-releases/pr110907_1.asp, February 6, 2008; "Gutierrez Honored by the Hispanic Association on Corporate Responsibility," www.sodexousa.com/ press-releases/pr111207_2.asp, February 6, 2008.

9. Principal.com—About the Principal, http://www.principal.com/about/index. htm?print, February 8, 2010.

10. 100 Best Companies to Work For 2008: Principal Financial Group snapshot/ FORTUNE, http://money.cnn.com/ magazines/fortune/bestcompanies/2008/ snapshots/21.html, February 8, 2010; 100 Best Companies to Work For 2009: Principal Financial Group—PFG— from *Fortune,* http://money.cnn.com/ magazines/fortune/bestcompanies/2009/ snapshots/17.html, February 8, 2010; Jessi Hempel, "In the Land of Women," *Fortune,* February 4, 2008, 68–69; Diversity: The Principal Financial Group Earns High Marks in 2010 Corporate Equality . . . , http://www.echelonmagazine.com/index. php?id=1123, February 8, 2010; Human Rights Campaign Foundation, Corporate Equality Index, 2010; HRC/Corporate Equality Index, http://www.hrc.org/issues/ workplace/cei.htm, February 22, 2010.

11. Hempel, "In the Land of Women."

12. Ibid.

13. Principal.com—Careers: Diversity, http:// www.principal.com/careers/workinghere/ diversity.htm?print, February 8, 2010; Principal.com—Careers at The Principal. http://www.principal.com/careers/work-inghere/benefits_main.htm?print, February 8, 2010.

14. Ibid.

15. "The Principal Financial Group is Once Again a Top 50 Company for Executive Women," February 9, 2012, http:// www.principal.com/about/news/2012/ crp-top50-nafe020912.htm?print, April 5, 2012.

16. D. McCracken, "Winning the Talent War for Women," *Harvard Business Review,* November–December 2000, 159–67.

17. W. B. Swann, Jr., J. T. Polzer, D. C. Seyle, and S. J. Ko, "Finding Value in Diversity: Verification of Personal and Social Self-Views in Diverse Groups," *Academy of Management Review* 29, no. 1 (2004), 9–27.

18. "Usual Weekly Earnings Summary," *News: Bureau of Labor Statistics,* April 16, 2004 (www.bls.gov/news.release/whyeng.nr0. htm); "Facts on Affirmative Action in Employment and Contracting," *Americans for a Fair Chance,* January, 28, 2004 (fair-chance.civilrights.org/research_center/

details.cfm?id=18076); "Household Data Annual Averages," www.bls.gov, April 28, 2004.

19. "Prejudice: Still on the Menu," *Business-Week,* April 3, 1995, 42.

20. "She's a Woman, Offer Her Less," *Business-Week,* May 7, 2001, 34.

21. "Glass Ceiling Is a Heavy Barrier for Minorities, Blocking Them from Top Jobs," *The Wall Street Journal,* March 14, 1995, A1.

22. "Catalyst Report Outlines Unique Challenges Faced by African-American Women in Business," *Catalyst news release,* February 18, 2004.

23. C. Gibson, "Nation's Median Age Highest Ever, but 65-and-Over Population's Growth Lags, Census 2000 Shows," *U.S. Census Bureau News,* May 30, 2001 (www. census.gov); "U.S. Census Press Releases: Nation's Population One-Third Minority," *U.S. Census Bureau News,* May 10, 2006 (www.census.gov/Press-Release/www/ releases/archives/population/006808. html); "The World Factbook," *Central Intelligence Agency,* https://www.cia.gov/ library/publications/the-world-factbook/ fields/2177.html, April 5, 2012.

24. "Table 2: United States Population Projections by Age and Sex: 2000–2050," *U.S. Census Board, International Data Base, 94,* April 28, 2004 (www.census.gov/ipc/ www.idbprint.html); "An Older and More Diverse Nation by Midcentury," August 14, 2008, Newsroom: Population, http:// www.census.gov/newsroom/releases/ archives/population/cb08-123.html, April 5, 2012.

25. U.S. Equal Employment Opportunity Commission, "Federal Laws Prohibiting Job Discrimination—Questions and Answers," www.eeoc.gov, June 20, 2001.

26. "Sex by Industry by Class of Worker for the Employed Civilian Population 16 Years and Over," *American FactFinder,* October 15, 2001 (factfinder.census. gov); "2002 Catalyst Census of Women Corporate Officers and Top Earners in the *Fortune* 500," www.catalystwomen. org, August 17, 2004; WB—Statistics & Data, http://www.dol.gov/wb/stats/main. htm?PrinterFriendly=true&, February 9, 2010; "Statistical Overview of Women in the Workplace," *Catalyst,* December 2011, http://www.catalyst.org/publication/219/ statistical-overview-of-women-in-the-workplace, April 4, 2012.

27. "Profile of Selected Economic Characteristics: 2000," *American FactFinder,* October 15, 2001 (factfinder.census.gov); "Usual Weekly Earnings Summary," www.bls.gov/ news.release, August 17, 2004; WB—Statistics & Data, http://www.dol.gov/wb/ stats/main.htm?PrinterFriendly=true&, February 9, 2010; "Usual Weekly Earnings of Wage and Salary Workers Fourth

Quarter 2011," January 24, 2012, *Bureau of Labor Statistics, U.S. Department of Labor (BLS),* http://www.bls.gov/news.release/ pdf/wkyeng.pdf, April 5, 2012.

28. "Women in Management in the United States, 1960–Present," July 2011, *Catalyst,* http://www.catalyst.org/publication/207/ women-in-management-in-the-united-states-1960-p, April 5, 2012.

29. "2000 Catalyst Census of Women Corporate Officers and Top Earners of the *Fortune* 500," www.catalystwomen.org, October 21, 2001; S. Wellington, M. Brumit Kropf, and P. R. Gerkovich, "What's Holding Women Back?" *Harvard Business Review,* June 2003, 18–19; D. Jones, "The Gender Factor," *USA Today.com,* December 30, 2003; "2002 Catalyst Census of Women Corporate Officers and Top Earners in the *Fortune* 500," www.cata-lystwomen.org, August 17, 2004; "2007 Catalyst Census of Women Corporate Officers and Top Earners of the *Fortune* 500," www.catalyst.org/knowledge/titles/ title.php?page=cen_COTE_07, February 8, 2008; "No News Is Bad News: Women's Leadership Still Stalled in Corporate America," December 14, 2011, *Catalyst,* http://www.catalyst.org/press-release/199/ no-news-is-bad-news-womens-leader-ship-still-sta . . . , April 5, 2012.

30. T. Gutner, "Wanted: More Diverse Directors," *BusinessWeek,* April 30, 2001, 134; "2003 Catalyst Census of Women Board Directors," www.catalystwomen.org, August 17, 2004; "2007 Catalyst Census of Women Board Directors of the *Fortune* 500," www.catalyst.org/knowledge/titles/ title.php?page+cen_WBD_07, February 8, 2008; "Statistical Overview of Women in the Workplace," *Catalyst,* December 2011, http://www.catalyst.org/publication/219/ statistical-overview-of-women-in-the-workplace, April 4, 2012.

31. Günter, "Wanted: More Diverse Directors"; "2003 Catalyst Census of Women Board Directors."

32. R. Sharpe, "As Leaders, Women Rule," *BusinessWeek,* November 20, 2000, 75–84.

33. Ibid.

34. "New Catalyst Study Reveals Financial Performance Is Higher for Companies with More Women at the Top," *Catalyst news release,* January 26, 2004.

35. P. Sellers, "Women on Boards (NOT!)," *Fortune,* October 15, 2007, 105.

36. United States Census 2010, U.S. Department of Commerce, U.S. Census Bureau; K. R. Hums, N. A. Jones, and R. R. Ramirez, "Overview of Race and Hispanic Original: 2010," *2010 Census Briefs,* March 2011, *United States Census Bureau,* http:// www.census.gov/prod/cen2010/briefs/ c2010br-02.pdf, April 5, 2012.

37. United States Census 2010.

38. B. Guzman, "The Hispanic Population," U.S. Census Bureau, May 2001; U.S. Census Bureau, "Profiles of General Demographic Characteristics," May 2001; U.S. Census Bureau, "Revisions to the Standards for the Classification of Federal Data on Race and Ethnicity," November 2, 2000, 1–19.

39. L. Chavez, "Just Another Ethnic Group," *The Wall Street Journal,* May 14, 2001, A22.

40. Bureau of Labor Statistics, "Civilian Labor Force 16 and Older by Sex, Age, Race, and Hispanic Origin, 1978, 1988, 1998, and Projected 2008," stats.bls.gov/emp, October 16, 2001.

41. "An Older and More Diverse Nation by Midcentury," August 14, 2008, http://www.census.gov/newsroom/releases/archives/population/cb08-123.html, April 5, 2012; Humes, Jones, and Ramirez, "Overview of Race and Hispanic Original: 2010."

42. Humes, Jones, and Ramirez, "Overview of Race and Hispanic Original: 2010."

43. "U.S. Census Bureau, Profile of General Demographic Characteristics: 2000," *Census 2000,* www.census.gov; "U.S. Census Press Releases: Nation's Population One-Third Minority," *U.S. Census Bureau News,* May 10, 2006 (www.census.gov/Press-Release/www/releases/archives/population/006808.html); Humes,. Jones, and Ramirez, "Overview of Race and Hispanic Original: 2010."

44. "An Older and More Diverse Nation by Midcentury," August 14, 2008, http://www.census.gov/newsroom/releases/archives/population/cb08-123.html, April 5, 2012.

45. "Usual Weekly Earnings of Wage and Salary Workers Fourth Quarter 2011," January 24, 2012, Bureau of Labor Statistics U.S. Department of Labor (BLS), http://www.bls.gov/news.release/pdf/wkyeng.pdf, April 5, 2012.

46. J. Flint, "NBC to Hire More Minorities on TV shows," *The Wall Street Journal,* January 6, 2000, B13.

47. J. Poniewozik, "What's Wrong with This Picture?" *Time,* June 1, 2001 (www.Time.com).

48. Ibid.

49. National Association of Realtors, "Real Estate Industry Adapting to Increasing Cultural Diversity," *PR Newswire,* May 16, 2001.

50. "Toyota Apologizes to African Americans over Controversial Ad," *Kyodo News Service,* Japan, May 23, 2001.

51. J. H. Coplan, "Putting a Little Faith in Diversity," *BusinessWeek Online,* December 21, 2000.

52. Ibid.

53. Ibid.

54. K. Holland, "When Religious Needs Test Company," *The New York Times,* February 25, 2007, BU17.

55. J. N. Cleveland, J. Barnes-Farrell, and J. M. Ratz, "Accommodation in the Workplace," *Human Resource Management Review* 7 (1997), 77–108; A. Colella, "Coworker Distributive Fairness Judgments of the Workplace Accommodations of Employees with Disabilities," *Academy of Management Review* 26 (2001), 100–16.

56. Colella, "Coworker Distributive Fairness"; D. Stamps, "Just How Scary Is the ADA," *Training* 32 (1995), 93–101; M. S. West and R. L. Cardy, "Accommodating Claims of Disability: The Potential Impact of Abuses," *Human Resource Management Review* 7 (1997), 233–46.

57. G. Koretz, "How to Enable the Disabled," *BusinessWeek,* November 6, 2000 (*BusinessWeek* Archives).

58. Colella, "Coworker Distributive Fairness."

59. "Notre Dame Disability Awareness Week 2004 Events," www.nd.edu/~bbuddies/daw.html, April 30, 2004.

60. P. Hewitt, "UH Highlights Abilities, Issues of the Disabled," *Houston Chronicle,* October 22, 2001, 24A.

61. "Notre Dame Disability Awareness"; Hewitt, "UH Highlights Abilities, Issues of the Disabled."

62. J. M. George, "AIDS/AIDS-Related Complex," in L. H. Peters, C. R. Greer, and S. A. Youngblood, eds., *The Blackwell Encyclopedic Dictionary of Human Resource Management* (Oxford, UK: Blackwell, 1997), 6–7.

63. J. M. George, "AIDS Awareness Training," 6.

64. S. Armour, "Firms Juggle Stigma, Needs of More Workers with HIV," *USA Today,* September 7, 2000, B1.

65. Armour, "Firms Juggle Stigma."

66. Armour, "Firms Juggle Stigma"; S. Vaughn, "Career Challenge; Companies' Work Not Over in HIV and AIDS Education," *Los Angeles Times,* July 8, 2001.

67. R. Brownstein, "Honoring Work Is Key to Ending Poverty," *Detroit News,* October 2, 2001, 9; G. Koretz, "How Welfare to Work Worked," *BusinessWeek,* September 24, 2001 (*BusinessWeek* Archives).

68. "As Ex-Welfare Recipients Lose Jobs, Offer Safety Net," *The Atlanta Constitution,* October 10, 2001, A18.

69. C. S. Rugaber, "Job Openings in a Squeeze," *Houston Chronicle,* February 10, 2010, D1.

70. Press Releases, U.S. Census Bureau, "Income, Poverty and Health Insurance Coverage in the United States: 2008," http://www.census.gov/Press-Release/www/releases/archives/income_wealth/014227.html, February 8, 2010; "The 2009 HHS Poverty Guidelines," http://aspe.hhs.gov/poverty/09poverty.shtml, February 8, 2010; "Income, Poverty and Health Insurance Coverage in the United States: 2010," September 13, 2011, http://www.census.gov/newsroom/releases/archives/income_wealth/cb11-157.html, April 5, 2012.

71. U.S. Census Bureau, "Poverty—How the Census Bureau Measures Poverty," *Census 2000,* September 25, 2001.

72. Press Releases, U.S. Census Bureau, "Income, Poverty and Health Insurance Coverage in the United States: 2008," http://www.census.gov/Press-Release/www/releases/archives/income_wealth/014227.html, February 8, 2010; "The 2009 HHS Poverty Guidelines," http://aspe.hhs.gov/poverty/09poverty.html, February 8, 2010; "Income, Poverty and Health Insurance Coverage in the United States: 2010," September 13, 2011, http://www.census.gov/newsroom/releases/archives/income_wealth/cb11-157.html, April 5, 2012.

73. I. Lelchuk, "Families Fear Hard Times Getting Worse/$30,000 in the Bay Area Won't Buy Necessities, Survey Says," *San Francisco Chronicle,* September 26, 2001, A13; S. R. Wheeler, "Activists: Welfare-to-Work Changes Needed," *Denver Post,* October 10, 2001, B6.

74. B. Carton, "Bedtime Stories: In 24-Hour Workplace, Day Care Is Moving to the Night Shift," *The Wall Street Journal,* July 6, 2001, A1, A4.

75. Carton, "Bedtime Stories"; Mission, Core Values, and Philosophy, *Children's Choice Features,* http://childrenschoice.com/AboutUs/MissionCoreValuesand Philosophy/tabid/59/Default.aspx, February 9, 2010.

76. Carton, "Bedtime Stories."

77. Ibid.

78. G. J. Gates, "How many people are lesbian, gay, bisexual, and transgender?" April 2011, *The William Institute,* http://williamsinstitute.law.ucla.edu/wp-content/uploads/Gates-How-Many-People-LGBT-Apr-2011.pdf, April 5, 2012.

79. S. E. Needleman, "More Programs Move to Halt Bias against Gays," *The Wall Street Journal,* November 26, 2007, B3.

80. K. Fahim, "United Parcel Service Agrees to Benefits in Civil Unions," *The New York Times,* July 31, 2007, A19.

81. J. Hempel, "Coming Out in Corporate America," *BusinessWeek,* December 15, 2003, 64–72; "LGBT Equality at the Fortune 500," *Human Rights Campaign,* http://www.hrc.org/resources/entry/lgbt-equality-at-the-fortune-500, April 5, 2012.

82. Hempel, "Coming Out in Corporate America."

83. J. Files, "Study Says Discharges Continue under 'Don't Ask, Don't Tell,'" *The New York Times,* March 24, 2004, A14; J. Files,

"Gay Ex-Officers Say 'Don't Ask' Doesn't Work," *The New York Times,* December 10, 2003, A14.

84. Hempel, "Coming Out in Corporate America"; "DreamWorks Animation SKG Company History," www.dreamworks-animation.com/dwa/opencms/company/history/index.html, May 29, 2006; J. Chng, "Allan Gilmour: Former Vice-Chairman of Ford Speaks on Diversity," www.harbus.org/media/storage/paper343/news/2006/04/18/News/Allan.Gilmour.Former.ViceChairman.Of.Ford.Speaks.On.Diversity-1859600.html?nore write200606021800&sourcedomain=www.harbus.org, April 18, 2006; "Allan D. Gilmour Profile," Forbes.com, http://people.forbes.com/profile/print/allan-d-gilmour/27441, April 11, 2012.

85. Needleman, "More Programs Move to Halt Bias."

86. Hempel, "Coming Out in Corporate America."

87. D. Kopecki, "JPMorgan, Goldman Rank Among Best Workplaces for Gays, Lesbians," December 9, 2011, *Bloomberg Business Week,* http://www.businessweek.com/news/2011-12-09/jpmorgan-goldman-rank-among-best-work. . ., April 5, 2012; "Best Places to Work 2012," http://www.hrc.org/resources/entry/best-places-to-work-2012, April 5, 2012; "Award for Workplace Equality Innovation," *Human Right Campaign,* http://www.hrc.org/resources/entry/award-for-workplace-equality-innovation, April 5, 2012.

88. Needleman, "More Programs Move to Halt Bias."

89. Ibid.

90. "Best Places to Work 2012."

91. "For Women, Weight May Affect Pay," *Houston Chronicle,* March 4, 2004, 12A.

92. V. Valian, *Why So Slow? The Advancement of Women* (Cambridge, MA: MIT Press, 2000).

93. S. T. Fiske and S. E. Taylor, *Social Cognition,* 2d ed. (New York: McGraw-Hill, 1991); Valian, *Why So Slow?*

94. Valian, *Why So Slow?*

95. S. Rynes and B. Rosen, "A Field Survey of Factors Affecting the Adoption and Perceived Success of Diversity Training," *Personnel Psychology* 48 (1995), 247–70; Valian, *Why So Slow?*

96. V. Brown and F. L. Geis, "Turning Lead into Gold: Leadership by Men and Women and the Alchemy of Social Consensus," *Journal of Personality and Social Psychology* 46 (1984), 811–24; Valian, *Why So Slow?*

97. Valian, *Why So Slow?*

98. J. Cole and B. Singer, "A Theory of Limited Differences: Explaining the Productivity Puzzle in Science," in H. Zuckerman, J. R. Cole, and J. T. Bruer, eds., *The Outer Circle: Women in the Scientific Community* (New York: Norton, 1991), 277–310; M. F. Fox, "Sex, Salary, and Achievement: Reward Dualism in Academia," *Sociology of Education* 54 (1981), 71–84; J. S. Long, "The Origins of Sex Differences in Science," *Social Forces* 68 (1990), 1297–1315; R. F. Martell, D. M. Lane, and C. Emrich, "Male–Female Differences: A Computer Simulation," *American Psychologist* 51 (1996), 157–58; Valian, *Why So Slow?*

99. Cole and Singer, "A Theory of Limited Differences"; Fox, "Sex, Salary, and Achievement"; Long, "The Origins of Sex Differences"; Martell, Lane, and Emrich, "Male–Female Differences: A Computer Simulation"; Valian, *Why So Slow?*

100. R. Folger and M. A. Konovsky, "Effects of Procedural and Distributive Justice on Reactions to Pay Raise Decisions," *Academy of Management Journal* 32 (1989), 115–30; J. Greenberg, "Organizational Justice: Yesterday, Today, and Tomorrow," *Journal of Management* 16 (1990), 399–402; O. Janssen, "How Fairness Perceptions Make Innovative Behavior More or Less Stressful," *Journal of Organizational Behavior* 25 (2004), 201–15.

101. Catalyst, "The Glass Ceiling in 2000: Where Are Women Now?" www.catalystwomen.org, October 21, 2001; Bureau of Labor Statistics, 1999, www.bls.gov; Catalyst, "1999 Census of Women Corporate Officers and Top Earners," www.catalystwomen.org; "1999 Census of Women Board Directors of the *Fortune* 1000," www.catalystwomen.org; Catalyst, "Women of Color in Corporate Management: Opportunities and Barriers, 1999," www.catalystwomen.org, October 21, 2001.

102. "Household Data Annual Averages," www.bls.gov, April 28, 2004; U.S. Bureau of Labor Statistics, Economic News Release, Table 7. *Median Usual Weekly Earnings of Full-Time Wage and Salary Workers by Occupation and Sex, Annual Averages,* http://data.bls.gov/cgi-bin/print.pl/news.release/wkyeng.t07.htm, February 9, 2010; "Household Data Annual Averages: 39. Median Weekly Earnings of Full-Time Wage and Salary Workers by Detailed Occupation and Sex," http://www.bls.gov/cps/cpsaat39.pdf, April 11, 2012.

103. "Household Data Annual Averages," www.bls.gov, April 28, 2004; "Household Data Annual Averages: 39."

104. A. M. Jaffe, "At Texaco, the Diversity Skeleton Still Stalks the Halls," *The New York Times,* December 11, 1994, sec. 3, p. 5.

105. Greenberg, "Organizational Justice"; M. G. Ehrhart, "Leadership and Procedural Justice Climate as Antecedents of Unit-Level Organizational Citizenship Behavior," *Personnel Psychology* 57 (2004), 61–94; A. Colella, R. L. Paetzold, and M. A. Belliveau, "Factors Affecting Coworkers' Procedural Justice Inferences of the Workplace Accommodations of Employees with Disabilities," *Personnel Psychology* 57 (2004), 1–23.

106. G. Robinson and K. Dechant, "Building a Case for Business Diversity," *Academy of Management Executive* 3 (1997), 32–47.

107. A. Patterson, "Target 'Micromarkets' Its Way to Success; No 2 Stores Are Alike," *The Wall Street Journal,* May 31, 1995, A1, A9.

108. "The Business Case for Diversity: Experts Tell What Counts, What Works," DiversityInc.com, October 23, 2001.

109. B. Hetzer, "Find a Niche—and Start Scratching," *BusinessWeek,* September 14, 1998 (*BusinessWeek* Archives). B. Hetzer, "Find a Niche—and Start Scratching," *BusinessWeek,* September 14, 1998 (*BusinessWeek* Archives).

110. K. Aaron, "Woman Laments Lack of Diversity on Boards of Major Companies," *The Times Union,* May 16, 2001 (www.timesunion.com).

111. "The Business Case for Diversity."

112. B. Frankel, "Measuring Diversity Is One Sure Way of Convincing CEOs of Its Value," DiversityInc.com, October 5, 2001.

113. A. Stevens, "Lawyers and Clients," *The Wall Street Journal,* June 19, 1995, B7.

114. J. Kahn, "Diversity Trumps the Downturn," *Fortune,* July 9, 2001, 114–16.

115. H. R. Schiffmann, *Sensation and Perception: An Integrated Approach* (New York: Wiley, 1990).

116. McDonald's Corporation, 2008 Annual Report.

117. A. E. Serwer, "McDonald's Conquers the World," *Fortune,* October 17, 1994, 103–16.

118. S. T. Fiske and S. E. Taylor, *Social Cognition* (Reading, MA: Addison-Wesley, 1984).

119. J. S. Bruner, "Going beyond the Information Given," in H. Gruber, G. Terrell, and M. Wertheimer, eds., *Contemporary Approaches to Cognition* (Cambridge, MA: Harvard University Press, 1957); Fiske and Taylor, *Social Cognition.*

120. Fiske and Taylor, *Social Cognition.*

121. Valian, *Why So Slow?*

122. D. Bakan, *The Duality of Human Existence* (Chicago: Rand McNally, 1966); J. T. Spence and R. L. Helmreich, *Masculinity and Femininity: Their Psychological Dimensions, Correlates, and Antecedents* (Austin: University of Texas Press, 1978); J. T. Spence and L. L. Sawin, "Images of Masculinity and Femininity: A Reconceptualization," in V. E. O'Leary, R. K. Unger, and B. B. Wallston, eds., *Women,*

Gender, and Social Psychology (Hillsdale, NJ: Erlbaum, 1985), 35–66; Valian, *Why So Slow?*

123. Valian, *Why So Slow?*

124. Serwer, "McDonald's Conquers the World"; P. R. Sackett, C. M. Hardison, and M. J. Cullen, "On Interpreting Stereotype Threat as Accounting for African American–White Differences on Cognitive Tests," *American Psychologist* 59, no. 1 (January 2004), 7–13; C. M. Steele and J. A. Aronson, "Stereotype Threat Does Not Live by Steele and Aronson," *American Psychologist* 59, no. 1 (January 2004), 47–55; P. R. Sackett, C. M. Hardison, and M. J. Cullen, "On the Value of Correcting Mischaracterizations of Stereotype Threat Research," *American Psychologist* 59, no. 1 (January 2004), 47–49; D. M. Amodio, E. Harmon-Jones, P. G. Devine, J. J. Curtin, S. L. Hartley, and A. E. Covert, "Neural Signals for the Detection of Unintentional Race Bias," *Psychological Science* 15, no. 2 (2004), 88–93.

125. M. Loden and J. B. Rosener, *Workforce America! Managing Employee Diversity as a Vital Resource* (Burr Ridge, IL: Irwin, 1991).

126. M. E. Heilman and T. G. Okimoto, "Motherhood: A Potential Source of Bias in Employment Decisions," *Journal of Applied Psychology* 93, no. 1 (2008), 189–98.

127. L. Roberson, B. M. Galvin, and A. C. Charles, "Chapter 13, When Group Identities Matter: Bias in Performance Appraisal," in J. P. Walsh and A. P. Brief, eds., *The Academy of Management Annals* 1 (New York: Erlbaum, 2008, 617–50).

128. A. Stein Wellner, "The Disability Advantage," *Inc.,* October 2005, 29–31.

129. A. Merrick, "Erasing 'Un' From 'Unemployable,'" *The Wall Street Journal,* August 2, 2007, B6; "2012 Spirit of Social Work Awards Luncheon – Public Citizen of the Year Award / Online. . . , http://www.event.com/events/2012-spirit-of-social-work-awards-luncheon/custom-19-a3be. . . , April 11, 2012.

130. Merrick, "Erasing 'Un' From 'Unemployable.'"

131. Ibid.

132. "Habitat International: Our Products," www.habitatint.com/products.htm, April 6, 2006; "Habitat International, Inc. Home Page," www.habitatint.com, April 6, 2006; "Habitat International, Inc. Home Page," http://www.habitatint.com/, April 11, 2012.

133. Wellner, "The Disability Advantage."

134. "Habitat International: Our People," Habitat International—Our People, http://www.habitatint.com/people.htm, February 10, 2010.

135. Wellner, "The Disability Advantage."

136. "Habitat International: Our People"; Wellner, "The Disability Advantage."

137. Ibid.

138. Ibid.

139. Ibid.

140. E. D. Pulakos and K. N. Wexley, "The Relationship among Perceptual Similarity, Sex, and Performance Ratings in Manager Subordinate Dyads," *Academy of Management Journal* 26 (1983), 129–39.

141. Fiske and Taylor, *Social Cognition.*

142. "Hotel to Pay $8 Million in Settlement," *The Houston Chronicle,* March 22, 2000, 3A; M. France and T. Smart, "The Ugly Talk on the Texaco Tape," *BusinessWeek,* November 18, 1996, 58; J. S. Lublin, "Texaco Case Causes a Stir in Boardrooms," *The Wall Street Journal,* November 22, 1996, B1, B6; T. Smart, "Texaco: Lessons from a Crisis-in-Progress," *BusinessWeek,* December 2, 1996, 44; "Ford Settling Bias Case, Will Hire More Women, Minorities," *The Houston Chronicle,* February 19, 2000, 8C; C. Salter, "A Reformer Who Means Business," *Fast Company,* April 2003, 102–11; A. Zimmerman, "Wal-Mart Appeals Bias-Suit Ruling," *The Wall Street Journal,* August 8, 2005, B5; C. H. Deutsch, "Chief of Unit Files Lawsuit Accusing G.E. of Racial Bias," *The New York Times,* May 18, 2005, C3; "Nike Settles Discrimination Suit for $7.6 Million," *The Wall Street Journal,* July 31, 2007, B9; R. Parloff, "The War over Unconscious Bias," *Fortune,* October 15, 2007, 90–102.

143. N. Alster, "When Gray Heads Roll, Is Age Bias at Work?" *The New York Times,* January 30, 2005, BU3.

144. "Nike Settles Discrimination Suit for $7.6 Million," *The Wall Street Journal,* July 31, 2007, B9.

145. Ibid.

146. Ibid.

147. M. Fackler, "Career Women in Japan Find a Blocked Path," *The New York Times,* August 6, 2007, A6.

148. Fackler, "Career Women in Japan"; www.un.org, February 11, 2008.

149. Fackler, "Career Women in Japan."

150. www.nissanusa.com.

151. Fackler, "Career Women in Japan."

152. Press Releases, U.S. Census Bureau, "Income, Poverty and Health Insurance Coverage in the United States: 2008," http://www.census.gov/Press-Release/www/releases/archives/income_wealth/014227.html, February 8, 2010.

153. Jennifer Levitz, "More Workers Cite Age Bias during Layoffs," *The Wall Street Journal,* March 11, 2009, pp. D1–2; "Age Discrimination in Employment Act (ADEA) Charges," U.S. Equal Employment Opportunity Commission, http://www1.eeoc.gov//eeoc/statistics/enforcement/adea.cfm?renderforprint=1, April 12, 2012.

154. "EEOC Issues Final Rule on 'Reasonable Factors Other than Age' Under the ADEA," http://www1.eeoc.gov//eeoc/newsroom/release/3-29-12.cfm?renderforprint=1, April 12, 2012.

155. Levitz, "More Workers Cite Age Bias."

156. Ibid.

157. Ibid.

158. A. Raghavan, "Terminated: Why the Women of Wall Street Are Disappearing," Forbes.com—Magazine Article, Forbes-Woman, by March 16, 2009, http://forbes.com/forbes/2009/0316-072_terminated_women_print.html, February 10, 2010.

159. Ibid.

160. G. Gross, "Dell Hit with Discrimination Class-Action Lawsuit," *The New York Times,* October 29, 2008, http://www.nytimes.com/external/idg/2008/10/29/29idg-Dell-hit-with-d.html?pagewanted . . . , February 10, 2010.

161. A. Shah, "Dell Settles Discrimination Suit for $9.1 Million," July 24, 2009, *PC World,* http://www.pcworld.com/printable/article/id,169046/printable.html, April 12, 2012; "Dell settles discrimination lawsuit for $9.1M," July 27, 2009, http://www.bizjournals.com/austin/stories/2009/07/27/daily1.html?s=print, April 12, 2012.

162. A. Gonsalves, "Dell Denies Discrimination In Layoffs," *InformationWeek,* November 3, 2008, http://www.informationweek.com/shared/printableArticleSrc.jhtml;jsessionid=5RQQTNK . . . , February 11, 2010.

163. A. G. Greenwald and M. Banaji, "Implicit Social Cognition: Attitudes, Self-Esteem, and Stereotypes," *Psychological Review* 102 (1995), 4–27.

164. A. Fisher, "Ask Annie: Five Ways to Promote Diversity in the Workplace," *Fortune,* April 23, 2004 (www.fortune.com/fortune/subs/print/0,15935,455997,00.html); E. Bonabeau, "Don't Trust Your Gut," *Harvard Business Review,* May 2003, 116–23.

165. A. P. Carnevale and S. C. Stone, "Diversity: Beyond the Golden Rule," *Training & Development,* October 1994, 22–39.

166. Fisher, "Ask Annie."

167. J. S. Lublin, "Top Brass Try Life in the Trenches," *The Wall Street Journal,* June 25, 2007, B1, B3; J.S. Lublin, "How to Be a Better Boss? Spend Time on the Front Lines, Wall Street Journal, February 9, 2012, http://online.wsj.com/article/SB10001424052970203824904577212951446826014.html.

168. www.davita.com, February 11, 2008; Company—About DaVita, http://www.davita.com/about/, February 11, 2010; J.S. Lublin, "How to Be a Better Boss? Spend Time on the Front Lines," February 9,

2012, *WSJ.com,* http://online.wsj.com/article/SB10001424052970203824904577212951446826014.html, April 12, 2012.

169. Lublin, "Top Brass Try Life in the Trenches."

170. Ibid.

171. Ibid.

172. Lublin, "Top Brass Try Life in the Trenches;" www.loews.com/loews.nsf/governance.htm, February 7, 2008; Lowes Hotel—Resorts, http://www.loewshotels.com/en/default.aspx?cm_mmc=Google-_-National-_-Paid%20Sea . . . , February 11, 2010.

173. B. De Lollis, "Lowes Hotels' new CEO advised Virgin Hotels," USAToday.com, January 4, 2012, http://travel.usatoday.com/hotels/post/2012/01/virgin-hotels-director-to-become-ceo-loews. . . , April 12, 2012.

174. Lublin, "Top Brass Try Life in the Trenches."

175. B. A. Battaglia, "Skills for Managing Multicultural Teams," *Cultural Diversity at Work* 4 (1992); Carnevale and Stone, "Diversity: Beyond the Golden Rule."

176. Swann et al., "Finding Value in Diversity."

177. Valian, *Why So Slow?*

178. A. P. Brief, R. T. Buttram, R. M. Reizenstein, S. D. Pugh, J. D. Callahan, R. L. McCline, and J. B. Vaslow, "Beyond Good Intentions: The Next Steps toward Racial Equality in the American Workplace," *Academy of Management Executive,* November 1997, 59–72.

179. Ibid.

180. Ibid.

181. Ibid.

182. Y. Cole, "Linking Diversity to Executive Compensation," *Diversity Inc.,* August–September 2003, 58–62.

183. B. Mandell and S. Kohler-Gray, "Management Development That Values Diversity," *Personnel,* March 1990, 41–47.

184. "Online Extra: UPS Delivers an Eye-Opener," by Bremen Leak, *Business-Week,* October 10, 2005, http://www.businessweek.com/print/magazine/content/05_41/b3954012.htm?chan=gl, February 11, 2010; Community Internship Program—UPS Corporate Responsibility, "Community Internship Program," http://www.community.ups.com/Community/Community+Internship+Program, February 11, 2010.

185. B. Filipczak, "25 Years of Diversity at UPS," *Training,* August 1992, 42–46.

186. D. A. Thomas, "Race Matters: The Truth about Mentoring Minorities," *Harvard Business Review,* April 2001, 99–107.

187. Thomas, "Race Matters."

188. "Chevron Settles Claims of 4 Women at Unit as Part of Sex Bias Suit," *The Wall Street Journal,* January 22, 1995, B12.

189. D. K. Berman, "TWA Settles Harassment Claims at JFK Airport for $2.6 Million," *The Wall Street Journal,* June 25, 2001, B6.

190. A. Lambert, "Insurers Help Clients Take Steps to Reduce Sexual Harassment," *Houston Business Journal,* March 19, 2004 (Houston.bizjournals.com/Houston/stories/2004/03/22/focus4.html).

191. L. M. Holson, "Chief of American Apparel Faces Second Harassment Suit," *New York Times,* March 24, 2011: B2.

192. T. Segal, "Getting Serious about Sexual Harassment," *BusinessWeek,* November 9, 1992, 78–82.

193. J. Green, "The Silencing of Sexual Harassment," *Bloomberg BusinessWeek,* November 21–27, 2011: 27–28.

194. U.S. Equal Employment Opportunity Commission, "Facts about Sexual Harassment," www.eeoc.gov/facts/fs-sex.html, May 1, 2004.

195. B. Carton, "Muscled Out? At Jenny Craig, Men Are Ones Who Claim Sex Discrimination," *The Wall Street Journal,* November 29, 1994, A1, A7.

196. R. L. Paetzold and A. M. O'Leary-Kelly, "Organizational Communication and the Legal Dimensions of Hostile Work Environment Sexual Harassment," in G. L. Kreps, ed., *Sexual Harassment: Communication Implications* (Cresskill, NJ: Hampton Press, 1993).

197. M. Galen, J. Weber, and A. Z. Cuneo, "Sexual Harassment: Out of the Shadows," *Fortune,* October 28, 1991, 30–31.

198. A. M. O'Leary-Kelly, R. L. Paetzold, and R. W. Griffin, "Sexual Harassment as Aggressive Action: A Framework for Understanding Sexual Harassment," paper presented at the annual meeting of the Academy of Management, Vancouver, August 1995.

199. B. S. Roberts and R. A. Mann, "Sexual Harassment in the Workplace: A Primer," www3.uakron.edu/lawrev/robert1.html, May 1, 2004.

200. "Former FedEx Driver Wins EEOC Lawsuit," *Houston Chronicle,* February 26, 2004, 9B.

201. Ibid.

202. J. Robertson, "California Jury Awards $61M for Harassment," http://news.Yahoo.com, June 4, 2006.

203. S. J. Bresler and R. Thacker, "Four-Point Plan Helps Solve Harassment Problems," *HR Magazine,* May 1993, 117–24.

204. "Du Pont's Solution," *Training,* March 1992, 29.

205. Ibid.

206. Ibid.

Chapter 6

1. www.nokia.com, 2011.

2. L. J. Bourgeois, "Strategy and Environment: A Conceptual Integration," *Academy of Management Review* 5 (1985), 25–39.

3. M. E. Porter, *Competitive Strategy* (New York: Free Press, 1980).

4. "Coca-Cola versus Pepsi-Cola and the Soft Drink Industry," Harvard Business School Case 9-391–179.

5. www.splenda.com, 2012.

6. A. K. Gupta and V. Govindarajan, "Cultivating a Global Mind-Set," *Academy of Management Executive* 16 (February 2002), 116–27.

7. "Boeing's Worldwide Supplier Network," *Seattle Post-Intelligencer,* April 9, 1994, 13.

8. I. Metthee, "Playing a Large Part," *Seattle Post-Intelligencer,* April 9, 1994, 13.

9. "Business: Link in the Global Chain," *The Economist,* June 2, 2001, 62–63.

10. www.hbi.com, 2012.

11. M. E. Porter, *Competitive Advantage* (New York: Free Press, 1985).

12. www.walmart.com, 2012.

13. Ibid.

14. T. Levitt, "The Globalization of Markets," *Harvard Business Review,* May–June 1983, 92–102.

15. "Dell CEO Would Like 40 Percent PC Market Share," www.dailynews.yahoo.com, June 20, 2001.

16. For views on barriers to entry from an economics perspective, see Porter, *Competitive Strategy.* For the sociological perspective, see J. Pfeffer and G. R. Salancik, *The External Control of Organization: A Resource Dependence Perspective* (New York: Harper & Row, 1978).

17. Porter, *Competitive Strategy;* J. E. Bain, *Barriers to New Competition* (Cambridge, MA: Harvard University Press, 1956); R. J. Gilbert, "Mobility Barriers and the Value of Incumbency," in R. Schmalensee and R. D. Willig, eds., *Handbook of Industrial Organization,* vol. 1 (Amsterdam: North Holland, 1989).

18. Press release, www.amazon.com, May 2001.

19. C. W. L. Hill, "The Computer Industry: The New Industry of Industries," in Hill and Jones, *Strategic Management: An Integrated Approach* (Boston: Houghton Mifflin, 2010).

20. J. Schumpeter, *Capitalism, Socialism and Democracy* (London: Macmillan, 1950), 68. Also see R. R. Winter and S. G. Winter, *An Evolutionary Theory of Economic Change* (Cambridge, MA: Harvard University Press, 1982).

21. N. Goodman, *An Introduction to Sociology* (New York: HarperCollins, 1991); C. Nakane, *Japanese Society* (Berkeley: University of California Press, 1970).

22. For a detailed discussion of the importance of the structure of law as a factor

explaining economic change and growth, see D. C. North, *Institutions, Institutional Change, and Economic Performance* (Cambridge: Cambridge University Press, 1990).

23. R. B. Reich, *The Work of Nations* (New York: Knopf, 1991).

24. J. Bhagwati, *Protectionism* (Cambridge, MA: MIT Press, 1988).

25. M. A. Carpenter and J. W. Fredrickson, "Top Management Teams, Global Strategic Posture, and the Moderating Role of Uncertainty," *Academy of Management Journal* 44 (June 2001), 533–46.

26. www.ikea.com, 2012.

27. Bhagwati, *Protectionism*.

28. For a summary of these theories, see P. Krugman and M. Obstfeld, *International Economics: Theory and Policy* (New York: HarperCollins, 1991). Also see C. W. L. Hill, *International Business* (New York: McGraw-Hill, 1997), chap. 4.

29. A. M. Rugman, "The Quest for Global Dominance," *Academy of Management Executive* 16 (August 2002), 157–60.

30. www.wto.org.com, 2004.

31. www.wto.org.com, 2012.

32. C. A. Bartlett and S. Ghoshal, *Managing across Borders* (Boston: Harvard Business School Press, 1989).

33. C. Arnst and G. Edmondson, "The Global Free-for-All," *BusinessWeek,* September 26, 1994, 118–26.

34. W. Konrads, "Why Leslie Wexner Shops Overseas," *BusinessWeek,* February 3, 1992, 30.

35. E. B. Tylor, *Primitive Culture* (London: Murray, 1971).

36. For details on the forces that shape culture, see Hill, *International Business,* chap. 2.

37. G. Hofstede, B. Neuijen, D. D. Ohayv, and G. Sanders, "Measuring Organizational Cultures: A Qualitative and Quantitative Study across Twenty Cases," *Administrative Science Quarterly* 35 (1990), 286–316.

38. M. H. Hoppe, "Introduction: Geert Hofstede's Culture's Consequences: International Differences in Work-Related Values," *Academy of Management Executive* 18 (February 2004), 73–75.

39. R. Bellah, *Habits of the Heart: Individualism and Commitment in American Life* (Berkeley: University of California Press, 1985).

40. R. Bellah, *The Tokugawa Religion* (New York: Free Press, 1957).

41. C. Nakane, *Japanese Society* (Berkeley: University of California Press, 1970).

42. Ibid.

43. G. Hofstede, "The Cultural Relativity of Organizational Practices and Theories," *Journal of International Business Studies,* Fall 1983, 75–89.

44. Hofstede et al., "Measuring Organizational Cultures."

45. J. Perlez, "GE Finds Tough Going in Hungary," *The New York Times,* July 25, 1994, C1, C3.

46. www.ge.com, 2004, 2010, 2012.

47. J. P. Fernandez and M. Barr, *The Diversity Advantage* (New York: Lexington Books, 1994).

48. www.ibm.com, 2012.

49. www.sony.com, press release, 2010, 2011.

50. www.sony.com, press release, 2012.

Chapter 7

1. S. Clifford, "Marc Shuman Was Determined to Expand Fast," *Inc.,* March, 2006, 44–50; D. Kocieniewski, "After $12,000, There's Even Room to Park the Car," *The New York Times,* February 20, 2006; "The World's Cleanest Garage," www.garagetek.com, May 30, 2006 (www.garagetek.com/nav.asp); "What Is Garagetek?" www.garagetek.com, May 30, 2006 (www.garagetek.com/content_CNBC.asp); L. Christie, "7 Franchises: Riding the Housing Boom," CNNMoney.com, March 7, 2006 (http://money.cnn.com/2006/03/07/smbusiness/homefranchises/index.htm); "745 Businesses to Start Now!" *Entrepreneur,* January 2005, 88, 192, 193; "Franchise Opportunities Available," http://www.garagetek.com/FranchiseOpportunities/February 16, 2010; GarageTek Inc.: Private Company Information—*BusinessWeek,* http://investing.businessweek.com/research/stocks/private/snapshot.asp?privcapId=126174. . ., February 15, 2010; "Garage Makover," *Inc.,* July 2007, p. 53.

2. "About Us," *Garagetek,* http://www.garagetek.com/AboutUs/, April 17, 2012.

3. Clifford, "Marc Shuman Was Determined to Expand Fast."

4. Ibid.

5. Clifford, "Marc Shuman Was Determined to Expand Fast;" "Franchise Opportunities," *Garage Tek,* www.garagetek.com/FranchiseOpportunities/GarageTek-Opportunities.aspx, February 14, 2008.

6. Clifford, "Marc Shuman Was Determined to Expand Fast."

7. Ibid.

8. "Franchise Opportunities Available," *Garagetek,* http://www.garagetek.com/FranchiseOpportunities/, April 17, 2012.

9. Clifford, "Marc Shuman Was Determined to Expand Fast."

10. GarageTek; GarageTek Investment Levels, http://www.garagetek.com/FranchiseOpportunities/Investments.aspx, April 17, 2012.

11. Ibid.

12. GarageTek; GarageTek Investment Levels; "Available Top 50 Markets," *GarageTek,* http://www.garagetek.com/Franchise Opportunities/Franchise-Available-Markets.aspx, April 17, 2012.

13. GarageTek; GarageTek Investment Levels; "Available Top 51-100 Markets," Garage Tek; GarageTek Franchises Available, http://www.garagetek.com/FranchiseOpportunities/Available-Markets-Express.aspx, April 17, 2012.

14. GarageTek; GarageTek Investment Levels.

15. "About Us..

16. Clifford, "Marc Shuman Was Determined to Expand Fast."

17. G. P. Huber, *Managerial Decision Making* (Glenview, IL: Scott, Foresman, 1993).

18. Clifford, "Marc Shuman Was Determined to Expand Fast."

19. Martin Cooper—History of Cell Phone and Martin Cooper, http://inventors.about.com/cs/inventorsalphabet/a/martin_cooper.htm?p=1, February 16, 2010; "Motorola Demonstrates Portable Telephone to Be Available for Public Use by 1976," April 3, 1973, www.motorola.com, February 17, 2009; "The Cellular Telephone Concept—An Overview," September 10, 1984, www.motorola.com, February 17, 2009;" "iPad," http://www.apple.com/, February 16, 2010.

20. H. A. Simon, *The New Science of Management* (Englewood Cliffs, NJ: Prentice-Hall, 1977).

21. N. A. Hira, "The Making of a UPS Driver," *Fortune,* November 12, 2007, 118–29.

22. Hira, "The Making of a UPS Driver"; J. Lovell, "Left-Hand Turn Elimination," *The New York Times,* December 9, 2007, www.nytimes.com/2007/12/09/magazine/09left-handturn.html?_r=2&oref=slogin&r, February 20, 2008.

23. Hira, "The Making of a UPS Driver."

24. L. Osburn, "Expecting the World on a Silver Platter," *Houston Chronicle,* September 17, 2007, D1, D6.

25. Hira, "The Making of a UPS Driver;" UPS Integrad—UPS Corporate Responsibility, http://www.community.ups.com/Safety/Training+For+Safety/UPS+Integrad, April 18, 2012.

26. Hira, "The Making of a UPS Driver"; Welcome to UPS Careers, https://ups.managehr.com/Home.htm, February 20, 2008; UPS Integrad—UPS Corporate Responsibility.

27. UPS Integrad—UPS Corporate Responsibility.

28. Hira, "The Making of a UPS Driver;" UPS Integrad—UPS Corporate Responsibility.

29. Hira, "The Making of a UPS Driver."

30. Hira, "The Making of a UPS Driver;" UPS Integrad—UPS Corporate Responsibility.

31. Hira, "The Making of a UPS Driver."

32. Ibid.

33. D. Kahneman, "Maps of Bounded Rationality: A Perspective on Intuitive Judgment and Choice," Prize Lecture, December 8, 2002; E. Jaffe, "What Was I Thinking? Kahneman Explains How Intuition Leads Us Astray," *American Psychological Society* 17, no. 5 (May 2004), 23–26; E. Dane and M. Pratt, "Exploring Intuition and Its Role in Managerial Decision Making," *Academy of Management Review* 32 (2007), 33–54.

34. One should be careful not to generalize too much here, however; for as Peter Senge has shown, programmed decisions rely on the implicit assumption that the environment is in a steady state. If environmental conditions change, sticking to a routine decision rule can produce disastrous results. See P. Senge, *The Fifth Discipline: The Art and Practice of the Learning Organization* (New York: Doubleday, 1990).

35. Kahneman, "Maps of Bounded Rationality"; Jaffe, "What Was I Thinking?"

36. Kahneman, "Maps of Bounded Rationality"; Jaffe, "What Was I Thinking?"

37. J. Lehrer, "The Science of Irrationality," *The Wall Street Journal,* October 15, 2011: C18.

38. J. Smutniak, "Freud, Finance and Folly: Human Intuition Is a Bad Guide to Handling Risk," *The Economist* 24 (January 2004), 5–6.

39. Kahneman, "Maps of Bounded Rationality"; Jaffe, "What Was I Thinking?"

40. Kahneman, "Maps of Bounded Rationality"; Jaffe, "What Was I Thinking?"

41. J. Pfeffer, "Curbing the Urge to Merge," *Business 2.0,* July 2003, 58; Smutniak, "Freud, Finance and Folly."

42. Kahneman, "Maps of Bounded Rationality"; Jaffe, "What Was I Thinking?"

43. Pfeffer, "Curbing the Urge to Merge"; Smutniak, "Freud, Finance and Folly."

44. M. Landler, "New Austerity for German Car Industry," *The New York Times,* September 29, 2005, C3; E. Taylor and C. Rauwald, "DaimlerChrysler to Cut 8,500 Jobs at Mercedes," *The Wall Street Journal,* September 29, 2005, A6; G. Edmondson, "On the Hot Seat at Daimler," *Business-Week Online,* February 17, 2006 (www.businessweek.com/autos/content/feb2006/bw20060217_187348.htm?campaign_id=search); Daimler AG News—*The New York Times,* http://topics.nytimes.com/topics/news/business/companies/daimler_ag/index.html., February 19, 2010.

45. "Hiring Freeze and Cost Cuts at Time Inc.," *The New York Times,* August 2005, B13.

46. Pfeffer, "Curbing the Urge to Merge."

47. J. Lehrer, "The Science of Irrationality," *The Wall Street Journal,* October 15, 2011: C18.

48. Pfeffer, "Curbing the Urge to Merge."

49. H. A. Simon, *Administrative Behavior* (New York: Macmillan, 1947), 79.

50. H. A. Simon, *Models of Man* (New York: Wiley, 1957).

51. K. J. Arrow, *Aspects of the Theory of Risk Bearing* (Helsinki: Yrjo Johnssonis Saatio, 1965).

52. Arrow, *Aspects of the Theory of Risk Bearing.*

53. R. L. Daft and R. H. Lengel, "Organizational Information Requirements, Media Richness and Structural Design," *Management Science* 32 (1986), 554–71.

54. R. Cyert and J. March, *Behavioral Theory of the Firm* (Englewood Cliffs, NJ: Prentice-Hall, 1963).

55. J. G. March and H. A. Simon, *Organizations* (New York: Wiley, 1958).

56. H. A. Simon, "Making Management Decisions: The Role of Intuition and Emotion," *Academy of Management Executive* 1 (1987), 57–64.

57. M. H. Bazerman, *Judgment in Managerial Decision Making* (New York: Wiley, 1986). Also see Simon, *Administrative Behavior.*

58. Scott G. McNealy Profile—Forbes.com, http://people.forbes.com/profile/scott-g-mcnealy/75347, February 16, 2010; Sun Oracle, "Overview and Frequently Asked Questions," www.oracle.com, February 16, 2010.

59. "Sun Microsystems—Investor Relations: Officers and Directors," www.sun.com/aboutsun/investor/sun_facts/officers_directors.html, June 1, 2004; "How Sun Delivers Value to Customers," *Sun Microsystems—Investor Relations: Support & Training,* June 1, 2004 (www.sun.com/aboutsun/investor/sun_facts/core_strategies.html); "Sun at a Glance," *Sun Microsystems—Investor Relations: Sun Facts,* June 1, 2004 (www.sun.com/aboutsun/investor/sun_facts/index.html); "Plug in the System, and Everything Just Works," *Sun Microsystems—Investor Relations: Product Portfolio,* June 1, 2004 (www.sun.com/aboutsun/investor/sun_facts/portfolio/html).

60. N. J. Langowitz and S. C. Wheelright, "Sun Microsystems, Inc. (A)," Harvard Business School Case 686–133.

61. R. D. Hof, "How to Kick the Mainframe Habit," *BusinessWeek,* June 26, 1995, 102–104.

62. Bazerman, *Judgment in Managerial Decision Making;* Huber, *Managerial Decision Making;* J. E. Russo and P. J. Schoemaker, *Decision Traps* (New York: Simon & Schuster, 1989).

63. M. D. Cohen, J. G. March, and J. P. Olsen, "A Garbage Can Model of Organizational Choice," *Administrative Science Quarterly* 17 (1972), 1–25.

64. Cohen, March, and Olsen, "A Garbage Can Model."

65. Bazerman, *Judgment in Managerial Decision Making.*

66. Senge, *The Fifth Discipline.*

67. E. de Bono, *Lateral Thinking* (London: Penguin, 1968); Senge, *The Fifth Discipline.*

68. Russo and Schoemaker, *Decision Traps.*

69. Bazerman, *Judgment in Managerial Decision Making.*

70. B. Berger, "NASA: One Year after *Columbia*—Bush's New Vision Changes Agency's Course Midstream," *Space News Business Report,* January 26, 2004 (www.space.com/spacenews/businessmonday_040126.html).

71. J. Glanz and J. Schwartz, "Dogged Engineer's Effort to Assess Shuttle Damage," *The New York Times,* September 26, 2003, A1.

72. M. L. Wald and J. Schwartz, "NASA Chief Promises a Shift in Attitude," *The New York Times,* August 28, 2003, A23.

73. J. Light, "Sustainability Jobs Get Green Light at Large Firms," *The Wall Street Journal,* July 11, 2011: B5.

74. Light, "Sustainability Jobs Get Green"; Scott Wicker—UPS Pressroom, http://www.pressroom.ups.com/Biography/ci.Scott+Wicker.print, April 18, 2012.

75. Scott Wicker—UPS Pressroom.

76. L. J. Fisher, DuPont.com: Meet the Executives, http://www2.dupont.com/Our_Company/en_US/executives/fisher.html, April 18, 2012.

77. "An Interview with Linda Fisher Chief Sustainability Officer, DuPont," February 13, 2012, http://www.globe.net.com/articles/2012/february/9/an-interview-with-linda-fisher-chief-su. . . , April 18, 2012.

78. Coca-Cola–Press Center–Press Kits—Beatriz Perez Named Chief Sustainability Officer, May 19, 2011, http://www.theoca-colacompany.com/dynamic/press_center/2011/05/new-chief-sustainab. . . , April 18, 2012.

79. M. Albanese, "How She Leads: Coca-Cola's Beatriz Perez," October 3, 2011, http://www.greenbiz.com/print/44395, April 18, 2012.

80. Ibid.

81. Russo and Schoemaker, *Decision Traps.*

82. D. Kahneman and A. Tversky, "Judgment under Uncertainty: Heuristics and Biases," *Science* 185 (1974), 1124–31.

83. C. R. Schwenk, "Cognitive Simplification Processes in Strategic Decision Making," *Strategic Management Journal* 5 (1984), 111–28.

84. An interesting example of the illusion of control is Richard Roll's hubris hypothesis of takeovers. See R. Roll, "The Hubris Hypothesis of Corporate Takeovers," *Journal of Business* 59 (1986), 197–216.

85. J. Pfeffer and R. I. Sutton, *Hard Facts, Dangerous Half-Truths, and Total Nonsense: Profiting from Evidence-Based Management* (Boston: Harvard Business School Press, 2006).

86. B. M. Staw, "The Escalation of Commitment to a Course of Action," *Academy of Management Review* 6 (1981), 577–87.

87. Russo and Schoemaker, *Decision Traps*.

88. Ibid.

89. I. L. Janis, *Groupthink: Psychological Studies of Policy Decisions and Disasters,* 2nd ed. (Boston: Houghton Mifflin, 1982).

90. C. R. Schwenk, *The Essence of Strategic Decision Making* (Lexington, MA: Lexington Books, 1988).

91. See R. O. Mason, "A Dialectic Approach to Strategic Planning," *Management Science* 13 (1969) 403–14; R. A. Cosier and J. C. Aplin, "A Critical View of Dialectic Inquiry in Strategic Planning," *Strategic Management Journal* 1 (1980), 343–56; I. I. Mitroff and R. O. Mason, "Structuring III—Structured Policy Issues: Further Explorations in a Methodology for Messy Problems," *Strategic Management Journal* 1 (1980), 331–42.

92. Mason, "A Dialectic Approach to Strategic Planning."

93. D. M. Schweiger and P. A. Finger, "The Comparative Effectiveness of Dialectic Inquiry and Devil's Advocacy," *Strategic Management Journal* 5 (1984), 335–50.

94. Mary C. Gentile, *Differences That Work: Organizational Excellence through Diversity* (Boston: Harvard Business School Press, 1994); F. Rice, "How to Make Diversity Pay," *Fortune,* August 8, 1994, 78–86.

95. B. Hedberg, "How Organizations Learn and Unlearn," in W. H. Starbuck and P. C. Nystrom, eds., *Handbook of Organizational Design,* vol. 1 (New York: Oxford University Press, 1981), 1–27.

96. Senge, *The Fifth Discipline*.

97. Ibid.

98. P. M. Senge, "The Leader's New Work: Building Learning Organizations," *Sloan Management Review,* Fall 1990, 7–23.

99. W. Zellner, K. A. Schmidt, M. Ihlwan, and H. Dawley, "How Well Does Wal-Mart Travel?" *BusinessWeek,* September 3, 2001, 82–84.

100. J. P. Walsh and A. P. Brief (eds.), "Creativity in Organizations," *The Academy of Management Annals,* Vol. 1 (New York: Erlbaum), 439–77.

101. Walsh and Brief, "Creativity in Organizations."

102. C. Saltr, "FAST 50: The World's Most Innovative Companies," *Fast Company,* March 2008, 73–117.

103. R. W. Woodman, J. E. Sawyer, and R. W. Griffin, "Towards a Theory of Organizational Creativity," *Academy of Management Review* 18 (1993), 293–321.

104. T. Evans, "Entrepreneurs Seek to Elicit Workers' Ideas," *The Wall Street Journal,* December 22, 2009, B7; D. Dahl, "Rounding Up Staff Ideas," Inc.com, February 1, 2010, http://www.inc.com/magazine/20100201/rounding-up-staff-ideas_Printer_Friendly.html, February 12, 2010; "About Borrego Solar," http://www.borregosolar.com/solar-energy-company/solar-contractor.php, February 15, 2010.

105. T. J. Bouchard Jr., J. Barsaloux, and G. Drauden, "Brainstorming Procedure, Group Size, and Sex as Determinants of Problem Solving Effectiveness of Individuals and Groups," *Journal of Applied Psychology* 59 (1974), 135–38.

106. M. Diehl and W. Stroebe, "Productivity Loss in Brainstorming Groups: Towards the Solution of a Riddle," *Journal of Personality and Social Psychology* 53 (1987), 497–509.

107. D. H. Gustafson, R. K. Shulka, A. Delbecq, and W. G. Walster, "A Comparative Study of Differences in Subjective Likelihood Estimates Made by Individuals, Interacting Groups, Delphi Groups, and Nominal Groups," *Organizational Behavior and Human Performance* 9 (1973), 280–91.

108. N. Dalkey, *The Delphi Method: An Experimental Study of Group Decision Making* (Santa Monica, CA: Rand Corp., 1989).

109. T. Lonier, "Some Insights and Statistics on Working Solo," www.workingsolo.com.

110. I. N. Katsikis and L. P. Kyrgidou, "The Concept of Sustainable Entrepreneurship: A Conceptual Framework and Empirical Analysis," *Academy of Management Proceedings,* 2007, 1–6, web.ebscohost.com/ehost/delivery?vid=7&hid=102&sid=434afdf5-5ed9-45d4-993b-, January 24, 2008; "What Is a Social Entrepreneur?" http://ashoka.org/social_entrepreneur, February 20, 2008; C. Hsu, "Entrepreneur for Social Change," *U.S.News.com,* October 31, 2005, www.usnews.com/usnews/news/articles/051031/31drayton.htm; D. M. Sullivan, "Stimulating Social Entrepreneurship: Can Support from Cities Make a Difference?" *Academy of Management Perspectives,* February 2007, 78.

111. Katsikis and Kyrgidou, "The Concept of Sustainable Entrepreneurship"; "What Is a Social Entrepreneur?"; Hsu, "Entrepreneur for Social Change"; Sullivan, "Stimulating Social Entrepreneurship."

112. N. Tiku, "Do-Gooder Finance: How a New Crop of Investors is Helping Social Entrepreneurs," *Inc.,* February 2008.

113. "World of Good Inc. Sells Brand and Related Assets to eBay; Wholesale Division Acquired by GreaterGood/Charity USA, February 25, 2010, *World of Good, Inc.,* http://www.worldofgood-inc.com/ April 19, 2012.

114. World of Good, Inc., "Message from World of Good," http://worldofgoodinc.com/about/transition.php, February 17, 2010; "World of Good Inc. Sells Brand and Related Assets to eBay; Wholesale Division Acquired by GreaterGood/Charity USA, February 25, 2010, World of Good, Inc., http://www.worldofgood-inc.com/, April 19, 2012.

115. Tiku, "Do-Gooder Finance"; "About World of Good," *World of Good, Inc.,* www.worldofgoodinc.com/about/, February 20, 2008; "What Is Fair Trade?" *World of Good,* originalgood, www.originalgood.com/FT/, February 20, 2008.

116. Tiku, "Do-Gooder Finance."

117. "World of Good Inc. Sells Brand and Related Assets to eBay; Wholesale Division Acquired; "Our Founding Story," Welcome to WorldofGood.com by eBay, http://worldofgood.ebay.com/ns/OurFoundingStory.html, April 19, 2012; "Our Collaboration," Welcome to WorldofGood.com by eBay, http://worldofgood.ebay.com/ns/OurCollaboration.html, April 19, 2012.

118. Tiku, "Do-Gooder Finance"; Mission Research, "Our Mission Is to Support Your Mission," http://www.missionresearch.com/company.html, February 17, 2010; "GiftWorks Fundraising Software," http://www.missionresearch.com/index.html, April 19, 2012.

119. Tiku, "Do-Gooder Finance."

120. Ibid.

Chapter 8

1. www.groupon.com, 2011.

2. Ibid.

3. www.groupon, press release, 2012.

4. A. Chandler, *Strategy and Structure: Chapters in the History of the American Enterprise* (Cambridge, MA: MIT Press, 1962).

5. Ibid.

6. H. Fayol, *General and Industrial Management* (1884; New York: IEEE Press, 1984).

7. Ibid., 18.

8. F. J. Aguilar, "General Electric: Reg Jones and Jack Welch," in *General Managers in Action* (Oxford: Oxford University Press, 1992).

9. Aguilar, "General Electric."

10. www.ge.com, 2012.

11. C. W. Hofer and D. Schendel, *Strategy Formulation: Analytical Concepts* (St. Paul, MN: West, 1978).

12. A. P. De Geus, "Planning as Learning," *Harvard Business Review,* March–April 1988, 70–74.

13. P. Wack, "Scenarios: Shooting the Rapids," *Harvard Business Review,* November–December 1985, 139–50.

14. R. Phelps, C. Chan, and S. C. Kapsalis, "Does Scenario Planning Affect Firm Performance?" *Journal of Business Research,* March 2001, 223–32.

15. J. A. Pearce, "The Company Mission as a Strategic Tool," *Sloan Management Review,* Spring 1992, 15–24.

16. D. F. Abell, *Defining the Business: The Starting Point of Strategic Planning* (Englewood Cliffs, NJ: Prentice-Hall, 1980).

17. G. Hamel and C. K. Prahalad, "Strategic Intent," *Harvard Business Review,* May–June 1989, 63–73.

18. D. I. Jung and B. J. Avolio, "Opening the Black Box: An Experimental Investigation of the Mediating Effects of Trust and Value Congruence on Transformational and Transactional Leadership," *Journal of Organizational Behavior,* December 2000, 949–64; B. M. Bass and B. J. Avolio, "Transformational and Transactional Leadership: 1992 and Beyond," *Journal of European Industrial Training,* January 1990, 20–35.

19. J. Porras and J. Collins, *Built to Last: Successful Habits of Visionary Companies* (New York: HarperCollins, 1994).

20. E. A. Locke, G. P. Latham, and M. Erez, "The Determinants of Goal Commitment," *Academy of Management Review* 13 (1988), 23–39.

21. www.ge.com, 2012.

22. K. R. Andrews, *The Concept of Corporate Strategy* (Homewood, IL: Irwin, 1971).

23. www.campbellsoup.com, 2001.

24. G. Mulvihill, "Campbell Is Really Cooking," *San Diego Tribune*.com, August 5, 2004.

25. W. D. Crotty, "Campbell Soup Is Not So Hot," www.MotleyFool.com, May 24, 2004.

26. A. Halperin, "Chicken Soup for the Investor's Soul," *BusinessWeek Online, May* 25, 2006 (www.businessweek.com).

27. A. Carter, "Lighting a Fire under Campbell," www.businessweek.com, *December* 4, 2006.

28. www.campbellsoupcompany.com, 2012.

29. "Campbell Completes $850M Godiva Sale," www.yahoo.com, March 18, 2008.

30. R. D. Aveni, *Hypercompetition* (New York: Free Press, 1994).

31. M. E. Porter, *Competitive Strategy* (New York: Free Press, 1980).

32. C. W. L. Hill, "Differentiation versus Low Cost or Differentiation and Low Cost: A Contingency Framework," *Academy of Management Review* 13 (1988), 401–12.

33. For details, see J. P. Womack, D. T. Jones, and D. Roos, *The Machine That Changed the World* (New York: Rawson Associates, 1990).

34. Porter, *Competitive Strategy.*

35. www.cott.com, 2012.

36. www.cocacola.com, 2012; www. pepsico.com, 2012.

37. www.zara.com, 2012.

38. C. Vitzthum, "Just-in-Time-Fashion," *The Wall Street Journal,* May 18, 2001, B1, B4.

39. www.zara.com, 2010.

40. M. K. Perry, "Vertical Integration: Determinants and Effects," in R. Schmalensee and R. D. Willig, *Handbook of Industrial Organization,* vol. 1 (New York: Elsevier Science, 1989).

41. "Matsushita Electric Industrial (MEI) in 1987," Harvard Business School Case 388–144.

42. P. Ghemawat, *Commitment: The Dynamic of Strategy* (New York: Free Press, 1991).

43. www.ibm.com, 2012.

44. E. Penrose, *The Theory of the Growth of the Firm* (Oxford: Oxford University Press, 1959).

45. M. E. Porter, "From Competitive Advantage to Corporate Strategy," *Harvard Business Review* 65 (1987), 43–59.

46. D. J. Teece, "Economies of Scope and the Scope of the Enterprise," *Journal of Economic Behavior and Organization* 3 (1980), 223–47.

47. M. E. Porter, *Competitive Advantage: Creating and Sustaining Superior Performance* (New York: Free Press, 1985).

48. www.3M.com, 2005, 2010, 2012.

49. www.3M.com, 2012.

50. C. Wyant, "Minnesota Companies Make *BusinessWeek*'s 'Most Innovative' List," *Minneapolis/St. Paul Business Journal,* April 18, 2008.

51. www.vfc.com, 2012.

52. Ibid.

53. www.timberland.com, 2012

54. Ibid.

55. For a review of the evidence, see C. W. L. Hill and G. R. Jones, *Strategic Management: An Integrated Approach,* 5th ed. (Boston: Houghton Mifflin, 2011), chap. 10.

56. C. R. Christensen et al., *Business Policy Text and Cases* (Homewood, IL: Irwin, 1987), 778.

57. C. W. L. Hill, "Conglomerate Performance over the Economic Cycle," *Journal of Industrial Economics* 32 (1983), 197–213.

58. V. Ramanujam and P. Varadarajan, "Research on Corporate Diversification: A Synthesis," *Strategic Management Journal* 10 (1989), 523–51. Also see A. Shleifer and R. W. Vishny, "Takeovers in the 1960s and 1980s: Evidence and Implications," in R. P. Rumelt, D. E. Schendel, and D. J. Teece, eds., *Fundamental Issues in Strategy* (Boston: Harvard Business School Press, 1994).

59. J. R. Williams, B. L. Paez, and L. Sanders, "Conglomerates Revisited," *Strategic Management Journal* 9 (1988), 403–14.

60. G. Marcial, "As Tyco Splits into Three," www.businessweek.com, March 12, 2007.

61. www.tyco.com, 2008.

62. C. A. Bartlett and S. Ghoshal, *Managing across Borders* (Boston: Harvard Business School Press, 1989).

63. C. K. Prahalad and Y. L. Doz, *The Multinational Mission* (New York: Free Press, 1987).

64. "Gillette Co.9s New $40 Million Razor Blade Factory in St. Petersburg, Russia," *Boston Globe, June* 7, 2000, C6.

65. D. Sewell, "P&G Replaces Ex-Gillette CEO at Operations," www.yahoo.com, May 24, 2006.

66. www.pg.com, 2005, 2008, 2010.

67. R. E. Caves, *Multinational Enterprise and Economic Analysis* (Cambridge: Cambridge University Press, 1982).

68. B. Kogut, "Joint Ventures: Theoretical and Empirical Perspectives," *Strategic Management Journal* 9 (1988), 319–33.

69. "Venture with Nestlé SA Is Slated for Expansion," *The Wall Street Journal,* April 15, 2001, B2.

70. B. Bahree, "BP Amoco, Italy's ENI Plan $2.5 Billion Gas Plant," *The Wall Street Journal,* March 6, 2001, A16.

71. N. Hood and S. Young, *The Economics of the Multinational Enterprise* (London: Longman, 1979).

72. www.samsung.com, 2010.

73. Ibid.

Chapter 9

1. www.zynga.com, 2011, 2012.

2. Ibid.

3. www.zynga, press release, 2012.

4. See D. Garvin, "What Does Product Quality Really Mean?" *Sloan Management Review* 26 (Fall 1984), 25–44; P. B. Crosby, *Quality Is Free* (New York: Mentor Books, 1980); A. Gabor, *The Man Who Discovered Quality* (New York: Times Books, 1990).

5. D. F. Abell, *Defining the Business: The Starting Point of Strategic Planning* (Englewood Cliffs, NJ: Prentice-Hall, 1980).

6. According to Richard D'Aveni, the process of pushing price–attribute curves to the right is a characteristic of the competitive process. See R. D'Aveni, *Hypercompetition* (New York: Free Press, 1994).

7. www.walmart.com, 2012.

8. www.southwest.com, 2012.

9. B. O'Brian, "Flying on the Cheap," *The Wall Street Journal,* October 26, 1992, A1; B. O'Reilly, "Where Service Flies Right," *Fortune,* August 24, 1992, 116–17;

A. Salukis, "Hurt in Expansion, Airlines Cut Back and May Sell Hubs," *The Wall Street Journal,* April 1, 1993, A1, C8.

10. www.fgx.com, 2012.

11. www.fgx.com, company overview, 2012.

12. www.ciu.com, 2012.

13. www.crm.com, 2012.

14. The view of quality as reliability goes back to the work of Deming and Juran; see Gabor, *The Man Who Discovered Quality.*

15. See Garvin, "What Does Product Quality Really Mean?"; Crosby, *Quality Is Free;* Gabor, *The Man Who Discovered Quality.*

16. www.jdpa.com, 2009, 2012.

17. www.ford.com, 2012.

18. J. Wernau, "Women Leave Their Stamp on Manufacturing," chicagotribune.com, May 30, 2010.

19. www.ford.com, 2012.

20. See J. W. Dean and D. E. Bowen, "Management Theory and Total Quality: Improving Research and Practice through Theory Development," *Academy of Management Review* 19 (1994), 392–418.

21. For general background information, see J. C. Anderson, M. Rungtusanatham, and R. G. Schroeder, "A Theory of Quality Management Underlying the Deming Management Method," *Academy of Management Review* 19 (1994), 472–509; "How to Build Quality," *The Economist,* September 23, 1989, 91–92; Gabor, *The Man Who Discovered Quality;* Crosby, *Quality Is Free.*

22. Bowles, "Is American Management Really Committed to Quality?" *Management Review,* April 1992, 42–46.

23. Gabor, *The Man Who Discovered Quality.*

24. www.starwood.com, 2012.

25. S.E. Ante, "Six Sigma Kick-Starts Starwood," www.businessweek.com, August 30, 2007.

26. Ibid.

27. "The Application of Kaizen to Facilities Layout," *Financial Times,* January 4, 1994, 12. Reprinted by permission of Financial Times Syndication, London.

28. R. Gourlay, "Back to Basics on the Factory Floor," *Financial Times,* January 4, 1994, 12.

29. P. Nemetz and L. Fry, "Flexible Manufacturing Organizations: Implications for Strategy Formulation," *Academy of Management Review* 13 (1988), 627–38; N. Greenwood, *Implementing Flexible Manufacturing Systems* (New York: Halstead Press, 1986).

30. M. Williams, "Back to the Past," *The Wall Street Journal,* October 24, 1994, A1.

31. For an interesting discussion of some other drawbacks of JIT and other "Japanese" manufacturing techniques, see S. M. Young, "A Framework for Successful Adoption and Performance of Japanese Manufacturing Practices in the United States," *Academy of Management Review* 17 (1992), 677–701.

32. G. Stalk and T. M. Hout, *Competing against Time* (New York: Free Press, 1990).

33. T. Stundza, "Massachusetts Switch Maker Switches to Kanban," *Purchasing,* November 16, 2000, 103.

34. B. Dumaine, "The Trouble with Teams," *Fortune,* September 5, 1994, 86–92.

35. See C. W. L. Hill, "Transaction Cost Economizing as a Source of National Competitive Advantage: The Case of Japan," *Organization Science,* 2 (1994); M. Aoki, *Information, Incentives, and Bargaining in the Japanese Economy* (Cambridge: Cambridge University Press, 1989).

36. J. Hoerr, "The Payoff from Teamwork," *BusinessWeek,* July 10, 1989, 56–62.

37. M. Hammer and J. Champy, *Reengineering the Corporation* (New York: HarperBusiness, 1993), 35.

38. Ibid., 46.

39. Ibid.

40. www.google.com, 2012.

41. Ibid.

Chapter 10

1. www.ups.com, 2012.

2. walmart.com, 2012.

3. G. R. Jones, *Organizational Theory, Design, and Change: Text and Cases* (Upper Saddle River: Prentice-Hall, 2011).

4. J. Child, *Organization: A Guide for Managers and Administrators* (New York: Harper & Row, 1977).

5. P. R. Lawrence and J. W. Lorsch, *Organization and Environment* (Boston: Graduate School of Business Administration, Harvard University, 1967).

6. R. Duncan, "What Is the Right Organizational Design?" *Organizational Dynamics,* Winter 1979, 59–80.

7. T. Burns and G. R. Stalker, *The Management of Innovation* (London: Tavistock, 1966).

8. D. Miller, "Strategy Making and Structure: Analysis and Implications for Performance," *Academy of Management Journal* 30 (1987), 7–32.

9. A. D. Chandler, *Strategy and Structure* (Cambridge, MA: MIT Press, 1962).

10. J. Stopford and L. Wells, *Managing the Multinational Enterprise* (London: Longman, 1972).

11. C. Perrow, *Organizational Analysis: A Sociological View* (Belmont, CA: Wadsworth, 1970).

12. F. W. Taylor, *The Principles of Scientific Management* (New York: Harper, 1911).

13. R. W. Griffin, *Task Design: An Integrative Approach* (Glenview, IL: Scott, Foresman, 1982).

14. www.ddir.com, 2012.

15. http://seattletimes.nwsource.com/html/obituaries/2001211576_dicks23m.html

16. Ibid.

17. Ibid.

18. J. R. Hackman and G. R. Oldham, *Work Redesign* (Reading, MA: Addison-Wesley, 1980).

19. J. R. Galbraith and R. K. Kazanjian, *Strategy Implementation: Structure, System, and Process,* 2nd ed. (St. Paul, MN: West, 1986).

20. Lawrence and Lorsch, *Organization and Environment.*

21. Jones, *Organizational Theory.*

22. Lawrence and Lorsch, *Organization and Environment.*

23. R. H. Hall, *Organizations: Structure and Process* (Englewood Cliffs, NJ: Prentice-Hall, 1972); R. Miles, *Macro Organizational Behavior* (Santa Monica, CA: Goodyear, 1980).

24. Chandler, *Strategy and Structure.*

25. G. R. Jones and C. W. L. Hill, "Transaction Cost Analysis of Strategy–Structure Choice," *Strategic Management Journal* 9 (1988), 159–72.

26. www.gsk.com, 2006.

27. www.gsk.com, 2012.

28. www.avon.com, 2012.

29. N. Byrnes, "Avon: More Than Just Cosmetic Changes," www.businessweek.com, March 12, 2007.

30. www.avon.com, 2012.

31. S. M. Davis and P. R. Lawrence, *Matrix* (Reading, MA: Addison-Wesley, 1977); J. R. Galbraith, "Matrix Organization Designs: How to Combine Functional and Project Forms," *Business Horizons* 14 (1971), 29–40.

32. L. R. Burns, "Matrix Management in Hospitals: Testing Theories of Matrix Structure and Development," *Administrative Science Quarterly* 34 (1989), 349–68.

33. C. W. L. Hill, *International Business* (Homewood, IL: Irwin, 2003).

34. Jones, *Organizational Theory.*

35. A. Farnham, "America's Most Admired Company," *Fortune,* February 7, 1994, 50–54.

36. P. Blau, "A Formal Theory of Differentiation in Organizations," *American Sociological Review* 35 (1970), 684–95.

37. S. Grey, "McDonald's CEO Announces Shifts of Top Executives," *The Wall Street Journal,* July 16, 2004, A11.

38. www.mcdonalds.com, 2012.

39. Child, *Organization.*

40. S. McCartney, "Airline Industry's Top-Ranked Woman Keeps Southwest's Small-Fry Spirit Alive," *The Wall Street Journal,* November 30, 1995, B1; www.swamedia.com, 2012.

41. www.plexus.com, 2012.

42. W. M. Bulkeley, "Plexus Strategy: Smaller Runs of More Things," *The Wall Street Journal,* October 8, 2003, B1, B12.

43. P. M. Blau and R. A. Schoenherr, *The Structure of Organizations* (New York: Basic Books, 1971).

44. Jones, *Organizational Theory.*

45. Lawrence and Lorsch, *Organization and Environment,* 50–55.

46. J. R. Galbraith, *Designing Complex Organizations* (Reading, MA: Addison-Wesley, 1977), chap. 1; Galbraith and Kazanjian, *Strategy Implementation,* chap. 7.

47. Lawrence and Lorsch, *Organization and Environment,* 55.

48. S. D. N. Cook and D. Yanow, "Culture and Organizational Learning." *Journal of Management Inquiry* 2 (1993), 373–90.

49. www.ford.com, 2012.

50. D. Kiley, "The New Heat on Ford," www.businessweek.com, June 4, 2007.

51. Ibid.

52. B. Schneider, "The People Make the Place," *Personnel Psychology* 40 (1987), 437–53.

53. J. E. Sheriden, "Organizational Culture and Employee Retention," *Academy of Management Journal* 35 (1992), 657–92.

54. M. Hannan and J. Freeman, "Structural Inertia and Organizational Change," *American Sociological Review* 49 (1984), 149–64.

55. C. A. O'Reilly, J. Chatman, and D. F. Caldwell, "People and Organizational Culture: Assessing Person–Organizational Fit," *Academy of Management Journal* 34 (1991), 487–517.

56. T. L. Beauchamp and N. E. Bowie, eds., *Ethical Theory and Business* (Englewood Cliffs, NJ: Prentice-Hall, 1979); A. MacIntyre, *After Virtue* (Notre Dame, IN: University of Notre Dame Press, 1981).

57. A. Sagie and D. Elizur, "Work Values: A Theoretical Overview and a Model of Their Effects," *Journal of Organizational Behavior* 17 (1996), 503–14.

58. G. R. Jones, "Transaction Costs, Property Rights, and Organizational Culture: An Exchange Perspective," *Administrative Science Quarterly* 28 (1983), 454–67.

59. C. Perrow, *Normal Accidents* (New York: Basic Books, 1984).

60. H. Mintzberg, *The Structuring of Organizational Structures* (Englewood Cliffs, NJ: Prentice-Hall, 1979).

61. G. Kunda, *Engineering Culture* (Philadelphia: Temple University Press, 1992).

62. www.google.com, 2012.

63. K. E. Weick, *The Social Psychology of Organization* (Reading, MA: Addison-Wesley, 1979).

64. Copyright © 2006, Gareth R. Jones.

Chapter 11

1. www.utc, 2012.

2. W. G. Ouchi, "Markets, Bureaucracies, and Clans," *Administrative Science Quarterly* 25 (1980), 129–41.

3. "Toyota Blames Rapid Growth for Quality Problems," www.iht.com, March 13, 2008.

4. Press release, www.toyota.com, March 30, 2010.

5. P. Lorange, M. Morton and S. Ghoshal, *Strategic Control* (St. Paul, MN: West, 1986).

6. H. Koontz and R. W. Bradspies, "Managing through Feedforward Control," *Business Horizons,* June 1972, 25–36.

7. E. E. Lawler III and J. G. Rhode, *Information and Control in Organizations* (Pacific Palisades, CA: Goodyear, 1976).

8. C. W. L. Hill and G. R. Jones, *Strategic Management: An Integrated Approach,* 6th ed. (Boston: Houghton Mifflin, 2011).

9. E. Flamholtz, "Organizational Control Systems as a Management Tool," *California Management Review,* Winter 1979, 50–58.

10. W. G. Ouchi, "The Transmission of Control through Organizational Hierarchy," *Academy of Management Journal* 21 (1978), 173–92.

11. W. G. Ouchi, "The Relationship between Organizational Structure and Organizational Control," *Administrative Science Quarterly* 22 (1977), 95–113.

12. Ouchi, "Markets, Bureaucracies, and Clans."

13. W. H. Newman, *Constructive Control* (Englewood Cliffs, NJ: Prentice-Hall, 1975).

14. J. D. Thompson, *Organizations in Action* (New York: McGraw-Hill, 1967).

15. R. N. Anthony, *The Management Control Function* (Boston: Harvard Business School Press, 1988).

16. eBay.com, 2010, 2012.

17. Ouchi, "Markets, Bureaucracies, and Clans."

18. Hill and Jones, *Strategic Management.*

19. R. Simons, "Strategic Orientation and Top Management Attention to Control Systems," *Strategic Management Journal* 12 (1991), 49–62.

20. G. Schreyogg and H. Steinmann, "Strategic Control: A New Perspective," *Academy of Management Review* 12 (1987), 91–103.

21. B. Woolridge and S. W. Floyd, "The Strategy Process, Middle Management Involvement, and Organizational Performance," *Strategic Management Journal* 11 (1990), 231–41.

22. J. A. Alexander, "Adaptive Changes in Corporate Control Practices," *Academy of Management Journal* 34 (1991), 162–93.

23. Hill and Jones, *Strategic Management.*

24. G. H. B. Ross, "Revolution in Management Control," *Management Accounting* 72 (1992), 23–27.

25. P. F. Drucker, *The Practice of Management* (New York: Harper & Row, 1954).

26. S. J. Carroll and H. L. Tosi, *Management by Objectives: Applications and Research* (New York: Macmillan, 1973).

27. R. Rodgers and J. E. Hunter, "Impact of Management by Objectives on Organizational Productivity," *Journal of Applied Psychology* 76 (1991), 322–26.

28. M. B. Gavin, S. G. Green, and G. T. Fairhurst, "Managerial Control—Strategies for Poor Performance over Time and the Impact on Subordinate Reactions," *Organizational Behavior and Human Decision Processes* 63 (1995), 207–21.

29. www.cypress.com, 2001, 2005, 2012.

30. B. Dumaine, "The Bureaucracy Busters," *Fortune,* June 17, 1991, 46.

31. D. S. Pugh, D. J. Hickson, C. R. Hinings, and C. Turner, "Dimensions of Organizational Structure," *Administrative Science Quarterly* 13 (1968), 65–91.

32. B. Elgin, "Running the Tightest Ships on the Net," *BusinessWeek,* January 29, 2001, 125–26.

33. P. M. Blau, *The Dynamics of Bureaucracy* (Chicago: University of Chicago Press, 1955).

34. J. McGregor, "The World's Most Innovative Companies," www.businessweek.com, May 4, 2007.

35. www.waltdisney.com, 2010, 2012.

36. D. Janoski, "Conohan, Ciavarella Face New Charges," www.thetimestribune.com, September 10, 2009.

37. D. Janoski, "Conohan, Ciavarella Deny New Charges," www.thetimestribune.com, September 15, 2009.

38. Ouchi, "Markets, Bureaucracies, and Clans."

39. Ibid.

40. This section draws heavily on K. Lewin, *Field Theory in Social Science* (New York: Harper & Row, 1951).

41. L. Chung-Ming and R. W. Woodman, "Understanding Organizational Change: A Schematic Perspective," *Academy of Management Journal* 38, no. 2 (1995), 537–55.

42. D. Miller, "Evolution and Revolution: A Quantum View of Structural Change in Organizations," *Journal of Management Studies* 19 (1982), 11–151; D. Miller, "Momentum and Revolution in Organizational Adaptation," *Academy of Management Journal* 2 (1980), 591–614.

43. C. E. Lindblom, "The Science of Muddling Through," *Public Administration Review* 19 (1959), 79–88; P. C. Nystrom and W. H. Starbuck, "To Avoid Organizational

Crises, Unlearn," *Organizational Dynamics* 12 (1984), 53–65.

44. L. Brown, "Research Action: Organizational Feedback, Understanding, and Change," *Journal of Applied Behavioral Research* 8 (1972), 697–711; P. A. Clark, *Action Research and Organizational Change* (New York: Harper & Row, 1972); N. Margulies and A. P. Raia, eds., *Conceptual Foundations of Organizational Development* (New York: McGraw-Hill, 1978).

45. W. L. French and C. H. Bell, *Organizational Development* (Englewood Cliffs, NJ: Prentice-Hall, 1990).

46. www.pfizer.com, 2012.

47. W. L. French, "A Checklist for Organizing and Implementing an OD Effort," in W. L. French, C. H. Bell, and R. A. Zawacki, eds., *Organizational Development and Transformation* (Homewood, IL: Irwin, 1994), 484–95.

Chapter 12

1. "Looking for Ideas in Shared Workspaces. Established Companies Hope Interaction with Others Will Spark Collaboration," *The Wall Street Journal* (http://www.zappos.com/streetwear), March 20, 2012, http://about.zappos.com/press-center/media-coverage/looking-ideas-shared-workspaces-est. . . , April 23, 2012.

2. D. Garnick, "CEO Takes a Walk on the Whimsical Side," *Boston Herald,* Wednesday, May 20, 2009, http://about.zappos.com/press-center/media-coverage/ceo-takes-walk-whimsical-side, February 22, 2010; C. Palmeri, "Zappos Retails Its Culture," *BusinessWeek,* December 30, 2009, http://www.businessweek.com/print/magazine/content/10_02/b4162057120453.htm, February 22, 2010; "On a Scale of 1 to 10, How Weird Are You?" *The New York Times,* January 10, 2010, http://www.nytimes.com/2010/01/10/business/10corner.html?pagewanted=print, February 22, 2010; M. Chafkin, "Get Happy," *Inc.,* May 2009, 66–73; "Keeper of the Flame," *The Economist,* April 18, 2009, 75; M. Rich, "Why Is This Man Smiling," *New York Times,* April 8, 2011.

3. 100 Best Companies to Work For 2010: Zappos.com—AMZN—from FORTUNE, "15. Zappos.com," http://money.cnn.com/magazines/fortune/bestcompanies/2010/snapshots/15.html, February 22, 2010; "Zappos.com, Best Companies to Work For 2012," *Fortune,* http://money.cnn.com/magazines/fortune/best-companies/2012/snapshots/11.html, April 23, 2012.

4. R. Wauters, "Amazon Closes Zappos Deal, Ends Up Paying $1.2 Billion," TechCrunch, November 2, 2009, http://techcrunch.com/2009/11/02/amazon-closes-zappos-deal-ends-up-paying-1-2-billion/, February 22, 2010.

5. J. McGregor, "Zappo's Secret: It's an Open Book," *BusinessWeek,* March 23 & 30, 2009, 62; "About.zappos .com," Tony Hsieh—CEO, http://about.zappos.com/meet-our-monkeys/tony-hsieh-ceo, February 22, 2010; Chafkin, "Get Happy."

6. Chafkin, "Get Happy"; "Keeper of the Flame."

7. "On a Scale of 1 to 10, How Weird Are You?"; Chafkin, "Get Happy."

8. Chafkin, "Get Happy."

9. Chafkin, "Get Happy"; "Keeper of the Flame."

10. In The Beginning—Let There Be Shoes/about.zappos.com, http://about.zappos.com/zappos-story/in-the-beginning-let-there-be-shoes, February 22, 2010; Looking Ahead—Let There Be Anything and Everything/about.zappos.com, http://about.zappos.com/zappos-story/looking-ahead-let-there-be-anything-and-everything, February 22, 2010; J. B. Darin, "Curing Customer Service," *Fortune,* May 20, 2009, http://about.zappos.com/press-center/media-coverage/curing-customer-service, February 22, 2010.

11. "Happy Feet—Inside the Online Shoe Utopia," *The New Yorker,* September 14, 2009, http://about.zappos.com/press-center/media-coverage/happy-feet-inside-online-shoe-utopia, February 22, 2010.

12. "Happy Feet—Inside the Online Shoe Utopia."

13. Chafkin, "Get Happy"; "Keeper of the Flame."

14. "After Zappos hack, some online shopping safety tips to consider, January 17, 2012, http://news.consumerreports.org/electronics/2012/01/after-zappos-hack-some-online-shopp. . . , April 23, 2012; M.C. White, "Zappos Hacked: Expert Says You Need a Better Password," January 18, 2012, http://moneyland.time.com/2012/01/18/zappos-hacked-expert-says-you-need-a-better-pass. . . , April 23, 2012; T. Bradley, "Zappos Hacked: What You Need to Know," *PCWorld,* January 16, 2012, http://www.pcworld.com/printable/article/id,248244/printable.html, April 23, 2012; D. Goldman, "Zappos hacked, 24 million accounts accessed," *CNNMoneyTech,* January 16, 2012, http://money.cnn.com/2012/01/16/technology/zappos_hack/index.htm, April 23, 2012; "Security Email," *Zappos.com,* http://blogs.zappos.com/securityemail, April 23, 2012; "Password Change," *Zappos.com,* http://www.zappos.com/passwordchange, April 23, 2012.

15. "Security Email," *Zappos.com,* http://blogs.zappos.com/securityemail, April 23, 2012.

16. Chafkin, "Get Happy"; "Keeper of the Flame."

17. "Zappos Core Values/about.zappos.com," http://about.zappos.com/our-unique-culture/zappos-core-values, February 22, 2010; "Zappos Family Core Values / about.zappos.com," http://about.zappos.com/our-unique-culture/zappos-core-values, April 23, 2012.

18. "From Upstart to $1 Billion Behemoth, Zappos Marks 10 Years," *Las Vegas Sun,* Tuesday, June 16, 2009, http://about.zappos.com/press-center/media-coverage/upstart-1-billion-behemoth-zappos- . . . , February 22, 2010; Chafkin, "Get Happy"; "Keeper of the Flame."

19. Chafkin, "Keeper of the Flame"; "Get Happy."

20. Chafkin, "Get Happy."

21. 100 Best Companies to Work For 2010: Zappos.com; Chafkin, "Get Happy."

22. Chafkin, "Get Happy"; "Keeper of the Flame"; 100 Best Companies to Work For 2010: Zappos.com; "Zappos.com, Best Companies to Work for 2012," *Fortune,* http://money.cnn.com/magazines/fortune/best-companies/2012/snapshots/11.html, April 23, 2012.

23. J. E. Butler, G. R. Ferris, and N. K. Napier, *Strategy and Human Resource Management* (Cincinnati: Southwestern Publishing, 1991); P. M. Wright and G. C. McMahan, "Theoretical Perspectives for Strategic Human Resource Management," *Journal of Management* 18 (1992), 295–320.

24. L. Clifford, "Why You Can Safely Ignore Six Sigma," *Fortune,* January 22, 2001, 140.

25. J. B. Quinn, P. Anderson, and S. Finkelstein, "Managing Professional Intellect: Making the Most of the Best," *Harvard Business Review,* March–April 1996, 71–80.

26. Quinn et al., "Managing Professional Intellect."

27. C. D. Fisher, L. F. Schoenfeldt, and J. B. Shaw, *Human Resource Management* (Boston: Houghton Mifflin, 1990).

28. Wright and McMahan, "Theoretical Perspectives."

29. L. Baird and I. Meshoulam, "Managing Two Fits for Strategic Human Resource Management," *Academy of Management Review* 14, 116–28; J. Milliman, M. Von Glinow, and M. Nathan, "Organizational Life Cycles and Strategic International Human Resource Management in Multinational Companies: Implications for Congruence Theory," *Academy of Management Review* 16 (1991), 318–39; R. S. Schuler and S. E. Jackson, "Linking Competitive Strategies with Human Resource Management Practices," *Academy of Management Executive* 1 (1987), 207–19; P. M. Wright and S. A. Snell, "Toward an Integrative View of Strategic Human

Resource Management," *Human Resource Management Review* 1 (1991), 203–225.

30. "Who's in Charge Here? No One," *The Observer,* April 27, 2003 (http://observer.guardian.co.uk/business/story/0,6903,944138,00.html); "Ricardo Semler, CEO, Semco SA," cnn.com, June 29, 2004 (http://cnn.worldnews.printthis.clickability.com/pt/cpt&title=cnn.com); D. Kirkpatrick, "The Future of Work: An 'Apprentice' Style Office?" *Fortune,* April 14, 2004 (www.fortune.com/fortune/subs/print/0,15935,611068,00.html); A. Strutt and R. Van Der Beek, "Report from HR2004," www.mce.be/hr2004/reportd2.htm, July 2, 2004; R. Semler, "Seven-Day Weekend Returns Power to Employees," workopolis.com, May 26, 2004 (http://globeandmail.workopolis.com/servlet/content/qprinter/20040526/cabooks26); "SEMCO," http://semco.locaweb.com.br/ingles, May 31, 2006; "Ricardo Semler, Semco SA: What Are You Reading?" cnn.com, May 31, 2006. (www.cnn.com/2004/BUSINESS/06/29/semler.profile/index.html); "About the Semco Group, *SEMCO,* http://www.semco.com.br/en/content.asp?content=1&contentID=610, April 24, 2012.

31. "Group Companies: Semco Capital Goods Division," *SEMCO,* http://www.semco.com.br/en/content.asp?content=7&contentID=611, April 24, 2012; "Group Companies: Pitney Bowes Semco," *SEMCO,* http://www.semco.com.br/en/content.asp?content=7&contentID=612, April 24, 2012.

32. R. Semler, *The Seven-Day Weekend: Changing the Way Work Works* (New York: Penguin, 2003); "SEMCO."

33. Semler, *The Seven-Day Weekend;* "SEMCO"; G. Hamel, *The Future of Management* (Cambridge, MA: Harvard Business Press, 2007).

34. A. Strutt, "Interview with Ricardo Semler," *Management Centre Europe,* April 2004 (www.mce.be/knowledge/392/35).

35. Semler, *The Seven-Day Weekend.*

36. Ibid.

37. R. Semler, "How We Went *Digital* without a *Strategy,*" *Harvard Business Review* 78, no. 5 (September–October 2000), 51–56.

38. Semler, *The Seven-Day Weekend.*

39. Equal Employment Opportunity Commission, "Uniform Guidelines on Employee Selection Procedures," *Federal Register* 43 (1978), 38290–315.

40. R. Stogdill II, R. Mitchell, K. Thurston, and C. Del Valle, "Why AIDS Policy Must Be a Special Policy," *BusinessWeek,* February 1, 1993, 53–54.

41. J. M. George, "AIDS/AIDS-Related Complex," in L. Peters, B. Greer, and S. Youngblood, eds., *The Blackwell Encyclopedic Dictionary of Human Resource Management* (Oxford, England: Blackwell Publishers, 1997).

42. George, "AIDS/AIDS-Related Complex."

43. George, "AIDS/AIDS-Related Complex"; Stogdill et al., "Why AIDS Policy Must Be a Special Policy"; K. Holland, "Out of Retirement and into Uncertainty," *The New York Times,* May 27, 2007, BU17.

44. S. L. Rynes, "Recruitment, Job Choice, and Post-Hire Consequences: A Call for New Research Directions," in M. D. Dunnette and L. M. Hough, eds., *Handbook of Industrial and Organizational Psychology,* vol. 2 (Palo Alto, CA: Consulting Psychologists Press, 1991), 399–444.

45. "Kelly Services—Background," http://www.kellyservices.com/web/global/services/en/pages/background.html, April 24, 2012.

46. R. L. Sullivan, "Lawyers a la Carte," *Forbes,* September 11, 1995, 44.

47. E. Porter, "Send Jobs to India? U.S. Companies Say It's Not Always Best," *The New York Times,* April 28, 2004, A1, A7.

48. D. Wessel, "The Future of Jobs: New Ones Arise; Wage Gap Widens," *The Wall Street Journal,* April 2, 2004, A1, A5; "Relocating the Back Office," *The Economist,* December 13, 2003, 67–69.

49. The Conference Board, "Offshoring Evolving at a Rapid Pace, Report Duke University and The Conference Board," August 3, 2009, http://www.conference-board.org/utilities/pressPrinterFriendly.cfm?press_ID=3709, February 24, 2010; S. Minter, "Offshoring by U.S. Companies Doubles," *Industry Week,* August 19, 2009, http://www.industryweek.com/PrintArticle.aspx?ArticleID=19772&SectionID=3, February 24, 2010; AFP, "Offshoring by U.S. Companies Surges: Survey," August 3, 2009, http://www.google.com/hostednews/afp/article/ALeqM5iDaq1D-2KZU16YfbKrM PdborD7 . . . , February 24, 2010; V. Wadhwa, "The Global Innovation Migration," *BusinessWeek,* November 9, 2009, http://www.businessweek.com/print/technology/content/nov2009/tc2009119_331698.htm, February 24, 2010; T. Heijmen, A. Y. Lewin, S. Manning, N. Perm-Ajchariyawong, and J. W. Russell, "Offshoring Research the C-Suite," 2007–2008 ORN Survey Report, *The Conference Board,* in collaboration with Duke University Offshoring Research Network.

50. The Conference Board, "Offshoring Evolving at a Rapid Pace"; Minter, "Offshoring by U.S. Companies Doubles"; AFP, "Offshoring by U.S. Companies Surges"; V. Wadhwa, "The Global Innovation Migration"; Heijmen et al., "Offshoring Research the C-Suite."

51. V. Wadhwa, "The Global Innovation Migration."

52. The Conference Board, "Offshoring Evolving at a Rapid Pace."

53. The Conference Board, "Offshoring Evolving at a Rapid Pace"; Minter, "Offshoring by U.S. Companies Doubles"; AFP, "Offshoring by U.S. Companies Surges"; Heijmen et al., "Offshoring Research the C-Suite."

54. "Outsourcing: A Passage Out of India," *Bloomberg Businessweek,* March 19–March 25, 2012.

55. "Outsourcing: A Passage Out of India"; "IBM Research—Brazil," http://www.research.ibm.com/brazil/, April 25, 2012.

56. "Outsourcing: A Passage Out of India."

57. Ibid.

58. "Outsourcing: A Passage Out of India"; "Senior Management—Copal Partners," http://www.copalpartners.com/Senior%20Management, April 25, 2012.

59. "Outsourcing: A Passage Out of India."

60. Ibid.

61. Ibid.

62. R. J. Harvey, "Job Analysis," in Dunnette and Hough, *Handbook of Industrial and Organizational Psychology,* 71–163.

63. E. L. Levine, *Everything You Always Wanted to Know about Job Analysis: A Job Analysis Primer* (Tampa, FL: Mariner Publishing, 1983).

64. R. L. Mathis and J. H. Jackson, *Human Resource Management,* 7th ed. (Minneapolis: West, 1994).

65. E. J. McCormick, P. R. Jeannerette, and R. C. Mecham, *Position Analysis Questionnaire* (West Lafayette, IN: Occupational Research Center, Department of Psychological Sciences, Purdue University, 1969).

66. Fisher et al., *Human Resource Management;* Mathis and Jackson, *Human Resource Management;* R. A. Noe, J. R. Hollenbeck, B. Gerhart, and P. M. Wright, *Human Resource Management: Gaining a Competitive Advantage* (Burr Ridge, IL: Irwin, 1994).

67. Fisher et al., *Human Resource Management;* E. J. McCormick, *Job Analysis: Methods and Applications* (New York: American Management Association, 1979); E. J. McCormick and P. R. Jeannerette, "The Position Analysis Questionnaire," in S. Gael, ed., *The Job Analysis Handbook for Business, Industry, and Government* (New York: Wiley, 1988); Noe et al., *Human Resource Management.*

68. Rynes, "Recruitment, Job Choice, and Post-Hire Consequences."

69. R. Sharpe, "The Life of the Party? Can Jeff Taylor Keep the Good Times Rolling at Monster.com?" *BusinessWeek,* June 4, 2001 (*BusinessWeek* Archives); D. H. Freedman, "The Monster Dilemma," *Inc.,* May 2007, 77–78; P. Korkki, "So Easy to Apply, So Hard to Be Noticed," *The New York Times,* July 1, 2007, BU16.

70. Jobline International—Resume Vacancy Posting, Employment Resources, Job Searches, http://www.jobline.net, February 25, 2010.

71. www.jobline.org, Jobline press releases, May 8, 2001, accessed June 20, 2001.

72. J. Spolsky, "There Is a Better Way to Find and Hire the Very Best Employees," *Inc.,* May 2007, 81–82; "About the Company," www.fogcreek.com, March 5, 2008; "Fog Creek Software," www.fogcreek.com, March 5, 2008; Fog Creek Software— About the company, http://fogcreek.com/ About.html, February 25, 2010.

73. Spolsky, "Better Way to Find and Hire"; "Fog Creek Software."

74. Ibid.

75. Ibid.

76. Spolsky, "Better Way to Find and Hire"; "Intern in Software Development," http:// www.fogcreek.com/jobs/summerintern. html, April 25, 2012.

77. Spolsky, "Better Way to Find and Hire."

78. Ibid.

79. Spolsky, "Better Way to Find and Hire"; "About the Company"; "Fog Creek Software."

80. Spolsky, "Better Way to Find and Hire."

81. S. L. Premack and J. P. Wanous, "A Meta-Analysis of Realistic Job Preview Experiments," *Journal of Applied Psychology* 70 (1985), 706–19; J. P. Wanous, "Realistic Job Previews: Can a Procedure to Reduce Turnover also Influence the Relationship between Abilities and Performance?" *Personnel Psychology* 31 (1978), 249–58; J. P. Wanous, *Organizational Entry: Recruitment, Selection, and Socialization of Newcomers* (Reading, MA: Addison-Wesley, 1980).

82. R. M. Guion, "Personnel Assessment, Selection, and Placement," in Dunnette and Hough, *Handbook of Industrial and Organizational Psychology,* 327–97.

83. T. Joyner, "Job Background Checks Surge," *Houston Chronicle,* May 2, 2005, D6.

84. Joyner, "Job Background Checks Surge"; "ADP News Releases: Employer Services: ADP Hiring Index Reveals Background Checks Performed More Than Tripled since 1997," *Automatic Data Processing, Inc.,* June 3, 2006 (www.investquest. com/iq/a/aud/ne/news/adp042505background.htm); "Employee Benefits Administration," *ADP,* http://www.adp. com/, April 25, 2012.

85. "Background Checks and Employment Screening from ADP," http:// www.adp-es.co.uk/employment-screening/?printpreview=1, April 25, 2012.

86. "ADP News Releases."

87. Noe et al., *Human Resource Management;* J. A. Wheeler and J. A. Gier, "Reliability and Validity of the Situational Interview for a Sales Position," *Journal of Applied Psychology* 2 (1987), 484–87.

88. Noe et al., *Human Resource Management.*

89. J. Flint, "Can You Tell Applesauce from Pickles?" *Forbes,* October 9, 1995, 106–8.

90. Ibid.

91. "Wanted: Middle Managers, Audition Required," *The Wall Street Journal,* December 28, 1995, A1.

92. I. L. Goldstein, "Training in Work Organizations," in Dunnette and Hough, *Handbook of Industrial and Organizational Psychology,* 507–619.

93. "Disney Workplaces: Training & Development," *The Walt Disney Company,* 2010 Corporate Citizenship Report, http:// corporate.disney.go.com/citizenship2010/ disneyworkplaces/overview/trainingandde. . . , April 25, 2012.

94. N. Banerjee, "For Mary Kay Sales Reps in Russia, Hottest Shade Is the Color of Money," *The Wall Street Journal,* August 30, 1995, A8.

95. T. D. Allen, L. T. Eby, M. L. Poteet, E. Lentz, and L. Lima, "Career Benefits Associated with Mentoring for Protégés: A Meta-Analysis," *Journal of Applied Psychology* 89, no. 1 (2004), 127–36.

96. P. Garfinkel, "Putting a Formal Stamp on Mentoring," *The New York Times,* January 18, 2004, BU10.

97. Ibid.

98. Allen et al., "Career Benefits Associated with Mentoring"; L. Levin, "Lesson Learned: Know Your Limits. Get Outside Help Sooner Rather Than Later," *BusinessWeek Online,* July 5, 2004 (www. businessweek.com); "Family, Inc.," *BusinessWeek Online,* November 10, 2003 (www.businessweek.com); J. Salamon, "A Year with a Mentor. Now Comes the Test," *The New York Times,* September 30, 2003, B1, B5; E. White, "Making Mentorships Work," *The Wall Street Journal,* October 23, 2007, B11.

99. Garfinkel, "Putting a Formal Stamp on Mentoring."

100. J. A. Byrne, "Virtual B-Schools," *BusinessWeek,* October 23, 1995, 64–68; Michigan Executive Education Locations around the Globe, http://exceed.bus.umich.edu/ InternationalFacilities/default.aspx, February 25, 2010.

101. Fisher et al., *Human Resource Management.*

102. Fisher et al., *Human Resource Management;* G. P. Latham and K. N. Wexley, *Increasing Productivity through Performance Appraisal* (Reading, MA: Addison-Wesley, 1982).

103. T. A. DeCotiis, "An Analysis of the External Validity and Applied Relevance of Three Rating Formats," *Organizational Behavior and Human Performance* 19 (1977), 247–66; Fisher et al., *Human Resource Management.*

104. L. Kwoh, "Rank and Yank," *The Wall Street Journal,* January 31, 2012: B6.

105. Ibid.

106. J. S. Lublin, "It's Shape-Up Time for Performance Reviews," *The Wall Street Journal,* October 3, 1994, B1, B2.

107. J. S. Lublin, "Turning the Tables: Underlings Evaluate Bosses," *The Wall Street Journal,* October 4, 1994, B1, B14; S. Shellenbarger, "Reviews from Peers Instruct—and Sting," *The Wall Street Journal,* October 4, 1994, B1, B4.

108. C. Borman and D. W. Bracken, "360 Degree Appraisals," in C. L. Cooper and C. Argyris, eds., *The Concise Blackwell Encyclopedia of Management* (Oxford, England: Blackwell Publishers, 1998), 17; D. W. Bracken, "Straight Talk about Multi-Rater Feedback," *Training and Development* 48 (1994), 44–51; M. R. Edwards, W. C. Borman, and J. R. Sproul, "Solving the Double Bind in Performance Appraisal: A Saga of Solves, Sloths, and Eagles," *Business Horizons* 85 (1985), 59–68.

109. M. A. Peiperl, "Getting 360 Degree Feedback Right," *Harvard Business Review,* January 2001, 142–47.

110. A. Harrington, "Workers of the World, Rate Your Boss!" *Fortune,* September 18, 2000, 340, 342; www.ImproveNow.com, June 2001.

111. Lublin, "It's Shape-Up Time for Performance Reviews."

112. S. E. Moss and J. I. Sanchez, "Are Your Employees Avoiding You? Managerial Strategies for Closing the Feedback Gap," *Academy of Management Executive* 18, no. 1 (2004), 32–46.

113. J. M. O'Brien, "100 Best Companies to Work For—A Perfect Season," *Fortune,* February 4, 2008, 64–66; "Four Seasons Employees Name Company to *Fortune* '100 Best Companies to Work For' List," www.fourseasons.com/about_us/ press_release_280.html, February 22, 2008; "Four Seasons Hotels and Resort Named to *Fortune* List of the '100 Best Companies to Work For,'" http://press. fourseasons.com/news-releases/four-seasons-hotels-and-resorts-named-to-fortu . . . , February 24, 2010; "Four Seasons Hotels & Resorts – Best Companies to Work For 2012," *Fortune,* http:// money.cnn.com/magazines/fortune/ best-companies/2012/snapshots/85.html, April 23, 2012.

114. "Four Seasons Employees Name Company to *Fortune* '100 Best Companies to Work For' List."

115. O'Brien, "100 Best Companies to Work For—A Perfect Season"; "Four Seasons Hotels & Resorts—Best Companies to Work For 2012," *Fortune,* http://money. cnn.com/magazines/fortune/best-companies/2012/snapshots/85.html, April 23, 2012.

116. Four Seasons Hotels and Resorts—About Us: Corporate Bios, http://www.fourseasons.com/about_us/corporate_bios/, February 24, 2010; "Four Seasons Hotels and Resorts Jobs / Hotel and Resort Career Search Site," http://jobs.fourseasons.com/Pages/Home.aspx, April 26, 2012.

117. O'Brien, "100 Best Companies to Work For—A Perfect Season."

118. O'Brien, "100 Best Companies to Work For—A Perfect Season;" "Creating the Four Seasons Difference," www.businessweek.com/print/innovate/content/jan2008/id20080122_671354.htm, February 22, 2008.

119. O'Brien, "100 Best Companies to Work For—A Perfect Season."; "Creating the Four Seasons Difference."

120. "Creating the Four Seasons Difference"; "Four Seasons Employees Name Company to *Fortune* '100 Best Companies to Work For' List."

121. M. Moskowitz, R. Levering, and C. Tkaczyk, "The List," *Fortune*, February 8, 2010, pp. 75–88.

122. O'Brien, "100 Best Companies to Work For—A Perfect Season."

123. Ibid.

124. O'Brien, "100 Best Companies to Work For—A Perfect Season"; "Creating the Four Seasons Difference"; "Four Seasons Employees Name Company to *Fortune* '100 Best Companies to Work For' List."

125. J. Flynn and F. Nayeri, "Continental Divide over Executive Pay," *Business Week*, July 3, 1995, 40–41.

126. J. A. Byrne, "How High Can CEO Pay Go?" *Business Week*, April 22, 1996, 100–106.

127. A. Borrus, "A Battle Royal against Regal Paychecks," *Business Week*, February 24, 2003, 127; "Too Many Turkeys," *The Economist*, November 26, 2005, 75–76; G. Morgenson, "How to Slow Runaway Executive Pay," *The New York Times*, October 23, 2005, 1, 4; S. Greenhouse, *The Big Squeeze: Tough Times for the American Worker* (New York: Alfred A. Knopf, 2008); "Trends in CEO Pay," *AFL-CIO*, http://www.aflcio.org/Corporate-Watch/CEO-Pay-and-the-99/Trends-in-CEO-Pay, April 26, 2012.

128. "Executive Pay," *Business Week*, April 19, 2004, 106–110.

129. "Home Depot Chief's Pay in 2007 Could Reach $8.9m," *The New York Times*, Bloomberg News, January 25, 2007, C7; E. Carr, "The Stockpot," *The Economist, A Special Report on Executive Pay*, January 20, 2007, 6–10; E. Porter, "More Than Ever, It Pays to Be the Top Executive," *The New York Times*, May 25, 2007, A1, C7.

130. K. Garber, "What Is (and Isn't) in the Healthcare Bill," *U.S. News & World Report*, March 22, 2010, http://www. usnews.com/articles/news/politics/2010/02/22/what-is-and-isnt-in-the-healthca . . . , March 29, 2010; S. Condon, "Health Care Bill Signed by Obama," Political Hotsheet-CBS News, http://www.cbsnews.com/8301-503544_162-20000981-503544.html, March 29, 2010; T. S. Bernard, "For Consumers, Clarity on Health Care Changes," *The New York Times*, March 21, 2010, http://www.nytimes.com/2010/03/22/your-money/health-insurance/22consumer.html?sq=h . . . , March 29, 2010; CBSNews.com, "Health Care Reform Bill Summary: A Look At What's in the Bill," March 23, 2009, http://www.cbsnews.com/8301-503544_162-20000846-503544.html, March 29, 2010; Reuters, "Factbox: Details of final healthcare bill", March 21, 2010, http://www.reuters.com/article/idUSTRE62K11V20100321, March 29, 2010.

131. E. Tahmincioglu, "Paths to Better Health (On the Boss's Nickel)," *The New York Times*, May 23, 2004, BU7.

132. Ibid.

133. K. K. Spors, "Top Small Workplaces 2007," *The Wall Street Journal*, October 1, 2007, R1–R6; K. K. Spors, "Guerra DeBerry Coody," *The Wall Street Journal*, October 1, 2007, R5; "Guerra DeBerry Coody Named One of the Nation's 15 Top Small Workplaces of 2007," *Business Wire*, http://findarticles.com/p/articles/mi_m0EIN/is_2007_Oct_1/ai_n20527510/print, March 6, 2008; "Guerra DeBerry Coody," www.gdc-co.com/, March 6, 2008; "Frank Guerra '83, Trish DeBerry-Mejia '87, and Tess Coody '93," *Trinity University, Alumni—Profiles*, www.trinity.edu/alumni/profiles/0503_guerra_deberry_coody.htm, March 6, 2008.

134. "Founder—Guerra DeBerry Coody," http://www.gdc-co.com/people/partners, April 26, 2012.

135. Spors, "Top Small Workplaces 2007"; Spors, "Guerra DeBerry Coody"; "Guerra DeBerry Coody Named One of the Nation's 15 Top Small Workplaces of 2007"; "Culture – Guerra DeBerry Coody," http://www.gdc-co.com/about-gdc/culture, April 26, 2012.

136. Spors, "Top Small Workplaces 2007"; Spors, "Guerra DeBerry Coody"; Guerra DeBerry Coody: Day Care, http://www.gdc-co.com/, February 25, 2010.

137. Spors, "Top Small Workplaces 2007"; Spors, "Guerra DeBerry Coody."

138. Spors, "Top Small Workplaces 2007"; Spors, "Guerra DeBerry Coody."

139. "Guerra DeBerry Coody Named One of the Nation's 15 Top Small Workplaces of 2007."

140. S. Shellenbarger, "Amid Gay Marriage Debate, Companies Offer More Benefits to Same-Sex Couples," *The Wall Street Journal*, March 18, 2004, D1.

141. S. Premack and J. E. Hunter, "Individual Unionization Decisions," *Psychological Bulletin* 103 (1988), 223–34.

142. M. B. Regan, "Shattering the AFL-CIO's Glass Ceiling," *Business Week*, November 13, 1995, 46; S. Greenhouse, "The Hard Work of Reviving Labor," *The New York Times*, September 16, 2009, pp. B1, B7.

143. S. Greenhouse, "Survey Finds Deep Shift in the Makeup of Unions," *The New York Times*, November 11, 2009, p. B5; "Union Members—2011," Union Members Summary, January 27, 2012, http://www.bls.gov/news.release/union2.nr0.htm, April 26, 2012.

144. www.aflcio.org, June 2001; About Us, AFL-CIO, http://www.aflcio.org/aboutus/, February 25, 2010; S. Greenhouse, "Most U.S. Union Members Are Working for the Government, New Data Shows," *The New York Times*, January 23, 2010, http://www.nytimes.com/2010/01/23/business/23labor.html?pagewanted=print, February 25, 2010; "About the AFL-CIO," http://www.aflcio.org/About, April 27, 2012.

145. Greenhouse, "Most U.S. Union Members Are Working for the Government"; "Union Members—2011," Union Members Summary, January 27, 2012, http://www.bls.gov/news.release/union2.nr0.htm, April 26, 2012.

146. Greenhouse, "Survey Finds Deep Shift in the Makeup of Unions"; "Union Members – 2011," Union Members Summary, January 27, 2012, http://www.bls.gov/news.release/union2.nr0.htm, April 26, 2012.

147. Greenhouse, "Most U.S. Union Members Are Working for the Government."

148. G. P. Zachary, "Some Unions Step Up Organizing Campaigns and Get New Members," *The Wall Street Journal*, September 1, 1995, A1, A2.

149. Regan, "Shattering the AFL-CIO's Glass Ceiling"; www.aflcio.org, June 2001; R. S. Dunham, "Big Labor: So Out It's Off the Radar Screen," *Business Week*, March 26, 2001 (*Business Week* Archives); "Chavez-Thompson to Retire as Executive Vice President," *AFL-CIO Weblog*, http://blog.aflcio.org/2007/09/13/chavez-thompson-to-retire-as-executive-vice-president/print/, March 6, 2008.

150. "Secretary of Labor Elaine L. Chao," *U.S. Department of Labor—Office of the Secretary of Labor Elaine L. Chao (OSEC)*, www.dol.gov/_sec/welcome.htm, March 6, 2008; S. Greenhouse, "Departing Secretary of Labor Fends Off Critics," *The New York Times*, January 10, 2009, http://www.nytimes.com/2009/01/10/washington/10chao.html?_r=1&pagewanted=print, February

25, 2010; "Biography," http://www.elainechao.com/index.php/biography/Print.html, April 27, 2012.

151. "The Honorable Elaine L. Chao, United States Secretary of Labor," www.dol.gov/dol/sec/public/aboutsec/chao.htm, June 25, 2001.

152. Greenhouse, "Survey Finds Deep Shift in the Makeup of Unions"; "Union Members—2011," News Release, *Bureau of Labor Statistics (BLS),* U.S. Department of Labor, January 27, 2012, www.bls.gov/news.release/pdf/union2.pdf, April 27, 2012.

Chapter 13

1. C. J. Loomis, "The Big Surprise Is Enterprise," *Fortune,* July 14, 2006, http://cnnmoney.printthis.clickability.com/pt/cpt?action=cpt&title=Fortune%3A+The+big . . . , March 31, 2008.

2. "Overview," *Enterprise Rent-A-Car Careers—Overview,* http://www.erac.com/recruit/about_enterprise.asp?navID=overview, March 27, 2008; "Enterprise Rent-A-Car Looks to Hire Student-Athletes, Partners with Career Athletes," April 25, 2012, http://www.enterpriseholdings.com/press-room/enterprise-rent-a-car-looks-to-hire-student- . . . , April 30, 2012.

3. A. Fisher, "Who's Hiring New College Grads Now," *CNNMoney.com,* http://cnnmoney.printthis.clickability.com/pt/cpt?action=cpt&title=Who%27s+hiring+coll . . . , March 31, 2008; Francesca Di Meglio, "A Transcript for Soft Skills, Wisconsin Is Considering a Dual Transcript—One for Grades and One to Assess Critical Areas Such As Leadership and Communication," http://www.businessweek.com/print/bschools/content/feb2008/bs20080221_706663.htm, March 28, 2008; "Enterprise Rent-A-Car Career Site," http://www.erac.com/opportunities/default.aspx, May 1, 2012.

4. "Enterprise Ranked in Top 10 of Business Week's 'Customer Service Champs,'" Thursday, February 22, 2007, *Enterprise Rent-A-Car Careers*—Enterprise in the News, http://www.erac.com/recruit/news_detail.asp?navID=frontpage&RID=211, March 27, 2008; L. Gerdes, "The Best Places to Launch a Career, *Business Week,* September 24, 2007, 49–60; P. Lehman, "A Clear Road to the Top," *Business Week,* September 18, 2006, 72–82.

5. Loomis, "The Big Surprise Is Enterprise"; "About Us," *Enterprise,* http://www.erac.com/pdf/ERAC_Fact_Sheet_2011_20110407120634.pdf, May 1, 2012; "Executive Bios," *Enterprise Holdings,* Press Room, http://www.enterpriseholdings.com/press-room/executive-bios/jo-ann-taylor-kindle, May 1, 2012.

6. "Enterprise Rent-A-Car's Pam Nicholson Named to FORTUNE's 50 Most Powerful Women in Business 2007," Monday, October 1, 2007, http://www.erac.com/recruit/news_details.asp?navID=frontpage&RID=234, March 27, 2008.

7. "Enterprise Ranked in Top 10"; L. Gerdes, "The Best Places to Launch a Career."

8. "It's Running a Business . . . Not Doing a Job," *Enterprise Rent-A-Car Careers—Opportunities,* http://www.erac.com/recruit/opportunities.asp, March 27, 2008.

9. Loomis, "The Big Surprise Is Enterprise"; Lehman, "A Clear Road to the Top."

10. Loomis, "The Big Surprise Is Enterprise"; Lehman, "A Clear Road to the Top."

11. Lehman, "A Clear Road to the Top."

12. Loomis, "The Big Surprise Is Enterprise."

13. Loomis, "The Big Surprise Is Enterprise"; Lehman, "A Clear Road to the Top."

14. "Enterprise Ranked in Top 10"; Gerdes, "The Best Places to Launch a Career."

15. Loomis, "The Big Surprise Is Enterprise." "Overview," Enterprise *Rent-A-Car Careers—Overview.*

16. Loomis, "The Big Surprise Is Enterprise." "Overview," Enterprise *Rent-A-Car Careers—Overview.*

17. J. A. Taylor Kindle, "Enterprise: Why We Give Where We Give," http://www.businessweek.com/print/investor/content/jun2007/pi20070628_339711.htm, March 28, 2008.

18. "Arbor Day Foundation, U.S. Forest Service to Plant 1 Million Trees with Gift from Enterprise Rent-A-Car Foundation," April 26, 2012, http://www.enterpriseholdings.com/press-room/arbor-day-foundation-us-forest-service-to- . . . , April 30, 2012.

19. Kindle, "Enterprise: Why We Give Where We Give."

20. "100,000 Jobs Mission Hires 12, 179 Veterans through First Quarter 2012," *Enterprise Holdings,* April 11, 2012, http://www.enterpriseholdings.com/press-room/100000-jobs-mission-hires-12179-veterans . . . , April 30, 2012.

21. M. Gunther, "Renting 'Green'? Not So Easy," Enterprise *CNNMoney*.com, "Enterprise-Rent-A-Car Goes Green, with Limits," January 17, 2008, http://cnnmoney.printthis.clickability.com/pt/cpt?action=cpt&title=Enterprise-Rent-A-Car . . . , March 3, 2008; "Enterprise Rent-A-Car Announces Most Comprehensive Environmental Platform in Its Industry," Wednesday, June 06, 2007, *Enterprise Rent-A-Car Careers—Enterprise in the News,* http://www.erac.com/recruit/news_detail.asp?navID=frontpage&RID=221, March 27, 2008; "New Clean Technology: Hybrids," *Enterprise,* http://drivingfutures.com/innovation/, May 1, 2012; "Most Fuel-Efficient Fleet," *Enterprise,* http://drivingfutures.com/innovation/, May 1, 2012.

22. Gunther, "Renting 'Green'? Not So Easy."

23. Loomis, "The Big Surprise Is Enterprise"; Lehman, "A Clear Road to the Top."

24. R. Kanfer, "Motivation Theory and Industrial and Organizational Psychology," in M. D. Dunnette and L. M. Hough, eds., *Handbook of Industrial and Organizational Psychology,* 2nd ed., vol. 1 (Palo Alto, CA: Consulting Psychologists Press, 1990), 75–170.

25. G. P. Latham & M. H. Budworth, "The Study of Work Motivation in the 20th Century," in L. L. Koppes, ed., *Historical Perspectives in Industrial and Organizational Psychology* (Hillsdale, NJ: Laurence Erlbaum, 2006).

26. S. Clark, "Finding Daring Jobs for Bored Bankers," *Bloomberg Businessweek,* June 6–June 12, 2011.

27. Clark, "Finding Daring Jobs for Bored Bankers"; S. Clark, "Ex-Banker Wants You to Trade Wall Street 'Misery' for Mongolia," *Bloomberg,* May 26, 2011, http://www.bloomberg.com/news/print/2011-05-26/ex-banker-wants-you-to-trade-wall-stree. . . , May 1, 2012; S. Clark, "Finding Adventurous Jobs for Bored Bankers," *Businessweek,* June 2, 2011, http://www.businessweek.com/print/magazine/content/11_24/b4232053145331.htm, May 1, 2012.

28. Team Esc, "How to use Escape the City, November 24, 2011, http://blog.escapethecity.org/categories/how-to-use-escape-the-city/, May 1, 2012.

29. Clark, "Finding Daring Jobs for Bored Bankers."

30. Clark, "Finding Daring Jobs for Bored Bankers"; "The Team—Escape the City," http://escapethecity.org/pages/team, May 1, 2012.

31. Clark, "Finding Daring Jobs for Bored Bankers."

32. Ibid.

33. N. Nicholson, "How to Motivate Your Problem People," *Harvard Business Review,* January 2003, 57–65.

34. A. M. Grant, "Does Intrinsic Motivation Fuel the Prosocial Fire? Motivational Synergy in Predicting Persistence, Performance, and Productivity," *Journal of Applied Psychology* 93, no. 1 (2008), 48–58.

35. Grant, "Does Intrinsic Motivation Fuel the Prosocial Fire?"; C. D. Batson, "Prosocial Motiviation: Is It Ever Truly

Altruistic?" in L. Berkowitz, ed., *Advances in Experimental Social Psychology,* vol. 20 (New York: Academic Press, 1987), 65–122.

36. Ibid.

37. J. P. Campbell and R. D. Pritchard, "Motivation Theory in Industrial and Organizational Psychology," in M. D. Dunnette, ed., *Handbook of Industrial and Organizational Psychology* (Chicago: Rand McNally, 1976), 63–130; T. R. Mitchell, "Expectancy Value Models in Organizational Psychology," in N. T. Feather, ed., *Expectations and Actions: Expectancy Value Models in Psychology* (Hillsdale, NJ: Erlbaum, 1982), 293–312; V. H. Vroom, *Work and Motivation* (New York: Wiley, 1964).

38. N. Shope Griffin, "Personalize Your Management Development," *Harvard Business Review* 8, no. 10 (2003), 113–119.

39. T. A. Stewart, "Just Think: No Permission Needed," *Fortune,* January 8, 2001 (www.fortune.com, June 26, 2001).

40. M. Copeland, "Best Buy's Selling Machine," *Business 2.0,* July 2004, 91–102; L. Heller, "Best Buy Still Turning on the Fun," *DSN Retailing Today* 43, no. 13 (July 5, 2004), 3; S. Pounds, "Big-Box Retailers Cash In on South Florida Demand for Home Computer Repair," *Knight Ridder Tribune Business News,* July 5, 2004 (gateway.proquest .com); J. Bloom, "Best Buy Reaps the Rewards of Risking Marketing Failure," *Advertising Age* 75, no. 25 (June 21, 2004), 16; L. Heller, "Discount Turns Up the Volume: PC Comeback, iPod Popularity Add Edge," *DSN Retailing Today* 43, no. 13 (July 5, 2004), 45; www.bestbuy.com, June 8, 2006.

41. T. J. Maurer, E. M. Weiss, and F. G. Barbeite, "A Model of Involvement in Work-Related Learning and Development Activity: The Effects of Individual, Situational, Motivational, and Age Variables," *Journal of Applied Psychology* 88, no. 4 (2003), 707–24.

42. J. Kaufman, "How Cambodians Came to Control California Doughnuts," *The Wall Street Journal,* February 22, 1995, A1, A8; H. Lee, "We Eat LA—Why there are no Dunkin' Donuts in Los Angeles," December 2002, http://we-eat-la.com/post/267302770/why-there-are-no-dunkin-donuts-in-los-angeles, May 1, 2012.

43. "Learn about Us"; The Container Store, "Welcome from Kip Tindell, Chairman & CEO," http://standfor.containerstore.com, March 3, 2010.

44. M. Duff, "Top-Shelf Employees Keep Container Store on Track," www.looksmart.com, www.findarticles.com, March 8, 2004; M. K. Ammenheuser, "The Container Store Helps People Think inside the Box," www.icsc.org, May 2004; "The Container Store: Store Location," www.

containerstore.com/find/index/jhtml, June 5, 2006; "Store Locations," *The Container Store,* www.containerstore.com/find/index.jhtml, April 1, 2008; The Container Store—What We Stand For—Our Story, http:/standfor.containerstore.com/our-story/, March 3, 2010; "CEO Maxine Clark, of Build-a-Bear, Traded in Her Kid-Filled Existence for a Day in the Orderly Aisles of the Container Store, Doing the 'Closet Dance,'" *Fortune,* February 8, 2010, 68–72; "Store Locator," *The Container Store,* http://www.containerstore.com/locations/index.htm, May 3, 2012.

45. "Learn about Us," www.containerstore.com, June 26, 2001.

46. Ibid.

47. J. Schlosser and J. Sung, "The 100 Best Companies to Work For," *Fortune,* January 8, 2001, 148–168; "Fortune 100 Best Companies to Work For 2006," cnn.com, June 5, 2006 (http://money.cnn.com/magazines/fortune/bestcompanies/snapshots/359.html); "Learn about Us."; "A Career at The Container Store," *The Container Store,* http://www.containerstore.com/careers/index.html, May 3, 2012.

48. "The Container Store," www.careerbuilder.com, July 13, 2004; "Tom Takes Re-imagine to PBS," Case Studies, www.tompeters.com, March 15, 2004; "2004 Best Companies to Work For," www.fortune.com, July 12, 2004; "*Fortune* 100 Best Companies to Work For 2006"; Levering and Moskowitz, "100 Best Companies to Work For: The Rankings"; Moskowitz, Levering, and Tkacyzk, "The List"; "100 Best Companies to Work for 2012," *Fortune,* http://money.cnn.com/magazines/fortune/bestcompanies/2012/snapshots/22.html, May 3, 2012.

49. The Container Store—What We Stand For."

50. D. Roth, "My Job at The Container Store," *Fortune,* January 10, 2000 (www.fortune.com, June 26, 2001); "*Fortune* 2004: 100 Best Companies to Work For," www.containerstore.com/careers/FortunePR_2004.jhtml?message=/repository/messages/fortuneCareer.jhtml, January 12, 2004; Levering, Moskowitz, and Adams, "The 100 Best Companies to Work For"; www.containerstore.com/careers/FortunePR_2004.jhtml?message=/repository/messages/fortuneCareer.jhtml, January 12, 2004.

51. Roth, "My Job at The Container Store."

52. "Learn about Us."

53. R. Yu, "Some Texas Firms Start Wellness Programs to Encourage Healthier Workers," *Knight Ridder Tribune Business News,* July 7, 2004 (gateway.proquest.com); Levering et al., "The 100 Best Companies to Work For."

54. Roth, "My Job at The Container Store"; "The Foundation Is Organization," *The Container Store,* June 5, 2006 (www.containerstore.com/careers/foundation.html).

55. A. H. Maslow, *Motivation and Personality* (New York: Harper & Row, 1954); Campbell and Pritchard, "Motivation Theory in Industrial and Organizational Psychology."

56. Kanfer, "Motivation Theory and Industrial and Organizational Psychology."

57. S. Ronen, "An Underlying Structure of Motivational Need Taxonomies: A Cross-Cultural Confirmation," in H. C. Triandis, M. D. Dunnette, and L. M. Hough, eds., *Handbook of Industrial and Organizational Psychology,* vol. 4 (Palo Alto, CA: Consulting Psychologists Press, 1994), 241–69.

58. N. J. Adler, *International Dimensions of Organizational Behavior,* 2nd ed. (Boston: P.W.S. Kent, 1991); G. Hofstede, "Motivation, Leadership, and Organization: Do American Theories Apply Abroad?" *Organizational Dynamics,* Summer 1980, 42–63.

59. C. P. Alderfer, "An Empirical Test of a New Theory of Human Needs," *Organizational Behavior and Human Performance* 4 (1969), 142–75; C. P. Alderfer, *Existence, Relatedness, and Growth: Human Needs in Organizational Settings* (New York: Free Press, 1972); Campbell and Pritchard, "Motivation Theory in Industrial and Organizational Psychology."

60. Kanfer, "Motivation Theory and Industrial and Organizational Psychology."

61. F. Herzberg, *Work and the Nature of Man* (Cleveland: World, 1966).

62. N. King, "Clarification and Evaluation of the Two-Factor Theory of Job Satisfaction," *Psychological Bulletin* 74 (1970), 18–31; E. A. Locke, "The Nature and Causes of Job Satisfaction," in Dunnette, *Handbook of Industrial and Organizational Psychology,* 1297–1349.

63. D. C. McClelland, *Human Motivation* (Glenview, IL: Scott, Foresman, 1985); D. C. McClelland, "How Motives, Skills, and Values Determine What People Do," *American Psychologist* 40 (1985), 812–25; D. C. McClelland, "Managing Motivation to Expand Human Freedom," *American Psychologist* 33 (1978), 201–10.

64. D. G. Winter, *The Power Motive* (New York: Free Press, 1973).

65. M. J. Stahl, "Achievement, Power, and Managerial Motivation: Selecting Managerial Talent with the Job Choice Exercise," *Personnel Psychology* 36 (1983), 775–89; D. C. McClelland and D. H. Burnham, "Power Is the Great Motivator," *Harvard Business Review* 54 (1976), 100–10.

66. R. J. House, W. D. Spangler, and J. Woycke, "Personality and Charisma in the U.S. Presidency: A Psychological Theory of Leader Effectiveness," *Administrative Science Quarterly* 36 (1991), 364–96.

67. G. H. Hines, "Achievement, Motivation, Occupations, and Labor Turnover in New Zealand," *Journal of Applied Psychology* 58

(1973), 313–17; P. S. Hundal, "A Study of Entrepreneurial Motivation: Comparison of Fast- and Slow-Progressing Small Scale Industrial Entrepreneurs in Punjab, India," *Journal of Applied Psychology* 55 (1971), 317–23.

68. R. A. Clay, "Green Is Good for You," *Monitor on Psychology,* April 2001, 40–42.

69. Schlosser and Sung, "The 100 Best Companies to Work For"; Levering et al., "The 100 Best Companies to Work For"; "Fortune 100 Best Companies to Work For 2006"; "Awards," *SAS,* http://www.sas.com/awards/index.html, April 1, 2008; R. Levering & M. Moskowitz, "100 Best Companies to Work For: The Rankings," *Fortune,* February 4, 2008, 75–94; "100 Best Companies to Work For 2012 : Full list—*Fortune,* http://money.cnn.com/magazines/fortune/best-companies/2012/full_list/, April 30, 2012.

70. E. P. Dalesio, "Quiet Giant Ready to Raise Its Profits," *Houston Chronicle,* May 6, 2001, 4D; Levering et al., "The 100 Best Companies to Work For"; J. Goodnight, "Welcome to SAS," www.sas.com/corporate/index.html, August 26, 2003; "SAS Press Center: SAS Corporate Statistics," www.sas.com/bin/pfp.pl?=fi, April 18, 2006; "SAS Continues Annual Revenue Growth Streak," www.sas.com/news/prelease/031003/newsl.html, August 28, 2003; R. Levering & M. Moskowitz, "100 Best Companies to Work For: The Rankings"; L. Buchanan, "No Doubt about It," *Inc.,* September 2011: 104–110; 'SAS Institute—Best Companies to Work For 2012," *Fortune,* http://money.cnn.com/magazines/fortune/best-companies/2012/snapshots/3.html, April 30, 2012.

71. J. Pfeffer, "SAS Institute: A Different Approach to Incentives and People Management Practices in the Software Industry," Harvard Business School Case HR-6, January 1998; "Saluting the Global Awards Recipients of Arthur Andersen's Best Practices Awards 2000," www.fortune.com, September 6, 2000; N. Stein, "Winning the War to Keep Top Talent," www.fortune.com, September 6, 2000.

72. J. Pfeffer, "SAS Institute: A Different Approach to Incentives and People Management Practices in the Software Industry," Harvard Business School Case HR-6, January 1998; "Saluting the Global Awards Recipients of Arthur Andersen's Best Practices Awards 2000," www.fortune.com, September 6, 2000; Stein, "Winning the War to Keep Top Talent."

73. J. Pfeffer, "SAS Institute: A Different Approach to Incentives and People Management Practices in the Software Industry," Harvard Business School Case HR-6, January 1998; "Saluting the Global Awards Recipients of Arthur Andersen's Best Practices Awards 2000," www.fortune.

com, September 6, 2000; Stein, "Winning the War to Keep Top Talent."

74. Goodnight, "Welcome to SAS"; "By Solution," www.sas.com/success/solution.html, August 26, 2003; www.sas.com, June 8, 2006.

75. S. H. Wildstrom, "Do Your Homework, Microsoft," *BusinessWeek Online,* August 8, 2005 (www.businessweek.com/print/magazine/content/05-b3946033-mz006.htm?chan); www.sas.com, June 8, 2006.

76. J. S. Adams, "Toward an Understanding of Inequity," *Journal of Abnormal and Social Psychology* 67 (1963), 422–36.

77. Adams, "Toward an Understanding of Inequity"; J. Greenberg, "Approaching Equity and Avoiding Inequity in Groups and Organizations," in J. Greenberg and R. L. Cohen, eds., *Equity and Justice in Social Behavior* (New York: Academic Press, 1982), 389–435; J. Greenberg, "Equity and Workplace Status: A Field Experiment," *Journal of Applied Psychology* 73 (1988), 606–13; R. T. Mowday, "Equity Theory Predictions of Behavior in Organizations," in R. M. Steers and L. W. Porter, eds., *Motivation and Work Behavior* (New York: McGraw-Hill, 1987), 89–110.

78. A. Goldwasser, "Inhuman Resources," Ecompany.com, March 2001, 154–55.

79. E. A. Locke and G. P. Latham, *A Theory of Goal Setting and Task Performance* (Englewood Cliffs, NJ: Prentice-Hall, 1990).

80. Locke and Latham, *A Theory of Goal Setting and Task Performance;* J. J. Donovan and D. J. Radosevich, "The Moderating Role of Goal Commitment on the Goal Difficulty–Performance Relationship: A Meta-Analytic Review and Critical Analysis," *Journal of Applied Psychology* 83 (1998), 308–15; M. E. Tubbs, "Goal Setting: A Meta Analytic Examination of the Empirical Evidence," *Journal of Applied Psychology* 71 (1986), 474–83.

81. E. A. Locke, K. N. Shaw, L. M. Saari, and G. P. Latham, "Goal Setting and Task Performance: 1969–1980," *Psychological Bulletin* 90 (1981), 125–52.

82. P. C. Earley, T. Connolly, and G. Ekegren, "Goals, Strategy Development, and Task Performance: Some Limits on the Efficacy of Goal Setting," *Journal of Applied Psychology* 74 (1989), 24–33; R. Kanfer and P. L. Ackerman, "Motivation and Cognitive Abilities: An Integrative/Aptitude–Treatment Interaction Approach to Skill Acquisition," *Journal of Applied Psychology* 74 (1989), 657–90.

83. W. C. Hamner, "Reinforcement Theory and Contingency Management in Organizational Settings," in H. Tosi and W. C. Hamner, eds., *Organizational Behavior and Management: A Contingency Approach* (Chicago: St. Clair Press, 1974).

84. "Our Story / Stella & Dot," http://www.stelladot.com/about, May 2, 2012; "Our

History / Stella & Dot," http://www.stelladot.com/about/our-history, May 2, 2012.

85. B. Kowitt, "Full-Time Motivation for Part-Time Employees," *Fortune,* October 17, 2011: 58.

86. "Learn How to be a Jewelry+Accessories Stylist/Stella & Dot," "Training Program," http://www.stelladot.com/stylist/training-program, May 2, 2012.

87. Kowitt, "Full-Time Motivation for Part-Time Employees."

88. Ibid.

89. "How to be a Jewelry+Accessories Stylist ."

90. Kowitt, "Full-Time Motivation for Part-Time Employees."

91. B. F. Skinner, *Contingencies of Reinforcement* (New York: Appleton-Century-Crofts, 1969).

92. H. W. Weiss, "Learning Theory and Industrial and Organizational Psychology," in Dunnette and Hough, *Handbook of Industrial and Organizational Psychology,* 171–221.

93. Hamner, "Reinforcement Theory and Contingency Management."

94. F. Luthans and R. Kreitner, *Organizational Behavior Modification and Beyond* (Glenview, IL: Scott, Foresman, 1985); A. D. Stajkovic and F. Luthans, "A Meta-Analysis of the Effects of Organizational Behavior Modification on Task Performance, 1975–95," *Academy of Management Journal* 40 (1997), 1122–49.

95. A. D. Stajkovic and F. Luthans, "Behavioral Management and Task Performance in Organizations: Conceptual Background, Meta Analysis, and Test of Alternative Models," *Personnel Psychology* 56 (2003), 155–94.

96. Stajkovic and Luthans, "Behavioral Management and Task Performance"; Luthans and A. D. Stajkovic, "Reinforce for Performance: The Need to Go beyond Pay and Even Rewards," *Academy of Management Executive* 13, no. 2 (1999), 49–56; G. Billikopf Enciina and M. V. Norton, "Pay Method Affects Vineyard Pruner Performance," www.cnr.berkeley.edu/ucce50/ag-labor/7research/7calag05.htm.

97. A. Bandura, *Principles of Behavior Modification* (New York: Holt, Rinehart and Winston, 1969); A. Bandura, *Social Learning Theory* (Englewood Cliffs, NJ: Prentice-Hall, 1977); T. R. V. Davis and F. Luthans, "A Social Learning Approach to Organizational Behavior," *Academy of Management Review* 5 (1980), 281–90.

98. A. P. Goldstein and M. Sorcher, *Changing Supervisor Behaviors* (New York: Pergamon Press, 1974); Luthans and Kreitner, *Organizational Behavior Modification and Beyond.*

99. Bandura, *Social Learning Theory;* Davis and Luthans, "A Social Learning Approach to Organizational Behavior";

Luthans and Kreitner, *Organizational Behavior Modification and Beyond.*

100. A. Bandura, "Self-Reinforcement: Theoretical and Methodological Considerations," *Behaviorism* 4 (1976), 135–55.

101. K. H. Hammonds, "Growth Search," *Fast Company,* April, 2003, 74–81.

102. B. Elgin, "Managing Google's Idea Factory," *BusinessWeek,* October 3, 2005, 88–90.

103. A. Bandura, *Self-Efficacy: The Exercise of Control* (New York: W.H. Freeman, 1997); J. B. Vancouver, K. M. More, and R. J. Yoder, "Self-Efficacy and Resource Allocation: Support for a Nonmonotonic, Discontinuous Model," *Journal of Applied Psychology* 93, no. 1 (2008), 35–47.

104. A. Bandura, "Self-Efficacy Mechanism in Human Agency," *American Psychologist* 37 (1982), 122–27; M. E. Gist and T. R. Mitchell, "Self-Efficacy: A Theoretical Analysis of Its Determinants and Malleability," *Academy of Management Review* 17 (1992), 183–211.

105. E. E. Lawler III, *Pay and Organization Development* (Reading, MA: Addison-Wesley, 1981).

106. P. Dvorak and S. Thurm, "Slump Prods Firms to Seek New Compact with Workers," *The Wall Street Journal,* October 19, 2009, A1, A18.

107. D. Mattioli, "Rewards for Extra Work Come Cheap in Lean Times," *The Wall Street Journal,* January 4, 2010, B7.

108. Mattioli, "Rewards for Extra Work Come Cheap"; http://www.rockwellcollins.com/, March 3, 2010.

109. Mattioli, "Rewards for Extra Work Come Cheap."

110. Ibid.

111. Lawler, *Pay and Organization Development.*

112. Ibid.

113. J. F. Lincoln, *Incentive Management* (Cleveland: Lincoln Electric Company, 1951); R. Zager, "Managing Guaranteed Employment," *Harvard Business Review* 56 (1978), 103–15.

114. Lawler, *Pay and Organization Development.*

115. M. Gendron, "Gradient Named 'Small Business of Year,'" *Boston Herald,* May 11, 1994, 35; Gradient—Environmental Consulting, http://www.gradientcorp.com/index.php, March 3, 2010.

116. W. Zeller, R. D. Hof, R. Brandt, S. Baker, and D. Greising, "Go-Go Goliaths," *BusinessWeek,* February 13, 1995, 64–70.

117. N. Byrnes, "A Steely Resolve" *BusinessWeek,* April 6, 2009, 54.

118. "Stock Option," *Encarta World English Dictionary,* June 28, 2001 (www.dictionary.msn.com); personal interview with Professor Bala Dharan, Jones Graduate School of Business, Rice University, June 28, 2001.

119. Personal interview with Professor Bala Dharan.

120. Ibid.

121. C. D. Fisher, L. F. Schoenfeldt, and J. B. Shaw, *Human Resource Management* (Boston: Houghton Mifflin, 1990); B. E. Graham-Moore and T. L. Ross, *Productivity Gainsharing* (Englewood Cliffs, NJ: Prentice-Hall, 1983); A. J. Geare, "Productivity from Scanlon Type Plans," *Academy of Management Review* 1 (1976), 99–108.

122. K. Belson, "Japan's Net Generation," *BusinessWeek,* March 19, 2001 (*BusinessWeek* Archives, June 27, 2001).

123. K. Belson, "Taking a Hint from the Upstarts," *BusinessWeek,* March 19, 2001 (*BusinessWeek* Archives, June 27, 2001); "Going for the Gold," *BusinessWeek,* March 19, 2001 (*BusinessWeek* Archives, June 27, 2001); "What the Government Can Do to Promote a Flexible Workforce," *BusinessWeek,* March 19, 2001 (*BusinessWeek* Archives, June 27, 2001).

Chapter 14

1. "Management Team," *Aricent Group,* http://www.aricent.com/about/management-team.html, May 14, 2012; "Management," *Frog,* http://www.frogdesign.com/about/management.html, May 14, 2012.

2. A. Bryant, "What's the Mission? Your Troops Want to Hear It From You," *The New York Times,* http://www.nytimes.com/2011/03/27/business/27corner.html?_r=1&pagewanted=print, May 14, 2012.

3. Ibid.

4. "Creative Change-Makers Invited to 'Reinvent Business' at Hackathon in San Francisco," May 9, 2012, http://www.frogdesign.com/archive/press-release/creative-change-makers-invited-reinvent . . . , May 14, 2012.

5. J. K. Glei, "Doreen Lorenzo: Clients Don't Deserve Surprises," http://the99percent.com/articles/6983/Doreen-Lorenzo-Clients-Dont-Deserve-Surprises/print, May 14, 2012; "Work," *frog,* http://frogdesign.com/work/, May 14, 2012.

6. Bryant, "What's the Mission?"; "About frog," *frog,* http://www.frogdesign.com/about, May 14, 2012; "Creative Change-Makers Invited to 'Reinvent Business.' "; Glei, "Clients Don't Deserve Surprises"; D. Lorenzo, "Why Conviction Drives Innovation More Than Creativity, *CNNMoney,* October 17, 2011, http://tech.fortune.cnn.com/2011/10/17/innovation-creativity/, May 14, 2012; "Work."

7. Bryant, "What's the Mission?".

8. Lorenzo, "Why Conviction Drives Innovation."

9. Ibid.

10. Bryant, "What's the Mission?"

11. Ibid.

12. Glei, "Doreen Lorenzo."

13. Ibid.

14. Bryant, "What's the Mission?"

15. Ibid.

16. Ibid.

17. Ibid.

18. G. Yukl, *Leadership in Organizations,* 2nd ed. (New York: Academic Press, 1989); R. M. Stogdill, *Handbook of Leadership: A Survey of the Literature* (New York: Free Press, 1974).

19. W. D. Spangler, R. J. House, and R. Palrecha, "Personality and Leadership," in B. Schneider and D. B. Smith, eds., *Personality and Organizations* (Mahwah, NJ: Lawrence Erlbaum, 2004), 251–90.

20. Spangler, House, and Palrecha, "Personality and Leadership"; "Leaders vs. Managers: Leaders Master the Context of Their Mission, Managers Surrender to It," www.msue.msu.edu/msue/imp/modtd/visuals/tsld029.htm, July 28, 2004; "Leadership," Leadership Center at Washington State University; M. Maccoby, "Understanding the Difference between Management and Leadership," *Research Technology Management* 43, no. 1 (January–February 2000), 57–59, www.maccoby.com/articles/UtDBMaL.html; P. Coutts, "Leadership vs. Management," www.telusplanet.net/public/pdcoutts/leadership/LdrVsMgnt.htm, October 1, 2000; S. Robbins, "The Difference between Managing and Leading," www.Entrepreneur.com/article/0,4621,304743,00.html, November 18, 2002; W. Bennis, "The Leadership Advantage," *Leader to Leader* 12 (Spring 1999), www.pfdf.org/leaderbooks/121/spring99/bennis.html.

21. Spangler et al., "Personality and Leadership"; "Leaders vs. Managers"; "Leadership"; Maccoby, "Understanding the Difference between Management and Leadership"; Coutts, "Leadership vs. Management"; Robbins, "The Difference between Managing and Leading"; Bennis, "The Leadership Advantage."

22. "Greenleaf: Center for Servant Leadership: History," *Greenleaf Center for Servant Leadership,* www.greenleaf.org/aboutus/history.html, April 7, 2008.

23. "What Is Servant Leadership?" *Greenleaf: Center for Servant Leadership,* http://www.greenleaf.org/whatissl/index.html, April 2, 2008.

24. "What Is Servant Leadership?"; Review by F. Hamilton of L. Spears and M. Lawrence, *Practicing Servant Leadership: Succeeding through Trust, Bravery, and Forgiveness* (San Francisco: Jossey-Bass,

2004), in *Academy of Management Review* 30 (October 2005), 875–87; R. R. Washington, "Empirical Relationships between Theories of Servant, Transformational, and Transactional Leadership," *Academy of Management,* Best Paper Proceedings, 2007, 1–6.

25. "Greenleaf: Center for Servant Leadership: History"; "What Is Servant Leadership?"; "Greenleaf: Center for Servant Leadership: Our Mission," *Greenleaf Center for Servant Leadership,* www.greenleaf.org/aboutus/mission.html, April 7, 2008.

26. B. Burlingham, "The Coolest Small Company in America," *Inc.,* January 2003, www.inc.com/magazine/20030101/25036_Printer_Friendly.html, April 7, 2008; A. Weinzweig, "Step into the Future," *Inc.,* February 2011: 85–91.

27. Burlingham, "The Coolest Small Company in America"; "Zingerman's Community of Businesses," *About Us,* www.zingermans.com/AboutUs.aspx, April 7, 2008; L. Buchanan, "In Praise of Selflessness," *Inc.,* May 2007, 33–35; Zingerman's Community of Businesses, http://www.zingermanscommunity.com, March 3, 2010; D. Walsh, "No secrets: Businesses find it pays to open books to employees," *Crain's Detroit Business,* January 28, 2010, http://www.crainsdetroit.com/article/20100117/FREE/301179994/no-secrets-businesses-fi. . . , May 17, 2012.

28. Burlingham, "The Coolest Small Company in America"; "Zingerman's Community of Businesses"; Buchanan, "In Praise of Selflessness."

29. Buchanan, "In Praise of Selflessness."

30. Ibid.

31. Burlingham, "The Coolest Small Company in America"; "In a Nutshell," *food gatherers,* www.foodgatherers.org/about.htm, April 7, 2008; Food Gatherers, "In a Nutshell," http://www.foodgatherers.org/about.htm, March 3, 2010; "About Us in a Nutshell," *Food Gatherers,* http://www.foodgatherers.org/?module=Page&sID=about-us, May 17, 2012.

32. "In a Nutshell."

33. Buchanan, "In Praise of Selflessness."

34. R. Calori and B. Dufour, "Management European Style," *Academy of Management Executive* 9, no. 3 (1995), 61–70.

35. Calori and Dufour, "Management European Style."

36. H. Mintzberg, *Power in and around Organizations* (Englewood Cliffs, NJ: Prentice-Hall, 1983); J. Pfeffer, *Power in Organizations* (Marshfield, MA: Pitman, 1981).

37. R. P. French, Jr., and B. Raven, "The Bases of Social Power," in D. Cartwright and A. F. Zander, eds., *Group Dynamics* (Evanston, IL: Row, Peterson, 1960), 607–23.

38. C. Frey, "Nordstrom Salesman's Million-Dollar Secret Is in His Treasured Client List," *Seattle Post-Intelligencer,* Saturday, March 27, 2004, http://www.seattlepi.com/business/166571_retail27.html, March 5, 2010; "Macy's Herald Square, New York, NY: Retail Commission Sales Associate—Women's Shoes," http://jobview.monster.com/Macy's-Herald-Square-New-York-NY-Retail-Commission-Sale . . . , March 5, 2010.

39. R. L. Rose, "After Turning Around Giddings and Lewis, Fife Is Turned Out Himself," *The Wall Street Journal,* June 22, 1993, A1.

40. "Company Overview," *Liberty Media,* http://www.libertymedia.com/company-overview.aspx, May 17, 2012; "Management," *Liberty Media Corporation,* http://ir.libertymedia.com/management.cfm, May 17, 2012; "Gregory B. Maffei Profile," Forbes.com, http://people.forbes.com/profile/print/gregory-b-maffei/28822, May 17, 2012.

41. "Company Overview"; "Management" *Liberty;* "Gregory B. Maffei Profile."

42. "Management"; "Gregory B. Maffei Profile"

43. A. Bryant, "Take Me On, You Might Get a Promotion," *The New York Times,* January 9, 2011: BU2.

44. "Management"; "Gregory B. Maffei Profile."

45. Bryant, "Take Me On."

46. Ibid.

47. Ibid.

48. Ibid.

49. A. Grove, "How Intel Makes Spending Pay Off," *Fortune,* February 22, 1993, 56–61; "Craig R. Barrett, Chief Executive Officer: Intel Corporation," *Intel,* July 28, 2004, www.intel.com/pressroom/kits/bios/barrett/bio.htm; Craig R. Barrett Bio, http://www.intel.com/pressroom/kits/bios/barrett.htm, March 3, 2010.

50. Craig R. Barrett Bio, www.intel.com/pressroom/kits/bios/barrett.htm, April 8, 2008; Microsoft Press Pass—Microsoft Board of Directors, www.microsoft.com/presspass/bod/default.mspx, April 8, 2008; "Tachi Yamada Selected to Lead Gates Foundation's Global Health Program," Announcements—Bill & Melinda Gates Foundation, February 6, 2006, www.gatesfoundation.org/GlobalHealth/Announcements/Announce-060106.htm, April 8, 2008; Microsoft PressPass—Microsoft Executives and Images, "Microsoft Board of Directors," http://www.microsoft.com/presspass/bod/bod.aspx, March 3, 2010; Tachi Yamada—Bill & Melinda Gates Foundation, http://www.gatesfoundation.org/leadership/Pages/tachi-yamada.aspx, March 3, 2010; "Microsoft PressPass—Microsoft Executives and Images,"

http://www.microsoft.com/en-us/news/exec/bod.aspx, May 17, 2012; L. Timmerman, "Tachi Yamada, Former Gates Foundation Leader, Joins Frazier for New VC Gig," http://www.xconomy.com/seattle/2011/06/27/tachi-yamada-former-gates-foundation-leade. . . , May 17, 2012.

51. M. Loeb, "Jack Welch Lets Fly on Budgets, Bonuses, and Buddy Boards," *Fortune,* May 29, 1995, 146.

52. T. M. Burton, "Visionary's Reward: Combine 'Simple Ideas' and Some Failures; Result: Sweet Revenge," *The Wall Street Journal,* February 3, 1995, A1, A5.

53. L. Nakarmi, "A Flying Leap toward the 21st Century? Pressure from Competitors and Seoul May Transform the Chaebol," *BusinessWeek,* March 20, 1995, 78–80.

54. B. M. Bass, *Bass and Stogdill's Handbook of Leadership: Theory, Research, and Managerial Applications,* 3rd ed. (New York: Free Press, 1990); R. J. House and M. L. Baetz, "Leadership: Some Empirical Generalizations and New Research Directions," in B. M. Staw and L. L. Cummings, eds., *Research in Organizational Behavior,* vol. 1 (Greenwich, CT: JAI Press, 1979), 341–423; S. A. Kirpatrick and E. A. Locke, "Leadership: Do Traits Matter?" *Academy of Management Executive* 5, no. 2 (1991), 48–60; Yukl, *Leadership in Organizations;* G. Yukl and D. D. Van Fleet, "Theory and Research on Leadership in Organizations," in M. D. Dunnette and L. M. Hough, eds., *Handbook of Industrial and Organizational Psychology,* 2nd ed., vol. 3 (Palo Alto, CA: Consulting Psychologists Press, 1992), 147–97.

55. E. A. Fleishman, "Performance Assessment Based on an Empirically Derived Task Taxonomy," *Human Factors* 9 (1967), 349–66; E. A. Fleishman, "The Description of Supervisory Behavior," *Personnel Psychology* 37 (1953), 1–6; A. W. Halpin and B. J. Winer, "A Factorial Study of the Leader Behavior Descriptions," in R. M. Stogdill and A. I. Coons, eds., *Leader Behavior: Its Description and Measurement* (Columbus Bureau of Business Research, Ohio State University, 1957); D. Tscheulin, "Leader Behavior Measurement in German Industry," *Journal of Applied Psychology* 56 (1971), 28–31.

56. S. Greenhouse, "How Costco Became the Anti-Wal-Mart," *The New York Times,* July 17, 2005, BU1, BU8; "Directors," *Costco Wholesale, Investors Relations,* http://phx.corporate-ir.net/phoenix.zhtml?c=83830&p=irol-govBoard, April 8, 2008; "Company Profile," *Costco Wholesale, Investor Relations,* http://phx.corporate-ir.net/phoenix.zhtml?c=83830&p=irol-homeprofile, May 17, 2012.

57. "Corporate Governance," *Costco Wholesale, Investor Relations,* April 28, 2006,

http://phx.corporate-ir.net/phoenix. zhtml?c=83830&p=irol-govhighlights; J. Wohl, "Costco CEO's legacy continues as he steps down," September 1, 2011, Business & Financial News, Breaking US & International News, *Reuters.com*, http:// www.reuters.com/assets/print?aid=USTR E7805VW20110901, May 10, 2012.

58. Greenhouse, "How Costco Became the Anti-Wal-Mart;" M. Allison, "Costco's colorful CEO, co-founder Jim Sinegal to retire," *The Seattle Times*, August 31, 2011, http://seattletimes.nwsource.com/ html/businesstechnology/2016072309_ costco01.html, May 10, 2012.

59. Greenhouse, "How Costco Became the Anti-Wal-Mart."

60. Ibid.

61. Greenhouse, "How Costco Became the Anti-Wal-Mart"; S. Clifford, "Because Who Knew a Big-Box Chain Could Have a Generous Soul," *Inc.*, April 2005, 88.

62. S. Holmes and W. Zellner, "Commentary: The Costco Way," *BusinessWeek Online*, April 12, 2004, www.businessweek.com/ print/magazine/content/04_15/b3878084_ mz021.htm? chan . . .; M. Herbst, "The Costco Challenge: An Alternative to Wal-Martization?" *LRA Online*, July 5, 2005, www.laborresearch.org/print.php?id=391.

63. Greenhouse, "How Costco Became the Anti-Wal-Mart."

64. Greenhouse, "How Costco Became the Anti-Wal-Mart;" "Company Profile," *Costco Wholesale, Investor Relations*, http://phx.corporate-ir.net/phoenix. zhtml?c=83830&p=irol-homeprofile, April 8, 2008; Costco—Company Profile, http://phx.corporate-ir.net/phoenix. zhtml?c=83830&p=irol-homeprofile, March 5, 2010; "Company Profile," *Costco Wholesale, Investor Relations*, http://phx.corporate-ir.net/phoenix. zhtml?c=83830&p=irol-homeprofile, May 17, 2012.

65. A. Martinez and M. Allison, "Costco, Other Warehouse Clubs Holding Their Own during Recession," *The Seattle Times*, February 1, 2010, http://seattle-times.nwsource.com/cgi-bin/PrintStory. pl?document_id=2010922094&zsection . . . , March 3, 2010; S. Skidmore, "Wholesale Clubs' Profit Grows as Grocery Supermarkets Slide," *USA TODAY*, http://www. usatoday.com/cleanprint/?1267669249262, March 3, 2010.

66. Costco—Company Profile; "Company Profile," *Costco Wholesale, Investor Relations*.

67. "Costco Wholesale Corporation Reports Second Quarter and Year-to-Date Operating Results Fiscal 2006 and February Sales Results," *Costco Wholesale, Investor Relations: News Release*, April 28, 2006, http://phx.corporate-ir.net/phoenix.

zhtml?c=83830&p=irol-newsArticle&I D=824344&highlight=; "Costco Wholesale Corporation Reports March Sales Results and Plans for Membership Fee Increase," *Costco Wholesale, Investor Relations: News Release*, April 28, 2006, http://phx.corporate-ir.net/phoenix. zhtml?c=83830&p=irol-newsArticle&ID =839605&highlight=; "Wal-Mart Stores Post Higher January Sales," *BusinessWeek Online*, February 2, 2006, www.business-week.com/print/investor/conent/feb2006/ pi2006022_0732_pi004.htm.

68. Martinez and Allison, "Costco, Other Warehouse Clubs Holding Their Own" ; M. Allison, "Costco's Colorful CEO, Co-Founder Jim Sinegal to Retire."

69. "Costco Class Action Discrimination Lawsuit: Women Sue Costco," http:// genderclassactionagainstcostco.com/ costco94.pl, March 3, 2010; M. C. Fisk and K. Gullo, "Costco Ignored Sex Bias Warnings, Employees Say," http://www.seattlepi. com/business/284317_costcobias08.html, March 3, 2010; "Costco Job-Bias Lawsuit Advances," *Los Angeles Times*, January 12, 2007, http://articles.latimes.com/2007/ jan/12/business/fi-costco12, March 3, 2010.

70. "Costco Job-Bias Lawsuit Advances"; M. Allison, "Q&A: Costco CEO Jim Sinegal Talks about Recession, Succession," *The Seattle Times*, http://seattle-times.nwsource.com/cgi-bin/PrintStory. pl?document_id=2010271409&zsection . . . , March 3, 2010.

71. E. A. Fleishman and E. F. Harris, "Patterns of Leadership Behavior Related to Employee Grievances and Turnover," *Personnel Psychology* 15 (1962), 43–56.

72. R. Likert, *New Patterns of Management* (New York: McGraw-Hill, 1961); N. C. Morse and E. Reimer, "The Experimental Change of a Major Organizational Variable," *Journal of Abnormal and Social Psychology* 52 (1956), 120–29.

73. R. R. Blake and J. S. Mouton, *The New Managerial Grid* (Houston: Gulf, 1978).

74. P. Hersey and K. Blanchard, *Management of Organizational Behavior: Utilizing Human Resources* (Englewood Cliffs, NJ: Prentice-Hall, 1982).

75. F. E. Fiedler, *A Theory of Leadership Effectiveness* (New York: McGraw-Hill, 1967); F. E. Fiedler, "The Contingency Model and the Dynamics of the Leadership Process," in L. Berkowitz, ed., *Advances in Experimental Social Psychology* (New York: Academic Press, 1978).

76. J. Fierman, "Winning Ideas from Maverick Managers," *Fortune*, February 6, 1995, 66–80; "Laybourne, Geraldine, U.S. Media Executive," *Laybourne, Geraldine*, http:// museum.tv/archives/etv/L/htmlL/laybour-nege/laybournege.htm, April 8, 2008.

77. M. Schuman, "Free to Be," *Forbes*, May 8, 1995, 78–80; "Profile—Herman Mashaba," *SAIE—Herman Mashaba*, www.entrepre-neurship.co.za/page/herman_mashaba, April 8, 2008.

78. House and Baetz, "Leadership"; L. H. Peters, D. D. Hartke, and J. T. Pohlmann, "Fiedler's Contingency Theory of Leadership: An Application of the Meta-Analysis Procedures of Schmidt and Hunter," *Psychological Bulletin* 97 (1985), 274–85; C. A. Schriesheim, B. J. Tepper, and L. A. Tetrault, "Least Preferred Co-Worker Score, Situational Control, and Leadership Effectiveness: A Meta-Analysis of Contingency Model Performance Predictions," *Journal of Applied Psychology* 79 (1994), 561–73.

79. M. G. Evans, "The Effects of Supervisory Behavior on the Path–Goal Relationship," *Organizational Behavior and Human Performance* 5 (1970), 277–98; R. J. House, "A Path–Goal Theory of Leader Effectiveness," *Administrative Science Quarterly* 16 (1971), 321–38; J. C. Wofford and L. Z. Liska, "Path–Goal Theories of Leadership: A Meta-Analysis," *Journal of Management* 19 (1993), 857–76.

80. S. Kerr and J. M. Jermier, "Substitutes for Leadership: Their Meaning and Measurement," *Organizational Behavior and Human Performance* 22 (1978), 375–403; P. M. Podsakoff, B. P. Niehoff, S. B. MacKenzie, and M. L. Williams, "Do Substitutes for Leadership Really Substitute for Leadership? An Empirical Examination of Kerr and Jermier's Situational Leadership Model," *Organizational Behavior and Human Decision Processes* 54 (1993), 1–44.

81. Kerr and Jermier, "Substitutes for Leadership"; Podsakoff et al., "Do Substitutes for Leadership Really Substitute for Leadership?"

82. J. Reingold, "You Got Served," *Fortune*, October 1, 2007, 55–58; "News on Women," *News on Women: Sue Nokes SVP at T-Mobile*, http://newsonwomen. typepad.com/news_on_women/2007/09/ sue-nokes-svp-a.html, April 8, 2008.

83. "Company Information," "T-Mobile Cell Phone Carrier Quick Facts," http:// www.t-mobile/Company/CompanyInfo. aspx?tp=Abt_Tab_CompanyOverview, April 8, 2008; "T-Mobile Cell Phone Carrier Quick Facts," http://www.t-mobile.com/Company/CompanyInfo. aspx?tp=Abt_Tab_CompanyOverview, March 5, 2010; "T-Mobile Company Information / Quick Facts," http://www.t-mobile.com/Company/CompanyInfo. aspx?tp=Abt_Tab_CompanyOverview, May 17, 2012.

84. Reingold, "You Got Served."

85. Reingold, "You Got Served"; "Company Information," "Highest Customer Satisfaction & Wireless Call Quality—J.D. Power Awards," http://www.t-mobile.com/

Company/CompanyInfo.aspx?tp=Abt_
Tab_Awards, April 8, 2008.

86. Reingold, "You Got Served."

87. Ibid.

88. B. M. Bass, *Leadership and Performance beyond Expectations* (New York: Free Press, 1985); Bass, *Bass and Stogdill's Handbook of Leadership*; Yukl and Van Fleet, "Theory and Research on Leadership."

89. Reingold, "You Got Served."

90. Ibid.

91. Ibid.

92. Ibid.

93. Ibid.

94. Ibid.

95. J. A. Conger and R. N. Kanungo, "Behavioral Dimensions of Charismatic Leadership," in J. A. Conger, R. N. Kanungo, and Associates, *Charismatic Leadership* (San Francisco: Jossey-Bass, 1988).

96. Bass, *Leadership and Performance beyond Expectations*; Bass, *Bass and Stogdill's Handbook of Leadership*; Yukl and Van Fleet, "Theory and Research on Leadership;" Reingold, "You Got Served."

97. Ibid.

98. Reingold, "You Got Served."

99. Bass, *Leadership and Performance beyond Expectations*.

100. Bass, *Bass and Stogdill's Handbook of Leadership*; B. M. Bass and B. J. Avolio, "Transformational Leadership: A Response to Critiques," in M. M. Chemers and R. Ayman, eds., *Leadership Theory and Research: Perspectives and Directions* (San Diego: Academic Press, 1993), 49–80; B. M. Bass, B. J. Avolio, and L. Goodheim, "Biography and the Assessment of Transformational Leadership at the World Class Level," *Journal of Management* 13 (1987), 7–20; J. J. Hater and B. M. Bass, "Supervisors' Evaluations and Subordinates' Perceptions of Transformational and Transactional Leadership," *Journal of Applied Psychology* 73 (1988), 695–702; R. Pillai, "Crisis and Emergence of Charismatic Leadership in Groups: An Experimental Investigation," *Journal of Applied Psychology* 26 (1996), 543–62; J. Seltzer and B. M. Bass, "Transformational Leadership: Beyond Initiation and Consideration," *Journal of Management* 16 (1990), 693–703; D. A. Waldman, B. M. Bass, and W. O. Einstein, "Effort, Performance, Transformational Leadership in Industrial and Military Service," *Journal of Occupation Psychology* 60 (1987), 1–10.

101. R. Pillai, C. A. Schriesheim, and E. S. Williams, "Fairness Perceptions and Trust as Mediators of Transformational and Transactional Leadership: A Two-Sample Study," *Journal of Management* 25 (1999), 897–933; "About us," HP, http://

www8.hp.com/us/en/hp-information/about-hp/index.html, May 14, 2012.

102. "50 Most Powerful Women—1. Indra Nooyi (1)—*Fortune*," http://money.cnn.com/galleries/2009/fortune/0909/gallery.most_powerful_ women.fortune/i . . . , March 5, 2010.

103. L. Tischler, "Where Are the Women?" *Fast Company*, February 2004, 52–60.

104. "2000 Catalyst Census of Women Corporate Officers and Top Earners of the *Fortune* 500," www.catalyst women.org, October 21, 2001; S. Wellington, M. Brumit Kropf, and P. R. Gerkovich, "What's Holding Women Back?" *Harvard Business Review*, June 2003, 18–19; D. Jones, "The Gender Factor," USA *Today.com*, December 30, 2003; "2002 Catalyst Census of Women Corporate Officers and Top Earners in the *Fortune* 500," www.catalystwomen.org, August 17, 2004; "2007 Catalyst Census of Women Corporate Officers and Top Earners of the *Fortune* 500," www.catalyst.org/knowledge/titles/title/php?page=cen_COTE_07, February 8, 2008; "No News Is Bad News: Women's Leadership Still Stalled in Corporate America," December 14, 2011, *Catalyst*, http://www.catalyst.org/press-release/199/no-news-is-bad-news-womens-leadership-still-sta. . . , April 5, 2012.

105. A. H. Eagly and B. T. Johnson, "Gender and Leadership Style: A Meta-Analysis," *Psychological Bulletin* 108 (1990), 233–56.

106. Eagly and Johnson, "Gender and Leadership Style: A Meta-Analysis."

107. The Economist, "Workers Resent Scoldings from Female Bosses," *Houston Chronicle*, August 19, 2000, 1C.

108. Ibid.

109. Ibid.

110. Ibid.

111. A. H. Eagly, S. J. Karau, and M. G. Makhijani, "Gender and the Effectiveness of Leaders: A Meta-Analysis," *Psychological Bulletin* 117 (1995), 125–45.

112. Ibid.

113. J. M. George and K. Bettenhausen, "Understanding Prosocial Behavior, Sales Performance, and Turnover: A Group-Level Analysis in a Service Context," *Journal of Applied Psychology* 75 (1990), 698–709.

114. T. Sy, S. Cote, and R. Saavedra, "The Contagious Leader: Impact of the Leader's Mood on the Mood of Group Members, Group Affective Tone, and Group Processes," *Journal of Applied Psychology* 90(2), (2005), 295–305.

115. J. M. George, "Emotions and Leadership: The Role of Emotional Intelligence," *Human Relations* 53 (2000), 1027–55.

116. George, "Emotions and Leadership."

117. J. Zhou and J. M. George, "Awakening Employee Creativity: The Role of Leader Emotional Intelligence," *The Leadership Quarterly* 14, no. 45 (August–October 2003), 545–68.

118. Ibid.

119. Ibid.

120. D. Fenn, "My Bad," *Inc.*, October 2007, 37–38; *Creative Display Solutions: About Us*, www.creativedisplaysolutions.com/pages/about/about.html, April 4, 2008; *Creative Display Solutions: About Us*, http://www.creativedisplaysolutions.com/pages/about/about.html, March 5, 2010.

121. Fenn, "My Bad"; *Creative Display Solutions: About Us*, www.creativedisplay solutions.com/pages/about/about.html, April 4, 2008.

122. Fenn, "My Bad."

123. Ibid.

124. Ibid.

125. Ibid.

126. Ibid.

127. Fenn, "My Bad"; C. Mason-Draffen, "Inside Stories," "Feeling Like a Million," *Creative Display Solutions: CDS News*, www.creativedisplaysolutions.com/pages/about/news6.html, April 4, 2008.

128. D. Sonnenberg, "Mother Load: How to Balance Career and Family," July 30, 2007, *Creative Display Solutions: CDS News*, www.creativedisplay solutions.com/pages/about/news8.html, April 4, 2008; C. Mason-Draffen, "Partnership at Work: Couples in Business Together Have Their Share of Sweet Rewards and Unique Challenges," February 13, 2007, *Creative Display Solutions, CDS News*, www.creativedisplaysolutions.com/pages/about/news7.html, April 4, 2008; "Client List," *Creative Display Solutions: About Us*, www.creativedisplaysolutions.com/pages/about/clients.html, April 8, 2008; Fenn, "My Bad;" "Client List," *Creative*, http://www.creativedisplaysolutions.com/pages/about/clients.html, March 5, 2010; "Creative Display Solutions—Who We Are," http://www.creativedisplaysolutions.com/who-we-are.shtml, May 17, 2012.

129. Fenn, "My Bad."

Chapter 15

1. D. Kesmodel, "Boeing Teams Speed Up 737 Output," *The Wall Street Journal*, February 7, 2012: B10; D. Gates, "Boeing Fetes Renton Workers for Higher 737 Output, *Seattle Times*, http://o.seattletimes.nwsource.com/html/businesstechnology/2017205845_boeing11.html, May 22, 2012.

2. D. Kesmodel, "Boeing Teams Speed Up 737 Output," *The Wall Street Journal*, February 7, 2012: B10.

3. Ibid.

4. Ibid.

5. Ibid.

6. Ibid.

7. Ibid.

8. Ibid.

9. Ibid.

10. Ibid.

11. Gates, "Boeing Fetes Renton Workers"; S. Ray, "Boeing to Build MAX Next to Current 737 With Efficiency Push," *Bloomberg,* January 10, 2012, http://www.bloomberg.com/news/print/2012-01-10/being-will-build-max-model-alongsid. . . , May 22, 2012.

12. Kesmodel, "Boeing Teams Speed Up 737 Output"; C. Drew, "Boeing Lifts Forecast after a Strong Quarter," *The New York Times,* April 25, 2012, http://www.nytimes.com/2012/04/26/business/boeing-lifts-forecast-after-a-srong-quarter.h. . . , May 22, 2012.

13. T. M. Mills, *The Sociology of Small Groups* (Englewood Cliffs, NJ: Prentice-Hall, 1967); M. E. Shaw, *Group Dynamics* (New York: McGraw-Hill, 1981).

14. R. S. Buday, "Reengineering One Firm's Product Development and Another's Service Delivery," *Planning Review,* March–April 1993, 14–19; J. M. Burcke, "Hallmark's Quest for Quality Is a Job Never Done," *Business Insurance,* April 26, 1993, 122; M. Hammer and J. Champy, *Reengineering the Corporation* (New York: HarperBusiness, 1993); T. A. Stewart, "The Search for the Organization of Tomorrow," *Fortune,* May 18, 1992, 92–98; "Hallmark Corporate Information/About Hallmark," http://corporate.hallmark.com/Company, March 15, 2010; "Hallmark Corporate Information / Hallmark Facts," http://corporate.hallmark.com/Company/Hallmark-Facts, May 24, 2012.

15. "Amazon.com Investor Relations: Officers & Directors," http://phx.corporate-ir.net/phoenix.zhtml?c=97664&p=irol-govManage, June 19, 2006; "Amazon.com Investor Relations: Press Release," http://phx.corporate-ir.net/phoenix.zhtml?c=97664&p=irol-newsArticle&ID=1102342&hi. . . , April 17, 2008; "Amazon.com Investor Relations: Officers & Directors," http://phx.corporate-ir.net/phoenix.zhtml?c=97664&p=irol-govmanage_pf, March 14, 2010; "Amazon.com Investor Relations: Officers & Directors," http://phx.corporate-ir.net/phoenix.zhtml?c=97664&p=irol.govmanage, May 24, 2012.

16. R. L. Brandt, "Birth of a Salesman," *The Wall Street Journal,* October 15, 2011: C1-2.

17. A. Deutschman, "Inside the Mind of Jeff Bezos," *Fast Company,* August 2004, 50–58.

18. Deutschman, "Inside the Mind of Jeff Bezos"; "Amazon.com Digital Media Technology," http://media-server.amazon.com/jobs/jobs.html, June 19, 2006.

19. "Amazon.com: Kindle: Amazon's New Wireless Reading Device: Kindle Store," www.amazon.com/gp/product/B000F173MA/ref=amb_link_6369712_2?pf_rd_m=A. . . , April 17, 2008; "Amazon.com: Kindle Wireless Reading Device (6" Display, U.S. Wireless): Kindle Store," http://www.amazon.com/Kindle-Wireless-Reading-Device-Display/dp/B00154JDAI, March 15, 2010; "Kindle Touch 3G: Touchscreen e-Reader with Free 3G + Wi-Fi, 6" E Ink Display, 3G Wo. . . , http://www.amazon.com/gp/product/B005890G8O/ref=famstripe_kt3g, May 24, 2012.

20. Deutschman, "Inside the Mind of Jeff Bezos."

21. "Online Extra: Jeff Bezos on Word-of-Mouth Power," *Business Week Online,* August 2, 2004, www.businessweek.com; R. D. Hof, "Reprogramming Amazon," *Business Week Online,* December 22, 2003, www.businessweek.com; "About Amazon.com: Company Information," www.amazon.com/exec/obidos/tg/browsw/-/574562/104-0138839-3693547, June 19, 2006; "Amazon.com Investor Relations: Press Release."

22. "RockBottom Restaurants," www.rockbottom.com/RockBottomWeb/RBR/index.aspx?PageName=/RockBottom. . . , April 15, 2008; "Craft Works Restaurants & Breweries Inc.," http://www.craftworksrestaurants.com/executive.html, May 24, 2012.

23. S. Dallas, "Rock Bottom Restaurants: Brewing Up Solid Profits," *Business Week,* May 22, 1995, 74.

24. J. A. Pearce II and E. C. Ravlin, "The Design and Activation of Self-Regulating Work Groups," *Human Relations* 11 (1987), 751–82.

25. B. Dumaine, "Who Needs a Boss?" *Fortune,* May 7, 1990, 52–60; Pearce and Ravlin, "The Design and Activation of Self-Regulating Work Groups."

26. Dumaine, "Who Needs a Boss?"; A. R. Montebello and V. R. Buzzotta, "Work Teams That Work," *Training and Development,* March 1993, 59–64.

27. C. Matlack, R. Tiplady, D. Brady, R. Berner, and H. Tashiro, "The Vuitton Machine," *Business Week,* March 22, 2004, 98–102; "America's Most Admired Companies," *Fortune.com,* August 18, 2004, www.fortune.com/fortune/mostadmired/snapshot/0,15020,383,00.html; "Art Samberg's Ode to Steel," *Big Money Weekly,* June 29, 2004, http://trading.sina/com/trading/rightside/bigmoney_weekly_040629.b5.shtml; "Nucor Reports Record Results for First Quarter of 2004," www.nucor.com/financials.asp?finpage=newsreleases, August 18, 2004; "Nucor Reports Results for First Half and Second Quarter of 2004," www.nucor.com/financials.asp?finpage=newsreleases; J. C. Cooper, "The Price of Efficiency," *Business Week Online,* March 22, 2004, www.businessweek.com/magazine/content/04_12/b3875603.htm; "LVHM—Fashion & Leather Goods," www.lvmh.com, June 18, 2006; C. Matlack, "Rich Times for the Luxury Sector," *Business Week Online,* March 6, 2006, www.businessweek.com/globalbiz/content/mar2006/gb20060306_296309.htm?campaign_id=search; N. Byrnes, "The Art of Motivation," *Business Week,* May 1, 2006, 56–62; "Nucor Steel," http://www.nucor.com/indexinner.aspx?finpage=aboutus, April 16, 2008; "Annual General Meetings—Group Investor Relations—Corporate Governance," http://www.lvmh.com/comfi/pg_home.asp?rub=6&srub=0, March 16, 2008; B. Sowray, "Louis Vuitton: the world's most valuable luxury brand," *Telegraph,* May 24, 2012, http://fashion.telegraph.co.uk/news-features/TMG9287478/Louis-Vuitton-the-world-most. . . , May 24, 2012; "Nucor Corporation / Our Story / Chapter 1: Corporate Overview," http://www.nucor.com/story/chapter1/, May 24, 2012.

28. Matlack et al., "The Vuitton Machine."

29. M. Arndt, "Out of the Forge and into the Fire," *Business Week,* June 18, 2001, *Business Week* Archives; Byrnes, "The Art of Motivation."

30. S. Baker, "The Minimill That Acts Like a Biggie," *Business Week,* September 30, 1996, 101–104; S. Baker, "Nucor," *Business Week,* February 13, 1995, 70; S. Overman, "No-Frills at Nucor," *HRMagazine,* July 1994, 56–60.

31. www.nucor.com, November 21, 2001; "Nucor: About Us."

32. Baker, "The Minimill That Acts Like a Biggie"; Baker, "Nucor"; Overman, "No-Frills at Nucor"; www.nucor.com; Byrnes, "The Art of Motivation"; "Nucor: About Us."

33. N. Byrnes, "A Steely Resolve," *Business Week,* April 6, 2009, 54.

34. Matlack et al., "The Vuitton Machine"; "About Nucor"; "America's Most Admired Companies"; "Art Samberg's Ode to Steel"; "Nucor Reports Record Results for First Quarter of 2004"; "Nucor Reports Results for First Half and Second Quarter of 2004"; Byrnes, "The Art of Motivation."

35. T. D. Wall, N. J. Kemp, P. R. Jackson, and C. W. Clegg, "Outcomes of Autonomous Work Groups: A Long-Term Field Experiment," *Academy of Management Journal* 29 (1986), 280–304.

36. A. Markels, "A Power Producer Is Intent on Giving Power to Its People," *The Wall*

Street Journal, July 3, 1995, A1, A12; "AES Corporation/The Power of Being Global," www.aes.com/aes/index?page=home, April 15, 2008.

37. J. S. Lublin, "My Colleague, My Boss," *The Wall Street Journal,* April 12, 1995, R4, R12.

38. W. R. Pape, "Group Insurance," *Inc.* (Technology Supplement), June 17, 1997, 29–31; A. M. Townsend, S. M. DeMarie, and A. R. Hendrickson, "Are You Ready for Virtual Teams?" *HR Magazine,* September 1996, 122–126; A. M. Townsend, S. M. DeMarie, and A. M. Hendrickson, "Virtual Teams: Technology and the Workplace of the Future," *Academy of Management Executive* 12, no. 3 (1998), 17–29.

39. Townsend et al., "Virtual Teams."

40. Pape, "Group Insurance"; Townsend et al., "Are You Ready for Virtual Teams?"; L. Gratton, "Working Together . . . When Apart," *The Wall Street Journal,* June 16–17, 2007, R4.

41. D. L. Duarte and N. T. Snyder, *Mastering Virtual Teams* (San Francisco: Jossey-Bass, 1999); K. A. Karl, "Book Reviews: Mastering Virtual Teams," *Academy of Management Executive,* August 1999, 118–19.

42. B. Geber, "Virtual Teams," *Training* 32, no. 4 (August 1995), 36–40; T. Finholt and L. S. Sproull, "Electronic Groups at Work," *Organization Science* 1 (1990), 41–64.

43. Geber, "Virtual Teams."

44. E. J. Hill, B. C. Miller, S. P. Weiner, and J. Colihan, "Influences of the Virtual Office on Aspects of Work and Work/Life Balance," *Personnel Psychology* 31 (1998), 667–83; S. G. Strauss, "Technology, Group Process, and Group Outcomes: Testing the Connections in Computer-Mediated and Face-to-Face Groups," *Human Computer Interaction,* 12 (1997), 227–66; M. E. Warkentin, L. Sayeed, and R. Hightower, "Virtual Teams versus Face-to-Face Teams: An Exploratory Study of a Web-Based Conference System," *Decision Sciences* 28, no. 4 (Fall 1997), 975–96.

45. S. A. Furst, M. Reeves, B. Rosen, and R. S. Blackburn, "Managing the Life Cycle of Virtual Teams," *Academy of Management Executive* 18, no. 2 (May 2004), 6–20.

46. Furst et al., "Managing the Life Cycle of Virtual Teams."

47. Gratton, "Working Together . . . When Apart."

48. Ibid.

49. Ibid.

50. Ibid.

51. A. Deutschman, "The Managing Wisdom of High-Tech Superstars," *Fortune,* October 17, 1994, 197–206.

52. J. D. Thompson, *Organizations in Action* (New York: McGraw-Hill, 1967).

53. Thompson, *Organizations in Action.*

54. Lublin, "My Colleague, My Boss."

55. "About ICU Medical, Inc.," www.icumed.com/about.asp, April 11, 2008.

56. Ibid.

57. "ICU Medical, Inc.—Fundamentals," http://phx.corporate-ir.net/phoenix.zhtml?c=86695&p=irol-fundamentals, April 11, 2008; "ICU Medical Inc. (ICUI): Stock Quote & Company Profile—BusinessWeek," *Business Week,* http://investing.businessweek.com/research/stocks/snapshot/snapshot_article.asp?symbol=. . . , April 11, 2008; "The 200 Best Small Companies #80 ICU Medical," *Forbes.com,* http://www.forbes.com/lists/2009/23/small-companies-09_ICU-Medical_J1UO.html, March 14, 2010; "2011 Annual Report to Shareholders and Form 10-K," ICU Medical, http://files.shareholder.com/downloads/ICUI/0x0x563714/664702F0-84A0-41B4-B90B-B8204D2437EC/ICU_WEB_READY_PDF.pdf, May 24, 2012.

58. "ICU Medical, Inc.—Investor Relations Home," http://phx.corporate-ir.net/phoenix.zhtml?c=86695&p=irol-IRHome, April 11, 2008; "The 200 Best Small Companies #80 ICU Medical."

59. "About ICU Medical, Inc."

60. "Clave Connector," ICU Medical, Inc., www.icumend.com, April 11, 2008; "2011 Annual Report to Shareholders and Form 10-K," *ICU Medical,* http://files.shareholder.com/downloads/ICUI/0x0x563714/664702F0-84A0-41B4-B90B-B8204D2437EC/ICU_WEB_READY_PDF.pdf, May 24, 2012.

61. E. White, "How a Company Made Everyone a Team Player," *The Wall Street Journal,* August 13, 2007, B1, B7.

62. Ibid.

63. Ibid.

64. Ibid.

65. Ibid.

66. Ibid.

67. Ibid.

68. R. G. LeFauve and A. C. Hax, "Managerial and Technological Innovations at Saturn Corporation," *MIT Management,* Spring 1992, 8–19.

69. B. W. Tuckman, "Developmental Sequences in Small Groups," *Psychological Bulletin* 63 (1965), 384–99; B. W. Tuckman and M. C. Jensen, "Stages of Small Group Development," *Group and Organizational Studies* 2 (1977), 419–27.

70. C. J. G. Gersick, "Time and Transition in Work Teams: Toward a New Model of Group Development," *Academy of Management Journal* 31 (1988), 9–41; C. J. G. Gersick, "Marking Time: Predictable Transitions in Task Groups," *Academy of Management Journal* 32 (1989), 274–309.

71. J. R. Hackman, "Group Influences on Individuals in Organizations," in M. D.

Dunnette and L. M. Hough, eds., *Handbook of Industrial and Organizational Psychology,* 2nd ed., vol. 3 (Palo Alto, CA: Consulting Psychologists Press, 1992), 199–267.

72. Hackman, "Group Influences on Individuals."

73. Ibid.

74. Lublin, "My Colleague, My Boss."

75. T. Kelley and J. Littman, *The Art of Innovation* (New York: Doubleday, 2001); "ideo.com: Our Work," www.ideo.com/portfolio, June 19, 2006; "About IDEO," *IDEO,* http://www.ideo.com/about/, May 24, 2012.

76. B. Nussbaum, "The Power of Design," *BusinessWeek,* May 17, 2004, 86–94; "ideo.com: About Us: Teams," www.ideo.com/about/index.asp?x=1&y=1, June 19, 2006.

77. "ideo.com: About Us: Teams," www.ideo.com/about/index.asp?x=1&y=1, June 19, 2006; "ideo.com: About Us: Teams," www.ideo.com/about/index.asp?x=1&y=1, April 18, 2008; "Teams—IDEO," http://www.ideo.com/culture/teams/ March 15, 2010.

78. Nussbaum, "The Power of Design."

79. Kelley and Littman, *The Art of Innovation.*

80. Kelley and Littman, *The Art of Innovation;* www.ideo.com; "1999 Idea Winners," *BusinessWeek,* June 7, 1999, *BusinessWeek* Archives.

81. Nussbaum, "The Power of Design; "ideo.com: About Us: Teams;" "About IDEO," *IDEO,* http://www.ideo.com/about/, May 24, 2012.

82. L. Festinger, "Informal Social Communication," *Psychological Review* 57 (1950), 271–82; Shaw, *Group Dynamics.*

83. Hackman, "Group Influences on Individuals in Organizations"; Shaw, *Group Dynamics.*

84. D. Cartwright, "The Nature of Group Cohesiveness," in D. Cartwright and A. Zander, eds., *Group Dynamics,* 3rd ed. (New York: Harper & Row, 1968); L. Festinger, S. Schacter, and K. Black, *Social Pressures in Informal Groups* (New York: Harper & Row, 1950); Shaw, *Group Dynamics.*

85. T. F. O'Boyle, "A Manufacturer Grows Efficient by Soliciting Ideas from Employees," *The Wall Street Journal,* June 5, 1992, A1, A5.

86. Lublin, "My Colleague, My Boss."

87. Kelley and Littman, "The Art of Innovation," 93.

88. Ibid.

89. "Shared Commitment," www.valero.com/Work/SharedCommitment.htm, April 18, 2008.

90. R. Levering and M. Moskowitz, "100 Best Companies to Work For: The Rankings," *Fortune,* February 4, 2008, 75–94.

91. J. Guyon, "The Soul of a Moneymaking Machine," *Fortune,* October 3, 2005, 113–20.

92. Ibid.

93. Ibid.

94. Ibid.

95. P. C. Earley, "Social Loafing and Collectivism: A Comparison of the United States and the People's Republic of China," *Administrative Science Quarterly* 34 (1989), 565–81; J. M. George, "Extrinsic and Intrinsic Origins of Perceived Social Loafing in Organizations," *Academy of Management Journal* 35 (1992), 191–202; S. G. Harkins, B. Latane, and K. Williams, "Social Loafing: Allocating Effort or Taking It Easy," *Journal of Experimental Social Psychology* 16 (1980), 457–65; B. Latane, K. D. Williams, and S. Harkins, "Many Hands Make Light the Work: The Causes and Consequences of Social Loafing," *Journal of Personality and Social Psychology* 37 (1979), 822–32; J. A. Shepperd, "Productivity Loss in Performance Groups: A Motivation Analysis," *Psychological Bulletin* 113 (1993), 67–81.

96. George, "Extrinsic and Intrinsic Origins"; G. R. Jones, "Task Visibility, Free Riding, and Shirking: Explaining the Effect of Structure and Technology on Employee Behavior," *Academy of Management Review* 9 (1984), 684–95; K. Williams, S. Harkins, and B. Latane, "Identifiability as a Deterrent to Social Loafing: Two Cheering Experiments," *Journal of Personality and Social Psychology* 40 (1981), 303–11.

97. S. Harkins and J. Jackson, "The Role of Evaluation in Eliminating Social Loafing," *Personality and Social Psychology Bulletin* 11 (1985), 457–65; N. L. Kerr and S. E. Bruun, "Ringelman Revisited: Alternative Explanations for the Social Loafing Effect," *Personality and Social Psychology Bulletin* 7 (1981), 224–31; Williams et al., "Identifiability as a Deterrent to Social Loafing"; Harkins and Jackson, "The Role of Evaluation in Eliminating Social Loafing"; Kerr and Bruun, "Ringelman Revisited."

98. M. A. Brickner, S. G. Harkins, and T. M. Ostrom, "Effects of Personal Involvement: Thought-Provoking Implications for Social Loafing," *Journal of Personality and Social Psychology* 51 (1986), 763–69; S. G. Harkins and R. E. Petty, "The Effects of Task Difficulty and Task Uniqueness on Social Loafing," *Journal of Personality and Social Psychology* 43 (1982), 1214–29.

99. B. Latane, "Responsibility and Effort in Organizations," in P. S. Goodman, ed., *Designing Effective Work Groups* (San Francisco: Jossey-Bass, 1986); Latane et al., "Many Hands Make Light the Work"; I. D. Steiner, *Group Process and Productivity* (New York: Academic Press, 1972).

Chapter 16

1. D. A. Kaplan, "Salesforce's Happy Workforce," *Fortune,* February 6, 2012: 101–12; "Salesforce Software: Welcome to the Social Enterprise," 2012 Annual Report, http://www2.sfdcstatic.com/assets/pdf/investors/AnnualReport.pdf.

2. Kaplan, "Salesforce's Happy Workforce"; "Salesforce Software"; "Trusted Clouds Apps and Platform for the Social Enterprise," http://www.salesforce.com/products/, May 30, 2012.

3. Kaplan, "Salesforce's Happy Workforce"; "Salesforce Service Cloud and Customers Take Home Four 2012 CRM Magazine Service Awards," http://www.salesforce.com/company/news-press/press-releases/2012/03/120319.jsp, May 30, 2012; "Salesforce Software: Welcome to the Social Enterprise," 2012 Annual Report, http://www2.sfdcstatic.com/assets/pdf/investors/AnnualReport.pdf.

4. "Salesforce Software."

5. "Salesforce.com Announces Fiscal 2013 First Quarter Results," http://www2.sfdcstatic.com/assets/pdf/investors/Q113_Earnings_Press_Release_w_financials.pdf, June 1, 2012.

6. Kaplan, "Salesforce's Happy Workforce"; "Careers #dreamjob," *Salesforce.com,* http://www.salesforce.com/careers/main/, June 5, 2012.

7. "What Does APP mean?"—APP Definition—Meaning of APP—InternetSlang.com, http://www.internetslang.com/APP-meaning-definition.asp, June 1, 2012.

8. Kaplan, "Salesforce's Happy Workforce."

9. Ibid.

10. Ibid.

11. Ibid.

12. Ibid.

13. Ibid.

14. Ibid.

15. Ibid.

16. Ibid.

17. Kaplan, "Salesforce's Happy Workforce"; "Salesforce Software."

18. C. A. O'Reilly and L. R. Pondy, "Organizational Communication," in S. Kerr, ed., *Organizational Behavior* (Columbus, OH: Grid, 1979).

19. "World's First Volume Computed Tomography (VCT) System, Developed by GE Healthcare, Scanning Patients at Froedtert," www.gehealthcare.com/company/pressroom/releases/pr_release_9722.html, June 18, 2004; "GE Healthcare Fact Sheet," *GE Healthcare Worldwide,* June 20, 2006, www.gehealthcare.com/usen/about/ge_factsheet.html; WTN News, "GE Healthcare Names New CEO," *Wisconsin Technology Network,* January 25, 2006, http://wistechnology.com/printarticle.php?id=2639, June 20, 2006; "About GE Healthcare," *GE Healthcare-Brochure—About GE Healthcare,* www.gehealthcare.com/usen/about/about.html, April 25, 2008; "About GE Healthcare," *GE Healthcare-Brochure—About GE Healthcare,* http://www.gehealthcare.com/usen/about/about.html, March 15, 2010; "GE Healthcare-Company Information—about GE Healthcare," http://www.gehealthcare.com/eueu/msabout/msabout.html, June 5, 2012.

20. "New CT Scanner by GE Healthcare Advances Imaging Technology," *Wisconsin Technology Network,* June 21, 2004, www.wistechnology.com; S. Kirsner, "Time [Zone] Travelers," *Fast Company,* August 2004, 60–66; "LightSpeed VCT Series," *GE Healthcare Worldwide,* June 20, 2006, www.gehealthcare.com/usen/ct/products/vct.html..

21. Kirsner, "Time [Zone] Travelers."

22. Ibid.

23. Ibid.

24. E. M. Rogers and R. Agarwala-Rogers, *Communication in Organizations* (New York: Free Press, 1976).

25. R. B. Schmitt, "Judges Try Curbing Lawyers' Body Language Antics," *The Wall Street Journal,* September 11, 1997, B1, B7.

26. D. A. Adams, P. A. Todd, and R. R. Nelson, "A Comparative Evaluation of the Impact of Electronic and Voice Mail on Organizational Communication," *Information & Management* 24 (1993), 9–21.

27. R. Winslow, "Hospitals' Weak Systems Hurt Patients, Study Says," *The Wall Street Journal,* July 5, 1995, B1, B6.

28. B. Newman, "Global Chatter," *The Wall Street Journal,* March 22, 1995, A1, A15.

29. M. L. Wald, "Details Are Added on Pilots in Overflight," *The New York Times,* December 17, 2009, A34; "Pilots Who Missed Airport OK Deal," *Houston Chronicle,* Tuesday, March 16, 2010, p. A6.

30. "Miscommunications Plague Pilots and Air Traffic Controllers," *The Wall Street Journal,* August 22, 1995, A1.

31. P. Reinert, "Miscommunication Seen as Threat to Space Station," *Houston Chronicle,* September 24, 2003, 6A.

32. W. E. Leary, "NASA Report Says Problems Plague Space Station Program," *The New York Times,* February 28, 2004, A12.

33. R. L. Daft, R. H. Lengel, and L. K. Trevino, "Message Equivocality, Media Selection, and Manager Performance: Implications for Information Systems," *MIS Quarterly* 11 (1987), 355–66; R. L. Daft and R. H. Lengel, "Information Richness: A New Approach to Managerial Behavior and

Organization Design," in B. M. Staw and L. L. Cummings, eds., *Research in Organizational Behavior* (Greenwich, CT: JAI Press, 1984).

34. R. L. Daft, *Organization Theory and Design* (St. Paul, MN: West, 1992).

35. "Lights, Camera, Meeting: Teleconferencing Becomes a Time-Saving Tool," *The Wall Street Journal,* February 21, 1995, A1.

36. Daft, *Organization Theory and Design.*

37. A. S. Wellner, "Lost in Translation," *Inc.,* September 2005, 37–38.

38. Ibid.

39. Wellner, "Lost in Translation"; R. McMillan, "Business Communication Expert and *New York Times* Bestselling Author," www.vitalsmarts.com, June 20, 2006.

40. Wellner, "Lost in Translation."

41. Ibid.

42. "Team," *Roberts Golden Consulting,* http://www.robertsgolden.com/about/team, June 5, 2012.

43. Wellner, "Lost in Translation"; S. Roberts, "Sara Roberts, President, Roberts Golden Consulting—Biographies," www.robertsgolden.com/bios.html, June 20, 2006; "Roberts Golden Consulting," www.robertsgolden.com, June 20, 2006; "Roberts Golden Consulting— About Us," "Management Team," http://www.robertsgolden.com/about_us/mgmt_team.html, March 15, 2010; "Roberts Golden Consulting—About Us," http://www.robertsgolden.com/about_us/index.html, March 15, 2010.

44. Wellner, "Lost in Translation."

45. S. Shellenbarger, "A Day without E-mail Is Like . . . ," *The Wall Street Journal,* October 11, 2007, D1, D2; D. Brady, "*!#?@ the E-Mail. Can We Talk?" *BusinessWeek,* December 4, 2006, 109; "No Email Friday Pays Off for Florida-based Bank," *Simply Communicate.com,* http://www.simplycommunicate.com/news/simply-news/no-email-Friday-pays-florida-base. . . , June 5, 2012.

46. P. Dvorak, "Frequent Contact Helps Bridge International Divide," *The Wall Street Journal,* June 1, 2009, B4.

47. T. J. Peters and R. H. Waterman, Jr., *In Search of Excellence* (New York: Harper & Row, 1982); T. Peters and N. Austin, *A Passion for Excellence: The Leadership Difference* (New York: Random House, 1985).

48. "Lights, Camera, Meeting."

49. R. Kirkland, "Cisco's Display of Strength," *Fortune,* November 12, 2007, 90–100; "Cisco TelePresence Overview," *Overview (TelePresence)—Cisco Systems,* www.cisco.com/en/US/solutions/ns669/networking_solutions_ products_genericcont. . . , April 25, 2008.

50. R. Kirkland, "Cisco's Display of Strength."

51. Kirkland, "Cisco's Display of Strength"; "Cisco TelePresence Overview."

52. Dvorak, "Frequent Contact Helps Bridge International Divide."

53. "Skype Technologies S.A. News," *The New York Times,* http://topics.nytimes.com/top/news/business/companies/skype_technologies_sa/index.html, June 5, 2012.

54. C. Hymowitz, "Missing from Work: The Chance to Think, Even to Dream a Little," *The Wall Street Journal,* March 23, 2004, B1.

55. D. Beizer, "Email Is Dead . . . ," *Fast Company,* July–August 2007, 46; "The Radicati Group, Inc.," www.radicati.com, April 28, 2008.

56. J. Sandberg, "Employees Forsake Dreaded E-mail for the Beloved Phone," *The Wall Street Journal,* September 26, 2006, B1.

57. Beizer, "Email Is Dead . . ."

58. Sandberg, "Employees Forsake Dreaded E-mail."

59. Ibid.

60. K. Byron, "Carrying Too Heavy a Load? The Communication and Miscommunication of Emotion by E-mail," *Academy of Management Review* 33, no. 2 (2008), 309–27.

61. "There's a Message in Every E-mail," *Fast Company,* September 2007, 43; Byron, "Carrying Too Heavy a Load?"

62. Byron, "Carrying Too Heavy a Load?"

63. "Telecommuters Bring Home Work and Broadband," www.emarketer.com/Article.aspx?1002943, July 20, 2004; "Annual Survey Shows Americans Are Working from Many Different Locations outside Their Employer's Office," *International Telework Association & Council,* May 10, 2006, www.workingfromanywhere.org/news; "Itac, the Telework Advisory Group for World at Work," www.workingfromanywhere.org, May 10, 2006; "Virtual Business Owners Community—FAQ Center: Telecommuting/Telework," www.vsscyberoffice.com/vfaq/25.html, May 10, 2006; T. Schadler, "US Telecommuting Forecast, 2009 to 2016: Telecommuting Will Rise to Include 43% of US Workers by 2016," March 11, 2009, http://www.forrester.com/rb/Research/us_telecommuting_forecast%2C_2009_to_2016/q/i. . . , March 15, 2010.

64. E. Baig, "Taking Care of Business—Without Leaving the House," *BusinessWeek,* April 17, 1995, 106–07.

65. "Life Is Good for Telecommuters, but Some Problems Persist," *The Wall Street Journal,* August 3, 1995, A1.

66. "E-Mail Abuse: Workers Discover High-Tech Ways to Cause Trouble in the Office," *The Wall Street Journal,* November 22, 1994, A1; "E-mail Alert: Companies Lag in Devising Policies on How It Should Be Used," *The Wall Street Journal,* December 29, 1994, A1.

67. Wellner, "Lost in Translation."

68. "The Most Important Part of an E-mail System Isn't the Software. It's the Rules You Make About Using It," *Inc. Magazine,* October 2005, 119–22.

69. "The Most Important Part of an E-mail System Isn't the Software."

70. Ibid.

71. American Management Association and the ePolicy Institute's N. Flynn, "2004 Workplace E-Mail and Instant Messaging Survey Summary," www.amanet.org, 2004; "2007 Electronic Monitoring & Surveillance Survey," *AMA/ePolicy Institute Research, American Management Association,* 2008.

72. J. Tyson, "How Instant Messaging Works," computer.howstuffworks.com, August 23, 2004.

73. "Study: Workers Are Surfing on Company Time," www.medialifemagazine.com/news2004/may04/may03/3_wed/news-8wednesday.html, May 5, 2004; "Company Profile," *Websense,* www.websense.com/global/en/AboutWebsense/, April 25, 2008.

74. "Study: Workers Are Surfing on Company Time."

75. Ibid.

76. ClikZ Stats staff, "U.S. Web Usage and Traffic, July 2004," www.clickz.com/stats/big_picture/traffic_patterns/article.php/3395351, August 23, 2004.

77. L. Guernsey, "Technology; Keeping Watch Over Instant Messages," April 15, 2002, http://www.nytimes.com/2002/04/15/business/technology-keeping-watch-over-instant-mess. . . , June 6, 2012; "About Smarsh," *Smarsh,* http://www.smarsh.com/about-smarsh, June 6, 2012; L. Petrecca, "More employers use tech to track workers," *USA Today.com,* http://www.usatoday.com/money/workplace/2010-03-17-workplaceprivacy15_CV_N.htm., June 6, 2012; "How to Monitor Your Employees' PCs without Going Too Far," *PCWorld,* http://www.pcworld.com/printable/article/id,222169/printable.html, June 5, 2012.

78. "Employers Spying on Staff: Big Brother Bosses," *The Economist,* http://www.economist.com/node/14413380/print, June 5, 2012.

79. "Is Your Employer Monitoring Your Internet Use? *World Law Direct,* August 14, 2011, http://www.worldlawdirect.com/article/451/your-employer-monitoring-your-internet-use.html, June 6, 2012.

80. Conley, "The Privacy Arms Race"; "2007 Electronic Monitoring & Surveillance Survey"; M. Villano, "The Risk Is All Yours

in Office E-Mail," *The New York Times,* March 4, 2007, BU17.

81. "2007 Electronic Monitoring & Surveillance Survey."

82. J. Pfeffer, "It's Time to Start Trusting the Workforce," *Business 2.0,* December 2006, 68.

83. Conley, "The Privacy Arms Race."

84. "P&G: Our Worldwide Business Conduct Manual, p.12, http://www.pg.com/en_US/downloads/company/governance/Policy_Worldwide_Business_Conduct_Manual.pdf, June 6, 2012.

85. "P & G Who We Are: Purpose, Values, and Principles," www.pg.com/company/who_we_are/ppv.jhtml, August 25, 2004; L. Conley, "Refusing to Gamble on Privacy," *Fast Company,* July 2004, http://pf.fastcompany.com/magazine/84.essay_hughes.html; "Who We Are," *P&G Global Operations,* June 20, 2006, www.pg.com/company/who_we_are/index.jhtml; "Company Who We Are," P&G, PG.com—Who *We Are,* www.pg.com/company/who_we_are/index.jhtml, April 28, 2008; "Fortune Global 500 2011: The World's Biggest Companies—Procter & Gamble PG," http://money.cnn.com/magazines/fortune/global500/2011/snapshots/334.html, June 6, 2012.

86. Conley, "The Privacy Arms Race;" "Privacy: Our Global Privacy Policy," *P&G,* http://www.pg.com/en_US/sustainability/point_of_view/privacy.shtml, March 15, 2010.

87. J. O'Neil, "E-Mail Doesn't Lie (That Much)," *The New York Times,* March 2, 2004, D6.

88. "Employee-Newsletter Names Include the Good, the Bad, and the Boring," *The Wall Street Journal,* July 18, 1995, A1.

89. W. M. Bulkeley, "Playing Well with Others," *The Wall Street Journal,* June 18, 2007, R10.

90. E. White, J. S. Lublin, and D. Kesmodel, "Executives Get the Blogging Bug," *The Wall Street Journal,* July 13, 2007, B1, B2.

91. *Blog—Wikipedia, the free encyclopedia,* http://en.wikipedia.org/wiki/Blog, April 28, 2008; White et al., "Executives Get the Blogging Bug."

92. *Blog—Wikipedia, the free encyclopedia;* White et al., "Executives Get the Blogging Bug;" "GM FastLane Blog: Lutz Biography," http://fastlane.gmblogs.com/archives/2005/01/lutz_biography_1.html, April 28, 2008.

93. "2006 Workplace E-Mail, Instant Messaging & Blog Survey: Bosses Battle Risk by Firing E-Mail, IM & Blog Violators," New York, July 11, 2006, *AMA Press Room,* http://press.amanet.org/press-releases/28/2006-workplace-e-mail-instant-messaging-blog-s. . . April 28, 2008.

94. Bulkeley, "Playing Well with Others."

95. Ibid.

96. D. M. Boyd and N. B. Ellison, "Social Network Sites: Definition, History, and Scholarship," *Journal of Computer-Mediated Communication* 13, no. 1 (2007), article 11, http://jcmc.indiana.edu/vol13/issue1/boyd.ellison.html, March 15, 2010; "Social Networking Site Definition from PC Magazine Encyclopedia," http://www.pcmag.com/encyclopedia_term/0,2542,t=social+networking&i=55316,00.asp, March 15, 2010; "Factsheet/Facebook," http://www.facebook.com/press/info.php?factsheet, March 15, 2010; "Statistics / Facebook," http://www.facebook.com/press/info.php?statistics, March 15, 2010; "Twitter News—*The New York Times,*" http://topics.nytimes.com/top/news/business/companies/twitter/index.html, March 15, 2010; "Twitter," http://twitter.com/about, March 15, 2010; "Facebook, Inc.: Private Company Information—*Business Week,*" http://investing.businessweek.com/research/stocks/private/snapshot.asp?privcapId=207654. . . , March 15, 2010.

97. J. E. Vascellaro, "Why E-mail No Longer Rules," *The Wall Street Journal,* October 12, 2009, R1–3.

98. "Study: 54 Percent of Companies Ban Facebook, Twitter at Work/Epicenter/Wired.com," October 9, 2009, http://www.wired.com/epicenter/2009/10/study-54-of-companies-ban-facebook-twitter-at-. . . March 16, 2010.

99. "Study: 54 Percent of Companies Ban Facebook, Twitter."

100. O. W. Baskin and C. E. Aronoff, *Interpersonal Communication in Organizations* (Santa Monica, CA: Goodyear, 1989).

101. T. Gutner, "Move Over, Bohemian Grove," *BusinessWeek,* February 19, 2001, 102.

102. "We've All Got Mail," *Newsweek,* May 15, 2001, 73K; "Diversity Deficit," *BusinessWeek Online,* May 14, 2001; "Dial-Up Users Converting to Broadband in Droves," www.emarketer.com/Article.aspx?1003009, August 23, 2004; "Top 20 Countries with the Highest Number of Internet Users," *Internet World Stats,* June 20, 2006, www.internetworldstats.com/top20.htm; "Top 20 Countries with the Highest Number of Internet Users," www.internetworldstats.com/top20.htm, April 29, 2008; "Top 20 Countries with the Highest Number of Internet Users," http://www.internetworldstats.com/top20.htm, March 15, 2010; "Internet Users—Top 20 Countries—Internet Usage," *Internet World Stats,* http://www.internetworldstats.com/top20.htm, June 6, 2012.

103. "Top 15 Countries in Internet Usage, 2002," www.infoplease.com/ipa/A0908185.html, August 25, 2004; "Top 20 Countries with the Highest Number of Internet Users," http://www.internetworldstats.com/top20.htm, April 29, 2008; "Top 20 Countries with the Highest Number of Internet Users," http://www.internetworldstats.com/top20.htm, March 15, 2010; "Internet Users—Top 20 Countries—Internet Usage," *Internet World Stats,* http://www.internetworldstats.com/top20.htm, June 6, 2012.

104. J. Sandberg, "Internet's Popularity in North America Appears to Be Soaring," *The Wall Street Journal,* October 30, 1995, B2.

105. "How to Research Companies," *Oxford Knowledge Company,* www.oxford-knowledge.co.uk, September 16, 2004.

106. "Survey: Denmark Is Web-Savviest Nation," MSNBC.com, April 19, 2004, www.msnbc.msn.com/id/4779944/1/displaymode/1098; L. Grinsven, "U.S. Drops on Lists of Internet Savvy," *Houston Chronicle,* April 20, 2004, 6B.

107. M. J. Cronin, "Ford's Intranet Success," *Fortune,* March 30, 1998, 158; M. J. Cronin, "Intranets Reach the Factory Floor," *Fortune,* June 10, 1997; A. L. Sprout, "The Internet inside Your Company," *Fortune,* November 27, 1995, 161–68; J. B. White, "Chrysler's Intranet: Promise vs. Reality," *The Wall Street Journal,* May 13, 1997, B1, B6.

108. White, "Chrysler's Intranet: Promise vs. Reality."

109. G. Rifkin, "A Skeptic's Guide to Groupware," *Forbes ASAP,* 1995, 76–91.

110. Ibid.

111. Ibid.

112. "Groupware Requires a Group Effort," *BusinessWeek,* June 26, 1995, 154.

113. M. Totty, "The Path to Better Teamwork," *The Wall Street Journal,* May 20, 2004, R4; "Collaborative Software," *Wikipedia,* August 25, 2004, en.wikipedia.org/wiki/Collaborative_software; "Collaborative Groupware Software," www.svpal.org/~grantbow/groupware.html, August 25, 2004.

114. Totty, "The Path to Better Teamwork"; "Collaborative Software."

115. Totty, "The Path to Better Teamwork"; "Collaborative Software"; "Collaborative Groupware Software."

116. Totty, "The Path to Better Teamwork"; "Collaborative Software."

117. Totty, "The Path to Better Teamwork"; "Collaborative Software."

118. Microsoft Windows SharePoint Services Developer Center, "Windows SharePoint Service," http://msdn .microsoft.com/sharepoint, June 21, 2006.

119. Totty, "The Path to Better Teamwork"; "Collaborative Software."

120. M. Conlin, "E-mail Is So Five Minutes Ago," *BusinessWeek,* November 28, 2005, 111–12; D. Dahl, "The End of E-mail," *Inc.,* February 2006, 41–42; "Weaving a Secure Web around Education: A Guide to Technology Standards and Security," http://nces.ed.gov/pubs2003/secureweb/glossary.asp, June 21, 2006; "Wikis Make Collaboration Easier," *InformationWeek,* June 20, 2006, www.informationweek.com/shared/printableArticleSrc.jhtml?articleID=170100392.

121. "Postini," www.postini.com, April 28, 2008.

122. Conlin, "E-mail Is So Five Minutes Ago."

123. Ibid.

124. Ibid.

125. Ibid.

126. Dahl, "The End of E-mail"; "Wikis Make Collaboration Easier;" V. Vara, "Wikis at Work," *The Wall Street Journal,* June 18, 2007, R11.

127. Dahl, "The End of E-mail."

128. D. Dahl, "Connecting the Dots," *Inc.,* June 2009, 103–4; "Project Management, Collaboration, and Task Software: Basecamp," http://basecamphq.com/, March 15, 2010; "Basecamp's exclusive single-page projects keep everything organized," http://basecamp.com/one-page-project, June 6, 2012.

129. Conlin, "E-mail Is So Five Minutes Ago"; "Soar Technology, Thinking inside the Box," *Soar Technology, Inc.,* www.soartech.com/home.php, April 28, 2008; "SoarTech—About—History," http://www.soartech.com/about/history/, June 6, 2012.

130. Conlin, "E-mail Is So Five Minutes Ago."

131. Ibid.

132. Ibid.

133. Bulkeley, "Playing Well with Others."

134. Ibid.

135. Conlin, "E-mail Is So Five Minutes Ago"; Dahl, "The End of E-mail"; "Weaving a Secure Web around Education."

136. Wakizaka, "Faxes, E-Mail, Help the Deaf Get Office Jobs," *The Wall Street Journal,* October 3, 1995, B1, B5.

137. S. E. Needleman, "Business Owners Try to Motivate Employees," *The Wall Street Journal,* January 14, 2010, B5.

138. Needleman, "Business Owners Try to Motivate Employees."

139. D. Tannen, "The Power of Talk," *Harvard Business Review,* September–October 1995, 138–48; D. Tannen, *Talking from 9 to 5* (New York: Avon Books, 1995).

140. Tannen, "The Power of Talk."

141. Ibid.

142. Ibid.

143. Ibid.

144. Tannen, "The Power of Talk"; Tannen, *Talking from 9 to 5.*

145. Tannen, *Talking from 9 to 5.*

146. J. Cohen, "He Writes, She Writes," *Houston Chronicle,* July 7, 2001, C1–C2.

147. Ibid.

148. Ibid.

149. Tannen, "The Power of Talk," 148.

Chapter 17

1. K. Wells, "Nature's Own Hedge Fund," *Bloomberg Businessweek,* June 4–June 10, 2012; B. Griscom, "New Study Finds That Loggers and Conservationists Can Be Allies," May 21, 2012, http://thinkprogress.org/climate/2012/05/21/487604/new-study-finds-that-loggers-and-con. . . , June 11, 2012; L. Kaufman, "Partnership Preserves Livelihoods and Fish Stocks," *The New York Times,* http://www.nytimes.com/2011/11/28/science/earth/nature-conservancy-partners-with-califor. . . , June 8, 2012.

2. Wells, "Nature's Own Hedge Fund."

3. Ibid.

4. Ibid.

5. Ibid.

6. Ibid.

7. P. Kareiva, "Our Scientists," *The Nature Conservancy,* http://www.nature.org/ourscience/ourscientists/conservation-science-at-the-nature-conserva. . . , June 8, 2012.

8. Wells, "Nature's Own Hedge Fund."

9. Ibid.

10. Ibid.

11. Ibid.

12. "Louisiana Bucket Brigade: Staff," http://www.labucketbrigade.org/article.php?list=type&type=138, June 11, 2012.

13. Wells, "Nature's Own Hedge Fund."

14. "Louisiana Bucket Brigade: About Us," http://www.labucketbrigade.org/article.php?list=type&type=136, June 11, 2012.

15. Wells, "Nature's Own Hedge Fund."

16. L. Kaufman, "Partnership Preserves Livelihoods and Fish Stocks," *The New York Times,* http://www.nytimes.com/2011/11/28/science/earth/nature-conservancy-partners-with-califor. . . , June 8, 2012.

17. P. Voosen, E&E reporter, "Conservation: Myth-busting scientist pushes greens past reliance on 'horror stories'" *Greenwire,* April 3, 2012, http://www.eenews.net/public/Greenwire/2012/04/03/1?page_type=print, June 8, 2012.

18. Ibid.

19. Ibid.

20. Wells, "Nature's Own Hedge Fund"; Voosen, "Conservation: Myth-busting Scientist Pushes Greens"; Griscom, "New Study Finds That Loggers and Conservationists Can Be Allies"; Kaufman, "Partnership Preserves Livelihoods and Fish Stocks."

21. J. A. Litterer, "Conflict in Organizations: A Reexamination," *Academy of Management Journal* 9 (1966), 178–86; S. M. Schmidt and T. A. Kochan, "Conflict: Towards Conceptual Clarity," *Administrative Science Quarterly* 13 (1972), 359–70; R. H. Miles, *Macro Organizational Behavior* (Santa Monica, CA: Goodyear, 1980).

22. S. P. Robbins, *Managing Organizational Conflict: A Nontraditional Approach* (Englewood Cliffs, NJ: Prentice-Hall, 1974); L. Coser, *The Functions of Social Conflict* (New York: Free Press, 1956).

23. K. A. Jehn, "A Qualitative Analysis of Conflict Types and Dimensions in Organizational Groups," Cornell University, 1997; K. A. Jehn, "A Multimethod Examination of the Benefits and Detriments of Intragroup Conflict," Cornell University, 1995.

24. L. L. Putnam and M. S. Poole, "Conflict and Negotiation," in F. M. Jablin, L. L. Putnam, K. H. Roberts, and L. W. Porter, eds., *Handbook of Organizational Communication: An Interdisciplinary Perspective* (Newbury Park, CA: Sage, 1987), 549–99.

25. M. Trottman and R. Whelan, "U.S. Hits Builders with Probe into Pay," *The Wall Street Journal,* September 12, 2011: B1, http://search.proquest.com.ezproxy.rice.edu/docprintview/887932566?accountid=7064, June 12, 2012.

26. Trottman, & Whelan, "U.S. Hits Builders with Probe Into Pay"; "Compliance Assistance—Fair Labor Standards Act (FLSA)," *U.S. Department of Labor,* Wage and Hour Division (WHD), http://www.dol.gov/whd/flsa, June 12, 2012.

27. "Welcome," *PulteGroup, Inc.,* http://pultegroupinc.com/, June 12, 2012.

28. R. Whelan and M. Trottman, "U.S. Battles Home Builder Over Pay Probe," *The Wall Street Journal,* March 23, 2012: B3.

29. Ibid.

30. Ibid.

31. Ibid.

32. Ibid.

33. "Directors & Officers," *PulteGroup, Inc.,* Pulte Homes, Investor Relations, http://phx.corporate-ir-net/phoenix.zhtml?c=77968&p=77968&p=irol-govmanage, June 12, 2012.

34. Whelan and Trottman, "U.S. Battles Home Builder Over Pay Probe."

35. L. R. Pondy, "Organizational Conflict: Concepts and Models," *Administrative Science Quarterly* 2 (1967), 296–320; R. E. Walton and J. M. Dutton, "The Management of Interdepartmental Conflict: A Model and Review," *Administrative Science Quarterly* 14 (1969), 62–73.

36. G. R. Jones and J. E. Butler, "Managing Internal Corporate Entrepreneurship: An Agency Theory Perspective," *Journal of Management* 18 (1992), 733–49.

37. T. Petzinger, Jr., "All Happy Businesses Are Alike, but Heirs Bring Unique Conflicts," *The Wall Street Journal,* November 17, 1995, B1.

38. J. A. Wall, Jr., "Conflict and Its Management," *Journal of Management* 21 (1995), 515–58.

39. Walton and Dutton, "The Management of Interdepartmental Conflict."

40. Pondy, "Organizational Conflict."

41. W. F. White, *Human Relations in the Restaurant Industry* (New York: McGraw-Hill, 1948).

42. R. L. Pinkley and G. B. Northcraft, "Conflict Frames of Reference: Implications for Dispute Processes and Outcomes," *Academy of Management Journal* 37 (February 1994), 193–206.

43. K. W. Thomas, "Conflict and Negotiation Processes in Organizations," in M. D. Dunnette and L. M. Hough, eds., *Handbook of Industrial and Organizational Psychology,* 2nd ed., vol. 3 (Palo Alto, CA: Consulting Psychologists Press, 1992), 651–717.

44. "Ravi Kant: Executive Profile & Biography," *BusinessWeek,* http://investing.businessweek.com/business week/research/stocks/people/person.asp?person. . . . , March 18, 2010; "Ravi Kant Profile," Forbes.com, http://people.forbes.com/profile/print/ ravi-kant/76754, March 18, 2010; "Board of Directors," *TATA Motors,* http://www.tatamotors.com/know-us/bod.php, June 12, 2012.

45. "Board of Directors," *TATA Motors,* http://www.tatamotors.com/know-us/bod.php, June 12, 2012.

46. M. Kripalana, "Tata: Master of the Gentle Approach," *BusinessWeek,* February 25, 2008; "Ravi Kant," *Tata Group,* www.tata.com/scripts/print.asp, May 2, 2008; "Ravi Kant: Executive Profile & Biography," *Business Week,* http://investing.businessweek.com/businessweek/research/stocks/people/person.asp?person . . . , March 18, 2010; "Ravi Kant Profile," Forbes.com, http://people.forbes.com/profile/print/ ravi-kant/76754, March 18, 2010.

47. Kripalana, "Tata: Master of the Gentle Approach"; "Profile," Tata Motors, www.tatamotors.com/our_world/profile.php, May 2, 2008; "Our Companies: Tata Motors," www.tata.com/tata_motors/index.htm, May 2, 2008.

48. Kripalana, "Tata: Master of the Gentle Approach."

49. Ibid.

50. Ibid.

51. K. Chae, "CEO Message," *Tata Daewoo,* www.tata-daewoo.com/ver3/ eng/03_company/01_ceo.html, May 7, 2008; "Events and Happenings," *Tata,* www.tata.com/scripts/print.asp, May 7, 2008.

52. Kripalana, "Tata: Master of the Gentle Approach."

53. Ibid.

54. Ibid.

55. Kripalana, "Tata: Master of the Gentle Approach"; Tata Group/ Our Businesses/ Tata Companies/ The Tata Daewoo Commercial Vehicle Co . . . , "Tata Daewoo Commercial Vehicle Company," http://www.tata.com/company/profile.aspx?sectid=HckEHljxqtM=, March 18, 2010.

56. "Sales Activities," *Tata Daewoo,* www.tata-daewoo.com/ver3/eng/08_center/ 01_faq.html, May 7, 2008; "Company," *Tata Daewoo,* www.tata-daewoo.com/ver3/eng/03_company/02_tata.html, May 7, 2008; "Tata Daewoo Commercial Vehicle Company," *TATA Group* / Our businesses / Tata companies, http://www.tata.com/company/profile.aspx?sectid=HckEH1jxqtM=, June 12, 2012.

57. Kripalana, "Tata: Master of the Gentle Approach."

58. Thomas, "Conflict and Negotiation Processes in Organizations."

59. Pinkley and Northcraft, "Conflict Frames of Reference."

60. G. Stoller, "Foreign Etiquette for Americans: A Guide to Dos and Don'ts abroad," March 29, 2011, http://travel.usatoday.com/news/story/2011/03/Foeign-etiquette-for-Americans-A-guide-t. . . , June 12, 2012.

61. Ibid.

62. E. Spitznagel, "Impress Your Chinese Boss," *Bloomberg Businessweek,* January 9, 2012: 80–81.

63. Ibid.

64. M-J Chen, "Inside Chinese Business: A Guide for Managers Worldwide," MA: Harvard Business School Press, 2001.

65. Ibid.

66. H. Seligson, "For American Workers in China, a Culture Clash, *The New York Times,* http://www.nytimes.com/2009/12/24/business/global/24chinawork.html?_r=1&pagewante. . . , June 12, 2012.

67. J. Sharkey, "On a Visit to Saudi Arabia, Doing What the Saudis Do," *The New York Times,* March 15, 2011: B8.

68. Ibid.

69. E. Shapiro, J. A. Trachtenberg, and L. Landro, "Time Warner Settles Feud by Pushing Out Music Division's Fuchs," *The Wall Street Journal,* November 17, 1995, A1, A6.

70. Shapiro et al., "Time Warner Settles Feud."

71. P. R. Lawrence, L. B. Barnes, and J. W. Lorsch, *Organizational Behavior and Administration* (Homewood, IL: Irwin, 1976).

72. R. J. Lewicki and J. R. Litterer, *Negotiation* (Homewood, IL: Irwin, 1985); G. B. Northcraft and M. A. Neale, *Organizational Behavior* (Fort Worth, TX: Dryden, 1994); J. Z. Rubin and B. R. Brown, *The Social Psychology of Bargaining and Negotiation* (New York: Academic Press, 1975).

73. C. Bendersky, "Organizational Dispute Resolution Systems: A Complementarities Model," *Academy of Management Review* 28 (October 2003), 643–57.

74. R. E. Walton, "Third Party Roles in Interdepartmental Conflicts," *Industrial Relations* 7 (1967), 29–43.

75. "Meaning of Arbitrator," www.hyperdictionary.com, September 4, 2004; "Definitions of Arbitrator on the Web," www.google.com, September 4, 2004.

76. L. Thompson and R. Hastie, "Social Perception in Negotiation," *Organizational Behavior and Human Decision Processes* 47 (1990), 98–123.

77. Thomas, "Conflict and Negotiation Processes in Organizations."

78. R. J. Lewicki, S. E. Weiss, and D. Lewin, "Models of Conflict, Negotiation, and Third Party Intervention: A Review and Synthesis," *Journal of Organizational Behavior* 13 (1992), 209–52.

79. Northcraft and Neale, *Organizational Behavior.*

80. Lewicki et al., "Models of Conflict, Negotiation, and Third Party Intervention"; Northcraft and Neale, *Organizational Behavior;* D. G. Pruitt, "Integrative Agreements: Nature and Consequences," in M. H. Bazerman and R. J. Lewicki, eds., *Negotiating in Organizations* (Beverly Hills, CA: Sage, 1983).

81. R. Fischer and W. Ury, *Getting to Yes* (Boston: Houghton Mifflin, 1981); Northcraft and Neale, *Organizational Behavior.*

82. P. J. Carnevale and D. G. Pruitt, "Negotiation and Mediation," *Annual Review of Psychology* 43 (1992), 531–82.

83. A. M. Pettigrew, *The Politics of Organizational Decision Making* (London: Tavistock, 1973); Miles, *Macro Organizational Behavior.*

84. D. J. Hickson, C. R. Hinings, C. A. Lee, R. E. Schneck, and D. J. Pennings, "A Strategic Contingencies Theory of Intraorganizational Power," *Administrative Science Quarterly* 16 (1971), 216–27; C. R. Hinings, D. J. Hickson, J. M. Pennings, and R. E. Schneck, "Structural Conditions of Interorganizational Power," *Administrative Science Quarterly* 19 (1974), 22–44; J. Pfeffer, *Power in Organizations* (Boston: Pitman, 1981).

85. Pfeffer, *Power in Organizations.*

86. Ibid.

87. M. Crozier, "Sources of Power of Lower Level Participants in Complex Organizations," *Administrative Science Quarterly* 7

(1962), 349–64; A. M. Pettigrew, "Information Control as a Power Resource," *Sociology* 6 (1972), 187–204.

88. Pfeffer, *Power in Organizations;* G. R. Salancik and J. Pfeffer, "The Bases and Uses of Power in Organizational Decision Making," *Administrative Science Quarterly* 19 (1974), 453–73; J. Pfeffer and G. R. Salancik, *The External Control of Organizations: A Resource Dependence View* (New York: Harper & Row, 1978).

89. Pfeffer, *Power in Organizations.*

90. Ibid.

91. Ibid.

92. L. Kramer, "Doing Well and Good: How Social Responsibility Helped One Coffee Grower Land a Deal with Starbucks," *Inc.,* June 2006, 55–56.

93. Kramer, "Doing Well and Good"; "Corporate Social Responsibility," www.starbucks.com/aboutus/csr.asp, June 25, 2006.

94. "The Exceptional Cup Participating Farms Finca El Faro," www.guatemalancoffees.com/GCContent/GCeng/auction_tec_fincas/FincaElFaro.asp, June 25, 2006; "Coca-Cola Years," *El Faro Estate Coffee,* http://www.elfaroestate.com/history/coca-ColaYears.php, June 13, 2012.

95. Kramer, "Doing Well and Good."

96. Ibid.

97. Ibid.

98. Ibid.

99. "Welcome to El Faro Estate Website," *El Faro Estate Coffee,* www.elfaroestate.com/default.htm, May 7, 2008; "El Faro Today," El Faro Estate Coffee, www.elfaroestate.com/history/elFaro/ElFaroToday.htm, May 7, 2008; "C.A.F.E. Practices (Coffee and Farmer Equity Practices)," *Starbucks Coffee,* The Business of Coffee, www.starbucks.com/aboutus/sourcingcoffee .asp, May 7, 2008; "Welcome to El Faro Estate Website," http://www.elfaroestate.com/default.php, March 18, 2010; "El Faro Today," *El Faro Estate Coffee,* http://www.elfaroestate.com/history/elFaro/elFaroToday.php, March 18, 2010; "El Faro Today," *El Faro Estate Coffee,* http://www.elfaroestate.com/history/elFaro/elFaroToday.php, June 13, 2012; "Welcome to El Faro Estate Website," *El Faro Estate Coffee,* http://www.elfaroestate.com/default.php, June 13, 2012.

100. Kramer, "Doing Well and Good."

Chapter 18

1. N. B. Macintosh, *The Social Software of Accounting Information Systems* (New York: Wiley, 1995).

2. C. A. O'Reilly, "Variations in Decision Makers' Use of Information: The Impact of Quality and Accessibility," *Academy of Management Journal* 25 (1982), 756–71.

3. G. Stalk and T. H. Hout, *Competing against Time* (New York: Free Press, 1990).

4. www.iata.com, 2012.

5. R. Cyert and J. March, *Behavioral Theory of the Firm* (Englewood Cliffs, NJ: Prentice-Hall, 1963).

6. E. Turban, *Decision Support and Expert Systems* (New York: Macmillan, 1988).

7. R. I. Benjamin and J. Blunt, "Critical IT Issues: The Next Ten Years," *Sloan Management Review,* Summer 1992, 7–19; W. H. Davidsow and M. S. Malone, *The Virtual Corporation* (New York: Harper Business, 1992).

8. Davidow and Malone, *The Virtual Corporation;* M. E. Porter, *Competitive Advantage* (New York: Free Press, 1984).

9. S. M. Dornbusch and W. R. Scott, *Evaluation and the Exercise of Authority* (San Francisco: Jossey-Bass, 1975).

10. J. Child, *Organization: A Guide to Problems and Practice* (London: Harper & Row, 1984).

11. www.ups.com, 2012.

12. Macintosh, *The Social Software of Accounting Information Systems.*

13. www.cypress.com, 2012.

14. www.hermanmiller.com, 2012.

15. www.fortune.com, 2012.

16. www.boeing.com, 2012.

17. P. Bradley, "Global Sourcing Takes Split-Second Timing," *Purchasing,* July 20, 1989, 52–58.

18. J. A. Schumpeter, *Capitalism, Socialism, and Democracy* (New York: Harper, 1942).

19. V. P. Buell, *Marketing Management* (New York: McGraw-Hill, 1985).

20. See M. M. J. Berry and J. H. Taggart, "Managing Technology and Innovation: A Review," *R & D Management* 24 (1994), 341–53; K. B. Clark and S. C. Wheelwright, *Managing New Product and Process Development* (New York: Free Press, 1993).

21. www.ebay.com, March 2010.

22. See Berry and Taggart, "Managing Technology and Innovation"; M. Gort and J. Klepper, "Time Paths in the Diffusion of Product Innovations," *Economic Journal,* September 1982, 630–53. Looking at the history of 46 products, Gort and Klepper found that the length of time before other companies entered the markets created by a few inventive companies declined from an average of 14.4 years for products introduced before 1930 to 4.9 years for those introduced after 1949—implying that product life cycles were being compressed. Also see A. Griffin, "Metrics for Measuring Product Development Cycle Time," *Journal of Production and Innovation Management* 10 (1993), 112–25.

23. www.sgi.com, 2012.

24. A. D. Chandler, *The Visible Hand* (Cambridge, MA: Harvard University Press, 1977).

25. C. W. L. Hill and J. F. Pickering, "Divisionalization, Decentralization, and Performance of Large United Kingdom Companies," *Journal of Management Studies* 23 (1986), 26–50.

26. O. E. Williamson, *Markets and Hierarchies: Analysis and Antitrust Implications* (New York: Free Press, 1975).

27. Turban, *Decision Support and Expert Systems.*

28. www.merck.com, 2008, 2010, 2012.

29. N. A. Nichols, "Scientific Management at Merck: An Interview with CFO Judy Lewent," *Harvard Business Review,* January–February 1994, 88–91.

30. Turban, *Decision Support and Expert Systems.*

31. E. Rich, *Artificial Intelligence* (New York: McGraw-Hill, 1983).

32. R. Brandt, "Agents and Artificial Life," *BusinessWeek,* June 13, 1994, 55–56.

33. Rich, *Artificial Intelligence.*

34. Ibid., 346.

35. G. R. Jones, "SAP and the Enterprise Resource Planning Industry," in C. W. L. Hill and G. R. Jones, *Strategic Management: An Integrated Approach,* 6th ed. (Boston: Houghton Mifflin, 2003).

36. B. Kogut, "Joint Ventures: Theoretical and Empirical Perspectives," *Strategic Management Journal* 9 (1988), 319–32.

37. G. S. Capowski, "Designing a Corporate Identity," *Management Review,* June 1993, 37–38.

38. J. Marcia, "Just Doing It," *Distribution,* January 1995, 36–40.

39. Davidow and Malone, *The Virtual Corporation.*

40. Ibid., 168.

41. J. Fulk and G. Desanctis, "Electronic Communication and Changing Organizational Forms," *Organizational Science,* 1995, vol. 6, 337–49.

42. Y. P. Shao, S. Y. Liao, and H. Q. Wang, "A Model of Virtual Organizations," *Academy of Management Executive,* 1998, 12, 120–28.

43. A. Williams, "Arthur Andersen-IT Initiatives Support Shifts in Business Strategy," *Informationweek,* September 11, 2000, 14–18.

44. T. Davenport and L. Prusak, *Information Ecology* (London: Oxford University Press, 1997).

45. www.accenture.com, 2012.

46. www.yahoo.com, 2012.

47. T. Stewart, "Managing in a Wired Company," *Fortune,* July 11, 1994, 44–56.

CREDITS

Photo Credits

Chapter 1

Page 3: Kevork Djansezian/Getty Images; p. 9: AP Photo/Harry Cabluck; p. 10: Michael Nagie/Getty Images; p. 11: Mark Peterson/Redux Pictures NYC; p. 19: Dan Lamont/Alamy; p. 21: Tracy Hayes/Bloomberg News/Landov; p. 25: © Jan Sochor/Alamy; p. 26: Courtesy of Accenture (top), Photo by James Berglie/ZUMA Press. © Copyright 2006 by James Berglie (bottom); p. 28: William Philpott/AFP/Getty Images.

Chapter 2

Page 35: Austrian Archives/CORBIS (top), © Imaginechina/CORBIS (bottom); p. 39: Bettmann/CORBIS; p. 40: Bettmann/CORBIS; p. 42: Bettmann/CORBIS (t), 20th Century Fox/Courtesy The Kobal Collection (b); p. 43: Hulton-Deutsch Collection/CORBIS; p. 46: The Granger Collection, New York; p. 48: Jacques Boyer/Roger Viollet/The Image Works; p. 51: Photo courtesy of Regina A. Greenwood, from the Ronald G. Greenwood Collection; p. 52: Fox Photos/Getty Images; P. 54: AP Photo/HO/Hewlett Packard.

Chapter 3

Page 65: © David Yellen/CORBIS; p. 71: Paul Drinkwater/NBCU Photo Bank via AP Images; p. 73: © Digital Vision; p. 74: Courtesy of Gentle Giant Moving Company; p. 78: Courtesy of Subaru of Indiana Automotive Inc; p. 79: © Jon Feingersh/Blend Images LLC; p. 82: Getty Images/OJO Images; p. 85: Courtesy of IDEO; p. 88: © Orjan F. Ellingvag/Dagbladet/CORBIS.

Chapter 4

Page 99: Bowen Liu/Apple Inc. via Bloomberg via Getty Images; p. 103: The Granger Collection, New York; p. 105: Spencer Platt/Getty Images; p. 108: Mark Wilson/Getty Images; p. 110: AP Photo/Damian Dovarganes, file; p. 118: Darren McCollester/Getty Images; p. 119: Robert K. Chin/Alamy; p. 122: AP Images/John Todd; p. 126: Courtesy of Google.

Chapter 5

Page 133: Courtesy of Sodexo; p. 137: Cultura Limited/Getty Images; p.138: © ColorBlind Images/Blend Images LLC; p.141: Ellen B. Senisi/The Image Works; p. 142: © Mikkel Bækhøj Christensen/Demotix/CORBIS; p. 149: Tannis Toohey/Toronto Star/ZUMA Press/

Newscom; p. 150: © Tim Pannell/CORBIS; p. 152: Bloom Productions/Digital Vision/Getty Images; p. 155: © Pittsburgh Post-Gazette, 2010, all rights reserved. Reprinted with permission; p. 157: Somos/Veer/Getty Images.

Chapter 6

Page 165: © Nokia 2010; p. 169: AP Photo/The News Tribune, Lui Kit Wong; p. 170: Simon Dawson/Bloomberg via Getty Images; p. 173: AP Photo/Itsuo Inouye; p. 176: Getty Images; p. 179: AP Photo/ Matt Houston; p. 186: Cornstock/Getty Images; p. 188: David Becker/Getty Images.

Chapter 7

Page 195: Courtesy of Garage Tek; p. 198: Andersen Ross/Blend Images/Getty Images; p. 199: AP Photo/Nati Hamik; p. 200: ASSOCIATED PRESS; p. 208: Chip East/Reuters/CORBIS; p. 211: © Digital Vision/Punchstock; p. 214: Morgan Lane Photography/Alamy; p. 217: Courtesy of World of Good, Inc; p. 218: Radius Images/Getty Images.

Chapter 8

Page 227: Chris Batson/Alamy; p. 231: Ryan McVay/Getty Images; p. 235: AP Images/Tom Mihalek; p. 239: AP Photo/Mel Evans; p. 243 (left): Courtesy of Cott Corporation, (right): The McGraw-Hill Companies, Inc/Jill Braaten, photographer; p. 245: Bloomberg via Getty Images; p. 249: Bill Varie/CORBIS; p. 250: Art Directors & TRIP/Alamy; p. 252 (l): AP Images/Kasumi Kasahara, (r): Pablo Bartholomew/Getty News/Liaison; p. 255: Gene Blevins/LA DailyNews/CORBIS.

Chapter 9

Page 263: John Lee/Aurora Photos/CORBIS; p. 269: Jeff Greenberg/PhotoEdit; p. 270: AP Images/Joseph Kaczmarek; p. 271: Andy Sotiriou/Photodisc/Getty Images; p. 277: CORBIS; p. 281: Junko Kimura/Getty Images; p. 282: Courtesy of United Electric Controls; p. 285: OJO Images Ltd/Alamy; p. 288: Erin Siegal/Redux Pictures.

Chapter 10

Page 296: ZUMA Press/Newscom; p. 300: Jeffrey Allan Salter/CORBIS; p. 301: Seattlepi/Joshua Trujillo; p. 305: Tim Boyle/Getty Images; p. 307: Kim Steele/Photodisc Green/

Getty Images; p. 308: Courtesy of AVON; p. 312: AP Images/Orlin Wagner; p. 313: Scott Olson/Getty Images; p. 316: Tom Raymond/Stone/Getty Images; p. 321: Fabrizio Constantini/The New York Times/Redux Pictures.

Chapter 11

Page 333: VisitBritain/Pawel Libera/Getty Images; p. 336: AP Photo/Eugene Hoshiko; p. 342: Tony Avelar/Bloomberg via Getty Images; p. 345: AP Images/Harry Cabluck; p. 352: AP Photo/Disney, Gene Duncan; p. 353: Mark Moran/ASSOCIATED PRESS; p. 360: Wendy Maeda/The Boston Globe via Getty Images.

Chapter 12

Page 367: Ronda Churchill/Bloomberg via Getty Images; p. 372: James Leynse/CORBIS; p. 376: David Pearson/Alamy; p. 377: Amy Etra/PhotoEdit; p. 378: Courtesy of Fog Creek Software; p. 380: Cabruken/Taxi/Getty Images; p. 381: CORBIS Bridge/Alamy; p. 382: Fuse/Getty Images; p. 383: Reza Estakhrian/Photographer's Choice/Getty Images; p. 389: Helen Ashford/Workbook Stock/Getty Images; p. 391: Mark Peterson 2007/Redux Pictures; p. 393: Photo by Jess Haessler/Courtesy Guerra DeBerry Coody.

Chapter 13

Page 403: AP Photo/Carlos Osorio; p. 407 (top): Simon Dawson/Bloomberg via Getty Images, (bottom): © LWA/Dann Tardif/Blend Images/CORBIS RF; p. 411: Courtesy of the Container Store; p. 413: Jim Esposito/Getty Images; p. 416: Jeremy M. Lange/The New York Times/Redux; p. 419: Stockbyte/Punchstock Images; p. 420: Courtesy of Stella & Dot; p. 424: vario images GmbH & Co.KG/Alamy.

Chapter 14

Page 433: Benjamin Sklar/The New York Times; p. 437: Courtesy of Zingerman's; p. 440: Matthew Staver/The New York Times; p. 442: Yun Suk Bong/Reuters/CORBIS; p. 444: Tim Boyle/Getty Images; p. 448: Stockbyte/Getty Images; p. 450: D. Clarke Evans/NBAE via Getty Images; p. 455: Courtesy of Creative Display Solutions, Inc.

Chapter 15

Page 465: Stephen Brashear/Getty Images; p. 468: image100/Alamy; p. 470: Brand X

622

Pictures/PunchStock; p. 472: Comstock Images/PictureQuest; p. 473: AP Images/ Alexandra Boulat/VII; p. 475: David P. Hall/ CORBIS; p. 478: Getty Images/Digital Vision; p. 479: LatinStock Collection/Alamy; p. 483: hana/Datacraft/Getty Images; p. 485: ASSOCI-ATED PRESS RF.

Chapter 16

Page 497: David Paul Morris/Bloomberg via Getty Images; p. 500: Doug Menuez/Getty Images; p. 502: Allan Danahar/Getty Images; p. 505: 2009 Jupiterimages Corporation; p. 506:

Blend Images/Getty Images; p. 509: David Lee/ Alamy; p. 511: Royalty-Free/CORBIS; p. 516: NetPhotos/Alamy; 520: Duncan Smith/Getty Images; p. 521: Photodisc/Alamy.

Chapter 17

Page 529: Photoshot/Newscom; p. 533: avatra images/Alamy; p. 534: © Hugh Sitton/CORBIS; p. 536: BananaStock/Jupiterimages; p. 537: Kim Jae-Hwan/AFP/Getty Images; p. 539: © Move Art Management/CORBIS; p. 541: Compassion-ate Eye Foundation/Robert Kent/Getty Images; p. 548: Courtesy of El Faro Estate Coffee.

Chapter 18

Page 557: NetPhotos/Alamy; p. 561: Bill Freeman/PhotoEdit; p. 563: Herman Miller, Inc; p. 566: © The McGraw-Hill Companies, Inc./Jill Braaten, photographer; p. 567: Website screenshot courtesy of Ebay; p. 568: Courtesy of Sun Microsystems, Inc; p. 573: REUTERS/ China Newsphoto/Landov; p. 574: Alexan-der Heimann/AFP/Getty Images; p. 580: Jeff Greenberg/Alamy.

INDEX

Names

A

Aaron, K., 594
Abell, D. F., 600
Abott, Ida, 384
Ackerman, P. L., 609
Acquah, B. B., 260
Adamo, M., 33
Adams, D. A., 616
Adams, J. S., 609
Adams, M., 608, 609
Adler, N. J., 608
Adler, P. S., 591
Agarwala-Rogers, R., 616
Aguilar, F. J., 599
Akerson, Dan, 584, 585
Albanese, M., 598
Alderfer, Clayton, 414, 608
Alexander, J. A., 602
Allen, T. D., 605
Allison, M., 612
Allman, Jan, 274
Alsever, J., 400
Alster, N., 595
Ammenheuser, M. K., 608
Amodio, D. M., 595
Amoruso, Cheryl, 140
Anand, Rohini, 134
Ancona, D. G., 586
Anderson, C., 586
Anderson, J. C., 601
Anderson, P., 603
Andrade, Jackie, 526
Andreessen, Marc, 552
Andrews, K. R., 591, 600
Anmuth, Doug, 365
Ante, S. E., 601
Anthony, R. N., 602
Aoki, M., 601
Aplin, J. C., 599
Argyris, C., 605
Ariishi, Takako, 152
Armour, S., 593
Armstrong, Bob, 501
Armstrong, Drew, 131
Arndt, M., 591, 614
Arnst, C., 597
Aronoff, C. E., 618
Aronson, J. A., 595
Arrow, K. J., 598
Aveni, R. D., 600
Aversa, J., 589
Avolio, B. J., 600, 613
Aylward, Colleen, 399
Ayman, R., 613

B

Bachelder, Cheryl, 261
Baetz, M. L., 611, 612
Bahree, B., 600
Baig, E., 617
Bailey, J. R., 588
Bain, Adam, 460
Bain, J. E., 596
Baird, L., 603
Bakan, D., 594
Baker, S., 610, 614
Ballmer, Steve, 441
Banaji, M., 595
Bandura, A., 609, 610
Banerjee, N., 605
Barbeite, F. G., 608
Barley, S. R., 591
Barnard, C. I., 591
Barnes, L. B., 620
Barnes-Farrell, J., 593
Barrett, Coleen, 127, 316
Barrett, Craig, 441, 611
Barrick, M. R., 588
Barry, V., 587, 591
Barsaloux, J., 599
Bart, M., 597
Bartlett, C. A., 597, 600
Bartz, Carol, 317, 318
Baskin, O. W., 618
Bass, B. M., 600, 611, 613
Batson, C. D., 607
Battaglia, B. A., 596
Baucus, M. S., 591
Baum, H. G., 586
Bazerman, M. H., 598, 620
Beauchamp, Katia, 553
Beauchamp, T. L., 591, 602
Beaudo, Daren, 27
Becker, T. E., 591
Bedecarre, Tom, 460–461
Begley, S., 590
Beizer, D., 617
Bell, C. H., 603
Bellah, R., 597
Belson, K., 610
Bender, Leon, 82
Bendersky, C., 620
Benioff, Marc, 497–499
Benjamin, R. I., 621
Bennis, W., 610
Bensen, Peter, 313
Bercovici, J., 590
Berger, B., 598
Berger, P. L., 590

Berkowitz, L., 608
Berman, D. K., 596
Bernard, T. S., 606
Berner, R., 614
Berns, Gregory, 494
Berry, L. L., 586
Berry, M. M. J., 621
Bessemer, Henry, 44
Bettenhausen, K., 589, 613
Beyer, J. M., 590
Beynon, H., 587
Bezos, Jeff, 71, 172, 469
Bhagwati, J., 597
Biegelsen, Lawrence, 131
Billikopf Encina, G., 609
Biyani, Gagan, 163
Black, Greg, 265
Black, K., 615
Blackburn, R. S., 615
Blackedge, B. J., 591
Blake, Frank, 293
Blake, Robert, 445, 612
Blanchard, Kenneth, 445, 612
Blankfein, Lloyd, 7
Blau, P., 601, 602
Bloom, J., 608
Bloomberg, Michael R., 120
Blunt, J., 621
Bogue, Zachary, 364
Bonabeau, E., 595
Bond, Ron, 133
Boone, Garrett, 409, 411
Borman, C., 605
Borman, W. C., 605
Borrus, A., 606
Borzacchiello, Maureen, 455
Bouchard, T. J., Jr., 599
Bourgeois, L. J., 596
Bowen, D. E., 601
Bowie, N. E., 591, 602
Bowles, J., 601
Boyd, D. M., 618
Boyle, Dennis, 89
Bracken, D. W., 605
Bradley, P., 621
Bradley, T., 603
Bradspies, R. W., 602
Brady, D., 614, 617
Brady, Diane, 261
Brandt, R., 610, 614, 621
Bresler, S. J., 596
Brickner, M. A., 616
Brief, Arthur P., 83, 589, 595, 596, 599
Brin, Sergey, 288, 289, 330, 354, 355
Brockner, J., 588

Organization Index

A

Accenture, 7, 18, 25–26, 172, 575, 579, 580
Acer, 9, 172
Adam's Mark, 151
Adidas, 578
AdMob, 163
Adobe, 167
Advantica, 147
AES Corporation, 474
AFL-CIO, 395
Air France, 271
Airbus Industries, 21
All American Window, 431
Amazon.com, 101, 172, 173, 229, 253, 469–470, 558, 566, 567, 569
AMD, 126, 167, 175, 340
American Apparel, 157
American Express, 11, 156
American Federation of Labor-Congress of Industrial Organizations (AFL-CIO), 395
American Greetings, 505, 506
American Journal of Public Health, 143
Ameritrade, 172
Andreessen Horowitz, 552
Apollo, 204
Apple, 3–5, 6, 7, 9, 11, 18, 23, 24, 55, 58, 99–101, 118, 165, 166, 169, 172, 187, 188, 203, 214, 245, 246, 266, 267, 284, 322, 323, 434, 459, 493, 557, 558
Armani, 244, 251
Army Research Institute, 545
Arthur Andersen, 122, 125
Artisan Business Group, 539
ASDA, 214
Asia Pacific Investment Partners, 407
AstraZeneca International, 393
Atos Origin, 525
AT&T, 19, 236, 381, 565, 566
Audi, 459
Automatic Data Processing (ADP), 380
Avis, 254
Avon, 308

B

Babson College, 384
Backbone Entertainment, 494
Bank of America, 142, 152, 514
Bank of Tokyo, 152
Bayer Corporation, 156
BBC, 182
Beech-Nut, 129–130
BellSouth, 151
Best Buy, 172, 410, 460, 558
Betterworks, 163
BIC, 241
Bill and Melinda Gates Foundation, 104
Black & Decker, 312
Blackberry, 9, 165
Blue Cross-Blue Shield, 116
Blue Oak Capital, 539
BMW, 243
Boeing, 20, 169, 253, 285, 465–467, 564

Borrego Solar Systems, 214
Bose, 564
BP, 27–28, 475
BP Amoco, 254
Brainvisa, 199
Bristol Myers Squib, 116
British Petroleum (BP), 27–28, 475
Brooks Brothers, 307
Buddy Media, 557
Budweiser, 459
Build-a-Bear, 95–96
Burger King, 147

C

Calvert Group, 146
Campell Soup Co., 238–242
Canon, 377
Cap Gemini, 172, 376, 575, 584
Capital One, 507
Carnegie Steel Company, 44
Catalyst, 137, 138
Caterpillar, 20, 170, 375
CCR, 258
Cedars-Sinai Medical Center, 82
Chanel, 244, 251
Charles Schwab, 172
Chesapeake Energy, 103, 105
Chevron Corporation, 157, 514
Chevron Information Technology Company, 157
Children Now, 139
Children's Choice Learning Center, 141
Chrysler, 37, 177, 268, 381, 514
Chubb Group of Insurance Companies, 142
Cisco Systems, 167, 172, 236, 242, 283, 377, 506
Citibank, 85, 274–275
Citigroup, 152
Citrix Systems, 526
CNN, 182
Coca-Cola, 147, 156, 168, 172, 176, 178, 207, 242–244, 247, 248, 254, 268, 377
Coca-Cola Enterprises, 376
Colgate, 171, 252
Comcast, 566
Computer Associates, 125
The Container Store, 409, 411
Continental Airlines, 271
Copal Partners, 376
Costco, 247, 443–444
Cott Corporation, 244
Coty, 308
Count Me In for Women's Economic Independence, 455
Countrywide Mortgage, 106
Creative Display Solutions, 455
Cypress Semiconductor, 349, 562, 572

D

D. R. Horton, 534
Daewoo, 442
Darden Restaurants, 146

DaVita Inc., 154
Dell Computer, 8–9, 11–12, 14, 17, 18, 19, 23, 26, 55, 101, 125, 153, 167–168, 169, 171, 172, 218, 251, 266, 284, 309, 345, 568
Delta Air Lines, 461
Deutsche Telekom, 450
DHL, 270
Dial, 251
Dick's Drive-In Restaurants, 301
Digital Equipment, 323
Dior, 244
Direct TV, 566
Disney. *See* Walt Disney Company
Documentum, 515
Dole Food Company, 393
Donna Karan, 567
Dow Chemical, 530, 531
Dresdner Kleinwort Wasserstein, 516
DST Global, 461
DuPont, 19, 125, 159, 207, 254, 319

E

E. & J. Gallo Winery, 246–247
E*Trade, 172
Eastman Kodak, 142, 269, 516, 579
Eaton Corporation, 486
eBay, 173, 216, 229, 341–342, 558, 566–567
The Economist, 118
EDS, 584
EEOC, 157
El Faro Estate Coffee, 548–549
Electronic Arts (EA), 263
Electronic Banking System (EBS), 62–63
Embraer, 21
Empire HealthChoice, 272
ENI, 254
Enron, 91, 116, 125
Enterprise Rent-A-Car, 403–405
Ernst & Young, 142, 146, 376, 377, 406
Escape the City, 406–407
ESPN, 182
E*Trade, 172
ExxonMobil, 85

F

Facebook, 214, 461, 510, 526
Fair Factories Clearinghouse, 118
FedEx, 158, 171, 268, 270, 307
Fiat, 177
Finca El Faro, 549
Fireman's Fund Insurance, 515
First Global Xpress (FGX), 270–271
Fog Creek Software, 377–378
Food Gatherers, 438
Ford Motor Company, 19, 36, 37, 57, 124, 151, 169, 204, 213, 273–274, 282–283, 320–321, 322, 352, 381, 439, 461, 472, 514, 584
Forman, 535
Four Seasons Hotels and Resorts, 384, 391–392
Foxconn, 99–101, 169
Franklin Motor Company, 41
Frog Design, 433–435

Subject Glindex